ESSENTIALS OF

HUMAN
BEHAVIOR

Note From the Author

The Educational Policy and Accreditation Standards of the Council on Social Work Education, adopted in 2008 and revised on March 27, 2010, lay out 10 core social work competencies that should guide curriculum design in social work education programs. Competencies are practice behaviors that integrate knowledge, values, and skills. The seventh competency, "Apply knowledge of human behavior and the social environment," is the explicit focus of this book.

We have presented material to assist the reader to engage in personal reflection related to social work values. Critical thinking questions appear in each chapter to assist the reader in ongoing critical examination of personal biases, conceptual frameworks, and empirical research. The content on diversity and social and economic justice includes attention to issues of global social justice. Material on the changing social contexts of social work practice is introduced, most notably in terms of changes in the physical environment, social policy initiatives, new technological developments, and global societal trends.

The 10 core competencies and the related practice behaviors are presented below, followed by a grid that indicates which of the core competencies are addressed in some fashion in each chapter. You might find it helpful to review these core competencies from time to time as you are learning more and more about what it means to be a social worker.

Council on Social Work Education's Educational Policy and Accreditation Standards

Educational Policy 2.1—Core Competencies

2.1.1—Identify as a professional social worker and conduct oneself accordingly. Social workers

- Advocate for client access to the services of social work;
- Practice personal reflection and self-correction to assure continual professional development;
- Attend to professional roles and boundaries;
- Demonstrate professional demeanor in behavior, appearance, and communication;
- Engage in career-long learning; and
- Use supervision and consultation.

2.1.2—Apply social work ethical principles to guide professional practice. Social workers

- Recognize and manage personal values in a way that allows professional values to guide practice;
- Make ethical decisions by applying standards of the National Association of Social Workers Code of Ethics and, as applicable, of the International Federation of Social Workers/International Association of Schools of Social Work Ethics in Social Work, Statement of Principles;
- Tolerate ambiguity in resolving ethical conflicts; and
- Apply strategies of ethical reasoning to arrive at principled decisions.

2.1.3—Apply critical thinking to inform and communicate professional judgments. Social workers

- Distinguish, appraise, and integrate multiple sources of knowledge, including research-based knowledge, and practice wisdom;
- Analyze models of assessment, prevention, intervention, and evaluation; and
- Demonstrate effective oral and written communication in working with individuals, families, groups, organizations, communities, and colleagues.

2.1.4—Engage diversity and difference in practice. Social workers

- Recognize the extent to which a culture's structures and values may oppress, marginalize, alienate, or create or enhance privilege and power;

- Gain sufficient self-awareness to eliminate the influence of personal biases and values in working with diverse groups;
- Recognize and communicate their understanding of the importance of difference in shaping life experiences; and
- View themselves as learners and engage those with whom they work as informants.

2.1.5—Advance human rights and social and economic justice. Social workers

- Understand the forms and mechanisms of oppression and discrimination;
- Advocate for human rights and social and economic justice; and
- Engage in practices that advance social and economic justice.

2.1.6—Engage in research-informed practice and practice-informed research. Social workers

- Use practice experience to inform scientific inquiry and
- Use research evidence to inform practice.

2.1.7—Apply knowledge of human behavior and the social environment. Social workers

- Utilize conceptual frameworks to guide the processes of assessment, intervention, and evaluation; and
- Critique and apply knowledge to understand person and environment.

2.1.8—Engage in policy practice to advance social and economic well-being and to deliver effective social work services. Social workers

- Analyze, formulate, and advocate for policies that advance social well-being; and
- Collaborate with colleagues and clients for effective policy action.

2.1.9—Respond to contexts that shape practice. Social workers

- Continually discover, appraise, and attend to changing locales, populations, scientific and technological developments, and emerging societal trends to provide relevant services; and
- Provide leadership in promoting sustainable changes in service delivery and practice to improve the quality of social services.

2.1.10(a)–(d)—Engage, assess, intervene, and evaluate with individuals, families, groups, organizations, and communities. Social workers

- Substantively and affectively prepare for action with individuals, families, groups, organizations, and communities;
- Use empathy and other interpersonal skills;
- Develop a mutually agreed-on focus of work and desired outcomes;
- Collect, organize, and interpret client data;
- Assess client strengths and limitations;
- Develop mutually agreed-on intervention goals and objectives;
- Select appropriate intervention strategies;
- Initiate actions to achieve organizational goals;
- Implement prevention interventions that enhance client capacities;
- Help clients resolve problems;
- Negotiate, mediate, and advocate for clients;
- Facilitate transitions and endings; and
- Critically analyze, monitor, and evaluate interventions.

Essentials of Human Behavior and Social Work Core Competencies

Chapter	Professional Identity	Ethical Practice	Critical Thinking	Engage Diversity	Human Rights & Justice	Research-Informed Practice	Human Behavior	Policy Practice	Practice Context	Engage, Assess, Intervene, & Evaluate
1	√	√	√	√	√	√	√		√	√
2	√	√	√	√	√	√	√	√	√	√
3	√		√	√	√	√	√	√	√	√
4	√	√	√	√		√	√		√	√
5	√	√	√	√	√	√	√		√	√
6	√	√	√	√	√	√	√	√	√	√
7	√		√	√	√	√	√	√	√	√
8	√	√	√	√	√	√	√	√	√	√
9	√	√	√	√	√	√	√	√	√	√
10	√	√	√	√	√	√	√	√	√	√
11	√	√	√	√	√	√	√	√	√	√
12	√	√	√	√	√	√	√	√	√	√
13	√	√	√	√	√	√	√	√	√	√
14	√	√	√	√	√	√	√	√	√	√
15	√		√	√	√	√	√	√	√	√
16	√	√	√	√	√	√	√	√	√	√
Total Chapters	16	13	16	16	15	16	16	13	16	16

ESSENTIALS OF
HUMAN
BEHAVIOR

Integrating Person, Environment, and the Life Course

Elizabeth D. Hutchison

Professor Emeritus
Virginia Commonwealth University

and Contributing Authors

Los Angeles | London | New Delhi
Singapore | Washington DC

Los Angeles | London | New Delhi
Singapore | Washington DC

FOR INFORMATION:

SAGE Publications, Inc.

2455 Teller Road

Thousand Oaks, California 91320

E-mail: order@sagepub.com

SAGE Publications Ltd.

1 Oliver's Yard

55 City Road

London EC1Y 1SP

United Kingdom

SAGE Publications India Pvt. Ltd.

B 1/I 1 Mohan Cooperative Industrial Area

Mathura Road, New Delhi 110 044

India

SAGE Publications Asia-Pacific Pte. Ltd.

33 Pekin Street #02-01

Far East Square

Singapore 048763

Acquisitions Editor: Kassie Graves

Associate Editor: Leah Mori

Editorial Assistant: Courtney Munz

Production Editor: Karen Wiley

Copy Editor: Teresa Herlinger

Typesetter: C&M Digitals (P) Ltd.

Proofreaders: Annie Lubinsky/Andrea Martin

Indexer: Molly Hall

Cover Designer: Bryan Fishman

Marketing Manager: Kelley McAllister

Permissions Editor: Adele Hutchinson

Printed in the United States of America

Library of Congress Cataloging-in-Publication Data

Hutchison, Elizabeth D.

Essentials of human behavior : integrating person, environment, and the life course / [compiled by] Elizabeth D. Hutchison.

p. cm.
Includes bibliographical references and index.

ISBN 978-1-4129-9884-0 (pbk. : acid-free paper)

1. Human behavior. 2. Psychology. 3. Social psychology. 4. Social service. I. Title.

HM1033.H87 2012
302—dc23   2011036142

This book is printed on acid-free paper.

11 12 13 14 15 10 9 8 7 6 5 4 3 2 1

BRIEF CONTENTS

PART III

The Changing Life Course 373

DETAILED CONTENTS

PART II

The Multiple Dimensions of Person and Environment   73

7. Social Structure and Social Institutions: Global and National   237

PART III

The Changing Life Course   373

16. Late Adulthood   639

Matthias J. Naleppa, Pamela J. Kovacs, and Rosa Schnitzenbaumer

CASE STORIES

(Continued)

PREFACE

I have always been intrigued with human behavior. I didn't know any social workers when I was growing up—or even that there was a social work profession—but I felt an immediate connection to social work and social workers during my junior year in college when I enrolled in an elective entitled Introduction to Social Work and Social Welfare. What attracted me most was the approach social workers take to understanding human behavior. I was a sociology major, minoring in psychology, and it seemed that each of these disciplines—as well as disciplines such as economics, political science, and ethics—added pieces to the puzzle of human behavior; that is, they each provided new ways to think about the complexities of human behavior. Unfortunately, it wasn't until several years later when I was a hospital social worker that I began to wish I had been a bit more attentive to my course work in biology, because that discipline holds other pieces of the puzzle of human behavior. But when I sat in that Introduction to Social Work and Social Welfare course, it seemed that the pieces of the puzzle were coming together. I was inspired by the optimism about creating a more humane world, and I was impressed with an approach to human behavior that clearly cut across disciplinary lines.

Just out of college, amid the tumultuous societal changes of the late 1960s, I became an MSW student. I began to recognize the challenge of developing the holistic understanding of human behavior that has been the enduring signature of social work. I also was introduced to the tensions in social work education, contrasting breadth of knowledge versus depth of knowledge. I found that I was unprepared for the intensity of the struggle to apply what I was learning about general patterns of human behavior to the complex, unique situations that I encountered in the field. I was surprised to find that being a social worker meant learning to understand my own behavior, as well as the behavior of others.

Since completing my MSW, I have provided services in a variety of social work settings, including hospitals, nursing homes, state mental health and mental retardation institutions, community mental health centers, a school-based program, public child welfare, and a city jail. Sometimes the target of change was an individual, and other times the focus was on bringing about changes in dyadic or family relationships, communities, organizations, or social institutions. I have also performed a variety of social work roles, including case manager, therapist, teacher, advocate, group facilitator, consultant, collaborator, program planner, administrator, and researcher. I love the diversity of social work settings and the multiple roles of practice. My varied experiences strengthened my commitment to the pursuit of social justice, enhanced my fascination with human behavior, and reinforced my belief in the need to understand human behavior holistically.

For almost 30 years, I taught courses in Human Behavior in the Social Environment to undergraduate students, MSW students, and doctoral students. The students and I struggled with the same challenges that I encountered as a social work student in the late 1960s: the daunting task of developing a holistic understanding of human behavior, the issue of breadth versus depth of knowledge, and discovering how to use general knowledge about human behavior in unique practice situations. And, increasingly, over time, my students and I recognized a need to learn more about human and social diversity, and to build a knowledge base that provided tools for promoting social justice. My experiences as student, practitioner, and teacher of human behavior led me, with the help of a dedicated and thoughtful group of contributing authors, to spend several years in the 1990s writing the two-volume *Dimensions of Human Behavior* books, which are now in their fourth edition.

I have appreciated hearing from faculty and students who use the *Dimensions of Human Behavior* books, and their feedback has been enormously helpful as the contributing authors and I revised and updated the books for subsequent editions. Over the years, I have been approached by faculty who would like to see a briefer, one-volume version of these books. Sometimes the requests came from faculty who are teaching in universities organized by quarters rather than semesters, and they wanted text material better suited for this shorter term. Other requests came from faculty who wanted a somewhat less comprehensive, but still multidimensional, textbook. The contributing authors and I have written this book to respond to these requests, out of respect for the great variety of social work educational programs and the diversity of ways of organizing the human behavior and the social environment curriculum.

This book retains the multidimensional, multitheoretical approach of the two-volume *Dimensions of Human Behavior*, and retains much of the content, as well, but it is organized into fewer chapters and is presented in a more simplified fashion. We have retained what we consider the essential themes of theory and research about human behavior and the social environment, which is in accord with the Council on Social Work Education's Educational Policy and Accreditation Standards for educational content on human behavior and the social environment. Educational Policy 2.1.7 states the following:

> Social workers are knowledgeable about human behavior across the life course; the range of social systems in which people live; and the ways social systems promote or deter people in maintaining or achieving health and well-being. Social workers apply theories and knowledge from the liberal arts to understand biological, social, cultural, psychological, and spiritual development. Social workers

- Utilize conceptual frameworks to guide the processes of assessment, intervention, and evaluation; and
- Critique and apply knowledge to understand person and environment.

MULTIDIMENSIONAL UNDERSTANDING OF HUMAN BEHAVIOR

Social work has historically used the idea of person-in-environment to develop a multidimensional understanding of human behavior. The idea that human behavior is multidimensional has become popular with most social and behavioral science disciplines. Recently, we have recognized the need to add the aspect of time to the person-environment construct, to capture the dynamic, changing nature of person-in-environment.

The purpose of this book is to help you to breathe life into the abstract idea of person-in-environment. I identify relevant dimensions of both person and environment, and my colleagues and I present up-to-date reports on theory and research about each of these dimensions in Part II of the book. All the while, we encourage you to link the micro world of personal experience with the macro world of social trends—to recognize the unity of person and environment. We help you make this connection by showing how several of the same theories have been used to understand dimensions of both person and environment.

THE CHANGING LIFE COURSE

Part III of the book builds on the multiple dimensions of person and environment analyzed in Chapters 3–9 and demonstrates how they work together with the dimension of time to produce patterns in unique life course journeys. The life course perspective puts equal value on individual agency and human connectedness; therefore, it serves as a good framework for social work's commitments to both the dignity and worth of the person as well as the importance of human relationships.

The contributing authors and I draw on the best available evidence about the life course to assist the reader to develop and enhance expertise in serving people at all life stages.

BREADTH VERSUS DEPTH

The most difficult challenge I have faced as a student and teacher of human behavior is to develop a broad, multidimensional approach to human behavior without unacceptable sacrifice of depth. It is indeed a formidable task to build a knowledge base both wide and deep. After years of struggle, I have reluctantly concluded that although both breadth and depth are necessary, it is better for social work to err on the side of breadth. Let me tell you why.

Social workers are doers; we use what we know to tell us what to do. If we have a narrow band of knowledge, no matter how impressive it is in its depth, we will "understand" the practice situations we encounter from this perspective. This will lead us to use the same solutions for all situations, rather than to tailor solutions to the unique situations we encounter. The emerging risk and resilience literature suggests that human behavior is influenced by the multiple risk factors and protective factors inherent in the multiple dimensions of contemporary social arrangements. What we need is a multidimensional knowledge base that allows us to scan widely for and think critically about risk factors and protective factors and to craft multipronged intervention programs to reduce risks and strengthen protective factors.

To reflect recent developments in the social and behavioral sciences, this book introduces dimensions of human behavior that are not covered in similar texts. Content on the biological and spiritual dimensions of person, the physical environment, social institutions, and social movements provide important insights into human behavior not usually covered in social work texts. In addition, we provide up-to-date information on the typically identified dimensions of human behavior.

GENERAL KNOWLEDGE AND UNIQUE SITUATIONS

The purpose of the social and behavioral sciences is to help us understand *general patterns* in person-environment transactions. The purpose of social work assessment is to understand *unique configurations* of person and environment dimensions. Those who practice social work must weave what they know about unique situations with general knowledge. To assist you in this process, as we did in the *Dimensions of Human Behavior* books, we begin each chapter with one or more case studies, which we then weave with contemporary theory and research. Most of the stories are composite cases and do not correspond to actual people known to the authors. Throughout the book, we call attention to the successes and failures of theory and research to accommodate human diversity related to gender, class, race and ethnicity, culture, sexual orientation, and disability. More important, we extend our attention to diversity by being very intentional in our effort to provide a global context for understanding person-environment transactions. This global perspective becomes increasingly necessary in our highly interconnected world. It also calls us to examine the impact of new technologies on all dimensions of the person and environment, and across the life course.

FEATURES OF THE BOOK

The task of developing a solid knowledge base for doing social work can seem overwhelming. For me, it is an exciting journey because I am learning about my own behavior as well as the behavior of others. What I learn enriches my personal life as well as my professional life. My colleagues and I wanted to write a book that gives you a state-of-the-art knowledge base, but we also wanted you to find pleasure in your learning. We have tried to write as we teach, with enthusiasm for the content and a desire to connect with your process of learning. We use some special features that we hope will aid your learning process.

- *Case Studies* put human faces on theory and research.
- *Key Terms* are presented in bold blue type in the chapters and defined in the Glossary.
- *Opening Questions* at the beginning of each chapter help the reader to begin to think about why the content of the chapter is important for social workers.
- *Key Ideas* are summarized at the beginning of each chapter to give readers an overview of what is to come.
- *Critical Thinking Questions* are presented throughout all chapters to encourage critical analysis of theory and research and assist the reader in recognizing and managing personal values.
- *Exhibits* are used throughout the chapters to summarize information in graphical or tabular form to help the reader understand and retain ideas.
- *Photographs* provide visual interest and human faces for abstract content.
- *Active Learning Exercises* are presented at the end of each chapter.
- *Implications for Social Work Practice* are included throughout the chapters and summarized as a set of practice principles at the end of each chapter to guide your use of general knowledge in social work practice.
- *Web Resources* appear at the end of each chapter to assist you with your further exploration of issues.

ONE LAST WORD _____

I imagine that you, like me, are intrigued with human behavior. That is probably a part of what attracted you to social work. I hope that reading this book reinforces your fascination with human behavior. I also hope that when you finish this book, and in the years to come, you will have new ideas about the possibilities for social work action.

Learning about human behavior is a lifelong process. You can help me in my learning process by letting me know what you liked or didn't like about the book.

—Elizabeth D. Hutchison
Rancho Mirage, California
ehutch@vcu.edu

ACKNOWLEDGMENTS

A project like this book is never completed without the support and assistance of many people. Steve Rutter, former publisher and president of Pine Forge Press, patiently shepherded every step of the many years of work to produce the first edition of the *Dimensions of Human Behavior* books. Along with Paul O'Connell, Becky Smith, and Maria Zuniga, he helped to refine the outline for the second edition of those books, and that outline continued to be used in the third and fourth editions.

The contributing authors and I are grateful for the assistance Dr. Maria E. Zuniga offered during the drafting of the second edition of the *Dimensions of Human Behavior* books. She contributed two case studies and provided many valuable suggestions of how to improve the coverage of cultural diversity in each chapter. Her suggestions have stayed with us as lasting lessons about human behavior in a multicultural society.

I am grateful once again to work with a fine group of contributing authors. They care about your learning and are committed to providing a state-of-the-art knowledge base for understanding the multiple dimensions of human behavior across the life course.

I am lucky to be working again with the folks at SAGE. It has been wonderful to have the disciplined and creative editorial assistance of Kassie Graves since she joined SAGE in early 2006. She has encouraged (gently nudged is more like it) me to bring this book to fruition for several years. She is a good friend to the authors with whom she works. Kassie has introduced me to a whole host of folks at SAGE that play a role in turning manuscripts into books and getting them into the hands of students and faculty. Associate Editor Leah Mori brought creative energy to some of the visual aspects of the book, and did so in a competent and pleasant way. I am happy to work with Karen Wiley as production editor again. I always look forward to the visual magic that she works. I am also happy to have the skillful assistance of Teresa Herlinger again; she is the best copy editor I know.

I am grateful to my former faculty colleagues at Virginia Commonwealth University (VCU), who set a high standard for scientific inquiry and teaching excellence. They also provided love and encouragement through both good and hard times. My conversations about the human behavior curriculum with colleagues Rosemary Farmer, Marcia Harrigan, Holly Matto, and Mary Secret over many years have stimulated much thinking and resulted in many ideas found in this book.

My students over almost 30 years also deserve a special note of gratitude. They taught me all the time, and many things that I have learned in interaction with them show up in the pages of this book. They also provided a great deal of joy to my life journey. Those moments when I learn of former students doing informed, creative, and humane social work are special moments indeed. I have also enjoyed receiving e-mail messages from students from other universities who are using the books and have found their insights to be very helpful.

My deepest gratitude goes to my husband, Hutch. Since the first edition of the *Dimensions of Human Behavior* books was published, we have weathered several challenging years and experienced many celebratory moments. He is constantly patient and supportive and often technically useful. But, more important, he makes sure that I don't forget that life can be great fun.

Finally, I am enormously grateful to a host of reviewers who provided very helpful feedback in the early stage of planning this briefer version of the *Dimensions of Human Behavior* books. Their ideas were very helpful in framing our work on this book.

Marian A. Aguilar, Texas A&M International University

Renee Daniel, Daemen College

Lawanna Lancaster, Northwest Nazarene University

Maria A. Spence, University of Akron

William D. Cabin, The Richard Stockton College

Jo Dee Gottlieb, Marshall University

Debra S. Norris, University of South Dakota

—*Elizabeth D. Hutchison*

To Juliet Rose Hutchison. I am so happy to share my life journey with you.

PART I

A Multidimensional, Multi-Theoretical Approach for Multifaceted Social Work

- Caroline O'Malley is knocking at the door of a family reported to her agency for child abuse.
- Sylvia Gomez and other members of her team at the rehabilitation hospital are meeting with the family of an 18-year-old man who is recovering from head injuries sustained in a motorcycle accident.
- Mark Bernstein is on the way to the county jail to assess the suicide risk of an inmate.
- Helen Moore is preparing a report for a legislative committee.
- Juanita Alvarez is talking with a homeless man about taking his psychotropic medications.
- Stan Weslowski is meeting with a couple who would like to adopt a child.
- Andrea Thomas is analyzing the results of a needs assessment recently conducted at the service center for older adults where she works.
- Anthony Pacino is wrapping up a meeting of a cancer support group.
- Sam Belick is writing a social history for tomorrow's team meeting at the high school where he works.
- Sarah Sahair has just begun a meeting of a recreational group of 9- and 10-year-old girls.
- Jane Kerr is facilitating the monthly meeting of an interagency coalition of service providers for substance-abusing women and their children.
- Ann Noles is planning a fund-raising project for the local Boys Club and Girls Club.
- Meg Hart is wrapping up her fourth counseling session with a lesbian couple.
- Chien Liu is meeting with a community group concerned about youth gang behavior in their neighborhood.
- Mary Wells is talking with one of her clients at the rape crisis center.
- Nagwa Nadi is evaluating treatment for post-traumatic stress disorder at a Veterans Administration Hospital.
- Devyani Hakakian is beginning her workday at an international advocacy organization devoted to women's rights.

What do these people have in common? You have probably guessed that they all are social workers. They work in a variety of settings, and they are involved in a variety of activities, but they all are doing social work. Social work is, indeed, a multifaceted profession. And because it is multifaceted, social workers need a multidimensional, multi-theoretical understanding of human behavior. This book provides such an understanding. The purpose of the two chapters in Part I is to introduce you to a multidimensional way of thinking about human behavior and to set the stage for subsequent discussion. In Chapter 1, you will be introduced to the multiple dimensions of person, environment, and time that serve as the framework for the book, and you will learn about social work's emphasis on diversity, inequality, and social justice. You also will be given some tools to think critically about the multiple theories and varieties of research that make up our general knowledge about these dimensions of human behavior. In Chapter 2, you will encounter eight theoretical perspectives that contribute to multidimensional understanding. You will learn about their central ideas and their scientific merits. Most important, you will consider the usefulness of these eight theoretical perspectives for social work.

CHAPTER 1

Setting the Stage

A Multidimensional Approach

Elizabeth D. Hutchison

 C3 ∞

C3 ∞

Opening Questions

What is it about people, environments, and time that social workers need to understand?

Why is it important for social workers to understand the roles that diversity and inequality play in human behavior?

Key Ideas

As you read this chapter, take note of these central ideas:

1. This book provides a multidimensional way of thinking about human behavior in terms of changing configurations of persons and environments.

2. Although person, environment, and time are inseparable, we can focus on them separately by thinking about the relevant dimensions of each.

3. Relevant personal dimensions include the biological, the psychological, and the spiritual.

4. Nine dimensions of environment that have relevance for social work are the physical environment, culture, social structure and social institutions, formal organizations, communities, social movements, small groups, families, and dyads. These dimensions have been studied separately, but they are neither mutually exclusive nor hierarchically ordered.

5. Social work puts special emphasis on diversity, inequality, and the pursuit of global social justice.

6. Knowledge about the case, knowledge about the self, values and ethics, and scientific knowledge are four important ingredients for moving from knowing to doing.

7. This book draws on two interrelated logical and systematic ways of building scientific knowledge: theory and empirical research.

CASE STUDY

Manisha's Quest for Dignity and Purpose

Manisha is a 57-year-old Bhutanese woman who resettled in the United States in early 2009. She is eager to tell her story, which she does with the help of an interpreter. Manisha describes her childhood as wonderful. She was the youngest of seven children born to a farming family in a rural village of Bhutan. Although there was little support for education in her community, especially for girls, Manisha's parents valued education, and she was one of five girls in her village school, where she was able to finish the second grade. As was tradition, she married young, at age 17, and became a homemaker for her husband, a contractor, and the four sons they later had. Manisha and her husband had a large plot of farmland and built a good life. They were able to develop some wealth and were sending their children to school. She says that they were managing well and living in peace.

In 1988, the political climate began to change and the good times ended. Manisha says she doesn't really understand how the problem started, because in Bhutan women were excluded from decision making and were given little information. As she talks, she begins to reflect that she has learned some things about what happened, but she still doesn't understand it. What she does recall is that the Bhutanese government began to discriminate against the Nepali ethnic group to which she belongs. News accounts indicate that the Druk Buddhist majority wanted to unite Bhutan under the Druk culture, religion, and language. The Nepalis had a separate culture and language and were mostly Hindu, while the Druks were Buddhist. Manisha says she does not know much about this, but she does recall that suddenly Nepalis were denied citizenship, were not allowed to speak their language, and could no longer get access to jobs. Within a family, different family members could be classified in different ways based on ethnicity.

Manisha recalls a woman who committed suicide as the discrimination grew worse. She also remembers that the Nepali people began to raise their voices and question what was happening. When this occurred, the Bhutanese government began to send soldiers to intimidate the villagers and undermine the Nepali resistance. It is evident that Manisha is controlling her emotions as she tells about cases of rape of Nepali women at the hands of the Bhutanese soldiers and recalls that the soldiers expected Nepali girls and women to be made available to them for sexual activity. She reports that government forces targeted Nepali families who had property and wealth, arresting them in the middle of the night and torturing and killing some. Families were forcefully evicted from their property. She recalls families who had to flee at night, sometimes leaving food on their tables.

One day when Manisha was at the market, the soldiers arrested her husband and took him to jail; she didn't know where he was for 2 days. He was in jail for 18 months. She remembers that she and her sons would hide out, carefully watch for soldiers, and sneak back home to cook. She was afraid to be at home. Finally, one day she was forced to report to the government office, and there she was told to leave and go to Nepal. She says that until then, she was just a simple housewife who was tending her gardens and cooking for her family. She told the government representative that she couldn't leave because her husband was in jail and she needed to care for her children. She tried to survive, living with other families, and she managed to live that way for a year.

Finally, Manisha heard that her husband would be released from jail on the condition that he leave the country. By this time, neighbors had started to flee, and only four households were left in her village. She sent her youngest son with friends and neighbors who were fleeing. A few days later, her husband was released. He said he was too afraid to stay in their home, and they too had to flee. Manisha did not want to leave, and as she tells her story, she still talks longingly of the property they had to leave behind. But the next morning, she and her husband and their other three sons fled the country. It was a 3-day walk to the Indian border, where the family joined the youngest son. Manisha and her family then lived on the banks of a river with other Nepalis who had fled. Her sons ranged in age from 6 to 19 at this time. Manisha recalls that many people died by the river and that there was "fever all around."

After 3 months, Manisha and her family were moved to a refugee camp in Nepal, the largest of seven Nepali refugee camps. They spent 17 years in the refugee camp before coming to the United States. The 18 months of imprisonment affected her husband such that he was not able to tolerate the close quarters of refugee camp living; he lived and worked in the adjacent Nepali community and came to visit his family. The four boys were able to attend school in the camp.

The camp was managed by the United Nations High Commissioner for Refugees (UNHCR), whose representatives started to build a forum for women. Manisha says that many of the women were, like her, from rural areas where they had been self-reliant, eating what they grew and taking care of their families. Now they were dependent on other people. The facilities at the camps were closely built and crowded. There was always a need for cash; the refugees were given food, but money was needed for other things, like clothes and personal hygiene items. Oxfam, an international aid organization, started a knitting program and the women were able to sell their knitted items, which provided much-needed cash. Manisha recalls that many of the women were emotionally disturbed and needed support. Some committed suicide. She began to provide moral support to other women and to disabled children, and she worked as the camp's Deputy Secretary for 3 years.

(Continued)

(Continued)

Manisha's family wanted desperately to get back to Bhutan, but they began to realize that that would not happen. They also learned that Nepal would not give citizenship to the refugees even though they had a shared culture. So, Manisha and her family decided to resettle in the United States where they had been assured by UNHCR workers that they would have a better life. The family resettled in three stages: First, Manisha and her husband came to the United States along with their youngest son and his wife. The older sons and their families resettled in two different waves of migration. They all live in close proximity. Some of Manisha's sons and daughters-in-law are working and some are not, but most are employed only part-time. Some work in hotel housekeeping, and one daughter-in-law works in a hospital. Manisha and her husband have not been able to find work, and she suggests that the language barrier is greater for them than for their sons and their families. She says they are all struggling financially and that they worry because they need to repay the costs of transportation from Nepal to the United States. But mostly, Manisha wants to find a job because she wants to make a contribution and have self-respect. In the camp in Nepal, she had been working and was on the go. Now, she says she lives behind closed doors. She and her husband are taking English as a second language (ESL) classes, but she feels strongly that she needs to be out at work so that she has a chance to practice English. She has given some thought to the type of work she could do, such as folding laundry or working in a school cafeteria. She thinks she could do those jobs, even with her limited English proficiency. She and her husband continue to practice their Hindu faith at home, but they are not able to attend the nearest Hindu Center, which is 15–20 miles from their apartment, as often as they would like. The social worker at the Refugee Resettlement Program is concerned about Manisha and other women like her who are isolated and unhappy.

—*Beverly B. Koerin and Elizabeth D. Hutchison*

SOCIAL WORK'S PURPOSE AND APPROACH: INDIVIDUAL AND COMMUNITY WELL-BEING

As eventful as it has been, Manisha's story is still unfolding. As a social worker, you will become a part of many unfolding life stories, and you will want to have useful ways to think about those stories and effective ways to be helpful to people like Manisha and her community of Bhutanese refugees. The purpose of this book is to provide ways for you to think about the nature and complexities of the people and situations that are at the center of social work practice. To begin to do that, we must first clarify the purpose of social work and the approach it takes to individual and collective human behavior. This is laid out in the 2008 *Educational Policy and Accreditation Standards* of the Council on Social Work Education (CSWE):

The purpose of the social work profession is to promote human and community well-being. Guided by a person and environment construct, a global perspective, respect for human diversity, and knowledge based on scientific inquiry, social work's purpose is actualized through its quest for social and economic justice, the prevention of conditions that limit human rights, the elimination of poverty, and the enhancement of the quality of life for all persons. (p. 1)

As noted in the preface, Section 2.1.7 of the policy lays out the guidelines for the human behavior and the social environment curriculum.

Social workers are knowledgeable about human behavior across the life course; the range of social systems in which people live; and the ways social systems promote or deter people in maintaining or achieving health and well-being. Social workers apply theories and knowledge from the liberal arts to understand biological, social, cultural, psychological, and spiritual development. (p. 6)

The first nine chapters of this book elaborate and update the person and environment construct that has guided social work intervention since the earliest days of the profession. The element of time is added to the person and environment construct to call attention to the dynamic nature of both people and environments. In the first nine chapters, the contributing authors and I identify multiple dimensions of both person and environment and draw on ongoing scientific inquiry, both conceptual and empirical, to examine the dynamic understanding of each dimension. Special attention is paid to globalization, diversity, human rights, and social and economic justice in examination of each dimension. The last seven chapters of the book (Chapters 10–16) have the specific purpose of presenting multidimensional understanding of human behavior across the life course, as mandated in Section 2.1.7.

In this chapter, the multidimensional approach to person and environment is presented, followed by a discussion of diversity, inequality, and the pursuit of social justice from a global perspective. After a brief description of the process by which professionals like social workers move from knowing to doing, the chapter ends with a discussion of how scientific knowledge from theory and research informs social work's multidimensional understanding of human behavior.

A MULTIDIMENSIONAL APPROACH

If we focus on the *person* in Manisha's story, it appears that she was born with a healthy biological constitution that allowed her to work on the family farms and nurture four sons. She describes no difficulty in managing the strenuous 3-day walk to the Indian border as she fled Bhutan. She survived while many people died by the river, and later, in the refugee camp, she survived and found new purpose when many others died of damaged bodies or broken spirits. We might wonder whether these hardships have taken their toll on her biological systems in ways that will show up later as health problems. We can wonder the same about the harsh conditions of her husband's 18-month imprisonment. Manisha appears to have emotional resilience, but she is struggling to maintain belief in her ability to find dignity and purpose in her new life in the United States. Her Hindu faith continues to be a source of comfort for her as she strives to maintain hope for the future.

If we focus on the *environment,* we see many influences on Manisha's story. Consider first the physical environment. Manisha lived in relative comfort, first on her father's and then on her husband's farm for almost 40 years, where she was able to spend much of her day outside, helping to turn farmland into food for her family. She still grieves the loss of land and the freedom she had to roam it. From there, she endured a long hike and a few months of survival in a poorly sheltered camp by the river. Her next stop was a crowded refugee camp where she faced a level of dependence she had not previously known. After 17 years, she left the camp with her family to establish a new life in the United States where she lives in a small apartment that leaves her feeling isolated.

Culture is an aspect of environment that exerts a powerful influence in Manisha's story. Culture influenced the fact that she received limited, if any, education and that she was married at what may appear to us to be an early age. Her culture also held that women should not have power and influence and are not to be involved in affairs outside the home, and yet Manisha assumed a powerful role in holding her family together after her husband was imprisoned. She also developed a very public role in the refugee camp and grieves the loss of that role in which she felt she was making a contribution to the public good. Although there were many challenges in the camp, she was living among people who shared her culture, language, and religion. She is struggling to adapt to a new, fast-moving culture where language is a constant barrier and her religious beliefs are in the minority. But culture is an important part of Manisha's story in another way. Culture clash and cultural imperialism led the Bhutanese government to discriminate against and then banish the Nepali ethnic group. Unfortunately, such cultural conflict is a source of great international upheaval.

Manisha's story has been powerfully influenced by the geopolitical unrest that began just as she was entering middle adulthood. Her relationships with social institutions have changed over time, and she has had to learn new rules based on her changing place in the social structure. Prior to 1988, she enjoyed high status in her village and the respect that comes with it. She lived in peace. She still does not understand why the Bhutanese government suddenly began to discriminate against her ethnic group, and she grieves the loss of property, status, and homeland that came out of this unrest. She is grateful to the United Nations for their support of the Bhutanese refugees and to the United States for welcoming some to resettle there. Unfortunately, she and her family resettled in the United States in the midst of the worst global economic recession since the Great Depression of the 1930s. They are all struggling to find work that will allow them to have some of the self-reliance they experienced in Bhutan.

Organizations and communities have been important forces in Manisha's life, but she has had little direct contact with social movements. Several organizations have been helpful to her and her family since they fled Bhutan. First, she is grateful to the UNHCR for all of the resources that they put into running the Nepali refugee camps. Second, she has high praise for Oxfam International that started the knitting program in the camps. In the United States, she is grateful for the assistance of the refugee resettlement program that sponsored her family, and is especially appreciative of the ESL program they run and the moral support provided by the social worker. She would like to have more contact with the Hindu Center, but the distance does not make that easy.

Manisha moved from a farming community, where she was surrounded by open land, extended family, and long-term friends, to a poorly sheltered camp by the river, where fear and confusion were the driving force of relationships and loss of loved ones was a much too common occurrence. Next, she moved to a crowded refugee camp, where disease and despair were common, but where she also found her voice and played an important role in helping other women and their children. She enjoyed her leadership position as Deputy Secretary of the camp and enjoyed the active life she created in this role. Now, she has moved to a city in the United States where many people are willing to help, but everything seems strange, and the language barrier is a serious impediment. She feels isolated and lonely in her small apartment.

Manisha is aware that some members of her Nepali ethnic group developed a resistance movement when the Bhutanese government began to discriminate against them. She is also aware that some refugees in the Nepali refugee camps have resisted the idea of resettlement to the United States and other countries because they think that resettlement will dilute the pressure on Bhutan to repatriate the Nepalis. As much as Manisha would love to be repatriated, she and her family decided that resettlement in the United States was their best chance for a good future.

Some small groups have been important to Manisha's adjustment to changing circumstances. In the refugee camp, she participated in some focus groups that the UNHCR conducted with the women in the camps. She is enjoying the relationships she is developing with her ESL class; she draws courage from the companionship and the collegial sense of "we are all in the same boat" that she gets from the weekly classes.

Family is paramount to Manisha. She is lucky to have her husband living with her again and all of her children nearby. None of her siblings was resettled in the same city, however, and they are spread across several countries at this time. Some are still in the Nepali camp awaiting resettlement. She is not even sure what has happened to much of her large extended family. Manisha's children and grandchildren are central to her life, and they give her hope for the future. Manisha and her husband are devoted to each other, but must adjust to living together again after living in separate quarters for many years. In some ways, Manisha led a much more independent life in the refugee camp than back in Bhutan, and she came to value that independence. She and her husband are still negotiating this change from traditional gender roles. Her husband has enormous sadness about all that the family lost after the situation changed for them in Bhutan, including the loss of social status and self-reliance.

Time is also an important part of Manisha's story, and there are many trace effects of earlier times in her current story. She thinks of her 40 years in Bhutan as a time that moved by too fast, but left her with many happy memories that she now cherishes. The 17 years in the refugee camp seemed to move very slowly at first, but Manisha was able to develop a rhythm to her life that kept time moving. These were also years when Manisha and her husband lived in separate quarters, and their relationship still suffers from having had such a long period of partial separation. Experiences with past environments have left them with a preference for rural environments and a discomfort with too much privacy, which they experience as isolation. Discrimination, imprisonment, escape, crowded camp conditions, and resettlement have been powerful life events for Manisha and her family and continue to affect their current life. Most notably, Manisha's husband is uncomfortable in situations involving confinement, food shortage, or harsh authority figures, which appears to be related to the 18 months he spent in jail, an experience he does not talk about, not even with Manisha. Both Manisha and her husband still grieve the loss of their farm and long to see it again. They also long for a time of life that was much simpler, living with their children on their farm with family and friends all around. The language barrier where they now live is the most persistent reminder that this is not home, but it takes on special meaning because it reminds them of the time when the Bhutanese government prohibited the use of the Nepali language in schools. Manisha sees that her children and grandchildren are living in the present rather than the past, and she is trying to do that as well.

Manisha's story is a good illustration of the dynamic nature of the person and environment over time. In addition, it illustrates why the person and environment must be put within the context of time. What made Manisha decide to take an active role in providing support and comfort to other women in the refugee camp? Was it something within her, something about her physical and social environment, or something about her life course phase? Or a combination of all three? What will her life be like in 10 years? How about the lives of her husband, her children, and her grandchildren? What factors will influence their futures? How will they look back on this time in their lives? It is impossible to focus on person, environment, and time independently; they are inseparable.

As suggested above, social work has historically recognized human behavior as an interaction of person with environment. The earliest social work practice book, *Social Diagnosis,* written by Mary Richmond in 1917, identified the social situation and the personality of the client as the dual foci of social work assessment. The settlement house movement put heavy emphasis on the environmental elements of person–environment interactions, but environment was deemphasized, and intrapsychic factors were emphasized when social work began to rely on psychodynamic theory in the 1920s. In the late 1960s, however, social work scholars began to focus on the environment again when general systems theory and other related formulations were incorporated into the way social work scholars think about human behavior (R. E. Anderson & Carter, 1974; M. Bloom, 1984; Germain, 1973; Hartman, 1970; G. Hearn, 1958, 1969; C. Meyer, 1976; Pincus & Minahan, 1973; Siporin, 1975).

In recent times, ecological theory, which addresses the relationships between organisms and their environments, has become the dominant theoretical approach across a number of behavioral science disciplines (Gardiner & Kosmitzki, 2008). These approaches have renewed social workers' interest in the social sciences and helped them to understand the processes and activities involved in the relationships between person and environment. The multidimensional approach of this book is rooted in the systems perspective.

Today, a vast multidisciplinary literature, of both theory and research, is available to help us in our social work efforts. The good news is that the multifaceted nature of this literature provides a broad knowledge base for the varied settings and roles involved in social work practice. The bad news is that this literature is highly fragmented, "scattered across more than thirty fields" (Kirk & Reid, 2002, p. 207). What we need is a structure for organizing our thinking about this multifaceted, multidisciplinary, fragmented literature.

The multidimensional approach provided in this book should help. This approach is built on the three major elements of human behavior: person, environment, and time. Although we focus on each of these elements separately, keep in mind that no single element can be entirely understood without attention to the other elements. Person, environment, and time are not simple concepts, and they can best be thought of as **multidimensional**,

that is, as having several identifiable dimensions. We can get a clearer picture of these three elements if we think about the important dimensions of each—about what it is that we should study about person, about environment, and about time. Exhibit 1.1 is a graphic overview of the dimensions of person, environment, and time discussed in this book. Exhibit 1.2 defines and gives examples for each dimension.

Keep in mind that **dimension** refers to a feature that can be focused on separately but that cannot be understood without also considering other features. The dimensions identified in this book are usually studied as detached or semidetached realities, with one dimension characterized as causing or leading to another. However, I do not see dimensions as detached realities, and I am not presenting a causal model here. I want instead to show how these dimensions work together, how they are embedded with each other, and how many possibilities are opened for social work practice when we think about human behavior this way. I am suggesting that humans engage in

Exhibit 1.1   Person, Environment, and Time Dimensions

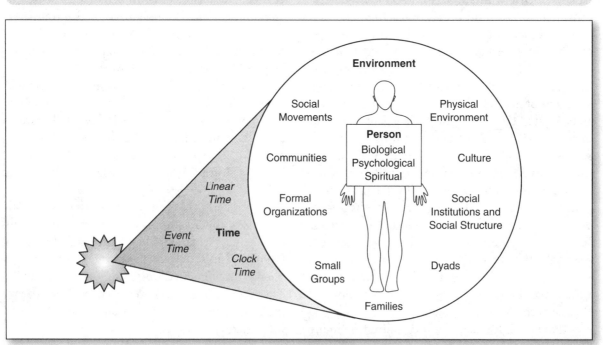

Exhibit 1.2 Definitions and Examples of Dimensions of Person, Environment, and Time

Dimension	Definition	Examples
Personal Dimensions		
The Biological Person	The body's biochemical, cell, organ, and physiological systems	Nervous system, endocrine system, immune system, cardiovascular system, musculoskeletal system, reproductive system
The Psychological Person	The mind and the mental processes	Cognitions (conscious thinking processes), emotion (feelings), self (identity)
The Spiritual Person	The aspect of the person that searches for meaning and purpose in life	Themes of morality; ethics; justice; interconnectedness; creativity; mystical states; prayer, meditation, and contemplation; relationships with a higher power
Environmental Dimensions		
The Physical Environment	The natural and human-built material aspects of the environment	Water, sun, trees, buildings, landscapes
Culture	A set of common understandings, evident in both behavior and material artifacts	Beliefs, customs, traditions, values
Social Structure and Social Institutions	Social structure: A set of interrelated social institutions developed by humans to impose constraints on human interaction for the purpose of the survival and well-being of the collectivity	Social structure: social class
	Social institutions: Patterned ways of organizing social relations in a particular sector of social life	Social institutions: government, economy, education, health care, social welfare, religion, mass media, and family
Formal Organizations	Collectivities of people, with a high degree of formality of structure, working together to meet a goal or goals	Civic and social service organizations, business organizations, professional associations
Communities	People bound either by geography or by network links (webs of communication), sharing common ties, and interacting with one another	Territorial communities such as neighborhoods; relational communities such as the social work community, the disability community, a faith community, a soccer league
Social Movements	Large-scale collective actions to make change, or resist change, in specific social institutions	Civil rights movement, poor people's movement, disability movement, gay rights movement

(Continued)

Exhibit 1.2 (Continued)

Dimension	Definition	Examples
Small Groups	Collections of people who interact with each other, perceive themselves as belonging to a group, are interdependent, join together to accomplish a goal, fulfill a need through joint association, or are influenced by a set of rules and norms	Friendship group, self-help group, therapy group, committee, task group, interdisciplinary team
Families	A social group of two or more persons, characterized by ongoing interdependence with long-term commitments that stem from blood, law, or affection	Nuclear family, extended family, chosen family
Dyads	Two persons bound together in some way	Parent and child, romantic couple, social worker and client
Time Dimensions		
Clock Time	Time in terms of clocks and calendars	Hours, days, workdays, weekends
Event Time	Time in terms of signals from the body and from nature	Hunger signals time to eat; natural signs signal time to plant and harvest
Linear Time	Time in terms of a straight line	Past, present, future

multidetermined behavior, that is, behavior that develops as a result of many causes. I do think, however, that focusing on specific dimensions one at a time can help to clarify general, abstract statements about person and environment—that is, it can put some flesh on the bones of this idea.

Personal Dimensions

Any story could be told from the perspective of any person in the story. The story at the beginning of this chapter is told from Manisha's perspective, but it could have been told from the perspective of a variety of other persons such as the Bhutanese king, Manisha's husband, one of her children, one of her grandchildren, a UNHCR staff member, one of the women supported by Manisha in the camp, the social worker at the refugee resettlement agency, or Manisha's ESL teacher. You will want to recognize the multiple perspectives held by different persons

involved in the stories of which you become a part in your social work activities.

You also will want tools for thinking about the various dimensions of the persons involved in these stories. For many years, social work scholars described the approach of social work as *psychosocial,* giving primacy to psychological dimensions of the person. Personality, ego states, emotion, and cognition are the important features of the person in this approach. Currently, however, social workers, like contemporary scholars in other disciplines (e.g., Bandura, 2001; E. Garland & Howard, 2009; C. MacDonald & Mikes-Liu, 2009; Sadock & Sadock, 2007; P. White, 2005), take a **biopsychosocial approach.** In this approach, human behavior is considered to be the result of interactions of integrated biological, psychological, and social systems. Psychology is seen as inseparable from biology; emotions and cognitions affect the health of the body and are affected by it (Adelman, 2006).

Increasingly, neurobiologists write about the "social brain," recognizing that the human brain is wired for social life, but also that the social environment has an impact on brain structure and processes (Cacioppo et al., 2007; Frith & Frith, 2010).

In recent years, social work scholars as well as scholars in the social and behavioral sciences and medicine have also argued for greater attention to the spiritual dimension of persons (Carley, 2005; Faull & Hills, 2006; Richards, 2005; Watts, Dutton, & Gulliford, 2006). Developments in neuroscience have generated new explorations of the unity of the biological, psychological, and spiritual dimensions of the person. For example, recent research has focused on the ways that emotions and thoughts, as well as spiritual states, influence the immune system (Kimura et al., 2005; Woods, Antoni, Ironson, & Kling, 1999) and health practices (C. Park, Edmondson, Hale-Smith, & Blank, 2009). One research team has explored the impact of spirituality and religiosity on mental health and found that thankfulness protects against major depression (Kendler et al., 2003). In this book, we give substantial coverage to all three of these personal dimensions: biological, psychological, and spiritual.

Environmental Dimensions

Social workers have always thought of the environment as multidimensional. As early as 1901, Mary Richmond presented a model of case coordination that took into account not only personal dimensions but also family, neighborhood, civic organizations, private charitable organizations, and public relief organizations (see Exhibit 1.3). Like contemporary social workers, Richmond saw the environment as multidimensional, including in her model many of the same dimensions of environment covered in this book and presented in Exhibit 1.1.

Several models for classifying dimensions of the environment have been proposed since Mary Richmond's time. Among social work scholars, Ralph Anderson and Irl Carter made a historic contribution to systemic thinking about human

behavior with the first edition of their *Human Behavior in the Social Environment: A Social Systems Approach* (1974), one of the earliest textbooks on human behavior authored by social workers. Their classification of environmental dimensions has had a significant impact on the way social workers think about the environment. Anderson and Carter divided the environment into five dimensions: culture and society, communities, organizations, groups, and families.

Social workers (see, e.g., Ashford, LeCroy, & Lortie, 2010) have also been influenced by Uri Bronfenbrenner's (1989, 1999) ecological perspective, which identifies four interdependent, nested categories or levels of systems:

1. *Microsystems* are systems that involve direct, face-to-face contact between members.

2. *Mesosystems* are networks of microsystems of a given person.

3. *Exosystems* are the linkages between microsystems and larger institutions that affect the system, such as the family system and the parent's workplace or the family system and the child's school.

4. *Macrosystems* are the broader influences of culture, subculture, and social structure.

Some recent models have added the physical environment (natural and designed environments) as a separate dimension. Failure to include the physical environment has most notably hampered social work's ability to respond to persons with physical disabilities. Recent research on the connection between the physical environment and healing has special relevance for social workers in many settings.

To have an up-to-date understanding of the multidimensional environment, social workers need knowledge about the eight dimensions of environment described in Exhibit 1.2 and discussed in Chapters 6–9 in this book: the physical environment, culture, social structure and social institutions, formal organizations, communities, social movements, small groups, and families.

Exhibit 1.3   Mary Richmond's 1901 Model of Case Coordination

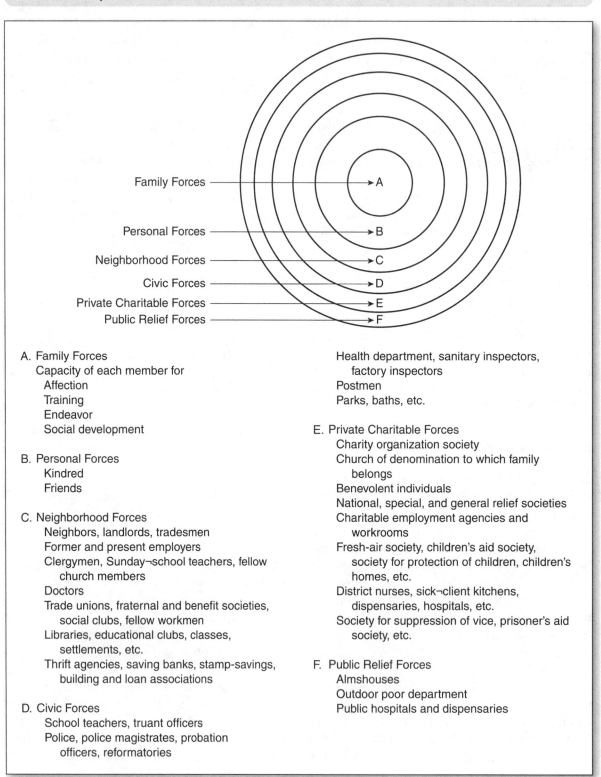

Family Forces → A

Personal Forces → B

Neighborhood Forces → C

Civic Forces → D

Private Charitable Forces → E

Public Relief Forces → F

A. Family Forces
  Capacity of each member for
    Affection
    Training
    Endeavor
    Social development

B. Personal Forces
    Kindred
    Friends

C. Neighborhood Forces
    Neighbors, landlords, tradesmen
    Former and present employers
    Clergymen, Sunday¬school teachers, fellow
      church members
    Doctors
    Trade unions, fraternal and benefit societies,
      social clubs, fellow workmen
    Libraries, educational clubs, classes,
      settlements, etc.
    Thrift agencies, saving banks, stamp-savings,
      building and loan associations

D. Civic Forces
    School teachers, truant officers
    Police, police magistrates, probation
      officers, reformatories

    Health department, sanitary inspectors,
      factory inspectors
    Postmen
    Parks, baths, etc.

E. Private Charitable Forces
    Charity organization society
    Church of denomination to which family
      belongs
    Benevolent individuals
    National, special, and general relief societies
    Charitable employment agencies and
      workrooms
    Fresh-air society, children's aid society,
      society for protection of children, children's
      homes, etc.
    District nurses, sick¬client kitchens,
      dispensaries, hospitals, etc.
    Society for suppression of vice, prisoner's aid
      society, etc.

F. Public Relief Forces
    Almshouses
    Outdoor poor department
    Public hospitals and dispensaries

We also need knowledge about dyadic relationships—relationships between two people, the most basic social relationships. Dyadic relationships receive attention throughout the book and are emphasized in Chapter 4 in discussion of the self in relationships. Simultaneous consideration of multiple environmental dimensions provides new possibilities for action, perhaps even new or revised approaches to social work practice.

These dimensions are neither mutually exclusive nor hierarchically ordered. For example, a family is sometimes referred to as a social institution, families can also be considered small groups or dyads, and family theorists write about family culture. Remember, dimensions are useful ways of thinking about person-environment configurations, but you should not think of them as detached realities.

Time Dimensions

When I was a doctoral student in a social work practice course, Professor Max Siporin began his discussion about social work assessment with the comment, "The date is the most important information on a written social work assessment." This was Siporin's way of acknowledging the importance of time in human behavior, of recognizing that person–environment transactions are ever-changing, dynamic, and flowing.

We are aware of the time dimension in the ongoing process of migration in Manisha's story. And, you may be interested, as I am, in the process of acculturation in which she and her family are now engaged. As will be discussed in Chapter 6, **acculturation** is a process of changing one's culture by incorporating elements of another culture. When the Bhutanese government tried to impose a different culture, religion, and language on the Nepali ethnic group, they, not surprisingly, resisted. In the refugee camps, their culture, religion, and language were practiced without conflict. Now that they have resettled in the United States, they must find a way to live in a multicultural society that is nevertheless dominated by Anglo culture, Christianity, and the English language. Think about the complexity of the developmental tasks involved in adapting to that culture change.

Photo 1.1 Three elements of human behavior are captured in this photo—person, environment, and time.

Acculturation happens over time, in a nonlinear process, with new situations and opportunities to learn, negotiate, and accommodate. Manisha recognizes that her development of English proficiency skills depends to a large degree on opportunities to be in situations where she must use those skills and observe other people using the English language. She is interested in learning about her new culture's roles while still keeping her culture of origin. No doubt she will become bicultural over time, given her adaptability in developing new gender roles in the refugee camp. Most likely, the different members of her family will acculturate at different paces, with her grandchildren leading the way (Bush, Bohon, & Kim, 2010). Twenty years ago, research indicated that men adapted to cultural change faster than women, but more recent research indicates that immigrant women often have a faster pace of acculturation than their spouses (Falicov, 2003).

When I think of time, I tend to think of clocks, calendars, and appointments. Moreover, I often seem to be racing against time, allowing the clock to tell me when an event should begin and end. This is the way most people in affluent countries with market economies think of time. This approach to time has been called *clock time* (Lauer, 1981; R. Levine, 2006). However, this approach to time is a relatively new invention, and many people in the contemporary world have a very different approach (Rosen, 2004). In nonindustrialized countries, and in subcultures within industrialized countries, people operate on *event time,* allowing scheduling to be determined by events. Robert Levine (2006) provides numerous examples of event time. Signals from the body, rather than the hour on the clock, dictate when to eat. Activities are guided by seasonal changes; when the rainy season comes, it is time for planting. Appointments are flexible: "I will see you tomorrow morning when the cows go out to graze." The length of an event may be explained by saying, for example, "The storm lasted as long as a rice-cooking." Monks in Burma have developed their own alarm clocks, knowing it is time to get up when there is enough light to see the veins in their hands (Thompson, 1967, cited in R. Levine, 2006). In agricultural societies, the most successful farmers are the ones who can be responsive to natural events rather than to scheduled events. Manisha's life was organized around cues from the natural world rather than the clock when she lived in Bhutan, just as my grandfather's was on his farm in rural Tennessee.

Anthropologists report that some event time cultures, such as that of the Hopi of the U.S. Southwest and some Arab cultures, have no language to distinguish past, present, and future time. However, clock time cultures often use the concept of **time orientation** to describe the extent to which individuals and collectivities are invested

Photo 1.2 Time is one of the three elements outlined in this text for studying human behavior. It recognizes that people and environments are ever-changing, dynamic, and flowing.

in three temporal zones—past, present, and future time—known as **linear time.** Research indicates that cultures differ in their time orientation. Traditional cultures are more invested in the past, and advanced industrial cultures are more invested in the future (Hofstede, 1998). In reality, some situations call for us to be totally immersed in the present, others call for historical understanding of the past and its impact on the present, and still others call for attention to future consequences and possibilities. Recently, Western behavioral scientists have begun to incorporate Eastern mindfulness practices of being more fully present in the current moment (present orientation) to help people buffer the persistent stresses of clock time and goal monitoring (future orientation) (see, e.g., Boyatzis & McKee, 2005). People in fast-paced clock time societies often berate those who are less attentive to the clock while at the same time bemoaning the hold the clock has on them. Research also indicates that there are age-related differences in time orientation, with older adults being more past oriented than younger age groups (Shmotkin, 1991). There are also individual variations in time orientation. For example, researchers have found that trauma survivors who experienced the most severe loss are more likely than other trauma survivors to be highly oriented to the past (Holman & Silver, 1998; E. Martz, 2004). This is something to keep in mind when we interact with refugees, military men and women who have served in war zones, and other groups who have an increased likelihood of having a history of trauma. It is also important for social workers to be aware of the meaning of time for the individuals and communities they serve.

Sometimes the pace of change is more rapid than at other times—for example, the pace of change accelerated in 1988 for Manisha and her family and again when they resettled in the United States. There is also a temporal scope, or duration, to social and personal change. In linear time, the scope of some events is brief, such as a birthday party, an automobile accident, termination from a job, winning the lottery, or a natural disaster. Werner, Altman, and Oxley (1985) refer to these brief events as *incidents;* in this book, they are

called *life events.* Although life events are brief in scope, they may produce shifts and have serious and long-lasting effects. It is important to note the role of perception when discussing both the pace of change and the duration of an event (Rappaport, Enrich, & Wilson, 1985). It is easy to imagine that the 3 months that Manisha and her family spent in the camp by the river seemed longer than 3 months in a more peaceful time on their farm in Bhutan.

Other events are long and complex transactions of people and environments. Werner et al. (1985) refer to these longer events as *stages;* it is this dimension of time that has been incorporated into life stage theories of human behavior. As will be explained in Chapter 2, however, life stage theories have been criticized for their overstatement of the universality of the sequence of stages and of the timing of human behavior. In contrast, a *life course perspective* assumes that each person's life has a unique long-term pattern of stability and change, but that shared social and historical contexts produce a number of commonalities. In some ways, Manisha's life journey is unique, but in other ways, her journey is similar to that of other members of the Nepali ethnic group from Bhutan. The life course perspective is the framework used in Part III of this book to discuss phases of human life.

Critical Thinking Questions 1.1

How would our understanding of Manisha's story change if we had no knowledge of her prior life experiences in Bhutan and the Nepali refugee camp—if we only assessed her based on her current functioning? What person and environment dimensions would we note in her current functioning?

DIVERSITY, INEQUALITY, AND THE PURSUIT OF SOCIAL JUSTICE: A GLOBAL PERSPECTIVE

The Council on Social Work Education requires that social work educational programs provide a global perspective to their students. What exactly does that mean, and why is it valued? We are increasingly aware that we are part of an interconnected world, and Manisha's story is one reminder of this. But just how connected are we? In her book *Beyond Borders: Thinking Critically about Global Issues,* Paula Rothenberg (2006) writes, "A not so funny, but perhaps sadly true, joke going around claims that people in the United States learn geography by going to war" (p. xv). Certainly, we in the United States have learned something about the maps of Afghanistan and Iraq, but what do we know about the map of Bhutan? A global perspective involves much more than geography, however. Here are some aspects of what it means to take a global perspective:

- To be aware that my view of the world is not universally shared, and that others may have a view of the world that is profoundly different from mine
- To have a growing awareness of the diversity of ideas and cultural practices found in human societies around the world
- To be curious about conditions in other parts of the world and how they relate to conditions in our own society
- To understand where I fit in global social institutions and social structure
- To have a growing awareness of how people in other societies view my society
- To have a growing understanding of how the world works, with special attention paid to systems and mechanisms of inequality and oppression around the world

We have always been connected to other peoples of the world, but those connections are being intensified by the process of **globalization,** a process by which the world's peoples are becoming more interconnected economically, politically, environmentally, and culturally. This increasing connectedness is, of course, aided by rapid advancements in communication technology. There is much debate about whether globalization is a good thing or a bad thing, a conversation that will be picked up in Chapter 7 as we consider the globalization of social institutions. What is important to note here is that globalization is increasing our experiences with social diversity and raising new questions about inequality, human rights, and social justice.

Diversity

Diversity has always been a part of the social reality in the United States. Even before the Europeans came, the Indigenous people were divided into about 200 distinct societies with about 200 different languages (Parrillo, 2009). Since the inception of the nation of the United States of America, we have been a nation of immigrants. We value our nation's immigrant heritage and take pride in the ideals of equality of opportunity for all who come. However, there have always been tensions about how we as a nation will handle diversity. Will we be a *melting pot* where all are melted into one indistinguishable model of citizenship, or will we be a *pluralist society* in which groups have separate identities, cultures, and ways of organizing but work together in mutual respect? Pioneer social worker Jane Addams was a prominent voice for pluralism during the early 20th century, and that stance is consistent with social work's concern for human rights.

However, it is accurate to say that some of the diversity in our national social life is new. Clearly, there is increasing racial, ethnic, and religious diversity in the United States, and the mix in the population stream has become much more complex in recent years (Parrillo, 2009). The United States was 87% White in 1925, it was 80% White in 1950, and was 72% White in 2000; by 2050, it is projected that we will be about 50% White (Prewitt, 2000). Why is this happening at this time? A major driving force is the demographic reality that native-born people are no longer reproducing at a replacement level in the wealthy postindustrial nations, which, if it continues, ultimately will lead to a declining population skewed toward advanced age. One solution used by some countries, including the United States, is to change immigration policy to allow new streams of immigration. The current number of foreign-born persons in the United States is lower than it has been throughout most of the past 150 years, but foreign-born persons are less likely to be White than when immigration policy, prior to 1965, strictly limited entry to persons of color. With the recent influx of immigrants from around the globe, the United States has become one of many ethnically and racially diverse nations in the world today. In many wealthy postindustrial countries, including the United States, there is much anti-immigrant sentiment, even though the economies of these countries are dependent on such migration. Waves of immigration have usually been accompanied by anti-immigrant sentiment. There appear to be many reasons for this, including fear that new immigrants will dilute the "purity" of the native culture, racial and religious bias, and fear of economic competition. Like other diverse societies, we must find ways to embrace the diversity and seize the opportunity to demonstrate the human capacity for intergroup harmony.

On the other hand, some of the diversity in our social life is not new but simply newly recognized. In the contemporary era, we have been developing a heightened consciousness of human differences—gender differences, racial and ethnic differences, cultural differences, religious differences, differences in sexual orientation, differences in abilities and disabilities, differences in family forms, and so on. We are experiencing a new tension in navigating the line between cultural sensitivity and stereotypical thinking about individuals and groups. It is the intent of this book to capture the diversity of human experience in a manner that is respectful of all groups, conveys the positive value of human diversity, and recognizes differences *within* groups as well as differences *among* groups.

As you seek to honor differences, keep in mind the distinction between heterogeneity and diversity (Calasanti, 1996). **Heterogeneity** refers to *individual-level* variations—differences among individuals. For example, as the social worker whom Manisha consults, you will want to recognize the ways in which she is different from you and from other clients you serve, including other clients of Bhutanese heritage. An understanding of heterogeneity allows us to recognize the uniqueness of each person and situation. **Diversity,** on the

other hand, refers to *patterns* of group differences. Diversity recognizes social groups—groups of people who share a range of physical, cultural, or social characteristics within a category of social identity. As a social worker, besides recognizing individual differences, you will also want to be aware of the diversity in your community, such as the distribution of various ethnic groups, including those of Bhutanese heritage. Knowledge of diversity helps us to provide culturally sensitive practice.

I want to interject a word here about terminology and human diversity. As the contributing authors and I attempted to uncover what is known about human diversity, we struggled with terminology to define identity groups. We searched for consistent language to describe different groups, and we were dedicated to using language that identity groups would use to describe themselves. However, we ran into challenges endemic to our time, related to the language of diversity. It is not the case that all members of a given identity group at any given time embrace the same terminology for their group. As I write this paragraph, I am listening to news reports about the political uproar over Senator Harry Reid's use of the word *Negro* to refer to President Barack Obama. Yesterday, I heard a news report about the U.S. Census Bureau using Negro as a racial category in the 2010 census. Staff at the Census Bureau argued that this is the term preferred by older African Americans. However, the young African American reporter said the word is not in his vocabulary. Similar examples could be found for other ethnic groups. As we reviewed literature from different historical moments, we recognized the shifting nature of terminology. In addition, even within a given historical era, we found that different researchers used different terms and had different decision rules about who composes the membership of identity groups. Add to this the changing way that the U.S. Census Bureau establishes official categories of people, and in the end, we did not settle on fixed terminology to consistently describe identity groups. Rather, we use the language of individual researchers when reporting their work, because we want to avoid distorting their work. We hope you will not find this too distracting. We also hope you will recognize that the ever-changing language of diversity has both constructive potential to find creative ways to affirm diversity and destructive potential to dichotomize diversity into *the norm* and *the other*.

Inequality

Attending to diversity involves recognition of the power relations between social groups and the patterns of opportunities and constraints for social groups. If we are interested in the Bhutanese community in our city, for example, we will want to note, among other things, the neighborhoods where they live, the quality of the housing stock in those neighborhoods, the comparative educational attainment in the community, the occupational profile of the community, and the comparative income levels. When we attend to diversity, we not only note the differences between groups, but we also note how socially constructed hierarchies of power are superimposed on these differences.

Recent U.S. scholarship in the social sciences has emphasized the ways in which three types of categorization—gender, race, and class—are used to develop hierarchical social structures that influence social identities and life chances (Rothenberg, 2007; Sernau, 2006). This literature suggests that these social categorizations create **privilege**, or unearned advantage, for some groups and disadvantage for other groups. In a much-cited article, Peggy McIntosh (2007, first printed in 1988) has pointed out the mundane daily advantages of White privilege that are not available to members of groups of color, such as, "can be sure that my children will be given curricular materials that testify to the existence of their race" and "Whether I use checks, credit cards, or cash, I can count on my skin color not to work against the appearance of financial reliability" (p. 179). We could also generate lists of advantages of male privilege, adult privilege, upper-middle-class privilege, heterosexual privilege, ability privilege, Christian privilege, and so on. McIntosh argues that members of privileged groups benefit from their privilege but have not been taught to think of themselves as privileged.

They take for granted that their advantages are "normal and universal" (L. Bell, 1997, p. 12). For survival, members of nonprivileged groups must learn a lot about the lives of groups with privilege, but groups with privileged status are not similarly compelled to learn about the lives of members of nonprivileged groups.

Michael Schwalbe (2006) argues that those of us who live in the United States also carry "American privilege," which comes from our dominant position in the world. (I would prefer to call this "U.S. privilege," since people living in Canada, Ecuador, and Brazil also live in America.) According to Schwalbe, among other things, American privilege means that we don't have to bother to learn about other countries or about the impact of our foreign policy on people living in those countries. Perhaps that is what Rothenberg (2006) was thinking of when she noted the ignorance of world geography among people living in the United States. American privilege also means that we have access to cheap goods that are produced by poorly paid workers in impoverished countries. As you will see in Chapter 7, the income and wealth gap between nations is mind-boggling. Sernau (2006) reports that the combined income of the 25 richest people in the United States is almost as great as the combined income of 2 billion of the world's poorest people. The average per capita income in Bhutan is $1,440 in U.S. dollars, compared to $46,040 in the United States (UNICEF, n.d.). It is becoming increasingly difficult to deny the costs of exercising American privilege to remain ignorant about the rest of the world and the impact our actions have on other nations.

As the contributing authors and I strive to provide a global context, we encounter current controversies about appropriate language to describe different sectors of the world. Following World War II, a distinction was made among First World, Second World, and Third World nations, with First World referring to the Western capitalist nations, Second World referring to the countries belonging to the socialist bloc led by the Soviet Union, and Third World referring to a set of countries that were primarily former colonies of the First World.

More recently, many scholars have used this same language to define global sectors in a slightly different way. *First World* has been used to describe the nations that were the first to industrialize, urbanize, and modernize. *Second World* has been used to describe nations that have industrialized but have not yet become central to the world economy. *Third World* has been used to refer to nonindustrialized nations that have few resources and are considered expendable in the global economy. However, this approach has begun to lose favor in the past few years (Leeder, 2004). Immanuel Wallerstein (1974, 1979) uses different language but makes a similar distinction; he refers to wealthy *core* countries, newly industrialized *semiperiphery* countries, and the poorest *periphery* countries. Other writers divide the world into *developed* and *developing* countries, referring to the level of industrialization, urbanization, and modernization. Still others divide the world into the *Global North* and the *Global South,* calling attention to a history in which the Global North colonized and exploited the resources of the Global South. Finally, some writers talk about the *West* versus the *East,* where the distinctions are largely cultural. We recognize that such categories carry great symbolic meaning and can mask systems of power and exploitation. As with diversity, we attempted to find a respectful language that could be used consistently throughout the book. Again, we found that different researchers have used different language and different characteristics to describe categories of nations, and when reporting on their findings, we have used their own language to avoid misrepresenting their results.

It is important to note that privilege and disadvantage are multidimensional, not one-dimensional. One can be privileged in one dimension and disadvantaged in another; for example, I have White privilege but not gender privilege, as a female. As social workers, we need to be attuned to our own *social locations,* where we fit in a system of social identities, such as race, ethnicity, gender, social class, sexual orientation, religion, ability/disability, and age. We must recognize how our own particular social locations shape how we see the world, what we notice, and how we interpret what we "see."

This is not easy for us, because in the United States, as a rule, we avoid the topic of class and don't like to admit that it shapes our lives (Sernau, 2006). It is important for social workers to acknowledge social inequalities, however, because our interactions are constantly affected by them. In addition, there is clear evidence that social inequalities are on the rise in the United States. In the last couple of decades, the United States gained the distinction as the most unequal society in the postindustrial world, and the gap continued to widen in the midst of the deep economic recession that officially began in December 2007 (Sernau, 2006).

The Pursuit of Social Justice

There is another important reason that social workers must acknowledge social inequalities. The National Association of Social Workers (NASW) Code of Ethics (1999) identifies social justice as one of six core values of social work and mandates that "Social Workers challenge social injustice" p. 3). To challenge injustice, we must first recognize it and understand the ways that it is embedded in a number of societal institutions. That will be the subject of Chapter 7.

Suzanne Pharr (1988) has provided some useful conceptual tools that can help us recognize injustice when we see it. She identifies a set of mechanisms of oppression, whereby the everyday arrangements of social life systematically block opportunities for some groups and inhibit their power to exercise self-determination. Exhibit 1.4 provides an overview of these mechanisms of oppression. As you review the list, you may recognize some that are familiar to you, such as stereotyping and perhaps blaming the victim. There may be others to which you have not previously given much thought. You may also recognize, as I do each time I look at the list, that while some of these mechanisms of oppression are sometimes used quite intentionally, others are not so intentional but occur as we do business as usual. For example, when you walk into your classroom, do you give much thought to the person who cleans that room, what wage this person is paid, whether this is the only job this person holds, and what opportunities

Exhibit 1.4 Common Mechanisms of Oppression

Economic Power and Control	Limiting of resources, mobility, education, and employment options to all but a few
Myth of Scarcity	Myth used to pit people against one another, suggests that resources are limited and blames people (e.g., poor people, immigrants) for using too many of them
Defined Norm	A standard of what is good and right, against which all are judged
The Other	Those who fall outside "the norm" but are defined in relation to it, seen as abnormal, inferior, marginalized
Invisibility	Keeping "the other's" existence, everyday life, and achievements unknown
Distortion	Selective presentation or rewriting of history so that only negative aspects of "the other" are included
Stereotyping	Generalizing the actions of a few to an entire group, denying individual characteristics and behaviors
Violence and the Threat of Violence	Laying claim to resources, then using might to ensure superior position
Lack of Prior Claim	Excluding anyone who was not originally included and labeling as disruptive those who fight for inclusion
Blaming the Victim	Condemning "the others" for their situation, diverting attention from the roles that dominants play in the situation
Internalized Oppression	Internalizing negative judgments of being "the other," leading to self-hatred, depression, despair, and self-abuse
Horizontal Hostility	Extending internalized oppression to one's entire group as well as to other subordinate groups, expressing hostility to other oppressed persons and groups rather than to members of dominant groups
Isolation	Physically isolating people as individuals or as a "minority" group
Assimilation	Pressuring members of "minority" groups to drop their culture and differences and become a mirror of the dominant culture
Tokenism	Rewarding some of the most assimilated "others" with position and resources
Emphasis on Individual Solutions	Emphasizing individual responsibility for problems and individual solutions rather than collective responsibility and collective solutions

SOURCE: Adapted from Pharr (1988).

and barriers this person has experienced in life? Most likely, the classroom is cleaned in the evening after it has been vacated by teachers and students, and the person who cleans it, like many people who provide services that make our lives more pleasant, is invisible to you. Giving serious thought to common mechanisms of oppression can help us to recognize social injustice and think about ways to challenge it.

In recent years, social workers have expanded the conversation about social justice to include global social justice. As they have done so, they have more and more drawn on the concept of *human rights* to organize thinking about social justice, but ideas about human rights are in the early stage of development (see Mapp, 2008; Reichert, 2006; Wronka, 2008). In the aftermath of World War II, the newly formed United Nations created a Universal Declaration of Human Rights (UDHR) (1948), which spelled out the rights to which all humans were entitled, regardless of their place in the world, and this document has become a point of reference for subsequent definitions of human rights. Joseph Wronka argues that human rights are the bedrock of social justice. He identifies five core notions of human rights as suggested by the UDHR:

- *Human dignity:* equality and freedom
- *Nondiscrimination:* based on race, color, sex, language, religion, political opinion, national or social origin, property, birth, or other status
- *Civil and political rights:* freedom of thought, religion, expression, access to information, privacy, and fair and public hearing
- *Economic, social, and cultural rights:* to meaningful and gainful employment, rest and leisure, health care, food, housing, education, participation in cultural life, special care for motherhood and children
- *Solidarity rights:* to a just social and international order, self-determination, peace

Mapp (2008) suggests that three main barriers prevent full access to human rights: poverty, discrimination, and lack of access to education. Manisha has experienced all three of these barriers at some point in her life.

Critical Thinking Questions 1.2

What impact is globalization having on your own life? Do you see it as having a positive or negative impact on your life? What about for Manisha? Do you think globalization is having a positive or negative impact on her life?

KNOWING AND DOING

Social workers, like other professional practitioners, must find a way to move from knowing to doing, from "knowing about" and "knowing that" into "knowing how to" (for fuller discussion of this issue, see Hutchison, Charlesworth, Matto, Harrigan, & Viggiani, 2007). We *know* for the purpose of *doing*. Like architects, engineers, physicians, and teachers, social workers are faced with complex problems and case situations that are unique and uncertain. You no doubt will find that social work education, social work practice, and even this book will stretch your capacity to tolerate ambiguity and uncertainty. That is important because, as Carol Meyer (1993) has suggested, "There are no easy or simple [social work] cases, only simplistic perceptions" (p. 63). There is evidence that social workers have a tendency to terminate the learning process too early, to quest for answers, as opposed to appreciating the complexity of the process that may lead to multiple possible solutions (Gambrill, 2006). There are four important ingredients of "knowing how" to do social work: knowledge about the case, knowledge about the self, values and ethics, and scientific knowledge. These four ingredients are intertwined in the process of doing social work. The focus of this book is on scientific knowledge, but all four ingredients are essential in social work practice. Before moving to a discussion of scientific knowledge, I want to say a word about the other three ingredients.

Knowledge About the Case

I am using *case* to mean the situation at hand, a situation that has become problematic for some person or collectivity, resulting in a social work intervention. Our first task as social workers is to develop as good an understanding of the situation as possible. Who is involved in the situation and how are they involved? What is the nature of the relationships of the people involved? What are the societal, cultural, and community contexts of the situation? What are the contextual constraints as well as the contextual resources for bringing change to the situation? What elements of the case are maintaining the problematic situation? How have people tried to cope with the situation? What preference do the involved people have about the types of intervention to use? What is the culture and what are the social resources of the social agency to whose attention the situation is brought? You might begin to think about how you would answer some of these questions in relation to Manisha's situation.

It is important to note that knowledge about the case is influenced by the quality of the relationship between the social worker and client(s). There is good evidence that people are likely to reveal more aspects of their situation if they are approached with commitment, an open mind, warmth, empathic attunement, authentic responsiveness, and mutuality. For example, as Manisha becomes comfortable in the interview, feeling validated by both the interviewer and the interpreter, she begins to engage in deeper reflection about what happened in Bhutan. At the end of the interview, she expresses much gratitude for the opportunity to tell her story, noting that this is the first chance she has had to put the story together and that telling the story has led her to think about some events in new ways. This can be an important part of her grieving process. The integrity of knowledge about the case is related to the quality of the relationship, and the capacity for relationship is related to knowledge about the self.

However, knowledge about the case requires more than simply gathering information. We must select and order the information at hand and decide if further information is needed. This involves making a series of decisions about what is relevant and what is not. It also involves searching for recurring themes as well as contradictions in the information. For example, it is important for the refugee resettlement social worker to note a strong theme of the desire for purpose and self-respect in Manisha's story. Equally important is the information that Manisha shares about the knitting project sponsored by Oxfam. This may provide a clue for further program development to meet the needs of the community of Bhutanese refugees. It is also important to note Manisha's lingering confusion about why her peaceful world in Bhutan got turned upside down. This suggests that Manisha and other Bhutanese refugees might benefit from narrative exercises that help them to make sense of these experiences.

To assist you in moving between knowledge about the case and scientific knowledge, each chapter in this book begins, as this one does, with one or more case studies. Each of these unique stories suggests which scientific knowledge is needed. For example, to work effectively with Manisha, you will want to understand some things about Bhutan, the Nepali ethnic group, Hinduism, grief reactions, the acculturation process, challenges facing immigrant families, and cross-cultural communication. Throughout the chapters, the stories are woven together with the relevant scientific knowledge. Keep in mind that scientific knowledge is necessary, but you will not be an effective practitioner unless you take the time to learn about the unique situation of each person or collectivity you serve. It is the unique situation that guides which scientific knowledge is needed.

Knowledge About the Self

In his book *The Spiritual Life of Children,* Robert Coles (1990) wrote about the struggles of a 10-year-old Hopi girl to have her Anglo teacher understand Hopi spirituality. Coles suggested to the girl that perhaps she could try to explain her tribal nation's spiritual beliefs to the teacher. The girl answered, "But they don't listen to hear *us;* they listen to hear themselves" (p. 25). This young girl has captured, in a profound way, a major challenge to our everyday personal and professional communications: the tendency to approach the world with preconceived notions that we seek to validate by attending to some information while ignoring other information. The capacity to understand oneself is needed to guard against this very human tendency.

Three types of self-knowledge are essential for social workers: understanding of one's own thinking processes, understanding of one's own emotions, and understanding of one's own social location. We must be able to think about our thinking, a process called *metacognition*. We also must be able to recognize what emotions get aroused in us when we hear stories like Manisha's and when we contemplate the challenges of the situation, and we must find a way to use those emotions in ways that are helpful and avoid using them in ways that are harmful. Although writing about physicians, Gunnar Biorck (1977) said it well when he commented that practitioners make "a tremendous number of judgments each day, based on inadequate, often ambiguous data, and under pressure of time, and carrying out this task with the outward appearance of calmness, dedication and interpersonal warmth" (p. 146).

In terms of social location, as suggested earlier, social workers must identify and reflect on where they fit in a system of social identities, such as race, ethnicity, gender, social class, sexual orientation, religion, ability/disability, and age.

The literature on culturally sensitive social work practice proposes that a strong personal identity in relation to important societal categories, and an understanding of the impact of those identities on other people, is essential for successful social work intervention across cultural lines (see Lum, 2007). This type of self-knowledge requires reflecting on where one fits in systems of privilege.

Values and Ethics

The process of developing knowledge about the case is a dialogue between the social worker and client system, and social workers have a well-defined value base to guide the dialogue. Six core values of the profession have been set out in a preamble to the Code of Ethics established by the National Association for Social Workers (NASW) in 1996 and revised in 1999. These values are service, social justice, dignity and worth of the person, importance of human relationships, integrity, and competence. The value of social justice was

---

Exhibit 1.5 Core Values and Ethical Principles in NASW Code of Ethics

1. **Value:** Service
   Ethical Principle: Social workers' primary goal is to help people in need and to address social problems.
2. **Value:** Social Justice
   Ethical Principle: Social workers challenge social injustice.
3. **Value:** Dignity and Worth of the Person
   Ethical Principle: Social workers respect the inherent dignity and worth of the person.
4. **Value:** Importance of Human Relationships
   Ethical Principle: Social workers recognize the central importance of human relationships.
5. **Value:** Integrity
   Ethical Principle: Social workers behave in a trustworthy manner.
6. **Value:** Competence
   Ethical Principle: Social workers practice within their areas of competence and develop and enhance their professional expertise.

SOURCE: Copyright 1999, National Association of Social Workers, Inc., NASW Code of Ethics.

discussed earlier in the chapter. As demonstrated in Exhibit 1.5, the Code of Ethics articulates an ethical principle for each of the core values. Value 6, competence, requires that we recognize what science there is to inform our work. It requires understanding the limitations of the available science for considering the situation at hand, but also that we use the strongest available evidence to make practice decisions. This is where scientific knowledge comes into the picture.

Critical Thinking Questions 1.3

What emotional reactions did you have to reading Manisha's story? What did you find yourself thinking about her story? Where do you see Manisha fitting in systems of privilege? Where do you see yourself fitting? How might any of this impact your ability to be helpful to Manisha?

SCIENTIFIC KNOWLEDGE: THEORY AND RESEARCH

Ethical social workers are always searching for/recalling what is known about the situations they encounter, turning to the social and behavioral sciences for this information. Scientific knowledge serves as a screen against which the knowledge about the case is considered. It suggests **hypotheses,** or tentative statements, to be explored and tested, not facts to be applied, in transactions with a person or group. Because of the breadth and complexity of social work practice, usable knowledge must be culled from diverse sources and a number of scientific disciplines. **Science,** also known as scientific inquiry, is a set of logical, systematic, documented methods for answering questions about the world. Scientific knowledge is the knowledge produced by scientific inquiry. Two interrelated approaches to knowledge building, theory and empirical research, fit the scientific criteria of being logical, systematic, and documented for the public.

Together, they create the base of knowledge that social workers need to understand commonalities among their clients and practice situations. In your course work on social work research, you will be learning much more about these concepts, so only a brief description is provided here to help you understand how this book draws on theory and research.

Theory

Social workers use theory to help organize and make sense of the situations they encounter. A **theory** is a logically interrelated set of concepts and propositions, organized into a deductive system, that explains relationships among aspects of our world. As Elaine Leeder (2004) so aptly put it, "To have a theory is to have a way of explaining the world—an understanding that the world is not just a random series of events and experiences" (p. 9). Theory is a somewhat imposing word, seemingly abstract and associated with serious scholars, but it has everyday utility for social workers:

> Scratch any social worker and you will find a theoretician. Her own theoretical perspectives about people and practice may be informed by theories in print (or formal theories) but are put together in her own way with many modifications and additions growing out of her own professional and personal experience. (W. Reid & Smith, 1989, p. 45)

Thus, theory gives us a framework for interpreting person and environment and planning interventions. Theories focus our attention on particular aspects of the person-environment-time configuration.

Other terms that you will often encounter in discussions of theories are model, paradigm, and perspective. *Model* usually is used to refer to a visual representation of the relationships between concepts. *Paradigm* is usually used to mean a way of seeing the world, and *perspective* is an emphasis or a view. Paradigms and perspectives are broader and more general than theory.

If you are to make good use of theory, you should know something about how it is constructed. **Concepts** are the building blocks of theory. They are symbols, or mental images, that summarize observations, feelings, or ideas. Concepts allow us to communicate about the phenomena of interest. Some relevant concepts in Manisha's story are culture, Hinduism, Buddhism, cultural conflict, refugee, acculturation, loss, grief, dignity, and self-reliance.

Theoretical concepts are put together to form **propositions** or assertions. For example, loss and grief theory proposes that loss of a person, object, or ideal leads to a grief reaction. This proposition, which asserts a particular relationship between the concepts of loss and grief, may help the refugee resettlement social worker understand some of the sadness, and sometimes despair, that she sees in her work with Bhutanese refugee families. They have lived with an accumulation of losses—loss of land, loss of livelihood, loss of roles, loss of status, loss of extended family members, loss of familiar language and rituals, and many more.

Theories are a form of **deductive reasoning,** meaning that they lay out general, abstract propositions that we can use to generate specific hypotheses to test in unique situations. In this example, loss and grief theory can lead us to hypothesize that many Bhutanese refugees are grieving the many losses they have suffered.

Social and behavioral science theories are based on **assumptions,** or beliefs held to be true without testing or proof, about the nature of human social life. These theoretical assumptions have raised a number of controversies, three of which are worth introducing at this point (Burrell & Morgan, 1979; P. Y. Martin & O'Connor, 1989; Monte & Sollod, 2003):

1. Do the dimensions of human behavior have an **objective reality** that exists outside a person's consciousness, or is all reality based on personal perception (**subjective reality**)?
2. Is human behavior determined by forces beyond the control of the person (**determinism**), or are

persons free and proactive agents in the creation of their behavior (**voluntarism**)?

3. Are the patterned interactions among people characterized by harmony, unity, and social cohesion or by conflict, domination, coercion, and exploitation?

The nature of these controversies will become more apparent to you in Chapter 2. The contributing authors and I take a middle ground on all of them: We assume that reality has both objective and subjective aspects, that human behavior is partially constrained and partially free, and that social life is marked by both cohesion and conflict.

Empirical Research

Traditionally, science is equated with empirical research, which is widely held as the most rigorous and systematic way to understand human behavior. Research is typically viewed, in simple terms, as a problem-solving process, or a method of seeking answers to questions. If something is empirical, we experience it through our senses, as opposed to something that we experience purely in our minds. The process of **empirical research** includes a careful, purposeful, and systematic observation of events with the intent to note and record them in terms of their attributes, to look for patterns in those events, and to make our methods and observations public. Like theory, empirical research is a key tool for social workers: "The practitioner who just conforms to ongoing practices without keeping abreast of the latest research in his or her field is not doing all possible to see that his or her clients get the best possible service" (A. Rubin & Babbie, 1993, p. xxv).

Just as there are controversies about theoretical assumptions, there are also controversies about what constitutes appropriate research methods for understanding human behavior. Modern science is based on several assumptions, which are together generally recognized as a **positivist perspective:** The world has an order that can be discovered, findings of one study should be applicable to other

Photo 1.3 Theories and research about human behavior are boundless and constantly growing. Active readers must question what they read.

groups, complex phenomena can be studied by reducing them to some component part, findings are tentative and subject to question, and scientific methods are value-free. **Quantitative methods of research** are the preferred methods from the positivist perspective. These methods use quantifiable measures of concepts, standardize the collection of data, attend only to preselected variables, and use statistical methods to look for patterns and associations (Schutt, 2009).

Over the years, the positivist perspective and its claim that positivism = science have been challenged. Critics argue that quantitative methods cannot possibly capture the subjective experience of individuals or the complex nature of social life. Although most of these critics do not reject positivism as *a way* of doing science, they recommend other ways of understanding the world and suggest that these alternative methods should also be considered part of science. Various names have been given to these alternative methods. We will be referring to them as the **interpretist perspective,** because they share the assumption that reality is based on people's definitions of it and that research should focus on learning the meanings that people give to their situations. This is also referred to as a *constructivist perspective.*

Interpretists see a need to replace existing methods with **qualitative methods of research,** which are more flexible, more experiential, and designed to capture how participants view social life rather than to ask participants to respond to categories preset by the researcher (Schutt, 2009). Participant observation, intensive interviewing, and focus groups are examples of qualitative methods of research. Interpretists assume that people's behavior cannot be observed objectively, that reality is created as researcher and research participants interact. Researchers using qualitative methods are more likely to present their findings in words than in numbers and to attempt to capture the settings of behavior. They are likely to report the transactions of researcher and participant as well as the values of the researcher, because they assume that value-free research is impossible.

In this controversy, it is our position that no single research method can adequately capture the whole, the complexity, of human behavior. In fact, "we must often settle for likely, approximate, or partial truths" (Kirk & Reid, 2002, p. 16). Both quantitative and qualitative research methods have a place in a multidimensional approach, and used together they may help us to see more dimensions of situations. Alvin Saperstein (1996) has stated our view well: "Science is a fabric: its ability to cover the world depends upon the existence of many different fibers acting together to give it structure and strength" (p. 163). This view has much in common with postpositivism, which developed in response to criticism of positivism. **Postpositivism** is a philosophical position that recognizes the complexity of reality and the limitations of human observers. It proposes that scientists can never develop more than a partial understanding of human behavior (Schutt, 2009). Nevertheless, science remains the most rigorous and systematic way to understand human behavior.

Critical Use of Theory and Research

You may already know that social and behavioral science theory and research have been growing at a fast pace in modern times, and you will often feel, as McAvoy (1999) aptly put it, that you are "drowning in a swamp of information" (p. 19), both case information and scientific information. Phillip Dybicz (2004) considers it a strength of the profession that social workers have been more willing than other social and behavioral scientists and professionals to wade into the swamp. Ironically, as you are drowning in a swamp of information, you will also be discovering that the available scientific information is incomplete. You will also encounter contradictory ideas that must be held simultaneously and, where possible, coordinated to develop an integrated picture of the situation at hand. That is, as you might guess, not a simple project. It involves weighing available evidence and analyzing its relevance to the situation at hand. That requires

critical thinking. **Critical thinking** is a thoughtful and reflective judgment about alternative views and contradictory information. It involves thinking about your own thinking and the influences on that thinking, as well as a willingness to change your mind. It also involves careful analysis of assumptions and evidence. Critical thinkers also ask, "What is left out of this conceptualization or research?" Throughout the book, we will call out critical thinking questions to support your efforts to think critically.

As you read this book and other sources of scientific knowledge, you will want to begin to think critically about the theory and research that they present. You will want to give careful thought to the credibility of the claims made. Let's look first at theory. It is important to remember that although theorists may try to put checks on their biases, they write from their own cultural frame of reference and from a particular location in the social structure of their society. So, when taking a critical look at a theory, it is important to remember that theories are generally created by people of privileged backgrounds who operate in seats of power. The bulk of theories still used today were authored by White, middle- to upper-class Western European men and men in the United States with academic appointments. Therefore, as we work in a highly diversified world, we need to be attentive to the possibilities of biases related to race, gender, culture, religion, sexual orientation, abilities/disabilities, and social class—as well as professional or occupational orientation. One particular concern is that such biases can lead us to think of disadvantaged members of society or of members of minority groups as pathological or deficient.

Social and behavioral science scholars disagree about the criteria for evaluating theory and research. However, I recommend the criteria presented in Exhibit 1.6 because they are consistent with the multidimensional approach of this book and with the value base of the social work profession. (The five criteria for evaluating theory presented in Exhibit 1.6 are also used in Chapter 2 to evaluate eight theoretical perspectives relevant to

Exhibit 1.6   Criteria for Evaluating Theory and Research

Criteria for Evaluating Theory

Coherence and conceptual clarity. Are the concepts clearly defined and consistently used? Is the theory free of logical inconsistencies? Is it stated in the simplest possible way, without oversimplifying?

Testability and evidence of empirical support. Can the concepts and propositions be expressed in language that makes them observable and accessible to corroboration or refutation by persons other than the theoretician? Is there evidence of empirical support for the theory?

Comprehensiveness. Does the theory include multiple dimensions of persons, environments, and time? What is included and what is excluded? What dimension(s) is (are) emphasized? Does the theory account for things that other theories have overlooked or been unable to account for?

Consistency with social work's emphasis on diversity and power arrangements. Can the theory help us understand diversity? How inclusive is it? Does it avoid pathologizing members of minority groups? Does it assist in understanding power arrangements and systems of oppression?

Usefulness for social work practice. Does the theory assist in the understanding of person-and-environment transactions over time? Can principles of action be derived from the theory? At what levels of practice can the theory be used? Can the theory be used in practice in a way that is consistent with the NASW Code of Ethics?

Criteria for Evaluating Research

Corroboration. Are the research findings corroborated by other researchers? Is a variety of research methods used in corroborating research? Do the findings fit logically with accepted theory and other research findings?

Multidimensionality. Does the research include multiple dimensions of persons, environments, and time? If not, do the researchers acknowledge the omissions, connect the research to larger programs of research that include omitted dimensions, or recommend further research to include omitted dimensions?

Definition of terms. Are major variables defined and measured in such a way as to avoid bias against members of minority groups?

Limitation of sample. Does the researcher make sufficient effort to include diversity in the sample? Are minority groups represented in sufficient number to show the variability within them? When demographic groups are compared, are they equivalent on important variables? Does the researcher specify the limitations of the sample for generalizing to specific groups?

Influence of setting. Does the researcher specify attributes of the setting of the research, acknowledge the possible contribution of the setting to research outcomes, and present the findings of similar research across a range of settings?

Influence of the researcher. Does the researcher specify his or her attributes and role in the observed person-environment configurations? Does the researcher specify his or her possible contributions of the researcher to research outcomes?

Social distance. Does the researcher attempt to minimize errors that could occur because of literacy, language, and cultural differences between the researcher and respondents?

Specification of inferences. Does the researcher specify how inferences are made, based on the data?

Suitability of measures. Does the researcher use measures that seem suited to, and sensitive to, the situation being researched?

social work.) There is agreement in the social and behavioral sciences that theory should be evaluated for coherence and conceptual clarity as well as for testability and evidence of empirical support.

The criterion of comprehensiveness is specifically related to the multidimensional approach of this book. We do not expect all theories to be multidimensional in nature, but critical analysis of a theory should help us identify deterministic and unidimensional thinking where they exist. The criterion of consistency with emphasis on diversity and power arrangements examines the utility of the theory for a profession that places high value on social justice. In addition, the criterion of usefulness for practice is essential for a profession.

Just as theory may be biased toward the experiences of members of dominant groups, so too may research be biased. The result may be "misleading and, in some cases, [may lead to] outright false conclusions regarding a minority" (Monette, Sullivan, & DeJong, 2008, p. 8). Bias can occur at all stages of the research process.

- Funding sources and other vested interests have a strong influence on which problems are selected for research attention. For example, several critics have suggested that governmental agencies were slow to fund research on acquired immune deficiency syndrome (AIDS) because it was associated in the early years with gay males (Shilts, 1987).

- Bias can occur in the definition of variables for study. For example, using "offenses cleared by arrests" as the definition of crime, rather than using a definition such as "self-reported crime involvement," leads to an overestimation of crime among minority groups of color, because those are the people who are most often arrested for their crimes (Hagan, 1994).

- Bias can occur in choosing the sample to be studied. Because of their smaller numbers, members of minority groups may not be included in sufficient numbers to demonstrate the variability within a particular minority group. Or a biased sample of minorities may be used (e.g., it is not uncommon to make Black vs. White comparisons on a sample that includes middle-class Whites and low-income Blacks).

- Bias can occur in data collection. The validity and reliability of most standardized measuring instruments have been evaluated by using them with White, non-Hispanic respondents, and their cultural relevance with ethnic minorities is questionable. Language and literacy difficulties may arise with both written survey instruments and interviews. Several potential sources of errors when majority researchers gather data from members of minority groups are minority group members' mistrust and fear, their motivation to provide what is perceived to be wanted, shame and embarrassment, joking or making sport of the researcher, answering based on the ideal rather than the real, and inadequacy of questions (e.g., asking about a monthly income with families that will have to do a complex computation of incomes of different family members: "income from selling fruit and Popsicles on weekends, income from helping another family make cheese once every two to three weeks, extra money brought in by giving haircuts and permanents to neighborhood women, or occasional childcare and sewing" [Goodson-Lawes, 1994, p. 24]).

As with theory evaluation, there is no universally agreed-upon set of criteria for evaluating research. We recommend the nine criteria presented in Exhibit 1.6 for considering the credibility of a research report. These criteria can be applied to either quantitative or qualitative research. Many research reports would be strengthened if their authors were to attend to these criteria.

A WORD OF CAUTION

In this book, Part I includes two stage-setting chapters that introduce the framework for the book and provide a foundation for thinking critically about the discussions of theory and research presented in Parts II and III. Part II comprises three chapters that analyze the multiple dimensions of persons—one chapter each on the biological person, the psychological person, and the spiritual person, and four chapters that discuss environmental dimensions, including the physical environment, culture, social structure and social institutions, formal organizations, communities, social movements, small groups, and families. Part III overviews the life course perspective and includes seven chapters that examine theory and research about phases of the human life course.

Presenting personal and environmental dimensions separately, as I do in Part II, is a risky approach. I do not wish to reinforce any tendency to think about human behavior in a way that camouflages the inseparability of person and environment. I have taken this approach, however, for two reasons. First, the personal and environmental dimensions, for the most part, have been studied separately, often by different disciplines, and usually as detached or semidetached entities. Second, I want to introduce some dimensions of persons and environments not typically covered in social work textbooks and provide updated knowledge about all the dimensions. However, it is important to remember that no single dimension of human behavior can be understood without attention to other dimensions. Thus, frequent references to other dimensions throughout Part II should help develop an understanding of the unity of persons, environments, and time. Part III illustrates the complex interaction of person and environment as we make the journey through the human life course.

Implications for Social Work Practice

The multidimensional approach outlined in this chapter suggests several principles for social work assessment and intervention, for both prevention and remediation services:

- In the assessment process, collect information about all the critical dimensions of the changing configuration of person and environment.
- In the assessment process, attempt to see the situation from a variety of perspectives. Use multiple data sources, including the person(s), significant others, and direct observations.
- Allow people to tell their own stories, and pay attention to how they describe the pattern and flow of their person-environment configurations.
- Use the multidimensional database to develop a dynamic picture of the person-environment configuration.
- Link intervention strategies to the dimensions of the assessment.
- In general, expect more effective outcomes from interventions that are multidimensional, because the situation itself is multidimensional.
- Pay particular attention to the impact of diversity and inequality on the unique stories and situations that you encounter.
- Allow the unique stories of people and situations to direct the choice of theory and research to be used.
- Use scientific knowledge to suggest tentative hypotheses to be explored in the unique situation.

Key Terms

acculturation	dimension	linear time
assumptions	diversity	multidetermined behavior
biopsychosocial approach	empirical research	multidimensional
concepts	globalization	objective reality
critical thinking	heterogeneity	positivist perspective
deductive reasoning	hypotheses	postpositivism
determinism	interpretist perspective	privilege

propositions	quantitative methods of research	theory
qualitative methods of research	science	time orientation
	subjective reality	voluntarism

Active Learning

1. We have used multiple dimensions of person, environment, and time to think about Manisha's story. If you were the social worker at the refugee resettlement agency that sponsored her family's resettlement, you would bring your own unfolding person-environment-time story to that encounter. With the graphic in Exhibit 1.1 as your guide, write your own multidimensional story. What personal dimensions are important? What environmental dimensions? What time dimensions? What might happen when these two stories encounter each other?

2. Select a social issue that interests you, such as child abuse or youth gangs. List five things that you "know" about this issue. Think about *how* you know what you know. How would you go about confirming or disproving your current state of knowledge on this topic?

Web Resources

Each chapter of this textbook contains a list of Internet resources and websites that may be useful to readers in their search for further information. Each site listing includes the web address and a brief description of the contents of the site. Readers should be aware that the information contained in websites may not be truthful or reliable and should be confirmed before the site is used as a reference. Readers should also be aware that Internet addresses, or URLs, are constantly changing; therefore, the addresses listed may no longer be active or accurate. Many of the Internet sites listed in each chapter contain links to other Internet sites containing more information on the topic. Readers may use these links for further investigation.

Information not included in the Web Resources sections of each chapter can be found by using one of the many search engines on the Internet. Below, we list the search engines first.

www.google.com
www.bing.com
www.cuil.com

www.ask.com
www.yahoo.com
www.excite.com
www.lycos.com

There are several Internet sites that are maintained by and for social workers, some at university schools of social work and some by professional associations:

Council on Social Work Education (CSWE)
www.cswe.org

CSWE is the accrediting body for academic social work programs; site contains information about accreditation, projects, publications, and links to a number of social work–related websites.

Information for Practice
www.nyu.edu/socialwork/ip/

Site was developed and is maintained by Professor Gary Holden of New York University's School of Social Work, contains links to many federal and state Internet sites as well as journals, assessment and measurement tools, and sites maintained by professional associations.

International Federation of Social Workers
www.ifsw.org

Site contains information about international conferences, policy papers on selected issues, and links to human rights groups and other social work organizations.

National Association of Social Workers (NASW)
www.naswdc.org

Site contains professional development material, press room, advocacy information, and resources.

Social Work Access Network (SWAN)
www.sc.edu/swan/

Site presented by the University of South Carolina College of Social Work, contains social work topics, list of schools of social work, upcoming conferences, and online chats.

Social Work and Social Services Web Sites
http://gwbweb/wustl.edu/Resources/Pages/social serviceresourcesintro.aspx

Site presented by the George Warren Brown School of Social Work, Washington University, St. Louis, Missouri, contains links to resources for a wide variety of social issues and social service organizations.

CHAPTER 2

Theoretical Perspectives on Human Behavior

Elizabeth D. Hutchison

Leanne W. Charlesworth

Opening Questions

What theories are needed to understand the multiple dimensions of person, environment, and time involved in human behavior?

What criteria should social workers use to evaluate theories of human behavior?

Key Ideas

As you read this chapter, take note of these central ideas:

1. The systems perspective sees human behavior as the outcome of reciprocal interactions of persons operating within linked social systems.

2. The conflict perspective draws attention to conflict, inequality, dominance, and oppression in social life.

3. The rational choice perspective sees human behavior as based on self-interest and rational choices about effective ways to accomplish goals.

4. The social constructionist perspective focuses on how people learn, through their interactions with each other, to understand the world and their place in it.

5. The psychodynamic perspective is concerned with how internal processes such as needs, drives, and emotions motivate human behavior.

6. The developmental perspective focuses on how human behavior unfolds across the life course.

7. The social behavioral perspective suggests that human behavior is learned as individuals interact with their environments.

8. The humanistic perspective emphasizes the individual's inherent value, freedom of action, and search for meaning.

CASE STUDY

Intergenerational Stresses in the McKinley Family

The hospice social worker meets three generations of McKinleys when she visits their home in an upper-midwestern city. She is there because the family has requested hospice services for Ruth McKinley, the 79-year-old mother of Stanley McKinley. Ruth is having a recurrence of breast cancer, which has metastasized to her lungs; she is no longer receiving aggressive treatment, and her condition is deteriorating. Upon entering the house, the social worker meets 50-year-old Stanley; his 51-year-old wife, Marcia; and their 25-year-old daughter, Bethany, who takes the social worker to a bedroom to meet her grandmother. Bethany gives Ruth a gentle pat and introduces the social worker. Ruth smiles at Bethany and greets the social worker. Bethany leaves the room to give some privacy to the social worker and her grandmother.

The social worker spends about 20 minutes with Ruth and finds her weak but interested in talking. Ruth says she knows that she is receiving hospice care because she is dying. She says she has lived a good life and is not afraid of dying. She goes on to say, however, that there are some things on her mind as she thinks about her life. She is thinking a lot about her estranged daughter who lives several states away, and she does not want to die with this "hardness between us." She also is thinking a lot about Stanley, who is unemployed, and hoping that he can find a spark in his life again. Bethany is very much on her mind as well. She says she worries that Bethany is sacrificing too much of her young life to the needs of the family. As Ruth grows tired, the social worker ends the conversation, saying that she would like to visit with Ruth again next week so that they can talk some more about Ruth's life and the things that are on her mind.

Back in the living room, the social worker talks with Stanley, Marcia, and Bethany. She learns that Ruth moved into Stanley and Marcia's home 5 years ago after she had a stroke that resulted in left-sided paralysis. At that time, Stanley and Marcia took out a second mortgage on their house to finance some remodeling to make the home more accessible for Ruth, providing her with a bedroom and bathroom downstairs. They also put in a much-needed new furnace at the same time. Bethany speaks up to say that her grandmother is the kindest person she knows and that they were all happy to rearrange their home life to make Ruth comfortable. Marcia notes that it seemed the natural thing to do, because Ruth had taken care of Bethany while Marcia worked during Bethany's early years. After Ruth came to live with them, Stanley continued to work at a print shop, and Marcia changed to the evening shift in her job as a police dispatcher. Bethany arranged her work and part-time community college studies so that she could be available to her grandmother between the time her mother left for work and her father returned from his workday. She took charge of preparing dinner for her dad and grandmother and for giving Ruth a daily bath.

This arrangement worked well for 4 years. Bethany speaks fondly of the good times she and her grandmother had together as Bethany provided direct care to her grandmother, and her grandmother showered her with stories of the past and took a lively interest in her life, often giving her advice about her romantic life. Marcia breaks in to say that life has been tough for the past year, however, and her voice cracks as she says this. She recounts that they learned of the recurrence of Ruth's breast cancer 11 months ago and of the metastasis 5 months ago. For a few months after learning of the recurrence, Stanley, Marcia, and Bethany juggled their schedules to get Ruth to doctor visits, chemotherapy treatments, and bone scans, until Ruth and the oncologist decided that it was time to discontinue aggressive treatment.

Then, 7 months ago, Stanley lost his job at the printing company where he had worked since getting out of the army, and he has been unsuccessful at finding new work. They were still managing financially with the help of unemployment checks until Marcia took a tumble down the stairs and injured her back and hip 4 months ago. She had surgery, which was followed by complications, and has been out of work on disability. She is expecting to go back to work next week. Bethany says she has wanted to work more to bring more money into the home, but she has also been needed at home more to fill in for Marcia. She lost one job because of too many absences and has pieced together two part-time jobs that give her a little more flexibility. She worries, however, about having no health insurance because she needs ongoing treatment for asthma. Marcia says that Stanley has been a wonderful caregiver to her and his mom, but she knows that the caregiving has interfered with his job search and is wearing him down.

Stanley enters the conversation to report that they have been unable to make mortgage payments for the past 3 months, and the bank has notified him that they are at risk of facing foreclosure. He becomes despondent as he tells this. He says they have been in the house for 15 years and had always paid the mortgage on time. The second mortgage for the remodeling is adding to the current financial pinch. He says he is in a quandary about what to do. Marcia is going back to work soon, but she is still not strong enough to provide much physical care to Ruth. In addition, he is not at all optimistic that he will find a job in the near future. His former boss has now closed the printing shop because she lost some of her large clients. Stanley wonders if he should retrain for another occupation, but knows that this is not a good time for him to try to do that, with his mother's deteriorating condition. Bethany suggests that she should take some time off from school and find a job working nights so that she can give her dad time to look for jobs during the day. She has graduated from community college and been accepted into a bachelor's degree program in nursing. She says she is feeling too sad about her grandmother and too worried about the family's future to do well in school anyway. And, besides that, she would like to be able to spend more time with her grandmother before she dies. At this point, Marcia breaks down and cries, sobbing that she just wants to give up: "We work so hard, but nothing goes our way. I don't know where we will go if we lose the house."

As the family talks about their problems and possible solutions, the social worker recalls that she has heard something about a community program that provides counseling to people who are in jeopardy of home foreclosure. She wonders if that could help the McKinley family.

MULTIPLE PERSPECTIVES FOR A MULTIDIMENSIONAL APPROACH _____

The unfolding story of the multigenerational McKinley family may be familiar to you in some ways, but it is also unique in the way these particular persons and environments are interacting over time. As a social worker, you need to understand the details about the family's situation. However, if you are to be helpful in improving the situation, you also need some scientific knowledge that will assist you in thinking about its unique elements. As suggested in Chapter 1, the range of knowledge offered by a multi-theoretical approach is necessary when taking a multidimensional approach to human behavior. The purpose of this chapter is to introduce you to eight theoretical perspectives that are particularly useful for thinking about changing situations of persons and environments: systems perspective, conflict perspective, rational choice perspective, social constructionist perspective, psychodynamic perspective, developmental perspective, social behavioral perspective, and humanistic perspective. In Chapter 1, we defined *theory* as a logically interrelated set of concepts and propositions, organized into a deductive system, which explains relationships among aspects of our world. We suggested that a *perspective,* in contrast to a theory, is broader and more general—an emphasis or view. Each of the perspectives discussed in this chapter is composed of a number of diverse theories. Each of these perspectives is European American in heritage, but, in recent years, each has been influenced by thinking in other regions of the world.

We have selected these eight theoretical perspectives because they have stood the test of time, have a wide range of applications across dimensions of human behavior, and are used in empirical research. Each has been reconceptualized and extended over time. Margin notes are used in the chapters in Part II to help you recognize ideas from specific perspectives as they are used to understand different dimensions of persons and environments. Our purpose in this chapter is to introduce the

"big ideas" of the eight perspectives, and not to present a detailed discussion of the various theories within the perspectives. We do call attention, however, to some of the most recent extensions of the perspectives. We want to lay the groundwork for your understanding of the variations of the perspectives discussed in chapters in Part II. If you are interested in a more in-depth look at these theoretical perspectives, you might want to consult an excellent book titled *Contemporary Human Behavior Theory: A Critical Perspective for Social Work* (Robbins, Chatterjee, & Canda, 2006a).

Besides presenting an overview of the big ideas, we analyze the scientific merit of the perspectives and their usefulness for social work practice. The five criteria for critical understanding of theory identified in Chapter 1 provide the framework for our discussion of the perspectives: coherence and conceptual clarity, testability and empirical support, comprehensiveness, consistency with social work's emphasis on diversity and power arrangements, and usefulness for social work practice. Four of the perspectives introduced in this chapter are based in sociology, four are based in psychology, and several have additional interdisciplinary roots. This diversity reflects the history of the social work profession: Social work scholars began with a preference for sociological knowledge, moved over time to a preference for psychological knowledge, and have recently come to seek knowledge of both environmental and personal factors. This recent trend is consistent with the multidimensional approach of this book.

As noted in Chapter 1, diversity and inequality are major themes of this book. In earlier versions of the eight perspectives, few theorists acknowledged the importance of looking at diverse persons in diverse environments. Each of the perspectives has continued to evolve, however, and the perspectives are being reconstructed to better accommodate diversity and address inequality. Some theory critics suggest that this shift to greater emphasis on diversity and inequality represents a paradigm, or worldview, shift (e.g., Schriver, 2011). Other theory critics, on the other hand, argue that the eight perspectives discussed here have undergone continual change, but not such revolutionary change as to be labeled a paradigm shift (e.g., Ritzer & Goodman, 2004). These critics suggest that the perspectives have stood the test of time because they have, over time, become much more attuned to issues of diversity and inequality. Whether or not the attention to diversity and inequality constitutes a paradigm shift, we agree that it has been a major and positive trend in behavioral science theorizing.

Another major trend in behavioral science theory is that, although much of recent theorizing fits within existing categories of theoretical perspectives, theoretical synthesizing is blurring the boundaries between perspectives (Ritzer & Goodman, 2004). Theorists are being influenced by each other, as well as by societal changes, and have begun to borrow ideas from each other to build new theory by combining aspects of existing theory. As you read about each of the perspectives, think about not only how it can be applied in social work practice, but also how well it represents the complexities of human behavior in its current form.

SYSTEMS PERSPECTIVE

When you read the case study at the beginning of this chapter, you probably thought of it as a story about a family system—a story about Ruth, Stanley, Marcia, and Bethany McKinley—rather than "Ruth McKinley's story," even though the hospice case file reads "Ruth McKinley." You may have noted how Ruth's, Stanley's, Marcia's, and Bethany's lives are interrelated, how they influence one another's behavior, and what impact each of them has on the overall well-being of the family. You may be thinking about the reciprocal roles of caregiver and care

recipient and how the family members keep adjusting their caregiving roles to accommodate changing care needs. You also may note that this family, like other families, has a **boundary** indicating who is in and who is out, and you may be wondering if the boundary around this family allows sufficient input from friends, extended family, neighbors, religious organizations, and so on. You may also have noted the influence of larger systems on this family, particularly the insecurities in the labor market and the gaps in the health care system. Medicare coverage for hospice care is an important resource for the family as they cope with the end-of-life care needs of Ruth. You can see, in Exhibit 2.1, how these observations about the McKinley family fit with the big ideas of the systems perspective.

The **systems perspective** sees human behavior as the outcome of reciprocal interactions of persons operating within linked social systems. Its roots are very interdisciplinary. During the 1940s and 1950s, a variety of disciplines—including mathematics, physics, engineering, biology, psychology, cultural anthropology, economics, and sociology—began looking at phenomena as the outcome of interactions within and among systems. Mathematicians and engineers used the new ideas about system **feedback mechanisms**—the processes by which information about past behaviors in a system is fed back into the system in a circular manner—to develop military technology for World War II; scientists at Bell Laboratories used the same ideas to develop transistors and other communication technology (Becvar & Becvar, 1996). Later, George Engel (1977) used the same ideas to develop a biopsychosocial model of disease.

Exhibit 2.1   Big Ideas of the Systems Perspective

- Systems are made up of interrelated members (parts) that constitute a linked whole.
- Each part of the system impacts all other parts and the system as a whole.
- All systems are subsystems of other larger systems.
- Systems maintain boundaries that give them their identities.
- The dynamic interactions within, between, and among systems produce both stability and change, sometimes even rapid, dramatic change.

Photo 2.1 The pieces of this globe come together to form a unified whole—each part interacts with and influences the other parts—but the pieces are interdependent, as suggested by the systems perspective.

Social workers were attracted to the systems perspective in the 1960s, as they shifted from a psychiatric model to a model more inclusive of environment. Social work has drawn most heavily on the work of sociologists Talcott Parsons and Robert Merton, psychologists Kurt Lewin and Uri Bronfenbrenner, and biologist Ludwig von Bertalanffy. The social workers who first adopted the systems perspective were heavily influenced by *functionalist sociology,* which was the dominant sociological theory during the 1940s and 1950s. In functionalism, social systems are thought to be orderly and to remain in a relatively stable state, also known as *homeostasis* or *equilibrium.* Each part of the system serves an essential function in maintaining it, and the functions of the various parts are coordinated to produce a well-functioning whole. System processes and structures such as rules and roles serve to maintain system stability. Although this systems approach did not deny the possibility of system change, it was more concerned with the mechanisms of system maintenance and stability.

In the systems perspective, the structure of roles has been an important mechanism for maintaining system balance. **Role** refers to the usual behaviors of persons occupying a particular social position. Consider the roles played by each person in the McKinley family and the stresses the family has faced as a result of role transitions over the past year. Stanley has lost his role as family provider and has needed to increase his caregiving role. He has struggled to find time and energy for the job search. Marcia took on the role of care recipient rather than caregiver. Bethany faced new challenges in juggling worker, student, and caregiver roles. She seems to be indicating that she is experiencing some role overload.

There was substantial growth in interest in the use of the systems perspective in social work during the 1970s, but by the end of the decade, social workers became dissatisfied with the perspective on two counts. First, the perspective was seen as too abstract, and second, the emphasis on stability seemed too conservative for a profession devoted to social change. Throughout the 1980s, some social work scholars tried to correct for these shortcomings with the continual development of ecological and dynamic systems approaches (e.g., Germain & Gitterman, 1980). Social workers (e.g., Bolland & Atherton, 1999; Hudson, 2000; K. Warren, Franklin, & Streeter, 1998) took renewed interest in the systems perspective in the 1990s as they began to make use of chaos theory and the related complexity theory. Chaos theory emerged in mathematics in the 1960s, took hold in a number of natural science disciplines in the 1970s, and revitalized the systems perspective in the social sciences, but interest in chaos theory waned somewhat in the first decade of the 21st century.

Whereas traditional systems theories emphasize systems processes that produce stability, **chaos theory,** and the closely related complexity theory, emphasize systems processes that produce change, even sudden, rapid, radical change. This difference in understanding about change and stability in social systems is explained by propositions central to chaos theory. Traditional systems theories proposed that system stability results from *negative feedback loops* that work like a thermostat to feed back information that the system is deviating from a steady state and needs to take corrective action. Chaos theory recognizes negative feedback loops as important processes in systems and acknowledges their role in promoting system stability. In addition, it proposes that complex systems produce *positive feedback loops* that feed back information about deviation, or should we say innovation, into the steady state in such a way that the deviation reverberates throughout the system and produces change, sometimes even rapid change. The change-producing feedback may come from within the system or from other systems in the environment.

Like earlier systems theories, chaos theory emphasizes that all systems are made up of subsystems, and all systems serve, as well, as subsystems in other systems. Subsystems are always adjusting to each other and their environments, and the resultant changes are continuously being fed back. This results in a constant state of flux, and sometimes small changes in systems can reverberate in such a way as to produce very sudden and dramatic changes. Recently, chaos theory has been recommended as a useful approach to be used by clinical social workers and clinical psychologists as they assist clients to try new solutions to long-standing problems (M. Lee, 2008) and to recreate themselves in times of transitions (Bussolari & Goodell, 2009).

One issue about which the various versions of the systems perspective disagree is the permeability, or openness, of systems' boundaries to the environment. Functionalist sociology seemed to assume that interactions take place within a *closed system* that is isolated from exchanges with other systems. The idea of systems as closed was challenged by dynamic systems theories, most recently chaos theory, which assumes a more *open system* as the healthy system. As Exhibit 2.2 illustrates, an open system is more likely than a closed system to receive resources from external systems.

Recently, *deep ecology* has emerged with an emphasis on the notion of the total interconnectedness of all elements of the natural and physical world (Besthorn & Canda, 2002; Ungar, 2002). Sociologist

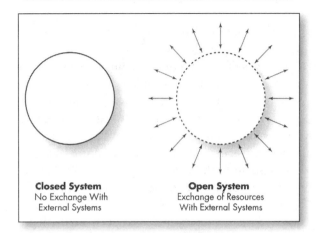

Exhibit 2.2   Closed and Open Systems

Closed System
No Exchange With
External Systems

Open System
Exchange of Resources
With External Systems

John Clammer (2009) suggests that deep ecology, with its addition of connections to the natural and physical worlds, can help to bridge Western and Eastern social science. The emerging *globalization theories* also emphasize the openness of systems, calling our attention, among other things, to how Stanley McKinley's job opportunities are connected to the increasingly globalized economy (Z. Bauman, 1998; U. Beck, 1999; Giddens, 2000).

On the other hand, recent theorizing in sociology has argued the case of the closed system. Niklas Luhmann's (1987) *general systems theory*, which has lately gained popularity in sociology, suggests that in highly complex societies, systems tend to become fragmented and closed to each other. They develop different languages and cultures and, consequently, cannot receive (hear and understand) feedback from each other. Luhmann calls such systems *autopoietic.* The terrorist attacks of September 11, 2001, and many other recent events, remind us that even in a context of rapid international communication and a global economy, cultures may remain very isolated from the feedback of other cultures. The seemingly impermeable cultural boundaries between the United States and Middle Eastern nations speak to this. Luhmann's theory of closed systems has not been used in the U.S. social work literature, but it has been a popular approach among European social workers (see Wirth, 2009).

This is how the criteria for evaluating theory apply to the systems perspective:

- *Coherence and conceptual clarity.* Although it has been popular over time, the systems perspective is often criticized as vague and somewhat ambiguous. Functional sociology has been particularly vulnerable to criticisms that its concepts are defined poorly or inconsistently. Although chaos theory and complexity theory have greater consistency in use of terms than earlier approaches did, concepts in these theories remain highly abstract and often confusing in their generality. In reality, chaos theory and complexity theory emerged in applied mathematics, and concepts from them are still being developed in the social sciences. There are recent attempts by social workers to extrapolate concepts from these theories (e.g., Bolland & Atherton, 1999; Hudson, 2000; K. Warren et al., 1998), but scholars have not yet stated or explained the concepts of these theories in the simplest and clearest way possible. A recent article by Mo Yee Lee (2008) makes great progress in this area.

- *Testability and evidence of empirical support.* Poorly defined and highly abstract concepts are difficult to translate into measurable variables for research. Nevertheless, a long tradition of research supporting a systems perspective can be found in anthropology and sociology (see J. White & Klein, 2008a, for a discussion of the use of the systems perspective to study family systems). The systems perspective has been greatly strengthened in recent years with developments in brain research and epidemiology, and a rapidly expanding empirical literature on ecological risk and resilience (J. Corcoran & Walsh, 2006; Fraser, 2004; Hutchison, Matto, Harrigan, Charlesworth, & Viggiani, 2007). Research methods, such as lengthy time series analyses, have been developed in the natural and social sciences for studying concepts of chaos and complexity, but these methods are still rarely used in social work.

- *Comprehensiveness.* Clearly, the systems perspective is devoted to the ideal of comprehensiveness, or holism. It can, and has, incorporated the various dimensions of human systems as well as various dimensions of environmental systems, nonhuman as well as human. Systems theorists recognize—even if they do not always make clear—the social, cultural, economic, and political environments of human behavior. They acknowledge the role of external influences and demands in creating and maintaining patterns of interaction within the system. Early theorizing in the systems perspective did not deal with the time dimension—the focus was always on the present. However, recent formulations have attempted to add a time dimension to accommodate both past and future influences on human behavior (see Bronfenbrenner, 1989; Ford & Lerner, 1992; Hannerz, 1992; Wachs, 1992). Certainly, chaos theory and complexity theory give implicit, if not always explicit, attention to time with their emphasis on dynamic change. Globalization theory calls attention to the impact of speedy communications on world systems (Giddens, 2000; Virilio, 2000).

- *Diversity and power.* Although diversity is not addressed in most systems theorizing, recent versions of the systems perspective, with their attention to complexity and continuous dynamic change, open many possibilities for diversity. Furthermore, while most systems theorists do not address the role of power in systems transactions, some can accommodate the idea of power differentials better than others. Traditional systems theories that were influenced by functionalist sociology assumed that social systems are held together by social consensus and shared values. The emphasis on system equilibrium and on the necessity of traditional roles to hold systems together can rightly be criticized as socially conservative and oppressive to those who lack power within the system. Contemporary systems theory has begun to recognize power and oppression; conflict is seen as necessary for change in chaos theory, and some versions of globalization theory call attention to how powerful nations exploit the cultures, economies, and political arrangements of less powerful nations (McMichael, 2008).

- *Usefulness for social work practice.* The systems perspective is more useful for understanding human behavior than for directing social work interventions, but several social work practice textbooks were based on the systems perspective in the 1970s and 1980s (see Germain & Gitterman, 1980; C. Meyer, 1983; Pincus & Minahan, 1973; Siporin, 1975). The primary value of the systems perspective is that it can be used at any level of practice. It also has merit because it surpasses other perspectives in suggesting that we should widen the scope of assessment and intervention and expect better outcomes from multidimensional interventions (Hutchison et al., 2007). Chaos theory can even be used by social workers to input information into a client system to facilitate rapid change, thereby enhancing possibilities for brief treatment, and group process can be used as reverberating feedback to produce change (K. Warren et al., 1998). In fact, social workers who work from a family systems perspective (e.g., Carter & McGoldrick, 2005a) have for some time used methods such as family genograms, and other forms of feedback about the family, as information that can produce change as it reverberates through the family system. Mo Yee Lee (2008) provides a number of examples of how clinical social workers can use chaos and turbulence to help clients open to new ways of looking at and resolving problems.

CONFLICT PERSPECTIVE

As she thinks about the McKinley family, the hospice social worker is struck by Stanley and Marcia's growing sense of powerlessness to manage the trajectories of their lives. A major theme in their story,

like the stories of so many other families under current economic conditions, is lack of power in both the labor market and the housing market. Worries about access to health care are another part of the story, and one is reminded of ongoing political debates about health care funding. It remains to be seen what impact the federal health insurance law passed in March 2010 will have on families like the McKinleys. While the systems perspective helps us think about how interdependent the family members are, you may be thinking that they have some competing interests in relation to scarce resources of time and money. For example, Bethany's educational goals are in competition with the caregiving needs of Ruth and Marcia. The hospice social worker knows that communications can become tense in families facing similar situations of scarce resources, as members assert their self-interests, and she wants to know more about how the McKinley family negotiates competing interests. She is also curious about the history of gender roles in this family and how they have been affected by Stanley's unemployment. Compare these observations with the central ideas of the conflict perspective, presented in Exhibit 2.3.

The **conflict perspective** has been popular over and over again in history, with roots that can be traced back to German philosopher Georg Hegel (1770–1831) and Italian philosopher Niccolo Machiavelli (1469–1527), and perhaps even further, drawing attention to conflict, dominance, and oppression in social life (R. Collins, 1994; Ritzer, 2008b). The conflict perspective typically looks for sources of conflict, and causes of human behavior,

Exhibit 2.3   Big Ideas of the Conflict Perspective

- Groups and individuals try to advance their own interests over the interests of others as they compete for scarce resources.
- Power is unequally divided, and some social groups dominate others.
- Social order is based on the manipulation and control of nondominant groups by dominant groups.
- Lack of open conflict is a sign of exploitation.
- Members of nondominant groups become alienated from society.
- Social change is driven by conflict, with periods of change interrupting long periods of stability.

in the economic and political arenas, and more recently in the cultural arena. In sociology, the conflict perspective has two traditions: a utopian tradition that foresees a society in which there is no longer a basis for social conflict, and a second tradition that sees conflict as inevitable in social life.

The roots of contemporary conflict theory are usually traced to the works of Karl Marx and his collaborator, Friedrich Engels, and to the works of Max Weber. Marx (1887/1967) and Engels (1884/1970) focused on economic structures, suggesting that the capitalist economic system is divided into capitalists and workers. Capitalists decide what is to be done and how to do it, and they own the products produced by the workers. Capitalists pay workers as little as they can get away with, and they, not the workers, reap the benefits of exploiting natural resources. According to Marx, this system produces *false consciousness:* Neither capitalists nor workers are aware that the system is based on exploitation; workers think they are getting a fair day's pay, and capitalists think workers are fairly rewarded. Marx proposed, however, that workers are capable of recognizing the exploitation and achieving *class consciousness,* but capitalists are incapable of recognizing the exploitation in the system.

Weber (1904–1905/1958) rejected this singular emphasis on economics in favor of a multidimensional perspective on social class that included prestige and power derived from sources other than economics. Contemporary conflict theory tends to support Weber's multidimensional perspective, calling attention to a confluence of social, economic, and political structures in the creation of inequality (Allan, 2007; Appelrouth & Edles, 2007; Ritzer, 2008b). Jürgen Habermas (1984, 1981/1987) and other **critical theorists** argue that as capitalism underwent change, people were more likely to be controlled by culture than by their work position. Our lives became dominated by the *culture industry,* which is controlled by mass media. Critical theorists suggest that the culture industry plays a major role in turning workers into consumers, calling attention to the role of advertising in exploiting consumers. They suggest that in the contemporary world, workers work very hard, sometimes with second and third jobs, in order to consume. They describe the exploitation of consumers as a pleasant kind of control. People spend more and more time working to be able to shop, and shopping becomes the major form of recreation. Working and shopping leave little time for reflective or revolutionary thinking. Of course, this approach to conflict theory continues to recognize the supremely important role of the economic system, which is a very important part of the McKinley family situation at the current time.

Immanuel Wallerstein (1974, 1979) is a neo-Marxist who focuses on international inequality. He proposed that the capitalist world system is divided into three geographic areas with greatly different levels of power. A *core* of nations dominates the capitalist worldwide economy and exploits the natural resources and labor in other nations. The *periphery* includes nations that provide cheap raw materials and labor that are exploited to the advantage of the core. The *semiperiphery* includes nations that are newly industrializing; they benefit from the periphery but are exploited by the core.

Power relationships are the focus of the conflict perspective. Some theorists in the conflict tradition limit their focus to the large-scale structure of power relationships, but many theorists, especially critical theorists, also look at the reactions and adaptations of individual members of nondominant groups. These theorists note that oppression of nondominant groups leads to their *alienation,* or a sense of indifference or hostility.

Lewis Coser (1956) proposed a **pluralistic theory of social conflict,** which recognizes that more than one social conflict is going on at all times, and that individuals hold cross-cutting and overlapping memberships in status groups. Social conflict exists between economic groups, racial groups, ethnic groups, religious groups, age groups, gender groups, and so forth. Thus, this theory seeks to understand life experience by looking at simultaneous memberships—for example, a White, Italian American, Protestant, heterosexual, male semiskilled worker, or a Black, African American, Catholic, lesbian, female professional worker. Feminist theorists have developed a pluralistic approach called *intersectionality theory,* which recognizes vectors of oppression and privilege, including not only gender, but also class, race, global location, sexual orientation, and age (see P. H. Collins 1990).

Although early social workers in the settlement house tradition recognized social conflict and structured inequality, and focused on eliminating oppression of immigrants, women, and children, most critics agree that social workers have not drawn consistently on the conflict perspective over time (Robbins et al., 2006a). Concepts of power and social conflict were revived in the social work literature in the 1960s (Germain, 1994). In the past decade or so, with renewed commitment to social justice in its professional code of ethics and in its curriculum guidelines, U.S. social work has drawn more heavily on the conflict perspective to understand dynamics of *privilege,* or unearned advantage, as well as discrimination and oppression. Social workers have used the conflict perspective as a base to develop practice-oriented **empowerment theories,** which focus on processes that individuals and collectivities can use to recognize patterns of inequality and injustice and take action to increase their own power (e.g., L. Gutiérrez, 1990, 1994; J. Lee, 2001; Rose, 1992, 1994; B. Solomon, 1976, 1987). Both in their renewed interest in domination and oppression and in their development of practice-oriented empowerment theories, social workers have been influenced by earlier **feminist theories,** which focus on male domination of the major social institutions and present a vision of a just world based on gender equity. Feminist theories emphasize that people are socialized to see themselves through the eyes of powerful actors. Like Marx, most feminist theorists are not content to ask, "Why is it this way?" but also ask, "How can we change and improve the social world?" Scanzoni and colleagues (Scanzoni & Szinovacz, 1980) have been interested in whether and, if so, how gender power arrangements change as women become the more stable provider in families, a situation that has now occurred in the McKinley family as well as many other families around the world.

Photo 2.2   This homeless woman on a street in prosperous Beverly Hills, California, is one of many examples of unequal power in the global economy, a focus of the conflict perspective.

Here is how the conflict perspective rates on the five criteria for evaluating social work theory:

- *Coherence and conceptual clarity.* Most concepts of the conflict perspective are straightforward—conflict, power, domination, inequality—at least at the abstract level. Like all theoretical concepts, however, they become less straightforward when we begin to define them for the purpose of measurement. Across the various versions of the conflict perspective, concepts are not consistently used. One major source of variation is whether power and privilege are to be thought of as objective material circumstances, subjectively experienced situations, or both. In general, theories in the conflict tradition are expressed in language that is relatively accessible and clear. This is especially true of many of the practice-oriented empowerment theories developed by social workers. On the other hand, most of the recent conflict theorizing in the critical theory tradition is stated at a high level of abstraction.

- *Testability and evidence of empirical support.* Conflict theory has developed, in the main, through attempts to codify persistent themes in history (R. Collins, 1990). The preferred research method is empirical historical research that looks at large-scale patterns of history (see Mann, 1986; McCarthy & Zald, 1977; McMichael, 2008; Skocpol, 1979; Wallerstein, 1974, 1979). As with other methods of research, critics have attacked some interpretations of historical data from the conflict perspective, but the historical analyses of Michael Mann, Theda Skocpol, and Immanuel Wallerstein are some of the most influential works in contemporary sociology. In addition to historical analysis, conflict theorists have used experimental methods to study reactions to coercive power (see Willer, 1987; Zimbardo, 2007) and naturalistic inquiry to study social ranking through interaction rituals (R. Collins, 1981). Contemporary conflict theorists are also drawing on network analysis, which plots the relationships among people within groups, and are finding support for their propositions about power and domination. Family researchers have used conflict theory, specifically the concept of power, to study family violence (J. White & Klein, 2008a).

- *Comprehensiveness.* Traditionally, the conflict perspective focused on large-scale social institutions and social structures, such as economic and political institutions. In the contemporary era, Randall Collins (1990) is a conflict theorist who has made great efforts to integrate conflict processes at the societal level with those at the community, small group, and family levels. Collins suggests that we should recognize conflict as a central process in social life at all levels. Family theorists propose a conflict theory of families (J. White & Klein, 2008d). Traditional conflict theories propose that oppression of nondominant groups leads to a sense of alienation, and recent empowerment theories give considerable attention to individual perceptions of power. The conflict perspective does not explicitly address biology, but it has been used to examine racial and social class health disparities. Most conflict theories do consider dimensions of time. They are particularly noteworthy for recommending that the behavior of members of minority groups should be put in historical context, and indeed, as discussed above, empirical historical research is the research method that many conflict theorists prefer.

- *Diversity and power.* The conflict perspective is about inequality, power arrangements, and systems of oppression. It helps us look at group-based patterns of inequality. In that way, it also assists us in understanding diversity. The pluralist theory of social conflict and feminist intersectionality theory, both of which recognize that individuals have overlapping memberships in a variety of status groups, are particularly useful for considering human diversity. A major strength of the conflict perspective is that it discourages pathologizing members of minority groups by encouraging recognition of the historical, cultural, economic, and political context of human behavior. Empowerment theories guide practice interventions that build on the strengths of members of minority groups.

- *Usefulness for social work.* Concepts from the conflict perspective have great value for understanding power dimensions in community, group, and family relationships, as well as the power differential between social worker and client. Clearly, the conflict perspective is crucial to social work because (a) it shines a spotlight on how domination and oppression might be affecting human behavior; (b) it illuminates processes by which people become estranged and discouraged; and (c) it encourages social workers to consider the meaning of their power relationships with clients, particularly non-voluntary clients (Cingolani, 1984). The conflict perspective is essential to the social justice mission of social work. In recent years, social workers have been in the forefront of developing practice-oriented empowerment theories, and the conflict perspective has become as useful for recommending particular practice strategies as for assisting in the assessment process. Empowerment theories provide guidelines for working at all system levels (e.g., individual, family, small group, community, and organization), but they put particular emphasis on group work because of the opportunities presented in small groups for solidarity and mutual support. With the addition of empowerment theories, the conflict perspective can not only help us to understand how the McKinley family came to feel powerless, but also help us think about how we can assist individual family members, as well as the family as a whole, to feel empowered to improve their situation. Social movement theories (see Chapter 8), which are based in the conflict perspective, have implications for the mobilization of oppressed groups, but the conflict perspective in general provides little in the way of specific policy direction.

RATIONAL CHOICE PERSPECTIVE _____

Another way to think about the McKinley family is to focus on the resources that each brings to the ongoing life of the family, and each member's sense of fairness in the exchange of those resources. You might note that Ruth has diminishing resources to offer to the family, but the rest of the family seems to derive satisfaction from caring for her. Marcia indicates that it is only fair that they care for her now because of the care Ruth provided to Bethany when she was a young child (not to mention the care she provided to Stanley in his formative years).

Stanley's ability to provide economic resources to the family has diminished, and we might wonder how this has affected his sense of providing his "fair share" of resources to the family. Marcia has gotten satisfaction over the years from her caregiving role in the family, and her ability to bring this resource to the family has been compromised. On the other hand, the economic resources she brings into the family have become more important since Stanley became unemployed. Bethany provides economic resources as well as caregiving resources, and there is no evidence that she considers her contributions to the family to be unfair. She is weighing the long-term rewards of education against the short-term costs of adding a rigorous educational program to an already overtaxed life. Exhibit 2.4 reveals a fit between these observations about the McKinley family and the central ideas of the rational choice perspective.

Exhibit 2.4 Big Ideas of the Rational Choice Perspective

- People are rational and goal-directed.
- Human interaction involves trade of social resources, such as love, approval, information, money, and physical labor.
- Social exchange is based on self-interest, with actors trying to maximize rewards and minimize costs.
- Values, norms, and expectations, as well as alternatives, influence the assessment of rewards and costs.
- Reciprocity of exchange is essential to social life.
- Power comes from unequal resources in an exchange.

The **rational choice perspective** sees human behavior as based on self-interest and rational choices about effective ways to accomplish goals. Human interaction is seen as an exchange of resources, and people make judgments about the fairness of the exchange. The perspective is inter-disciplinary, with strong roots in utilitarian philosophy, economics, and social behaviorism. Social workers are most familiar with the rational choice perspective as it is manifested in social exchange theory in sociology, rational choice models of organizations, public choice theory in political science, and the emerging social network theory. The rational choice perspective comes out of a very old tradition in social thought (J. White & Klein, 2008c), but the roots of contemporary sociological theories of rational choice are generally traced to Claude Lévi-Strauss, George Homans, and Peter Blau. Other major theorists include John Thibaut and Harold Kelley, James March and Herbert Simon, Michael Hechter, James Coleman, James Buchanan, Richard Emerson, and Karen Cook.

Social exchange theory starts with the premise that social behavior is based on the desire to maximize benefits and minimize costs. A basic belief is that social relationships occur in a social marketplace in which people give in order to get. Persons with greater resources in a social exchange hold what is often unacknowledged power over other actors in the exchange. In the early development of social exchange theory, Homans (1958) insisted that behavior could be understood only at the psychological level, denying the relevance of the cultural and social environments. Homans was particularly forceful in attacking the view that individual behavior is influenced by role expectations that emanate from sociocultural systems. More recent formulations of social exchange theory have moved from this position toward a greater emphasis on the social, economic, political, and historical contexts of social exchanges (see Levi, Cook, O'Brien, & Faye, 1990; Markovsky, 2005). These formulations would emphasize how relationships in the McKinley family are influenced by the structure of the labor market and political decisions about governmental support systems, including health care. Beginning with the work of Peter Blau (1964), social exchange theorists and researchers have taken a strong interest in how power is negotiated at all levels, from interactions between two people to *Realpolitik,* or balance of power, among nations. Particularly noteworthy in this regard are Emerson's (1972a, 1972b) power-dependency theory and Cook's (1987) exchange network theory.

Rational choice theory is currently popular in sociology, health promotion, and family studies. In sociology, James Coleman (1990) used rational choice theory to explore possible incentives to encourage actors to behave in ways that are more beneficial to others. For example, he has proposed lifting the legal immunity of members of corporate boards to encourage them to act in a more prosocial manner. In the health promotion literature, a number of rational models have been proposed to understand risky health behaviors and to extrapolate prevention strategies from them. Two of those models are the *health belief model* (HBM) (M. Becker, 1974; M. Becker & Joseph, 1988) and the *theory of reasoned action* (Ajzen & Fishbein, 1977; Hornik, 1991). In family studies, social exchange theory has been used to understand mate selection, divorce, and caregiver burden (Dainton & Zelley, 2006).

Some feminists have criticized exchange theory on the grounds that its emphasis on rational calculation of personal advantage is a male attitude and does not represent the female perspective (Ritzer, 2008b). This criticism might be shared by ethnic groups who have traditionally been more collectivist, and less individualist, than White Anglo-Saxon Protestant Americans. In fact, Homans developed his American version of exchange theory partially in reaction to Lévi-Strauss's French collectivist version, which argued that social exchange is driven by collective, cultural, symbolic forces and is not based simply on self-interest (Ekeh, 1974). Karen Cook and her colleagues (Cook, O'Brien, & Kollock, 1990) have undertaken a synthesis of social exchange and symbolic interaction theories (see the discussion of the social constructionist perspective), recognizing the possibility that different people hold different definitions of fairness and positive outcomes in social exchange. We can imagine, for example, that some young adults in Bethany McKinley's position would consider it unfair to be involved in provider and caregiving roles in their family of origin.

Thibaut and Kelley's concepts of comparison level and comparison level alternatives are also useful in understanding different definitions of rewards and costs (Kelley & Thibaut, 1978; Thibaut & Kelley, 1959). *Comparison level,* a standard for evaluating the rewards and costs of a given relationship, is based on what the evaluator expects from the relationship. It has been used to understand why some people stay in abusive relationships. *Comparison level alternative* is the lowest level of outcomes a person will accept in light of alternative opportunities. This concept has been used to understand how people make decisions about seeking divorce. Some rational choice theorists have used the concept of *opportunity costs* to refer to the cost of forgoing the next most attractive alternative when choosing a particular action. Researchers across a wide range of disciplines are using statistical methods to calculate the opportunity costs of particular courses of action, such as conserving natural habitats (Naidoo & Adamowicz, 2006) or prescribing antidepressant medications instead of cognitive behavioral therapy (Hollinghurst, Kessler, Peters, & Gunnell, 2005).

Theorists in the rational choice tradition are also advancing **social network theory,** which actually has intellectual roots in the systems perspective. Still in the early stages of development, social network theory already provides useful tools for person-environment assessments and holds great promise for the future. Social networks are typically presented visually as sociograms, which illustrate the relations among network members (see Hartman, 1995; C. Meyer, 1993). Members of the network—individuals, groups, or organizations—are represented as points, and lines are drawn between pairs of points to demonstrate a relationship between them. Arrows are often used to show the flow of exchanges in a relationship. These graphic displays illuminate such issues as network size, density of relationships, strength of relationships, reciprocity of relationships, and access to power and influence. Sociograms are usually called **ecomaps** in the social work literature. An ecomap of the McKinley family is presented in Exhibit 2.5.

Here is an analysis of how well the rational choice perspective meets the criteria for judging social work theory:

- *Coherence and conceptual clarity.* As the rational choice perspective has developed, two conceptual puzzles have emerged, one at the individual level and one at the collective level. At the individual level, there is a question about the individual's capacity to process information and make rational decisions. At the collective level, the question is how collective action is possible if each actor maximizes rewards and minimizes costs. To their credit, recent theorists have embraced these puzzles. Developments in the rational choice perspective emphasize the limits to rational choice in social life (see Cook et al., 1990; Emerson, 1972a, 1972b; Levi, Cook, O'Brien, & Faye, 1990; March & Simon, 1958). James Coleman (1990) is particularly noted for his attempts to employ rational choice theory to activate collective action for the purpose of social justice. There is still much internal inconsistency among most rational choice theories, however, about the nature and extent of rationality, with some theorists more willing than others to recognize the limits of human rationality.

- *Testability and empirical support.* The rational choice perspective has stimulated empirical research at several levels of analysis, with mixed results. Cognitive psychologists Daniel Kahneman and Amos Tversky (1982, 1984) dealt a blow to the rational choice perspective in the 1980s. They reported research findings that individual choices and decisions are often inconsistent with assumed rationality and that, indeed, situations are often too complicated for individuals to ascertain what is the most rational choice. On the other hand, more than modest support for the perspective has been found in research on dyads and families (see G. Becker, 1981; Nomaguchi & Milkie, 2005; Sprecher, 2005). A number of scholars have pointed out the difficulty of measuring rewards, costs, and fairness, because they are subjectively evaluated—what is rewarding to one person may not be rewarding to another. In response, researchers have developed tools such as the Marital Comparison Level Index (Sabatelli, 1984) and Parental Comparison Level Index (Waldron-Hennessey & Sabatelli, 1997). Researchers in a number of disciplines are attempting to find precise ways of measuring opportunity costs of alternative policies.

Exhibit 2.5   Ecomap of the McKinley Family

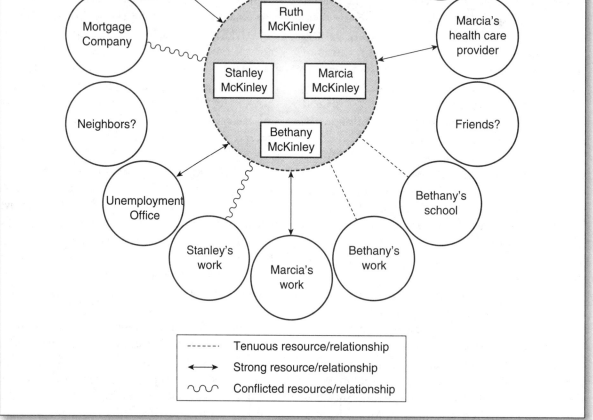

Exhibit 2.5   Ecomap of the McKinley Family

- *Comprehensiveness*. Although all strains of the rational choice perspective are interested in human interactions, the various strains focus on different dimensions of those configurations. Homans as well as Thibaut and Kelley were primarily interested in dyads. Ivan Nye (1982) has used the rational choice perspective to understand family life. Peter Blau (1964) came to be interested in larger structures. Coleman (1990) is interested in how individual actions get aggregated into collective action at the organizational and societal level. Network theory focuses on social interactions at the community, organizational, and institutional levels. In general, the rational choice perspective is weak in exploration of personal dimensions. The rational choice perspective has also ignored the time dimension, except to respect the history of rewards and costs in past exchanges.

- *Diversity and power.* Although they were looking for patterns, not diversity, early rational choice theories provided some tools for understanding diversity in behaviors that come out of particular social exchanges. All theories in this perspective recognize power as deriving from unequal resources in the exchange process. Some versions of rational choice theory emphasize the ways in which patterns of exchange lead to social inequalities and social injustices. Although the rational choice perspective does not explicitly pathologize members of minority groups, those versions that fail to put social exchanges in historical, political, and economic contexts may unintentionally contribute to the pathologizing of these groups.

- *Usefulness for social work practice.* Some versions of rational choice theory serve as little more than a defense of the rationality of the marketplace of social exchange, suggesting a noninterventionist approach. In other words, if all social exchanges are based on rational choices, then who are we to interfere with this process? This stance, of course, is inconsistent with the purposes of social work. However, some theorists in this tradition, most notably James Coleman, have begun to propose solutions for creating social solidarity while recognizing the self-interestedness that is characteristic of Western, capitalistic societies. These attempts have led Randall Collins (1994) to suggest that, out of all current social theories, contemporary rational choice theories have the greatest chance of informing social policy. On the other hand, Deborah Stone (2002) has skillfully demonstrated that the rational choice model is not a sufficient fit, and maybe not even a good fit, with the messy, nonlinear policy-making process. Family therapists use social exchange theory to guide prevention and intervention in marital and parent–child

relationships, assisting family members to increase rewarding interactions and decrease unrewarding exchanges (J. White & Klein, 2008c). Social workers make use of social network theory at the micro level, to assess and enhance the social support networks of individual clients and families (K. D. Johnson, Whitbeck, & Hoyt, 2005; Pinto, 2006; Tracy & Johnson, 2007). Social work administrators and planners use social network theory to understand and enhance the exchange of resources in networks of social service providers (see Streeter & Gillespie, 1992).

SOCIAL CONSTRUCTIONIST PERSPECTIVE

As the hospice social worker drives back to the office, the McKinley family is on her mind. She thinks about Ruth and her end-of-life reflections about her life and social relationships. She hopes that she can be a good listener and a partner with Ruth as she makes meaning of her life. She recalls other clients who have made some changes in their stories as they had a chance to reflect on them with her. She is curious about the story of the estrangement between Ruth and her daughter and wants to hear more about that from Ruth. She wonders if Ruth has been able to talk with Stanley and Bethany about her concerns for them and what meaning they might make of those concerns. The social worker also thinks about the story she heard from Stanley, Marcia, and Bethany. She thinks of Marcia's words, "nothing goes our way," and wonders whether this understanding of the world is shared by Stanley and Bethany—and, if so, how she might help them construct a different ending to the story they are telling themselves. The social worker also reflects on the way gender roles are defined in the family and would like to know more about how these roles have been negotiated over time in the family. You can see how her reflections are consistent with the social constructionist perspective by exploring Exhibit 2.6.

To understand human behavior, the **social constructionist perspective** focuses on how people

Exhibit 2.6   Big Ideas of the Social Constructionist Perspective

- Human consciousness, and the sense of self, is shaped by continual social interaction.
- Social reality is created when people, in social interaction, develop a common understanding of their world.
- People perform for their social audiences, but they are also free, active, and creative.
- Social interaction is grounded in language customs, as well as cultural and historical contexts.
- People can modify meanings in the process of interaction.
- Society consists of social processes, not social structures.

learn, through their interactions with each other, to classify the world and their place in it. People are seen as social beings who interact with each other and the physical world based on *shared meanings*, or shared understandings about the world. In this view, people develop their understandings of the world and themselves from social interaction, and these understandings shape their subsequent social interactions.

The intellectual roots of the social constructionist perspective are usually traced to the German philosopher Edmund Husserl, as well as to the philosophical pragmatism of John Dewey and early theorists in the symbolic interaction tradition, including Charles Horton Cooley, W. I. Thomas, and George Herbert Mead. More recent theorists include Herbert Blumer, Erving Goffman, Alfred Schutz, Harold Garfinkel, Peter Berger, and Thomas Luckmann. Randall Collins (1994) suggests that social constructionist theorizing is the type of sociology that American sociologists do best.

To the social constructionist, there is no singular objective reality, no true reality that exists "out there" in the world. There are, instead, the shared subjective realities that are created as people interact. Constructionists emphasize the existence of multiple social and cultural realities. Both persons and environments are dynamic processes, not static structures. The sociopolitical environment and history of any situation play an important role in understanding human behavior. The social constructionist would call attention to how Stanley's understanding of himself as a worker is being influenced by current economic conditions.

The importance of subjective rather than objective reality has often been summed up by the words of W. I. Thomas (Thomas & Thomas, 1928): "If men [sic] define situations as real, they are real in their consequences" (p. 128). Actually, social constructionists disagree about whether there is, in fact, some objective reality out there. Radical social constructionists believe there is not. They believe that there is no reality beyond our personal experiences. Most *postmodern theorists* fall in this category, arguing that there are no universals, including no universal truth, reality, or morality (Danto, 2008; Lyotard, 1984). The postmodernists accept that the world is "messy" and see no need to impose order on it. More moderate social constructionists believe that there are "real objects" in the world, but those objects are never known objectively. Rather, they are only known through the subjective interpretations of individuals and collectivities (C. Williams, 2006).

Social constructionists also disagree about how constraining the environment is. Some see individual actors in social interactions as essentially free, active, and creative (Gergen, 1985). Others suggest that individual actors are always performing for their social audiences, based on their understanding of community standards for human behavior (Berger & Luckmann, 1966; Goffman, 1959). The dominant position is probably the one represented by Schutz's (1932/1967) *phenomenological sociology*. While arguing that people shape social reality, Schutz also suggests that individuals and groups are constrained by the preexisting social and cultural arrangements created by their predecessors.

The social constructionist perspective sees human understanding, or human consciousness, as both the product and the driving force of social interaction. Some social constructionists focus on individual consciousness, particularly on the human capacity to interpret social interactions and to have an inner conversation with oneself about them (Cooley, 1902/1964; Ellis, 1989; G. H. Mead, 1934). They see the self as developing from interpretation of social interaction. Cooley introduces the concept of the "looking-glass self," which can be explained as "I am what I think you think I am." The looking-glass self has three components: (1) I imagine how I appear to others, (2) I imagine their judgment of me, and (3) I develop some feeling about myself that is a result of imagining their judgments of me. George Herbert Mead (1959) suggests that one has a self only when one is in community and that the self develops based on our interpretation of the *generalized other*, which is the attitude of the entire community. Cynthia Franklin (1995) suggests that these cognitively oriented versions of social constructionism are best known as *constructivism*.

Other social constructionists put greater emphasis on the nature of social interactions, calling attention to gestures and language that are used as symbols in social interaction (Charon, 1998). These symbols take on particular meaning in particular situations. These social constructionists also see social problems as social constructions, created through claims making, labeling, and other social processes (Best, 1989).

The McKinley family is coping with a great deal of change in the external world as well as within their family system. The social constructionist perspective would encourage us to be interested in how they are describing and explaining these changes. For example, how do they understand their struggles in the labor market and the housing market? How much do they attribute their struggles to personal failings, to being victims of a globalized world economy that is creating more privilege for some and more disadvantage for others, or perhaps to corporate greed that caused a meltdown in the housing and financial markets? How do their attributions affect their sense of self-worth? The social constructionist perspective would also be interested in how the McKinley family understands the meaning of family and how they have developed this understanding in their ongoing interactions with each other and the world.

This is how the social constructionist perspective measures against the criteria for judging theories:

- *Coherence and conceptual clarity.* Social constructionism, both the original phenomenological and symbolic interactional concepts as well as the contemporary postmodern conceptualizations, is often criticized as vague and unclear. Over the past few decades, a great diversity of theorizing has been done within this broad theoretical perspective, and there is much fragmentation of ideas. Sociologists in the conflict and rational choice traditions have begun to incorporate social constructionist ideas, particularly those related to meaning making, which has further blurred the boundaries of this perspective. One challenge to the consistency of the social constructionist perspective is that it denies the one-absolute-truth, objective approach to reality while arguing that it is absolutely true that reality is subjective. It criticizes grand theorizing while presenting a grand theory of human behavior.

- *Testability and evidence of empirical support.* Because of the vagueness of concepts, the social constructionist perspective has been criticized for being difficult to operationalize for empirical research. Social constructionists have responded in two different ways to this criticism. Some social constructionists argue that it is naïve to think that any theory can be evaluated based on empirical evidence (S. Cole, 1992). However, many social constructionist proponents have challenged the criticism and offered alternative criteria for evaluating theory (see Witkin & Gottschalk, 1988). They also propose an alternative research methodology, constructivist research (Lincoln & Guba, 1985), which is sensitive to the context of the research, seeks the views of key parties, and takes into account the interactions involved in the research process (Schutt, 2009; C. Williams, 2006). Research in the postmodern tradition is interested in stories, not facts (Danto, 2008). Social constructionism has stimulated a trend in the behavioral sciences to use a mix of quantitative and qualitative research methodologies to accommodate both objective and subjective reality.

- *Comprehensiveness.* Social constructionism pays little attention to the role of biology in human behavior, with the exception of a few constructivist biologists (Maturana, 1988; J. Stewart, 2001; Varela, 1989). In some versions of social constructionism, cognitive processes are central (M. Mahoney, 1991), and the social construction of emotions is considered in others (A. Ellis, 1989). With the emphasis on meaning making, social constructionism is open to the role of religion and spirituality in human behavior. With its emphasis on social interaction, the social constructionist perspective is strong in attention to the social environment. It has been criticized, however, for failing to pay attention to the macro world of social institutions and social structure. Time, and the role of history, is respected in the social constructionist perspective, with many authors drawing attention to the historical era in which behavior is constructed. Reality, to the social constructionist, is a moving target (C. Williams, 2006).

- *Diversity and power.* With its emphasis on multiple social realities, the social constructionist perspective is strong in its ability to accommodate diversity. It has been criticized, however, for failure to provide the theoretical tools necessary for the analysis of power relationships (Coser, 1975; Ritzer, 2008b; C. Williams, 2006). Some critics have suggested that many contemporary postmodern versions of social constructionism, by ignoring power while focusing on multiple voices and multiple meanings in the construction of reality, reduce oppression to mere difference (C. Williams, 2006). These critics suggest that this reduction of oppression to difference masks the fact that some actors have greater power than others to privilege their own constructions of reality and to disadvantage the constructions of other actors. This criticism cannot be leveled at all versions of social constructionism, however. Social work scholars have been attracted to those versions of the social constructionist perspective that have incorporated pieces of the conflict tradition (E. Freeman & Couchonnal, 2006; Laird, 1994; Saleebey, 1994), particularly the early work of Michel Foucault (1969) on the relationship between power and knowledge. They propose that in contemporary society, minority or "local" knowledges are denied credibility in majority-dominated social arenas and suggest that social work practitioners can bring credibility to minority viewpoints by allowing oppressed individuals and groups to tell their own stories.

- *Usefulness for social work practice.* Social constructionism gives new meaning to the old social work adage, "Begin where the client is." In the social constructionist perspective, the social work relationship begins with developing an understanding of how the client views the situation and what the client would like to have happen. The current strong interest in solution-focused and narrative and storytelling therapies is based on the social constructionist perspective. Solution-focused approaches attempt to help clients construct solutions rather than solve problems. They are based on the assumption that clients want to change and are capable of envisioning the change they would like to see. Narrative therapy starts with the assumption that we all tell ourselves stories about our lives, developing dominant story lines and forgetting material that does not fit into them. A goal of therapy is to help clients see more realities in their story lines, with other possible interpretations of events (J. Walsh, 2010). The social worker should engage the client in thinking about the social, cultural, and historical environments in which his or her version of reality was constructed, which, for members of oppressed groups, may lead to empowerment through *restorying,* or revision of the story line (R. R. Greene & Cohen, 2005; Laird, 1994; Saleebey, 1994). Joseph Walsh suggests that narrative therapy can be particularly helpful to hospice patients who are reflecting on their life stories. That is, indeed, the approach of the hospice social worker who is working with Ruth McKinley and her family. At the level of groups and organizations, the social constructionist perspective recommends getting discordant groups to engage in sincere discussion of their disparate constructions of reality and to negotiate lines of action acceptable to all (C. Fox & Miller, 1995).

Critical Thinking Questions 2.1

The systems, conflict, rational choice, and social constructionist perspectives all pay attention to the environment that is external to individuals. It could be argued that the hospice social worker should only be focusing on Ruth McKinley's personal needs and reactions. How would you argue in favor of that approach? How would you argue against it?

PSYCHODYNAMIC PERSPECTIVE

Both Stanley and Marcia McKinley's despondence and loss of hope are apparent in their first meeting with the hospice social worker—and easy to understand. Think about the losses they have faced in the past year: loss of job (Stanley), loss of income (Stanley and Marcia), loss of valued roles (provider for Stanley and caregiver for Marcia), and loss of health (Marcia). They also face the impending loss of Ruth, the last surviving parent for them, and the possible loss of their home. This rapid accumulation of loss would challenge, even overwhelm, the adaptive capacities of most any human. Bethany is thinking of dropping out of school, a decision that will involve loss of a dream, at least temporarily.

In the midst of all that loss, we also note the deep attachment that all four family members—Ruth, Stanley, Marcia, and Bethany—have for each other. This suggests that early nurturing environments supported the development of secure attachments. As you explore the McKinley family's situation from the psychodynamic perspective (see Exhibit 2.7), these and other ideas emerge.

The **psychodynamic perspective** is concerned with how internal processes such as needs, drives, and emotions motivate human behavior. The perspective has evolved over the years, moving from the classical psychodynamic emphasis on innate drives and unconscious processes toward greater emphasis on the adaptive capacities of individuals and their interactions with the environment. The origins of all psychodynamic theories are in the work of Sigmund Freud; other prominent theorists in the evolving psychodynamic perspective include Carl Jung, Anna Freud, Melanie Klein, Margaret Mahler, Karen Horney, Heinz Hartmann, Robert W. White, Donald Winnicott, Otto Kernberg, Heinz Kohut, and Erik Erikson. More recent formulations of the perspective include ego psychology, object relations, self psychology, and relational-cultural theories. We will say more about these more recent developments later.

To trace the evolution of the psychodynamic perspective, it is essential to begin with its Freudian roots. Sigmund Freud looked at the human personality from a number of interrelated points of view; the most notable are his drive or instinct theory, topographical theory, structural theory, and psychosexual stage theory, summarized below.

Exhibit 2.7   Big Ideas of the Psychodynamic Perspective

- Emotions have a central place in human behavior.
- Unconscious, as well as conscious, mental activity serves as the motivating force in human behavior.
- Early childhood experiences are central in the patterning of an individual's emotions and, therefore, are central to problems of living throughout life.
- Individuals may become overwhelmed by internal or external demands.
- Individuals frequently use ego defense mechanisms to avoid becoming overwhelmed by internal or external demands.

Freud revised each of these approaches to human personality over time, and different followers of Freud have attended to different aspects of his theoretical works, further revising each of them over time.

Drive or instinct theory. This theory proposes that human behavior is motivated by two basic instincts: *thanatos,* or the drive for aggression or destruction, and *eros,* or the drive for life (through sexual gratification). Recent revisions of drive theory have suggested that human behavior is also motivated by drives for mastery (see D. Goldstein, 1996) and for connectedness (Borden, 2009).

Topographical theory of the mind. Topographical theory proposes three states of mind: conscious mental activities of which we are fully aware; preconscious thoughts and feelings that can be easily brought to mind; and unconscious thoughts, feelings, and desires of which we are not aware but which have a powerful influence on our behavior. Although all psychodynamic theorists believe in the unconscious, the different versions of the theory put different emphases on the importance of the unconscious in human behavior.

Structural model of the mind. This model proposes that personality is structured around three parts: the *id,* which is unconscious and strives for satisfaction of basic instincts; the *superego,* which is made up of conscience and ideals and is the censor of the id; and the *ego,* which is the rational part of personality that mediates between the id and the superego. Freud and his early followers were most interested in the id and the pathologies that emanate from it, but later followers have focused primarily on ego strengths and the drive for adaptation. Both ego psychology and self psychology are in this later tradition.

Psychosexual stage theory. This theory proposes a five-stage model of child development, based on sexual instincts: the oral phase (birth to about 18 months), when the search for pleasure is centered in the mouth; the anal phase (from about 18 months to 3 years), when the search for pleasure is centered in the anus; the phallic phase (ages 3–6), when the search for pleasure is centered in the genitals; the latency phase (ages 6–8), when erotic urges are repressed; and the genital phase (adolescence onward), when the search for pleasure is centered in the genitals and sexual intimacy. Freud asserted that there was no further personality development in adulthood. Recent revisions of psychodynamic theory, starting with the work of Erik Erikson (1963), have challenged that idea. Although they still give primacy to the childhood years, they suggest that personality continues to develop over the life course. Recent theories also put less emphasis on sexual instincts in stage development.

Let's turn now to some revisions of Freudian theory. *Ego psychology* gives primary attention to the rational part of the mind and the human capacity for adaptation. It recognizes conscious as well as unconscious attempts to cope, and the importance of both past and present experiences. Defense mechanisms, unconscious processes that keep intolerable threats from conscious awareness, play an important role in ego psychology (see E. Goldstein, 2001). *Object relations theory* studies how people develop attitudes toward others in the context of early nurturing relationships, and how those attitudes affect the view of the self as well as social relationships. In this tradition, John Bowlby's attachment theory has become the basis for a psychobiological theory of attachment (Barnekow & Kraemer, 2005; Kraemer, 1992). *Self psychology* focuses on the individual need to organize the personality into a cohesive sense of self and to build relationships that support this sense of self (see E. Goldstein, 2001). *Relational-cultural theory,* also known as relational feminist theory, proposes that the basic human drive is for relationships with others. The self is understood to develop and mature through emotional connectedness in mutually empathic relationships, rather than through a process of separation and independence as proposed by traditional object relations theory. Human connectedness is emphasized, human diversity acknowledged, and human difference normalized rather than pathologized (Borden, 2009; Freedberg, 2007). You will read more about the psychodynamic perspective in Chapter 4.

Here are the criteria for evaluating theories as applied to the psychodynamic perspective:

- *Coherence and conceptual clarity.* Criticisms that the psychodynamic perspective lacks logical consistency are directed primarily at Freud's original concepts and propositions, which were not entirely consistent because they evolved over time. Ego psychology and object relations theorists strengthened the logical consistency of the psychodynamic perspective by expanding and clarifying definitions of major concepts. Theories in the psychodynamic perspective are also criticized for the vague and abstract nature of their concepts.

- *Testability and evidence of empirical support.* Later psychodynamic theorists translated Freud's ideas into more measurable terms. Consequently, much empirical work has been based on the psychodynamic perspective. Contradictions in the research findings may be due in large part to the use of different definitions and measures. Some concepts, such as mastery or competence, have strong empirical support, but this support has been generated primarily by other schools of thought, such as developmental psychology and Albert Bandura's social behaviorism. Recent long-term longitudinal studies support the importance of childhood experiences, but also indicate that personality continues to develop throughout life (see E. Werner & Smith, 2001). There is growing evidence of the supremely important role that attachment plays in shaping development over the life course (see Trees, 2006).

- *Comprehensiveness.* Early psychodynamic theories were primarily concerned with internal psychological processes. Strong attention is paid to emotions, and in recent formulations, cognitions are also acknowledged. Although Freud assumed that biology determines behavior, he developed his theory several decades before neurological science began to uncover the biological base of emotions. Recently, however, psychodynamic theorists have begun to incorporate new developments in neurological sciences about early brain development into their formulations (see, e.g., Applegate & Shapiro, 2005). With the exception of Carl Jung,

early psychodynamic theorists were not interested in the spiritual aspects of human behavior, typically viewing them as irrational defenses against anxiety. Recently, psychodynamically oriented social workers have attempted to integrate spirituality into their practice (see Northcut, 2000). As for environments, most psychodynamic theory conceptualizes them as sources of conflicts with which the individual must struggle. Relational-cultural theory, with its emphasis on supporting the growth of relationships and community, takes exception to that view. Overall, however, environments beyond the family or other close interpersonal relationships are ignored. This has led to criticisms of "mother blaming" and "family blaming" in traditional psychodynamic theories. Social, economic, political, and historical environments of human behavior are probably implied in ego psychology, but they are not explicated. As for time, the focus is on how people change across childhood. There has traditionally been little attempt to account for change after childhood or to recognize the contributions of historical time to human behavior, but the relational-cultural theory looks at relationships across the life course.

- *Diversity and power.* Traditional psychodynamic theories search for universal laws of behavior and their applicability to unique individuals. Thus, diversity of experience at the group level has been quite neglected in this tradition until recently. Moreover, in the main, "universal" laws have been developed through analysis of heterosexual men of White, Anglo-Saxon, middle-class culture. Feminists, as well as members of racial and ethnic minority groups, have criticized the psychodynamic bias toward thinking of people as autonomous individuals (Freedberg, 2007). These critics suggest that viewing this standard as "normal" makes the connectedness found among many women and members of racial and ethnic minority groups seem pathological. Recently, proponents of the psychodynamic perspective have tried to correct for these biases and develop a better understanding of human diversity (E. Goldstein, 1995). Psychodynamic theories are strong in their recognition of power dynamics in parent–child relationships and in exploration of the life worlds of children. They are weaker, overall, in looking at power issues in other relationships, however, including gender relationships. Early on, Freud recognized gender differences, even gender inequality, but attributed them to moral deficits within women. Erik Erikson's theory of psychosocial development has a somewhat greater emphasis on social forces. However, Erikson's work has been criticized for its lack of attention to the worlds of women, racial minorities, and sexual minorities. It did not take into account the persistently hostile environments in which minority group members interact or the extraordinary coping strategies needed to negotiate those environments. In the contemporary era, psychoanalytic feminists have reworked Freud's ideas to focus on patriarchy, asking the question, "Why do men work so hard to maintain patriarchy and why do women put so little energy into challenging patriarchy?" (Lengermann & Niebrugge-Brantley, 2007). They propose that the answer to this question is found in the gender-based early child-rearing environment. African American social workers have proposed that social workers can help to empower African American clients by integrating empowerment theory and an Afrocentric perspective with the ego-strengthening aspects of ego psychology (Manning, Cornelius, & Okundaye, 2004). Relational-cultural theory was developed out of concerns about the male bias in existing psychodynamic theories.

- *Usefulness for social work practice.* Most versions of the psychodynamic perspective have included clinical theory as well as human behavior theory. Differences of opinion about principles of practice reflect the theoretical evolution that has occurred. Practice principles common to all versions of the psychodynamic perspective include the centrality of the professional–client relationship, the curative value of expressing emotional conflicts and understanding past events, and the goals of self-awareness and self-control. In contrast to the classical psychodynamic approach, recent formulations include directive as well as nondirective

intervention, short-term as well as long-term intervention, and environmental manipulations—such as locating counseling regarding possible mortgage foreclosure for the McKinley family—along with intrapsychic manipulations such as emotional catharsis. Ego psychology has also been used to develop principles for prevention activities in addition to principles of remediation (D. Goldstein, 1996). In general, however, the psychodynamic perspective does not suggest practice principles at the level of communities, organizations, and social institutions. Thus, it would not help you to think about how to influence public policy related to housing, income security, or access to health care.

DEVELOPMENTAL PERSPECTIVE

Another way to think about the McKinley family is to view their situation in terms of the developmental tasks that they face. You might note that Ruth McKinley is in late adulthood and engaged in a review of her life journey, attempting to make peace with the life she has lived. You might also note that Stanley and Marcia assumed caregiving responsibilities for Ruth 5 years ago while also continuing to provide support to Bethany as she moved into young adulthood. At the current time, their struggles to stay employed and hold onto their house are situations that were once thought to be "off time" for individuals in middle adulthood, but have become more common for the current cohort of midlife adults. Bethany assumed a caregiving role with Ruth as she emerged into adulthood, and that also may seem off time. We can think about where she stands with the developmental markers typically associated with young adulthood: education/work, intimate relationship, leaving home, and starting a career. These observations are consistent with the central ideas of the developmental perspective, summarized in Exhibit 2.8.

The focus of the **developmental perspective** is on how human behavior unfolds across the life course, how people change and stay the same over time. Human development is seen to occur in clearly

Exhibit 2.8   Big Ideas of the Developmental Perspective

- Human development occurs in clearly defined, age-graded stages.
- Each stage of life is qualitatively different from all other stages.
- Each stage builds on earlier stages.
- Human development is a complex interaction of biological, psychological, and social factors.
- Moving from one stage to the next involves new tasks and changes in statuses and roles.

defined stages based on a complex interaction of biological, psychological, and social processes. Each new stage involves new tasks and brings changes in social roles and statuses. Currently, there are two streams of theorizing in the developmental perspective, one based in psychology and one based in sociology.

Life span or *life cycle theory,* based in psychology, focuses on the inner life during age-related stages. The study of life span development is rooted in Freud's (1905/1953) theory of psychosexual stages of childhood development, but Erikson (1963) has been the most influential developmental theorist to date because his model of development includes

Photo 2.3   Families are composed of people in different life stages, occupying different statuses and playing different roles, as suggested by the developmental perspective.

adult as well as child stages of development. Other early life cycle theorists include Margaret Mahler, Harry Stack Sullivan, and Jean Piaget. More recent developmental theorists include Daniel Levinson, George Vaillant, Roger Gould, Lawrence Kohlberg, Robert Havighurst, Joan Borysenko, Barbara Newman, and Philip Newman.

Erikson (1963) proposed an *epigenetic model of human development,* in which the psychological unfolding of personality takes place in sequences. Healthy development depends on the mastery of life tasks at the appropriate time in the sequence. Although life span theorists tend to agree with this epigenetic principle, there is also growing agreement that the stages are experienced in a more flexible way than Erikson proposed, with cultural, economic, and personal circumstances leading to some differences in timing and sequencing (Sollod, Wilson, & Monte, 2009). For example, Bethany McKinley is thinking of postponing school and career development to be a support to her extended family in a stressful period in the life of the family. Stanley McKinley is faced with a need to rethink his occupational career at the age of 50.

Erikson divided the life cycle into eight stages, each with a special psychosocial crisis:

Stage 1 (birth–1 year): basic trust versus mistrust

Stage 2 (ages 2–3): autonomy versus shame, doubt

Stage 3 (ages 3–5): initiative versus guilt

Stage 4 (ages 6–12): industry versus inferiority

Stage 5 (ages 12–18 or so): identity versus role confusion

Stage 6 (early–late 20s): intimacy versus isolation

Stage 7 (late 20s–50s): generativity versus stagnation

Stage 8 (late adulthood): integrity versus despair

Early life span theorists, including Erikson, saw their models of development as universal, applying equally well to all groups of people. This idea has been the target of much criticism, with suggestions that the traditional models are based on the experiences of Anglo, White, heterosexual, middle-class men and do not apply well to members of other groups. This criticism has led to a number of life cycle models for specific groups, such as women (Borysenko, 1996), gay and lesbian persons (e.g., Troiden, 1989), and African Americans (Cross, Parham, & Black, 1991). Life span theories have also been criticized for failing to deal with historical time and the cohort effects on human behavior that arise when groups of persons born in the same historical time share cultural influences and historical events at the same period in their lives.

These criticisms have helped to stimulate development of the *life course perspective* in sociology. This relatively new perspective conceptualizes the life course as a social, rather than psychological, phenomenon that is nonetheless unique for each individual, with some common life course markers, or transitions, related to shared social and historical contexts (George, 1993). Glen Elder, Jr. (1998), and Tamara Hareven (2000) have been major forces in the development of the life course perspective. In its current state, there are six major themes in the life course perspective: interplay of human lives and historical time; biological, psychological, and social timing of human lives; linked or interdependent lives; human capacity for choice making; diversity in life course trajectories; and developmental risk and protection. As you may recall, the life course perspective is the conceptual framework for Part III of this book.

The life course perspective would suggest that the timing of young adult transition markers for Bethany McKinley has been influenced by historical trends toward increasing levels of education and delayed marriage. It would also call attention to the impact of the global economic recession that began in December 2007 on Stanley's occupational trajectory. The life course perspective would emphasize how the life course trajectories of Stanley, Marcia, Bethany, and Ruth are intertwined, and how what happens in one generation reverberates up and down the extended family line. For example, Stanley, Marcia, and Bethany reorganized their work and family lives to care for Ruth after her stroke. Give some thought to how their life journeys might have been different if Ruth had not required care at that time. Or imagine what decision Bethany might be making about school if Marcia was in stronger health. This notion that families are linked across generations by both opportunity and misfortune is a central idea of the life course perspective, but you may also recognize it as consistent with the system perspective's emphasis on interdependence. The evolving life course model respects the idea of role transition that is so central to the developmental perspective, but it also recognizes the multiplicity of interacting factors that contribute to diversity in the timing and experience of these transitions.

Here is how the criteria for evaluating theories apply to the developmental perspective:

- *Coherence and conceptual clarity.* Classical developmental theory's notion of life stages is internally consistent and conceptually clear. Theorists have been able to build on each other's work in a coherent manner. Still in its early stages, the life course perspective has developed some coherence and beginning clarity about the major concepts. When viewing these two developmental streams together, contradictions appear in terms of universality versus diversity in life span/life course development.

- *Testability and evidence of empirical support.* Many of Erikson's ideas have been employed and verified in empirical research, but until recently, much of developmental research has been based on White, heterosexual, middle-class males. Another concern is that by defining normal as average, developmental research fails to capture the life worlds of groups who deviate even moderately from the average, or even to capture the broad range of behavior considered normal. Thus, empirical support for the developmental perspective is based to some extent on statistical masking of diversity. The life course perspective has offered a glimpse of diversity, however, because it has been developed, in the main, from the results of longitudinal research, which follows the same people over an extended period of time. The benefit of longitudinal research is that it clarifies whether differences between age groups are really based on developmental differences or whether they reflect cohort effects from living in particular cultures at

particular historical times. There is a growing body of longitudinal research in the life course tradition (see Elder & Giele, 2009a).

- *Comprehensiveness.* The developmental perspective, when both theoretical streams are taken together, gets relatively high marks for comprehensiveness. Both the life span and the life course streams recognize human behavior as an outcome of complex interactions of biological, psychological, and social factors, although most theorists in both streams pay little attention to the spiritual dimension. The traditional life span approach pays too little attention to the political, economic, and cultural environments of human behavior; the life course perspective pays too little attention to psychological factors. Both approaches attend to the dimension of time, in terms of linear time, but the life course perspective attends to time in a more comprehensive manner, by emphasizing the role of historical time in human behavior. Indeed, the developmental perspective is the only one of the eight perspectives discussed here that makes time a major focus.

- *Diversity and power.* The early life span models were looking for universal stages of human development and did not attend to issues of diversity. More recent life span models have paid more attention to diversity, and diversity of pathways through life is a major theme in the life course perspective. Likewise, the traditional life span approach did not take account of power relationships, with the possible exception of power dynamics in the parent–child relationship. Moreover, traditional life span models are based on the average White, middle-class, heterosexual, Anglo-Saxon male and ignore the worlds of members of nondominant groups. Newer models of life span development have attempted to correct for that failure. Daniel Levinson's (1996) study of women's lives is noteworthy in that regard; it includes a sample of women diversified by race and social class and acknowledges the impact of gender power differentials on women's development. The life course perspective recognizes patterns of advantage and disadvantage in life course trajectories, and life course researchers have done considerable research on the accumulation of advantage and disadvantage over the life course (see Ferraro & Shippee, 2009).

- *Usefulness for social work practice.* Erikson's model has often been used for assessment purposes in social work practice, and in a positive sense, the model can aid indirectly in the identification of potential personal and social developmental resources. Traditional life span theories should be applied, however, only with recognition of the ethnocentrism expressed in them. They have traditionally suggested, for example, that there is one right way to raise a child, one "appropriate" type of relationship with the family of origin, and one "healthy" way to develop intimate relationships in adulthood. Although it is harder to extrapolate practice principles from the more complex, still-emerging life course perspective, it seems more promising for understanding diverse persons in diverse environments. It suggests that individuals must always be assessed within familial, cultural, and historical contexts. Overall, the developmental perspective can be viewed as optimistic. Most people face difficult transitions, life crises, and developmental or other challenges at some point, and many people have been reassured to hear that their struggle is "typical." Because the developmental perspective sees individuals as having the possibility to rework their inner experiences, as well as their family relationships, clients may be assisted in finding new strategies for getting their lives back on course. For example, Stanley McKinley could explore untapped talents and interests that might be used to get his occupational career moving again.

SOCIAL BEHAVIORAL PERSPECTIVE

The hospice social worker observed Bethany McKinley's warm and gentle interaction with her grandmother, Ruth. Therefore, she wasn't surprised later to hear Bethany describe Ruth as kind. She imagined that Ruth modeled kind behavior as she cared for Bethany when Bethany was a young child.

She also observed that Stanley, Marcia, and Bethany seemed to reinforce kind behavior in each other. She noticed how Stanley and Bethany put their arms around Marcia when she began to cry. The social worker was also struck by statements by both Stanley and Marcia that seem to indicate that they have lost their confidence in their ability to make things happen in their lives. She understood how recent events could have undermined their confidence, but she was curious whether she had simply caught them on a down day or if, indeed, they no longer have expectations of being able to improve their situation. Viewing the McKinley family from a social behavioral perspective (see Exhibit 2.9) can lead to such assessment and questions.

| Exhibit 2.9 | Big Ideas of the Social Behavioral Perspective |

- Human behavior is learned when individuals interact with the environment.
- All human behavior is learned by the same principles: association of environmental stimuli, reinforcement, imitation, and personal expectations and meaning.
- All human problems can be formulated as undesirable behavior.
- All behavior can be defined and changed.

Theories in the **social behavioral perspective,** sometimes called the social learning perspective, suggest that human behavior is learned as individuals interact with their environments. But behaviorists disagree among themselves about the processes by which behavior is learned. Over time, three major versions of behavioral theory have been presented, proposing different mechanisms by which learning occurs:

Classical conditioning theory, also known as *respondent conditioning,* sees behavior as learned through association, when a naturally occurring stimulus (unconditioned stimulus) is paired with a neutral stimulus (conditioned stimulus). This approach is usually traced to a classic experiment by Russian physiologist Ivan Pavlov, who showed, first, that dogs naturally salivate (unconditioned response) in response to meat powder on the tongue (unconditioned stimulus). Then, a ringing bell (conditioned stimulus) was paired with the meat powder a number of times. Eventually, the dog salivated (conditioned response) to the ringing of the bell (conditioned stimulus). In other words, an initially neutral stimulus comes to produce a particular behavioral response after it is repeatedly paired with another stimulus of significance. Classical conditioning plays a role in understanding many problems that social work clients experience. For example, a woman with an alcohol abuse problem may experience urges to drink when in a location where she often engaged in drinking alcohol before getting sober. Anxiety disorders are also often conditioned; for example, a humiliating experience with public speaking may lead to a deep-seated and long-lasting fear of it, which can result in anxiety attacks in situations where the person has to speak publicly. This approach looks for antecedents of behavior—stimuli that precede behavior—as the mechanism for learning.

Photo 2.4 Classical conditioning is traced to an experiment Russian physiologist Ivan Pavlov performed with dogs.

Operant conditioning theory, sometimes known as *instrumental conditioning,* sees behavior as the result of reinforcement. It is built on the work of two American psychologists, John B. Watson and B. F. Skinner. In operant conditioning, behavior is learned as it is strengthened or weakened by the reinforcement (rewards and punishments) it receives or, in other words, by the consequences of the behavior. Behaviors are strengthened when they are followed by positive consequences and weakened when they are followed by negative consequences. A classic experiment demonstrated that if a pigeon is given a food pellet each time it touches a lever, over time the pigeon learns to touch the lever to receive a food pellet. This approach looks for *consequences* of behavior—what comes after the behavior—as the mechanism for learning the behavior. We all use operant conditioning as we go about our daily lives. We use *positive reinforcers,* such as smiles or praise, to reward behaviors that we find pleasing, in the hopes of strengthening those behaviors. *Negative reinforcers* are also used regularly in social life to stop or avoid unpleasant behavior. For example, the adolescent girl cleans her room to avoid parental complaints. Avoiding the complaints reinforces the room-cleaning behavior.

Cognitive social learning theory, also known as *cognitive behavioral theory* or *social cognitive theory,* with Albert Bandura as its chief contemporary proponent, suggests that behavior is also learned by imitation, observation, beliefs, and expectations. In this view, the "learner" is not passively manipulated by elements of the environment but can use cognitive processes to learn behaviors. Observing and imitating models is a pervasive method for learning human behavior. Bandura (1977a, 1986) proposes that human behavior is also driven by beliefs and expectations. He suggests that **self-efficacy** (a sense of personal competence) and **efficacy expectation** (an expectation that one can personally accomplish a goal) play an important role in motivation and human behavior. Bandura (2001, 2002) has recently extended his theory of self-efficacy to propose three models of agency (the capacity to intentionally make things happen): *personal agency* of the individual actor, *proxy agency* in which people reach goals by influencing others to act on their behalf, and *collective agency* in which people act cooperatively to reach a goal.

Although the different streams of social behavioral theorizing disagree about the mechanisms by which behavioral learning occurs, there is agreement that differences in behavior occur when the same learning processes happen in different environments. In this perspective, all human problems of living can be defined in terms of undesirable behaviors, and all behaviors can be defined, measured, and changed.

This is how social behavioral perspectives rate on the criteria for evaluating theories:

• *Coherence and conceptual clarity.* Although there are disagreements about the mechanisms of learning among the various streams of the social behavioral perspective, within each stream, ideas are logically developed in a consistent manner. The social behavioral perspective gets high marks for conceptual clarity; concepts are very clearly defined in each of the streams.

• *Testability and evidence of empirical support.* Social behavioral concepts are easily measured for empirical investigation because theorizing has been based, in very large part, on laboratory research. This characteristic is also a drawback of the social behavioral perspective, however, because laboratory experiments by design eliminate much of the complexity of person-environment configurations. Furthermore, all versions have had their "share of confirmations and disconfirmations" (Monte & Sollod, 2003, p. 578). In general, however, it seems fair to say that all streams of the social behavioral perspective have attained a relatively high degree of empirical support.

• *Comprehensiveness.* Overall, the social behavioral perspective sacrifices multidimensional understanding to gain logical consistency and testability. Although it accepts biology's impact on learning, little attention is paid to biology, except for recent work of Bandura (2001, 2002), which recognizes

the role of biology in human behavior, noting that in most spheres, while biology sets constraints on behavior, it also permits a wide range of behaviors. It is also important to note that contemporary research on neurophysiology and the immune system indicate that classical conditioning plays a role in physiological functioning (Pert, 1997). Cognition and emotion are not included in theories of classical and operant conditioning, but they do receive attention in social cognitive theory. Spiritual factors are considered immeasurable and irrelevant in classical and operant conditioning theories. They would be relevant only to the extent that they reinforce behavior. For this reason, many theorists and social workers see social behaviorism as dehumanizing. Although environment plays a large role in the social behavioral perspective, the view of environment is quite limited in classical and operant conditioning. Typically, the social behavioral perspective searches for the one environmental factor, or contingency, that has reinforced one specific behavior. The identified contingency is usually in the micro system (such as the family) or sometimes in the meso system (e.g., a school classroom), but these systems are not typically put in social, economic, political, or historical contexts. One exception is Bandura's social cognitive theory, which acknowledges broad systemic influences on the development of gender roles. Social work scholars applying behavioral principles have also made notable efforts to incorporate a broader view of the environments of human behavior (Mattaini, 1997). Time is important in this perspective only in terms of the juxtaposition of stimuli and reinforcement. The social behaviorist is careful to analyze antecedents and consequences of behavior.

• *Diversity and power.* The social behavioral perspective receives low marks in terms of both diversity and power issues. Very little attention has been paid to recognizing diversity in human behaviors, and it is assumed that the same mechanisms of learning work equally well for all groups. Likewise, the social behavioral perspective attends little to issues of power and oppression. Operant behavioral theory recommends rewards over punishment, but it does not account for the coercion and oppression inherent in power relationships at every system level. It is quite possible, therefore, for the professional behavior modifier to be in service to oppressive forces. On the other hand, behavioral methods can be used in service to social work values (Thyer & Wodarski, 2007). Bandura (1986) writes specifically about power as related to gender roles. He and other theorists note that persons in nondominant positions are particularly vulnerable to **learned helplessness** (see Mikulincer, 1994; Seligman, 1992), in which a person's prior experience with environmental forces has led to low self-efficacy and expectations of efficacy. You may find the concepts of self-efficacy and learned helplessness particularly useful in thinking about both Stanley and Marcia McKinley's situations. Both have experienced some setbacks that may be leading them to expect less of themselves.

- *Usefulness for social work practice.* A major strength of the social behavioral perspective is the ease with which principles of behavior modification can be extrapolated, and it is probably a rare person who has not used social behavioral principles of action at some point. Social workers and psychologists have used social behavioral methods primarily to modify undesirable behavior of individuals. For example, systematic desensitization techniques are used to diminish or eradicate anxiety symptoms. Parent training programs often teach parents how to make more effective use of reinforcements to strengthen positive behaviors and weaken negative behaviors in their children. Social workers often model how to enact new behaviors for their clients. Dialectical behavior therapy teaches adaptive coping related to emotion regulation, distress tolerance, cognitive distortions, and interpersonal communication (J. Walsh, 2010). However, behavioral methods have not been used effectively to produce social reform. Richard Stuart (1989) reminds us that behavior modification was once a "social movement" that appealed to young social reformers who were more interested in changing social conditi... that produce atypical behaviors than in ... systems for managing atypical beha... *Walden Two* (1948) was the imp...

by these young reformers to build nonpunitive communities, which represented significant modification of social conditions (see Kinkade, 1973; Wheeler, 1973). And, indeed, Bandura's (2002) recent conceptualization of proxy agency and collective agency has implications for social reform.

HUMANISTIC PERSPECTIVE

Consistent with the social work code of ethics, the hospice social worker who is making contact with the McKinley family believes in the dignity and worth of all humans. Her experiences as a hospice social worker have reinforced her belief that each person is unique, and even though she has worked with over 100 hospice patients, she expects Ruth McKinley's story to be in some ways unlike any other story she has heard. She is eager to hear more about how Ruth sees her situation and whether there are any things she would like to change in the limited time she has left. The social worker takes note of strengths she sees in the McKinley family, their love and kindness toward each other, and their courage in the face of an accumulation of stress. She wants to hear more about how Stanley, Marcia, and Bethany are thinking about their relationships with Ruth and whether there are any changes they would like to make in those relationships during Ruth's final days. Her thoughts and planned course of action reflect the humanistic perspectiv... marized in Exhibit 2.10.

The humanistic ... "third force" ... oped in rea... versions ... as intrap... perspecti... (Sollod ... **istic p...** and e... siz...

Exhibit 2.10   Big Ideas of the Humanistic Perspective

- Each person is unique and has value.
- Each person is responsible for the choices he or she makes within the limits of freedom.
- People always have the capacity to change themselves, even to make radical change.
- Human behavior can be understood only from the vantage point of the "phenomenal self"—from the internal frame of reference of the individual.
- Behaving in ways that are not consistent with the true self causes anxiety.
- Human behavior is driven by a desire for growth, personal meaning, and competence, and by a need to experience a bond with others.

theme the idea that people are simultaneously free and constrained, both active and passive agents; and the growing movement of positive psychology.

Like social constructionism, the humanistic perspective is often traced to the German phenomenological philosopher Edmund Husserl (Krill, 1996). It is also influenced by a host of existential philosophers, beginning with Søren Kierkegaard and including Friedrich Nietzsche, Martin Heidegger, Jean-Paul Sartre, Albert Camus, Simone de Beauvoir, Martin Buber, and Paul Tillich. Other early contributors to existential psychology include Viktor Frankl, Rollo May, Carl Jung, R. D. Laing, Karen Horney, and Erich Fromm. Perhaps the most influential contributions to humanistic psychology were made by Carl Rogers (1951) and Abraham Maslow (1962). Maslow is considered one of the founders *personal psychology,* which he labeled as the ____ gy, and Ken Wilber (2006) ____ fluential transper- ____ apter 5.

____ eloped out ____ uring and ____ ry themes

____ wth.

It is the emphasis on the necessity for suffering that sets existentialism apart from humanism.

Abraham Maslow (1962), a humanistic psychologist, was drawn to understand "peak experiences," or intense mystical moments of feeling connected to other people, nature, or a divine being. Maslow found peak experiences to occur often among self-actualizing people, or people who were expressing their innate potentials. Maslow developed a theory of **hierarchy of needs,** which suggests that higher needs cannot emerge in full motivational force until lower needs have been at least partially satisfied. Physiological needs are at the bottom of the hierarchy and the need for self-actualization at the top. The needs are listed below, in order from the bottom to the top of Maslow's hierarchy:

1. *Physiological needs:* hunger, thirst, sex

2. *Safety needs:* avoidance of pain and anxiety; desire for security

3. *Belongingness and love needs:* affection, intimacy

4. *Esteem needs:* self-respect, adequacy, mastery

5. *Self-actualization:* to be fully what one can be; altruism, beauty, creativity, justice

Carl Rogers (1951), another major humanistic psychologist, was interested in the capacity ____ humans to change in therapeutic relation- ____ began his professional career at the ____ ld Guidance Center, where he worked with social workers who had been trained at the Philadelphia School of Social Work. He has acknowledged Otto Rank, Jessie Taft, and the social workers at the Rochester agency, for their influence on his thinking about the importance of responding to client feelings (J. Hart, 1970). He came to believe that humans have vast internal resources for self-understanding and self-directed behavior. He emphasized, therefore, the dignity and worth of each individual, and presented the ideal interpersonal conditions under which people come to use their vast internal resources to become "more fully functioning." These conditions have become known as the core conditions of the therapeutic process: empathy, warmth, and genuineness.

Maslow is said to have coined the term "positive psychology" when he used it as a chapter title in his 1954 book, *Motivation and Personality*. **Positive psychology** is a relatively recent branch of psychology that undertakes the scientific study of people's strengths and virtues and promotes optimal functioning of individuals and communities. Proponents of positive psychology argue that psychology has paid too much attention to human pathology and not enough attention to human strengths and virtues (see C. Snyder & Lopez, 2007). Martin Seligman (1991, 1998, 2002), one of the authors of the concept of "learned helplessness," has been at the forefront of positive psychology, contributing the important idea of "learned optimism." Positive psychologists argue that prevention of mental illness is best accomplished by promoting human strength and competence. They have identified a set of human strengths that promote well-being and buffer against mental illness, including optimism, courage, hope, perseverance, honesty, work ethic, and interpersonal skills (C. Snyder & Lopez, 2007). The positive psychology approach draws on both Western and Eastern worldviews. The large focus on hope is rooted in Western thinking (McKnight, Snyder, & Lopez, 2007), whereas emphasis on balance, compassion, and harmony comes more from Eastern thinking (Pedrotti, Snyder, & Lopez, 2007).

This is how the humanistic perspective rates on the criteria for evaluating theories:

- *Coherence and conceptual clarity.* Theories in the humanistic perspective are often criticized for being vague and highly abstract, with concepts such as "being" and "phenomenal self." The language of transpersonal theories is particularly abstract, with discussion of self-transcendence and higher states of consciousness. Indeed, theorists in the humanistic perspective, in general, have not been afraid to sacrifice coherence to gain what they see as a more complete understanding of human behavior. The positive psychology movement is working to bring greater consistency and coherence to humanistic concepts.

- *Testability and evidence of empirical support.* As might be expected, empirically minded scholars have not been attracted to the humanistic perspective, and consequently until recently there was little empirical literature to support the perspective. A notable exception is the clinical side of Carl Rogers' theory. Rogers began a rigorous program of empirical investigation of the therapeutic process, and such research has provided strong empirical support for his conceptualization of the necessary conditions for the therapeutic relationship: warmth, empathy, and genuineness (Sollod et al., 2009). The positive psychology movement is focusing, with much success, on providing support for the role of human in human well-being

- *Comprehe... individual is th... tive, and it... psychologi... person. W... the hum... presented... the role... theories... In additi... of satisfac... be expec...

tradition give limited attention to the environments of human behavior. Taking the lead from existential philosophers, R. D. Laing sees humans as interrelated with their worlds and frowns on the word *environment* because it implies a fragmented person. In discussions of human behavior, however, Laing (1967, 1969) emphasizes the insane situations in which human behavior is enacted. Erich Fromm was heavily influenced by Karl Marx and is much more inclusive of environment than other theorists in the humanistic perspective, emphasizing industrialization, Protestant reformation, capitalism, and technological revolution as alienating contexts against which humans search for meaning (Fromm, 1941). Although existential sociologists emphasize the importance of feelings and emotions, they also focus on the problematic nature of social life under modernization (see Fontana, 1984). A dehumanizing world is implicit in the works of Maslow and Rogers, but neither theorist focuses explicitly on the environments of human behavior, nor do they acknowledge that some environments are more dehumanizing than others. The positive psychology movement has begun to examine positive environments that can promote human strengths and virtues, including school, work, and community environments (C. Snyder & Lopez, 2007).

* *Diversity and power.* The humanistic per- ...most singular consideration of ...nce, devotes more atten- ...than to differences ...romm and Horney ...tatement. Karen ...gender differ- ...her ignored ...approach. ...dynamic ...alization ...psychol- ...rspective ...tle atten- ...o the pro- ...influences ...bjectively ...m." Like

the social constructionist perspective, however, the humanistic perspective is sometimes quite strong in giving voice to experiences of members of nondominant groups. With the emphasis on the phenomenal self, members of nondominant groups are more likely to have preferential input into the telling of their own stories. The social worker's intention to hear and honor the stories of each member of the McKinley family may be a novel experience for each of them, and she may, indeed, hear very different stories from what she expects to hear. Erich Fromm and Michael Maccoby (1970) illustrate this emphasis in their identification of the different life worlds of members of groups of different socioeconomic statuses in a Mexican village. Most significantly, Rogers developed his respect for the personal self, and consequently his client-centered approach to therapy, when he realized that his perceptions of the lifeworlds of his low-income clients in the Child Guidance Center were very different from their own perceptions (J. Hart, 1970).

* *Usefulness for social work.* If the social constructionist perspective gives new meaning to the old social work adage, "Begin where the client is," it is social work's historical involvement in the development of the humanistic perspective that gave original meaning to the adage. It is limited in terms of providing specific interventions, but it is consistent with social work's value for the dignity and worth of the individual. The humanistic perspective suggests that social workers begin by developing an understanding of how the client views the situation and, with its emphasis on the individual drive for growth and competence, it recommends a "strengths" rather than "pathology" approach to practice (Saleebey, 2006). George Vaillant (2002), a research psychiatrist, suggested that this attention to strengths is what distinguishes social workers from other helping professionals. From this perspective, then, we might note the strong commitment to helping one another displayed by the McKinley family, which can be the basis for successful intervention. At the organizational level, the humanistic perspective has been used by organizational theorists, such as Douglas McGregor (1960), to prescribe administrative actions that focus on employee well-being as the

best route to organizational efficiency and effectiveness. Positive psychology is beginning to propose guidelines for developing positive environments in schools, workplaces, and communities.

Critical Thinking Questions 2.2

When it comes to theory/perspective, some people are one-theory/perspective people and find that one theory/perspective does an adequate job of explaining the world. Other people can be described as cluster people; they can identify about three theories (or perspectives) that work well for them in most situations. Still other people can best be described as multi-theoretical; they think the world calls for a larger range of theories (perspectives) than the cluster folks. After reading this chapter, how would you characterize your current thinking about which of those groups you fall into? What factors do you think influence your theoretical preferences?

THE MERITS OF MULTIPLE PERSPECTIVES

You can see that each of these perspectives puts a different lens on the unfolding story of the McKinley family, and that each has been used to guide social work practice over time. But do these different ways of thinking make you more effective when you meet with clients like the McKinleys? We think so. It was suggested in Chapter 1 that each situation can be examined from several perspectives, and that using a variety of perspectives brings more dimensions of the situation into view.

Eileen Gambrill (2006) has suggested that all of us, whether new or experienced social workers, have biases that predispose us to do too little thinking, rather than too much, about the practice situations we confront. We are, she asserts, particularly prone to ignore information that is contrary to our hypotheses about situations. Consequently, we tend to end our search for understanding prematurely. One step we can take to prevent this premature closure is to think about practice situations from multiple theoretical perspectives.

The fields of psychology and sociology offer a variety of patterned ways of thinking about changing person-environment configurations, ways that have been worked out over time to assist in understanding human behavior. They are tools that can help us make sense of the situations we encounter. We do not mean to suggest that all eight of the perspectives discussed in this chapter will be equally useful, or even useful at all, in all situations. But each of these perspectives will be useful in some situations that you encounter as a social worker, and therefore should be in your general knowledge base. As a competent professional, you must view the quest for adequate breadth and depth in your knowledge base as an ongoing, lifelong challenge and responsibility. We hope that over time you will begin to use these multiple perspectives in integrated fashion so that you can see the dimensions—the contradictions consistencies—in stories li ily's. We encourag in your think your career. knowledge in specific

Implications for Social Wor

The eight perspectives on human behavior discussed in this chapt work assessment and intervention:

- In assessment, consider any recent role transitions that may be to renegotiate unsatisfactory role structures. Develop netwo lenging role transitions.

- In assessment, consider power arrangements and forces of oppression, and the alienation that emanates from them. Assist in the development of advocacy efforts to challenge patterns of dominance, when possible. Be aware of the power dynamics in your relationships with clients; when working with nonvoluntary clients, speak directly about the limits and uses of your power.
- In assessment, consider the patterns of exchange in the social support networks of individual clients, families, and organizations, using ecomaps for network mapping when useful. Assist individuals, families, and organizations to renegotiate unsatisfactory patterns of exchange, when possible. Consider how social policy can increase the rewards for prosocial behavior.
- Begin your work by understanding how clients view their situations. Engage clients in thinking about the environments in which these constructions of self and situations have developed. When working in situations characterized by differences in belief systems, assist members to engage in sincere discussions and to negotiate lines of action.
- Assist clients in expressing emotional conflicts and in understanding how these are related to past events, when appropriate. Help them develop self-awareness and self-control, where needed. Assist clients in locating and using needed environmental resources.
- In assessment, consider the familial, cultural, and historical contexts in the timing and experience of developmental transitions. Recognize human development as unique and lifelong.
- In assessment, consider the variety of learning processes by which behavior is learned. Be sensitive to the possibility of learned helplessness when clients lack motivation for change. Consider issues of social justice and fairness before engaging in behavior modification.
- Be aware of the potential for significant differences between your assessment of the situation and the client's own assessment; value self-determination. Focus on strengths rather than pathology.

Key Terms

boundary
chaos theory
...sical conditioning theory
...cial learning theory

feedback mechanism
feminist theories
hierarchy of needs
humanistic perspective
learned helplessness
operant conditioning theory
phenomenal self
pluralistic theory
    of social conflict
...sitive psychology

psychodynamic perspective
rational choice perspective
role
self-efficacy
social behavioral perspective
social constructionist
    perspective
social exchange theory
social network theory
systems perspective

Active Learning

...onal stresses in the McKinley family. Next, review the big ideas of the
...2.1, 2.3, 2.4, 2.6, 2.7, 2.8, 2.9, and 2.10. Choose three specific big ideas
...t helpful in thinking about the McKinley family. For example, you might
...spective: Each part of the system affects all other parts and the system
...idea from the humanistic perspective: Human behavior is driven by a
...ompetence, and by a need to experience a bond with others. Likewise,

you might choose another specific idea from any of the perspectives. The point is to find the three big ideas that you find most useful. Now, in a small group, compare notes with three or four classmates about which big ideas were chosen. How do you understand the similarities and differences in thinking about this?

2. Break into eight small groups and assign each group one of the theoretical perspectives described in the chapter. Each group's task is to briefly summarize the assigned theoretical perspective and then explain the group's interpretation of the perspective's usefulness when applied to the McKinley family or another case scenario.

3. Choose a story that interests you in a current edition of a daily newspaper. Read the story carefully and then think about which of the eight theoretical perspectives discussed in this chapter are most reflected in the story.

Web Resources

Conflict Theory(ies) of Deviance

http://www.umsl.edu/~keelr/200/conflict.html

Site presented by Robert O. Keel at the University of Missouri at St. Louis, contains information on the basic premises of conflict theory as well as specific information on radical conflict theory and pluralistic conflict theory.

Humanistic Psychology

www.ahpweb.org/aboutahp/whatis.html

Site maintained by the Association of Humanistic Psychology, contains the history of humanistic psychology, information on Carl Rogers, the humanistic view of human behavior, methods of inquiry, and humanistic psychotherapies.

Narrative Therapy Centre of Ontario

www.narrativetherapycentre.com/index_files/Page1733.htm

Site contains information on narrative therapy, events and training, articles and books, and links to other websites on narrative therapy.

Personality Theories

www.webspace.ship.edu/~cgboer/perscontents.html

Site maintained by C. George Boeree at the Psychology Department of Shippensburg University, provides an electronic textbook on theories of personality, including the theories of Sigmund Freud, Erik Erikson, Carl Jung, B. F. Skinner, Albert Bandura, Abraham Maslow, Carl Rogers, and Jean Piaget.

Sociological Theories and Perspectives

www.sociosite.net/topics/theory.php

Site maintained at the University of Amsterdam, contains general information on sociological theory and specific information on a number of theories, including chaos theory, interaction theory, conflict theory, and rational choice theory.

William Alanson White Institute

www.wawhite.org

Site contains contemporary psychoanalysis journal articles, training programs, and professional meetings.

PART II

The Multiple Dimensions of Person and Environment

The multiple dimensions of person, environment, and time have unity; they are inseparable and embedded. That is the way I think about them and the way I am encouraging you to think about them. However, you will be better able to think about the unity of the three aspects of human behavior when you have developed a clearer understanding of the different dimensions encompassed by each one. A review of theory and research about the different dimensions will help you to sharpen your thinking about what is involved in the changing configurations of persons and environments.

The purpose of Chapters 3–5 is to provide you with an up-to-date understanding of theory and research about the dimensions of person. Part II begins with a chapter on the biological dimension, is followed by a chapter on the complex psychological dimension, and ends with a chapter on the spiritual dimension.

With a state-of-the-art knowledge base about the multiple dimensions of persons, you will be prepared to consider the interactions between persons and environments. Social workers have always recognized the important role the environment plays in human behavior and, equally important, have always understood the environment as multidimensional. The social work literature has not been consistent in identifying the important dimensions of environment, however. Although all dimensions of environment are intertwined and inseparable, social scientists have developed specialized literature on several specific dimensions. Both the environment and the study of it become more complex with each new era of technological development, making our efforts to understand the environment ever more challenging.

The purpose of Chapters 6–9 is to provide you with an up-to-date understanding of the multidisciplinary theory and research about dimensions of environment. Chapter 6 examines two important dimensions that are present but not always recognized in every person-environment configuration: culture and the physical environment. Chapter 7 explores the macro environment, focusing on contemporary trends in social institutions and social structure, placing U.S. trends in a global context. Chapter 8 focuses on the moderate-sized configurations of formal organizations, communities, and social movements. Chapter 9 covers the smaller-scale configurations of families and small groups. When you put knowledge about these person and environment dimensions together, you will be better prepared to understand the situations you encounter in social work practice. This knowledge base also prepares you well to think about the changing configurations of persons and environments across the life course—the subject of Part III. Margin notes are used in the chapters in Part II to help you recognize the major theoretical perspectives covered in Chapter 2 as they are applied specifically to dimensions of person and environment.

CHAPTER 3

The Biological Person

Stephen French Gilson

Opening Questions

What do social workers need to know about the interior environment of human biology?

How does knowledge of biology contribute to important roles that social workers play in individual and community health and illness?

ACKNOWLEDGMENTS: The author wishes to thank Elizabeth DePoy and Elizabeth Hutchison for their helpful comments, insights, and suggestions for this chapter.

1. One way to think about our bodies is as the interior environment, with environment defined as a "set of conditions" (DePoy & Gilson, 2007).

2. There is strong evidence of relationships among physical health, psychological health, and exterior environmental conditions. Biological functioning is the result of complex transactions among interior and exterior systems. No biological system operates in isolation from these other phenomena.

3. The nervous system is responsible for processing and integrating incoming information, and it influences and directs reactions to that information. It is divided into three major subsystems: central nervous system, peripheral nervous system, and autonomic nervous system.

4. The endocrine system plays a crucial role in growth, metabolism, development, learning, and memory.

5. The immune system is made up of organs and cells that work together to defend the body against disease. Autoimmune diseases occur when the immune system mistakenly targets parts of the interior environment.

6. The cardiovascular system is made up of the heart and the blood circulatory system. The circulatory system supplies cells of the body with the food and oxygen that they need for functioning.

7. The musculoskeletal system supports and protects the body and its organs and provides motion. The contraction and relaxation of muscles attached to the skeleton is the basis for voluntary movements.

8. The reproductive system is composed of both internal and external structures that are different for males and females.

CASE STUDY 3.1

Cheryl's Brain Injury

Cheryl grew up in rural Idaho in a large extended family of Anglo heritage and enlisted as a private in the army just after she finished her third year of high school. After basic training, she was deployed to Iraq for active combat duty. Traveling en route to Baghdad, Cheryl's Humvee contacted an improvised explosive device (IED), causing Cheryl to sustain a closed head injury and multiple fractures. She was in a coma for 3 weeks.

Over a 6-month period, all of Cheryl's external bodily injuries, including the fractures, healed, and she was able to walk and talk with no apparent residual impairments. Cognitively and socially, however, Cheryl experienced change. Although able to read, she could not retain what she had just read a minute ago. She did not easily recall her previous knowledge of math and was not able to compute basic math such as addition and subtraction without the use of a calculator. She was slow in penmanship, taking at least 5 minutes to write her own name. Dissimilar to her social behavior prior to the accident, Cheryl was often blunt in her comments, even to the point of becoming confrontational with friends without provocation.

Because of her observable recovery, everyone expected Cheryl to return to active duty, but 2 years after the accident, her family knows that she is not going to return to military service. Cheryl's ex-boyfriend, Sean, is about to get engaged to another woman, but Cheryl thinks that she is still dating Sean and thinks that he will soon marry her. People who knew Cheryl before the accident cannot understand why her personality has changed so markedly, and they even say, "She's a completely different person!"

CASE STUDY 3.2

A Diabetes Diagnosis for Bess

Bess, a 52-year-old Franco-American woman who lives in rural Maine, was enjoying her empty nest just before the social worker met her. The youngest of her three children had married 6 months ago, and although Bess was proud of what she had accomplished as a single mother, she was now ready to get on with her life. Her first order of business was to get her body back into shape, so she started on a high-carbohydrate, low-fat diet that she had read about in a magazine. Drinking the recommended eight glasses of water or more each day was easy, because it seemed that she was always thirsty. But Bess was losing more weight than she thought possible on a diet, and she was always cheating! Bess had thought that she would have to get more exercise to lose weight, but even walking to and from her car at the grocery store tired her out.

One morning, Bess did not show up at the country store where she worked. Because it was very unusual for her not to call and also not to answer her phone, a coworker went to her house. When there was no response to the knocking, the coworker and one of Bess's neighbors opened the door to Bess's house and walked in. They found Bess sitting on her couch, still in her nightclothes, which were drenched with perspiration. Bess was very confused, unable to answer simple questions with correct responses. Paramedics transported Bess to the local community hospital.

In the emergency room, after some blood work, a doctor diagnosed diabetes mellitus (diabetes). Because diabetes is common among middle-aged and older Franco Americans in this poor rural town, a social worker had already established an educational support group for persons with diabetes that Bess now attends.

CASE STUDY 3.3

Melissa's HIV Diagnosis

Melissa's "perfect life" has just fallen apart. As a young, Jewish, urban professional who grew up in a middle-class suburb, Melissa had always dreamed of a big wedding at her parents' country club, and her dreams were coming true. All the plans had been made, invitations sent out, bridesmaids' dresses bought and measured, and

(Continued)

her wedding dress selected. All that remained was finalizing the menu and approving the flower arrangements. Because Melissa and her fiancé planned to have children soon after their marriage, she went to her physician for a physical exam 2 months before her wedding. As the doctor does with all of her patients, she asked if Melissa had ever been tested for HIV. Melissa said no, and gave her permission for an HIV test to be run with all the other routine blood work.

One week after her physical, the doctor's office called and asked Melissa to return for more blood work because of what was thought to be an inaccuracy in the report. Melissa went back to the office for more blood tests. Another week passed, but Melissa did not think again about the tests because she was immersed in wedding plans. Her physician called her at home at 8:00 one morning and asked her to come to her office after work that day. Because she was distracted by the wedding plans and a busy schedule at work, Melissa did not think anything of the doctor's request.

When she arrived at the doctor's office, she was immediately taken to the doctor's private office. The doctor came in, sat down, and told Melissa that two separate blood tests had confirmed that she was HIV positive. Melissa spent over 3 hours with her physician that evening, and soon thereafter she began to attend an HIV support group.

Melissa has never used illicit drugs, and she has only had two sexual partners. She and her fiancé had decided not to have unprotected intercourse until they were ready for children, and because they used a condom, he was not a prime suspect for passing along the infection. Melissa remembered that the man with whom she was involved prior to meeting her fiancé would not talk about his past. She has not seen this former lover for the past 3 years, ever since she moved away from New York.

CASE STUDY 3.4

Lifestyle Changes for Thomas

Thomas is a 30-year-old African American man who lives with his parents, both of whom are obese, as are his two older sisters. Thomas loves his mom's cooking, but some time ago realized that its high-fat and high-sodium content was contributing to his parents' obesity and high blood pressure.

In contrast, Thomas takes pride in watching his diet (when he isn't eating at home) and is pretty smug about being the only one in the family who is not obese. Being called "the thin man" is, to Thomas, a compliment. He also boasts about being in great physical shape, and exercises to the point of being dizzy.

After one of his dizziness episodes, a friend told him that he should get his blood pressure checked. Although Thomas knew of the high incidence of heart disease among African Americans, he never considered that he would have a problem. After all, he is young and in good physical shape. Out of curiosity, the next time Thomas stopped at his local drug store, he decided to use one of those self-monitoring blood pressure machines to check his blood pressure. To his astonishment, the reading came back 200/105, which is quite high. Thomas now seeks a social worker's help to adopt some major lifestyle changes.

Max's Post-Polio Syndrome

Max is from an Eastern European immigrant family that settled in a midwestern city in the United States. When he was 2 years old, he contracted polio that affected only his legs. He never had any breathing difficulties, nor was there any involvement in his arms. In fact, after 6 months in the hospital and another 6 months of therapy when he returned home, Max appeared to be "cured." Afterward, as he was growing up, there were no visible signs of previous illness. He clearly could keep up with his friends, except he could never run very long distances.

Forty-three years later, Max developed early symptoms of post-polio syndrome. He began to notice increasing weakness in his legs, unusual fatigue, and a lot of pain all over his body. A recent evaluation at a university clinic confirmed the diagnosis of post-polio syndrome, and the clinicians who saw him recommended that he consider getting the type of brace that is inserted in his shoes to support both ankles, as well as use forearm crutches for walking long distances. Max has earned his living all his life as a house painter. He needs help figuring out how to cope with these new developments and how to support his growing family.

Juan and Belinda's Reproductive Health

Juan and Belinda, now both 17 years old, grew up in the same neighborhood of a southwestern city in the United States and attend the same church, St. Joseph's Catholic Church. They do not attend the same school, however. Belinda has received all of her education at the schools at St. Joseph's; Juan attended J. F. Kennedy Elementary School and John Marshall Junior High, and he now attends Cesar Chavez High School. Since seventh grade, Juan has met Belinda after school and walked her home.

They both live in small, well-kept homes in a section of the community that is largely Spanish speaking with very strong influences from the wide variety of countries of origin represented by community residents: Mexico, Honduras, El Salvador, and Nicaragua, among others. The Catholic Church here is a dominant exterior environmental force in shaping community social, political, economic, and personal values and behaviors.

Both Juan's and Belinda's parents immigrated to the United States from Mexico, seeking to improve the opportunities for their future families. Juan's mother found a job as a housekeeper at a local hotel, where she now manages the housekeeping staff. His father began as a day laborer and construction worker, eventually moving up to become foreman of the largest construction company in the area. He anticipates beginning his own construction company within the next year. Belinda's mother was a skilled seamstress and was able to start her own tailoring business shortly after immigrating. Belinda's father, with a background in diesel mechanics, was able to find work at a large trucking company where he continues to work today.

(Continued)

(Continued)

Like many teenagers today, Juan and Belinda face the difficulties of seeking to sort out the complexities and the intricacies of their relationship. They feel very much in love, knowing in their hearts that they want to get married and raise a family. At 17, they are at a crossroads, because they face conflicts about their future sexual intimacy with limited information and strong prohibitions against premarital sex. Following many of the teachings of their church and the urgings of their parents, Juan and Belinda have avoided much physical contact except for kissing and holding each other.

Like many communities in the United States, their community struggled with the question of just what information should be given to students about physical health and sexuality. Their community's school board decided to limit the amount and type of information to the basics of female and male sexual anatomy and physiology. The result of this decision for Juan and Belinda was that they learned very little about sexual response and behavior, conception, pregnancy, childbirth, contraception, safe sex practices, or other areas that are critical in today's world. The decision by the school board was based on a belief that it was the families' responsibility to provide this information to their children. The school social worker at Cesar Chavez High School is aware of the moral conflicts that arise for youth in this community that in part result from limited sex education.

AN INTEGRATIVE APPROACH FOR UNDERSTANDING THE INTERSECTION OF INTERIOR BIOLOGICAL HEALTH AND ILLNESS AND EXTERIOR ENVIRONMENTAL FACTORS

As we think about the stories of Cheryl, Bess, Melissa, Thomas, Max, Juan, and Belinda, we can see that biology is an important dimension of their behavior. But despite growing agreement of the importance of biology in influencing human behavior and thus the need for social workers to be well informed in this arena, the profession is struggling to articulate exactly what social workers need to know about human biology, or what DePoy and Gilson (2008) refer to as a substantial part of the interior environment. Because social workers deal with people, and people comprise the corpus of human biology, social workers encounter biology and its reciprocal influence with exterior environment conditions such as poverty, chronic illness, addictions, violence, reproductive problems, and child abuse each time they interact with individuals. For instructive purposes, we distinguish interior from exterior environments on the basis of corporeality, or material that relates to the body (DePoy & Gilson, 2007). However, the division between the corporeal and non-corporeal is not always clear. Consider for example a knee replacement. While it is not organic in composition, it is located beneath the skin and functions as integral to body stability and movement. But is it interior or exterior? What about eyeglasses, prostheses, or even clothes that preserve body temperature?

Returning to the cases of Cheryl, Bess, Melissa, Thomas, Max, Juan, and Belinda, their interior environments are the central reason they are seeking social work assistance. To be effective in meeting professional goals, social workers must have a working knowledge of the body's systems and the ways these systems interact with each other and with other interior and exterior environmental dimensions. Social workers also must be sufficiently informed about interior environment theory and knowledge in order to discuss details of biological functioning with clients when indicated (H. C. Johnson, 2001; Tangenberg & Kemp, 2002).

While the knowledge of biological structures and their function is foundational to understanding the interior environment, it is insufficient for social workers, in that social work professional decision making and activity require a complex mastery of knowledge about the interactions of interior and exterior environments. Moreover, understanding of how the interior environment contributes to human behavior (what people do and do not do and how they do what they do), appearance, and experience (DePoy & Gilson, 2004) is critical for informed social work practice as exemplified by each of the case studies above.

Approaching social work practice from well accepted explanatory models such as biopsycho-social-spiritual and legitimacy (DePoy & Gilson, 2008) requires depth of knowledge not only of interior parts, but also of their complex, context-embedded interaction. Consistent with post-postmodern thinking, which colocates multiple fields of knowledge adjacent to and informing one another (DePoy & Gilson, 2008), social work's growing interest in human biology is essential for framing effective social work responses that consider the interstices of "mind–body interactions."

Systems frameworks describe and explain human phenomena as a set of interrelated parts. There are many variations and applications of systems approaches ranging from those that look at embodied or interior systems, to those that examine human systems composed of both humans and their exterior environments, and even extending to systems that do not contain embodied elements (DePoy & Gilson, 2008). At this point, there is a well-developed theory supported by rigorously conducted empirical evidence of the complex relationships among physical health, psychological health, and social experiences (DePoy & Gilson, 2008; Epel et al., 2006; Weitz, 2009). This is an exciting and rapidly changing knowledge base.

Systems perspective

In March of 2001, the National Institutes of Health sponsored a conference titled Vital Connections: The Science of Mind–Body Interactions (MacArthur Network on Mind–Body Interactions, 2001). This event was one of the most important in influencing new theory and knowledge linking interior and exterior systems and environments. Renowned scholars reported on several topics focusing on the interaction of exterior and interior environments that have been receiving and continue to receive intense research scrutiny—for example, the neurobiology of human emotions, early care and brain development, the biology of social interactions, socioeconomic status (SES) and health, neuroendocrinology of stress, and the role of sleep in health and cognition. Scholarship at this conference revealed further evidence of the critical connections between external environmental conditions and embodied phenomena, which were previously thought to be only tangentially related to one another. Throughout the 3-day conference, presenters theorized about the "integrative mechanisms" that link social and psychological dimensions to the brain and the rest of the body. Researchers were clear that we are just beginning to understand these mechanisms, and we need to be cautious not to exceed our data in any claims or beliefs about systems interactivity. Much of the current evidence emerged from animal studies and is now conducted with advanced computer modeling software. Its accuracy in explaining the human body remains probable but cautiously applied.

Although these attempts to understand mind–body connections have led to many important theories about health and illness, they may also be misinterpreted. Social workers therefore would be advised to heed the warning of a number of medical researchers and social critics against explaining behavior and emotion through a medicalized lens (see Conrad, 2007; Fischbach, quoted in MacArthur Network on Mind–Body Interactions, 2001; Lane, 2007; Watters, 2010). Such a reductionist perspective may undermine our ability to consider the full range of exterior environmental influences on embodied phenomena. Moreover, medicalization serves to pathologize typical daily experience.

On the flipside of this caution, over attribution of physical experiences to psychological and social conditions fails to consider the interior environmental causes of illness. While we cannot forget that health and illness are influenced by

Photo 3.1 A medical researcher examines data to test a hypothesis.

and economic exterior environments (Albrecht, Seelman, & Bury, 2001; Barnett & Scotch, 2002; DePoy & Gilson, 2004; Gilson & DePoy, 2000, 2002). Thus, using social construction as explanatory, the experience of having atypical low vision can be interpreted as influenced by shared cultural understandings of the "expected roles" for persons with atypical vision, or by actions or inactions of political institutions to promote or impede this subpopulation's access to physical and social environments. We may automatically assume that an individual with atypical low vision is in need of professional intervention, when that person may in fact have his or her life well organized and function well in all chosen living and working environments. Thus, rather than being explained by the biological condition itself, limitation associated with an atypical biological condition may be a function of the exterior environment; the characteristics of the task; personal attitude; and available resources such as technology; assistance from family, friends, or employers; accessible transportation; and welcoming, fully accessible communities (DePoy & Gilson, 2010).

As an example, although social workers do not diagnose medical explanations for embodied conditions in the scope of our practice, the social work administrator who is developing or operating a shelter, a food kitchen, or an advocacy center may integrate medical and mental health services with employment, housing, financial, and companionship services (Gelberg & Linn, 1988; Nyamathi, Leake, Keenan, & Gelberg, 2000) within the larger considerations of the meaning of those services to the users and community context. Lowe (1997) has recommended a model of social work practice that promotes healthy communities as well as working with individuals, families, and groups to help them identify and advocate for their own health needs if they so choose. DePoy and Gilson (2004, 2010) have built on this model by proposing *legitimate communities,* defined as those that practice acceptance of ideas and appreciate and respond to the full range of human diversity.

exterior social, political, cultural, and economic environmental conditions (DePoy & Gilson, 2007; Saleebey, 2001), these are often invoked as one-way streets rather than being seen as part of a more complex interactive picture. While the efficiency of a single framework is seductive, such thinking may limit our ability to expansively identify the broad nature of problems, needs, and a range of appropriate interventions to resolve the problems (DePoy & Gilson, 2004, 2010).

The social constructionist perspective suggests that human phenomena are pluralistic in meaning. As an example, rather than being a singular scientifically supported entity, through the lens of social construction, a physically disabling medical condition, such as paralysis or low vision, is defined in large part by its meaning from interior views as well as from political, social, cultural,

Social constructionist perspective

A LOOK AT SIX INTERIOR ENVIRONMENT SYSTEMS _____

Now we turn to the six biological systems discussed in this chapter: the nervous system, the endocrine system, the immune system, the cardiovascular system, the musculoskeletal system, and the reproductive system. All the other biological systems (such as the digestive system, the respiratory system, and the urinary system) also warrant our attention, but with the limitations of space, we have chosen these six because they are commonly involved in many of the biologically based issues that social workers encounter, and thus can serve as a model for thinking about other systems as well.

As you read the descriptions of these six interior environment systems, keep in mind their connect-

Systems perspective

edness with each other as well as with all environmental conditions. As we emphasize throughout, just as human behavior is a complex transaction of person and environment, biological functioning is the result of complex interactions among all biological systems and the environments in which they function. No one system operates in isolation from other systems.

Nervous System

In the first case study, you met Cheryl, who is like the more than 235,000 people in the United States hospitalized each year with a **brain injury (BI)**. In Cheryl's case, we are referring to what is commonly termed a *traumatic brain injury* (TBI), defined as an insult to the brain caused by an external physical force that may result in a diminished or altered state of consciousness (Brain Injury Association of America, 2001). Included here are what might be classified as mild brain injuries or concussions. Traumatic brain injuries include head injuries that result from falls, automobile accidents, infections and viruses, insufficient oxygen, and poisoning. Explosions caused by landmines and improvised explosive devices (IEDs) have been identified as

one of the primary causes of TBI and interior environment problems in military personnel.

According to the Centers for Disease Control and Prevention (CDC, 2006b), approximately 1.4 million individuals sustain traumatic brain injury in the United States each year, creating $60 billion yearly in hospital and injury-related costs (direct medical costs and indirect costs such as lost economic productivity). It is estimated that 2% of the population in the United States, or 5.3 million people, live with the atypical results of traumatic brain injuries. For children and young adults, TBI is the type of injury most often associated with deaths due to unintended injuries. The rates of TBI among African American children ages 0–4 are about 40% higher than those for White children. It is estimated that 1 in 4 adults with TBI is unable to return to work within one year after the injury.

Although the symptoms may be similar, *acquired brain injury* (ABI) is a different classification of brain injury. It does not result from traumatic injury to the head; is not hereditary, congenital, or degenerative; and occurs after birth. Included in this category are oxygen deprivation (anoxia), aneurysms, infections to the brain, and stroke (Brain Injury Association of America, 2001).

Each type of BI may provoke specific atypical issues and behaviors for the individual. However, brain injury in general can affect cognitive, physical, and psychological skills. Atypical cognitive function may present as atypical language and communication, information processing, memory, and perception. Cheryl's atypical writing is an example, as well as a reflection of atypical fine motor skill. Atypical physical functioning often occurs, such as walking differently or not at all, and changes in balance and coordination, strength, and endurance. Atypical psychological changes may come from two different sources. They may be *primary* or directly related to the BI, such as irritability and judgment errors, or they may be *reactive* to the adjustments required to live with the atypical function caused by BI and its consequences, typically resulting in a diagnosis of depression and changes in self-esteem. Cheryl's difficulty in recognizing that Sean is not going to marry her and her misjudgments in other social situations are symptoms of the psychological consequences of her BI.

The **nervous system** provides the structure and processes for communicating sensory, perceptual, and autonomically generated information throughout the body. Three major subsystems compose the nervous system:

1. *Central nervous system* (CNS): the brain and the spinal cord

2. *Peripheral nervous system* (PNS): spinal and cranial nerves

3. *Autonomic nervous system* (ANS): nerves controlling cardiovascular, gastrointestinal, genitourinary, and respiratory systems

The brain sends signals to the spinal cord, which in turn relays the message to specific parts of the body by way of the PNS. Messages from the PNS to the brain travel back by way of a similar pathway (J. Carey, 1990; R. Carter, 2009). Note that Cheryl's brain injury affects only a part of her nervous system—in fact, only part of the CNS. Damage to other parts of the nervous system can have significant atypical effects, but here we focus on her brain injury because it is so closely linked with behavioral changes.

The human brain, which constitutes only about 2% of total body weight, may contain as many as 10 million neurons. Its three major internal regions are referred to as the forebrain, midbrain, and hindbrain. Viewed from the side (see Exhibit 3.1), the largest structure visible is the *cerebral cortex*, part of the forebrain. The cerebral cortex is the seat of higher mental functions, including thinking, planning, and problem solving. This area of the brain is more highly developed in humans than in any other animal. It is divided into two hemispheres—left and right—that are interconnected by nerve fibers. The hemispheres are thought to be specialized, one side for language and the other for processing of spatial information such as maps and pictures. Each hemisphere controls the opposite

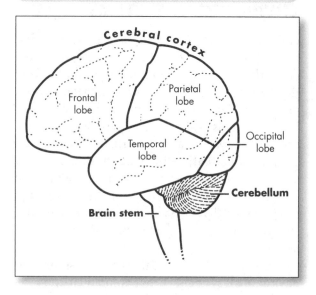

Exhibit 3.1 Selected Areas of the Brain

side of the body, so that damage to one side of the brain may cause numbness or paralysis of the arm and leg on the opposite side.

The cerebral cortex has four lobes, which are depicted in Exhibit 3.1. As Exhibit 3.2 explains, functions such as vision, hearing, and speech are distributed in specific regions, with some lobes being associated with more than one function. The frontal lobe is the largest, making up nearly one third of the surface of the cerebral cortex. Lesions of any one of the lobes can have a dramatic impact on the functions of that lobe (M. B. Carpenter, 1991; R. Carter, 2009; Earle, 1987). Other forebrain structures process information from the sensory and perceptual organs and structures and send it to the cortex, or receive orders from cortical centers and relay them on down through central nervous system structures to central and peripheral structures throughout the body. Also in the forebrain are centers for memory and emotion, as well as control of essential functions such as hunger, thirst, and biological sex drive.

The midbrain is a small area, but it contains important centers for sleep and pain as well as relay centers for sensory information and control of movement.

Exhibit 3.2 Regions of the Cerebral Cortex

Brain Region	Function
Frontal lobe	Motor behavior
	Expressive language
	Social functioning
	Concentration and ability to attend
	Reasoning and thinking
	Orientation to time, place, and person
Temporal lobe	Language
	Memory
	Emotions
Parietal lobes	Intellectual processing
	Integration of sensory information
Left parietal lobe	Verbal processing
Right parietal lobe	Visual/spatial processing
Occipital lobe	Vision

Exhibit 3.3 Features of a Typical Neuron

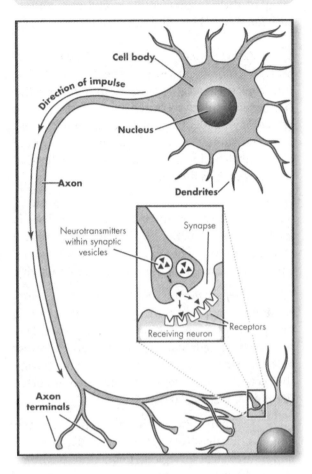

In Exhibit 3.1, part of the hindbrain, including the cerebellum, can also be seen. The *cerebellum* controls complex motor programming, including maintaining muscle tone and posture. Other hindbrain structures are essential to the regulation of basic physiological functions, including breathing, heart rate, and blood pressure. The brain stem connects the cerebral cortex to the spinal cord.

The basic working unit of all the nervous systems is the **neuron,** or nerve cell. The human body has a great diversity of neuronal types, but all consist of a cell body with a nucleus and a conduction fiber, an **axon.** Extending from the cell body are *dendrites,* which conduct impulses to the neurons from the axons of other nerve cells. Exhibit 3.3 shows how neurons are linked by axons and dendrites.

The connection between each axon and dendrite is actually a gap called a **synapse.** Synapses use chemical and electrical **neurotransmitters** to communicate. As the inset box in Exhibit 3.3 shows, nerve impulses travel from the cell body to the ends of the axons, where they trigger the release of neurotransmitters. The adjacent dendrite of another neuron has receptors distinctly shaped to fit particular types of neurotransmitters. When the neurotransmitter fits into a slot, the message is passed along.

Although neurotransmitters are the focus of much current research, scientists have not yet articulated all that positivist research reveals about what neurotransmitters do. Essentially, they may either excite or inhibit nervous system responses.

But medical research has revealed very little about many of the neurotransmitters, and may not yet have identified them all. Here are a few:

- *Acetylcholine* (ACh): The first neurotransmitter identified (in 1914 by Henry Hallett Dale and confirmed as a neurotransmitter by Otto Loewi; they jointly received the Nobel Prize in Physiology or Medicine in 1936) is an excitatory neurotransmitter active in both the CNS and the PNS. Acetylcholine may be critical for intellectual activities such as memory.

- *Dopamine* (DA): This neurotransmitter, which is widely present in the CNS and PNS, is implicated in regulation of the endocrine system. Dopamine is thought to play a role in influencing emotional behavior, cognition, and motor activity.

- *Norepinephrine* (NE): Like dopamine, norepinephrine appears in many parts of the body. It may play a role in learning and memory and is also secreted by the adrenal glands in response to stress or events that produce arousal. Norepinephrine connects the brain stem with the cerebral cortex (Bentley & Walsh, 2006).

- *Serotonin:* Present in blood platelets, the lining of the digestive tract, and in a tract from the midbrain to all brain regions, this neurotransmitter is thought to be a factor in many body functions. Serotonin plays a role in sensory processes, muscular activity, thinking, states of consciousness, mood, depression diagnoses, and anxiety diagnoses (Bentley & Walsh, 2006).

- *Amino acids:* Some types of these molecules, which are found in proteins, are distributed throughout the brain and other body tissues. One amino acid, gamma aminobutyric acid (GABA), is thought to play a critical role in inhibiting the firing of impulses of some cells. Thus, GABA is believed to be instrumental in many functions of the CNS, such as locomotor activity, cardiovascular reactions, pituitary function, and anxiety diagnoses (Bentley & Walsh, 2006).

- *Peptides:* Amino acids that are joined together have only recently been studied as neurotransmitters.

Opioids, many of which are peptides, play an important role in activities ranging from moderating pain to causing sleepiness. Endorphins help to minimize pain and enhance adaptive behavior (J. Carey, 1990; Sadock & Sadock, 2007).

Biologically, behavior is affected by not only the levels of a neurotransmitter, but also the balance between two or more neurotransmitters. Psychotropic medications impact behaviors and symptoms associated with diagnoses of mental illness by affecting the levels of specific neurotransmitters and altering the balance among neurotransmitters. Social workers working from a medical diagnostic perspective would be well advised to keep up on medical research about the effects of neurotransmitters on human behavior when working with individuals who are typically referred for medications evaluation and when following up with individuals who have been placed on medication treatment regimens (Bentley & Walsh, 2006).

For Cheryl, as for many people living with traumatic brain injury, her skills, abilities, and atypical changes may be affected by a variety of interior and exterior environment circumstances—including which parts of the brain were injured, her achievements prior to injury, her social and psychological supports, and the training and education that she is offered following her accident. Tremendous advances are being made in rehabilitation following brain injuries (W. Gordon et al., 2006). The better that social workers understand brain functions and brain plasticity, the more they can understand and communicate with medical personnel. We may be able to help with adjustment or adaptation to atypical changes as well as the recovery of functions. Cheryl could benefit from cognitive retraining, support in finding and maintaining employment, family counseling, and individual counseling that will help her end her relationship with Sean. A key to recovery for many individuals who have experienced similar trauma is an opportunity to interact with peers and other individuals with similar experiences. Such peer networks may provide the individual with access to new skills and a key link to exterior environment social support.

A social worker working with Cheryl may fill several roles: case manager, advocate, counselor, resource coordinator, and referral source.

Endocrine System

Remember Bess, the middle-aged woman diagnosed with diabetes? If you had first met her in a nonhospital setting, you might have interpreted her behaviors quite differently. Because of the recent rural health initiative in Bess's town, which has a number of residents who have relocated from French Canada, it was not unusual to hear women speaking in both French and English about their diets and exercises, and initially you may have been quite pleased for Bess's success. If Bess had told you that she was tired, you might have suggested that she slow down and get more rest, or perhaps that she include vitamins in her diet. Sitting in the morning in her nightclothes on her couch and missing work might suggest alcohol or other drug use. Confusion, switching back and forth between speaking French and English in the same sentence, and inability to answer simple questions could signal stroke, dementia, or a diagnosis of mental illness such as schizophrenia. But only a thorough medical assessment of her interior environment revealed the cause

of Bess's behaviors: a physical health condition traceable to a malfunction in the endocrine system.

The **endocrine system** plays a crucial role in our growth, metabolism, development, learning, and memory. It is made up of *glands* that secrete hormones into the blood system; those hormones bind to receptors in target organs, much as neurotransmitters do in the brain, and affect the metabolism or function of those organs (Besser & Thorner, 1994; Kapit, Macey, & Meisami, 2000; Mader, 2003; Rosenzweig, Breedlove, & Watson, 2004; Rosenzweig & Leiman, 1989). Distinguishing differences between hormones and neurotransmitters are often the distance of travel from the point of release to the target, as well as the route of travel. Hormones travel long distances through the bloodstream; neurotransmitters travel shorter distances from cell to cell, across the synaptic cleft.

Endocrine glands include the pineal, pituitary, thyroid, parathyroid, pancreas, and adrenal. Endocrine cells are also found in some organs that have primarily a non-endocrine function: the hypothalamus, liver, thymus, heart, kidney, stomach, duodenum, testes, and ovaries. Exhibit 3.4 lists some of the better-known glands and organs, the hormones they produce, and their effects on other body structures.

Exhibit 3.4   Selected Endocrine Glands and Their Effects

Gland	Hormone	Effect
Hypothalamus	Releasing and release-inhibiting factors	• Targets pituitary gland, which affects many hormonal activities
Pituitary	Adrenocorticotropic (ACTH) Growth (GH, somatotropic) Vasopressin Prolactin	• Stimulates adrenal cortex • Stimulates cell division, protein synthesis, and bone growth • Stimulates water reabsorption by kidneys • Stimulates milk production in mammary glands
Testes	Androgens (testosterone)	• Stimulates development of sex organs, skin, muscles, bones, and sperm • Stimulates development and maintenance of secondary male sex characteristics

(Continued)

Exhibit 3.4 (Continued)

Ovaries	Estrogen and progesterone	• Stimulates development of sex organs, skin, muscles, bones, and uterine lining • Stimulates development and maintenance of secondary female sex characteristics
Adrenal	Epinephrine Adrenal Cortical Steroids	• Stimulates fight-or-flight reactions in heart and other muscles • Raises blood glucose levels • Stimulates sex characteristics
Pancreas	Insulin Glucagon	• Targets liver, muscles, adipose tissues • Lowers blood glucose levels • Promotes formation of glycogen, proteins, and fats
Thymus	Thymosins	• Triggers development of T lymphocytes, which orchestrate immune system response
Pineal	Melatonin	• Maintains circadian rhythms (daily cycles of activity)
Thyroid	Thyroxin	• Plays role in growth and development • Stimulates metabolic rate of all organs

The most basic form of hormonal communication is from an endocrine cell through the blood system to a target cell. A more complex form of hormonal communication is directly from an endocrine gland to a target endocrine gland.

The endocrine system regulates the secretion of hormones through a **feedback control mechanism.** Output consists of hormones released from an endocrine gland; input consists of hormones taken into a target tissue or organ. The system is self-regulating. Similar to neurotransmitters, hormones have specific receptors, so that the hormone released from one gland has a specific target tissue or organ (Mader, 2003).

A good example of a feedback loop is presented in Exhibit 3.5. The hypothalamus secretes the gonadotropin-releasing hormone (GnRH), which binds to receptors in the

Systems perspective

anterior pituitary and stimulates the secretion of luteinizing hormone (LH). LH binds to receptors in the ovaries to stimulate the production of estrogen. Estrogen has a negative effect on the secretion of LH and GnRH at both the pituitary and hypothalamus,

Exhibit 3.5   An Example of a Feedback Loop

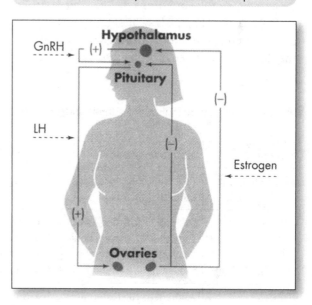

thus completing the loop. Loops like these allow the body to finely control the secretion of hormones.

Another good way to understand the feedback control mechanism is to observe the results when it malfunctions. Consider what has happened to

Bess, who has been diagnosed with the most common illness caused by hormonal imbalance: **diabetes mellitus.** Insulin deficiency or resistance to insulin's effects is the basis of diabetes. Insulin and glucagon, which are released by the pancreas, regulate the metabolism of carbohydrates, the source of cell energy. They are essential for the maintenance of blood glucose levels (blood sugar). High blood glucose levels stimulate the release of insulin, which in turn helps to decrease blood sugar by promoting the uptake of glucose by tissues. Low blood sugar stimulates the release of glucagon, which in turn stimulates the liver to release glucose, raising blood sugar. In individuals with insulin deficiency, muscle cells are deprived of glucose. As an alternative, those muscle cells tap fat and protein reserves in muscle tissue as an energy source. The results include wasting of muscles; weakness; weight loss; and *metabolic acidosis,* a chemical imbalance in the blood. The increase in blood acidity suppresses higher nervous system functions, leading to coma. Suppression of the respiratory centers in the brain leads to death (Kapit et al., 2000).

Epidemiologists report a dramatic increase in the incidence of diabetes worldwide in recent years (Zimmet, Alberti, & Shaw, 2001). There are currently 25.8 million persons (8.3% of the population) in the United States who have diabetes. There are 18.8 million persons who have been diagnosed with diabetes, with an estimated 7.0 million persons having undiagnosed diabetes (National Institute of Diabetes and Digestive and Kidney Diseases [NIDDK], 2011). Nearly 800,000 new cases of diabetes are diagnosed each year, or 2,200 per day. The number of persons who have been diagnosed with diabetes has shown a steady increase over the past 15 years. It is estimated that $1 out of every $10 spent on health care in the United States is spent on diabetes and its consequences (American Diabetes Association, n.d.). Juvenile-onset diabetes (type 1) is found in children and young adults; risk factors may be autoimmune, genetic, or environmental. Non-Hispanic Whites are at greater risk of developing type 1 diabetes than other racial and ethnic groups. No known way to prevent type 1 diabetes exists. Maturity-onset diabetes (type 2),

non-insulin-dependent diabetes mellitus, most commonly arises in individuals over the age of 40 who are also obese. Type 2 diabetes is associated with older age, obesity, family history of diabetes, history of gestational diabetes, impaired glucose metabolism, physical inactivity, and race/ethnicity. Latinos, Native Americans, Asian Americans, and non-Hispanic Blacks are twice as likely to have type 2 diabetes as non-Hispanic Whites. Gestational diabetes is a third type, a form of glucose intolerance diagnosed during pregnancy. This form of diabetes occurs more frequently among African Americans, Hispanic/Latino Americans, and Native Americans, than among other populations (NIDDK, 2011).

For Bess, as for many individuals with symptoms indicating the presence of a medical condition, a crucial role for the social worker is to facilitate access to and comprehension of information

| Rational choice perspective |

and knowledge about the symptoms and the diagnosed condition. Social workers can also aid in the translation of this information, so clients such as Bess, whose first language is French and who might not understand medical jargon, can grasp what is happening to them. The social worker may also help Bess begin to examine the lifestyle changes that may be suggested by this diagnosis. What might it mean in terms of diet, exercise, home and work responsibilities, and so forth? Bess may need assistance in working with her insurance company to plan how her care will be financed. She may also need counseling as she works to adjust to life with this new medical diagnosis.

Immune System

Melissa (Case Study 3.3) is far from alone in testing positive for HIV. The Centers for Disease Control and Prevention (2009c) estimated that approximately 56,300 people were newly infected with HIV in 2006 (the most recent year that such diagnostic data was recorded). Nearly 1 out of every 250, or about 1 million Americans, is infected with the **human immunodeficiency virus (HIV),** the virus that causes **acquired immunodeficiency syndrome (AIDS).** In 2005, Glynn and Rhodes estimated that 24% to 27% of the people in the United States infected with HIV are not aware of their infection. It is estimated that the number of diagnoses of AIDS through 2007 in the United States and dependent areas was 1,051,875; the estimated number of people newly diagnosed with AIDS in 2007 in the United States and dependent areas was 35,962 (CDC, 2009c).

It has been estimated that 33.4 million (31.1–35.8 million) people are living with HIV worldwide, that 2.7 million (2.4–3.0 million) people were newly infected in 2008, and that 2 million (1.7–2.4 million) people died of AIDS-related illness in 2008 (Joint United Nations Programme on HIV/AIDS [UNAIDS], 2009). The good news is that, according to the 2009 AIDS epidemic update by UNAIDS, new infections of HIV have been reduced 17% over the past 8 years. In addition, the number of AIDS-related deaths has declined 10% over the past 5 years.

Cumulatively, the estimated number of adults and adolescents diagnosed with AIDS in the United States and dependent areas is 1,009,200, with 810,676 cases in males, 198,544 cases in females, and 9,200 cases estimated in children under age 13. These numbers represent point estimates, which result from adjustments of reported case counts (CDC, 2009c). Persons of all ages and racial and ethnic groups are affected. The cumulative estimates of the number of AIDS cases from the beginning of the epidemic through 2007 include 404,465 cases of AIDS among Whites (not Hispanic), 426,003 cases among Black African Americans (not Hispanic), 169,138 cases among Hispanic/Latinos, 7,511 cases among Asian/Pacific Islanders, 3,492 cases among American Indians/Alaska Natives, and 721 among Native Hawaiians/Other Pacific Islanders.

HIV/AIDS is a relatively new disease, and early in its history, it was assumed to be terminal. The introduction of highly active antiretroviral therapy (HAART) that became widespread in the United States in 1996 altered the perception of AIDS. It came to be seen as a chronic instead of terminal disease. The reality is that, although some are living

longer with the disease, others are still dying young. In 2002, HIV/AIDS was the leading cause of death in the United States for Black (not Hispanic) females ages 25–44 (R. Anderson, 2002). The CDC estimated that cumulative number of deaths due to AIDS in the United States and dependent areas through 2007 was 583,298. This report further states that when considering only the 50 states and the District of Columbia, cumulative estimated number of deaths included 557,902 adults and adolescents, and 4,891 children under age 13 (CDC, 2009c).

The Centers for Disease Control and Prevention (2009c) has reported that the six common transmission categories for HIV are male-to-male sexual contact, injection drug use, male-to-male sexual contact *and* injection drug use, high-risk heterosexual (male–female) contact, mother-to-child (perinatal) transmission, and other (includes blood transfusions and unknown causes). According to the CDC (2005a), the fastest growing groups of persons reported with HIV have been men and women who acquire HIV through heterosexual contact, a group to which Melissa now belongs. Although HIV is more easily transmitted from men to women, it can be transmitted from women to men. Heterosexual transmission occurs mainly through vaginal intercourse.

Once a person is infected with HIV, the disease-fighting immune system gradually weakens. This weakened immune system lets other diseases begin to attack the body. Over the next few years, Melissa will learn a great deal about how her body does or does not protect itself against disease and infection. The **immune system** is made up of organs and cells that work together to defend the body against disease (Kennedy, Kiecolt-Glaser, & Glaser, 1988; E. P. Sarafino, 2008). When operating in an optimal manner, the immune system is able to distinguish our own cells and organs from foreign elements (E. P. Sarafino, 2008). When the body recognizes something as exterior or foreign, the immune system mobilizes body resources and attacks. Remember that we cautioned you about the arbitrary distinction between exterior and interior environments? Here is a good example. The foreign substance (which may be organic in composition and thus fit the definition of interior environment) that can trigger an immune response may be a tissue or organ transplant or, more commonly, an antigen. **Antigens** include bacteria, fungi, protozoa, and viruses.

Sometimes, however, the immune system is mistakenly directed at parts of the body it was designed to protect, resulting in **autoimmune diseases.** Examples include rheumatoid arthritis, rheumatic fever, and lupus erythematosus. With rheumatoid arthritis, the immune system is directed against tissues and bones at the joints. In rheumatic fever, the immune system targets the muscles of the heart. With lupus erythematosus, the immune system affects various parts of the interior environment, including the skin and kidneys (E. P. Sarafino, 2008).

Organs of the immune system are located throughout the body. They have primary involvement in the development of **lymphocytes,** or white blood cells (E. P. Sarafino, 2008), which fight infection. The main lymphatic organs include the following:

- *Bone marrow:* This is the soft tissue in the core of bones. There are two types of bone marrow, red and yellow. Yellow bone marrow stores fat, which the body consumes only as a last resort in cases of extreme starvation. At birth, all bone marrow is red, but as the body ages, more and more red bone marrow is converted to yellow. In adults, red bone marrow is found in the sternum, ribs, vertebrae, skull, and long bones. The bone marrow produces both red (erythrocytes) and white (leukocytes and lymphocytes) blood cells.

- *Lymph nodes:* These are small oval or round spongy masses distributed throughout the body (E. P. Sarafino, 2008). Lymph nodes are connected by a network of lymphatic vessels that contain a clear fluid called *lymph,* whose job is to bathe cells and remove bacteria and certain proteins. As the lymph passes through a lymph node, it is purified of infectious organisms. These vessels ultimately empty into the bloodstream.

- *Spleen:* This organ is located in the upper left quadrant of the abdomen. The spleen functions much like a very large lymph node, except

that instead of lymph, blood passes through it. The spleen filters out antigens and removes ineffective or worn-out red blood cells from the body (E. P. Sarafino, 2008). An injured spleen can be removed, but the individual becomes more susceptible to certain infections (Mader, 2003).

- *Thymus:* Located along the trachea in the chest behind the sternum, the thymus secretes *thymosins,* hormones believed to trigger the development of T cells. *T cells,* white blood cells that mature in the thymus, have the task of slowing down, fighting, and attacking antigens (Mader, 2003).

The immune system's response to antigens occurs in both specific and nonspecific ways. **Nonspecific immunity** is more general. "Scavenger" cells, or *phagocytes,* circulate in the blood and lymph, being attracted by biochemical signals to congregate at the site of a wound and ingest antigens (Safyer & Spies-Karotkin, 1988; E. P. Sarafino, 2008). This process, known as *phagocytosis,* is quite effective but has two limitations: (1) Certain bacteria and most viruses can survive after they have been engulfed, and (2) because our bodies are under constant attack and our phagocytes are constantly busy, a major assault on the immune system can easily overwhelm the nonspecific response. Thus, specific immunity is essential (Safyer & Spies-Karotkin, 1988).

Specific immunity, or acquired immunity, involves the lymphocytes. They not only respond to an infection, but they also develop a *memory* of that infection and allow the body to make rapid defense against it in subsequent exposure. Certain lymphocytes produce **antibodies,** protein molecules designed to attach to the surface of specific invaders. The antibodies recruit other protein substances that puncture the membrane of invading microorganisms, causing the invaders to explode. The antibodies are assisted in this battle by T cells, which destroy foreign cells directly and orchestrate the immune response. Following the *primary response,* the antibodies remain in the circulatory system at significant levels until they are no longer needed. With reexposure to the same antigen, a *secondary immune response* occurs, characterized by a more rapid rise in antibody levels—over a period of hours rather than days. This rapid response is possible because, during initial exposure to the antigen, memory cells were created. *Memory T cells* store the information needed to produce specific antibodies. They also have very long lives (Safyer & Spies-Karotkin, 1988; Sprent & Surth, 2001).

The immune system becomes increasingly effective throughout childhood and declines in effectiveness in older adulthood. Infants are born with relatively little immune defense, but their immune system gradually becomes more efficient and complex. Thus, as the child develops, the incidence of serious illness declines. During adolescence and most of adulthood, the immune system, for most individuals, functions at a high level of effectiveness. As we age, although the numbers of lymphocytes and antibodies circulating in the lymph and blood do not decrease, their potency diminishes.

Developmental perspective

The functioning of the immune system can be hampered by a diet low in vitamins A, E, and C and high in fats and cholesterol, and by excess weight (E. P. Sarafino, 2008). There are also far more serious problems that can occur with the immune system, such as HIV, that are life-threatening. HIV, like other viruses, infects "normal" cells and "hijacks" their genetic machinery. These infected cells in essence become factories that make copies of the HIV, which then go on to infect other cells. The hijacked cells are destroyed. A favorite target of HIV is the T cells that tell other cells when to start fighting off infections. HIV thus weakens the immune system and makes it increasingly difficult for the body to fight off other diseases and infections. Most of us host organisms such as fungi, viruses, and parasites that live inside us without causing disease. However, for people with HIV, because of the low T cell count, these same organisms can cause serious infection. When such a disease occurs or when the individual's number of T cells drops below a certain level, the person with HIV is considered to have AIDS (Cressey & Lallemant, 2007).

Melissa's life may undergo significant changes as symptoms of HIV infection begin to emerge.

Melissa may be at increased risk of repeated serious yeast infections of the vagina, and she may also be at increased risk for cancer of the cervix and pelvic inflammatory disease. Both men and women are vulnerable to opportunistic diseases and infections such as Kaposi's sarcoma, cytomegalovirus (CMV), AIDS retinopathy, pneumocystis carinii pneumonia (PCP), mycobacterium tuberculosis, and Candida albicans (thrush); atypical functioning such as AIDS dementia, loss of memory, loss of judgment, and depression; and other symptoms such as gastrointestinal dysfunction/distress, joint pain, anemia, and low platelet counts. The social worker may help to educate Melissa about these increased risks. In order to protect her health and the health of others, Melissa will most likely be advised to take special precautions. She can be supported in staying well by getting early treatment, adopting a healthy lifestyle, and remaining hopeful and informed about new treatments (Patterson et al., 1996).

The social worker also may have a role to play in working with Melissa as she tells her family and fiancé about her diagnosis. Melissa and her fiancé may need advice about how to practice safe sex. The social worker should also be available to work with Melissa, her fiancé, and her family as they adjust to her diagnosis and the grief frequently associated with it. The social worker may explore reactions and responses of Melissa, her fiancé, and her parents to this health crisis.

Because of the tremendous costs for medications, particularly HAART, the social worker may link Melissa to sources of financial support. This aid will become increasingly critical if she gets sicker, her income declines, and her medical expenses increase. Given recent advances in medical diagnostics and therapeutics, recent estimates indicate that the lifetime costs of health care associated with HIV may be more than $385,200 per person who is diagnosed as an adult (Schackman et al., 2006). Treatment with HAART is not a cure, but it allows the individual with HIV to fight off other infections and live longer (Markowitz, 1997). However, side effects of some of the drugs are just as debilitating as the effects of AIDS.

In addition to providing Melissa with information about her immune system, HIV, AIDS, and other physical health issues, the social worker can advise Melissa of the protections she qualifies for under the Americans with Disabilities Act of 1990. Melissa has joined an HIV support group, but the social worker may also offer to provide her with or refer her to counseling. The social worker may also have a role to play on behalf of all people with HIV/AIDS, working to address prevention and public health in part by providing HIV/AIDS education to business groups, schools, civic and volunteer associations, and neighborhood groups and by influencing policy to support public health HIV prevention initiatives.

Critical Thinking Questions 3.1

How important is it for Cheryl, Bess, and Melissa to be well informed about their medical conditions? How would you advise them about possible sources of information for their specific conditions? How should their social workers go about becoming better informed about their medical conditions?

Cardiovascular System

According to current estimates, 80 million people in the United States, or more than 1 in 5, have one or more types of *cardiovascular disease* (CVD), the most common cause of death in this country (American Heart Association, 2009).

An estimated 73,600,000 people in the United States ages 6 and over have high blood pressure, over 17 million (17,600,000) have a history of coronary heart disease ("heart attack"), and 6.4 million have a history of having had a stroke. CVD claimed 831,272 lives (34.3% of all deaths, or 1 of every 2.9) in 2006. Over 151,000 Americans killed by CVD in 2005 were under the age of 65. The final death rates from CVD per 100,000 population in the United States in 2006 were 306.6 for White males, 422.8 for Black males, 215.5 for White females, and 298.2 for Black females (American Heart Association, 2010). In 2006, strokes killed 137,119. Stroke is

the third leading cause of death (American Heart Association, 2006, 2009; U.S. Department of Health and Human Services, 2000a). In the United States, stroke is the leading cause of serious, long-term disability (American Heart Association, 2009). The death rates per 100,000 population for stroke in 2006 were 41.7 for White males, 67.1 for Black males, 41.1 for White females, and 57.0 for Black females (American Heart Association, 2009). In 2003, the rates of stroke among Mexican Americans were 2.6% for males and 1.8% for females; among Hispanic persons or Latinos (male and female), the rate was 2.2%; it was 1.8% among Asians (male and female) and 3.1% among American Indians/Alaska Natives (males and females) (American Heart Association, 2006). In the United States, the death rate from heart disease has been consistently higher in males than in females and higher among African Americans than among Whites (U.S. Department of Health and Human Services, 2000a). The rate of nonfatal strokes for Blacks in the United States is 1.3 times that of non-Hispanic Whites, the rate of fatal stroke is 1.8 times greater, and the rate of heart disease death is 1.5 times greater (American Heart Association, 2006).

Thomas's cardiovascular diagnosis is **high blood pressure (hypertension),** defined as a systolic blood pressure equal to or greater than ($\geq$) 140 mm Hg and/or a diastolic blood pressure $\geq$ 90 mm Hg (his was 200/105). Blacks, Puerto Ricans, Cubans, and Mexican Americans are all more likely to suffer from high blood pressure than are Whites, and the number of existing cases of high blood pressure is nearly 40% higher among Blacks than among Whites. An estimated 6.4 million Blacks have high blood pressure, with more frequent and severe effects than in other population subgroups (U.S. Department of Health and Human Services, 2000a). The prevalence of hypertension among Blacks in the United States is among the highest rates in the world.

In 2006, it was estimated that 1 in 3 adults had high blood pressure, with 77.6% of those individuals being aware of their condition. In 90% to 95% of the cases of individuals with high blood pressure, the cause is unknown. The death rate from high blood pressure has steadily increased (19.5%) from 1996 to 2006, with the actual number of deaths having risen 48.1%. The death rates per 100,000 population from high blood pressure in 2006 were 15.6 for White males, 51.1 for Black males, 14.3 for White females, and 37.7 for Black females (American Heart Association, 2009). High blood pressure also tends to be more common in people with lower education and income levels (N. Adler, 2006).

The cost of cardiovascular disease and stroke in 2005 was estimated to exceed $394 billion, including $242 billion for health care expenses and $152 billion for lost productivity (CDC, 2005b). According to the American Heart Association (2006), the estimated combined direct and indirect cost associated with high blood pressure for 2006 is $63.5 billion.

To better understand cardiovascular disease, it is first important to gain insight into the functioning of the **cardiovascular system,** which consists of the heart and the blood circulatory system (Kapit et al., 2000; Mader, 2003). The heart's walls are made up of specialized muscle. As the muscle shortens and squeezes the hollow cavities of the heart, blood is forced in the directions permitted by the opening or closing of valves. Blood vessels continually carry blood from the heart to the rest of the body's tissues and then return the blood to the heart. Exhibit 3.6 shows the direction of the blood's flow through the heart.

There are three types of blood vessels:

1. Arteries: These have thick walls containing elastic and muscular tissues. The elastic tissues allow the arteries to expand and accommodate the increase in blood volume that occurs after each heartbeat. *Arterioles* are small arteries that branch into smaller vessels called capillaries.

2. Capillaries: A critical part of this closed circulation system, they allow the exchange of nutrients and waste material with the body's cells. Oxygen and nutrients transfer out of a capillary into the tissue fluid surrounding cells, and blood absorbs carbon dioxide and other wastes from the cells.

3. Veins: These take blood from the capillaries and return it to the heart. Some of the major veins in the arms and legs have valves allowing the blood to flow only toward the heart when they are open and blocking any backward flow when they are closed (Kapit et al., 2000; Mader, 2003).

The heart has two sides (right and left) separated by the septum. Each side is divided into an upper and a lower chamber. The two upper, thin-walled chambers are called **atria (singular: atrium).** The atria are smaller than the two lower, thick-walled chambers, called **ventricles.** Valves within the heart direct the flow of blood from chamber to chamber, and when closed, prevent its backward flow (Kapit et al., 2000; Mader, 2003).

As Exhibit 3.6 shows, the right side of the heart pumps blood to the lungs, and the left side of the heart pumps blood to the tissues of the body. Blood from body tissues that is low in oxygen and high in carbon dioxide (deoxygenated blood) enters the right atrium. The right atrium then sends blood through a valve to the right ventricle. The right ventricle then sends the blood through another valve and the pulmonary arteries into the lungs. In the lungs, the blood gives up carbon dioxide and takes up oxygen. Pulmonary veins then carry blood that is high in oxygen (oxygenated) from the lungs to the left atrium. From the left atrium, blood is sent through a valve to the left ventricle. The blood is then sent through a valve into the aorta for distribution around the body (Kapit et al., 2000; Mader, 2003).

Contraction and relaxation of the heart moves the blood from the ventricles to the lungs and to the body. The right and left sides of the heart contract together—first the two atria, then the two ventricles. The heart contracts ("beats") about 70 times per minute when the body is at rest. The contraction and relaxation cycle is called the *cardiac cycle.* The sound of the heartbeat, as heard through a stethoscope, is caused by the opening and closing of the heart valves.

Although the heart will beat independently of any nervous system stimulation, regulation of the heart is primarily the responsibility of the ANS. *Parasympathetic activities* of the nervous system, which tend to be thought of as normal or routine

Exhibit 3.6   The Direction of Blood Flow Through the Heart

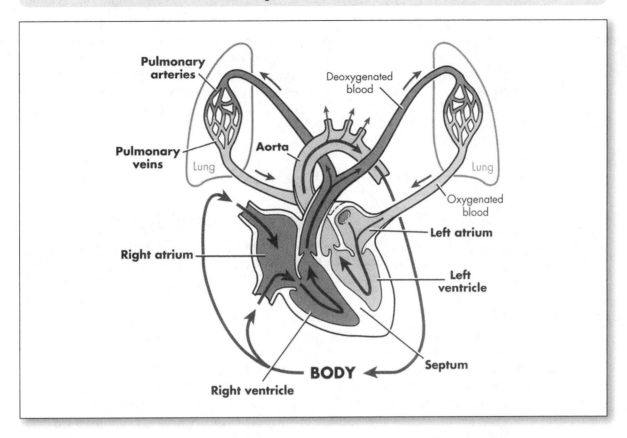

activities, slow the heart rate. *Sympathetic activities,* associated with stress, increase the heart rate. As blood is pumped from the aorta into the arteries, their elastic walls swell, followed by an immediate recoiling. The alternating expansion and recoiling of the arterial wall is the pulse. The normal pulse rate at rest for children ages 6–15 is 70–100 beats per minute; for adults age 18 and over, the normal pulse rate at rest is 60–100 beats per minute (Cleveland Clinic, 2005–2009).

Blood pressure is the measure of the pressure of the blood against the wall of a blood vessel. A *sphygmomanometer* is used to measure blood pressure. The cuff of the sphygmomanometer is placed around the upper arm over an artery. A pressure gauge is used to measure the *systolic blood pressure,* the highest arterial pressure, which results from ejection of blood from the aorta. *Diastolic blood pressure,* the lowest arterial pressure, occurs while the ventricles of the heart are relaxing. Medically desired and healthy blood pressure for a young adult is 120 mm Hg systole over 80 mm Hg diastole, or 120/80 (Kapit et al., 2000; Mader, 2003).

Blood pressure accounts for the movement of blood from the heart to the body by way of arteries and arterioles, but skeletal muscle contraction moves the blood through the venous system. As skeletal muscles contract, they push against the thin or weak walls of the veins, causing the blood to move past valves. Once past the valve, the blood cannot return, forcing it to move toward the heart.

High blood pressure has been called the silent killer, because many people like Thomas have it without noticeable symptoms. It is the leading cause of strokes and is a major risk factor for heart attacks and kidney failure.

Suddenly faced with startling information, such as a dramatic change in what was believed to be good health, Thomas might experience a range of responses, including but not limited to denial, questioning, self-reflection, self-critique, and even anger. The social worker can play many critical roles with Thomas. Perceptions of exterior conditions such as racial discrimination, daily hassles, and stressful life events place him at increased risk for having a stroke or dying as a result of his high blood pressure (Paradies, 2006). Social workers are uniquely positioned to see the links between external environment issues—such as vocational and educational opportunities, economics and income, housing, and criminal victimization—and interior environment health issues.

Conflict perspective

On an individual level, possession of knowledge to access the benefits of medical examination and treatment would be warranted for Thomas. The social worker can participate in medical care by helping Thomas learn the essential elements of effective health practice, including knowledge of what it means to have high blood pressure, the causes, and strategies for decreasing the health risks. If medication is prescribed, the social worker can support the medication regimen and Thomas's decision about how to follow it.

The social worker also can process with Thomas a strategy for identifying and deciding on his preferred lifestyle changes to help lower his blood pressure. These may include examination of sources of stress and patterns of coping, diet, how much exercise he gets on a regular basis, and his social and economic external environmental conditions.

Because high blood pressure has been shown to run in families, the social worker can also work with Thomas's family to discuss lifestyle factors that might contribute to high blood pressure, such as exposure to stress, cigarette/tobacco use, a diet high in cholesterol, physical inactivity, and excess weight.

Because African Americans and some other minorities have been shown to be at increased risk for high blood pressure, the social worker may work with community organizations, community centers, and religious organizations to advance policy and public health practices to support education and prevention programs as well as a physician and health care provider referral program. These health issues have been shown to be related to exterior environment experiences of discrimination and prejudice, and thus the social worker should pay attention to the external environment issues that negatively affect groups and individuals.

Systems perspective

Musculoskeletal System

Today, polio, a viral infection of the nerves that control muscles, has been nearly eradicated in industrialized countries. But in the middle of the 20th century, the disease was much more common, and it temporarily or permanently paralyzed both children and adults. The first outbreak of polio in the United States occurred in 1843 (University of Cincinnati, 2001–2010). According to the College of Medicine at the University of Cincinnati, in 1952 there were 21,000 cases of polio paralysis in the United States, with the last case of wild-virus acquired polio in the United States being diagnosed in 1979. By 1991, new cases of wild-virus acquired poliomyelitis syndrome had disappeared from the Western Hemisphere; by 1997, the Western Pacific was polio free; and by 2002, the European region was polio free (University of Cincinnati, 2001–2010). As of 2008, only four countries remain polio-endemic. This is down from more than 125 countries in 1998. The four remaining countries are Afghanistan, India, Nigeria, and Pakistan (World Health Organization [WHO], 2010). According to the World Health Organization (2006c), the total confirmed cases of polio diagnosed in 2006, as of July 27, were 597 for Africa, 0 for the Americas, 58 for the Eastern Mediterranean, 0 for Europe, 134 for Southeast Asia, and 1 for the Western Pacific (WHO, 2006c). Of the 440,000 people living with polio in the United States, about 25% to 50% may be affected by **post-poliomyelitis syndrome (PPS),** progressive atrophy of muscles in those who once had polio (National Institute of Neurological Disorders and Stroke, 2006). Case Study 3.5, at the beginning of the chapter, involves Max, who has PPS.

PPS has many causes. Some of the symptoms may be the result of the natural aging of muscles and joints damaged by polio or by overuse of unaffected muscles. Unrelated medical conditions may lead to new symptoms in people who have had polio and a progression of earlier weaknesses. Unexplained atypical muscle atrophy and weakness may also develop. The overuse or repetitive use of weakened muscle fibers and tissues may lead to musculoskeletal pain, which in turn may lead to further atrophy, a need for increased rest, and possibly an increasing level of impairment (Gevirtz, 2006).

For Max, as for many people who have had polio, this onset of new symptoms is unexpected. It may signal increasing physical impairment, which may require new adjustments and adaptations. A social worker who is working with Max should first acquire a knowledge base and then work to identify his strengths, resources, and perceived needs for intervention.

At the center of PPS is dysfunction in the **musculoskeletal system,** which supports and protects the body and enables motion. The contraction and relaxation of muscles attached to the skeleton is the basis for all voluntary movements. Over 600 skeletal muscles in the body account for about 40% of our body weight (Mader, 2003). When a muscle contracts, it shortens; it can only pull, not push. Therefore, for us to be able to extend and to flex at a joint, muscles work in "antagonistic" pairs. As an example, when the hamstring group in the back of the leg contracts, the quadriceps in the front relax; this allows the leg to bend at the knee. When the quadriceps contract, the hamstring relaxes, allowing the leg to extend.

The contraction of a muscle occurs as a result of an electrical impulse passed to the muscle by a controlling nerve that releases acetylcholine. When a single stimulus is given to a muscle, it responds with a twitch, a contraction lasting only a fraction of a second. But when there are repeated stimulations close together, the muscle cannot fully relax between impulses. As a result, each contraction benefits from

the previous contraction, giving a combined contraction that is greater than an individual twitch. When stimulation is sufficiently rapid, the twitches cease to be jerky and fuse into a smooth contraction/movement called *tetanus.* However, tetanus that continues eventually produces muscle fatigue due to depletion of energy reserves.

Skeletal muscles exhibit tone when some muscles are always contracted. Tone is critical if we are to maintain body posture. If all the muscle fibers in the neck, trunk, and legs were to relax, our bodies would collapse. Nerve fibers embedded in the muscles emit impulses that communicate to the CNS the state of particular muscles. This communication allows the CNS to coordinate the contraction of muscles (Kapit et al., 2000; Mader, 2003). In its entirety, the musculoskeletal system both supports the body and allows it to move. The skeleton, particularly the large heavy bones of the legs, supports the body against the pull of gravity and protects soft body parts. Most essential, the skull protects the brain, the rib cage protects the heart and lungs, and the vertebrae protect and support the spinal cord.

Bones serve as sites for the attachment of muscles. It may not seem so, but bone is a very active tissue, supplied with nerves and blood vessels. Throughout life, bone cells repair, remold, and rejuvenate in response to stresses, strains, and fractures (Kapit et al., 2000). A typical long bone, such as an arm or leg bone, has a cavity surrounded by a dense area. The dense area contains compact bone; the cavernous area contains blood vessels and nerves surrounded by spongy bone. Far from being weak, spongy bone is designed for strength. It is the site of red marrow, the specialized tissue that produces red and white blood cells. The cavity of a long bone also contains yellow marrow, which is a fat-storage tissue (Kapit et al., 2000; Mader, 2003).

Most bones begin as cartilage. In long bones, growth and calcification (hardening) begin in early childhood and continue through adolescence. Growth hormones and thyroid hormones stimulate bone growth during childhood. Androgens, which are responsible for

Developmental perspective

the adolescent growth spurt, stimulate bone growth during puberty. In late adolescence, androgens terminate bone growth.

Bones are joined together at joints. Long bones and their corresponding joints are what permit flexible body movement (Mader, 2003). Joints are classified according to the amount of movement they permit. Bones of the cranium, which are sutured together, are examples of immovable joints. Joints between the vertebrae are slightly movable. Freely movable joints, which connect two bones separated by a cavity, are called *synovial joints.* Synovial joints may be hinge joints (knee and elbow) or ball-and-socket joints (attachment of the femur to the hipbone). Exhibit 3.7 shows the structure of the knee joint. Synovial joints are prone to arthritis because the bones gradually lose their protective covering and grate against each other as they move (Mader, 2003).

The bones in a joint are held together by *ligaments,* while *tendons* connect muscle to bone. The ends of the bones are capped by cartilage, which gives added strength and support to the joint. Friction between tendons and ligaments and between tendons and bones is eased by fluid-filled sacs called *bursae.* Inflammation of the bursae is called bursitis.

Although overuse is damaging to the musculoskeletal system, underuse is too. Without a certain amount of use, muscles atrophy and bone density declines. Thus, the advice given to many individuals who were diagnosed with polio has been to "use it or lose it." Unfortunately, this advice may have inadvertently contributed to Max's post-polio symptoms.

Because of the commonly held perspective that individual independence is most desirable, it is not unusual for social workers and other health care professionals to discourage a person with a medical explanation for atypical function from using exterior environmental modifications and resources when they are not essential. These may include ramps, elevators, and electrically operated doors or assistive devices. **Assistive devices** are those products that are designated by the medical community to help a person to communicate, see, hear, or maneuver. Examples that have been used by individuals with atypical activity include manual wheelchairs, motorized wheelchairs, motorized scooters, and other aids that enhance mobility; hearing aids, telephone communication devices, assistive listening devices, visual and audible signal systems, and other aids that enhance an individual's ability to hear; and voice-synthesized computer modules, optical scanners, talking software, Braille printers, and other devices that enhance an individual's ability to communicate.

Those who believe that working to "overcome" challenges is a helpful approach in adjusting to or working with atypical function are well meaning. But hidden within this belief system is the impression that being labeled as "disabled" ascribes deficiency that makes an individual less than whole, less than competent, and less than capable. Having attended school before the Rehabilitation Act of 1973, the Individuals with Disabilities Education Act of 1975, and the Americans with Disabilities Act of 1990, Max's early years were spent in a world with little understanding or acceptance of his atypical gait. For Max, as for many people considered to be "disabled" on the basis of an atypical function,

---

Exhibit 3.7 Structure of the Knee Joint

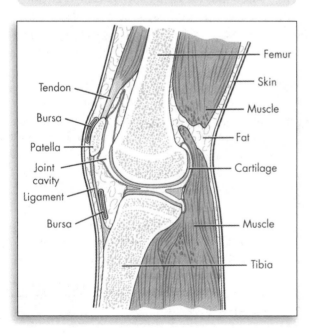

Labels: Femur, Skin, Muscle, Fat, Cartilage, Muscle, Tibia, Tendon, Bursa, Patella, Joint cavity, Ligament, Bursa

the pressure was and often is to "overcome" or to succeed in spite of a disability. Possibly, that interior and exterior environment pressure may have contributed to Max's current post-polio exacerbation.

The social worker has many options or none for working with Max. Max may choose to receive a thorough examination by a physician knowledgeable about polio and PPS and stop there. If Max seeks social services, the social worker will then be able to serve as a resource and referral agent. He or she may work with other rehabilitation professionals, such as physical therapists and occupational therapists, in identifying useful adaptations in Max's home and work environment that he could choose to use if he so desired. The social worker can provide counseling but could also refer Max to a PPS peer support group. Because Max may choose to acquire new technology, the social worker may also intervene with insurance companies reluctant to purchase expensive equipment.

Reproductive System

Juan and Belinda are at the age when an understanding of reproduction and sexuality is critical. In the United States, as in many countries around the globe, the typical age for the first experience of sexual intercourse is approximately 17, with 75% of high school seniors reporting having had sexual intercourse. Moreover, on average, there are almost 9 years for women and 10 years for men between first intercourse and first marriage (Guttmacher Institute, 2006). According to the CDC (2007), 47.8% of high school students reported having had sexual intercourse during their life, 45.9% for females and 49.8% for males. For high school students, 43.7% of White students reported that they had ever had sexual intercourse during their life; the percentage among Black students was 66.5%, and 52.0% among Hispanic students.

Contraception use has been increasing among sexually active teens in the United States. In 2006, an estimated 74% of sexually active females and 82% of sexually active males used contraception during the first experience with sexual intercourse (Guttmacher Institute, 2006). This is an encouraging trend, but sexually active U.S. teens still lag behind sexually active teens in other wealthy countries in contraceptive use. This contributes to a higher incidence of teen pregnancy and sexually transmitted disease (STD) in the United States than in other wealthy countries (Guttmacher Institute, 2002b). Annually, between 750,000 and 850,000 teenage females become pregnant in the United States, with between 75% and 95% of the teen pregnancies being unintended (Moss, 2004). The teen pregnancy rate in the United States declined 28% between 1990 and 2002. Among Black teenagers aged 15–19, the pregnancy rate fell by 40% during the same period; among White teenagers 15–19, the rate of decline was 34%; and among Hispanic teenagers 15–19, of any race, the pregnancy rate decreased by 19% (Guttmacher Institute, 2006). The teen birth rate began to rise again for females between the ages of 15 and 19 in 2006 (CDC, 2009i). The CDC (2004) estimates that nearly 19 million new STD infections occur each year, with nearly half occurring among youth and young adults ages 15 to 24.

Sex education is very much related to these statistics. As of 2002, research indicates that 2 out of 3 public school districts in the United States required some education about human sexuality. The great majority, 86%, of school districts that have sex education policies require that abstinence be promoted, and 35% require that abstinence be taught as the *only option*. The remaining school districts require that abstinence be taught as the *preferred option* and permit content on contraception and STDs. Ninety percent of sex education teachers believe that students should receive instruction on contraception, but 1 in 4 report that they are prohibited from providing such instruction. At least 75% of parents indicate they believe that sex education should include information about abstinence, abortion, sexual orientation, pressures to have sex, emotional reactions to having sex, and how to use condoms and other forms of birth control (Guttmacher Institute, 2002a).

If adolescents are to make responsible decisions about their sexuality, they would be wise to develop an understanding of the structures and functions of the reproductive system as well as a value base.

For some individuals, this information may come from the home; for others, from their schools or community activity centers; and for others, from family planning centers where social workers may work. The discussion that follows focuses on the interior environmental aspects of heterosexual sexuality and reproduction, but before beginning this discussion, we raise several important points.

First, recent theory and research have advanced concepts that suggest that gender and sexuality are multifaceted. Some theorists identify ways in which

Social constructionist perspective	culture influences gender definitions, beliefs, and attitudes about sexuality, as well as sexual behav-

iors (Rathus, Nevid, & Fichner-Rathus, 1998). Second, many contemporary definitions of gender, and thus of sexuality, move beyond the binary of male and female to the assertion that experience itself is a major element in ascribing gender. Moreover, experience does not have to be consistent with one's biology (S. Davies, 2006; Siragusa, 2001). Third, according to progressive approaches, rather than being a biological phenomenon, gender is considered by some to be a function of comfort as a member of a particular gendered group (Siragusa, 2001).

Finally, although we may typically think of gender as male or female, more recently the number of biologically described genders has expanded to five (heterosexual male, heterosexual female, homosexual male, homosexual female, and transsexual) (S. Davies, 2006), and six (McDermott, 1997): the feminine, masculine, androgynous, transsexual, cross-dresser, and culturally specific genders (DePoy & Gilson, 2007). It is possible for a person to be a chromosomal male with female genitals or vice versa. Chromosomal, genetic, anatomical, and hormonal aspects of sex are sometimes not aligned (Rudacille, 2005).

Let us now return to our discussion of the interior environment of heterosexual sexuality and gender. In humans, the reproductive system comprises internal and external structures. After conception, the sex-determining chromosome produced by the father unites with the mother's egg,

and it is this configuration that determines the child's sex. At birth, boys and girls are distinguished by the presence of specific genitalia.

As Exhibit 3.8 shows, the external male organs are the penis and scrotum. Internal organs consist of the testes, the tubes and ducts that serve to transfer the sperm through the reproductive system, and the organs that help nourish and activate sperm and neutralize some of the acidity that sperm encounter in the vagina. The penis functions as a conduit for both urine and semen.

Externally, the shaft and the glans (often referred to as the head or tip) of the penis are visible. The shaft contains three cylinders. The two largest are called the *corpa cavernosa* (singular: corpus cavernosum). During sexual arousal, these become engorged with blood and stiffen. The *corpus spongiosum*, the third cylinder, contains the urethra. It enlarges at the tip of the penis to form a structure called the *glans*. The ridge that separates the glans from the shaft of the penis is called the *corona*. The *frenulum* is the sensitive strip of tissue connecting the underside of the glans to the shaft. At the base of the penis is the *root*, which extends into the pelvis.

Three glands are part of the feedback loop that maintains a constant level of male hormones in the bloodstream. The primary functions of the **testes,** or male gonads, are to produce sperm (mature germ cells that fertilize the female egg) and to secrete male hormones called *androgens. Testosterone* is one of the most important hormones in that it stimulates the development of the sex organs in the male fetus and the later development of secondary sex characteristics such as facial hair, male muscle mass, and a deep voice. The two other glands in the feedback loop are the hypothalamus and the pituitary gland. Both secrete hormones that serve a regulatory function, primarily maintaining a constant testosterone level in the blood.

In the early stages of their development, sperm cells are called *spermatocytes.* Each contains 46 chromosomes, including both an X and a Y chromosome that determine sex. As the spermatocytes mature and divide, chromosomes are reduced by half, and only one (either the X or Y) sex-determining

Exhibit 3.8   The Male Reproductive System

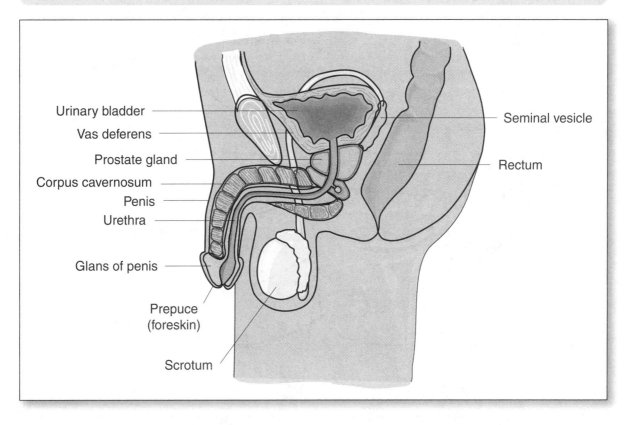

Urinary bladder

Vas deferens

Prostate gland

Corpus cavernosum

Penis

Urethra

Glans of penis

Prepuce
(foreskin)

Scrotum

Seminal vesicle

Rectum

chromosome is retained. The mature sperm cell is called the *spermatozoan*. This cell fertilizes the female egg (ovum), which contains only X chromosomes. Thus, the spermatozoan is the determining factor for the child's sex. (Females have two X chromosomes, and males have one X and one Y chromosome.)

Before ejaculation, the sperm pass through a number of tubes and glands, beginning with a testis, proceeding through a maze of ducts, and then to an epididymis, which is the convergence of the ducts and serves as the storage facility for sperm in a testicle. Each epididymis empties into the vas deferens, which brings the mature sperm to the seminal vesicles, small glands that lie behind the bladder. In these glands, a nourishing and activating fluid combines with the sperm before the mixture is carried through the urethra to the outside of the penis. The *prostate gland*, through which the urethra passes, produces and introduces the milky

fluid that preserves the sperm and neutralizes the alkalinity that is met in the female reproductive system. Cowper's glands also make their contribution to the seminal fluid before it leaves the male.

However, even if there is early ejaculation and the Cowper's glands do not have time to secrete fluid, viable sperm exist in the ejaculate and can fertilize the female egg. Early withdrawal of the penis from a woman's vagina therefore does not prevent the passage of some viable sperm cells. It is also important to know that sperm only compose about 1% of the ejaculate (3 to 5 milliliters of fluid total), but that this small percentage contains between 200 million and 400 million sperm. The number of sperm decreases with frequent ejaculation and advancing age.

Exhibit 3.9 shows the external female sex organs. They include the pudendum, also called the vulva, which consists of the mons veneris, the fatty tissue below the abdomen that becomes

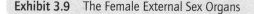

Exhibit 3.9 The Female External Sex Organs

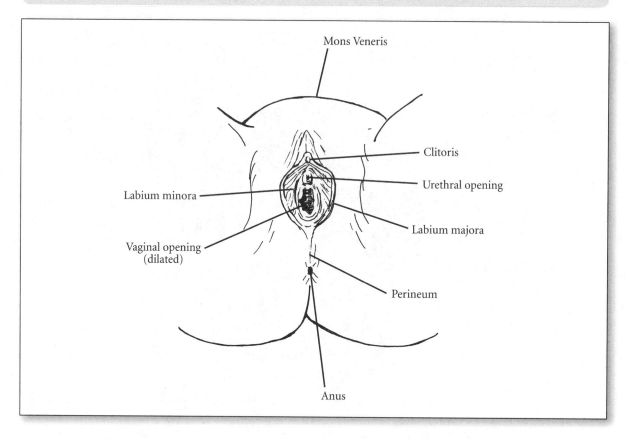

covered with hair after puberty; the labia majora and minora; the clitoris; and the vaginal opening. Unlike the male, the female has a physical separation between excretory and reproductive organs. Urine passes from the bladder through the urethra to the urethral opening, where it is expelled from the body. The urethra is located immediately before the vaginal opening and is unconnected to the vaginal opening.

The labia majora, large folds of skin, contain nerve endings that are responsive to stimulation and protect the inner genitalia. Labia minora join the prepuce hood at the top that covers the clitoris. These structures, when stimulated, engorge with blood and darken, indicating sexual arousal. Resembling the male penis and developing from the same embryonic tissue, the clitoris is about 1 inch long and ¼ inch wide. However, unlike the

penis, the clitoris is not directly involved in reproduction but serves primarily to produce sexual pleasure. The vestibule located inside the labia minora contains openings to the urethra and the vagina. It is also a site for arousal because it is rich in nerve endings that are sensitive to stimulation.

Internal structures of the female reproductive system, which are shown in Exhibit 3.10, include the vagina, ovaries, fallopian tubes, cervical canal (cervix), and uterus. The vagina is the structure that connects with the external sexual structures. Composed of three layers and shaped cylindrically, the vagina both receives the penis during intercourse and functions as the birth canal through which the child passes from the uterus to the world outside the mother. Because of its multiple functions, the vagina is flexible in size and changes climate from dry to lubricated. The cervix is the

Exhibit 3.10 The Female Internal Sex Organs

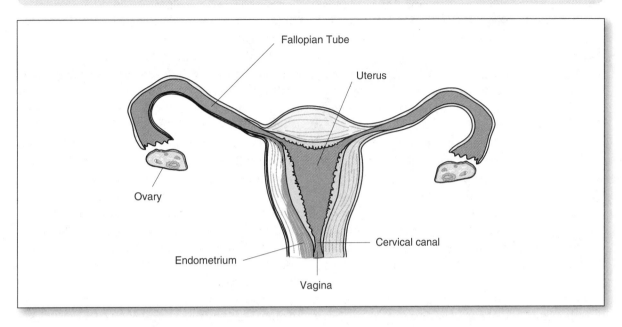

lower end of the uterus and protrudes into the vagina. It maintains the chemical balance of the vagina through its secretions.

The **uterus,** also called the womb, serves as the pear-shaped home for the unborn child for the 9 months between implantation and birth. The innermost of its three layers, the endometrium, is the tissue that builds to protect and nourish the developing fetus. If pregnancy does not occur, the endometrium is shed monthly through the process of menstruation. If pregnancy does occur, the well-muscled middle layer of the uterus produces the strong contractions necessary at birth to move the fetus out of the uterus, into the vaginal canal, and then into the world. The external layer protects the uterus within the body.

The fallopian tubes connect the ovaries to the uterus and serve as a conduit for the ova (egg cells) from the ovaries to the uterus. Located on either side of the uterus, the ovaries have two major functions: the production of ova and the production of the female sex hormones, progesterone and estrogen.

Unlike males, who produce an unlimited number of sperm throughout their lives, females are born with the total number of ova (eggs) that they will ever possess. At birth, the female baby's ovaries contain hundreds of thousands of eggs, but the eggs remain inactive until puberty begins. Toward the end of puberty, girls begin to release one egg each month during ovulation.

Estrogen facilitates sexual maturation and regulates the menstrual cycle in premenopausal women. The benefits of estrogen replacement in postmenopausal women are debatable. Some argue that estrogen maintains cognitive function and cardiac well-being in older women. However, estrogen supplements (also called hormone replacement therapy [HRT]) have been associated with increasing breast and uterine cancer risk, among other problems. Progesterone, though less discussed in the popular media, is critically important in preparing the uterus for pregnancy. It also is a regulator of the menstrual cycle.

Women's breasts are considered to be secondary sex characteristics because they do not have a direct function in reproduction. Mammary glands contained in the breast produce milk that is discharged through the nipple. The nipples are surrounded by the aureoles and become erect when stimulated. The size of the mammary glands is incidental to breast size and milk production. Rather, breast size is a function of the fatty tissue within the breast.

The social worker who is knowledgeable about interior environment mechanisms can clarify the specifics of male and female sexuality for Juan and Belinda. In the school setting or a local community agency, young couples may come to talk about their feelings for each other and ask questions regarding sexual and emotional intimacy. Young people in the United States often have inaccurate information about heterosexual and other types of sexuality and the biological aspects of sexual intimacy. Accurate information about sexuality could provide a basis for Juan and Belinda to make informed decisions about exercising their options related to sexuality.

While it is beyond the scope of this chapter to discuss sexual activity among diverse genders, we urge you to consider this important area of knowledge and social work practice.

Critical Thinking Questions 3.2

What are the available sources of information about the reproductive system in contemporary societies? What sources of information have you used to learn about the reproductive system? At what age did you begin to gather information about the reproductive system? How did you sort out accurate from inaccurate information? How would you like your little sister or brother—or one of your children—to learn about the reproductive system?

EXTERIOR SOCIOECONOMIC ENVIRONMENT/INTERIOR HEALTH ENVIRONMENT

Public health experts have long noted the association of poor health outcomes, in all body systems, with low income, low education, unsanitary housing, inadequate health care, unstable employment, and unsafe physical environments (Auerbach & Krimgold, 2001a; Engels, 1892). Until recently, however, researchers have made little attempt to understand the reasons behind this empirically supported connection of SES and health.

But by the mid-1990s, researchers in several countries began to try to understand how health is related to SES. In the United States, that research effort became much more focused in 1997, when the MacArthur Foundation established the Network on Socioeconomic Status and Health (N. Adler, 2001). This network is interdisciplinary, including scholars from the fields of anthropology, biostatistics, clinical epidemiology, economics, medicine, neuroscience, psychoimmunology, psychology, and sociology. Beginning in 2000, there was a big jump in research on health inequalities related to SES, oppression, and discrimination in the United States (N. Adler, 2006).

The relationship between SES and health is turning out to involve complex interactions of interior and exterior environments, and researchers are finding some surprises. For example, immigrants to the United States have a longer life expectancy than native U.S.–born persons, and this difference increased between 1979 and 2003 (G. Singh & Hiatt, 2006). This increase may be at least partially explained by U.S. immigration policies, which have been favoring immigrant populations with skill sets that are well suited for contemporary global capitalism.

One of the most consistent, but also most controversial, findings is that the level of income inequality in a country, and not purely SES, is associated with health (N. Adler, 2001). Residents | Conflict perspective
in more egalitarian countries, like Sweden and Japan, are healthier on average than residents in countries like Great Britain and the United States, where disparities in the incomes of the poor and the rich are larger (Wilkinson, 2001). Likewise, within the United States, residents in states with the greatest levels of inequality are 25% more likely to report their health to be fair or poor than residents in states with less inequality (Kawachi & Kennedy, 2001). High levels of perceived inequality are particularly

associated with heart attack, cancer, homicide, and infant mortality. A significant body of empirical inquiry has suggested that individuals in the lowest SES group are those hardest hit with the negative health effects of inequality (J. Chen et al., 2006).

Recent research is indicating that the mechanisms of this health-and-wealth connection involve a complex interaction of biological, psychological, and social factors. Several factors are consistently showing up in the research, however, including the following:

• Persons with lower incomes engage in disproportionately high-risk health behaviors and lifestyles. Persons with low income may be more likely than higher-SES individuals to smoke, use alcohol excessively, and eat high-fat diets. There is some evidence that these behaviors are used as coping strategies in the face of stress (J. Jackson, 2006). Researchers are also noting that people with low incomes who live in geographic areas with a high concentration of low-income families are less likely than those who live in more affluent areas to have access to health-related information, to health clubs and other facilities that foster good health, and to safe places to walk or jog. They are more likely than their affluent counterparts to be targeted by advertisers for fast food restaurants and to work in jobs with less flexibility. For example, one study of health among a sample of bus drivers found that many with hypertension did not take prescribed medications because the diuretics would increase the frequency of their need to visit a bathroom. Their rigid bus schedules did not allow for bathroom breaks (Ragland, Krause, Greiner, & Fisher, 1998).

• Persons with lower incomes are more likely than those with more substantial incomes to be exposed to carcinogens, pathogens, and other hazards in the physical environment. There is evidence that toxic waste sites are most likely to be located in neighborhoods with a high concentration of low-income residents (Kozol, 2000). Rapid urbanization in Africa and some parts of Asia is producing a number of hazards in the physical environment, including crowding, poor sanitation, and unsafe water (Curtis, 2004).

• Persons with lower incomes as compared to their wealthier counterparts are exposed to more

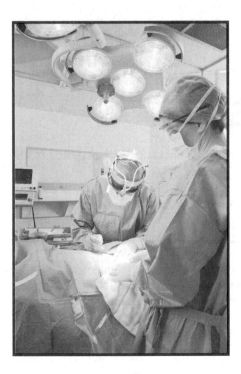

Photo 3.2a & 3.2b Biological health and illness greatly impact human behavior. Here, contrast how medical care is delivered in two very different situations, one in a high-tech operating room in the United States and the other in a temporary clinic in Haiti.

stressors and have fewer resources for coping with stress. Persons with low incomes often have less control over their work situations, a circumstance that has been found to have a powerful negative impact on health (Wilkinson, 2001). It is well documented that stress increases as SES decreases, and recent research indicates that high levels of stress are associated with cellular aging (Epel et al., 2006). It has also been found that "subjective social status," or an individual's evaluation of where she or he stands in the social hierarchy, is strongly related to health status (Sapolsky, 2005; Singh-Manoux, Marmot, & Adler, 2005). The subjective experience of being disadvantaged has been found to be highly correlated with endocrine response to stressors and with respiratory illness when exposed to a virus. These findings are in line with the emerging idea that the degree of the difference in wealth among a population has a greater effect than low SES alone. In addition, perceived racism is associated with ill health (Paradies, 2006).

The research so far supports the notion that the health care system alone cannot offset the effects of other external environment forces on health. Therefore, an important social work domain is public health research and practice. One recent study found that governmental policies aimed at reducing social inequalities result in lowering infant mortality rates and increasing life expectancy at birth (Navarro et al., 2006).

An additional critical factor in health status (positive and negative) involves health literacy. In *Tracking Healthy People 2010,* health literacy was defined by the U.S. Department of Health and Human Services as "The degree to which individuals have the capacity to obtain, process, and understand basic health information and services needed to make appropriate health decisions" (quoted in National Network of Libraries of Medicine, 2008, p. 1). Health literacy involves much more than simply translating health information into multiple languages. It also involves consideration of reading and listening skills; analytic and decision-making skills; and the freedom to be able to engage in dialogue, questioning, and critical evaluation of health information and health care options.

> ## Critical Thinking Questions 3.3
>
> What could be some reasons that the incidence of heart attack, cancer, homicide, and infant mortality increases as the level of societal inequality increases? What are the implications of this for public health policies?

Implications for Social Work Practice

This discussion of the interior biological person suggests several principles for social work assessment and intervention.

- Develop a working knowledge of the body's interior environmental systems, their interconnectedness, and the ways they interact with other dimensions of human behavior.
- In assessments and interventions, recognize that interior environmental conditions of health and illness are influenced by the exterior environmental social, political, cultural, and economic context.
- Recognize that the exterior environmental meanings attached to health and illness may influence not only the physical experience, but also the values and socio-emotional response assigned to health and illness.
- In assessment and intervention activities, look for the ways that behavior affects biological functions and the ways biological systems affect behaviors.
- In assessment and interventions, evaluate the influence of health status on cognitive performance, emotional comfort, and overall well-being.

- In assessment and intervention, consider the ways in which one person's interior environment health status is affecting other people in the person's exterior environment.
- Where appropriate, incorporate multiple social work roles into practice related to the health of the biological system, including the roles of researcher, clinician, educator, case manager, service coordinator, prevention specialist, and policy advocate.

Key Terms

acquired immunodeficiency
   syndrome (AIDS)
antibodies
antigens
assistive devices
atria (singular: atrium)
autoimmune disease
axon
blood pressure
brain injury (BI)

cardiovascular system
diabetes mellitus
endocrine system
feedback control mechanism
high blood pressure (hypertension)
human immunodeficiency
   virus (HIV)
immune system
lymphocytes
musculoskeletal system

nervous system
neuron
neurotransmitters
nonspecific immunity
post-poliomyelitis syndrome (PPS)
specific immunity
synapse
testes
uterus
ventricles

Active Learning

1. You have been asked by the local public middle school to teach youth about the experiences of living with one of the following conditions: brain injury, diabetes, HIV, high blood pressure, or post-polio syndrome. Locate literature and web resources on your chosen topic, select the material that you wish to present, and prepare a presentation in lay terms that will be accessible to the youth audience.

2. Working in small groups, prepare two arguments, one supporting and one opposing sex education in public school. Give some consideration to content that should or should not be included in sex education programs in public school and the ages at which such education should occur. Provide evidence for your arguments.

Web Resources

American Diabetes Association

www.diabetes.org

Site contains basic diabetes information as well as specific information on type 1 diabetes, type 2 diabetes, community resources, and healthy living.

American Heart Association

www.americanheart.org

Site contains information on diseases and conditions, healthy lifestyles, health news, and a heart and stroke encyclopedia.

Centers for Disease Control and Prevention (CDC) Division of HIV/AIDS Prevention

www.cdc.gov/hiv

Site contains basic science information on HIV/AIDS, basic statistics, fact sheets, and links to other resource sites.

Guttmacher Institute

www.guttmacher.org

Site presented by the Guttmacher Institute (formerly the Alan Guttmacher Institute), a nonprofit organization that focuses on sexual and reproductive health research, policy analysis, and public education, contains information on abortion law and public policy, pregnancy and birth, disease prevention and contraception, sexual behavior, sexually transmitted infections and HIV, and sexuality and youth.

MacArthur Network SES & Health

www.macses.ucsf.edu

Site has overviews of questions of interest to four working groups: social environment group, psychosocial group, allostatic load (physiological wear and tear on the body resulting from chronic stress) group, and developmental group.

National Center for Health Statistics

www.cdc.gov/nchs

Site contains FASTATS on a wide range of health topics as well as news releases and a publication listing.

Neuroscience for Kids

faculty.washington.edu/chudler/introb.html

Site maintained by faculty at the University of Washington, presents basic neuroscience information, including brain basics, the spinal cord, the peripheral nervous system, the neuron, sensory systems, effects of drugs on the nervous system, and neurological and mental disorders.

Post-Polio Syndrome Central

www.skally.net/ppsc

Site maintained by a group of volunteers, contains a post-polio syndrome survey and links to other web resources about PPS.

The Psychological Person

Joseph Walsh

Opening Questions

How is human behavior influenced by cognitions, emotions, and relationships?

What are some different approaches to coping with stress?

Key Ideas

As you read this chapter, take note of these central ideas:

1. Cognition and emotion are different but interrelated internal processes, and the nature of their relationship has long been debated.

2. Cognition includes the conscious thinking processes of taking in relevant information from the environment, synthesizing that information, and formulating a plan of action based on that synthesis. Cognitive theory in social work practice asserts that thinking, not emotion, should be the primary focus of intervention.

3. Emotions can be understood as feeling states characterized by appraisals of a stimulus, changes in bodily sensations, and displays of expressive gestures.

4. The symptoms of psychological problems may be primarily cognitive or emotional, but both cognition and emotion influence the development of problems.

5. Understanding the nature of a person's relationship patterns is important for evaluating his or her susceptibility to stress and potential for coping and adaptation. A variety of psychological (object relations, relational, and feminist) and social (Afrocentric, social identity development) theories are useful toward this end.

6. Stress, an event that taxes adaptive resources, may be biological, psychological, or social in origin; psychological stress can be categorized as harm, threat, or challenge.

7. Our efforts to master the demands of stress are known as coping.

CASE STUDY

Sheila's Difficult Transition to University Life

Sheila, age 22 and in her first semester at the state university, experienced a crisis during the seventh week of classes. It was the midpoint of the semester, when instructors were required to give interim grades so that students would clearly understand their academic status before the final date for course drops passed. Sheila knew that she was having trouble in all four of her courses but was shocked to receive two C's and two D's. Her chronic sense of sadness became worse; she starting having the occasional thoughts of suicide that she had experienced in the past. Sheila knew that she needed to study that weekend, but instead she made the 5-hour drive to her parents' home, feeling a need to be around familiar faces. She had no close friends at school. Distraught, Sheila considered dropping out, but her parents convinced her to talk to her academic adviser first. The adviser immediately became more involved in helping Sheila manage her dyslexia. Sheila learned to become more assertive with her instructors so that they understood her special challenges with the course work. The academic adviser also encouraged Sheila to begin seeing a counselor at the university counseling center.

The social worker at the counseling center learned that Sheila had been a troubled young woman for quite some time. In fact, Sheila said that she had felt depressed and inferior to her peers since childhood. The patterns of negative thinking and feeling that influenced Sheila's current crisis had been in place for 10 years. At this moment, Sheila believed that she simply did not have the intelligence to succeed in college. She did, in fact, have a diagnosed learning disability, a type of dyslexia that made it difficult for her to read and write. A special university adviser was helping her manage this problem, although not all her professors seemed sympathetic to her situation. Sheila also did not believe she had the social competence to make friends, male or female, or the strength of will to overcome her negative moods and outlook. She believed her depression was a basic part of her personality. After all, she couldn't recall ever feeling different.

Sheila grew up in a rural county in Virginia, several miles from the nearest small town. She was accustomed to spending time with her family and relatives, including her sister, Amy, who is 2 years older. During the previous 2 years, Sheila had commuted from her family home to a nearby community college. She had stayed home and worked for a year after high school graduation, without the motivation or direction to continue with schooling.

Amy was, in contrast, the star child who attended a major university to pursue a career in commercial art after winning academic awards throughout her high school years. Sheila watched Amy, so polished and popular, make her way easily and independently into the world. Sheila, by comparison, knew that she could not function so well. Eventually, she decided to enroll in the community college for general education studies. She felt awkward around the other students, as usual, but liked the small size of the school. It was peaceful and kept Sheila near her parents.

After Sheila completed her studies at the community college, she applied for admission to the state university. She decided to major in art preservation, an area of study similar to Amy's. Sheila's adjustment to the state university had been difficult from the beginning. She was intimidated by the grand scale of the institution: the size of the classes; the more distant, formal manner of her professors; the large numbers of students she saw on the campus streets; and the crowds in the student union. The university seemed cold and the students unfriendly. Sheila was a White, middle-class student like the majority at her campus, but she believed that the other students saw her as a misfit. She didn't dress in the latest styles, was not interesting or sophisticated, and was not intelligent enough to stand out in her classes. Even as she sat in the back of her classrooms, she believed that others were thinking of her, in her own words, as a geek. Sheila even felt out of place in her off-campus living quarters. A cousin had found her a basement apartment in a house in which a married couple resided. The walls were thin, and Sheila felt that she lacked privacy. She enjoyed perusing Facebook, the social networking website, but admitted that she felt a marginal connection to her few dozen "friends" there.

Many students experience a difficult transition to college. The counseling center social worker, however, was struck by several family themes that seemed to contribute to Sheila's low self-esteem. Sheila's paternal grandmother, a powerful matriarch, had always lived near the family. She disapproved of much of her grandchildren's behavior, and was frequently critical of them to the point of cruelty. She valued good social graces, and thus was particularly unhappy with Sheila's lack of social competence. Sheila's mother was always reluctant to disagree with her mother-in-law or defend her children. This passivity made Sheila angry at her mother, as did the fact that her mother argued with her father quite often and was known to have had several affairs.

Sheila was closer to her father, who was also fond of her, but he maintained a strict work ethic and believed that productive people should have no time for play. He felt that his children showed disrespect to him when they

(Continued)

(Continued)

"wasted time" with recreation. Amy seemed able to take her father's admonitions in stride and was closer in spirit and personality to her exuberant mother. Sheila, however, felt guilty when violating her father's wishes. They did have a special relationship, and her father tended to confide in Sheila, but he sometimes did so inappropriately. He told her on several occasions that he was thinking of divorcing his wife, and that in fact Sheila might have been fathered by one of his wife's boyfriends.

Thus, during her transition to the university, Sheila was faced with the task of making her way with a learning disability, a work ethic that did not permit her to enjoy college life and young adulthood, a personal history of being criticized with little balancing support, and even a lack of identity. Sheila was also living in an unfamiliar cultural environment, vastly different from the quiet rural community in which she was raised.

Over several months, the social worker at the university counseling center helped Sheila focus her thoughts and feelings in ways that were productive for her problem solving. First, Sheila found an apartment that afforded her some privacy and personal space. Then she got a part-time job at a shop on the campus perimeter to help keep busy and involved with people. With the social worker's encouragement, Sheila also joined some small university clubs focused on academic topics as a way for her to feel more comfortable on campus and to begin interacting with other students. She made a couple of good friends whose attention helped her believe that she was a person of worth. The social worker also helped her learn not to bury her emotions by escaping to her apartment, into her work, or back to her parents' home; rather, Sheila learned to experience her emotions as valid indicators that she was feeling threatened. This new way of coping was frightening to Sheila, but the social worker's support is helping her develop a greater sense of competence to manage stress.

By the end of her first year at the university, Sheila was still mildly depressed but feeling significantly better than she had been a few months before. She felt surer of herself, had more friends, and was looking forward to her second year at the university.

COGNITION AND EMOTION

Sheila's difficult transition to college life reflects her personal **psychology**, a term used here to mean her mind and her mental processes. Her story illustrates the impact on social functioning of a person's particular patterns of cognition and emotion. **Cognition** can be defined as our conscious or preconscious thinking processes—the mental activities of which we are aware or can become aware with probing. Cognition includes taking in relevant information from the environment, synthesizing that information, and formulating a plan of action based on that synthesis (Ronen & Freeman, 2007). *Beliefs,* key elements of our cognition, are ideas that we hold to be true. Our assessment of any idea as true or false is based on the synthesis of information. Erroneous beliefs, which may result from misinterpretations of perceptions or from conclusions based on insufficient evidence, frequently contribute to social dysfunction.

Emotion can be understood as a feeling state characterized by our appraisal of a stimulus, by changes in bodily sensations, and by displays of expressive gestures (Parkinson, Fischer, & Manstead, 2005). The term *emotion* is often used interchangeably in the study of psychology with the term *affect*, but the latter term refers only to the physiological manifestations of feelings. Affect may be the result of *drives* (innate compulsions to gratify basic needs). It generates both conscious and **unconscious** feelings (those of which we are not aware but which influence our behavior). In contrast, emotion is always consciously experienced. Nor is emotion the same as *mood*, a feeling disposition that is more stable than emotion, less intense, and less tied to a specific situation.

The evolution of psychological thought since the late 1800s has consisted largely of a debate about the origins of cognition and emotion, the nature of their influence on behavior, and their influence on each other. The only point of agreement seems to be that cognition and emotion are complex and interactive.

THEORIES OF COGNITION

Theories of cognition, which emerged in the 1950s, assume that conscious thinking is the basis for almost all behavior and emotions. Emotions are defined within these theories as the physiological responses that follow our cognitive evaluations of input. In other words, thoughts produce emotions.

Cognitive Theory

Jean Piaget's cognitive theory is the most influential theory of cognition in social work and psychology (Lightfoot, Lalonde, & Chandler, 2004). In his system, our capacity for reasoning develops in stages, from infancy through adolescence and early adulthood. Piaget identified four stages (summarized in Exhibit 4.1), which he

Developmental perspective

saw as sequential and interdependent, evolving from activity without thought to thought with less emphasis on activity—from doing, to doing knowingly, and finally to conceptualizing. He saw physical and neurological development as necessary for cognitive development.

A central concept in Piaget's theory is **schema (plural: schemata),** defined as an internalized representation of the world or an ingrained and systematic pattern of thought, action, and problem solving. Our schemata develop through *social learning* (watching and absorbing the experiences of others) or *direct learning* (our own experiences). Both of these processes may involve **assimilation** (responding to experiences based on existing schemata) or **accommodation** (changing schemata when new situations cannot be incorporated within an existing one). As children, we are motivated to develop schemata as a means of maintaining psychological *equilibrium*, or balance. Any experience that we cannot assimilate creates anxiety, but if our schemata are adjusted to accommodate the new experience, the desired state of equilibrium will be restored. From this perspective, you might interpret Sheila's difficulties in college as an inability to achieve equilibrium by assimilating new experience within her existing schemata. As a shy person from

Exhibit 4.1   Piaget's Stages of Cognitive Operations

Stage	Description
Sensorimotor stage (birth to 2 years)	The infant is egocentric; he or she gradually learns to coordinate sensory and motor activities and develops a beginning sense of objects existing apart from the self.
Preoperational stage (2 to 7 years)	The child remains primarily egocentric but discovers rules (regularities) that can be applied to new incoming information. The child tends to overgeneralize rules, however, and thus makes many cognitive errors.
Concrete operations stage (7 to 11 years)	The child can solve concrete problems through the application of logical problem-solving strategies.
Formal operations stage (11 to adulthood)	The person becomes able to solve real and hypothetical problems using abstract concepts.

a rural background, Sheila was accustomed to making friends very slowly in environments where she interacted with relatively small numbers of peers. She could not easily adjust to the challenge of initiating friendships quickly in a much larger and more transient student population.

Another of Piaget's central ideas is that cognitive development unfolds sequentially. Infants are unable to differentiate between "self" and the external world; the primary task in early cognitive development is the gradual reduction of such egocentricity, or self-centeredness. The child gradually learns to perform *cognitive operations*—to use abstract thoughts and ideas that are not tied to situational sensory and motor information.

Information Processing Theory

Social behavioral perspective; Systems perspective

Cognitive theory has been very influential but, as you might guess, leaves many aspects of cognitive functioning unexplained.

Whereas Piaget sought to explain how cognition develops, *information processing theory* offers details about how our cognitive processes are organized (G. Logan, 2000). Information processing is a *sensory theory* in that it depicts information as flowing passively from the external world inward through the senses to the mind. It views the mind as having distinct parts—including the sensory register, short-term memory, and long-term memory—that make unique contributions to thinking in a specific sequence. Interestingly, information processing theory has become important in designing computer systems! In contrast, a *motor theory* such as Piaget's sees the mind as playing an active role in processing—not merely recording but actually constructing the nature of the input it receives. In Sheila's case, information processing theory would suggest that she simply has not experienced a situation like her current one and thus lacks the schemata required to adapt. In contrast, cognitive theory would suggest that a faulty processing of input established somewhere in Sheila's past is making her adjustment difficult.

Photo 4.1 Information processing theory would suggest that the information these children are receiving from the computer flows through their senses to their minds, which operate much like computers.

Social Learning Theory

According to *social learning theory,* we are motivated by nature to experience pleasure and avoid pain. Social learning theorists acknowledge that thoughts and emotions exist but understand them as behaviors in need of explaining rather than as primary motivating factors. Social learning theory relies to a great extent on social behavioral

Social behavioral perspective

principles of conditioning, which assert that behavior is shaped by its reinforcing or punishing consequences (operant conditioning) and antecedents (classical conditioning). Albert Bandura (1977b) added the principle of vicarious learning, or *modeling,* which asserts that behavior is also acquired by witnessing how the actions of others are reinforced.

Social learning theorists, unlike other social behavioral theorists, assert that thinking takes place between the occurrence of a stimulus and our response. They call this thought process *cognitive mediation.* The unique patterns we learn for evaluating environmental stimuli explain why each of us may adopt very different behaviors in response to the same stimulus—for example, why Sheila's reaction to the crowds in the student union is very different from the reactions of some of her peers. Bandura (1977b, 1986, 2001) takes this idea a step further and asserts that we engage in self-observations and make self-judgments about our competence and mastery. We then act on the basis of these self-judgments. Bandura (2001) criticizes information processing theory for its passive view of human agency, arguing that it omits important features of what it means to be human, including subjective consciousness, deliberative action, and the capacity for self-reflection. It is clear that Sheila made very negative self-judgments about her competence as she began her studies at the university.

Theory of Multiple Intelligences

Howard Gardner's (1999, 2006) theory of **multiple intelligences** constitutes a major step forward in our understanding of how people come to possess different types of cognitive skills and how the same person is able to effectively use cognitive skills in some areas of life but not others. In this theory, which is based on anthropological and neuroscientific research, intelligence is defined as a "biopsychosocial potential to process information that can be activated in a cultural setting to solve problems or create products that are of value in a culture" (Gardner, 1999, p. 23).

The brain is understood not as a single cognitive system but as a central unit of neurological functioning that houses relatively separate cognitive faculties. During

Systems perspective

its evolution, the brain has developed separate organs, or modules, as information-processing devices. Thus, all people have a unique blend of intelligences derived from these modules. Gardner has delineated eight intelligences, which are overviewed in Exhibit 4.2, although in his ongoing research he is considering additional possibilities. Two intelligences, the *linguistic* (related to spoken and written language) and the *logical-mathematical* (analytic), are consistent with traditional notions of intelligence. The six others are not, however. You may be interested to note that in one study, social work educators rated intrapersonal, interpersonal, and linguistic intelligences as the most important for social work practice, and the same educators rated bodily-kinesthetic, musical, and spatial intelligences as important for culturally sensitive practice (Matto, Berry-Edwards, Hutchison, Bryant, & Waldbillig, 2006).

One of the most positive implications of the theory of multiple intelligences is that it helps us see strengths in ourselves that lie outside the mainstream. For example, Sheila, so self-critical, might be encouraged to consider that she has a strong spatial intelligence that con-

Humanistic perspective

tributes to her artistic sensibilities. She needs help, however, in further development of both her intrapersonal and interpersonal intelligences.

Exhibit 4.2   Gardner's Eight Intelligences

Linguistic Intelligence: The capacity to use language to express what is on your mind and to understand other people. Linguistic intelligence includes listening, speaking, reading, and writing skills.

Logical-Mathematical Intelligence: The capacity for mathematical calculation, logical thinking, problem solving, deductive and inductive reasoning, and the discernment of patterns and relationships. Gardner suggests that this is the type of intelligence addressed by Piaget's model of cognitive development, but he does not think Piaget's model fits other types of intelligence.

Visual-Spatial Intelligence: The ability to represent the spatial world internally in your mind. Visual-spatial intelligence involves visual discrimination, recognition, projection, mental imagery, spatial reasoning, and image manipulation.

Bodily-Kinesthetic Intelligence: The capacity to use your whole body or parts of your body to solve a problem, make something, or put on some kind of production. Gardner suggests that our tradition of separating body and mind is unfortunate because the mind can be trained to use the body properly and the body trained to respond to the expressive powers of the mind. He notes that some learners rely on tactile and kinesthetic processes, not just visual and auditory processes.

Musical Intelligence: The capacity to think in musical images, to be able to hear patterns, recognize them, remember them, and perhaps manipulate them.

Intrapersonal Intelligence: The capacity to understand yourself, to know who you are, what you can do, what you want to do, how you react to things, which things to avoid, which things to gravitate toward, and where to go if you need help. Gardner says we are drawn to people who have a good understanding of themselves because those people tend not to make mistakes. They are aware of their range of emotions and can find outlets for expressing feelings and thoughts. They are motivated to pursue goals and live by an ethical value system.

Interpersonal Intelligence: The ability to understand and communicate with others, to note differences in moods, temperaments, motivations, and skills. Interpersonal intelligence includes the ability to form and maintain relationships and to assume various roles within groups, and the ability to adapt behavior to different environments. It also includes the ability to perceive diverse perspectives on social and political issues. Gardner suggests that individuals with this intelligence express an interest in interpersonally oriented careers, such as teaching, social work, and politics.

Naturalist Intelligence: The ability to recognize and categorize objects and processes in nature. Naturalist intelligence leads to talent in caring for, taming, and interacting with the natural environment, including living creatures. Gardner suggests that naturalist intelligence can also be brought to bear to discriminate among artificial items such as sneakers, cars, and toys.

SOURCE: Based on Gardner (1999, 2006).

Theories of Moral Reasoning

Morality is our sensitivity to, and knowledge of, what is right and wrong. It develops from our acquired principles of justice and ways of caring for others. Theories of moral reasoning are similar to those of cognitive development in that a sequential process is involved. Familiarity with these theories can help

Developmental perspective

social workers understand how clients make decisions and develop preferences for action in various situations. Both of these issues are important in our efforts to develop goals with clients. The best-known theories of moral reasoning are those of Lawrence Kohlberg and Carol Gilligan. In reviewing these theories, it is important to keep in mind that they are based on studies of men and women in the United States. It is likely that moral development unfolds differently in other cultures, even though more research is needed to investigate these differences (Gardiner & Kosmitzki, 2008).

Kohlberg (1969b) formulated six stages of moral development, which begin in childhood and unfold through adolescence and young adulthood (see Exhibit 4.3). The first two stages represent *preconventional morality,* in which the child's primary motivation is to avoid immediate punishment and receive immediate rewards. *Conventional morality* emphasizes adherence to social rules. A person at this level of morality might be very troubled, as Sheila is, by circumstances that make him or her different from other people. Many people never move beyond this level to *postconventional morality,* which is characterized by a concern with moral principles transcending those of their own society.

One limitation of Kohlberg's theory is that it does not take into account gender differences (as his participants were all male). In fact, he claims that women do not advance through all six stages as often as men. Addressing this issue, Gilligan (1982, 1988) notes that boys tend to emphasize independence, autonomy, and the rights of others in their moral thinking, using a *justice-oriented* approach. Girls, on the

Conflict perspective

other hand, develop an *ethic of care* that grows out of a concern for the needs of others rather than the value of independence. To account for this difference, Gilligan proposed the three stages of moral development listed in Exhibit 4.4. Her stages place greater emphasis than Kohlberg does on the ethic of care and are meant to more accurately describe the moral development of females. The research findings on gender differences in moral reasoning are inconsistent, however (e.g., Galotti, 1989; Hauser, Cushman, Young, Mikhail, & Jin, 2007; Malti, Gasser, & Buchmann, 2009; M. Ryan, David, & Reynolds, 2004). With her great concern about what her parents and grandmother want her to do, Sheila seems to fall into Kohlberg's stage of conventional morality and Gilligan's stage of conventional care.

Researchers have also found evidence that culture may have a greater influence on moral reasoning than gender does, with Anglo-Americans putting less emphasis on an ethic of care than members of other ethnic groups (Al-Ansari, 2002; Gardiner & Kosmitzki, 2008; L. Gump, Baker, & Roll, 2000). Gardiner and Kozmitzki argue that moral development may not follow a universal script across cultures and suggest that the ecological system in which

Exhibit 4.3 Kohlberg's Stages of Moral Development

Stage	Description
Preconventional	
Heteronomous morality	Accepting what the world says is right
Instrumental purpose	Defining the good as whatever is agreeable to the self and those in the immediate environment
Conventional	
Interpersonal experiences	Seeking conformity and consistency in moral action with significant others
The societal point of view	Seeking conformity and consistency with what one perceives to be the opinions of the larger community
Postconventional	
Ethics	Observing individual and group (societal) rights
Conscience and logic	Seeking to apply universal principles of right and wrong

Exhibit 4.4   Gilligan's Three Stages of Moral Development

Stage	Description
Survival orientation	Egocentric concerns of emotional and physical survival are primary.
Conventional care	The person defines as right those actions that please significant others.
Integrated care	A person's right actions take into account the needs of others as well as the self.

early social interactions occur shapes moral thought and behavior. For understanding moral reasoning across cultures, they recommend a social constructionist theory of moral development proposed by Norma Haan (1991), in which she suggests that moral reasoning comes from the understanding of the interdependence of self and others that develops through social interactions. She proposes that the most mature moral reasoner is the one who makes moral decisions that balance the person's own needs and desires with those of others who are affected by the issue at hand. Haan found that people who are able to control their own emotions in order to think about possible solutions engage in higher levels of moral action than people who are not able to control their own emotions.

Theories of Cognition in Social Work Practice

When theories of cognition first emerged, they represented a reaction against psychodynamic theories, which focused on the influence of unconscious thought. Many practitioners had come to believe that although some mental processes may be categorized as unconscious, they have only a minor influence on behavior. Rather, conscious thinking is the basis for almost all behavior and emotions (J. Walsh, 2010).

According to cognitive theory, we are "rational" as long as our schemata accommodate available evidence and our decisions do not rely solely on preconceived notions of the external world. So long as a person's cognitive style helps to achieve his or her goals, it is considered healthy. However, a person's thinking patterns can become distorted, featuring patterns of bias that dismiss relevant environmental information from judgment, which can lead in turn to the maladaptive emotional responses described in Exhibit 4.5. These *cognitive errors* are habits of thought that lead people to distort input from the environment and experience psychological distress (A. T. Beck, 1976; J. S. Beck, 1995).

As a social worker, you could use cognitive theory to surmise that Sheila feels depressed because she subjectively assesses her life situations in a distorted manner. For example, *arbitrary inferences* may lead her to conclude that because the university students do not approach her in the crowded student union, they are not friendly. Because she mistakenly concludes that they are not friendly, she may also conclude that she will continue to be lonely at the university, and this thought produces her emotional response of sadness.

To adjust her emotions and mood, Sheila needs to learn to evaluate her external environment differently. She needs to change some of the beliefs, expectations, and meanings she attaches to events, because they are not objectively true. She might conclude, for example, that the union is simply not an appropriate place to meet people, because it is crowded and students tend to be hurrying through lunch and off to classes. Sheila can either change her perceptions or change the troubling environments by seeking out new situations. In either case, cognitive theorists would make Sheila's thinking the primary target of change activity, assuming that cognitive change will in turn produce changes in her emotional states.

Exhibit 4.5   Common Cognitive Distortions

Cognitive Error	Description
Absolute thinking	Viewing experience as all good or all bad, and failing to understand that experiences can be a mixture of both
Overgeneralization	Assuming that deficiencies in one area of life necessarily imply deficiencies in other areas
Selective abstraction	Focusing only on the negative aspects of a situation, and consequently overlooking its positive aspects
Arbitrary inference	Reaching a negative conclusion about a situation with insufficient evidence
Magnification	Creating large problems out of small ones
Minimization	Making large problems small, and thus not dealing adequately with them
Personalization	Accepting blame for negative events without sufficient evidence

Cognitive theory is a highly rational approach to human behavior. Even though the theory assumes that many of a person's beliefs are irrational and distorted, it also assumes that human beings have great potential to correct these beliefs in light of contradictory evidence. In clinical assessment, the social worker must assess the client's schemata, identify any faulty thinking patterns, and consider the evidence supporting a client's beliefs. During intervention, the social worker helps the client adjust his or her cognitive process to better facilitate the attainment of goals. As a result, the client will also experience more positive emotions. It is important to emphasize at the same time that clients are not encouraged to rationalize all of their problems as involving faulty assumptions, as many challenges people face are due to oppressive external circumstances. Still, Sheila's belief that other students in the busy union have critical thoughts about her as she passes by is an arbitrary inference, based on her own inclination to think poorly of herself. To help her overcome this cognitive error, the social worker could review the available evidence, helping Sheila to understand that the other students probably did not notice her at all.

Social learning theory takes the tendency in cognitive theory to deemphasize innate drives and unconscious thinking even further. Some practitioners in the social learning tradition make no attempt to understand internal processes at all and avoid making any inferences about them. Social workers who practice from the behavioral approach conceptualize thoughts and emotions as behaviors subject to *reinforcement contingencies* (Thyer, 2005). That is, we tend to behave in ways that produce rewards (material or emotional) for us. Thus, behaviors can be modified through the application of specific action-oriented methods, such as those listed in Exhibit 4.6. If Sheila is depressed, the social worker would help to identify the things that reinforce her depressed behavior and adjust them so that her emotional states (as revealed in behaviors) will change in response. Through desensitization and behavioral rehearsal, for example, Sheila could learn step-by-step to approach a small group of students at a lunch table and ask to join them. Her positive reinforcers might include success in these measured experiences, a new sense of efficacy, reduced anxiety, and the affirmation of her social worker.

The combination of assessing and intervening with a person's thought processes, and then helping the client to identify and develop reinforcers for new ways of thinking and behaving, is known as

Exhibit 4.6   Four Behavioral Change Strategies

Strategy	Description
Desensitization	Confronting a difficult challenge through a step-by-step process of approach and anxiety control
Shaping	Differentially reinforcing approximations of a desired but difficult behavior so as to help the person eventually master the behavior
Behavioral rehearsal	Role-playing a desired behavior after seeing it modeled appropriately and then applying the skill to real-life situations
Extinction	Eliminating a behavior by reinforcing alternative behaviors

cognitive-behavioral therapy. Most cognitive practitioners actually use cognitive-behavioral methods, because it is important to help the client experience rewards for any changes he or she risks.

THEORIES OF EMOTION

Emotion is physiologically programmed into the human brain (see Chapter 3). Its expression is primarily mediated by the hypothalamus, whereas the experience of emotion is a limbic function. But emotion also involves a cognitive labeling of these programmed feelings, which is at least partially a learned process. For example, two students might feel anxious walking into the classroom on the first day of a semester. The anxiety would be a normal reaction to entering a new and unfamiliar situation. However, one student might interpret the anxiety as a heightened alertness that will serve her well in adjusting to the new students and professor, whereas the other student might interpret the same emotion as evidence that she is not prepared to manage the course material. The first student may become excited, but the second student becomes distressed. Many theorists distinguish between primary and secondary emotions (Parkinson et al., 2005). The **primary emotions** may have evolved as specific reactions with survival value for the human species. They mobilize us, focus our attention, and signal our state of mind to others. There is no consensus on what the primary emotions are, but they are usually limited to anger, fear, sadness, joy,

and anticipation (Panksepp, 2008). The **secondary emotions** are more variable among people and are socially acquired. They evolved as humans developed more sophisticated means of learning, controlling, and managing emotions to promote flexible cohesion in social groups. The secondary emotions may result from combinations of the primary emotions (Plutchik, 2005). These emotions include (but are not limited to) envy, jealousy, anxiety, guilt, shame, relief, hope, depression, pride, love, gratitude, and compassion (Lazarus, 2007).

The autonomic nervous system is central to our processing of emotion (Bentley & Walsh, 2006). This system consists of nerve tracts running from the base of the brain, through the spinal cord, and into the internal organs of the body. It is concerned with maintaining the body's physical homeostasis. Tracts from one branch of this system, the sympathetic division, produce physiological changes that help make us more alert and active. These changes are sustained by the release of hormones from the endocrine glands into the bloodstream. As part of the feedback control mechanism, parasympathetic system nerve tracts produce opposite, or calming, effects in the body. The two systems work together to maintain an appropriate level of physical arousal.

Systems perspective

Still, psychologists have debated for more than a century the sources of emotion. Theories range from those that emphasize physiology to those that emphasize the psychological or the purely social context, and they give variable weight to the role of cognition.

Physiological Theories of Emotion

A theory of emotion (W. James, 1890) developed over a century ago speculated that our bodies produce automatic physiological reactions to any stimulus. We notice these reactions after the fact and then attempt through cognition to make sense of them. This "making sense" involves labeling the emotion. Thus, emotion follows cognition, which itself follows the physiological reaction to a stimulus. The original theory stated that a distinct emotion arises from each physiological reaction.

A few decades later, another theory was developed (Cannon, 1924) that argued that physiological arousal and the experience of emotion are unrelated. Our physiological responses to a stimulus are nonspecific and only prepare us for a general fight-or-flight response (to confront or avoid the stimulus). This response in itself has nothing to do with the experience of emotion, because any particular physiological activity may give rise to different emotional states and may not even involve our emotions at all. Thus, a separate process of perception produces our feeling of emotion. Emotion derives from the associations we make based on prior attempts to understand the sensation of arousal.

Physiology-based theories of emotion lost favor in the mid-20th century, but recent brain research is once again suggesting a strong link between physiological processes and emotion. *Differential emotions theory* (Magai, 2001) asserts that emotions originate in our neurophysiology and that our personalities are organized around "affective biases." All of us possess five primary human emotions: happiness, sadness, fear, anger, and interest/excitement. These emotions are instinctual, are in a sense hardwired into our brains, and are the source of our motivations. When our emotions are activated, they have a pervasive influence on our cognition and behavior. A key theme in this theory is that emotions influence cognition, a principle opposite to that stressed in cognitive theory.

For example, Sheila has a persistent bias toward sadness, which may reflect some personal or material loss long before she started college. Her sadness has a temporary physical response: a slowing down and a decrease in general effort. It also leads her to withdraw in situations where her efforts to recover the loss would likely be ineffective. The sadness thus allows Sheila time to reevaluate her needs and regain energy for more focused attempts to reach more achievable goals. It is also a signal for others to provide Sheila with support. The sadness of others promotes our own empathic responses. Of course, it is likely that "appearing sad" may have been more functional for Sheila in her home community, where she was more consistently around people who knew and took an interest in her. In contrast, anger tends to increase a person's energy and motivate behavior that is intended to overcome frustration. Furthermore, it is a signal to others to respond with avoidance, compliance, or submission so that the person may resolve the problem.

Researchers have speculated for decades about the precise locations of emotional processing in the brain. Much has been learned about structures that participate in this process, but many areas of the brain have a role (LeDoux & Phelps, 2008). The physiology of emotion begins in the *thalamus,* a major integrating center of the brain. Located in the forebrain, the thalamus is the site that receives and relays sensory information from the body and from the environment to other parts of the brain. Any perceived environmental event travels first to the thalamus and then to the sensory cortex (for thought), the basal ganglia (for movement), and the hypothalamus (for feeling). The *amygdala,* part of the limbic system, is key in the production of emotional states. There are in fact two routes to the amygdala from the thalamus. Sensations that produce the primary emotions described above may travel there directly from the thalamus, bypassing any cognitive apparatus, to produce an immediate reaction that is key

Social constructionist perspective

to survival. Other inputs first travel through the cortex, where they are cognitively evaluated prior to moving on to the limbic system and amygdala to be processed as the secondary emotions.

Culture and the characteristics of the individual may influence the processing of stimulation because the cognitive structures (schemata) that interpret this stimulation may, through feedback loops to the thalamus, actually shape the neural pathways that will be followed by future stimuli (J. Kagan, 2007). In other words, neural schemata tend to become rigid patterns of information processing, shaping subsequent patterns for making sense of the external world.

| Systems perspective |

Psychological Theories of Emotion

Perhaps the most contentious debates about the role of cognition in emotion have taken place among psychological theorists. Some psychologists have considered emotion as primary, and others have considered cognition as primary. Psychological theories in the social behavioral perspective, somewhat like physiology-based theories, assume an automatic, programmed response that is then interpreted as emotion, perhaps first consciously but eventually (through habit) unconsciously.

Psychoanalytic Theory

Freud's landmark work, *The Interpretation of Dreams,* first published in 1899, signaled the arrival of **psychoanalytic theory.** Freud's theories became prominent in the United States by the early 1900s, immediately influencing the young profession of social work, and were a dominant force through the 1950s. Psychoanalytic thinking continues to be influential in social work today, through the theories of ego psychology, self psychology, and object relations, among others.

| Psychodynamic perspective |

The basis of psychoanalytic theory is the primacy of internal drives and unconscious mental activity in human behavior. Sexual and aggressive drives are not "feelings" in themselves, but they motivate behavior that will presumably gratify our impulses. We experience positive emotions when our drives are gratified and negative emotions when they are frustrated.

Our conscious mental functioning takes place within the **ego,** that part of the personality responsible for negotiating between internal drives and the outside world. It is here that cognition occurs, but it is driven by those unconscious thoughts that are focused on drive satisfaction.

In psychoanalytic thought, then, conscious thinking is a product of the drives from which our emotions also spring. By nature, we are pleasure seekers and "feelers," not thinkers. Thoughts are our means of deciding how to gratify our drives. Defense mechanisms result from our need to indirectly manage drives when we become frustrated, as we frequently do in the social world, where we must negotiate acceptable behaviors with others. The need to manage drives also contributes to the development of our unconscious mental processes. According to psychoanalytic theory, personal growth cannot be achieved by attending only to conscious processes. We need to explore all of our thoughts and feelings to understand our essential drives. Change requires that we uncover unconscious material and the accompanying feelings that are repressed, or kept out of consciousness.

Let us grant, for example, that Sheila has a normal, healthy drive for pleasure. She may thus be angry with her father for the manner in which he discourages her from developing a social life and also burdens her with his personal problems. This feeling of anger might be repressed into unconsciousness, however, because Sheila is close to her father in many ways and may believe that it is not permissible for a daughter to be angry with a well-meaning parent. Sheila's unconscious anger, having been turned onto herself, may be contributing to her depression. A psychoanalytically oriented social worker

| Psychodynamic perspective |

might suspect from Sheila's presentation that she experiences this anger. The social worker might try to help Sheila uncover this by having her reflect on her feelings about her father in detail, in a safe clinical environment. With the insights that might result from this reflection, Sheila's feeling may become conscious, and she can then take direct measures to work through her anger.

Ego Psychology

Ego psychology, which emerged in the 1930s (E. Goldstein, 2008), shifted to a more balanced perspective on the influences of cognition and emotion in social functioning. As an adaptation of psychoanalytic theory, it signaled a reaction against Freud's heavy emphasis on drives and highlighted the ego's role in promoting healthy social functioning. Ego psychology represents an effort to build a holistic psychology of normal development. It was a major social work practice theory throughout much of the 20th century because of its attention to the environment as well as the person, and it continues to be taught in many schools of social work.

In ego psychology, the ego is conceived of as present from birth and not as derived from the need to reconcile drives within the constraints of social living, as psychoanalytic theory would say. The ego is the source of our attention, concentration, learning, memory, will, and perception. Both past and present experiences are relevant in influencing social functioning. The influence of the drives on emotions and thoughts is not dismissed, but the autonomy of the ego, and thus conscious thought processes, receives greater emphasis than in psychoanalytic theory. The ego moderates internal conflicts, which may relate to drive frustration, but it also mediates the interactions of a healthy person with stressful environmental conditions.

If we experience sadness, then, it is possible that we are having conflicts related to drive frustration that are internal in origin. However, it is also possible that we are experiencing person-environment conflicts in which our coping efforts are not effective;

Social behavioral perspective

the negative emotion may result from a frustration of our ability to manage an environmental stressor and thus may arise from cognitive activities. Sheila may be experiencing both types of conflict. Her anger at the lack of adequate nurturance in her early family history may have been turned inward to produce a depression that has persisted in all of her environments. At the same time, the mismatch between her personal needs for mastery and the demands of this particular academic environment may be contributing to her frustration and depression.

Attribution Theory (A Cognitive Perspective)

Attribution theory was the first of the psychological theories of emotion to give primacy to cognition as a producer of emotions (Schacter & Singer, 1962). Attribution theory holds that our experience of emotion is based on conscious evaluations we make about physiological sensations in particular social settings. We respond to situations as we understand them cognitively, which leads directly to our experience of a particular emotion. For example, Sheila has often experienced anxiety, but she interprets it differently in dealing with her strict father (who makes her feel guilty about enjoying life) and her fellow students (who make her feel ashamed of who she is). The nature of the social setting is key to the process of emotional experience.

A further refinement of attribution theory states that our initial reactions to any stimulus are limited to the sense of whether it will have positive or negative consequences for us (Weiner, 2008). This is an automatic, preconscious process. Afterward, we consider what has caused the event, which leads to modification of the emotion we feel. Our perceptions of internal versus external cause determine in part the type of emotion that we experience. For example, if we experience frustration, the emotion of shame may emerge if we decide that it is due to our own behavior. However, we may experience anger if we decide that the frustration is due to the actions of someone else.

Richard Lazarus (2001) has proposed a three-part psychological theory of emotion based on appraisals of situations. He suggests that emotion develops when we assess a situation as somehow relevant to a personal value or life concern. First, we make an unconscious appraisal of whether a situation constitutes a threat. This appraisal is followed by coping responses, which may be cognitive, physiological, or both, and may be conscious or unconscious. Once these coping mechanisms are in place, we reappraise the situation and label our associated emotion. This process implies that our feelings originate with an automatic evaluative judgment. We decide whether there is a threat, take immediate coping action to deal with it, and then take a closer look to see exactly what was involved in the situation. At the end of this process, we experience a specific emotion.

A major life concern for Sheila is feeling secure in her interpersonal environments. She feels secure in familiar environments (such as her hometown) but feels threatened in unfamiliar places. When she walks into a new classroom, she experiences anxiety. The feeling seems to Sheila to be automatic, because her need for security is threatened in the situation. Her means of coping is to ignore the other students, neither speaking to nor making eye contact with them, and to sit in a relatively isolated area of the room. Sheila then makes at least a partly conscious appraisal that the room is not only occupied with strangers, but that they will quickly judge her in negative ways. Sheila labels her emotion as shame, because she concludes (erroneously, we would think) that her classmates are correct in perceiving her as socially inferior.

Theory of Emotional Intelligence

Emotional intelligence is a person's ability to process information about emotions accurately and effectively and consequently to regulate emotions in an optimal manner (Goleman, 2005). It includes self-control, zest and persistence, ability to motivate oneself, ability to understand and regulate one's own emotions, and ability to read and deal effectively with other people's feelings. This is a

Systems perspective

relatively new concept in psychology. The idea of integrating the emotional and intellectual systems was considered contradictory for many years, but recently psychologists have determined that emotional stimulation is necessary for activating certain schematic thought patterns.

Emotional intelligence involves recognizing and regulating emotions in ourselves and other people. It requires emotional sensitivity, or the ability to evaluate emotions within a variety of social circumstances. A person who is angry but knows that certain expressions of anger will be counterproductive in a particular situation, and as a result constrains his or her expressions of anger, is emotionally intelligent. On the other hand, a person with this same knowledge who behaves angrily in spite of this awareness is emotionally unintelligent.

People are not necessarily equally emotionally intelligent about themselves and other people. We may be more emotionally intelligent about other people than we are about ourselves, or vice versa. The first possibility helps to explain why some people, social workers included, seem to be better at giving advice to others than they are to themselves.

Emotional intelligence requires an integration of intellectual and emotional abilities. Recognizing and regulating emotions requires emotional self-awareness and empathy, but it also requires the intellectual ability to calculate the implications of different behavioral alternatives. To understand how and why we feel as we do, and other people feel as they do, requires emotional awareness and intellectual reasoning. Emotional intelligence is more important to excellence in many aspects of life than pure intellect (as measured by IQ tests), because it includes intellect plus other capacities.

One of Sheila's great assets, and one that she herself can "own," is her sensitivity to preadolescent children. She likes them and is always attuned to the nuances of their thoughts and emotions. Sheila functions exceptionally well as a sitter for her friends and neighbors because children pick up on her sensitivity and reciprocate those positive feelings. On the other hand, as we have already seen, Sheila generally lacks emotional self-awareness and intensity. It seems that her negative moods and attitudes contribute to her generally flat emotional style with most people. She is able to engage emotionally with children because, unlike her peers and older persons, they do not constitute any kind of threat to her.

Social Theories of Emotion

Social theories of emotion take the view that perception, or the interpretation of a situation, precedes emotion. These interpretations are learned, and as such they become automatic (unconscious or preconscious). Social theories emphasize the purpose of emotion, which is to sustain shared interpersonal norms and social cohesion. Two social theories are considered here.

Social constructionist perspective

James Averill's (1997) theory states that emotions can be understood as socially constructed, transitory roles. They are socially constructed because they originate in our appraisals of situations. They are transitory in that they are time limited. Finally, emotions are roles because they include a range of socially acceptable actions that may be performed in a certain social context. We organize and interpret our physiological reactions to stimuli with regard to the social norms involved in the situations where these reactions occur. Emotions permit us, in response to these stimuli, to step out of the conventional social roles to which people not experiencing the emotion are held. For example, in our culture, we generally would not say that we wish to harm someone unless we were feeling anger. We would generally not lash out verbally at a friend or spouse unless we felt frustrated. We would generally not withdraw from certain personal responsibilities and ask others for comfort unless we felt sad. Because of the social function of emotions, we often experience them as passions, or feelings not under our control. Experiencing passion permits unconventional behavior because we assume that we are somehow not "ourselves," not able to control what we do at that moment. Our society has adopted this mode of thinking about emotions because it allows us to distance ourselves

from some of our actions. Emotions are thus legitimized social roles or permissible behaviors when in particular emotional states.

George Herbert Mead (1934), the originator of symbolic interaction theory, took a somewhat different view. He suggested that emotions develop as symbols for communication. He also believed that humans are by nature more sensitive to visual than to verbal cues. Emotional expressions are thus particularly powerful in that they are apprehended visually rather than verbally. Our emotional expression is a signal about how we are inclined to act in a situation, and others can adjust their own behavior in response to our perceived inclinations. Sheila's lack of eye contact, tendency to look down, and physical distancing from others are manifestations of her sadness. Other persons, in response, may choose either to offer her support or, more likely in a classroom setting, to avoid her if they interpret her expressions as a desire for distance. Sheila was accustomed to people noticing her sadness at home, and responding to it in helpful ways, but in the faster-paced, more impersonal context of the university culture, this was not happening.

Theories of Emotion in Social Work Practice

The preceding theories are useful in assessment and intervention with clients because they enhance the social worker's understanding of the origins of emotional experiences and describe how negative emotional states may emerge and influence behavior. The social worker can help the client develop more positive emotional responses by providing insight or corrective experiences. What follows, however, is a theory that is even more precise in identifying the processes of emotional experience.

L. S. Greenberg (2008) has offered an emotion-focused practice theory, similar to psychoanalytic theory, that promises to help in social work interventions. Greenberg asserts that all primary emotions—those that originate as biologically based rapid responses—are adaptive. Every primary emotion we experience has the purpose of helping us adjust our relationship with an environmental situation to enhance coping. Secondary emotions emerge from these primary emotions as a result of cognitive mediation. Problems in social functioning may occur in one of four scenarios, summarized in Exhibit 4.7.

From this perspective, it is the unconscious or **preconscious** (mental activity that is out of awareness but can be brought into awareness with prompting) appraisal of situations in relation to our needs that creates emotions. Furthermore, as Mead (1934) pointed out, we experience our emotions as images, not as verbal thoughts. Emotions are difficult to apprehend cognitively, and in our attempts to do so, we may mistake their essence. The bad feelings that trouble us come not from those primary emotional responses, which, if experienced directly, would tend to dissipate, but from defensive distortions of those responses. We tend to appraise situations accurately with our primary emotions, but our frustration in achieving affective goals can produce distortions. Thus, in contrast to the assumptions of cognitive theory, distortions of thought may be the result of emotional phenomena rather than their cause.

Consider Sheila's depression as an example. Perhaps she is interpersonally sensitive by nature and accurately perceives aloofness in others. Her affective goals of closeness are threatened by this appraisal, and the intensity of her reaction to this frustration becomes problematic. Her emotional patterns evoke tendencies to withdraw temporarily and to become less active in response to discouragement or sadness. To this point, the process may be adaptive, as she may be able to rest and regain energy during her temporary withdrawal. This particular feeling state, however, may become a cue for negative thoughts about herself, which then prevent her from actively addressing her frustrations.

In emotion-focused practice, the social worker would attempt to activate the person's primary emotional reactions, making them more available to awareness within the safety of the social worker–client relationship and making secondary emotional reactions amenable to change when necessary. Emotional reactions, cognitive appraisals, and action tendencies may then be identified more clearly by the client.

From this perspective, a social worker could help Sheila understand that she carries much anger at her family because of their long-term lack of adequate support for her emotional development. Sheila could be encouraged within the safety of the social worker–client relationship to experience and ventilate that anger, and gain insight into her pattern. Once Sheila can consciously identify and experience that negative emotion, she may be less incapacitated by the depression, which is a secondary emotion resulting from her suppression of anger. She would then have more energy to devote to her own social and academic goals and to develop new ways of interacting with others in the university setting.

Exhibit 4.7   Four Sources of Emotion-Based Problems in Social Functioning

1. A primary emotion may not achieve its aim of changing our relationship with the environment to facilitate adaptation.

2. We may, prior to awareness of a primary emotion, deny, distort, avoid, or repress it and thus become unable to constructively address our person-environment challenge.

3. We may develop cognitive distortions, or irrational "meaning construction" processes, that produce negative secondary emotions.

4. We may regulate our appropriate emotional experiences poorly, by either minimizing or not maintaining control over them.

COGNITIVE/EMOTIONAL "DISORDERS"

As social workers, we are reluctant to label people as having cognitive or emotional "disorders." Instead, we conceptualize problems in social functioning as mismatches in the fit between person and environment.

Still, in our study of the psychological person, we can consider how problems are manifested in the client's cognitive and emotional patterns.

Many social workers are employed in mental health agencies and use the fourth edition of the *Diagnostic and Statistical Manual of Mental Disorders* (*DSM-IV-TR* [text revision]; American Psychiatric Association, 2000) to make diagnoses as part of a comprehensive client assessment. The *DSM* has been the standard resource for clinical diagnosis in the United States for more than half a century. The manual states that its purpose is to "provide clear descriptions of diagnostic categories in order to enable clinicians and investigators to diagnose, communicate about, study, and treat people with various mental disorders" (p. xi). The *DSM* includes 16 chapters that address, among others, disorders diagnosed in infancy, childhood, or adolescence; cognitive disorders; substance-related disorders; psychotic disorders; mood disorders; anxiety disorders; sexual disorders; eating disorders; personality disorders; and adjustment disorders. As summarized in Exhibit 4.8, the diagnostic system includes five

Exhibit 4.8 *DSM-IV* Classification of Mental Disorders

Axis I	Clinical or mental disorders
	Other conditions that may be a focus of clinical attention
Axis II	Personality disorders
	Mental retardation
Axis III	General medical conditions
Axis IV	Psychosocial and environmental problems

Axis IV		
	Primary support group	Economic
	Social environment	Access to health care services
	Educational	Interaction with the legal system
	Occupational	Other psychosocial and
	Housing	environmental problems

Axis V	Global assessment of functioning (based on the clinician's judgment):	
	90–100	Superior functioning in a wide range of activities
	0–10	Persistent danger of severely hurting self or others, persistent inability to maintain personal hygiene, or serious suicidal acts with clear expectation of death

SOURCE: *Diagnostic and Statistical Manual of Mental Disorders* (4th ed., Text Rev.), copyright © 2000 American Psychiatric Association. Reprinted with permission

categories, or "axes," for each client. Axis I includes clinical or mental disorders, Axis II includes personality disorders and mental retardation, Axis III lists any medical conditions the client may have, Axis IV pertains to psychosocial and environmental problems, and Axis V includes a global assessment of functioning.

It is important to recognize that the *DSM* provides a medical perspective on human functioning. There is tension between the social work profession's person-in-environment perspective and the requirement in many settings that social workers use the *DSM* to "diagnose" mental, emotional, or behavioral disorders in clients (J. Corcoran & Walsh, 2006). More will be said about this later in the chapter.

With this brief introduction, we can consider four examples of disorders selected from the *DSM* to illustrate how either cognitive or emotional characteristics may predominate in a client's symptom profile, even though both aspects of the psychological person are always present:

- Two disorders that feature cognitive symptoms are obsessive-compulsive disorder and anorexia nervosa. Obsessive-compulsive disorder is an anxiety disorder that, when featuring obsessions, is characterized by persistent thoughts that are experienced as intrusive, inappropriate, unwelcome, and distressful. The thoughts are more than excessive worries about real problems, and the person is unable to ignore or suppress them. In anorexia nervosa, an eating disorder, the person becomes obsessive about food, thinking about it almost constantly. The person refuses to maintain a reasonable body weight because of distorted beliefs about physical appearance and the effects of food on the body.

- Two disorders that feature emotional symptoms are dysthymia and agoraphobia. Dysthymia, a mood disorder, is characterized by a lengthy period of depression. It features the emotion of sadness, which persists regardless of external events. Agoraphobia is an anxiety disorder characterized by fear. The person is afraid to be in situations (such as crowds) or places (such as large open areas) from which escape might be difficult or embarrassing. The person must restrict his or her range of social mobility out of fear of having a panic attack (being overwhelmed by anxiety) for reasons that are not consciously clear.

As a social worker, you might note that Sheila is depressed and also has a mild form of agoraphobia. She feels uncomfortable and insecure on the large, crowded campus, and developed fears of having panic attacks when in the student union. This building includes several large open areas that are highly congested at certain times of the day. Sheila is concerned that people there look at her critically. You might conclude that Sheila's problems are primarily emotional. However, Sheila's cognitive patterns have contributed to the development of her negative emotions. Her overall negative self-assessment sustains her depression, and her distorted beliefs about the attitudes of others contribute to her fears of being in the crowded union. It is rarely the case that only cognitive factors or only emotional factors are behind a client's problems.

THE SELF

It remains for us to integrate cognition and emotion into a cohesive notion of the self. This is a difficult task—one that may, in fact, be impossible to achieve. All of us possess a sense of self, but

| Humanistic perspective |

it is difficult to articulate. How would you define *self*? Most of us tend to think of it as incorporating an essence that is more or less enduring. But beyond that, what would you say? Thinkers from the fields of philosophy, theology, sociology, psychology, and social work have struggled to identify the essence of the **self**, and they offer us a range of perspectives (Levin, 1992):

- *The self as soul.* A constant, unchanging self, existing apart from its material environment and material body, perhaps transcending the life of the physical body

- *The self as organizing activity.* The initiator of activity, organizer of drives, and mediator of both internal and person-environment conflicts; an evolving entity in the synthesizing of experiences
- *The self as cognitive structure.* The thinker and definer of reality through conscious activities that support the primacy of thought
- *The self as verbal activity.* The product of internal monologues (self-talk) and shared conversation with others; the product of what we tell ourselves about who we are
- *The self as experience of cohesion (self psychology).* The sense of cohesion achieved through action and reflection; the three-part self (grandiose self based on positive affirmation, idealized parent image, and twinship or connected self)
- *The self as flow of experience.* The self-in-process, the changing self

Photo 4.2 Some see the self as an ongoing process of experience. The play and exploration of these schoolgirls in Bhutan contribute to their developing self-concepts.

THEORIES OF THE SELF IN RELATIONSHIPS

Cultural psychologists suggest that all of the above perspectives on the self assume an independent self, but in many cultures of the world, the self is an interdependent self that cannot be detached from the context of human relationships (Markus & Kitayama, 2009). And, indeed, as Sheila learned, the ability to form, sustain, and use significant relationships with other people is a key to the process of successful coping and adaptation. With this theme in mind, we turn to examination of several theories that address the issue of how we exist in the context of relationships, including the object relations, feminist, relational, Afrocentric, and social identity theories.

Object Relations Theory

The basic assumption of object relations theory is that all people naturally seek relationships with other people. The question is how well an individual forms interpersonal relationships and how any deficiencies in social functioning might have arisen. The term *object relations* is synonymous with *interpersonal relations*. An "object" is another person but may also be the mental image of a person that we have incorporated into our psychological selves.

Object relations theory is a psychodynamic theory of human development that considers our ability to form lasting attachments with others based on early experiences of separation from

> Psychodynamic perspective

and connection with our primary caregivers. Many social workers see this theory as an advance over psychoanalytic theory because it considers people in the context of relationships rather than as individual entities. We internalize our early relationship patterns, meaning that our first relationships make such an impression on us that they determine how we approach relationships from that point on.

These early relationships are a primary determinant of our personality and the quality of our interpersonal functioning (L. M. Flanagan, 2008; E. Goldstein, 2001).

The ideal is to be raised by caregivers who help us gradually and appropriately move away from their physical and emotional supervision while communicating their availability for support. In such conditions, we acquire the capacity to form trusting attachments with others. This is known as *object constancy.* If, on the other hand, we learn (because of loss or negative caregiver behavior) that we cannot count on others for support as we take risks to move away, we might "internalize" an emotional schema that other people cannot be counted on. Stable object relations result in our ability to form stable relationships, to trust others, and to persist in positive relationships during times of conflict. This idea of internalization is very important, as it implies that we carry our attachments with us. Those significant others in our lives not only exist as memories but are also part of our psychological makeup—they are a part of who we are.

Object relations theorists have suggested a variety of stages in this process of developing object constancy, but we need not get into that level of detail. Suffice it to say that, in addition to the process of developing object relations in early childhood, we also experience a second such process in early adolescence. At that time (at least in Anglo-American society), we begin to move away from the pervasive influence of our families and test our abilities to develop our own identity. This is another time of life in which we need to feel that we can trust our primary caregivers as we experiment with independence.

If you are concerned that your own early relationships might have been problematic, don't worry. Object relations theorists do not assert that caregivers need to be perfect (whatever that might be), only that they communicate a sense of caring and permit the child to develop a sense of self (Winnicott, 1975). Even if early object relations are problematic, a person's ability to develop trusting relationships can always be improved, sometimes with therapy.

It may be useful for us to consider one model of parent–child attachment here (Shorey &

Photo 4.3 Object relations theory proposes that our first relationships make such an impression on us that they determine how we approach relationships from that point on.

Snyder, 2006). All children seek close proximity to their parents, and they develop attachment styles suited to the types of parenting they encounter. Ainsworth and her colleagues (Ainsworth, Blehar, Waters, & Wall, 1978) identified three infant attachment styles—secure, anxious-ambivalent, and avoidant types. A fourth attachment style has been identified more recently—the disorganized type (Madigan, Moran, & Pederson, 2006).

Securely attached infants act somewhat distressed when their parent figures leave, but greet them eagerly and warmly upon return. Parents of secure infants are sensitive and accepting. Securely attached children are unconcerned about security needs and are thus free to direct their energies toward non-attachment-related activities in the environment. Infants who are not securely attached must direct their attention to maintaining their attachments to inconsistent, unavailable, or rejecting parents, rather than engaging in exploratory behaviors. Because these children are only able to maintain proximity to the parents by behaving as if the parents are not needed, the children may learn not to express needs for closeness or attention.

Anxious-ambivalently attached infants, in contrast, are distraught when their parent figures leave. Upon their parents' return, these infants continue to be distressed even as they want to be comforted and held. Their parents, while not overtly rejecting, are often unpredictable and inconsistent in their responses. Fearing potential caregiver abandonment, the children maximize their efforts to maintain close parental attachments and become hypervigilant for threat cues and any signs of rejection.

Avoidantly attached infants seem to be relatively undisturbed both when their parent figures leave and when they return. These children want to maintain proximity to their parent figures, but this attachment style enables the children to maintain a sense of proximity to parents who otherwise may reject them. Avoidant children thus suppress expressions of overt distress, and rather than risk further rejection in the face of attachment figure unavailability, may give up on their proximity-seeking efforts.

The *disorganized attachment* style is characterized by chaotic and conflicted behaviors. These children exhibit simultaneous approach and avoidance behaviors. Disorganized infants seem incapable of applying any consistent strategy to bond with their parents. Their conflicted and disorganized behaviors reflect their best attempts at gaining some sense of security from parents who are perceived as frightening. When afraid and needing reassurance, these children have no options but to seek support from a caregiver who is frightening. The parents may be either hostile or fearful and unable to hide their apprehension from their children. In either case, the child's anxiety and distress are not lessened, and one source of stress is merely traded for another.

Although the children with disorganized attachments typically do not attain a sense of being cared for, the avoidant and anxious-ambivalent children do experience some success in fulfilling their needs for care.

Relational Theory

In recent years, there has been an integration of the psychoanalytic, object relations, and interpersonal theoretical perspectives, and this is broadly termed **relational theory** (Borden, 2009). In relational theory, as with object relations, the basic human tendency (or drive) is relationships with others, and our personalities are structured through ongoing interactions with others in the social environment. In this theory, however, there is a strong value of recognizing and supporting diversity in human experience, avoiding the pathologizing of differences, and enlarging traditional conceptions of gender and identity. It is assumed that all patterns of human behavior are learned in the give-and-take of relational life and thus they are all adaptive, reasonable ways to negotiate experience in the context of circumstances and our need to elicit care from others. Also consistent with object relations concepts, serious problems in living are seen as self-perpetuating because we all have a tendency to preserve continuity, connections, and familiarity in our interpersonal worlds. Our problematic ways of being and relating are perpetuated because they preserve our ongoing experience of the self. What is new is threatening because it lies beyond the bounds of our experience in which we recognize ourselves as cohesive, continuous beings. That is, problematic interpersonal patterns are repeated because they preserve our connections to significant others in the past.

The relational perspective provides contexts of understanding for social workers in their ongoing efforts to connect biological, psychological, and social domains of concern and to enlarge conceptions of persons in their environments. If this sounds to the reader like social work's long-standing focus on person-in-environment, it should! It seems in this sense that social work was ahead of some other disciplines. Relational practitioners encourage a variety of activities familiar to social workers including brief intervention, case management, environmental development, and advocacy.

The relational approach enriches the concept of practitioner empathy by adding the notion of mutuality. The ability to participate in a mutual relationship through the use of empathic communication is seen as a goal for the client's growth and development. Current social work literature reflects different views regarding the degree to which workers should remain emotionally detached from clients, but the general consensus calls for the worker to maintain a neutral, objective persona and a sense of separateness. In relational theory, the more the worker expends energy on keeping parts of himself or herself out of the process, the more rigid, and less spontaneous and genuine, he or she will be in relating to the client system. The worker–client relationship runs the risk of becoming organized into dominant and subordinate roles.

Feminist Theories of Relationships

The term *feminism* does not refer to any single body of thought. It refers to a wide-ranging system of ideas about human experience developed from a woman-centered perspective. Feminist theories may be classified as liberal,

Conflict perspective

radical, Marxist, socialist, existential, postmodern, multicultural, and ecofeminist (Lengermann & Niebrugge-Brantley, 2007). Among the psychological theories are psychoanalytic feminism (Angers, 2008) and gender feminism (Marecek, Kimmel, Crawford, & Hare-Mustin, 2003). We focus on these two as we consider how feminism has deepened our capacity for understanding human behavior and interaction. All of these theorists begin from the position that women and men approach relationships differently, and that patriarchal societies consider male attributes to be superior.

Psychoanalytic feminists assert that women's ways of acting are rooted deeply in women's unique ways of thinking. These differences may be biological, but they are certainly influenced by cultural and psychosocial conditions. Feminine behavior features gentleness, modesty, humility, supportiveness, empathy, compassion, tenderness, nurturance, intuitiveness, sensitivity, and unselfishness. Masculine behavior is characterized by strength of will, ambition, courage, independence, assertiveness, hardiness, rationality, and emotional control. Psychoanalytic feminists assert that these differences are largely rooted in early childhood relationships. Because women are the primary caretakers in our society, young girls tend to develop and enjoy an ongoing relationship with their mothers, which promotes their valuing of relatedness as well as the other feminine behaviors. For young boys, on the other hand, the mother is eventually perceived as fundamentally different, particularly as they face social pressures to begin fulfilling male roles. The need to separate from the mother figure has long-range implications for boys: They tend to lose what could otherwise become a learned capacity for intimacy and relatedness.

Psychodynamic perspective

Gender feminists tend to be concerned with values of separateness (for men) and connectedness (for women) and how these lead to a different morality for women. Carol Gilligan is a leading thinker in this area. As reported earlier, she elucidated a process by which women develop an ethic of care rather than an ethic of justice, based on the value they place on relationships. Gender feminists believe that these female ethics are equal to male ethics, although they have tended in patriarchal societies to be considered inferior. Gilligan (1982, 1988) asserts that all of humanity would be best served if both ethics could be valued equally. Other gender feminists go further, however, arguing for the superiority of women's ethics. For example, Noddings (2002, 2005) asserts that war will never be discarded in favor of the sustained pursuit of peace until the female ethic of caring, aimed at unification, replaces the male ethic of strenuous striving, aimed at dividing people.

Afrocentric Relational Theory

The origins of Afrocentric relational theory (which can be considered a type of the broader relational theory discussed above) are in traditional Africa, before the arrival of European and Arabian

Humanistic perspective

influences. The Afrocentric worldview values cultural pluralism and, in fact, values difference in all of its forms. It does not accept hierarchies based on social differences, however. Eurocentric thinking, emphasizing mastery rather than harmony with the environment, is seen as oppressive. The three major objectives of Afrocentric theory are to provide an alternative perspective that reflects African cultures; to dispel negative distortions about African people held by other cultures; and to promote social transformations that are spiritual, moral, and humanistic.

Afrocentric relational theory assumes a collective identity for people rather than valuing individuality (Y. R. Bell, Bouie, & Baldwin, 1998; R. L. Jackson, 2004). It places great value on the spiritual or nonmaterial aspects of life, understood broadly as an "invisible substance" that connects all people. It values an affective approach to knowledge, conceptualizing emotion as the most direct experience of the self. This is of course in contrast to the Western emphasis on cognition and rationality. In its emphasis on the collective, Afrocentrism does not distinguish

between things that affect the individual and things that affect larger groups of people, and it sees all social problems as related to practices of oppression and alienation. Personal connection and reciprocity are emphasized in helping relationships such as the social worker–client relationship. Like feminism, Afrocentrism counters the object relations emphasis on individuality and independence with attention to collective identity and human connectedness.

Social Identity Theory

Social identity theory is a stage theory of socialization that articulates the process by which we come to identify with some social groups and develop a sense of difference from other social groups (Hornsey, 2008; Nesdale, 2004). Social identity development can be

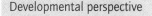
Developmental perspective

an affirming process that provides us with a lifelong sense of belonging and support. I might feel good to have membership in a Roman Catholic or Irish American community. Because social identity can be exclusionary, however, it can also give rise to prejudice and oppression. I may believe that my race is more intelligent than another, or that persons of my cultural background are entitled to more benefits than those of another.

Social identity development proceeds in five stages. These stages are not truly distinct or sequential, however; people often experience several stages simultaneously.

1. *Naïveté.* During early childhood, we are not aware of particular codes of behavior for members of our group or any other social group. Our parents or other primary caregivers are our most significant influences, and we accept that socialization without question. As young children, we do, however, begin to distinguish between ourselves and other groups of people. We may not feel completely comfortable with the racial, ethnic, or religious differences we observe, but neither do we feel fearful, superior, or inferior. Children at this stage are mainly curious about differences.

2. *Acceptance.* Older children and young adolescents learn the distinct ideologies and belief systems of their own and other social groups. During this stage, we learn that the world's institutions and authority figures have rules that encourage certain behaviors and prohibit others, and we internalize these dominant cultural beliefs and make them a part of our everyday lives. We come to believe that the way our group does things is normal, makes more sense, and is better. We regard the cultures of people who are different from us as strange, marginal, and perhaps inferior.

3. *Resistance.* In adolescence, or even later, if at all, we become aware of the harmful effects of acting on social differences. We have new experiences with members of other social groups that challenge our prior assumptions. We begin to reevaluate those assumptions and investigate our own role in perpetuating harmful differences. We may feel anger at others within our own social group who foster these irrational differences. We begin to move toward a new definition of social identity that is broader than our previous definition. We may work to end our newly perceived patterns of collusion and oppression.

4. *Redefinition.* Redefinition is a process of creating a new social identity that preserves our pride in our origins while perceiving differences with others as positive representations of diversity. We may isolate from some members of our social group and shift toward interactions with others who share our level of awareness. We see all groups as being rich in strengths and values. We may reclaim our own group heritage but broaden our definition of that heritage as one of many varieties of constructive living.

5. *Internalization.* In the final stage of social identity development, we become comfortable with our revised identity and are able to incorporate it into all aspects of our life. Life continues as an ongoing process of discovering vestiges of our old biases, but now we test our integrated new identities in wider contexts than our limited reference group. Our appreciation of the plight of all oppressed people, and our enhanced empathy for others, is a part of this process. For many people, the internalization stage is an ongoing challenge rather than an end state.

RESEARCH ON THE IMPACT OF EARLY NURTURING

Turning to the empirical research, we can find evidence that, as suggested by object relations theory, the quality of our *early* relationships is crucial to our lifelong capacity to engage in healthy relationships, and even to enjoy basic physical health. There is a large body of research devoted to studying the links between early life experiences and physical and mental health risks

Psychodynamic perspective; Developmental perspective

(e.g., Gerhardt, 2004; Gunnar, Broderson, Nachimas, Buss, & Rigatuso, 1996; Stansfeld, Head, Bartley, & Fonagy, 2008). This work demonstrates that negative infant experiences such as child abuse, family strife, poverty, and emotional neglect correlate with later health problems ranging from depression to drug abuse and heart disease. Relational elements of our early environments appear to permanently alter the development of central nervous system structures that govern our autonomic, cognitive, behavioral, and emotional responses to stress.

Although much of this research is being conducted on rats, monkeys, and other animals, it has clear implications for human development. The concept of **neural plasticity,** which refers to the capacity of the nervous system to be modified by experience, is significant here (Knudsen, 2004; Nelson, 2000). Humans may have a window of opportunity, or a critical period, for altering neurological development, but this window varies, depending on the area of the nervous system. Even through the second decade of life, for example, neurotransmitter and synapse changes are influenced by internal biology but by external signals as well.

There is also much research underway that is exploring the relationship between the processes of attachment and specific neurological development in young persons (Schore, 2001, & 2002). Persistent stress in the infant or toddler results in an overdevelopment of areas of the brain that process anxiety and fear, and the underdevelopment of other areas of the brain, particularly the cortex. Of particular concern to one leading researcher (Schore, 2002) is the impact of the absence of nurturance on the orbital frontal cortex (OFC) of the brain. Chronic levels of stress contribute to fewer neural connections between the prefrontal cortex and the amygdala, a process that is significant to psychosocial functioning. The OFC is particularly active in such processes as concentration and judgment as well as the ability to observe and control internal subjective states. Further, the frontal cortex is central to our emotional regulation capacity and our experience of empathy. The amygdala, part of the limbic system, is attributed with interpreting incoming stimuli and information and storing this information in our implicit (automatic) memory. The amygdala assesses threat and triggers our immediate responses to it (the fight, flight, or freeze behaviors). A reduction in neural connections between these two areas suggests that the frontal cortex is not optimally able to regulate the processing of fear, resulting in exaggerated fear responses.

Stress can clearly affect brain development, but there is little evidence that the first 3 years of life are all-important (Nelson, 1999). A study of 2,600 undergraduate students found that even in late adolescence and early adulthood, satisfying social relationships were associated with greater autonomic activity and restorative behaviors when confronting acute stress (Cacioppo, Bernston, Sheridan, & McClintock, 2000).

In summary, the research evidence indicates that secure attachments play a critical role in shaping the systems that underlie our reactivity to stressful situations. At the time when infants begin to form specific attachments to adults, the presence of caregivers who are warm and responsive begins to buffer or prevent elevations in stress hormones, even in situations that distress the infant. In contrast, insecure relationships are associated with higher levels of stress hormones in potentially threatening situations. Secure emotional relationships with adults appear to be at least as critical as individual differences in temperament in determining stress reactivity and regulation (Eagle & Wolitzky, 2009).

Still, there is much to be learned in this area. Many people who have been subjected to serious early life traumas become effective, high-functioning adolescents and adults. Infants and children are resilient and have many strengths that can help them overcome these early-life stresses. Researchers are challenged to determine whether interventions such as foster care can remedy the physical, emotional, and social problems seen in children who have experienced poor nurturing and early problems in separation.

Critical Thinking Questions 4.2

How important is culture in influencing the nature of the self? Does religion or spirituality play a role in the development of self? If so, how? Give some thought to social identity theory. With what social groups do you identify? How did you come to identify with these groups? How might your social identities affect your social work practice?

THE CONCEPT OF STRESS

One of the main benefits of good nurturing is, as you have seen, the way it strengthens the ability to cope with stress. **Stress** can be defined as any event in which environmental or internal demands tax the adaptive resources of an individual. Stress may be biological (a disturbance in bodily systems), psychological (cognitive and emotional factors involved in the evaluation of a threat), and even social (the disruption of a social unit). Sheila experienced psychological stress as evidenced by her troublesome thoughts and feelings of depression, but she also experienced other types of stress. She experienced biological stress because, in an effort to attend classes, study, and work, she did not give her body adequate rest. As a result, she was susceptible to colds and the flu, which kept her in bed for several days each month and compounded her worries about managing course work. Sheila also experienced social stress, because she had left the slow-paced, interpersonally comfortable environments of her rural home and community college to attend the university.

Three Categories of Psychological Stress

Psychological stress, about which we are primarily concerned in this chapter, can be broken down into three categories (Lazarus, 2007):

1. *Harm:* A damaging event that has already occurred. Sheila avoided interaction with her classmates during much of the first semester, which may have led them to decide that she is aloof and that they should not try to approach her socially. Sheila has to accept that this happened and that some harm has been done to her as a result, although she can learn from the experience and try to change in the future.

2. *Threat:* A perceived potential for harm that has not yet happened. This is probably the most common form of psychological stress. We feel stress because we are apprehensive about the possibility of the negative event. Sheila felt threatened when she walked into a classroom during the first semester because she anticipated rejection from her classmates. We can be proactive in managing threats to ensure that they do not in fact occur and result in harm to us.

3. *Challenge:* An event we appraise as an opportunity rather than an occasion for alarm. We are mobilized to struggle against the obstacle, as with a threat, but our attitude is quite different. Faced with a threat, we are likely to act defensively to protect ourselves. Our defensiveness sends a negative message to the environment: We don't want to change; we want to be left alone. In a state of

challenge, however, we are excited, expansive, and confident about the task to be undertaken. In her second year at the university, Sheila may feel more excited than before about entering a classroom full of strangers at the beginning of a semester. She may look forward with more confidence to meeting some persons who may become friends.

Stress has been measured in several ways (Aldwin & Yancura, 2004; Lazarus, 2007). One of the earliest attempts to measure stress consisted of a list of *life events,* uncommon events that bring about some change in our lives—experiencing the death of a loved one, getting married, becoming a parent, and so forth. The use of life events to measure stress is based on the assumption that major changes involve losses and disrupt our behavioral patterns.

More recently, stress has also been measured as *daily hassles,* common occurrences that are taxing—standing in line waiting, misplacing or losing things, dealing with troublesome coworkers, worrying about money, and many more. It is thought that an accumulation of daily hassles takes a greater toll on our coping capacities than do relatively rare life events.

Sociologists and community psychologists also study stress by measuring *role strain*—problems experienced in the performance of specific roles, such as romantic partner, caregiver, or worker. Research on caregiver burden is one example of measuring stress as role strain (Bowman, 2006).

Social workers should be aware that as increasing emphasis is placed on the deleterious effects of stress on the immune system, our attention and energies are diverted from the project of changing societal conditions that create stress toward individual methods of stress management (D. Becker, 2005). With the influence of the medical model, we should not be surprised when we are offered individual or biomedical solutions to such different social problems as working motherhood, poverty, and road rage. It may be that the appeal of the stress concept is based on its attention away from the environmental causes of stress. This is why social workers should always be alert to the social nature of stress.

Photo 4.4 This woman is experiencing psychological stress; she is challenged by the task at hand but she feels equal to the task.

Stress and Crisis

A **crisis** is a major upset in our psychological equilibrium due to some harm, threat, or challenge with which we cannot cope (R. K. James & Gilliland, 2001). The crisis poses an obstacle to achieving a personal goal, but we cannot overcome the obstacle through our usual methods of problem solving. We temporarily lack either the necessary knowledge for coping or the ability to focus on the problem, because we feel overwhelmed. A crisis episode often results when we face a serious stressor with which we have had no prior experience. It may be biological (major illness), interpersonal (the sudden loss of a loved one), or environmental (unemployment or a natural disaster such as flood or fire). We can regard anxiety, guilt, shame, sadness, envy, jealousy, and disgust as stress emotions (Zautra, 2003). They are the emotions most likely to emerge in a person who is experiencing crisis. Crisis episodes occur in three stages:

1. Our level of tension increases sharply.

2. We try and fail to cope with the stress, which further increases our tension and contributes to our sense of being overwhelmed. We are particularly receptive to receiving help from others at this time.

3. The crisis episode ends, either negatively (unhealthy coping) or positively (successful management of the crisis).

Crises can be classified into three types (Lantz & Walsh, 2007). *Developmental* crises occur as events in the normal flow of life create dramatic changes that produce extreme responses. Examples include going off to college, college graduation, the birth of one's child, a midlife career change, and retirement from work. *Situational* crises refer to uncommon and extraordinary events that a person has no way of forecasting or controlling. Examples include physical injuries, sexual assault, loss of a job, illness, and the death of a loved one. *Existential* crises are characterized by escalating inner conflicts related to issues of purpose in life, responsibility, independence, freedom, and commitment. Examples include remorse over past life choices, a feeling that one's life has no meaning, and a questioning of one's basic values or spiritual beliefs.

Sheila's poor midterm grades during her first semester illustrate some of these points. First, she was overwhelmed by the negative emotions of shame and sadness. Then she retreated to her parents' home, where she received much-needed support from her family. With their encouragement, she sought additional support from her academic adviser and a counselor. Finally, as the crisis situation stabilized, Sheila concluded that she could take some actions to relieve her feelings of loneliness and incompetence (a positive outcome).

Traumatic Stress

Although a single event may pose a crisis for one person but not another, some stressors are so severe that they are almost universally experienced as crisis. The stress is so overwhelming that almost anyone would be affected. The term **traumatic stress** is used to refer to events that involve actual or threatened severe injury or death, of oneself or significant others (American Psychiatric Association, 2000). Three types of traumatic stress have been identified: natural (such as flood, tornado, earthquake) and technological (such as nuclear) disasters; war and related problems (such as concentration camps); and individual trauma (such as being raped, assaulted, or tortured) (Aldwin, 2007). People respond to traumatic stress with helplessness, terror, and horror.

Some occupations—particularly those of emergency workers such as police officers, firefighters, disaster relief workers, and military personnel in war settings—involve regular exposure to traumatic events that most people do not experience in a lifetime. Emergency workers, particularly police officers and firefighters, may experience threats to their own lives and the lives of their colleagues, as well as encounter mass casualties. Emergency workers may also experience *compassion stress*, a feeling of deep sympathy and sorrow for another who is stricken by misfortune, accompanied by a strong desire to alleviate the pain (Figley, 2002). Any professionals who work regularly with trauma survivors are susceptible to compassion stress. Many social workers fall into this category.

Vulnerability to Stress

Our experience of stress is in part related to our individual biological constitutions and our previous experiences with stress. Research from the field of mental illness underscores this point. In an attempt to understand the causes of many mental disorders, several researchers have postulated *stress/diathesis models* of mental illness (Ingram & Luxton, 2005). These models are based on empirical data indicating that certain disorders (psychotic and mood disorders, for example) develop from the interaction of environmental stresses and a *diathesis*, or vulnerability, to the disorders. The diathesis may be biological (a genetic or biochemical predisposition), environmental (history of severe stressors), or both. Most models, however, emphasize biological factors.

Systems perspective

Stress/diathesis models suggest that all persons do not have an equal chance of developing mental disorders, because it depends in part on one's chemical makeup. A person at risk may have an innate inability to manage high levels of stimulation from the outside world. For example, one model postulates that the onset of schizophrenia is 70% related to innate predisposition and 30% related to external stress (S. Jones & Fernyhough, 2007).

The stress/diathesis view highlights a probable interaction between constitutional and environmental factors in our experience and tolerance of stress. It suggests that a single event may pose a crisis for one person but not another. In its broadest versions, it also suggests that vulnerability to stress is related to one's position in the social structure, with some social positions exposed to a greater number of adverse situations—such as poverty, racism, and blocked opportunities—than others (Ingram & Luxton, 2005).

COPING AND ADAPTATION

Our efforts to master the demands of stress are referred to as **coping.** Coping includes the thoughts, feelings, and actions that constitute these efforts.

One method of coping is **adaptation,** which may involve adjustments in our biological responses, in our perceptions, or in our lifestyle.

Biological Coping

The traditional biological view of stress and coping, developed in the 1950s, emphasizes the body's attempts to maintain physical equilibrium, or *homeostasis,* which is a steady state of functioning (Selye, 1991). Stress is considered the result of any demand on the body (specifically, the nervous and hormonal systems) during perceived emergencies to prepare for fight (confrontation) or flight (escape). A stressor may be any biological process, emotion, or thought.

In this view, the body's response to a stressor is called the *general adaptation syndrome* (explained in Exhibit 4.9). It occurs in three stages:

1. *Alarm:* The body first becomes aware of a threat.

2. *Resistance:* The body attempts to restore homeostasis.

3. *Exhaustion:* The body terminates coping efforts because of its inability to physically sustain the state of disequilibrium.

In this context, *resistance* means an active, positive response of the body in which endorphins and specialized cells of the immune system fight off stress and infection. Our immune systems are constructed for adaptation to stress, but cumulative wear and

Exhibit 4.9 The General Adaptation Syndrome

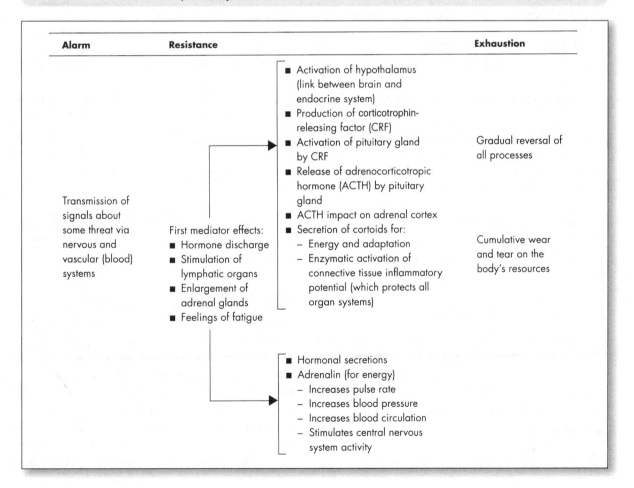

tear of multiple stress episodes can gradually deplete our body's resources. Common outcomes of chronic stress include stomach and intestinal disorders, high blood pressure, heart problems, and emotional problems. If only to preserve healthy physical functioning, we must combat and prevent stress.

This traditional view of biological coping with stress came from research that focused on males, either male rodents or human males. Since 1995, the U.S. federal government has required federally funded researchers to include a broad representation of both men and women in their study samples. Consequently, recent research on stress has included female as well as male participants, and gender differences in responses to stress have been found. Research by Shelley Taylor and colleagues (S. E. Taylor et al., 2002; S. E. Taylor & Stanton, 2007) found that females of many species, including humans, respond to stress with "tend-and-befriend" rather than the "fight-or-flight" behavior described in the general adaptation syndrome. Under stressful conditions, females have been found to turn to protecting and nurturing their offspring and to seek social contact. The researchers suggest a possible biological basis for this gender difference in the coping response. More specifically, they note a large role for the hormone oxytocin, which plays a role in childbirth but also is secreted in both males and females in response to stress. High levels of oxytocin in animals are associated with calmness and increased sociability. Although males as well as females secrete oxytocin in response to stress, there is evidence that male hormones reduce the effects of oxytocin. Taylor and colleagues believe this explains the gender differences in response to stress.

Psychological Coping

The psychological aspect of managing stress can be viewed in two different ways. Some theorists consider coping ability to be a stable personality characteristic, or **trait**; others see it instead as a transient **state**—a process that changes over time, depending on the context (J. Y. E. Lau, Eley, & Stevenson, 2006).

Psychodynamic perspective

Those who consider coping to be a *trait* see it as an acquired defensive style. **Defense mechanisms** are unconscious, automatic responses that enable us to minimize perceived threats or keep them out of our awareness entirely. Exhibit 4.10 lists the common defense mechanisms identified by ego psychology. Some defense mechanisms are considered healthier, or more adaptive, than others. Sheila's denial of her need for intimacy, for example, did not help her meet her goal of developing relationships with peers. But through the defense of sublimation (channeling the need for intimacy into alternative and socially acceptable outlets), she has become an excellent caregiver to a friend's child.

Those who see coping as a *state,* or process, observe that our coping strategies change in different situations. From this perspective, Sheila's use of denial would be adaptive at some times and maladaptive at others. Perhaps her denial of loneliness during the first academic semester helped her focus on her studies, which would help her achieve her goal of receiving an education. During the summer, however, when classes are out of session, she might become aware that her avoidance of relationships has prevented her from attaining interpersonal goals. Her efforts to cope with loneliness might also change when she can afford more energy to confront the issue.

Systems perspective

The trait and state approaches can usefully be combined. We can think of coping as a general pattern of managing stress that allows flexibility across diverse contexts.

Coping Styles

Another way to look at coping is by how the person responds to crisis. Coping efforts may be problem-focused or emotion-focused (Sideridis, 2006). The function of **problem-focused coping** is to change the situation by acting on the environment. This method tends to dominate whenever we view situations as controllable by action. For example, Sheila was concerned about her professors' insensitivity to her learning disability. When she took action to

Exhibit 4.10 Common Defense Mechanisms

Defense Mechanism	Definition	Example
Denial	Negating an important aspect of reality that one may actually perceive	A woman with anorexia acknowledges her actual weight and strict dieting practices, but firmly believes that she is maintaining good self-care by dieting.
Displacement	Shifting feelings about one person or situation onto another	A student's anger at her professor, who is threatening as an authority figure, is transposed into anger at her boyfriend, a safer target.
Intellectualization	Avoiding unacceptable emotions by thinking or talking about them rather than experiencing them directly	A person talks to her counselor about the fact that she is sad but shows no emotional evidence of sadness, which makes it harder for her to understand its effects on her life.
Introjection	Taking characteristics of another person into the self in order to avoid a direct expression of emotions. The emotions originally felt about the other person are now felt toward the self.	An abused woman feels angry with herself rather than her abusing partner, because she has taken on his belief that she is an inadequate caregiver. Believing otherwise would make her more fearful that the desired relationship might end.
Isolation of Affect	Consciously experiencing an emotion in a "safe" context rather than the threatening context in which it was first unconsciously experienced	A person does not experience sadness at the funeral of a family member, but the following week weeps uncontrollably at the death of a pet hamster.
Projection	Attributing unacceptable thoughts and feelings to others	A man does not want to be angry with his girlfriend, so when he is upset with her, he avoids owning that emotion by assuming that she is angry at him.
Rationalization	Using convincing reasons to justify ideas, feelings, or actions so as to avoid recognizing true motives	A student copes with the guilt normally associated with cheating on an exam by reasoning that he was too ill the previous week to prepare as well as he wanted.
Reaction Formation	Replacing an unwanted unconscious impulse with its opposite in conscious behavior	A person cannot bear to be angry with his boss, so after a conflict he convinces himself that the boss is worthy of loyalty and demonstrates this by volunteering to work overtime.
Regression	Resuming behaviors associated with an earlier developmental stage or level of functioning in order to avoid present anxiety. The behavior may or may not help to resolve the anxiety	A young man throws a temper tantrum as a means of discharging his frustration when he cannot master a task on his computer. The startled computer technician, who had been reluctant to attend to the situation, now comes forth to provide assistance.

(Continued)

Exhibit 4.10 (Continued)

Defense Mechanism	Definition	Example
Repression	Keeping unwanted thoughts and feelings entirely out of awareness	A son may begin to generate an impulse of hatred for his father, but because the impulse would be consciously unacceptable, he represses the hatred and does not become aware of it.
Somatization	Converting intolerable impulses into somatic symptoms	A person who is unable to express his negative emotions develops frequent stomachaches as a result.
Sublimation	Converting an impulse from a socially unacceptable aim to a socially acceptable one	An angry, aggressive young man becomes a star on his school's debate team.
Undoing	Nullifying an undesired impulse with an act of reparation	A man who feels guilty about having lustful thoughts about a coworker tries to make amends to his wife by purchasing a special gift for her.

educate them about it and explain more clearly how she learns best in a classroom setting, she was using problem-focused coping. In contrast, the function of **emotion-focused coping** is to change either the way the stressful situation is attended to (by vigilance or avoidance) or the meaning to oneself of what is happening. The external situation does not change, but our behaviors or attitudes change with respect to it, and we may thus effectively manage the stressor. When we view stressful conditions as unchangeable, emotion-focused coping may dominate. If Sheila learns that one of her professors has no empathy for students with learning disabilities, she might avoid taking that professor's courses in the future, or decide that getting a good grade in that course is not as important as being exposed to the course material.

U.S. culture tends to venerate problem-focused coping and the independently functioning self and to distrust emotion-focused coping and what

Conflict perspective

may be called relational coping. **Relational coping** takes into account actions that maximize the sur-

vival of others—such as our families, children, and friends—as well as ourselves (Zunkel, 2002).

Feminist theorists propose that women are more likely than men to employ the relational coping strategies of negotiation and forbearance, and Taylor's recent research (S. E. Taylor et al., 2002; S. E. Taylor & Stanton, 2007) gives credence to the idea that women are more likely than men to use relational coping. As social workers, we must be careful not to assume that one type of coping is superior to the other. Power imbalances and social forces such as racism and sexism affect the coping strategies of individuals (Lippa, 2005). We need to give clients credit for the extraordinary coping efforts they may make in hostile environments.

We might note that Sheila did not initially employ many problem-focused coping strategies to manage stressors at the university, and she over-used emotion-focused methods. For example, she accepted responsibility (that is, blamed herself) for her difficulties at first and tried without success to control her moods through force of will. Later, she distanced herself from her emotions and avoided stressors by spending more time away from campus working, and she was in fact quite skilled at this job. When she began seeking social support, she became more problem-focused.

Photo 4.5 Meditation is an emotion-focused method for dealing with stress. This woman is using meditation to change the way she attends to stress.

Coping and Traumatic Stress

People exhibit some similarities between the way they cope with traumatic stress and the way they cope with everyday stress. For both types of stress, they use problem-focused action, social support, negotiation skills, humor, altruism, and prayer (Aldwin, 2007). However, coping with traumatic stress differs from coping with everyday stress in several ways (Aldwin & Yancura, 2004):

- Because people tend to have much less control in traumatic situations, their primary emotion-focused coping strategy is emotional numbing, or the constriction of emotional expression. They also make greater use of the defense mechanism of denial.
- Confiding in others takes on greater importance.
- The process of coping tends to take a much longer time. Reactions can be delayed, for months or even years.
- A search for meaning takes on greater importance, and transformation in personal identity is more common.

Although there is evidence of long-term negative consequences of traumatic stress, trauma survivors sometimes report positive outcomes as well. Studies have found that 34% of Holocaust survivors and 50% of rape survivors report positive personal changes following their experiences with traumatic stress (Burt & Katz, 1987; Kahana, 1992).

However, many trauma survivors experience a set of symptoms known as *post-traumatic stress disorder* (PTSD) (American Psychiatric Association, 2000). These symptoms include the following:

- *Persistent reliving of the traumatic event:* intrusive, distressing recollections of the event; distressing dreams of the event; a sense of reliving the event; intense distress when exposed to cues of the event
- *Persistent avoidance of stimuli associated with the traumatic event:* avoidance of thoughts or feelings connected to the event; avoidance of places, activities, and people connected to the event; inability to recall aspects of the trauma; loss of interest in activities; feeling detached from others; emotional numbing; no sense of a future

- *Persistent high state of arousal:* difficulty sleeping, irritability, difficulty concentrating, excessive attention to stimuli, exaggerated startle response

Symptoms of post-traumatic stress disorder have been noted as soon as 1 week following the traumatic event, or as long as 30 years after (Sadock & Sadock, 2007). It is important to understand that the initial symptoms of post-traumatic stress are normal and expectable, and that PTSD should only be considered a disorder if those symptoms do not remit over time and present the person with serious long-term limitations in social functioning (D. Becker, 2004). Complete recovery from symptoms occurs in 30% of the cases, mild symptoms continue over time in 40%, moderate symptoms continue in 20%, and symptoms persist or get worse in about 10%. Children and older adults have the most trouble coping with traumatic events. A strong system of social support helps to prevent or to foster recovery from post-traumatic stress disorder. Besides providing support, social workers may be helpful by encouraging the person to discuss the traumatic event and by providing education about a variety of coping mechanisms.

Social Support

In coping with the demands of daily life, our social supports—the people we rely on to enrich our lives—can be invaluable. **Social support** can be defined as the interpersonal interactions and relationships that provide us with assistance or feelings of attachment to persons we perceive as caring (Hobfoll, 1996). Three types of social support resources are available (J. Walsh, 2000): *material support* (food, clothing, shelter, and other concrete items); *emotional support* (interpersonal support); and *instrumental support* (services provided by casual contacts, such as grocers, hairstylists, and landlords). Some authors add "social integration" support to the mix, which refers to a person's sense of belonging (Wethington, Moen, Glasgow, & Pillemer, 2000).

Our **social network** includes not just our social support, but also all the people with whom we regularly interact and the patterns of interaction that result from exchanging resources with them (Moren-Cross & Lin, 2006). Network relationships often occur in clusters (distinct categories such as nuclear family, extended family, friends, neighbors, community relations, school, work, church, recreational groups, and professional associations). Network relationships are not synonymous with support; they may be negative or positive. But the scope of the network does tend to indicate our potential for obtaining social support. Having supportive others in a variety of clusters indicates that we are supported in many areas of our lives, rather than being limited to relatively few sources. Our *personal network* includes those from the social network who, in our view, provide us with our most essential supports (Bidart & Lavenu, 2005).

How Social Support Aids Coping

The experience of stress creates a physiological state of emotional arousal, which reduces the efficiency of cognitive functions (Caplan & Caplan, 2000). When we experience stress, we become less effective at focusing our attention and scanning the environment for relevant information. We cannot access the memories that normally bring meaning to our perceptions, judgment, planning, and integration of feedback from others. These memory impairments reduce our ability to maintain a consistent sense of identity.

Social support helps in these situations by acting as an "auxiliary ego." Our social support, particularly our personal network, compensates for our perceptual deficits, reminds us of our sense of self, and monitors the adequacy of our functioning. Here are ten characteristics of effective support (Caplan, 1990; Caplan & Caplan, 2000):

1. Nurtures and promotes an ordered worldview
2. Promotes hope
3. Promotes timely withdrawal and initiative
4. Provides guidance

5. Provides a communication channel with the social world

6. Affirms one's personal identity

7. Provides material help

8. Contains distress through reassurance and affirmation

9. Ensures adequate rest

10. Mobilizes other personal supports

Some of these support systems are formal (service organizations), and some are informal (such

| Systems perspective |

as friends and neighbors). Religion, which attends to the spiritual realm, also plays a distinctive support role (Caplan, 1990). This topic is explored in Chapter 5.

How Social Workers Evaluate Social Support

There is no consensus about how social workers can evaluate a client's level of social support. The simplest procedure is to ask for the client's subjective perceptions of support from family and friends (Procidano & Smith, 1997). One of the most complex procedures uses eight indicators of social support: available listening, task appreciation, task challenge, emotional support, emotional challenge, reality confirmation, tangible assistance, and personal assistance (Richman, Rosenfeld, & Hardy, 1993). One particularly useful model includes three social support indicators (Uchino, 2009):

1. *Listing of social network resources.* The client lists all the people with whom he or she regularly interacts.

2. *Accounts of supportive behavior.* The client identifies specific episodes of receiving support from others in the recent past.

3. *Perceptions of support.* The client subjectively assesses the adequacy of the support received from various sources.

In assessing a client's social supports from this perspective, the social worker first asks the client to list all persons with whom he or she has interacted in the past 1 or 2 weeks. Next, the social worker asks the client to draw from that list the persons he or she perceives to be supportive in significant ways (significance is intended to be open to the client's interpretation). The client is asked to describe specific recent acts of support provided by those significant others. Finally, the social worker asks the client to evaluate the adequacy of the support received from specific sources, and in general. On the basis of this assessment, the social worker can identify both subjective and objective support indicators with the client and target underused clusters for the development of additional social support.

NORMAL AND ABNORMAL COPING

Most people readily assess the coping behaviors they observe in others as "normal" or "abnormal." But what does "normal" mean? We all apply different criteria. The standards we use to classify coping thoughts and feelings as normal or abnormal are important, however, because they have implications for how we view ourselves and how we behave toward those different from us. For example, Sheila was concerned that other students at the university perceived her as abnormal because of her social isolation and her inadequacy. Most likely, other students did not notice her at all. It is interesting that, in Sheila's view, her physical appearance and her demeanor revealed her as abnormal. However, her appearance did not stand out, and her feelings were not as evident to others as she thought.

Social workers struggle just as much to define *normal* and *abnormal* as anybody else. And their definitions may have greater consequences. Misidentifying someone as normal may forestall needed interventions; misidentifying someone as abnormal may create a stigma or become a self-fulfilling prophecy. To avoid such problems, social workers may profitably consider how four different disciplines define normal.

The Medical (Psychiatric) Perspective

One definition from psychiatry, a branch of medicine, states that we are normal when we are in harmony with ourselves and our environment. Normality is characterized by conformity with our community and culture. We can be deviant from some social norms, so long as our deviance does not impair our reasoning, judgment, intellectual capacity, and ability to make personal and social adaptations (Bartholomew, 2000).

The current definition of *mental disorder* used by the American Psychiatric Association (2000), which is intended to help psychiatrists and many other professionals distinguish between normality and abnormality, is a

> significant behavioral or psychological syndrome or pattern that occurs in an individual and that is associated with present distress (e.g., a painful symptom) or disability (i.e., impairment in one or more important areas of functioning) or with significantly increased risk of suffering death, pain, disability, or an important loss of freedom. (p. xxiii)

The syndrome or pattern "must not be an expectable and culturally sanctioned response to a particular event" (p. xxiii). Whatever its cause, "it must currently be considered a manifestation of behavioral, psychological, or biological dysfunction in the individual" (p. xxiii). Neither deviant behavior nor conflicts between an individual and society are to be considered mental disorders unless they are symptomatic of problems within the individual. As noted earlier, the *DSM* is the standard resource for diagnosing mental disorders.

Psychological Perspectives

One major difference between psychiatry and psychology is that psychiatry tends to emphasize biological and somatic interventions to return the person to a state of normalcy, whereas psychology emphasizes various cognitive, behavioral, or reflective interventions for individuals, families, or small groups.

The field of psychological theory is quite broad, but some theories are distinctive in that they postulate that people normally progress through a sequence of life stages. The time context thus becomes important. Each new stage of personality development builds on previous stages, and any unsuccessful transitions can result in abnormal behavior—that is, a deviant pattern of coping with threats and challenges. An unsuccessful struggle through one stage implies that the person will experience difficulties in mastering subsequent stages.

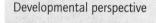

Developmental perspective

One life-stage view of normality very well known in social work is that of Erik Erikson (1968), who proposed eight stages of normal *psychosocial development* (see Exhibit 4.11). Sheila, although 22 years old, is still struggling with the two developmental stages of adolescence (in which the issue is identity vs. diffusion) and young adulthood (in which the issue is intimacy vs. isolation). Common challenges in adolescence include developing a sense of one's potential and place in society by negotiating issues of self-certainty versus apathy, role experimentation versus negative identity, and anticipation of achievement versus work paralysis. Challenges in young adulthood include developing a capacity for interpersonal intimacy as opposed to feeling socially empty or isolated within the family unit. According to Erikson's theory, Sheila's difficulties are related to her lack of success in negotiating one or more of the four preceding developmental phases.

From this perspective, Sheila's experience of stress would not be seen as abnormal, but her inability to make coping choices that promote positive personal adaptation would signal psychological abnormality. For example, in her first semester at the university, she was having difficulty with role experimentation (identity vs. identity diffusion). She lacked the necessary sense of competence and

Exhibit 4.11   Erikson's Stages of Psychosocial Development

Life Stage	Psychosocial Challenge	Significant Others
Infancy	Trust versus mistrust	Maternal persons
Early Childhood	Autonomy versus shame and doubt	Parental persons
Play Age	Initiative versus guilt	Family
School Age	Industry versus inferiority	Neighborhood
Adolescence	Identity versus identity diffusion	Peers
Young Adulthood	Intimacy versus isolation	Partners
Adulthood	Generativity versus self-absorption	Household
Mature Age	Integrity versus disgust and despair	Humanity

self-efficacy to allow herself to try out various social roles. She avoided social situations such as study groups, recreational activities, and university organizations in which she might learn more about what kinds of people she likes, what her main social interests are, and what range of careers she might enjoy. Instead, she was stuck with a negative identity, or self-image, and could not readily advance in her social development. From a stage theory perspective, her means of coping with the challenge of identity development would be seen as maladaptive, or abnormal.

The Sociological Approach: Deviance

The field of sociology offers a variety of approaches to the study of abnormality, or deviance. As an example, consider one sociological perspective on deviance derived from symbolic interactionism. It states that those who cannot constrain their behaviors within role limitations acceptable to others become labeled as deviant. Thus, *deviance* is a negative labeling that is assigned when one is considered by a

Social constructionist perspective

majority of significant others to be in violation of the prescribed social order (Downes & Rock, 2003). Put more simply, we are unable to grasp the perspective from which the deviant person thinks and acts; the person's behavior does not make sense to us. We conclude that our inability to understand the other person's perspective is due to that person's shortcomings rather than to our own rigidity, and we label the behavior as deviant. The deviance label may be mitigated if the individual accepts that he or she should think or behave otherwise and tries to conform to the social order.

From this viewpoint, Sheila would be perceived as abnormal, or deviant, only by those who had sufficient knowledge of her thoughts and feelings to form an opinion about her allegiance to their ideas of appropriate social behavior. She might also be considered abnormal by peers who had little understanding of rural culture. Those who knew Sheila well might understand the basis for her negative thoughts and emotions and in that context continue to view her as normal in her coping efforts. However, it is significant that Sheila was trying to avoid intimacy with her university classmates and work peers so that she would not become well-known to them. Because she still views herself as somewhat deviant, she wants to avoid being seen as deviant (or abnormal) by others, which in her view would lead to their rejection of her. This circular reasoning poorly serves Sheila's efforts to cope with stress in ways that promote her personal goals.

The Social Work Perspective: Social Functioning

The profession of social work is characterized by the consideration of systems and the reciprocal impact of persons and their environments (the biopsychosocial-spiritual perspective) on human behavior. Social workers tend not to classify individuals as abnormal. Instead, they consider the person-in-environment as an ongoing process that facilitates or blocks one's ability to experience satisfactory social functioning. In fact, in clinical social work, the term *normalization* refers to helping clients realize that their thoughts and feelings are shared by many other individuals in similar circumstances (Hepworth, Rooney, Rooney, Strom-Gottfried, & Larsen, 2010).

Social systems perspective

Three types of situations are most likely to produce problems in social functioning: stressful life transitions, relationship difficulties, and environmental unresponsiveness (Gitterman, 2009). Note that all three are related to transitory interactions of the person with other persons or the environment and do not rely on evaluating the client as normal or abnormal.

Social work's *person-in-environment (PIE) classification system* formally organizes the assessment of individuals' ability to cope with stress around the four factors shown in Exhibit 4.12: social functioning problems, environmental problems, mental health problems, and physical health problems. Such a broad classification scheme helps ensure that Sheila's range of needs will be addressed. James Karls and Maura O'Keefe (2008), the authors of the PIE system, state that it "underlines the importance of conceptualizing a person in an interactive context" and that "pathological and psychological limitations are accounted for but are not accorded extraordinary attention" (p. x). Thus, the system avoids labeling a client as abnormal. At the same time, however, it offers no way to assess the client's strengths and resources.

With the exception of its neglect of strengths and resources, the PIE assessment system is appropriate for social work because it was specifically developed to promote a holistic biopsychosocial perspective on human behavior. For example, at a mental health center that subscribed to psychiatry's *DSM-IV* classification system, Sheila might be given an Axis I diagnosis of adjustment disorder or dysthymic disorder, and her dyslexia might be diagnosed on Axis III. In addition, some clinicians might use Axis IV to note that Sheila has some school adjustment problems. With the PIE, the social worker would, in addition to her mental and physical health concerns, assess Sheila's overall social and occupational functioning, as well as any specific environmental problems. For example, her problems with the student role that might be highlighted on PIE Factor I include her ambivalence and isolation, the high severity of her impairment, its 6 months' to a year's duration, and the inadequacy of her coping skills. Her environmental stressors on Factor II might include a deficiency in affectional support, of high severity, with a duration of 6 months to a year. Assessment with PIE provides Sheila and the social worker with more avenues for intervention, which might include personal interventions, interpersonal interventions, and environmental interventions.

Critical Thinking Questions 4.3

What biases do you have about how people should cope with discrimination based on race, ethnicity, gender, sexual orientation, and so on? How might the coping strategy need to change in different situations, such as receiving service in a restaurant, being interviewed for a job, or dealing with an unthinking comment from a classmate?

Exhibit 4.12   The Person-in-Environment (PIE) Classification System

Factor I: Social Functioning Problems

A. Social role in which each problem is identified

   1. Family (parent, spouse, child, sibling, other, significant other)

   2. Other interpersonal (lover, friend, neighbor, member, other)

   3. Occupational (worker/paid, worker/home, worker/volunteer, student, other)

B. Type of problem in social role

1. Power	4. Dependency	7. Victimization
2. Ambivalence	5. Loss	8. Mixed
3. Responsibility	6. Isolation	9. Other

C. Severity of problem

1. No problem	4. High severity
2. Low severity	5. Very high severity
3. Moderate severity	6. Catastrophic

D. Duration of problem

1. More than five years	4. Two to four weeks
2. One to five years	5. Two weeks or less
3. Six months to one year	

E. Ability of client to cope with problem

1. Outstanding coping skills	4. Somewhat inadequate
2. Above average	5. Inadequate
3. Adequate	6. No coping skills

Factor II: Environmental Problems

A. Social system where each problem is identified

1. Economic/basic need	4. Health, safety, social services
2. Education/training	5. Voluntary association
3. Judicial/legal	6. Affectional support

B. Specific type of problem within each social system

C. Severity of problem

D. Duration of problem

Factor III: Mental Health Problems

A. Clinical syndromes (Axis I of DSM)

B. Personality and developmental disorders (Axis II of DSM)

Factor IV: Physical Health Problems

A. Disease diagnosed by a physician

B. Other health problems reported by client and others

Implications for Social Work Practice

The study of the psychological person as a thinking and feeling being and as a self in relationship has many implications for social work practice:

- Be alert to the possibility that practice interventions may need to focus on any of several systems, including family, small groups, organizations, and communities. The person's transactions with all of these systems affect psychological functioning.
- Where appropriate, help individual clients to develop a stronger sense of competence through both ego-supportive and ego-modifying interventions.
- Where appropriate, help individual clients to enhance problem-solving skills through techniques directed at both cognitive reorganization and behavioral change.
- Where appropriate, help individual clients strengthen the sense of self by bringing balance to emotional and cognitive experiences.
- Help clients consider their strengths in terms of the unique sets of intelligences they may have, and show how these intelligences may help them address their challenges in unique ways.
- Always assess the nature, range, and intensity of a client's interpersonal relationships.
- Help clients identify their sources of stress and patterns of coping. Recognize the possibility of particular vulnerabilities to stress, and to social and environmental conditions that give rise to stress.
- Help clients assess the effectiveness of particular coping strategies for specific situations.
- Where appropriate, use case management activities focused on developing a client's social supports through linkages with potentially supportive others in a variety of social network clusters.
- When working with persons in crisis, attempt to alleviate distress and facilitate a return to the previous level of functioning.

Key Terms

accommodation (cognitive)	emotion-focused coping	relational theory
adaptation	multiple intelligences	schema (schemata)
assimilation (cognitive)	neural plasticity	secondary emotions
cognition	object relations theory	self
coping	preconscious	social network
crisis	primary emotions	social support
defense mechanisms	problem-focused coping	state
ego	psychoanalytic theory	stress
ego psychology	psychology	trait
emotion	relational coping	traumatic stress
emotional intelligence		unconscious

Active Learning

1. Reread the case study at the beginning of this chapter. As you read, what do you see as the driving force of Sheila's behavior as she makes the transition to the university? Is it cognition? Is it emotion? What patterns of thinking and feeling might Sheila have developed from her rural background? What theories presented in the chapter are most helpful to you in thinking about this?

2. What is your own perspective on the nature of the self? How does this affect your work with clients, when you consider their potential for change?

3. Consider several recent situations in which you have utilized problem-focused or emotion-focused coping strategies. What was different about the situations in which you used one rather than the other? Were the coping strategies successful? Why or why not?

Web Resources

The Consortium for Research on Emotional Intelligence in Organizations

www.eiconsortium.org

Site contains recent research and model programs for promoting the development of emotional intelligence in the work setting.

Institute of Contemporary Psychotherapy ad Psychoanalysis

www.icpeast.org/index.html

Site contains information on conferences, training, and links to other resources on contemporary self and relational psychologies.

Lawrence Kohlberg's Stages of Moral Development

www.xenodocy.org/ex/lists/moraldev.html

Site maintained by Ralph Kenyon, contains an overview and critique of Kohlberg's stage theory of moral development.

MEDLINEplus: Stress

www.nlm.nih.gov/medlineplus/stress.html

Site maintained by the National Institute of Mental Health, includes links to latest news about stress research; coping; disease management; specific conditions; and stress in children, seniors, teenagers, and women.

Multiple Intelligences for Adult Literacy and Education

http://literacyworks.org/mi/home.html

Site presented by Literacyworks, contains a visual overview of Howard Gardner's theory of multiple intelligences, guidelines for assessment, and suggestions for putting the theory to practice in adult literacy programs.

National Center for Posttraumatic Stress Disorder

www.ncptsd.org

Site presented by the National Center for PTSD, a program of the U.S. Department of Veterans Affairs, contains facts about PTSD, information about how to manage the traumatic stress of terrorism, and recent research.

Object Relations Theory and Therapy

www.objectrelations.org

Site maintained by Thomas Klee, Ph.D., clinical psychologist, contains information on object relations theory, a method of object relations psychotherapy, and current articles on object relations theory and therapy.

Piaget's Developmental theory

www.learningandteaching.info/learning/piaget.htm

Site maintained by James Atherton of the United Kingdom overviews Jean Piaget's key ideas and developmental stages.

Self Psychology Page

www.selfpsychology.com

Site maintained by David Wolf contains a definition of the self psychology of Heinz Kohut, bibliography, papers, discussion groups on self psychology, and links to other Internet sites.

Stone Center

www.wcwonline.org

Site presented by the Stone Center of the Wellesley Centers for Women, the largest women's research center in the United States, contains theoretical work on women's psychological development and model programs for the prevention of psychological problems.

Stress Management

http://mentalhealth.about.com/od/stress/stress_management.htm

Site presented by About.com, which is owned by the *New York Times,* includes a large number of articles and links about topics related to stress management in a variety of contexts.

CHAPTER 5

The Spiritual Person

Michael J. Sheridan

☙❧

☙❧

Opening Questions

How does the inclusion of the spiritual dimension in the existing biopsychosocial framework expand and enhance our understanding of human behavior? What challenges does it bring to this understanding?

How can social workers effectively tap into the universals (e.g., love, compassion, service, justice) found in most spiritual perspectives—both religious and nonreligious—while recognizing and honoring diversity among various spiritual paths?

CASE STUDY 5.1

Caroline's Challenging Questions

Caroline, who grew up in a large, close-knit family from North Carolina, is in her first year of college at a university in another state where she is encountering all kinds of new experiences. A devout Christian, Caroline is a member of a Baptist church back home, where her family has attended for generations. She was very involved in her home church, singing in the choir and actively engaged in several youth programs. Most of her high school friends attended her church, so she was more than a little uncomfortable when she learned that her roommate, Ruth, was Jewish. Caroline has met a number of other students who are from different faiths or who say that they don't belong to a church at all. This has been a new and challenging experience for her.

At first she tried to stay away from anyone who wasn't Christian, but struggled with this because so many of her non-Christian classmates seemed like nice people and she really wanted to have friends. All sorts of questions began to emerge in her mind, like "How can they not believe in Jesus Christ?" and "What *do* they believe?" and "What will happen to them in the afterlife if they are not saved?" These questions only grew as she took a comparative religions class where she learned about faiths that she had never heard of before. In one class exercise, she was paired with a student from Turkey who said she was Muslim. At first, Caroline was anxious about talking with her, but as they moved through the exercise, she began to feel that they were more alike than different. They both were from very religious families, their faith was important to them personally, and they both were struggling with all the different perspectives that they were encountering in college. Later that day, Caroline realized that if she had been born in Turkey, she would probably be a Muslim too. This thought both intrigued and unsettled her. More and more she is asking herself, "What *do* I really believe and why?"

CASE STUDY 5.2

Naomi's Health Crisis

Naomi is a 42-year-old mother of three children who are 10, 7, and 3 years old. Naomi discovered a lump in her breast a couple of weeks ago, and she and her husband, David, have been anxiously awaiting news regarding test results. When the diagnosis of cancer finally comes, they are both stunned and frightened, but pull themselves together for the sake of the children. Naomi begins the long journey of doctors, surgery, chemotherapy, and radiation treatments while simultaneously trying to maintain family life and a part-time job as best she can. David takes on new duties as a more active parent and homemaker while still going to his full-time job. He struggles with his own fears and anger about what is happening, initially not sharing these with Naomi because he is determined to be her "rock."

Naomi and David are members of Temple Shalom, a local Reform Jewish congregation, which they joined after their first child was born. When they were growing up, Naomi's family were members of a Reform congregation, while David's family expressed their Jewish heritage in more secular and cultural terms, gathering annually for a Passover Seder but not attending services except occasionally on Yom Kippur. Naomi had not regularly attended services after her bat mitzvah, but both she and David decided that they wanted to be part of a spiritual community for their children. They had heard good things about the temple in their neighborhood and decided to explore it. They liked its open, welcoming atmosphere; its liberal viewpoints on social issues; and its active engagement in social action in the community. They both enjoy the weekly connection with other adults and are happy with the religious classes that their children attend. Recently, Naomi and David have been engaged in weekly Shabbat Torah study sessions, to deepen their understanding of Jewish sacred texts.

Now that Naomi is facing this health crisis, both she and David are feeling a bit lost and are searching for answers. Although friends have been supportive, both of their families live far away, and their short visits and phone calls only provide minimal comfort. One night, when they both can't sleep, Naomi and David begin to share their doubts and fears with one another, even admitting that they feel angry with God and are wondering if there is such a thing as God at all. Naomi finally suggests, "I think it would help to talk with Rabbi Shapiro and some of the people we've met at Temple Shalom." David agrees and adds that they should also explore the Jewish Healing Network that was described in the bulletin the previous week.

CASE STUDY 5.3

Matthew's Faith Journey

Matthew will be 70 next month—a fact that is hard for him to believe. He's been a widower for 5 years now since his wife, Betty, died of a sudden heart attack. The first few years following her death were rough, but Matthew made it through with the help of his sons and their families, and members of his Catholic parish, which he has been attending for 40 years. His faith has always been very important to him, even though he has struggled with periods of doubt and confusion—the latest following Betty's death. At one point when he was younger, he considered leaving the church, when disagreements about doctrine and rumblings about the new priest were causing uproar in the congregation. He even visited several other denominations to see if they were a better fit for him. But after much reflection and conversation with Betty, Matthew decided to stick with his commitment to the Catholic faith and his parish, saying, "No church is perfect, and this is where I truly belong."

For the past couple of years, he has been actively involved with the outreach activities of the church, working on the Food Bank and Affordable Housing committees. Recently, he has been a member of the Interfaith Dialogue Program, which promotes respect and mutual understanding across religious and cultural perspectives. Matthew finds the panel discussions, conferences, and interfaith community projects both challenging and invigorating. He's particularly looking forward to an upcoming conference on the role of interfaith dialogue in advancing world peace. He's also been involved with the National Religious Partnership for the Environment (NRPE), a Judeo-Christian association composed of many faiths that focuses on environmental stewardship. As a result of all of these activities, Matthew has also been reading a number of books on different religions and is struck by the similar themes that are reflected in the teachings of very diverse traditions. He is beginning to feel a new sense of purpose for his life, which both surprises and delights him as he heads into his seventies. Some of his friends have asked him if his involvement with the Interfaith Dialogue Program is making him question his own religion, but Matthew says, "No, quite the opposite. I feel more deeply connected to my faith as I understand more about other religions. It's not that I think mine is right and theirs is wrong, but I appreciate and respect other religions, while still knowing that mine is right for me."

CASE STUDY 5.4

Trudy's Search for the Sacred

Trudy is a 35-year-old single woman living in Berkeley, California—which is a long way from the little town in Arkansas where she lived until she left home at 18. She's moved several times since then, searching for a new home that feels right to her. She thinks she may have finally found it. A new job in a health food store; a small, but comfortable and affordable apartment; a great yoga class; and a welcoming Buddhist Sangha (community) of like-minded people all make her feel like she's finally found what she's been looking for.

Trudy's early years were not easy ones. Her father was an alcoholic who flew into rages when drunk, which happened more often as the years went by. It was not an unusual event for someone in her family to be physically hurt during these episodes. Trudy, her mother, and her two sisters were afraid of her father and "walked around on eggshells" most of the time to avoid triggering his angry spells. Trudy found refuge in the woods in back of her house and in books, which she devoured as they took her to places beyond her current reality. She could stay curled up in a nook of her favorite tree for hours, transporting herself to somewhere else—anywhere else. She promised herself she would leave as soon as she finished high school.

Life since then has not been easy either. Trudy was briefly married in her twenties to a man who also had a hard time controlling his anger and began to drink more and more as problems in the marriage started to emerge. Trudy even found herself turning to alcohol as a way of numbing her pain, which really scared her. With the support of some friends, she finally left the marriage and was off again, searching for a new home. After a couple of other relationships that didn't work out, Trudy decided to avoid men and increasingly became isolated from all social ties. But in her new home in Berkeley, she finds that she likes the people who attend her Sangha and likes even more the fact that they don't share a lot of personal information, focusing more on spiritual practices. She loves the group meditation and the dharma talks and has made a commitment to increased periods of solitary meditation when she is at home. Trudy is now rising at 4:00 AM to meditate for 3 hours before work, and she meditates an additional 2 hours most evenings. Her reading is now totally focused on books about spirituality, which support her quest to rise above personal concerns and ego to become an enlightened being. Although Trudy was not exposed to a particular religious tradition during childhood, her spiritual development is now her highest priority.

CASE STUDY 5.5

Leon's Two Worlds

Leon is a 23-year-old man who is feeling torn in two. He is the oldest son in a family with five kids and the mainstay of his mother's life. Regina became a widow 8 years ago when her husband, Rodney, was killed in an accident at the mill yard where he worked. Since then, she's leaned heavily on Leon for help with his brothers and sisters and as a major contributor to the family's finances. He is also the one she confides in the most, sharing things with him that she once shared with her husband. The whole family also relies heavily on their African Methodist Episcopal (AME) church for both social support and spiritual nurturance.

Leon has grown up in the church and loves the fellowship and the joyous feeling that comes over him as he sings and worships on Sundays. But it is also a place that increasingly troubles him, as he has finally admitted to himself that he is gay. He has denied this for years, trying hard to follow church teachings about homosexuality being a sin and something that can be overcome with the help of God. He has prayed and prayed to God to change him, but this has not worked. Leon is now battling despair, as he fears that he will always be caught between his love for his faith and his church and a longing to be who he truly is. The idea of telling his mother about his sexual orientation seems unthinkable, but he's not sure how long he can go on living a lie. He knows he will have to leave the church if it ever becomes known that he is gay. That possibility also seems unthinkable. He has been feeling more and more depressed, to the point where his mother keeps asking him what's wrong. He's even had thoughts of suicide, which frighten him. In his nightly prayers to God he asks, "Why must I lose you to be who I am?"

Jean-Joseph's Serving the Spirits

Jean-Joseph is a 50-year-old man, originally from Haiti, who came with his family to the United States 10 years ago. He and his family were adherents of the Roman Catholic faith in Haiti and now attend a Catholic church near their new home. Jean-Joseph's family are also believers in Vodoun (known by most Westerners as Voodoo), which is widely practiced in Haiti and often integrated with belief in Catholicism. Most Roman Catholics who are active in this spiritual tradition refer to it as "serving the spirits." Although this belief system holds that there is only one God, Bondje, who created the universe, he is considered to be too far away for a personal relationship with humans. Instead, believers in Vodoun center on *Loa,* or spirits of ancestors and animals, natural forces, and good and evil spirits. Family Loa are spirits who are seen to protect their "children"—the Haitian people—from misfortune. Jean-Joseph and his family regularly participate in rituals to feed the Loa food and drink, and offer them other gifts.

Recently, a Loa visited Jean-Joseph in a dream, telling him that his youngest son was ill and needed healing. His son Emmanuel had indeed been listless for days, not wanting to eat or play, and his parents were very worried about him. Jean-Joseph decided that they needed to take him to a *Mambo,* a Vodoun priestess, who could mediate between the human and spirit worlds to diagnose and treat Emmanuel's illness. The Mambo agreed to perform a healing ceremony, which was held at a *hounfour,* or Vodoun temple, around a *poteau-mitan,* a center pole where the spirits can communicate with people. A *veve,* or pattern of cornmeal unique to the Loa who was the focus of the ceremony, was created on the floor, and an altar was decorated with candles, pictures of Christian saints, and other symbolic items. A goat was also sacrificed for the ceremony. The Mambo and her assistants began to chant and dance, accompanied by the shaking of rattles and beating of drums. Finally, the Mambo was possessed by the Loa and fell down. The Lao then spoke through the Mambo and told the family how to treat the distressed spirit that was causing Emmanuel's illness. After the ceremony, the Mambo gave Jean-Joseph an herbal remedy to give to his son and instructions on how to continue feeding the spirit of the Lao until Emmanuel was healed. The family also prayed to the Christian God and Catholic saints to bring healing to Emmanuel.

THE SPIRITUAL DIMENSION

All of the stories presented in the six case studies could be viewed through many different lenses.

Systems perspective

Social work's biopsychosocial framework would be helpful in understanding many facets of these cases. Knowledge of the biological components of health certainly would be useful in understanding the circumstances of Naomi's health crisis and Jean-Joseph's attempts at healing his son's illness. Psychological perspectives would shed light on Caroline's discomfort with encountering different beliefs, Matthew's deepening faith perspective, Trudy's search for a home and a different sense of self, and Leon's despair at being torn between his faith and his sexual identity. Social theories on family dynamics, ethnicity and culture, social movements, socioeconomic class, and social institutions would yield invaluable information about all of the subjects of these cases, providing a wider frame for understanding their individual lives. This use of multiple perspectives to understand human behavior is consistent with social work's focus on changing configurations of person and environment.

However, the biopsychosocial framework omits an important dimension of human existence:

spirituality. This omission seems antithetical to social work's commitment to holistic practice. What would be gained if we added a spiritual lens in our attempt to understand Caroline's challenging questions, Naomi's health crisis, Matthew's faith journey, Trudy's search for the sacred, Leon's two worlds, and Jean-Joseph's serving of the spirits? And how would this perspective help you as a social worker provide holistic and effective service in working with them? Keep these questions and all of the stories in mind as you read the rest of the chapter.

The Meaning of Spirituality

The concept of spirituality is often confused with religion, and writers in social work and related fields point to a number of attempts to delineate these terms and distinguish them from one another (Bullis, 1996; Canda, 1997; Carroll, 1998; D. MacDonald, 2000; Sheridan, 2004; Wuthnow, 2003; Zinnbauer et al., 1997). Canda and Furman (2010) provide a detailed discussion of how the two terms are understood in social work and related fields, including medicine, nursing, and psychology. They also report findings from a series of national studies that they have conducted in the United States, the United Kingdom, Norway, and New Zealand, which show relative consistency across countries. Specifically, the top six descriptors of *spirituality* across geographic locales were "meaning, personal, purpose, values, belief, and ethics." Similar congruence was found for the term *religion,* where the top six descriptors selected in all of the countries were "belief, ritual, community, values, prayer, and scripture" (p. 67). Drawing from these studies and additional research in the helping professions, Canda and Furman propose the following definitions for these two concepts.

Spirituality is "a process of human life and development

- Focusing on the search for a sense of meaning, purpose, morality, and well-being;
- In relationship with oneself, other people, other beings, the universe, and ultimate

reality however understood (e.g., in animistic, atheistic, nontheistic, polytheistic, theistic, or other ways);
- Orienting around centrally significant priorities; and
- Engaging a sense of the transcendence (experienced as deeply profound, sacred, or transpersonal)." (p. 75)

Religion is "an institutionalized (i.e., systematic and organized) pattern of values, beliefs, symbols, behaviors, and experiences that involves

- Spirituality;
- A community of adherents;
- Transmission of traditions over time; and
- Community support functions (e.g., organizational structure, material assistance, emotional support, or political advocacy) that are directly or indirectly related to spirituality." (p. 76)

Thus, the term *spirituality* is generally used in the social work literature to mean a broader concept than religion in that spiritual expression may or may not involve a particular religious faith or religious institution. But some writers have pointed out that for persons affiliated with certain faith perspectives, the two terms cannot be separated from one another, or *religion* is considered to be the broader construct, subsuming spirituality (Pals, 1996; Praglin, 2004). Others propose that the separation of the two terms in social work has resulted in discrimination against particular religious worldviews, especially those of evangelical or conservative faiths (Hodge, 2002, 2003; Ressler & Hodge, 2003). Clearly, there is a need for continued exploration and dialogue about definitional issues. Regardless of how the scholarly definition of these terms evolves, it is important as social workers to always inquire about and honor the client's definition of spirituality and religion, and use the term that is most acceptable and relevant for that person, family, or community.

For the sake of clarity, it should be noted that when the term *spirituality* is used in the current chapter, it is meant to convey spirituality as the broader concept, inclusive of both religious and nonreligious expressions. Occasionally, the two terms are used together in the same sentence (e.g., "gathering religious or spiritual information"). In this case, the reader should recognize that both are included in order to be applicable regardless of whether persons identify themselves as primarily religious, primarily spiritual, both religious and spiritual, or neither.

Regardless of the precise words that are used to capture the meaning of spirituality, the term brings to mind many related themes. Exhibit 5.1 lists 20 symbolic themes of spirituality identified by Patrick O'Brien (1992). Which themes do you think are most applicable to the six case studies presented at the beginning of this chapter?

Spirituality in the United States and Globally

The current spiritual landscape in the United States reveals both common threads and a colorful array of unique patterns. A number of polls have consistently reported that between 92% and 96% of people in the United States say they believe in God or a universal spirit, and 80% report that religion is either "very important" or "fairly important" in their life (Gallup, 2008). In another intriguing survey of how Americans experience spirituality in everyday life, George Gallup and Timothy Jones (2000) asked participants about their activities during the previous 24 hours. Two thirds said that they had prayed during that time, and almost half stated that they had experienced "a strong sense of God's presence" (p. 17). These statistics indicate a strong thread of spirituality in the United States. However, expressions of both religious and nonreligious spirituality have become increasingly diverse, making the United States likely the most religiously diverse country in the world today, with more than 1,500 different religious groups (Parrillo, 2009; Pew Forum on Religion & Public Life, 2008).

This diversity is due, in part, to ongoing schisms and divisions among many of the organized religions historically present within the United States.

Photo 5.1 Spirituality is understood and expressed differently by individuals but is generally associated with a person's search for meaning.

Exhibit 5.1   Symbolic Themes of Spirituality

1. Morality, ethics, justice, and right effort

2. The nature and meaning of self and the intention and purpose of human existence

3. Interconnection; wholeness; alignment; and integration of persons, place, time, and events

4. Creativity, inspiration, and intuition

5. Altruistic service for the benefit of others

6. The mystery and wonder that are woven into nature, the universe, and the unknown

7. Sociocultural-historical traditions, rituals, and myths

8. Virtues (such as compassion, universal love, peace, patience, forgiveness, hope, honesty, trust, faith)

9. Mystical, altered states of consciousness

10. Sexuality

11. Openness, willingness, surrender, and receptivity

12. The power of choice, freedom, and responsibility

13. Special wisdom or revealed knowledge

14. Prayer, meditation, and quiet contemplation

15. Answers to pain, suffering, and death

16. Identity and relation to the metaphysical grounds of existence, ultimate reality, and life force

17. The relationship of cause and effect regarding prosperity or poverty

18. Beliefs or experiences related to intangible reality or the unobstructed universe

19. The path to enlightenment or salvation

20. Sensitive awareness of the earth and the nonhuman world

SOURCE: Adapted from O'Brien (1992).

For example, the number of Christian denominations alone grew from 20 to more than 900 from 1800 to 1988 (Melton, 1993). In addition, there has been a significant rise in other spiritual traditions with each new influx of immigrants from other parts of the world. They have brought not only faiths recognized as major religions (e.g., Islam, Buddhism, Confucianism, Hinduism), but also various forms of spiritualism, folk healing, and shamanism (e.g., Santeria, *espiritismo*, Vodoun, *curanderismo, krou khmer, mudang*). This trend is further augmented by a growing interest in Eastern and Middle Eastern religions (e.g., Islam, Buddhism, and Hinduism) and earth-based spiritualities (e.g., neo-paganism, goddess worship, and deep ecology). There has also been a revived or more visible involvement in traditional spiritual paths within Indigenous communities, as increasing numbers of Native Americans or First Nations peoples explore their tribal traditions or combine these traditions with faith in Christianity. Many of these "new" religions are among the fastest growing in the United States, although their overall numbers are still relatively small. Exhibit 5.2 shows the self-identification of the U.S. adult population by religious tradition in 1990, 2001, and 2008.

Exhibit 5.2   Self-Identification of U.S. Adult Population by Religious Tradition, 1990, 2001, 2008

Religious Tradition	1990 Estimate	1990 percent of U.S. Population	2001 Estimate	2001 percent of U.S. Population	2008 Estimate	2008 percent of U.S. Population
Christianity	151,225,000	86.2	159,514,000	76.7	173,402,000	76.0
Jewish	3,137,000	1.8	2,837,000	1.4	2,680,000	1.2
Eastern Religions	687,000	0.4	2,020,000	1.0	1,961,000	0.9
Muslim	527,000	0.3	1,104,000	0.5	1,349,000	0.9
No Religion	14,331,000	8.2	29,481,000	14.1	34,169,000	15.0

SOURCE: Kosmin & Keysar (2009).

It should be noted that estimates of members of any particular religious group vary widely depending on the source, data collection methods, and definition of "adherents" (e.g., self-identified, formal membership, or regular participant). For example, in the United States, figures for adherents of Islam range from 1 million to 8 million; adherents of Judaism from 1 million to 5 million; adherents of Buddhism from 1 million to 5 million; and adherents of neo-paganism from 10,000 to 770,000 (Canda & Furman, 1999; *Major Branches of Religions,* 2005; Parrillo, 2009).

As tempting as it is to make overarching statements based on statistics concerning belief in God and religious identification—for example, that the U.S. population is highly religious—we must be cautious in drawing specific conclusions, as the picture changes depending on the particular indicator. During generally the same time period, 1990–2001, the percentage of U.S. adults who regularly attend religious services decreased from 49% to 36%, reflecting a worldwide trend among industrialized countries (Reeves, 1998). More recent data drawn from Gallup Polls (2008) reveal only 30% reporting that they attend religious services on a weekly basis. Furthermore, the 2001 American Religious Identification Survey (Kosmin & Keysar, 2009)

reports that respondents who did not subscribe to any religious identification showed the greatest increase in both absolute numbers and percentages of the U.S. population. Specifically, this group grew from 14.3 million (8%) in 1990 to 20.4 million (over 14%) in 2001. More recent data from the Pew Forum on Religion & Public Life (2008; hereafter "Pew Forum") reveal that 16.1% of adults report being unaffiliated, making them a substantial category second only to Christians in the United States.

In addition, there appears to be increasing fluidity in religious affiliation. Data on changes from one major religious tradition to another (e.g., from Protestantism to Catholicism, or from Judaism to no religion) show that 28% of U.S. adults have changed their affiliation from that of their childhood. When changes within affiliations are examined (e.g., from Baptist to Methodist), an even larger percentage (44%) of American adults report shifts in religious affiliation. The two affiliations showing the greatest net gains are the unaffiliated, increasing from 7.3% to 16.1%, and nondenominational Protestantism, increasing from 1.5% to 4.5% (Pew Forum, 2008).

Groups that show a net loss due to changes in affiliation include Baptists, Methodists, and other Protestant groups, which show decreases ranging from less than 1 percentage point to 3.7 percentage points. Judaism also shows a small loss due to changing affiliations (0.2 percentage points). But the group that has experienced the greatest decrease is the Catholic Church, with 31.4% reporting being raised as Catholic, but only 23.9% identifying as Catholic today, a net loss of 7.5 percentage points (Pew Forum, 2008). It should be noted, however, that the overall proportion of the U.S. population that is Catholic is roughly the same as it was in the early 1970s. This can be explained in part by the number of converts, but the greatest contributor to replacing those who have left the Catholic Church has been immigrants coming into the United States who are adherents of this faith.

Overall, it is noteworthy that the percentage of respondents moving from "some" religious affiliation to "none" (12.7%) is greater than that of people moving from "none" to "some" religious affiliation (3.9%) (Pew Forum, 2008). All of this suggests that the current phenomenon of "religion switching" may be a reflection of deeper cultural changes within our society, perhaps in part explained by what Roof (1993) calls the "generation of seekers," referring to the substantial numbers of the baby boomer cohort in the United States.

Interestingly, these figures concerning shifts and declines in organized religious affiliation or identification emerge at a time when people in the United States are expressing an unprecedented interest in spirituality in general. In 1994, an estimated 58% of the U.S. population said they "feel the need . . . to experience spiritual growth in their lives"; just 4 years later, in 1998, a total of 82% of those polled made the same claim (Gallup & Lindsay, 1999, p. 1). It is apparent that this interest in spiritual growth may or may not be expressed within traditional religious institutions and is increasingly focused on a spirituality that is more subjective, experiential, and personalized (Roof, 1993, 1999). This reflects Ulrich Beck's (1992) understanding of spirituality as attending to the development of positive human qualities—such as generosity, gratitude, a capacity for awe and wonder, an appreciation of the interconnectedness among all beings, and deeper awareness and insight—as much as or even more than a search for any divine form of transcendence.

It is important to consider all of these data within the context of global statistics (see Exhibit 5.3). Although adherents of Christianity remain the highest proportion of the population in the United States, worldwide they compose only 33% of all religious adherents, with the remainder being composed of those who self-identify with some other perspective, including Islam (21%); Hinduism (14%); nonreligious (16%); Buddhism, Chinese traditional, and primal-Indigenous faiths (6% each); and Sikhism and Judaism (less than 1% each) (*Major Religions of the World*, 2005).

It is important to understand the impact of globalization on religious or spiritual diversity both within and outside of the United States. *Globalization* is used here to refer to "the worldwide diffusion of practices, expansion of relations across continents, reorganization of social life on a global scale, and a growth of a shared global consciousness" (Lechner, as quoted in Swatos, 2005, p. 320). Simply put, it is our growing sense of the world being "a single place" (R. Robertson, 1992). As with other aspects of human life, globalization is also increasing our awareness of the many different religious and spiritual traditions in the world and the role they play in various conflicts, both between and within countries.

Lester Kurtz (2007) posits that there are three factors—modernism, multiculturalism, and modern technologies of warfare—that are significant in understanding religious conflict today. First, *modernism,* based on scientific, industrial, and technological revolutions, has had an ongoing contentious relationship with religious perspectives and institutions beginning in the 17th century, when church authorities charged Galileo with heresy because he stated that the earth revolved around the sun. Present-day examples include debates regarding evolution versus creationism and intelligent design; the question of when life begins and ends; the ethics of stem-cell research and genetic manipulation; the

Conflict perspective

Exhibit 5.3   Major Religions of the World Ranked by Number of Adherents

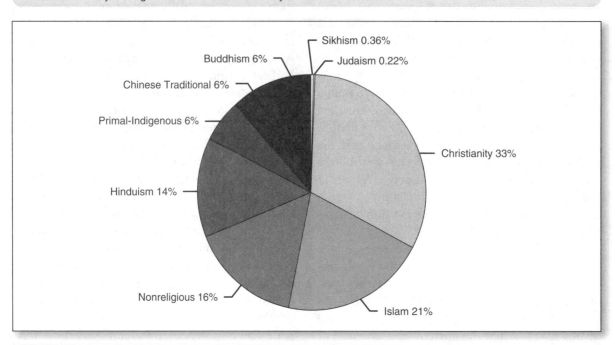

SOURCE: Data drawn from www.adherents.com.

Photos 5.2a & 5.2b   Religion involves the patterning of spiritual beliefs and practices into social institutions; different cultures focus their beliefs around different central figures.

proper codes of behavior, especially sexual behavior; the rightful roles of women in society and the correct way to raise children; and the appropriate place of religion in the political sphere. Thus, this tension between science and religion continues during our current postmodern times as scientific and secular thought compete with religious traditions and doctrine as the authority for "truth" and moral guidelines for contemporary life.

Second, *multiculturalism* increasingly requires us to recognize that there are myriad worldviews and ways of life, within the United States as well as globally. This pluralistic reality stands in contrast to unilateral belief systems, both religious and cultural, that have historically provided what Peter Berger (1969) calls a "sacred canopy," or the security and certainty of one view of the universe, one answer to profound and mundane questions, and one approach to organizing individual and collective life. Such a unified perspective is difficult to maintain as individuals and whole cultures are increasingly exposed to a religious and spiritual "marketplace" (Warner, 1993) of diverse belief systems and practices, which often challenge the basic tenets previously held as absolute.

The potential for conflict is inherent in both modernism and multiculturalism, conflict that becomes especially deadly when combined with the third aspect of globalization—the dispersion of *modern technological advances in warfare.* Violent conflict, often intertwined with religious issues, has been part of human history for thousands of years. But in the current period of globalization, the cost of such conflict has grown unimaginably high in that our arsenal now includes nuclear, biological, and chemical weapons of mass destruction as opposed to stones, clubs, and other primitive weapons. As Lester Kurtz (2007) succinctly states, "Given the destructive capabilities of modern weaponry and the consequent necessity for peaceful coexistence, the potential for religious traditions to promote either chaos or community becomes a crucial factor in the global village" (p. 243).

In light of this complex and ever-changing picture, social workers gain very little real understanding of a person by simply knowing his or her primary religious affiliation. First, religious affiliation may or may not hold great significance for the person, and identification with a religion alone does not indicate depth of involvement. Second, belief, practice, and involvement can be quite varied, even among adherents of the same spiritual tradition or among members of the same family, kinship group, or faith community—even if they all self-identify as Methodist or Muslim or Wiccan. Third, some people feel connected to multiple spiritual perspectives simultaneously, such as a combination of Judaism and Buddhism or traditional Indigenous spiritual beliefs and Christianity. Fourth, the meaning of religious or spiritual affiliation may change across the life course; a person may feel more or less connected to a particular tradition at different points in his or her life. And finally, the meaning of a person's religious or spiritual affiliation must be understood within his or her broader historical, sociopolitical, and cultural context in order for its full significance to be realized. It is important to understand the range of spiritual influences (both religious and nonreligious) that may contribute to anyone's life story and the larger collective realities that impact that story at any particular point in time.

Critical Thinking Questions 5.1

At the beginning of the chapter, you read the spiritual and religious beliefs of six people. With which of the stories were you most comfortable? For what reasons? With which of the stories were you least comfortable? For what reasons? How comfortable are you with the idea of including the spiritual person in social work's understanding of human behavior? What do you like about the idea? What don't you like about the idea?

TRANSPERSONAL THEORIES OF HUMAN DEVELOPMENT _____

The idea that spirituality is an important dimension of human behavior is not a new one in social work or in other helping professions. Although Sigmund Freud (1928) asserted that all religious and spiritual beliefs were either illusions or projections of unconscious wishes, many other early behavioral science theorists viewed the role of spirituality differently.

Notably, Carl Jung, a student of Freud's, differed with his former teacher and mentor in regard to the

topic of spirituality. Jung's (1933a) theory of personality includes physical, mental, and spiritual selves, which all strive for unity and wholeness within each person. In Jung's (1959/1969) view, an important *archetype* (a universal unconscious idea) is "the Spirit" (p. 214). Jung further proposed that the evolution of consciousness and the struggle to find a spiritual outlook on life were the primary developmental tasks in midlife. If this task is successfully accomplished, the result is *individuation,* which Jung defined as "the moment when the finite mind realizes it is rooted in the infinite" (as quoted in Keutzer, 1982, p. 76).

Robert Assagioli (1965, 1973) also emphasized the spiritual dimension in his approach known as *psychosynthesis.* His understanding of the human psyche included the constructs of "higher unconscious" or "superconscious" as the source of creativity and spirituality. In Assagioli's view, some psychological disturbances are best understood as crises of spiritual awakening rather than symptoms of psychopathology. In such cases, the responsibility of the therapist is to facilitate the client's exploration of spiritual possibilities while dealing with the difficulties that such awakenings can engender. As Assagioli (1989) defined it, "'spiritual' refers not only to experiences traditionally considered religious but to *all* the states of awareness, all the human functions and activities which have as their common denominator the possession of *values* higher than average" (p. 30).

A third major contributor to early formulations on spirituality and human behavior was Abraham

Maslow, founding father of humanistic psychology. Maslow (1971) described spirituality as an innate and key element in human nature. In his study of optimally functioning people, he characterized people at the top of his hierarchy as "transcendent self-actualizers" and described them as having (among other traits) a more holistic view of life; a natural tendency toward cooperative action; a tendency to be motivated by truth, goodness, and unity; a greater appreciation for peak experiences; an ability to go beyond their ego self to higher levels of identity; and more awareness of the sacredness of every person and every living thing. Maslow later came to believe that even this definition was not adequate to explain the highest levels of human potential. Near the end of his life, he predicted the emergence of a more expansive understanding of human behavior: "a still 'higher' Fourth Psychology; transpersonal, trans-human, centered in the cosmos, rather than in human needs and interests, going beyond humanness, identity, self-actualization, and the like" (as quoted in Wittine, 1987, p. 53).

Describing this evolution of forces within psychology, Au-Deane Cowley (1993, 1996) delineates four major therapeutic approaches that have emerged over the past century, each developed in response to our understanding of human behavior and human needs at the time:

1. **First Force therapies** are based on dynamic theories of human behavior. The prime concern of these therapies is dealing with repression and resolving instinctual conflicts by developing insight.

2. **Second Force therapies** evolved from behavioral theories. These therapies focus on learned habits and seek to remove symptoms through various processes of direct learning.

3. **Third Force therapies** are rooted in existential/humanistic/experiential theories. They help the person deal with existential despair and seek the actualization of the person's potential through techniques grounded in immediate experiencing.

4. **Fourth Force therapies**, based on transpersonal theories, specifically target the spiritual dimension. They focus on helping the person let go of ego attachments—identifications with the mind, body, and social roles—and transcend the self through various spiritually based practices (Cowley, 1996).

The Fourth Force builds upon the previous three forces and thus incorporates existing knowledge concerning human behavior within its framework. What differentiates the Fourth Force—the **transpersonal approach**—from other theoretical orientations is the premise that some states of human consciousness and potential go beyond our traditional views of health and normality. These states explicitly address the spiritual dimension of human existence (Cowley & Derezotes, 1994).

The term *transpersonal* literally means "beyond" or "through" the "persona" or "mask" (Wittine, 1987). When applied to theories of human behavior, transpersonal means going beyond identity tied to the individual body, ego, or social roles to include spiritual experience or higher levels of consciousness. The self is experienced as in unity with all others. A major focus of transpersonal theory is on "humanity's highest potential" (Lajoie & Shapiro, 1992, p. 91). Increasingly, there has been recognition of the relevance of a transpersonal orientation to the realm of everyday life as well, including the "lower end" of human functioning. Thus, transpersonal practice approaches must "include the whole—not just the high end of human experience but the very personal realm of ordinary consciousness as well" (Cortright, 1997, p. 13). There are several branches of transpersonal thought that are currently recognized, including Jungian psychology; depth or archetypal psychology; spiritual psychology; positive psychology; psychosynthesis; and approaches based on the writings of Abraham Maslow, Stanislav Grof, Ken Wilber, Michael Washburn, Frances Vaughan, Roger Walsh, Jorge Ferrer, and Charles Tart, among others. A major objective of all transpersonal theories is to integrate spirituality within a larger framework of human behavior. One key application of transpersonal theory is as a conceptual underpinning for theories that address spiritual development.

Two theorists who have developed comprehensive perspectives on spiritual development are James Fowler and Ken Wilber. Although these two theorists are not the only contributors to this area, they have produced two of the best-known approaches in the field today. The following sections give an overview of these two theories of spiritual development, providing key concepts and discussion of their respective models. Along the way, we will consider the people you read about in the case studies at the beginning of this chapter and see how these two perspectives enhance our understanding of their current life situations and spiritual journeys.

Fowler's Stages of Faith Development

James Fowler's (1981, 1995) theory of faith development grew out of 359 in-depth interviews conducted between 1972 and 1981 in Boston, Chicago, and Toronto. The sample was overwhelmingly White (97.8%), largely Christian (over 85%), evenly divided

| Developmental perspective |

by gender, and widely distributed in terms of age (3.5 years to 84 years). Each semi-structured interview consisted of more than 30 questions about life-shaping experiences and relationships, present values and commitments, and religion. After the responses were analyzed, interviewees were placed in one of 6 **faith stages.** Fowler found a generally positive relationship between age and stage development; as age increased, so did the tendency for persons to be in higher stages. However, only a minority of persons revealed characteristics of Stages 5 or 6, regardless of age.

To Fowler (1996), **faith** is broader than religious faith, creed, or belief. It can, in fact, be expressed even by people who do not believe in God. Instead, faith is viewed as a universal aspect of human existence,

> an integral, centering process, underlying the formation of beliefs, values, and meanings that (1) gives coherence and direction to people's lives, (2) links

them in shared trusts and loyalties with others, (3) grounds their personal stances and communal loyalties in a sense of relatedness to a larger frame of reference, and (4) enables them to face and deal with the limited conditions of life, relying upon that which has the quality of ultimacy in their lives. (p. 56)

Thus, Fowler's definition of faith is more aligned with the definition of spirituality given at the beginning of this chapter and is clearly distinguished from more specific notions of particular beliefs or religious traditions.

Another important concept in Fowler's theory is the **ultimate environment** (also known as the ultimate reality or simply the ultimate)—the highest level of reality. Faith is not only your internal image of the ultimate environment, but also your relationship with that image. Your view of the ultimate environment—as personal or impersonal, trustworthy or not dependable, capable of dialogue or silent, purposeful or based on chance—and your relationship with it is an evolving, dynamic process that is strongly influenced by your experiences throughout the life course. Thus, Fowler's faith is best understood as a verb, or a way of being, versus a noun, or a thing that is unchangeable.

Fowler's stages of faith development should not be viewed as goals to be achieved or as steps necessary for "salvation." Rather, they help us understand a person's values, beliefs, and sense of meaning and help us better appreciate the tasks, tensions, and challenges at various points in life. They also reveal increasing capacity in terms of cognitive functioning; moral reasoning; perspective taking; critical reflection and dialectical thought; understanding of symbols, myths, and rituals; deeper faith commitments; and openness to and acceptance of difference. Here is a brief description of Fowler's faith stages:

Pre-stage: Primal Faith (infancy): If consistent nurturance is experienced, the infant develops a sense of trust and safety about the universe and the divine. Negative experiences produce images of the ultimate as untrustworthy, punitive, or arbitrary.

Stage 1: Intuitive-Projective Faith (early childhood, beginning about age 2): The young child's new tools of speech and symbols give rise to fluid and magical thoughts, based on intuition and imagination. Faith is fantasy-filled and imitative and can be powerfully influenced by examples, actions, stories of significant others, and familial and cultural taboos.

Stage 2: Mythic-Literal Faith (middle childhood, beginning about age 6 and beyond): The child begins to take on stories, beliefs, and practices that symbolize belonging to his or her community. There is a high degree of conformity to community beliefs and practices. The ability to participate in concrete operational thinking allows distinction between fantasy and reality. There is increased capacity to take the perspective of others, and ideas about reciprocity and fairness become central.

Stage 3: Synthetic-Conventional Faith (adolescence and beyond): For many adolescents, the capacity for abstract thinking and manipulation of concepts affects the process of developing faith as well as overall identity. Authority is perceived as external and is found in traditional authority figures, but there is an increased influence of peers, school and work associates, the media, and popular culture. Beliefs and values are often deeply felt, but not critically examined or systematically reflected on. Symbols are not perceived as literally as in Stage 2.

Stage 4: Individuative-Reflective Faith (young adulthood and beyond): Beginning in young adulthood, many people experience an increased responsibility for their own commitments, lifestyles, beliefs, and attitudes. Previously held creeds, symbols, and stories are demythologized through critical analysis. The ultimate becomes more explicit and personally meaningful, and symbols are reshaped into more powerful conceptualizations.

Stage 5: Conjunctive Faith (midlife and beyond): A minority of adults begin in midlife to rework the past and become open to voices of the "deeper self." They develop the capacity for "both/and" versus "either/or" thinking and come to tolerate ambiguity and paradox, taking into account and looking for balance in such polarities as independence and connection and determinism and free will. They recognize that there are many truths and engage in critical examination of their own beliefs, myths, and prejudices. They expand their definition of community and their sense of connection and responsibility to others.

Stage 6: Universalizing Faith (midlife and beyond): A very small minority of adults develop the capacity to truly embrace paradox. They develop an enlarged awareness of justice and injustice. The vision of truth is expanded to recognize partial truths. Symbols, myths, and rituals are appreciated and cherished at a deeper level. Divisions within the human family are felt with vivid pain because of the recognition of the possibility of the inclusive union of all beings. They lead selfless lives of service and action for justice. They live sacrificial lives aimed at transformation of humankind.

Now let us consider the stories revealed in the six case studies through the lens of Fowler's faith stages, based on both his early research and later theoretical refinements. In Fowler's model, our early experiences set the stage for later faith development. Given what we know about our six people described in the case studies, it is probably safe to assume that most of them were able to develop at least a "good enough" fund of basic trust and mutuality during the *Pre-stage: Primal Faith* for later development of a relationship with the ultimate. A possible exception to this is Trudy, whose early years were marked by parental substance abuse and violence. It would be important to know when these problems first appeared within her family and how much they interfered with her initial bonding with her mother and father, as these factors would be influential in both her ability to trust and her internal sense of the ultimate as she moves through her life.

None of the six case studies tells us much about the development of early images of the ultimate environment during *Stage 1: Intuitive-Projective Faith*. However, we can speculate that these images were probably drawn from each person's particular faith affiliation. For Caroline, Matthew, and Leon, these initial conceptions of the divine would have been grounded within their particular Christian denominations, while Naomi would have developed her sense of the ultimate as it was reflected in her Jewish faith. Caroline's partner in the comparative religions class exercise would most likely have developed her sense of the divine based on examples, modes, actions, and stories that she experienced

in her family's belief in Islam. Jean-Joseph's sense of the ultimate would have been influenced by a combination of Catholic symbols, narratives, and rituals, and the spiritual beliefs and practices of Vodoun. Trudy was not raised in any particular faith tradition, but found her solace in nature. It would be important to talk with her about how these early experiences affected her sense of the sacred and to not assume that her lack of exposure to organized religion meant that she had no early images or experiences with the ultimate, as spirituality is experienced and expressed through both religious and nonreligious means. In working with all six people, we would want to understand how this process of image making was handled by their families and others in their lives, and how much support they were given for their own intuition and imagination during this time.

If Fowler had interviewed any of the six during middle childhood, they more than likely would have reflected many of the aspects of *Stage 2: Mythic-Literal Faith*. It would be important to understand the role of their childhood spiritual communities in shaping each person's sense of the world and his or her place in it. It would be particularly useful to explore the stories and narratives that they remember from that time, especially as they transmitted values, attitudes, and norms for behavior. For example, discussing with Leon what he understood as his church's core principles relative to sin and redemption would be invaluable in comprehending his current struggle. It would also be important to understand the messages that Caroline received regarding her own religion as the only true faith. For Naomi and Jean-Joseph, it would be key to talk about how their communities handled being believers of a nondominant (or "other") religion, in a culture where Christianity is the dominant faith and is generally seen as "the norm." For all six people, it would be vital to explore what helped create a sense of order and meaning at this stage of life and what provided a sense of guidance and belonging.

The events that occur during adolescence generally have a significant effect on faith development during *Stage 3: Synthetic-Conventional Faith*, as this is the point where people are heavily engaged in the process of identity development, including spiritual identity. It is also a time when the person's world is greatly expanded, bringing diverse and complex ideas and experiences regarding all of life. Adolescents must make coherent meaning from all of the different messages that they receive from family, school, work, media, and the larger sociocultural realm. A person's faith understanding can help synthesize various values and viewpoints and provide a basis for forming a stable identity and worldview. There is a tendency to construct one's faith through conforming to a set of values and beliefs that are most familiar and to defer to whatever authority is most meaningful. As the two people most recently in this life stage, both Caroline and Leon illustrate the strong impetus to form a faith identity that provides a solid sense of self and a feeling of belonging to a particular group. For both of them, the faith of their families and their home churches were highly instrumental in this process. And for both of them, entry into the next stage of life brought questions regarding the beliefs and values of these key social institutions and an urge to explore beyond what they had previously known.

If we look at Caroline's and Leon's lives as they move into *Stage 4: Individuative-Reflective Faith,* we see young people grappling with key questions about themselves and their belief systems. Caroline's experiences at college have opened the door to considering different worldviews, which she handles with an approach-avoidance strategy. On the one hand, she is troubled by her experience with others who believe and practice differently from the way she does, but on the other hand, she is increasingly curious about these differences. For Leon, the struggle is more difficult, as he is attempting to live with values, attitudes, and beliefs that tell him that a core aspect of his identity is unacceptable. For both of these young adults, the task ahead is to construct a unique, individual self (identity) and outlook (**ideology**) from previously held conventional beliefs and develop an approach to faith that is both personal and workable. This requires a level of critical reflection and a capacity to struggle with conflicts and tensions that were not

yet fully developed in the previous stage. As a social worker, you would want to facilitate this process while being mindful of the social work principles of self-determination and empowerment.

Naomi and David provide another example of *Individuative-Reflective Faith,* even though they are considerably older than Caroline and Leon. When they were in their late teens and early twenties, their identity formation led them to a more secular worldview, as Naomi lessened her involvement with her faith and David continued to base his identity and outlook on more humanistic understandings of self and the world. But the creation of a family caused them both to reconsider the role of Judaism in their lives as they realized their desire for a spiritual community. As their children grew, their involvement with their temple has provided the personal and workable framework that is characteristic of this phase. That framework is now being challenged by Naomi's illness and is leading both her and David to a deeper reflection of their faith. Social work with this couple would involve supporting this reflection, as well as exploring with them possible supports they could receive from their rabbi and larger faith community in dealing with Naomi's health crisis.

According to Lownsdale (1997), only 1 in 6 adults reflects characteristics of *Stage 5: Conjunctive Faith.* Of our six life stories, only Matthew's provides glimpses of this faith stage. Although there is not much information about Matthew's internal reflection on the paradoxes of life (a key criterion of *Conjunctive Faith*), we do know that he was able to work through the loss of his wife, and other losses that inevitably come with aging, to embrace a new chapter in his life. As a social worker, it would be useful to explore with Matthew his understanding of life's paradoxes (such as God being both personal and abstract, and life being both rational and mysterious), and talk with him about any previously unrealized parts of himself that are now emerging. What is apparent in Matthew's story is his enthusiastic willingness to acknowledge and honor multiple faith perspectives, while being open to new depths within his own spirituality. We also see him engaging in service for others and concern for the natural world. All of these activities suggest a perspective that goes beyond egocentric and ethnocentric views to a more **worldcentric** (identification with the entire global human family) and **ecocentric** (identification with the whole ecosphere, of which humans are only one part) way of being in the world. As a result of these commitments, he is experiencing a renewed sense of purpose, meaning, and connection in his life. All of these are characteristic of persons of *Conjunctive Faith,* which brings a broader social consciousness, a passion for social justice, and a wider and deeper understanding of the sacred.

It is clear that none of the six people reflects the self-sacrificial life of Fowler's *Stage 6: Universalizing Faith.* Persons at this stage are exceedingly rare, perhaps 2 to 3 individuals per thousand (Lownsdale, 1997). Given the exceptional nature of such persons, it is not surprising that the six case studies do not reveal examples of this faith stage. Some might point to Trudy's total immersion in spiritual practices as evidence of this stage, but another perspective on her development will be offered later in this chapter during discussion of the second theorist, Ken Wilber, and his integral theory of consciousness.

Finally, we must address Jean-Joseph's spiritual path, which includes a syncretism (combination) of Catholicism and Vodoun, or "serving the spirits." If a social worker embedded in dominant Western culture assessed his faith development solely from the standpoint of this context, he or she may determine that Jean-Joseph falls within an early stage, either *Mythic-Literal* or perhaps even *Intuitive-Projective.* This determination would no doubt lead to a conclusion that this 50-year-old man is an example of underdeveloped faith and may lead to interventions aimed at helping him give up his "primitive and immature" beliefs and practices for a worldview seen as more appropriate for mature adults. If this was the stance taken by a practitioner, he or she would be showing ethnocentric and religiocentric bias, as well as cultural insensitivity. Viewed within his sociocultural context, Jean-Joseph is exhibiting a faith stage that could be more accurately determined to be at least

Synthetic-Conventional, given its congruence with the spiritual beliefs and practices of his Haitian culture. Upon further exploration with him—with an open mind, respect, and humility for the limits of one's knowledge about his religion—a social worker may discover that Jean-Joseph displays characteristics of higher stages of faith development. This highlights the need for social workers to constantly be aware of their own lack of knowledge and their internalized biases when working with religious and spiritual traditions that are unfamiliar to them, in order to engage in culturally sensitive service that is respectful of those traditions (Weaver, 1999).

Wilber's Integral Theory of Consciousness

Ken Wilber first published his transpersonal theory of development in 1977 in *The Spectrum of Consciousness,* but has continued to develop and refine his model in numerous writings. His work reflects a unique integration of biology, history, psychology, sociology, philosophy, and religion.

Developmental perspective

It is rooted in both conventional Western knowledge and contemplative-mystical traditions of Eastern religions and other spiritual perspectives. Wilber currently refers to his approach as an "Integral Theory of Consciousness" (2006). He identifies it as "integral" because it explores human development across **four quadrants** or vantage points (interior-individual, exterior-individual, interior-collective, and exterior-collective), as well as through *three levels of consciousness* (pre-personal, personal, and transpersonal). He posits that human development must be understood through the lenses of subjective awareness of *personal meaning and sense of self* (the interior of individuals), objective knowledge of the *physical body and observable behaviors* (the external part of individuals), intersubjective understanding of *sociocultural values and shared meanings* (the interior of collectives), and interobjective knowledge of *institutional structures and systemic forces* (the external part of collectives). Within each quadrant, the three levels of consciousness unfold in a way that reflects the unique properties of that particular quadrant (see Exhibit 5.4). According to Wilber, integrated knowledge of all of these areas is required for an accurate and complete understanding of human behavior.

Wilber sees the ultimate goal of human development (at the individual and collective levels) as being to evolve to a higher, nondual level of consciousness that is well-integrated into personal and societal functioning. This requires movement through the three stages of spiritual development, marked by increasingly complex, comprehensive, and inclusive understandings of spirituality and expanded consciousness about reality. We will look closer at Wilber's description of transpersonal levels within the *interior of individuals,* as this is a major contribution of his model to theories of spiritual development. But first we need to review some key concepts underpinning integral theory.

As already noted, Wilber agrees with other transpersonal theorists

that consciousness spans from pre-personal to personal to transpersonal (Wilber, 1995, 2000a, 2000b, 2006). This overall spectrum is reflected in the world's major spiritual traditions and is referred to as the "great chain of being" (matter to body to mind to soul to spirit). Wilber points out that because this process is not strictly a linear one, it is best understood as a "great nest of being" in that it is really a series of enfolding and unfolding spheres or spirals. In other words, spirit transcends but includes soul, which transcends but includes mind, which transcends but includes body, which transcends but includes matter. This process of incorporation is rooted in the concept of a *holon,* or "that which, being a *whole* in one context, is simultaneously a *part* in another" (Wilber, 1995, p. 18). Thus, Wilber refers to his spectrum of consciousness

Exhibit 5.4   Wilber's Integral Theory: Four Quadrants and Three Levels of Consciousness

	Interior	Exterior
Individual	Upper Left Quadrant	Upper Right Quadrant
	(Individual Interior)	(Individual Exterior)
	"I"	"IT"
	INTENTIONAL	BEHAVIORAL
	(Personal meaning and sense of self)	(Physical body and observable behaviors)
	subjective truthfulness	*objective truth*
Collective	Lower Left Quadrant	Lower Right Quadrant
	(Collective Interior)	(Collective Exterior)
	"WE"	"ITS"
	CULTURAL	SOCIAL
	(Culture and shared values)	(Institutions, systems, nature)
	intersubjective justness	*intersubjective functional fit*

SOURCES: Wilber (1996, 2006).

as a *holarchy* (rather than a hierarchy), because it reflects an ordering of holons (or increasing levels of complexity and wholeness) throughout the developmental process. It may be helpful to visualize this as a set of Russian nesting dolls, with each larger doll both including and going beyond the smaller ones. With each larger level (or doll), one expands his or her awareness of reality and develops a larger repertoire of individual and social functioning.

There are five major components relative to the development of interior individual consciousness in Wilber's theory. The following gives an overview of each of these components, leading to a more detailed discussion of the higher or transpersonal levels of consciousness.

1. **Levels** (or waves) **of consciousness** refers to various developmental milestones that unfold within the human psyche. As our discussion of holarchy suggests, this is not a strictly linear process. Rather, it involves "all sorts of regressions, spirals, temporary leaps forward, peak experiences, and so on" (Wilber, 1996, p. 148). A person does not have to master all the competencies of one level to move on to the next; in fact, most people at any given level will often respond about 50% from one level, 25% from the level above, and 25% from the level below. However, levels cannot be skipped over, as each level incorporates the capacities of earlier levels. Drawing from various cross-cultural sources, Wilber posits several major levels of consciousness, all of which are *potentials*—but not *givens*—at the onset of development. We will consider these in more detail following introduction of the other major components.

2. Multiple **lines** (or streams) **of consciousness** flow through the basic levels of consciousness. Wilber (2000a) identifies the following developmental lines as areas for which we have empirical evidence: "morals, affects, self-identity, psychosexuality, ideas of the good, role taking, socio-emotional capacity, creativity, altruism, several lines that can be called 'spiritual' (care, openness, concern, religious faith, meditative stages), joy,

communicative competence, modes of space and time, death-seizure, needs, worldviews, logico-mathematical competence, kinesthetic skills, gender identity, and empathy" (p. 28). He proposes that these lines or streams are relatively independent of one another in that they can develop at different rates within the same individual. Thus, a person can be at a relatively high level of development in some lines (such as cognition), medium in others (such as morals), and low in still others (such as spirituality). Thus, although most *individual* lines unfold sequentially, *overall development* does not, and can be a relatively uneven process.

3. Wilber also includes in his model **states of consciousness,** which include both ordinary (e.g., waking, sleeping, dreaming) and non-ordinary experiences (e.g., peak experiences, religious experiences, altered states, and meditative or contemplative states). He points out that research has shown that a person at virtually any *level* of consciousness can have an altered *state* of consciousness, including a peak or spiritual experience. Whatever the actual experience, individuals can only interpret these experiences at their current level of consciousness and may have to grow and develop further to really accommodate the full depth or meaning of the experience. In order for these *temporary* experiences or states to become *permanent* aspects of a person's level of consciousness, they must become fully realized through continual development.

4. Wilber proposes that levels, lines, and states of consciousness are all navigated by the self or **self-system.** He posits that there are at least two parts to the self: (a) an observing self (an inner subject or watcher) and (b) an observed self (the object that is watched and can be known in some way). As a person negotiates each unfolding *level* and various *lines* of consciousness and integrates experiences from various *states* of consciousness, he or she moves from a narrower to a deeper and wider sense of self and self-identity.

5. At each point of development, the self goes through a **fulcrum,** or switch point. Specifically,

each time the self moves to a different level on the developmental spiral, it goes through a three-step process. First, the self becomes comfortable and eventually identifies with the basic functioning of that level. Second, new experiences begin to challenge the way of being at this level, and the self begins to differentiate or "dis-identify" with it. Third, the self begins to move toward and identify with the next level while integrating the functioning of the previous basic structure into the sense of self. If the person is able to negotiate these fulcrum points successfully, development is largely non-problematic. However, disturbances at different fulcrum points tend to produce various pathologies.

As noted earlier, Wilber's spectrum of consciousness can be further categorized into the three phases of development: the Pre-personal (Pre-egoic) phase, the Personal (Egoic) phase, and the Transpersonal (Transegoic) phase. The specific levels of consciousness at both the Pre-personal and Personal phases in Wilber's theory are very similar to the first five of Fowler's faith stages and will not be presented in detail here. (See Wilber [1995, 1996, 1997a, 1997b] for a detailed discussion of these levels.) A review of the levels of Pre-personal and Personal phases of consciousness should sound familiar to students of conventional approaches to human development. In contrast, the levels of the Transpersonal phase (and the language used to describe them) are most likely unfamiliar to those who are not well versed in contemplative Eastern ideas about human development. However, this synthesis of both conventional and contemplative approaches and the inclusion of higher-order levels of development is Wilber's primary contribution to our attempts to understand human behavior.

As one moves into the Transpersonal or Transegoic phase, the world and life in general are perceived in more holistic and interconnected terms. There is movement from an egocentric and ethnocentric perspective to a worldcentric and eco-centric grasp of the complete interdependence of all things in the cosmos. There is also the realization that the self is more than a body, mind, and culture-bound social roles, and awareness that there is a self that exists beyond time-space limits or ego boundaries. This realization facilitates a growing awareness of how all beings are unified within a singular or nondual ultimate reality. As people move further into the Transpersonal or Transegoic phase, they retain all the capacities developed during previous levels and incorporate these functions into expanded consciousness experienced at higher, transpersonal levels. The three Transpersonal levels are described below. As you read through each one, focus on what the descriptions are saying about a person's *level of consciousness* at each level. In other words, what is the person perceiving or what is he or she aware of beyond the ordinary states of reality (waking, sleeping, dreaming) that are common to most people?

Level 7 (Psychic) is characterized by a continuing evolution of consciousness as the observing self develops more and more depth. Wilber refers to this evolving inner sense as the *Witness,* because it represents an awareness that moves beyond ordinary reality (sensorimotor, rational, existential) into the transpersonal (beyond ego) levels. A distinguishing spiritual experience at this level is a strong interconnectedness of self with nature. For example, a person may temporarily become one with a mountain or bird or tree. This type of experience is not psychotic fusion—the person is still very clear about his or her own personal boundaries—but it is a strong awareness of communion with the natural world. At this point, one's higher self becomes a *World Soul* and experiences *nature mysticism.* Because of this powerful experience of connection and identification, there is a natural deepening of compassion for all living things, including nature itself.

Level 8 (Subtle) is characterized by an awareness of more subtle processes than are commonly experienced in gross, ordinary states of waking consciousness. Examples of such processes are interior light and sounds; awareness of transpersonal archetypes; and extreme states of bliss, love, and compassion. At this point, even nature is transcended, yet it is understood as a manifest expression of the ultimate. One's sense of connection and identification is extended to communion with the Deity, or union with God, by whatever name. Thus, consciousness at this level is not just nature mysticism—union with the natural world—but gives way to *deity mysticism.* This level of consciousness can be experienced in many forms, often rooted in the person's personal or cultural history. For example, a Christian may feel union with Christ, while a Buddhist might experience connection with the Buddha.

Level 9 (Causal) transcends all distinctions between subject and object (even self and God). The Witness is experienced as pure consciousness and pure awareness, prior to the manifestation of anything. Thus, this level is said to be timeless, spaceless, and objectless. As Wilber (1996) describes it, "Space, time, objects—all of those merely parade by. But you are the Witness, the pure Seer that is itself pure Emptiness, pure Freedom, pure Openness, the great Emptiness through which the entire parade passes, never touching you, never tempting you, never hurting you, never consoling you" (p. 224). This level is pure *formless mysticism,* in that all objects, even God as a perceived form, vanish into pure consciousness. This level of consciousness is sometimes referred to as "full Enlightenment, ultimate release, pure nirvana" (Wilber, 1996, p. 226). But it is still not the final story.

Wilber also proposes a *Level 10 (Nondual),* which is characterized by dis-identification with even the Witness. The interior sense of *being* a Witness disappears, and the Witness turns out to be everything that is witnessed. At this level, Emptiness becomes pure Consciousness itself. There is no sense of two, there is only one (hence the name Nondual). Essentially, the person's awareness has moved beyond nature, Deity, and formless mysticism to *nondual mysticism.* Furthermore, it is not really a level among other levels, but is rather the condition or reality of *all* levels. It is simultaneously the source, the process, and the realization of consciousness. Wilber does not depict the Nondual as a separate level in his illustration of the structures of consciousness, because it represents the ground or origin of all the other levels—the paper on which the figure is drawn.

With this model, Wilber is proposing that the Personal phase of development, with its achievement of strong ego development and self-actualization, is not the highest potential of human existence, although a necessary point along the way. Rather, the ultimate goal of human development is the Transpersonal or Transegoic phase—beyond ego or self to self-transcendence and unity with the ultimate reality. The capacity for attaining the highest levels of consciousness is innate within each human being, although Wilber acknowledges that very few people reach the higher transpersonal levels.

As for the characteristic pathologies, or problems in development at each level, all the disorders or conditions that Wilber identifies at the lower phases of development are well recognized within conventional diagnostic approaches (albeit with different labels). It is again at the Transpersonal phase that Wilber strikes new ground, by including what he calls psychic disorders and subtle or causal pathologies. Examples of such problems in living include unsought spiritual awakenings, psychic inflation, split life goals, integration-identification failure, pseudo nirvana, and failure to differentiate or integrate. Wilber states that although these conditions are not well-known, because most people do not reach these higher levels of development, they must be understood in order to be treated properly when they do occur.

Likewise, the treatment modalities that Wilber identifies at the Pre-personal and Personal phases are well-known to most social workers. However, the approaches that Wilber proposes for Transpersonal phase disorders—nature mysticism, deity mysticism, and formless mysticism—are largely unknown (and sound a bit strange) to the majority of helping professionals. But they have been used in non-Western cultures for centuries. Furthermore, they are becoming more widely accepted in the United States as effective, complementary treatment approaches (e.g., prayer and meditation, yoga, visualization and spiritual imagery, focusing, dreamwork, dis-identification techniques, bodywork, acupuncture, journaling, intuition techniques). Wilber (1996, 2000a) stresses that practitioners should be able to correctly identify the level of development in order to provide the most appropriate treatment. If not correctly identified, there is the probability of what Wilber (1995, 2000b) calls the "pre/trans fallacy," which occurs when a problem at a Transpersonal level (such as a spiritual awakening) may be treated as if it were a Pre-personal or Personal disorder (a psychotic episode or existential crisis), or vice versa.

Let's revisit Trudy's story to better understand what Wilber is talking about here. Trudy is currently focusing most of her time and energy toward developing her spiritual self in order to achieve enlightenment. She is meditating 5 hours a day, is engaged with a daily yoga practice, and limits her reading and interpersonal contacts to those that she identifies as spiritual. Given that most transpersonal theorists and spiritual leaders would agree that engagement in some type of spiritual practice is necessary for spiritual growth, one might characterize Trudy's behavior as that of a disciplined, spiritual seeker. But there is evidence in her story that Trudy is caught up in **spiritual bypassing,** a term first coined by John Welwood (2000), which he describes as "the tendency to use spiritual practice to bypass or avoid dealing with certain personal or emotional 'unfinished business'" (p. 11). He states that persons who are struggling with life's developmental challenges are particularly susceptible to spiritual bypassing, as they attempt to *find themselves by giving themselves up*—or prematurely trying to move beyond their ego to self-transcendence, ignoring their personal and emotional needs. This attempt to create a new "spiritual" identity in order to avoid the pain of working through unresolved psychosocial issues does not work and frequently causes additional problems. As Trudy's social worker, you would want to do a thorough assessment, taking into account the substantial unresolved trauma and losses in her life. To ignore these issues and focus only on supporting her quest for enlightenment would be to commit Wilber's "pre/trans fallacy." As a responsible and ethical social worker, you

would help her address these unresolved issues at the personal, and perhaps even pre-personal, level while maintaining respect for her spiritual perspective. You would also help her discern the appropriate role of her spiritual practices in support of her overall growth and development. Consulting with a spiritual teacher or a transpersonal practitioner, with Trudy's permission, also might be helpful in this case.

Likewise, if a practitioner identifies a client's spiritual practices as signs of a serious problem simply because they are unfamiliar or seem "strange," he or she would be moving to the other side of the "pre/trans fallacy"—treating potentially spiritual or transpersonal experiences as if they were psychological disorders. The potential for this type of error is evident in the case of Jean-Joseph and his family. If this family sought help from conventional health care services, while also following traditional spiritually based healing processes, as a social worker your task would be to help the family and the medical professionals find a way to work together. This is not always an easy task, as is poignantly illustrated in Anne Fadiman's (1998) book, *The Spirit Catches You and You Fall Down*, which tells the tragic story of a Hmong child with epilepsy who becomes brain dead because of the failure of professionals to understand unfamiliar spiritual worldviews and negotiate cultural differences. This true account highlights the critical need for social workers to develop the knowledge, values, and skills of spiritually sensitive practice in order to serve clients from diverse spiritual traditions.

Summary and Critique of Fowler's and Wilber's Theories

Both Fowler's and Wilber's models of individual spiritual development reflect Fourth Force theory in that they incorporate the first three forces (dynamic, behavior, and existential/humanistic/experiential theories). In fact, Fowler and Wilber use many of the same theorists as foundations for their own work (e.g., Piaget, Kohlberg, Maslow), and both are delineating higher and more transcendent levels of human development than have been previously proposed by Western theories. In later writings, both theorists also offer additional conceptual formulations at the larger sociocultural levels (Fowler, 1996; Wilber, 2000b).

The major difference between the two models in terms of individual development is that Wilber provides more substance and specification than Fowler does about what transpersonal levels of development look like and how they evolve. Wilber also provides more detailed descriptions of the potential pitfalls of spiritual development than Fowler, who provides only a general overview of the possible dangers or deficits of development at each of his faith stages. However, Fowler provides more specification about the content and process of spiritual development at the Pre-personal and Personal phases. In terms of their utility for social work practice, we could say that Fowler's model is more *descriptive* and Wilber's is more *prescriptive*. Both theories have been critiqued in a number of areas. An overview of these critiques is presented next.

First, as developmental models, Fowler's and Wilber's models are open to the criticisms of all developmental perspectives, including charges of dominant group bias. Such perspectives do not pay enough attention to social, economic, political, and historical factors and the role of power dynamics and oppression in human development. Developmental perspectives are also said to convey the idea that there is only one right way to proceed down the developmental path, and thus display an ethnocentrism often rooted in middle-class, heterosexual, Anglo-Saxon male life experience.

Both Fowler and Wilber might counter by pointing out that familial, cultural, and historical contexts are considered in their models. Wilber, in particular, would highlight the extensive use of cross-cultural knowledge in the development of his theory and point to the cessation of ethnocentrism as a major characteristic of his later stages of consciousness. He would also stress the integral nature of his more current theoretical developments, which pay equal attention to *exterior* impacts on spiritual development as to *interior* aspects (Wilber, 2000b,

Conflict perspective

2001, 2006). Both theorists would also support the notion of many paths in spiritual development, although they would say that these many paths have common features in their evolution.

A second critique of both theories is their relative lack of attention to the spiritual capacities and potentialities of children, focusing more on the emergence of spiritual issues in adulthood. This is due to the assertion that higher levels of cognitive functioning (capacity for formal operations and abstract thought) are necessary to fully experience and incorporate spiritual experience. A number of writers have contested this assertion, proposing that childhood is a unique time of enhanced, not diminished, spiritual awareness (R. Coles, 1990; Hay, Nye, & Murphy, 1996; S. Levine, 1999; R. Nye & Hay, 1996). They base this viewpoint on in-depth interviews with children, which often revealed a richness and depth regarding spirituality that is generally not expected of people of this age (see Hay & Nye, 2006). They point to a variety of spiritual experiences and epiphanies that the children shared with them, including archetypical mythical dreams; visionary experiences; profound insights about self-identity, life, and death; and heightened capacities for compassion for all living things. Interestingly, results from a recent national survey of seasoned social workers who work with children and adolescents reveal that practitioners generally see the relevance of religion and spirituality in the lives of children and that they encounter youth who present spiritual issues in practice (Kvarfordt & Sheridan, 2007).

Wilber (2000a) concedes that children can have a variety of spiritual experiences, including peak experiences that provide glimpses of the Transpersonal realm, but he states that these incidents are experienced and incorporated within the child's Pre-personal or Personal stage of development. Regardless of the particular developmental level, there clearly is a need for further exploration of children's spirituality in order to understand their unique spiritual experiences, developmental processes, and needs. Similarly, there is also a need to revisit assumptions about the spiritual experiences and capacities of adults who have lower cognitive functioning, either congenitally or as a result of injury.

A third critique concerns empirical investigation of the theories. Although Fowler's model was developed through an inductive research process and Wilber's formulations are grounded in a synthesis of many lines of research, there is a need for empirical verification of both models. Limited empirical exploration of Fowler's faith stages has provided partial support for his framework (Das & Harries, 1996; Furushima, 1983; Mischey, 1981; Swenson, Fuller, & Clements, 1993), while a number of research projects are currently underway as part of Wilber's Integral Institute. The fact that such research is still in its beginning stage is somewhat understandable, given the difficulties of empirical investigation in such an abstract realm. It is difficult enough to operationalize and measure such concepts as formal operational cognition or self-esteem; the challenge of investigating transcendence is even more daunting. Nonetheless, strategies from both positivist and constructivist research approaches are currently available to study interior states and subjective experiences of meaning as well as biophysical manifestations of different states of consciousness. (See Chapters 1 and 2 for a review of positivist and constructivist research approaches.) As is true for all theories of human behavior, transpersonal models such as Fowler's and Wilber's need to be specifically tested and refined through the research process. This research also must be replicated with different groups (defined by sex and gender, age, race, ethnicity, socioeconomic status, geopolitical membership, and the like) in order to explore the universality of the models.

In conclusion, both Fowler and Wilber provide perspectives beyond our traditional biopsychosocial framework that allow us to better understand human development and functioning, and they suggest a direction for working with people from diverse spiritual perspectives. Their theories are major contributions to human behavior theory. However, we also need viable practice theories and practice models that explicitly address the spiritual dimension. There have been promising developments in this area. Examples include E. D. Smith's (1995) transegoic model for dealing with death and other losses; Cowley's (1999) transpersonal approach for working with couples and families; Hickson and Phelp's (1998) model for facilitating women's spirituality; and J. L. Clark's (2007) model for working with spirituality, culture, and diverse worldviews. There are also practice models that directly integrate spirituality within biopsychosocial approaches. Examples are Almaas's (1995, 1996) Diamond approach, which incorporates object relations and body sensing within Sufism, and Grof's (1988, 2003; Grof & Bennett, 1992) Holotropic Breathwork model, which combines bodywork and altered states of consciousness to address unresolved psychological issues from earlier points in development. Finally, Cortright (1997) provides a good overview of how a transpersonal orientation can be generally incorporated within psychoanalytic and existential therapies, and Mikulas (2002) offers a practice approach that integrates a transpersonal perspective with behavioral approaches. All of these developments reflect a synthesis of transpersonal with earlier therapeutic modalities (First, Second, and Third Force therapies). As with human behavior theories of spiritual development, these practice theories and models also must be tested and continually refined to determine their utility and applicability for a wide range of client situations.

> ### Critical Thinking Questions 5.2
>
> Fowler and Wilber both think of spirituality in terms of development to higher levels of faith over time. Do you think this is a helpful way to think about spirituality? Is it a helpful way to think about your own spiritual life? Do you see any cultural biases in either of the theories?

THE ROLE OF SPIRITUALITY IN SOCIAL WORK

Canda and Furman (2010) outline five broad historical phases that trace the development of linkages between spirituality and social work in the United States. An overview of these phases is presented next.

1. *Indigenous Pre-colonial Period:* This period includes the thousands of years when Indigenous cultures in North America employed a variety of spiritually based approaches to healing and mutual support. These practices, which will be discussed in greater detail later in the chapter, focused beyond human welfare to include the well-being of other living beings and the earth itself. Many of these traditional ways continue into the present, both outside of and within social work (Baskin, 2006; Brave Heart, 2001; Bucko & Iron Cloud, 2008; Deloria, 1994).

2. *Sectarian Origins:* This phase began with the colonial period and lasted through the first 20 years of the 20th century. Early human services, institutions, and social welfare policy were significantly influenced by Judeo-Christian worldviews on charity, communal responsibility, and social justice (Fauri, 1988; Leiby, 1985; Lowenberg, 1988; Marty, 1980; Popple & Leighninger, 2005). At this time, there were also competing explanations of human behavior: on the one hand, an emphasis on distinguishing individual moral blame or merit (e.g., the worthy vs. unworthy poor), and on the other hand, a focus on social reform and social justice (e.g., Jewish communal service and Christian social gospel). Human service providers typically had a strong spiritual foundation for their work, but offered service through non-sectarian means (e.g., Jane Addams and the settlement house movement). Indigenous, African American, and Spanish and French Catholic spiritual perspectives also contributed to the evolution of social work during this time frame (E. P. Martin & Martin, 2002; Van Hook, Hugen, & Aguilar, 2001).

3. *Professionalization and Secularization:* Beginning in the 1920s and continuing through the 1970s, social work began to distance itself from its early sectarian roots. This movement mirrored a shift within the larger society, which began to replace moral explanations of human problems with a scientific, rational understanding of human behavior. The social work profession increasingly relied on scientific empiricism and secular humanism as the major foundations for its values, ethics, and practice approaches (Imre, 1984; Siporin, 1986). This period also witnessed social work's reliance on a variety of emerging psychological and sociological theories (such as psychoanalytic, behavioral, and social functionalism), which did not recognize the spiritual dimension as significant for either understanding human behavior or as a focus for practice. However, several religiously affiliated agencies continued to provide social services (e.g., Catholic Social Services, Jewish Family Services, Lutheran Social Services, the Salvation Army). Non-sectarian spiritual influences were also felt, including principles of 12-step programs; humanistic, existential, and Jungian thought; and ideas about human development drawn from Eastern religions (Robbins et al., 2006a).

4. *Resurgence of Interest in Spirituality:* A renewed interest in the spiritual dimension began in the 1980s through 1995 (Canda, 1997; Russel, 1998). Indicators of this new phase within the profession included a marked increase in the numbers of publications and presentations on the topic; the development of a national Society for Spirituality and Social Work (SSSW); and the first national conference on spirituality and social work, held in 1994. As part of this substantial activity, there was infusion of new and diverse perspectives on spirituality that influenced the profession, including Buddhism, Confucianism, Hinduism, Shamanism, Taoism, and transpersonal theory. This period differed from the earlier sectarian period in that it emphasized the need to address spirituality in a way that recognizes the value of diverse spiritual traditions and respects client self-determination (Canda, 1988; Sheridan, Bullis, Adcock, Berlin, & Miller, 1992). This trend toward reexamination and reintegration of spirituality within the profession corresponded with increased interest within the larger culture (Gallup & Lindsay, 1999).

5. *Transcending Boundaries:* From 1995 to the present, the profession has witnessed an elaboration and expansion of prior trends. This includes the reintroduction of references to religion and spirituality in the Council on Social Work Education's (CSWE) 1995 Curriculum

Policy Statement and 2000 Educational Policy and Accreditation Standards after an absence of more than 20 years. The first international conference of the SSSW was held in 2000, with other national and international conferences increasingly including presentations on spirituality (e.g., National Association of Social Workers [NASW], CSWE's Annual Program Meeting, International Federation of Social Workers [IFSW], International Association of Schools of Social Work [IASSW]). The Canadian Society for Social Work was established in 2002 and cohosts conferences with the U.S. SSSW. New postmodern perspectives on spirituality have also entered the arena, including feminist, ecophilosophical, postcolonial, and expanded transpersonal frameworks, which have broadened the focus of spirituality to include all peoples, all nations, all beings, and the planet itself, with special concern for marginalized and oppressed groups (Besthorn, 2001; Canda, 2005; Coates, 2003; Meinert, Pardeck, & Murphy, 1998). There has also been exponential growth in empirical work during this period, including over 50 studies of social work practitioners, faculty, and students (see Sheridan, 2004 and 2009, for reviews of this literature) and growing numbers of studies of social work clients (see, for example, Beitel et al., 2007; Margolin, Beitel, Shuman-Olivier, & Avants, 2006; Nelson-Becker, 2006; C. Stewart, Koeske, & Pringle, 2007). Clearly, the focus has shifted from *whether* the topic should be included in the profession to *how* to integrate spirituality within social work practice in an ethical, effective, and spiritually sensitive manner (Canda & Furman, 2010; Canda, Nakashima, & Furman, 2004; Derezotes, 2006; Sheridan, 2009; Van Hook, Hugen, & Aguilar, 2001).

In regards to social work education, two major rationales have been proposed for including content on spirituality within undergraduate and graduate studies. Studies of social work educators (Sheridan, Wilmer, & Atcheson, 1994) and students (Sheridan & Amato-von Hemert, 1999) reveal general endorsement of these two rationales, as reflected in the following statements:

- Religious and spiritual beliefs and practices are part of multicultural diversity. Social workers should have knowledge and skills in this area in order to work effectively with diverse client groups (90% of educators "strongly agree/agree"; 93% of students "strongly agree/agree").
- There is another dimension of human existence beyond the biopsychosocial framework that can be used to understand human behavior. Social work education should expand this framework to include the spiritual dimension (61% of educators "strongly agree/agree"; 72% of students "strongly agree/agree").

A number of publications address the relevance of spirituality for the profession in these two domains, and the range of this literature has become extensive. Thus, the following sections provide examples of writings that examine the role of spirituality relative to human diversity or the human condition. Readers are encouraged to use these as a starting place for further exploration.

Spirituality and Human Diversity

Commitment to issues of human diversity and to oppressed populations is a hallmark of the social work profession. At various times in history, some branches of organized religion have played

| Conflict perspective |

a negative or impeding role in the attainment of social justice for various groups. Examples include the use of religious texts, policies, and practices to deny the full human rights of persons of color; women; and gay, lesbian, bisexual, and transgendered persons. At the same time, organized religion has a rich heritage of involvement in myriad social justice causes and movements, including the civil rights movement, the peace movement, the women's movement, the gay rights movement, abolition of the death penalty, the antipoverty movement, and the deep ecology movement.

It is beyond the scope of this chapter to do an overall analysis of the role of religion in the struggle for social and economic justice. However, the following sections provide examples of the impact of both religious and nonreligious spirituality in the lives of oppressed groups as defined by race and ethnicity, sex and gender, sexual orientation, and other forms of human diversity.

Race and Ethnicity

Spirituality expressed in both religious and nonreligious forms has been pivotal in the lives of many persons of color and other marginalized ethnic groups. This brief discussion of spirituality and race/ethnicity emphasizes common experiences and themes in order to provide a general overview. However, remember that a great deal of diversity exists within these groups and that every person's story will be unique.

African Americans. Religious affiliation for African Americans is generally high, and this racial group is most likely to report a specific affiliation. Data from the General Social Surveys from 1972 to 2004 show the majority of African Americans as Protestant (75.7%), followed by Catholic (6.5%), and Jewish (less than 1%). Seven percent reported some other type of affiliation, and 10.6% do not identify with a religious group (*A Guide to African Americans and Religion,* 2007). African Americans account for about one-fourth of adherents to Islam in the United States (Pew Forum, 2008), including membership in Sunni Islam or other mainstream Islamic denominations, the Nation of Islam, or smaller Black Muslim sects (Haddad, 1997). Black churches, in particular, have historically been a safe haven for African Americans facing racism and oppression, as well as an important source of social support, race consciousness and inspiration, leadership training, human services, and empowerment and social change (R. M. Franklin, 1994; S. L. Logan, 2001; R. J. Taylor, Ellison, Chatters, Levin, & Lincoln, 2000). The legacy of slavery and the integrated heritage of African and African American spiritual values have emphasized collective unity and the connection of all beings (Nobles, 1980, p. 29). Afrocentric spirituality stresses the interdependence among God,

community, family, and the individual. Its central virtues include beneficence to the community, forbearance through tragedy, wisdom applied to action, creative improvisation, forgiveness of wrongs and oppression, and social justice (Paris, 1995). *Kwanzaa* is an important nonsectarian Afrocentric spiritual tradition, which was developed by Maulana Karenga in the 1960s as a mechanism for celebrating and supporting African and African American strengths and empowerment. Seven principles represent the core values of Kwanzaa: Umoja (Unity), Kujichagulia (Self-Determination), Ujima (Collective Work and Responsibility), Ujamaa (Collective Economics), Nia (Purpose), Kuumba (Creativity), and Imani (Faith) (Karenga, 1995). Many writers stress the importance of paying attention to the role of spirituality in its various forms when working with African American clients, families, and communities (see, for example, Banerjee & Canda, 2009; Burke, Chauvin, & Miranti, 2005; D. R. Freeman, 2006; C. Stewart et al., 2007).

Latino(a) Americans. This category includes people with ties to 26 countries in North, South, and Central America; the Caribbean; and Europe (Spain). Thus, the categorizing of these peoples under a reductionist label such as Latino(a) or Hispanic denies the considerable diversity within this population. Keeping this in mind, the majority (58%) of Latino(a) Americans are Roman Catholic, but there is also a large and growing number (23%) of Protestants among this group. Almost 5% report other religious affiliations, including Muslim and Jewish, and 14% are unaffiliated (Pew Forum, 2008). In addition, many Latino(a) people follow beliefs and practices that represent a blending of Christian, African, and Indigenous spiritual traditions (Castex, 1994; Canda & Furman, 2010). Latino(a) American spirituality has been strongly affected by factors related to colonialism (Costas, 1991). This history includes military, political, economic, cultural, and religious conquest, forcing many Indigenous peoples to take on the Catholicism of their conquerors. Many traditional places of worship, spiritual texts, beliefs, and practices were destroyed, repressed, or blended with Catholic traditions (Canda & Furman, 2010). Today, Christian Latino(a) faith has several central features: a personal relationship with God that encompasses love and reverence as well as fear and dread; an emphasis on both faith and ritual behavior; belief in the holiness of Jesus Christ as savior, king, and infant God; special reverence shown to Mary as the mother of God; recognition of saints as models of behavior and as benefactors; significance of sacred objects as both symbols of faith and transmitters of luck or magic; and special events and celebrations, such as saints' feast days, Holy Week, Christmas Eve, feasts of the Virgin, and life passages (e.g., baptisms, first communions, confirmations, coming-of-age ceremonies, weddings, and funerals) (Aguilar, 2001; Ramirez, 1985). In addition to mainstream religions, a number of African and Indigenous spiritual healing traditions continue to be practiced by some Latino(a) groups today, including curanderismo, santiguando, espiritismo, Santeria, and Vodoun (M. Delgado, 1988; Paulino, 1995; Torrez, 1984). Social workers need to understand the importance of both religious institutions and folk healing traditions when working with Latino(a) populations. These various expressions of spirituality serve as important sources for social support, coping strategies, means of healing, socialization and maintenance of culture, and resources for human services and social justice efforts (Burke et al., 2005; M. Delgado & Humm-Delgado, 1982; Faver & Trachte, 2005; Paulino, 1998).

Asian Americans and Pacific Islanders. This population represents many different cultures, including Chinese, Filipino, Japanese, Korean, Asian Indian, Vietnamese, Hawaiian, Cambodian, Laotian, Thai, Hmong, Pakistani, Samoan, Guamanian, Indonesian, and others (Healey, 2010). These different peoples are affiliated with a wide range of spiritual traditions, including Hinduism, Buddhism, Islam, Confucianism, Sikhism, Zoroastrianism, Jainism, Shinto, Taoism, and Christianity (Tweed, 1997). In the United States, recent data show that 27% of this group is Protestant, 17% Catholic, 14% Hindu, 9% Buddhist, and 4% Muslim. Approximately 6% report other religious affiliations, and

23% are unaffiliated (Pew Forum, 2008). There is much diversity within these various religious traditions as well, making it particularly difficult to discuss common elements of spiritual beliefs or practices. However, several themes can be discerned: the connection between and the divinity of all beings; the need to transcend suffering and the material world; the importance of displaying compassion, selflessness, and cooperation; the honoring of ancestors; a disciplined approach to life and spiritual development; and a holistic understanding of existence (Canda & Furman, 1999; D. K. Chung, 2001; R. Singh, 2001). Both religious institutions and traditional practices have been helpful to a variety of Asian and Pacific Islander immigrants and refugees and their descendants. For example, many Southeast Asian refugee communities have established Buddhist temples and mutual assistance associations, which provide social, physical, mental, and spiritual resources (Canda & Phaobtong, 1992; Morreale, 1998; Timberlake & Cook, 1984), and the Korean church has been an essential provider of social services (G. Choi & Tirrito, 1999). Some Asian Americans and Pacific Islanders also use Indigenous healers, such as the Cambodian krou khmer, the Korean mudang, the Hmong spirit medium, and the Hawaiian kahuna (Canda & Furman, 1999; Canda, Shin, & Canda, 1993; D. E. Hurdle, 2002). As with other groups, there is an emerging literature stressing the importance of attending to spirituality in practice with clients from this large and diverse cultural population (Canda, 2001; D. K. Chung, 2001; Hodge, 2004; D. E. Hurdle, 2002; R. Singh, 2001; P. P. Tan, 2006). In addition, several writers have proposed incorporating concepts and practices from Asian spiritual traditions into mainstream social work practice, including meditation (Keefe, 1996; S. L. Logan, 1997), Zen-oriented practice (Brandon, 1976), and yoga (Fukuyama & Sevig, 1999).

Native Americans. Native Americans, or First Nations, people originally numbered in the millions and were members of hundreds of distinct tribes or nations, each with its own language, heritage, and spiritual traditions (Healey, 2010; Swift, 1998). As part of

Photo 5.3 Native American dance is a cultural and highly spiritual form of expression.

rest of life; connection to and responsibility for the Earth and all her creatures; the sacredness of all things, including animals, plants, minerals, and natural forces; the values of balance, harmony, and connectedness; the importance of extended family and community; and the use of myth, ritual, and storytelling as spiritual practices (Duran & Duran, 1995; Matheson, 1996; Yellow Bird, 1995). Many of these values are of increasing appeal to non-Indigenous people, producing great concern among First Nations people regarding appropriation of their customs, ceremonies, rituals, and healing practices (Kasee, 1995; LaDue, 1994). This cross-tradition borrowing of spiritual practices requires sensitivity, respect, competence, and permission in such matters (Canda & Yellow Bird, 1996). Many service providers also call for sensitivity and awareness of the effects of historical trauma on Native Americans and recommend the integration of traditional practices for more effective service delivery (Brave Heart, 2001; Burke et al., 2005; L. A. French & White, 2004; Limb & Hodge, 2008; Skye, 2002; Weaver, 1999). In addition, Indigenous worldviews and spiritual practices have application to social work in general (Canda, 1983; R. W. Voss, Douville, Little Soldier, & Twiss, 1999).

the effort to "humanize and civilize" First Nations people, Congress regularly appropriated funds for Christian missionary efforts beginning in 1819 (U.S. Commission on Human Rights, 1998). American Indian boarding schools were a major component of these efforts, where children were forbidden to wear their native attire, eat their native foods, speak their native language, or practice their traditional religion, and were often severely punished for failure to adhere to these prohibitions (Haig-Brown, 1988; Snipp, 1998). Through a long history of resistance and renewal, however, Indigenous spiritual traditions have persisted and currently are being restored and revitalized (Swift, 1998). Various expressions of First Nations spirituality have several common themes: the inseparability of spirituality from the

It is important to remember the experience of other groups that have been more extensively assimilated into the dominant culture of the United States (e.g., Irish, Italian, and Jewish Americans). Many of these groups also have histories of discrimination and religious intolerance, the effects of which are felt by succeeding generations. Currently, in the decade since the terrorist attacks of September 11, 2001, we in the United States have witnessed increased discrimination and oppressive acts against Muslim Americans, especially those of Middle Eastern descent (Crabtree, Husain, & Spalek, 2008; New York City Commission on Human Rights, 2003). Given this atmosphere and the growing Muslim population within the United States, it is imperative that social workers develop sensitivity and competence in working with Muslim clients (Carolan, Bagherinia, Juhari, Himelright, & Mouton-Sanders, 2000;

Hodge, 2005a). Indeed, social workers must be sensitive to the particular history and spiritual traditions of all racial and ethnic groups.

Sex and Gender

Women are more likely than men to report that they are religious, church-affiliated, and frequent users of prayer; are certain in their belief of God; feel close to God; hold a positive view of their church; and are more religiously engaged (Cornwall, 1989; Felty & Poloma, 1991; Pew Forum, 2008). Women also are the majority of members in most religious bodies in the United States and play important roles in the life of many religious communities (Braude, 1997).

However, in several denominations, women's participation has been significantly restricted, prohibiting them from holding leadership positions or performing certain religious rites and ceremonies (Burke et al., 2005; J. Holm & Bowker, 1994; Reilly, 1995). In addition, women members of traditional Judeo-Christian-Islamic faiths generally experience conceptualizations and symbols of the divine as masculine, suggesting that men are closer to (and thus more like) God than women (Reuther, 1983). In response to this, some scholars are calling for increased ordination of women and more women in leadership positions in order to create a more woman-affirming environment within religious institutions (K. A. Roberts, 2004).

Although most women who belong to mainstream denominations report being generally satisfied with their affiliations (Corbett, 1997), some struggle with the patriarchal aspects of their faith. One study conducted in-depth interviews of 61 women between the ages of 18 and 71 who were affiliated with Catholic, United Methodist, Unitarian Universalist, or Jewish congregations (Ozorak, 1996). Most (93%) perceived gender inequality within their religions. Sixteen percent viewed these inequalities as appropriate, and thus accepted them; 8% left their faith in reaction to this issue and others. The remainder coped by using behavioral strategies (e.g., requesting equal treatment; requesting gender-inclusive language; substituting feminine words, images, or interpretations; participating in feminist activities), cognitive strategies (e.g., focusing on positive aspects of the religion, comparing their faith favorably to others, emphasizing signs of positive change), or a combination of both behavioral and cognitive mechanisms.

Christian and Jewish feminist theologians have made efforts to emphasize the feminine heritage of conventional faiths, and some Christian and Jewish denominations have increased opportunities for women in both lay leadership roles and clerical positions (Canda & Furman, 1999). There also has been a movement toward alternative women's spiritualities. Some women have become involved in spiritual support groups or explored other religious traditions, such as Buddhism (Carnes & Craig, 1998; J. Holm & Bowker, 1994). Others have pursued feminist-identified theology, such as Goddess worship (Bolen, 1984; Christ, 1995; Kruel, 1995), Wicca (Starhawk, 1979; Warwick, 1995), Jewish feminism (Breitman, 1995), or Christian womanist spirituality (M. A. Jackson, 2002). These spiritual traditions emphasize the feminine aspect of the divine; the sacredness of women's bodies, rhythms, and life cycles; the power and creativity of women's spirituality; a connection to earth-centered practices; and the care of all people and the planet (Kidd, 1996; J. G. Martin, 1993; Ochshorn & Cole, 1995; Warwick, 1995). Some men are also turning to alternative spiritual traditions to overcome religious experiences and conceptions of God and masculinity that they feel have been detrimental to them (Kivel, 1991; Warwick, 1995).

Sexual Orientation

Nonheterosexual persons are often linked together as the GLBT community (gay, lesbian, bisexual, and transgendered persons). It should be noted, however, that transgendered persons may identify themselves as heterosexual, bisexual, or homosexual; therefore, transgendered status is a matter of sex and gender, not sexual orientation. However, as a group, transgendered persons have much in common with gay men, lesbians, and bisexual persons when it comes to experiences with oppression, and thus will be included with these groups in this discussion of spirituality.

As an oppressed population, GLBT persons have suffered greatly at the hands of some groups affiliated with organized religion. Some egregious examples are the pronouncement by certain religious leaders that AIDS is a "punishment for the sins" of GLBT persons and the picketing of Matthew Shepard's (victim of an antigay hate crime) funeral by religiously identified individuals. More pervasively, many GLBT members of various faiths have had to struggle with religious teachings that tell them their feelings and behaviors are immoral or sinful.

Every major religious and spiritual tradition has GLBT adherents. Furthermore, there are religious rationales within Christianity, Islam, Judaism, Buddhism, Confucianism, and Taoism for tolerance of nonheterosexual orientations, even though historically these religions have privileged heterosexuality (J. W. Ellison & Plaskow, 2007). There are also associations within every major religion that go beyond tolerance to work for full inclusion of GLBT persons. Examples include the following: Affirmation—United Methodists for Lesbian, Gay, Bisexual & Transgender Concerns; Association of Welcoming & Affirming Baptists; Integrity (Episcopal); Lutherans Concerned; More Light Presbyterians; United Church of Christ Coalition for Lesbian, Bisexual, Gay and Transgender Concerns; World Congress of Gay, Lesbian, Bisexual, and Transgender Jews: Keshet Ga'ayah; Al-Fatiah (Muslim); Gay Buddhist Fellowship; the Gay and Lesbian Vaishnava Association (Hindu); and Seventh Day Adventist Kinship. There are also denominations that generally identify themselves as "open and gay-affirming," including Dignity (Catholic), Metropolitan Community Church (Protestant), Society of Friends (Quakers), United Church of Christ, Unitarian Universalism, and Reform and Reconstructionist branches of Judaism.

GLBT persons who grow up in less tolerant religious communities experience considerable tension between their faith and their sexuality. They, and others close to them, must decide how to respond to this tension. Canda and Furman (2010) identify four alternative ideological responses that are evident within Christianity, but are also applicable to other faiths. The first three refer to the faith's stance on nonheterosexual orientation, and the fourth refers to a possible stance that GLBT persons or GLBT allies may take regarding organized religion:

1. Condemn homosexuality and homosexual persons.

2. Accept homosexual persons, but reject homosexual behavior.

3. Affirm and accept GLBT persons at every level.

4. Reject the faith's position relative to GLBT persons, and depart from the faith.

These four responses have implications for both GLBT persons and social work practitioners. For GLBT persons, involvement with religious institutions characteristic of the first response exacerbates both the direct and internalized oppression that most experience as a result of living in a society that privileges heterosexual orientation and views any other sexual expression as deviant or "less than." At the other end of the spectrum, involvement with congregations that display the third response of affirmation and acceptance would allow the GLBT person to honor both his or her sexual identity and faith commitments. The middle position of accepting the person but rejecting the behavior would most likely maintain the tension and internal conflict that a GLBT person experiences when an important part of his or her identity is "not welcome at the table." The final reaction, leaving one's faith, is unsatisfactory for many GLBT persons who want to be involved with communal religious experiences and desire a spiritual community that is welcoming of their whole self. For others, it represents a choice that is self-affirming and liberating.

Regarding social work practitioners, Canda and Furman (2010) point out that the first response is clearly antithetical to social work values and ethics, while the third position is congruent with ethical standards of practice. The second response brings up questions concerning how this stance will affect the practitioner's work with GLBT clients. It is challenging enough to affirm a positive self-identity and possess confidence and self-assurance as a GLBT person in a heterosexist and homophobic society without experiencing negative attitudes from one's social worker. If the practitioner cannot transmit the level of empathy and respect for GLBT persons and their sexual orientation that is required by the NASW Code of Ethics, referral to another practitioner is warranted. Furthermore, the practitioner needs to engage in a process of reflection and self-examination in order to be able to move toward a more positive and ethical response to GLBT clients. Social workers who themselves have left a faith tradition (the fourth response) due to disagreement with teachings on sexual orientation, or any other issue, also need to be vigilant that they are not transmitting negative and disrespectful attitudes toward religious clients, whether they are GLBT or heterosexual.

It also is important to respect the unique spiritual journeys that individual GLBT persons may take. If you were working with Leon as he struggles with the conflict between his church and his sexual identity, it would be important to work collaboratively with him to discern what option was best for him, providing him information about alternatives while maintaining respect for his self-determination. As Barret and Barzan (1996) point out, regardless of the individual decisions that GLBT persons make regarding religion, the process of self-acceptance is a spiritual journey unto itself.

Other Aspects of Diversity

The issues and implications relative to spirituality that pertain to race and ethnicity, sex and gender, and sexual orientation apply to other forms of human diversity as well. For example, some religious teachings have interpreted disability as a punishment for the sins of the person or family (Miles, 1995; Niemann, 2005), or as a means for nondisabled persons to acquire spiritual status through expressions of pity and charity (Fitzgerald, 1997). Conversely, spirituality has been noted as both a significant means of coping and a vehicle toward positive self-definition for persons with disabilities (Fitzgerald, 1997; Hurst, 2007; Niemann, 2005; Parish, Magana, & Cassiman, 2008; Swinton, 1997).

Spirituality and age is another area that has been widely addressed. Both religious and nonreligious forms of spirituality are important sources of social support for older persons and a pathway for coping, ongoing development, and successful aging (Burke et al., 2005; Hedberg, Brulin, & Alex, 2009; Yoon & Lee, 2004). In addition, spirituality is viewed as an essential foundation for healthy development among young people (Hay & Nye, 2006; Myers, 1997; Roehlkepartain, King, Wagener, & Benson, 2006). Research has shown spirituality to be a significant protective factor against substance abuse, premature sexual activity, and delinquency for children and adolescents (Holder et al., 2000; Johnson, Jang, Larsen, & De Li, 2001; Miller, Davies, & Greenwald, 2000; C. Smith & Denton, 2005). As our understanding of the interaction between religious and nonreligious spirituality and other forms of human diversity increases, social work will be in a better position to work sensitively, competently, and ethically with many diverse groups and communities.

Spirituality and the Human Experience

Social workers deal with every aspect of the human experience. They simultaneously focus on solving problems in living while supporting optimal human functioning and quality of life. The literature regarding spirituality in these two areas is immense, with significant development in social work, psychology, nursing, medicine, rehabilitation counseling, pastoral counseling, marital and family counseling, and other helping disciplines. The following discussion highlights examples of this continually evolving knowledge base. Similar to the previous discussion of spirituality and diversity, readers can use this brief overview as an entry point to this expanding literature.

Problems in Living

It is difficult to find an area related to problems in living in which spirituality is not being explored. For example, much has been written about the link between spirituality and mental health. Various indicators of spirituality—such as religious commitment, involvement in spiritual or religious practices, level of religiosity or spirituality—have been shown to have an inverse relationship with depression, anxiety, hopelessness, suicide, and other mental health problems while showing a positive relationship with self-esteem, self-efficacy, hope, optimism, life satisfaction, and general well-being (Koenig, 2005; Mueller, Plevak, & Rummans, 2001; Pargament, 1997).

Similar influences are found between spirituality and physical health, with spirituality linked to a variety of better health outcomes (C. G. Ellison & Levin, 1998; Koenig, 2001a; Koenig, McCullough, & Larson, 2000; Matthews et al., 1998). Various propositions have been investigated to explain the exact mechanisms of this relationship. Findings suggest that religion and spirituality benefit physical health through their support of health-promoting behaviors and discouragement of risk behaviors, while others indicate possible biological processes that mediate the negative impacts of stress and support healthy immune functioning (Koenig, 1999; P. C. Mueller, Plevak, & Rummans, 2001; O. Ray, 2004; Segerstrom & Miller, 2004). Specific spiritual practices, such as mindfulness-based stress-reduction techniques, have shown positive outcomes in several areas, including chronic pain, anxiety disorders, recurrent depression, psoriasis, and general psychological well-being (Grossman, Niemann, Schmidt, & Walach, 2004; Williams, Teasdale, Segal, & Kabat-Zinn, 2007), as well as benefits to the immune system (Davidson et al., 2003).

For both mental and physical health problems, religion and spirituality have been noted as major

means of coping (Koenig, 2005; Koenig, Larson, & Larson, 2001; Koenig et al., 2000; Pargament, 1997). In an extensive review of the social and behavioral science literature, Oakley Ray (2004) cites spirituality as one of four key factors that are significantly linked to positive coping, along with knowledge, inner resources, and social support. The specific benefits of spiritually based coping include relieving stress, retaining a sense of control, maintaining hope, and providing a sense of meaning and purpose in life (Koenig, 2001b, 2005).

Higher levels of social support through religious and spiritual networks also play a significant role in positive coping with health issues (C. G. Ellison & Levin, 1998; B. G. F. Perry, 1998; Reese & Kaplan, 2000). Both religious and nonreligious forms of spirituality have proven helpful to persons coping with caregiving demands related to health problems of family members (Koenig, 2005; Sanders, 2005; Tolliver, 2001; Vickrey et al., 2007). Similar effects are noted for coping with poverty (Black, 1999; Greeff & Fillis, 2009; Parish et al., 2008) and homelessness (Ferguson, Wu, Dryrness, & Spruijt-Metz, 2007; Lindsey, Kurtz, Jarvis, Williams, & Nackerud, 2000).

Still another body of scholarship explores spirituality and substance abuse. Both religiosity and spirituality have been noted as protective factors in this area for both adults and children (Kendler, Gardner, & Prescott, 1997; Hodge, Cardenas, & Montoya, 2001; C. Smith & Denton, 2005; Wills, Yaeger, & Sandy, 2003). In addition, the spiritual dimension as a key factor in recovery from substance abuse has long been recognized in self-help groups such as Alcoholics Anonymous, Narcotics Anonymous, and other treatment approaches (Hsu, Grow, Marlatt, Galanter, & Kaskutas, 2008; Pardini, Plante, Sherman, & Stump, 2000; Streifel & Servaty-Seib, 2009).

There is also a growing literature addressing the role of spirituality in understanding and dealing with the effects of various types of trauma—including physical abuse and violence (Garbarino & Bedard, 1997; Parappully, Rosenbaum, van den Daele, & Nzewi, 2002; P. L. Ryan, 1998);

sexual abuse and sexual assault (Galambos, 2001; T. L. Robinson, 2000; D. F. Walker, Reid, O'Neill, & Brown, 2009); severe accidents and serious injury (Ashkanani, 2009; Johnstone, Yoon, Rupright, & Reid-Arndt, 2009); incarceration (P. O'Brien, 2001; Redman, 2008; Sheridan, 1995); and ethnic trauma, war, displacement, and terrorism (Drescher et al., 2009; Markovitzky & Mosek, 2005; Meisenhelder & Marcum, 2009; Schuster et al., 2001). Certain spiritually oriented interventions, such as the use of ceremony and ritual, appear to have particular utility in helping persons recover from trauma and loss (M. J. Barrett, 1999; Cairns, 2005; Lubin & Johnson, 1998).

Finally, nowhere has spirituality been viewed as more relevant than in the area of death and dying. Religious and spiritual issues often arise at the end of life, and thus practitioners need to be able to deal with these issues effectively (G. R. Cox, 2000; MacKinlay, 2006; J. P. Morgan, 2002; Nelson-Becker, 2006). Spiritual sensitivity is also needed in working with those who are grieving the loss of loved ones (Angell, Dennis, & Dumain, 1998; Golsworthy & Coyle, 1999; Winston, 2006) or facing other kinds of loss, such as divorce (Nathanson, 1995; E. D. Smith & Gray, 1995).

Individual and Collective Well-Being

Spirituality also has a role to play in regard to the second major focus of social work: supporting and enhancing optimal human functioning and quality of life. This role is evident at all levels of human systems, including the individual, family, community, organizational, and societal spheres. The following discussion identifies key points of this influence on well-being at both individual and collective levels.

At the individual level, interest in wellness, holistic health, and the mind–body connection has exploded in recent years, as evidenced by increasing numbers of workshops and retreats, weekly groups, self-help books, and media reports on the topic. Furthermore, there has been a marked increase in the use of complementary and

alternative medicine (CAM), defined as "a group of diverse medical and healthcare systems, practices, and products that are not generally considered to be part of conventional medicine" (National Center for Complementary and Alternative Medicine [NCCAM], n.d., ¶2). These approaches, which often are grounded in spiritual traditions and a holistic understanding of the human condition, include homeopathy and naturopathic medicine; traditional Chinese and Ayurveda medicine; chiropractic and osteopathic manipulation; massage and other relaxation techniques; acupuncture and acupressure; herbal therapy; yoga and Tai Chi; energy medicine such as Qigong, Reiki, and healing touch; reflexology; and bioelectromagnetic-based therapies (NCCAM, n.d.).

Over 1,200 research projects have been funded by NCCAM, which is the lead agency under the National Institutes of Health (NIH) charged with investigating the efficacy of these approaches for both physical and mental health. Many of these studies have found positive effects of various CAM modalities, while also identifying approaches that are ineffective. Regardless of the scientific results, Americans are increasingly using CAM processes and products. Findings from a 2007 national survey reveal that approximately 50% of Americans (38% of adults and 12% of children) used some form of alternative or complementary medicine (P. M. Barnes, Bloom, & Nahin, 2008), compared to 34% in 1990 (Williamson & Wyandt, 2001). There is a rise in the use of CAM by physical health and mental health practitioners as well. In a study of social work practitioners, over 75% of the sample reported either direct use or referral to mind–body techniques or community health alternatives in work with their clients (L. Henderson, 2000).

In related research, investigations are uncovering the specific mechanisms of the mind–body connection. In a meta-analysis of 30 years of research, findings show clear linkages between psychological stress and lowered immune system functioning, the major biological system that defends the body against disease (Segerstrom &

Miller, 2004). In another review of 100 years of research, Oakley Ray (2004) reports mounting evidence that stressors that affect the brain are harmful to the body at both a cellular and molecular level, and they diminish a person's health and quality of life. In addition, intriguing results are coming out of research on the "neurobiology of consciousness." Several studies have shown demonstrable links between subjective experiences reported during meditation and noted alterations in brain function (e.g., EEG patterns, gamma activity, phase synchrony), as well as evidence of neuroplasticity (transformations of the brain) in long-term meditators (Lutz, Dunne, & Davidson, 2007). Taken together, these investigations suggest that many of our core mental and emotional processes are not only pivotal in maintaining optimal health, but also affect our capacity for personal happiness and compassion for others. Results from the consciousness studies suggest that positive workings of the mind are trainable skills through practices such as meditation. This possibility has significant implications for both individual and communal well-being.

As a result of this research, a growing number of articles in the professional literature also promote the use of wellness or mind–body approaches for both clients and practitioners. Examples include the development of specialized wellness programs (C. C. Clark, 2002; Kissman, & Maurer, 2002; Neufeld & Knipemann, 2001; Plasse, 2001; A. H. Scott et al., 2001), the use of stress management and relaxation techniques (Finger & Arnold, 2002; McBee, Westreich, & Likourezos, 2004; R. A. Payne, 2000), and the use of mindfulness meditation and yoga (L. Bell, 2009; Brantley, Doucett, & Lindell, 2008; Lee, Ng, Leung, & Chan, 2009; Vohra-Gupta, Russell, & Lo, 2007; Wisniewski, 2008). Many of these approaches are rooted in spiritual traditions, especially Eastern traditions.

There also has been a great deal of recent development concerning spirituality and work. Much of this literature focuses on the search for "right livelihood," or the conscious choice of work that is consistent with one's spiritual values and supportive of ongoing spiritual growth (Bloch & Richmond, 1998; M. Fox, 1994; L. S. Hansen, 1997). Other writers exploring the role of spirituality in the workplace discuss such issues as use of power, management style, workplace environment, and integrating spiritual values with overall work goals (DePree, 1997; Natale & Neher, 1997; Roberson, 2004; N. R. Smith, 2006). The social work enterprise itself has been the subject of such interest. Edward Canda and Leola Furman (2010) identify principles for spiritually sensitive administration of human service organizations.

The connection between spirituality and creativity is another area being addressed by a variety of writers. Much of this writing emphasizes the potential that linking spirituality and creativity has for healing as well as nurturing self-expression and optimal development. Examples include use of the visual arts (Cohn, 1997; Farrelly-Hansen, 2009); journaling, poetry, and creative writing (J. Cameron, 1992; Wright, 2005); music and sound (D. Campbell, 1997; Goldman, 1996); and movement and dance, drama, and other performing arts (J. Adler, 1995; Pearson, 1996; Wuthnow, 2001). Engaging in the creative process seems to facilitate spiritual growth and well-being by encouraging the person to go beyond ego limitations, surrender to process, and tap into spiritual sources of strength and self-expression (Fukuyama & Sevig, 1999; K. R. Mayo, 2009).

Spirituality is also emerging as an important factor in the optimal functioning of various human collectives. In social work with couples and families, paying attention to the spiritual dimension of family life is viewed as important not only for the religiously affiliated, but for the nonaffiliated as well (Dosser, Smith, Markowski, & Cain, 2001; Duba & Watts, 2009; F. Walsh, 2009a). It has been identified as an important component in working with couples and families relative to a wide range of problems, including discord (Cowley, 1999; Derezotes, 2001; Hunler & Gencoz, 2005), challenges of adoption and parenting (Belanger, Copeland, & Cheung, 2009; C. J. Evans, Boustead, & Owens, 2008), health issues (Cattich, & Knudson-Martin, 2009), death and loss (F. Walsh, 2009b), and other issues that arise as part of family functioning (H. Anderson, 2009; Gale, 2009; Hames & Godwin, 2008).

The literature also notes the role of spirituality in community-based initiatives. Examples include community health-promotion programs (K. A. Brown, Jemmott, Mitchell, & Walton, 1998; C. C. Clark, 2002), collective action and social justice efforts (A. V. Perry & Rolland, 2009; Staral, 2000; Tripses & Scroggs, 2009), services to rural communities (Furman & Chandy, 1994; S. K. Johnson, 1997), and other types of community-focused practice (D. R. Garland, Myers, & Wolfer, 2008; Obst & Tham, 2009; Pargament, 2008; Tangenberg, 2008). Social workers are also becoming acquainted with the newly emerging "spiritual activism" movement, which goes beyond a focus on political and economic forces as primary mechanisms for social change to incorporate a spiritual framework for activism. Emerging principles of this new model include such themes as "awareness, compassion, and love"; "interdependence"; "mindfulness and presence"; "paradox and mystery"; "seeking balance"; and "living our values" (C. Goldstein, n.d., ¶6). This more holistic approach is viewed as having greater potential for achieving liberation and social justice than previous efforts embedded in a conflict perspective.

Attention to religious and spiritual resources is also being identified in organizational practice. President Obama announced the newly configured White House Office of Faith-based and Neighborhood Partnerships on the 17th day of his new administration. This office is charged with four priorities: "involving faith-based and neighborhood groups in the economic recovery, promoting responsible fatherhood, fostering interfaith cooperation, and building common ground to reduce unintended pregnancies and the need for abortion" (Office of Faith-based and Neighborhood Partnerships, 2009, ¶3). The proliferation of congregational and faith-based social services, which began with the George W. Bush administration in 2001, is being closely followed

and evaluated by social work scholars. Some note positive opportunities and outcomes as a result of this trend, while others point to negative and unanticipated consequences (Belcher, Fandetti, & Cole, 2004; Boddie & Cnaan, 2006; Netting, O'Connor, & Singletary, 2007; M. L. Thomas, 2009). NASW's (2002) response to the federal faith-based initiative remains cautious, stressing the need for services to be delivered in a way that makes them clearly voluntary and emphasizing the central role and responsibility of government in providing social services. There is a need for ongoing research on the impact of the faith-based services for both clients and social workers employed in such agencies.

At the larger policy and societal levels, both conservative and progressive religious perspectives have a significant voice in a host of issues that impact the well-being of individuals, families, and communities. The Pew Forum (n.d.) has identified four arenas where religion plays a role in public life, often creating controversy and debate due to differing visions of the common good:

1. Religion and politics (e.g., the influence of religion and religious organizations on political behavior, including political campaigns and voting);

2. Religion and the law (e.g., church–state controversies, such as legal battles over the Ten Commandments and public displays of nativity scenes, the Pledge of Allegiance, suicide, the death penalty, and school vouchers);

3. Religion and domestic policy (e.g., issues such as abortion; gay rights, including marriage and adoption; stem cell research, genetic engineering, and cloning; and faith-based initiatives);

4. Religion and world affairs (e.g., appropriate role for religion in foreign policy, international initiatives, and climate change and environmental issues).

Social workers should keep abreast of these issues, particularly as they impact the client populations they serve.

Finally, spirituality is being increasingly identified as a needed force in nurturing and sustaining life beyond the circle of the human family to include all living beings and our planet that is home to all. Growing numbers of religious congregations, both conservative and progressive, are identifying "stewardship of the planet" as part of their commitment to God's creation (The National Religious Partnership for the Environment, n.d.). Many writers are pointing to the critical link between our capacity to view all of nature as sacred and the mounting issues of environmental degradation, climate change, and eco-justice for vulnerable and marginalized populations (Berry, 2009; Coates, 2003, 2007; W. Jenkins, 2008; McFague, 2001). This spiritually grounded perspective challenges us to redefine the meaning of community and re-envision our rightful place in the "sacred hoop" of life.

In sum, spirituality in both its religious and nonreligious forms holds much potential for promoting well-being and quality of life at all levels of the human experience, as well as for helping the profession address the problems and possibilities inherent in the human condition.

Spiritual Assessment

Given the important role of spirituality in understanding both human diversity and human experience, it has become evident that gathering information about a client's religious or spiritual history and assessing spiritual development and current interests are as important as learning about biopsychosocial factors. Assessment needs to go beyond the surface features of faith affiliation (such as Protestant, Catholic, Jewish, or Muslim) to include deeper facets of a person's spiritual life (Sheridan, 2002). For example, talking with Caroline about where she is in her unfolding spiritual development would be helpful in supporting her exploration of different faith perspectives. Asking Matthew what brings him meaning, purpose, and connection right now would be valuable in assisting him in the next chapter of his life. And in working with Leon, it would be useful to know

what aspects of his current religious affiliation are the most important and meaningful to him as he struggles with the conflicts regarding his faith and his sexual identity. None of this knowledge would be gleaned by a simple response to "What is your current religious affiliation?"

Social workers also need to assess both the positive and negative aspects of clients' religious or spiritual beliefs and practices (Canda & Furman, 2010; M. V. Joseph, 1988; Lewandowski & Canda, 1995; Sheridan & Bullis, 1991). For example, Naomi and David's understanding of the meaning of illness may be either helpful or harmful in dealing with Naomi's health crisis; Trudy's current spiritual practices may be supportive or detrimental to her physical, emotional, and social well-being; and Jean-Joseph's synthesis of Catholic and Vodoun beliefs and practices may be very positive for his personal and family life, but may be problematic in his interactions with the wider social environment. Assessing the role and impact of all of these factors would be important areas for exploration in developing a spiritually sensitive relationship with any of these individuals.

A growing number of assessment instruments and approaches are available to help social workers. These include brief screening tools, which can provide an initial assessment of the relevance of religion or spirituality in clients' lives. Examples include the HOPE (Anandarajah & Hight, 2001), the FICA (Puchalski, & Romer, 2000), the MIMBRA (Canda & Furman, 2010), and the Brief RCOPE (Pargament, Koenig, & Perez, 2000). There are also several more comprehensive assessment tools that focus on religious/ spiritual history and current life circumstances. For example, Bullis (1996) developed a spiritual history that includes questions about individuals, their parents or guardians, and their spouses or significant others. Canda and Furman (2010) provide a discussion guide for a detailed spiritual assessment, which covers spiritual group membership and participation; spiritual beliefs, activities, experiences, and feelings; moral and value issues; spiritual development; spiritual sources of support and transformation; spiritual well-being; and extrinsic/intrinsic styles of spiritual propensity.

There are also examples of more implicit assessment approaches, which do not directly include a reference to "religion" or "spirituality," but are composed of open-ended questions that tap into spiritual themes, such as those identified by Titone (1991) and Canda and Furman (2010). (See Exhibit 5.5 for examples of these kind of questions.) A number of other creative, nonverbal strategies for gathering such information have also been developed, including the use of spiritual timelines (Bullis, 1996); spiritual lifemaps, genograms, ecomaps, and ecograms (Hodge, 2005b); and spiritual trees (Raines, 1997). Finally, Lewandowski and Canda (1995) and Canda and Furman (2010) provide questions for assessing the helpful or harmful impacts of participating in spiritual groups or organizations (e.g., satisfaction with leadership style, methods of recruitment, response to members leaving the group).

Assessment must also be able to distinguish between a religious/spiritual problem and a mental disorder. The fourth edition of the *Diagnostic and Statistical Manual of Mental Disorders,* Text Revision (*DSM-IV-TR*) (American Psychiatric Association, 2000) provides guidance in this area. "Religious or spiritual problem" is now included as a condition (*not* a mental disorder) that is appropriate for clinical attention. Types of religious problems under this category include difficulties resulting from a change in one's denomination or conversion to a new religion, intensified adherence to beliefs or practices, loss or questioning of faith, guilt, or involvement in destructive religious groups. Spiritual problems may include distress due to mystical experiences, near-death experiences, spiritual emergence/ emergency, or separation from a spiritual teacher (R. P. Turner, Lukoff, Barnhouse, & Lu, 1995). This framework would be helpful in understanding any extraordinary or mystical experiences that Trudy, Jean-Joseph, or any of the other people in the case

---

Exhibit 5.5   Examples of Questions for Implicit Spiritual Assessment

1. What nourishes you spiritually—for example: music, nature, intimacy, witnessing heroism, meditation, creative expression, sharing another's joy?

2. What is the difference between shame and guilt? What are healthy and unhealthy shame and guilt?

3. What do you mean when you say your spirits are low? Is that different from being sad or depressed?

4. What is an incident in your life that precipitated a change in your belief about the meaning of life?

5. What helps you maintain a sense of hope when there is no immediate apparent basis for it?

6. Do you need forgiveness from yourself or someone else?

7. What currently brings a sense of meaning and purpose to your life?

8. Where do you go to find a sense of deep inspiration or peace?

9. For what are you most grateful?

10. What are your most cherished ideals?

11. In what way is it important or meaningful for you to be in this world (or in this situation)?

12. What are the deepest questions your situation raises for you?

SOURCES: Canda & Furman (2010); Titone (1991).

studies might share with you. Accurate assessment of such an occurrence can help determine whether the experience needs to be integrated and used as a stimulus for personal growth or whether it should be recognized as a sign of mental instability.

Assessment is just one component of spiritually sensitive social work practice. The field is accumulating a number of publications that provide more comprehensive discussion of spiritually sensitive practice (see, for example, Bullis 1996; Canda & Furman, 2010; Derezotes, 2006; Frame, 2003; Mijares & Khalsa, 2005; Pargament, 2007; Scales et al., 2002; and Sheridan, 2002).

Critical Thinking Questions 5.3

With globalization, we have more regular contact with people of diverse religious and spiritual beliefs. How much religious and spiritual diversity do you come in contact with in your everyday life? How comfortable are you with honoring different religious and spiritual beliefs? How have you seen religious and spiritual beliefs used to discriminate against some groups of people? How have you seen religious and spiritual beliefs used to promote social justice?

Implications for Social Work Practice

Spiritually sensitive social work practice involves gaining knowledge and skills in the areas discussed in this chapter, always keeping in mind that this approach must be grounded within the values and ethics of the profession. The following practice principles are offered as guidelines for effective and ethical social work practice in this area.

- Maintain clarity about your role as a spiritually sensitive practitioner, making a distinction between being a social worker who includes a focus on the spiritual dimension as part of holistic practice and being a religious leader or spiritual director.
- Be respectful of different religious or spiritual paths, and be willing to learn about the role and meaning of various beliefs, practices, and experiences for various client systems (individuals, families, groups, communities).
- Critically examine your own values, beliefs, and biases concerning religion and spirituality, and be willing to work through any unresolved or negative feelings or experiences in this area that may adversely affect your work with clients.
- Inform yourself about both the positive and negative role of religion and spirituality in the fight for social justice by various groups, and be sensitive to this history in working with members of oppressed and marginalized populations.
- Develop a working knowledge of the beliefs and practices frequently encountered in your work with clients, especially those of newly arriving immigrants/refugees or nondominant groups (for example, Buddhist beliefs of Southeast Asian refugees, spiritual traditions of First Nations peoples).
- Conduct comprehensive spiritual assessments with clients at all levels, and use this information in service planning and delivery.
- Acquire the knowledge and skills necessary to employ spiritually based intervention techniques appropriately, ethically, and effectively.
- Seek information about the various religious and spiritual organizations, services, and leaders pertinent to your practice, and develop good working relationships with these resources for purposes of referral and collaboration.
- Engage in ongoing self-reflection about what brings purpose, meaning, and connection in your own life, and make disciplined efforts toward your own spiritual development, however you define this process.

ecocentric	ideology (personal)	spirituality
faith	levels of consciousness	states of consciousness
faith stages	lines of consciousness	Third Force therapies
First Force therapies	religion	transpersonal approach
Four quadrants	Second Force therapies	ultimate environment
Fourth Force therapies	self-system	worldcentric
fulcrum	spiritual bypassing	

Active Learning

1. Consider any of the case studies presented at the beginning of the chapter. Using either Fowler's stages of faith development or Wilber's integral theory of consciousness as the conceptual framework, construct a timeline of the person's spiritual development. Trace the overall growth patterns through the different stages, including any ups and downs, as well as plateau periods. Identify the significant points or transitions that you consider as pivotal to the person's spiritual development.

   • How would this information help you to better understand the person's story and overall development? How would this information help you work with him or her as a social worker at various points in his or her life?
   • What would your own spiritual timeline look like, including patterns throughout various stages and significant points or transitions that were particularly significant for your own growth and development?

2. Select a partner for this exercise. This chapter provides a brief overview of the spiritual diversity present within the United States. Given both your knowledge and experiences with different spiritual traditions, both religious and nonreligious, address the following questions. Take a few moments to reflect on each question before answering it. Partners should take turns answering the questions.

   • To which spiritual perspectives do you have the most *positive reactions* (e.g., are in the most agreement with, feel an appreciation or attraction toward, are the most comfortable with, find it easiest to keep an open mind and heart about)? What is it about you that contributes to these reactions (e.g., previous knowledge, personal experiences, messages from family or larger culture)?
   • To which perspective do you have the most *negative reactions* (e.g., are in the most disagreement with, feel a repulsion or fear about, are the most uncomfortable with, find it most difficult to keep an open mind and heart about)? What is it about you that contributes to these reactions (e.g., previous knowledge, personal experiences, messages from family or larger culture)?
   • What impact(s) might your reactions (both positive and negative) have on work with clients (especially with those who may hold different spiritual perspectives from yourself)? What personal and professional "work" on yourself is suggested by your positive and/or negative reactions?

3. Select a partner for this exercise. Together select one of the open-ended questions listed in Exhibit 5.5 to consider as it applies to your own lives. After a few moments of quiet reflection, write your response to the question, allowing yourself to write freely without concern for the proper mechanics of writing (e.g., spelling, grammar). Then sit with what you've written, reading it over with fresh eyes. When you're ready, share this experience with your partner, sharing as much or as little of what you've written as you feel comfortable with. Then talk together about the following questions:

- What was the experience like of answering this question and then reading the response to yourself (e.g., easy, difficult, exciting, anxiety-producing, confirming)?
- Are there previous times in your life when you considered this question? Did you share your thoughts about it with others? If so, what was that like? What is it like to do that now with your partner?
- Can you see yourself asking this kind of a question with a client? What do you think that experience might be like for both the client and yourself?

Web Resources

Adherents.com

www.adherents.com

Site not affiliated with any religious, political, educational, or commercial organization. Contains a comprehensive collection of over 41,000 statistics on religious adherents, geography citations, and links to other major sites on diverse religious and spiritual traditions.

Association of Religion Data Archives

www.thearda.com

Site sponsored by the Lilly Endowment, the John Templeton Foundation, and Pennsylvania State University. Provides over 350 data files on U.S. and international religions using online features for generating national profiles, maps, overviews of church memberships, denominational heritage trees, tables, charts, and other summary reports.

Canadian Society for Spirituality and Social Work

http://w3.stu.ca/stu/sites/spirituality/index.html

Site includes information about the activities of this society, links to other websites, and other resources.

Pew Forum on Religion & Public Life

http://pewforum.org/

Site sponsored by the larger Pew Research Center. Functions as both a clearinghouse for research and other publications related to issues at the intersection of religion and public affairs, and also as a virtual town hall for discussion of related topics.

Religious Tolerance

www.religioustolerance.org

Site presented by the Ontario Consultants on Religious Tolerance, an agency that promotes religious tolerance as a human right. Contains comparative descriptions of world religions and diverse spiritual paths from Asatru to Zoroastrianism, and links to other related sites.

Society for Spirituality and Social Work

http://soceityforspiritualityandsocialwork.com

Site includes information about joining the U.S. Society for Spirituality and Social Work, a selected bibliography, and other resources.

Virtual Religion Index

www.virtualreligion.net/vri/

Site presented by the Religion Department at Rutgers University. Contains analysis and highlights of religion-related websites and provides links to major sites for specific religious groups and topics.

CHAPTER 6

Culture and the Physical Environment

Linwood Cousins

Elizabeth D. Hutchison

CX 8O

CX 8O

Opening Questions

How does culture produce variations in human behavior and play a role in social inequality?

What is the relationship between the physical environment and human behavior?

CASE STUDY 6.1

Stan and Tina at Community High School

Community High School in Newark, New Jersey, has approximately 1,300 students, the majority of whom are Black (African American, Afro-Caribbean, and West African). Most of the students live in the community of Village Park, which has a total population of approximately 58,000 people, also predominantly Black. Village Park has a distinct social history and identity as well as distinct physical boundaries that distinguish it from less prosperous communities and schools in Newark.

Village Park evolved from a middle- and working-class Jewish community that centered around its academic institutions, such as Community High. The school generated a national reputation for academic excellence as measured by the number of graduates who went on to become doctors, lawyers, scientists, professors, and the like. But after the Newark riots of the late 1960s, Jews and other Whites started moving out. By the early 1970s, upwardly mobile middle- and working-class Black families had become the majority in Village Park. The same process has occurred in other communities, but what's interesting about Village Park is that its Black residents, like the Jewish residents who preceded them, continued to believe in the ethic of upward mobility through schooling at Community High.

Since the mid-1980s, however, Village Park and Community High have undergone another transformation. Slumps in the economy and ongoing patterns of racial discrimination in employment have reduced the income base of the community's families. Many families who were able to maintain a middle-class income moved to the suburbs as crime and economic blight encroached on the community. Increasingly, Village Park was taken over by renters and absentee landlords, along with the social problems—drug abuse, crime, school dropouts—that accompany economically driven social despair.

By 1993, the population profile of Newark had become simultaneously Black and multiethnic. In the 1990s, the majority of Newark's residents were African American, but the city had a considerable population of other ethnic groups: Hispanics (Puerto Ricans, Colombians, Mexicans, Dominicans, etc.), Italians, Portuguese, Africans (from Nigeria, Sierra Leone, Liberia, Ghana, and other countries), Polish, and small groups of others. At the same time, the governing bodies of the city, the school system, and Community High in particular were predominantly composed of Black people. With an estimated population of 278,000 in 2008, Newark remains an ethnically diverse urban community.

The intermingling of such history and traditions has had an interesting impact on the students at Community High. Like many urban high schools all over the nation, Community High has suffered disproportionate levels of dropouts, low attendance, and violence. Yet a few parents, teachers, school staff, and community officials have tried hard to rekindle the spirit of academic excellence and social competence that are the school's tradition.

In this context, many of the students resist traditional definitions of academic success but value success nonetheless. Consider the behaviors of Stan and Tina, both students at Community High. Stan is the more troubled and more academically marginal of the two students. He is 17 years old, lives with his girlfriend who has recently had a baby, and has made a living selling drugs (which he is trying to discontinue). Stan was arrested (and released) for selling drugs some time ago. He was also under questioning for the drug-related murder of his cousin, because the police wanted him to identify the perpetrator. However, Stan has considerable social prestige at school and is academically successful when he attends school and is focused. Stan's mother—who has hammered into his head the importance of education—is a clerical supervisor, his stepfather works in a meat factory, and his biological father sells drugs.

Among his male and female peers, Stan is considered the epitome of urban maleness and style. He is an innovator. He mixes and matches the square-toe motorcycle boots normally associated with White bikers with the brand-name shirts and jeans commonly associated with urban, rap-oriented young people of color. At the same time, Stan is respected by teachers and administrators because he understands and observes the rules of conduct preferred in the classroom and because he can do his work at a level reflecting high intelligence. Before the end of his senior year, Stan visited Howard University in Washington, D.C., and was smitten by the idea that young Black men and women were participating in university life. He says he will try very hard to go to that school after he graduates, but the odds are against him.

Tina is also 17 years old, but she is more academically successful than Stan. She ranks in the top 25 of her senior class and has been accepted into the pre-med program of a historically Black university. Tina talks about the lower academic performance of some of her Black peers. She sees it as a manifestation of the social distractions that seem to preoccupy Black youths—being popular and cool. On the other hand, Tina sees her successful academic performance, level of motivation, and assertive style of interacting in the classroom as part of being Black too—taking care of business and trying to make it in this world.

Tina is an only child. Her father is an engineer, and her stepmother is a restaurant manager. Tina has never known her biological mother, and she was raised primarily by her father until about 6 years ago. They moved to Village Park from Brooklyn, New York, around that time. Tina's is the kind of family that is likely to leave Village Park not for the suburbs, but for a more productive and less hostile urban community. Tina has been raised in a community that, despite its ills, centers around Black identity and culture.

(Continued)

(Continued)

Like Stan, Tina is an innovator. She adopted modes of language, demeanor, and clothing that are seen by some as decidedly mainstream in their origins. In fact, however, Tina mixes the aesthetics of Black and mainstream White culture as well as the contemporary urban flavor that textures the lives of many youths today. Perhaps the results are most apparent in the way Tina mixes and matches hip-hop–influenced clothing, attitudes, and hairstyles with mainstream clothing styles and the mannerisms associated with the norms and standards of professional, middle-class occupations.

However, anyone who would approach Tina as an ally of "the system"—defining the system as the White establishment—would meet with disappointment. He or she would discover that in Tina's view, and perhaps in Stan's, there is nothing generally wrong with Black people and their behavior. But there is something wrong with Black individuals who do things that are not in their own best interest and consequently not in the best interest of the Black community.

Furthermore, he or she would hear Tina, Stan, and other students at Community High describe academic success and failure not just in terms of students' actions. The person would hear these students indict uninterested and complacent teachers and staff, and schools that do not understand "how to educate Black people."

SOURCE: Based on an ethnographic study of culture, race, and class during the 1992–1993 academic year in Cousins (1994). See Fordham (1996) and Ogbu (2003) for similar studies of Black high school students that confirm the persistence of the characteristics described here.

CASE STUDY 6.2

Ben Watson's Changing Experience With the Physical Environment

AUTHOR'S NOTE: *The following is told in Ben's own words.*

I finished my final semester in the Bachelor of Architecture Program, and a couple of friends and I decided to spend a few days doing some rock climbing before graduation. I already had a job lined up with a small architecture firm down in North Carolina. Things were looking good, but it doesn't take but a minute to change things forever. I fell 500 feet and knew, as soon as I came to, that something was very wrong. My legs were numb, I couldn't move them, and I had terrific pain in my back. My friends knew not to move me, and one stayed with me while the other went for help.

I don't remember much about the rescue, the trip to the nearest hospital, or the medivac to the closest trauma center. In my early days at the trauma hospital, I saw lots of medical people, but I vividly remember the doc who told me that I had an incomplete spinal cord injury, that I would have some sensation below my lesion but no movement. I didn't really believe it. Movement was what I was all about. I spent 5 months in the hospital and rehabilitation center, and I gradually began to understand that my legs were not going to move. I was depressed, I was angry (furious, really), and for one week I wanted to give up. My parents and my brothers pulled me through. They showered me with love but were firm when I tried to refuse rehabilitation treatments. Oh yeah, some of my friends were terrific also. When things get rough, you learn who your real friends are. I also appreciated a chance to talk with the rehab social worker about my grief over this unbelievable turn in my life. It was good to talk with him because he wasn't dealing with his own grief about my situation the way my family and friends were.

I left rehab with my new partner, a sophisticated titanium wheelchair, and went home to live with my parents. They rearranged the house so that I could have the first-floor bedroom and bath. I appreciated the assistance from my parents and brothers, and my friends made heroic efforts to get me out of the house. As we did so, I began to learn the importance of the word *access.* The first time my friends took me out, we wanted to go to a bar; after all, that's what 20-something guys do. My friends called around to find a nearby bar that would be accessible to me and my wheelchair. That turned out to be tougher than they thought. Did you ever notice how many bars require dealing with stairs? Finally, they were assured that one bar was accessible—well, actually, nobody wanted to say their place wasn't accessible, given the law and all, plus most folks haven't given any thought to what that really means. So, my friends had to go through a set of questions about stairs, ramps, size of doors, etc., to make their own determination about accessibility. One question they didn't think to ask was whether there were stairs leading to the bathroom. So, we went out drinking, but I was afraid to drink or eat because I couldn't get to the bathroom.

After several months at home, I began to get restless and wanted to get on with my life. After my accident, the architecture firm down in North Carolina had told my parents that they would still be interested in having me work for them when I was strong enough. So, I began to talk with my parents about making the move to North Carolina. They understood that I needed to get on with my life, but they worried about me moving 350 miles away. I was still dependent on them for a lot of personal care, but I was gradually learning to do more for myself.

I knew from my interviews that the architecture firm was accessible by wheelchair—it was in a relatively new building with ground-level entrance, spacious elevator, wide doors, and accessible bathrooms. With some trepidation, my dad drove me down to look for housing. There were plenty of new apartment complexes, but we found that everybody, not just people with disabilities, wanted ground-floor apartments with the open architectural features that make wheelchair mobility so much easier. After a lot of calls, we found a one-bedroom apartment that I could afford. I immediately loved the location, in a part of the city where there was a lot happening on the streets, with shops, restaurants, and a movie theater. The apartment was attractive, convenient, and accessible, but most important, it was mine. I was finally beginning to feel like an adult. I would have my privacy, but the open floor plan would allow me to have friends over without feeling cramped. And, I loved the abundance of windows that would allow for good natural lighting from the sun. I couldn't afford to get my own car with hand controls yet, but the apartment luckily was only a short cab ride from my office.

My father and brothers helped me make the move, and my grandmother came for a visit to add some charming decorating touches. I hired a personal assistant to help me get ready in the mornings—well, actually, my parents paid him for the first few months, until I could get my finances worked out.

Given my profession, it is good that I still have excellent function of my upper body, particularly my hands. My colleagues at work turned out to be good friends as well as good colleagues. And, I never paid much attention to issues of accessibility in my design studios at school, but I have become the local expert on accessible design.

I learned a lot about accessible design from some of my own frustrating experiences. I have been lucky to develop a close set of friends, and we have an active life. My friends and I have learned where the streets are that don't have curb cuts, which bars and restaurants are truly accessible, places where the "accessible" entry is really some dark alley back entrance, and to watch out for retail doorways blocked by displays of goods.

My friends and I travel, and I find some airline personnel handle me and my wheelchair well and some are disastrous—imagine being rolled over on the ramp, and with an audience, no less. The natural environment was always an important part of my life—it provides beauty and serenity—and my friends and I could write a book about all the wonderful hiking trails that are wheelchair accessible. Hey, that's a good idea!

In the last three chapters, we focused on internal dimensions of the person—biological, psychological, and spiritual. These two cases illustrate well the multiple dimensions of the external environment that influence our moment-to-moment behavior—and how our behavior influences those environments. We see evidence of the mutual influence of human behavior with culture, the physical environment, social institutions and social structure, formal organizations, communities, social movements, small groups, and families. In this chapter, we focus on two aspects of the environment that are present, but not often recognized, in all other dimensions: culture and the physical environment.

THE CHALLENGE OF DEFINING CULTURE

The case of Tina and Stan has been selected because it makes a point we often miss in the United States in general and in social work and human services in particular: Culture is right under our noses and therefore often concealed from our awareness. We are more likely to think of immigrants and non-Americans as the real examples of culture because they represent peoples who appear to be more different from us than perhaps they are. We may also think of Tina and Stan as more like you (or people you know) and me than perhaps they are. The case example highlights not only race and ethnicity, but also social class, power relations, gender, popular culture, and other significant features of interactions between people and their environments. In our everyday lives, we think we know what we see, but our life experiences lead us to see some things and not others. It is incredibly hard for us to take a detached viewpoint about our person–environment interactions.

The U.S. Census Bureau (2009d) tells us that there are now over 7 billion people in the world. Just over 300 million of them live in the United States. The United States is the third most populated country, behind China (just over 1.3 billion) and India (just over 1 billion), with the smallest population being in Montserrat, a small Caribbean island of 5,097 people. The U.S. population includes 199 million White (non-Hispanic) people of various ancestries, just over 46 million Hispanics/Latinos, just over 37 million African Americans/Blacks, more than 13 million Asians, and over 3 million American Indians and Alaska Natives, with Native Hawaiian, other Pacific Islanders, and other peoples constituting the rest (U.S. Census Bureau, 2009d). Finally, approximately 34.2 million, or 12% of the civilian, non-institutionalized U.S. population, are foreign born (U.S. Census Bureau, 2004a).

Much diversity is concealed in this numerical portrait, but it is a good place to begin our discussion of the diverse society we live in. Given this scenario, how should we as social workers interpret the multifaceted contexts of Tina's and Stan's lives? Economics, race/ethnicity, traditions and customs, gender, political processes, immigration, popular culture, psychology, academic processes, and a host of other factors are all involved. All this and more must be considered in our discussion of culture.

But let me caution you. Defining **culture** is a complex and arbitrary game. It is a word we use all the time but have trouble defining (Gardiner & Kosmitzki, 2008; Griswold, 2008). Long ago, Alfred Kroeber and Clyde Kluckhohn (1963, 1952/1978), two renowned anthropologists, catalogued more than 100 definitions of culture (see Exhibit 6.1). Definitions and discussions of culture tend to reflect the theoretical perspectives and purposes of the definers. Like other views of culture, the one presented here has its biases. In keeping with the emphasis in this book on power arrangements, a view of culture is presented that will expose not only social differences or human variation, but also the cultural bases of various forms of inequality. We look at the ways in which variations in human behavior have led to subjugation and have become the basis of, among other things, racial, ethnic, economic, and gender oppression and inequality.

> Social constructionist perspective

Exhibit 6.1   Categorical Definitions of Culture

Enumeration of Social Content

- That complex whole that includes knowledge, belief, art, morals, law, custom, and any other capabilities and habits acquired by humans as members of society; the sum total of human achievement

Social Heritage/Tradition

- The learned repertoire of thoughts and actions exhibited by members of a social group, independently of genetic heredity from one generation to the next
- The sum total and organization of social heritages that have acquired social meaning because of racial temperament and the historical life of the group

Rule or Way of Life

- The sum total of ways of doing and thinking, past and present, of a social group
- The distinctive way of life of a group of people; their complete design for living

Psychological and Social Adjustment and Learning

- The total equipment of technique—mechanical, mental, and moral—by use of which the people of a given period try to attain their ends
- The sum total of the material and intellectual equipment whereby people satisfy their biological and social needs and adapt themselves to their environment
- Learned modes of behavior that are socially transmitted from one generation to another within a particular society and that may be diffused from one society to another

Ideas and Values

- An organized group of ideas, habits, and conditioned emotional responses shared by members of a society
- Acquired or cultivated behavior and thought of individuals; the material and social values of any group of people

Patterning and Symbols

- A system of interrelated and interdependent habit patterns of response
- Organization of conventional understandings, manifest in act and artifact, that, persisting through tradition, characterizes a human group
- Semiotics—those webs of public meaning that people have spun and by which they are suspended
- A distinct order or class of phenomena—namely, those things and events that are dependent upon the exercise of a mental ability peculiar to the human species—that we have termed symboling; or material objects (such as tools, utensils, ornaments, amulets), acts, beliefs, and attitudes that function in contexts characterized by symboling

SOURCE: Adapted from Kroeber and Kluckhohn (1952/1978), pp. 40–79.

According to Raymond Williams (1983), "Culture is one of the two or three most complicated words in the English language" (p. 87), partly because of its intricate historical development in several European languages, but also because it is used as a concept that sometimes has quite different meanings in several incompatible systems of thought. For example, early German intellectual traditions merged with English traditions to define culture as general processes of intellectual, spiritual, and aesthetic development. A modified version of this usage is found in the contemporary field of arts and humanities, which describes culture in terms of music, literature, painting, sculpture, and the like. By contrast, U.S. tradition has produced the use of culture as we know it in contemporary social sciences to describe a particular way of life of a people, a period of time, or humanity in general. But even in this tradition, anthropologists have used the concept to refer to the material production of a people, whereas historians and cultural studies have used it to refer to symbolic systems such as language, stories, and rituals. Currently, and with the rise of postmodern theorizing, these uses of the concept overlap considerably.

| Systems perspective; |
| Psychodynamic perspective |

One useful postmodern approach to human behavior sees culture as

> a set of common understandings, manifest in act and artifact. It is in two places at once: inside some-body's head as understandings and in the external environment as act and artifact. If it isn't truly present in both spheres, it is only incomplete culture. (Bohannan, 1995, p. 47)

Culture, in other words, includes both behavior (act or actions) and the material outcomes of that behavior (artifacts, or the things we construct from the material world around us—such as houses, clothing, cars, nuclear weapons, jets, and the like). It both constrains and is constrained by nature, biology, social conditions, and other realities of human existence. But at the same time, it is "inside our heads," or part of our thoughts, perceptions, and feelings. It is expressed through our emotions and thought processes, our motivations, intentions, and meanings as we live out our lives.

It is through culture that we construct meanings associated with the social and material world. Art, shelter, transportation, music, food, and clothing are material examples. The meanings we give these products influence how we use them. Some women's clothing is considered provocative,

and pork for some people is considered "polluted." In interaction with the social world of things around us, we construct religion, race and ethnicity, family and kinship, gender roles, sexuality, ability/disability, and complex modern organizations and institutions.

Here's an example from U.S. history of how human beings construct meaning in a cultural context. Slaves of African descent tended to interpret their plight and quest for freedom in terms of Judeo-Christian religious beliefs, which were pressed on them by the slaveholders but which were also adapted for better fit with their oppressive situations. They likened their suffering to that of the crucifixion and resurrection of Jesus Christ. Just like the biblical "children of Israel" who had to make it to the Promised Land, so it was that slaves had to find freedom in the promised land of Northern cities in the United States and Canada. The association of the plight of Christians and Jews in the Bible with racial oppression lives on today in the lives of many African Americans.

You may encounter clients who believe that their social, economic, and psychological difficulties are the result of God's will, or issues of spirituality, rather than of the biopsychosocial causes we study and apply as social workers. Should a social work assessment include the various meanings that people construct about their circumstances? Applying a cultural perspective that considers this question will help you find more empowering interpretations and solutions to issues you face as a social worker, especially when working with members of oppressed communities.

Here is another example. Disability in our culture seems to be about its opposite: being normal, competent, "properly human" (R. Jenkins, 1998, p. 2). It is also about the desire for sameness or similarity (Ingstad & Whyte, 1995). But decisions about what is normal are embedded in culture. We may think that physical, mental, or cognitive disabilities are purely biological or psychological and therefore real in a scientific sense. But like race and gender, what they mean to the person possessing them and to those looking on and judging is a matter of the meanings derived from culture (S. Snyder

& Mitchell, 2001; R. G. Thomson, 1996). These meanings play out in social, economic, and political relations that determine the distribution of resources and generate various types of inequality.

What are your emotional responses to thinking about Ben Watson in his wheelchair? How do you suppose he feels? Can you imagine his sexual attractiveness? Do you suppose he sees himself as a sexual being? What are the bodily images we hold for being "handsome" or "beautiful"? Do they correspond with the images that others, including Ben, hold? The point is that if the culturally diverse people who reside in the United States see life in various ways, we must expect no less regarding those with different types and levels of ability.

The above examples about African Americans and disability occur in a historical context. But history is about more than dates, names, inventions, and records of events. Rather, history is an ongoing story about the connections among ideas, communities, peoples, nations, and social transformations within the constraints of the natural world (Huynh-Nhu et al., 2008; McHale, Updegraff, Ji-Yeon, & Cansler, 2009). Think about how the historical plight of Native Americans, Asian Americans, or Hispanic Americans in the United States influences how they perceive their lives today. Think about the historical development of the terms and ideas associated with disability: "crippled," "handicapped," "disabled," "differently abled," and so on.

Think about the history of social work. It is about more than mere dates and events. Think of the people involved in social work, such as Mary Richmond, a leader in the early charity movement, and Jane Addams, a leader in the early settlement house movement. Think about the philosophy and social practices they espoused in working with the disadvantaged people of their time. What do you know about their ethnic identity, socioeconomic status, gender, and living conditions? What about the dominant thinking and political, social, and economic trends of their time? What do you know about what may have influenced their very different conceptions of social

Conflict perspective

work and how those influences connect to the ideas and practices of contemporary social work? Now, think about Ida B. Wells-Barnett, former slave, contemporary of Jane Addams, and founder of an African American settlement house. How much do you know about her achievements? This line of thought reveals a lot about U.S. culture and how it has interacted with the development of social work.

To sum up, culture includes multiple levels of traditions, values, and beliefs, as well as social, biological, and natural acts. These processes are driven by the meanings we give to and take from them. These meanings are fortified or changed in relations between people, as history unfolds. Culture affects all of us.

Among those who are affected by culture are the students and staff at Community High School. Culture affects what curriculum is delivered, how, and by whom. A cultural interpretation would reveal competition and *strain,* or unequal power relations in this process. For example, many Village Park residents and Community High students have cultural frames of reference that give adversarial meanings to requirements that students act "studiously and behave a certain way" in class. These community members and students do not necessarily dismiss education and classroom rules, but they may see education and some of its rules as part of a system of mainstream institutions that have been oppressive and insensitive toward Blacks. They see schools as dismissing their norms and points of view, and the power to change things eludes them. When a teacher at Community High asks Black students like Stan and Tina to stop talking out of turn in class, these students hear more than an impartial and benign request. Of course, any adolescent student might resent being told to stop talking by an adult authority. However, the interpretation of that request by Black students is likely to reflect their understanding about what it means to be "put down" or "dissed" in front of one's peers by an "outsider" who represents the dominant White society and does not respect the Black community.

These are complex issues, but they are part of the everyday problems social workers encounter. Further examination of what culture is and how

Photo 6.1 Family life is structured by meanings, values, and beliefs that fit our desires and imaginations about what is right and appropriate.

ideas about it have changed over time helps in our quest for multidimensional knowledge and skills.

Changing Ideas About Culture and Human Behavior

Ideas about culture have changed over time, in step with intellectual, social, economic, and political trends. Exhibit 6.2 provides an overview of the evolution of culture as a concept since the 18th century.

Some of the influential ideas that have remained with us from the past come from the Enlightenment and Romantic intellectual traditions, dating back to the 18th century. Enlightenment thinking in the early 18th century ranked cultures and civilizations according to their developed logic, reason, and technology (or mastery and use of the physical environment). Africans and Native Americans, for example, were seen as less civilized and less valuable than Europeans because their technology was not on the same scale as some European countries. Can you think of situations that demonstrate Enlightenment

biases today? Is this the same framework that justifies interpreting the actions of Tina and Stan as less developed, less mature, and less rational than the actions of more mainstream students?

Another set of ideas comes from a Romantic orientation dating from the late 18th century. This orientation suggests that all people and their cultures are relatively equal in value. Differences in culture reflect different frameworks of meaning and understanding and thus result in different

Conflict perspective

lifestyles and ways of living (Benedict, 1946, 1934/1989; Shweder, 1984/1995). From this tradition comes the idea of **cultural relativism** that frames contemporary multiculturalism. For example, at some point you may have been asked which is superior, Islam or Christianity, Black culture or White culture, African culture or European culture. These religions and cultures differ in content and meaning, but is one better than the other? If so, what is the standard of measure, and in whose interest is it developed and enforced?

Exhibit 6.2 Ideas and Processes Influencing the Evolution of Culture as a Concept

Time Period	Ideas and Human Processes
18th and 19th centuries: Enlightenment and Romanticism	Rankings of logic, reason, art, technology Culture seizing nature Psychic unity of humankind
19th and 20th centuries: Variation in human behavior and development	Cultural relativism Culture as patterns and structures Culture and personality Symbols as vehicles of culture
Contemporary understandings: Integration and synthesis of processes of human development and variation since 1950s	Cultural psychology (cognitive psychology and anthropology) Meaning, ecology, and culture Political and economic systems and culture Culture as private and public Physical environment, biology, and culture Ideology, history, common sense, tradition as cultural systems

Some today dismiss cultural relativism as "politically correct" thinking, but it does have practical value. For instance, as a social worker, you could contrast the behavior of Tina and Stan with that of successful White students to identify differences between them. How will doing so help Tina, Stan, or the successful White students—or any other students, for that matter? In the context of the recent conflict between the United States and Iraq, one may question the value of Islam compared to Christianity or Eastern culture compared to Western. Perhaps it is more productive to measure each of these against some mutually relevant standard, such as how well the students will be able to succeed in their own communities, or how well a religion or culture serves humanity. The point here is not that we should apply different standards to different people. Rather, in social work at least, to start where individuals are, to understand their points of view and the context of their lives, has been an effective method of helping them gain control of their lives.

In the United States today, we still see conflicts between Enlightenment thinking and the cultural relativism of Romanticism. Romanticism is reflected by those who call for respect for diversity in our multicultural society. But the premises of Enlightenment thinking have a great influence on our everyday understanding of culture. Consider recent public debates over crime, welfare, health insurance, Islam, and other issues that associate historical and contemporary social problems with people's race/ethnicity, religion, and socioeconomic status. Some social scientists and the popular media frequently express mainstream, Enlightenment-oriented values, attitudes, and morals in examining these issues, assigning more value to some things than to others (Huntington, 1996; Lakoff, 2006; McWhorter, 2000; C. Murray & Herrnstein, 1994; O'Reilly, 2007; J. Q. Wilson, 1995).

One outcome of such thinking is a belief in *biological determinism*—the attempt to differentiate social behavior on the basis of biological and genetic endowment. One form of biological determinism is based on racial identity. For example, a person's intellectual performance is associated with skin color and other physical differences believed to be related to race. **Race,** however, is a social construction based on biological differences in appearance. No racial differences in cognitive and intellectual capacities have been found to be biologically based. There is no verifiable evidence that the fundamental composition and functioning of the brain differs between Blacks and Whites, Asians and Hispanics, or whatever so-called racial groups you can identify and compare (S. Gould, 1981; Mullings, 2005). Yet many still believe that race makes people inherently different. Such false associations are a vestige of Enlightenment thinking.

As a social work student, you can recognize the power and influence of such tendencies. Thinking in terms of natural, ordained, and inevitable differences based on race reinforces the social tendency to think in terms of "we-ness" and "they-ness," which often has unfortunate effects (Jandt, 2010). It leads to what has come to be called *othering*, or labeling people who fall outside of your own group as abnormal, inferior, or marginal. In your personal and professional lives, pay attention to the images and thoughts you use to make sense of the economic, social, and behavioral difficulties of Black people or other ethnic groups. Pay attention to the characterizations of English-speaking and non–English-speaking immigrants, or of legal and illegal immigrants.

The 20th- and 21st-century scholars of culture inherited both advances and limitations in thought from scholars of previous centuries. With these challenges in mind, anthropologist Franz Boas (1940/1948) encouraged us to understand cultural differences as environmental differences interacting with the accidents of history.

Before we go further, it is important to note that many contemporary culture scholars suggest

| Social constructionist perspective; Social behavioral perspective |

that environmental differences interacting with accidents of history have produced three major types of culture in recent centuries (see Griswold, 2008; Leeder, 2004). They suggest the name *traditional culture,* or *premodern culture,* to describe preindustrial societies based on subsistence agriculture. They argue that this type of culture was markedly different from *modern culture,* which arose with the 18th-century Enlightenment and is characterized by rationality, industrialization, urbanization, and capitalism. **Postmodernism** is the term many people use to describe contemporary culture. They suggest that global electronic communications is the foundation of postmodern culture, exposing people in advanced capitalist societies to media images that span place and time and allow them to splice together cultural elements from these different times and places (Griswold, 2008). Exhibit 6.3 presents the primary characteristics usually attributed to these three types of culture. While culture scholars who make these distinctions often present these three types as a historical timeline, running from traditional to modern to postmodern culture, we suggest that traits of all three types of culture can be found in advanced capitalist societies today, and often become the source of contemporary culture wars within societies. Furthermore, many nonindustrial and newly industrializing societies can be characterized as either traditional or modern cultures, or some mixture of the two.

Some Important Culture Concepts

The following concepts are central to contemporary thinking about culture.

- *Ideology.* Ideology is the dominant ideas about the way things are and should work. Problems of inequality and discrimination arise when ideology supports social, economic, and political exploitation and subjugation of some people. Ideologies that justify exploitation and inequality get built

| Conflict perspective |

into the everyday, taken-for-granted way the culture's members live their lives.

- *Ethnocentrism.* Through cross-cultural comparisons, anthropologists have demonstrated that Western culture is not universal. They have exposed our tendency to elevate our own ethnic group and its culture over

| Social constructionist perspective; Psychodynamic perspective |

Exhibit 6.3 Characteristics of Traditional, Modern, and Postmodern Culture

Characteristic	Traditional Culture	Modern Culture	Postmodern Culture
Role of Rationality	Positive value for irrational aspects of life; religious traditions superior to reason	Supreme value of rationality; rational control of nature	Questions the limits of rationality
Status	Status based on blood line; hierarchy as natural order; patriarchy	Status based on achievement; egalitarianism	Emphasis on difference, not power
Source of Authority	Religious authority	Nation-state; science	Globalization; national authority breaks down
Stability and Change	Stability and order valued; order based on religion	Progress valued	Unpredictability and chaos
Unit of Value	Communal values	Individualism	Diversity: multiplicity of perspectives and voices
Life Structure	Agrarian, subsistence agriculture	Industrialization, urbanization, capitalism, commodity fetishism, specialization of function	Electronic communications, simulation, mass consumption

others, a tendency known as **ethnocentrism.** For instance, theories of personality development are based on Western ideals of individuality and reliance on objective science rather than Eastern ideals of collective identity and reliance on subjective processes such as spirituality (Kottak, 2008; Matsumoto, 2007; Shweder & LeVine, 1984/1995; B. Whiting & Whiting, 1975).

• *Cultural symbols.* A **symbol** is something, verbal or nonverbal, that comes to stand for something else. The letters *d-o-g* have come to stand for the animal we call *dog;* golden arches forming a large *M* stand for McDonald's restaurants or hamburgers; water in baptism rites stands for something sacred and holy and moves a person from one state of being to another (D'Andrade, 1984/1995; Kottak, 2008). Race, ethnicity, and gender are symbols that can be thought of in this way as well. For instance, beyond biological differences, what comes to mind when you think of a girl or woman? What about a boy or man? How do the images,

thoughts, and feelings you possess about gender influence how you interact with boys and girls, men and women? Gendered thinking undoubtedly influences your assessment of persons, even those you have not actually met. In short, symbols shape perception, or the way a person sees, feels, and thinks about the world, and they communicate a host of feelings, thoughts, beliefs, and values that people use to make sense of their daily lives and to guide their behavior (Ortner, 1973; Wilkin, 2009). The idea that symbols express meaning within a culture is part of many recent models of practice in social work and psychology. For example, social constructionists focus on narratives and stories as emotional and behavioral correctives in clinical social work practice.

• *Worldview and ethos. Worldview* is associated with the cognitive domain—what we think about things; *ethos* is associated more with the emotional or affective and stylistic dimensions of behavior— how we feel about things (Ortner, 1984, p. 129).

Like Stan and Tina, recent Hispanic/Latino and African immigrants are adept at using symbols such as clothing, language, and music to convey specific feelings and perceptions that express their world-view and ethos.

- *Cultural innovation.* Culture is not static; it is adapted, modified, and changed through interactions over time. This process is known as **cultural innovation.** For example, Stan and Tina were described earlier as innovators. Both restyle mainstream clothing to fit with their sense of meaning and with the values of their peers and their community. In addition, in the classroom and with peers, Stan and Tina can switch between Standard English and Black English. The mode of language they use depends on the social and political message or identity they want to convey to listeners. We see economic cultural innovation with immigrants, both recent and in the past.

- *Cultural conflict.* The symbols we use can mean one thing to you and something different to others. Therefore, cultural conflict over meanings can easily arise. For example, jeans that hang low on the hips of adolescents and young adults generally signify an ethos of hipness, toughness, and coolness. This is the style, mood, and perspective of a particular generation. However, the clothing, music, and language of politically and economically disadvantaged Black and Hispanic/Latino adolescents convey a different symbolic meaning to law enforcers, school officials, parents, and even social workers. In today's sociopolitical climate, these authority figures are likely to perceive low-slung jeans not only as signs of hip-hop culture, but also as signs of drug and gang culture or as a form of social rebellion, decadence, or incivility.

Conflict perspective

In sum, culture is both public and private. It has emotional and cognitive components, but these play out in public in our social actions. Symbols are a way of communicating private meaning through public or social action. Furthermore, people's actions express their worldview (how they think about the world) and their ethos (how they feel about the world)—just as Tina and Stan do when they alternate between Black and mainstream styles.

These concepts have great relevance to social work. For example, arguments accompanying welfare reform legislation in the United States in the late 1990s represented shifting meanings regarding poverty, single parenting, and work. During the 1960s, it was considered society's moral duty to combat poverty by assisting the poor. Today, poverty does not just mean a lack of financial resources for the necessities of life; to many people, it symbolizes laziness, the demise of family values, and other characteristics that shade into immorality. Thus, to help people who are poor is now often purported to hurt them by consigning them to dependency and immoral behavior.

As social workers, we depend on the NASW Code of Ethics for professional guidance in negotiating these shifts. But what is the source of the values and beliefs that guide our personal lives? And what happens when what we believe and value differs from our clients' beliefs and values? Exhibit 6.4 demonstrates several cultural conflicts that may arise as our personal social habits confront our principles, values, and ethics as professional social workers.

Critical Thinking Questions 6.1

When you think of your day-to-day life, do you think you live in a traditional, modern, or postmodern culture? Explain. What do you see as the benefits and costs of each of these types of culture?

A POSTMODERN VIEW OF CULTURE

Forty or more years ago, the problems of Village Park and Community High School would have been explained largely in terms of a **culture of poverty.** The term *culture of poverty* was originally used to bring attention to the way of life developed by poor

What are your beliefs about the following interactions with clients and colleagues?		
Continuum		
Most Professional (Formal)		*Least Professional (Informal)*
Greetings by handshake .... hugging... kissing		
Use of last name/title .... first name .... nickname (Mr., Ms., Dr.)		
Authority by credentials .... age, experience, ... religion/politics (BSW, MSW, etc.) gender, marital status		
Sharing no personal .... pertinent information .... open-ended, information mutual sharing		
Confidentiality .... sharing with professionals/ .... sharing with friends/ family community members		

people to adapt to the difficult circumstances of their lives. Proponents of this theoretical orientation twisted it to suggest that Black schools and communities were impoverished because of Black people's own beliefs, values, traditions, morals, and frames of reference. Mainstream culture's racism and discrimination were not considered to be decisive factors. That Black people faced *redlining,* a practice that forced them to buy or rent homes only in Black communities, was not considered to be a factor. That Black people were working in low-income jobs despite qualifications for better ones was not considered to be a factor. That major colleges and universities were denying admission to qualified Black applicants was not considered to be a factor either. The list could go on. The culture of poverty orientation was used to argue both for and against publicly financed social programs. Even today, in public discourse, a culture of poverty line of reasoning is often used to explain people on welfare, poor single parents, and other problems of inner cities.

Contemporary and postmodern culture scholars (anthropologists, sociologists, psychologists, political scientists, social workers, economists) have also adopted some of the tenets of past theorizing. They have taken parts of it to develop what has come to be called postmodern and **practice orientations** (Berger & Luckmann, 1966; Bourdieu, 1977; Giddens, 1979; Ortner, 1989, 1996, 2006; Sahlins, 1981). *Practice* as used here is different from its use in social work. This theoretical orientation seeks to explain what people do as thinking, intentionally acting persons who face the impact of history and the constraints of structures that are embedded in our society and culture. It asks how social systems shape, guide, and direct people's values, beliefs, and behavior. But it also asks how people, as human actors or agents, perpetuate or shape social systems.

History, social structure, and human agency are key elements in a practice orientation. *History* is made by people, but it is made within the constraints of the social, economic, political, physical, and biological systems in which people are living. To understand human diversity, especially as it relates to oppression, exploitation, and subjugation, we must listen to the memories of both official and unofficial observers. We must listen to clients as much as to social workers.

> Social constructionist perspective; Conflict perspective

Structure refers to the ordered forms and systems of human behavior existing in public life (e.g., capitalism, family, public education). It also includes cognitive, emotional, and behavioral frameworks that are mapped onto who we are as people. We carry forth meanings, values, and beliefs through social, economic, and political practices in our everyday personal lives and the institutions in which we participate. We reproduce structures when we assume the rightness of our values, beliefs, and meaning and see no need to change them. When one set of values, beliefs, and meanings dominates, **cultural hegemony** results—the dominance of a particular way of seeing the world. Most observers of culture in the United States would agree that it is based on the hegemony of a Euro-American, or Anglo, worldview. People in many other parts of the world have observed a hegemony of the U.S. worldview. And there is much evidence that those whose cultures are overtaken by another culture often resent the hegemony. Chapter 7 deals with trends and patterns in contemporary social institutions and social structures, at the national and global levels.

Human agency asserts that people are not simply puppets, the pawns of history and structure; people are also active participants, capable of exercising their will to shape their lives. Thus, although racism is structured into society, it is not so completely dominant over Tina and Stan that they have no room for meaningful self-expression in their social and political lives. Human agency is a major source of hope and motivation for social workers who encounter people, organizations, and systems that seem unable to break away from the constraints of daily life. Human agency helps to counteract cultural hegemony as well. However, no individual or group is a fully free agent. All are constrained by external factors such as the climate, disease, natural resources, and population size and growth—although we may be able to modify these constraints through technology (J. Diamond, 1999). Examples of technologies that modify facts of biology and nature are medicines, agricultural

Humanistic perspective

breakthroughs, climate-controlled homes, telecommunications, transportation, and synthetic products that replace the use of wood in furniture and related items.

The issue of poverty offers one example of how the practice orientation can be applied. The practice orientation would not blame poverty's prevalence and influence in Tina and Stan's community solely on the failings of individuals. Rather, it would seek to identify the structural factors—such as low-income jobs, housing segregation, and racism—that impede upward mobility. It would also seek to understand how poor African Americans perceive and contribute to their conditions; how nonpoor, non-Black Americans perceive and contribute to the conditions of poor African Americans; and how all of these perceptions and actions shape the lives and influence the upward mobility of poor African Americans. Is there a "culture" of poverty, or do people in dire circumstances adapt their values and beliefs to the demands of survival?

We can use the practice orientation to ask, how have the values, beliefs, and practices of the social work profession helped to maintain the profession and society as they are? When we label the people we have failed to help as resistant, unmotivated, and pathological, are we carelessly overlooking the ineffectiveness of our modes of understanding and intervention? Are we blaming the victim and reproducing his or her victimization? These and other questions are important for all of us to ponder.

Cultural Maintenance, Change, and Adaptation

Tina's and Stan's experiences with mainstream schooling provide a good example of how cultural structures are maintained, how they change, and how they adapt. School systems are centered on the norms, values, and beliefs preferred by those who have had the power to decide what is or is not appropriate to learn and use in our lives. Some things we learn in school fit well with the needs of industry. Other things we learn fit well with the needs of our social and political institutions. From the outside looking in, schools look like benign or innocent institutions that are simply about academics and education. Yet which academic subjects are taught, how they are taught, who teaches them, and how they are to be learned involve an assertion of someone's values and beliefs, whether right or wrong, whether shared by many or few. Even in the face of evidence that schools do not work for many of us, they persist. Education is strongly correlated with economic and social success.

Culture provides stability to social life, but it does change over time. It does not change rapidly, however. First, we will look at some ideas about how culture produces stability, and then we will turn to how culture changes over time through immigration and processes of negotiating multicultural community life.

Common Sense, Customs, and Traditions

Over time, the ways in which families, schools, cities, and governments do things have come to seem natural to us. They seem to fit with the common sense, customs, and traditions of most people in our society.

Keep in mind, however, that **common sense** is a cultural system. It is what people have come to believe everyone in a community or society should know and understand as a matter of ordinary, taken-for-granted social competence. It is based on a set of assumptions that are so unself-conscious that they seem natural, transparent, and an undeniable part of the structure of the world (Geertz, 1983; Swidler, 1986).

Yet not everyone—especially not members of oppressed, subjugated, or immigrant groups within a society—is likely to share these common schemes of meaning and understanding. Thus, common sense becomes self-serving for those who are in a position of power to determine what it is and who has it. We believe common sense tells us what actions are appropriate in school or in any number of other contexts. But, as a part of culture, common sense is subject to historically defined standards of judgment related to maleness and femaleness, parenting, poverty, work, education, and psychosocial functioning, among other categories of social

being. For better or worse, common sense helps to maintain cultures and societies as they are.

We need to approach customs and traditions with the same caution with which we approach common sense. **Customs,** or cultural practices, come into being and persist as solutions to problems of living (Goodenough, 1996). **Tradition** is a process of handing down from one generation to another particular cultural beliefs and practices. Traditions become so taken for granted that they seem "natural" parts of life, as if they have always been here and as if we cannot live without them (Hobsbawm, 1983; Swidler, 1986; R. Williams, 1977). They are not necessarily followed by everyone in the culture, but they seem necessary and ordained, and they stabilize the culture. They are, in a sense, collective memories of the group. They reflect meanings at a particular moment in time and serve as guides for the present and future (I. W. Chung, 2006; McHale et al., 2009).

Customs and traditions are selective, however. They leave out the experiences, memories, and voices of some group members while highlighting and including others. African American, Latino/Hispanic, and Native American students generally do not experience schooling as reflecting their traditions and customs. To reflect Village Park residents' traditions and customs, Community High would have to respect and understand the use of Nonstandard English as students are learning Standard English. Literature and history classes would make salient connections between European traditions and customs and those of West Africans, Afro-Caribbeans, and contemporary African Americans. In addition, processes for including a student's family in schooling processes would include kinship bonds that are not based on legalized blood ties or the rules of state foster care systems. What do you think a school social worker would have to learn to assist schools and to help immigrant families in your community to have a more successful experience in school?

Customs and traditions, moreover, play a role in the strain that characterizes shifts from old patterns and styles of living to new ones in schools and other institutions in society. To survive, groups of

Photo 6.2 These mothers from different cultural backgrounds may have some different traditions and customs about child rearing, but they find their toddlers to have much in common.

people have to bend their traditions and customs without letting them lose their essence. Nondominant ethnic, gender, religious, and other groups in the United States often have to assimilate or accommodate their host culture if they are to share in economic and political power. In fact, the general survival of the traditions and customs of nondominant groups requires adaptability.

Customs and traditions are parts of a cultural process that are changing ever so subtly and slowly but at times abruptly. Sometimes groups disagree about these changes, and some members deny that they are occurring because they believe they should still do things the old way. Social workers have to understand a group's need to hold onto old ways. They do this to protect their worldview about what life means and who they are as a people.

Immigration

It is hard to deny that the United States is a nation of immigrants (Parrillo, 2009). Immigration to

this land began with the gradual migration of prehistoric peoples reported by anthropologists, and picked up speed when Columbus and other Europeans arrived from across the Atlantic Ocean. It continued with the involuntary arrival of Africans and the voluntary and semi-voluntary arrivals of various European ethnic groups. Later came Asian people and others. Forceful extension of the nation's borders and political influence incorporated Hispanics and Pacific Islanders. There have been many subsequent waves of immigration, with a great influx late in the 20th century that continues today. Now, more than ever, people are coming to the United States from all over the world. Today we define cultural diversity as a relatively new issue, but the nation's fabric has long included a rich diversity of cultures (Hing, 2004).

Although diversity has been a feature of life in the United States for centuries, immigration is an especially prominent feature of society today. According to U.S. Census estimates, 34.2 million foreign-born residents now reside in the United

States (U.S. Census Bureau, 2002a, 2002b, 2004). They represent 12% of the total U.S. population of 300 million. Over 53% of these immigrants were born in Latin America in general, and 37.7% were born in Central America in particular. They constitute what the media have called the "browning" of the United States. As for the remaining immigrants, 25.4% of all foreign-born U.S. residents were born in Asia, 13.6% in Europe, and 7.5% in other regions of the world. One of every three foreign-born people is a naturalized citizen (U.S. Census Bureau, 2002a, 2002b).

These population profiles represent relatively recent immigration trends. For example, 18% of immigrants alive today entered the United States since 2000, 39.5% in the 1990s, 28.3% entered in the 1980s, 16.2% in the 1970s, and the remaining 16.0% arrived before 1970 (U.S. Census Bureau, 2002a, 2002b). Each group brings with it its own cultural traditions and languages, which influence its worldview; ethos; and social, economic, and political beliefs and values. Nevertheless, foreign-born people have a few characteristics in common. For example, they are more likely to live in central cities of metropolitan areas and to live in larger households than nonimmigrants, those age 25 and over are roughly 67% as likely as nonimmigrants to have graduated from high school, and 6 million (17.1%) are in poverty (U. S. Census Bureau, 2002a, 2002b, 2004a).

Although a large number of immigrants realize their dream of economic opportunity, many (but not all) encounter resistance from the native-born. Let us consider the case of immigrants from Latin American countries (Central and South America and the Caribbean). This group recently surpassed African Americans as the largest minority in the United States and is therefore the group that social workers are increasingly likely to encounter. New York City, Los Angeles, Chicago, San Antonio, Houston, and other southwestern cities are traditional sites for the settlement of Hispanic/Latino immigrants. However, they are also settling in increasing numbers in growing metropolitan areas.

Like other Americans, many Hispanic/Latino immigrants come to the United States to get a piece of the economic pie. However, Hispanic/Latino immigrants face a unique set of circumstances. One often hears complaints about "foreigners taking our jobs." African Americans and Latinos/Hispanics face social conflicts over lifestyles in the low-income neighborhoods they share. Social service and law enforcement agencies scramble for Spanish-language workers and interpreters. Banks decry the fact that many new Spanish-language residents don't trust banks and consequently don't open checking and savings accounts. An understanding of cultural processes helps social workers interpret such issues when they encounter them in practice.

Processes of Cultural Change

In multicultural societies, cultural change can be understood in terms of four processes: assimilation, accommodation, acculturation, and bicultural socialization. They describe the minority individual's or group's response to the dominant culture and may have implications for clients' well-being.

- *Assimilation.* **Assimilation** is the process in which the cultural uniqueness of the minority is abandoned, and its members try to blend invisibly into the dominant culture (Kottak, 2008). Some culture scholars have noted a prevailing assimilation ideology that asserts the ideal of Anglo conformity (M. Gordon, 1964). In keeping with this view, some people have argued that the root of the problems faced by African Americans and by economically marginal immigrants is that they have not assimilated successfully. This argument is oversimplified. First, to the extent that discrimination is based on obvious features such as skin color or lack of facility with Standard English, the ability to assimilate is limited. Second, capitalist economies and societies arbitrarily select different group characteristics as desirable at different times. Historically, we have done this in part through immigration policies that admit some groups but not others. For example, the Chinese Exclusion Act of 1882, which was not repealed until 1943, suspended the right of people from China to immigrate to the United States. Many minorities, especially first-generation immigrants, often resist giving up parts of their ethnic identity in order to protect their sense of meaning and purpose in life.

- *Accommodation.* This process is more common than assimilation in multicultural, multiethnic society in the United States. **Accommodation** is the process of partial or selective cultural change. Nondominant groups follow the norms, rules, and standards of the dominant culture only in specific circumstances and contexts. When Punjabi Sikh children attended school in Stockton, California, in the 1980s, they generally followed the rules of the school (Gibson, 1988). They did not, however, remove their head coverings, socialize with peers of both sexes as is normal in mainstream U.S. society, or live by U.S. cultural standards at home. Some of the Muslim students at Community High could be compared to the Punjabis. Black Muslim girls at Community High, for example, continue to wear their head coverings and their customary long gowns to attend school, even though the school asks them not to do so. Similar stories continue to turn up in local and national newspapers about students whose Islamic religious attire conflicts with school norms and rules, in Europe as well as the United States. Increasingly, Latino/Hispanic immigrants and native citizens are opting to retain their Spanish in many settings, even though they can and will speak English when necessary.

- *Acculturation.* As noted in Chapter 1, acculturation is a mutual sharing of culture (Kottak & Kozaitis, 2008). Although cultural groups remain distinct, certain elements of their culture change, and they exchange and blend preferences for foods, music, dances, clothing, and the like. As cities and towns grow in diversity, Mexican, Vietnamese, Asian Indian, and other cuisines are becoming more common. At the same time, these diverse cultural groups are incorporating parts of regional cultures into their lives.

- *Bicultural socialization.* The process of **bicultural socialization** involves a nonmajority

group or its members mastering both the dominant culture and their own (Robbins, Chatterjee, & Canda, 2006b). Bicultural socialization is necessary in societies that have relatively fixed notions about how a person should live and interact in school, work, court, financial institutions, and so on. A person who has achieved bicultural socialization has, in a sense, a dual identity. Mainstream economic, political, and social success requires nonmajority musicians, athletes, intellectuals and scholars, news anchors, bankers, and a host of others to master this process of cultural change and adaptation.

Social workers who conduct multidimensional cultural analyses should seek to uncover the processes by which culture is being maintained, changed, and adapted in the lives of the individuals and groups with whom they work. We must also be alert to the fact that the process of cultural change is not always voluntary, or a free and open exchange of culture. We must also pay attention to the political, social, and economic practices that undergird institutional norms and values. If these processes are harmful and oppressive for some people, we have a professional obligation, through our code of ethics, to facilitate change.

Women, people of color, immigrants, poor people, and other nondominant groups have historically not had a significant say in how cultural change proceeds. But having a limited voice does not eliminate one's voice altogether. As social workers, we must comprehend the process of cultural change affecting our clients and act in accord with such knowledge. We cannot accept only dominant notions about the meaning of the actions of exploited and subjugated groups. We cannot look only to mainstream culture and traditions of knowledge to determine the actions we take with nonmajority people. If we do, we are merely reproducing inequality and subjugation and limiting our effectiveness as human service providers.

Keep this discussion of culture in mind as we turn to discuss the physical environment and how it influences and is influenced by human behavior.

> Conflict perspective

As you do so, recall that culture is both inside our heads as understandings and in the external environment—as behavior and the things we construct from the material world around us. Anthropologists are particularly interested in the role of the material culture in shaping behavior and societies. That is the driving force of the multidisciplinary literature on the physical environment and human behavior.

> ### Critical Thinking Questions 6.2
>
> How much human agency do you think you have to take charge of your life? Do all people have the same level of human agency? What factors make a difference in how much human agency people have?

THE RELATIONSHIP BETWEEN THE PHYSICAL ENVIRONMENT AND HUMAN BEHAVIOR

As with most stories we hear as social workers, Ben Watson's story, as told at the beginning of the chapter, provides information about a number of interacting dimensions of human behavior. It presents issues of life course development, family and friend relationships, physical disability, and a struggle for emotional well-being. And, of course, a supremely important dimension of this unfolding story is the physical environment. Ben's story reminds us that all human behavior occurs not only in a cultural context, but also in a physical one.

Systems perspective

Perhaps the most obvious aspect of Ben's relationship with his physical environment is *accessibility*—the amount of ease with which he can act in his environment. But accessibility is only one relevant aspect. Gerald Weisman (1981) has identified 11 key concepts that unify the multidisciplinary study of the relationship between human behavior and the physical environment. (A slightly revised version of these concepts appears in Exhibit 6.5.) In addition to accessibility, Ben's story addresses another 7 of Weisman's 11 concepts: *activity* (a lot happening on the streets); *adaptability* (house rearranged to provide a first-floor bedroom and bath); *comfort* (attractive; charming decorating touches); *control* (It was *mine*); *crowding* (friends can come over without feeling cramped); *privacy* (I would have my privacy); and *sensory stimulation* (good natural lighting from the sun). We are also aware that the physical environment of the new apartment may hold very different *meanings* for the storyteller, for his parents, and for friends who visit. *Sociality* will be discussed later in the chapter. *Legibility* refers to the ease with which people can find their way in the environment. Legibility can be especially challenging in large regional hospitals, like the one where Ben was treated for his injury.

When we as social workers make person-in-environment assessments, we ought to pay attention to the physical environment, which has an inescapable influence on human behavior (see Germain, 1978, 1981; Gutheil, 1991, 1992; M. Kahn & Scher, 2002; Resnick & Jaffee, 1982; Seabury, 1971). The relationship between human behavior and the physical environment is a multidisciplinary study that includes contributions from the social and behavioral sciences of psychology, sociology, geography, and anthropology as well as from the design disciplines of architecture, landscape architecture, interior design, and urban and regional planning. Recently, it has also included contributions from neuroscience research (E. Sternberg, 2009; Zeisel, 2006) and public health (H. Frumkin, 2003; Northridge & Sclar, 2003). This discussion gives you some ways of thinking about the relationship between human behavior and the physical environment as you begin to consider the role it plays in the stories of the people you encounter in practice.

Most theorists start from an assumption that person and physical environment are separate entities and emphasize the ways in which the physical environment influences behavior. Some theorists,

Systems perspective

however, start from an assumption of person-environment unity and propose interlocking and

Exhibit 6.5 Key Concepts for Understanding Physical Environment–Behavior Relationships

Concept	Definition
Accessibility	Ease in movement through and use of an environment
Activity	Perceived intensity of ongoing behavior within an environment
Adaptability	Extent to which an environment and its components can be reorganized to accommodate new or different patterns of behavior
Comfort	Extent to which an environment provides sensory and mobility fit and facilitates task performance
Control	Extent to which an environment facilitates personalization and conveys territorial claims to space
Crowding	Unpleasant experience of being spatially cramped
Legibility	Ease with which people can conceptualize key elements and spatial relationships within an environment and effectively find their way
Meaning	Extent to which an environment holds individual or cultural meaning(s) for people (e.g., attachment, challenge, beauty)
Privacy	Selective control of access to the self or to one's group
Sensory stimulation	Quality and intensity of stimulation as experienced by the various sensory modalities
Sociality	Degree to which an environment facilitates or inhibits social interaction among people

SOURCE: Adapted from Weisman (1981). Reproduced with permission of the author.

ongoing processes of coexistence between people and physical environments—people shape their environment just as the physical environment influences them—an approach called *transactionalism* (see Minami & Tanaka, 1995; Wapner, 1995; Werner & Altman, 2000; C. Werner, Brown, & Altman, 2002). This transactional approach is consistent with the assumption of person-environment unity of this book.

Three broad categories of theory about human behavior and the physical environment are introduced in this chapter: stimulation theories, control theories, and behavior settings theories. Each of these categories of theory, and the research it has stimulated, provides useful possibilities for social workers to consider as they participate in

person-environment assessments, although stimulation theories and control theories have been more widely used than behavior settings theories. Exhibit 6.6 presents the key ideas and important concepts of these three types of theory.

Stimulation Theories

Have you thought about how you would react to the abundance of sunlight in Ben Watson's new apartment or the activity on his street? That question is consistent with **stimulation theories,** which focus on the physical environment as a source of sensory information that is essential for human well-being. The stimulation may be light, color, heat, texture, or scent, or it may be buildings,

Exhibit 6.6 Three Categories of Theories About the Relationship Between the Physical Environment and Human Behavior

Theories	Key Ideas	Important Concepts
Stimulation Theories	The physical environment is a source of sensory information essential for human well-being. Patterns of stimulation influence thinking, emotions, social interaction, and health.	Stimulus overload Stimulus deprivation
Control Theories	Humans desire control over their physical environments. Some person-environment configurations provide more control over the physical environment than others.	Personal space Territoriality Crowding Privacy
Behavior Settings Theories	Consistent, uniform patterns of behavior occur in particular settings. Behaviors of different persons in the same setting are more similar than the behaviors of the same person in different settings.	Behavior settings Programs Staffing

streets, and parks. Stimulation theorists propose that patterns of stimulation influence thinking, feelings, social interaction, and health.

Stimulation varies by amount—intensity, frequency, duration, number of sources—as well as by type. Stimulation theories that are based on theories of psychophysiological arousal assume that moderate levels of stimulation are optimal for human behavior (Gifford, 2007). However, both *stimulus overload* (too much stimulation) and *restricted environmental stimulation* (once called *stimulus deprivation*) have a negative effect on human behavior. Theorists interested in the behavioral and health effects of stimulus overload have built on Han Selye's work regarding stress (see Chapter 4).

Some stimulation theories focus on the direct, concrete effect of stimulation on behavior; others focus on the meanings people construct regarding particular stimuli (Gifford, 2007). In fact, people respond to both

Social behavioral perspective; Social constructionist perspective

the concrete and the symbolic aspects of their physical environments. A doorway too narrow to accommodate a wheelchair has a concrete effect on the behavior of a person in a wheelchair; it will also have a symbolic effect, contributing to the person's feelings of exclusion and stigma. Stimulation theories alert social workers to consider the quality and intensity of sensory stimulation in the environments where their clients live and work.

Environmental design scholars have begun to incorporate recent advances in neuroscience research to understand how the human brain responds to different types of stimulation in physical environments. Their goal is to use this knowledge to design environments that support brain development and functioning for the general population as well as for groups with special needs, such as premature newborns and persons with Alzheimer's disease (Zeisel, 2006). Neuroscientists are also working with architects and environmental psychologists to learn what aspects of the physical environment stimulate emotional and physical healing (E. Sternberg, 2009).

Control Theories

The ability to gain control over his physical environment is a central theme of Ben Watson's story.

Psychodynamic perspective;
Social behavioral
perspective

In that way, the story is a good demonstration of the ideas found in **control theories,** which focus on the issue of how much control we have over our physical environments and the attempts we make to gain control (Gifford, 2007). Four concepts are central to the work of control theorists: privacy, personal space, territoriality, and crowding. Personal space and territoriality are *boundary regulating mechanisms* that we use to gain greater control over our physical environments.

Privacy

Altman (1975) defines *privacy* as "selective control of access to the self or to one's group" (p. 18).

Psychodynamic perspective

This definition contains two important elements: Privacy involves control over information about oneself as well as control over interactions with others. Virginia Kupritz (2003) has extended Altman's work by making a distinction between speech or conversational privacy (being able to hold conversations without being overheard) and visual privacy (being free of unwanted observation). Contemporary innovations in communication technologies have introduced new concerns about having control over information with respect to oneself and one's group and about how to balance national security with rights to privacy (B. Friedman, Kahn, Hagman, Severson, & Gill, 2006).

Some of us require more privacy than others, and some situations stimulate privacy needs more than other situations. Ben Watson was accustomed to sharing a house with his university pals and didn't

Social constructionist
perspective

mind the lack of privacy that came with that situation. He felt differently about lack of privacy in his parents' home after rehab and was eager for a more private living situation, even though his privacy in some areas would be compromised by his need for a personal care assistant.

It appears that people in different cultures use space differently to create privacy. Susan Kent (1991) theorizes that the use of partitions, such as walls or screens, to create private spaces increases as societies become more complex. She particularly notes the strong emphasis that European American culture places on partitioned space, both at home and at work (see Duvall-Early & Benedict, 1992). More recent research supports this idea; for example, college students in the United States have been found to desire more privacy in their residence halls than Turkish students (Kaya & Weber, 2003).

Kupritz (2003) is interested in the physical attributes of workplace offices that satisfy the privacy needs of the U.S. workforce. She argues that in recent decades, employers have limited personal space of employees, using open-plan cubicles, based on the belief that such arrangements will facilitate communication among employees. Her research indicates that often the open cubicles have the opposite impact, because employees tend to communicate less when they feel they cannot control the privacy of communications.

Have you given much thought to your need for private space? How about the needs of your clients? Personal space and territoriality are two mechanisms for securing privacy.

Personal Space

Personal space, also known as *interpersonal distance,* is the physical distance we choose to maintain in interpersonal relationships. Robert Sommer (1969) has defined it as "an area with invisible boundaries surrounding a person's body into which intruders may not come" (p. 26). More recent formulations (Gifford, 2007) emphasize that personal space is not stable, but contracts and expands with changing interpersonal circumstances and with variations in physical settings. The distance you desire when talking with your best friend is likely to be different from the distance you prefer when talking with a stranger, or even with a known authority figure like your professor. The desired distance for any of these interpersonal situations is likely to expand in small spaces (Sinha & Mukherjee, 1996). We will want to recognize our own personal space requirements in different work situations and be sensitive to the personal space requirements of our coworkers and clients.

Variations in personal space are also thought to be related to age, gender, attachment style, previous victimization, and culture. The size of personal space has been found to increase with age until early adulthood (Gifford, 2007). One recent research project found that, in shopping malls in the United States and Turkey, adolescents interacting with other adolescents kept the largest interpersonal distance of any age group (Ozdemir, 2008). When encountering strangers, personal space has been found to increase again in late adulthood if there are declines in mobility (J. Webb & Weber, 2003). Males have often been found to require greater personal space than females, but research indicates that the largest interpersonal distances, on average, are kept in male–male pairs, followed by female–female pairs, with the smallest interpersonal distances kept in male–female pairs (Akande, 1997; Kilbury, Bordieri, & Wong, 1996; Ozdemir, 2008). One research project found no gender differences in personal space among children ages 7 to 9 (Vranic, 2003). There is also evidence that adults with insecure attachment style require a larger personal space than children and adults with secure attachments (Kaitz, Bar-Haim, Lehrer, & Grossman, 2004). Physically abused children have also been found to keep significantly larger personal space than non-abused children, suggesting that personal space provides a protective function for these children (Vranic, 2003).

In *The Hidden Dimensions,* Edward Hall (1966) reported that his field research indicated that members of contact-oriented, collectivist cultures (e.g., Latin, Asian, Arab) prefer closer interpersonal distances than members of non–contact-oriented,

Social constructionist perspective; Developmental perspective

individualist cultures (e.g., Northern European, North American). More recent research has supported this suggestion; for example, pairs in Turkish malls have been observed to interact more closely than pairs in U.S. malls (Ozdemir, 2008), but within-culture differences in interpersonal distance preferences have also been noted (G. W. Evans, Lepore, & Allen, 2000). Hirofumi Minami and Takiji Yamamoto (2000) suggest that communal space is more important than personal space in Japan and other Asian cultures that value intimate community life.

Previous research (Langer, Fiske, Taylor, & Chanowitz, 1976; Stephens & Clark, 1987) found that people maintain larger interpersonal distances when interacting with people with disabilities. However, a more recent study found that research participants sat closer to a research assistant in a wheelchair than to one without a visible disability (Kilbury et al., 1996). These researchers conjectured that recent legislation is reducing the stigma of disability. Some of this legislation will be discussed later in this chapter.

Sommer (2002) has updated his discussion of personal space by raising questions about how personal space is affected by digital technology. For example, how much personal space do we need to have intimate conversations on our cell phones? Sommer also raises questions about the impact of the computer on personal space, noting that at work people sometimes communicate by e-mail with coworkers sitting beside them in the same office. Other researchers have examined how much personal space people need when using automated teller machines and other technology where private information is stored and found that people report larger desired space than the space actually provided (Shu & Li, 2007).

Territoriality

Personal space is a concept having to do with individual behavior and about the use of space to control the interpersonal environment. **Territoriality** refers primarily to the behavior of individuals and small groups as they seek control over physical space

(R. B. Taylor, 1988), but recently, the concept has also been used to refer to attempts to control objects, roles, and relationships (G. Brown, Lawrence, & Robinson, 2005; Gifford, 2007). Territoriality leads us to mark, or personalize, our territory to signify our "ownership," and to engage in a variety of behaviors to protect it from invasion. The study of animal territoriality has a longer history than the study of human territorial behavior. For humans, there is much evidence that males are more territorial than females, but there is also some contradictory evidence (Kaya & Burgess, 2007; Kaya & Weber, 2003). For example, in crowded living conditions in Nigerian university residence halls, female students appeared to use more territorial strategies to cope, while male students used more withdrawal strategies (Amole, 2005). Other research shows that by their mid-teens, many youth in the United States want some territory of their own, as is sometimes demonstrated with graffiti, tagging, and gang behavior (Childress, 2004).

Irwin Altman (1975) classifies our territories as primary, secondary, and public. A *primary territory* is one that evokes feelings of ownership that we control on a relatively permanent basis and that is vital to our daily lives. For most of us, our primary territories would include our home and place of work. *Secondary territories* are less important to us than primary territories, and control of them does not seem as essential to us; examples might be our favorite table at Starbucks or our favorite cardio machine at the gym. *Public territories* are open to anyone in the community, and we generally make no attempt to control access to them—places such as public parks, public beaches, sidewalks, and stores. For people who are homeless and lack access to typical primary territories, however, public territories may serve as primary territories.

Much of the literature on territoriality draws on the functionalist sociological tradition (discussed in Chapter 2), emphasizing the positive value of territorial behavior to provide order to

---
Systems perspective;
Conflict perspective
---

the social world and a sense of security to individuals (R. Taylor, 1988). We know, however, that

territorial behavior can also be the source of conflict, domination, and oppression. Recently, it has been suggested that globalization is reducing territoriality among nation-states (Raustiala, 2005). And, indeed, globalization does blur national boundaries, but current national conversations about "securing our borders" are prime examples of territorial behaviors.

Crowding

The term *crowding* has sometimes been used interchangeably with *density,* but environmental psychologists make important distinctions between these terms. **Density** is the ratio of persons per unit area of a space. **Crowding** is the subjective feeling of having too many people

---
Social constructionist
perspective
---

around. Crowding is not always correlated with density; the feeling of being crowded seems to be influenced by an interaction of personal, social, and cultural as well as physical factors. For example, in one study the perception of crowding was associated with density among older adults living with extended families in India, but perceived social support in high-density environments buffered the perception of crowding and decreased personal space requirements (Sinha & Nayyar, 2000). Researchers (G. W. Evans et al., 2000) have compared different ethnic groups that live in high-density housing in the United States and found that Latin American and Asian American residents tolerate more density before feeling crowded than Anglo Americans and African Americans. These researchers also found, however, that all four ethnic groups experienced similar psychological distress from crowding. Another research team found that Middle Eastern respondents were less likely to perceive high-density retail situations as crowded than their North American counterparts (Pons, Laroche, & Mourali, 2006).

Research has also found gender differences in response to crowding. Women living in crowded homes are more likely to be depressed, while men living in crowded homes demonstrate higher levels of withdrawal and violence (Regoeczi, 2008). In crowded elementary school classrooms, girls' academic achievement and boys' classroom behavior are adversely affected (Maxwell, 2003).

Crowding has been found to have an adverse effect on child development (G. W. Evans & Saegert, 2000), and to be associated with elevated blood pressure and neuroendocrine hormone activity (Gifford, 2007), poor compliance with mental health care (Menezes, Scazufca, Rodrigues, & Mann, 2000), increased incidence of tuberculosis (Baker, Das, Venugopal, & Howden-Chapman, 2008; Wanyeki et al., 2006), and aggressive behavior in prison inmates (C. Lawrence & Andrews, 2004).

Behavior Settings Theories

Would you expect to see the same behaviors if you were observing Ben Watson in different settings—

| Social behavioral perspective; Systems perspective |

for example, his parents' home, his apartment, running errands in his neighborhood, at work, at a party with friends, or on an outing in the natural environment? My guess is that you would not. A third major category of theories about the relationship between human behavior and the physical environment is **behavior settings theories.** According to these theories, consistent, uniform patterns of behavior occur in particular places, or *behavior settings*. Behavior is *always* tied to a specific place, and the setting may have a more powerful influence on behavior than characteristics of the individual (Bechtel, 2000; M. Scott, 2005).

Behavior settings theory was first developed by Roger Barker (1968), who was searching for the factors that influence different individuals to behave differently in the same environment. He and his colleagues studied human behavior in public settings, rather than in the laboratory, where individual differences were usually studied. They unexpectedly noted that observations of different persons in the same setting, even when substantial time elapsed between the observations, were more similar than observations of the same person in different settings, even when there was only a short time between observations. For example, your behavior at a musical festival is more similar to the behavior of other festival attendees than it is to your own behavior in the classroom or at the grocery store.

Barker suggested that *programs*—consistent, prescribed patterns of behavior—develop and are maintained in many specific settings. For example, when you enter a grocery store, you grab a cart, travel down aisles collecting items and putting them in the cart, and take the cart to a checkout counter where you wait while store employees tabulate the cost of the items and bag them (or you take your items to a self-serve checkout counter). Imagine how surprised you would be if you went into the grocery store to find everybody kicking soccer balls! You might argue that behavior settings theory is more about the social environment than the physical environment—that behavioral programs are socially constructed, developed by people in interaction, and not determined by the physical environment. According to this theory, however, behavioral programs are created conjointly by individuals and their inanimate surroundings, and behavior settings are distinctive in their physical-spatial features as well as their social rules. The relationships of the social and physical environments to behavior can be summarized in these words: "*It is the social situation that influences people's behavior, but it is the physical environment that provides the cues*" (Rapoport, 1990, p. 57).

However, in recent years, behavior settings theory has been extended to explain behavior in non-place settings, more specifically to explain behavior in *virtual behavior settings* such as online chat rooms and blogs (Stokols & Montero, 2002). This line of inquiry is interested in how interaction in such virtual behavior settings is integrated, or not, with the place-based settings in which it occurs, such as the home, workplace, or Internet café.

Behavior settings as conceptualized by Barker had a static quality, but Allan Wicker (1987) has more recently written about the changing nature— the life histories—of behavior settings. Some settings disappear (Have you been to a barn raising lately?), and some become radically altered. These days, that trip to the grocery store often involves getting your own reusable grocery bags from the car before entering the store (or making a trip back to the car to get them when you are almost at the store door).

Behavior settings theory has implications for social work assessment and intervention. It suggests that patterns of behavior are specific to a setting and, therefore, we must assess settings as well as individuals when problematic behavior occurs. Ben Watson was feeling restless at his parents' home, but we do not see behaviors that suggest he was feeling the same way once he got settled in North Carolina. The behavior setting may not be the only factor involved in this change, but it should be considered as one possible factor. Behavior settings theory also suggests that the place where we first learn a new skill helps recreate the state necessary to retrieve and enact the skill. When we are assisting clients in skill development, we should pay particular attention to the discontinuities between the settings where the skills are being "learned" and the settings where those skills must be used.

Another key concept in behavior settings theory is the level of *staffing* (R. G. Barker, 1968; L. Brown, Shepherd, Wituk, & Meissen, 2007; Wicker, 1979). Different behavior settings attract different numbers of participants, or staff. It is important to have a good fit between the number of participants and the behavioral program for the setting. Overstaffing occurs when there are too many participants for the behavioral program of a given setting; understaffing occurs when there are too few participants. A growing body of research suggests that larger settings tend to exclude more people from action, and smaller settings put pressure on more people to perform (Bechtel, 2000). The issue of appropriate staffing, in terms of number of participants, for particular behavioral programs in particular behavior settings has great relevance for the planning of social work programs. Indeed, behavior settings theory and the issue of optimal staffing have been used to understand the benefits of member participation in consumer-run mental health organizations (L. Brown et al., 2007).

THE NATURAL ENVIRONMENT __

Do you find that you feel refreshed from being in the natural environment—walking along the beach, hiking in the mountains, or even walking in your neighborhood? Research findings suggest that you may, and that you should consider the benefits of time spent in the **natural environment**—the portion of the environment influenced primarily by geological and nonhuman biological forces—for both you and your clients. The natural environment has always been a place of serenity for Ben Watson. Most of the research on the relationship between human behavior and the natural environment has been in the stimulation theory tradition—looking for ways in which aspects of the natural environment affect our thinking, feeling, social interaction, and health. In general, this research identifies a strong human preference for elements of the natural world and finds many positive outcomes of time spent in the natural environment (H. Frumkin, 2001, 2003; P. Kahn, 1999; R. Kaplan & Kaplan, 1989; Newell, 1997; Sebba, 1991). These benefits are summarized in Exhibit 6.7. Sociobiologists

Exhibit 6.7 Benefits of Time Spent in the Natural Environment (Based on Stimulation Theory Research)

- Engaging children's interest
- Stimulating children's imagination
- Stimulating activity and physical fitness
- Increasing productivity
- Enhancing creativity
- Providing intellectual stimulation
- Aiding recovery from mental fatigue
- Improving concentration
- Enhancing group cohesiveness and community cooperation
- Fostering serenity
- Fostering a sense of oneness or wholeness
- Fostering a sense of control
- Fostering recovery from surgery
- Improving physical health
- Improving emotional state

propose that humans have a genetically based need to affiliate with nature; they call it **biophilia** (Kellert & Wilson, 1993; E. Wilson, 1984, 2007). They argue that humans have a 2 million–year history of evolving in natural environments and have only lived in cities for a small fraction of that time; therefore, we are much better adapted to natural environments than built environments.

In recent years, practitioners in various disciplines have taken the age-old advice of poets, novelists, and philosophers that natural settings are good for body, mind, and spirit, and have developed programs that center on activities in both wilderness and urban natural settings. Researchers who have studied the effects of such programs have found some positive gain and no evidence of negative effects (see Burton, 1981; P. Kahn, 1999; R. Kaplan & Kaplan, 1989). Studies on the impact of wilderness programs have reported three positive outcomes: recovery from mental fatigue with improved attention (Hartig, Mang, & Evans, 1991; R. Kaplan & Kaplan, 1989), enhanced group cohesiveness (Cumes, 1998; Ewert & Heywood, 1991), and spiritual benefits such as serenity and a sense of oneness or wholeness (Cumes, 1998; R. Kaplan & Kaplan, 1989).

But it may not be necessary to travel to wilderness areas to benefit from activity in natural settings. Urban community gardening projects have been found to contribute to the development of cooperation and to improved self-esteem among the participants (C. Lewis, 1979, 1996). The presence of trees and grass in the neighborhood has been found to stimulate social activity in common spaces (Sullivan, Kuo, & DePooter, 2004). Research with individuals involved in both community gardening and backyard gardening indicates benefits that include a sense of tranquility, sense of control, and improved physical health (R. Kaplan, 1983; S. Kaplan, 1995). Playing in outdoor green spaces has been found to improve attention among children and adolescents with attention deficit/hyperactivity disorder (ADHD) (Kuo & Faber Taylor, 2004). Opportunities to walk in outdoor urban green spaces have been found to increase longevity in a sample of older adults in Tokyo, even when controlling for social class, age, gender, marital status, and functional status (Takano, Nakamura, & Watanabe, 2002).

One does not have to be active in the natural environment to derive benefits from it. Surgery patients with views of nature from their hospital windows have been found to recover more quickly than patients whose window views have no nature content (Ulrich, 1984). Two studies in prison settings found that inmates who had views of nature from their cells sought health care less often than those without such views (E. Moore, 1981; West, 1986). In a psychiatric ward renovation project that included changes in or additions of paint, wallpaper, carpet, lighting, furniture, curtains, plants, and bathtubs, staff rated the addition of plants to be the most positive change (Devlin, 1992). Patients in a short-term psychiatric hospital were found to respond favorably to wall art that involved nature but negatively to abstract wall art (Ulrich, 1993). For 7- to 12-year-old girls living in inner-city high-rise apartments, having a view of nature from the home was associated with greater self-discipline; this association was not found for boys in the same environments, and the researchers speculate that boys spend more time in more distant green spaces than girls (A. Taylor, Kuo, & Sullivan, 2002). University students with a view of nature while taking a test scored better on the test than students who did not have a view of nature (Tennessen & Cimprich, 1995). Commuter drivers with nature-dominated drives demonstrate quicker recovery from stress than drivers whose drives have minimal nature scenery (Parsons, Tassinary, Ulrich, Hebl, & Grossman-Alexander, 1998). Several recent research projects report that views of natural settings stimulate recovery from stress (Hartig, Evans, Jamner, Davis, & Gärling, 2003; Hartig & Staats, 2006; Staats, Kieviet, & Hartig, 2003). Office workers have been found to experience less anger and stress when art posters with nature paintings are present (Byoung-Suk, Ulrich, Walker, & Tassinary, 2008).

Three features of the natural environment have been found to be particularly influential on emotional states: *water* (see Herzog, Herbert, Kaplan,

& Crooks, 2000; Yang & Brown, 1992); *trees* (see Sheets & Manzer, 1991; Kuo, Bacaicoa, & Sullivan, 1998; A. Taylor, Wiley, Kuo, & Sullivan, 1998); and *sunlight* (see Boubekri, Hull, & Boyer, 1991; Brawley, 2006; Sadock & Sadock, 2007; Westrin & Lam, 2007). These features of the natural environment have been found, across cultures, to have positive impact on emotional states, with water being the preferred element of the natural environment in both Eastern and Western cultures.

Given the strong evidence of the psychological benefits of time spent in nature, there is a growing call for **ecotherapy,** exposure to nature and the outdoors as a component of psychotherapy, as a major agenda for mental health promotion and treatment (see Buzzell, 2009; M. Jordan, 2009; Maller, Townsend, Pryor, Brown, & St. Leger, 2005; Mind, 2007). The combination of green spaces with physical exercise has been found to be a particularly potent program for mood elevation in people with major depression (Mind, 2007). This is important in light of estimates that major

depression will constitute one of the largest health problems worldwide by 2020 (Maller et al., 2005). Ecotherapy includes time spent with domestic and companion animals.

Although the natural environment can be a positive force, it also has the potential to damage mental, social, and physical well-being. For example, benefit comes from exposure to sunlight until a certain optimum point, after which increasing amounts damage rather than benefit emotional states. The natural environment provides sensory stimulation in an uncontrolled strength, and the patterns of stimulation are quite unstable. Extremely stimulating natural events are known as natural disasters, including such events as hurricanes, tornadoes, floods, earthquakes, volcanic eruptions, landslides, avalanches, tsunamis, and forest fires. Natural disasters are considered to be cataclysmic events—a class of stressors with great force, sudden onset, excessive demands on human coping, and large scope. These events are considered to be almost universally stressful (Kobayashi & Miura, 2000). Social workers play active roles in services to communities that have experienced natural disasters.

There is currently great international concern about the damage that is being done to the natural environment by human endeavors and about the need to protect the natural environment. In 2000, United Nations Secretary-General Kofi Annan called for an assessment of the consequences of natural environment change on human well-being. The report, presented in 2005, included four major findings (Millennium Ecosystem Assessment, 2005):

- In response to growing demands for food, fresh water, timber, and fuel, humans have changed ecosystems more over the last 50 years than in any other historical period. The result is a sizable and mostly irreversible loss of diversity of life.
- Although there are, to date, net gains for human well-being from these changes, they have exacerbated poverty for some groups of people. In addition, many costs of the changes will be deferred to future generations.

Photo 6.3 The physical environment (both natural and humanmade) impacts our behavior. Researchers have found a strong preference for elements of the natural environment and positive outcomes of time spent in nature.

- It is likely that the degradation of world ecosystems will grow significantly worse in the first half of the 21st century.
- Reversing the degradation of ecosystems will require major changes in policies across the globe.

THE BUILT ENVIRONMENT _____

It is the uncontrollable quality of the natural environment that humans try to overcome in constructing the **built environment**—the portion of the physical environment attributable solely to human effort. The built environment is intended to create comfort and controllability, but unfortunately, technological developments often have negative impacts as well. The toxic waste problem is but one example of the risks we have created but not yet learned to control. Social workers have called attention to the fact that the risks of environmental hazards are falling disproportionately on minority and low-socioeconomic communities (M. Kahn & Scher, 2002; Rogge, 1993). A very current concern is the dumping of electronic waste on developing nations. The U.S. Environmental Protection Agency estimates that the United States produces 300 million tons of electronic waste (e-waste) each year, and about 80% of it ends up in landfills overseas in conditions that are hazardous (Bennion, 2009).

For several decades, environmental psychologists have been studying the impact of the physical environment on such factors as mood, problem solving, productivity, and violent behavior. They have examined physical designs that encourage social interaction, *sociopetal spaces,* and designs that discourage social interaction, *sociofugal spaces.* As Exhibit 6.5 shows, Weisman (1981) refers to this social interaction aspect of the physical environment as *sociality.* Researchers have studied design features of such institutional settings as psychiatric hospitals, state schools for persons with cognitive disabilities, college dormitories, and correctional facilities. Late 20th- and early 21st-century developments in biomedical science, particularly new understandings of the brain and the immune system, have allowed more

sophisticated analysis of how the built environment affects physical and mental health and can be a source of healing (see E. Sternberg, 2009; Ulrich, 2006; Ulrich & Zimring, 2005).

Healing Environments

By many accounts, Roger Ulrich (1984) was the first researcher to measure the effects of the physical environment on physical health of hospital patients. He studied patients who had undergone gall bladder surgery and had rooms with two different types of view out their hospital windows. One group had views of a brown brick wall, and the other group had views of a small stand of trees. On average, the patients who had views of the trees left the hospital almost a day sooner than the patients with views of a brick wall. They also required less pain medication, received fewer negative comments from the nurses, and had slightly fewer postoperative complications.

The idea that nature is important to healing is not new; indeed, it has been around for thousands of years (E. Sternberg, 2009). Furthermore, there is a long tradition in architecture that proposes a connection of health with nature and building design (Joye, 2007). In the 19th century, hospitals were built with large windows, even skylights, and often in beautiful natural settings (Joye, 2007; E. Sternberg, 2009). Clinics and hospitals were particularly designed to take advantage of natural light because it was thought that sunlight could heal. Some public health scholars argue, however, that as medical technology became more sophisticated, hospital design began to focus more on care of the equipment than on care of the patient (Maller et al., 2005; E. Sternberg, 2009). These public health scholars are calling attention to biomedical research that links physical environments and human health.

Based on his early research, Roger Ulrich, a behavioral scientist, has collaborated with architects, environmental psychologists, and public and private agencies and foundations to develop a field called *evidence-based design,* which uses physiological and health-outcome measures to

Photo 6.4   There is a long tradition in architecture that proposes a connection of health with nature and building design.

evaluate the health benefits of hospital design features (Ulrich, 2006). Following on the earlier work of Ulrich, researchers use such measures as length of stay; amount of pain medication; rates of health complications; and patient satisfaction, stress, and mood to evaluate design innovations. By 2006, a total of 700 rigorous studies had been identified (Ulrich, 2006), and the Center for Health Design (2006) had been established to engage in ongoing hospital design innovations and evaluations. Two foci of this research are discussed here: noise and sunlight.

A great deal of international research has focused on hospital noise as an impediment to healing. This research consistently finds that hospital noise exceeds the guidelines recommended by the World Health Organization (E. Sternberg, 2009). Hospital noise comes from a variety of sources, for example, overhead paging, moving of bedrails, medical equipment, and staff shift changes. The problem is exacerbated in hospitals that have hard, sound-reflecting floors and ceilings. It is also intensified in multi-bed rooms because of the activity of

caring for multiple patients. Noise has been associated with high blood pressure and elevated heart rates, sleep loss, slower recovery from heart attack, and negative physiological responses such as apnea and fluctuations in blood pressure and oxygen saturation in infants in neonatal intensive care (G. Brown, 2009; Hagerman et al., 2005; Ulrich, 2006; Ulrich & Zimring, 2005). Preterm infants exposed to prolonged high levels of noise are at risk for hearing loss, impaired brain development, and speech and language problems (G. Brown, 2009). Excessive noise also contributes to staff fatigue (Ulrich, 2006). A number of design innovations have been found to be effective in reducing hospital noise. These include single-bed rooms, replacing overhead paging with a noiseless system, covering neonatal incubators with blankets, and installing high-performance sound-absorbing ceiling tiles and floor carpets (G. Brown, 2009; Ulrich, 2006). These innovations have been found to be related to improved health outcomes and fewer rehospitalizations for patients as well as improved staff satisfaction and home sleep quality (E. Sternberg, 2009).

There is also growing evidence that 19th-century hospital designers were accurate in their belief that sunlight can heal. Beauchemin and Hays (1998) found that patients recovering from heart attacks in sunny hospital rooms had significantly shorter hospital stays than patients recovering in rooms without natural light. Another research team studied patients recovering from spinal surgery in one hospital and compared the experiences of patients in sunny rooms with the experiences of patients in rooms without sunlight. Patients in sunny rooms took 22% less pain medication and had 21% lower medication costs than similar patients recovering in rooms without sunlight (Walch, Day, & Kang, 2005). The patients in the sunny rooms also reported less stress than patients in the rooms without sunlight. Hospital rooms with morning sunlight have also been found to reduce the hospital stays of patients with unipolar and bipolar depression (Beauchemin & Hays, 1996; Benedetti, Colombo, Barbini, Campori, & Smeraldi, 2001).

Urban Design and Health

Prior to the early 20th century in the United States, public health experts focused on what they called "the urban penalty" for health and mortality. As city size increased, so did the death rate. Infectious diseases, such as tuberculosis, measles, smallpox, and influenza, were the main cause of the urban penalty. Such diseases spread quickly in high-density environments. By the 1920s, improved sanitation and other public health measures had eliminated the urban penalty in the United States and other wealthy nations, but it still exists in very large cities in poorer nations, and in the poorest sections of cities in wealthy nations. The biggest threats to urban populations in the United States at the current time are violent crime and pollution, the latter of which contributes to high rates of asthma (E. Sternberg, 2009).

In recent years, some public health officials have begun to suggest an increasing rural and suburban penalty, and an urban advantage (see Vlahov, Galea, & Freudenberg, 2005). To illustrate, in 2007, public health data indicated that New York City was the healthiest location in the United States as indicated by longevity (the most commonly used measure of a geographical area's health). Life expectancy increased there by 6.2 years between 1990 and 2007, compared to 2.5 years for the rest of the country (E. Sternberg, 2009).

Considerable research has focused in recent years on urban sprawl and design features of suburban built environments that contribute to decreased physical activity. The researchers note the long distances that suburban dwellers need to travel to work and to amenities, requiring more time spent in the car. These researchers have been particularly interested in whether suburban built environments contribute to obesity and the related health problems of cardiovascular disease and diabetes. The evidence is mixed on this question. Some researchers have found that urban sprawl is associated with weight problems and obesity (Ewing, Schmid, Killingsworth, Zlot, & Raudenbush, 2003; L. Frank, Andresen, & Schmid, 2004; Garden & Jalaludin, 2009; Lopez, 2004). The Centers for Disease Control and Prevention (CDC, 2006d) has mapped obesity across the United States and found that it is a perfect match for the map of urban sprawl, both of which are greatest in the Southeast and Midwest. Others have found that aspects of the built environment contribute to neighborhood walkability, but no conclusive evidence that these design features contribute to obesity (Berke, Koepsell, Moudon, Hoskins, & Larson, 2007). The new urbanist designers are designing suburban towns with several features that are known to contribute to walkability: houses with front porches; neighborhood spots for congregation; sidewalks; short blocks; good lighting; amenities that are accessible by foot; public transportation; mixed-use areas, including residences, businesses, offices, and recreation centers; and bike paths, tennis courts, parks, and golf courses (WebUrbanDesign, 2009). The hope is that these design features will contribute to resident activity and health.

Lopez and Hynes (2006) enter this conversation with a more complicated story. They report that although it is true that obesity is associated with urban sprawl, inner-city populations have higher rates of obesity and inactivity than suburban dwellers. They suggest that different aspects of the physical environment are contributing to ill health for inner-city residents and making their neighborhoods unwalkable. Inner-city neighborhoods have some of the design features recommended by the new urbanist designers, features such as sidewalks, short blocks, and public transportation, but they have a set of barriers to walking that do not exist in suburbs, such as hazardous waste sites, abandoned buildings, decaying sidewalks, disappearing tree canopies, and dilapidated school playgrounds and parks. For example, one study found that low-income neighborhoods are 4 times as likely as high-income neighborhoods to have hazardous waste facilities, power plants, and polluting industrial plants, and low-income *minority* neighborhoods are 20 times as likely as high-income neighborhoods to have these facilities (Faber & Krieg, 2005, cited in Lopez & Hynes, 2006). Public health officials also warn that with the new types of infectious diseases whose spread is fueled by global warming, dense cities contribute to contagion (E. Sternberg, 2009).

Behavior Settings and Addictions

An emerging line of research suggests that behavior settings are an important element in substance addiction. For instance, Winifred Gallagher (1993) reports that large numbers of American soldiers who used heroin during the Vietnam conflict left the drug behind when they returned to an environment that they did not associate with heroin.

| Social behavioral perspective |

Shepard Siegel's research (Kim, Siegel, & Patenall, 1999; Ramos, Siegel, & Bueno, 2002; S. Siegel, 1991, 2001, 2005; S. Siegel & Allan, 1998; S. Siegel, Hinson, Krank, & McCully, 1982) also supports the idea that behavior settings play an important role in substance addiction. Siegel and colleagues found that when a person with a heroin addiction takes a customary dose of heroin in an environment where he or she does not usually take the drug, the reaction is much more intense, and an overdose may even occur. This consistent finding over time has led Siegel to suggest that *tolerance*—the ability to take increasing amounts of the drug without feeling increased effects—is embedded in the environment in which the drug is usually taken. He has also found that behavior settings stimulate craving, even when the person has been in recovery for some time. Siegel recommends that treatment include systematic exposure to cues from the behavior setting, with no reinforcement of drug ingestion, to provide environmental deconditioning. You may recognize that this approach to treatment comes from classical conditioning.

Maybe the concept of behavior setting also explains why many people with addictions attempt to shake them by moving to a new environment. Siegel reports that "studies from all over the world show that after a year, most of those who don't relapse after drug treatment have relocated" (cited in Gallagher, 1993, p. 138).

PLACE ATTACHMENT

Have you ever been strongly attached to a specific place—a beloved home, a particular beach or mountain spot, or a house of worship? **Place attachment**— the process in which people and groups form bonds with places—is the subject of a growing literature (Devine-Wright, 2009; Hidalgo & Hernandez, 2001; Kyle, Graefe, Manning, & Bacon, 2004; Manzo & Perkins, 2006). Although place attachment is usually discussed in terms of emotional bonding, an interplay of emotions, cognitions, and behaviors and actions is what forges the people–place bond (Low & Altman, 1992). Researchers have looked at attachment to places of different scale, including outdoor recreational areas (Kyle et al., 2004).

In the context of place attachment, *place* is defined as a "space that has been given meaning through personal, group, or cultural processes" (Low & Altman, 1992, p. 5). The literature on place attachment emphasizes emotional bonding to environmental settings that are satisfying in terms of one or more of the aspects of physical environment–behavior relationships presented in Exhibit 6.5, with different researchers focusing on different aspects. Those who focus on sociality emphasize that attachment to places may be based largely on our satisfying relationships with people in those places—once again reminding us of the inseparability of people and environments.

When a strong place attachment develops, it has been suggested that the place has become an important part of the self, that we can't think of who we are without some reference to the place (Gifford, 2007). When a particular place becomes an important part of our self-identity, this merger of place and self is known as **place identity.** Place identity can develop where there is strong negative, as well as positive, place attachment, as a boy named Kareem observes:

> Psychodynamic perspective; Social behavioral perspective

> It's strange, but I really like when the lights go off in the movies because then I'm no longer a "homeless kid." I'm just a person watching the movie like everyone else. A lot of the children at the hotel believe that they are "hotel kids." They've been told by so many people for so long that they are not important, that they live up to what is expected of them. It gets so some children have no dreams and live in a nightmare because they believe that they are "hotel kids." It's worse than being in jail. In jail you can see the bars and you know when you're getting out. In the hotel you can't see the bars because they're inside of you and you don't know when you're getting out. (Quoted in Berck, 1992, p. 105)

Home and work are the settings most likely to become merged with our sense of self, but recent research has focused on attachment to the neighborhood (Altman, 1993; Devine-Wright, 2009; Manzo & Perkins, 2006). Place attachment can also play a strong role in group and cultural identity (Low & Altman, 1992). One study found that many Cambodian American and Filipino American older adults expressed a desire to die in their homelands (G. Becker, 2002).

Researchers have been particularly interested in what happens to people when a place of identity is lost. Certainly, we should pay attention to issues of place identity when we encounter people who have relocated, particularly when working with immigrant and refugee families. We should also consider the long-term consequences of early experiences, such as homelessness or frequent movement between foster homes, in which no stable place attachment forms, or that result in a negative place attachment.

HOMELESSNESS

As suggested above, place attachment can be quite problematic for people without homes. The official U.S. definition of homelessness is found in Exhibit 6.8. The National Coalition for the Homeless (NCH, 2009a) points out that this definition does not apply as well in rural areas as it does in urban areas, because there are few shelters in rural areas. Many homeless rural people live in crowded situations with relatives or in substandard housing.

It is difficult to count the number of people who are homeless in the United States and worldwide, but there are widely accepted estimates of both. In 2005, a United Nations (UN) report estimated 100 million homeless people worldwide and 1.6 billion inadequately housed people (National Alliance to End Homelessness [NAEH], 2005). Economic globalization, poverty, and lack of affordable housing are thought to be the major causes of global homelessness. The UN report emphasized the contributing role of inequality in home ownership, noting that, worldwide, almost 75% of private land is controlled by 2.5% of landowners.

There are several national estimates of the number of people who are homeless in the United States and different methods for deriving estimates (NCH, 2009b). Some researchers count the number of people who are homeless at a given point in time, on a given day or during a given week, and others count the number of people who have a spell of homelessness over a given period of time, usually a year. One problem in counting the number of homeless persons is that many people without homes stay in places where researchers cannot easily find them, for example, in automobiles or campgrounds. In 2009, the National Alliance to End Homelessness (NAEH, 2009) estimated that over a month's time, there are 671,859 homeless people in the United States. The NCH (2009a) estimates that between 2.3 and 3.5 million people are homeless in the United States each year. In most cases, homelessness is temporary, and the average stay in an emergency shelter is 70 days for families, 69 days for single men, and 51 days for single women.

In 2008 and 2009, housing foreclosures, eroding work opportunities, and the declining value of public assistance increased the number of people who experience homelessness (NCH, 2009c). A 2007 survey found that half of the cities surveyed had to turn people away from emergency shelters (U.S. Conference of Mayors, 2007). About 75% of

homeless people in the United States are from urban areas (NAEH, 2009). Families with children are one of the fastest growing segments of the homeless population, constituting 23% in 2007. Males make up 68% of the single segment of the homeless population but are represented in only 35% of homeless families with children. Approximately half of all women and children experiencing homelessness are escaping from domestic violence. Twenty-six percent of sheltered homeless persons have severe mental illness, and among surveyed homeless persons, sheltered and unsheltered, 38% report an alcohol problem and 26% report problems with other drugs. African Americans are overrepresented in among the homeless, accounting for 42% of the sheltered homeless population (NCH, 2009b).

ACCESSIBLE ENVIRONMENTS FOR PERSONS WITH DISABILITIES

Accessibility is one of the key concepts for the study of human behavior and the physical environment (see Exhibit 6.5). In recent years, we have been reminded that environments, particularly built environments, can be disabling because of their inaccessibility to many persons, including most people with disabilities. Ben Watson provides us with several examples of how the physical environment curtailed his activity at times, and he is now in a professional position to try to minimize the barriers that people with disabilities experience in the world. The *social model of disability* emphasizes the barriers that people with impairments face as they interact with the physical and social world, arguing that disability is a result of the relationship between the individual and the environment (see Swain, French, Barnes, & Thomas, 2004).

This way of thinking about disability was the impetus for development of the Disabled Peoples' International (2005), a network of national organizations that promotes the rights of people with disabilities worldwide. In the United States, the social model of disability led to legislation at all levels of government during the 1970s and 1980s, most notably two pieces of federal legislation (Gilson, 1996). The Rehabilitation Act of 1973 (Public Law 93–112) was the first federal act to recognize the need for civil rights protection for persons with disabilities. It required all organizations receiving federal assistance to have an affirmative action plan to ensure accessibility of employment to persons with disabilities. The Americans with Disabilities Act of 1990 (ADA) (Public Law 101–336) extended the civil rights of persons with disabilities to the private sector. It seeks to end discrimination against persons with disabilities and promote their full participation in society.

Conflict perspective

The five titles of the ADA, listed below, seek to eliminate environmental barriers to the full participation of persons with disabilities. You will want to be aware of the legal rights of your clients with disabilities. Ben Watson has discovered that, in spite of the law, he still encounters many physical barriers to his full participation in society.

- Title I addresses discrimination in the workplace. It requires reasonable accommodations, including architectural modification, for disabled workers.
- Title II requires that all public services, programs, and facilities, including public transportation, be accessible to persons with disabilities.
- Title III requires all public accommodations and services operated by private organizations to be accessible to persons with disabilities. It specifically lists 12 categories of accommodations: hotels and places of lodging; restaurants; movies and theaters; auditoriums and places of public gathering; stores and banks; health care service providers, hospitals, and pharmacies; terminals for public transportation; museums and libraries; parks and zoos; schools; senior centers and social service centers; and places of recreation.
- Title IV requires all intrastate and interstate phone companies to develop telecommunication relay services and devices for persons with speech or hearing impairments to allow them to communicate in a manner similar to that of persons without impairments.
- Title V covers technical guidelines for enforcing the ADA.

Under industrial capitalism, wages are the primary source of livelihood. People who cannot earn wages, therefore, tend to be poor. Research by staff at the World Bank indicates that, around the world, poverty and disability are inextricably linked (Elwan, 1999). In the United States, people with disabilities are disproportionately represented in poverty statistics. In 2000, an estimated 17.6% of people with disabilities were poor, compared to 10.6% of people without disabilities (U.S. Census Bureau, 2005). In January 2010, an estimated 15.2% of adults with disabilities were unemployed, compared to an overall unemployment rate of 9.7% (U.S. Bureau of Labor Statistics, 2010). People with disabilities who lobbied for passage of the ADA argued that government was spending vast sums of money for what they called "dependency programs," but was failing to make the investments required to make environments accessible so that people with disabilities could become employed (M. Johnson, 1992; Roulstone, 2004).

Social workers need to keep in mind the high prevalence of disabilities among older persons, the fastest growing group in the United States. More accessible environments may be an important way to buffer the expected deleterious effects of a large elderly population. As the baby boomers age, they will benefit from the earlier activism of the disability community.

Exhibit 6.9 lists some of the elements of environmental design that improve accessibility for persons with disabilities. It is important to remember, however, that rapid developments in assistive technology are likely to alter current guidelines about what is optimal environmental design. For example, the minimum space requirements in the ADA's guidelines for wheelchairs are already too tight for the new styles of motorized wheelchairs like the one used by Ben Watson.

Critical Thinking Questions 6.3

Have you noticed ways that your behavior is affected by the physical environment? Have you given much thought to the impact of the physical environment on your behavior and the behavior of others? How well do any of the categories of theories discussed above—stimulation theory, control theory, or behavior settings theory—account for the influence of the physical environment on your behavior? How might social workers incorporate ecotherapy into their practice in different settings? How easy would it be for Ben Watson to visit your home, your favorite restaurant, or your classroom?

Exhibit 6.9 Elements of Accessible Environments for Persons With Disabilities

- Create some close-in parking spaces widened to 8 feet to accommodate unloading of wheelchairs (1 accessible space for every 25 spaces).
- Create curb cuts or ramping for curbs, with 12 inches of slope for every inch of drop in the curb.
- Make ramps at least 3 feet wide to accommodate wheelchairs and provide a 5-by-5-foot square area at the top of ramps to entrances to allow space for door opening.
- Remove high-pile carpeting, low-density carpeting, and plush carpeting, at least in the path of travel. Put nonslip material on slippery floors.
- Avoid phone-in security systems in entrances (barriers for persons who are deaf).
- Make all doorways at least 32 inches wide (36 is better).
- Use automatic doors or doors that take no more than 5 pounds of force to open.
- Use door levers instead of doorknobs.
- Create aisles that are at least 3 feet wide (wider is better). Keep the path of travel clear.
- Connect different levels in buildings with ramps (for small level changes) or a wheelchair-accessible elevator.
- Place public phones no higher than 48 inches off the ground (35–42 is optimal).
- Place other things that need to be reached at this optimal height.
- Brightly light foyers and areas with directories to assist persons with low vision. Use 3-inch-high lettering in directories.
- Install Braille signs about 5 feet off the ground.
- Make restroom stalls at least 3 feet deep by 4 feet wide (5 feet by 5 feet is optimal).
- Install toilets that are 17–19 inches in height. Provide grab bars at toilets.
- Hang restroom sinks with no vanity underneath, so that persons in wheelchairs can pull up to them.
- Avoid having low seats, and provide arm supports and backrests on chairs.
- Apply nonslip finish to tub and shower. Install grab bars in tub and shower.
- Use both visual and audible emergency warning systems.

SOURCES: Based on Brawley (2006); M. Johnson (1992).

Implications for Social Work Practice

This discussion of culture and the physical environment suggests several professional principles of action:

- Recognize the categories of knowledge—social science theories and orientations, folk or common everyday theories and orientations—that you rely on to understand human behavior in the social environment.

- Embrace the traditions, customs, values, and behaviors of disparate groups identified by race, ethnicity, sexual orientation, gender, physical differences, age, nationality, and religion. Avoid approaching these groups in a cookbook, stereotyped, or one-size-fits-all fashion.
- Examine culture through the lens of the practice orientation using a "strengths" and person-in-environment perspective that allows you to assess the simultaneous forces of history, social structure, human agency, and the political context in which all of these forces work themselves out in the lives of your clients.
- Pay attention to processes of cultural change, including assimilation, accommodation, acculturation, and bicultural socialization, in the lives of individuals and groups with whom you work.
- Work to ensure that members of nondominant groups have a significant say in how cultural change proceeds.
- Assess the physical environment of your social service setting. Do clients find it accessible, legible, and comfortable? Do they find that it provides adequate privacy and control? Does it provide optimal quality and intensity of sensory stimulation? If it is a residential setting, does it promote social interaction?
- Routinely evaluate the physical environments of clients—particularly those environments where problem behaviors occur—for accessibility, legibility, comfort, privacy and control, and sensory stimulation. Check your evaluation against the clients' perceptions. If you have no opportunity to see these environments, have the clients evaluate them for you. Provide space on the intake form for assessing the physical environments of clients.
- Know the physical environments of the organizations to which you refer clients. Assist referral agencies and clients in planning how to overcome any existing environmental barriers. Maximize opportunities for client input into design of their built environments.
- Keep the benefits of the natural environment in mind when planning both prevention and remediation programs. When possible, help clients gain access to elements of the natural environment, and where appropriate, help them plan activities in the natural environment.
- Become familiar with technology for adapting environments to make them more accessible.

Active Learning

1. *The cultural construction of schooling.* Compare and contrast Stan's and Tina's experiences at Community High School with your own high school experience, considering the following themes:

   - Material and behavioral cultural symbols
   - Processes of cultural change (assimilation, accommodation, acculturation, bicultural socialization)
   - Ways in which race, ethnicity, social class, and gender play out in the school setting
   - Cultural conflict

   Next, imagine that you spend a day as a student at Community High, and Stan and Tina spend a day at your high school. How do you think you might react to the cultural symbols at Community High? How might Stan and Tina react to the cultural symbols at your high school? How do you account for these reactions?

2. Compare and contrast Ben Watson's place of his own with your own living space using the 11 concepts found in Exhibit 6.5.

Key Terms

accommodation (cultural)	biophilia	cultural hegemony
assimilation (cultural)	built environment	cultural innovation
behavior settings theories	common sense	cultural relativism
	control theories	culture
	crowding	culture of poverty

customs	personal space	race
density	place attachment	stimulation theories
ecotherapy	place identity	symbol
ethnocentrism	postmodernism	territoriality
natural environment	practice orientation	tradition

Web Resources

Academy of Neuroscience for Architecture
www.anfarch.org

Site contains information about the academy and its projects, upcoming workshops on neuroscience and specific design environments, and links to neuroscience and architecture organizations.

American Association of People With Disabilities
www.aapd.com

Site maintained by the American Association of People With Disabilities, a national nonprofit cross-disability organization. Contains information on benefits, information on disability rights, news, and links to other disability-related sites.

The Center for Health Design
www.healthdesign.org

Site maintained by the Center for Health Design, a research and advocacy organization committed to using architectural design to transform health care settings into healing environments.

Electronic Magazine of Multicultural Education
www.eastern.edu/publications/emme

An open access e-journal published twice a year by Eastern University, St. Davids, Pennsylvania. Includes articles on multicultural education for an international audience.

Environmental Justice in Waste Programs
www.epa.gov/oswer/ej/ejndex.html

Site maintained by the U.S. Environmental Protection Agency, contains special topics in environment justice, action agenda, resources, laws and regulations, and news and events.

Internet Resources for Ethnic Studies
www2.ib.udel.edu/subj/ethst/internet.htm

Site maintained by University of Delaware Library, contains links to information on a wide range of materials on ethnic issues.

Job Accommodation Network
www.jan.wvu.edu

Site maintained by the Job Accommodation Network of the Office of Disability Employment Policy of the U.S. Department of Labor. Contains ADA statutes, regulations, guidelines, technical sheets, and other assistance documents.

Multicultural Pavilion
www.edchange.org/multicultural/

Site maintained by Paul C. Gorski at Hamline University, contains resources, research, awareness activities, and links to multicultural topics.

National Alliance to End Homelessness
www.endhomlessness.org

Site contains facts about and policy issues related to homeless families, chronic homelessness, rural homelessness, homeless youth, homeless veterans, domestic violence, and mental health and physical health; also contains case studies and best practices for ending homelessness.

Social Structure and Social Institutions

Global and National

Elizabeth D. Hutchison

cs so

cs so

Opening Questions

What are the key social institutions that give pattern to social life?

What are the major global and U.S. trends in each of these social institutions?

What are the positions in the contemporary debate about social inequality?

CASE STUDY

The Meza Family's Struggle to Make It in the United States

The Meza family had been getting along well in the United States until the birth of their daughter, Minerva, now age 2, who was born premature and experienced some developmental delays. Mr. and Mrs. Meza are immigrants from Mexico. Mr. Meza has legal status, but Mrs. Meza does not. Their three oldest children, Enrique, age 17; Myra, age 15; and Jesus, age 11, are all U.S. citizens, having been born here.

Mr. Meza is grateful for the health insurance coverage he receives from the construction company that employs him; it covered much of the extensive hospitalization expense demanded by Minerva's premature birth. However, Mrs. Meza is not covered because she is not documented. Her lack of legal status often causes stress both for her and her family, especially when she becomes ill and they have to pay for all her medical expenses. Also, the children are aware of other situations where parents are forced to return to Mexico due to lack of legal immigration status, and in many cases children are left in the United States with relatives. They fear that their mother can be deported if the U.S. Citizenship and Immigration Services (USCIS) finds out. The family also has been afraid to report unethical landlords who failed to return rental deposits as agreed or who had failed to address hazardous plumbing problems that violated housing codes and jeopardized their health. They were afraid that the landlords would report them to the USCIS.

Mrs. Meza, now 44, worked until Minerva's birth, at a dry cleaning establishment where she was exposed to the fumes of toxic cleaning fluids. She feels that she should have obtained a safer job when she discovered she was pregnant. However, her undocumented status prevented her from easily finding other employment.

In addition, her employer knew about her lack of documentation, yet paid her as well as others who worked there and were citizens. Moreover, the family had just recently purchased their first home, and she was hesitant to seek new employment because she felt that no one would hire a pregnant woman.

Minerva has been hospitalized several times this year, just recently due to pneumonia. The doctor has also recently informed Mrs. Meza that Minerva very likely has cerebral palsy, and Mrs. Meza needs to attend meetings of the multidisciplinary team that oversees Minerva's care, which includes a social worker. Mrs. Meza feels that this disability is a way for God to punish her for not placing the health of her unborn child over her concern about making house payments. Although she took good care of herself—took vitamins regularly, watched her diet, and tried not to work too hard—she only saw a doctor twice during her pregnancy.

Two months ago, Mrs. Meza returned to work because the family desperately needed her income. Mr. Meza's mother, age 65, came from Mexico to babysit Minerva and help out with housework and meals. Although Grandma has really helped to lift the caregiving burden from Mom, there have been communication issues and conflicts about methods of child care between Mrs. Meza and her mother-in-law. These problems are now causing marital conflict between Mr. and Mrs. Meza because he often sides with his mother. His mother raised 10 children according to her health care beliefs, all of whom are healthy, so he argues that she knows what she is doing.

Recently, a real problem arose when Mom picked up Minerva from Grandma, who had been asked to bathe and ready Minerva for a late afternoon appointment Mom had scheduled with the doctor, so she would not lose too much work. When the nurse asked Mom to undress Minerva, Mom discovered that Minerva's chest had been wrapped in a poultice that smelled quite strongly. When the doctor asked what the poultice consisted of, Mom was embarrassed that she could not tell him. When the mustard-like substance was wiped away, the physician noted bruising on Minerva's rib cage. Mom was just as surprised as the physician and was not able to explain how the bruising occurred. A referral to Child Protective Services (CPS) resulted in a home call to the Meza household. Both Mr. and Mrs. Meza stayed home from work to try to sort out this embarrassing situation and to explain what had happened.

When Mrs. Meza returned from the doctor's office, she nervously grilled the grandmother about the poultice. She discovered that the senior Mrs. Meza had taken it upon herself to take Minerva to a *huesero* in a nearby barrio. This man is essentially a masseur. The grandmother felt that if Minerva's chest was massaged, the phlegm that was causing so much congestion would be loosened and Minerva could breathe more easily. Mr. and Mrs. Meza went to visit the *huesero,* and he explained that he had only rubbed her chest as he normally would any client. He claimed that the child's lack of weight resulted in the bruising.

When all this information was shared with the CPS worker, he informed the family that they could never use this *huesero* again, and if they did, they would be charged with child abuse. Mr. Meza has informed his mother that she cannot undertake any kind of intervention without his knowledge. Mrs. Meza fears that more interactions with CPS might cause her to be identified as undocumented.

Although Mr. Meza is now more supportive of his wife, Mrs. Meza is constantly fearful about the care of Minerva. She calls home several times during the day and has demanded that both Enrique and Myra come home immediately after school each day to attend to Minerva's care. Enrique is a top student and is hoping that his grades and extracurricular activities, including his membership in the Science Club, will result in scholarship opportunities for college. He has a Saturday job tutoring children, which provides a little income. He understands his parents' concerns about Minerva but feels it should be enough if Myra takes care of Minerva after school. He feels that he has been a good son and has not caused any problems for his parents. He also feels that his parents are not concerned about intruding on his college plans, and he has become irritable and almost disrespectful to his parents and to his grandmother.

(Continued)

Myra, on the other hand, is scared to take care of Minerva by herself, especially when Minerva is ill. She feels that she cannot depend on her grandmother to make correct choices about Minerva's care, particularly if Minerva starts to cough a lot. She also feels that Enrique is trying to dump all responsibility on her and that her parents have always let him get away with not doing household chores because he is a boy. She has always had to do more around the house, like care for her younger brother, Jesus. She feels it is really unfair that Mexican families do that with their children. The one time she voiced this sentiment, her father told her she was acting like she no longer wanted to be Mexican.

Mrs. Meza has lost 8 pounds in the 6 weeks since the child abuse report. She has noticed that the night sweats she was already experiencing have increased; she wakes up three to four times a night soaked with perspiration and finds herself exhausted at work the next day. She also feels overwhelmed and has had crying spells both at work and at home. She has tried to hide her feelings from her husband, but he is concerned that something is wrong with her. He wants her to see a doctor, but she says she does not want to call any attention to herself after what happened with the child abuse report. Often when she wakes up at night, she thinks about what would happen to her family if she were forced to return to Mexico. She feels that this would destroy her family. Meanwhile, the visitor's permit the grandmother has used to come to the United States will expire soon. Should they try to renew it? Should Mrs. Meza stop working? How will they pay their expenses with less income, especially now with the extracurricular activities of the two oldest children costing more money? Maybe buying their home was a bad decision. Maybe the family is becoming too Americanized.

—Maria E. Zuniga

PATTERNS OF SOCIAL LIFE

As you read this story, you are probably aware of both the people and the environments involved. A number of people are involved in the story, and you may be observing how they are interacting with each other and what each contributes to the current situation. Although you do not want to lose sight of the personal dimensions of the Mezas' story, in this chapter we consider the broad patterns of social life that they have encountered and continue to encounter. I want you to see the connections between the personal troubles of the Meza family and social conditions.

A good way to begin to think about broad patterns of social life is to imagine that you and 100 other people have made a space journey to a new planet that has recently, thanks to technological breakthroughs, become inhabitable to humans. You are committed to beginning a new society on this new frontier. How will you work together to be successful in this endeavor? What will you need to do to ensure your survival? Now imagine that your society of 100 has grown to include over 7 billion people, spread across six continents, with news and ideas being carried around the globe instantly through multiple media outlets, billions of dollars moving across continents with the click of a computer mouse, and products being manufactured and services being provided by a dispersed global labor force. How would you suggest that people work together to ensure the survival of this global society? One way to think about the Meza family story is as a globalization story. In Chapter 1, we defined globalization as a process by which the world's people are becoming more interconnected economically, politically, environmentally, and culturally.

Sociologists and anthropologists have given much thought to how people work together to try to ensure the survival of a society. They have identified two concepts— social structure and social institution—as central to

Systems perspective

understanding those endeavors. Social structure and social institution are among the more abstract concepts used by sociologists. In the broadest sense, social structure is another term for *society,* or simply an acknowledgment that social life is patterned, not random. It provides the framework within which individual behavior is played out in daily life. **Social structure** is a set of interrelated social institutions developed by human beings to impose constraints on human interaction for the purpose of the survival and well-being of the collectivity. Certainly, we can see some of the constraints that various social institutions impose on members of the Meza family.

Our understanding of social institutions is complicated by the casual, everyday use of the term *institution* to cover a variety of meanings. In this book, however, we use the definition of **social institutions** as "patterned ways of solving the problems and meeting the requirements of a particular society" (D. Newman, 2008, p. 27). To provide stability, social institutions organize rights and duties into statuses and roles and the expected behaviors that accompany them. **Status** refers to a specific social position; roles, as suggested in Chapter 2, are the behaviors of persons occupying particular statuses. Sociologists have identified a set of interrelated social institutions—such as family, religion, government, economy, education—with each institution organizing social relations in a particular sector of social life. We see evidence of each of these institutions in the lives of the Meza family.

Sociological treatment of social structure and social institutions emphasizes the ways in which they persist and contribute to social stability. But often they persist despite unintended consequences and evidence that they are ineffective. In addition, although social institutions are relatively stable, they also change—whether by accident, by evolution, or by design (McMichael, 2008; W. R. Scott, 2008). Social institutions persist only when they are carried forward by individual actors and only when they are actively monitored. This view of social structure and social institutions as relatively stable but also changing is consistent with the multidimensional

perspective of this book. This view seems justified, given the extraordinary changes in several major social institutions since 1970 in societies around the world (McMichael, 2008).

W. Richard Scott (2008) suggests that there are three different types of processes that contribute to the stability of social institutions: regulatory processes, normative processes, and cultural-cognitive processes. Different types of processes are at work in different social institutions. *Regulatory processes* involve rules, monitoring, and enforcement through rewards and punishment. *Normative processes* involve values and norms about how things should be done. *Cultural-cognitive processes* involve beliefs, internalized understandings about the world and how to behave in it.

Eight interrelated social institutions will be discussed in this chapter: government and politics, economy, education, health care, social welfare, religion, mass media, and family and kinship. We can see how important each of these institutions is in the current lives of the Meza family. Exhibit 7.1 presents these social institutions and the major functions that they perform for society.

CONTEMPORARY TRENDS IN GLOBAL AND U.S. SOCIAL INSTITUTIONS _____

To function effectively as social workers, we need accurate information about how social institutions are both changing and staying the same. As Philip McMichael (2004) suggests, when speaking about U.S. society, "we can no longer understand the changes in our society without situating them globally" (p. xxxiii). Indeed, the process of globalization has been stimulating changes in all eight of the social institutions for several decades, but in a pronounced way for the past two decades. The discussion that follows positions trends in U.S. social institutions within a global context. Doing so illuminates how U.S. society is both different from and the same as other societies, and aids critical thinking about the question, why do we do things the way we do?

Exhibit 7.1   Key Social Institutions and the Functions They Perform

Social Institution	Functions Performed
Government and politics	Making and enforcing societal rules Resolving internal and external conflicts Mobilizing collective resources to meet societal goals
Economy	Regulating production, distribution, and consumption of goods and services
Education	Passing along formal knowledge from one generation to next Socializing individuals
Health care	Promoting the general health
Social welfare	Promoting interdependence Dealing with issues of dependence
Religion	Answering questions about meaning and purpose of life Socializing individuals Maintaining social control Providing mutual support
Mass media	Managing the flow of information, images, and ideas
Family and kinship	Regulating procreation Conducting initial socialization Providing mutual support

Perhaps the most important and troubling trend in contemporary life is the continued extremely high level of social inequality, both between nations and within nation-states.

Conflict perspective

Although globalization has brought some improvements in literacy, health, and living standards for many, we pay particular attention to trends in social inequality because the profession of social work has historically made a commitment to persons and groups who are disadvantaged in the distribution of resources by social institutions. To carry out this commitment, we must have a way of understanding social inequality and its influence on human behavior. Throughout this chapter, we demonstrate how social inequality is created and maintained in eight major interrelated social institutions. But first we take a closer look at inequality globally and in the United States.

There are many debates about whether globalization is leading to increased or decreased global inequality, and the answer depends on how the question is asked. McMichael (2008) argues that global inequality is deepening; he reports that the gap between the richest 20% of the world's people and the poorest 20% has doubled since 1970, now standing at 89 to 1. He further reports that in 2000, there were 3 people in the world whose total wealth was more than the total of the wealth of the people in the 48 poorest countries. The best available data indicate that the *average* gap in income among peoples of the world has closed slightly in the past two decades, with the estimated decrease ranging from 4% to 24% (Firebaugh & Goesling, 2004; Melchior & Telle, 2001; United Nations

Development Program, 2005). This reverses a trend of increasing global inequality that began in the 1820s, but leaves us with much greater global income inequality than existed 200 years ago. It is estimated that average incomes in the world's richest regions were 3 times greater than average incomes in the poorest regions 200 years ago, 9 times greater 100 years ago, and 20 times greater in 1998 (Firebaugh & Goesling, 2004). Although different data sources report different numbers, there is agreement that we are talking about comparatively huge disparities in the contemporary world.

It is clear that not all regions of the world have shared equally in the benefits of globalization. One analysis suggests that the regions of the world can be divided into three groups with different recent income trends (Firebaugh & Goesling, 2004):

- Group 1: Rich regions that have been growing richer (Western Europe, Northern America, and Japan)
- Group 2: Regions with lower-than-average per capita but rapidly growing income (South Asia, East Asia, and China)
- Group 3: Poor regions with slower-than-average growth, or decline, in average income (Latin America, Middle East and North Africa, Eastern Europe and Russia, and sub-Saharan Africa)

Because 40% of the world's population lives in China and South Asia, the rapid increase in incomes in these areas carries great weight in calculating overall global inequality and produces the decline noted above. During a time of massive income growth worldwide, average incomes fell in most of sub-Saharan Africa, leading to a growing disparity between this region and the rest of the world. For example, the average U.S. resident was 38 times richer than the average Tanzanian in 1990 and 61 times richer in 2005 (United Nations Development Program, 2005). That same report estimated that if incomes in high-income countries were to stop growing in 2005, and incomes in Latin America and sub-Saharan Africa were to continue at their current rate, Latin America would not catch up with high-income countries until 2177, and sub-Saharan Africa would not catch up until

2236. So, while available data show a slight average decline in global inequality, they also indicate that income inequality is growing between the poorest 10% and the richest 10% of the world's people (Melchior & Telle, 2001).

Although most of the global inequality is due to inequality *between* countries, it is important to understand the patterns of inequality *within* a given country. In the period 1947 to 1973, income inequality in the United States declined slightly. Since 1974, however, income inequality has grown substantially (Burtless, 2001; DeNavas-Walt, Proctor, & Hill Lee, 2006). The most commonly used measure of income inequality is the **Gini index,** which measures the extent to which the distribution of income within a country deviates from a perfectly equal distribution. Gini index scores range from 0 (perfect equality) to 100 (perfect inequality). As Exhibit 7.2 shows, the Gini index in the United States grew from 39.4 in 1970 to 46.9 in 2005, with most of that growth occurring between 1980 and 2000 (DeNavas-Walt et al., 2006). U.S. Census data show no change in the U.S. Gini index between 2005 and 2008 (DeNavas-Walt, Proctor, & Smith, 2009). Emmanuel Saez (2009) reports that the incomes of the top 1% of earners in the United States captured half of the overall economic growth in the country in the period from 1993–2007. There has been much controversy about the very large bonuses paid to executives of financial companies that received government aid in the economic crisis that began in December 2007. Unfortunately, there is a 2-year lag in the most reliable data on income inequality, and it is too early to tell what impact the recession that resulted from this crisis, with its high rate of unemployment, has had on income inequality, in either the short term or the long term.

When per capita income is adjusted for cost of living, the United States is the highest-income country in the world (Sernau, 2006), but in recent years it has earned the distinction of being the most unequal society in the advanced industrial world. Exhibit 7.3 shows the ranking of 19 advanced industrial countries in terms of income inequality, based on the Gini index, moving from the country

Exhibit 7.2   Gini Index of Inequality in the United States, 1970–2005

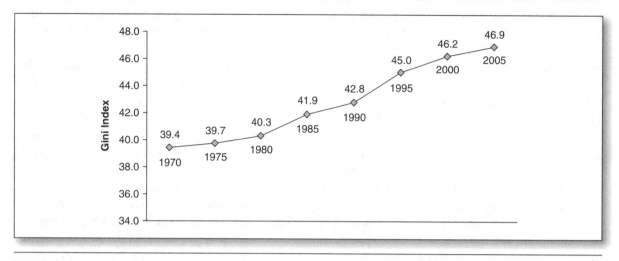

SOURCE: DeNavas-Walt, Proctor, and Hill Lee (2006).

Exhibit 7.3   Ranking of Social Inequality in 19 Advanced Industrial Countries

Most Inequality	United States
	United Kingdom, Italy
	Ireland
	Israel
	Australia
	Switzerland, Canada
	France
	Spain
	Netherlands
	Austria
	Germany
	Finland
	Norway
	Belgium
	Sweden
	Japan
Least Inequality	Denmark

SOURCE: United Nations Development Program (2005).

with least inequality at the bottom (Denmark) to the country with greatest inequality at the top (United States).

Of course, the United States does not have more inequality than all countries in the world. In a general sense, highly industrialized, high-income countries have much lower levels of inequality than nonindustrial or newly industrializing countries. The rate of inequality is much lower in the United States than in many low- to middle-income countries. Overall, the highest rates of inequality can be found in some Latin American countries and African countries, but the rate of inequality is not consistent within these regions. For example, the Gini index is 70.7 in Namibia and 30.0 in Ethiopia.

The Mezas came to the United States to escape brutal poverty in Mexico. In recent years, Mexico has developed trade agreements with a number of other countries and has moved from being the world's 26th largest economy to being the 9th largest. However, real wages in Mexico have declined by about 20% in this period of growth. A large percentage of workers, about 40% of Mexico's workforce, are poorly paid and have few employment options (McMichael, 2008; Sernau, 2006). Half of Mexican families live in poverty, a poverty rate that has not changed since the early 1980s. Half of the country's rural population earns less than $1.40 per day (McMichael, 2008). Mexico's ratio of inequality (a Gini index of 54.6) is lower than that of Brazil (59.3) and Guatemala (59.9), but it is still much higher than that in most advanced or postindustrial countries. Although the Mezas are struggling for economic survival in the United States, they do not wish to return to Mexico.

Some social analysts argue that social inequality is the price of economic growth and suggest that the poorest families in the United States enjoy a much higher standard of living than poor families in other countries (Rector & Hederman, 1999). In other words, "Rising tides lift all boats." Indeed, the growing number of immigrant families taking great risks to come to the United States from the Latin American countries would seem to support this idea.

But a comparison of the United States with other advanced industrialized countries suggests that societal health is best maintained when economic growth is balanced with attention to social equality. A growing international research literature points to the idea that high levels of inequality are bad for the social health of a nation. Let's look at three social indicators for the 19 industrial countries in Exhibit 7.3: childhood mortality (probability of dying before age 5), life expectancy, and secondary school enrollment. In 1960, the United States had a lower childhood mortality rate than 10 of the other countries listed in Exhibit 7.3. By 2008, the United States had the highest childhood mortality rate of the 19 countries. Indeed, the cross-national continuum for childhood mortality looks almost exactly like the continuum of inequality. All but two of the advanced industrialized countries have longer life expectancies than the United States, and 10 have higher rates of completion of secondary education, with data unavailable for four of the countries (UNICEF, 2009b).

Observers have noted that a culture of inequality develops in countries with high rates of inequality. The interests of the rich begin to diverge from the interests of the average family. There is good cross-national evidence that societies with high levels of inequality make smaller investments in public education and other social supports. These societies also have higher levels of violence, less trust and more hostility, and lower levels of involvement in community life (Wilkinson, 2001).

Marc and Marque-Luisa Miringoff and colleagues (M. Miringoff, 2003; M. L. Miringoff & Miringoff, 1999; M. L. Miringoff, Miringoff, & Opdycke, 1996; M. L. Miringoff & Opdycke, 2008) developed an index that can be used to monitor the social health of the United States. They suggest that we in the United States are highly attentive to economic performance and have access to minute-by-minute reports on the economic health of the country through the Dow Jones Industrial Index. However, it is much harder to get indicators of social health. Although there has been some revision of their index over time, Miringoff and colleagues most recently recommend the 16 indicators found in Exhibit 7.4, and they suggest that these indicators should not be measured against an ideal standard, but rather in comparison to the best year this nation has achieved—a model year. In their research covering the years from 1970 to 2005, they found five main phases in the social health of the United States (M. L. Miringoff & Opdycke, 2008):

(1) 1970–1976: social health at a record high

(2) 1976–1983: social health declined rapidly

(3) 1983–1993: social health stagnated at low level

(4) 1993–2000: period of progress, highest score since 1978

(5) 2000–2005: social health stalled again

It is too early to know what happened to the social health of the nation during the recession that began in December 2007, but the preliminary evidence is not good.

Until the mid-1970s, the Index of Social Health tracked well with the Dow Jones Industrial Average. After the mid-1970s, however, the social health of the United States stagnated while the economic health began a rapid upturn. From 1970 to 2001, the gross domestic product (GDP) in the United States grew by 158%, and the nation's social health declined by 38% (M. Miringoff, 2003).

Exhibit 7.4	Indicators of Social Health

Children:	Infant mortality
	Child abuse
	Child poverty
Youth:	Teenage suicide
	Teenage drug abuse
	High school dropouts
Adults:	Unemployment
	Wages
	Health care coverage
Older Adults:	Poverty, ages 65 and older
	Out-of-pocket health costs, ages 65 and older
All Ages:	Homicides
	Alcohol-related traffic fatalities
	Food stamp coverage
	Affordable housing
	Income inequality

SOURCE: Based on M. L. Miringoff & Opdycke (2008).

Poverty rates in the United States, one measure of social inequality, demonstrate that social inequality is related to race and ethnicity, age, gender, family structure, and geographic location (DeNavas-Walt et al., 2009). The overall poverty rate in 2008 was 13.2%, up from 12.5% in 2007. Unfortunately, there are no available official data to describe how the deep recession that began in December 2007 affected the poverty rate. Although the majority of people living below the poverty level are White, and people of color can be found in all income groups, Blacks and Hispanics are almost 3 times as likely as Whites to be poor. The poverty rate in 2008 was 24.7% for Blacks, 23.2% for Hispanics, 11.8% for Asians, and 8.6% for White non-Hispanics. The good news is that the differential between Whites and groups of color has decreased in recent years. The bad news is that the differential remains quite large. For example,

in the 1940s, the median income of Black families was about 50% of the median income of White families, and in 2005, the median income of Black families was 61% of non-Hispanic White families (Bradshaw, Healey, & Smith, 2001; DeNavas-Walt et al., 2006). Foreign-born noncitizens have a higher poverty rate (23.3%) than natives (12.2%), but foreign-born citizens have a lower poverty rate (10.2%) than natives (12.1%) (DeNavas-Walt et al., 2009). You can see from the Mezas' story how lack of citizenship makes people particularly vulnerable in the labor market. Moreover, recent immigration policy has favored well-educated, highly skilled workers for legal immigration.

Over the past 50 years, vulnerability to poverty has shifted from older adults to children. Between 1959 and 2008, the percentage of the U.S. population 65 years and older living in poverty decreased from about 35% to about 9.7% (DeNavas-Walt et al., 2006, 2009). The proportion of the population under 18 years old living in poverty showed a smaller decrease in this same period, from about 27% to about 19%. Since 1974, the poverty rate for persons under 18 has been higher than for the group 65 and over.

Women are more likely than men to be poor in the United States as well as globally. Women's poverty rate (12.9%) is higher than men's (10.4%), and this difference continues to grow across the life course, rising to 12.4% of women 65 and over compared to 7.0% of men of the same age (U.S. Census Bureau, 2002b). Single-parent, mother-only families (28.7%) are more likely to live in poverty than two-parent families (5.5%) or single-parent, father-only families (13.8%) (DeNavas-Walt et al., 2009).

In 1970, poverty was primarily a rural problem in the United States. By 1990, poverty was much more of an urban problem. In 2000, an estimated 17.0% of people living inside principal cities were poor, compared to 14.5% of people in rural areas and 9.3% of people in suburbs (DeNavas-Walt et al., 2006). Poverty rates also vary by geographical region in the United States, with 11.6% in the Northeast, 12.4% in the Midwest, 13.5% in the West, and 14.3% in the South living in poverty in 2008 (DeNavas-Walt et al., 2009).

We turn now to analysis of trends in eight major social institutions, both globally and in the United States. We look for the good news in these trends, but we also pay close attention to how social inequality and social conflict are created or maintained in each institution.

Trends in Government and Politics

At the current time, Mrs. Meza lives in fear of agents of the government, whether they come from the U.S. Citizenship and Immigration Services or Child Protective Services. She sees the government as a coercive force rather than a supportive force in her life. The **government and political institution** is responsible for how decisions get made and enforced for the society as a whole. It is expected to resolve both internal and external conflicts and mobilize collective resources to meet societal goals.

Systems perspective; Conflict perspective

Political systems around the world vary widely, from authoritarian to democratic. Authoritarian systems may have a hereditary monarchy or a dictator who seized power; sometimes democratically elected leaders become dictators. Leaders in democratic systems are elected by their citizens and are accountable to them; they must govern in the context of written documents (Ballantine & Roberts, 2009). Evidence suggests that the government institution is in a transition period globally as well as in the United States. There is much complexity in global trends in government and politics, but three historical factors are supremely important for beginning to understand current complexities.

1. *Colonialism.* The contemporary global political landscape must be understood in the historical context of **colonialism** (L. Kurtz, 2007; McMichael, 2008). Eight European countries (Belgium, Britain, France, Germany, Italy, the Netherlands, Portugal, and Spain) were involved over several centuries in setting up colonial empires, which allowed them to strengthen their own economies by exploiting the raw materials and labors of the colonized countries. Colonial governments took power away from local governance and prevented the localities from establishing stable political systems. Most of these empires came to a rather abrupt end after World War II, but they left a disorganized political legacy in their wake in much of Africa, Central and South America, and parts of Asia and the Middle East (McMichael, 2008; T. R. Reid, 2004). After the colonized countries established their independence, the United States and other Western powers advanced a new institutional framework that called for free trade and transformation of the

Photos 7.1a & 7.1b State, local, and federal governments are social institutions that are responsible for making and enforcing societal rules. Here we see the U.S. Federal Reserve building and the capitol building in Sacramento, California.

formerly colonized countries into democracies (Aronowitz, 2003). This new institutional framework, sometimes referred to as **neocolonialism,** is promoted by such international organizations as the World Bank, the International Monetary Fund (IMF), and the World Trade Organization (WTO). These organizations, which are led by the United States and Western Europe, regulate relations between countries, and this role carries much power over political and economic institutions. The United States and Western Europe also played a major role in coercing former colonies to organize into nation-states, and imposed national boundaries that were inconsistent with age-old ethnic divisions. This has resulted in ongoing ethnic clashes throughout the former colonies (McMichael, 2008).

2. *Aftermath of hot and cold wars.* Two bloody world wars in the 20th century, both initiated between European countries, left Europe weakened and wary of war as a viable solution to conflicts between nations. With the European states weakened after World War II, the United States and the Soviet Union emerged as competing superpowers. These became competing spheres of influence, each trying to promote its political and economic interests around the world in a struggle known as the Cold War. The collapse of the Soviet Union in 1989 produced political instability in the former Soviet Union, and that country is no longer considered a superpower. In the meantime, after World War II, the nations of Europe began a process of unification, a process that has not always been smooth but has produced the European Union (EU), with "a president, a parliament, a constitution, a cabinet, a central bank, a bill of rights, a unified patent office, and a court system," as well as a currency system (the euro) used by 22 countries plus Vatican City to date (T. R. Reid, 2004, p. 2). T. R. Reid suggests that the EU has become a second superpower and may well be joined by China as a third superpower in the near future.

3. *Economic globalization.* Changes in the government institution are very intertwined with changes in the economic institution, and these changes taken together are playing a large role in global inequality. Beginning in the 1970s, economic globalization began to present serious challenges to nationally based democracies (McMichael, 2008). For a number of centuries, political and economic life had been organized into nation-states with bureaucracies for maintaining order and mobilizing resources to meet societal needs. With the start of the 1970s, however, new information and transportation technologies made possible the development of **transnational corporations (TNCs),** which carry on production and distribution activities in many nations. These corporations cross national lines to take advantage of cheap labor pools, lax environmental regulations, beneficial tax laws, and new consumer markets. It is hard for any nation-state to monitor or get control over the TNCs (Alperovitz, 2005; McMichael, 2008). Under these circumstances, governments began to retrench in their efforts to monitor and control the economic institution. A **neoliberal philosophy** that governments should keep their hands off the economic institution took hold, perhaps nowhere more than in the United States. Neoliberalism led to the abolition of many government regulations that attempted to control actions in the economic system, a process known as *deregulation.* Neoliberalism also promotes transferring control of many government functions from the public to the private sector, with the belief that privatization will result in more efficient government and improve the economic health of the nation. It also promotes trade liberalization, or free trade across national boundaries.

Countries around the world have attempted to adapt to the challenges of economic globalization by changing the way that government does business. One common adaptation is to make change in the level of government that assumes power in particular situations. These common adaptations have been to move federal power upward, downward, or outward (Bradshaw et al., 2001).

Upward movement. The United States played a leadership role in the development of several transnational political and economic organizations and policies at the end of World War II. These organizations and policies have been significant in helping to move power upward from nation-states. The United Nations (UN) was developed to ensure international peace and security. The World Bank was developed to promote reconstruction in war-torn nations but has, in recent years, taken on a concern for poverty. The World Bank president is appointed by the U.S. president. The IMF was developed to promote international monetary cooperation and a fair balance of trade. The managing director of the IMF is appointed by the United Kingdom, France, and Germany. The General Agreement on Tariffs and Trade (GATT) was designed to provide an international forum for developing freer trade across national boundaries; the World Trade Organization (WTO) was developed under GATT in 1995 to regulate the global economy according to principles of free trade. More recently, the United States, Canada, and Mexico signed the North American Free Trade Agreement (NAFTA) in 1994. European nations joined together as the EU, adopting a common currency, a set of common legal and economic structures, and other joint endeavors. Similar organizations are in various stages of development in Latin America, Asia, and Africa.

These trends are not without controversy. In recent years, there have been conflicts among rich and poor nations at meetings of the WTO and IMF and activist demonstrations at their meetings. The last decade has seen growth of a number of antiglobalization social movements that are challenging neoliberal principles and the ways they are being enforced around the world. The World Bank, IMF, and WTO, all governed by unelected officials, have become very powerful in dictating how nation-states should govern. For example, when making loans, the World Bank requires that borrowing nations follow the principles of neoliberalism, including reducing their social welfare programs, privatizing their public services, and becoming more open to imports. The IMF has enforced these principles, sometimes overriding decisions made at the national level. The deliberations of the WTO are secret; members can lodge complaints, but the decision of the WTO's dispute settlement program is binding unless every member of the WTO votes to reverse it. There is much evidence that the decisions of the World Bank, IMF, and WTO have been more favorable to some nations than to others (McMichael, 2008).

Downward movement. In a period of rising doubt about the ability of nation-states to govern, many of them, including the United States, have been passing policy responsibilities down to regional and local governments. This downward movement has been called the **new federalism.** The stated intent is to improve the responsiveness and efficiency of government. The U.S. federal government has used several different mechanisms for moving responsibilities downward, including block grants (large grants to regional, state, or local governments) and increased flexibility for states in complying with federal mandates. As pressures increase on states, some are beginning to pass responsibilities to local governments. On the other hand, some states are beginning to tackle tough issues like environmental and immigration policy that are not being addressed by federal policy.

Outward movement. Growing faith across the world in the wisdom and efficiency of the economic institution led many nation-states to withdraw from direct control of activities that they have hitherto controlled. They do this in several ways:

- *Privatization:* The government sells enterprises that produce goods or deliver services to the private sector. This can be done at any level of government. Between 1986 and 1992, monetary policies of the World Bank and IMF required former colonial countries to engage in massive privatization in exchange for rescheduling their debts (McMichael, 2008).
- *Contracting out.* The government retains ultimate control over a program but contracts with private organizations for some activities. The most notable example of this type of government retrenchment is state contracts with the private prison industry that have increased in recent years in the United States, but also in other countries such as Australia (Wettenhall, 1999). Governmental social service agencies

also contract out many social service programs to both nonprofit and for-profit organizations. Some school systems have experimented with contracting out public schools to the private sector, in the hopes that the result will be more effective teaching and learning.

- *Deregulation.* Governments give up their claims to the right to regulate particular activities that they have previously regulated but not controlled. The expectation is that deregulation will lead to greater economic growth and lower cost to the consumer. Deregulation of the telephone system is often credited with the proliferation of new services, including wireless telephones. U.S. states followed the global trend to deregulate electricity and other utilities. As the financial system in the United States and other countries began to collapse in late 2007, much attention was paid to the lax regulation of the financial system, particularly the U.S. system, and the role that deregulation played in the crisis.

The future of the neoliberal philosophy is not clear. For a number of decades, it served wealthy nations and wealthy individuals well. However, the global economic crisis that began in late 2007 called into question its primary premise that the market has its own wisdom and should not be interfered with. It is unclear whether the wisdom of neoliberalism is getting serious review, but for some time now, poor nations and social justice advocates have engaged in growing resistance to the neoliberal philosophy and its implementation by the World Bank, IMF, and WTO. There has been much concern about the unfair advantage given to wealthy nations and the exploitation of labor and natural resources in poor nations. But there is also much resolve by rich and powerful individuals and societies to hold onto neoliberal principles.

Economic globalization combined with war and political strife have produced mass cross-national migration. Most of this migration has occurred within regions; for example, most refugees fleeing Iraq have fled to other Middle Eastern countries. But there is also a trend of migration from low-wage to high-wage countries (McMichael, 2008). This has led to considerable political attention to immigration issues around the globe. In the United States and Europe, immigration issues are the source of intense political debate, and more restrictive immigration policies are being proposed across these two regions.

As we think about the trials of the Meza family, we are reminded of this increased attention to immigration issues. Some observers (Teeple, 2000) have suggested that nation-states compensate for their

| Rational choice perspective |

inability to control the business processes that cross their borders by heightening their attempts to control the human movement across their borders. By controlling borders, a nation-state can get some control of the flow of labor across national boundaries.

Although the United States and the EU share a commitment to democracy and a free market economy, they have some important differences in political theory that come out of their different experiences in the 20th century. The United States puts much more emphasis on military power than the EU, or any other part of the world, for that matter. European countries devote more of their GDP to overseas development aid (ODA) to poor nations than the United States does. European countries also devote more of their GDP to social welfare programs than does the United States. The EU's European Convention on Human Rights is more expansive than the U.S. Bill of Rights. The EU has been more willing than the United States to regulate TNCs. In recent years, the EU has enacted policies for greater personal privacy at the same time that the United States has enacted policies like the Patriot Act that added limitations to personal privacy (T. R. Reid, 2004).

Michael Reisch (1997) reminds us that social work has been "at the mercy of political forces throughout its history" (p. 81). He argues that social workers cannot afford to ignore processes and trends in the political arena. In the United States, social workers must be attuned to the important role that money plays in providing access to government and politics, and to continuing underrepresentation of women and people of color among elected officials.

Trends in the Economy

As you read the Mezas' story, their economic struggles seem paramount, and yet, both Mr. and Mrs. Meza are employed full time and working hard to provide for their family. The **economic institution** has the primary responsibility for regulating the production, distribution, and consumption of goods and services. In a capitalistic market economy, like the one in the United States, what one consumes is dependent on how much one is paid for selling goods and services in the economic marketplace. Most people, if they are not self-employed or independently wealthy, exchange labor for wages, which they then use for consumption. The nature of the economy has been ever changing since premodern times, but the *rate* of change has accelerated wildly since the beginning of the industrial revolution, particularly in recent decades under neoliberalism and economic globalization.

Before further discussion, we should have some clarity about what we mean by *economic globalization*. The primary ingredients are a global production system, a global labor force, and global consumers. Much of what we wear, eat, and use has global origins. If you look around your room, you will see many examples of economic globalization, but much of the global process will be invisible to you. A few examples, taken from the work of Philip McMichael (2008), will demonstrate some of the complexity of current globalization. First, let's look at the U.S.-based athletic shoe industry. The design and marketing of the shoes are typically done at headquarters in the United States by workers earning relatively high wages. The materials are produced, dyed, cut, stitched, and assembled, and then packed and transported in work sites in South Korea, Taiwan, China, Indonesia, and the Philippines, primarily by women earning very low wages. The shoes are sold globally, but disproportionately to consumers in wealthy advanced industrialized countries.

A second example involves the food we eat. In wealthy countries, we have become accustomed to having our favorite fruits and vegetables year round. We can have this because of the global food market. During the winter months, if we live in the United States, we can get grapes, apples, pears, apricots, cherries, peaches, and avocados from Chile; and tomatoes, broccoli, bell peppers, cucumbers, and cantaloupe from Mexico. If we live in Japan, we might get pineapples and asparagus from Thailand; and if we live in Europe, we can buy strawberries, mangoes, and chilies grown in Kenya as well as organic fruits and vegetables from China. For a final example, we can look at the production of the Ford Escort car, which uses parts from 14 countries and is assembled at work sites in several different countries.

The global economy is driven by corporate desire for the bigger profits that come from cheap raw materials and cheap labor, and by consumer desire for cheap and novel products. Corporations are constantly seeking cheaper labor sites to stay competitive. Much of the global economy is controlled by TNCs, also called multinational corporations, which are very large companies with production and marketing departments in multiple countries. TNCs have become very powerful over the past several decades; in fact, UN data indicate that TNCs account for two thirds of world trade and hold most product patents (cited in McMichael, 2008). Most TNCs are headquartered in France, Germany, the United Kingdom, and the United States.

> Conflict perspective

Proponents of economic globalization argue that in time it will bring modernity and prosperity to all regions of the world. Critics argue that it is just an unsustainable pyramid scheme that must end because prosperity of victors is always paid for by the losses of latecomers, or because the physical environment can no longer sustain the economic activities (Sernau, 2006). This is a good place to point out that not all peoples of the world put a high value on consumerism and chasing economic growth, values that are central to globalization. Unfortunately, however, policies of the World Bank, IMF, and WTO have made it impossible to make a living on subsistence farms and small

Photo 7.2 Walmart is a growing symbol of economic globalization.

craft enterprises. The future of globalization is not certain, but several trends can be identified at its current stage of development.

1. *Regional disparities.* Rich nations have been getting richer, a few nations have made impressive gains, most poor nations have made few gains, and the poorest nations have lost ground. Consumers in high-income countries benefit from the cheap labor of workers in newly industrializing countries. For example, much of the clothing in the stores in the United States has "Made in China" on its labels, and this clothing is often produced by people working 12-hour shifts and 7-day weeks (McMichael, 2008). Current regional disparities must be put into

historical context. Globalization gained speed just as European colonialism collapsed, at the end of World War II. Formerly colonized countries began the global era in a compromised position created by colonial exploitation. The newly created World Bank made large loans to the former colonies to improve their infrastructures, and much of the money was used to import technology from wealthy industrial countries. In the 1980s, a combination of factors, including recession in the United States and other wealthy Western nations, produced a debt crisis in many previously colonized countries. They began taking out new loans to pay for previous loans. As a condition for restructuring the loans, the World Bank and IMF imposed austerity measures. Some countries have not been able to recover from the debt crisis, especially those facing a massive AIDS epidemic. More recently, beginning in late 2007, low-income countries were severely affected by the global economic recession, which originated in the financial systems of the wealthy countries of the world. Poor countries entered the recession in already weak fiscal positions, and there have been several negative impacts of the recession on their already fragile economies: a decline of foreign aid, restricted access to credit, lost trade, and loss of remittances from family members who have migrated to wealthy countries (UNESCO, 2010). Sub-Saharan Africa has been the most vulnerable global region to these economic losses, but low-income countries in Eastern Europe, Asia Pacific, and Latin America have also been at risk.

2. *Labor force bifurcation.* As globalization progressed, wage labor began to **bifurcate,** or divide into two branches. One branch is the *core* of relatively stable, skilled, well-paid labor. The other branch is the *periphery* of periodic or seasonal (often referred to as casual), low-wage labor. The upper tier of jobs is found disproportionately in the wealthy advanced industrial countries, and the lower tier of jobs is found disproportionately in the previously colonized countries. The athletic shoe industry provides one of the most extreme examples of this bifurcation: Vietnamese workers earn about US$400 a year stitching the sneakers,

and celebrity athletes in the United States are paid US$10–$20 million to market them. Recently, bifurcation of labor has occurred all over the world, in advanced industrial societies as well as in poor, newly industrializing societies (McMichael, 2008). Work in the core is usually full-time and comes with nonwage compensation such as sick leave, health insurance, and retirement benefits. Work in the periphery is usually part-time and/or temporary, with many working on a contract basis, and it provides few if any nonwage benefits. Use of such casual, irregular, low-wage labor provides employers with a lot of flexibility as they try to stay competitive. Workers in the periphery often work very long hours in crowded and unsafe workplaces, and, if they are women, they may cope with sexual harassment on the job. Women have been reported to compose 70% to 90% of the temporary workers in advanced industrial societies, but recently, many jobs historically performed by middle-class men are being filled by contract workers who do not receive the nonwage benefits once associated with these jobs (McMichael, 2008).

3. *Corporate downsizing.* Another way that corporations in advanced industrial societies have responded to global competition is by **downsizing** for greater efficiency. Increasingly, high-wage workers are almost as vulnerable to layoffs as low-wage workers. Exhibit 7.5 demonstrates the large increase in downsizing in the United States since 1990. This trend, coupled with the increasing use of casual labor discussed above, has resulted in low job security for many workers. This situation was exacerbated by the recession that began in December 2007. It is estimated that 2.6 million jobs were lost in the United States in 2008, and the unemployment rate rose to 10% by December 2009. The rates of unemployment vary by major worker groups. In January 2010, a total of 10% of adult men and 7.9%

Exhibit 7.5 U.S. Job Cut Announcements

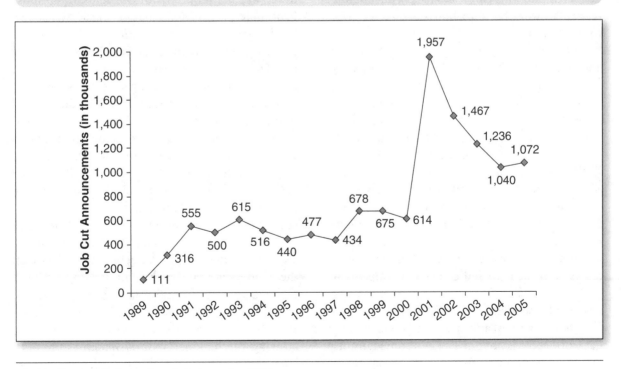

SOURCE: Based on Challenger, Gray, & Christmas, Inc. (2006).

of adult women were unemployed; the unemployment rate was 16.5% among Blacks, 12.6% among Hispanic Americans, 8.7% among Whites, and 8.4% among Asian Americans. The unemployment rate for veterans from the Gulf War era II (since September 2001) was 12.6%, and the unemployment rate for persons with disabilities was 15.2%. The unemployment rate for the foreign born was 11.8% compared to 10.3% for the native born (U.S. Bureau of Labor Statistics [BLS], 2010). Unfortunately, the unemployment rate is predicted to stay at a high level at least through 2011.

4. *Work intensification.* J. Walsh and Zacharias-Walsh (2008) suggest that since the beginning of capitalism, there has been a constant struggle between workers and employers over the length of the workday, with a constant pressure from employers to increase it. They provide evidence that in the contemporary global era, the length of the working day is increasing, but there is also much evidence that the length of the working day varies across national lines as well as within national borders. For example, migrant workers in some settings reportedly work 12- to 16-hour days, 7 days a week. In sweatshops around the world, workers have been found to work as many as 84 hours a week, and sometimes 22 hours a day, at very low wages, producing products for major U.S. retailers such as Nordstrom, Gymboree, and J. Crew (McMichael, 2008; J. Walsh & Zacharias-Walsh, 2008). But it is not just in newly industrializing countries that such long workweeks can be found. J. Walsh and Zacharias-Walsh argue that there was a "return of the 12-hour day" in the United States during the 1990s, with a number of major U.S. corporations instituting the 12-hour shift and enforced overtime during that period. By some reports, the average workweek increased in the United States between 1990 and 2000 (Berg, Appelbaum, Bailey, & Kalleberg, 2004), and by other reports it remained essentially steady (Mishel, Bernstein, & Shierholz, 2006). At any rate, the trend toward longer workweeks is not universal. In some European and Scandinavian countries, and in Japan, the workweek grew shorter rather than longer during the 1990s (Berg et al., 2004). In 2006, the average annual hours worked in the United States was 1,804, compared to 1,669 in the United Kingdom, 1,564 in France, and 1,436 in Germany (Mishel et al., 2006). The average annual work hours do not tell the full story about the intensification of work in contemporary societies, however. The increased labor force participation of women in recent decades has resulted in a significant increase in family work hours (Crompton, 2006). For example, the average middle-class family with two wage earners worked a total of 3,932 hours in 2000 (Berg et al., 2004). This extra time spent in the economic institution has a major impact on the family and kinship institution as well as community life. The Mezas are a good example of a family struggling to balance their work life with family needs.

5. *Limited protection by organized labor.* Since the beginning of industrial capitalism, labor unions have been the force behind governmental protection of worker's rights, lobbying successfully for such protection as workplace safety, a minimum wage, a reduced workweek, and pensions. Economic globalization has seriously weakened the bargaining power of nationally based labor unions, because companies can always threaten to take their business somewhere else. However, labor unions are still strong in some countries, and this helps to explain much of the differences in annual work hours across national lines. For example, 13.5% of the workers in the United States are union members, compared to 30.4% of the workers in the EU and 80% in Sweden (Berg et al., 2004). In addition, labor unions play a strong role in negotiating working conditions in India (Rai, 2006), but there is a ban on independent labor unions in China (Pan, 2002). South Korea accomplished much of its economic growth in the contemporary era by suppressing unions. Unionization has been on the decline in Mexico, where 1 in 3 workers held union membership in 1984, but only 1 in 5 did in 1998 (Hilger, 2003). A growing international labor movement is attempting to forge networks of labor organizations across national lines (McMichael, 2008).

Social workers who participate in policy development must be informed about the serious challenges to job security in the contemporary era. Social workers are also called on to deal with many of the social problems arising out of these changes in the economic institution—problems such as inadequate resources for family caregiving, domestic violence, substance abuse, depression, and anxiety. Social workers attached to the workplace need to be skillful in influencing organizational policy and linking the work organization to the wider community, as well as in assessing specific work situations affecting their clients.

Trends in Education

As young as they are, Enrique and Myra Meza understand that educational attainment is becoming increasingly important in the labor market, but Myra complains that their parents take Enrique's education more seriously than hers. Traditionally, the primary purpose of the **educational institution** has been to pass along formal knowledge from one generation to the next—a function that was largely performed by the family, with some help from religion, until the 19th century. Formal education, schooling that includes a predetermined curriculum, has expanded dramatically around the world in the past several decades. In the process, there has been a trend toward convergence in educational curricula, especially in mathematics and science (Ballantine & Roberts, 2009).

The Education for All movement is an international effort to meet the basic learning needs of children, youth, and adults of the world (UNESCO, 2010). However, in an era of a knowledge-based

Conflict perspective

global economy, there continue to be large global gaps in opportunities for education. In both low-income and wealthy nations, children from low-income families have less access to early childhood education than other children (UNESCO, 2010). Although educational participation is almost universal between the ages of 5 and 14 in affluent countries, 115 million of the world's children, most

residing in Africa or South Asia, do not receive even a primary education (United Nations Development Program, 2005). This situation was worsened by conditions the World Bank set on debt refinancing in the late 1980s, which mandated reductions in education expenditure. The result was reduced educational levels in Asia, Latin America, and Africa, and a widening gap in average years of education between rich and poor countries (McMichael, 2008). The global financial crisis that began in late 2007 continues to have an impact; both nations and families are finding it necessary to cut back on education spending. This is happening in wealthy nations like the United States, but the impact is greatest in low-income nations (UNESCO, 2010). The average child born in Mozambique in 2005 will receive 4 years of formal education, compared to the child in South Asia who will receive 8 years, and the child in France who will receive 15 years (United Nations Development Program, 2005). About 40% of college-age people in affluent countries go to college, but this opportunity is afforded to only 3% in poor countries (D. Newman, 2006). There are gender disparities in educational attainment across the globe, but there is a difference in the direction of this disparity between poor and affluent nations. Females still receive 1 year less education than males in African and Arab countries, and 2 years less in South Asia (United Nations Development Program, 2005), but females receive higher levels of education than males in most affluent industrialized countries (Sen, Partelow, & Miller, 2005). Women still make up nearly two thirds of the world's adults who lack literacy (UNESCO, 2010).

There are also inequalities in the resources available for schooling across the world. In low-income countries, and also in impoverished neighborhoods in the United States, children attend schools with leaking roofs, poor sanitation, bad ventilation, and inadequate materials, or go to school under a tree in some parts of the world. There is a shortage of trained teachers in many areas around the globe. In countries such as Madagascar, Mozambique, Sierra Leone, and Togo, the pupil-to-teacher ratio is 80:1 (UNESCO, 2010).

Photos 7.3a & 7.3b The contrast between these two classrooms—one in a well-resourced suburban school in the United States and another one on a footpath in Ahmedabad, India—demonstrates global inequality in resources for education.

In this era of global economic competition, the U.S. Department of Education (DOE) has been interested in tracking how education in the United States compares to that in other affluent industrialized countries. The DOE's most recent comparisons focus on the United States, Canada, France, Germany, Italy, Japan, the Russian Federation, and the United Kingdom (England, Scotland, Wales, and Ireland) (Sen et al., 2005). There are some similarities and some differences in the education institutions in these countries. All of these countries have compulsory education, and participation in formal education is high until the end of the compulsory period, which is age 18 in Germany; age 17 in the United States; age 16 in Canada, France, and the United Kingdom; and age 15 in Italy, Japan, and the Russian Federation (Sen et al., 2005). China's compulsory education law requires 9 years of education rather than stipulating a compulsory age, but also indicates age 6 as the age of school entry (China Education and Research Network, 2000).

Universal early childhood enrollment, defined as a 90% enrollment rate, begins later in the United States than in several other countries: age 5 in the United States, compared to age 3 in France and Italy and age 4 in Japan and the United Kingdom. In France, a large number of children below the age of 3 are enrolled in formal education.

The ratio of the average annual teacher salary to GDP per capita, a measure of how teachers are paid relative to other salaried employees, is lower in the United States than it is in the United Kingdom, Germany, Japan, and Scotland, and on par with France and Italy, where primary and secondary education are funded primarily at the federal level. The federal government plays a very large role in the funding of higher education in several countries, including the United Kingdom where the government provides 100% of higher education funding, Italy (92%), France (91%), and Japan (84%) (Sen et al., 2005). This is not the case in the United States.

In the 20th century, average educational attainment increased spectacularly in the United States. For a time after the 1954 *Brown v. Board of Education* Supreme Court ruling that "separate but equal" has no place in public education, there was a serious attempt to desegregate many urban school systems, and racial and ethnic differences in educational attainment were reduced (Kozol, 2005). In the past 15 years, however, courts at both the state and federal level have been lifting desegregation orders, arguing that separate can be equal or at least "good enough," and African American and Latino/Hispanic students are now more segregated than they were 30 years ago (D. Newman, 2008). Jonathan Kozol, a long-time equal education advocate, describes the current situation as "the

| Conflict perspective |

restoration of apartheid schooling in America" in the subtitle of his 2005 book.

In the current climate, the education institution in the United States is becoming a prime force in perpetuating, if not exacerbating, economic inequalities. A 2006 report by Kati Haycock of the Education Trust indicates that current trends in the education institution are the principal reason that there is less upward mobility in the social class structure in the United States today than there was 20 years ago, and less mobility in the United States than in any European nation except England. Trends at every educational level are involved in this situation.

Conflict perspective

Before summarizing some of those trends, it is important to note that the stated goal of the No Child Left Behind (NCLB) Act of 2001 was to raise academic achievement for all students, out of concern that U.S. students were falling behind those in other wealthy nations, and to close the achievement gaps that divide low-income students and students of color from their White and higher-income peers. There has been much state-level opposition to aspects of this federal legislation across the political spectrum, and some negotiated changes to the law over time (Sunderman, 2006). In November 2006, the U.S. Department of Education proclaimed NCLB to be a major success, but a 2006 study by The Civil Rights Project (which was then at Harvard University) reported that NCLB had not improved reading and mathematical achievement, nor had it reduced achievement gaps (J. Lee, 2006). Some critics argue that NCLB relies heavily on testing to accomplish its goals without providing the increased resources necessary for schools serving low-income and minority youth to raise test scores or to approximate the education provided in wealthy communities (Kozol, 2005).

Let's return now to discussion of some of the trends in education that perpetuate societal inequalities:

1. *Trends in early childhood education.* As noted earlier, the United States has no universal early childhood education program, and there is much evidence that low-income and racial minority students have less access to quality early childhood education than their White and higher-income peers (Education Trust, 2006b). Many poorer school districts do not provide prekindergarten programs, and many low-income children are placed on a waiting list for Head Start programs. Some low- to middle-income districts are canceling full-day kindergarten, and some public school districts have begun to provide for-pay preschool and full-day kindergarten, a practice that clearly disadvantages low-income children. Wealthy families are competing for slots for their young children in expensive preschool programs, called the "baby ivies," that provide highly enriched early learning environments, further advancing the opportunities for children in privileged families (Kozol, 2005).

2. *Trends in primary school education.* In 35 states, school districts that educate the greatest number of low-income and minority children receive much less state and local money per pupil than other school districts (Education Trust, 2006b; Habash Rowan, Hall, & Haycock, 2010). Nationally, the average difference is $1,100 per child, but in some states the difference is much larger. Kozol (2005) reports that a high-poverty elementary school with 400 students in New York receives over $1 million less per year than a school of equal size in a district where there are few impoverished children. The result is usually poor building infrastructures, lower salaries for teachers, and less technology in the lower-funded schools. Although NCLB requires equity in teacher quality for poor and minority students, very few states have developed methods to evaluate progress on this requirement, and much evidence suggests that these students are disproportionately taught by inexperienced and poorly qualified teachers (Education Trust, 2006a; Habash Rowan et al., 2010). In addition, parents in affluent communities often supplement public funds to enhance the school library, to provide art and music programs, and even to hire extra teachers to reduce class size. There is little wonder that the longer children of

color stay in school, the larger their achievement gap becomes (Education Trust, 2006b).

3. *Trends in secondary education.* High school graduation rates are a key measure of whether schools are making adequate yearly progress (AYP) under the provisions of NCLB. As it turns out, most school districts do not have a system for calculating graduation rates, and there are major holes in their reported data (Habash, 2008). Furthermore, researchers at the Education Trust have analyzed the reported state data and found that all states inflated their graduation rates, ranging from a 1% to a 33% inflation rate (as reported in D. Hall, 2005). These researchers estimate that graduation rates for students who entered high school in 2000 ranged from 51% in South Carolina to 86% in New Jersey. More than half of the nongraduates were African American, Latino, or Native American, indicating an overrepresentation because these groups together compose about one third of students in public school nationally. African Americans have made gains in high school completion in the past 30 years, however. In 2008, 94% of Whites age 25–29 had completed high school, compared to 87% of Blacks and 75% of Hispanics. National data indicate that in 1972, 86% of White, 72% of Blacks, and 56% of Hispanics age 25–29 had completed high school (National Center for Education Statistics, 2011). Even when students in impoverished rural and urban neighborhoods graduate, their high schools may not have offered the types of courses that college admissions departments require (Habash Rowan et al., 2010; Kozol, 2005). There is also a critical shortage of teachers who are trained to teach English language learners, who often must navigate very large high school settings (Hood, 2003).

4. *Trends in higher education.* The costs to attend college have been escalating rapidly in recent years, and financial aid for low-income students has not been keeping pace. Consequently, the rate of completion of a bachelor's degree by age 24 for students from the top income quartile increased from 40% in the 1970s to 75% in 2003, compared to an increase from 6% to 9% for low-income students.

Between 1970 and 2008, the race and ethnic gap in college education closed but remains quite high, as demonstrated in Exhibit 7.6. There are many factors that contribute to these disparities, including rising tuition, but changes in the pattern of financial aid distribution are important. There was a strong increase in financial aid over the past 20 years, but the biggest increases went to affluent students rather than to low-income students. By 2005, a total of 34% of federal financial aid went to families with annual incomes over $100,000. Between 1995 and 2005, state need-based grants increased by 95%, while state non–need-based grants increased by 350%. In that same period, private colleges and universities increased their grants to low-income students by 52% and their grants to students from families with incomes over $100,000 by 254% (Haycock, 2006). Some colleges and universities are doing better than others in improving the graduation rate of minority students (see Engle & Theokas, 2010).

It is important to remember that many immigrants, like Mr. and Mrs. Meza, had limited education in their home country but manage to instill in their children the value of a college education. Social workers should become active partners in efforts at educational reform, particularly in those that equalize educational opportunities. To be effective in these efforts, we need to be informed about trends in the educational institution.

Trends in Health Care

Health and health care costs are important issues for the Meza family. Mrs. Meza didn't receive much prenatal care, which is relatively inexpensive, when she was pregnant with Minerva because she lacked health insurance. Luckily, Mr. Meza had insurance coverage for Minerva's long postnatal care, which was very expensive. Health is important to this family, but health is also important to a society. Child development, adult well-being, and family stability are all affected by health. The **health care institution** is the primary institution for promoting the general health of a society. At one time, health care was addressed primarily in the home by families. Today, in wealthy countries, health care is a major

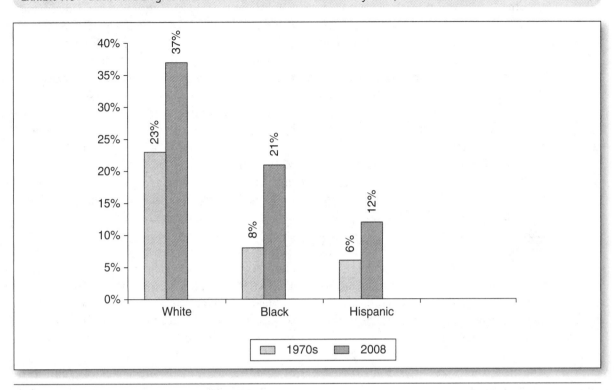

SOURCE: Based on Child Trends Data Bank (2010); Haycock (2006).

social institution, and health care organizations are major employers (Ballantine & Roberts, 2009).

Unfortunately, there is much disparity in the global health care institution, both between and within countries (WHO, 2008c). Global inequalities in child and adult mortality are large and growing. They are highly influenced by factors in the economic and health care institution, but also by factors in the education and family institutions (J. P. Ruger & Kim, 2006). Almost 10 million children in the world die each year before they are 5 years old (UNICEF, 2009a). Every 2 minutes, 4 people in the world die from malaria, 3 of them children. Almost all (98%) of the children who die each year live in poor countries. The sad story is that these children "die because of where they are born" (United Nations Development Program, 2005, p. 24).

Conflict perspective

In poor countries, basic health prevention and treatment services are almost nonexistent. The World Health Organization (2006d) reports that the African Region has 24% of the world's health burden but only 3% of the world's health workers, and it attracts only 1% of world health expenditure. People living in extreme poverty typically lack access to safe drinking water, adequate housing, adequate sanitation, adequate nutrition, health education, and professional health care. Infectious and parasitic diseases are rampant; they account for 77% of child deaths in Africa and 57% of those in Southeast Asia, compared to about 5% of child deaths in the United States and Western Europe (D. Newman, 2008). And yet, only 1% of the drugs introduced by pharmaceutical companies between 1975 and 1999 target the tropical diseases that kill or disable millions of people in Africa, Asia, and South America each year (D. Newman, 2008). In sub-Saharan Africa, only 17% of those in need of antiretroviral therapy for HIV/AIDS had access to it in December 2005, even though there was an eightfold increase in coverage between December 2003 and December 2005. In the Sudan, less than 1% of those in need had access (WHO, 2006b).

Within-country health disparities are very prominent in the United States, where deep inequalities are related to socioeconomic status, race, and ethnicity, and poverty is seen as the driving force behind these growing gaps (J. Chen et al., 2006). A baby born to a family in the top 5% of the U.S. income distribution has an average life expectancy that is 25% longer than a baby born to a family in the bottom 5% (United Nations Development Program, 2005). As a result of poor health, impoverished children are at risk for poor school attendance and thus low educational attainment, increasing the odds of poor health and its consequences across the life course (L. Bauman, Silver, & Stein, 2006). However, it is clear that race as well as social class critically impact health disparities in the United States. Even at higher ends of education, there are large health disparities between African Americans and Whites (J. Jackson, 2006).

Although much of the health disparities are related to factors in other social institutions, aspects of the health care institution play a large role. The United States is currently the only affluent country with no universal health plan. In 2008, a total of 46.3 million people in the United States (15.4% of the population) were without health insurance coverage (DeNavas-Walt et al., 2009). It is likely that the number of uninsured grew during the recession that began in December 2007, as the rate of unemployment grew. The uninsured rate varied by race and ethnicity for the 3-year period 2006–2008. American Indian/Alaska Natives (31.7%) and Latinos (30.7%) were about 3 times as likely to be uninsured as Whites/Not Hispanic (10.7%), and Native Hawaiian and Other Pacific Islanders (18.5%), Asian Americans (16.6%), and African Americans (19.7%) were close to twice as likely (DeNavas-Walt et al., 2009). Over 40% of the uninsured have no usual source of health care, and almost half (49%) of uninsured adults with chronic conditions reported going without needed health care because of the cost in 2003 (Davidoff & Kenney, 2005; United Nations Development Program, 2005).

The level of uninsured individuals is only part of the story. Recent research indicates that bankruptcies related to health care costs have been increasing, and one study found that 62.1% of all bankruptcies in the United States in 2007 were caused by illness and medical bills, up 49.6% since 2001. Three-quarters of the people involved in medical bankruptcies had health insurance. Many faced bankruptcy because they lost income due to illness or mortgaged their home to pay for medical bills. Most people facing medical bankruptcy owned their own homes, were well educated, and had middle-class occupations (Himmelstein, Thorne, Warren, & Woolhandler, 2009).

Jeanne Ballantine and Keith Roberts (2009) suggest that the United States has both the best and the worst health care system in the industrialized world. It is one of the best in terms of quality of care, trained practitioners, facilities, and technology. However, it is the worst in terms of costs, inefficiency, equality of access, and fragmentation. The United States spends a greater percentage of its gross domestic product (GDP) on health care than any other industrial country, for example, 15.2% of GDP compared to 6.2% in Mexico, 7.5% in Austria, 8.0% in the United Kingdom, and 10.1% in France. It also has the greatest concentration of advanced medical technology. Even so, the World Health Organization ranks the United States 37th among all nations in performance of its health care system (Auerbach & Krimgold, 2001a). Public satisfaction with the health care system does not seem to reflect the percentage of the national GDP spent on health. In 1999–2000, public satisfaction was highest in Austria, with 83% of the public reporting that they were fairly or very happy with their health care system. This compares to 40% in the United States. Indeed, satisfaction levels were lower than those in the United States in only three countries—Italy, Portugal, and Greece (Organisation for Economic Co-operation and Development [OECD], 2006a).

The major causes of dissatisfaction in the United States relate to costs and system fragmentation. One solution that some U.S. patients are choosing is to become what is called "medical tourists." They are traveling to countries such as India, Thailand, Singapore, and Malaysia for surgery and other procedures, where the costs are typically 20% to 25% of those in the United States (Kher, 2008).

The reasons why the health care institution is so costly in the United States are quite complex, but two contributing factors are discussed here. First, compared to the health care systems in other countries, the U.S. approach to financing health care is extremely complex, and the administrative cost of this complex system is greater than in the more streamlined universal systems in other industrialized countries (Reinhardt, Hussey, & Anderson, 2004). Second, the health care institution is influenced by culture. Health care in the United States reflects the aggressive, can-do spirit of the mainstream culture (Gardiner & Kosmitzki, 2008; D. Newman, 2008). For example, compared to European physicians, U.S. physicians recommend more routine examinations and perform many more bypass surgeries and angioplasties than European doctors. These are both examples of a more aggressive approach to treatment that could be attributed to a reimbursement system that rewards such aggressiveness, as much as to a cultural bias toward aggressive treatment (Reinhardt, Hussey, & Anderson, 2002). The rapid growth in **therapeutic medicine**—diagnosing and treating disease—has drained resources from the U.S. *public health system,* which focuses on disease prevention and health promotion (Coombs & Capper, 1996). Researchers in the United States and the United Kingdom agree that the impressive decline in mortality in the 20th century was more the result of improvements in the social and physical environments in which people lived than of advances in medical treatment. They note that medical advancements such as therapeutic drugs, immunizations, and surgical procedures were introduced several decades after significant declines in the diseases that they targeted (Auerbach & Krimgold, 2001a).

Societies around the world struggle with health care costs, quality, and access to care and medical technology. Most governments in Europe made a decision in the late 1800s and early 1900s to support health care as a human right and put some form of national health care system into place. It appears that they were operating out of a belief that maintaining a healthy population was necessary to maintain a strong society. In contrast, the health care system in the United States developed with less direction and made piecemeal policies over time. Medical research has been a major strength in the developing U.S. health care system, but the two biggest challenges in the past three decades have been lack of universal access to care and continuously escalating costs. Several attempts have been made to develop federal legislation to address these problems for a number of decades, but these efforts failed because politicians had different philosophical positions on the role of government in health care delivery and because of considerable opposition from private insurance companies, physicians, and pharmaceutical companies.

After a year-long debate, the U.S. Congress passed the Patient Protection and Affordable Care Act and the Health Care and Education Reconciliation Act of 2010, and both bills were signed into law in March 2010. It is projected that 95% of people in the United States will be covered by the new health reform plan once it is fully implemented by the end of 2018 (Whitehouse. gov, 2010). This legislation has led to contentious public debate, and some states are challenging its constitutionality. Its impact, if and when it is fully implemented, remains to be seen. Proponents of the legislation argue that it will make health insurance more affordable (Whitehouse.gov, 2010).

Like many other families, the Meza family may need social work assistance to navigate the very complex, quite fragmented, health care system as they seek ongoing care for Minerva. Social workers need to be particularly sensitive to the situation of immigrant families who try to integrate traditional healing practices with Global North, technology-oriented medical practices.

Trends in Social Welfare

The Meza family is facing a number of stressors that are beginning to overwhelm them and tear at their relationships with one another. Although Mrs. Meza is becoming desperate about her situation, because of her undocumented immigrant status she is fearful about trusting anyone outside the family in terms of seeking help. Her understanding of what social workers do is to "take children away," and her social worker will have a challenge to win her trust. A good understanding of the special stressors of undocumented immigrants will be essential. As social workers, we are well aware of the network of social welfare agencies and programs that could help the Meza family; we are also aware of the gaps in the contemporary social welfare institution.

Different writers have presented various definitions of the **social welfare institution,** but the definition provided by Philip Popple and Leslie Leighninger (2001) is particularly compatible with the definition of social institution used in this chapter: The social welfare institution functions to promote *interdependence* and to deal with issues of *dependence*. Individuals are interdependent with institutions, as well as with other individuals, for survival and for satisfactory role performance. We depend on our doctors, day care centers, families, friends, neighbors, and so on, and they depend on us. Sometimes, situations occur that increase our need for assistance or decrease the assistance available to us. For example, we may

Systems perspective

become sick or injured, lose our job, or take on a caregiving role for a newborn infant or a frail parent. In these situations, our ability to successfully fulfill role expectations is jeopardized—a situation that Popple and Leighninger refer to as dependence. In analyzing such problematic situations, social workers must pay attention not only to the behavior of individuals, but also to how well social institutions are supporting people in their role performance.

In the contemporary era, there are several major challenges facing the social welfare institution around the globe.

- *Aging population.* The prosperous advanced industrial societies in the United States, Europe, and Japan face a crisis involving aging populations produced by recent trends of mass longevity and low fertility rates, a situation commonly referred to as "the graying of the population." In the United States, that has translated into policy debates about "tightening" our Social Security and Medicare programs. Japan, the world's most rapidly graying nation, has begun to respond by cutting back its safety net for older adults (Faiola, 2006).

- *Labor market insecurities.* Global labor market insecurities are undermining the ability of families, even middle-income families, to avoid dependence. This situation intensified during the deep economic recession that began in December 2007.

- *Debt in low-income countries.* The World Bank and IMF have required many impoverished countries to reduce social spending as a condition for rescheduling their debt during a time when these countries face rising numbers of orphans of the AIDS pandemic (McMichael, 2008).

- *Increasing evidence of the importance of the early years.* Behavioral science research is finding increasing evidence of the important role that the early social environment plays in long-term physical and mental health.

The social welfare institution developed in all industrialized countries in the 19th and 20th centuries as these nations tried to cope with the alienation and disruption caused by social inequalities of industrial capitalism (Teeple, 2000). However, the social welfare institution, like any other social institution, reflects the culture of the society. Public expenditure on social welfare (including old age, survivors, disability, health, family, unemployment, housing and other policies), as a percentage of GDP, varies among affluent societies. For example, Sweden spent 31.3% of its GDP on social welfare in 2003, compared to 16.2% spent in the United States. Of the wealthy advanced industrial countries, only Ireland spent less of its GDP on social welfare than the United States (15.9%). Expenditures on social welfare increased in most affluent societies, including the United States, between 1980 and 2003. It is important to note, however, that as societies gray, expenditures on old age benefits are increasing at a much faster rate than those in other social welfare sectors (UNICEF, 2005a). Consequently, in many affluent countries, there was an increase in child poverty rates but not older adult poverty rates in the 1990s (UNICEF, 2005a). Given what we are learning about the long-term negative health consequences of early deprivation, this may pose serious challenges for the social welfare institution in the future (N. Adler, 2006).

The differences in cultural attitudes toward social welfare are best illustrated by the approaches of the United States and Europe. In the United States, the neoliberal political philosophy led to a diminishing sense of public responsibility, and an increasing emphasis on individual responsibility, for the social well-being of the nation. U.S. officials have boasted in recent years about how much the welfare rolls have been reduced since the passage of welfare reform in 1996. In a period of declining security in the labor market, the governmental welfare safety net for families with children has become more short-term (Sennett, 2006). The overall goal of U.S. policy is to prevent dependency.

In contrast, European officials tend to speak with pride about their "European Social Model" and their "welfare state" (T. R. Reid, 2004). Their goal is to promote interdependence and social inclusion, rather than preventing dependence, and paying for the social health of the society is seen as everyone's responsibility. Indeed, the expansive cradle-to-grave programs in the European welfare states are costly and paid for by high taxes, particularly high sales taxes, which run from a low of 16% in Germany to a high of 25% in Denmark and Sweden (T. R. Reid, 2004). European countries have higher minimum wages and more generous unemployment compensation than the United States. A worker who becomes unemployed in the United States will receive an average of 50% wage replacement from public assistance. In Europe, a laid-off worker receives a housing benefit, heat and light benefit, food benefit, child care benefit, as well as a monthly unemployment payment, in addition to continued access to public health care. This results in the family of an unemployed person in France receiving approximately 86% of his or her former earnings, while the family of an unemployed person in Sweden or the Netherlands receives approximately 90% of the former earnings. European countries provide birth or maternity grants, family allowances, and generous paid parental leave to care for children. Many European countries treat the monthly payment to parents as a salary, withholding income and social security taxes as would happen with any paycheck (T. R. Reid, 2004).

The European countries are not alone in providing more generous public support to families than is offered in the United States. Parental leave policies are a good example. The United States and Australia are the only affluent countries of the world that do not offer some *paid* parental leave at the time of birth and adoption. Australia does, however, provide families with a universal, flat-rate maternity grant of $5,000 for each new child to assist with the costs of birth or adoption (Australian Government, 2006). Many low- and middle-income countries also offer paid parental leave; for example, Afghanistan offers 3 months at 100% of wages, the Bahamas offers 13 weeks at 60% of wages, Brazil offers 17 weeks at 100% of wages, the Congo offers 15 weeks at 50% of wages, and Libya offers 3 months at 100% of wages (Clearinghouse on International Developments in Child, Youth and Family Policies, 2004). If the Mezas lived in Sweden, they might have made use of a family policy that allows 1 year of parental leave at 80% of wage replacement as well as up to 60 days of sick child leave at the same wage-replacement level. The sick child leave could give them time to work with the multidisciplinary team to stabilize the situation at home.

The social welfare institution in the United States has been influenced by the call to move federal power both downward and outward. The Personal Responsibility and Work Opportunity Reconciliation ACT (PRWORA) of 1996 passed to the states most of the responsibility for public assistance to needy families and children. The Temporary Assistance to Needy Families (TANF) block grant gives states more flexibility to design their own public assistance programs (Urban Institute, 2006). This is a downward movement of power. However, in 2006, Congress and the George W. Bush administration wrote new rules that tightened the federal reins on state definitions of work requirements for people on welfare, demonstrating some continued negotiations about the role of federal and state governments (A. Goldstein, 2006).

Since the 1970s, there has also been a growing global trend for government at all levels to develop "purchase of service" contract agreements with private, nonprofit organizations to provide social welfare services in "public–private partnerships." These nonprofit organizations are coming to be known as *nongovernmental organizations* (NGOs). This trend has accelerated since the 1980s, particularly in affluent societies. In recent natural disasters, such as the Asian Tsunami caused by an Indian Ocean earthquake in December 2004, the earthquake in Haiti in January 2010, and the Japanese earthquake and tsunami in 2011, large numbers of NGOs provided aid, but coordination among the NGOs was a major challenge. In 2004, it was estimated that 2 million NGOs operate in the United States, with 70% of them established since the 1970s (Roff, 2004).

Historically, the social welfare institution has had a mix of governmental and nongovernmental monies and activities, but the nature of this mix

has changed over time. The U.S. government is now playing a smaller role in delivering social service programs, but it continues to play a large role in the funding of services through contract agreements (Schmid, 2004). The nonprofit sector is larger in affluent countries than in low- and middle-income countries, and it is most highly developed in Western Europe (Roff, 2004; Salamon, Anheier, List, Toepler, & Sokolowski, 1999). Increasingly, NGOs are becoming multinational organizations, and there is some evidence that social welfare is higher in poor countries when multinational NGOs are involved (Aldashev & Verdier, 2009).

There is also a long history of faith-based organizations providing social welfare services in the United States. Currently, much controversy exists about the "charitable choice provision" of PRWORA, which allows states to contract with religious organizations, as well as other private organizations, for service provision. President George W. Bush (2000–2008) introduced a "faith-based initiative" to expand the role of faith-based organizations in social service delivery. When he took office in 2009, President Barak Obama developed the White House Office of Faith-based and Neighborhood Partnerships to build bridges between the federal government and both secular and faith-based nonprofits. Some critics have been concerned that the religious freedom of clients would not be honored with such arrangements. However, a 2009 public opinion poll showed that 69% of the U.S. public favors allowing religious organizations to apply for government funding to provide social services, but 63% oppose allowing groups that encourage religious conversion to seek such funding (Pew Research Center, 2009).

The most controversial trend in the social welfare institution is the entrance of for-profit organizations into the mix of public–private partnerships, beginning in the 1980s. The for-profit share of social welfare services continued to grow, and by the early 1990s, nearly half of social welfare agencies in the United States were for-profit, and they accounted for 22% of all social service employees (P. Frumkin, 2002; Lynn, 2002). The for-profit organizations continue to expand their business lines into new service sectors. America Works, Maximus, Children's Comprehensive Services, and Youth Services International are just a few of the large, for-profit social welfare organizations on the contemporary scene. Among the serious questions that have been raised by the entrance of for-profit organizations into the social welfare institution is whether these organizations will choose to serve only "easy to serve" client groups, avoiding those with entrenched problems related to poverty (Lynn, 2002; W. Ryan, 1999). For-profit agencies have greater access to capital and can take advantage of efficiencies of scale if they are part of a national chain (S. Smith, 2010).

The Meza family is struggling to reorganize itself to cope with Minerva's special needs. They could use help in this effort, but to date, they have experienced the social welfare institution only as a coercive institution, one that tries to control their behavior rather than provide compassionate support. Indeed, the social welfare institution in the United States has always played a social control function as well as a social reform function (Hutchison, 1987). In recent times, it has moved toward greater attention to social control than to social reform (Hutchison & Charlesworth, 2000; Teeple, 2000). Social workers cannot be active participants in moving that balance back to social reform unless they clearly understand trends in the interrelated social institutions discussed in this chapter.

| Conflict perspective |

Trends in Religion

Mrs. Meza believes that Minerva's health problems are God's way of punishing her for not placing the health of her unborn child over other concerns. This is how she makes meaning of the situation. The **religious institution** is the primary institution for addressing spiritual and ethical issues. It also serves important socialization, social control, and mutual support functions.

Although there is a long history of conflict and adaptation as the major world religions confronted each other in the same political and geographic areas, globalization has urgently increased the need for religious communities to find ways to coexist globally as well as locally. A religious belief system helps people to feel secure, and exposure to different belief systems can be unsettling and sometimes perceived as a threat to the integrity of one's own beliefs and identity. Today, however, it is almost impossible for believers in one religious tradition to be isolated from other religious traditions. We are increasingly exposed to the beliefs, rituals, and organizations of diverse religious groups, and this is not a trend that is likely to be reversed. There are few choices about how to cope with this trend. We can attempt to impose one belief system on the world and commit genocide if that doesn't work. Or we can attempt to find a unified ethical code consistent with all religious traditions, and respectfully agree to disagree if that doesn't work, giving legal protections to all groups. In the past, all of these choices have been put into practice at one time or another.

We are living in a time of much religious strife. Serbian Orthodox Christians engaged in ethnic cleansing of Muslims in the former Yugoslavia. Catholics and Protestants have waged a long and often violent battle in Northern Ireland. The Ku Klux Klan in the United States uses religious arguments to vilify and sometimes persecute Jews, African Americans, and other groups. Terrorists have killed and injured thousands in the name of Islam. The United States has called on the name of God, and the language of good and evil, to justify the war on terror and the invasions of Afghanistan and Iraq. Hindus and Muslims kill each other in India. When religious differences are woven with other forms of struggle, such as social class, ethnic, or political struggle, the conflict is likely to be particularly intense (L. Kurtz, 2007).

On the other hand, there are also historical and current stories of peaceful coexistence of religious groups. In 1893, representatives of a wide range of religions were brought together to create the Parliament of the World's Religions. The second meeting of the Parliament did not convene until a century later, in 1993 (L. Kurtz, 2007). It met again in 1999, 2004, and 2009. The mission of the parliament is "to cultivate harmony among the world's religious and spiritual communities and foster their engagement with the world and its other guiding institutions in order to achieve a just, peaceful and sustainable world" (Council for a Parliament of the World's Religions, 2010). Among the issues discussed and debated at the 2009 parliament were healing the earth, reconciling with Indigenous people, overcoming poverty in a patriarchal world, increasing social cohesion in village and city, sharing wisdom in the search for inner peace, securing food and water for all people, and building peace in pursuit of justice. Many predict that access to safe water will become the next major battle over scarce resources (McMichael, 2008).

It is not surprising that both violence and nonviolence have been used in the name of religion. The texts of all of the major world religions include what Lester Kurtz (2007) calls both a "warrior motif" and a "pacifist motif" (p. 247). All major religions justify violence on occasion, but no religion justifies terrorism. They also include norms of mercy, compassion, and respect. In the contemporary era, Islam is sometimes characterized as a violent religion, but Christianity was seen as the most violent world religion during the Crusades and the Inquisition. All of the major world religions have proven that they are capable of perpetrating violence in the name of religion, and all have also demonstrated compassion and tolerance.

It is good to get a sense of the global religious landscape. Consider a group of 10 people that represent the distribution of world religions. Three will be Christian, two will be Muslim, two will be unaffiliated or atheists, one will be Hindu, one will be Buddhist or another East Asian religion, and the remaining one will represent every other religion of the world (L. Kurtz, 2007). This landscape includes two Eastern religions (Hinduism and Buddhism) and three Western religions (Judaism, Christianity, and Islam). The Western religions are *monotheistic,* believing that there is only one God, while the Eastern religions are either *polytheistic,* believing in multiple Gods (e.g., Hinduism, some forms of Buddhism) or not believing in a deity (e.g., some forms of Buddhism). Eastern religions are less insistent on the primacy of their "Truth" than the Western religions and are more likely to embrace nonviolence. Eastern religions have also tended to be less centrally organized than the Western religions.

Each of the major world religions has changed over time and place and become more diverse, a "patchwork of contradictory ideas stitched together over the centuries" (L. Kurtz, 2007, p. 190). Lester Kurtz suggests that we should speak of all of the major world religions in the plural: Hinduisms, Buddhisms, Judaisms, Christianities, and Islams. He also argues that some of the most violent contests occur *within* these religious traditions and not *between* them, as witnessed by the Christian Catholics and Protestants in Northern Ireland, and the Muslim Sunnis and Shias in Iraq.

Each of the major world religions, but especially the Western religions, has internal struggles, sometimes called culture wars (J. D. Hunter, 1994), between a branch of traditionalists and a branch of modernists (L. Kurtz, 2007). The *traditionalists* believe that moral obligations are rigid, given, and | Conflict perspective

absolute. The *modernists* believe that moral commitment is voluntary, conditional, and fluid. These two branches often engage in a struggle for the heart and soul of the religious tradition, sometimes using violence to press their case.

Although many religious peoples around the world fear that modernism and postmodernism are destroying religion, there is clear evidence that the religious institution is quite resilient. As noted in Chapter 5, public opinion polls consistently report that religion is important in the lives of a great majority of people in the United States (Gallup, 2008). International data indicate that people in the United States have much higher weekly attendance at religious services than Europeans; they spend more time in private devotions and more money on religious activities than residents of other advanced industrial countries. This is an aspect of U.S. life that has been very appealing to the Meza and many other immigrant families. In the 1990s, about 60% of the U.S. population were church members, compared with about 10% in 1776 (L. Kurtz, 2007). As suggested in Chapter 5, diversity is the hallmark of the religious institution in the United States today, with between 1,500 and 2,000 religious groups represented, about half of them Christian (L. Kurtz, 2007; Parrillo, 2009).

Christianity remains dominant within the United States, but there are intense culture wars between the traditionalists and the modernists, with the conflict centering on such issues as the definition of family, the role of women, the beginning and end of life, same-sex relationships, prayer in school, and theories of the creation of the world. Both the traditionalists and the modernists base their arguments on their understanding of biblical texts, but each tends to see the other as immoral. Some examples will help to clarify the competing moral precepts regarding some of these questions. Traditionalists see the push for women's rights as destructive to the traditional family and motherhood. Modernists see women's rights as necessary in a just society. Likewise, traditionalists see the gay rights movement as a particularly vicious attack on the traditional family, and modernists see it as a struggle for dignity. Traditionalists argue that school prayer is essential to help students develop a moral code, and modernists argue that it is an intrusion on religious freedom and tolerance. The culture wars are intense because both groups wish for dominance in the political institution.

| Conflict perspective |

Given the clear evidence of the central importance of religion in the lives of billions of people in the world, social workers must become comfortable in assessing the role of religion and spirituality in the lives of their client systems at the individual, family, and community levels. Certainly, we cannot be helpful to Mrs. Meza without understanding the role religion plays in the way she views her situation or her connectedness to a religious community. We should not assume that all persons of a religious group hold the same beliefs on social issues. But we must be aware of religious beliefs—both our own and those of clients—when working with controversial social issues.

Trends in Mass Media

The **mass media institution** is the primary institution for managing the flow of information, images, and ideas among all members of society. Mass media serves an entertainment role for society, but it also influences how we understand ourselves and the world. Mass media technology is the engine of globalization, giving people worldwide immediate access to other cultures and other markets. Rapid advances in electronic communication technology since the 1950s have resulted in widespread access to multiple forms of mass communication—"old media," such as newspapers, magazines, books, radio, television, and film, and "new media" such as the Internet, digital television and radio, MP3 players, ever more elaborate multifunctional cellular telephones, and video games (Devereux, 2008). Electronic media now allow two-way communication as well as one-way communication, and they can store and manipulate vast amounts of information. The mass media is thoroughly embedded in our daily lives and constitutes a larger focus of our leisure time than any other social institution (Devereaux, 2008).

Like other families around the world, the Meza family is saturated with images from these media. Some of these images are negative portrayals of Mexican immigrants, which add to the family's distress, but others, like those shown on the television networks Univision and Telemundo, allow them to be in touch with their Latino heritage, and Telemundo (a U.S. network that broadcasts in Spanish with closed captions in both English and Spanish) can help make connections between the English and Spanish languages.

There are several important trends in the mass media landscape:

1. *Growth in media outlets and media products.* For most of the latter half of the twentieth century, U.S. households had access to 3 television channels, but by 2002, the average number of television channels receivable by U.S. family reached over 100, and some predict that we may well be coming into an era of over 500 cable channels (D. Croteau

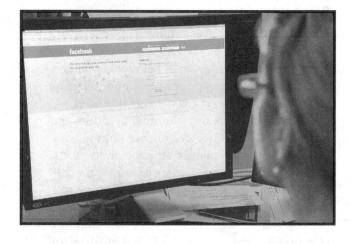

Photo 7.4a & 7.4b Mass media technology is the engine of globalization, and people around the world are saturated with images from multiple media forms. In photo 7.4a, a man sits next to a billboard promoting Chinese wine in Chengdu. In Photo 7.4b, a woman logs in to her Facebook page.

& Hoynes, 2006). New media products have been coming at a very fast clip for more than a decade.

2. *More time and money spent on media products.* There were 650,000 cable television subscribers in the United States in 1960, but the number had grown to 74 million by 2003. In an even newer media sector, the number of cellular telephone subscribers in the United States was 5 million in 1990, and by 2010, 83% of adults reported having a cell phone. (There are over 220 million adults in the United States, and some own more than one cell phone.) (D. Croteau & Hoynes, 2006; Rainie, 2010). Indeed, by the end of 2007, half of the world's people had a mobile phone, including 1 out of 4 in Africa and 1 out of 3 in Asia (International Telecommunications Union, 2008). Widespread use of the Internet did not begin until the early 1990s, but by 2010, the Pew Internet & American Life Project found that 74% of U.S. adults over the age of 18 used the Internet (Rainie, 2010).

3. *Integration of media functions.* Increasingly, one media product is expected to provide several functions. Computers can be used to word process; surf the Internet; communicate by e-mail, instant message, social networking sites, or Skype; participate in chat rooms and blogs; shop; play music; watch DVDs; or read online newspapers. Cellular phones can now send text messages, take and transmit photographs, browse the Internet, communicate by e-mail or on social networking sites, and more. Newspapers have stagnated or lost readership, but large newspapers are developing online versions (Oates, 2008).

4. *Globalization.* Media companies are increasingly targeting a global market to sell products. For example, by 2004 the Viacom corporation reported that it had been able to export the MTV (Music Television) network to 166 countries and territories, to 400 million households, in more than 25 languages, making it the most widely distributed television network in the world (D. Croteau & Hoynes, 2006). The great majority of households receiving MTV are outside the United States. The Arabic news channel, Al-Jazeera, is based in Qatar, but its broadcasts are carried worldwide (D. Newman, 2006). Some critics suggest that the global reach of media companies based in North America and

Europe, particularly in the United States, is a form of cultural imperialism by which U.S. cultural values are spread around the world (Devereux, 2008). As this book is being prepared in March of 2011, it appears that social networking sites like Facebook and Twitter are playing a major role in the mobilization of citizen uprisings in Middle Eastern and Northern African countries.

5. *Concentration of ownership.* The mass media institution has been experiencing a merger mania. In 1983, the majority of all media products in the United States was controlled by 50 media companies. By 2004, although there were many new media products, five global conglomerates controlled the media business in the United States: Time Warner (U.S.), Disney (U.S.), News Corporation (Britain), Viacom (U.S.), and Bertelsmann (Germany) (Bagdikian, 2004). In the United States, this concentration of ownership was enabled by the 1996 Telecommunications Act and a subsequent round of deregulatory actions by the Federal Communications Commission in 2003 (D. Croteau & Hoynes, 2006). It is interesting to note that these policy changes received scant coverage by large media companies. News Corporation CEO Rupert Murdoch argues that his company is the most international mass media provider in the world. News Corp owns several movie studios, including Twentieth Century Fox, and has released such blockbusters as *Star Wars* and *Titanic.* It owns satellite systems and television channels in North America, Europe, and Asia. News Corp is the leading publisher of English-language newspapers, owning more than 100 in the United States, the United Kingdom, Australia, Fiji, Papua New Guinea, and across Europe and Asia. The *Wall Street Journal* was bought by News Corp in 2007. HarperCollins Publishers, with more than 20 imprints, is News Corp's book publishing division (News Corporation, 2006, 2010).

In totalitarian societies, like North Korea, the flow of information, images, and ideas is controlled by the government. In the United States, we have a long tradition of freedom of the press—a belief that the media must be free to serve as a public watchdog. Traditionally, the emphasis has been on the watchdog role in relation to the government and political institution—in other words, a press that is not controlled by the government. Exposure of the Watergate cover-up during the Nixon presidency is considered a high point in U.S. media history. However, the relationship between government and media is controversial, with some groups calling for more government censorship (e.g., to limit children's access and exposure to pornography) and other groups calling for strict adherence to freedom of the press. In the current era of media mergers and acquisitions, concerns have centered on censorship by the economic institution (Bagdikian, 2004; D. Croteau & Hoynes, 2006). Critics suggest that powerful multinational media corporations censor the coverage of news to protect their economic or political interests. Organizations that analyze freedom of the press report that after two decades of improvement of freedom of the press around the world, there was a decline in press freedom in 2009, with only 17% of the world's population living in countries with a free press. These organizations rated the United States as 21st in freedom of the press in 2009. The highest marks went to the Nordic countries (Freedom House, 2010; Reporters Without Borders, 2010).

Social psychologists have been interested in the effects of the media on human behavior, focusing particularly on the effects of television, which has become the dominant form of mass media communication globally. Research on the effects of the media on human behavior is difficult to design because it is hard to isolate the effects of specific media forms and to capture the cumulative effect of multiple forms. Although it is possible for the media to influence human behavior in both positive and negative ways, the research has focused, for the most part, on negative effects. Social workers and other professionals have been particularly concerned that television provides more models of antisocial than prosocial behavior. Feminists have been concerned about the influence of gender role

Conflict perspective

stereotypes presented in the media. Members of racial and ethnic minority groups; the disability community; and the gay, lesbian, bisexual, and transgender community have also been concerned about stereotypical media presentations of their groups (D. Newman, 2008). The Mezas have grown increasingly concerned about the negative portrayal of immigrant issues on U.S. television.

Mass media critics also suggest that control of the media by political and economic elites results in control of cultural meanings to benefit elites and silence dissident views. The mass media has historically been controlled by White, middle- and upper-class men, who have presented their worldviews. Mass media owners are interested in attracting affluent consumers and choose content with this aim in mind (D. Croteau & Hoynes, 2006). As a partial corrective, David Croteau and William Hoynes argue that privately owned media should be required to provide a minimum amount of substantive public affairs programming. Social work advocates can collaborate with other professionals toward this goal.

It is estimated that there were 1.7 billion Internet users around the world in September of 2009, but they are concentrated in the wealthy industrialized nations. The latest cross-national data indicate that the largest number of users (738 million) are in Asia, 418 million in Europe, 252 million in North America, 179 million in Latin America/Caribbean, 67 million in Africa, 57 million in the Middle East, and 20 million in Oceania/Australia. Although Asia has the most Internet users, North America has the highest percentage of its population online (74.2%), compared to 60.4% in Oceania/Australia, 52.0% in Europe, 30.5% in Latin America/Caribbean, 28.3% of the Middle East, 19.4% in Asia, and 6.8% in Africa (Internet World Stats, 2010). When interpreting these data, it is important to note that the European data include both wealthy Western European countries and the less wealthy Eastern European countries. Unequal access perpetuates advantage and disadvantage in life chances. Writing about the United States, D. Croteau and Hoynes (2006) argue that we must work toward publicly funded universal access to the

Internet to prevent "hardening of the digital divide" (p. 239). They suggest that Internet services should be made available to schools, community centers, and libraries, particularly in low-income neighborhoods. Increasing access to the Internet has also raised new questions about the need to prevent minors from gaining access to sexually explicit material and from being exploited by predators on the Internet. These are issues that call for social work advocacy.

Trends in Family and Kinship

You undoubtedly would agree that family and kinship relationships are a very important part of the unfolding story of the Meza family. Family and kinship is the most basic social institution, and in simple societies it fulfills many of the functions assigned to other social institutions in complex societies. Although the functions of family and kinship have been the subject of some controversy in the contemporary era, most societies generally agree that the **family and kinship institution** is primarily responsible for the regulation of procreation, for the initial socialization of new members of society, and for mutual support.

As the primary unit of every society, families are altered as the result of social change, and globalization is changing family life in some extraordinary ways around the world (B. Adams & Trost, 2005; Leeder, 2004). There are many ways of being family around the globe, and there seems to be an exception for almost every family trend that can be identified. However, we can identify three global trends in family life.

1. *Modified extended family form.* Historically, the extended family has been more important in Latin America, Asia, and Africa than in Europe and North America. Globalization appears to be leading to some convergence toward a *modified extended family,* a family system in which family members are highly involved with each other but maintain separate dwellings (Leeder, 2004). This is the current family form for the Meza family, where family members maintain households across national

lines, making them one of the growing numbers of *transnational families*. Within this general pattern, there are many variations. In wealthy, advanced, industrial societies, governmental programs augment the care of dependent family members, but such programs are not typically available in nonindustrial or newly industrializing societies. Marriages continue to be arranged by the elders in many parts of the world, particularly in African and Asian societies, but they are based on love matches in Western societies. *Monogamy,* or marriage to one person at a time, is the norm in Western societies, but *polygamy,* or marriage to multiple partners, is still followed in some parts of the world.

2. *Mass migration.* Migration for a better life is not new; indeed, it is the history of the United States. Between 1810 and 1921, a total of 34 million people emigrated from Europe to the United States (McMichael, 2008). With economic globalization, numerous rural peasants in nonindustrialized and newly industrializing countries have been displaced by large agricultural corporations, many headquartered in the United States; some move to the cities in their own countries, and others immigrate to countries with greater economic opportunities. Many migrate because their labor became obsolete in a constantly reorganizing global market. Still others migrate to escape war or political persecution. By one account, 75% of refugees and displaced persons are women and children (McMichael, 2008). Often families are separated, with some members migrating and others staying behind, sometimes to migrate at a later stage. Migrants seek to earn money for families back home, and it is estimated that 100 million people globally depend on the remittances from family members who have migrated (McMichael, 2008). Indeed, the Mezas regularly send money to relatives in Mexico. In affluent societies like the United States, corporations welcome the cheap labor of undocumented immigrants, and wealthy households welcome the access to cheap household servants. Yet there is ongoing backlash and there are political fear campaigns against immigrants from low-income nations. Anti-immigrant sentiment has been particularly strong in Europe in recent years (Klapper, 2006).

3. *Feminization of wage labor.* In many parts of the world, women are increasingly involved in wage labor, in newly industrializing as well as highly industrialized societies (Leeder, 2004). For example, women make up 80% of the labor force in the export processing zones of Taiwan, the Philippines, Sri Lanka, Mexico, and Malaysia. In these export zones, women typically work longer hours at lower wages than men (McMichael, 2008). In the United States, both parents work outside the home for wages in 78% of married-couple families with children, up from 32% in 1976 (D. Newman, 2008). And yet, there is a global gender wage gap. In the United States, women involved in full-time wage labor earn about 76 cents for every dollar earned by men. In other late industrial societies, such as Australia, Denmark, France, New Zealand, and the United Kingdom, women earn 80 to 90% of what men earn (D. Newman, 2008). Multinational corporations often pay female factory workers in newly industrializing countries as little as half of what they pay men (D. Newman, 2008). In many parts of Latin America, Africa, and Asia, women earn 25% or less of what men earn (McMichael, 2008).

Two other trends are more characteristic of the United States and other late industrial societies than of the preindustrial and newly industrializing societies, but are occurring, nevertheless, across societies around the world (B. Adams & Trost, 2005):

1. *A rise in divorce rates.* Increase in divorce and separation are well-documented in Argentina, China, Cuba, India, Iran, Kenya, and Kuwait. The divorce rate in the United States is nearly twice what it was in 1960. The divorce rate peaked in 1981, began to decline slightly, and leveled off at the high rate of nearly 50% for first marriages. Divorce rates are highest for couples who married as teens, for high school dropouts, and for the nonreligious (National Marriage Project, 2006). There has been an increase in the divorce rate in almost every advanced industrial nation since 1960, but the United States leads most others in divorce (B. Adams & Trost, 2005).

2. *Declining fertility rates.* Declining fertility rates have been documented in Argentina, India, Iran, Kenya, Kuwait, South Africa, and Turkey (Adams & Trost, 2005). The birthrate in the United States dropped from 23.7 births per 1,000 population in 1960 to 14.3 in 2007 (B. E. Hamilton, Martin, & Ventura, 2009). People are waiting longer to have children and are having fewer children. In 1970, an estimated 73.6% of women between the ages of 25 and 29 had given birth to at least one child; this had fallen to 48.7% by 2000. In 1976, an estimated 1 in 10 women over 40 was childless; this increased to almost 1 in 5 by 2004. Fertility rates decrease with education; in 2004, it is estimated that 24% of college-educated women between the ages of 40 and 44 were childless, compared to 15% of women of the same age who lacked a high school education (National Marriage Project, 2006). This means that those with the fewest economic resources are raising a disproportionate number of children in the United States. Another important trend is for more children to be raised in single-parent families; the percentage of children being raised in such families increased from 9% of children in the United States in 1960 to 28% in 2005. Although the total fertility rate in the United States was slightly below the replacement level of 2.1 in 2004, it is one of the highest birth rates in advanced industrial societies (National Marriage Project, 2006). In China, a one-child policy, initiated in 1979, has resulted in low birthrates.

Two other long-term trends in family relationships are likely to continue: greater valuing of autonomy and self-direction in children, as opposed to obedience and conformity, and equalization of power between men and women. These trends have been found to be almost universal, but they are more problematic in some societies than others (B. Adams & Trost, 2005). Not all people agree that these trends are good, and some point to them as causes of the weakening of the family. Other people see these trends as providing possibilities for stabilizing the family in a time of great change in all major social institutions.

The average life expectancy is increasing in all of the advanced industrial societies. In the United States, it increased from 68.2 years in 1950 to 77.7 years in 2009 (CDC, 2009e). This increase in longevity, added to the decrease in fertility rates, is changing the shape of families in the late industrial societies. Families now have more generations but fewer people in each generation. The increase in longevity has also led to an increase in chronic disease and the need for families to provide personal care for members with disabilities.

Social service programs serving families, children, and older adults need to be responsive to these changing trends. The confluence of declining family size, increasing numbers of single parents, increasing numbers of women in the paid labor force, and an aging population calls for a reexamination, in particular, of our assumptions about family caregiving for dependent persons. Social workers should lead the way in discussions about social policies that can strengthen families and alleviate family stressors. We must pay particular attention to the needs of immigrant families like the Mezas.

Critical Thinking Questions 7.2

What would life be like without the mass media? How would you find out about national and global events? Where would you get your ideas about politics, social welfare, religion, and family? How would your daily life be different?

THEORIES OF SOCIAL INEQUALITY

Throughout this chapter, we have presented information on how social inequality is created and maintained in eight interrelated major social institutions. **Social class** is the term generally used by sociologists to describe contemporary structures of inequality. Perhaps no question regarding the human condition has generated more intense and complex controversies and conflicts than the related issues of inequality and distributive justice. Unequal distribution of resources is probably as old as the human species and certainly has existed in all complex societies. Long before the discipline of sociology arose, thoughtful people constructed explanations and justifications for these inequalities (Lenski, 1966; Sernau, 2006). Although social class has been an important topic for sociology, by no means do sociologists agree about the role that social class plays in human behavior.

The contributing authors and I have presented inequality as a problem, but as you have probably noted, not everyone agrees with this view. Gerhard Lenski (1966) did a careful study of how societies over time have answered the question, is inequality a good thing or a bad thing? He divided the way that societies have responded to this question into a conservative thesis and a radical antithesis. In the **conservative thesis,** inequality is the natural, divine order, and no efforts should be made to alter it. In the **radical antithesis,** equality is the natural, divine order; inequality is based on abuse of privilege and should be minimized.

Classical Sociological Theories of Social Inequality

When social inequality is considered to be the natural order and divinely ordained, there is no need to search further for explanations of inequality. But as this traditional assumption gave way to a belief that human beings are born equal, persistent social inequalities required explanation and justification. Explanation of inequality and its relationship to human behavior became central questions for the emerging social and political sciences. Two classical theorists, Karl Marx (1818–1883) and Max Weber (1864–1920), have had lasting impact on the sociological analysis of social inequality.

Karl Marx was both a social theorist and a committed revolutionary. He was interested in explaining the social inequalities of industrial capitalism, but his interests went beyond explanation of inequality to promotion of a more just and equitable society. Marx (1887/1967) emphasized

Conflict perspective

the economic determinants of social class relationships and proposed that class lines are drawn according to roles in the capitalist production system. Although he did not propose a strict two-class system, he suggested a social class division based on a dichotomy of owners and controllers of production (bourgeoisie), on the one hand, and workers who must sell their labor to owners (proletariat), on the other. Marx saw the relationship between the classes as based on exploitation and domination by the owners and controllers of production and on alienation among the workers. He saw social class as a central variable in human behavior and a central force in human history, and he believed that *class consciousness*—not only the awareness of one's social class, but also hostility toward other classes—is what motivates people to transform society.

In contrast to Marx, Max Weber argued for a value-free social science. Weber differed from Marx in other ways as well. Marx saw a class division based on production roles (owners of production and workers); Weber (1947) saw a class division based on "life chances" in the marketplace. *Life chances* reflect the distribution of power within a community, including economic power, social prestige, and legal power. Instead of Marx's dichotomous class system, Weber proposed that life chances fall on a continuum, and that the great variability found along the continuum reflects the multiple sources of power. He suggested that social class is an important variable in human behavior, but not, as Marx believed, the primary variable.

This difference in perspective on the causal importance of social class reflects the theorists' disagreement about the inevitability of class consciousness or class action. Marx saw class consciousness and communal action related to class as inevitable. Weber saw social class as a possible, but not inevitable, source of identity and communal action.

The Contemporary Debate

Attempts to determine the cause of persistent social inequalities have led to debate among sociologists who embrace functional theories and sociologists who embrace conflict theories. *Functional theories* of social stratification present structural inequality (social classes) as necessary for society. According to this view, unequal rewards for different types of work guarantee that the most talented persons will work hard and produce technological innovation to benefit the whole society. *Conflict theorists* (see Chapter 2 for more discussion of conflict theories), on the other hand, emphasize the role of power, domination, and coercion in the maintenance of inequality. According to this view, persons with superior wealth and income also hold superior social and political power and use that power to protect their privileged positions.

Sociological functionalism was dominant in U.S. sociology during the 1940s and 1950s, but it faded in importance after that. However, functionalism was the root for *modernization theory,* which attempted, in the 1960s, to explain on the global level why some countries are poor and others are rich (Rostow, 1990). Modernization theorists suggested that poverty is caused by traditional attitudes and technology—by the failure to modernize. The conflict perspective counterargument to modernization theory was *dependency theory,* which argued that poor societies are created by worldwide industrial capitalism, which exploits natural resources and labor (A. Frank, 1967). These theorists emphasized the tremendous power of foreign multinational corporations to coerce national governments in poor nations. They called attention to colonial imperialism as the historical context of contemporary global inequalities (Sernau, 2006).

The most recent debate has been between neoliberalism and the world systems perspective. *Neoliberalism* is based in classic economics and argues that free trade and free markets, with limited government interference, will result in a fair distribution of resources. As suggested earlier, this philosophy has been dominant across the world for the past few decades but is currently being challenged on several fronts. Economists at the World Bank and IMF have been strong voices in favor of neoliberalism, which informed the ideals of their structural adjustment program for dealing with the debts of impoverished nations. *Structural adjustment* called for poor countries to

"clean house" by reducing government spending and bureaucracy and increasing exportation and entrepreneurship. To counter this view, the *world systems perspective* suggests that inequality is created and maintained by economic globalization (I. Wallerstein, 1974, 1980, 1989). As mentioned in Chapter 1, under this perspective, the world is divided into three different sectors: a *core sector* that dominates the capitalist world economy and exploits the world's resources, a *peripheral sector* that provides raw material to the core and is heavily exploited by it, and a *semiperipheral sector* that is somewhat independent but very vulnerable to the financial fluctuations of the core states. The core currently includes the United States, Western Europe, and Japan; the periphery includes much of Africa, South Asia, and Latin America; and the semiperiphery includes such places as Spain, Portugal, Brazil, Mexico, Venezuela, and oil-producing countries in the Middle East (Leeder, 2004; McMichael, 2008). According to the world systems perspective, the hegemony of the core sector is reinforced by neocolonial practices of such transnational institutions as the World Bank, the IMF, and the WTO.

Structural Determinism Versus Human Agency

Will knowledge of my social class position help you to predict my attitudes and behaviors? That question has become a controversial one for contemporary social science. Social scientists who see human behavior as highly determined by one's position in the social class structure (*structural determinism*) are challenged by social scientists who emphasize the capacity of humans to create their own realities and who give central roles to human actors, not social structures (*human agency*).

Macro-oriented sociologists have taken Émile Durkheim's lead in arguing that human action is a by-product of social institutions that are external to human consciousness. Micro-oriented sociologists have taken Max Weber's lead in the counterargument that humans are proactive agents who construct meaning in interaction with others. In a position that is more consistent with the multidimensional framework of this book, Anthony Giddens (1979) has proposed *structuration theory,* a theory of the relationship between human agency and social structure. Giddens observes that social practices repeat themselves in patterned ways over time and in space, structured by the rules and resources embedded in social institutions. While acknowledging the constraints that rules and resources place on human action, he also notes that human agents have the ability to make a difference in the social world. Human actions produce social structure, and at all times human action is serving either to perpetuate or to transform social structure. You may recognize that this is very similar to the practice approach to culture presented in Chapter 6. Some critics have suggested that Giddens is too optimistic about how much agency humans have, but Giddens acknowledges that those with the most power have a disproportionate opportunity to reinforce institutional arrangements that perpetuate their positions of power.

Structuration theory is a good framework for social workers. It calls our attention to power arrangements that constrain the behaviors of some actors more than others in a way that perpetuates social injustice. But it also calls our attention to the possibilities for human action to transform social institutions. Mary Ellen Kondrat (1999) suggests that structuration theory poses two questions that, when raised, provide critical consciousness, a necessary ingredient for progressive change agents. **Critical consciousness** can be defined as an ongoing process of reflection and knowledge seeking about mechanisms and outcomes of social, political, and economic oppression that requires taking personal and collective action toward fairness and social justice. The first question raised by Kondrat is, "How aware are we of the ways in which social institutions and social structure condition our behaviors?" The second question is, "How aware are we of the ways in which our day-to-day activities over time perpetuate or transform social structure?" Just as individual agency is essential for individual change, collective agency is essential for changing social institutions. That is the central point of social movements, which will be discussed in the next chapter.

Critical Thinking Questions 7.3

Which social institutions have the greatest impact on your day-to-day life? What are some ways that your day-to-day activities perpetuate the existing social structure? What are some ways that your day-to-day activities have a potential to change social structure?

Implications for Social Work Practice

The trends in social institutions and social structure discussed in this chapter suggest several principles for social work practice. These practice principles have greatest relevance for social work planning and administration, but some are relevant for direct social work practice as well.

- Develop adequate information retrieval skills to keep abreast of trends in the interrelated social institutions and the impact of these trends on human interdependence and dependence.
- Monitor the impact of public policies on poverty and inequality.
- Learn to use political processes to promote social services that contribute to the well-being of individuals and communities.
- Be particularly aware of the impact of trends in the economic institution on client resources and functioning.
- Collaborate with other social workers and human service providers to advocate for greater equality of opportunity in the educational institution.

- Work to ensure that the voices of poor and other oppressed people are included in public dialogue about health care reform.
- Take the lead in public discourse about the fit between the current social welfare institution and trends in the other major social institutions.
- Be aware of the role that religious organizations play in social service delivery and the role that religion plays in the lives of clients.
- Collaborate with other social workers and human service providers to influence media coverage of vulnerable populations and patterns of social inequality.
- Review social service programs serving children, older adults, and other dependent persons to ensure that they are responsive to changes in the family and kinship institution as well as the economic institution.

Key Terms

bifurcate
colonialism
conservative thesis
critical consciousness
downsizing
economic institution
educational institution
family and kinship institution

Gini index
government and political institution
health care institution
mass media institution
neocolonialism
neoliberal philosophy
new federalism
radical antithesis

religious institution
social class
social institution
social structure
social welfare institution
status
therapeutic medicine
transnational corporation (TNC)

Active Learning

1. In the case study at the beginning of the chapter, Mrs. Meza has been eager to legalize her immigrant status to ensure that the family can stay in the United States rather than return to their native Mexico. One way to begin to understand their motivation to stay in the United States is to do a comparative analysis of social indicators in the two countries. To do this, you can make use of some of the many web resources that contain statistics on global well-being, including the following:

   - *www.census.gov.* Official site of the U.S. Census Bureau. Under People & Households, click on International, which will take you to International Programs Center. Click on International Data Base (IDB). Click on World Population Information. Click on Data Access. You can select specific countries and years and get key summary information about the social health of the countries.
   - *www.unicef.org.* Official site of the United Nations Children's Fund. By going to Info by Country and clicking on a specific country and Statistics under that country, you can access data on the status of children by country.
   - *www.undp.org.* Site of the United Nations Development Program. Click on Regions, select Full List of Countries, and click on specific country. You will get updated material on the country, including the latest report on efforts to meet the Millennium Development Goals.

   Use these three resources, or other relevant resources, to prepare a statistical overview of the social health of the United States and Mexico. What are the areas of similarity? Main areas of difference? What indicators seem to be the most important in understanding Mr. and Mrs. Meza's motivation to stay in the United States?

2. We have looked at the conservative thesis and the radical antithesis in an ongoing debate about the role of inequality in social life. Talk to at least five people about this issue, including at least one member of your family and at least one friend. Ask each person the following questions:

- Is inequality a good thing for a society?
- If so, in what way, and good for whom?
- If we accept inequality as inevitable, how much inequality is necessary? Should society try to maximize or minimize the amount of inequality?
- On what criteria do we measure inequality?
- If we seek equality, is it equality of opportunity or of outcomes?

What kinds of positions did people take? How did they support their arguments? Did you find more support for the conservative thesis or the radical antithesis in the responses you heard?

Web Resources

Center for Responsive Politics

www.opensecrets.org

Site maintained by the nonpartisan Center for Responsive Politics, contains information on the money collected and spent by major political candidates, major organizational and individual contributors, and political news and issues.

The Civil Rights Project at Harvard University

www.civilrightsproject.ucla.edu/

Site presented by the Civil Rights Project, which was founded at Harvard University in 1997 and in 2007 moved to UCLA, presents data that track racial achievement gaps in the United States.

Pew Research Center's Internet & American Life Project

www.pewinternet.org/

Site presented by the Pew Research Center's Internet & American Life Project, presents reports on the impact of the Internet on families, communities, work and home, daily life, education, health care, and civic and political life.

United Nations Children's Fund

www.unicef.org

Site contains cross-national information on the well-being of children.

U.S. Census Bureau

www.census.gov

Official site of the U.S. Census Bureau, contains statistics on a wide variety of topics, including race and ethnicity, gender, education, birthrates, disabilities, and many other subjects.

The World Health Organization (WHO)

www.who.int

Site contains information on the health and the health care institutions of countries around the world.

CHAPTER 8

Formal Organizations, Communities, and Social Movements

Elizabeth D. Hutchison

☙ ❧

☙ ❧

CASE STUDY 8.1

Changing Leadership at Beacon Center

Beacon Center (BC) has a short but proud history of providing innovative services to persons who are homeless in River Run, the midsize Midwestern city where it is located. It was established in 1980, thanks to one woman, Martha Green, and her relentless pursuit of a vision.

While serving as executive director of the YWCA, Martha became increasingly concerned about the growing homeless population in River Run. During the late 1960s and 1970s, she had worked in several positions in River Run's antipoverty agency, and she was well-known throughout the city for her uncompromising advocacy efforts for families living in poverty. Martha was also a skilled advocate and service planner, and she soon pulled together supporters for a new social service agency to address the special needs of homeless persons. A mix of private and public, federal, and local funds were secured, and BC opened with Martha Green as director, working with the assistance of one staff social worker. The agency grew steadily, and within a decade it had a staff of 15, as well as several subcontracted programs.

Martha valued client input into program development and made sure that client voices were heard at all levels: at city council meetings, in community discussions of program needs, in BC discussions of program needs and issues, in staff interviews, and at board meetings. She remained uncompromising in advocacy efforts, and she often angered city officials because she was unyielding in her demands for fair treatment of homeless persons. She advocated for their right to receive resources and services from other social service organizations as well as for their right to congregate in public places.

Martha also had a vision regarding staff relationships. She was committed to working collaboratively, to trusting frontline workers to make their own decisions, and to securing the participation of all staff on important policy decisions. Rules were kept to a minimum, and staff relationships were very personal. Martha believed in hiring the best-trained and most experienced staff for frontline positions and, over the years, hired and retained a highly skilled, committed core staff. She had high expectations of her staff, particularly in terms of their commitment to the rights of homeless persons, but she was also a nurturing administrator who was concerned about the personal well-being and professional development of each staff member. She established a climate of mutual respect where people could risk disagreeing.

She kept staff fully informed about economic and political pressures faced by BC and about her actions in regard to these issues. She regularly sought their input on these issues, and decisions were usually made by consensus. On occasion, however, around really sensitive issues—such as the choice between forgoing a salary increase and closing a program—she asked staff to vote by secret ballot to neutralize any potential power dynamics.

Martha had a vision, as well, about how a board of directors can facilitate a successful client-centered program. She saw the board as part of the BC system, just as staff and clients were part of the system. She worked hard to ensure that members chosen for the board shared the BC commitment to the rights of homeless persons, and she developed warm, personal relationships with them. She kept the board fully informed about issues facing BC, and she was successful in securing their support and active involvement in advocacy and resource development activities.

Over the years, BC became known as an innovative, client-centered service center, as well as a hardheaded advocacy organization. Staff and board members took pride in being part of what they considered to be a very special endeavor—one that outstripped other social service organizations in its expertise, commitment, and compassion. Clients were not always satisfied with the services, but generally acknowledged among themselves that they were lucky to have the dedication of BC.

Reactions from the community were more mixed, however. The respect offered up was, in many circles, a grudging one. Many city officials as well as staff of other social service organizations complained about the self-righteous attitudes and uncompromising posture of Martha and the staff at BC. These detractors acknowledged that the tactics of BC staff were successful in countering discrimination against homeless persons, but suggested that BC succeeded at much cost of goodwill.

Martha retired 15 years ago and relocated with her husband to be closer to their children. An acting director was appointed at BC while a search for a permanent director was under way. The acting director had worked several years at BC and shared much of Martha's administrative and service philosophy. She was not as good,

(Continued)

(Continued)

however, at juggling the multiple demands of the position. Staff and clients felt a loss of support, board members lost some of their enthusiasm and confidence, and antagonists in the community saw an opportunity to mute some of BC's advocacy efforts. Staff maintained a strong commitment to the rights of homeless persons, but they lost some of their optimism about making a difference.

After eight months, Helen Blue, a former community college administrator, was hired as the new executive director. Like Martha Green, she was of European American heritage but had only lived in River Run for a few years. She was excited about this new professional challenge, but she had a vision for BC that was somewhat different from Martha's. She was concerned about the alienation that had resulted, in some circles, from BC's hard-hitting advocacy stance, and she favored a more conciliatory approach. For example, after meeting with city officials, she assigned staff social workers the task of convincing clients to quit congregating in the city park near BC and to stay out of the business district during business hours. After meeting with directors of other social service organizations, she directed staff to be less demanding in their advocacy for clients.

Helen was also concerned about the lack of rules and the looseness of attention to the chain of command, and she began to institute new rules and procedures. Staff meetings and open community meetings with clients became presentations by Helen. Staff were no longer allowed to attend board meetings and were not informed about what happened at them. Frontline staff often found their decisions overturned by Helen. When the first staff resignation came, Helen hired the replacement with no input from staff, clients, or board members.

Helen stayed a few years at BC and then decided to return to community college administration. Since she left BC, two executive directors have come and gone. In the recession of 2008 and 2009, funding streams became more restricted at a time of growing homelessness caused by home foreclosures and a weakened economy. Needs increased and resources declined. The board of directors has recently hired a consultant to assist them in beginning a strategic planning process.

CASE STUDY 8.2

Filipina Domestic Workers Creating Transnational Communities

Filipina domestic workers scattered around the globe read the multinational magazines *Tinig Filipino* and *Diwaliwan,* and many contribute articles to *Tinig Filipino* describing the realities of their lives as overseas domestic workers. Sometimes their children back in the Philippines write articles about the pain of separation from their mothers or about the heroic sacrifices their mothers make to provide much-needed economic resources to their families back home. Filipino women (Filipinas) are employed as domestic workers in more than 130 countries, working in elder care, child care, and housecleaning in private homes. They are among the ranks of service workers of globalization.

Globalization has created both a pull and a push for Filipinas to become global domestic workers. It has created a heightened demand (pull) for low-wage service workers in major global cities of affluent nations to maintain the lifestyles of professional and managerial workers. It has also produced large geographical economic inequalities, and many poor countries, like the Philippines, are depending on the export of labor to help with debt repayment. Over 6 million Filipinos work overseas as contract workers, and the money and goods these workers send home to families, known as remittances, are an important source of revenue at home. In 1999, the Philippines ranked second among countries receiving the largest remittances from overseas workers (McMichael, 2008). The large outflow of labor also helps to decrease very high unemployment and underemployment rates. In the Philippines, about 70% of families live in poverty. There is thus quite a "push" for exporting Filipino labor.

Since the early 1990s, women have made up over half of Filipino contract workers. Filipino men work as seamen, carpenters, masons, and mechanics, many in the Middle East. Two thirds of the migrant Filipinas are domestic workers, and they work in cities around the world. Many of them have a college education, but they earn more as domestic workers in affluent nations than they would as professional workers in the Philippines. They migrate for economic gain, but also, in many instances, to escape domestic violence or other domestic struggles. Most migrate alone. The Philippine government has applauded the legion of female migrant workers as "modern-day heroes." The remittances they send home allow families to buy houses; computers; and college educations for siblings, children, and other relatives.

The two most popular destinations for Filipina domestic workers are Rome and Los Angeles, both of which are difficult to access. In Italy, Filipina domestic workers are restricted to the status of guest worker, but they are allowed to stay for as long as 7 years, longer than in many other countries. A majority of Filipina domestic workers in Rome entered the country clandestinely, and often faced much danger and trauma on the journey. In contrast, most Filipina domestic workers in Los Angeles entered the country with valid legal documents. Migrants to both cities used their social networks to learn about the opportunities and the process for migrating.

The community life of the Filipina domestic workers in Rome and Los Angeles is alike in a number of ways; most importantly, both groups see themselves as simultaneously members of more than one community. They see themselves as part of a global community of Filipina domestic workers across geographic territories. They also see themselves as part of their Philippine communities and only temporarily part of their receiving communities, referring to their sending communities as "home." While they are doing domestic work for class-privileged women in their receiving communities, they purchase the domestic services of even lower-paid women left behind in the Philippines to help care for their own families. They leave children, who are often very young, at home to be cared for by the extended family that benefits from the remittances that they send. They keep contact with their families in the Philippines by mail and by telephone. Both in Rome and in Los Angeles, they face anti-immigrant sentiment in their receiving communities.

There are great differences, however, in the local cultures of community life among Filipina domestic workers in Rome and Los Angeles. These differences seem to reflect the larger social and political contexts of the migration experience. Let's look first at the community of domestic workers in Rome. There, Filipina migrants are restricted to domestic work, and they live segregated lives in a society that is not welcoming. Consequently, they have built a community of much solidarity that congregates in multiple private and public gathering places. The domestic workers are residentially dispersed throughout the city, and gathering places are likewise geographically dispersed. Specific gathering places are associated with specific regions of the Philippines.

On their days off, the workers tend to congregate in private gathering places in church centers and apartments. Several churches, mostly Catholic, have opened day-off shelters or church centers where the workers can spend time watching television or listening to music, visiting, and purchasing Filipino food. These centers are often developed out of the joint efforts of churches in the Philippines and in Rome. The Filipino Chaplaincy, a coalition of 28 Roman Catholic churches, is the strongest advocate for Filipino workers in Rome. It publishes a directory of religious, government, and civic organizations relevant to the Filipino workers. The Santa Prudenziana parish, besides offering regular spiritual activities, also offers a variety of social services, including job placement referrals,

(Continued)

(Continued)

free medical care, legal assistance, and Italian language classes. The migrant workers can also participate in choirs, dance groups, and a theater group.

Apartments are another site of private gathering for the Filipinas in Rome. Domestic workers who can navigate the barriers to rent their own apartments sometimes rent out rooms or beds to other migrant workers. They also rent access to their apartments to live-in workers on their days off. Apartments are furnished with televisions and equipment for watching Filipino movies, and at night, renters congregate in the kitchen, eating and relaxing, playing card games and mahjong.

There are also particular train stations and bus stops that are known as public gathering places for Filipinos in Rome. However, the city authorities have discouraged congregating in such public places. After much harassment at one bus stop, the Filipino migrants moved to a spot under an overpass, near the Tiber River. They subsequently turned the spot into a shopping bazaar that includes food shops, restaurants, hair salons, and tailoring shops.

These gathering spots allow for network building, sharing information, and providing a variety of assistance to new migrants. The domestic workers often discuss their work-related problems and share information about housing. There is an ethic of mutual assistance and solidarity, although occasionally, some migrants take advantage of others in activities such as money lending.

The community of Filipina domestic workers in Los Angeles is not nearly as cohesive as the one in Rome. In contrast to Rome, the Los Angeles Filipino population is class stratified. There has been a long stream of migration from the Philippines to the United States, going back a century, and many earlier streams involved professional workers, particularly in the medical fields. Although many of the Filipina domestic workers have connections to more economically privileged Filipinos in Los Angeles, often securing work through these connections, they perceive the class distinctions as impeding cohesion in the Filipino community and do not feel supported by the middle-class Filipinos. This is the case even though they often spend their days off with relatives or friends in middle-class homes, or even live alongside middle-class neighbors. The domestic workers perceive the Filipino enclaves as middle-class spaces.

A subcommunity of Filipina domestic workers does seem to form from time to time, however. Live-in workers often congregate in the parks and playgrounds of the wealthy communities where they work. Those who are employed as part-time rather than live-in workers often meet on the buses traveling to and from work. Like their counterparts in Rome, they talk about work situations, but these gatherings are neither as large nor as regular as they are in Rome. The domestic workers also often participate in parties in the homes of middle-class Filipinos, but these associations do not seem to lead to the type of solidarity that occurs among the workers in Rome (Parrenas, 2001).

CASE STUDY 8.3

Fighting for a Living Wage

Greg Halpern was in his senior year at Harvard University in 1998 when Aaron Bartley, his labor activist roommate and childhood friend, "dragged" him to a meeting of the Harvard Living Wage Campaign (Terkel, 2003). Greg remembers that he was in the lunch line a few days later when a friend made a joke about how bad the food was.

Greg laughed, and then he looked up and exchanged glances with one of the young women working behind the lunch counter. He saw her anger and hurt. He was deeply embarrassed and realized that most Harvard students had never been taught about the people who clean the bathrooms, serve the food, or clean the chalkboards. Greg became active in the living wage campaign at Harvard, attending weekly rallies and sending letters to the university president, calling for the custodians, security guards, and food service workers at Harvard to be paid a living wage. In March of 1999, the campaign presented the university president with the "Worst Employer in Boston" award while he was addressing a group of high school students. At graduation, some students chartered an airplane to pull a sign that read, "Harvard Needs a Living Wage" (Tanner, 2002).

That same spring, just before graduating from Harvard, Greg Halpern did an independent study in which he interviewed and photographed university workers. He decided to blow the interviews up on 10-foot pages and stick them up in the public space provided for students, so that other students could know the stories of the low-wage workers. Greg had never been an activist, but he was dismayed at what he was hearing from workers, and he remained active in the Harvard Living Wage Campaign after he graduated. The campaign had been holding rallies for 3 years, but nothing was happening. During the spring of 2001, 2 years after Greg graduated, there was growing interest among the members of the Harvard Living Wage Campaign to engage in a sit-in. As they discussed this option, Greg remembered the custodian he had interviewed 2 years earlier. Bill Brook, who cleaned the room in which they were meeting, was 65 years old, worked two full-time jobs, and slept 4 hours per night (Terkel, 2003).

Greg became one of the leaders of the Harvard Living Wage Campaign sit-in strike that occupied Massachusetts Hall, the president's building, for 21 days, demanding that the university raise the wages for 1,400 employees who were making less than a living wage. Throughout the strike, the students, who had never participated in such an event before, kept in touch with the media by cell phones and e-mail (sent and received on their laptops).

There were 50 students inside Massachusetts Hall and a growing group of students on the outside. Three hundred professors or more took out a full-page ad in the *Boston Globe* in support of the students. The dining hall workers and food workers began to deliver pizzas to the students on the inside, and many workers took the risk to wear buttons on the job that said, "We Support the Living Wage Campaign." Every local labor union in Cambridge, Massachusetts, endorsed the students, and national labor leaders came to speak. The AFL-CIO union sent one of its top lawyers to negotiate with the university administration. Several high-profile religious leaders made appearances to support the students. On the 15th day of the sit-in, the Cambridge mayor and city council, along with other sympathizers, marched from City Hall to Harvard Yard in support of the students. During the second week of the sit-in, between 30 and 40 Harvard Divinity School students held a vigil, chanting, "Where's your horror? Where's your rage? Div School wants a living wage." On the last night of the sit-in, there was a rally of about 3,000 people outside Massachusetts Hall (Gourevitch, 2001; Tanner, 2002; Terkel, 2003).

In the end, the Harvard administration agreed to negotiate higher wages with the unions. Higher wages were paid, but the students were not fully satisfied with the results of their campaign. Two of the student activists later coproduced an advocacy film based on the sit-in, *Occupation: The Harvard University Living Wage Sit-In,* narrated by Ben Affleck (Raza & Velez, 2002).

The sit-in at Harvard was neither the beginning nor the end of the gathering living wage movement in the United States. It built on the momentum that had started in Baltimore, Maryland, in 1994, and it fueled new actions on other university campuses. It was one piece of a story of a rapidly growing social movement.

In 1994, religious groups in Baltimore were seeing an increase in the use of soup kitchens and food pantries by the working poor (Quigley, 2001; Tanner, 2002). They were angry that working people could not afford to

(Continued)

(Continued)

feed their families. A coalition of 50 religious groups joined forces with the American Federation of State, County, and Municipal Employees (AFSCME) and low-wage service workers to create a local campaign, which they called Baltimoreans United in Leadership Development (BUILD). BUILD worked to develop a law that would require businesses with contracts with the city to pay their workers a "living wage," a pay rate that would lift a family of four over the federal poverty level. At the time, the federal minimum wage was $4.25 an hour, a wage that could not lift a family out of poverty. Both the religious groups and AFSCME provided people and funds to educate the public about the problem of low wages and to lobby for signing of the living wage bill. The living wage law was enacted in July 1996, requiring city contractors with municipal contracts over $5,000 to pay a minimum wage of $6.16 an hour in 1996, with increments to reach $7.70 an hour in 1999. The law is estimated to have affected 1,500 to 2,000 workers.

The BUILD coalition had no intention of sparking a national social movement, but their success helped to trigger a nationwide alliance of religious and labor groups that has come to be known as the living wage movement. Local grassroots coalitions of activists have used a variety of tactics, including lobbying, postcard campaigns, rallies, door-knocking, leafleting, workshops, and sit-ins to achieve their goals in over 120 localities by 2004, just 10 years after BUILD began work in Baltimore. The policy solutions have varied by locality, with some bolder than others, but all have established a wage above the federal minimum wage for some group of workers. Some of the local living wage ordinances, like the one in Baltimore, cover only municipal workers. Others have been more expansive in their approach, like the Chicago ordinance passed on July 26, 2006, which requires "big box" stores—those making over $1 billion per year—to pay a wage of $10 plus $3 in benefits per hour, beginning in 2010. The living wage movement has also helped to enact legislation at the state rather than local level. By the end of 2006, a total of 22 states plus the District of Columbia had enacted laws that set the minimum wage higher than the federal requirement (Vanden Heuvel & Graham-Felsen, 2006).

Each local coalition is different, but these campaigns benefited from much assistance from the Living Wage Resource Center established by the Association of Community Organizations for Reform Now (ACORN). ACORN developed a 225-page guide to assist local activists in organizing a successful living wage campaign, written by labor economist David Reynolds. ACORN, a now-defunct organization that once had neighborhood chapters in over 90 cities, organized national training conferences and also regularly dispatched staff to consult to local coalitions. In 2006, a documentary called *Waging a Living* (Weisberg, 2006), which chronicles the daily struggles of four low-wage workers, premiered on public television and became available for sale and rental. The documentary was produced by Public Policy Productions in association with Thirteen/WNET New York, with funding from the Annie E. Casey Foundation, Ford Foundation, David and Lucille Packard Foundation, and the Corporation for Public Broadcasting.

Along the way, the living wage movement has benefited from the support of a number of organizations. The Economic Policy Institute developed a guide to living wage initiatives and their economic impacts on its website. The National Low Income Housing Coalition compiled a report that calculated the amount of money a household needs to afford a rental unit in specific localities. The Brennan Center for Justice, located at the New York University School of Law, provided assistance to design and implement living wage campaigns, including economic impact analysis, legislative drafting, and legal analysis and defense. Responsible Wealth, a national network of business-people, investors, and affluent citizens, developed a living wage covenant for businesses who are interested in economic fairness. The Political Economy Research Institute (PERI), at the University of Massachusetts at Amherst, collected a number of research reports on the effects of living wage laws.

One of the more promising developments in the living wage social movement is the entry of university and high school students into the movement. The Living Wage Action Coalition (LWAC), made up of university students and recent graduates who have participated in living wage campaigns around the country, was created in the summer of 2005. LWAC has been touring around colleges and universities in the United States, running workshops about strategies for successful living wage campaigns for low-wage workers on campus. In May 2005, Brookline, Massachusetts, passed Article 19 to amend the town's living wage bylaws to be more inclusive. Article 19 was researched and proposed by the Student Action for Justice and Education group at Brookline High School (Living Wage Resource Center, 2006).

The living wage movement started in the United States, but by 2001, it had crossed national lines to London, England, where it spread to hospitals, finance houses, universities, art galleries, and hotels. The movement there has also secured agreements that all new jobs at the Olympic site for the 2012 Summer Olympics will be living wage jobs (J. Willis, 2010). In October of 2009, activists in 11 European countries participated in events to demand that retailers pay a living wage to all garment workers in their supply chains. The events included leafleting, public debates, visiting corporate headquarters, and hosting film screenings. These events were organized by a coalition of activists involved in a "clean clothes campaign" (fighting for the rights of workers in the global garment industry) (Clean Clothes Campaign, 2009).

These three case studies illustrate some of the many ways that contemporary social life is shaped by and also shapes human behavior. In Chapter 7, we read about how patterns of human social life are structured through eight major social institutions. In this chapter, we look at how humans, in their attempt to work together for stability, survival, and a just world, create formal organizations, communities, and social movements, and how these social creations subsequently influence individual and collective behavior. See Exhibit 8.1 for definitions of formal organization, community, and social movement.

Exhibit 8.1 Definitions of Formal Organization, Community, and Social Movement

Formal Organization: A collectivity of people, with a high degree of formality of structure, working together to meet a goal or goals

Community: People bound either by geography or by webs of communication, sharing common ties, and interacting with one another

Social Movement: Large-scale collective actions to make change, or resist change, in specific social institutions

---

FORMAL ORGANIZATION DEFINED

Martha Green, in Case Study 8.1, saw a social condition that she thought needed a remedy, and she envisioned a formal organization as at least part of the remedy. For those of us who live in contemporary complex societies, formal organizations are pervasive in our lives, a most important but usually taken-for-granted part of life. **Formal organization** can be defined as a collectivity of people with a high degree of formality of structure, working together to meet a goal or goals. This definition, like most found in the organization literature (see Greenwald, 2008) has three key components: a collectivity of people, a highly formal structure, and the common purpose of working together to meet a goal or goals.

The above definition leaves a lot of room for variation. Formal organizations differ in size, structure, culture, and goals. They also perform a variety of functions in contemporary society and influence human behavior in many ways. Formal organizations are intricately woven into the fabric of life in contemporary society, but they can be both functional and dysfunctional for society or for specific groups. They meet our needs, help us fulfill goals, and nurture our development. They also make stressful demands, thwart our goals, inhibit our holistic development, and constrain our behavior. And, of course, some members of organizations benefit more than others from organizational goals and structure.

PERSPECTIVES ON FORMAL ORGANIZATIONS

Over the past few decades, ways of thinking about organizational life have become numerous and fragmented (Pfeffer, 1982; J. Walsh, Meyer, & Schoonhoven, 2006). Likewise, the research on organizations and the related prescriptions for organizational administration reflect great variety, as you can see from the changing approaches at Beacon Center. Several people have attempted to organize U.S. organizational theory—to bring some order to the diversity of viewpoints without denying the complexity and multifaceted nature of contemporary formal organizations (e.g., Garrow

& Hasenfeld, 2010; Greenwald, 2008; G. Morgan, 2006). Here we use a classification system that includes four perspectives: the rational perspective, systems perspective, interpretive perspective, and critical perspective. Each perspective encompasses both classical and contemporary theories, and each has relevance for social work practice.

As you read about these perspectives, you may want to keep in mind a suggestion (J. Walsh et al., 2006) that to be useful, contemporary research on organization theory needs to address three basic questions: (1) How can we understand current changing organizations (the theory question)? (2) How can we live *in* these organizations? and (3) How can we more healthily live *with* these organizations? James Walsh and colleagues argue that existing theories of organizations fail to consider the powerful impact that contemporary organizations have on "human's social and material lives and on our planet's ecosystem," (p. 661) and that new theorizing is needed that takes these issues into account (see I. Marti, Etzion, & Leca, 2008, for a similar argument). This argument is consistent

Photo 8.1 Formal organizations are defined as a collectivity of people, with a high degree of formality, working together to meet a common goal.

with social work's interest in social justice, and in the discussion below, I have tried to incorporate contemporary theories that are beginning to address these issues.

Please keep the important role of culture in mind as you read the following discussion of theoretical perspectives, which focuses primarily on organization theory developed in the United States and Europe. National culture has a great influence on the theories that are developed, and this is nowhere more true than in theorizing about formal organizations (Hofstede, 1996, 2001). Recently, organization theorists have suggested the possibility of developing a more globally relevant theory of organizations (see Soulsby & Clark, 2007). They note that existing theories of organizations have been developed and studied in stable market economic systems, usually in North America and Europe. They propose that study of the transformation of organizations in former socialist countries as they transitioned to market economies is a fruitful area for beginning to develop a more globally relevant theory (see Uhlenbruck, Meyer, & Hitt, 2003). However, at the moment, it appears that around the world, in Asia, Arab countries, Eastern Europe, and Russia, business schools are using translations of North American books on organization theory (Czarniawska, 2007). It is possible that the scholars in other countries will develop original theory as they try to adapt existing theory to fit their unique situations.

Rational Perspective

When Helen Blue became the executive director at Beacon Center, she was concerned about, among other things, the lack of administrative formality, the lack of rules, and the

---
Rational choice perspective
---

ambiguous chain of command. She also wanted greater authority over planning and decision making. These concerns reflect the **rational perspective on organizations**, which views the formal organization as a "goal-directed, purposefully designed machine" (Garrow

& Hasenfeld, 2010, p. 34). It assumes that organizations can be designed with structures and processes that maximize efficiency and effectiveness, concepts that are highly valued in this perspective. *Efficiency* means obtaining a high ratio of output to input, achieving the best outcome from the least investment of resources. *Effectiveness* means goal accomplishment. Exhibit 8.2 summarizes the central theories in this perspective, as well as the other perspectives discussed below.

The Ideal-Type Bureaucracy

In the modern era, formal organization is often equated with bureaucracy. Indeed, Max Weber (1947), the German sociologist who formulated a theory of bureaucracy at the beginning of the 20th century, saw bureaucracy and capitalism as inseparable. Weber proposed a **bureaucracy** as the most efficient form of organization for goal accomplishment. The characteristics of Weber's ideal-type bureaucracy include a clear hierarchy and chain of command, clear division of labor based on specialized skills, formal rules of operation, formal and task-oriented communications, merit-based recruitment and advancement, and keeping files and records for administrative action. Although Weber was enthusiastic about the advantages of the ideal-type bureaucracy over other ways of organizing for goal accomplishment, he was concerned about the dehumanizing potential of bureaucracies—their potential to become an *iron cage of rationality*, trapping people and denying many aspects of their humanity. Researchers have noted that the excessive use of rules and procedures often limits the efficiency and effectiveness of bureaucratic organizations, but bureaucracies continue to be the predominant form of organization in contemporary modern and postmodern societies.

There is evidence, however, that some newer organizations are using less bureaucratic structures. This is true for human service organizations as well as those formed for other purposes (Hasenfeld, 2010a). Indeed, as Mary Katherine

Exhibit 8.2 Summary of Perspectives on Formal Organizations

Rational Perspective: The organization is a goal-directed, purposefully designed machine (closed system).

Theory	Central Idea
The ideal-type bureaucracy (Weber)	Formal rationality—rules, regulations, and structures—is essential to goal accomplishment.
Scientific management (Taylor)	The most effective organizations maximize internal efficiency, the "one best way."
Human relations theory	Human relationships are central to organizational efficiency and effectiveness.

Systems Perspective: The organization is in constant interaction with multiple environments.

Theory	Central idea
Political economy model	The organization depends on the environment for political and economic resources.
Learning organization theory	The organization must be able to learn and change in a rapidly changing environment.

Interpretive Perspective: The organization is a social construction of reality.

Theory	Central idea
Social action model (Silverman)	The organization is defined by individual actors.
Organizational culture model	Organizations are cultures with shared experiences and shared meanings.
Managing diversity model	Organizational systems and practices should maximize the potential advantages of diversity in organizational membership.

Critical Perspective: Organizations are instruments of domination

Theory	Central Idea
Organizations as multiple oppressions	Organizations exclude and discriminate against multiple groups.
Nonhierarchical organizations	Organizations run by consensus, with few rules and with informality, are least likely to oppress employees.

O'Connor and F. Ellen Netting (2009) suggest, most of the organizations that employ social workers have been influenced by the rational perspective but do not typically operate purely from this perspective. And, as is the case with other types of organizations, their research has found that newer social service organizations are less likely than older social service organizations to have traditional bureaucratic cultures.

Helen Blue and the two executive directors who followed her wanted to move Beacon Center closer to the ideal-type bureaucracy than it was under Martha Green's leadership. Both Martha Green and Helen Blue might be interested in one researcher's findings that client satisfaction decreased as the level of bureaucracy increased in transitional housing programs for homeless families (Crook, 2001). In addition, conflict among residents increased as the level of organizational bureaucracy increased. The indirect impact of organizational bureaucracy on clients is called *trickle-down bureaucracy.*

Scientific Management

Another early 20th-century approach to formal organizations has had lasting influence. Frederick W. Taylor's (1911) *scientific management,* sometimes referred to as Taylorism, was directed toward maximizing internal efficiency. The set of principles that Taylor developed to guide the design of organizations was widely adopted by both industry and government, first in the United States and then worldwide. These principles are as follows: the conducting of time and motion studies to find the "one best way" to perform each organizational task; scientific selection and training of workers; training focused on performing tasks in the standardized one best way; close managerial monitoring of workers to ensure accurate implementation of task prescriptions and to provide appropriate rewards for compliance; and managerial authority over planning and decision making, with no challenge from workers.

In his provocative book *The McDonaldization of Society* (2008a), George Ritzer proposes that McDonald's Corporation is a prototype organization, whose organizational style is coming to dominate much of the world. This new type of organization, which operates on the combined principles of bureaucratization and scientific management, has four key traits:

1. *Efficiency,* which is valued in a fast-paced society

2. *Calculability,* with an emphasis on saving time and money rather than on quality of product

3. *Predictability,* with the assurance that a Big Mac will be the same in San Francisco as in Washington, D.C., or Hong Kong

4. *Control,* with workers trained to do a limited number of things exactly as they are told to do them, and with maximum use of nonhuman technology

Principles of scientific management are frequently followed in social service organizations. For example, some organizations undertake task and workload analyses to improve effectiveness and efficiency, and managers develop procedures, regulations, and decision trees to be implemented by direct service workers. The recent emphasis on *best practices* and *evidence-based practice* is derivative of scientific management thinking, but they do not typically conceive of "one best way." Although Helen Blue initiated more procedures and regulations and believed in managerial authority over planning and decision making, she did not share scientific management's enthusiasm for "one best way" of delivering services.

Human Relations Theory

Human relations theory introduced a new twist on maximizing organizational efficiency and effectiveness. Based on several research projects, this new theory emphasized the heretofore unrecognized importance of human interaction in organizational efficiency and effectiveness. As the theory developed, it also proposed that democratic leadership is more effective than authoritarian management in securing worker cooperation.

The human relations approach has been a favorite theory in social service organizations because it calls attention to how staff attitudes about the work situation can influence the way they relate to clients (see Garrow & Hasenfeld, 2010). The social workers at Beacon Center did indeed respond more cooperatively to Martha Green's democratic leadership than to Helen Blue's more authoritarian leadership. And it appears that the staff cohesion did "trickle down" to improve consumer satisfaction as well.

It is important to note, however, that human relations theory is still in the rational tradition. Like scientific management, it focuses on maximizing efficiency and effectiveness, and it endorses the interests of owners and managers. Managers must become leaders capable of securing the cooperation of workers, but they are still in control of the organization. Human relations theorists still assume that, with "leadership skills," human interactions can be as rationally managed as structures and procedures. After losing ground during the 1950s, human relations theory was reinvigorated in the 1960s by *organizational humanism* and a subfield called organizational development. These theories suggest that organizations can maximize efficiency and effectiveness while also promoting individual happiness and well-being (McGregor, 1960).

Conflict perspective;
Humanistic perspective

Although the rational perspective on organizations has been dominant in the design of organizations, including social service organizations, and has had some positive impact on productivity, it has been criticized on a number of grounds. It fails to consider external pressures on organizational decision makers. It overstates the rational capacity of organizational actors, assuming too much about their ability to understand all possible alternatives for action and the consequences of those actions. It fails to attend to the issue of power in organizational life. Garrow and Hasenfeld (2010) suggest that the rational perspective fails to take the moral basis of human service organizations into account.

Systems Perspective

Martha Green and Helen Blue had different styles of managing what happened inside Beacon Center, but they also had different styles of managing external pressures and resources. Martha focused on giving homeless persons a voice in efforts to secure political and economic resources for Beacon Center; Helen focused on conciliation with community and political leaders. In her own way, however, each was attentive to Beacon Center's relationship with its environment. In this respect, they negated the rational perspective's view of the organization as a closed system that can be controlled by careful attention to internal structure and processes. During the 1950s and 1960s, the rationalist view of organizations was challenged by the systems perspective, which seems to inform the efforts of both Martha Green and Helen Blue. All subsequent theorizing about organizations has been influenced by the systems perspective.

Systems perspective

The **systems perspective on organizations** builds on the fundamental principle that the organization is in constant interaction with its multiple environments—social, political, economic, cultural, technological—and must be able to adapt to environmental change. Some systems theorists suggest mutual influence between organizations and their environments; other theorists see the influence as unidirectional, with organizational structure and processes being determined by the environment. A second important principle of the systems perspective is that organizations are composed of interrelated subsystems that must be integrated in order to achieve the organization's goals and meet environmental demands. Finally, in contrast to the rational approach, the systems perspective holds that there are many different ways, rather than one best way, to reach the same ends. The idea that a system can attain its goals in a variety of ways is known as *equifinality*.

Several systems theories of organizations have been developed over time, but we look at only two here: the political economy model and learning organization theory. These two theories are summarized in Exhibit 8.2.

Political Economy Model

The *political economy model* focuses on the dependence of organizations on their environments for necessary resources and on the impact of organization–environment interactions on the internal structure and processes of the organization (Wamsley & Zald, 1973). More specifically, it focuses on two types of resources necessary to organizations: political resources (legitimacy and power) and economic resources. The greater the dependence of the organization on the environment for either of these types of resources, the greater the influence the environment will have on the organization. Likewise, the greater control one unit of the organization has over resources, the more power that unit has over the organizational processes.

The political economy model is particularly potent for clarifying how social service organizations resolve such important issues as which clients to serve, which services to provide, how to organize service provision, and how to define staff and client roles (Garrow & Hasenfeld, 2010). Both Martha Green and Helen Blue were trying to read their political and economic environments as they made these kinds of decisions, but their different ways of thinking led them to attend to different aspects of the environment. The political economy model recognizes clients as resources and as potential players in the political arena. Social workers have an important role to play in facilitating their inclusion in the political process, a role that was part of Martha Green's vision for Beacon Center.

Learning Organization Theory

The *learning organization theory* was developed on the premise that rational planning is not sufficient for an organization to survive in a rapidly changing environment such as the one in which we live. Formal organizations must become complex systems that are capable of constant learning (Argyris, 1999; Argyris & Schön, 1978, 1996; Senge, 1990). The learning organization is one that can

- Scan the environment, anticipate change, and detect "early warning" signs of trends and patterns.
- Question, challenge, and change customary ways of operating.
- Allow the appropriate strategic direction to emerge.
- Evolve designs that support continuous learning.

Theories in the systems perspective have advanced organizational understanding by calling attention to the influence of the external environment on organizations. They provide useful concepts for considering how organizations survive in turbulent environments, and, indeed, Uhlenbruck et al. (2003) suggest that learning organization theory is an appropriate theoretical approach for understanding how organizations in former socialist countries successfully adapted to the transition to market economies. But the systems perspective has little to say about the moral purposes of social service organizations, or how organizations can be positive rather than negative forces in society. Recently, however, Stephen Gill (2010) has proposed learning organization theory as an appropriate model for nonprofit organizations. As we can see from the experience of Beacon Center, we live in a world that values the kind of order that Helen Blue wants to bring to Beacon Center, and there can be much environmental resistance to the development of learning organizations. But if nothing else, the idea of the learning organization serves as a bridge between the systems perspective and the interpretive perspective.

Interpretive Perspective

As I have been suggesting, when Helen Blue became executive director at Beacon Center, she wanted to introduce more "rational order" and have fewer internal voices speaking about

Social constructionist perspective

the kind of place the center should be. It might be said that she found Martha Green's vision for Beacon Center to be too "interpretive." Theories of organizations within the **interpretive perspective on organizations** are quite diverse, but they all share one basic premise: Organizations are creations of human consciousness and reflect the worldviews of the creators; they are social constructions of reality.

The interpretive perspective rejects both the rational and the systems perspectives. Contrary to the rational perspective, the interpretive perspective focuses on processes rather than goals, emphasizes flexibility rather than control and reason, and is interested in a diversity of approaches rather than one right way. From this perspective, organizations are seen as increasingly fragmented into multiple realities, and they should be studied through multiple voices rather than through the unitary voice of the manager. Contrary to the systems perspective, the interpretive perspective emphasizes human agency in creating organizations and challenges the constraining influence of external forces.

Different interpretive theorists focus on different themes in relation to the basic premises stated above. The three separate approaches summarized in Exhibit 8.2 will give you some sense of these differences.

Social Action Model

One of the most influential contributions to the interpretive study of organizations is that of British sociologist David Silverman, presented in his 1971 book *The Theory of Organizations: A Sociological Framework*. Criticizing both rational and systems perspectives, Silverman proposed an approach to organizations that emphasizes the active role of individual organizational actors in creating the organization—an approach known as *Silverman's social action model*.

In a more recent work, David Silverman (1994) criticized the singular emphasis on organizational actors in his earlier model. He suggested that in reacting against deterministic theories of

environmental constraints, he failed to acknowledge the influence of history and social structure. He further suggested that his portrayal of human behavior as free and undetermined failed to acknowledge the influence of cultural scripts and the tendency of humans to see their behavior as freer than it is. This self-critique is consistent with other criticisms of the limitations of the interpretive perspective (e.g., M. Reed, 1993; P. Thompson, 1993).

Organizational Culture Model

In contrast to David Silverman's de-emphasis of culture, Edgar Schein (1992) focuses on organizations as cultures whose members have shared experiences that produce shared meanings, or interpretations. Organizations, therefore, exist as much in the heads of their members as in policies, rules, and procedures. The *organizational culture model* views organizations as ongoing, interactive processes of reality construction, involving many organizational actors. Organizational culture is made up of language, slogans, symbols, rituals, stories, and ceremonies (G. Morgan, 2006), but also of mundane, routine, day-to-day activities. For example, under Martha Green's leadership, the slogan "client input" was an important feature of the Beacon Center culture, buttressed by the day-to-day practice of soliciting client opinions.

Organizational culture is always evolving, and it is not always unitary. In many organizations, like Beacon Center under the administration of Helen Blue, competing beliefs and value systems produce subcultures. Given the evolution of organizational culture and rapid societal changes, it is not unusual to find a split between the old guard and the new guard or to find cultural divisions based on organizational function. The result may be cultural fragmentation or cultural warfare.

Criticisms of the organizational culture approach are twofold (G. Morgan, 2006). One criticism is leveled at theorists who write about managing organizational culture. These theorists are sometimes criticized for being biased in favor of management and potentially exploitative of employees. They are also criticized for overstating managers' potential to control culture, negating the role of multiple actors in the creation of shared meaning. The second criticism of the organizational culture approach is that it fails to take account of the fact that some members have more power than others to influence the construction of culture.

Managing Diversity Model

In the 1990s, organizational theorists developed an approach to organizational management called the *managing diversity model*. Given the trend toward greater diversity in the labor force, several social scientists (e.g., T. Cox, 1993, 2001; Kossek, Lobel, & Brown, 2006; Mor Barak, 2005; Mor Barak & Travis, 2010) have suggested that contemporary organizations cannot be successful unless they can learn to manage diverse populations. Diversity is a permanent, not transitory, feature of contemporary life.

The purpose in managing diversity is to maximize the advantages of diversity while minimizing its disadvantages. Taylor Cox (1993), a leading proponent of the model, says, "I view the goal of managing diversity as maximizing the ability of all employees to contribute to organizational goals and to achieve their full potential unhindered by group identities such as gender, race, nationality, age, and departmental affiliation" (p. 11). He argues that this goal requires that a new organizational culture must be institutionalized, a culture that welcomes diversity (T. Cox, 2001).

Mor Barak & Travis (2010) analyzed a decade of research about the linkages between organizational diversity and organizational performance. This research can be divided into the study of individual outcomes, workgroup outcomes, and organizational outcomes. The results were mixed in terms of individual outcomes, with some researchers finding that job satisfaction improves when workers find a higher proportion of people similar to them in values and ethnicity, and other researchers finding no such association. Likewise, mixed results were found in regard to diversity and workgroup outcomes. Some researchers found that the quality of ideas produced by workgroups increased as racial and ethnic diversity increased, other researchers found that racially diverse groups had more emotional conflict than racially homogeneous workgroups, and still other researchers found no relationship between extent of diversity and workgroup cohesion and performance. The results were also mixed regarding the relationship between diversity and organizational performance, but the majority of studies report positive relationships in both the corporate sector and the human service sector, meaning that organizational performance improves as diversity in the workforce increases.

Critical Perspective

Although it may appear that Martha Green administered Beacon Center from an interpretive perspective, it is probably more accurate to describe her worldview as a **critical perspective on organizations.** She tried to minimize the power differences in her organization, and when she asked her staff to vote on sensitive issues, she invoked the secret ballot to neutralize any possible power dynamics.

Conflict perspective

Critical theorists share the interpretive perspective's bias about the role of human consciousness in human behavior, but critical theory undertakes, as its central concern, a critique of existing power arrangements and a vision for change suggested by this critique. More specifically, critical theories of organizations see them as instruments of exploitation and domination, where conflicting interests are decided in favor of the most powerful members. This focus distinguishes the critical perspective from the interpretive perspective, which generally ignores or negates issues of power and the possibility that persons in power positions can privilege their own versions of reality and marginalize other versions, thus controlling the organizational culture. Exhibit 8.2 summarizes the two contemporary critical approaches to formal organizations discussed here: organizations as multiple oppressions and nonhierarchical organizations.

Organizations as Multiple Oppressions

Have you ever felt oppressed—voiceless, powerless, abused, manipulated, unappreciated—in any of the organizations of which you have been a member? Do you think that whole groups of people have felt oppressed in any of those organizations? In the contemporary era, the critical perspective has taken a more focused look at who is oppressed in organizations and the ways in which they are oppressed. This approach was influenced by feminist critiques, during the 1970s and 1980s, of the failure of traditional organization theories to consider gender issues (J. Hearn & Parkin, 1993). Feminist critiques led to the recognition that other groups besides women had also been marginalized by formal organizations and by organization theory.

Jeff Hearn and Wendy Parkin (1993) recommend viewing *organizations as multiple oppressions*—social constructions that exclude and discriminate against some categories of people. They indicate that oppression happens through a variety of processes, including "marginalization, domination and subordination, degradation, ignoring, harassment, invisibilizing, silencing, punishment, discipline and violence" (p. 153). These processes may also be directed at a variety of organizational actors, including "staff, members, employees, residents, patients and clients" (p. 153). Organizational domination can become compounded by multiple oppressions. This idea that multiple oppressions are usually embedded in organizational life has been addressed in a book by Sharon Kurtz (2002), who argues that addressing the situation of only one oppressed group will never get to the heart of the matrix of domination in organizations.

The critical perspective on organizations has special relevance to social workers. It helps us recognize the ways in which clients' struggles are related to oppressive structures and processes in the formal organizations with which they interact.

It can help us to understand the ways in which social service organizations are gendered, with women constituting the majority of human service workers and men assuming key administrative roles. It also calls our attention to the power imbalance between clients and social workers and helps us think critically about how we use our power. We must be constantly vigilant about the multiple oppressions within the organizations where we work, as well as those with which we interact, as we try to promote social justice.

Nonhierarchical Organizations

Helen Blue preferred a more hierarchical organizational structure than the one developed at Beacon Center under Martha Green's leadership. A constant theme in critical theory is that hierarchical organizational structures lead to alienation and internal class conflict. Critical theorists directly challenge the rational perspective argument that hierarchy is needed to maximize efficiency; they point out that in fact hierarchy is often inefficient, but that it is maintained because it works well to protect the positions of persons in power. For example, the staff at Beacon Center wasted much time and energy trying to find ways to thwart Helen Blue's decisions.

The idea of the *nonhierarchical organization* is not new. Human relations theorists have recommended "participatory management," which involves lower-level employees in at least some decision making, for several decades. Historical evidence indicates that since the 1840s, experiments with nonhierarchical organizations have accompanied every wave of antimodernist social movements in the United States (Rothschild-Whitt & Whitt, 1986). Beginning in the 1970s, feminist critiques of organizational theory helped to stimulate renewed interest in nonhierarchical organizations (Kravetz, 2004). Nevertheless, such organizations constitute only a small portion of the population of formal organizations, and research on nonhierarchical organizations

Humanistic perspective

constitutes a very small part of the massive body of research on organizations (Garrow & Hasenfeld, 2010; Iannello, 1992).

Studies of nonhierarchical organizations summarize some of the special challenges, both internal and external, faced by them (Ferree & Martin, 1995; Kravetz, 2004; Rothschild-Whitt & Whitt, 1986). Internal challenges include increased time needed for decision making, increased emotional intensity due to the more personal style of relationships, and difficulty incorporating diversity. External challenges are the constraints of social, economic, and political environments that value and reward hierarchy (Garrow & Hasenfeld, 2010).

On the basis of her study of two successful feminist organizations, Iannello (1992) proposed that the internal challenges of the nonhierarchical organization could be addressed by what she calls a "modified consensual organization" model. Critical decisions continue to be made by the broad membership, but routine decisions are made by smaller groups; members are recognized by ability and expertise, but not by rank and position; there are clear goals, developed through a consensual process. Similarly, reporting on the life course of five feminist organizations initiated in the 1970s, Diane Kravetz (2004) found that these organizations developed "modified hierarchies" as they grew and faced new external challenges. They gradually delegated authority to individuals and committees but retained some elements of consensus decision making.

One trend to watch is the trend toward worker-owned corporations, both in the United States and Europe. Sometimes, these corporations are not truly democratic, with strong worker input into decisions, but there is evidence that they are moving toward greater democratization (Alperovitz, 2005). The fact that the number of worker-owned companies in the United States increased from 1,600 in 1975 to 11,000 in 2003 seems to be a sign that the idea of shared leadership is gaining in popularity (Alperovitz, 2005).

Given the increasing diversity of the workforce in the United States, management of difference and conflict can be expected to become an increasing challenge in organizational life. This is as true for social work organizations as for other organizations. To date, the literature on nonhierarchical organizations has failed to address the difficult challenges of diverse ideological and cultural perspectives among organizational members—issues that are the focus of the managing diversity model. This is an area in which social work should take the lead.

In Canada, one notable exception has occurred. Feminist critiques of social service organizations have led to growing interest in *anti-oppressive* social work practice at both the direct practice and organizational practice levels. The anti-oppression model seeks to develop social service organizations that are free from all types of domination and privilege (Barnoff & Moffatt, 2007).

Critical Thinking Questions 8.1

Think of a formal organization of which you have been a part, for which you have positive feelings. What words come to mind when you think of this organization? Which of the theoretical perspectives discussed above seem to best describe this organization? Can you use specific theoretical concepts to talk about this organization? Now, think of a formal organization of which you have been a part, for which you have negative feelings. What words come to mind when you think of this organization? Which of the theoretical perspectives seem to best describe this organization? Can you use specific theoretical concepts to describe this organization?

COMMUNITY: TERRITORIAL AND RELATIONAL

As summarized in Case Study 8.2, Rhacel Salazar Parrenas (2001) chronicled the lives of Filipina domestic workers between June 1995 and August 1996, a period before the wide use of the Internet and cell phones. We can wonder how these technologies might have changed the lives of these women. Although the circumstances of their lives are different in some important ways, the Filipinas in Rome and Los Angeles both appear to see themselves as members of multiple communities. But exactly what is community?

Historically, community had a geographic meaning in sociology. More recently, however, two different sociological meanings of community have developed: community as a geographic or territorial concept, and community as an interactional or relational concept. Both meanings of community have relevance for human behavior in the contemporary era, and recently, researchers are finding more similarities than differences between these two types of community (Obst & White, 2004; Obst, Zinkiewicz, & Smith, 2002a, 2002b). The following definition can be used to cover both territorial and relational communities: **Community** is people bound either by geography or by webs of communication, sharing common ties, and interacting with one another. Communities can be distinguished from formal organizations in two ways: Communities have less formal structures, and they are not organized around specific goals.

The field of community psychology has been interested in how people develop a **sense of community,** which Seymour Sarason (1974) defined in this way:

> the perception of similarity with others, an acknowledged interdependence with others, a willingness to maintain this interdependence by giving to or doing for others what one expects from them, the feeling that one is part of a larger dependable and stable structure. (p. 157)

These characteristics of sense of community are very similar to the "common ties" element of the definition of community. Does it appear to you that the Filipina domestic workers in Rome have a sense of community with other domestic workers in the city? What about the Filipina domestic workers in Los Angeles?

Some would argue that community in the contemporary era is based on voluntary interaction (**relational community**), not on geography or territory (**territorial community**). For the Filipina domestic workers, community seems to be both relational and territorial. They are a part of a growing trend of transnational families who are also creating *transnational communities*. They maintain a sense of community connection to their sending communities in the Philippines as well as to other Filipina domestic workers in their territorial communities. In addition, they imagine themselves as a part of a global community of Filipina domestic workers, especially when they read magazines such as *Tinig Filipino*. Their sense of belonging to this global community is based on common ties but does not include much interaction. They do, however, draw support from feeling a part of this community. What about for you? Are your strongest supports based on territorial or relational community?

In premodern times, human groups depended, by necessity, on the territorial community to meet their human needs. But each development in communication and transportation technology has loosened that dependency somewhat. Electronic communications now connect people over distant spaces, with a high degree of both immediacy and intimacy. The development of the World Wide Web in the early 1990s allowed rapid growth in the use of e-mail; beginning in the mid-1990s, hundreds of millions of people around the world began to use e-mail to communicate with other individuals and to develop e-mail discussion groups. Toward the end of 2004, Web 2.0 technologies, a second generation of the World Wide Web that allows people to collaborate and share information online, came to prominence. Web 2.0 technologies include blogs, wikis, podcasting, multimedia sharing sites, and social networking sites (SNSs). By 2008, a major research study of the use of digital technologies by adults in 17 industrialized nations found an average use of these technologies for one third of leisure time (Harrison & Thomas, 2009). The SNS Facebook reportedly has more than 175 million users worldwide. Other SNSs have sprung up in specific countries, for example, Cyworld (Korea), Hyves (Holland), LunarStorm (Sweden), Mixi (Japan),

Orkut (Brazil), QQ (China), and Skyrock (France). SNSs have been defined as web-based services that allow individuals to "construct a public or semi-public profile within a bounded system, articulate a list of other users with whom they share a connection, and view and traverse their list of connections and those made by others within the system" (Boyd & Ellison, 2007, ¶ 5). This definition is consistent with the aspects of the above-stated definition of community: linked by webs of communication, common ties, and interaction.

For a number of years, researchers have been finding that local ties make up a decreasing portion of our social connections, and they have interpreted that finding to mean that territorial community is no longer important in our lives (A. Hunter & Riger, 1986; Wellman, 1982; Wellman & Wortley, 1990). A more careful look at this research suggests, however, that even highly mobile people continue to have a lot of contacts in their territorial communities. One study in Toronto (Wellman, 1996) found that if we study *ties,* the number of people with whom we have connections, it is true that the majority of ties for most of us are nonterritorial. However, when we study *contacts,* our actual interactions, two thirds of all contacts are local, in the neighborhood or work setting. This may well be the case for the Filipina domestic workers who often complain about how isolating their domestic work is.

When technology opens the possibilities for relational communities, it does not necessarily spell the death of territorial community, but there have been conflicting findings about this. One research team found that Internet-wired sub-urbanites were more likely than their nonwired neighbors to engage in "active neighboring," actually using the Internet to support neighboring (Hampton & Wellman, 2003). A widely publicized 2006 study by McPherson et al. found the opposite. This study found that since 1985, people in the United States have become more socially isolated, the size of their discussion networks has declined, and the diversity of their networks has decreased. More specifically, the researchers found that people had fewer close ties in their neighborhoods and from voluntary associations (clubs, etc.). They suggested that use of the Internet and mobile phones pulls people away from neighborhood and other locally based social settings. To address the inconsistencies in prior research, the most comprehensive study of social isolation and new technology in the United States to date was reported by researchers with the Pew Internet & American Life Project (Hampton, Sessions, Her, & Rainie, 2009). These researchers undertook a study to compare the social networks of people who use particular technologies with those of demographically similar people who do not use

Photo 8.2a & 8.2b   Two contrasting communities: (left) a tribal community in Ethiopia and (right) a member of the Second Life (online) community

these technologies. Here are their major findings about the trends in social networks since 1985:

- There has been a small-to-modest drop in the number of people reporting that they have no one to talk to about important matters; 6% of adults report they have no one with whom they can discuss such matters.
- The average size of people's core discussion networks has declined, with a drop of about one confidant.
- The diversity of people's core discussion network has markedly declined.

However, the research indicates that use of technology is not the driving force behind these changes. Here are the findings about the relationship between new technology and social networks:

- People who own a cell phone and use the Internet for sharing photos and messages have larger core discussion networks than those who do not use this technology.
- People who use these technologies have more non-kin in their networks than people who do not.
- People who use the Internet to share photos are more likely to have discussion partners that cross political lines.
- People who use Internet social networking sites have social networks that are about 20% more diverse.
- In-person contact remains the most frequent way to have contact in the geographical community.
- The mobile phone has replaced the landline as the most frequently used medium for communication.
- Text messaging tied with the land line as the third most popular way to communicate.
- Those who use SNSs are 25% less likely to use neighbors for companionship, but use of other technologies is associated with higher levels of neighborhood involvement.
- Internet users are less likely to depend on neighbors to provide concrete services.

Wendy Griswold (2008) proposes that people can have ties to both relational and territorial communities at the same time, and this does seem to be the case for the Filipina domestic workers in both Rome and Los Angeles. They maintain relationships with their sending communities while also building community in local gathering places in their receiving communities. Griswold recognizes the possibility that the new technologies will simply allow us to develop and maintain a larger network of increasingly superficial relationships. But she also points out the possibility that the new capacity to be immediately and intimately connected across space could help us to develop more shared meanings and become more tolerant of our differences. We can imagine that e-mail and Internet SNSs are now helping the Filipina mothers maintain more intimate contact with their children and other family members back in the Philippines.

As social workers concerned about social justice, however, we must understand the multiple implications of inequality of access to the new technologies. These technologies open opportunities for relational community and the multitude of resources provided by such communities. Skills in using the new technologies are also increasingly rewarded in the labor market. Unless access to these technologies is equalized, however, territorial community will remain central to the lives of some groups—most notably, young children and their caregivers; older adults; poor families; and many persons with disabilities, who have their own special technological needs. On the other hand, the new technologies may make it easier for some people with disabilities to gain access to relational community, even while inaccessible physical environments continue to block their connections to territorial community. One of my former African American students has told me that she likes the Internet because it is color-blind, and she can have encounters of various kinds without feeling that race got in the way.

Although both territorial and relational communities are relevant to social work, social work's commitment to social justice has led to continued concern for territorial communities. That same commitment also requires social workers to work toward equalization of access to both territorial and relational community.

THEORETICAL APPROACHES TO COMMUNITY _____

Five theoretical approaches to community seem particularly relevant for social work: the contrasting types approach, spatial arrangements approach, social systems approach, social capital approach, and conflict approach (see Exhibit 8.3 for a summary of the main ideas of these approaches). The second of these approaches, the spatial arrangements approach, applies only to territorial communities, but the other four can be applied equally well to both relational and territorial communities. In combination, these five approaches to community should enable you to scan more widely for factors contributing to the problems of living among vulnerable populations, to recognize community resources, and to think more creatively about possible interventions. Using approaches that are not only varied but even discordant should assist you in thinking critically about human behavior and prepare you for the often ambiguous practice situations that you will encounter.

Contrasting Types Approach

The Filipina domestic workers in Rome and Los Angeles are concerned about commitment, identification, and relationships within their communities.

The Los Angeles Filipinas seem especially concerned about the nature of their relationship to the wider Filipino community in their area. These concerns are at the heart of the oldest theory of community, Ferdinand Tonnies' (1887/1963) concepts of *gemeinschaft* and *gesellschaft* (translated as community and society). Actually, Tonnies was trying to describe contrasting types of societies, rural preindustrial societies (gemeinschaft) versus urban industrial societies (gesellschaft), but his ideas continue to be used by community sociologists today to understand differences between communities, both territorial communities and online communities (Ballantine & Roberts, 2009; Memmi, 2006). In *gemeinschaft* communities, relationships are personal and traditional; in *gesellschaft* communities, relationships are impersonal and contractual.

Tonnies (1887/1963) saw gemeinschaft and gesellschaft as ideal types that will never exist in reality. However, they constitute a hypothetical dichotomy against which the real world can be compared. Although Tonnies' work is more than a century old, the gemeinschaft–gesellschaft dichotomy has proven to be a powerful analytical construct, and it continues to be used and validated in community research.

Tonnies shared the view of other early European sociologists, such as Max Weber and Émile Durkheim, that modernization was leading

Exhibit 8.3   Approaches to Community

Approach	Central Idea
Contrasting Types Approach	Communities can be dichotomized as either *gemeinschaft* (personal and traditional) or *gesellschaft* (impersonal and contractual).
Spatial Arrangements Approach	Territorial communities can be understood by considering their spatial arrangements.
Social Systems Approach	Communities can be understood by studying their patterns of social interaction, their cultures and social structures.
Social Capital Approach	Communities can be understood by examining their levels of social cohesion.
Conflict Approach	Communities can be understood by examining their power structure and patterns of domination and coercion.

us away from gemeinschaft and toward gesellschaft. Capitalism, urbanization, and industrialization have all been proposed as causes of the movement toward gesellschaft. Many typology theorists lament the "loss of community" that occurs in the process. But some theorists suggest that electronic technology is moving us into a third type of community—sometimes referred to as a *postgesellschaft,* or postmodern, community—characterized by diversity and unpredictability (Griswold, 2008; Lyon, 1987; G. Smith, 1996). This view has become more prominent with increasing globalization, and it is well illustrated by the Filipina domestic workers and their families back in the Philippines. Back home in their rural, newly industrializing sending communities, children, relatives, and friends talk about the loss of emotional intimacy in their relationships with the migrant workers. Although the Filipina domestic workers feel the pain of separation from family and friends back home, they talk about relationships based on goal attainment, meeting the goal of improving the financial situation of their families.

Howard Becker (1957) saw the evolution of community in a different light. He suggested that modern society does not always move in one direction, but instead moves back and forth a great deal on the gemeinschaft–gesellschaft continuum (which Becker called the *sacred–secular continuum*).

Tonnies and other theorists who have studied communities as contrasting types have focused their attention on territorial communities. Indeed, empirical research supports the idea that territorial communities vary along the gemeinschaft–gesellschaft continuum (Cuba & Hummon, 1993; A. Hunter & Riger, 1986; Keane, 1991; Woolever, 1992). More recently, however, Barry Wellman (1999) and research associates have attempted to understand contrasting types of relational communities that are based on networks of interaction rather than territory. In his early work, Wellman (1979) identified three contrasting types of communities:

1. *Community lost:* Communities that have lost a sense of connectedness, social support, and traditional customs for behavior

2. *Community saved:* Communities that have retained a strong sense of connectedness, social support, and customs for behavior

3. *Community liberated:* Communities that are loosely knit, with unclear boundaries and a great deal of heterogeneity

Wellman (1999) suggested that as societies change, community is not necessarily lost but becomes transformed, and new forms of community develop. Daniel Memmi (2006) argues that online communities are just another form of community and another example of the long-term evolution of looser social relationships. There are differences of opinion about whether community is lost or merely transformed in the exportation of labor around the world.

Wellman and associates have continued to study the idea of contrasting types of relational communities for over 20 years, seeking to understand multiple dimensions of communities. Their work (e.g., Wellman & Potter, 1999) suggests that it is more important to think in terms of *elements* of communities rather than *types* of communities. Using factor analytic statistical methods, they have identified four important elements of community—contact (level of interaction), range (size and heterogeneity of community membership), level of intimacy, and proportion of community membership composed of immediate kin versus friends. These elements are configured in different ways in different communities, and in the same community at different times.

Social workers might benefit by recognizing both the gemeinschaft and gesellschaft qualities of the communities they serve as well as the histories of those communities. Approaches like Wellman and Potter's multiple elements of communities could be helpful in this regard.

Spatial Arrangements Approach

If we think about the Filipina community in Rome in terms of spatial arrangements, we note the dispersed gathering places where they congregate.

We think about how their gathering places are segregated from the public space of the dominant society. We also think about the crowded apartments that sometimes hold as many as four residents in a small room. If we think about the Filipinas in Los Angeles, we think of domestic workers isolated in houses in wealthy neighborhoods and visiting middle-class Filipino neighborhoods where they feel like outsiders on their days off. We also think about their lack of transportation to get beyond their live-in and day-off neighborhoods.

Beginning with Robert Park's (1936) human ecology theory, a diverse group of sociological theorists have focused on community as spatial arrangements. Their interests have included city placement; population growth; land use patterns; the process of suburbanization; the development of "edge" cities (newly developed business districts of large scale located on the edge of major cities); and the relationships among central cities, suburbs, and edge cities. They are also interested in variations in human behavior related to the type of spatial community, such as rural area, small town, suburb, or central city, and more recently, in how human health and well-being are related to physical features of the community (E. Sternberg, 2009).

Symbolic interactionists have studied how symbolic images of communities—the way people think about their communities—are related to spatial arrangements (G. Wilson & Baldassare, 1996). A survey of a random sample of Denver employees found that a large majority thought of themselves as either a "city person" or a "suburbanite" (Feldman, 1990). Participants largely agreed about the spatial attributes that distinguish cities from suburbs. On the whole, both city people and suburbanites reported a preference for the type of spatial community in which they resided.

Social constructionist perspective

One research team set out to discover the meanings that residents of seven distressed neighborhoods in one midwestern city make of the physical aspects of their neighborhoods (Nowell, Berkowitz, Deacon, & Foster-Fishman, 2006).

They used a *photovoice* methodology, putting cameras in the hands of participants and asking them to use the cameras to tell a story about their community. They found that physical aspects of the neighborhood carry many meanings for the residents. Positive physical landmarks, such as parks and monuments, communicate a message of pride and identity, but physical conditions such as dilapidated houses, graffiti, and overflowing garbage convey negative meaning that invites frustration and shame. The researchers concluded that community physical conditions are important because they carry symbolic meanings for the residents. We are reminded that the Los Angeles Filipina domestic workers interpret the middle-class neighborhoods where they visit on their days off as "middle-class spaces."

The multidisciplinary theory on human behavior and the physical environment, discussed in Chapter 6, has also been extended to the study of community as spatial arrangements. Social scientists have focused on elements of environmental design that encourage social interaction as well as those that encourage a sense of control and the motivation to look out for the neighborhood.

Systems perspective

They have identified such elements as large spaces broken into smaller spaces, personalized spaces, and spaces for both privacy and congregation. One research team that studied the spatial arrangements in a suburban region found that people who had a sense of adequate privacy from neighbors' houses also reported a greater sense of community (G. Wilson & Baldassare, 1996). Another researcher found that opportunities to visit nearby shared space and having views of nature from home are correlated with increased neighborhood satisfaction (Kearney, 2006). Still another researcher found that neighborhood physical environments that provide opportunity for physical activity are particularly valued by children and recommends that social work assessment with children should include aspects of the child–neighborhood relationship (Nicotera, 2005). Recently, the new urbanist designers have been interested in aspects of community design that encourage physical activity for people of all ages; they are thinking of the health benefits of physical activity (see discussion in Chapter 6).

Early settlement house social workers at Hull House in Chicago developed community maps for assessing the spatial arrangements of social and economic injustices in local neighborhoods (Wong & Hillier, 2001). Social work planners and administrators have recently returned to the idea of geographical mapping, making use of advancements in *geographic information system (GIS)* computer technology, which can map the spatial distribution of a variety of social data. Social workers have used GIS to map (1) the distribution of child care facilities in a geographic region (Queralt & Witte, 1998a, 1998b); (2) prior residences of persons admitted to homeless shelters (Culhane, Lee, & Wachter, 1997); (3) the geographical distribution of rates of child physical abuse, neglect, and sexual abuse (Ernst, 2000); and (4) the geographical areas of greatest unmet service needs (Wong & Hillier, 2001). GIS is also being used to map public health risk factors and to examine the match of physicians to community needs (see Cervigni, Suzuki, Ishii, & Hata, 2008); to target neighborhoods for community-building initiatives (Huber, Egeren, Pierce, & Foster-Fishman, 2009); to understand the match of welfare recipients, child care providers, and potential employers (M. Chen, Harris, Folkoff, Drudge, & Jackson, 1999); and to study race disparities in the national distribution of hazardous waste treatment, storage, and disposal facilities (Mohai & Saha, 2007). Huber et al. emphasize that community resources as well as community risk factors can be identified through the use of GIS.

GIS holds much promise for future social work planning, administration, and research (see Lohmann & McNutt, 2005). Amy Hillier (2007), a leading proponent of the use of GIS by social workers, emphasizes the important role that GIS can play in identifying where social work clients live in relation to both resources and hazards. She also argues that GIS has the potential to empower community groups, particularly disenfranchised groups, but that it is rarely used this way by social

workers. If you have access to GIS technology, you might want to do some mapping of your territorial community: its ethnic makeup, socioeconomic class, crime rate, libraries, parks, hospitals, social services, and so on. If you do not have access to GIS, you can accomplish the same task with a good map blowup and multicolored pushpins.

Thinking about territorial communities as spatial arrangements can help social workers decide which territorial communities to target, for which problems, and with which methods. An interdisciplinary literature has recently focused on the compounding and interrelated nature of problems in deteriorating, impoverished neighborhoods in central cities. Philanthropic funders have responded with comprehensive community initiatives (CCIs) to fund multifaceted community-building programs that address the economic and physical conditions, as well as social and cultural issues, of these impoverished communities (Huber et al., 2009; Nowell et al., 2006). Typical elements of CCIs are economic and commercial development, education, health care, employment, housing, leadership development, physical revitalization, neighborhood security, recreation, social services, and support networks. Although CCIs have been thought of as a development strategy for impoverished urban neighborhoods, Lori Messinger (2004) argues that the model is also relevant for work in rural communities. She suggests, however, that in rural communities, it is particularly important to pay attention to both current and historical points of tension and conflict. Another recent development is that many communities are using neighborhood youth for neighborhood cleanup and revitalization (L. Ross & Coleman, 2000; Twiss & Cooper, 2000).

> Systems perspective

Social Systems Approach

A third way to think about communities is as social systems with cultures and patterns of interaction. We have looked at some of the ways that the cultures and patterns of

> Systems perspective

interactions of the Filipina community in Rome are similar to and different from those in Los Angeles. A closer look at these communities as social systems might help us understand both the differences and similarities. The social systems perspective focuses on social interaction rather than on the physical, spatial aspects of community. Social interaction in a community can be understood in two different ways: as culture and as structure (Griswold, 2008). Community culture includes patterns of meanings; enduring patterns of communication; and symbols that guide thinking, feelings, and behaviors. Community structure includes patterns of interaction, institutions, economic factors, and political factors.

For thinking about community in terms of its culture, symbolic interaction theory is promising

| Social constructionist perspective |

because of its emphasis on the development of meaning through interaction. *Ethnography* is also particularly useful for studying community culture. The goal of ethnographic research is to understand the underlying rules and patterns of everyday life, in a particular location or among a particular group, from the native point of view rather than the researcher's point of view. One example of this is work by Italian community psychologists Donata Francescato and Manuela Tomai (2001). Their method of building a profile of a territorial community of interest combines demographic data with ethnographic methods that include "environmental walks, drawings, movie scripts, narratives, and telling jokes" (p. 376). For the movie script, they ask different target groups in the community to develop a plot for a movie script about the future they imagine for the neighborhood; sometimes these different groups perform parts of their "movies" for each other. Francescato and Tomai have used the movie script method to build understanding among Blacks, Afrikaners, and Indians in a college town in South Africa, between old farmers and young students in an Austrian town, and between immigrants and locals in several neighborhoods in Italy.

Community can also be studied in terms of its structure. Roland Warren (1963, 1978, 1987) made significant contributions to the understanding of patterns of interactions in communities. Warren pointed out that members of communities have two distinctive types of interactions. The first are those that create *horizontal linkage,* or interactions with other members of the community. The second are interactions that create *vertical linkage,* or interaction with individuals and systems outside the community. Warren suggested that healthy communities must have both types of interactions. Communities with strong horizontal linkage provide a sense of identity for community members, but without good vertical linkage they cannot provide the necessary resources for the well-being of community members. Communities with strong vertical linkage but weak horizontal linkage may leave community members searching and yearning for a sense of community.

More recently, a similar distinction has been made by scholars who write about community as social capital (to be discussed later; see Putnam, 2000). They differentiate between bonding social capital and bridging social capital. **Bonding social capital** is inward looking and tends to mobilize solidarity and in-group loyalty, and it leads to exclusive identities and homogenous communities. It may also lead to strong out-group hostilities. This type of social capital is often found in minority ethnic conclaves that provide psychological, social, and economic support to members. **Bridging social capital** is outward looking and diverse, and it links community members to assets and information across community boundaries. Robert Putnam (2000) describes the difference between the two types of social capital this way: "Bonding social capital constitutes a kind of sociological superglue, whereas bridging social capital provides a sociological WD-40" (p. 23). One research team (N. Ellison, Steinfield, & Lampe, 2007) found that the SNS Facebook is particularly useful for bridging social capital but much less useful for bonding social capital. Tomai et al. (2010) studied high school students outside Rome, Italy, and found that both bridging and bonding social capital were increased by joining an online community; however, increased intensity of use was associated with increased bridging social capital but not with increased bonding social capital.

Researchers have found support for the advantages and disadvantages of horizontal and vertical linkage discussed above. But consider also the experiences of the Filipina domestic workers in Rome and Los Angeles. We see much evidence that the workers in Rome have built strong horizontal linkages, but their opportunities to build vertical linkages are hampered by anti-immigrant sentiment. Unfortunately, the Filipina domestic workers in Los Angeles seem to be limited in both horizontal and vertical linkages, although middle-class Filipinos appear to be a source of bridging social capital for them.

For almost three decades, network theorists and researchers have been using network analysis to study community structure. They suggest that communities, like small groups and organizations, should be thought of as networks of social interaction (Wellman, 1999, 2001, 2005). They have tended to define community as *personal community*, which is composed of ties with friends, relatives, neighbors, workmates, and so on. Community is personal because the makeup of community membership varies from person to person. Another name for personal community is *network*, which has been defined as "the set of social relations or social ties among a set of actors" (Emirbayer & Goodwin, 1994). Network theorists suggest that the new communication technologies, particularly the Internet, have played a large role in transforming community from *solidary community*, which seeks the participation of all members in an integrated fashion, to what Barry Wellman has called community as *networked individualism*, where individuals operate in large, personalized, complex networks (Boase, Horrigan, Wellman, & Rainie, 2006). Some network theorists value this transformation (see, e.g., Boase et al., 2006). Others argue that communication technologies, and particularly the Internet, can and should be used to develop solidary community, which is friendlier, richer, and more socially binding than networked individualism, which they argue is a

North American idea (see, e.g., Day & Schuler, 2004). It seems that both sides are correct. Certainly, we know that the Internet has been used to develop support groups as one form of solidary community. It is interesting to note that the Los Angeles Filipina domestic workers seem to be closer to a network individualism model, while the Rome Filipinas seem to have built solidary community.

In the mid-1990s, when Parrenas (2001) did her study of Filipina domestic workers, the Internet was a tool that was accessible only to the technically elite, but a decade later, it was a part of everyday life for a large majority of people. That represents an unusually rapid diffusion of innovation, which has been accompanied by debates about whether it is helping to build or destroy community. In 2004–2005, the PEW Internet & American Life Project undertook a research project to study this question (Boase et al., 2006). Calling a random digit sample of telephone numbers in the United States, the researchers studied two types of connection people have in their social networks: *core ties*, or our closest relationships, and *significant ties*, or relationships that are only somewhat closely connected. They found surprisingly large networks among the respondents, a median of 15 core ties and 16 significant ties. There was no difference in the number of core ties between Internet users and nonusers, but Internet users were found to have larger numbers of significant ties.

In-person encounters continued to be the most common form of interaction, followed by landline phone, cell phone, e-mail, and instant messaging (IM). E-mail was not found to be replacing other forms of contact, either with core ties or significant ties. In fact, higher levels of e-mail communication were associated with higher levels of other forms of contact, and with both local and distant ties. This latter finding led the researchers to conclude that e-mail is a tool of "glocalization," a term that has been invented to emphasize the bringing together of the global and the local. Finally, as found in earlier research, the amount of support offered to network members increases as the *range* of the network—size and heterogeneity—increases. In interpreting these results, it is important to note that 74% of respondents are cell phone users, 63% are e-mail users, and 27% (mostly teens) are instant messaging (IM) users (Boase et al., 2006). This raises important concerns about the digital divide discussed in Chapter 7.

Network analysis has been used to study social ties in both territorial and relational communities. In doing so, researchers have found that for many people, community is based more on relationships than territory. One research team (B. Lee & Campbell, 1999) did find, however, that barriers of segregation and discrimination make neighborhood relationships more important for Blacks than for Whites. They found that Blacks have more intimate and long-standing ties with neighbors than Whites do in similar neighborhoods, and they engage in more frequent contact with neighbors. Similarly, it would seem that the network of relationships built in Filipina gathering places in Rome is highly important to the Filipinas who face much segregation and anti-immigrant discrimination.

Social Capital Approach

When the Filipinas in Rome talk about solidarity in their migrant community, they are talking about the quality of the connections that community members make with each other and the commitment they feel to one another. They are thinking about community as a social bond that unifies people. Similarly, when the Filipinas in Los Angeles talk about the lack of camaraderie in the Los Angeles Filipino community, they are talking about a lack of a social bond in the community.

In the midst of globalization, it is not unusual to hear both the general public and social scientists lamenting the weakening of community bonds and talking longingly about searching for community, strengthening community, or building a sense of community. These concerns have been consistently voiced in public opinion polls for some time in the United States, and they were the subject of Robert Putnam's (2000) best-selling book, *Bowling Alone: The Collapse and Revival of American Community.* To be sure, concerns about the waxing and waning of community are not new, but the nature of those

concerns has shifted over time. In the past decade, community psychologists and sociologists have turned to the concept of social capital to conceptualize this social bond aspect of community. This approach has been reinforced by the World Bank (2009b), which has endorsed such an approach for international development work.

In simplest terms, **social capital** is community cohesion, which is thought to be based in dense social networks, high levels of civic engagement, a sense of solidarity and equality among members, and norms of reciprocity and trustworthiness (see Kay, 2006; Putnam, 1993). The World Bank (2009b) identifies five components of its social capital implementation framework: groups and networks, trust and solidarity, collective action and cooperation, social cohesion and inclusion, and information and communication. In *Bowling Alone,* Putnam argues that for the first two-thirds of the 20th century, social capital was expanding in the United States, but that tide reversed in the final decades of the century. He calls for reconnection and revitalization of networks, civic engagement, solidarity and equality, and reciprocity and trustworthiness.

Putnam (2000) presents large amounts of empirical evidence to build a powerful argument for the loss of community in the United States. Here is some of that evidence: a 25% decline in voting and large declines in other forms of political participation in recent decades, a steep decline in face-to-face involvement in civic associations, a 25% to 50% decline in involvement in religious activities, less stable work settings and less involvement in unions, and less time socializing with friends and neighbors. He also provides evidence that we are relying increasingly on formal systems, such as the legal system, to regulate reciprocity and trustworthiness. On the other hand, he reports an increase in volunteering during this same time period. Putnam also draws on a variety of data to consider what is driving the above trends and identifies four contributing factors: pressures of time and money (about 10% of the decline); suburbanization, commuting, and sprawl (about 10% of the decline); electronic communication (about 25%

of the decline); and generation change (perhaps 50% of the decline). Factors that he did not find to be associated with the decline in social capital are changing family structure and larger government. Finally, Putnam argues, with supportive data, that social capital has an important impact on human well-being in several domains, including economic, educational, and physical and mental health (see also C. Campbell & Jovchelovitch, 2000).

While respecting his empirical analysis, researchers engaged in network analysis are critical of Putnam's conceptual analysis. They argue that community has been *changing* rather than declining and that, while people in the United States may not be participating in group-based community activities to the same extent as in the past, their networks remain large and strong (Boase et al., 2006). They see no inherent disadvantage to the more fragmented nature of contemporary social networks, while Putnam (2000) suggests that it takes dense, integrated networks that exist over time to build cohesion and trust. The work of Robert Sampson and colleagues (see Sampson, 2003; Sampson, Morenoff, & Earls, 1999) seems to support and expand this concern of Putnam's. They have proposed a theory of **collective efficacy**, which is "the capacity of community residents to achieve social control over the environment and to engage in collective action for the common good" (Sampson, 2003, p. S56). Collective efficacy involves a working trust, a shared belief in the neighborhood's ability for action, and a shared willingness to intervene to gain social control. Research to date indicates that as collective efficacy in a neighborhood decreases, a host of individual and social ills increase (Odgers et al., 2009; Sampson, 2003). It is important to note, however, that Sampson and colleagues (1999) have found that the spatial dynamics and quality of the physical environment of the neighborhood have an impact on collective efficacy. The Filipinos in Rome showed a great deal of collective efficacy when they developed their shopping bazaar by the Tiber River after the city authorities challenged their right to congregate in public spaces.

This idea of a social bond among community members is what Seymour Sarason (1974) had in mind when he declared the enhancement of a *psychological sense of community* (PSOC) as the mission of community psychology. Community psychologists David McMillan and David Chavis (McMillan, 1996; McMillan & Chavis, 1986) turned to the literature on group cohesiveness to understand how to enhance the social bonds of community. They presented a theory of PSOC that identified four essential elements:

1. *Membership* is a sense of belonging, of being part of a collective, something bigger than oneself.

2. *Influence* is bidirectional.

3. *Integration and fulfillment of needs* refers to individual reinforcement or reward for membership.

4. *Shared emotional connection* is based on a shared history and identification with the community.

On the basis of this definition of PSOC, D. McMillan and Chavis (1986) developed a 12-item Sense of Community Index (SCI) that has been used extensively for research on sense of community in such diverse settings as religious communities (Miers & Fisher, 2002), the workplace (Pretty & McCarthy, 1991), student communities (Pretty, 1990; Obst & White, 2007), Internet communities (Obst et al., 2002a), immigrant communities (Sonn, 2002), political groups (Sonn & Fisher, 1996), and residential and geographic communities (Brodsky & Marx, 2001; Brodsky, O'Campo, & Aronson, 1999). Recently, researchers have suggested the need to make minor revisions to the SCI (Obst & White, 2004). One research team cautioned that SCI was developed and validated in Western societies and may not be a good fit for the meaning of community for non-Western people (Mak, Cheung, & Law, 2009). Another research team developed separate measures for each of the four components of POSC and tested their psychometric properties in the first known study of POSC in a community of gay men (Proescholdbell, Roosa, & Nemeroff, 2006). They found that membership could not be distinguished from integration and need fulfillment.

An Australian research team (Obst et al., 2002a, 2002b) has used D. McMillan and Chavis's (1986) theory of PSOC to compare PSOC in territorial and relational communities. More specifically, the researchers asked 359 science fiction aficionados attending a World Science Fiction Convention to complete questionnaires rating PSOC both for their fandom community and for their territorial community. Research participants reported significantly higher levels of PSOC in their fandom communities than in their territorial communities. They also found that although the ratings on all dimensions of McMillan and Chavis's four theorized dimensions of PSOC were higher in the fandom communities than in the geographical communities, the dimensions received essentially the same rank ordering in both communities. The researchers also suggest that a fifth dimension, *conscious identification* with the community, should be added to McMillan and Chavis's theory of PSOC. They found this cognitive identification to be an important component of PSOC. Other researchers have found that social bonding and intimacy takes time to mature in computer-mediated communication (Harrison & Thomas, 2009).

In recent years, the social work literature has paid much attention to the issue of community building. This literature often focuses broadly on community revitalization, in terms of the economic and physical, as well as the social relationship dimensions of communities (e.g., E. Beck & Eichler, 2000; Halperin, 2001; C. Hendricks & Rudich, 2000; Zachary, 2000). The literature on youth leadership development is particularly noteworthy for its attention to building a sense of community among youth in neighborhoods (J. L. Finn & Checkoway, 1998; Tilton, 2009; Twiss & Cooper, 2000). Recent social work literature on community youth development has returned to its settlement house roots, recommending the use of arts, humanities, and sports to build a sense of community, as well as to empower youth and help them build skills (M. Delgado, 2000; Tilton, 2009). Building social capital has been an especially popular public health strategy in the United Kingdom and Australia (F. Baum, 1999; C. Campbell & Jovchelovitch, 2000).

Social capital theorists acknowledge that social capital can be used for antisocial as well as prosocial purposes. Think of the elements of social capital and sense of community, and you will have to agree that they apply equally well to the Ku Klux Klan (KKK) and a neighborhood committee formed to welcome the influx of new immigrants. The literature on networks often suggests that birds of a feather flock together. It is quite possible, as the KKK example demonstrates, that groups can be socially cohesive and yet quite exclusionary, distrustful, and hostile (even violently so) to outsiders. That has led Putnam (2000) and others (F. Baum, 1999; Potocky-Tripodi, 2004) to accede to the dark side of social capital. Putnam notes that in the same time period that social capital was declining in the United States, social tolerance was growing. On another dark note, Australian public health educator Fran Baum (1999) states a fear that has also been presented by European community psychologists (see Riera, 2005):

> Social capital may come to be seen as a shorthand way of putting responsibility on communities that do not have the economic, educational or other resources to generate social capital. Networks, trust and cooperation are not substitutes for housing, jobs, incomes and education even though they might play a role in helping people gain access to them. (p. 176)

I would suggest that the dark side of social capital calls for a conflict approach to understanding community.

Conflict Approach

The Filipina domestic workers in Rome and Los Angeles have confronted anti-immigrant sentiment. They often feel exploited by their privileged employers. They feel shut out of all sectors of the labor market except for low-status domestic work. In Los Angeles, they have felt marginalized by and alienated from middle-class Filipinos. Back in the Philippines, many were abused or abandoned by their husbands. They blame the Philippines government for providing so little security to its

Conflict perspective

residents, but they seldom blame the inequities of economic globalization for their limited options. Conflict theory's emphasis on dissension, power, and exploitation adds another dimension to our understanding of their story.

Writing about how European approaches to community psychology differ from U.S. community psychology, Francescato and Tomai (2001) suggest that European theorizing is much more in the conflict tradition than U.S. theorizing. They propose that particularly in continental Europe (Germany, Italy, Spain, and Portugal), the work of community psychologists shows that they "do not believe in the myth of the self-made man" (p. 372) that undergirds much of the work in the United States. They further suggest that the longer historical view in Europe leads to more critical emphases in European theory on social and economic inequalities, the historical interpretations that have been presented by power elites to legitimize existing social hierarchies, and the historical collective struggles by which groups of people have become empowered. Indeed, they report that European textbooks on community psychology typically devote chapters to historical social struggles that have led to greater empowerment for specific groups. Francescato and Tomai argue that Putnam's findings of declining social capital in the United States can be explained by U.S. fascination with neoliberal economics and individual success, which has led to increasing inequality. They insist that social capital cannot exist at the community level without state policy that supports it. In their view, community practice should involve strategies that focus on unequal power distribution and stimulate community participants to challenge community narratives that legitimize the status quo.

Writing from the United Kingdom, Isabelle Fremeaux (2005) criticizes the social capital approach on several fronts. She argues that it typically romanticizes community and fails to recognize the internal coercion and divisions that often are at play in communities. Failure to recognize the power politics operating in communities does damage to the least powerful members. And, much like Francescato and Tomai, she criticizes Putnam and other social capital theorists for neglecting to analyze the impact of the macro political and economic contexts on local networks. The story of the Filipinas in Rome and Los Angeles is an excellent example of the influence of macro political and economic contexts on social networks among migrant domestic workers.

Other European social scientists argue that community is "as much about struggle as it is about unity" (Brent, 1997, p. 83). Community workers are often faced with heterogeneous settings with diverse opinions, attitudes, and emotional attachments (Dixon, Dogan, & Sanderson, 2005). Carles Riera (2005), community development specialist from Spain, argues that managing the conflicts in such diversity should be the focus of community theorists and practitioners. Riera notes that European society, like U.S. society, is becoming more and more multicultural, caused by migrations from non-European countries as well as by the loosening of the borders of the European Union. Migrating groups often have strong internal cohesion, but the receiving communities are often fragmented. The task for community workers is to work for both inclusion and equality of opportunities in a framework of coexistence.

Riera (2005) describes a model of practice developed in Barcelona, Spain, called the Intercultural Mediation Programme. The program is three-pronged: It strives (1) to facilitate the resolution of intercultural community conflicts that occur in public spaces, (2) to facilitate the resolution of intercultural conflict situations among neighbors living in the same buildings, and (3) to provide information and advice to service professionals struggling with intercultural conflicts. The program is carried out by community mediator teams who use both linguistic and sociocultural interpreters. Perhaps such mediation could have helped when the Filipinos in Rome were being harassed to stop congregating in public spaces, and it might also be helpful to bridge divisions in the Los Angeles Filipino community.

Conflict theory is not new to U.S. social workers and social scientists, but its popularity has waxed and waned over time. Like European theorists, Robert Fisher and Eric Shragge (2000) argue that the worldwide spread of neoliberal faith in the free market (see discussion in Chapter 7) has "dulled the political edge" (p. 1) of community social workers. They argue for renewed commitment to a form of community social work that is willing to build opposition and use a range of confrontational tactics to challenge privilege and oppression. Given economic globalization, Fisher and Shragge recommend that effective community organizing in the current era will need to be tied to a global social movement. To work effectively with community conflict, social workers must be able to analyze the structure of community power and influence (Martinez-Brawley, 2000). They must understand who controls which types of resources and how power brokers are related to one another. That means understanding the power held internally in the community as well as the power that is external to the community. This type of analysis allows social workers to understand both the possibilities and limits of community empowerment. Emilia Martinez-Brawley suggests that social workers working in small communities should keep in mind that memories are usually long in such places, and conflictual relationships established on one issue may have an impact on future issues. Historical understanding is important.

Contemporary life also calls for the type of mediation programs recommended by Riera (2005). In many areas of life, from race relations to family relations, the mediator role is becoming more prominent for social workers. We will have to become more comfortable with conflict if we are to take leadership roles in healing these social fractures. In recent years, some rural communities have faced sudden influxes of refugees from a particular trouble spot in the world. Some of these communities have responded in exclusionary and punitive ways, while others have responded in inclusive and collaborative ways. It is more than likely that communities in the United States and other affluent countries will continue to face such influxes, and social workers should be able to assist communities in managing such change. One suggestion recently forwarded is that restorative justice programs similar to the ones used in criminal justice could be used to heal friction and conflict within neighborhoods (Verity & King, 2007). Restorative justice gatherings would allow storytelling and dialogue about social fractures and allow communities to move toward a more just future. This suggestion is consistent with Riera's Intercultural Mediation Programme.

Critical Thinking Questions 8.2

Which technologies have you used in the past week to keep in touch with people you know? Which type of technology do you use the most these days to build and maintain relationships? Do you use different types of technologies to keep in touch with different people or for different types of situations? How important is territorial community to you? What methods do you use to stay in touch with your territorial community?

SOCIAL MOVEMENTS: A DEFINITION

Conflict theory leads us to ask, so what happens when a group of people, like the many people involved in living wage campaigns, think that certain arrangements are unjust and need to be changed? Sometimes they work together to try to bring about the desired changes—not just for themselves but for a larger group of people. These joint efforts are **social movements**—ongoing, large-scale, collective efforts to bring about (or resist) social change.

We can think of social movements as either offensive or defensive (L. Ray, 1993). **Offensive social movements** seek to "try out new ways of cooperating and living together" (Habermas, 1981/1987, p. 394). The living wage and Amnesty International movements are examples of offensive social movements. **Defensive social movements,** on the other hand, seek to defend traditional values and social arrangements. Christian and Islamic fundamentalist and property rights movements are examples of defensive social movements.

Both types of social movements are common today in the United States and across the world.

Mario Diani (della Porta & Diani, 2006) identifies the following properties that distinguish social movements from other social collectivities. They

- Are involved in conflictual relations with clearly identified opponents
- Are linked by dense informal networks
- Share a distinct collective identity (p. 20).

It is protest that distinguishes social movements from other types of social networks, but a single episode of protest is not a social movement unless it is connected to a longer-lasting network of public action (della Porta & Diani, 2006; Tarrow, 2006).

PERSPECTIVES ON SOCIAL MOVEMENTS

Theory and research about social movements have flourished in the past four decades. Throughout the 1970s, social movement scholars in the United States and Europe worked independently of each other and developed different theories and different research emphases (McAdam, McCarthy, & Zald, 1996). In the past 20 years, however, U.S. and European social movement scholars have begun to work together and to engage in comparative analysis of social movements across place and time. Originally, these collaborative efforts focused only on social movements in the United States and Western Europe. Since the momentous political events in Eastern Europe in the late 1980s, however, Eastern European social movements have received extensive and intensive investigation. Social movement scholarship has begun to extend comparative analysis beyond the United States and Europe to nonindustrialized countries as well as to social movements that cross national lines (J. Smith, Chatfield, & Pagnucco, 1997; Tarrow, 2006).

Three perspectives on social movements have emerged out of this lively interest. I will be referring to these perspectives as the political opportunities perspective, the mobilizing structures perspective, and the cultural framing perspective (see Exhibit 8.4

for a summary of the main ideas of these perspectives). There is growing agreement among social movement scholars that none of these perspectives taken alone provides adequate tools for understanding social movements (della Porta & Diani, 2006; Goodwin & Jasper, 2004; McAdam et al., 1996; Tarrow, 1994, 1998, 2006). Each perspective adds important dimensions to our understanding of social movements, however, and taken together they provide a relatively comprehensive theory of social movements. Social movement scholars recommend research that synthesizes concepts across the three perspectives. The recent social movement literature offers one of the best examples of contemporary attempts to integrate and synthesize multiple theoretical perspectives to give a more complete picture of social phenomena.

Political Opportunities Perspective

Many advocates have been concerned about the deteriorating economic situation of low-wage workers in the United States for some time. After Republicans regained control of Congress in 1994, advocates saw little hope for major increases in the federal minimum wage. The federal minimum wage was increased slightly in 1996, from $4.25 an hour to $5.15 an hour, with a Democratic president and the Republican Congress. However, under the circumstances, advocates of a living wage decided it was more feasible to engage in campaigns at the local rather than the federal level to ensure a living wage for all workers. A shift occurred at the federal level when the Democrats regained control of Congress in November 2006. After being stalled at $5.15 for 10 years, Congress voted in a three-step increase in the minimum wage on May 24, 2007, and Republican President George W. Bush signed the new wage bill into law. The law called for an increase of the federal minimum wage to $5.85 in the summer of 2007, $6.55 in the summer of 2008, and $7.25 in the summer of 2009 (Labor Law Center, 2009).

These observations are in line with the **political opportunities (PO) perspective,** which begins with the assumption that social institutions—particularly

Exhibit 8.4 Perspectives on Social Movements

Perspective	Main Ideas
Political Opportunities Perspective	Social movements emerge when political opportunities are open.
	Political systems differ from each other, and change over time, in their openness to social movements.
	A given political system is not equally open or closed to all challengers.
	Success of one social movement can open the political system to challenges from other social movements.
	A given political system's openness to social movements is influenced by international events.
	Opportunities for social movements open at times of instability in political alignments.
	Social movements often rely on elite allies.
Mobilizing Structures Perspective	Social movements must be able to mobilize various kinds of formal and informal networks.
	Resource mobilization theory focuses on the coordination of movement activists through social movement organizations (SMOs).
	The network model focuses on mobilization of the movement through informal networks.
	Mobilizing structures have a strong influence on the life course of social movements.
	To survive, social movements must be able to attract new members and sustain the involvement of current members.
Cultural Framing Perspective	Social movements must be able to develop shared understandings that legitimate and motivate collective action.
	Social movements actively participate in the naming of grievances and injustices.
	Social movement leaders must construct a perception that change is possible.
	Social movements must articulate goals.
	Social movements must identify and create tactical choices for accomplishing goals.
	Contests over cultural frames are common in social movements.
	Social movements must be able to create cultural frames to appeal to diverse audiences.

Conflict perspective

political and economic institutions—benefit the more powerful members of society, often called *elites,* and disadvantage many. The elites typically have routine access to institutionalized political channels, whereas disadvantaged groups are denied access. Power disparities make it very difficult for some groups to successfully challenge existing institutions, but the PO perspective suggests that institutions are not consistently invulnerable to challenge by groups with little power. Social movements can at times take advantage of institutional arrangements that are vulnerable to challenge. The BUILD coalition (Case Study 8.3) was convinced that it was morally unjust for workers to receive wages that kept them below the federal poverty line, but they astounded even themselves by setting in motion a process that would spark a national social movement. Theories of social movements often underestimate the ability of challengers to mount and sustain social movements (A. Morris, 2000).

The political system itself may influence whether a social movement will emerge at a given time, as well as the form the movement will take. Social movement scholars have identified several influential dimensions of political systems and analyzed the ways in which changes in one or more of these dimensions make the political system either receptive or vulnerable to challenges (della Porta & Diani, 2006; Tarrow, 2006). Here we examine four of those dimensions: openness of the political system, stability of political alignments, availability of elite allies, and international relations.

Openness of the Political System

It might seem reasonable to think that activists will undertake collective action when political systems are open and avoid such action when political systems are closed. The relationship of system openness or closure to social movement activity is not that simple, however. They have instead a curvilinear relationship: Neither full access nor its total absence encourages the greatest degree of collective action. Some resistance stimulates movement solidarity, but too much resistance makes collective action too costly for social movement participants (D. Meyer, 2004). The nature of the political structure will also affect the types of social movement activities that emerge in a given society (Koopmans, 2004).

More generally, but in a similar vein, democratic states facilitate social movements and authoritarian states repress them (della Porta & Diani, 2006). However, because democratic states invite participation, even criticism, many challenging issues that might spark social movements are "processed" out of existence through electoral processes. It is hard to mount a social movement if it seems that the political system is easily influenced without serious collective action. On the other hand, the repression found in authoritarian states may serve to radicalize social movement leaders (della Porta, 1996). Furthermore, as was evident in Eastern Europe in the late 1980s and more recently in Middle Eastern and Northern African countries, authoritarian states are not always effective in repressing challenges. The political leadership's efforts to appease the population by offering small liberties can have a snowball effect. Relaxation of social control in a previously repressive political system often has the unintended consequence of fueling the fire of long-held grievances (G. Marx & McAdam, 1994).

Social movement researchers are interested in how police handle protest events. They have identified two contrasting styles of policing: the escalated force model and the negotiated control model. The *escalated force model* puts little value on the right to protest, has low tolerance for many forms of protest, favors little communication between the police and demonstrators, and makes use of coercive and even illegal methods to control protests. The *negotiated control model* honors the right to demonstrate peacefully, tolerates even disruptive forms of protest, puts high priority on communication between police and demonstrators, and avoids coercive control as much as possible (della Porta & Diani, 2006).

A given political system is not equally open or closed to all challengers at a given time; some social movements are favored over others. Even in a democracy, universal franchise does not mean equal access to the political system; wealth buys access not easily available to poor people's movements (A. Bornstein, 2009; della Porta & Diani, 2006; Piven & Cloward, 1977). Indeed, the rapid success and growth of the living wage movement has been a surprise to many who support it ideologically, because it has been hard to sustain poor people's movements in the past.

The success of one social movement can open the political system to the challenge of other social movements. For example, successful legislative action by the Black civil rights movement during the 1960s opened the way for other civil rights movements, particularly the women's movement, which benefited from the targeting of women in Title VII of the Civil Rights Act of 1964 (McAdam, 1996a). But the successful movement may also open the way for opponent movements, called **counter-movements,** as well as for allied movements. The living wage movement has engendered opposition coalitions that have launched intensive lobbying campaigns to convince state legislators in several states to bar cities from establishing their own minimum wages (B. Murray, 2001; Quigley, 2001).

Stability of Political Alignments

PO theorists agree that the routine transfer of political power from one group of incumbents to another, as when a different political party takes control of the U.S. presidency or Congress, opens opportunities for the development or reactivation of social movements (Tarrow, 2006). At such times, some social movements lose favor and others gain opportunity. In both the 1930s and 1960s, changes in political party strength appear to have been related to increased social movement activity among poor people. Some observers note that social movements on the Left mobilized during the Kennedy and Johnson administrations, and social movements on the Right mobilized during the Reagan and Bush administrations and again when the Republicans took over Congress in 1994 (McAdam et al., 1996); social movements on the Right also appear to have gained momentum when George W. Bush became president in 2000. That did not mean, however, that local grassroots movements for a living wage could not be mounted.

Disruption of political alliances also occurs at times other than political elections, for both partisan and nonpartisan reasons, and such disruptions produce conflicts and divisions among elites. When elites are divided, social movements can sometimes encourage some factions to take a stand for the disenfranchised and support the goals of the movement. The Harvard Living Wage Campaign garnered the support of the mayor and city council in Cambridge, Massachusetts. Disruptions in political alliances also occur when different branches of the government—such as the executive branch and the legislative branch—are at odds with each other. New coalitions may be formed, and the uncertainty that ensues may encourage groups to make new or renewed attempts to challenge institutional arrangements, hoping to find new elite allies.

The events in Eastern Europe in the late 1980s represent another type of political opportunity—one that has received little attention by social movement scholars: the opportunity that opens when a political regime loses legitimacy with those it governs. A political regime that has lost both legitimacy and effectiveness "is skating on very thin ice" (Oberschall, 1996, p. 98). This seems to be the situation leading to citizen uprisings in a number of Middle Eastern and North African countries in early 2011.

Availability of Elite Allies

Participants in social movements often lack both power and resources for influencing the political process. But they may be assisted by influential allies who play a variety of supportive roles. These elite allies may provide financial support, or they may provide name and face recognition that attracts media attention to the goals and activities of the movement. Research indicates a strong correlation between the presence of elite allies and social movement success (della Porta & Diani, 2006). The Harvard students, who mostly came from elite families themselves, were able to attract a number of elite allies, including the late Congressman Edward M. Kennedy, former Labor Secretary Robert Reich, Chairman of the NAACP Julian Bond, high profile religious leaders, and actors Ben Affleck and Matt Damon. Social movement participants often have ambivalent relationships with their elite allies, however. On the one hand, powerful allies provide needed resources; on the other hand, they may limit or distort the goals of the movement (della Porta & Diani, 2006; Kriesi, 1996).

International Relations

Since the 18th century, social movements have diffused rapidly across national boundaries, and the fate of national social movements has been influenced by international events. In the 19th century, the antislavery movement spread from England to France, the Netherlands, and the Americas (Tarrow, 2006). The mid-20th century Black civil rights movement in the United States was influenced by international attention to the gap between our national image as champion of human rights and the racial discrimination that permeated our social institutions (McAdam, 1996a). The fight for women's right to vote was first won in New Zealand in the 1880s; the United States followed almost 40 years later in 1920. It took some time, but gradually the movement for women's suffrage spread around the world (Sernau, 2006).

The recent revolution in communication technology, coupled with the globalization of market systems, is quickening the diffusion of collective action, as evidenced by peace and global social justice movements (della Porta & Diani, 2006; Tarrow, 2006). The protest against corporate globalization that took place at the 1999 meeting of the World Trade Organization (WTO) in Seattle was only one

action in several years of work by an international coalition of more than 1,200 labor, religious, consumer, environmental, farm, academic, and human rights groups from over 90 nations (D. Newman, 2006). On February 15, 2003, an estimated 16 million people around the world marched in protest of the impending U.S.-led war in Iraq, including 2.5 million in Italy, 1.75 million in London, 1.3 million in Barcelona, 1 million in Madrid, 500,000 in Berlin, 500,000 in New York City, and 250,000 in Paris. This was probably the largest international protest in history (Tarrow, 2006).

Mobilizing Structures Perspective

Most analysts would agree that much of the success of the living wage movement can be attributed to strong existing networks of local progressive

Photos 8.3a, 8.3b, 8.3c People around the world marched to protest the U.S.-led war in Iraq, including in China, Indonesia, and the Philippines.

advocates. The movement has also benefited from strong advocacy organizations like the now-defunct ACORN that developed and provided resources to grassroots organizers. These views are consistent with the **mobilizing structures (MS) perspective**, which starts from this basic premise: Given their disadvantaged position in the political system, social movement leaders must seek out and mobilize the resources they need—people, money, information, ideas, and skills—in order to reduce the costs and increase the benefits of movement activities (G. Davis, McAdam, Scott, & Zald, 2005; della Porta & Diani, 2006; A. Morris, 2004). In the MS perspective, social movements have no influence without effective organization of various kinds of *mobilizing structures*—existing informal networks and formal organizations through which people mobilize and engage in collective action. Mobilizing structures are the collective building blocks of social movements.

Informal and Formal Structures

MS scholars agree that social movements typically do not start from scratch but build on existing structures. They disagree, however, on the relative importance of informal versus formal structures. The MS perspective has two theoretical building blocks, one that emphasizes formal mobilizing structures and the other that emphasizes informal mobilizing structures.

Resource mobilization theory focuses on the organization and coordination of movement activities through formal organizations called *social movement organizations (SMOs)* (G. Davis et al., 2005). Theorists in this tradition are particularly interested in professional social movement organizations, staffed by leaders and activists who make a professional career out of reform causes (della Porta & Diani, 2006; A. Morris, 2004). The professional staff engages in fund-raising and attempts to speak for the constituency represented by the movement. There are advantages to professional SMOs, because social movements are more likely to meet their goals when they have a well-structured organization to engage in continuous fund-raising and lobbying. There are also problems, however. Professional SMOs must respond to the wishes of the benefactors who may be comfortable with low-level claims only. Theda Skocpol (2003) argues that professionalization can lead to movement defeat by taming protest.

Global social movements are being supported by growing numbers of *transnational social movement organizations (TSMOs),* or social movement organizations that operate in more than one nation-state. The number of TSMOs grew each decade of the 20th century, with particularly rapid growth in the last three decades of the century. There were fewer than 200 TSMOs in the 1970s but nearly 1,000 by the year 2000 (A. Bornstein, 2009; G. Davis et al., 2005). Some examples of TSMOs are Green Peace and Amnesty International.

In contrast to resource mobilization theory, the *network model* focuses on everyday ties between people, in grassroots settings, as the basic structures for the communication and social solidarity necessary for mobilization (della Porta & Diani, 2006; Tindall, 2004). The focus is thus on naturally existing networks based in family, work, religious, educational, and neighborhood relationships, or such networks as those that can be found at alternative cafés and bookshops and social and cultural centers. Naturally existing social networks facilitate recruitment to movement activities and support continued participation. These natural networks are hard to repress and control because, in a democratic society, people have the right to congregate in their private homes and other informal settings.

Although resource mobilization theory and the network model disagree about the relative merits of formal and informal structures, they do agree that the costs of mobilizing social movements are minimized by drawing on preexisting structures and networks (G. Davis et al., 2005; Tindall, 2004). The living wage campaign in Baltimore got its start in an existing coalition of religious leaders, and the growing living wage movement was able to generate support from existing social movement organizations and university students. The global justice movement depends on a broad coalition of organizations with a strong background in activism, including trade unions and other worker organizations, ethnic organizations, farmers, religious organizations, consumer groups, environmental groups, women's groups, and youth groups (della Porta & Diani, 2006; Tarrow, 2006).

The Life Course of Social Movements

Social movements are by definition fluid in nature. The MS perspective asserts that mobilizing structures have a strong influence on the life course of a social movement. Although most social movements fade relatively soon, some last decades.

| Developmental perspective |

Movements typically have brief periods of intense activity and long latent periods when not much is happening. One pattern for the movements that persist is as follows: At the outset, the movement is ill-defined, and the various mobilizing structures are weakly organized (Kriesi, 1996; G. Marx & McAdam, 1994). Once the movement has been in existence for a while, it is likely to become larger, less spontaneous, and better organized. The mature social movement is typically led by the SMOs that were developed in the course of mobilization. The living wage movement seems to be in this position currently, with several organizations, including some transnational ones, playing a major role, but it was not always so.

Social movement scholars disagree about whether the increasing role of formal organizations as time passes is a good thing or a bad thing. Many suggest that movements cannot survive without becoming more organized and taking on many of the characteristics of the institutions they challenge (Tarrow, 2006). On the other hand, this tendency of social movements to become more organized and less spontaneous has often doomed them—particularly poor people's movements—to failure (Skocpol, 2003). Organizations that become more formal commonly abandon the oppositional tactics that brought early success and fail to seize the window of opportunity created by the unrest those

tactics generated. But that is not always the case. Sometimes SMOs become more radical over time, and most current large-scale social movements are strengthened by the support of a number of different types of organizations (della Porta & Diani, 2006). One of the most important problems facing social movement organizers is to create mobilizing structures that are sufficiently strong to stand up to opponents, but also flexible enough to respond to changing circumstances (Tarrow, 2006). The living wage movement appears to have managed that tension in its first decade, but it is still a work in progress, and it is too early to tell what the long-term trajectory of this movement will be.

Computer-Mediated Social Movement Communication

Increasingly, social movements are being mounted and maintained by use of computer technology. Both progressive and conservative social movements have benefited from the use of e-mail Listservs, Internet blogs, organizational websites, social networking sites, cell phones, and text messaging to communicate with potential members. These methods are used to provide information, solicit funds, recommend political action, and organize activities. They provide easy entry into activism. Communication scholars suggest that the Internet is a rich resource for social movements because it can be used to bypass mainstream media, which often ignores or distorts movement activity.

The widespread use of computer-mediated communication (CMC) in social movement mobilization is raising new questions for social movement scholars. Are dense, face-to-face networks still necessary to mobilize social movements? How essential is shared direct experience and face-to-face interaction to keep activists involved? To date, the answers to these questions appear mixed. It is true that the Internet can connect diverse communities that would never be connected otherwise. In addition, there are clear instances of solidarity and mutual trust developed by people who only know each other on the Internet (della Porta & Diani, 2006). Transnational computer-based networks contribute to efficient coordination of international campaigns, as demonstrated by the February 15, 2003, worldwide demonstrations against the impending Iraq war. On the other hand, participants on Listservs often hide their personal identity, participate only occasionally and typically only with one other person, and do not have a strong sense of loyalty to the network as a whole (Tilly, 2004). It appears that the best results come from a combination of local grassroots organizing and CMC (Bennett, 2004; Van Aelst & Walgrave, 2004).

Cultural Framing Perspective

The **cultural framing (CF) perspective on social movements** asserts that a social movement can succeed only when participants develop shared understandings and definitions of the situation. These shared meanings develop through a transactional process of consciousness raising, which social movement scholars call cultural framing. *Cultural framing* involves "conscious strategic efforts by groups of people to fashion shared understandings of the world and of themselves that legitimate and motivate collective action" (McAdam et al., 1996, p. 6).

Social constructionist perspective

Social movement leaders and participants engage in a delicate balancing act as they construct cultural frames. To legitimate collective action, cultural frames must impel people to feel aggrieved or outraged about some situation they consider unjust. But to motivate people to engage in collective action, cultural frames must be optimistic about the possibilities for improving the situation. Consider the chant developed by the divinity students at Harvard: "Where's your horror? Where's your rage? Div School wants a living wage." The chant dramatized the severity of the situation and the fairness of their cause, but it also expressed hope for a solution. Simultaneously, social movements want to draw heavily on existing cultural symbols so that the movement frame will resonate with people's cultural understandings while they add new frames to the cultural stock, thus sponsoring new ways of thinking about social conditions. The challenge of this balancing act is, "how to put forward a set of unsettling demands for unconventional people in ways that will not make enemies out of potential allies" (Tarrow, 1994, p. 10). The BUILD coalition was wise in choosing to call their cause a "living wage" rather than a "minimum wage." The notion that workers should draw a wage that allows them to "live" is morally persuasive, and even those who oppose the living wage movement have suggested that it is hard to take a public stance that you are opposed to such an idea (Malanga, 2003).

Cultural frames are "metaphors, symbols, and cognitive cues that cast issues in a particular light and suggest possible ways to respond to these issues" (G. Davis et al., 2005, pp. 48–49). A complication in the process of constructing frames is that frames attractive to one audience are likely to be rejected by other audiences. Activists desire media attention because that is the most effective way to reach wide audiences, but they also know that they cannot control the way the movement will be framed by the media. The media are attracted to dramatic, even violent, aspects of a movement, but these aspects are likely to be rejected by other audiences (L. Stein, 2009). The media are often more interested in scandal than in providing substantive information on movement issues (della Porta & Diani, 2006). ACORN, a now-defunct SMO that had been very helpful to the living wage campaign in the United States, became the subject of a highly publicized scandal in September of 2009 regarding the behavior of a few local staff caught in what appeared to be unethical behavior on hidden camera (Farrell, 2009). This scandal led to loss of federal funding and private donations, and by March 2010, ACORN announced that it was closing its offices after 40 years of successful advocacy efforts (Urbina, 2010). Indeed, it was their success in fighting for the rights of poor people that led to a backlash from conservative forces that wanted to destroy them. That is a possibility with which successful social movements must always contend. It remains to be seen how ACORN's demise will affect that living wage movement.

Social movement framing is never a matter of easy consensus building, and intense *framing contests* may arise among a variety of actors, particularly in the later stages. Representatives of the political system and participants in countermovements influence framing through their own actions and public statements, and internal conflicts may become more pronounced. Leaders and followers often have different frames for the movement (G. Marx & McAdam, 1994), and there are often splits between moderate and radical participants. It is not at all unusual for movements to put forth multiple frames, with different groups sponsoring different frames. For example, Bill Hughes (2009) suggests that disability activism in the UK is splitting into two branches, the Disabled People's Movement (DPM) and the "biological citizens." The DPM takes the position that disability is a social phenomenon created by discrimination and oppression, and suggests that impairment is irrelevant to disability. In contrast, the "biological citizens" organize politically around specific diagnostic labels and embrace medical and scientific knowledge associated with their "condition," with the goal of enhancing their ability to exercise citizenship. When a movement captures media attention, there is often an intense struggle over who speaks for the movement and which cultural frame is put forward.

Frames for Understanding That a Problem Exists

Social movements are actively involved in the "naming" of grievances and injustices. They do so in part by drawing on existing cultural symbols, but they also underscore, accentuate, and enlarge current understanding of the seriousness of a situation. In essence, they call attention to contradictions between cultural ideals and cultural realities. For example, the living wage movement calls attention to the discrepancy between working and receiving a wage that does not allow a person to rise out of poverty. Calling attention to this discrepancy is important in the United States, where the public tends to believe that people are poor because they don't work.

In the United States, movement frames are often articulated in terms of rights—civil rights, disability rights, GLBT rights, animal rights, children's rights. In Europe, where there is less emphasis on individual liberty, rights frames are far less common in social movements (Hastings, 1998; Tarrow, 1994).

In the past decade, fundamentalist religious movements have sprung up in many countries, including the United States. These movements have used morality frames, focusing on good and evil rather than justice versus injustice. Compared to Europe, the United States has historically produced a high number of such movements (G. Marx & McAdam, 1994). Prohibition, abolition, anticommunism, and antiabortionism have all had religious roots. A contemporary religious frame that crosses national boundaries as well as liberal and conservative ideologies is "reverence for life," expressed in such disparate movements as the environmental, health, antiabortion, animal rights, and anti–capital punishment movements.

Frames for Recognizing a Window of Opportunity

The perception of opportunity to change a troublesome situation is also culturally framed to some extent (della Porta & Diani, 2006; Gamson & Meyer, 1996; Polletta, 2004). On occasion, it is easy to develop a shared frame that opportunity exists or does not exist, but most situations are more ambiguous. Social movement leaders must successfully construct a perception that change is possible, because an opportunity does not exist unless it is recognized. They typically attempt to overcome concerns about the dangers and futility of activism by focusing on the risks of inaction, communicating a sense of urgency, and emphasizing the openness of the moment.

Calibrating this type of frame is a difficult task. On the one hand, overstating an opportunity can be hazardous (Piven & Cloward, 1977). Without "fortifying myths," which allow participants to see defeats as mere setbacks, unrealistically high expectations can degenerate into pessimism about possibilities for change (K. Voss, 1996). On the other hand, "movement activists systematically overestimate the degree of political opportunity, and if they did not, they would not be doing their job wisely" (Gamson & Meyer, 1996, p. 285). Unrealistic perceptions about what is possible can actually make change more possible. The Harvard students were not happy with the size of the worker raise that came out of their sit-in, but their expectations led them to bold action, which brought some improvements in the lives of workers and has been an inspiration for students at other universities around the country.

Frames for Establishing Goals

Once it has been established that both problem and opportunity exist, the question of social movement goals arises. Is change to be narrow or sweeping, reformist or revolutionary? Will the emphasis be on providing opportunities for individual self-expression or on changing the social order? U.S. social movements have generally set goals that are more reformist than revolutionary (G. Marx & McAdam, 1994).

Typically, goals are poorly articulated in the early stages of a movement but are clarified through ongoing negotiations about the desired changes. Manuals for social activism suggest that modest and winnable objectives in the early stages of a movement help to reinforce the possibility of change (Gamson & Meyer, 1996). Indeed, the early goals for the living wage movement were quite modest. The wage increase secured by BUILD only covered 1,500 to 2,000 workers. By 2001, it was estimated that the combined efforts of all local living wage campaigns now brought the number to only about 100,000 workers. Some progressives were critical of a movement that was yielding so little, but other analysts argued that it was the modest and winnable nature of the early campaigns that neutralized opposition and built a momentum

of success (B. Murray, 2001). Certainly, it is true that the movement has become more ambitious in its goals over time, moving from improving the wages of a small number of municipal contract workers to large-scale citywide ordinances like the one in Chicago, as well as to statewide minimum wage laws. Likewise, the European activists' demands that all garment workers in the retail supply chain be paid a living wage would have far-reaching results across national lines (Clean Clothes Campaign, 2009).

Frames for Identifying Pathways for Action

Some of the most important framing efforts of a social movement involve tactical choices for accomplishing goals. Social movement scholars generally agree that each society has a repertoire of forms of collective action that are familiar to social movement participants as well as the elites they challenge (Tarrow, 2006). New forms are introduced from time to time, and they spread quickly if they are successful. In the United States, for example, marches on Washington have come to be standard fare in collective action, and activist groups exchange information on the logistics of organizing such a march. On the other hand, the sit-down strike is no longer as common as it once was, although university students in the living wage movement have brought it back in the form of sit-in strikes in recent years (Gourevitch, 2001; McAdam, 1996b). Contemporary social movements draw power from the large selection of forms of collective action currently in the cultural stock, and many movements have wisely used multiple forms of action (della Porta & Diani, 2006; Tarrow, 2006). As noted in Case Study 8.3, the living wage movement has made use of lobbying, postcard campaigns, door-knocking campaigns, leafleting, rallies, sit-ins, workshops, newspaper ads, and advocacy videos.

The repertoire of collective action is handed down, but there is some improvisation by individual movements. For example, public marches are a standard part of the repertoire, but there have been innovations to the march in recent years, such as closing rallies and the incorporation of theatrical forms. Participants in the global justice movement are using some long-standing action forms such as petitions, reports and press releases, sit-ins, marches, lobbying, blockades, and boycotts. They are also using recent action innovations as well as developing new action forms. Their repertoire includes concerts, vigils, theatrical masks, puppets, electronic advocacy, documentaries, and "buycotts" (active campaign to buy the products) of fair trade products. Computer technology is being used in two new forms of disruptive action. *Net striking* is an action form in which a large number of people connect to the same website at a prearranged time. This jams the site and makes it impossible for other users to reach the site. *Mailbombing* is an action form in which large numbers of e-mails are sent to a web address or a server until it overloads (della Porta & Diani, 2006).

Just as social movement goals fall on a continuum from reform to revolution, forms of collective action can be arranged along a continuum from conventional to violent. Nonviolent forms of collective action are the core of contemporary U.S. movements. Nonviolent disruption of routine activities is today considered the most powerful form of activism in the United States and in other Western democracies with relatively stable governments (della Porta & Diani, 2006). The power of nonviolent disruption is that it creates uncertainty and some fear of violence, yet provides authorities in democratic societies with no valid argument for repression. Violent collective action, on the other hand, destroys public support for the movement. Dr. Martin Luther King, Jr., was ingenious in recognizing that the best path for the U.S. civil rights movement was "successfully courting violence while restraining violence in his followers" (McAdam, 1996b, p. 349). Consequently, it was the police who lost public favor for their brutality, not the demonstrators.

Some action forms, such as marches, petitions, and Net strikes, are used to demonstrate numerical strength. Other action forms, such as conferences, concerts, documentaries, and buycotts of fair trade

products, are used to bear witness to the substantive issues. Still other action forms are designed to do damage to the parties reputed to be at blame for an unfair situation. Small-scale violence does this, as do boycotts. Not only do these latter action forms run the risk of escalating repression and alienating sympathizers, boycotts run the risk of damaging workers (della Porta & Diani, 2006).

In an interesting development, a new organizing tactic has been used in peace and justice campaigns. The proponents of this tactic call it "creative play." They argue that "changing entrenched systems of oppression requires shifts in emotional as well as intellectual attitudes" (Shephard, 2005, p. 52). Furthermore, "culture-poems, songs, paintings, murals, chants, sermons, quilts, stories, rhythms, weavings, pots, and dances can make such emotional and visceral breakthroughs possible" (Si Kahn, quoted in Shephard, 2005, p. 52). Paul Bartlett suggests that "Performance with humor can disarm fear. When we laugh, we can listen, we can learn. . . . When people participate in a play, opportunities for new perspectives and transformation emerge" (quoted in Shepherd, 2005, p. 55).

Emerging Perspectives on Social Movements

Some social movement scholars have suggested that the three dominant perspectives discussed above, political opportunities, mobilizing structures, and cultural framing, fail to attend to some important dimensions of social movements. Two emerging perspectives are discussed here.

First, Deborah Gould (2004) argues that social movement researchers should take another look at the role of emotions in motivating people to participate in social movement activities. She contends that the social movement literature has fallen short by attending to rationality but not emotions of movement participants. She applauds the rejection of earlier attempts to understand social movement actors in terms of psychopathologies but suggests that social movements are passionate political processes and emotions must be considered. She proposes that social movement researchers should study the role that emotions such as anger, indignation, hope, and pride play in motivating social movement involvement. She recounts her own qualitative research with lesbians and gays who participate in the movement called ACT UP, noting the important role that grief and anger about AIDS and the slow response to it played in moving participants to action.

When reconsidering the living wage campaign, it seems that Gould has a point. Certainly, it appears that Greg Halpern was touched emotionally as well as intellectually by the stories he heard from workers at Harvard. The divinity students who participated in the vigil chanted, "Where's your horror? Where's your rage?" Perhaps they were thinking that such strong emotions move people to action. We know that the religious leaders who started the action in Baltimore were angry at the plight of the working poor. This raises an important question for social movement leaders: Should they appeal to both emotional and intellectual understanding of injustice? If so, what are the best methods to do this? These are the questions that Gould recommends that social movement researchers investigate.

Second, Richard Flacks (2004) suggests that the literature on resource mobilization has failed to consider the fundamental differences in the way that different members participate in social movements. He asserts that there may be very different explanations for the participation of leaders, organizers, and mass participants. He thinks we should be more interested in why some people come to see societal change as a major priority in their lives while others don't, and he suggests that social movement scholars should study the biographies of activists to learn more about that. Studs Terkel was an activist, not a social movement scholar, but he was interested in exactly the same question that Flacks raises. For his book *Hope Dies Last* (2003), he interviewed 55 activists about what motivated them to activism. As the title of the book indicates, he found hope to be a major motivator.

From another perspective, Robert Putnam (2000) notes that many people are participating at a very superficial level in contemporary social movements, responding to direct mail campaigns with a one-time contribution but making no greater commitment to the cause. Putnam argues that this type of involvement in social movements fails to build the social capital that is built in grassroots coalitions like those driving the living wage movement. There are, indeed, different ways to participate in social movements, and social movement leaders need to understand the different motivations involved.

Critical Thinking Questions 8.3

Think of a social justice issue that you have some passion about. How would you talk about this issue in terms of social justice? How global is the issue? How open is the political system (in the United States or internationally) to social action about the issue? What existing networks might be available to organize reform efforts regarding this issue? Think of two to three cultural frames that would motivate people to engage in collective action on this issue?

Implications for Social Work Practice

Several principles for social work action are recommended by this discussion of formal organizations, communities, and social movements:

- Be alert to the influence of formal organizations on the client's behavior. Be particularly alert to the ways in which the social service organization where you work, as well as other social service organizations to which you frequently refer clients, influences the client's behavior.
- Develop an understanding of the organizational goals of the social service organization where you work and how the tasks that you perform are related to these goals.

- Develop an understanding of the shared meanings in the social service organization where you work and of the processes by which those meanings are developed and maintained.
- Develop an understanding of the social, political, economic, cultural, and technological environments of the social service organization where you work.
- Be informed about the communities you serve; learn about their readiness to change, their spatial arrangements (for territorial communities), their cultures, their patterns of internal and external relationships, their social capital, and their conflicts.
- Where appropriate, strengthen interaction within the community (horizontal linkages) to build a sense of community and maximize the use of internal resources. Strengthen intercommunity interactions (vertical linkages) to ensure there are adequate resources to meet the community's needs.
- Where appropriate, collaborate with others to challenge exploitation and oppression in communities. Use consciousness-raising tactics to help oppressed groups understand their situations.
- Where appropriate, assist communities to negotiate differences and resolve conflicts.
- Become skillful in assessing political opportunities for social reform efforts.
- Become skillful in recognizing and mobilizing formal and informal networks for social reform activities.
- Become skillful in developing cultural frames that legitimate and motivate collective action.
- Assist social workers in the traditional social welfare institution to recognize the important role that reform social movements play in identifying new or previously unrecognized social injustices and social service needs.

Key Terms

bonding social capital
bridging social capital
bureaucracy
collective efficacy
community
countermovement
critical perspective on organizations
cultural framing (CF) perspective
    on social movements

defensive social movement
formal organization
interpretive perspective on
    organizations
mobilizing structures (MS)
    perspective on social movements
offensive social movement
political opportunities (PO)
    perspective on social movements

rational perspective on
    organizations
relational community
sense of community
social capital
social movements
systems perspective on
    organizations
territorial community

Active Learning

1. In Case Study 8.1 at the beginning of the chapter, you read about the transition in leadership at Beacon Center. You have also read about four theoretical perspectives on formal organizations. Imagine that you, and not Helen Blue, succeeded Martha Green as executive director at Beacon Center. What vision would you have for Beacon Center? What would you want to keep the same as it had been and what would you want to change? Use theory to back up your position.

2. You have read about two communities with geographical properties, one based in Rome and one based in Los Angeles. Now think about your own geographic community. Compare and contrast it with the communities of Filipina domestic workers in Rome and in Los Angeles according to the following characteristics:

   a. Sense of community

   b. Physical environment

   c. Horizontal and vertical linkages

3. In this chapter, I suggested that successful social movements often open the way for countermovements. I also suggested that social movements may be either offensive or defensive. In considering these ideas, it is helpful to look at two social movements that hold competing views on issues related to women. Go to the websites of the National Organization for Women (NOW) at www.now.org and the National Right to Life Committee (NRLC) at www.nrlc.org. Study carefully the positions that each of these social movement organizations takes on the issue of abortion. What language and symbols does each organization use for framing the issue?

Web Resources

ARNOVA

www.arnova.org

Site presented by the Association for Research on Nonprofit Organizations and Voluntary Action (ARNOVA), contains member directory, conference information, publications, partners, and links.

Association for Community Organization and Social Administration (ACOSA)

www.acosa.org

Site includes recent paper presentations, hot topics, important news about community organizing, and links to other Internet sites.

Center on Nonprofits & Philanthropy

www.urban.org/nonprofits/index.cfm

Site maintained by the Center on Nonprofits & Philanthropy at the Urban Institute, contains fact sheets, state profiles, resources, and databases.

Critical Social Work

www.criticalsocialwork.com

Site organized at the University of Windsor in Ontario, Canada, is an international, interdisciplinary e-journal whose goal is to promote dialogue about methods for achieving social justice.

The National Community Action Foundation (NCAF)

www.ncaf.org

Site maintained by NCAF, an advocacy group for community action agencies, contains news, events, and current issues.

National Organizers Alliance (NOA)

www.noacentral.org

Site maintained by NOA, a nonprofit organization with the mission to advance progressive organizing for social, economic, environmental, and racial justice, contains information about national gatherings, a job bank, a newsletter, a calendar of events, and links to other activist organizations.

New Organizing Institute (NOI)

www.neworganizing.com

Site maintained by NOI, a grassroots program that trains young political organizers for progressive campaigns, contains information about training programs, internships, and jobs as well as a blog.

CHAPTER 9

Small Groups and Families

Elizabeth P. Cramer

Elizabeth D. Hutchison

Opening Questions

People find themselves a part of many different formal and informal small groups during their lifetimes. What theoretical perspectives are available to help social workers understand and make use of small groups to promote individual and group well-being?

What theoretical perspectives are available to help social workers understand family life and provide avenues for positive changes in families?

Key Ideas

As you read this chapter, take note of these central ideas:

1. Small groups and families play important roles in human lives.

2. Small groups are typically defined as collections of individuals who interact with each other, perceive themselves as belonging to a group, are interdependent, join together to accomplish a goal or fulfill a need through joint association, and are influenced by a set of rules and norms.

3. Social work practitioners work with a variety of types of small groups to enhance the lives of individuals and improve social conditions, including therapy, mutual aid, psychoeducational, self-help, and task groups.

4. Small groups vary in structure, composition, and process.

5. To understand small group processes, social workers may draw on psychodynamic theory, symbolic interaction theory, status characteristics and expectation states theory, exchange theory, and self-categorization theory.

6. How we define family shapes our view of family membership and our approach to working with different types of families. In this chapter, we use the following definition: "a social group of two or more persons, characterized by ongoing interdependence with long-term commitments that stem from blood, law, or affection" (Baxter & Braithwaite, 2006, p. 2).

7. A number of theoretical "lenses" for understanding families have been proposed, including the psychodynamic perspective, family systems perspective, family life cycle perspective, feminist perspective, family stress and coping perspective, and family resilience perspective.

8. Social workers encounter a diversity of family structures in their work with families, including nuclear families, extended families, cohabiting heterosexual couples, couples with no children, lone-parent families, stepfamilies, same-sex partner families, and military families. Family structure is influenced by economic and cultural patterns, as well as immigration status.

CASE STUDY 9.1

Terry's Support Group

As she drove to a meeting of her Wednesday night support group, Terry popped a Melissa Etheridge CD into the player. A year ago, she would have barely recognized the singer's name. Now she listens to her music incessantly. But much more has changed in Terry's life these past several months. Last year at this time, she was married—to a man. Terry and Brad had an amiable 2-year marriage, but Terry had felt a sense of loneliness and discomfort throughout their marriage. She loved Brad, but could not commit to him deep in her heart. She also felt an unhappiness beyond her marriage to Brad. Terry realized she had to discover what was contributing to her unhappiness. After some serious soul-searching, she joined a support group run for women much like her. The group members have gradually learned much of Terry's history.

In sixth grade, Terry was inseparable from her best friend, Barb. Barb and Terry shared a similar family background—White, middle class, Protestant—and shared many of the preteen rites of passage together: starting menstruation, kissing boys for the first time, being picked on as the youngest children in the middle school, and wearing shirts that show your belly button. Barb loved Terry and Terry loved Barb in that very special way that best friends do.

One night when Terry was sleeping over at Barb's house, Barb suggested that they play the dating game. Terry had played the game before at a boy–girl party. The lights go out, and the boys pair up with the girls to plan a make-believe date. At Barb's house, when Terry protested because there were no boys to play the game with them, Barb suggested that they could switch off playing boys and girls. So Terry and Barb enacted the date themselves, including a long good-night kiss. That was the first and last time Barb and Terry played the dating game. They did not discuss this incident ever again.

Terry went through her preteen and adolescent years dating boys and imagining the kind of guy she might marry. In college, Terry had another sexual experience with a female. She had been at a party with some friends where heavy drinking occurred. The group of friends with whom she went to the party decided to spend the night at the home of the hostess instead of trying to drive home drunk. Bed space was sparse, so beds needed to be shared. Terry and Patricia shared a twin-size bed in a private room. The two women crawled into bed and giggled about the fact that the two of them were sharing this tiny space. The giggling turned into tickling, and the tickling turned into kissing and touching. The next morning, Terry blamed this sexual experience on the alcohol.

After college, Terry worked as a loan officer in a bank. A few years into her job, at age 26, she met Brad. After several relationships with men, she was ready to leave the dating scene. Brad and Terry developed a close relationship quickly and were engaged within 9 months of meeting each other. They bought a house, combined their possessions, and began what they both thought would be the rest of their lives together. But that scenario didn't work out.

When Terry came to the women's Coming Out Support Group for the first time, she was petrified. Beverly, a woman on Terry's softball team, promised she would meet Terry in the parking lot and they'd go together. Sure enough, Beverly was in the parking lot with a big smile and hug: "Hey, girl. You'll be all right," she told Terry. They walked to the front of the building, past the sign that read "Gay and Lesbian Community Center." (Terry was sure the sign must have been at least as big as a Ping-Pong table.) Beverly rang the doorbell and gave Terry a reassuring look. An African American woman who looked to be in her fifties answered the door: "Hi, Beverly. Nice to meet you, Terry. . . . I'm Doris. I'm so glad you could make it here tonight. Come on in."

What was so new that evening is now familiar. Terry has told the group that she looks forward to seeing the faces of those faithful members who return each week; she sympathizes with the nervousness and shyness of the new members. Each of the group members' stories is unique. The group includes bisexual women and women questioning their sexual orientation, as Terry did when first attending the group. "Temperature reading"—a review of group members' excitements, concerns, and hopes and wishes—begins each group session. Sometimes, temperature reading is short and superficial; other times, it goes on for nearly the whole meeting, with much disclosure, intensity, and sometimes crying. The facilitators, both lesbians, plan activities for each session but are flexible enough to allow the members to control the flow of the session. They share a good deal about themselves and their own coming out processes (e.g., how they came to identify themselves as lesbians and to whom they've disclosed their sexual orientation and experiences).

(Continued)

(Continued)

One of the first people in the group to befriend Terry was Kathy, another woman who had been heterosexually married. Kathy approached Terry during social time, an informal gathering after the meeting to schmooze and have refreshments. Kathy shared that she, too, had questioned her sexual orientation during the time she was married. Kathy and Terry became friends outside the group; in fact, much of Terry's current friendship network has grown out of the group. She often sees group members at gay and lesbian functions that she has begun to attend, such as the gay/lesbian theater company and the monthly women's potlucks.

Terry still feels like a "baby dyke" (a woman who has newly emerged in her lesbian identity) around her friends, most of whom have been "out" (open as lesbians/bisexuals) for much longer than she. She still has many questions about lesbian and gay culture, but she feels comfortable to ask them in the group. She has also found that she can help other women who are just beginning to come out by sharing her experiences. Sometimes she is embarrassed by the discussion in the group, however. For example, the facilitators keep an envelope marked "sex questions," where group members can anonymously submit questions about lesbian sex; the facilitators periodically read them to the group to open a discussion. The frankness of such discussions makes Terry blush sometimes, but she's glad she has a place to find answers about these things. Terry also didn't realize some of the differences between the predominantly White lesbian community and the Black lesbian community, and has now learned from her friends about some of the issues faced by African American lesbians.

Terry is consistently amazed at the diversity within the group—women of different races, educational backgrounds, socioeconomic classes, disabilities, religions, and ages. Just last week, for example, seven women attended the group: three African Americans, two women who self-identify as bisexual, one who identifies herself as disabled, one woman who is Jewish, and two women who are younger than 21. How different her circle of friends has become, compared to when she and Brad were together and they socialized primarily with other White, childless, heterosexual couples.

Tonight, as she pulled into the parking lot and got out of the car, a woman pulled into the space next to her. Terry hadn't seen her before. The woman stepped out of the car and looked around nervously. Terry walked over to her: "Hi, have you been to the group before?" she asked. "No," the woman responded. "C'mon," Terry said, "I'll walk in with you." And now Terry is introducing the new woman to the rest of the group.

CASE STUDY 9.2

The Sharpe Family Prepares for Deployment

Bobby Sharpe's Army National Guard Unit is preparing for a 12-month deployment to Afghanistan, and they have been spending more than the usual 1 weekend per month in drills and training. Bobby has 2 months to help his family prepare for his deployment, and then his unit will train in Texas for 2 months before leaving for Afghanistan. This is not the first time his family has needed to prepare for Bobby's deployment to a war zone, but the preparations are more complicated this time.

Bobby Sharpe is a 36-year-old African American man who lives in a small southwestern town. He has been married to Vivian for 13 years, and they have a 12-year-old daughter, Marcie, and a 3-year-old son, Caleb, who has cerebral palsy. Back when Bobby finished high school, he served in the Army for 4 years. He received some good training, enjoyed making friends with people from diverse backgrounds, and had two tours overseas but never served in a war zone. After 4 years, he was eager to return home to be near his close-knit family. Soon after coming home, he ran into Vivian, who had grown up in his neighborhood, and they were soon spending a lot of time together. A year later, they were married, and a year after that, Marcie was born.

Bobby wasn't sure what work he could do after he left the Army, but a few months after he returned home, he got in touch with a high school friend who was working as a heating and air conditioning technician. After another technician was fired, Bobby got a job where his friend worked, and his friend helped him learn the technical aspects of the business. When Marcie was born, Vivian cared for her at home and also cared for her sister's small children while her sister, a single mother, worked. When Bobby's father had an automobile accident and had to miss work for 6 months, Bobby and Vivian provided some financial aid to Bobby's mother and younger siblings. Finances were tight, and Bobby and Vivian were afraid they would not be able to keep up with the mortgage on their house, which was a source of great pride to them. Bobby decided to join the Army National Guard to bring in some extra money. He also looked forward to the type of camaraderie he had experienced in the Army. He went to drills 1 weekend per month and took time off from work for a 2-week training each year. His unit was mobilized on two occasions to assist with floods in the state. The extra money helped to stabilize the family finances, and he enjoyed the friendships he developed, even though only one other person in his unit was from his small town. When Marcie entered public school, Vivian took a job in the school cafeteria, which allowed Bobby and Vivian to start a college fund for Marcie.

Bobby grew up in a close-knit family that included his mother and father and three younger sisters, as well as a maternal grandmother who lived with them. Several aunts, uncles, and cousins lived nearby. Both parents were hardworking people, and they created a happy home. Bobby's grandmother provided child care when the children were small and helped to keep the household running smoothly.

Vivian grew up a few blocks from Bobby. Her father had died in Vietnam a few months before she was born, and her mother had moved her two daughters back to the town where she had grown up. She struggled to raise her two daughters while working two jobs, with some help from her mother who lived in town but also worked two jobs. Vivian was lucky that a neighborhood couple became her godparents and played an active role in her life. This couple was never able to have children of their own, and they were happy to include Vivian in their leisure activities. Vivian often turned to them for support and encouragement, and she continues to consider them family.

During Bobby's deployment to Iraq 5 years ago, Vivian and Marcie were able to get on fine, with the love and support of Bobby's family; Vivian's mother, sister, and godparents; and Bobby's boss. They missed Bobby and worried about him, but Marcie was very good about picking up more responsibilities to help Vivian with the chores usually performed by Bobby. When the furnace broke, Bobby's boss was generous about doing the repair. One of Bobby's sisters helped Vivian juggle taking Marcie to her after-school activities and picking her up. Bobby was injured by shrapnel in his last week in Iraq and spent 2 weeks in the hospital in the nearest city when he returned home. The family and friend network took care of Marcie while Vivian juggled trips to the hospital with her work schedule.

But things are more complicated as Bobby and Vivian prepare for the impending deployment to Afghanistan. Bobby's beloved grandmother had a stroke 2 years ago and is cared for in his parents' home. His mother and father are working opposite shifts at the local nursing home so that someone is always at home to care for her. Bobby's aunts, uncles, and cousins take turns providing a few hours of care so that his mom and dad can get a break and run errands. One of Bobby's sisters stayed in the city after she completed college and has a busy life there. Another sister, a single mother of a 2-year-old daughter, is serving in the Army in Iraq. Her daughter has

(Continued)

(Continued)

been living with Bobby and Vivian while she is deployed. Caleb is the joy of the family, but he requires extra care. Vivian's mother has moved in with Bobby and Vivian and cares for Caleb and the 2-year-old niece during the day while Vivian works, and then turns their care over to Vivian so that she can do a 6-hour shift caring for an older woman with dementia. Work has been very slow for Bobby lately, and his boss has talked about closing the business down and retiring, so there is some anxiety about whether he will have work when he returns from Afghanistan. To help stabilize the family finances, Vivian recently accepted the offer to take a supervisory position in the school department's lunch program. She is excited about the new responsibilities but also concerned about whether the added stress is manageable in this time of great family upheaval. She is especially concerned about monitoring Marcie's after-school activities now that she is approaching adolescence. Her godparents have promised to help with that, just as they did for Vivian during her adolescent years. Vivian has heard that the National Guard has family support groups, but there is nothing in the small town where she lives.

As you can see in these two case studies, small groups and families both play significant roles in our lives. The coming out support group provided much-needed support and information as Terry made a difficult decision about her personal life; it also gave her the opportunity to begin to build a new social network as she lost contact with the heterosexual couples with whom she and Brad had socialized together. It appears that the group may be serving as family for Terry in this phase of her life. Family is supremely important to Bobby and Vivian Sharpe, and to their extended family, in good times and bad. The National Guard family support groups are valuable resources for many families facing deployment to war zones, but that is a resource that will not be available to Vivian Sharpe.

SMALL GROUPS AND SOCIAL WORK

Most of us become involved in many types of small groups: friendship groups, task groups at work, self-help groups, or sports teams, to name but a few. In a mobile society, where family members may live in different parts of the country and community gathering places (such as a community center) may be

Humanistic perspective

few, small groups serve a useful function. They offer individuals an opportunity to meet others and work together to achieve mutual goals. Exhibit 9.1 shows how group members may benefit from belonging to a small group. Groups may provide the social support, connection, and healing that various persons (such as neighbors) or institutions (such as houses of worship) did in the past (Specht & Courtney, 1994). In the words of Specht and Courtney, identifying with a group is one way that people can "try to find a sense of purpose or meaning" in life (p. 48). In the hustle and bustle of everyday lives, the warmth and sense of "realness" of a productive and healthy group is inviting. Robert Putnam (2000) suggests that in our rapidly changing globalized society, small groups are an important source of *social capital*, or connections among individuals based on reciprocity and trustworthiness.

Small groups may be formally defined in a number of ways, but there is general agreement that small groups are more than a collection of individuals who may have similar traits or be in physical proximity. Persons who live on the same block may be in close proximity but have little social interaction and may not perceive themselves as a group. Thus, we may define a **small group** as a collection of individuals who interact with each other, perceive themselves as belonging to a group, are interdependent, join together to

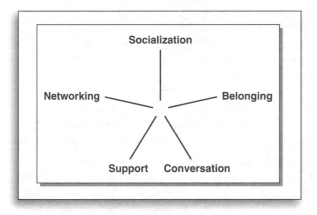

accomplish a goal or fulfill a need, and are influenced by a set of rules and norms (D. W. Johnson & Johnson, 1994).

A significant element of social work practice today is **group work,** which serves people's needs by bringing them together in small groups. Group work emerged in the United States in the late 1800s and early 1900s.

Social behavioral perspective

Early group work took place within the settlement houses, YMCA/YWCAs, Jewish community centers, and the Boy Scouts and Girl Scouts. These groups focused primarily on recreation, social integration, immigration issues, character building, and social reform. We are now seeing a resurgence in recreation and social skill–building groups, reminiscent of early group work. Social skills groups with elementary-age children (LeCroy, 1992), hoops (basketball) groups with adolescent males (Pollio, 1995), physical activity and reminiscence and motivation groups for older adults (S. Hughes et al., 2005; Link, 1997) are three examples.

Today, groups are viewed as a financially prudent method of service delivery (S. Hurdle, 2001; Roller, 1997). In addition, empirical studies have shown the effectiveness of groups in addressing a number of social, health, and emotional problems, such as mental illness (Yalom, 1995) and cancer (Spiegel & Classen, 2000). One researcher (K. Garrett, 2004)

found that a small sample of school social workers make extensive use of group work methods.

A number of scholars have established classifications for groups encountered in social work (see, e.g., Corey & Corey, 2006; Kottler & Englar-Carlson, 2010; Toseland & Rivas, 2009). Exhibit 9.2 compares five types of groups (therapy groups, mutual aid groups, psychoeducational groups, self-help groups, and task groups) on several major features of small groups—purpose, leadership, size of membership, duration—and gives examples of each. Groups may not fall exclusively into one category; rather, they may share elements of several group types. For example, a group for parents and friends of seriously mentally ill persons may include psychoeducational material about the nature of mental illness and its impact on family members, provide mutual aid to its members through discussion of taboo areas, and offer a therapeutic component in the examination of family patterns and dynamics.

Any of the above group types can and have utilized technology, either as the primary format for running the group or as a supplement to a group that meets face-to-face. For example, use of telephone technology in agency-led groups has been recommended for persons who have transportation challenges (such as in rural areas or locales without public transportation systems), persons with disabilities, people with financial limitations who cannot afford to travel to a location for a group, and those who lack time or child care (Mallon & Houtstra, 2007). Computer technology offers several potential support group outlets including chat rooms, news groups, videoconferencing, and discussion forums. Yet studies have shown that social workers express some discomfort with facilitation of groups that utilize telephone and computer technology (Galinsky, Schopler, & Abell, 1997). Based on their experience leading telephone-based groups for patients who are survivors of brain injury, spinal cord injury, and stroke, Mallon and Houtstra note that the skills needed to lead such groups do not differ from the skills required for face-to-face group facilitation. The skills need to be *altered* for

Exhibit 9.2 Types of Groups

Type of Group	Main Purpose	Leadership	Typical Number of Members	Duration	Examples
Therapy	Uses group modality to assist individuals to resolve emotional and behavioral problems	Typically led by a trained clinician or psychotherapist	Typically small in size; sometimes six or fewer members	Brief therapy groups usually meet for 6 weeks or less. Long-term psychotherapy groups can last years.	Groups for college students run by university counseling centers; groups for male adolescents who engage in sexual harm
Mutual Aid	Uses mutual aid processes to create a helping environment within the group milieu	Typically led by a facilitator who may be a professional or a layperson trained to lead the group. The leader may or may not have experienced the issue on which the group is focused.	These groups may be small (less than 5 persons) or large (12 or more), especially if run in a drop-in format.	Drop-in mutual aid groups may be ongoing for a number of years with members coming in and out of the group. Time-limited mutual aid groups typically run for between 4 and 12 weeks.	Groups for cancer survivors; groups in schools for children whose parents are going through a divorce
Psycho-educational	Focuses on the provision of information about an experience or problem	Typically led by a trained professional who is knowledgeable about the subject	Limiting the group size is usually not as critical with these types of groups because of their purpose.	One-time meetings of psychoeducation groups may be offered on a regular schedule; they might be offered in a series of sessions (e.g., a 4-week educational series); or they might be offered on an as-needed basis.	Groups for couples preparing to adopt a child; groups to teach parents how to use adaptive equipment for children with disabilities
Self-Help	Uses the commonality of the problem or issue to build social support among members	Typically led by a layperson who has experience with the problem (e.g., a person in recovery from alcohol and drug addiction)	Typically, since self-help groups operate on a drop-in basis, the group size is not limited.	Most often, self-help groups are run on a drop-in basis; however, some self-help groups may be offered in a time-limited format.	Twelve-step groups (e.g., Alcoholics Anonymous, Adult Children of Alcoholics, Narcotics Anonymous)
Task	Created to accomplish a specific task or to advocate around a particular social issue or problem	These groups may be led by professionals or nonprofessionals; leaders may be appointed or elected.	Often limited in size to successfully accomplish the task. When advocating for change, membership may be larger.	Meet until the task has been accomplished or the desired social change has been accomplished	A committee to examine low-income housing needs that is instructed to submit a report of their findings to the city council

Photo 9.1 Therapy group—Members in therapy groups share experiences and obstacles they have encountered. Through openness and self-disclosure, members feel supported and encouraged.

telephone group work, however. For example, group leaders may need to inquire more about silences and the feelings that participants may be experiencing because of the inability to observe group members' nonverbal cues. According to the Association for the Advancement of Social Work with Groups' publication, *Standards for Social Work Practice With Groups* (2005), when utilizing technology for group work, "issues such as member interaction, decision making, group structure, mutual aid, and, particularly, confidentiality are of vital concern" (p. 26).

It is also important to remember that there are a considerable number of persons who do not own a telephone or have a computer with private Internet access. According to the U.S. Census Bureau, about 62% of U.S. households have Internet access in their homes (cited in M. Martz, 2009). Those with a college education and Caucasians and Asians have the highest home Internet use. Those who are in the top three quarters of earnings in the United States are also more likely to have a home Internet connection, while persons living below the poverty level tend to use the Internet at public centers such as libraries (M. Martz, 2009). Computer and Internet use among persons with disabilities also significantly lags behind those without disabilities (Kaye, 2000). Thus, social service organizations that are considering Internet-based group intervention should assess whether their client population would have private access to the Internet as well as the technological skills to benefit from web-based groups.

Some people enjoy the anonymity of web-based groups. In some of these groups, the use of pseudonyms and the withholding of other identifying information are appealing for persons who desire support but don't want to feel too vulnerable. Social workers who refer clients to web-based groups may want to discuss the potential negative consequences of using such groups. For example, because of the anonymity of the site, participants may engage in hostile or bullying behavior to an extent that they would not do in person. A good group moderator will intervene in such behavior. Also, *cyberstalking* is another danger for those who desire to participate in web-based groups (Hitchcock, 2006).

SMALL GROUP STRUCTURE, COMPOSITION, AND PROCESSES

Terry's coming out group serves a variety of functions. However, that one group cannot provide for all of Terry's needs. She also belongs to a group of friends with whom she attends social functions, a group of coworkers, and a softball team. Each group plays a unique part in Terry's life. For example, the softball team provides an outlet for competition and team building, and the work group offers a context for achievement and accomplishment. But there is much variation among these groups in structure, composition, and processes.

Group structures can be categorized along three dimensions:

1. *How they develop.* Some groups are formed specifically to meet a defined purpose. Other groups develop spontaneously based on friendship, physical location, or some naturally occurring event (K. E. Reid, 1997).

2. *How long they last.* Some groups have a set time for termination, while other groups have no defined endpoint.

3. *How they determine membership.* Some groups permit the addition of new members throughout the group's life. Other groups limit the size of the group at the outset and do not add new members once the group is formed.

Another important element of small groups is their composition—the types of people who are members. Some groups are welcoming of a wide range of member characteristics, and other groups are more exclusive in member selection. Groups vary in the degree of heterogeneity/homogeneity among the membership, along dimensions such as age, race, sexual orientation, gender, level of education, coping style, religion, socioeconomic status, disabilities, and problem areas or strengths.

One important variable related to group composition is **group cohesiveness**—group identity, commitment, and sense of belonging. Groups that are cohesive tend to have higher rates of attendance, participation, and mutual support. But cohesiveness does not mean the absence of conflict or dislike among group members. Even a cohesive group may sometimes experience bickering, frustration, or alienation. It is important for group leaders to try to prevent heterogeneous groups from splitting into coalitions that are not committed to the interest of the whole group (T. Jones, 2005). Some groups may develop rituals or habits to increase cohesiveness among members.

To be effective, group workers need tools for understanding the group processes in which they participate. *Group processes* are those unique interactions between group members that result from being in a group together. How people behave in groups is of interest to us because we spend much of our time in groups, and groups have a strong influence on our behaviors.

THEORIES OF SMALL GROUP PROCESSES

The fields of social psychology and sociology have been in the forefront of empirical research on group processes. Five of the major theories of group processes are discussed in this section: psychodynamic theory, symbolic interaction theory, status characteristics and expectation states theory, exchange theory, and self-categorization theory. Each one helps us understand, among other things, the emotions involved in group interactions, group culture, and why and how certain members of a group develop and maintain more power than other members to influence the group's activities.

Psychodynamic Theory and Small Groups

You were introduced to the psychodynamic theoretical perspective in Chapter 2. When applied to small groups, **psychodynamic theory** "focuses on the relationship between the emotional unconscious processes and the

| Psychodynamic perspective |

Photo 9.2   Mothers support group—Here, mothers join together to share stories, struggles, and insights about the adjustment of becoming a parent.

rational processes of interpersonal interaction" (P. McLeod & Kettner-Polley, 2005, p. 63). It is assumed that understanding the emotional processes in the group is essential for accomplishing the group's task. The psychodynamic theoretical perspective is especially important to therapy groups where understanding emotional processes is the central task of the group, but some group leaders argue that it is an important perspective for increasing the effectiveness of any type of group. Small groups can be frustrating because we want to belong but they also arouse our fears about social acceptance and social competence (Geller, 2005).

McLeod and Kettner-Polley (2005) identify three broad assumptions of psychodynamic theory for understanding small groups.

1. Emotional, unconscious processes are always present in every group.

2. Emotional, unconscious processes affect the quality of interpersonal communication and task accomplishment.

3. Group effectiveness depends on bringing emotional, unconscious processes to group members' conscious awareness.

Group leaders in a psychodynamic therapy group would look for opportunities to assist group members in identifying how their interactions within the group may mirror their patterns of interactions with others outside of group; in other words, the group experience becomes a microcosm of members' lives outside group. For example, a female group member who tends to defer to the opinions of male group members and who is afraid to confront them may be demonstrating a general theme in her life of being intimidated by males because of childhood experiences of severe physical abuse by her father.

Symbolic Interaction Theory and Small Groups

Symbolic interaction theory is used to understand the development of the self, but it is also used to understand what happens in small groups. According to **symbolic interaction theory,** humans are symbol-using creatures. We make meaning of the world by interacting with others through symbols—words, gestures, and objects. Some small group theorists find it helpful to think about the small group as a place where symbols are created, exchanged, and interpreted, and to think about individual and social change happening as meanings are made and changed through the use of symbols (Frey & Sunwolf, 2005). In fact, they think that a "group" is itself a symbol that is used to describe a relationship that people understand themselves to have with each other. Group members create a sense of being a "group" through their symbolic actions with each other, through their language and their behaviors over time. Groups may use such symbols as metaphors, stories, and rituals to communicate and build cohesion. In this way, they also build a culture with its own symbols and meanings. The symbols provide group identity and stimulate commitment to struggle with the tensions of group life.

The symbols used in a group, and the meaning made of those symbols, are influenced by the environments in which the group is embedded (Frey & Sunwolf, 2005). Group members are also members of other groups and bring symbolic meanings with them from these groups. This may lead to tension and conflict in the group as the group members struggle to develop shared meaning about who they are as a group, what their goals are, and how they will operate as a group.

An example of symbolic interaction within a group is a ritual developed by one of the chapter authors and a cofacilitator for a support group for incarcerated battered women. At the beginning and end of each session, the group would light five candles and recite five affirmations related to the group's theme, loving and healing ourselves: "I am worthy of a good life," "I am worthy of positive friendship," "I am a loveable person," "I desire inner healing," and "I will recognize the good things about myself and others." The lighting of the candles symbolized

bringing to awareness the inner strength and healing power of each woman in the group.

Status Characteristics and Expectation States Theory and Small Groups

Status characteristics and expectation states theory proposes that the

influence and participation of group members during initial interactions are related to their status and to expectations others hold about their ability to help the group accomplish tasks (Fisek, Berger, & Moore, 2002; Oldmeadow, Platow, Foddy, & Anderson, 2003). **Status characteristics** are any characteristics that are evaluated in the broader society as associated with competence. **Performance expectations,** or the expectations that group members have of other group members in terms of how they will act or behave in the group or how well they will perform a task, are influenced by status characteristics.

In Terry's coming out group, Beverly carries some influence. She has attended for quite a long time and is one of the core members who come to the group consistently. As an influential member, she is expected to articulate and enforce the group's rules and to assist new members in acclimating to the group. Group members expect Beverly to share her insights about the coming out process, and they perceive her as a knowledgeable person, especially when discussing issues faced by African American lesbians.

But in another setting, the color of Beverly's skin might negatively influence how she is perceived by other people. Stereotypes about African Americans may cause other people to question Beverly's interests, skills, or values. Such stereotypes are the basis of *diffuse status characteristics* whereby the power and prestige of group members are correlated with their status in the external world, regardless of their specific characteristics relative to

the task at hand. For example, if people expect that someone using a wheelchair is incapable of playing basketball for a charity fund-raiser, then they will act as if a person using a wheelchair is unable to play basketball. They may disqualify that person from playing, thereby demoralizing the individual with the disability and preventing the person from contributing to the success of the fund-raiser.

Gender is an influential diffuse status characteristic in our society, perhaps because it is so easily discerned. In mixed-gender groups, males have greater participation and influence than females (Balkwell, 1994; C. D. Garvin & Reed, 1983), and males or females with traditionally masculine personality traits are likely to exhibit more dominant behavior (Seibert & Gruenfeld, 1992). In same-sex groups,

---

Conflict perspective

---

gender is not an initial status differential; instead, members develop expectations of each other based on other status characteristics, such as education, race, or experience. Regardless of gender, a person's perceived ability also affects performance expectations. For example, a female may be perceived as incapable of handling a complex mechanical problem in a work group, but she may be able to develop influence if she shows that she can accomplish the task successfully (J. Schneider & Cook, 1995).

One assumption of status characteristics and expectation states theory is that people rely on their stereotypes in the absence of proof that those characteristics are irrelevant (Balkwell, 1994). In our example of assumptions people may make about persons using wheelchairs, the burden of proof would be on the persons using wheelchairs to demonstrate that they could indeed play basketball, thus establishing the inapplicability of others' assumptions about the disability.

Exchange Theory and Small Groups

Sometimes in coming out groups, those who have been out for the longest time have implicit power over those newly out—the "baby dykes"

Rational choice perspective

---

in a women's coming out group. A "let me show you the ropes and tell you what this is about" attitude can be used to gain power and influence over another person and to create dependency: "You need me to help you understand what you are getting yourself into." But social power can also be used in a positive way in a coming out group, as when those who have been in the lesbian community for a long time offer support and information to others with the intention of providing mutual aid. To understand power as a social commodity, we can look to exchange theory (Thibaut & Kelley, 1959; Lovaglia, Mannix, Samuelson, Sell, & Wilson, 2005), which assumes that human interactions can be understood in terms of rewards and costs.

According to **exchange theory,** social power is what determines who gets valued resources in groups and whether those resources are perceived as being distributed in a just manner. Conflicts within the group often revolve around power issues among members—those who want the power in the group, those who have power and don't want to give it up, and those who don't want others to have power over them.

Small groups are particularly vulnerable to conflicts over power because social power arises within the context of the group itself rather than being an innate quality of an individual. "Sometimes it [power] works within a relationship between two people, but often it works within the complex relationships among a set of three, four, or many more people" (Stolte, 1994, p. 173).

Power not only determines the distribution of group resources, but it also influences people's expectations of others' abilities, even when the power results from conditions such as luck and not from innate personal ability (Lovaglia, 1995). Emotion also has an impact on perceived power and influence, regardless of status. If a person has negative emotions toward a high-status person, the power of the high-status person will lessen (Lovaglia, 1995).

The exercise of social power often brings with it a concern about justice, fairness, and equality. Most of us would agree that power should not be exercised to the special benefit or detriment of some group members. However, justice is a relative rather than absolute term. Any two persons may have quite different ideas about what constitutes justice. For some, justice would be an equal distribution of resources; for others, justice would be an equitable (but not necessarily equal) distribution.

How persons evaluate the equity of a situation depends on such factors as cultural values, self-interest, the relationships between those affected, and personal characteristics (Hegtvedt, 1994). People tend to operate more from self-interest in impersonal conditions than when they have personal bonds with others. The status of the person for whom justice claims are being considered also affects the definition of justice, the perception of injustice, and the resolution of injustices. In addition, what may be perceived as fair on an individual level may be perceived as unfair when viewed from a group perspective. For example, suppose a group member is in crisis and asks for extended time in the group. The other five group members agree to give the person an extra 10 minutes because of the crisis. This extension, however, requires each group member to give up 2 minutes of his or her floor time. Giving one individual an extra 10 minutes may not seem like much, but that one action has a cost for five other group members. And what if one group member decides that he or she has a pressing issue to discuss and does not want to give up the 2 minutes? How the group would resolve this dilemma relates to its spoken and unspoken guidelines for handling matters of justice within the group.

| Conflict perspective |

Self-Categorization Theory and Small Groups

This theory builds on social identity theory, which, as discussed in Chapter 4, is a stage theory of socialization that articulates the process by which we come to identify with some social groups and develop a sense of difference from other social groups. **Self-categorization theory** expands social identity theory by suggesting that in this process, we come to divide the world into *in-groups* (those to which we belong) and *out-groups* (those to which we do not belong). We begin to stereotype the attributes of in-groups and out-groups by comparing them to each other,

with bias toward in-groups. When we encounter new group situations, we are more likely to be influenced by in-group members than by out-group members. We give more credence to those who are similar to us than to those who are different from us, particularly when situations are conflictual or unclear. Doing so is consistent with our categorization schemes, but it also helps us maintain distinctive and positive social identities (Abrams, Hogg, Hinkle, & Otten, 2005; Hogg, 2005; Oldmeadow et al., 2003). So, in this approach, we are influenced in group situations by members of our in-groups whether or not they hold high status in society.

An example of the above is Katie, a member of Terry's support group, who was raised in an Evangelical Protestant church. Katie struggled with her sexuality and what she was taught in church about homosexuality. She accompanied another group member to a Metropolitan Community Church one day and immediately "felt at home" there. She felt she had found a place where both her sexual orientation and her faith could be affirmed—a place where she could belong.

Researchers have studied the impact of both status characteristics and self-categorization on social influence in group settings, recording who agrees with whom and who defers to whom. They have found that group members are influenced by both status characteristics and social identity. More specifically, they found that group members are more highly influenced by high-status members who also belong to the in-group than by either a low-status in-group member or a high-status out-group member (Kalkhoff & Barnum, 2000).

Critical Thinking Questions 9.1

Think about a small group in which you have participated that was particularly effective. What factors do you think contributed to this effectiveness? Now, think of a small group in which you have participated that was particularly ineffective. What factors do you think contributed to this ineffectiveness? Which of the above theories help to explain the effective group? The ineffective group?

FAMILY DEFINED _____

The psychodynamic perspective on small groups suggests that the roles we play in small groups

_____
| Social constructionist |
| perspective |
_____

are roles we developed in our families of origin. We know that families are one of the key institutions in almost every society, past and present. Perhaps no other relationships contribute as much to our identity and have such pervasive influence on all dimensions of our lives as our family relationships (Floyd & Morman, 2006). Families address personal needs, but they also contribute to the public welfare by caring for each other and socializing responsible members of society (D. Newman, 2008).

Families in every culture address similar societal needs, but there are many variations in family structure, family customs, and power arrangements (D. Newman, 2008). Around the globe, families are expected to provide economic security, emotional support, and a place in society for each family member; they also fulfill the critical social roles of bearing, providing for, and socializing children and youth (Benokraitis, 2004). Families respond to these challenges in different ways, due in no small part to different cultures and different political and economic circumstances. Family situations and their access to resources differ as a function of their socioeconomic location. As suggested in Chapter 7, social, cultural, and economic globalization are changing families in the United States and around the world (Gardiner & Kosmitzki, 2008; Leeder, 2004).

So, what is a family? We were all born into some sort of family and may have created a similar or different sort of family. Take a break from reading and think about who is family to you. Who is in your family, and what functions does your family perform for you? We hear a lot of talk about family and family values, but *family* means different things to different people. Even family scholars struggle to define how family is different from other social groups. J. White and Klein (2002) argue that family differs from other social groups in degree only.

They suggest that nonfamily groups such as friend networks and coworkers often have some of the same properties as families, but usually to a lesser degree. Family research is hampered by the lack of consensus about how to define family (Baxter & Braithwaite, 2006). This lack of consensus was consistent in family science throughout the 20th century (Chibucos & Leite, 2005).

The family literature includes many different definitions of family, but the many definitions center on three ways to form a family: biologically, legally, or socially (Floyd & Morman, 2006; Lepoire, 2006). *Biologically,* family refers to people who are related by blood and are genetically bound to each other, however distantly. Examples of biological family relationships include parents, children, aunts, uncles, cousins, grandparents, and great-grandparents. Families are created *legally* by marriage, adoption, or formalized fostering. There are many ways that families can be created *socially,* by social interaction, when there is no biological or legal relationship. Sometimes neighbors, godparents, or longtime friends are considered "family." These have been called "fictive kin," but we prefer to refer to them as chosen family. Vivian Sharpe clearly thinks of her godparents as family, and it is possible that Terry (Case Study 9.1) thinks of her support group as family. Family is increasingly being created by cohabiting romantic partners of either the opposite sex or same sex. Family may also be created by informal fostering.

Different definitions of family include different configurations of biological, legal, and social relationships. Exhibit 9.3 provides a selection of definitions that have been developed by family scholars in the United States, as well as the definition used by the U.S. Census Bureau. It is very difficult to develop one definition that includes all forms of families, but family scholars have attempted to develop inclusive definitions. As you can see, the Census Bureau definition includes families formed biologically and legally, but not those that are formed socially without legal sanction. Think about what types of family would not be considered family by this definition. In contrast to the Census Bureau, the definitions of family

Exhibit 9.3 Selected Definitions of Family

Baxter & Braithwaite (2006)	A social group of two or more persons, characterized by ongoing interdependence with long-term commitments that stem from blood, law, or affection
Galvin, Bylund, & Brommel (2003)	Networks of people who share their lives over long periods of time bound by ties of marriage, blood, or commitment, legal or otherwise, who consider themselves as family and who share a significant history and anticipated future of functioning in a family relationship
Leeder (2004)	A group of people who have intimate social relationships and have a history together
Seccombe & Warner (2004)	A relationship by blood, marriage, or affection, in which members may cooperate economically, may care for any children, and may consider identity to be intimately connected to the larger group
U.S. Census Bureau (2009a)	A group of two or more people who reside together and who are related by birth, marriage, or adoption

scholars Baxter and Braithwaite (2006); Galvin, Bylund, and Brommel (2003); and Seccombe and Warner (2004) include families formed socially along with families formed biologically and legally. Leeder (2004) goes even further with a purely social definition of family. Which of these definitions is the best fit for those you call family?

How do the definitions fit for Bobby and Vivian Sharpe's family? The Census Bureau definition would certainly include Bobby, Vivian, Marcie, and Caleb as they prepare for deployment. It also can embrace Vivian's mother now that she lives in the household. Would it still include Bobby once he is deployed and not living in the household? It is clear that he and other family members will think of him as family. But what about Bobby's 2-year-old niece? Is she family? Could Vivian legally sign for permission if she needs medical care? Whom do you think Bobby, Vivian, and Marcie consider to be family? How would they define family?

For the purposes of our discussion, I will use the Baxter & Braithwaite (2006) definition: **Family**

_____

Conflict perspective

_____

is "a social group of two or more persons, characterized by ongoing interdependence with long-term commitments that stem from blood, law, or affection" (p. 2). Increasingly, we exercise the freedom to

use the word *family* to describe the social group with whom we have emotional closeness (a social definition). However, our freedom to define our own families is limited (D. Newman, 2008). We must interact with organizations that have their own definitions of family and sometimes have the power to impose those definitions on us. Local, state, and federal governments have definitions of family and also have the power to enforce those definitions when providing goods, services, and legal sanctions. Examples include legal standards about who can marry, who inherits from whom, who can benefit from filing joint tax returns, who receives survivor benefits, and who can make medical decisions for another person.

In the United States, the most contentious and public struggle over the tension between legal definitions and social definitions of family involves families formed by same-sex couples. As social workers, we should be most interested in who a person considers to be family, because that is where resources can be tapped, but we must also be alert to situations where legal definitions do not recognize a given form of family and how enforcement of those definitions impinges on the lives of particular individuals and families. This is an area that calls for social work activism.

In the United States and other Western societies, *monogamy*, or one spouse at a time, is the legal way to start a biological family. But it is estimated that 75% of the world's societies prefer some type of *polygamy*, or having more than one spouse at a time (D. Newman, 2008). Polygamy can take the form of either polygyny (one man and multiple wives) or polyandry (one woman and multiple husbands). Polyandry is much less common than polygyny, however. Polygyny is found on every continent, but is most common in Islamic countries, African countries, and parts of Asia (Gardiner & Kosmitzki, 2008). All societies allow monogamy, and, indeed, most people of the world cannot afford multiple spouses.

There are cultural variations in the process of mate selection. In most societies, mate selection is governed by both exogamy and endogamy rules. *Exogamy rules* require that mates must be chosen from *outside* the group. Most societies have either formal or informal rules prohibiting mating with specified family members, often referred to as the "incest taboo," but there are differences across cultures about which family members are prohibited. In the United States, 24 states prohibit marriage of first cousins, but 6 states allow it under some circumstances where the couple cannot reproduce, and North Carolina allows first-cousin marriage but prohibits double-cousin marriage (such as sister and brother marrying cousins who are sister and brother; National Conference of State Legislatures, 2009). There are also some informal exogamy taboos against mating with people within other groups, such as in the same university dorm (dormcest) and with people in the workplace (workcest) (D. Newman, 2008). *Endogamy rules*, on the other hand, require that mates should be selected from within the group on characteristics such as religion, race and ethnicity, and social class. Bobby and Vivian were honoring these rules when they chose each other, but endogamy rules are loosening in many places.

In the United States and other Western societies, mate selection is a culmination of romantic love, and it is often assumed that there is one true love in the world for each one of us. In many Eastern societies, marriages are arranged, and it is generally assumed that there are several possible mates with whom one can establish a successful long-term relationship. It is also assumed that parents will make wiser decisions about their children's mates than young people will make for themselves. In countries like Japan, however, love marriages are beginning to replace arranged marriages (Gardiner & Kosmitzki, 2008).

THE FAMILY IN HISTORICAL PERSPECTIVE

We often hear people lament the demise of the family. Maybe you hear this as well. To understand whether there is reality in this lament, it is necessary to place the contemporary family in historical context. This is a daunting task, however. For one thing, the family has never been a monolithic institution. The structure and functions of families always varied according to race, ethnicity, religion, sexual orientation, social class, and so on. Most of what has been written about the family historically was written from the perspective of dominant members of society. It is only since the 1960s, when the discipline of social history began to describe the lives of women and other marginalized groups, that we have a more complete understanding of the varieties of ways that families adapted to the challenges they faced in their lives. When people in the United States talk about the "golden age of the traditional family," they are typically talking about one particular group of families: White, middle-class, heterosexual, two-parent families living in the 1950s. Moreover, social historians argue that the rosy picture usually painted about this group is really something that never existed. It is important to remember that a great diversity of family structures and functions has existed in the United States and around the world over time.

For another thing, in the United States, because we are a very young country, we tend to have a very short view of history. A tracing of the history of families worldwide over longer-term

> Social constructionist perspective; conflict perspective

historical time would be the subject of multiple books. So, for the longer-term global view, we will simply note two important themes. First, it seems clear that families have adapted both their structures and their functions over time to cope with the changing nature of societies, as hunting and gathering societies gave way to horticultural societies, which gave way to agrarian societies, which gave way to industrial societies, which are giving way to postindustrial societies focused on information, services, and technology. Second, a global understanding of the family in contemporary times must take account of the effects of colonialism. As the United States and European countries exploited local people in colonized countries, family life was directly impacted in both the colonizing and colonized countries. Most recently, families have been separated as some members relocate to find work, sometimes relocating from the rural areas to the cities within their own country, and other times, moving to wealthier countries where work is more plentiful.

Any discussion of the history of the family in the United States should begin with the Native peoples who predated the White settlers from Europe. The Native peoples included over 2,000 cultures and societies, each with its own set of family customs and lifestyles (Leeder, 2004). There were some similarities across these societies, however. As with other societies, social life was organized around the family. Affection was lavished on children, and they were never spanked or beaten. There was a clear gender division of labor, with women growing crops, building homes, and caring for the home, and men hunting, fishing, and waging war. In many Native societies, women were afforded a great deal of respect and power (Colonial Williamsburg, n.d.).

The White settlers established small, privately owned agricultural enterprises, and families performed many of the functions that have since been turned over to other institutions such as hospitals, schools, and social welfare agencies. David Fischer's (1989) historical analysis found that there were regional differences in the organization of

family life among the White settlers. Between 1629 and 1775, four major waves of English-speaking immigrants settled in what became the United States of America. Each wave of immigrants came from a different part of what is now the United Kingdom and brought their own family customs with them. Family customs differed along several dimensions, including gender power arrangements, child-rearing practices, appropriate marriage partners, and nuclear versus extended family. Different attitudes about social inequality were also transmitted through the family. Subsequently, new waves of immigration increased the diversity of family customs. Fischer argues that in spite of later waves of immigration and much inter-region mobility, regional differences in family customs have endured to some degree over time.

During the industrial revolution, the economy of the United States and other newly industrializing nations shifted from the family-based economy of small, privately owned farms to a wage-based economic system of large-scale industrial manufacturing. The functions of the family changed to accommodate the changes in the economic system. In the upper and middle classes, men went out to work and women ran the household, but less advantaged women engaged in paid labor as well as family labor. By 1900, one fifth of U.S. women worked outside the home (D. Newman, 2008). The great majority of African American women engaged in paid labor, often serving as domestic servants in White households where they were forced to leave their own families and live in the employer's home. Women in other poor families took in piecework so they could earn a wage while also staying at home. Poorer families also took in boarders to assist the family financially, something that also happened in the earlier agrarian period. Schools took over education, and family life began to be organized around segments of time: the workweek and weekends, and summers off from school for children (Leeder, 2004). Rather than the center of work, the family home became a place to retreat from economic activities, and the primary role of the family was to provide emotional support to its members.

A new ideal of marriage developed, based on sexual satisfaction, companionship, and emotional support (Zimmerman, 2001). Family togetherness was never more emphasized than in the 1950s, a period of strong economic health in the United States.

Since the 1950s, personal fulfillment has become a strong value in the United States and a number of other information/service/technology societies, but the great majority of people still view loving, committed relationships to be the most important source of happiness and well-being (Kamp Dush, & Amato, 2005; C. Snyder & Lopez, 2007). Family members are often scattered across state and national lines, but the new technologies allow for continued connection. Recently, work and family time is once again comingled in many families as the new technologies allow more work from home. Unfortunately, this often means that the workday is expanded.

As the above discussion suggests, diversity of family structures is not new, but family forms have become increasingly varied in recent decades. Marriage rates and birthrates have declined, and more adults are living on their own. More children are born to unmarried parents. Divorce and remarriage are creating complex remarried families. Perhaps the biggest change in family structure in recent decades is the increase in dual-earner families, as women increased their involvement in paid labor (F. Walsh, 2006).

There is general agreement that the most pronounced change in family life in the United States in the past 50 years is the change in gender roles. By 1960, one third of all workers were women (N. Gibbs, 2009), but employers typically paid women less than men performing the same job. In addition, as the current cable TV series *Mad Men* illustrates, women were often treated in a demeaning manner at work. Females were about half as likely as males to go to college, and less than 10% of students playing high school sports were girls (N. Gibbs, 2009). When women needed surgery or other medical treatment, they often needed the signed consent from husbands or fathers. In many settings, they were not allowed to wear pants in public. (For a comprehensive review of the changes in gender roles in the United States since 1960, see G. Collins, 2009.) By 2007, women made up 47% of the labor force, and during the 2008–2009 recession, 82% of job losses affected men, resulting in women outnumbering men in the labor force by February of 2010 for the first time in U.S. history (Rampell, 2010). In 2008, on average, women earned 80% of what men earned, up from 62% in 1979, but during the recession, women were increasingly the sole support of families (E. Galinsky, Aumann, & Bond, 2009; U.S. Department of Labor, 2008). In Bobby Sharpe's family (Case Study 9.2), as in many African American families, women have always been in the paid labor force, often working more than one job. In fact, research indicates that gender roles in African American families have typically been applied flexibly to manage work and family demands.

There is evidence that attitudes about women in the labor force are changing. In 1977, 74% of men and 52% of women agreed with the statement that "men should earn the money and women should take care of the children and family"; in 2008, 42% of men and 39% of women agreed with the statement (E. Galinsky et al., 2009, p. 9). The attitudes of men in dual-earner couples have changed the most. In 2008, an estimated 26% of women in dual-earner couples had annual earnings that were at least 10% higher than the earnings of their spouses/partners. In the 2005–2006 academic year, women earned 58% of all bachelor's degrees and 60% of master's degrees (E. Galinsky et al., 2009). The rate of girls participating in high school sports is approaching that of males. In addition, women have a larger presence in the public arena, serving in leadership positions in both the private and public sectors. However, women are still underrepresented on university faculties, and in boardrooms and legislatures. They have also been charged higher insurance premiums than men, and this became a part of the debate about health care reform in 2009 (N. Gibbs, 2009). Although men are increasing their participation in child care and household labor, women still provide a larger share of this domestic work (E. Galinsky et al., 2009).

Unfortunately, business and government in the United States have been slow to respond to the changing needs of families who do not have a full-time mother at home. The Family and Medical Leave Act (FMLA) of 1993 requires employers with more than 50 employees to provide up to 12 weeks of *unpaid* sick leave per year for the birth or adoption of a child or to care for a sick child, parent, or spouse, excluding temporary and part-time workers. With the exemptions, about 40% of U.S. workers are not eligible for FMLA leave, but a good feature of the FMLA is that it covers both male and female workers (Ray, Gornick, & Schmitt, 2009). Compare this to the way that most other countries have responded to the increasing numbers of dual-earner families. One research project found that of 168 countries studied, 163 guarantee *paid* leave to women for childbirth, and 45 guarantee paid paternity leave (cited in D. Newman, 2008). The combined leave employers must provide for both mothers and fathers in the five most generous countries ranges from 18 to 47 weeks. It is important to note, however, that the number of paid leave weeks offered to fathers ranges from 2–7 in these same five countries (Ray et al., 2009).

Not all people in the United States agree that the above-noted changes in gender roles are a good trend. Certainly, around the world, there are many societies that have not embraced these changes, even though economic globalization has depended on women in poor societies working long hours in low-wage jobs (McMichael, 2008).

Critical Thinking Questions 9.2

Where have you gotten your ideas about what it means to be family? Have those ideas changed over time? If so, what influenced those changes? What beliefs do you have about appropriate gender relationships, child-rearing practices, appropriate marriage partners, and nuclear versus extended family? How might those beliefs affect your ability to work with different types of families and families facing different types of challenges?

THEORETICAL PERSPECTIVES FOR UNDERSTANDING FAMILIES

With an understanding of societal trends affecting families as background, you can use a number of theoretical "lenses" to understand family functioning and avenues for positive change. There are a number of theoretical perspectives on the family. This section introduces six of these: the psychodynamic perspective, family systems perspective, family life cycle perspective, feminist perspective, family stress and coping perspective, and family resilience perspective.

Psychodynamic Perspective and Families

Social workers who make use of the **psychodynamic perspective on families** assume that current personal and interpersonal problems are the result of unresolved problems in the **family of origin,** the family into which we were born and/or in which we were raised (Nichols & Schwartz, 2006; J. Walsh, 2010). They suggest that these unresolved problems continue to be acted out in our current intimate relationships. Patterns of family relationships are passed on from generation to generation, and intergenerational relationship problems must be resolved to improve current problems.

Psychodynamic perspective

Some social workers who employ the psychodynamic perspective draw heavily on Murray Bowen's (1978) concept of differentiation of self. Bowen suggested that there are the following two aspects of differentiation of self in the family system (see B. Carter & McGoldrick, 2005a; J. Walsh, 2010):

1. *Differentiation between thinking and feeling.* Family members must learn to own and recognize their feelings. But they must also learn to think about and plan their lives rather than reacting emotionally at times that call for clear thinking. It is assumed that many family problems are based on family members' emotional reactivity to each other.

2. *Differentiation between the self and other members of the family.* While recognizing their interdependence with other family members, individuals should follow their own beliefs rather than make decisions based on reactivity to the cues of others or the need to win approval. They should do that, however, without attacking others or defending themselves. A clear sense of self allows them to achieve some independence while staying connected to other family members.

Another key concept in the psychodynamic perspective on families is triangulation. *Triangulation* occurs when two family members (a family subsystem) inappropriately involve another family member to reduce the anxiety in the dyadic relationship. For example, if a couple is having marital problems, they may focus their energy on a child's school problems to relieve the tension in the marital relationship. The child's school problems then become the stabilizing factor in the marriage, and this problem will not improve until the parents look at their relationship problem (and the origins of it in their own families of origin). In recent years, proponents of this approach have noted that it is not always another family member that gets "triangulated in." It may be an addiction, an over-involvement in work, or an extramarital affair—all used to ease tension in a dyadic relationship.

The psychodynamic perspective has been criticized for its Anglo American emphasis on individualism versus collectivism. To some, it pathologizes the value of connectedness that prevails in some cultures. There is some merit to this criticism if the theory is misused to interpret a strong sense of familial responsibility as seen in the Sharpe family, and many ethnic minority families, to be a sign of lack of differentiation. A strong separate self is not a value in many cultures. The psychodynamic perspective can alert us, however, to any problematic triangles that emerge when the parental subsystem is expanded in times of stress, such as in a military family when one parent is deployed.

If you use a psychodynamic perspective for thinking about the Sharpe family, you might want to do a multigenerational **genogram,** or a visual representation of a family's composition and structure (see Exhibit 9.4), to get a picture of the multigenerational family's patterns of relationships. (Females are indicated by circles, males by squares; lines indicate marriages and births.) The Sharpe family genogram helps you to visualize the extended family relationships in Bobby Sharpe's family and Vivian's more limited extended family system in her family of origin. It may lead you to think about whether Bobby's impending deployment will stir unresolved grief about the loss of father and husband for Vivian and her mother, respectively.

Family Systems Perspective

A **family systems perspective** adds another lens— that of the family as a social system. As you might imagine, this approach requires a focus on relationships within the family rather than on individual family members. Persons are not thought of as individuals but as parts of overall patterns of roles and interactions (Galvin, Dickson, & Marrow, 2006). All parts of the family system are interconnected. Family members both affect and are affected by other family members; when change occurs for one, all are affected. Certainly, we can see that Bobby's deployment, as well as that of his sister, and his grandmother's stroke, affect the entire extended kinship system.

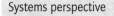
Systems perspective

From the family systems perspective, families develop boundaries that delineate who is in the family at any given time. In the Sharpe family, the boundaries have shifted over time to cope with stressors of various kinds. Among members, families develop organizational structures and roles for accomplishing tasks, commonly shared beliefs and rules, and verbal and nonverbal communication patterns (J. White & Klein, 2008d). Like all systems, family systems have subsystems, such as a parental subsystem, sibling subsystem, or parent–child subsystem. When problems occur, the focus for change is the family system itself, with the assumption that changing the patterns of interaction between and among family members will address whatever

Exhibit 9.4   Sharpe Family Genogram

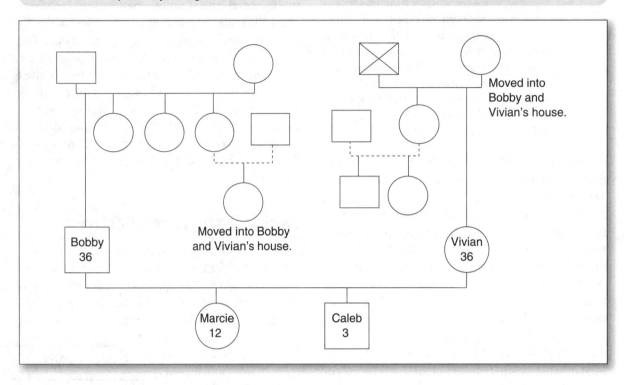

Moved into
Bobby and
Vivian's house.

Bobby
36

Moved into Bobby
and Vivian's house.

Vivian
36

Marcie
12

Caleb
3

problem first brought a family member to the attention of a social worker. Intervention may focus on helping to open communication across subsystems, on helping the family explore the stated and unstated rules that govern interactions, or on teaching members to communicate clearly with each other (Vetere, 2005; J. Walsh, 2010).

The *multilevel family practice model* (Vosler, 1996) widens the social worker's theoretical framework to include the larger systems in which the family system is embedded—including the neighborhood, the local community, the state, the nation, and the current global socioeconomic system. Thus, the multilevel model is broadly focused, acknowledging the economic, political, and cultural factors that affect resources available to the family and how family members view their current situation and future challenges. This model recognizes, as suggested in Chapter 7, that the family institution is interrelated with other social institutions—religious, political, economic, educational, social

welfare, health care, and mass media. Among other things, this perspective would call our attention to how the Sharpe family is affected by terrorism and war, the global economic meltdown, and health and social welfare policies related to elder care and children with disabilities. They are also influenced by mass media coverage of race issues and the U.S. involvement in war.

A *family ecomap* can be used to assess the way the Sharpe family is connected to larger social systems. The family ecomap uses circles, lines, and arrows to show family relationships and the strength and directional flow of energy and resources to and from the family (Hartman & Laird, 1983; see also Vosler, 1996). Ecomaps, which were discussed in Chapter 2, help the social worker and the family to identify external sources of stress, conflict, and social support. Exhibit 9.5 is an example of an ecomap for the Sharpe family. It shows that Bobby and Vivian's nuclear family has both external stressors and external resources.

Exhibit 9.5   Sharpe Family Ecomap

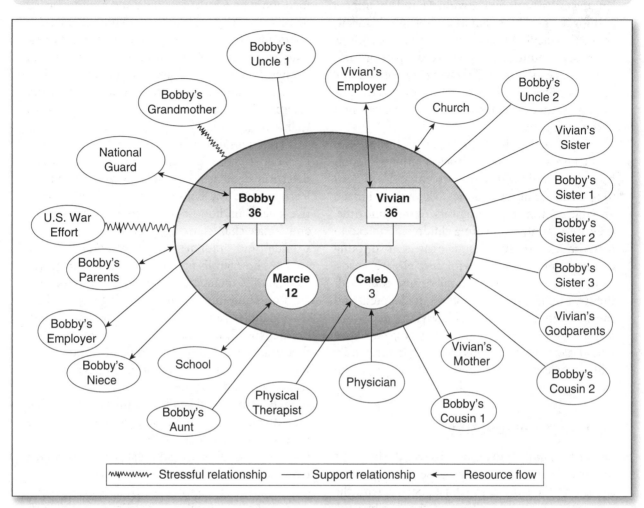

Family Life Cycle Perspective

The **family life cycle perspective** expands the concept of family system to look at families over time (B. Carter & McGoldrick, 2005c). Families are seen as multigenerational systems moving through time, composed of people who have a shared history and a shared future. Relationships in families go through transitions as they move along the life cycle; boundaries shift, rules change, and roles are constantly redefined. The family moving through time is influenced by cultural factors and by the

Developmental perspective

historical era in which they live. The family life cycle perspective proposes that *transition points,* when the family faces a transition in family life stage or in family composition, are particularly stressful for families. Such transition points are especially stressful to families with a family or cultural history of trauma or disruption. B. Carter and McGoldrick recognize that contemporary families are undergoing changes and have many forms, but they delineate six stages that many U.S. families seem to pass through: single young adults, new couples, families with young children, families with adolescents, families launching children and moving on, and families in later life. Each of these stages involves normative changes and challenging tasks, both for individual family members and for the family system as a whole. In this view, change is inevitable in families, and transitions offer opportunities for positive adaptation and growth. The identified life stages may not fit many of the families in today's society, however, including divorced and remarried families and families without children.

From the family life cycle perspective, we can see that Bobby and Vivian's nuclear family will soon become a family with an adolescent and will need to open the family boundaries to allow for Marcie's growing relationships with peers. At the same time, they are a family with young children and need to focus inward to ensure adequate care for two young children, including one with special care needs. This is happening as the family must cope with the stressful transition of Bobby's deployment and the stress that will come with Vivian's new work responsibilities. The family life cycle perspective would alert us to the possibility that the family will struggle under the pressure of these stressful transitions.

Feminist Perspective

Unlike the family systems perspective, the **feminist perspective on families** proposes that families should not be studied as whole systems, with the lens on the family level, because such attention results in failure to attend to patterns of domination, subjugation, and oppression in families (Chibucos & Leite, 2005). As suggested in Chapter 2, the focus of the feminist perspective is on how patterns of domination in major social institutions are tied to gender, with women devalued and oppressed. When applied to the family, the feminist perspective proposes that gender is the primary characteristic on which power is distributed and misused in the family (K. Allen, Lloyd, & Few, 2009). Although the Sharpe family, like many African American families, has relatively egalitarian approaches to

Conflict perspective

enacting gender roles, they live in a world that gives men more power than women and are influenced by that bias. Men and women are both involved in nurturing care, but women are considered the primary caregivers. Bobby and Vivian have nieces and nephews whose fathers have taken no responsibility for their children, leaving the mothers to take full responsibility for their economic and emotional well-being.

The feminist perspective makes a distinction between sex and gender: Sex is biologically determined, but gender is socially constructed and learned from the culture. The feminist perspective questions how society came to assign male and female characteristics; seeks understanding of women's and children's perspectives on family life; analyzes how family practices create advantages for some family members and disadvantages for others; raises questions about caregiving responsibilities in families; and questions why the state should decide who should marry and receive a range of financial, legal, and medical rights (Wood, 2006). It argues that a diversity of family forms should be recognized and that the strengths and weaknesses of each form should be thoughtfully considered. It calls attention to the family as a site of both love and trauma (K. Allen et al., 2009). Although gender is the starting point of the feminist perspective, most feminist theories focus on disadvantage based on other characteristics as well, including race, ethnicity, social class, sexuality, age, religion, nationality, and ability status (S. Lloyd, Few, & Allen, 2009).

The feminist perspective includes a variety of feminist theories—we should speak of *feminisms*, not feminism—such as liberal, radical, interpretive, critical, cultural, and postmodern feminism. These different varieties of feminism may disagree on important issues. For example, liberal feminists support the inclusion of women in all military positions, because of their focus on equality of opportunity, while the cultural feminists oppose women in the military because they see the valuing of life and nurturing, rather than destroying, as a central part of female culture (J. White & Klein, 2008b). Bobby Sharpe's sister who is in the U.S. Army in Iraq does not consider herself a feminist, but she has been among the many women who are taking advantage of career opportunities in the military.

The emerging **intersectionality feminist theory**, which was discussed in Chapter 2, is consistent with the multidimensional approach proposed in this book. Feminists of color introduced the concept of *intersectionality* to challenge the idea that gender is a monolithic category (P. H. Collins, 2000). They suggested that no singular category is sufficient to understand social oppression, and categories such as gender, race, and class intersect to produce different experiences for women of various races and classes. Bobby Sharpe's sister could probably embrace this version of feminist theory, based on the observation that her e-mails from Iraq often include musings about what she is learning about how different her life experiences and life chances have been from other women in her unit, both White women and other African American women. She has also been shocked at the level of sexual harassment and sexual violence she is finding in the military.

Intersectionality theory has also been used to look at other intersections in women's lives—for example, those related to sexuality, religion, disability, age, and nationality. From this perspective, a person may experience oppression based on gender or some other attribute, but also experience privilege based on a different attribute. Some people may experience oppression related to several social categories. Intersectionality theory is being expanded to consider transnational contexts, considering the consequences for women of colonialism and capitalism (K. Allen et al., 2009). Intersectionality theory would call attention to the ways that Bobby Sharpe and members of his family have experienced oppression related to race. However, it would also suggest that Bobby has been able to build a middle-class life that has given him some class privilege compared to poor African American families. He also carries male privilege, heterosexual privilege, age privilege, and Christian privilege.

Family Stress and Coping Perspective

You read about theories of individual stress and coping in Chapter 4, and research on stress and coping at the individual level is incorporated into theorizing about stress and coping at the family level. The primary interest of the family stress and coping perspective is the entire family unit (S. J. Price, Price, & McKenry, 2010).

| Systems perspective; |
| Psychodynamic perspective |

The theoretical foundation of this perspective is the **ABC-X model of family stress and coping**, based on Rueben Hill's (1949, 1958) classic research on war-induced separation and reunion. It theorizes that to understand whether an event in the family system (A) becomes a crisis (X), we also need to understand both the family's resources (B) and the family's definitions (C) of the event. The main idea is that the impact of stressors on the family (the X factor) is influenced by other factors, most notably the internal and external resources available to the family and the meaning the family makes of the situation. With some updating, this theory continues to be the basis for examining family stress and coping (see Boss, 2006; S. J. Price et al., 2010).

The ABC-X model describes a family transition process following a stressful event. A period of disequilibrium is followed by three possible outcomes: (1) *recovery* to the family's previous level of functioning; (2) *maladaptation,* or permanent deterioration in the family's functioning; or (3) *bonadaptation,* or improvement in the family's functioning over and above the previous level.

| Systems perspective |

Thus, under certain circumstances, a stressor event can actually be beneficial, if the family's coping process strengthens the family in the long term. They might, for instance, come together to deal with the stressors. Vivian and Marcie Sharpe often talk about how their relationship was strengthened by the way they pulled together during Bobby's earlier deployment.

A more complex *double* ABC-X model incorporates the concept of *stress pileup* (McCubbin & Patterson, 1983). Over time, a series of crises may deplete the family's resources and expose the family to increasing risk of very negative outcomes (such as divorce, violence, or removal of children from the home). In this view, the balance of stressors and resources is an important consideration. Where there are significant numbers of stressors, positive outcomes depend on a significant level of resources being available to family members and the family as a whole. A **family timeline,** or chronology depicting key dates and events in the family's life (Satir, 1983; Vosler, 1996), can be particularly helpful in identifying times when events have piled up. Family timelines can be used to begin to identify the resources that have been tapped successfully in the past, as well as resource needs in the present. Exhibit 9.6 presents a family timeline for the Sharpe family. It suggests that there has been a recent pileup of stressors for the family; consequently, they will need a significant number of resources in the coming year to allow for continued healthy individual and family functioning.

Two types of stressors are delineated in the ABC-X model (McCubbin & Figley, 1983). *Normative stressors* are the typical family life cycle transitions, such as the birth of a first child. *Nonnormative stressors* are potentially catastrophic events, such as natural disasters, medical trauma, drug abuse, unemployment, and family violence. These nonnormative events can quickly drain the family's resources and may leave family members feeling overwhelmed and exhausted. Lower-level but persistent stress—such as chronic illness or chronic poverty—can also create stress pileup, resulting in instability within the family system and a sense of being out of control on the part of family members.

Family Resilience Perspective

The **family resilience perspective** extends the family stress and coping perspective by seeking to identify and strengthen family processes that allow families to bear up

Humanistic perspective

under and rebound from distressing life experiences. From this perspective, distressed families are seen as challenged, not damaged, and they have the potential for repair and growth (F. Walsh, 2006). In her book *Strengthening Family Resilience,* Froma Walsh draws on existing research on risk and resilience to present a family resilience model for intervention and prevention, one that focuses on the family system as the target for intervention. She defines *resilience* as "the capacity to rebound from adversity strengthened and more resourceful" (p. 4). She describes this as "bouncing forward," rather than bouncing back. She assumes that all families face adversity, but resilient families "struggle well" and experience "both suffering and courage" (p. 6). She cautions social workers to avoid the tendency to pathologize the families that they encounter in the midst of transitional distress, assessing families, instead, in the context of the situations they face, and looking for family strengths.

Froma Walsh (2006) has taken the research on risk and resilience and organized the findings into a conceptual framework for targeting interventions to strengthen core processes of family resilience, whatever form the family takes. She organizes this framework into three dimensions: family belief systems, organizational patterns, and communication processes. Each dimension is summarized below:

- *Family belief systems.* How families view problems and possibilities is crucial to how they cope with challenges. Resilient families make meaning of adversity by viewing it as a shared challenge. They find a way to hold onto a shared confidence that they can overcome the challenge. They act on this shared hope by taking initiative and persevering. They draw on a spiritual value system to see their situation as meaningful, and to imagine future possibilities.
- *Organizational patterns.* Resilient families have organizational patterns that serve as shock absorbers. They maintain flexibility in family structure and are able to make changes in roles and rules to respond to the demands of the moment, but, in the midst of change, they hold onto some rituals and routines to provide stability and continuity. Strong family leaders provide

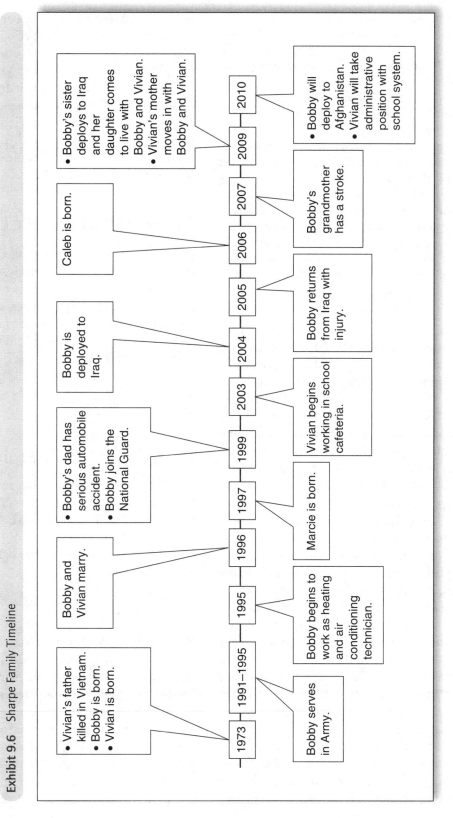

Exhibit 9.6   Sharpe Family Timeline

nurturance and protection to children and other vulnerable family members, but they also leave some room to negotiate rules and roles, based on the situation at hand, and exercise leadership with warmth. Resilient families provide mutual support and commitment while honoring individual differences. They are able to mobilize extended kin and community resources.

- *Communication processes.* Good communication is vital to family resilience. Resilient families send clear, consistent, and genuine messages. They share a wide range of feelings and show mutual empathy and tolerance for differences. They can use humor to lighten threatening situations. They also engage in collaborative problem solving, identifying problems and possible solutions, sharing decision making, and taking concrete steps.

Froma Walsh (2003b) cautions that the concept of family resilience should not be misused to blame families that are unable to rise above harsh conditions, by simply labeling them as not resilient. Just as individuals need supportive relationships to thrive, family resilience must be supported by social and institutional policies and practices that encourage the ability to thrive, such as flexible work schedules for parents and quality, affordable health care, child care, and elder care services (pp. 412–413).

The Sharpe family has weathered a number of challenges along the way: health problems, war zone deployments for Bobby and his sister, the birth of a baby with special care needs, and intense elder care needs. According to Froma Walsh's model of family resilience, they are a resilient family. They view each adversity as a shared challenge for the extended kinship network, and they move forward with confidence that they can overcome each challenge. They take the initiative to devise plans for handling difficult situations, and they draw on a deeply held faith that makes meaning of their challenges. In terms of organizational patterns, they are flexible in the assignment of roles and resourceful in mobilizing extended family care resources. They have not made similar use of community resources in the past, but they may

need to reach out more to the community during the coming highly stressful period. They communicate well for the most part, often using humor to lighten stressful situations. Vivian, her sister, and her mother might benefit from more open communication about the struggles they had after Vivian's father was killed in Vietnam. They have never been able to talk about this, and it may well play a role in Vivian's sister's clinical depression and her mother's pervasive sadness.

DIVERSITY IN FAMILY LIFE

One question that must be asked about each of the above theoretical perspectives on families is how well it applies to different types of families. As suggested earlier, diversity has always existed in the structures and functions of families, but that diversity is clearly increasing, and the reality today is that a great deal of diversity exists among families, both in the United States and globally. There is diversity in family structures, as well as economic and cultural diversity.

Diversity in Family Structures

It is difficult, if not impossible, to catalogue all of the types of family structures represented in the world's families. The discussion below is not meant to be exhaustive, but rather to overview some relatively common structures that social workers might encounter.

Nuclear Families

There is a worldwide trend toward the nuclear family structure as societies become more industrialized and more people live in urban areas where smaller families are more practical (Ballantine & Roberts, 2009). The nuclear family is an adaptation to industrialization and urbanization. Some of the White settlers to the United States preferred the extended family structure, and others preferred the nuclear family, but the nuclear family has been the preferred family structure throughout most of U.S. history. Consequently, we would expect *nuclear family* to be easy to define. Actually, the family literature presents different definitions of this family structure. Some definitions specify that the nuclear family is composed of two parents and their biological or adopted offspring (LePoire, 2006). Others specify that a nuclear family is composed of at least one parent and one child (Leeder, 2004; D. Newman, 2008). This definition would include a broader range of families, including lone-parent families and same-sex partners with children. But for the purpose of this discussion, we will use the definition that the *nuclear family* is composed of two biological parents and their biological or adopted offspring, because we think it is important to distinguish this idealized family structure from other family structures. Although, as mentioned, the nuclear family has been the preferred model throughout U.S. history, it has always been an ideal that was difficult to accomplish (Hareven, 2000). Families in colonial days and later were often marked by unplanned pregnancies and untimely death. Early parental death led to remarriage and stepfamilies, and to children being placed with extended family, or in foster care or orphanages. Non-kin boarders were brought in to provide income and companionship.

In 2007, according to the U. S. Census Bureau (2009a), 22.5% of households in the United States were married couples with children, down from 40.3% in 1970 (U.S. Census Bureau, 2009b). We don't know a lot about the functioning of nuclear families because they are not often studied, except to compare other types of families to them. For example, children in lone-parent families are often compared to children in two-parent families, with the finding that children benefit from the resources—material and social—that come with two parents (see Shore & Shore, 2009). Recent U.S. Census Bureau (2009a) data indicate that adults in married-couple families are older, more likely to have a bachelor's degree, more likely to own their own homes, and have higher incomes than lone-parent families. Both government (through marriage initiative programs) and religious groups are actively involved in trying to promote more two-parent families. Some social scientists see risk in nuclear families as compared to extended families, suggesting that they can easily become too isolated with too much pressure put on the spousal relationship to fill each other's needs (F. Walsh, 2003a; A. Williams & Nussbaum, 2001).

The often idealized nuclear family has a father in the labor force and a stay-at-home mother. That type of nuclear family peaked in the 1950s but was already beginning to decline by 1960. In 2007, a total of 66% of married couples with children under the age of 18 had two parents in the labor force (U.S. Census Bureau, 2009a). Having two parents in the labor force puts married couples at an economic advantage over single parents, but also raises concerns about who will provide child care and other domestic labor.

Nuclear families may involve adopted children (as may lone-parent families, same-sex partner families, and stepfamilies). The 2000 U.S. Census found that 2.5% of children under 18 were adopted, and 12.6% of those were foreign-born children (cited in Galvin, 2006). Adoptive families face the same challenges as other families, but they also face some additional ones. Every adopted child has two families, and disclosure about and navigation of this complexity must be addressed. The adoptive family must also develop a coherent story about how they came to be family and cope with issues of loss, grief, and attachment.

Extended Families

An *extended family* has traditionally been thought of as one in which the parent-child nuclear family lives along with other relatives, such as grandparents, adult siblings, aunts, uncles, or cousins. This is a common pattern in agricultural societies around the world. In the United States, this pattern exists in some rural families, as well as in some ethnic groups, particularly among Mexican Americans and some Asian American groups. This is financially practical, and it also allows family groups to practice their ethnic traditions (Ballantine & Roberts, 2009). However, there are some downsides to the extended family.

Sometimes, family members will exploit the labor of other family members. In other cases, the emotional and economic obligations to the extended family may come at the expense of individual development (Leeder, 2004).

At the moment, there is a great debate about the appropriate role for the extended family in the care of children orphaned by AIDS in southern Africa (see Mathambo & Gibbs, 2009). In societies where extended families share in the care of children, poor families are being challenged by the prolonged illness and death of family members at the prime working age. There is a growing interest in the capacity of the extended family to care for the increasing number of children orphaned by AIDS. Some argue, however, that the extended family network is collapsing under the strain of the devastation caused by AIDS. Where resources are scarce, both support and misery are shared.

Some family scholars suggest that it is more appropriate to speak of the contemporary family in the United States and other industrialized nations as a *modified extended family* than as a nuclear family (Leeder, 2004). Members of the extended family network may not reside together, but they are involved with each other in ongoing emotional and economic action. They stay connected. This is clearly the pattern in the Sharpe family. It is also the pattern in the current migrations across national lines. Family members are often separated across thousands of miles, but money is shared and the new technologies allow ongoing communication. Often, immigrant groups travel together in *kin networks* and live very close to each other when not living together. The extended kin network is a source of support in times of crisis. For example, children may be transferred from one nuclear family to another within the extended kin network as need arises. The extended kin system also influences values and behaviors. For instance, Vivian Sharpe has expectations that her extended kinship system will have a positive influence on Marcie's values and behaviors as she grows into an adolescent. Extended family ties are usually stronger in Asian and Pacific Islander Americans, Native Americans, African Americans, and Latino Americans than among middle-class White Americans (Ho, Rasheed, & Rasheed, 2004).

Cohabiting Heterosexual Couples

Cohabiting is living together without marriage. This method of forming a romantic partnership has been on the increase in the United States and other Western societies since 1960. Cohabitation is now recognized as a family form by family scholars. Sociologists Patrick Heuveline and Jeffrey Timberlake (2004) examined data from almost 70,000 women from 17 nations to learn how nonmarital cohabitation in the United States compares with that in 16 other industrialized nations. They examined the percentage of women in each of the nations estimated to experience at least one cohabitating relationship before the age of 45, and found a very large cross-nation range, from 4.4% in Poland to 83.6% in France. Spain and Italy were at the low end, with less than 15% of women in each country reporting cohabitation. The United States fell in the middle of the range, with about 50% of women estimated to ever cohabit before age 45. Heuveline and Timberlake suggest that the cross-national differences in rates of cohabitation are influenced by a number of sociocultural factors, including religion, the economy, partnership laws and benefits, and availability of affordable housing. Besides differences in rates of cohabitation, they also found different types of cohabiting relationships occurring in different nations. For example, cohabitation can be a prelude to marriage or an alternative to marriage. Heuveline and Timberlake found that cohabitating relationships are less stable in the United States than in other countries.

Although the estimates vary, there is agreement that the rate of unmarried cohabiting partners in the United States has increased dramatically since the 1960s, and that, currently, a majority of couples getting married are already living in a cohabiting relationship (Bjorklund & Bee, 2008). The increase in cohabitation is related to the increasing age at marriage. In the United States and other Western industrialized countries, cohabitation is most frequent among young adults between the ages of 20 and 34 (OECD Family Database, 2008a).

A number of researchers have found that cohabiting partners who marry are more likely to divorce than couples who married without cohabiting, and the first group also reports lower levels of marital satisfaction (see Kline et al., 2004; J. Phillips & Sweeny, 2005). Other researchers, however, have found that the increased risk of divorce applies only to those women who have cohabited with more than one partner. In other words, if a woman has cohabited with only her husband before marriage, she is no more likely to divorce than women who never cohabited before marriage (Teachman, 2003).

Two things are important to note about research on cohabitation. Because of the time that passes between data collection and publication of findings, the samples studied are typically people who cohabited in the late 1980s to the mid-1990s, and the nature of the cohabiting population appears to be changing. Second, the researchers are focusing on cohabiting women. Less is known about the relationship trajectory of cohabiting men, but some researchers find that cohabiting men report more time spent in domestic work than married men across 28 nations, a suggestion that traditional gender roles may be less common in cohabiting than in married romantic partnerships (S. Davis, Greenstein, & Marks, 2007; Kurdek, 2006). Lichter and Qian (2008) speculate that serial cohabitation by women may "reflect demographic shortages of men who are good providers or companions (e.g., men with good jobs, who are faithful, or who are drug free)" (p. 874).

Couples With No Children

Over the past three decades, the United States and other wealthy nations have seen an increase in the proportion of married couples who are childless. Interestingly, relatively high rates of childlessness were experienced in these same societies between 1890 and 1920, followed by the lowest recorded prevalence of childlessness during the 1950s and early 1960s (Abma & Martinez, 2006; Kohli & Albertini, 2009). Thus, the current high rates of

childlessness are a return to a trend started in the late 19th century. Couples may be temporarily childless or permanently childless. Permanently childless couples may be voluntarily or involuntarily childless. Although childlessness is a growing type of family structure, there is very little research on childless couples; the research that has been done focuses on childless women, with little or no attention to childless men (fertility of men is much harder to study) or to the childless couple system, except in cases of infertility. The research often does not distinguish between married and unmarried women.

The most comprehensive study of childless women in the United States to date was conducted by Joyce Abma and Gladys Martinez (2006) at the National Center for Health Statistics. Their study examined three types of childlessness: temporarily childless, voluntarily childless, and involuntarily childless. They studied both married and unmarried women and did not make distinctions between these two groups. They found that from 1976 to 2002, the percentage of women aged 35–39 who were childless increased from 11% to 20%, and the percentage of women aged 40–44 who were childless increased from 10% to 18%. The voluntarily childless was the largest group of childless women in 2002, making up 42% of all childless women; 30% were temporarily childless, and 28% were involuntarily childless. As might be expected, given declining fertility between the ages of 35 and 44, women who were temporarily childless were more likely to be in the younger cohort, ages 35–39, and women who were involuntarily childless were more likely to be in the older group, ages 40–44.

All three groups of childless women were found to have more egalitarian views on family relationships than the women who were parents. There were some differences in the profiles of these three groups of childless women, however. Consistent with earlier research, the voluntarily childless women, compared to parenting women and other childless women, were disproportionately White, tended to be employed full time, had the highest incomes, and were more likely to be nonreligious. However, between 1995 and 2002, the percentage of Black women among the voluntarily childless increased to where it was equivalent to their share of the total population of women between the ages of 35 and 44. From 1976 to 2002, Hispanic women were consistently underrepresented among the voluntarily childless (Abma & Martinez, 2006).

One finding from the Abma and Martinez (2006) study is that there was a slight downturn in the percentage of women who were voluntarily childless and a slight upturn in the percentage who were involuntarily childless between 1995 and 2002. They speculate that this change is probably related to the trend toward later marriage and childbearing, resulting in some couples discovering that they had fertility problems when they decided to become parents. Infertility can be caused by problems in the reproductive systems of the man, the woman, or both. It is a global problem, but in countries with low resources, it is most likely to be caused by infection-related tubal damage. Although there are currently many assistive technologies for dealing with fertility problems, these are inaccessible to most women in low-resource countries (Sharma, Mittal, & Aggarwal, 2009). In many countries of the world, childlessness is often highly stigmatizing (Chachamovich et al., 2009).

Research on the emotional impact of infertility indicates that it is a major source of stress. Infertility has been consistently associated with decreased scores in quality of life, affecting mental health, physical vitality, and social functioning (Drosdzol & Skrzypulec, 2008; El-Messidi, Al-Fozan, Lin Tan, Farag, & Tulandi, 2004; J. T. Lau et al., 2008). When both members of a couple experience similar levels of distress, they are more able to communicate about it and support each other (Peterson, Newton, & Rosen, 2003). However, it is not unusual for husbands and wives to have different reactions to infertility. The stressors related to infertility may go on over a long period of time. Treatments can be very costly and are often unsuccessful.

Although attitudes are changing, some social stigma is still attached to childlessness. Little is known about the lives of childless couples. In a recent attempt to understand the life trajectories of childless adults, an entire issue of the British journal *Ageing & Society* was devoted to research on childless older adults. One researcher (Wenger, 2009) found that by the time they reached old age, childless people in rural Wales had made adaptations to their childless situation and developed closer relationships with kin and friends. This is the way that Vivian Sharpe's godparents adjusted to involuntary childlessness, and they draw great pleasure from being a part of the lively extended kin network in which Vivian and Bobby are embedded. On average, however, childless older adults in Wales entered residential care at younger ages than older adults who had children.

Lone-Parent Families

Lone-parent families are composed of one parent and at least one child residing in the same household. They are headed by either a divorced or an unmarried parent. Lone-parent families are on the increase in all wealthy industrialized nations, but nowhere more than in the United States (UNICEF, 2007). In 2007, nearly one third (32%) of children in the United States lived with only one parent, 82% with the mother and 18% with the father (Shore & Shore, 2009). This compares with less than 10% in Greece and Italy (UNICEF, 2007). Around the world, lone mothers are the great majority of parents in lone-parent families. In the United States, 65% of non-Hispanic Black children, 49% of Native American children, 37% of Hispanic children, 23% of non-Hispanic White children, and 17% of Asian American and Pacific Islander children live with one parent. The share of children living with one parent in the United States tripled since 1970 when the rate was 11% (Shore & Shore, 2009). It is important to exercise caution with these statistics, however. Sometimes those who get counted as being lone-parent families reside with other family members and/or may have the support of a romantic partner.

Single mothers around the world have some common challenges: They are playing the dual roles of mother and worker with no partner assistance, receive lower earnings than men, and receive irregular paternal support. If they became lone parents after divorce, they and their children must cope with loss and grief, may have to relocate, and face an average of a 37% decline in their standard of living (Stirling & Aldrich, 2008). Lone-parent families headed by mothers are especially vulnerable to economic insecurity and poverty. Cross-national differences in government policies result in different circumstances for single mothers and their children, however. Some countries provide universal child allowances, paid maternity leave, and free child care. Children of single mothers have higher rates of poverty than children from two-parent families around the world, but the poverty rates among children of single parents are much lower in countries that provide such supports (D. Lindsey, 2004).

In 2000, the poverty rate for single-parent families in the United States was 55.4%, compared to 6.7% in Sweden (UNICEF, 2000). This is a very large range and primarily reflects differences in child and family policies in the two countries. Three other countries had poverty rates of over 45% for single-parent families: Canada, Germany, and the United Kingdom. At the other end of the continuum, three other countries had poverty rates of less than 15% for single-parent families: Denmark, Norway, and Hungary.

In the United States, social policy has focused on two priorities to improve the living situation of children in lone-parent families, as well as to decrease public expenditures on these families: improved child support payment by the nonresidential parent and marriage of the lone parent. The first of these priorities is to step up the enforcement of child support payment by the nonresidential parent. The research to date indicates that if non-residential parents paid the child support required, the economic situation of the children would indeed improve, although not to the level they would experience if both parents resided together. However, for impoverished families, the payment of child support is not sufficient to bring them out of poverty (see Stirling & Aldrich, 2008).

The second policy direction proposed in the United States in recent years is to encourage marriage of the lone parent. Some policy analysts

conclude that this would, indeed, improve the economic situation of children currently being raised in lone-parent families (see Rector, Johnson, & Fagan, 2008). Others conclude that while this might be a good solution for some lone-parent families, male unemployment and marginal employment present serious barriers to marriage for many low-income couples (Edin & Reed, 2005; Gibson-Davis, Edin, & McLanahan, 2005). These latter researchers have found that men and women in impoverished neighborhoods often value marriage highly, but do not see themselves as economically stable enough to have a viable marriage. Impoverished lone mothers have reported that they do not have a pool of attractive marriage partners who are economically stable, not addicted to drugs and alcohol, not involved with the criminal justice system, and able to be loving and kind parents to their children (Edin, Kefalas, & Reed, 2004).

It is important to note that in the United States and other wealthy nations, the number of lone-parent families is growing across all socioeconomic groups, and in the United States, many affluent and well-educated women and men are choosing to become lone parents because they want to be a parent but do not have a partner with whom to share parenting (C. M. Anderson, 2005). These lone parents have the resources to afford full-time child care, private schools, and other domestic assistance.

One more point is important. Much of the research on lone-parent families has taken a deficit approach in looking at family interaction and functioning. Other researchers have attempted to look at lone parents from a strengths perspective and document how they function to adapt to the challenges they face. One example of this is a qualitative research project that asked low-income African American mothers and members of their families (who were sometimes not biologically related to them) to identify components of effective and ineffective family functioning (McCreary & Dancy, 2004). They found that all but 1 of the 40 respondents reported that they see or talk daily with at least one family member other than their children, a coping strategy that increases the effectiveness of family functioning by preventing isolation.

Stepfamilies

Stepfamilies have always been a relatively common family form in the United States, but they have changed over time. In colonial days, stepfamilies were typically the result of one parent dying and the other parent remarrying. Today, most stepfamilies are formed after biological parents divorce or dissolve their relationship, and go on to form new romantic partnerships. We don't have good current data on the number of stepfamilies in the United States, but it is estimated that between 10% and 20% of children under the age of 18 reside in stepfamilies (Saint Louis Healthy Families, 2009).

The U.S. Census Bureau defines *stepfamilies* as those with two adults and children, where one adult is not the biological parent (cited in Pasley & Lee, 2010). Stepfamilies can be of several different types. The most common is the stepfather family in which the mother has children from a previous relationship in the household. Another type is the stepmother family in which the father has children from a previous relationship living in the household. Some stepfamilies have children from both partners' prior relationships living with them. Any of these family forms can become more complex when children are born to the new partnership. Stepfamilies are also formed by same-sex partners where one or both partners have children from prior heterosexual (or other) relationships living in the household. Although not counted by the U.S. Census Bureau as living in stepfamilies, many children reside with a single mother and make visits to the biological father and his new wife.

Stepfamilies are complex family structures. They involve complicated networks of relationships that include biological parents; stepparents; perhaps siblings and stepsiblings; and multiple sets of grandparents, aunts, uncles, and cousins. Children in stepfamilies may move back and forth between two homes and maintain connections with the nonresident parent. There are a number of subsystems in the stepfamily, including the couple, the parent-child, the stepparent-stepchild, the child-nonresidential parent, the biological parents, the parent-stepparent and nonresidential parent, and sometimes the sibling and/or stepsibling subsystem. The parent-child subsystem is a more long-standing form than the new couple subsystem.

The new stepfamily must negotiate rules, roles, rituals, and customs. Things as simple as foods served in the households, bedtimes, chores, and methods of discipline may become points of tension. This works best when the issues and expectations are made explicit. It is quite common for loyalty conflicts to arise involving several subsystems, with family members feeling torn and caught between people they love (Pasley & Lee, 2010). The biological parent often feels torn between loyalty to the child(ren) and love for the new spouse or partner. Children may aggravate this situation by testing the biological parent's loyalty to them. They may feel a conflict between their loyalty to the nonresidential parent and the need to form a relationship with the stepparent. Children can easily get triangulated into conflict between the parent and stepparent, between the residential parent and the nonresidential parent, or between the stepparent and the nonresidential parent. Events such as Parent Night at school can become a knotty situation.

The more children there are in the stepfamily situation, the more complicated the negotiations can become. First-marriage couples report that the biggest source of stress is finances, followed by child rearing. For stepfamilies, the biggest sources of stress are reversed, with child rearing coming first, followed by finances (Stanley, Markman, & Whitton, 2002). Stepparents are often treated as outsiders by children, and this is a difficult position from which to attempt to parent. Research indicates that stepfathers are less likely than stepmothers to try to engage in active parenting of stepchildren, no doubt because of expectations of gendered behavior; consequently, stepfathers tend to be perceived more positively than stepmothers (Pasley & Lee, 2010). There is also evidence that stepdaughters are more difficult to parent than stepsons (Hetherington & Kelly, 2002).

Same-Sex Partner Families

Long-term relationships between same-sex partners are becoming more visible, if not more common, in the United States and around the world. It is possible for gay and lesbian partners to be married or to enter into other legally sanctioned partnerships in some countries and some parts of the United States. As of March of 2011, ten countries have federal laws to legalize same-sex marriage: The Netherlands (2001), Belgium (2003), Spain (2005), Canada (2005), South Africa (2006), Norway (2009), Sweden (2009), Argentina (2010), Iceland (2010), and Portugal (2010) (Belge, 2011). A number of other countries of the world have some sort of federal civil union laws that grant partner registration and some rights and benefits of marriage.

In the United States, the federal Defense of Marriage Act (DOMA), enacted in 1996, defines *marriage* as a legal union between one man and one woman and makes two stipulations: (1) States are not required to recognize same-sex marriages performed in other states; and (2) the federal government will not acknowledge same-sex marriages even if they are recognized by states. In spite of this law, as of August 2011, six states and the District of Columbia issue marriage licenses to same-sex couples: Massachusetts (2004), Connecticut (2008), Iowa (2009), Vermont (2009), District of Columbia (2010), New Hampshire (2010), and New York (2011). Maryland (2010) recognizes marriages of same-sex couples legalized in other jurisdictions. Seven states provide the equivalent of spousal rights to same-sex couples in the state: California, Hawaii, Illinois, Nevada, New Jersey, Oregon, and Washington. Three other states have laws that provide some spousal rights to same-sex couples: Colorado, Maine, and Wisconsin (Human Rights Campaign, 2011b).

But the issue of marriage equality for same-sex couples is hotly debated in the United States at this time. Same-sex partnerships are openly condemned by some religious and political leaders as well as segments of society that think these partnerships are a threat to the family institution. Twenty-nine states have passed constitutional amendments restricting marriage to one man and one woman. Eleven other states have state laws, instead of constitutional amendments, that restrict marriage to one man and one woman (Human Rights Campaign, 2009). Given the current state of debate about same-sex marriage, it is quite likely that there will be other action by nations and states by the time you read this. In early 2011, legislation was introduced in both the U.S. House of Representatives and the Senate to repeal DOMA, and the Obama administration announced that it is dropping its legal defense of DOMA (Human Rights Campaign, 2011a).

Same-sex partnerships share many characteristics with heterosexual partnerships, but they also have some that are unique: The partners are of the same gender, they must navigate a social world that continues to stigmatize same-sex relationships, and in many places they lack legal recognition. Some researchers have found that same-sex partners report about the same frequency of arguments as heterosexual couples (Peplau & Fingerhut, 2007), but other researchers have found that same-sex couples report less conflict, more relationship satisfaction, and better conflict resolution than heterosexual couples (Balsam, Beauchaine, Rothblum, & Solomon, 2008; Kurdek, 2004). There is evidence that both same-sex and heterosexual partners tend to disagree about similar topics, such as sex, money, and household tasks (Kurdek, 2006). Some studies find that members of same-sex partnerships are more likely than married heterosexual couples to separate when they are unhappy, but the one longitudinal study that has followed the first same-sex partners to take advantage of Vermont's civil union laws found that same-sex couples in civil unions are less likely to separate than same-sex couples not in civil unions (Balsam et al., 2008). Same-sex partners have been found to engage in less traditional division of labor than heterosexual married couples with children, but this finding must be interpreted in the context of considerable research that shows that heterosexual couples become more traditional and less egalitarian when they become parents (Kurdek, 2006). Same-sex partners report receiving more support from friends and less support from biological family than heterosexual couples (Kurdek, 2006).

Many lesbians and gay men became parents in earlier heterosexual relationships, before coming out as gay or lesbian. Increasingly, lesbians and gay men are also becoming parents in the context of their same-sex relationships, with the assistance of reproductive technology or by adoption (Savin-Williams, 2008). The U.S. Census Bureau estimates that about 1 in 5 gay male couples and 1 in 3 lesbian couples were raising children in 2000 (Gates & Ost, 2004). Lesbian couples may choose artificial insemination and gay male couples may choose to use a surrogate mother; each method results in the child sharing a bloodline with one partner but not the other. Some lesbian and gay couples become parents through adoption. Each of these options involves challenges and decisions.

Considerable research attention has been given to the question of how children fare in families of same-sex partners. This research consistently finds that children who grow up with same-sex parents do not differ in any important way from children raised in families of heterosexual couples. They have similar emotional and behavioral adjustment; no differences are found in self-esteem, depression, or behavioral problems (Wainright, Russell, & Patterson, 2004). This is remarkable, given the stigma that such families often have to face. Children of same-sex parents have also been found to be no more likely than the children of heterosexual couples to identify as homosexual. The school setting may present challenges, however; children may face harassment, and their parents may find that they are not accepted on parent committees (A. Goldberg, 2010).

Thomas Johnson and Patricia Colucci (2005) argue that lesbians and gays are bicultural. They have been reared and socialized in the dominant heterosexual culture and have internalized the norms, values, and beliefs learned in that culture. For the most part, they are members of heterosexually oriented families, and they have heterosexual models of family life. At the same time, lesbians and gays participate in a gay culture that copes with homophobia and develops a set of norms and roles for the special circumstances of same-sex partnerships. They must often deal with family-of-origin reactivity to their sexual orientation and romantic relationships. Johnson and Colucci suggest that

> following this track, we believe that gays and lesbians are part of a complex multigenerational family system consisting of a family of origin, a multigenerational lesbian/gay community, and/or a family of choice that consists of friends, partners, and/or children. (p. 347)

Military Families

Military families may have any of the family structures discussed above. They are included in this discussion of diversity of family structures, however, because of some special challenges they face in times of deployment to war zones. In the United States, military members may serve in either the active-duty or reserve components of the military. Active-duty members serve in the U.S. Army, Navy, Marine Corps, or Air Force. Reservists serve either in the Army National Guard or Air National Guard. Compared to other recent conflicts, deployments to Afghanistan and Iraq have been more frequent and lengthier, usually lasting 12 to 15 months. Another dramatic difference is that reservists have made up almost one third of the military force being deployed during these wars (Faber, Willerton, Clymer, MacDermid, & Weiss, 2008). Historically, the National Guard has been a domestic 9-1-1 force responding to local, state, and sometimes national emergencies. Since 2003, they have been an important component of the armed forces, fighting in two theaters of war. Reservist deployments are typically longer than active-duty deployments, because reservists usually must be away from home for pre-deployment training for as long as 3 months before deployment (J. A. Martin & Sherman, 2010).

Photo 9.3 This father and son enjoy a moment of joy during a welcome home ceremony when the Arkansas National Guard's 39th Infantry Brigade Combat Team returned from deployment to Iraq.

Approximately one third of both active-duty and reservist members have children; children of reservist members are a little older, on average, than children of active-duty members. The circumstances of reservist families are different in some ways from those of active-duty families. Active-duty military families typically live on or near military installations where the active-duty member receives daily military training. Reservist families live and work in a civilian community, and the reservist receives military training 1 weekend per month (Faber et al., 2008).

Research indicates that active-duty families usually cope well with temporary separations during peacetime (Flake, Davis, Johnson, & Middleton, 2009). Active-duty military spouses are accustomed to managing as single parents for periods of time, and then readjusting to operating in their pre-deployment family structure again when the deployment ends. Reservists and their families, on the other hand, are accustomed to occasional brief deployments to respond to state, local, and even national emergencies. They are not as prepared to deploy quickly for long periods of time, and must deal with the break in civilian employment, as well as prepare the family for the coming separation. Consequently, active-duty families and reservist families face both similar and different challenges in the current system of deployment to Iraq and Afghanistan.

Spouses of both active-duty soldiers and reservists have reported loneliness, loss of emotional support, role overload, and worry about the safety and well-being of the deployed spouse

(Faber et al., 2008). Parents who are spouses or partners of soldiers deployed to war zones report higher levels of stress than the national average for parents. Communication with the military member in the war zone is spotty at best, as the deployed soldier is in and out of the range of adequate communications systems. During his earlier deployment to Iraq, Bobby Sharpe could only have infrequent contact with his family, but his sister is much luckier and has been able to be in regular e-mail communication. Both the family members at home and the deployed family member may try to avoid alarming each other about what is happening in their worlds, and together they must gauge how involved the deployed family member can be in making decisions about what is happening at home. Bobby Sharpe did not know his furnace was broken until he returned home from his first deployment, because Vivian did not want to bother him with that kind of family problem.

As the end of the deployment draws near, family members report that they begin to worry about what to expect when the soldier returns, in terms of possible war wounds or personality or behavior changes (Faber et al., 2008). Marcie Sharpe had heard scary stories of parents coming home with completely changed personalities. She worried about this during Bobby's first deployment and has already begun to worry about it again. Although it is often a joyous time, the military member's return home can be very stressful for families. Family members have to readjust to one another and realign family roles. Three out of every four families report that the first 3 months after coming home can be the most stressful period of the deployment process (Flake et al., 2009). Soldiers have to reacclimate to life away from the war zone and renegotiate roles, responsibilities, and boundaries with family members who had made adjustments in their absence (Faber et al., 2008). This readjustment is particularly difficult when there have been physical or mental injuries, such as traumatic brain injury or post-traumatic stress disorder (PTSD) (J. A. Martin & Sherman, 2010). Families tend to stabilize over time, but many families must prepare for another deployment that can come as quickly as in 1 year.

Children of both active-duty and reservist families involved in the current wars have been found to be at increased risk for a range of problems in psychosocial functioning. In the time just before a parent's deployment, children may become withdrawn or engage in regressive behavior. Early in the deployment, they may be overwhelmed, sad, and anxious, and have more somatic (physical) symptoms, but these symptoms usually diminish once children adjust to the deployment. They are usually excited and relieved when the soldier parent comes home, but may experience conflict about the readjustments being made at home (Flake et al., 2009). A recent study of children of deployed National Guard members found that they reported missing their deployed parent as the biggest difficulty of the deployment. Their biggest worry was that their deployed parent would be injured or killed. The biggest change in their lives involved increased responsibility at home, including more chores and more responsibility for younger siblings. They reported concern about trying to avoid upsetting the parent at home. The children also indicated some positive aspects of deployment. Some reported being proud of what their deployed parents were doing for the country, although this pride was tempered when they heard talk from television, classmates, and other sources suggesting that the war is bad. Some children also reported pride in themselves for their ability to be more responsible while the deployed parent was away (Houston et al., 2009).

There is one important difference in the experiences of active-duty versus reservist families. A large portion of active-duty military families continue to live in or near military installations during the family member's deployment. This allows them to have ongoing support from other military families as well as from military programs. Reservist families, on the other hand, are scattered across all 50 states and the U.S. territories, many of them living in rural communities. This is especially the case for National Guard members because the National Guard has a strong tradition in rural communities, where it serves as a point of pride as well as a supplement to the low wages often found in these communities (J. A. Martin & Sherman, 2010). Sometimes a National Guard family will be the only one in the area experiencing deployment at a given time. This is problematic because of the lack of access to other families facing similar experiences. Children of deployed reservists have reported that a chance to talk to other children with a deployed parent would be a big help (Houston et al., 2009). Likewise, the returning reservist soldier may be isolated from other returning soldiers, as well as from some of the medical and psychiatric resources available in and near military installations. Recognizing some of these challenges, the National Guard has instituted the Yellow Ribbon Program to provide support for families throughout the cycle of deployment. The challenge is to maintain the same level of services throughout the state.

As of March of 2011, both Operation Iraqi Freedom and Operation Enduring Freedom are winding down. It is hard to say what the future of these wars is, but it is clear that military families involved in them, both active-duty and reservist families, will experience multiple challenges in the aftermath of the wars. According to a large-scale study by the RAND Corporation, many service members from the wars in Iraq and Afghanistan have undergone prolonged periods of combat stress (Tanielian & Jaycox, 2008). In the aftermath of the trauma, many service members and veterans are experiencing horrific combat injuries; others are experiencing substance abuse, PTSD, relationship problems, and work problems. Social workers in all practice settings should be alert to possibilities to engage these families in supportive services.

Economic Diversity, Cultural Diversity, and Immigrant Families

Family structure is influenced by economic and cultural patterns, as well as immigration status. As you read the following sections on economic diversity, cultural diversity, and immigrant families, think about how family structure is affected by the family's position in the economic structure, its cultural heritage, and experience with immigration.

Economic Diversity

Economic inequality exists in all societies, historical and contemporary, but the number of social classes and the amount of inequality varies from society to society. As indicated in Chapter 7, the United States has less inequality than some nations of the world, but it has more inequality than any other advanced industrial nation. And, unfortunately, since 1970, the gap between the richest and poorest U.S. citizens has been growing. As I write this in March of 2011, the worst recession in the United States since the Great Depression of the 1930s has lifted, but the national unemployment rate remains near 9%. A number of wealthy families have lost millions, even billions, of dollars in fraud schemes and investments gone bad. Middle-class families have been devastated by job cutbacks, home foreclosures, and high debt, with middle-class men over the age of 55 being particularly hard hit by job loss. Moreover, the poorest of families are barely surviving, not able to meet basic needs for food and shelter. Large numbers of U.S. families report feeling a sense of financial insecurity (Bartholomae & Fox, 2010).

The question to be addressed here is, what impact do economic resources have on family life? How do family economic circumstances affect parental relationships, parent–child relationships, and child development? A large volume of research has found that individual physical and mental health, marital relationships, parent–child relationships, and child outcomes decline as economic stress increases. Two theoretical models have been proposed to explain the connection between economic resources and individual and family functioning: the family economic stress model and the family investment model.

The family economic stress model is based on Glen Elder's (1974) research on the impact of the Great Depression on parents and children. This research found that severe economic hardship disrupted family functioning in ways that negatively affected marital quality, parenting quality, and child outcomes. Similar results have been found in more recent studies of Iowa farm families facing a severe downturn in the agricultural economy in the 1980s (Conger & Elder, 1994), and of economic pressure in African American families (Conger et al., 2002). In the **family economic stress model** based on this research, economic hardship leads to economic pressure, which leads to parent distress, which leads to disrupted family relationships, which leads to child and adolescent adjustment problems (Conger & Conger, 2008).

There is a great deal of research to support the family economic stress model. Economic stress, such as unemployment, low income, and high debt, have been found to have negative effects on physical and mental health of parents (J. Kahn & Pearlin, 2006; Mckee-Ryan, Song, Wanberg, & Kinicki, 2005; Mistry, Vandewater, Huston, & McLoyd, 2002). Research has also found that psychological distress about economic pressures takes its toll on marital quality (Gudmunson, Beutler, Israelsen, McCoy, & Hill, 2007; Kinnunen & Feldt, 2004). Couple disagreements and fighting increase with financial strain. Parental psychological distress and marital conflict have been shown to affect parenting practices, leading to less parental warmth and more inconsistent, punitive, and controlling discipline (Mistry, Lowe, Renner, & Chin, 2008; Waanders, Mendez, & Downer, 2007).

Family economic hardship has also been found to be associated with a number of child outcomes. Children in families experiencing economic hardship tend to have higher levels of depression and anxiety (Gutman, McLoyd, & Tokoyawa, 2005). They also demonstrate more aggressive and antisocial behaviors (Solantaus, Leinonen, & Punamaki, 2004). Economic disadvantage is associated with lower self-esteem and self-efficacy in children (Shek, 2003) and poorer school performance (Gutman et al., 2005). Adolescents who report worrying about the family's finances also report more somatic complaints, such as stomachaches, headaches, and loss of appetite (Wadsworth & Santiago, 2008).

Where the family economic stress model focuses on the impact of low income and economic hardship on family life, the **family investment model** focuses on the other end of the economic continuum, on how economic advantage affects family life and child outcomes. This theoretical model proposes that families with greater economic resources can afford to make large investments in the development of their children (M. Bornstein & Bradley, 2003; R. Bradley & Corwyn, 2002).

Families with abundant economic resources are able to make more learning materials available in the home; spend more time engaged in intellectually stimulating activities, such as visiting museums and traveling; secure education in enriched educational environments; secure outside assistance such as tutoring and specialized training; provide a higher standard of living in such areas as housing, clothing, nutrition, transportation, and medical care; and reside in a safe, clean, and roomy environment. They also are able to open doors to social networks that provide educational and career opportunities. This seems to go without saying, but there is empirical support for the proposal that family income affects the types of investments parents make in their children (Bradley & Corwyn, 2002), and this investment has been demonstrated to be associated with child cognitive development (Linver, Brooks-Gunn, & Kohen, 2002).

Cultural Diversity

The world over, we are living in a time when people are moving about from society to society and increasing the level of cultural diversity in small towns, suburbs, and cities. As suggested earlier, there has always been cultural diversity in the United States, but with the new waves of immigration in recent years, the United States has become a microcosm of the whole world in terms of the complex mix of ethnic heritages and religions. Across cultural groups, families differ in how they define family; in how they organize family life; and in their customs, traditions, and communication patterns (Hines, Preto, McGoldrick, Almeida, & Weltman, 2005). Social workers face a daunting challenge in responding sensitively and appropriately to each and every family they encounter.

In the past, many of the clinical models for family practice were based on work with primarily middle-class and often two-biological-parent European American families. Working from these models often led to thinking of racial and ethnic minority families as deviant or deficient. One of the best examples of the damage that this way of thinking can do is illustrated in Ann Fadiman's (1998) story about the experience of a Hmong family with the health care and child protective systems in California. (If you haven't read that book yet, I suggest you put it on your to-do list for your next break between terms.) In recent years, however, there has been a concerted call for social workers and other professionals to practice in a culturally sensitive manner that moves from culturally aware to culturally competent practice (Fong & Furuto, 2001; Lum, 2007; J. Rothman, 2008).

We prefer to talk in terms of culturally sensitive practice, because we doubt that we can ever be truly competent in a culture other than the one in which we were raised, and certainly not in the multiple cultures we are likely to encounter in our work over time. In light of the great diversity in contemporary life, the goal should be to remain curious and open-minded, taking a stance of "informed not knowing" (Dean, 2001).

Consequently, we do not present a cookbook approach to working with cultural differences, but rather a process by which we can develop cultural awareness about the family groups with which we work. The first step, as suggested above, is to develop an intense understanding of the limitations of our own cultural perspective and a healthy respect for the integrity of all cultures. Starting from this position, we can set out to become as well-informed as possible about the cultural groups represented by the families we serve. One thing that social workers are particularly good at, when we are at our best, is putting people and situations into context. We will want to use that strength to learn as much as

Photo 9.4 It is important for social workers to understand ethnic differences in family beliefs, rules, communication patterns, and organizational norms.

possible about the context of the culturally variant families we encounter. Juliet Rothman (2008, p. 38) suggests the types of knowledge needed to practice in a culturally sensitive manner; they are presented in modified form here:

- The group's history prior to arriving in the United States, if relevant
- The group's experience with immigration, if relevant
- The group's experience with settlement in the United States, if relevant
- The group's experience with oppression, discrimination, bias, and prejudice
- The group's relationship to the country of origin, if relevant
- The group's relationship to the country of residence
- The group's worldviews and beliefs about child rearing, family relationships, dating and marriage, employment, education, recreation, health and illness, aging, death and bereavement, and other life course issues
- Variations and differences within the group, particularly those related to social class
- Generational issues about acculturation within the group, if relevant

Some of this information may be more important than others for specific practice situations. There are a number of ways to learn this information: through Internet research, history books, biographies and autobiographies of members of the group, films and documentaries about the group, conversations with friends or colleagues who are members of the group, attendance at cultural festivals, and by asking your clients what you need to know to be helpful to them.

Even though we want to learn as much as we can about the cultural group, we must realize that there are many variations within all cultural groups. When the authors of this chapter need to avoid stereotypical application of knowledge about a cultural group, it helps us to think about how many variations there are within our own cultural groups, and how well or poorly generalizations about our groups apply to us. It is also helpful to hear different stories from members of the group, through books, videos, or personal conversations. It is particularly important to remember that there are social class differences among all cultural groups. You will want to consider whether the African American woman you are working with is middle class or working class, and know something about her experiences with oppression. You will want to keep in mind that over 500 distinct Native American nations exist within the United States, and they differ in language, religion, social structure, and many other aspects of culture (Weaver, 2007). You will want to know how a specific nation coped with attempts to eradicate its cultural practices. You will want to note whether the Latino immigrant family came from a rural or urban environment and what level of education they received in their home country; you will also want to note their country of origin and whether they are of documented or undocumented status. When working with an Asian or Pacific Island family, you will want to know not only the country of origin (out of 60 represented in the United States), but also the social class and education level of the family, religious beliefs, and when the family first migrated to the United States. You will want to note how integrated the family from North Africa or the Middle East is into U.S. mainstream culture, as well as how traditional they are in religious and cultural beliefs. These are only a few examples of how you will need to individualize families while also putting them into cultural context.

Immigrant Families

The United States is built on successive waves of immigration. Recent census data indicate that approximately 37.5 million immigrants are currently living within the United States, making up 12.5% of the U.S. population (Bush et al., 2010). *Immigrants* are foreign-born people who plan to settle permanently in the United States. They may be economic migrants who are seeking better jobs and pay, family migrants who come to join family members already here, or refugees who are involuntarily fleeing political violence or extreme environmental distress. Current immigrants to the United States are more diverse than earlier immigrants in terms of country of origin, language, religion, and socioeconomic status. The places from which immigrants come have changed over time, influenced by immigration policies. For example, 1965 amendments to the Immigration and Nationality Act of 1952 created a "family reunification" category and gave preference to immigrants who had family members already in the United States. The 1986 Refugee Assistance Extension Act made it easier for families facing political persecution and extreme environments in their home countries to enter the United States. The Immigration Act of 1990 shifted policy away from family reunification to individuals with specific education and credentials and to wealthy individuals who could invest in the U.S. economy (Bush et al., 2010).

Immigrants may be *first-generation* (moved from another country to the United States), *second-generation* (children of first-generation immigrants), or *third-generation* (grandchildren of first-generation immigrants). In general, first-generation immigrants will experience more loss and grief than second- and third- generation immigrants, but the reaction to immigration differs by the degree of choice about migration, accessibility to the country of origin, gender and age, stage of family life cycle, number of family members immigrating and left behind, community social supports, and experiences with discrimination in the country of origin and the country of adoption (Falicov, 2003). Many losses are involved with migration, including loss of the family members and friends left behind, loss of familiar language, and loss of customs and traditions. Involuntary immigrants often have been traumatized in their country of origin and have no option to visit home. Other immigrants are able to make frequent visits home and maintain transnational families who are in frequent contact. Families may migrate together or in sequential

stages, whereby one or two family members immigrate first, followed by others at later times.

In cases of sequential migration, family roles and relationships must be reorganized over time. The first immigrating family member must now perform some roles not carried out in the home country, whether they be domestic chores, paid labor, or managing finances. Likewise, the spouse left in the home country must now take on roles that had been filled by the immigrating family member. If the trailing spouse later immigrates, the spousal roles will have to be renegotiated, as happens when military families reunite. One difference between the reunifications of immigrant and military families is that sequential immigration may happen over a period of years and have unexpected delays, and the separations can be much longer than for military families. When children are left behind for a number of years, they may have trouble reattaching to the parents.

Immigrant families face various challenges. If they come from a non–English-speaking country, the language barrier will be a serious impediment to becoming comfortable in the new country. They will be unable to read street signs, job announcements and applications, food labels, and communications from the children's schools, unless they live where language translations are commonly used. Because children learn new languages more easily than adults, parent and child roles often are reversed as children become the language and cultural brokers. Children also learn the new cultural norms more quickly than parents, and this can cause intergenerational tension about the appropriate level of acculturation, how much of the old to maintain and how much of the new to adopt. Parents may not understand the new culture's norms about child rearing and find themselves at odds with the school system, and perhaps with the child protective system. Immigrant wives often come from cultures with traditional gender roles but need to engage in paid work in the United States to keep the family afloat. This often results in more independence and status for wives than they were accustomed to in their home countries, and can cause marital conflict if men want to hold onto the traditional gender hierarchy. Research has found increased male-to-female violence in Asian families when wives earn as much as or more than their husbands (G. Chung, Tucker, & Takeuchi, 2008). Many immigrant families come from collectivist cultures where harmony is valued over individual ambition and may feel a great deal of tension about how to respond to cultural pressures toward individualism. They may have had both the support and control of the extended family in the home country and find themselves struggling to maintain family stability with a much more limited support network.

Critical Thinking Questions 9.3

Which one of the theoretical perspectives on family discussed in this chapter do you find most useful for thinking about the multigenerational Sharpe family? Which perspective do you think offers the least insight into this family? Which of the perspectives do you find most useful for thinking about your own family? The least useful? Which perspective might be particularly useful for working with impoverished families? Immigrant families? Families facing family violence? Divorcing families? Families struggling with substance abuse?

Implications for Social Work Practice

This discussion of small groups and families, in the context of larger social systems, suggests several practice principles:

- In the assessment process with individuals or families, identify any small groups to which the person or family belongs.
- In the assessment process, determine whether the group modality or another intervention modality would be most appropriate for the client.
- Be aware of various groups in your community for referral and networking purposes.
- Develop and implement small groups when it is clear that a group would benefit the population that you serve. Determine what type(s) of groups would be most appropriate for that population. Consider groups for prevention when appropriate.
- In the groups that you facilitate, understand the stated and unstated purposes and functions of the group, and pay careful attention to issues of group structure, development, composition, and dynamics.
- Assess families from a variety of theoretical perspectives. Given recent economic shifts, be particularly aware of the impact of changes in larger systems on families' resources and functioning.
- Recognize the diversity of family structures represented by the families with whom you work, and be sensitive to the relative strengths and weaknesses of each of these family structures.
- Develop awareness of economic diversity among families and the different economic and other resources available to the families you serve.
- Develop awareness of cultural diversity among families and a commitment to culturally sensitive practice that involves ongoing learning both about and from families that are different from your own.
- Use appropriate family assessment tools, including the genogram, ecomap, and timeline, to help you develop a more comprehensive understanding of families with which you work.

Key Terms

ABC-X model of family stress and coping	family	family life cycle perspective
exchange theory (small groups)	family economic stress model	family of origin
	family investment model	family resilience perspective

family systems perspective
family timeline
feminist perspective on families
genogram
group cohesiveness
group work
intersectionality feminist theory

performance expectations
psychodynamic
  perspective (family)
psychodynamic theory
  (small groups)
self-categorization theory
  (small groups)

small group
status characteristics
status characteristics and
  expectation states theory
  (small groups)
symbolic interaction theory
  (small groups)

Active Learning

1. In personal reflection, think about your behavior and your roles in important groups throughout your life to date, groups such as family of origin, friendship groups, social groups, sports teams, work groups, therapy groups, and so forth. What roles have you played in these different groups? Are there any patterns to the roles you have played across various types of groups? Do you notice any changes in roles over time or in different types of groups? How do you understand both the patterns and the changes?

2. Sometimes we learn new things about families when we prepare visual representations of them. There are several tools available for doing this. You will use three of them here to visualize your own family.

   • Referring back to Exhibit 9.5, prepare a family ecomap of your *current* family situation.
   • Referring to Exhibit 9.4, prepare a multigenerational genogram of your family, going back to your maternal and paternal grandparents.
   • Referring to Exhibit 9.6, prepare a family timeline beginning at the point of your birth, or earlier if you think there were significant earlier events that need to be noted.

   After you have prepared these materials, work in small groups in class to discuss how useful each tool was in helping you think about your family of origin. Were any new insights gained from using these visual tools? What is your overall reaction to using tools like these to understand your family?

Web Resources

American Self-Help Group Clearinghouse, Self-Help Group Sourcebook

www.mentalhelp.net/selfhelp/

Provides a guide to locate self-help and support groups in the United States and other countries.

The Association for the Advancement of Social Work With Groups (AASWG)

www.aaswg.org

Professional organization advocating in support of group work practice, education, research, and publication; includes links to newsletters, discussion lists, bibliographies, chapter information, syllabi, social work links, and other group work links. To order the association's bibliography on group work, write to Raymie H. Waysen, General Secretary, AASWG, Inc., 36 Rocklyn Drive, West Simsbury, CT 06092–2628.

Council on Contemporary Families

www.contemporaryfamilies.org

Official site of the Council on Contemporary Families, a nonprofit organization that promotes an inclusive view of families; contains information and research on families, along with links to other Internet resources.

Forum on Child and Family Statistics

www.childstats.gov

Official website of the Federal Interagency Forum on Child and Family Statistics, offers easy access to federal and state statistics and reports on children and families, including international comparisons.

Google Groups

Groups.google.com/

Site for creating or finding groups on the Internet, including support-related groups.

National Council on Family Relations (NCFR)

www.ncfr.org

The Public Policy section of this site contains NCFR Fact Sheets and NCFR Policy Briefs on a variety of family issues.

PART III

The Changing Life Course

"How old are you?" You have probably been asked that question many times, and no doubt you find yourself curious about the age of new acquaintances. Every society appears to use age as an important variable, and many social institutions in advanced industrial societies are organized, in part, around age—the age for starting school, the age of majority, retirement age, and so on. In the United States, our speech abounds with expressions related to age: "terrible 2s," "sweet 16," "20-something," "life begins at 40," "senior discounts," and lately "60 is the new 40." This interest in how humans change and stay the same across time is one important way that behavioral scientists introduce the idea of time into the understanding of person and environment.

We have chosen a life course perspective to capture the dynamic, changing nature of person-environment transactions. In the life course perspective, human behavior is not a linear march through time, nor is it simply played out in recurring cycles. Rather, the life course journey is a moving spiral, with both continuity and change, marked by both predictable and unpredictable twists and turns. It is influenced by changes in the physical and social environment as well as by changes in the personal, biological, psychological, and spiritual dimensions.

The life course perspective recognizes *patterns* in human behavior related to biological age, psychological age, and social age norms. The life course perspective also recognizes *diversity* in the life course related to historical time, gender, race, ethnicity, social class, and so forth, and we emphasize group-based diversity in our discussion of age-graded periods. Finally, the life course perspective recognizes the *unique life stories* of individuals—the unique configuration of specific life events and person-environment transactions over time.

The remaining chapters of the book will examine theory and research in relation to specific phases of the human life course. These chapters consider how the human life course is shaped by the constant interaction of persons and their environments. Chapter 10 overviews the important concepts and major themes of the life course perspective and considers the beginning of the life course, focusing on issues of conception, pregnancy, and childbirth. Chapter 11 examines infancy and toddlerhood, Chapter 12 looks at early childhood, Chapter 13 at middle childhood, Chapter 14 at adolescence, Chapter 15 at young and middle adulthood, and Chapter 16 at late adulthood. In these chapters, margin notes are used differently than in Chapters 3–9; here they are used to help you think critically about the major themes of the life course perspective.

CHAPTER 10

The Human Life Course

The Journey Begins

Marcia P. Harrigan

Suzanne M. Baldwin

Elizabeth D. Hutchison

C8 80

C8 80

Opening Questions

Why do social workers need to understand how people change from conception to death?

What biological, psychological, social, and spiritual factors influence the beginning of the life course?

As you read this chapter, take note of these central ideas:

1. The life course perspective attempts to understand the continuities as well as the twists and turns in the paths of individual lives.

2. Cohorts, transitions, trajectories, life events, and turning points are basic concepts of the life course perspective.

3. The life course perspective presents six major themes: the interplay of human lives and historical time, timing of lives, linked or interdependent lives, human agency in making choices, diversity in life course trajectories, and developmental risk and protection.

4. All elements of childbearing have deep meaning for a society, but the social meaning of childbearing changes over time and is influenced by factors such as social class, race, and ethnicity.

5. Genetic factors are an important way that we are linked with our families over time.

6. One way that humans exercise agency is by attempting to get control over conception and pregnancy.

7. The 40 weeks of gestation, during which the fertilized ovum becomes a fully developed infant, are a remarkable time for the parents as well as for the new life taking form.

8. Major congenital anomalies (commonly referred to as birth defects), prematurity, and low birth weight present challenges to the newborn and his or her family and can serve as risk factors throughout the life course.

CASE STUDY 10.1

David Sanchez's Search for Connections

David Sanchez has a Hispanic name, but he explains to his social worker, as he is readied for discharge from the hospital, that he is a member of the Navajo tribe. He has spent most of his life in New Mexico but came to Los Angeles to visit his son, Marco, age 29, and his grandchildren. While he was visiting them, he was brought to the emergency room and then hospitalized for what has turned out to be a diabetic coma. He had been aware of losing weight during the past year, and felt ill at times, but thought these symptoms were just signs of getting older or, perhaps, the vestiges of his alcoholism from the ages of 20 to 43. Now in his fifties, although he has been sober for over a decade, he is not surprised when his body reminds him how he abused it.

The social worker suggests to Mr. Sanchez that he will need to follow up in the outpatient clinic, but he indicates that he needs to return to New Mexico. There he is eligible—because he is a Vietnam veteran—for health services at the local Veterans Administration (VA) hospital outpatient clinic. He also receives a disability check for a partial disability from the war. He has not been to the VA since his rehabilitation from alcohol abuse, but he is committed to seeing someone there as soon as he gets home.

During recent visits with Marco and his family, David started to recognize how much his years of alcohol abuse hurt his son. After Mrs. Sanchez divorced David, he could never be relied on to visit Marco or to provide child support. Now that Marco has his own family, David hopes that by teaching his grandchildren the ways of the Navajo, he will pay Marco back a little for neglecting him. During the frequent visits of this past year, Marco has asked David to teach him and his son how to speak Navajo. This gesture has broken down some of the bad feelings between them.

David has talked about his own childhood during recent visits, and Marco now realizes how much his father suffered as a child. David was raised by his maternal grandmother after his father was killed in a car accident when David was 7. His mother had been very ill since his birth and was too overwhelmed by her husband's death to take care of David.

Just as David became attached to his grandmother, the Bureau of Indian Affairs (BIA) moved him to a boarding school. His hair was cut short with a tuft left at his forehead, which gave the teachers something to pull when he was being reprimanded. Like most Native American/First Nations children, David suffered this harshness in silence. Now, he feels that it is important to break this silence. He has told his grandchildren about having his mouth washed out with soap for speaking Navajo. He jokes that he has been baptized in four different religions—Mormon, Catholic, Lutheran, and Episcopalian—because these were the religious groups running the boarding schools he attended. He also remembers the harsh beatings for not studying, or for committing other small infractions, before the BIA reformed its policies for boarding schools and the harsh beatings diminished.

David often spent holidays at the school because his grandmother had no money for transportation. He remembers feeling so alone. When David did visit his grandmother, he realized he was forgetting his Navajo and saw that she was aging quickly.

He joined the Marines when he was 18, like many high school graduates of that era, and his grandmother could not understand why he wanted to join the "White man's war." David now recognizes why his grandmother questioned his decision to go to war. During his alcohol treatments, especially during the use of the Native sweat lodge, he often relived the horrible memories of the bombings and killings in Vietnam; these were the memories he spent his adult life trying to silence with his alcohol abuse. Like many veterans, he ended up on the streets, homeless, seeking only the numbness his alcoholism provided. But the memories were always there. Sometimes his memories of the children in the Vietnam villages reminded him of the children from the boarding schools who had been so scared; some of the Vietnamese children even looked like his Native American friends.

It was through the Native American medicine retreats during David's rehabilitation that he began to touch a softer reality. He began to believe in a higher order again. Although his father's funeral had been painful, David experienced his grandmother's funeral in a more spiritual way. It was as if she was there guiding him to enter his new role. David now realizes this was a turning point in his life.

At his grandmother's funeral, David's great-uncle, a medicine man, asked him to come and live with him because he was getting too old to cut or carry wood. He also wanted to teach David age-old cures that would enable him to help others struggling with alcohol dependency, from Navajo as well as other tribes. Although David is still learning, his work with other alcoholics has been inspirational, and he finds he can make special connections to Vietnam veterans.

David is thankful that his son has broken the cycle of alcoholism and did not face the physical abuse to which he was subjected. But he is sad that his son was depressed for many years as a teen and young man. Now, both he and Marco are working to heal their relationship. They draw on the meaning and strength of their cultural and spiritual rituals. David's new role as spiritual and cultural teacher in his family has provided him with respect he never anticipated. Finally, he is able to use his grandmother's wise teachings and his healing apprenticeship with his great-uncle to help his immediate family and his tribe.

A social worker working with a situation like this—helping Mr. Sanchez with his discharge plans—must be aware that discharge planning involves one life transition that is a part of a larger life trajectory.

—*Maria E. Zuniga*

Mahdi Mahdi's Shared Journey

Social workers involved in refugee resettlement work are eager to learn all they can about the refugee experience. Social workers in these scenarios are learning from their clients, but they will also find it helpful to talk with other resettlement workers who have made a successful adjustment after entering the United States as a refugee. In this particular case, the social worker has been particularly grateful for what she has learned from conversations with Mahdi Mahdi. Mahdi works as an immigration specialist at Catholic Social Services in Phoenix, providing the kind of services that he could have used when he came to Phoenix as a refugee in 1992.

Mahdi was born in Baghdad, Iraq, in 1957. His father was a teacher, and his mother stayed at home to raise Mahdi and his four brothers and two sisters. Mahdi remembers the Baghdad of his childhood as a mix of old and new architecture and traditional and modern ways of life. Life in Baghdad was "very good" for him until about 1974, when political unrest and military control changed the quality of life.

Mahdi and his wife were married after they graduated from Baghdad University with degrees in fine arts in 1982. Mahdi started teaching high school art when he graduated from college, but he was immediately drafted as an officer in the military to fight in the Iran–Iraq War. He was supposed to serve for only 2 years, but the war went on for 8 years, and he was not able to leave the military until 1989. Mahdi recalls that many of his friends were killed in the war.

By the end of the war, Mahdi and his wife had two daughters, and after the war Mahdi went back to teaching. He began to think, however, of moving to the United States, where two of his brothers had already immigrated. He began saving money and was hoping to emigrate in November 1990.

But on August 2, 1990, Iraq invaded Kuwait, and war broke out once again. Mahdi was drafted again to fight in the war, but this time, he refused to serve. According to the law in Iraq, anyone refusing the draft would be shot in front of his house. Mahdi had to go into hiding, and he remembers this as a very frightening time.

After a few months, Mahdi took his wife, two children, and brother in a car and escaped from Baghdad. He approached the American army on the border of Iraq and Kuwait. The Americans took Mahdi and his family to a camp at Rafha in northern Saudi Arabia and left them there with the Saudi Arabian soldiers. Mahdi's wife and children were very unhappy in the camp. The sun was hot, there was nothing green to be seen, and the windstorms were frightening. Mahdi also reports that the Saudi soldiers treated the Iraqi refugees like animals, beating them with sticks.

Mahdi and his family were in the refugee camp for a year and a half. He was very frightened because he had heard that some members of the Saudi Arabian army had an unofficial agreement with the Iraqi army to drop any refugees that they wanted at the Iraq border. One day he asked a man who came into the camp to help him get a letter to one of his brothers. Mahdi also wrote to the U.S. Embassy. Mahdi's brother petitioned to have him removed from the camp, and Mahdi and his family were taken to the U.S. Embassy in Riyadh. Mahdi worked as a volunteer at the embassy for almost a month, and then he and his family flew to Switzerland, on to New York, and finally to Arizona. It was now September of 1992.

Mahdi and his family lived with one of his brothers for about 6 weeks, and then they moved into their own apartment. Mahdi worked as a cashier in a convenience store and took English classes at night. He wanted to be able to help his daughters with their schoolwork. Mahdi reports that although the culture was very different from what he and his family were accustomed to, it did not all come as a surprise. Iraq was the first Middle Eastern country to get television, and Mahdi knew a lot about the United States from the programs he saw.

After a year and a half at the convenience store, Mahdi decided to open his own business, USA Moving Company. He also went to school half-time to study physics and math. He kept the moving company for 2 years, but it was hard. Some customers didn't like his accent, and some of the people he hired didn't like to work for an Iraqi.

After he gave up the moving company, Mahdi taught seventh grade fine arts in a public school for a couple of years. He did not enjoy this job because the students were not respectful to him.

For the past several years, Mahdi has worked as an immigration specialist for Catholic Social Services. He enjoys this work very much, and has assisted refugees and immigrants from many countries, including Somalia, Vietnam, and the Kosovo region of the former Yugoslavia. Mahdi has finished 20 credits toward a master's degree in art education, and he thinks he might go back to teaching someday.

Mahdi's father died in 1982 from a heart attack; Mahdi thinks that worrying about his sons' safety killed his father. Mahdi's mother immigrated to Arizona in 1996 and lives about a mile from Mahdi and his family, next door to one of Mahdi's brothers. (Three of Mahdi's brothers are in Phoenix and one is in Canada. One sister is in Norway and the other is in Ukraine.) Mahdi's mother loves being near the grandchildren, but she does not speak English and thus has a hard time meeting new people. In 1994, Mahdi and his wife had a third daughter. About 11 months ago, Mahdi's mother- and father-in-law immigrated to the United States and came to live with Mahdi and his family. His wife now stays home to take care of them. Mahdi is sensitive to how hard it is for them to move to a new culture at their age.

Mahdi and his family live in a neighborhood of Anglo Americans. His daughters' friends are mostly Anglo Americans and Hispanic Americans. Although Mahdi and his family are Muslim, Mahdi says that he is not a very religious person. They do not go to mosque, and his wife does not wear a veil—although his mother does. Mahdi says that his faith is a personal matter, and he does not like to draw attention to it. It is much better, he says, to keep it personal.

This part of the conversation brings Mahdi to mention the aftermath of September 11, 2001, and what it is like living in the United States as an Iraqi American since the terrorist attack. He says that, overall, people have been very good to him, although he has had some bad experiences on the street a few times, when people have stopped him and pointed their fingers angrily in his face. His neighbors and colleagues at work have offered their support.

A social worker who will assist many refugee families has a lot to gain from learning stories like this—about Mahdi Mahdi's pre-immigration experience, migration journey, and resettlement adjustments. We must realize, however, that each immigration journey is unique.

CASE STUDY 10.3

Jennifer Bradshaw's Experience With Infertility

Jennifer Bradshaw always knew that she would be a mom. She remembers being a little girl and wrapping up her favorite doll in her baby blanket. She would rock the doll and dream about the day when she would have a real baby of her own. Now, at 36, the dream of having her own baby is still just a dream as she struggles with infertility.

Like many women in her age group, Jennifer spent her late teens and twenties trying not to get pregnant. She focused on education, and finding the right relationship, finances, and a career. As an African American woman, and the first person in her family to earn a PhD, she wanted to prove that she could be a successful clinical

(Continued)

psychologist. She thought that when she wanted to get pregnant, it would just happen, that it would be as easy as scheduling anything else on her calendar. When the time finally was right and she and her husband, Allan, decided to get pregnant, they couldn't.

With every passing month and every negative pregnancy test, Jennifer's frustration grew. First, she was frustrated with herself, and had thoughts like, "What is wrong with me?" "Why is this happening to us?" and "We don't deserve this." She would look around and see pregnant teens and think, "Why them and not me?" She also was frustrated with her husband for not understanding how devastating this was to her and wondered to herself, "Could he be the one with the problem?" In addition, she was frustrated with her family and friends and started avoiding them to escape the comments and the next baby shower. Now, she is babyless and lonely. She thinks having an infertility problem is even worse for African American women because of the "Black fertility" myth. She gets so tired of hearing, "No one else in the family has had a problem getting pregnant," "When my husband just breathed on me, I got pregnant," and "Just relax, and you will get pregnant." It has also been hard for Allan. For many men, virility is a symbol of masculinity; Allan would not even consider that he might be the one with the fertility problem, even though it is a male-factor issue in about 50% of infertility cases.

After months of struggling to get pregnant; multiple visits to the obstetrician/gynecologist; a laparoscopic surgery; a semen analysis; timed intercourse (which began to feel like a chore); and after taking Clomid, a fertility drug that made Jennifer feel horrible, she and Allan finally accepted that they might need to see a specialist. She will never forget the first visit with the reproductive endocrinologist (RE). She was expecting a "quick fix," thinking that the RE would give her some special pills and then she would get pregnant. But instead, he casually said to her, "I think your only option is *in vitro fertilization* (IVF), which runs about $16,000 per cycle including medications." The RE also told her that for someone in her age range, the success rate would be about 35% to 40%.

From her clinical practice, and her friendship circle, Jennifer knows that many women think of IVF as being a backup plan when they delay pregnancy. But she is learning that IVF is a big deal. First, it is expensive. The $16,000 per cycle does not include the preliminary diagnostic testing, and in Jennifer's age group, the majority of women pursuing IVF will need at least two IVF cycles, $32,000 for two tries; three tries brings the bill up to $48,000. Jennifer has heard of couples spending close to $100,000 for infertility treatments.

Although about 15 states in the United States mandate insurance companies to cover fertility treatments, in the state where Jennifer lives, there is no fertility coverage mandate; consequently, her insurance company does not cover any infertility treatments. So at the very least, Jennifer and Allan would need to come up with $16,000 to give one IVF cycle a try. It's heartbreaking for them because they don't have $16,000, and their parents can't help them out. So to give IVF even one try, they need to borrow the money. They are considering taking out a home equity loan to cover the cost and know that they are lucky to be in a position to do that. They have heard of people packing up and moving to states with mandated fertility coverage or quitting their jobs to find those that carry specific insurance that will cover fertility treatments. Some couples are even traveling abroad for fertility treatments that can be had for much less than in the United States.

Jennifer has heard that IVF is physically and emotionally exhausting. First, the IVF patient is forced into menopause, and then the ovaries are hyperstimulated to release numerous eggs (up to 15 to 17 instead of 1), which can be painful. The eggs are surgically extracted, and finally the fertilized embryos are introduced into the IVF patient's body. Throughout this process, various hormone treatments are given via daily injections and multiple blood tests are taken. In addition, at any point during the procedure something could go wrong and the IVF cycle could be called off. If all goes well, the IVF patient is left to keep her fingers crossed for the next 2 weeks, waiting for a positive pregnancy test. If the test is negative, the treatment starts over again.

She has heard that most women are an emotional wreck during the entire process due to the high stakes and the artificial hormones.

Jennifer and Allan decided to go the IVF route 7 months after visiting the RE. Before they made this decision, however, Jennifer carefully tracked her BBT (basal body temperature), purchased a high-tech electronic fertility monitor, used an ovulation microscope, took multiple fertility supplements, and used sperm-friendly lubricant during intercourse. Still nothing helped. When she heard that acupuncture has been found to increase the success rate of IVF, she started seeing a fertility acupuncturist on a weekly basis for both herbal formulas and acupuncture treatments. The acupuncture treatments/herbs are averaging about $100 per week, which is also not covered by her insurance.

Jennifer and Allan have decided to give IVF three tries, and if they are not successful, they will move on to the next plan, adoption. They adore each other and want more than anything to have their own little one, but if they cannot have that, they will adopt, and Jennifer will realize her dream of being a mom.

—*Nicole Footen Bromfield*

CASE STUDY 10.4

The Thompsons' Premature Birth

The movement of her growing fetus drew Felicia into an entrancing world of hope and fantasy. Within days of discovering she was pregnant, her husband, Will, was suddenly deployed to a conflict zone. Through e-mails and occasional cell phone calls, Felicia told Will details about the changes she was experiencing with the pregnancy, but more and more, it seemed as if she and her baby were inhabiting a different world from that of her husband. His world was filled with smoke, dirt, bombs, and danger, punctuated with periods of boredom. Although she was only 6 months into the pregnancy, she had selected muted colors for the nursery and soft baby clothes in anticipation of the birth. Her changing figure was being noticed by her coworkers in the office where she worked part-time as a secretary. With weeks of nausea and fatigue behind her, a general sense of well-being pervaded Felicia's mind and body. She avoided all news media as well as "war talk" at the office to protect her from worry and anxiety. Yet even the sound of an unexpected car pulling up to the front of her home produced chills of panic. Was this the time when the officers would come to tell her that Will had been killed or wounded in combat? Her best friend only recently had experienced what every military wife fears may happen. The growing life within her and the constant threat of death filled her waking and sleeping hours.

Then, one night when dawn was still hours away, Felicia woke to cramping and blood. With 14 more weeks before her delivery date, Felicia was seized with fear. Wishing that Will were there, Felicia fervently prayed for herself and her fetus. The ambulance ride to the hospital became a blur of pain mixed with feelings of unreality. When she arrived in the labor and delivery suite, masked individuals in scrubs took control of her body while demanding answers to a seemingly endless number of questions. Felicia knew everything would be fine if only she could feel her son kick. Why didn't he kick?

As the pediatrician spoke of the risks of early delivery, the torrent of words and images threatened to engulf her. Suddenly, the doctors were telling her to push her son into the world—her fragile son who was too small and

(Continued)

(Continued)

vulnerable to come out of his cocoon so soon. Then the pain stopped. Oblivious to the relief, Felicia listened for her baby's cry. It didn't come. Just a few hours earlier, she had fallen asleep while the fetus danced inside her. Now there was only emptiness. Her arms ached for the weight of her infant, and her heart broke with what she believed was her failure as a mother.

In the neonatal intensive care unit (NICU), a flurry of activity revolved around baby boy Thompson. Born weighing only 1 pound 3 ounces, this tiny red baby's immature systems were unprepared for the demands of the extrauterine world. He was immediately connected to a ventilator, intravenous lines were placed in his umbilicus and arm, and monitor leads were placed on all available surfaces. Nameless to his caregivers, the baby, whose parents had already named him Paul, was now the recipient of some of the most advanced technological interventions available in modern medicine.

About an hour after giving birth, Felicia saw Paul for the first time. Lying on a stretcher, she counted 10 miniature toes and fingers. Through a film of tears, trying to find resemblance to Will, who is of Anglo heritage, or herself, a light-skinned Latina, in this tiny form, Felicia's breathing synchronized to Paul's as she willed him to keep fighting.

Alone in her room, she was flooded with fear, grief, and guilt. What had she done wrong? Could Paul's premature birth have been caused by paint fumes from decorating his room? From her anxiety and worry about Will?

The Red Cross sent the standard message to Will, telling him of the birth of his son. Was he in the field? Felicia wondered. Was he at headquarters? It mattered because Paul may not even be alive by the time Will found out he was born. How would he receive the news? Who would be nearby to comfort him? Would the command allow him to come home on emergency leave? If he were granted permission for emergency leave, it could be days of arduous travel, waiting for space on any military plane, before he landed somewhere in the United States. Felicia knew that Will would be given priority on any plane available; even admirals and generals step aside for men and women returning home to meet a family crisis. But, then again, the command may consider his mission so essential that only official notification of Paul's death would allow him to return home. Although Felicia told herself she was being unreasonable, she was angry that Will was not there to comfort her. After all, she had supported his decision to join the military and had accepted that she would deliver her child alone. Then why was this so overwhelming?

Thirteen days after his arrival, Paul took his first breath by himself. His hoarse, faint cry provoked both ecstasy and terror in his mother. A few days earlier Felicia had been notified by the Red Cross that her husband was on his way home, but information was not available regarding his arrival date. Now that Paul was off the ventilator, she watched him periodically miss a breath, which would lead to a decreased heart rate, then monitors flashing and beeping. She longed for Will's physical presence and support.

Will arrived home 2 days later. He walked into the neonatal intensive care unit (NICU) 72 hours after riding in an armed convoy to the airport. Although Paul would spend the next 10 weeks in the hospital, Will had 14 days before starting the journey back to his job, a very different battlefield from the one on which Paul was fighting.

Paul's struggle to survive was the most exhilarating yet terrifying roller-coaster ride of his parents' lives. Shattered hopes were mended, only to be re-shattered with the next telephone call from the NICU. Now Felicia dreaded the phone as well as the sound of an unfamiliar car. For Felicia, each visit to Paul was followed by the long trip home to the empty nursery. For Will, stationed thousands of miles away, there was uncertainty, guilt, helplessness, and sometimes an overwhelming sense of inadequacy. Felicia feared the arrival of a car with officers in it, and Will dreaded a Red Cross message that his son had died.

Great joy and equally intense anxiety pervaded Paul's homecoming day. After spending 53 days in the NICU and still weighing only 4 pounds, 13 ounces, Paul was handed to his mother. She made sure that a video was made so that Will could share in this moment. How she wished he could participate, but she also knew that his heart and thoughts spanned the distance between war on the other side of the world and Paul's quiet victory at home. With more questions than answers about her son's future and her ability to take care of him, Felicia took their baby to his new home.

As the NICU social worker at a military hospital, the major goal must be to support the family as they face this challenging transition to parenthood. In the past 53 days, the social worker has helped Felicia answer her questions, understand the unfamiliar medical language of the health care providers, and understand and cope with the strong emotions she is experiencing. The social worker also helped during the transition of Will's arrival from war and his departure back to war. Understanding the dynamics of an NICU, families in crisis, and the needs of the military family separated by an international conflict is critical to providing this family with the level of support they need to manage the multifaceted role transitions.

THE LIFE COURSE PERSPECTIVE

Although it is more obvious in some of the stories than others, the stories of David Sanchez, Mahdi Mahdi, Jennifer Bradshaw, and even little Paul Thompson have unfolded over time, across multiple generations. We all have stories that unfold as we progress through life. A useful way to understand this relationship between time and human behavior is the **life course perspective,** which looks at how chronological age, relationships, common life transitions, and social change shape people's lives from conception to death. Of course, time is only one dimension of human behavior; but it is common and sensible to try to understand a person by looking at the way that person has developed throughout different periods of life.

You could think of the life course as a path. But note that it is not a straight path; it is a path with both continuities and twists and turns. Certainly, we see twists and turns in the life stories of David Sanchez, Mahdi Mahdi, Jennifer Bradshaw, and Felicia Thompson. Think of your own life path. How straight has it been to date?

If you want to understand a person's life, you might begin with an *event history,* or the sequence of significant events, experiences, and transitions in

a person's life from conception to death. An event history for David Sanchez might include suffering his father's death as a child, moving to live with his grandmother, being removed to a boarding school, fighting in the Vietnam War, getting married, becoming a father, divorcing, being treated for substance abuse, participating in medicine retreats, attending his grandmother's funeral, moving to live with his great-uncle, and reconnecting with Marco. Mahdi Mahdi's event history would most likely include the date he was drafted, the end of the Iran–Iraq War, escape from Baghdad, and resettlement in the United States. It appears that the visit to the reproductive endocrinologist has become a significant event in Jennifer Bradshaw's life, and Paul Thompson's premature birth is a significant event for him, as well as for his mom and dad. We can try to understand a person not only in terms of his or her own event history, but also in terms of how that person's life has been synchronized with family members' lives across time.

Another way to think about the life course is in terms of how culture and social institutions shape the pattern of individual lives. David Sanchez's life course was shaped by cultural and institutional preferences for placing Native American children in boarding schools during middle childhood and adolescence and for a policy of military draft for male youth and young adults. Mahdi Mahdi's life course was heavily influenced by cultural expectations about soldiering, and Jennifer Bradshaw's was affected by changing norms for education and childbearing. Like that of David Sanchez and Mahdi Mahdi, little Paul Thompson's life course is impacted by his country's involvement in war.

The life course perspective (LCP) is a theoretical model that has been emerging over the last 45 years, across several disciplines. Sociologists, anthropologists, social historians, demographers, and psychologists—working independently and, more recently, collaboratively—have all helped to give it shape.

Glen Elder Jr., a sociologist, was one of the early authors to write about a life course perspective, and he continues to be one of the driving forces behind its development. In the early 1960s, he began to analyze data from three pioneering longitudinal studies of children that had been undertaken by the University of California, Berkeley. As he examined several decades of data, he was struck by the enormous impact of the Great Depression of the 1930s on individual and family pathways (Elder, 1974). He began to call for developmental theory and research that looked at the influence of historical forces on family, education, and work roles.

At about the same time, social history emerged as a serious field. Social historians were particularly interested in retrieving the experiences of ordinary people, from their own vantage point, rather than telling the historical story from the vantage point of wealthy and powerful persons. Tamara Hareven (1978, 1982b, 1996, 2000) has played a key role in developing the subdiscipline of the history of the family. She is particularly interested in how families change and adapt under changing historical conditions and how individuals and families synchronize their lives to accommodate to changing social conditions.

The life course perspective also draws on traditional theories of developmental psychology, which look at the events that typically occur in people's lives during different stages. The life course perspective differs from these psychological theories in one very important way, however. Developmental psychology looks for universal, predictable events and pathways, but the life course perspective calls attention to how historical time, social location, and culture affect the individual experience of each life stage.

The life course perspective is still relatively young, but its popularity is growing. In recent years, it has begun to be used to understand the pathways of families (Huinink & Feldhaus, 2009; MacMillan & Copher, 2005), organizations (W. King, 2009), and social movements (Della Porta & Diani, 2006). We suggest that it has potential for understanding patterns of stability and change in all types of social systems. Gerontologists increasingly use the perspective to understand how old age is shaped by events experienced earlier in life (Browne, Mokuau, & Braun, 2009; Ferraro & Shippee, 2009). The life course perspective has become a major theoretical framework in criminology (X. Chen, 2009; Haynie, Petts, Maimon, & Piquero, 2009) and the leading perspective driving longitudinal study of health behaviors and outcomes (B. Evans, Crogan, Belyea, & Coon, 2009; Osler, 2006). It has also been proposed as a useful perspective for understanding patterns of lifetime drug use (Hser, Longshore, & Anglin, 2007).

Basic Concepts of the Life Course Perspective

Scholars who write from a life course perspective and social workers who apply the life course perspective in their work rely on a handful of staple concepts: cohorts, transitions, trajectories, life events, and turning points. As you read about each concept below, imagine how it applies to the lives of David Sanchez, Mahdi Mahdi, Jennifer Bradshaw, and Felicia Thompson, as well as to your own life. (For a more detailed discussion of the concepts and themes of the life course perspective, see Hutchison, 2011.)

- *Cohort.* A **cohort** is a group of persons who were born during the same time period and who experience particular social changes within a given culture in the same sequence and at the same age (Alwin & McCammon, 2003; Bjorklund & Bee, 2008; D. Newman, 2008; Settersten, 2003a).

Generation is another term used to convey a similar meaning. Generation is usually used to refer to a period of about 20 years, but a cohort may be shorter than that. Life course scholars often make a distinction between the two terms, suggesting that a birth cohort becomes a generation only when it develops some shared sense of its social history and a shared identity (see Alwin, McCammon, & Hofer, 2006).

- *Transitions.* A life course perspective is stage-like because it proposes that each person experiences a number of **transitions,** or changes in roles and statuses that represent a distinct departure from prior roles and statuses (Elder & Kirkpatrick Johnson, 2003; Hagestad, 2003; Hser et al., 2007). Life is full of such transitions: starting school, entering puberty, leaving school, getting a first job, leaving home, getting married, retiring, and so on.
- *Trajectories.* The changes involved in transitions are discrete and bounded; when they happen, an old phase of life ends and a new phase begins. In contrast, **trajectories** involve a longer view of long-term patterns of stability and change in a person's life, involving multiple transitions (Elder & Kirkpatrick Johnson, 2003; George, 2003; Heinz, 2003). For example, getting married is a transition, but it is a transition that leads to a longer marital trajectory that will have some stability but will probably involve other transitions along the way. Transitions are always embedded in trajectories. We do not necessarily expect trajectories to be a straight line, but we do expect them to have some continuity of direction.

- *Life events.* Specific events predominate in the stories of David Sanchez, Mahdi Mahdi, Jennifer Bradshaw, and Felicia Thompson: death of a parent, escape from a homeland, visit to a reproductive endocrinologist, premature birth. A **life event** is a significant occurrence involving a relatively abrupt change that may produce serious and long-lasting effects (Settersten, 2003a). The term refers to the happening itself and not to the transitions that will occur because of the happening. For example, participating in one's own wedding is a common life event in all societies. The wedding is the life event, but it precipitates a transition that involves changes in roles and

Photo 10.1 The life course is full of transitions in roles and statuses; graduation from college or university is an important life transition that opens opportunities for future statuses and roles.

statuses in relation to the family of origin as well as the marriage family.

- *Turning points*. David Sanchez describes becoming an apprentice medicine man as a turning point in his life. For Mahdi Mahdi, the decision to refuse the draft was a turning point. A **turning point** is a time when major change occurs in the life course trajectory. It may involve a transformation in how the person views the self in relation to the world or a transformation in how the person responds to risk and opportunity (Cappeliez, Beaupré, & Robitaille, 2008; Ferraro & Shippee, 2009). It serves as a lasting change and not just a temporary detour. As significant as they are to individuals' lives, turning points usually become obvious only as time passes (Rönkä, Oravala, & Pulkkinen, 2003). According to traditional developmental theory, the developmental trajectory is more or less continuous, proceeding smoothly from one phase to another. But life course trajectories are seldom so smooth and predictable. They involve many discontinuities, or sudden breaks, and some special life events become turning points that produce a lasting shift in the life course trajectory.

Major Themes of the Life Course Perspective

Nearly two decades ago, Glen Elder (1994) identified four dominant, and interrelated, themes in the life course approach: interplay of human lives and historical time, timing of lives, linked or interdependent lives, and human agency in making choices. The meaning of these themes is presented below, along with the meaning of two other related themes that Elder (1998) and Michael Shanahan (2000) have more recently identified as important: diversity in life course trajectories and developmental risk and protection.

- *Interplay of human lives and historical time.* Persons born in different years face different historical worlds, and individual and family development must be understood in historical context. Historical time may produce **cohort effects** when distinctive formative experiences

are shared at the same point in the life course and have a lasting impact on a birth cohort (Alwin & McCammon, 2003).

- *Timing of lives.* Age is also a prominent attribute in efforts by social scientists to bring order and predictability to our understanding of human behavior. Particular roles and behaviors are associated with particular age groups, based on biological age, psychological age, social age, and spiritual age (Dannefer, 2003a, 2003b; Settersten, 2003b; Z. Solomon, Helvitz, & Zerach, 2009).

- *Linked or interdependent lives.* The life course perspective emphasizes the interdependence of human lives and the ways in which people are reciprocally connected on several levels. The family is seen as the primary arena for experiencing and interpreting wider historical, cultural, and social phenomena (Barajas, Philipsen, & Brooks-Gunn, 2008; Conger & Conger, 2008; Elder, 1974; E. E. Werner & Smith, 2001). But individual and family life trajectories are also linked with the wider world, to situations in the labor market, the housing market, the education system, and the welfare system (K. Newman, 2008; Scherger, 2009). It is also important for social workers to remember that lives are linked in systems of institutionalized privilege and oppression.

- *Human agency in making choices.* One of the most positive contributions of the life course perspective is its proposal that humans participate in constructing their own life courses through the exercise of **human agency,** or the use of personal power to achieve one's goals. The individual life course is thought to be constructed by the choices and actions individuals take within the opportunities and constraints of history and social circumstances (Bandura, 2002, 2006; Hareven, 2000; Hitlin & Elder, 2007). Cultural psychology critics of the concept of human agency have argued, however, that it is a culture-bound concept that does not apply as well in collectivist societies as it does in individualistic societies (Markus & Kitayama, 2003).

- *Diversity in life course trajectories.* Life course researchers have long had strong evidence of diversity in individuals' life patterns. In our contemporary globalized world, there is much diversity in life course pathways as a result of cohort variations, social class, culture, gender, individual

Photo 10.2 Parents' and children's lives are linked—when parents experience stress or joy, so do children, and when children experience stress and joy, so do parents.

agency, and other types of human diversity (Dannefer, 2003a, 2003b; Settersten, 2003b).

- *Developmental risk and protection.* As the life course perspective has continued to evolve, it has more clearly emphasized the links between the life events and transitions of childhood, adolescence, and adulthood (McLeod & Almazan, 2003; O'Rand, 2009). There is clear research evidence that experiences with one life transition or life event have an impact on subsequent transitions and events and may either protect the life course trajectory or put it at risk. **Risk factors** are personal or social factors that increase the likelihood of a problem occurring. **Protective factors** are personal and societal factors that reduce or protect against risk. In the research on developmental risk and protection, **resilience** has been identified as healthy development in the face of risk factors. It is thought to be the result of protective factors that shield the individual from the consequences of potential hazards.

Keeping in mind this overview of the important concepts and major themes of the life course

perspective, we turn now to a discussion of the beginning of the life course, focusing on issues of conception, pregnancy, and childbirth.

Critical Thinking Questions 10.1

Think of the stories of David Sanchez, Mahdi Mahdi, Jennifer Bradshaw, and Felicia Thompson. How are their life course trajectories influenced by the historical times in which they live? How are their lives influenced by norms and expectations about how people are to behave at particular ages? How are their lives linked with other family members across generations? How are their lives linked with people outside the family? What examples do you see that they have exercised or are exercising human agency? What are the sources of diversity in their life course trajectories? What risk factors do you see? What protective factors? Would you describe any of them as resilient? If so, to what do you attribute their resilience?

SOCIOCULTURAL ORGANIZATION OF CHILDBEARING _____

All elements of childbearing have deep meaning for a society and are experienced in different ways by different people. Procreation allows a culture to persist, as children are raised to follow the ways of their predecessors. Procreation may also allow a culture to expand if the birthrate exceeds the rate at which the society loses members. As Valsiner (1989) reminds us,

> Human procreation is socially organized in all its aspects. In any cultural group around the world, society regulates the conditions under which a woman is to become pregnant, how she and her husband [family] should conduct themselves during the pregnancy, how labor and delivery take place, and how the newborn child is introduced into society. (p. 117)

But, consistent with the life course perspective, pregnancy and childbearing practices change with historical time. Globalization, changes in gender roles and in the labor market, and reproductive technologies are current sources of such change.

In the United States, the social meaning of childbearing has changed rather dramatically over the past 30 years, in several ways (Carter & McGoldrick, 2005a; F. Walsh, 2006):

> In what ways might culture provide diversity in the childbearing experience?

- Marriage and childbirth are more commonly delayed.
- Most people want smaller families.
- There are approximately 80 million involuntarily childless persons in the world (Bos, van Balan, & Visser, 2005).
- Various options for controlling reproduction are more available and accessible but oftentimes only to the economically advantaged.
- Sexual freedom has increased, along with more couples seeking infertility treatment.
- Single women of all ages get pregnant and keep the baby; after a decade-long decline in adolescent pregnancy, teen pregnancy began to increase again in 2006 (Landau, 2008).

- Family values and sexual mores vary more compared to previous generations.
- Parents are less subject to gender role stereotyping—Mom takes care of the baby while Dad earns a paycheck, and so on.
- Fathers have been found to be more important in the baby's life, beyond their genetic contributions.
- Military spouses return home unexpectedly from a war zone more often due to wives experiencing problematic pregnancies than to other family crises (Schumm, Bell, & Knott, 2000).
- Medical advances and cultural globalization are raising new ethical issues.

As suggested in Chapter 9, these trends and others have prompted considerable debate over how our society should define family. We continue to witness what family historians call *family pluralism,* or recognition of the many viable types of family structures. Such pluralism is nothing new, but our tolerance for all types of families has grown over the past few decades. Consider your own family beliefs about favorable and unfavorable circumstances of conception, pregnancy, and childbirth. Perhaps these views vary across generations, but the views, forged by experiences of past generations, can still create an expectation for certain circumstances and behaviors.

Sociocultural Organization of Conception and Pregnancy

The Thompsons' conception brought joy, in contrast to Jennifer Bradshaw's frustration and lost dreams, followed by her rising hopefulness that in vitro fertilization might allow her to conceive. There is much diversity in the conception experience today. It is influenced by expectations the parents learned growing up in their own families regarding birth or adoption, as well as by many other factors: the parents' ages, health, marital status, social status, cultural expectations, peer expectations, school or employment circumstances, the social-political-economic context, and prior experiences with conception and childbearing, as well as the interplay of these factors with those of other people significant to the mother and father.

The conception experience may also be influenced by organized religion. The policies of religious groups reflect different views about the purpose of human sexual expression: pleasure, procreation, or perhaps both (Bullis & Harrigan, 1992). These beliefs are usually strongly held and have become powerful fodder for numerous social, political, economic, and religious debates related to conception, such as the continued debates about abortion legislation in the United States and around the globe.

Just as the experience of conception has varied over time and across cultures, so has the experience of pregnancy. It, too, is influenced by religious orientations, social customs, changing values, economics, and even political ideologies. For example, societal expectations of pregnant women in the United States have changed, from simply waiting for birth, to actively seeking to maintain the mother's—and hence the baby's—health, preparing for the birth process, and sometimes even trying to influence the baby's cognitive and emotional development while the baby is in the uterus.

Sociocultural Organization of Childbirth

So, too, have childbirth practices changed over time. Throughout history, families—and particularly women—have passed on to young girls the traditions of childbirth practices. These traditions have been shaped by cultural and institutional changes. Until the early 20th century, 95% of births in the United States occurred at home with a midwife (a trained birthing specialist) (Rothman, 1991). As formalized medical training developed, so did the medicalization of childbirth. By 1940, over 50% of deliveries occurred in hospitals (R. Campbell & MacFarlane, 1986). To further the trend away from home births, the American Congress of Obstetricians and Gynecologists (ACOG) issued a policy statement in 1975 that protested in-home births

> What historical trends are related to these changes in the view of childbirth?

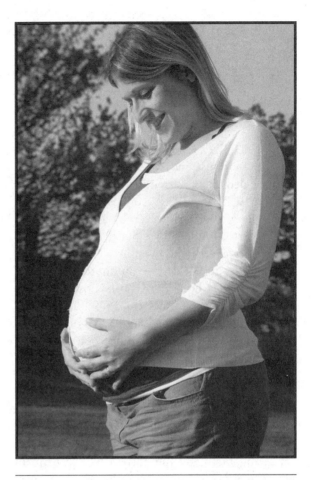

Photo 10.3 Societal views of pregnancy in the United States have changed from simply waiting, to being actively involved in nurturing the mother's and baby's health.

and asserted that acceptable levels of safety were only available in the hospital. This policy statement was affirmed in 1999 and again in 2007; it was supported in 2008 by the American Medical Association (ACOG, 2008; American Medical Association House of Delegates, 2008). In fact, a former president of ACOG labeled home births as child abuse (Hosmer, 2001). In contrast, the American College of Nurse-Midwives (2005) and the American Public Health Association (APHA, 2001) support planned home births. One recent study that used a small randomized sample in the Netherlands, where home births are endorsed, showed no statistical difference in maternal and neonatal outcomes between home births with trained midwives and hospital births (Janssen, et al., 2009; McLachlan & Forster, 2009). Recent studies in the United States have shown that home births for identified low-risk women offer no increased risks for mortality and morbidity if there are adequate support structures such as trained midwives and referral sources available (de Jonge et al., 2009; K. C. Johnson & Davis, 2005).

The feminist movement advocated for less invasive deliveries in friendlier environments during the 1960s and 1970s (Johanson, Newburn, & Macfarlane, 2002). However, by 1998, a study of 26,000 births in the United States found that only 1% occurred at home (Ventura, Martin, Curtin, & Mathews, 1998), despite an approximate 75% cost savings for home births over hospital births (R. E. Anderson & Anderson, 1999). This rate is declining, with less than 1% (0.59%) of all births in the United States in 2006 ($n = 38,568$) occurring in the home.

We are living in an era that values cost-effective, innovative, comprehensive health services. Thus, policies regarding the length of the new mother's stay in the hospital are also changing. Forty years ago, women remained hospitalized for 7 to 10 days following birth. By the early 1990s, the norm was 2 to 3 days. During the mid-1990s, however, controversial managed-care policies pushed for women with uncomplicated deliveries to be discharged within 24 hours, a savings of 2 hospital days. During the period following delivery, both the mother and infant undergo rapid transitions. The infant must adjust to a new environment, learn to nurse, and begin the process of bonding with parents. Potentially serious or life-threatening problems, such as heart problems, jaundice, or infections, may not be detected until the second or third day of life. Some research has shown, however, that early discharge of the mother and baby does not increase negative outcomes, and many women prefer to leave the hospital shortly after giving birth. Yet many women also appreciate continued assistance of health care workers and midwives after birth (L. Baker, 2006). Over a 10-year period, there has been a 50% increase in cesarean births, from 20.7% in 1996 to 31.1% in 2006 (MacDorman, Menacker, & Declercq, 2008; Menacker & Martin, 2009). Women who have had a cesarean birth have a higher rate of readmission with early discharge. With the increased incidence of cesarean birth, there also are increased hospital costs (S. Liu et al., 2002). A more recent trend is that employer-sponsored health care policies can require higher deductibles and copays (Wilde-Mathews, 2009), a trend that transfers even more of the cost of the necessary longer hospitalization to the parent(s).

Childbirth practices have changed in other ways as well. Many mothers are using the assistance of *doulas* (laywomen who are employed to stay with the woman through the entire labor, encouraging her and providing comfort measures) (Bain, Gau, & Reed, 1995; Hodnett, Downe, Edwards, & Walsh, 2005). Studies have shown that women who use doulas experience shorter labors, less pain, fewer medical interventions, higher rates of initiation of breastfeeding, and decreased postpartum depression (American Pregnancy Association, 2009; DONA International, n.d.; K. D. Scott, Klaus, & Klaus, 1999). Another development is the recent growth of birthing centers located close to a major hospital or within the hospital itself. Birthing centers offer an alternative to home delivery in a "home-like" freestanding facility with medical support. Recent research reveals that birthing centers reduce the number of medical interventions and increase maternal satisfaction (Hodnett et al., 2005; Oliver, 2005).

A major change over time is the role of fathers in childbirth. During the 16th century, law and custom excluded men from observing deliveries, because labor was viewed as "something to be endured by women under the control of other experienced and knowledgeable women" (M. P. Johnson, 2002, p. 165). During the 1960s, when childbirth moved out of the home, hospitals still excluded fathers from participating in the labor process (Kayne, Greulich, & Albers, 2001), and some continue to do so if there are complications (Koppel & Kaiser, 2001). This began to change in the 1970s. As more women were subjected to episiotomies (incisions to enlarge the opening for the baby during birth), enemas, and anesthesia in a male-dominated arena, often without their full knowledge or consent (Ashford, LeCroy, & Lortie, 2010), fathers were first invited in by physicians to serve as witnesses to avoid litigation (Odent, 1998, 1999). A 1995 survey in the United Kingdom found that fathers were present at 80% of all births, often serving as a "coach" (Woollett et al., 1995). There is still resistance to fathers' presence in the delivery room in some cultures, but when agreed upon by the couple, it has been shown that the father's involvement in the birthing process increases attachment, paternal satisfaction, nurturing behaviors, and positive feelings about the process (Pestvenidze & Bohrer, 2007; R. K. Reed, 2005), outcomes that are further enhanced if the father has attended childbirth classes (Wockel, Schafer, Beggel, & Abou-Dakn, 2007). Father-supported childbirth has also been found to increase the mother's satisfaction with the birth process and decrease the amount of pain medication needed (M. A. Smith et al., 1991). Increasing attention is being given to restrictive policies of some hospitals that will not allow the father to be present if the baby is being delivered by cesarean birth or if the mother has general anesthesia (Koppel & Kaiser, 2001). Reflect on the Thompsons' situation with Will in Afghanistan, unaware of the pending birth of his first child, and Felicia in premature labor without any family present.

Another change in the organization of childbirth over time was the formalization of childbirth education in the early 1900s, when the Red Cross set up hygiene and health care classes for women as a public health initiative. In 1912, the U.S. Children's Bureau, created as a new federal agency to inform women about personal hygiene and birth, published a handbook titled *Prenatal Care*, emphasizing the need for medical supervision during pregnancy (K. K. Barker, 1998). However, when Dr. Grantley Dick-Read published

How does childbirth education support human agency in making choices?

Childbirth Without Fear in 1944, the medical establishment rejected the idea that women who were educated about childbirth would have less fear and therefore less need for pain medication (Lindell, 1988). The idea of childbirth education did not gain credibility until the 1950s, after French obstetrician, Dr. Fernand Lamaze, published his book *Painless Childbirth* (1958). Lamaze proposed that women could use their intellect to control pain if they had information about their bodies and used relaxation techniques (DeHart, Sroufe, & Cooper, 2000; Lindell, 1988; J. C. Novak & Broom, 1995).

Childbirth education changed again in the 1980s as more women went back to work soon after birth and juggled multiple roles; technological interventions also increased at this time. The role of childbirth educator began to be filled by a professional from within the health care system (Zwelling, 1996). Childbirth education became a governmental priority as the gap widened between African Americans and other ethnic groups regarding the incidence of low birth weight and prematurity (Armstrong, 2000). In 2002, 17.7% of live African American births were preterm, compared to 11.0% of White live births, 12.0% of Native American live births, 10.4% of Asian/Pacific Islander live births, and 11.6% of Hispanic live births (March of Dimes, 2005). There are also significant socioeconomic and racial disparities in the utilization of childbirth classes, with one study finding that 76% of Caucasian women attended a childbirth class compared to 44% of African American women. In addition, there are racial differences in the utilization of prenatal care, with 89% of Caucasian women receiving first-trimester prenatal care compared to 75% of African American women (M. C. Lu et al., 2003). With increased racial and ethnic diversity in births, childbirth educators must engage more minority women and a broader range of ethnicities (Morton & Hsu, 2007). Research has demonstrated that lower minority participation in childbirth classes is most affected by lack of transportation and child care problems (Berman, 2006), both of which can be addressed by social workers.

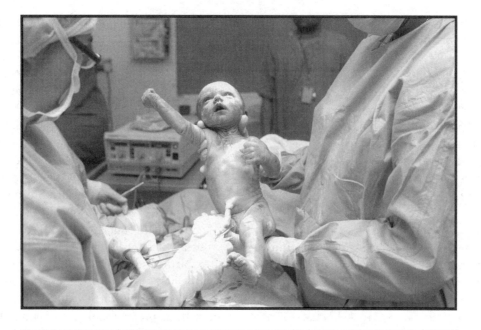

Photo 10.4 A typical delivery—Here, a newborn baby is delivered by medical professionals in a hospital delivery room.

REPRODUCTIVE GENETICS

When do you think your life story began? Did it begin at conception? At birth? At the birth of your parents? The birth of your grandparents? The life course perspective reminds us that we are linked back in time with our ancestry, as well as with our culture. Genetic factors are one important way that we are linked to our ancestry. Recognition of the need for genetics knowledge is not new to social work. In fact, Mary Richmond (1917) advocated that a social worker "get the facts of heredity" in the face of marriage between close relatives, miscarriage, tuberculosis, alcoholism, mental disorder, nervousness, epilepsy, cancer, deformities or abnormalities, or an exceptional ability.

Almost 50 years later, James Watson and Francis Crick (1953) first described the mechanisms of genetic inheritance. But it was not until 1970 that our knowledge of genetics began to explode. In 1990, the Human Genome Project (HGP) was funded by the U.S. Department of Energy and the National Institutes of Health as an international effort to map all the human genes by 2003. By June 2000, the first working draft of the human genome was completed, and in 2003 this project ended. The knowledge that resulted from the HGP has altered social work practice in many areas, primarily in working with persons of reproductive age. Genetic research continues around the world, with future findings that will continue to impact social work practice.

Chromosomes and genes are the essential components of the hereditary process. Genetic instructions are coded in **chromosomes** found in each cell; each chromosome carries **genes,** or segments of deoxyribonucleic acid (DNA), that contain the codes producing particular traits and dispositions. Each mature *germ cell*—ovum or sperm—contains 23 chromosomes, half of the set of 46 present in each parent's cells. As you can see in Exhibit 10.1, when the sperm penetrates the ovum (**fertilization**), the parents' chromosomes combine to make a total of 46 chromosomes arrayed in 23 pairs.

Exhibit 10.1   Germ Cell Division, Fertilization, and Chromosome Pairs

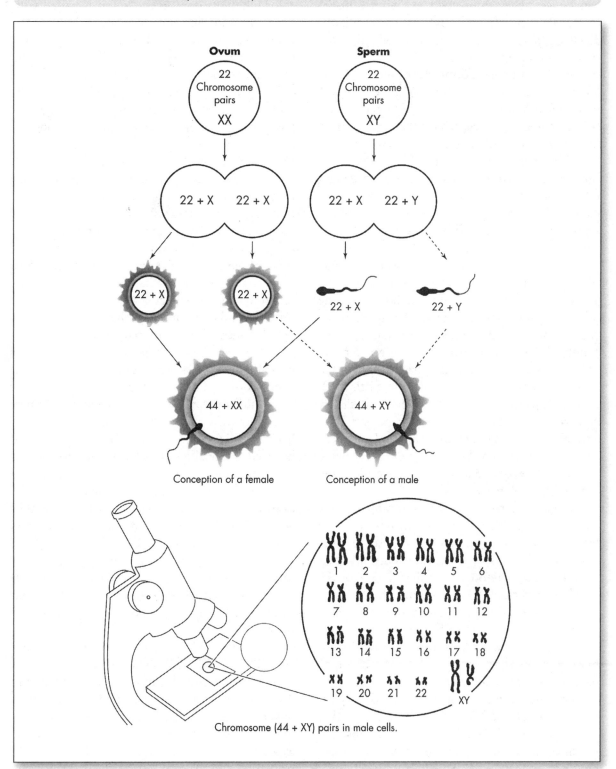

Ovum

22 Chromosome pairs XX

22 + X   22 + X

22 + X   22 + X

Sperm

22 Chromosome pairs XY

22 + X   22 + Y

22 + X   22 + Y

44 + XX

44 + XY

Conception of a female   Conception of a male

Chromosome (44 + XY) pairs in male cells.

The Human Genome Project (1990–2003) genetic researchers estimated that there are 20,000 to 25,000 genes in human DNA, with an average of 3,000 to 5,000 genes per chromosome, slightly more than the number mice have (HGP, 2009b). The goal now is to determine the complete sequencing of the 3 billion subunits of the human genome, an effort of global proportions involving both public and privately funded projects in more than 18 countries, including some developing countries (HGP, 2009b).

The genes constitute a "map" that guides the protein and enzyme reactions for every subsequent cell in the developing person and across the life course. Thus, every physical trait and many behavioral traits are influenced by the combined genes from the ovum and sperm.

Every person has a unique **genotype,** or array of genes, unless the person is an identical twin. Yet the environment may influence how each gene pilots the growth of cells. The result is a **phenotype** (observable trait) that differs somewhat from the genotype. Thus, even a person who is an identical twin has some unique characteristics. On initial observation, you may not be able to distinguish between identical twins, but if you look closely enough, you will probably find some variation, such as differences in the size of an ear, hair thickness, or temperament.

A chromosome and its mate have the same types of genes at the same location. The exception is the last pair of chromosomes, the *sex chromosomes,* which, among other things, determine sex. The ovum can contribute only an X chromosome to the 23rd pair, but the sperm can contribute either an X or a Y and therefore determines the sex of the developing person. A person with XX sex chromosomes is female; a person with XY sex chromosomes is male (refer to Exhibit 10.1).

Genes on one sex chromosome that do not have a counterpart on the other sex chromosome create *sex-linked traits.* A gene for red/green color-blindness, for example, is carried only on the X chromosome. When an X chromosome that carries this gene is paired with a Y chromosome, which could not carry the gene, red/green color-blindness is manifested. So, almost all red/green color-blindness is found in males. This gene for color-blindness does not manifest if paired with an X chromosome unless the gene is inherited from both parents, which is rare. However, if a woman inherits the gene from either parent, she can unknowingly pass it on to her sons.

Whether genes express certain traits depends on their being either dominant or recessive. Traits governed by **recessive genes** (e.g., hemophilia, baldness, thin lips) will only be expressed if the responsible gene is present on each chromosome of the relevant pair. In contrast, traits governed by **dominant genes** (e.g., normal blood clotting, curly hair, thick lips) will be expressed if one or both paired chromosomes have the gene. When the genes on a chromosome pair give competing, yet controlling, messages, they are called *interactive genes,* meaning that both messages may be followed to varying degrees. Hair, eye, and skin color often depend on such interactivity. For example, a light-skinned person with red hair and hazel eyes may mate with a person having dark skin, brown hair, and blue eyes and produce a child with a dark complexion, red hair, and blue eyes.

Although Mary Richmond noted in 1917 that many physical traits, medical problems, and mental health problems have a genetic basis, only recently has technology allowed us to identify the specific genes governing many of these traits. Now that the initial mapping of the human genome is complete, as further research is done, the goal is to develop genetic interventions to prevent or cure various diseases or disorders as well as affect conception, pregnancy, and childbirth in other ways. More than 1,000 genetic tests are available, ranging in cost from $200 to $3,000; they are seldom covered by insurance, and there is no federal regulation of them (HGP, 2009a).

Our quickly expanding ability to read a person's genetic code and understand the impact it could have on the person's life has resulted in increasing use of *genetic counseling.* The interdisciplinary field of genetic counseling acknowledges social work as one of its essential disciplines, thereby making at least a rudimentary understanding of genetics and related bioethical issues essential for social work practice (Garver, 1995; HGP, 2009a; Rauch, 1988; G. B. Reed, 1996). Social workers need to understand the rising and complex bioethical concerns that genetic research fosters and to use such knowledge to help clients faced with genetically related reproductive decisions. As increasing numbers of persons gain the ability to control conception, plan pregnancy, and control pregnancy outcomes, social workers need to protect the interests of those who lack the knowledge and other resources to do so.

CONTROL OVER CONCEPTION AND PREGNANCY _____

> How are decisions about timing of childbearing related to biological age, psychological age, social age, and spiritual age?

One way that humans exercise human agency is to attempt to get control over conception and pregnancy. The desire to plan the timing of childbearing is an ancient one, as is the desire to stimulate pregnancy in the event of infertility. Contraception and induced abortion have probably always existed in every culture. Effective solutions for infertility are more recent. But it is important to remember that not all methods of controlling conception and pregnancy are equally acceptable to all people. Cultural and religious beliefs, as well as personal circumstances, make some people more accepting of certain methods than others. Social workers must be aware of this diversity of attitudes and preferences related to the control of conception and pregnancy.

Contraception

Without any contraception, an estimated 85% of heterosexual couples who engage in regular intercourse will conceive within 1 year (Dirubbo, 2006; Trussell, 2004), but the range of birth control options available today provides women and men with the ability to plan pregnancy and childbirth more than ever before. Of the approximately 120 million women who become pregnant worldwide each year, approximately 38% of these pregnancies are unplanned, due to contraceptive failure or lack of pregnancy planning, and about 25% are unwanted (Ahman & Shah, 2006). It has been demonstrated that the rate of abortion increases as the availability of contraceptive use decreases, and abortion is often illegal and unsafe in nonindustrialized countries (Ahman & Shah, 2006; World Health Organization, 2004). In Eastern, Western, and Middle Africa, there is minimal use of contraceptives and abortion, resulting in high fertility rates (e.g., about 6 children per woman). However, in South America and Southeastern Asia, where there is limited access to contraceptives, abortion is often used as the primary regulator of fertility (Ahman & Shah, 2006). With the projected 7.4 to 10.6 billion people in the world by 2050, mostly born in countries with poor access to contraceptives, there is an urgent need to provide inexpensive, safe, convenient, and appropriate contraceptive devices to women and men worldwide. There is also a need to increase knowledge of these contraceptives (Goldenberg & Jobe, 2001; Prata, 2009).

Although adolescence is seen as the appropriate time for childbearing in many nonindustrialized societies, adolescent pregnancy is seen as a problem in advanced industrial societies. And, indeed, teen pregnancy carries medical risks. European countries have responded by providing comprehensive sex education and open access to birth control. In contrast, in the United States, there has been a push to encourage adolescents to engage in total abstinence with educational systems being required, in some situations, to teach abstinence as the only form of birth control.

With approximately half of all pregnancies in the United States being unintended (J. Miller & Holman, 2006; Van der Wijden, Kleijnen, & Van den Berk, 2003), it is important for social workers to be familiar with the choices women have; the potential impact of their choices; and how women of various cultural, racial, and ethnic groups may vary in their use of such options, if available. Complete sexual abstinence is the only certain form of contraception, but a recent review indicated that half of all averted pregnancies were stopped by oral contraceptives, about 20% by injectable methods, and 10% by barrier and patch methods (Foster et al., 2009, p. 446), with the implant and intrauterine devices being the most cost-effective. Each birth control option needs to be considered in light of its cost, failure rate, potential health risks, and probability of use, given the user's sociocultural circumstances. Female and male contraception options include the following:

- *Breastfeeding.* Women who are exclusively breastfeeding and are *amenorrheic* (not menstruating) are less likely than other women to conceive during the first 6 months postpartum (Hale, 2007). Breastfeeding without the use of other contraceptives carries a pregnancy risk of less than 2% during this time. For breastfeeding to be an effective contraceptive during those first 6 months, a woman must not be having menstrual periods, must nurse at least every 4 hours during the day and every 6 hours at night, and must not introduce the infant to other foods, a practice known as the lactational amenorrhea method (LAM) (Tilley, Shaaban, Wilson, Glasier, & Mishell, 2009; Van der Wijden et al., 2003).

- *Coitus interruptus.* Primarily seen as a male form of contraception, premature withdrawal of the penis from the vagina before ejaculation is probably the oldest form of birth control (Draper, 2006). However, the failure rate (proportion of method users who experienced failure within first year of use) is approximately 19 to 27% a year (4% if used perfectly) (Bachmann, 2007; Freundl, Sivin, & Batár, 2010). Coitus interruptus offers no protection from sexually transmitted infections (STIs) and HIV, and it may be unsatisfying in terms of sexual pleasure (Fu, Darroch, Haas, & Ranjit, 1999; Hatecher et al., 1994; Mahendru, Putran, & Khaled, 2009).

- *Periodic abstinence.* Natural family planning, or the *rhythm method,* is a term used for birth control that does not employ drugs or devices (Freundl et al., 2010). It involves daily tracking of changes in the woman's body associated with the menstrual cycle and an avoidance of intercourse during fertile periods. The effectiveness rate is 90%

to 98% if used perfectly, but if not practiced diligently, the failure rate rises to between 20 and 30% (American Academy of Family Physicians, 2005; Bachmann, 2007; Freundl et al., 2010).

- *Barrier methods.* The male condom (failure rate 2% when used correctly, 15% when used incorrectly or inconsistently over a 12-month period), the diaphragm (6–20% failure rate), and the cervical cap (20–36% failure rate) provide some protection against STIs, with the male condom having the highest protection rate against HIV and hepatitis B (Freundl et al., 2010; Mahendru et al., 2009). Dissatisfaction with condom use is lower than for any other form of birth control, leading to a lower rate of discontinuance (12%) (Moreau, Cleland, & Trussell, 2007). The female condom that was introduced in 1992 consists of two flexible rings, a soft sponge, or a dissolvable capsule (Rowlands, 2009), and also provides some protection against STIs (Freundl et al., 2010). It has approximately a 5% failure rate when used correctly, 21% when used incorrectly or inconsistently (Family Health International, 2006), and costs between $2.50 and $5 per use. The female condom is visible after insertion (some women are requesting colored condoms), and may cause crackling or popping sounds. Originally thought to be a good contraceptive option for low-income women internationally, it has not been well accepted (Severy & Spieler, 2000). Approximately 52% of women discontinue use of the diaphragm and cervical cap because they are dissatisfied (Moreau et al., 2007). Both male and female condoms are used with a spermicide that provides a chemical barrier against pregnancy but not STIs (Freundl et al., 2010). Spermicides can damage the skin of the male and increase the risk of infections, including HIV. Research is underway to develop spermicides that both kill sperm and lower the risk of STIs. Vaginal gels have also been found to have a wide variance in failure rates; many women are reluctant to use them, and often discontinue their use (Grimes et al., 2005).

- *Oral contraceptives.* The introduction of birth control pills in the United States in 1960 precipitated major changes in reproduction. With a failure rate of only about 0.3% to 8.0%, they revolutionized family planning (Freundl et al., 2010; Guttmacher Institute, 2005). Approximately 29% of women who start an oral contraceptive discontinue it due to dissatisfaction (Moreau et al., 2007). The progesterone-only pill has been shown to be safe for women who are breastfeeding (Mahendru et al., 2009). Using a combined estrogen and progesterone pill continuously (versus 3 out of 4 weeks a month to induce menstruation), most women will cease menstruation (experience amenorrhea) after several months. Using oral contraceptives that have estrogen can increase the risk of breast cancer, but the new regimen that does not include the use of estrogen may actually reduce this risk (Rowlands, 2009). Smoking while using oral contraceptives is contraindicated because there is a higher risk of serious cardiovascular problems, and smoking can lower the levels of estrogen, affecting the efficiency of the contraceptive (Kroon, 2007; J. A. Ruger, Moser, & Frisch, 2000). The use of oral contraceptives can lead to the development of inflammatory bowel disease (Cornish et al., 2008) and may be contraindicated in women who are obese (e.g., BMI > 35) (Mahendru et al., 2009).

• *Intramuscular injections.* In 1992, the introduction in the United States of depot medroxyprogesterone acetate (Depo-Provera), a drug used for many years in Europe, allowed women protection against pregnancy for 3 months per injection. There have been concerns that Depo-Provera leads to irregular bleeding, decreased bone density, headaches, dizziness, significant weight gain, and breast tenderness (M. K. Clark, Dillon, Sowers, & Nichols, 2005; S. Haider & Darney, 2007; Upadhyay, 2005). In addition, some research has shown that Depo-Provera negatively affects a woman's sense of well-being and her sleep cycle (Brown, Morrison, Larkspur, Marsh, & Nicolaisen, 2008). There is a 0.05% to 3.0% failure rate over 12 months (Guttmacher Institute, 2005; Upadhyay, 2005). The drug Lunelle is given by injection every month compared with the every-3-month injection of Depo-Provera (S. Freeman, 2004). New research is underway to develop a self-injectable

form that will counteract the high discontinuance rates and make it more accessible for those without access to a clinic (Prabhakaran, 2008). This may increase access for rural populations as well as for low-income women, but also will require increased education about proper administration.

• *Implants and patches.* Implants are tiny capsules inserted under the skin by a physician. Older systems consisted of six capsules that made insertion and removal difficult and increased the likelihood of complications (Rowlands, 2009). Implanon, a new single-rod implant, has been shown to be highly effective (i.e., a failure rate of less than 0.05%) and does not carry the risks of multiple-rod implants (Freundl et al., 2010; "Single-Rod Etonogestrel Implant Safe," 2009). In addition, women are given the option to select a transdermal patch, which is changed weekly for 3 weeks per monthly cycle (Hale, 2007; Rowlands, 2009). The patch has the same effectiveness as oral contraceptives in women who are not obese, but about 3% of women discontinue it due to skin irritation (Rowlands, 2009). In populations that are at high risk for unintended pregnancies and abortions, the patch has lower continuation and effectiveness rates than do oral contraceptives, but in low-risk populations, women are more compliant using the patch than oral contraceptives (Bakhru & Stanwood, 2006; J. Miller & Holman, 2006).

• *Vaginal rings.* The vaginal ring remains in place for 3 weeks and then is removed for 1 week. The continuous release of hormones is similar to oral contraceptives, but there are steadier levels of the contraceptive hormones in the blood (Serrant-Green, 2008). The vaginal ring can be removed up to 2 hours before intercourse (Rowlands, 2009). Recent studies have shown that women are more satisfied with the vaginal ring than with oral contraceptives (Schafer, Osborne, Davis, & Westhoff, 2006). They report less depression and irritability (Hollander, 2008), and experience less bleeding than with the pill (Roumen, Op Ten Berg, & Hoomans, 2006), but some women report problems with vaginal discomfort, coital problems, and expulsion (Rowlands, 2009). One study has shown that the vaginal ring can be used as emergency contraception (Croxatto et al., 2005). Another study showed that it was the most effective form of birth control for obese women (L. Gordon, Thakur, & Atlas, 2007).

- *Intrauterine devices (IUDs).* The use of IUDs has been marked by controversy and legal disputes for a number of years. They were introduced in the early 1900s, but high rates of infection and tissue damage discouraged their use until the 1960s. Most manufacturers discontinued production in the 1980s following expensive legal settlements. However, newer IUDs are widely used and are considered safe and reliable. No discernable difference exists in efficacy or side effects related to the copper levels in the IUDs or to the type of insertion used by the physician. Research is currently underway to develop an IUD whose insertion is easier and that can be used in women who are not anatomically suited for insertion of current types (Rowlands, 2009). Approximately 15% of women discontinue use of the IUD within 1 year because of complications, but IUDs have a contraceptive failure rate over 1 year of only between 0.6% and 0.8% for those devices made of copper and 1.5% to 2% for hormonal IUDs (Freundl et al., 2010; Population Reports, 2005). The copper IUD does not protect against STIs. Approximately 2% to 10% are expelled during the first year, but if there are no complications, they can be worn for up to 10 years (Bachmann, 2007). Although IUDs are chosen as a contraceptive by only 2% of women (Guttmacher Institute, 2005), conception after discontinuing for the first 3 months is higher than after stopping the pill (71–80% for the IUD and 60% for women stopping the pill) (B. Kaplan et al., 2005). The IUD has been found to be the optimal contraceptive for women approaching menopause (Bhathena & Guillebaud, 2006) and can be used by women who are breastfeeding (Hale, 2007).

- *Voluntary surgical sterilization.* Tubal ligation, surgical sterilization for women, is considered permanent and has an effectiveness rate of approximately 99.5% (Guttmacher Institute, 2005). A relatively new approach, which allows for a device to be inserted in the fallopian tubes, provides a barrier to the fertilized egg traveling to the uterus, but there is about a 6% failure rate and a risk of tubular rupture; it also requires verification of placement 3 months after placement (Rowlands, 2009). A hysterectomy, the removal of the uterus, is only done if there is a medical need and may involve the removal of the ovaries and fallopian tubes as well (H. Tan & Loth, 2010). For women who want to reverse the tubal ligation, there are new methods including robotic surgery, which reduce the hospital and recovery time significantly from the traditional surgical procedure (Patel, Patel, Steinkampf, Whitten, & Malizia, 2008). In one study, the success rate for robotic surgery was 62.5% compared with the pregnancy rate of 50% for earlier reversal methods (Patel et al., 2008). Vasectomy, or male sterilization, likewise is considered the most reliable method of contraception, with a failure rate of 0.015% to 0.08% in the first year (Hepp & Meuleman, 2006). Recent advances in microsurgery have increased the success rates for reversal procedures, especially if the vasectomy was performed less than 10 years ago. The resultant pregnancy rates within 2 years of reversal are approximately 50% (Busato & Wilson, 2009; Simon & Zieve, 2008).

- *Emergency contraception (EC).* In August of 2006, the U.S. Food and Drug Administration (FDA) approved the "morning-after pill," otherwise known as "Plan B," to be available to women 18 years and older who have a government-issued identification card. It may be purchased without a prescription, but the drug is behind the pharmacist's counter and must be requested (R. H. Allen & Goldberg, 2007; Kavanaugh & Schwarz, 2008; Krisberg, 2006). A two-dose regimen and a one-dose administration have been shown to be equally effective (L. B. Hansen, Saseen, & Teal, 2007), with an 89% effectiveness rate (Melby, 2009). Plan B contains the same ingredients as oral contraceptives, but higher doses are taken. Significant controversy exists regarding this medication, and some pharmacists have refused to provide it to women (Karpa, 2006). Advocates who oppose Plan B call for women under the age of 18 to have a prescription and for all women to talk to a pharmacist to obtain the contraceptive

(Krisberg, 2006). The U.S. Agency for International Development (USAID) has recommended EC for women who have been raped, whose partner's condom breaks, who run out of other forms of contraceptives, who have forgotten to take several consecutive oral contraceptives doses, and who did not expect to have sexual relations (Severy & Spieler, 2000). The American Academy of Pediatrics (AAP) has also supported the over-the-counter availability of EC (AAP—Committee on Adolescence, 2005). However, concerns have been expressed that women may rely on EC as a routine method of contraception rather than as an emergency form, leading to increased risk behaviors, and it offers no protection from STIs (Harvey, Beckman, Sherman, & Petitti, 1999). The cost is low, but there may be side effects, including nausea, vomiting, and bleeding (American Medical Association, 2002). In addition, the Copper T380A, an intrauterine contraceptive, has been used effectively for emergency contraception (R. H. Allen & Goldberg, 2007; Hale, 2007). It is important for the social worker to be familiar with these forms of birth control, especially if they work with populations who have a high rate of undesired fertility and low rates of contraceptive use.

- *New contraceptive methods.* Numerous clinical trials are being conducted, focusing on providing contraceptives to those most in need, using easily delivered methods. Steroidal compounds are in clinical trials, and it is expected that they will help to prevent pregnancy even when women miss doses of their oral contraceptives. Mirena is one new intrauterine device that may reduce the negative effects found with Depo-Provera. In addition, a weekly hormonal injection for men (testosterone enanthate), which suppresses sperm production, has been found to reduce pregnancy rates, but the required frequency of injection is problematic. Contraceptive vaccines continue to be tested, but the focus is moving from vaccinations for women and toward developing a vaccine for men. Other studies are focusing on the proteins in the sperm, changing the cervical mucus to make it less hospitable to sperm, and new implants. The use of vaginal or transdermal gels, nasal sprays, and oral medications is being explored. Generally,

it takes 10–15 years for development of a new contraceptive (Aitken et al., 2008), but hopefully with new research techniques, the demands of affordable, accessible, effective, low-risk, and culturally acceptable contraceptive availability will be met. In addition, emphasis on providing services to special populations—such as women who suffer from a seizure disorder, developmental disability, movement limitations, or mental disorders—must receive attention. As women with disabilities are living longer, this has become an area of interest to social workers (Diekema, 2003; C. Kaplan, 2006; Welner, 1997).

Medical Abortion

Abortion may be the most politicized, hotly debated social issue related to pregnancy today. But it was not always so controversial. Prior to the mid-1800s, abortion was practiced in the United States but was not considered a crime if performed before the fetus *quickened* (or showed signs of life). After 1860, however, physicians advocated banning abortion because of maternal harm caused by the use of dangerous poisons and practices (Figueira-McDonough, 1990). Legislators also wanted to see growth in the U.S. population. By 1900, all states had legislation prohibiting abortion except in extreme circumstances, typically medically related. Over the years, moral issues increasingly became the basis for debate.

In 1973, in *Roe v. Wade,* the U.S. Supreme Court legalized abortion in the first trimester and left it to the discretion of the woman and her physician. Three years later, in 1976, the Hyde Amendment limited federal funding for abortion, and the Supreme Court ruled in 1989, in *Webster v. Reproductive Health Services,* that Medicaid could no longer fund abortions, except in cases of rape, incest, or life endangerment (Kaiser Family Foundation, 2008), and that much of the decision making related to abortion should return to the states. Today, states vary considerably in who has access to abortion, when, how, and at what cost. In some states, new rules are effectively decreasing access, particularly for poor and minority populations. Eighty-seven percent of U.S. counties have no abortion provider, and over one third of women aged 15–44 live in these counties (Kaiser Family Foundation, 2008), resulting in rural disparities in access to abortion.

It is estimated that 42% of unintended pregnancies in the United States end in abortion (Finer & Henshaw, 2006; Kaiser Family Foundation, 2008). Globally, abortion incidence fell from 45.5 million in 1995 to 41.6 million in 2003, a change attributed to increased contraception availability and use. The most dramatic decrease (from 90 to 44 per 1,000 women aged 15–44) was in Eastern Europe. In 2003, Western Europe had the lowest abortion rate in the world (12 per 1,000 women, aged 15–44) (Guttmacher Institute, 2009). In spite of technological advances and improved accessibility, in 2003, there were an estimated 70,000 maternal deaths due to unsafe abortions worldwide; these were found most prevalently in nonindustrialized countries (Guttmacher Institute, 2009).

During the first trimester and until **fetal viability** (the point at which the baby could survive outside the womb) in the second trimester, U.S. federal law allows for a pregnant woman to legally choose an abortion, although states can narrow this option. Approximately 89% of abortions in the United States are performed during the first 12 weeks of pregnancy, 9.9% from 13 to 20 weeks, and 1% after 21 weeks (Kaiser Family Foundation, 2008; Strauss et al., 2002). Recent controversy regarding procedures for terminating a pregnancy after fetal viability has raised ethical and legal dilemmas that are being addressed in the legal system, by most religions, and in other parts of U.S. culture. Global comparisons suggest that there is little to no relationship between legal restrictions on abortion and incidence (Guttmacher Institute, 2009). However, there is a social class disparity in abortion rates, with poor women being less likely to have abortion and 5 times as likely as affluent women their age to have unintended births (Finer & Henshaw, 2006).

Abortion procedures fall into three categories:

1. *Chemical abortion,* also known as medical or nonsurgical abortion, uses the drugs methotrexate, misoprostol, and/or mifepristone (Mifeprex or RU-486, "abortion pill"), followed by prostaglandin. This procedure was used in 13% of all U.S. abortions in 2005 and rose to 25% by 2008, with 98.5% effectiveness for Mifeprex (Fjerstad, Truissell, Sivin, Lichtenberg, & Cullins, 2009). The combined regimen has 92% efficacy if used within the first 49 days of gestation. Prostaglandin can be used alone but has lower efficacy (Spitz, Bardin, Benton, & Robbins, 1998).

2. *Instrumental or surgical evacuation.* One of two types of procedures was used in 87% of all U.S. surgical abortions as of 2005 (R. K. Jones, Zolna, Henshaw, & Finer, 2008). The standard first-trimester vacuum curettage, also called manual vacuum aspiration or MVA, is the one most frequently performed in an outpatient clinic. A suction device is threaded through the cervix to remove the contents of the uterus. It is fairly safe, but because it is invasive, it introduces greater risks than the use of prostaglandin. The second-trimester curettage abortion, accounting for 2.4% of U.S. abortions in 2002 (Strauss et al., 2002), requires even greater dilation of the cervix to allow passage of a surgical instrument to scrape the walls of the uterus. If curettage abortion is performed on an outpatient basis, a second visit is required. With both types of instrumental evacuation, the woman faces risks of bleeding, infection, and subsequent infertility. Abortion between 18 and 26 weeks of gestation is referred to as "late-term abortion" and continues to be hotly debated. The Partial-Birth Abortion Ban Act was introduced in the United States in 1995, passed in 2003, and was reaffirmed in federal court in 2007. This legislation does not prohibit abortion, as sometimes thought, but bans a procedure called intact dilation and extraction, with no health exceptions (Gosten, 2007). Since its passage, 31 states have banned partial-birth abortion, and the debate continues (Kaiser Family Foundation, 2008).

3. *Amnioinfusion.* In the second trimester, a saline solution can be infused into the uterus to end the pregnancy. Amnioinfusion is used in only 0.4% of abortions and requires the greatest medical expertise and follow-up care.

Regardless of the timing or type of abortion, all women should be carefully counseled before and after the procedure. Unplanned pregnancies typically create considerable psychological stress, and social workers can help pregnant women consider all alternatives to an unwanted pregnancy—including abortion—consistent with the client's personal values and beliefs. Following an abortion, most women experience only mild feelings of guilt, sadness, or regret that abate fairly soon, followed by relief that the crisis is resolved (David, 1996). Nevertheless, some women may have a more severe response and may require ongoing counseling, particularly those women who had faced pre-abortion trauma such as sexual abuse and intimate violence (Charles, Polis, Sridhara, & Blum, 2008; G. E. Robinson, Stotland, Russo, Lang, & Occhiogrosso, 2009). Some researchers have found that as many as 40% of women undergoing abortion have prior unwanted sexual experiences (Rue, Coleman, Rue, & Reardon, 2004). Social workers need to be mindful of their personal views about abortion in order to help a client make an informed decision that reflects the client's values, religious beliefs, and available options. In addition, it is important to assess for prior traumatic experiences.

Infertility Treatment

Infertility is usually defined as the inability to create a viable embryo after 1 year of intercourse without contraception, but can also include situations where women can get pregnant but are unable to stay pregnant (P. A. Clark, 2009; Jordon & Ferguson, 2006; National Women's Health Information Center, 2009). It is estimated that about 10% of women in the United States between the ages of 15 and 44 have infertility problems. About one-third of these problems result from women's health issues, another one-third result from men's health issues, and another one-third are the result of health issues of both the woman and the man—or of some unknown issue (National Women's Health Information Center, 2009).

How does infertility affect the multigenerational family?

Most cases of infertility in women are caused by problems with ovulation. Polycystic ovarian syndrome (PCOS), impaired ovulation caused by a hormone imbalance, is the most common cause of infertility in women (Hahn et al., 2006; McGovern et al., 2007; Pasquali, Gambineri & Pagotto, 2006). Infertility can also occur if a woman's ovaries stop functioning normally prior to menopause, a condition known as primary ovarian insufficiency (POI); if the fallopian tubes are blocked due to pelvic inflammatory disease, endometriosis, or surgery for ectopic pregnancy; of if there are physical problems with the uterus, including uterine fibroids (Chavarro, Rich-Edwards, Rosner, & Willett, 2007; Kelly-Weeder & O'Connor, 2006; Khawaja et al., 2009; A. Taylor, 2003).

A number of other factors have been found to increase a woman's risk of infertility. These include older age, stress, poor diet, being either underweight or overweight, smoking, excessive use of alcohol, intensive athletic training, sexually transmitted diseases, or environmental toxins (Al-Hasani & Zohni, 2008; Al-Saleh et al., 2008; Grainger, Frazier, & Rowland, 2006; Kelly-Weeder & O'Connor, 2006; Mendola, Messer, & Rappazzo, 2008; National Women's Health Information Center, 2009; Wilkes & Murdoch, 2009). Black women have been shown to have twice the rate of infertility of White women, even when risk factors such as smoking and obesity are controlled for (Jain, 2006; D. B. Seifer, Frazier, & Grainger, 2008; Wellons et al., 2008).

Defective sperm function is a leading cause of infertility in men (Aitken, Wingate, De Iullis, Koppers, & McLaughlin, 2006; D. A. Bloom et al., 2009). Approximately 67% of men undergoing surgery for infertility had a diagnosis of varicocele, a condition in which the veins on a man's testicles are too large (Meacham, Joyce, Wise, Kparker, & Niederberger, 2007). Male infertility can also be caused by the production of too few or no sperm, or by problems in the movement of sperm (National Women's Health Information Center, 2009). About 10 to 15% of male infertility is due to genetic problems (an important issue when IVF is considered) (Ferlin, Arredi, & Foresta, 2006). Other factors that may impair the health of sperm or reduce their number are age, smoking, heavy alcohol use, some drugs, environmental toxins, radiation treatment or chemotherapy, sitting for extended periods of time, and some health problems (Aitken, Skakkebaek, & Roman, 2006; Boggia et al., 2009; Giudice, 2006; Kefer, Agarwal, & Sabenegh, 2009; K. P. Phillips & Tanphaichitr, 2008; Sheiner, Sheiner, Hammei, Potashnik, & Carel, 2003; Sloter et al., 2006).

As reported in Chapter 9, and clearly demonstrated by Jennifer Bradshaw's story (Case Study 10.3), infertility is a major source of stress for those trying to conceive. Social workers can give increased attention to building resilience in this population (Sexton, Byrd, & Von Kluge, 2010). It is particularly important to help couples like the Bradshaws to keep open lines of communication and to provide mutual support as they consider their options and pursue a line of action.

In the past, infertile couples could keep trying and hope for the best, but medical technology has given today's couples a variety of options, including medication, surgery, artificial insemination, or assisted reproductive technology (see Exhibit 10.2 for a summary of causes of infertility and corresponding treatments). The primary treatment for male infertility, diagnosed by a sperm analysis, is artificial insemination, using fresh or frozen donor sperm injected into the uterus. Artificial insemination is also a treatment choice for lesbian couples and single parents (De Brucker et al., 2009). The success rate varies with age of both the male and female (Kdous et al., 2007), the duration of infertility, previous pregnancy history (Pandian, Bhattacharya, Vale, & Templeton, 2005), and the number of cycles the couple goes through. Overall, it is expected that a woman would become pregnant after 1 cycle 14% of the time and after 12 cycles 77% of the time, but

Exhibit 10.2   Causes of and Treatments for Infertility

Male Infertility		Female Infertility	
Problem	Treatment	Problem	Treatment
Low sperm count	Change of environment; antibiotics; surgery; hormonal therapy; artificial insemination	Vaginal structural problem Abnormal cervical mucus	Surgery Hormonal therapy
Physical defect affecting transport of sperm	Microsurgery	Abnormal absence of ovulation	Antibiotics for infection; hormonal therapy
Genetic disorder	Artificial insemination	Blocked or scarred fallopian tubes	Surgery; IVF
Exposure to work environment substances	Early detection and changes in work environment	Uterine lining unfavorable to implantation	Hormone therapy; antibiotics; surgery
Alcohol and caffeine use and cigarette smoking	Reduction or abstinence pre-conception	Obesity	Weight reduction
Advancing age	Sperm banking at younger age; artificial insemination	Alcohol and caffeine use and cigarette smoking	Abstinence pre-conception (and post- to maximize pregnancy outcome)

this drops to 52% in 12 cycles for women between the ages of 40 and 45 (De Brucker et al., 2009). The cost is approximately $300 to $500 per cycle. Ethical and legal questions have been raised regarding the legal status of the sperm donor (What parental rights does he have?) and the psychosocial impact on the mother. Sperm donors are routinely screened for genetic defects and physical suitability, but psychological screening remains controversial—in large part because it is non-standardized and thus easily misinterpreted.

A number of fertility medicines are used to treat women's ovulation problems, but they carry possible dangers (such as the increased possibility of multiple births) and side effects as well as benefits (National Women's Health Information Center, 2009). It is important that women make informed decisions about their use.

The birth of the first "test tube baby," in 1978, demonstrating the first of many **assisted reproductive technologies (ART),** initiated a new era in infertility management and research. The first test tube baby was conceived in the United States in 1983, and by 2006 over 1% of all babies born in the United States were a result of ART (Van Voorhis, 2006). ART involves the recovery of eggs following hormonal treatment to induce ovulation. Previously frozen eggs may be used, a less expensive and less invasive technique because it does not require removal or hyperstimulation, but the rates of success decrease (B. Davis & Jocoy, 2008). Donor eggs are often used for women over the age of 40 because the rate of live births using ART decreases with age, from over 40% for a woman in her late twenties, to 30% at the age of 38, and 10% at the age of 40 (B. Davis & Jocoy, 2008). However, recent research shows that the use of luteinizing hormone (LH), growth hormones, and gonadotropic hormones may support successful later pregnancies (Alviggi, Humaidan, Howles, Tredway, & Hillier, 2009; Derman & Seifer, 2003).

The most common types of ART are the following:

- *IVF.* Many clinics now inject the sperm directly into the egg(s) that is (are) surgically retrieved (known as intracytoplasmic sperm injection),

especially when there is low sperm motility. This has been found to increase success rates, but coverage of this procedure varies among states, and so its utilization is often dictated by insurance plans (Check, 2007; Jain & Gupta, 2007). Treatment costs may vary among clinics, with one cycle of IVF costing approximately $10,000. Some clinics allow partial or complete refunds if pregnancy does not occur with higher-priced multiple-cycle plans, a practice that is sometimes referred to as "shared risk" (Advanced Fertility Center of Chicago, 2009). Success rates vary, but most clinics suggest that with a single cycle of IVF, there is a 30 to 40% success rate for women under the age of 34, with a live birth rate of 28.3% per cycle (B. Davis & Jocoy, 2008; Toner, 2002), odds slightly lower than what Jennifer Bradshaw was told. Obviously, in impoverished countries where childlessness is a "crippling social taboo," this procedure is beyond the reach of most of the population ("Cheap IVF Needed," 2006; Inhorn, 2003).

- *Gamete intrafallopian tube transfer* (GIFT). At one time, GIFT was used in about 25% of infertility cases, but now that IVF has the same success rate, it only represents 1% of ART procedures (CDC, 2009a; Jain & Gupta, 2007). Success rates are not well documented because this procedure is used so infrequently (B. Davis & Jocoy, 2008), but some estimate a 25–30% success rate with many GIFT treatments resulting in multiple pregnancies (S. Wilson, 2009). GIFT requires the same procedure as IVF, except that the fertilized ova are surgically returned to the woman's fallopian tubes (Jain & Gupta, 2007).

- *Intrauterine insemination* (IUI). IUI involves bypassing the cervix (usually altered by antibodies or infection) and surgically implanting the ovum and spermatozoa into the uterus. It is a costly procedure, often used during the early stages of endometriosis. Pregnancy success rates are less than with GIFT (Lodhi et al., 2004).

- *Preservation and gestational surrogacy.* Fertility preservation is the harvesting of embryos to preserve for future use. It is often used when women face surgery because of cancer and will not be able to conceive in the future (Plante, 2000). Gestational surrogacy is the implantation of an embryo that contains egg and sperm of the intended parents into a surrogate mother. In 2007, there were 10,321 transfers of fresh donor embryos (gestational surrogacy) and 5,632 of frozen donor embryos in the United States (fertility preservation), resulting in success rates of 55.1% and 31.9% of live births, respectively (CDC, 2009a). Cervical cancer is the fourth most frequent cancer diagnosed in women between the ages of 15 and 39, and it directly affects fertility. Recent surgical procedures that avoid hysterectomy to treat cervical cancer have led to increased fertility, but women treated by these procedures have a 33% rate of miscarriage in the first two trimesters (Plante, 2006).

Each procedure carries risks. These include multiple gestations, which carry higher risks of maternal and neonate complications. There is a 50 times greater likelihood of having three or more babies with a pregnancy resulting from ART. Multiple births from ART represent about 50% of all multiple-birth pregnancies (V. M. Allen, Wilson, & Cheung, 2006; Gurgan & Demiro, 2007; Van Voorhis, 2006). There is an increased rate of birth defects; 6.2% of IVF-conceived children have major birth defects compared to 4.4% of naturally conceived children (Van Voorhis, 2006, p. 193).

Uterine transplant is on the frontier of infertility treatment. This was first done in 2000 but did not lead to a successful pregnancy. It has been successful in animals and is being explored, especially to assist younger women who have had a hysterectomy (Nair, Stega, Smith, & Del Priore, 2008).

Adoption is another alternative for the infertile couple. In 2002, an estimated 2% of adults aged 18–44 adopted children, while the percentage of infants given up for adoption by never-married mothers declined to only 1% (J. Jones, 2009). Adoption is not much less daunting than infertility treatment, however. A time-consuming multiphase evaluation, which includes a home study, is required before finalization of custody. The idea of parenting an infant with an unknown genetic heritage may be a challenge for some people, particularly because an increasing number of medical and behavioral problems previously thought to be environmentally induced are being linked—at least in part—to genetics. On the positive side, however, some individuals and couples prefer adoption to the demands and uncertainties of ART, and some adoptive parents are also committed to giving a home to children in need of care.

Critical Thinking Questions 10.2

What do you know about your own genetic makeup? How important do you think genetics are in human behavior? How comfortable would you be in discussing birth control options with clients? How would you go about learning which birth control methods tend to be more acceptable to a particular cultural group? How comfortable would you be in exploring abortion as an option for a troubled pregnancy? If you were to face the challenge of infertility, what alternatives would you be willing to consider? How comfortable would you be in helping clients explore options that would not be acceptable to you?

NORMAL FETAL DEVELOPMENT _____

The 40 weeks of **gestation,** during which the fertilized ovum becomes a fully developed infant, are a remarkable time for both the parents as well as the new life taking form. *Gestational age* is calculated from the date of the beginning of the woman's last menstrual period, a fairly easy time for the woman to identify. In contrast, *fertilization age* is measured from the time of fertilization, approximately 14 days after the beginning of the last menstrual period. The average pregnancy lasts 280 days when calculated from gestational age and 266 days from the time of fertilization. Conventionally, the gestation period is organized by trimesters of about 3 months each. This is a convenient system, but note that these divisions are not supported by clearly demarcated events.

First Trimester

In some ways, the first 12 weeks of pregnancy are the most dramatic. In an amazingly short time, sperm and ovum unite and are transformed into a being with identifiable body parts. The mother's body also undergoes dramatic changes.

Fertilization and the Embryonic Period

Sexual intercourse results in the release of an average of 200 million to 300 million sperm. Their life span is relatively short, and their journey through the female reproductive tract is fraught with hazards. Thus, only about 1 or 2 in 1,000 of the original sperm reach the fallopian tubes, which lead from the ovaries to the uterus (refer back to Exhibit 3.10 for a visual representation of the female internal sex organs). Typically, only one sperm penetrates the ripened ovum, triggering a biochemical reaction that prevents entry of any other sperm. The **zygote** (fertilized egg) continues to divide and begins about a 7-day journey to the uterus.

Following implantation in the uterine wall, the zygote matures into an **embryo.** The placenta, which acts like a filter between the mother and the growing embryo, also forms. The umbilical cord connects the fetus to the placenta. Oxygen, water, and glucose, as well as many drugs, viruses, bacteria, vitamins, and hormones, pass through the placenta to the embryo. Amniotic fluid in the uterus protects the embryo throughout the pregnancy.

By the third week, tissue begins differentiating into organs. During this period, the embryo is vulnerable to **teratogens**—substances that may harm the developing organism—but most women do not know they are pregnant at this point. Exhibit 10.3 shows how some relatively common drugs may

Exhibit 10.3 Potential Teratogens During the First Trimester

Substance	Effects on Fetal Development
Acetaminophen (Tylenol)	None
Amphetamines	Cardiac defects, cleft palate
Antacids	Increase in anomalies
Antianxiety medications	Increase in anomalies
Antiepileptic medications	Neural tube defects, especially facial
Antihistamines	None
Barbiturates	Increase in anomalies
Gentamycin (antibiotic)	Cranial nerve damage
Glucocorticoids (steroids)	Cleft palate, cardiac defects
Haloperidol	Limb malformations
Insulin	Skeletal malformations
Lithium	Goiter, eye anomalies, cleft palate
LSD	Chromosomal abnormalities
Penicillin	None
Phenobarbital	Multiple anomalies
Podophyllin (in laxatives)	Multiple anomalies
Tetracycline (antibiotic)	Inhibition of bone growth, discoloration of teeth
Tricyclic antidepressants	Central nervous system and limb malformations

have a teratogenic effect in the earliest stage of fetal development. Research is also showing that maternal diet has an influence on brain development. Studies have found that nutritional deficiency in the first trimester results in an increase in brain abnormalities. High-fat diets negatively affect the development of the hippocampus, which helps control long-term memory and spatial navigation. Protein deficiency causes global deficits and problems in the hippocampus and cortex. Iron deficiencies affect processing speed, recognition memory, and motor development, and can cause irreversible behavioral and learning deficits. Zinc deficiency affects cognitive development, cerebellum development, and attention (Georgieff, 2007; Massaro, Rothbaum, & Aly, 2006; Niculescu & Lupu, 2009). Nutritional deficiencies also are thought to be a potential risk for later development of schizophrenia (Rifas-Shiman et al., 2006). Research has also shown that thyroid hormones play an important role in brain development and that deficiencies, such as iodine deficiency, during the first and third trimesters may lead to later learning disabilities (de Escobar, 2004; de Escobar, Ares, Berbel, Obregon, & del Rey, 2008; Rifas-Shiman et al., 2006; Sethi, 2004).

The Fetal Period

After the eighth week, the embryo is mature enough to be called a **fetus** (meaning "young one") (J. C. Novak & Broom, 1995), and the mother is experiencing signs of her pregnancy. Usually, the mother has now missed one menstrual period, but if her cycle was irregular, this may not be a reliable sign. Approximately 50% of women experience nausea and vomiting (morning sickness) during the first trimester, as was the case for Felicia Thompson. A few experience vomiting so severe that it causes dehydration and metabolic changes requiring hospitalization. *Multigravidas,* women who have had a previous pregnancy, often recognize the signs of excessive fatigue and soreness in their breasts as signs of pregnancy.

Between the 7th and 12th week, the fetal heart rate can be heard using a Doppler device that affords a three- or four-dimensional view leading to early diagnosis of maternal and fetal problems (Kurjak et al., 2005; Merce, Barco, Alcazar, Sabatel, & Trojano, 2009). At 12 weeks, the gender of the fetus can be detected, and the face is fully formed. The fetus is moving within the mother, but it is still too early for her to feel the movement.

Newly pregnant women often feel ambivalence. Because of hormonal changes, they may experience mood swings and become less outgoing. Concerns about the changes in their bodies, finances, the impact on their life goals, lifestyle adjustments, and interpersonal interactions may cause anxiety. Often, the father experiences similar ambivalence, and he may be distressed by his partner's mood swings. Parents who have previously miscarried may have a heightened concern for the well-being of this fetus.

Second Trimester

By the 16th week, the fetus is approximately 19 centimeters (7.5 inches) long and weighs about 100 grams (3.3 ounces). The most rapid period of brain development is during the second trimester

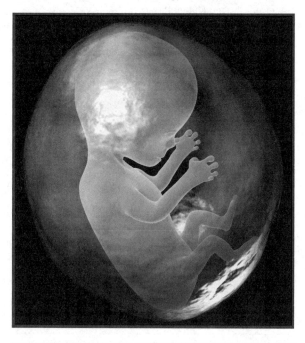

Photo 10.5 After week 8, the embryo is mature enough to be called a fetus.

(van de Beek, Thijssen, Cohen-Kettenis, van Goozen, & Buitelaar, 2004). Recent evidence cautions pregnant women to monitor the eating of fish with higher levels of mercury to avoid negative impact on the infant's cognitive skills (McDiarmid, Gardiner, & Jack, 2008; Oken et al., 2005). The second trimester is generally a period of contentment and planning for most women, as it seems to have been for Felicia Thompson. For problem pregnancies, or in troubled environments, quite the opposite may occur. However, the fatigue, nausea and vomiting, and mood swings that often accompany the first few weeks usually disappear in the second trimester.

Hearing the heartbeat and seeing the fetus via ultrasound often bring the reality of the pregnancy home. As seen in the story of the Thompsons, *quickening*—the experience of feeling fetal movement—usually occurs around this time, further validating the personhood of the fetus. *Fetal differentiation*, whereby the mother separates the individuality of the fetus from her own personhood, is usually completed by the end of this trimester. Many fathers also begin to relate to the fetus as a developing offspring.

Some fathers enjoy the changing shape of the woman's body, but others may struggle with the changes. Unless there are specific contraindications, sexual relations may continue throughout the pregnancy, and some men find the second trimester a period of great sexual satisfaction. Often during the second trimester, the pregnant woman also experiences a return of her pre-pregnancy level of sexual desire.

Third Trimester

By 24 weeks, the fetus is considered viable in many hospitals. Today, neurosonography can visualize the fetal brain anatomy when central nervous system (CNS) anomalies are suspected (Malinger, Lev, & Lerman-Sagie, 2006). In spite of fetal viability, parents are not usually prepared for childbirth early in the third trimester. Felicia Thompson, for instance, was not prepared for the birth of her son, Paul, who at 26 weeks' gestation, struggled to survive. Not only are parents not prepared, but the risks

to newborns are very great if birth occurs prior to the 26th week of pregnancy. Recent research indicates another caution for mothers during the third trimester: Smoking during this period can affect critical brain development, lead to higher rates of preterm delivery and low birth weight infants, and contribute to subsequent behavioral problems (Baler, Vakow, Fowler, & Benveniste, 2008; Huang & Winzer-Serhan, 2006; Jaddoe et al., 2008).

The tasks of the fetus during the third trimester are to gain weight and mature in preparation for delivery. As delivery nears, the increased weight of the fetus can cause discomfort for the mother, and often she looks forward to delivery with increasing anticipation. Completion of preparations for the new arrival consume much of her attention.

Labor and Delivery of the Neonate

Predicting when labor will begin is impossible. However, one indication of imminent labor is *lightening* (the descent of the fetus into the mother's pelvis). For a *primipara*—a first-time mother—lightening occurs approximately 2 weeks before delivery. For a *multipara*—a mother who has previously given birth—lightening typically occurs at the beginning of labor. Often, the mother experiences *Braxton Hicks contractions,* brief contractions that prepare the mother and fetus for labor (sometimes referred to as "false labor"). Usually, true labor begins with a show or release of the mucous plug that covered the cervical opening.

Labor is divided into three stages:

1. In the first stage, the cervix thins and dilates. The amniotic fluid is usually released during this stage ("water breaking"), and the mother feels regular contractions that intensify in frequency and strength as labor progresses. Many factors determine the length of this stage, including the number of pregnancies the mother has experienced, the weight of the fetus, the anatomy of the mother, the strength of the contractions, and the relaxation of the mother in the process. Despite the stories that abound, most mothers have plenty of time to prepare for the

upcoming birth. Near the end of this phase, "transition" occurs, marked by a significant increase in the intensity and frequency of the contractions and heightened emotionalism. The head crowns (is visible at the vulva) at the end of this stage.

2. The second stage is delivery, when the **neonate** (newborn) is expelled from the mother. If the newborn is born breech (feet or buttocks first) or is transverse (positioned horizontally in the birth canal) and cannot be turned prior to birth, the mother may require a cesarean section.

3. Typically, within 1 hour after delivery, the placenta, the remaining amniotic fluid, and the membrane that separated the fetus from the uterine wall are delivered with a few contractions. If the newborn breastfeeds immediately, the hormone oxytocin is released to stimulate these contractions.

Following birth, the neonate undergoes rapid physiological changes, particularly in its respiratory and cardiac systems. Prior to birth, oxygen is delivered to the fetus through the umbilical vein, and carbon dioxide is eliminated by the two umbilical arteries. Although the fetus begins to breathe prior to birth, breathing serves no purpose until after delivery. The neonate's first breath, typically in the form of a cry, creates tremendous pressure within the lungs, which clears amniotic fluid and triggers the opening and closing of several shunts and vessels in the heart. The blood flow is rerouted to the lungs.

Many factors, such as maternal exposure to narcotics during pregnancy or labor, can adversely affect the neonate's attempts to breathe—as can prematurity, congenital anomalies, and neonatal infections. Drugs and other interventions may be administered to maintain adequate respiration. To measure the neonate's adjustment to extrauterine life, *Apgar scores*—rather simple measurements of physiological health—are assessed at 1, 5, and 10 minutes after birth. Apgar scores determine the need for resuscitation, indicate the effectiveness of resuscitation efforts, and predict long-term problems that might arise. The other immediate challenge to the newborn is to establish a stable temperature. Inadequately maintained body

temperature creates neonatal stress and thus increased respiratory and cardiac effort, which can result in respiratory failure. Close monitoring of the neonate during the first 4 hours after birth is critical to detect any such problems in adapting to extrauterine life.

MISCARRIAGE AND STILLBIRTH _____

Not all pregnancies proceed smoothly and end in routine deliveries. *Miscarriage* is the naturally occurring loss of a fetus prior to 20 weeks of gestation—a *spontaneous abortion*. Approximately 10 to 20% of all clinically recognized pregnancies end in spontaneous abortion, often without a discernible cause and often unrecognized by the mother (Neugebauer et al., 2006). Recurrent miscarriage, three or more consecutive miscarriages, occur in 2 to 3% of women and are usually caused by chromosomal abnormalities, metabolic disorders, immune factors, problems with the woman's reproductive anatomy, or metabolic disorders (A. W. Horn & Alexander, 2005). Approximately 70% of these women ultimately are able to conceive (Kiwi, 2006; "New Concepts," 2006). Recent research focusing on the causes of miscarriage point to multiple potential factors, including fetal chromosomal anomalies (Christiansen, Nielsen, & Kolte, 2006), sickle cell trait (M. Y. Taylor et al., 2006), uterine cancer (Critchley & Wallace, 2005), PCOS (van der Spuy & Dyer, 2004), rubella (Edlich, Winters, Long, & Gubler, 2005), number of members in a household, coffee consumption, number of pregnancies, history of abortion (Nojomi, Akbarian, & Ashory-Moghadam, 2006), stress (Nepomnaschy et al., 2006), and obesity (Yu, Teoh, & Robinson, 2006). At greater risk are those women who are African American; have less education; and are of lower socioeconomic status, especially with income below the poverty level (S. K. Price, 2006).

An estimated 20.9% of threatened spontaneous abortions become complete abortions (Buss et al., 2006). Any vaginal bleeding other than spotting during pregnancy is considered a threatened spontaneous abortion (miscarriage), but about 1 in 4 women experience some bleeding in the first few months of pregnancy and many stop bleeding and have a normal pregnancy. If the abortion is incomplete, any placenta or fetus that is not expelled must be surgically removed or the mother risks hemorrhage and infection. Counseling of women who struggle with miscarriages focuses on genetics and the biopsychological needs of the woman and her family (Laurino et al., 2005; Neugebauer et al., 2006).

Stillbirth is defined as fetal loss at 20 weeks or later and accounts for 60% of all perinatal mortality. More than 4 million stillbirths occur annually, most in impoverished countries (E. M. McClure, Nalubamba-Phiri, & Goldenberg, 2006; Nhu et al., 2006). In the United States, approximately 25,000 stillbirths occur annually, 37.9 per 10,000 births with 3.2 per 1,000 occurring at between 20 and 27 weeks and 4.3 per 1,000 after 28 weeks (Ananth, Liu, Joseph, Kramer, & Fetal and Infant Health Study Group of the Canadian Perinatal Surveillance System, 2008; Barclay, 2009). Approximately 8 to 13% of fetal deaths at this gestational period are caused by chromosomal and genetic abnormalities, with other risks including obesity, advanced maternal age, and women with no previous pregnancies. African American women experience 2.2 times greater chance of stillbirth than non-Hispanic White women, with higher education reducing the hazard for stillbirth more for Caucasian women than for Black women (Willinger, Ko, & Reddy, 2009). Women who had a preexisting mental illness prior to pregnancy have a greater rate of fetal loss (Gold, Dalton, Schwenk, & Hayward, 2007), and women who have been victims of domestic violence are also at greater risk. There is a greater chance of subsequent pregnancies ending in stillbirth once one has occurred (Barclay, 2009). In cases of stillbirth, the pregnancy may continue for several days following cessation of movement. Although this wait can be distressing for the mother, labor generally proceeds and is allowed to occur naturally. Cesarean sections are usually avoided due to the high number of complications for the mother (Barclay, 2009). Stillbirths are often unexpected, resulting in great stress and anguish for parents, who blame themselves and struggle with unresolved guilt. Social workers can help parents to understand and cope with the strong emotions they are experiencing.

AT-RISK NEWBORNS

There is growing evidence from longitudinal research on developmental risk and protection that conditions during pregnancy and delivery influence what happens at later points in life. For example,

> What do social workers need to know about the effects that different aspects of fetal development can have on subsequent development?

recent biomedical research indicates that fetal undernutrition is a contributing factor in late-life health conditions such as coronary heart disease, type 2 diabetes, and hypertension (see Joss-Moore & Lane, 2009). Major congenital anomalies (commonly referred to as birth defects), prematurity, and low birth weight present challenges to the newborn and his or her family and can serve as risk factors throughout the life course.

Major Congenital Anomalies

Overall, only 2 to 4% of all surviving newborns have a birth defect. However, the number of neonates born with anomalies due to genetics, exposure to teratogens, or nonhereditary factors that affect development of the fetus does not reflect the number of abnormal embryos. Fewer than half of all fertilized ova result in a live birth; the rest of all fertilized ova are spontaneously aborted. The probability that a fertilized ovum with a genetic anomaly will abort spontaneously ranges from 80 to 90% (Opitz, 1996). The American College of Medical Genetics with the March of Dimes has established a recommended list of 28 metabolic, endocrine, and hemoglobin disorders for which newborns should be screened because early intervention for these hereditary yet rare diseases is essential. As of March 2006, only five U.S. states met all of these recommendations. The National Newborn Screening and Genetics Resource Center (www.nccrcg.org/about.asp) provides the list of mandatory screenings by a specific state. Each state's health department has this information as well. You can visit the website www.ornl.gov/sci/techresources/Human_Genome/medicine/genetest.shtml#testsavailable to obtain a list of diseases for which genetic tests are available.

It is important to remember that not all congenital anomalies have a genetic basis, but preventing, diagnosing, and predicting the outcome of genetic disorders are very difficult because of the complexities of genetic processes. Here are some examples of that complexity:

- *Variable expressivity.* Genes manifest differently in different people. For example, persons with cystic fibrosis, caused by a recessive gene, display wide variability in the severity of symptoms. The expression of the disorder appears to be influenced by the interplay of psychological, social, political, economic, and other environmental factors. The effects can be exacerbated by maternal substance abuse, inadequate maternal nutrition, and birth trauma. Children with cystic fibrosis born into poverty may not have benefited from early diagnosis, may live in an inner city that exposes them to increased levels of pollution, or may lack adequate home medical care because the primary caregiver is also responsible for meeting the family's economic needs.

- *Genetic heterogeneity.* The same characteristic may be a consequence of mutations or other defects in more than one gene. Genetic heterogeneity is common in many human diseases, including Alzheimer's and polycystic kidney diseases (Medical Glossary, 2011; National Institute on Aging, 2011).

- *Pleiotropy principle.* The same gene may influence seemingly unrelated systems (Vansteelandt et al., 2009). One example is the disease phenylketonuria (PKU), which is caused by a mutation in a single gene but causes such disparate traits as mental retardation and reduced hair and skin pigmentation.

- *Epigenetics.* More recently, researchers have focused on another dimension of heritability that points to environmental factors that influence gene expression (phenotype) without changing the genetic makeup of a person (genotype). These factors influence the chemicals that trigger (methyl groups) or inhibit (acetyl groups) genetic expression. Furthermore, these chemicals appear to have a generational influence without genetic alterations. Examples of these epigenetic environmental influences include nutrition, trauma such as childhood abuse, and teratogens (Lederberg, 2001). The epigenetic influences in many cases are preventable and treatable, especially if identified early in development.

Congenital anomalies fall into four main categories, summarized in Exhibit 10.4 (Opitz, 1996; G. B. Reed, 1996; Vekemans, 1996).

Exhibit 10.4   Four Categories of Genetic Anomalies

Inheritance of Single Abnormal Gene		
Recessive	**Dominant**	**Sex-Linked**
Sickle-cell anemia	Neurofibromatosis	Hemophilia
Tay-Sachs disease	Huntington's disease	Duchenne muscular dystrophy
Cystic fibrosis		
Multifactorial Inheritance		
Possible mental illness	Alcoholism	

Chromosomal Aberration		
Down syndrome (additional 21st chromosome)	Turner's syndrome (X)	Klinefelter's syndrome (XXY)
Exposure to Teratogens			
---	---	---	---
Radiation	Infections	Maternal Metabolic Imbalance	Drugs and Environmental Chemicals
Neural tube defects	Rubella: deafness, glaucoma Syphilis: neurological, ocular, and skeletal defects	Diabetes: neural tube defects Folic acid deficiency: brain and neural tube defects Hyperthermia (at 14–28 days)	Alcohol: mental retardation Heroin: attention deficit/ hyperactivity disorder Amphetamine: congenital defects

1. *Inheritance of a single abnormal gene.* An inherited anomaly in a single gene may lead to a serious disorder. The gene may be recessive, meaning that both parents must pass it along, or it may be dominant, in which case only one parent needs to have the gene in order for it to be expressed in the child. A third possibility is that the disorder is sex-linked, meaning that it is passed along by either the father or the mother.

2. *Multifactorial inheritance.* Some genetic traits, such as height and intelligence, are influenced by environmental factors such as nutrition. Their expression varies because of *multifactorial inheritance,* meaning that they are controlled by multiple genes. Multifactorial inheritance is implicated in traits that predispose a person to mental illnesses, such as depression. However, these traits are merely predisposing factors, creating what is called *genetic liability.* Siblings born with the same genetic traits thus may vary in the likelihood of developing a specific genetically based disorder, such as alcoholism or mental illness (E. A. Takahashi & Turnbull, 1994).

3. *Chromosomal aberration.* Some genetic abnormalities are not hereditary but rather are caused by a genetic mishap during development of the ovum or sperm cells. Sometimes the cells end up missing chromosomes or having too many. When the ovum or sperm cell has fewer than 23 chromosomes, the probability of conception and survival is minimal. But in the presence of too many chromosomes in the ovum or the sperm, various anomalies occur. Down syndrome, or trisomy 21, the most common chromosomal aberration, is the presence of 47 chromosomes—specifically, an extra chromosome in the 21st pair. Its prevalence is 1 in 600 to 1,000 live births, but increases to 1 in 350 for women over age 35 (Vekemans, 1996). Other chromosome anomalies include Turner's syndrome (a single sex chromosome, X) and Klinefelter's syndrome (an extra sex chromosome, XXY).

4. *Exposure to teratogens.* Teratogens can be divided into four categories: radiation, infections, maternal metabolic imbalance, and drugs and environmental chemicals. Possible effects of commonly abused legal and illegal substances are presented in Exhibit 10.5. In the Thompson story, Felicia wondered if Paul's premature birth was a result of prenatal exposure to paint fumes. It may have been, depending on what specific chemicals were involved when exposure occurred, and to what degree. Parents who, like the Thompsons, are experiencing considerable guilt over their possible responsibility for their newborn's problems may take comfort from the knowledge that the impact of exposure to teratogens can vary greatly. Much depends on the timing of exposure. The various organ systems have different critical or *sensitive periods,* summarized in Exhibit 10.6.

Exhibit 10.5 Commonly Abused Drugs and Fetal Effects

	Alcohol	Cocaine	Amphetamines	Cigarettes	Heroin
Abortion	X	X	X		X
Stillbirth	X	X	X		X
Prematurity	X	X	X	X	X
Intrauterine growth retardation	X	X	X	X	X
Respiratory distress	X	X			X
Withdrawal	X	X	X		X
Fine motor problems	X				X
Malformations	X	X	X		X
Developmental delays	X	X	X		X

Exhibit 10.6 Sensitive Periods in Prenatal Development

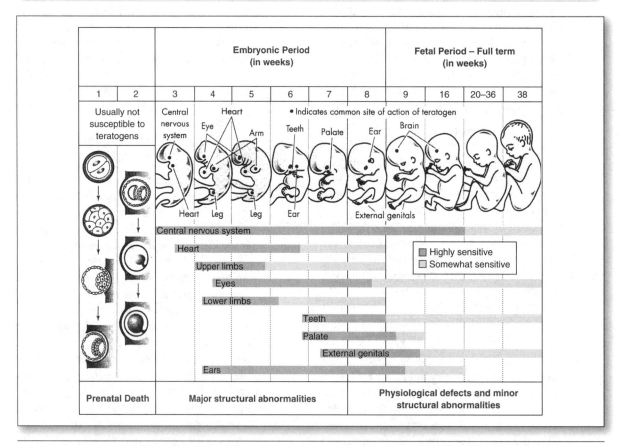

SOURCE: K. L. Moore & Persend (1993). ©Elsevier. Reprinted with permission.

Parents who have reason to fear these congenital anomalies often opt for diagnosis during pregnancy. *Chorionic villi testing* (CVT) involves the insertion of a catheter through the cervix into the uterus to obtain a sample of the developing placenta; it can be done as early as 8 weeks but carries a slightly higher risk of causing *spontaneous abortion* (miscarriage) compared to amniocentesis. *Amniocentesis* is the extraction of amniotic fluid for chromosomal analysis; it involves inserting a hollow needle through the abdominal wall during the second trimester. A frequent procedure is *ultrasonography* (ultrasound), which produces a visual image of the developing fetus, typically done at 18–22 weeks of pregnancy. Risk factors for any pre-birth genetic testing include mothers over the age of 35, carriers of sex-linked genetic disorders and single-gene defects, parents with chromosomal disorders, and women who have had previous and recurring pregnancy loss (American Pregnancy Association, 2009).

If an anomaly is detected, the decisions that need to be made are not easy ones. The possibility of false readings on these tests makes the decisions even more complicated. Should the fetus be aborted? Should fetal surgery be undertaken? Could gene replacement therapy, implantation of genetic material to alter the genotype—still a costly experimental procedure—prevent an anomaly or limit its manifestation? Do the parents have the financial and psychological means to care for a neonate with a disability? What is the potential impact on the marriage and extended family system? What is the potential long-term impact of knowing one's genetic makeup? For example, the 2008 Genetic Information Nondiscrimination Act (GINA) prohibits insurance companies and employers from using genetic information in discriminatory ways (HGP, 2009b).

Prematurity and Low Birth Weight

Prematurity is the leading cause of illness and death in obstetrics (Reedy, 2008) and can have a profound long-term effect on the newborn and the family (Carvalho, Linhares, Padovani, & Martinez, 2009).

In the United States, the rate of premature birth rose 31% between 1981 and 2007, and in 2007, a total of 12.7% of all births were early (Cantor, 2007; Gaylord, Greer, & Botti, 2008; B. Johnson & Chavkin, 2007; M. M. Kent, 2009; March of Dimes, 2009). This is one of the highest rates in industrialized countries (B. Johnson & Chavkin, 2007) and much higher than the targeted rate of 7.6% proposed in the Healthy People's Initiative goal for 2010 (Rabin, 2009). In 2007, Mississippi led the country with a premature birth rate of 18.3%, and Puerto Rico's rate was 19.4% (March of Dimes, 2009; Rabin, 2009). There is a disparity in the rates of prematurity among different ethnic groups. An estimated 1 in 5 births to African American women is premature, compared to 1 in 8 for non-Hispanic White infants. The African American infant has a mortality rate that is 2 to 3 times higher than non-Hispanic White infants, (M. M. Kent, 2009; MacDorman & Mathews, 2009), but there is some question as to whether the number of Black deaths is accurately reported (Wingate & Alexander, 2006). The rates for American Indian, Alaska Native, and Puerto Rican premature births are also higher than those for the non-Hispanic White woman, but Asian, Pacific Islander, Central and South American, Mexican, and Cuban rates are lower than for non-Hispanic White women (Damus, 2008; Grady, 2009; Reedy, 2007). Increased research attention is being given to the interplay between biological determinants and social patterns that may contribute to prematurity (M. R. Kramer & Hogue, 2009).

Approximately 70% of preterm births occur at 34 to 36 weeks' gestation (40 weeks is full gestation) and are referred to as *late-preterm births* (March of Dimes, 2010). These newborns may weigh more than 2,500 grams (see below) but are still premature. Between 1990 and 2006, the rate of late preterm births rose 20% with about 900 late preterm babies born each day in the United States. There appears to be minimal difference in this rate based on race or maternal age (J. A. Martin, Kirmeyer, Osterman, & Shepherd, 2009). Previously, it was considered that babies born within a few weeks of their due date had fewer complications, but new evidence shows that they are at risk for possible neurodevelopmental problems, feeding and respiratory difficulties, and poor temperature regulation (Darcy, 2009; Reedy, 2008). They have increased rates of readmission to the hospital during their first year of life, higher health costs, and greater morbidity than full-term infants (McLaurin, Hall, Jackson, Owens, & Mahadevia, 2009).

Low birth weight (LBW) infants—those weighing less than 2,500 grams (5 pounds, 8 ounces) at birth—account for 65% of all premature births (Darcy, 2009). Infants under 2,500 grams account for 7.9% of births, those between 2,000 grams (4.4 pounds) and 2,499 grams (5.5 pounds) account for 4.9% of births, and those between 1,500 grams (3.3 pounds) and 1,999 grams (4.4 pounds) account for 1.4% of births (CDC, 2009d). In the past, it was postulated that LBW infants had fewer long-term complications than those born at even lower weights and at earlier stages of development, but there may be more risk than expected (Reedy, 2007). LBW infants are 6 times more likely to die in the first week of life compared to a full-term infant and have a mortality rate in the first year that is 3 times greater (March of Dimes, 2009).

The rate of *very low birth weight (VLBW)* infants—those weighing less than 1,500 grams (3 pounds, 3 ounces)—has increased from 1.15% of all births in 1980 to 1.4% in 2007, primarily due to multiple births (often a complication of ART) (CDC, 2009d; Hoyert, Mathews, Menacker, Strobino, & Guyer, 2006; Lucille Packard Children's Hospital, 2010). Children born at this weight have a greater risk for poor physical growth (Datar & Jacknowitz, 2009), learning disabilities, and behavioral problems (March of Dimes, 2010). Infants born in rural areas have lower success rates than those born in urban areas, possibly due to less access to neonatal intensive care units (NICUs) (Abdel-Latif et al., 2006). There are significant racial differences in the number of VLBW infants born, with African American women having a higher premature delivery rate (Reedy, 2008).

Extremely low birth weight (ELBW) infants—those weighing less than 1,000 grams (2.2 pounds)—experience approximately a 50 to 80% survival rate (Gargus et al., 2009). Delivery rates decrease as the neonate's weight decreases, with those between 500 grams (1.1 pounds) and 999 grams (2.2 pounds) representing 0.6% of those born prematurely and those under 500 grams (less than 1.1 pounds) only representing 0.2% (CDC, 2009d). One large study found that 18 months after birth, 40% of ELBW infants had died, 16% were unimpaired, 22% had mild impairments, and the same percentage had moderate to severe neurodevelopmental impairments. Less than 1% of infants born weighing less than 500 grams survived free of impairments (Gargus et al., 2009). Paul Thompson is considered an ELBW newborn, and at approximately 540 grams, he has a 50% chance of survival.

About 30% of LBW births can be attributed to perinatal environmental factors, such as maternal stress or illness (e.g., genital infections), some maternal working conditions, smoking, poor maternal weight gain during pregnancy along with being underweight before the pregnancy, intrauterine infections, and maternal short stature (Goldenberg, Hauth, & Andrews, 2000; Heck, Schoendorf, & Chavez, 2002; N. Spencer & Logan, 2002). More than 50% of children are born to mothers who work during their pregnancy, and some work conditions pose risk of premature birth. Women who have high job stress, moderate or low social support, a demanding posture for 3 or more hours per day, and whole-body vibrations have an increased risk of premature delivery (A. Croteau, Marcoux, & Brisson, 2007).

One of the greatest risk factors for the infant's decreased birth weight (LBW, VLBW, ELBW, or intrauterine growth retardation) is maternal smoking. Women who smoke have smaller babies, with female neonates more negatively affected than males (Ling, Lian, Ho, & Yeo, 2009; Suzuki et al., 2008; Volgt, Hermanussen, Wittwer-Backofen, Fusch, & Hesse, 2006). Other risk factors for prematurity, LBW, and VLBW include alcohol and other drug use (especially polydrug and cocaine use) (Bada et al., 2005; Sokol et al., 2007). Also, advanced maternal age (greater than 30), high blood pressure, and a nontechnical/nonprofessional paternal occupation (perhaps a measure of lower socioeconomic status) are associated with repetitive premature deliveries (Sclowitz & Santos,

2006). Obesity, adolescent pregnancy, diabetes, late or inadequate prenatal care, a male infant, a multiple pregnancy, or a previous cesarean section also increase the risk of prematurity (Guillory, Cai, & Hoff, 2008). Finally, mothers enrolled in Medicaid have increased rates of prematurity and infant death compared to mothers enrolled in non-public insurance plans (G. D. Brandon et al., 2009). The mother's adequate nutrition prior to conception, as well as during pregnancy, is another important factor in fetal health. Risk is decreased by gaining between 20 and 35 pounds with a singleton (rather than multiple) pregnancy if the mother's pre-pregnancy weight was normal. If the mother was underweight, a gain of 28–40 pounds is recommended compared to 11–20 pounds if the mother was obese (Hitti, 2009; Institute of Medicine of the National Academies, 2009).

Children born prematurely are at risk for lower IQ scores (Narberhaus et al., 2007; Weisglas-Kuperus et al., 2009) and more impairments in language and visual motor skills (Ortiz-Mantilla, Choudhury, Leevers, & Benasich, 2008). Prematurity also contributes to developmental delays (C. E. F. Delgado, Vagi, & Scott, 2007; Kalia, Visintainer, Brumberg, Pici, & Kase, 2009) and cognitive disabilities (Petrini et al., 2009), as well as attention problems and self-regulatory problems (Aarnoudse-Moens, Weisglas-Kuperus, van Goudoever, & Oosterlaan, 2009). Preterm birth accounts for one third of all cases of cerebral palsy (Wenstrom, 2009) and carries a higher risk of neonatal seizures (Petrini et al., 2009). Thus, the Thompsons have reason to wonder what the future holds for their baby. In spite of the risks associated with preterm birth, the first cohort of survivors is now reaching early adulthood, and early studies are heartening because their high school graduation rates are equal to those of their normal birth weight peers (Saigal et al., 2006).

The survival rates of premature infants have improved largely because of explosive growth in the field of neonatal medicine and the establishment of regional NICUs. Studying the long-term effects of prematurity is difficult because today's 5-year-old who was LBW received significantly less sophisticated care than the current patients in NICUs. There is evidence that the vulnerability of the premature brain during this critical period of development is negatively affected by the stressful neonatal environmental conditions (Elley, 2001; J. M. Perlman, 2001). Therefore, neonatal environmental conditions may be as much of a risk factor for negative pregnancy outcomes as prematurity (Als, Heidelise, & Butler, 2008).

As the Thompsons know all too well, parents' expectations for a healthy newborn are shattered when their child is admitted to an NICU. Their fear and anxiety often make it hard for them to form a strong emotional bond with their newborn. About 90% of mothers and 80% of fathers report that they develop an attachment to the infant during the third trimester of pregnancy. But when an infant is premature, the parents have not had the same opportunity. In addition, the fear that a sickly newborn may die inhibits some parents from risking attachment. Mothers of VLBW infants visit the newborn significantly less than do mothers of infants who weigh more; for fathers, visitation is influenced by geographical distance and the number of other children in the home (Latva, Lehtonen, Salmelin, & Tamminen, 2007). Some parents are consumed with guilt about their baby's condition and believe that they will only harm the newborn by their presence. The NICU experience places the mother at risk of depression, but it also has been found that short-term psychotherapy can reduce stress and promote visitation (S. H. Friedman, Kessler, & Martin, 2009). Felicia and Will Thompson had to work hard to contain their anxiety about Paul's frailties.

Early disruption in bonding may have a larger long-term impact on the child than the infant's actual medical condition (Wigert, Johannson, Berg, & Hellstrom, 2006). The response has been a movement toward family-centered NICU environments, which are structured to promote interaction between the infant and the parents, siblings, and others in the family's support system. Mothers seem to more readily engage in caring for their infants in this environment than fathers (A. N. Johnson, 2008). Ample opportunity to interact with Paul facilitated Felicia and Will Thompson's attempts to bond with him.

Neuroscientists have recently called attention to the physical environment needs of prematurely born babies, noting the competing needs of these vulnerable infants and the medical staff that care for them in NICUs. The medical staff needs lights, equipment that is often noisy, and alarms to signal physiological distress. The vulnerable baby needs a physical environment that more nearly approximates the uterus, without bright lights and stressful noise stimulation (D. H. Brandon, Ryan, & Barnes, 2008; Zeisel, 2006). With this discrepancy in mind, NICUs are being modified to accommodate the neurological needs of vulnerable newborns.

Neonatology, the care of critically ill newborns, has only recently been recognized as a medical specialty. It is a much-needed specialty, however. Since the advent of the NICU in the 1970s, the survival rate of critically ill neonates has continued to increase. It is highly unlikely that Paul Thompson would have survived in 1970. Social workers in an NICU must negotiate a complex technological environment requiring specialized skill and knowledge while attempting to respond with compassion, understanding, and appropriate advocacy. Research has clearly shown the need for social work intervention that enables the parents to bond with their children and decrease the level of stress (Spielman & Taubman-Ben-Ari, 2009). It helps to remember that the effort could affect a neonate's long-term life course.

Critical Thinking Questions 10.3

Pregnancy is a powerful experience for the pregnant woman as well as for her partner. What are the biological needs of the pregnant woman? The psychological needs? The social needs? Where there is an involved father, what are his biological needs? The psychological needs? The social needs? What might be the special needs of the parents in situations involving major congenital anomalies? Situations of prematurity and low birth weight?

Implications for Social Work Practice

The life course perspective has many implications for social work practice:

- Help clients make sense of their unique life's journeys and to use that understanding to improve their current situations.
- Try to understand the historical contexts of clients' lives and the ways that important historical events have influenced their behavior.
- Recognize the ways that the lives of family members are linked across generations and the impact of circumstances in one generation on other generations.
- Be aware of the unique systems of support developed by members of various cultural groups, and encourage the use of those supports in times of crisis.
- Support and help to develop clients' sense of personal competence for making life choices.
- Respond to the complex interplay of biological, psychological, social, and spiritual factors related to conception, pregnancy, and childbirth.
- Support the attempts of clients, both females and males, to exercise human agency to get control over conception and pregnancy.
- Assume a proactive stance when working with at-risk populations to limit undesirable reproductive outcomes and to help meet their reproductive needs. At-risk groups include adolescents, low-income women, women involved with substance abuse, women with eating disorders, and women with disabilities, among others.

- Assist parents faced with a potential genetic anomaly to gain access to genetic screenings, prenatal diagnosis, postnatal diagnosis, treatment, and genetic counseling.
- Involve childbearing parents in decision making to the greatest extent possible by delaying nonurgent decisions until parents have had a chance to adjust to any crisis and acquire the necessary information to make informed decisions.

Key Terms

assisted reproductive technologies (ART)	genes	recessive genes
chromosomes	genotype	resilience
cohort	gestation	risk factors
cohort effects	human agency	teratogen
dominant genes	infertility	trajectories
embryo	life course perspective	transitions
fertilization	life event	turning point
fetal viability	neonate	zygote
fetus	phenotype	
	protective factors	

Active Learning

1. Think of someone you think of as resilient, someone who has been successful against the odds. This may be you, a friend, a coworker, a family member, or a character from a book or movie. If the person is someone you know and to whom you have access, ask the person to what he or she owes this success. If it is you or someone to whom you do not have access, speculate about the reasons for the success. What developmental risk and protective factors do you see in the person's life journey?

2. Locate the National Association of Social Workers Code of Ethics on the organization's website at www.naswdc .org. Choose an ethical issue from the list below. Using the Code of Ethics as a guide, what values and principles can you identify to guide decision making related to the issue you have chosen?

   - Should all women and men, regardless of marital status or income, be provided with the most current technologies to conceive when they wish to but are unable to do so?
   - What are the potential issues of preservation and gestational surrogacy in terms of social justice and diversity?
   - Should pregnant women who abuse substances be incarcerated to protect the developing fetus?
   - Do adoptive parents have the right to know the genetic background of an adoptee?
   - Under what conditions is abortion an acceptable option?
   - Will persons who are poor be hampered in their ability to get access and make use of genetic information?

3. What variations of conception, pregnancy, and childbirth would you anticipate for teen mothers? For lesbian mothers? For immigrant families? For women with a substance abuse problem? For mothers with eating disorders? For HIV-infected mothers? For incarcerated pregnant women? For parents with any type of disability—mental, emotional, or physical? What research findings can you identify that relate to such special populations?

A number of Internet sites provide information on theory and research on the life course, and on issues related to conception, pregnancy, and childbirth:

The American Pregnancy Association
www.americanpregnancy.org

Site contains information on a number of pregnancy-related topics, including infertility, adopting, pregnancy options, multiples pregnancy, and the developing baby.

Bronfenbrenner Life Course Center (BLCC)
www.blc.cornell.edu

Site presented by the Bronfenbrenner Life Course Center at Cornell University contains information on the center, current research, working papers, and links to work/family, demography, and gerontology websites.

Childbirth.org
www.childbirth.org

Award-winning site maintained by Robin Elise Weiss contains information on conception, pregnancy, and birth, including recommended pregnancy books and access to a free online childbirth class.

The German Life History Study (GLHS)
www.mpib-berlin.mpg.de/en/forschung/bag

Site presented by the Max Planck Institute for Human Development in Berlin, Germany, contains information on comprehensive research on social structure and the institutional contexts of the life course.

Human Genome Project
www.ornl.gov/hgmis

Site of the Human Genome Project of the U.S. Department of Energy that has sequenced the genes present in human DNA provides quick access to recent news, including related legislation. Available in both English and Spanish.

Twin Study at University of Helsinki
www.twinstudy.helsinki.fi/

Site presented by the Department of Public Health at the University of Helsinki contains information on an ongoing project begun in 1974 to study environmental and genetic factors in selected chronic diseases, with links to other related resources.

CHAPTER 11

Infancy and Toddlerhood

Debra J. Woody

 CR ℞

CR ℞

ACKNOWLEDGMENTS: The author wishes to thank Suzanne Baldwin, PhD, for her contributions to the discussion of breastfeeding.

CASE STUDY 11.1

Holly's Early Arrival

Although Marilyn Hicks had been very careful with her diet, exercise, and prenatal care during pregnancy, Holly arrived at 26 weeks' gestation, around 6 months into the pregnancy. Initially she weighed 3 pounds, 11 ounces, but she quickly lost the 11 ounces. Immediately after birth, Holly was whisked away to the neonatal unit in the hospital, and her parents had just a quick peek at her. The assigned social worker's first contact with Marilyn and Martin Hicks, an Anglo couple, was in the neonatal unit. Although Marilyn Hicks began to cry when the social worker first spoke with her, overall both parents seemed to be coping well and had all their basic needs met at that time. The social worker left his business card with them and instructed them to call if they needed anything.

Despite her early arrival and low birth weight, Holly did not show any signs of medical problems, and after 6 weeks in the neonatal unit, her parents were able to take her home. The social worker wisely allowed the newly formed Hicks family time to adjust, and in keeping with the policy of the neonatal program, scheduled a follow-up home visit within a few weeks.

When the social worker arrives at the house, Marilyn Hicks is at the door in tears. She states that taking care of Holly is much more than she imagined. Holly cries "constantly" and does not seem to respond to her mother's attempts to comfort her. In fact, Marilyn Hicks thinks that Holly cries even louder when she picks her up or tries to cuddle with her. Mrs. Hicks is very disappointed because she considers herself to be a nurturing person. She is unsure how to respond to Holly's "rejection" of her. The only time Holly seems to respond positively is when Mrs. Hicks breastfeeds her.

Marilyn has taken Holly to the pediatrician on several occasions and has discussed her concerns. The doctor told her that nothing is physically wrong with Holly and that Mrs. Hicks has to be more patient.

Mrs. Hicks confides during this meeting that she read some horrifying material on the Internet about premature infants. According to the information she read, premature infants often have difficulty bonding with their caretaker, which in some children may ultimately result in mental health and emotional problems. Mrs. Hicks is concerned that this is the case with Holly.

The social worker must take into consideration that in addition to her fears, Mrs. Hicks must be exhausted. Her husband returned to work shortly after the baby came home, and Marilyn has not left the house since then. She tried taking a break once when her aunt came for a visit, but Holly cried so intensely during this time that her aunt refused to be left alone with Holly again. The social worker must now help Mrs. Hicks cope with the powerful feelings that have been aroused by Holly's premature birth, get any needed clarification on Holly's medical condition, and find ways to get Mrs. Hicks a break from caregiving. He will also want to help her to begin to feel more confident about her ability to parent Holly.

CASE STUDY 11.2

Sarah's Teen Dad

Chris Johnson is the only dad in the teen fathers group facilitated by the social worker at a local high school who has sole custody of his infant daughter. Initially, Sarah, Chris's daughter, lived with her mom and maternal grandparents. Chris was later contacted by the social worker from Child Protective Services (CPS), who informed him that Sarah had been removed from the mom's care due to physical neglect. The referral to CPS was made when Sarah was seen in a pediatric clinic, and the medical staff noticed that she had not gained weight since the last visit and was generally unresponsive in the examination. Further investigation by the CPS worker revealed that Sarah was left in her crib for most of the day, and few of Sarah's basic daily care needs were being fulfilled.

(Continued)

(Continued)

Although Chris's contact with Sarah had been sporadic since her birth, he did not hesitate to pursue custody, especially given that the only other alternative was Sarah's placement in foster care. Chris's parents were also supportive of Chris's desire to have Sarah live with all of them. However, although they were willing to help, they were adamant that the responsibility for Sarah's care belonged to Chris, not them. They were unwilling to raise Sarah themselves and in fact required Chris to sign a written statement indicating that he, not they, would assume primary responsibility for Sarah's care. Chris's parents also insisted that he remain in school and earn his high school diploma.

Thus far, the situation seems to be working well. At the last medical appointment, Sarah's weight had increased significantly, and she responded to the nurse's attempts to play and communicate with her. Chris is continuing his education at the alternative high school, which also has a day care for Sarah. Chris admits that it is much more difficult than he anticipated. He attends school for half the day, works a part-time job the other half, and then has to care for Sarah in the evenings. Chris has shared several times in the group that it is a lot for him to juggle. He still mourns the loss of his freedom and "carefree" lifestyle. Like most of the other teen dads in the group, whether they physically live with the child or not, Chris is concerned about doing the best he can for Sarah; he states that he just wants to be a good dad.

CASE STUDY 11.3

Overprotecting Henry

Irma Velasquez is still mourning the death of her little girl, Angel, who was 2 years old when she was killed by a stray bullet that entered their home through the living room window. Although it has been about a year since the incident, no one has been arrested. The police do know, however, that neither Irma's daughter nor another family member was the intended victim. The stray bullet was the result of a shoot-out between two rival drug dealers in the family's neighborhood.

Irma is just glad that 14-month-old Henry was in his crib in the back of the house instead of in the living room on that horrible evening. He had fallen asleep in her lap a few minutes before, but she had just returned from laying him in his crib when the shooting occurred. Irma Velasquez confides in her social worker at Victim Services that her family has not been the same since the incident. For one, she and her husband barely speak. His method of dealing with the tragedy is to stay away from home. She admits that she is angry with her husband because he does not make enough money for them to live in a safer neighborhood. She thinks that he blames her because she did not protect Angel in some way.

Irma admits that she is afraid that something bad will also happen to Henry. She has limited their area in the home to the back bedroom, and they seldom leave the house. She does not allow anyone, even her sister, to take care of him, and confesses that she has not left his side since the shooting. Even with these restrictions, Irma worries. She is concerned that Henry will choke on a toy or food, or become ill. She still does not allow him to feed himself, even dry cereal. He has just begun walking, and she severely limits his space for movement. Irma looks worn and exhausted. Although she knows these behaviors are somewhat irrational, she states that she is determined to protect Henry. She further states that she just could not live through losing another child.

HEALTHY DEVELOPMENT IN INFANTS AND TODDLERS____

What must social workers know about biological age, psychological age, and social age to understand whether an infant's or toddler's behavior is healthy or problematic?

What happens during the prenatal period and the earliest months and years of a child's life has lasting impact on the life course journey. From the earliest moments, interactions with parents, family members, and other adults and children influence the way the brain develops, as do such factors as nutrition and environmental safety. Although it is never too late to improve health and well-being, what happens during infancy and toddlerhood sets the stage for the journey through childhood, adolescence, and adulthood. We were all infants and toddlers once, but sometimes, in our work as social workers, we may find it hard to understand the experience of someone 2 years old or younger. (Young children are typically referred to as **infants** in the first year, but as they enter the second year of life and become more mobile, they are usually called **toddlers,** from about 12 to 36 months of age.) As adults, we have become accustomed to communicating with words, and we are not always sure how to read the behaviors of very young children. Moreover, we are not always sure how we are to behave with them. The best way to overcome these limitations, of course, is to learn what we can about the lives of infants and toddlers.

In all three of the case studies at the beginning of this chapter, factors can be identified that may adversely affect children's development. However, we must begin by understanding what is traditionally referred to as "normal" development. But because *normal* is a relative term with some judgmental overtones, we will use the term *healthy* instead.

Social workers employed in schools, hospitals, community mental health centers, and other public health settings are often approached by parents and teachers with questions about development in young children. To assess whether any of the children they bring to your attention require intervention, you must be able to distinguish between healthy and problematic development in three

Photo 11.1   Babies depend on others for basic physical and emotional needs. Family support and affection are important factors in healthy development.

areas: physical, cognitive, and socio-emotional development. As you will see, young children go through a multitude of changes in all three areas simultaneously. Inadequate development in any one of them—or in multiple areas—may have long-lasting consequences for the individual.

Keep in mind, however, that what is considered to be healthy is relative to environment and culture. Every newborn enters a world with distinctive features structured by the social setting that he or she encounters (Gardiner & Kosmitzki, 2008; Rogoff, 2003; Valsiner, 2000). Therefore, all aspects of development must be considered in their cultural context. Each newborn enters a **developmental niche,** in which culture guides every aspect of the developmental process (Harkness & Super, 2003, 2006). Parents get their ideas about parenting and about the nature of children from the cultural milieu, and parents' ideas are the dominant force in how the infant and toddler develop. Harry Gardiner and Corinne Kosmitzki identify three interrelated components of the developmental niche: physical and social settings of everyday life, child-rearing customs, and caretaker psychology. Exhibit 11.1 provides an overview of these three important components of the developmental niche encountered by every newborn. As you review this exhibit, think about the developmental niches encountered by Holly Hicks, Sarah Johnson, and Henry Velasquez as they begin their life journeys.

In the United States and other wealthy postindustrial societies, many newborns enter a developmental niche in which families have become smaller than in earlier eras. This results in a great deal of attention being paid to each child. Parents take courses and read books about how to provide the best possible care for their infants and toddlers. Infant safety is stressed, with laws about car seats, guidelines about the position in which the baby should sleep, and a "baby industry" that provides a broad range of safety equipment (baby monitors, baby gates, and so on) and toys, books, and electronics to provide sensory stimulation. Of course, this developmental niche requires considerable resources, and many families in wealthy nations cannot afford the regulation car seat or the baby

Exhibit 11.1   Components of the Developmental Niche

Physical and Social Settings of Daily Life

Size, shape, and location of living space

Objects, toys, reading materials

Ecological setting and climate

Nutritional status of children

Family structure (e.g., nuclear, extended, single-parent, blended)

Presence of multiple generations (e.g., parents, grandparents, other relatives)

Presence or absence of mother or father

Presence of multiple caretakers

Role of siblings as caretakers

Presence and influence of peer group members

Customs of Child Care and Child Rearing

Sleeping patterns (e.g., co-sleeping vs. sleeping alone)

Dependence vs. independence training

Feeding and eating schedules

Handling and carrying practices

Play and work patterns

Initiation rites

Formal vs. informal learning

Psychology of the Caretakers

Parenting styles (e.g., authoritarian, authoritative, laissez-faire)

Value systems (e.g., dependence, independence, interdependence)

Parental cultural belief systems or ethnotheories

Developmental expectations

SOURCE: Gardiner & Kosmitzki (2008, Table 2.1, p. 29). ©2008. Printed and electronically reproduced by permission of Pearson Education, Inc., Upper Saddle River, New Jersey.

monitor. Chris Johnson is attending school, working, and caring for Sarah; he probably would be hard-pressed to find time to read parenting books, but he does find time to attend a group for teen fathers. Irma Velasquez's concern for Henry's safety focuses on protecting him from stray bullets rather than on baby monitors and baby gates. And, of course, the developmental niches in nonindustrial and newly industrializing countries are very different from the niche described above. For example, African pygmy newborns are introduced to multiple caregivers who will help protect them from danger and prepare them to live an intensely social life (Gardiner & Kosmitzki, 2008). Unfortunately, many infants of the world live in developmental niches characterized by infection and malnutrition. Please keep these variations in mind as you read about infant and toddler development.

To make the presentation of ideas about infancy and toddlerhood manageable, this chapter follows a traditional method of organizing the discussion by type of development: physical development, cognitive development, emotional development, and social development. In this chapter, emotional development and social development are combined under the heading Socio-Emotional Development. Of course, all these types of development and behavior are interdependent, and often the distinctions blur.

Physical Development

Newborns depend on others for basic physical needs. They must be fed, cleaned, and kept safe and comfortable until they develop the ability to do these things for themselves. At the same time, however, newborns have an amazing set of physical abilities and potentials right from the beginning.

In Case Study 11.2, the pediatrician and CPS social worker were concerned that Sarah Johnson was not gaining weight. With adequate nourishment and care, the physical growth of the infant is quite predictable. Infants grow very rapidly throughout the first 2 years of life, but the pace of growth slows a bit in toddlerhood. The World Health Organization (WHO) undertook a project, called the Multicentre Growth Reference Study (MGRS), to construct standards for evaluating children from birth through 5 years of age. One part of that project was to construct growth standards

to propose how children *should* grow in *all* countries, of interest because of WHO's commitment to eliminate global health disparities. MGRS collected growth data from 8,440 affluent children from diverse geographical and cultural settings, including Brazil, Ghana, India, Norway, Oman, and the United States. To be eligible for the study, mothers needed to be breastfeeding and not smoking, and the environment needed to be adequate to support unconstrained growth.

The researchers found that there were no differences in growth patterns across sites, even though there were some differences in parental stature. Given the striking similarity in growth patterns across sites, they concluded that the data could be used to develop an international standard. Across sites, the average length at birth was 19.5 inches (49.5 cm), 26.3 inches (66.7 cm) at 6 months, 29.5 inches (75.0 cm) at 12 months, and 34.4 inches (87.4 cm) at 24 months (WHO Multicentre Growth Reference Study Group, 2006a). By 1 year of age, infant height was about 1.5 times birth height, and by 2 years, the toddler had nearly doubled his or her birth height.

In terms of weight, most newborns weigh between 5 and 10 pounds at birth. Infants triple their weight in the first year, and by age 2 most infants are quadruple their birth weight. Thus, the average 2-year-old weighs between 20 and 40 pounds. Evidently, the size of individual infants and toddlers can vary quite a bit. Some of the difference is the result of nutrition, exposure to disease, and other environmental factors; much of it is the result of genetics. Some ethnic differences in physical development have also been observed. For example, Asian American children tend to be smaller than average, and African American children tend to be larger than average (Tate, Dezateux, Cole, & the Millennium Cohort Study Child Health Group, 2006). In recent years, there has been a great deal of concern about rapid weight gain during the first 6 months, which has been connected to children being overweight by age 4 and to several chronic diseases in adulthood. Researchers have found Latino American infants to be twice as likely as other infants in the United

States to have this pattern of early rapid weight gain (Dennison, Edmunds, & Stratton, 2006). The WHO child weight growth standards, calculated by multiple methods, can be found at www.who.int/childgrowth/standards.

The importance of nutrition in infancy cannot be overstated. Nutrition affects physical stature, motor skill development, brain development, and most every other aspect of development. A recent report by UNICEF (2009b) indicated that approximately 200 million children under the age of 5 in the developing world suffer from stunted growth because of chronic maternal and child undernutrition. Undernutrition accounts for more than a third of the deaths of children under the age of 5. Nutritional deficiencies during the first 1,000 days of the child's life can result in damage to the immune system and impair social and cognitive capacities (UNICEF, 2009b).

Self-Regulation

Before birth, the bodily functions of the fetus are regulated by the mother's body. After birth, the infant must develop the capacity to engage in self-regulation (D. Davies, 2004; Shonkoff & Phillips, 2000). At first, the challenge is to regulate bodily functions, such as temperature control, sleeping, eating, and eliminating. That challenge is heightened for the premature or medically fragile infant, as Holly Hicks's mother is finding. Growing evidence indicates that some self-regulatory functions that allow self-calming and organize the wake-sleep cycles get integrated and coordinated during the third trimester, between 30 and 34 weeks of gestation (Institute of Medicine of the National Academies, 2006). Born at 26 weeks' gestation, Holly Hicks did not have the benefit of the uterine environment to support the development of these self-regulatory functions.

As any new parent will attest, however, infants are not born with regular patterns of sleeping, eating, and eliminating. With maturation of the central nervous system in the first 3 months, and with lots of help from parents or other caregivers, the infant's rhythms of sleeping, eating, and eliminating become much more regular (D. Davies, 2004). A newborn usually sleeps about 16 hours a day, dividing that time fairly evenly between day and night. Of course, this is not a good fit with the way adults organize their sleep lives. At the end of 3 months, most infants are sleeping 14 to 15 hours per day, primarily at night, with some well-defined nap times during the day. Parents also gradually shape infants' eating schedules so that they are eating mainly during the day.

There are cultural variations in, and controversies about, the way caregivers shape the sleeping and eating behaviors of infants. The management of sleep is one of the earliest culturally influenced parenting behaviors. In some cultures, infants sleep with parents, and in other cultures, infants are put to sleep in their own beds and often in their own rooms. In some cultures, putting an infant to sleep alone in a room is considered to be neglectful (Gardiner & Kosmitzki, 2008). Co-sleeping, the child sleeping with the parents, is routine in most of the world's cultures (McKenna, 2002). Japanese and Chinese children often sleep with their parents throughout infancy and early childhood (Z. Liu, Liu, Owens, & Kaplan, 2005). There are also cultural variations and controversies about breastfeeding versus bottle feeding. It is interesting to note that both breastfeeding and sleeping with parents induce shorter bouts of sleep and less sound sleep than the alternatives (Shonkoff & Phillips, 2000). Some researchers have speculated that the infant's lighter and shorter sleep pattern may protect against sudden infant death syndrome (SIDS). Of course, parents sleeping with infants must be aware of the hazard of rolling over and suffocating the infant. Luckily, parents have also been found to sleep less soundly when they sleep with infants (Shonkoff & Phillips, 2000).

Parents become less anxious as the infant's rhythms become more regular and predictable. At the same time, if the caregiver is responsive and dependable, the infant becomes less anxious and begins to develop the ability to wait to have needs met.

> What have you observed about how culture influences the parenting of infants and toddlers?

Cultural variations exist in beliefs about how to respond when infants cry and fuss, whether to soothe them, or leave them to learn to soothe themselves. When parents do attempt to soothe infants, interestingly, they seem to use the same methods across cultures: "They say something, touch, pick up, search for sources of discomfort, and then feed" (Shonkoff & Phillips, 2000, p. 100). Infants who have been consistently soothed usually begin to develop the ability to soothe themselves after 3 or 4 months. This ability is the precursor to struggles for self-control and mastery over powerful emotions that occur in toddlerhood. More will be said about emotion self-regulation in a later section.

Sensory Abilities

Full-term infants are born with a functioning **sensory system**—the senses of hearing, sight, taste, smell, touch, and sensitivity to pain—and these abilities continue to develop rapidly in the first few months. Indeed, in the early months the sensory system seems to function at a higher level than the motor system, which allows movement. The sensory system allows infants, from the time of birth, to participate in and adapt to their environments. A lot of their learning happens through listening and watching (B. Newman & Newman, 2009; G. Novak & Pelaez, 2004). The sensory system is an interconnected system, with various sensory abilities working together to give the infant multiple sources of information about the world.

Hearing is the earliest link to the environment; the fetus is sensitive to auditory stimulation in the uterus (Porcaro et al., 2006). The fetus hears the mother's heartbeat, and this sound is soothing to the infant in the early days and weeks after birth. Newborns show a preference for their mother's voice over unfamiliar voices (Reis, 2006). Young infants can also distinguish changes in loudness, pitch, and location of sounds, and they can use auditory information to differentiate one object from another and to track the location of an object (Bahrick, Lickliter, & Flom, 2006; Wilcox, Woods, Tuggy, & Napoli, 2006). These capacities grow

increasingly sensitive during the first 6 months after birth. Infants appear to be particularly sensitive to language sounds, and the earliest infant smiles are evoked by the sound of the human voice (Benasich & Leevers, 2003).

The newborn's vision improves rapidly during the first few months of life. By about the age of 4 months, the infant sees objects the same way that an adult would. Of course, infants do not have cognitive associations with objects as adults do. Infants respond to a number of visual dimensions, including depth, brightness, movement, color, and distance. Human faces have particular appeal for newborns. At 1 to 2 days after birth, infants are able to discriminate among—and even imitate—happy, sad, and surprised expressions, but this ability wanes after a few weeks (Field, Woodson, Greenberg, & Cohen, 1982). Between 4 and 7 months, however, infants have been found to be able to recognize some expressions, particularly happiness, fear, and anger (E. B. McClure, 2000). Infants show preference for certain faces, and by 3 months, most infants are able to distinguish a parent's face from the face of a stranger (Nelson, 2001). Some researchers have found that infants are distressed by a lack of facial movement in the people they look at, showing that they prefer caregivers to have expressive faces (Muir & Lee, 2003).

Taste and smell begin to function while the baby is still in the uterus, and newborns can differentiate sweet, bitter, sour, and salty tastes. Sweet tastes seem to have a calming effect on both preterm and full-term newborns (Blass & Ciaramitaro, 1994; B. Smith & Blass, 1996). Recent research suggests that the first few minutes after birth is a particularly sensitive period for learning to distinguish smells (Delaunay-El Allam, Marlier, & Schaal, 2006). Breastfed babies are particularly sensitive to their mother's body odors. One research team found that newborns undergoing a heel prick were soothed by the smell of breast milk, but only if the milk came from the mother's breast (Nishitani et al., 2009).

Both animal and human research tells us that touch plays a very important role in infant development. In many cultures, swaddling, or wrapping a baby snugly in a blanket, is used to soothe a fussy newborn. We also know that gentle handling, rocking, stroking, and cuddling are all soothing to an infant. Regular gentle rocking and stroking are very effective in soothing low birth weight (LBW) babies, who may have underdeveloped central nervous systems. Skin-to-skin contact between parents and their newborns has been found to have benefit for both infants and their parents. Preterm babies who have lots of skin contact with their parents, including gentle touching and massage, gain weight faster, have better temperature regulation, and are more alert compared to preterm babies who do not receive extensive skin contact (Feldman, 2004; Feldman & Edelman, 2003). Infants also use touch to learn about their world and their own bodies. Young infants use their mouths for exploring their worlds, but by 5 or 6 months of age, infants can make controlled use of their hands to explore objects in their environment. They learn about the world and keep themselves entertained by exploring small details, transferring objects from one hand to the other, and examining the differences in surfaces and other features of the object (Streri, 2005).

Clear evidence exists that from the first days of life, babies are able to feel pain. Recently, pediatric researchers have been studying newborn reactions to medical procedures such as heel sticks, the sticks used to draw blood for lab analysis. One researcher found that newborns who undergo repeated heel sticks learn to anticipate pain and develop a stronger reaction to pain than other infants (Taddio, Shah, Gilbert-Macleod, & Katz, 2002). These findings are leading pediatricians to reconsider their stance against the use of pain medications with newborns (Mathew & Mathew, 2003).

Reflexes

Although dependent on others, newborns are equipped from the start with tools for survival that are involuntary responses to simple stimuli, called **reflexes.** Reflexes aid the infant in adapting to the environment outside the womb. The presence and strength of a reflex is an important sign of neurological development, and the absence of reflexes can indicate a serious developmental disorder (K. Lee, 2009). Given Holly Hicks's early arrival, her reflex responses were thoroughly evaluated.

Newborns have two critical reflexes:

1. *Rooting reflex.* When infants' cheeks or the corners of their mouth are gently stroked with a finger, they will turn their head in the direction of the touch and open their mouths in an attempt to suck the finger. This reflex aids in feeding because it guides the infants to the nipple.

2. *Sucking reflex.* When a nipple or some other suckable object is presented to the infant, the infant sucks it. This reflex is another important tool for feeding.

Many infants would probably perish without the rooting and sucking reflexes. Imagine the time and effort it would require for one feeding if they did not have them. Instead, infants are born with the ability to take in nutriment.

A number of reflexes disappear at identified times during infancy (see Exhibit 11.2), but others persist throughout adulthood (K. Lee, 2009). Both the rooting reflex and sucking reflex disappear at between 2 and 4 months. By this time, the infant has mastered the voluntary act of sucking and is therefore no longer in need of the reflexive response. Several other infant reflexes appear to have little use now, but probably had some specific survival purposes in earlier times. The presence of an infant reflex after the age at which it typically disappears can be a sign of brain damage or stroke (K. Lee, 2009).

Motor Skills

The infant gradually advances from reflex functioning to motor functioning. The development of **motor skills**—the ability to move and manipulate—occurs in a more or less orderly, logical sequence. It begins with simple actions such as lifting the chin and progresses to more complex acts such as walking, running, and throwing. Infants usually crawl before they walk.

Exhibit 11.2 Infant Reflexes

Reflex	Description	Visible
Sucking	The infant instinctively sucks any object of appropriate size that is presented to it.	First 2 to 4 months
Rooting	The head turns in the direction of a stimulus when the cheek is touched. The infant's mouth opens in an attempt to suck.	First 3 months
Moro/Startle	The arms thrust outward when the infant is released in midair, as if attempting to regain support.	First 5 months
Swimming	When placed face down in water, the infant makes paddling, swim-like motions.	First 3 months
Stepping	When the infant is held in an upright position with the feet placed on a firm surface, the infant moves the feet in a walking motion.	First 3 months
Grasping	The infant grasps objects placed in its hand.	First 4 months
Babinski	The toes spread when the soles of the feet are stroked.	First year
Blinking	The eyes blink when they are touched or when sudden bright light appears.	Lifetime
Cough	Cough occurs when airway is stimulated.	Lifetime
Gag	Gagging occurs when the throat or back of mouth is stimulated.	Lifetime
Sneeze	Sneezing occurs when the nasal passages are irritated.	Lifetime
Yawn	Yawning occurs when the body needs additional oxygen.	Lifetime

Motor development is somewhat predictable in that children tend to reach milestones at about the same age and in the same sequence. As a part of the MGRS, WHO undertook a project to construct standards for evaluating the motor development of children from birth through 5 years of age. MGRS collected longitudinal data on six gross motor milestones of children ages 4 to 24 months in Ghana, India, Norway, Oman, and the United States. The milestones studied were sitting without support, standing with assistance, hands-and-knees crawling, walking with assistance, standing alone, and walking alone. Because WHO was trying to establish standards for evaluating child development,

> How do these motor skills help to promote a sense of human agency in making choices?

healthy children were studied in all five study sites. The researchers found that 90% of the children achieved five of the six milestones, in the same sequence, but 4.3% of the sample never engaged in hands-and-knees crawling (WHO Multicentre Growth Reference Study Group, 2006b).

Based on the data collected, MGRS developed "windows of milestone achievement" for each of the six motor skills, with achievement at the 1st and 99th percentiles as the window boundaries. All motor achievement within the windows is considered normal variation in ages of achievement for healthy children. The windows of achievement for the six motor skills studied are reported in Exhibit 11.3. The results reveal that the windows vary from 5.4 months for sitting without support to 10.0 months for standing alone. This is quite a

Photo 11.2 Fine motor skills, the ability to move and manipulate objects, develop in a logical sequence.

wide range for normal development and should be reassuring to parents who become anxious if their child is not at the low end of the window. Many parents, for example, become concerned if their child has not attempted to walk unassisted by age 1. However, some children walk alone at age 9 months; others do not even attempt to walk until almost 18 months.

Culture and ethnicity appear to have some influence on motor development in infants and toddlers. MGRS found that girls were slightly ahead of boys in gross motor (large muscle) development, but the differences were not statistically significant. They did find small, but statistically significant, differences among sites of the study, however. The researchers speculate that these differences probably reflect culture-based child care behaviors, but the cause cannot be determined from the data, and a genetic component is possible. The earliest mean age of achievement for four of the six milestones occurred in the Ghanaian sample, and the latest mean age of achievement for all six milestones occurred in the Norwegian sample (WHO Multicentre Growth Reference Study Group, 2006c). The U.S. sample mean was in the middle range on all milestones except for hands-and-knees crawling, where it had the lowest mean achievement.

A longitudinal study of almost 16,000 infants in the United Kingdom took up this issue of cultural differences in developmental motor milestones. In this study, Black Caribbean infants, Black African infants, and East Indian infants were, on average, more advanced in motor development than White infants. Pakistani and Bangladeshi infants were more likely than White infants to show motor delays. While the delays among Pakistani and Bangladeshi infants might appear to be explained by factors associated with poverty, the earlier development of Black Caribbean, Black African, and East Indian infants could not be explained by economic advantage. The researchers suggest that parental expectations and parenting practices play a role in cultural differences in motor development (Kelly, Sacker, Schoon, & Nazroo, 2006).

The development of motor skills (and most other types of skills, for that matter) is a continuous

Exhibit 11.3   Windows of Milestone Achievement in Months

Motor Milestone	Window of Milestone Achievement
Sitting without support	3.8–9.2 months
Standing with assistance	4.8–11.4 months
Hands-and-knees crawling	5.2–13.5 months
Walking with assistance	5.9–13.7 months
Standing alone	6.9–16.9 months
Walking alone	8.2–17.6 months

SOURCE: Taken from WHO Multicentre Growth Reference Study Group (2006c).

process. Children progress from broad capacities to more specific, refined abilities. For example, toddlers progress from eating cereal with their fingers to eating with a spoon.

Parents are usually quite patient with their child's motor development. However, toilet training (potty training) is often a source of stress and uncertainty for new parents. Every human culture has mechanisms for disposing of human waste and socializes infants and toddlers to that method. One of the basic issues in this socialization is whether it should be in the hands of the child or the caregiver (Valsiner, 2000). In the United States until recently, many child development experts recommended that babies be potty trained during the first year of life. Consequently, many parents exercised strong measures, including scolding and punishment, to ensure timely toilet training. Even now, many grandparents proudly report that they tied their infants to the potty chair at times of predicted elimination (after eating, for example) until the child was able to master the skill. T. Berry Brazelton (1983), one of the best-known pediatricians in the United States, endeavored to change this negative perspective. He advocated that parents begin potty training during the second year of life, during the lull time after standing and walking have been accomplished. Only then, he says, is the infant

physiologically and psychologically ready to master this skill. That is the current position of the American Academy of Pediatrics (1999), which recommends waiting until the child is ready and guiding toilet training in a systematic way, beginning with bowel training. By age 3, most children have mastered toilet training, but even 5-year-olds are still prone to soiling accidents. It should be noted, however, that in some parts of the world there is a perception of readiness for this training at a much earlier age (Valsiner, 2000).

The Growing Brain

We are living in the midst of a neuroscientific revolution that is clarifying the important role of the brain in helping to shape human behavior (see, for example, Farmer, 2009; B. Garrett, 2009). Like the brains of other primates, human brains contain *neurons*, or specialized nerve cells that store and transmit information; they carry sensory information to the brain, and they carry out the processes involved in thought, emotion, and action. Between the neurons are *synapses*, or gaps, which function as the site of information exchange from one neuron to another. (You might want to review the discussion of the nervous system in Chapter 3.) During the prenatal period, the brain overproduces neurons in massive numbers. In fact, the human newborn has more synapses than the human adult. During infancy and toddlerhood, each neuron joins with thousands of other neurons to form a colossal number of synapses or connections. During the first 3 years of life, the human brain triples in weight and creates about 1,000 trillion new connections among neurons (B. Newman & Newman, 2009). The period of overproduction of synapses, or **blooming,** is followed by a period of reduction, or **pruning,** of the synapses to improve the efficiency of brain functioning. It is through this process of creating elaborate communication systems between the connecting neurons that more and more complex skills and abilities become possible. Thus, during these early years of life, children are capable of rapid new learning. The blooming and pruning of synapses process continues well into childhood and adolescence on different timetables in different regions of the brain. For example, overproduction of synapses in the visual cortex of the brain peaks in the fourth month after birth, and pruning in that region continues until sometime toward the end of the early childhood period (Huttenlocher & Kabholkar, 1997). By contrast, in the medial prefrontal cortex part of the brain, where higher-level cognition and self-regulation take place, synaptic blooming peaks at about 1 year of age, and pruning continues until middle to late adolescence.

The available evidence suggests that both genetic processes and early experiences with the environment influence the timing of brain development (R. A. Thompson & Nelson, 2001). Brain plasticity has been a major finding of neuroscientific research of the past few decades. There are two elements of **brain plasticity:** First, research indicates that the brain changes throughout life; and second, the brain changes in response to what it experiences—it is shaped by experience (Farmer, 2009). The human brain is genetically designed to accommodate an incredibly wide range of human experiences, and the environmental context helps to shape the brain for life in a particular developmental niche. What

is used gets strengthened, and what is not used gets pruned. The infant and toddler contribute to their own brain development by repeating certain actions, attending to certain stimuli, and responding in particular ways to caregivers (Shonkoff & Phillips, 2000).

Exposure to speech in the first year expedites the discrimination of speech sounds; exposure to patterned visual information in the first few years of life is necessary for normal development of some aspects of vision. Some suggest that the entire infancy period is a crucial and sensitive time for brain development, given the quantity and speed at which the neurons develop and connect (Zigler, Finn-Stevenson, & Hall, 2002). Positive physical experiences (feeding, safety, and so on) and positive psychological experiences (touching, cooing, and playing) activate and stimulate brain activity (Shonkoff & Phillips, 2000). So, good nutrition and infant stimulation are essential for brain development, and exposure to environmental toxins, abuse, emotional trauma, and deprivation is hazardous (Shonkoff & Phillips, 2000; Teicher, 2002; Zigler et al., 2002). Persistent stress for the infant or toddler has been found to result in overdevelopment of areas of the brain that process anxiety and fear, and underdevelopment of other brain areas, particularly the frontal cortex (Schore, 2002).

Certain risks to brain development are associated with prematurity. Premature infants, like Holly Hicks, born at 24 to 28 weeks' gestation, have high rates of serious intracranial hemorrhage, which can lead to problems in cognitive and motor development, including cerebral palsy and intellectual disability. Less serious intracranial hemorrhage can lead to later behavioral, attentional, and memory problems (Shonkoff & Phillips, 2000). Also, the premature infant faces the challenging environment of the neonatal intensive care unit (NICU) at a time when the brain is developing rapidly (refer back to Chapter 10). With this in mind, architects and neonatalists have been working together in recent years to make the NICU a more nurturing environment for this rapid brain development (Zeisel, 2006). It is not yet clear whether Holly Hicks suffered any type of brain hemorrhage and what impact it will have on her future development if she did.

Recent research has focused on the relationship between infant–parent attachment and brain development. One of the most popular perspectives on this issue is presented in a book entitled *Why Love Matters: How Affection Shapes a Baby's Brain,* by Sue Gerhardt (2004). The premise here is that without affection and bonding, the frontal cortex of the brain cannot develop. The connection between attachment and brain development is discussed in more detail later in this chapter.

Cognitive Development

As the brain develops, so does its ability to process and store information and to solve problems. These abilities are known as *cognition.* When we talk about how fast a child is learning, we are talking about cognitive development. Researchers now describe the infant as "wired to learn," and agree that infants have an intrinsic drive to learn and to be in interaction with their environments (Shonkoff & Phillips, 2000). A central element of cognition is language, which facilitates both thinking and communicating. Exhibit 11.4 lists some milestones in cognitive development.

> How do the drives to learn and be in interaction with the environment promote interdependence?

Piaget's Stages of Cognitive Development

To assess children's cognitive progress, many people use the concepts developed by the best-known cognitive development theorist, Jean Piaget (1936/1952). Piaget believed that cognitive development occurs in successive stages. His overall contention was that as a child grows and develops, cognition changes not only in quantity but also in quality.

Exhibit 11.4 Selected Milestones in Cognitive Development

Milestone	Age of Onset
Coos responsively	Birth–3 months
Smiles responsively	3–4 months
Smiles at self in mirror	3–4 months
Laughs out loud	3–4 months
Plays peek-a-boo	3–4 months
Shows displeasure	5–6 months
Babbles	6–8 months
Understands simple commands	12 months
Follows directions	2 years
Puts two or three words together	2 years
Uses sentences	2 to 3 years

Piaget used the metaphor of a slow-motion movie to explain his theory, which is summarized in Exhibit 4.1 (found in Chapter 4) as follows:

1. **Sensorimotor stage** (ages birth to 2 years). Infants at this stage of development can look at only one frame of the movie at a time. When the next picture appears on the screen, infants focus on it and cannot go back to the previous frame.

2. **Preoperational stage** (ages 2 to 7). Preschool children and children in early grades can remember (recall) the sequence of the pictures in the movie. They also develop **symbolic functioning**—the ability to use symbols to represent what is not present. However, they do not necessarily understand what has happened in the movie or how the pictures fit together.

3. **Concrete operations stage** (ages 7 to 11). Not until this stage can children run the pictures in the movie backward and forward to better understand how they blend to form a specific meaning.

4. **Formal operations stage** (ages 11 and beyond). Children gain the capacity to apply logic to various situations and to use symbols to solve problems. Adding to Piaget's metaphor, one cognitive scientist describes formal operations as the ability of the adolescent not only to understand the observed movie, but also to add or change characters and create an additional plot or staging plan (C. Edwards, 1992).

The first of Piaget's stages applies to infants and toddlers. During the sensorimotor period, they respond to immediate stimuli—what they see, hear, taste, touch, and smell—and learning takes place through the senses and motor activities. Piaget suggests that infant and toddler cognitive development occurs in six substages during the sensorimotor period.

Substage 1: *Reflex Activity (birth to 1 month)*. Because reflexes are what the infant can "do," they become the foundation to future learning. Reflexes are what infants build on.

Substage 2: *Primary Circular Reactions (1 to 4 months)*. During this stage, infants repeat (thus the term *circular*) behaviors that bring them a positive response and pleasure. The infant's body is the

focus of the response, thus the term *primary*. If, for example, infants by chance hold their head erect or lift their chest, they will continue to repeat these acts because they are pleasurable. Infants also have limited anticipation abilities.

Substage 3: *Secondary Circular Reactions (4 to 8 months)*. As in the second substage, the focus is on performing acts and behaviors that bring about a response. In this stage, however, the infant reacts to responses from the environment. If, for example, 5-month-old infants cause the rattle to sound inadvertently as their arms move, they will continue attempts to repeat this occurrence.

Substage 4: *Coordination of Secondary Circular Reactions (8 to 12 months)*. The mastery of **object permanence** is a significant task during this stage. Piaget contended that around 9 months of age, infants develop the ability to understand that an object or a person exists even when they don't see it. Piaget demonstrated this ability by hiding a favored toy under a blanket. Infants are able to move the blanket and retrieve the toy. Object permanence is related to the rapid development of memory abilities during this period (Rovee-Collier, 1999). Two other phenomena are related to this advance in memory. **Stranger anxiety**, in which the infant reacts with fear and withdrawal to unfamiliar persons, has been found to occur at about 9 months across cultures. Many first-time parents comment, "I don't know what has gotten into her; she has always been so outgoing." Babies vary in how intensely they react to the strange situation and in how they express their anxiety (Rieser-Danner, 2003). **Separation anxiety** also becomes prominent in this period. The infant is able to remember previous separations and becomes anxious at the signs of an impending separation from parents. With time, the infant also learns that the parent always returns.

Substage 5: *Tertiary Circular Reactions (12 to 18 months)*. During this stage, toddlers become more creative in eliciting responses and are better problem solvers. For example, if the first button on the talking telephone does not make it talk, they will continue to press other buttons on the phone until they find the correct one.

Substage 6: *Mental Representation (18 months to 2 years)*. Piaget described toddlers in this stage as actually able to use thinking skills in that they retain mental images of what is not immediately in front of them. For example, the toddler will look in a toy box for a desired toy and move other toys aside that prohibit recovery of the desired toy. Toddlers can also remember and imitate observed behavior. For example, toddlers roll their toy lawn mower over the lawn, imitating their parents' lawn mowing.

As much as Piaget's work has been praised, it has also been questioned and criticized. Piaget constructed his theory based on his observations of his own three children. Thus, one question has been how objective was he and whether the concepts can really be generalized to all children. Also, Piaget has been criticized for not addressing the influence of environmental factors—such as culture, family, and significant relationships and friendships—on cognitive development. However, for the past 30 years, researchers around the world have put Piaget's theory to the test. This research literature is immense but has been summarized by several reviewers (see, for example, Bronfenbrenner, 1993; Rogoff & Chavajay, 1995; Segall, Dasen, Berry, & Poortinga, 1999). Piaget's sensorimotor stage has been studied less than his other cognitive stages, but the existing research tends to support Piaget's theory, even though some minor cultural differences are noted (Gardiner & Kosmitzki, 2008). For example, some research has found that African infants receive more social stimulation and emotional support than European and American infants, while European and American infants get more experience with handling objects. This leads to African infants and toddlers developing more social intelligence and European and American children developing more technological intelligence (Mundy-Castle, 1974, cited in Gardiner & Kosmitzki, 2008). This supports the idea of the importance of the developmental niche, but, overall, suggests much more similarity than difference in cognitive development across developmental niches during infancy and toddlerhood.

Research findings have called into question some aspects of Piaget's theory. For example, Piaget described young children as being incapable of object permanence until at least 9 months of age. However, infants as young as 3½ and 4½ months of age have been observed who are already

proficient at object permanence (Baillargeon, 1987; Ruffman, Slade, & Redman, 2005). Other researchers (Munakata, McClelland, Johnson, & Siegler, 1997) have found that although infants seem aware of hidden objects at 3½ months, they fail to retrieve those objects until about 8 months of age. These researchers suggest that cognitive skills such as object permanence may be multifaceted and gradually developed (Baillargeon, 2004).

Cognitive researchers have been interested in the development of object permanence in children with very low birth weight and in children with a range of intellectual and physical disabilities. One research team found that toddlers who were born full-term were more than 6 times more likely to have developed object permanence than children born prematurely with very low birth weight (Lowe, Erickson, MacLean, & Duvall, 2009). Susan Bruce and Zayyad Muhammad (2009) reviewed the research on the development of object permanence in children with intellectual disability, physical disability, autism, and blindness. They concluded that this research indicates that children with these disabilities develop object permanence in a similar sequence as children without disabilities, but at a slower rate. They also found evidence that children with severe disability benefit from systematic instruction in object permanence. It is interesting to note that much of the recent research on object permanence studies nonhuman animals. For example, one research team that studied Piagetian object permanence in Eurasian jays found support for Piagetian stages of cognitive development in this avian species (Zucca, Milos, & Vallortigara, 2007).

Categorization is a cognitive skill that begins to develop in the first year of life. *Categorization,* or recognizing similarities in groups of objects, is a fundamental element of information processing. There is evidence that by 6 months, infants begin to see patterns in and make distinctions regarding human faces (Nelson, 2001; Ramsey, Langlois, Hoss, Rubenstein, & Griffin, 2004). There is also evidence that by 3 months of age, infants can make a distinction between people and inanimate objects. They have been observed to smile and vocalize more and become more active when they are interacting with people than when interacting with inanimate objects (Rakison & Poulin-Dubois, 2001). Research has also found that 4½-month-old babies indicate recognition when two objects are different from each other (Needham, 2001). As toddlers develop language skills, they use language as well as visual cues to categorize objects (Nazzi & Gopnick, 2001).

Pre-Language Skills

Some of the developmental milestones for language development are listed in Exhibit 11.4. Although infants communicate with their caretakers from the beginning (primarily by crying), language development truly starts around 2 months of age. The first sounds, cooing, are pleasing to most parents. By age 4 months, infants babble. Initially, these babbles are unrecognizable. Eventually, between 8 and 12 months, infants make gestures to indicate their desires. The babble sounds and gestures together, along with caretakers' growing familiarity with the infant's "vocabulary," make it easier for infants to communicate their desires. For example, 12-month-old infants may point to their bottle located on the kitchen cabinet and babble "baba." The caretaker soon learns that "baba" means "bottle."

By the age of 18 to 24 months, the toddler can speak between 50 and 200 words. Piaget (1936/1952) asserts that children develop language in direct correlation to their cognitive skills. Thus, most of the words spoken at this age relate to people and significant objects in the toddler's environment. These include words such as "mama," "dada," "cat," and "sissy" (sister), for example. There is an overall bias in infancy to use nouns (Gardiner & Kosmitzki, 2008). Toddlers' first words also include situational words such as "hot," "no," and "bye." Between 20 and 26 months, toddlers begin to combine two words together, also in tandem with growing cognitive abilities. For example, children can say "all gone" as they develop an understanding of object permanence (Berk, 2005).

Even with these skills, toddlers may be difficult to understand on occasion. Cindy, the mom of 24-month-old Steven, describes collecting her son from day care. During the trip home, Steven initiated conversation with Cindy by calling out "Mama." He began to "tell" her about something that Cindy assumes must have occurred during the day. Steven continued to babble to his mother with animation and laughs and giggles during the story. Although Cindy laughed at the appropriate moments, she was unable to understand most of what Steven was sharing with her.

The most important thing that adults can do to assist with language development is to provide opportunity for interactions. Adults can answer questions, provide information, explain plans and actions, and offer feedback about behavior. Adults can also read to infants and toddlers and play language games. The opportunity for interaction is important for deaf children as well as hearing children, but deaf children need interaction that involves the hand and eye, as with sign language (Shonkoff & Phillips, 2000). Researchers have found that when talking with infants and toddlers, adults and even older children will engage in behaviors that facilitate language development; they tend to speak in a high pitch, use shorter sentences, and speak slowly (L. Singh, Morgan, & Best, 2002). However, there appear to be cultural differences in how adults communicate with infants and toddlers, though it is not clear how these differences affect language acquisition (Sabbagh & Baldwin, 2001).

Research indicates that all early infants are capable of recognizing and making sounds from a wide range of languages. However, as they have repeated interactions with caregivers and family members, they strengthen the neural connections for the sounds of the language(s) spoken in the home environment, and the neural connections for sounds from other languages are lost (Hoff, 2009). Miraculously, infants and toddlers who are bilingual from birth learn two languages as fast as monolingual infants learn one (Á. Kovács & Mehler, 2009). Of course, ability in any language is not retained unless the environment provides an opportunity for using the language.

Socio-emotional Development

Infants and toddlers face vital developmental tasks in the emotional arena (some of which are listed in Exhibit 11.5), as well as in the social arena.

Exhibit 11.5   Selected Milestones in Emotional Development

Milestone	Age
Emotional life is centered on physical states. Exhibits distress, fear, and rage	Newborn
Emotional life begins to be centered on relationships. Exhibits pleasure and delight	3 months
Emotional life continues to be relational, but distinctions are made between those relationships, as in stranger anxiety and separation anxiety. Exhibits joy, fear, anxiety, and anger	9 months
Emotional life becomes sensitive to emotional cues from other people. Exhibits a range of emotion from joy to rage	End of first year
Emotional life becomes centered on regulation of emotional states.	Second and third year

SOURCE: Based on D. Davies (2004); Shonkoff & Phillips (2000).

Development during these early ages may set the stage for socio-emotional development during all other developmental ages. This section addresses these tasks.

Erikson's Theory of Psychosocial Development

Erik Erikson's (1950) theory explains socio-emotional development in terms of eight consecutive, age-defined stages. Each stage requires the mastery of a developmental task. Mastery at each stage depends on mastery in the previous stages. If the "task facilitating factors" for a stage are absent, the individual will become stuck in that stage of development.

Each of Erikson's stages is overviewed in Exhibit 4.11 (in Chapter 4) and discussed in the chapter about the part of the life course to which it applies. The following two stages are relevant to infants and toddlers:

1. *Trust versus mistrust* (ages birth to 1½). The overall task of this stage is for infants to develop a sense that their needs will be met by the outside world and that the outside world is an okay place to be. In addition, the infant develops an emotional bond

with an adult, which Erikson believes becomes the foundation for being able to form intimate, loving relationships in the future. Erikson asserts the need for one consistent mother figure. The most important factor facilitating growth in this stage is consistency in having physical and emotional needs met: being fed when hungry, being kept warm and dry, and being allowed undisturbed sleep. In addition, the infant has to be protected from injury, disease, and so on, and receive adequate stimulation. Infants who develop mistrust at this stage become suspicious of the world and withdraw, react with rage, and have deep-seated feelings of dependency. These infants lack drive, hope, and motivation for continued growth. They cannot trust their environment and are unable to form intimate relationships with others. Given Irma Velasquez's view that the outside world is not a safe place, described in Case Study 11.3, her young son, Henry, is at risk of developing feelings of mistrust.

> How does the development of trust during infancy affect future relationships?

2. *Autonomy versus shame and doubt* (ages 1½ to 3). A child with autonomy has a growing sense of self-awareness and begins to strive for independence and self-control. These children feel proud that they can perform tasks and exercise

control over bodily functions. They relate well with close people in the environment and begin to exercise self-control in response to parental limits. To develop autonomy, children need firm limits for controlling impulses and managing anxieties, but at the same time they still need the freedom to explore their environment. Exhibit 11.6 summarizes possible sources of anxiety for toddlers (D. Davies, 2004). Toddlers also need an environment rich with stimulating and interesting objects and with opportunities for freedom of choice. Adults must accept the child's bodily functions as normal and good and offer praise and encouragement to enhance the child's mastery of self-control. At the other end of the spectrum are children who doubt themselves. They fear a loss of love and are overly concerned about their parents' approval. These children are ashamed of their abilities and develop an unhealthy kind of self-consciousness.

How does the toddler's experience with autonomy contribute to the capacity for human agency?

Erikson does not address whether tasks that should be mastered in one stage can be mastered later if the facilitating factors—such as a dependable, nurturing caregiver—are introduced. For example, we know that Sarah suffered some neglect until Chris Johnson and his parents provided a dependable, nurturing environment for her. At what point is it too late to undo psychosocial damage? Critics also question Erikson's emphasis on the process of individuation, through which children develop a strong identity separate from that of their family. Many believe this to be a North American, Western value and therefore not applicable to collectivistic societies such as many African, Latin, and Asian societies or to collectivistic subcultures in the United States.

Emotional Control

Researchers have paid a lot of attention to the strategies infants develop to cope with intense emotions, both positive and negative ones. They have noted that infants use a range of techniques to cope with intense emotions, including turning the head away, sucking on hands or lips, and closing their eyes. By the middle of the second year, toddlers have built a repertoire of ways to manage strong emotions. They make active efforts to avoid or disregard situations that arouse strong emotions; they move away or they distract themselves with objects. They soothe themselves by thumb sucking, rocking, or stroking; they also engage in reassuring self-talk. In addition, they develop substitute goals if they become thwarted in goal-directed behavior (Shonkoff & Phillips, 2000). However, researchers who do experimental infant research note that a number of infants have had to be discontinued

---

Exhibit 11.6   Some Possible Sources of Anxiety for Toddlers

Difficulty understanding what is happening

Difficulty communicating

Frustration over not being able to do what others can do or what they imagine others can do

Conflicts between wanting to be independent and wanting their parents' help

Separation or threat of separation from caregivers

Fears of losing parental approval and love

Reactions to losing self-control

Anxieties about the body

SOURCE: Adapted from D. Davies (2004).

Photo 11.3 Toddlers begin to build a repertoire of ways to manage strong emotions. The ability to control the intensity of emotional states has important implications for early childhood school performance and social relationships.

from the research process because they cannot be calmed enough to participate (B. Newman & Newman, 2009). The ability to control the intensity of emotional states has important implications for early childhood school performance and social relationships (Calkins, 2004).

It will come as no surprise that researchers have found that one of the most important elements in how an infant learns to manage strong emotions is the assistance provided by the caregiver for emotion management (D. Siegel, 1999). Caregivers may offer food or a pacifier, or they may swaddle, cuddle, hug, or rock the infant. By the time the infant is 6 months old, caregivers often provide distraction and use vocalization to soothe. One research team found that for all levels of infant distress, the most effective methods of soothing were holding, rocking, and vocalizing. Feeding and offering a pacifier were effective when the infant was moderately distressed but not at times of extreme distress (Jahromi, Putnam, & Stifter, 2004). The child's temperament also makes a difference, as you will see in the next section.

Finally, there are cultural differences in expectations for management of emotions in infants. For example, Japanese parents try to shield their infants from the frustrations that would invite anger. In other words, some emotions are regulated by protecting the child from situations that would arouse them (Kitayama, Karasawa, & Mesquita, 2004; Miyake, Campos, Kagan, & Bradshaw, 1986). Cultural differences also exist in how much independence infants and toddlers are expected to exercise in managing emotions. In one study comparing Anglo and Puerto Rican mothers, Harwood (1992) found that Anglo mothers expected their infants to manage their stranger anxiety and separation anxiety without clinging to the mother. The Puerto Rican mothers, on the other hand, expected their infants to rely on the mother for solace.

Temperament

Another way to look at emotional development is by evaluating **temperament**—the individual's innate disposition. The best-known study of temperament in infants and young children was conducted by Alexander Thomas, Stella Chess, and Herbert Birch (1968, 1970). They studied nine components of temperament: activity level, regularity of biological functions, initial reaction to any new stimulus, adaptability, intensity of reaction, level of stimulation needed to evoke a discernible response, quality of mood, distractibility, and attention span or persistence. From their observations, the researchers identified three types of temperament: easy, slow to warm up, and difficult. The *easy* baby is characterized by good mood, regular patterns of eating and sleeping, and general calmness. The *slow to warm up* baby has few intense reactions, either positive or negative, and tends to be low in activity level. The *difficult* baby is characterized by negative mood, irregular sleeping and eating patterns, and difficulty adapting to new experiences and people. There is a tendency for recent researchers to focus on two clusters of temperamental traits, negative emotions (irritability, fear, sadness, shyness, frustration, and discomfort) and regulatory capacity (ability to self-regulate behavior and engage in self-soothing), as important to parent–infant relationships as well as to future personality and behavior development (see Bridgett et al., 2009).

For an idea of the differences in infant temperament, consider the range of reactions you might see at a baptism service. One infant might scream when passed from one person to the other and when water is placed on his or her forehead. The mother might have difficulty calming the infant for the remainder of the baptism service. At the other extreme, another infant might make cooing noises throughout the entire service and seem unbothered by the rituals. The slow-to-warm-up infant might cautiously check out the clergy administering the baptism and begin to relax by the time the ritual is completed.

Thomas and his colleagues believed that a child's temperament appears shortly after birth and is set, or remains unchanged, throughout life. Recent research indicates, however, that a stable pattern of temperament is not evident until about 4 months, when the central nervous system is

further developed (Shonkoff & Phillips, 2000). Whether temperament is permanent or not is still unresolved. There is growing agreement, however, about two aspects of temperament: (1) There is some stability to a child's positive or negative reactions to environmental events, and (2) this stability of reaction leads to patterned reactions from others (Vaughn & Bost, 1999).

Thomas, Chess, and Birch (1968, 1970) cautioned that a difficult temperament does not necessarily indicate future childhood behavior problems, as one might logically assume. More significant than an infant's temperament type is the "goodness of fit" between the infant and the expectations, temperament, and needs of those in the child's environment (Thomas & Chess, 1986). In other words, how well the infant's temperament matches with that of parents, caregivers, and siblings is crucial to the infant's emotional development. For example, there appears to be a "problematic fit" between Holly Hicks and her mother. Although Mrs. Hicks is able to meet Holly's basic needs, she feels rejected and overwhelmed by Holly's "difficult" temperament. Holly seems to get irritated with her mother's nurturing style. Thomas and Chess suggest that regardless of a child's temperament, caregivers and others in the child's environment can learn to work with the child. Thus, helping Marilyn Hicks develop a better fit between herself and Holly will help Holly develop toward healthy functioning.

Recent research provides some insight about what could happen between Holly and her mother, as well as between Mr. and Mrs. Hicks, over time. Researchers are finding that negative emotion in the first 3 months is related to decreases in regulatory capacity between 4 and 12 months. Moreover, decreases in regulatory capacity in the infant between the ages of 4 and 12 months predict poor parent–child relationships when the child is 18 months old (Bridgett et al., 2009). Another research team found a relationship between infant regulatory capacity and marital satisfaction of the parents. Following a group of

How are the lives of parents linked with the temperament of their infants?

infants and their families from the time the infants were 7 months old until they were 14 months, these researchers found that marital satisfaction increased as infants developed greater regulatory capacity and decreased when infants failed to gain in regulatory capacity (Mehall, Spinrad, Eisenberg, & Gaertner, 2009). As parents discipline infants and toddlers to help them gain self-control, different methods of discipline are indicated for children of different temperaments. Infants and toddlers who are fearful and inhibited respond best to gentle, low-power discipline techniques, but these techniques do not work well with fearless infants and toddlers who do best when positive feelings between the mother and child are emphasized (Kochanska, Aksan, & Joy, 2007).

Researchers have also been interested in whether there are cultural and socioeconomic differences in infant temperament. Several studies have found small to moderate cross-cultural differences in infant temperament and have attributed these differences mainly to genetics (see Gartstein, Knyazev, & Slobodskaya, 2005; Gartstein et al., 2006). To begin to examine the contributions of the role of genetics and environment to temperament, one research team compared three groups of Russian infants between the ages of 3 and 12 months: infants living in Russia, infants of parents who immigrated to Israel, and infants of parents who immigrated to the United States. They found some differences in temperament across these three situations, and concluded that the differences in temperament between the Russian-Israeli infants and the Russian-American immigrants probably reflect the different acculturation strategies used to adapt to the host societies (Gartstein, Peleg, Young, & Slobodskaya, 2009).

Findings about the relationship between socioeconomic status and temperament are contradictory. Some researchers find no socioeconomic differences (Bridgett et al., 2009), while other researchers find that infants in more economically disadvantaged families have more difficult temperaments and conclude that this difference is largely explained by family stress (Jansen et al., 2009). The difference in findings about socioeconomic status and temperament could be caused by different samples, with socioeconomic variations in temperament more likely to show up when the sample includes greater income variability.

Recent research indicates that temperament is a more complex concept than once thought and that it is influenced by both genetics and the developmental niche. Another implication is that families like the Hicks family who have an infant with negative emotion and poor regulatory capacity may be in special need of social work interventions to prevent a troubling developmental trajectory for the infant and the relationship between the parents.

Attachment

Another key component of emotional development is **attachment**—the ability to form emotional bonds with other people. Many child development scholars have suggested that attachment is one of the most important issues in infant development, mainly because attachment is the foundation for emotional development and a predictor of later functioning. Note that this view of attachment is similar to Erikson's first stage of psychosocial development. This perspective is similar to the one Mrs. Hicks found on the Internet, which raised issues of concern for her.

> How important is the early attachment relationship for the quality of future relationships?

The two most popular theories of attachment were developed by John Bowlby (1969) and Mary Ainsworth and colleagues (Ainsworth et al., 1978).

Bowlby's theory of attachment. Bowlby (1969), who initially studied attachment in animals, concluded that attachment is natural, a result of the infant's instinct for survival and consequent need to be protected. Attachment between infant and mother ensures that the infant will be adequately nurtured and protected from attack or, in the case of human infants, protected from a harsh environment. The infant is innately programmed to emit stimuli (smiling, clinging, and so on) to which the mother responds. This exchange between infant and mother creates a bond of attachment. The infant initiates the attachment process, but later the mother's behavior is what strengthens the bond.

Bowlby (1969) hypothesized that attachment advances through four stages: pre-attachment, attachment in the making, clear-cut attachment, and goal-corrected attachment. This process begins in the first month of life, with the infant's ability to discriminate the mother's voice. Attachment becomes fully developed during the second year of life, when the mother and toddler develop a partnership. During this later phase of attachment, the child is able to manipulate the mother into desired outcomes, but the child also has the capacity to understand the mother's point of view. The mother and the child reach a mutually acceptable compromise.

Bowlby contends that infants can demonstrate attachment behavior to others; however, attachment to the mother occurs earlier than attachment to others and is stronger and more consistent. It is thought that the earliest attachment becomes the child's **working model** for subsequent relationships (Bowlby, 1982).

Attachment explains the child's anxiety when the parents leave. However, children eventually learn to cope with separation. Toddlers often make use of **transitional objects,** or comfort objects, to help them cope with separations from parents and to handle other stressful situations. During such times, they may cuddle with a blanket, teddy bear, or other stuffed animal. The transitional object is seen as a symbol of the relationship with the caregiver, but toddlers also see it as having magic powers to soothe and protect them (D. Davies, 2004).

Ainsworth's theory of attachment. One of the most widely used methods to investigate infant attachment, known as the strange situation procedure, was developed by Ainsworth and colleagues (Ainsworth et al., 1978). The Ainsworth group believed that the level of infant attachment to the mother could be assessed through the infant's response to a series of "strange" episodes. Basically, the child is exposed over a period of 25 minutes to eight constructed episodes involving separation from and reunion with the mother. The amount of child attachment to the mother is measured by how the child responds to the mother following the "distressing" separation.

As presented in Chapter 4, Ainsworth and her colleagues (1978) identified three types of attachment:

1. *Secure attachment.* The child uses the mother as a home base and feels comfortable leaving this base to explore the playroom. The child returns to the mother every so often to ensure that she is still present. When the mother leaves the room (act of separation), the securely attached child will cry and will seek comfort from the mother when she returns. But this child is easily reassured and soothed by the mother's return.

2. *Anxious attachment.* The child is reluctant to explore the playroom and clings to the mother. When the mother leaves the room, the child cries for a long time. When the mother returns, this child seeks solace from the mother but continues to cry and may swat at or pull away from the mother. Ainsworth and colleagues described these infants as somewhat insecure and doubted that their mothers would ever be able to provide the security and safety they need.

3. *Avoidant attachment.* Some infants seem indifferent to the presence of their mother. Whether the mother is present or absent from the room, these children's responses are the same.

More recent scholars have added a fourth response, known as the *insecure disorganized/disoriented* response (Belsky, Campbell, Cohn, & Moore, 1996; Main & Hesse, 1990). These children display contradictory behavior: They attempt physical closeness, but retreat with acts of avoidance. These infants often have mothers who are depressed, have a history of being abused, or continue to struggle with a traumatic experience in their own lives. Observations of mothers of infants with disorganized attachment style reveal two patterns of parenting. Some mothers are negative and intrusive and frighten their babies with intense bursts of hostility. Other mothers are passive or helpless; they rarely comfort their babies and may actually appear afraid of their babies (Lyons-Ruth, Lyubchik, Wolfe, & Bronfman, 2002). As a result, the infants become confused in the "strange" situation. They fear the unknown figure and seek solace from the mother, but retreat because they are also fearful of the mother. Some authors have suggested that the behavior associated with the disorganized style is actually an adaptive response to harsh caregiving (Stovall & Dozier, 1998). Research also suggests a link between disorganized attachment and serious mental health problems in later childhood and beyond (Lyons-Ruth et al., 2002; Fonagy, 2003).

According to Ainsworth's attachment theory, children whose mothers are consistently present and responsive to their needs and who exhibit a warm, caring relationship develop an appropriate attachment. Findings from studies indicate that this is true, even when there are negative family issues such as alcoholism by the father (E. Edwards, Eiden, & Leonard, 2006). However, the implication is that only mother–infant attachment exists or is relevant to healthy infant development. This assumption probably seemed unquestionable when these theories were constructed. Today, however, many fathers have prominent, equal, and/or primary responsibilities in child rearing and child care, sometimes by choice, and other times because of necessity. Sarah Johnson's dad, for example, became the primary caretaker for Sarah out of necessity. The gender of the parent is irrelevant in the development of secure infant attachment. Rather, it is the behavior of the primary caregiver, regardless of whether it is the mother or father, which has the most influence on infant attachment (Geiger, 1996). When fathers who are the primary caregivers are able to provide infants with the warmth and affection they need, the infants develop secure attachments to their fathers. In fact, under stress, the fathers become a greater source of comfort to their infants than the mothers who are the secondary caregivers (Geiger, 1996). Perhaps the best scenario is when infants develop secure attachments to both parents. In one study, infants with secure attachments to both parents demonstrated less behavioral difficulties as toddlers, even less problems than toddlers with only secure mother–infant attachment (Volling, Blandon, & Kolak, 2006).

In addition to a more prominent role by fathers over the past 20 to 30 years, more women have entered the workforce, and many more children experience alternative forms of child care, including day care. The effect day care has on the development of attachment in young children continues to be a hotly debated topic. Some argue that day care has a negative effect on infant attachment and increases the risk of the infant developing insecure and avoidant forms of attachment (see, e.g., Belsky, 1987; Belsky & Braungart, 1991). The risks are thought to be especially high if the infant attends day care during the first year of life. Others argue that day care does not have a negative effect on infant and early childhood attachment (Griffith, 1996; Shonkoff & Phillips, 2000). A study in the Netherlands found that professional caregivers may be alternative attachment figures for children when their parents are not available, but it is the professional caregivers' group-related sensitivity, rather than the child's individual relationship with one professional caregiver, that promotes a sense of security and safety in children. Girls were found to be more securely attached to their professional caregivers than boys, however (De Schipper, Tavecchio, & Van IJzendoorn, 2008). In one study in the United States, day care was found to mitigate the adverse effects of insecure mother–infant attachment (Spieker, Nelson, & Petras, 2003).

The question of how day care attendance affects attachment is probably not as simplistic as either side contends. Many factors appear to be associated with the development of attachment for children in day care. The overriding factor is the quality of the relationship between the infant and parents, regardless of the child's care arrangements. For example, mothers who have a positive attitude toward their infant, are emotionally available to their infant, and encourage age-appropriate levels of independence produce infants with secure attachment (Clarke-Stewart, 1988; Shonkoff & Phillips, 2000). Also, infants whose parents have a stable and loving marriage and whose father is significantly involved in their nurturing and care tend to develop secure attachment, even if they spend a significant portion of the day in child care (Schachere, 1990).

Recently, researchers have begun to study attachment among children in foster care. Almost a half million children are in foster care in the United States (Child Trends, 2011). Most of these children come into foster care without secure attachments. Once in foster care, many children are subjected to frequent changes in their foster homes (D. Smith, Stormshak, Chamberlain, & Whaley, 2001). Problems with attachment may contribute to foster home disruptions, but foster home disruptions also contribute to attachment problems. Others conclude that institutional care can have similarly devastating effects on attachment (R. Johnson, Browne, & Hamilton-Giachritsis, 2006). Regardless of these findings, the child welfare system has historically paid too little attention to issues of attachment.

Let's look at one other issue concerning attachment. The manner in which infant attachment is measured raises some concerns. Most studies of attachment have used the Ainsworth group's strange situation method. However, this measure may not yield valid results with some groups or under certain conditions. For example, the avoidant pattern of attachment some investigators have noted among children in day care may not indicate lack of attachment, as some have concluded (Clarke-Stewart, 1989). These children may be securely attached but seem indifferent to the exit and return of the mother simply because they have become accustomed to routine separations and reunions with their mother.

The appropriateness of using the strange situation method with certain ethnic groups has also been questioned. In many parts of Asia, Africa, and South America, infants sleep with their parents and are carried on their mother's back or side throughout the day, and how well these infants tolerate separation from the mother may not be a good measure of their emotional health (P. Greenfield, Keller, Fuglini, & Maynard, 2003). One researcher found that Japanese mothers leave their babies in the care of others an average of 2.2 times in a given month, and only in the care of an immediate relative such as the father or grandmother. They also keep their infants in close proximity; they often sleep in the same room, and infants are carried on the mother's back (K. Takahashi, 1990). As a result, Japanese infants tend to be highly anxious when their mothers leave the room. The response to the mother leaving is so intense that these infants are not easily comforted when the mother returns. Some might label the response by these infants as a sign of insecure attachment, although the response is consistent with the environment they have experienced. Quite likely, the infants in fact have a secure and appropriate attachment to their mother (Takahashi, 1990).

Conversely, in many cultures, infants are cared for by a collective of mothers, older siblings, cousins, fathers, aunts, uncles, and grandparents. The level of sense of security in these infants depends on coordinated care of a number of caregivers. The strange situation does not capture the fluid nature of caregiving and the degree to which it supports infants' feelings of security and safety (M. Lewis, 2005). One study found that in Israeli kibbutz-reared children, one negative caregiving relationship could negatively affect other attachment relationships (Sagi, Koren-Karie, Gini, Ziv, & Joels, 2002). In spite of these concerns, findings from a large number of studies using the strange situation in Europe, Africa, Asia, the Middle East, as well as North America indicate that the attachment patterns identified by Ainsworth occur in many cultures (Gardiner & Kosmitzki, 2008). It is important to remember that attachment theory was developed by Euro-American theorists who conceptualized attachment as the basis for developing subsequent independence. However, in more collectivist cultures, attachment is seen as the basis for developing obedience and harmony (Weisner, 2005).

Attachment and brain development. Attachment directly affects brain development (Gerhardt, 2004; B. Perry, 2002a; Zigler et al., 2002). Gerhardt concludes that without emotional bonding with an adult, the orbitofrontal cortex in the brain of infants (the part of the brain that allows social relationships to develop) cannot develop well.

In what other ways does culture contribute to diversity in infant and toddler development?

During the first year of life, the infant must develop the capacity to tolerate higher and higher levels of emotional arousal. The caregiver helps the infant with this by managing the amount of stimulation that the infant receives. As the right orbitofrontal cortex develops, the infant is able to tolerate higher levels of arousal and stimulation. However, when the caregiver is not attuned to the needs of the infant regarding the management of stimulation during the first year of life, negative emotions result, and growth of the right orbitofrontal cortex is inhibited (Farmer, 2009). This process has been called the development of the *social brain*. Advocates of this perspective cite several studies to support these conclusions, including an investigation of infants reared in orphanages in Romania conducted by Chugani et al. (2001). The infants had little contact with an adult, were left in their cots for most of the day, were fed with propped-up bottles, and were never smiled at or hugged. Research with these infants found that their brain development was severely impaired.

One question of concern is whether these deficiencies in brain development are permanent. Some suggest that the brain impairments can be reversed if changes in care and attachment occur early enough (Zigler et al., 2002). They highlight the strides in brain development made by the Romanian orphans who were adopted into caring homes before they were 6 months of age. Perhaps Sarah Johnson's improvement was due to early intervention and moving her quickly to live with her dad. Others suggest that the brain impairments caused by lack of attachment with a primary caregiver are permanent (B. Perry, 2002a). Regardless, the implication is that future brain growth is seriously jeopardized if brain development is not adequately nurtured in the first 2 to 3 years. We have clear evidence that the human brain is generally plastic and changes over time with new experiences, but we also know that it is not completely plastic; brain vulnerabilities in early childhood predispose one to difficulties in managing social relationships, and social relationship problems affect ongoing brain development (Farmer, 2009). Gerhardt (2004) concludes that the best advice we can offer parents of newborns is to forget about holding flashcards in front of the baby, and instead, just hold and cuddle the infants and simply enjoy them.

The Role of Play

Historically, play was thought to be insignificant to development, especially for infants and toddlers. However, we now know that play allows infants and toddlers to enhance motor, cognitive, emotional, and social development.

Because of their differences in development in all areas, infants and toddlers play in different ways. Exhibit 11.7 describes four types of infant play and three types of play observed in very young children. These latter types of play begin in toddlerhood, and develop in union with cognitive and motor

Exhibit 11.7 Types of Play in Infancy and Toddlerhood

	Types of Infant Play
Vocal play	Playful vocalizing with grunts, squeals, trills, vowels, and so on to experiment with sound and have fun with it
Interactive play	Initiating interactions with caregivers (at about 4–5 months), by smiling and vocalizing, to communicate and make connection
Exploratory play with objects	Exploring objects with eyes, mouth, and hands to learn about their shape, color, texture, movement, and sounds and to experience pleasure

(Continued)

Exhibit 11.7 (Continued)

	Types of Infant Play
Baby games	Participating in parent-initiated, ritualized, repetitive games, such as peek-a-boo, that contain humor, suspense, and excitement and build an emotional bond
	Types of Toddler Play
Functional play	Engaging in simple, repetitive motor movements
Constructive play	Creating and constructing objects
Make-believe play	Acting out everyday functions and tasks and playing with an imaginary friend

SOURCES: Types of infant play based on D. Davies, 2004; types of toddler play based on Rubin, Fein, & Vandenberg (1983).

development. For example, young toddlers will play with a mound of clay by hitting and perhaps squishing it. More developed toddlers will mold the clay into a ball, and older toddlers will try to roll or throw the molded ball.

One zealous mother describes joining the "toy of the month club" in which she received developmental toys through the mail each month for the first 2 years of her child's life. This mother wanted to be sure that her child had every opportunity to advance in terms of motor and cognitive skills. Although this mother's efforts are to be applauded, she admits that these toys were very costly and that perhaps she could have achieved the same outcome with other less expensive objects. For example, there is no evidence that a store-bought infant mobile is any more effective than a homemade paper one hung on a clothes hanger. The objective is to provide stimulation and opportunities for play. Fergus Hughes (2010, p. 68) makes the following suggestions about the appropriate toys for infants and toddlers during the first 2 years of life:

- Birth to 3 months: toys for sensory stimulation, such as rattles, bells, colorful pictures and wallpaper, crib ornaments, mobiles, music boxes, and other musical toys
- 3–6 months: toys for grasping, squeezing, feeling, and mouthing, such as cloth balls, soft blocks, and teething toys

- 6–12 months: colorful picture books, stacking toys, nesting toys, sponges for water play, mirrors, toy telephones, toys that react to the child's activity
- 12–18 months: push toys; pull toys; balls; plain and interlocking blocks; simple puzzles with large, easy-to-handle pieces; stacking toys; riding toys with wheels close to the ground
- 18–24 months: toys for the sandbox and water play; spoons, shovels, and pails; storybooks; blocks; dolls, stuffed animals, and puppets

Another important aspect of play is parent–child interaction. Parent–infant play may increase the likelihood of secure attachment between the parent and child (D. Davies, 2004; F. Hughes, 2010; Scarlett, Naudeau, Salonius-Pasternak, & Ponte, 2005). The act of play, at the very least, provides the opportunity for infants and parents to feel good about themselves by enjoying each other and by being enjoyed. Even before infants can speak or understand language spoken to them, play provides a mechanism of communication between parents and infants. Infants receive messages about themselves through play, which promotes their sense of self (Scarlett et al., 2005).

Many similarities exist in the way that mothers and fathers play with infants and toddlers, but also some differences. Both mothers and fathers are teachers and sensitive communicators, and both generally enjoy rough-and-tumble play with their babies (Roggman, Boyce, Cook, Christiansen, & Jones, 2004). However, fathers tend to engage in more rough-and-tumble play; they are more likely to lift their babies, bounce them, and move their legs and arms. Mothers are more likely to offer toys, play conventional games of peek-a-boo and pat-a-cake, and engage in constructive play. Moreover, mothers have been found to play differently with infant sons than with infant daughters, engaging in more conversation with daughters and making more statements about the baby's feelings when talking with daughters; conversely, they engage in more direction with sons and make more comments to call the baby's attention to his surroundings (Clearfield & Nelson, 2006). Mothers have also been found to be more likely to follow the child's lead, while fathers are more likely to steer play activity according to their preferences. It is important to note, however, that these mother/father differences have not been found in Sweden and Israel, both societies with more egalitarian gender roles than those found in the United States (F. Hughes, 2010).

Play also is a vehicle for developing peer relations. A few decades ago, it was thought that babies really aren't interested in other babies and cannot form relationships with each other. Recent research challenges this view (F. Hughes, 2010; Shonkoff & Phillips, 2000). The peer group becomes more important at earlier ages as family size decreases and siblings are no longer available for daily social interaction. Researchers have found that very young infants, as young as 2 months old, get excited by the sight of other infants; by 6 to 9 months, infants appear to try to get the attention of other infants; and by 9 to 12 months, infants imitate each other (F. Hughes, 2010). Although toddlers are capable of establishing relationships, their social play is a struggle, and a toddler play session is quite a fragile experience. Toddlers need help in structuring their play with each other. And yet, researchers have found that groups of toddlers in preschool settings develop play routines that they return to again and again over periods of months (Corsaro, 2005). These toddler play routines are primarily nonverbal, with a set of ritualized actions. For

example, Corsaro notes a play routine in one Italian preschool in which a group of toddlers would rearrange the chairs in the room and work together to move them around in patterns. They returned to this routine fairly regularly over the course of a year, modifying it slightly over time. Peer relations are thus being built by "doing things together."

DEVELOPMENTAL DISRUPTIONS

Providing interventions to infants and toddlers with disabilities is mandated by the Developmental Disabilities Assistance and Bill of Rights Act. However, accurately assessing **developmental delays** in young children is difficult (Zipper & Simeonsson, 2004). One reason is that although we have some guidelines for healthy development in infants and toddlers, development varies by individual child. Young children walk, master potty training, and develop language skills on different timetables. It is therefore difficult to assess whether a particular child has a case of delayed development—and if so, which faculties are delayed. Premature infants like Holly Hicks, for example, often need time to catch up in terms of physical, cognitive, and emotional development. At what point does Holly's social worker decide that she is not developing fast enough, and think of her as developmentally delayed?

The other reason that accurate assessment of developmental difficulties in infants and toddlers is hard is that although many physical and cognitive disabilities have been found to be genetic and others to be associated with environmental factors, the cause of most disabilities is unknown. Anticipating what the risk factors might be for a particular child and how they might influence developmental delays is therefore difficult. Assessment should be multidimensional, including the child, the family, and the broader environment (Zipper & Simeonsson, 2004).

Autism spectrum disorders (also known as ASDs; pervasive developmental disorders, PDDs; or autism), for example, are a group of developmental disorders in which the main features are pervasive impairment in the nature and quality of social and communication development and the presence of restricted and repetitive behaviors. (Specific criteria are described in the *Diagnostic and Statistical Manual of Mental Disorders,* or *DSM-IV-TR.*) However, autism is often difficult to detect because children with the disorder exhibit a wide range of symptoms. Crane and Winsler (2008) observe, for example, that some children with autism are very verbal and interactive with family and friends but exhibit peculiar repetitive behaviors, while other children with the disorder never develop verbal skills, prefer social isolation, and have moderate to severe mental retardation.

Usually, autism is not diagnosed until age 3 or 4, but results from recent research indicate that signs of autism are detectable at birth and increase throughout the first 2 years of life. For example, results from retrospective interviews of parents with children diagnosed with autism indicate the presence of symptoms within the first 2 years (Wimpory, Hobson, Williams, & Nash, 2000). In another study, infants between ages 8 and 10 months diagnosed with autism were unable to orient when their name was called and were less likely to look at another person while smiling (E. Werner, Dawson, Osterling, & Dinno, 2000). From their research, Wetherby et al. (2004) identify the following additional warning signs of autism in children at age 2: a delay in verbal skills; lack of response to instructions; delay in using conventional toys in play; display of repetitive movements; and delay in social behaviors such as eye contact, sharing affect, pointing, and facial expression.

Since early detection and diagnosis is associated with improved outcomes for infants and toddlers with developmental delays in general (Shonkoff, Hauser-Cram, Krauss, & Upshur, 1992), the Centers for Disease Control and Prevention (CDC) recommend screening for all types of developmental delays and disabilities at 9, 18, and 24 or 30 months of age, and the CDC along with the American Academy of Pediatrics recommend the universal screening for autism specifically at 18 and 24 months of age (CDC, 2009b). Interventions for autism include behavior modification techniques, interventions to improve communication skills, dietary approaches, and use of medications.

CHILD CARE ARRANGEMENTS IN INFANCY AND TODDLERHOOD

Human infants start life in a remarkably dependent state, in need of constant care and protection. On their own, they would die. Toddlers are full of life and are making great strides in development in all areas, but they are also "not ready to set out for life alone in the big city" (B. Newman & Newman, 2009, p. 187). Societal health is dependent on finding good solutions to the question, who will care for infants and toddlers?

With large numbers of mothers and fathers of infants and toddlers in the paid workforce, and not at home, this question becomes a challenging one. The United States seems to be responding to this challenge more reluctantly than other highly industrialized countries are. This difference becomes clear in comparative analysis of two solutions for early child care: family leave and paid child care.

Family Leave

Because of changes in the economic institution in the United States between 1975 and 1999, the proportion of infants with mothers in paid employment

What impact might this trend have over time on the current cohort of infants and toddlers?

increased from 24% to 54% (Shonkoff & Phillips, 2000). A similar trend is occurring around the world.

In response, most industrialized countries have instituted social policies that provide for job-protected leaves for parents to allow them to take off from work to care for their young children. Sweden was the first country to develop such a policy in 1974. The Swedish policy guaranteed paid leave.

By the early 1990s, the United States was the only industrialized country without a family leave policy (Kamerman, 1996). But in 1993, the U.S. Congress passed the Family and Medical Leave Act (FMLA) (P.L. 103–3). FMLA requires businesses with 50 or more employees to provide up to 12 weeks of unpaid, job-protected leave during a 12-month period for workers to manage childbirth, adoption, or personal or family illness. Eligible workers are entitled to continued health insurance coverage during the leave period, if such coverage is a part of their compensation package.

Exhibit 11.8 highlights the family leave policies in selected countries. The United States and Australia are the only affluent countries of the world that do not offer some paid parental leave at the time of birth and adoption. But, as noted in Chapter 7, Australia does provide families with a universal, flat-rate maternity grant of $5,000 for each new child, to assist with the costs of birth or adoption (Australian Government: Department of Family and Community Services, Office for Women, 2006). European countries also provide birth or maternity grants and family allowances. This is an area where social work advocacy is needed in the United States.

Exhibit 11.8 Maternity and Parental Leave Policies in Selected Countries, 1999–2002

Country	Duration of Leave	Percentage of Wage Replaced
Afghanistan	3 months	100%
Australia	1 year	Unpaid
Belgium	15 weeks	75%–80%
Canada	1 year	55%
Denmark	1 year	60%
Greece	2 weeks paternity	60%
Italy	16 weeks	50%
Mexico	5 months	80%
Norway	12 weeks	100%
Peru	52 weeks (or 42 weeks at 100%)	80%
Sweden	First 3 months	100%
	Subsequent 1 year	80%
United States	12 weeks	Unpaid

SOURCE: Based on Clearinghouse on International Developments in Child, Youth and Family Policies at Columbia University (2002).

Paid Child Care

Historically in the United States, mothers were expected to provide full-time care for infants and toddlers at home. If mothers were not available, it was expected that children would be cared for by domestic help or a close relative but still in their home setting. Even in the 1960s, with the development of Head Start programs, the focus was on preschool-age children; infants and toddlers were still expected to be cared for at home (Kamerman & Kahn, 1995). Thus, historically there was very little provision of alternative child care for most children below school age.

This phenomenon has changed dramatically, however, over the last 30 years. In 1999, about 61% of women in the United States with children age 6 and under worked outside the home, and 54% with children age 1 year and younger worked outside the home (Shonkoff & Phillips, 2000). Therefore, alternative child care has become a necessity in the United States. In 2005, an estimated 74% of U.S. children under the age of 6 were receiving some type of nonparental care (B. Newman & Newman, 2009).

Many advocates for day care refer to the European model as an ideal for the United States. Countries in Europe provide "universal" child care for all children, regardless of the parents' income, employment status, race, age, and so forth. These programs are supported through national policy and funded through public monies. If they pay at all, parents pay no more than a quarter of the monies needed. Parents in Europe thus pay far less than parents in the United States typically pay.

Currently, there are some innovative programs in Europe in which the focus is on providing alternative group care for toddlers in group settings outside the home (Kamerman & Kahn, 1995). The thought is that the cognitive and social skills of children age 2 and older can be enhanced in a group setting. This care is also paid for and regulated through public funds. Workers who provide this care are well trained in child development and are paid well (by United States' standards) for their services. Most important, this care is available to all families and children.

As suggested earlier, there are controversies about whether day care centers are harmful to infants and toddlers, but there is growing consensus that day care in general is not harmful to them (Shonkoff & Phillips, 2000). The primary concern is the quality of the day care provided. Researchers conclude that quality day care can even enhance cognitive development among 9-month-old infants (Schuetze, Lewis, & DiMartino, 1999). The National Research Council (1990) has identified three factors essential to quality day care: a staff–child ratio of 1:3 for infants, 1:4 for toddlers, and 1:8 for preschoolers; group size of no larger than 6 for infants, 8 for toddlers, and 16 for preschoolers; and staff training on child development and age-appropriate child care. The Canadian Council on Learning (2006) suggests that a staff–child ratio of 1:6 constitutes quality child care for children 2 and 3 years old (compared to 1:4 specified by the National Research Council). They also propose that quality group child care must include well-defined spaces, well-planned curriculum, and significant parental involvement.

INFANTS AND TODDLERS IN THE MULTIGENERATIONAL FAMILY __

Maria, a new mom, describes the first visit her mother and father made to her home after the birth of Maria's new infant:

> What have you observed about how family relationships change when a baby is born?

> Mom and Dad walked right past me as if I was not there, even though we had not seen each other for 6 months. I quickly realized that my status as their "princess" was now replaced with a new little princess. During their visit, my husband and I had to fight to see our own child. When she cried, they immediately ran to her. And my mother criticized everything I did—she didn't like the brand of diapers I used, she thought the color of the room was too dreary for an infant—and she even scolded my husband at one point for waking the baby when he went to check on her. I appreciated their visit, but I must admit that I was glad when it was time for them to leave.

Maria's description is not unique. The involvement of grandparents and other extended family members in the care of infants and toddlers may be experienced either as a great source of support or as interference and intrusion (and sometimes as a little of each). And, of course, cultures of the world have different norms about who is involved, and in what ways, in the care of infants and toddlers.

Yet the specific roles of grandparents and other extended family members are rarely discussed within the family, which is why conflicts often occur. When these roles are clearly articulated and agreed upon, extended family members can provide support that enhances infant and toddler development (Hines et al., 2005). Family involvement as a form of social support is further discussed as a "protective factor" later in this chapter.

The birth of a child, especially of a first child, brings about a major transition not only for parents, but also for the entire kin network. Partners become parents, sons and daughters become fathers and mothers, fathers and mothers become grandfathers and grandmothers, and brothers and sisters become uncles and aunts. The social status of the extended family serves as the basis of the social status of the child, and the values and beliefs of the extended family will shape the way they care for and socialize the child (Carter & McGoldrick, 2005c; B. Newman & Newman, 2009). In addition, many child-rearing rituals, decisions, and behaviors, as well as children's names, are passed from one generation to the next.

To illustrate this point, there is an old joke about a mother who prepared a roast beef for most Sunday family dinners. She would always cut the roast in half and place it in two pans before cooking it in the oven. Observing this behavior, her young daughter asked her why she cut the roast in half. After some thought, she told her daughter that she did not know for sure, but her mother had always cut her roast in half. Later, the mother asked her mother why she had cut her roast in half before cooking it. The senior mother explained that she did not have a pan large enough for the size roast she needed to feed her family. Thus, she would cut the roast in half in order to fit it into her two smaller pans.

Similar behavior affects decisions regarding infants and toddlers. One mother reports giving her infant daughter herb tea in addition to an ointment provided by her physician for a skin rash. It seems that this skin rash was common among infant girls in each generation in this family. A specific herb tea was traditionally used to treat the rash. This mother confesses that she did not tell her mother or grandmother that she used the ointment prescribed by her doctor. It is interesting for us to note that although the mother did not have complete faith in the tea, she also did not have complete faith in the ointment. The mother states that she is not sure which one actually cured the rash. Violation of family and cultural rituals and norms can be a source of conflict between new parents and other family members (Hines et al., 2005). For example, differences of opinion about baptism, male circumcision, and even child care arrangements can create family disharmony. One decision that often involves the multigenerational family is that of whether to breastfeed or bottle feed the infant.

The Breastfeeding Versus Bottle Feeding Decision

Throughout history, most infants have been breastfed. However, alternatives to breastfeeding by the mother have always existed, sometimes in the form of a wet nurse (a woman employed to breastfeed someone else's infant) or in the form of animal milks. Following World War II, breastfeeding ceased to be the primary nutritional source for infants because of the promotion of manufactured formula in industrialized and nonindustrialized countries. Since the 1980s, cultural attitudes have shifted again in favor of breastfeeding. However, in the United States, only 39% of infants are breastfed at 6 months, 40% less than the Healthy People 2010 goal (CDC, 2006a). Employer support, including on-site day care centers, is needed to expand breastfeeding among working mothers, especially for women at risk of discontinuing breastfeeding early (Pascoe, Pletta, Beasley, & Schellpfeffer, 2002).

It is important to note that in many impoverished countries, it is hazardous to use formula because of the lack of access to a safe water supply for mixing with the formula.

In European American and Mexican American families, the mother often seeks the opinion of the baby's father and maternal and paternal grandparents, whereas in African American families, the maternal grandmother and peers tend to be most influential in the decision to breastfeed (Baranowski, 1983). Korean mothers-in-law care for the new mother and are a powerful influence in choices about breastfeeding. In Saudi Arabia, a woman may breastfeed her infant openly and receive no notice, although otherwise she is fully veiled. In France, topless swimming is culturally acceptable, but breastfeeding in public is not (Riordan & Auerbach, 1999).

Most women decide to nurse primarily for infant health benefits. One benefit is increased immunity—which begins in the third trimester of pregnancy, with nutrients received from the placenta—to viruses such as mumps, chicken pox, and influenza (K. M. Jackson & Nazar, 2006). Breastfeeding has also been demonstrated to decrease the risk of obesity during childhood and adolescence, especially if infants are exclusively breastfed for the first 6 months of life (Weyermann, Beermann, Brenner, & Rothenbacher, 2006). Contraindications to breastfeeding are few, but they include maternal medical conditions such as untreated tuberculosis, leukemia, breast cancer diagnosed during lactation, drug abuse, and sexually transmitted diseases (Dickason, Silverman, & Kaplan, 1998). Mothers who are positive for HIV are often advised to avoid breastfeeding because it is a risk factor for mother-to-infant transmission (Mbori-Ngacha et al., 2001). However, in poor countries, the contaminated water supply may pose more risk than breastfeeding (Piwoz, Ross, & Humphrey, 2004).

Postpartum Depression

Family dynamics are often altered when mothers are depressed following childbirth. There is evidence that, around the world, between 10 and 15% of mothers will have postpartum depression in the first year of the infant's life (Posmontier & Horowitz, 2004; Wisner, Chambers, & Sit, 2006). Although social factors no doubt contribute to postpartum depression, it is generally accepted that the precipitous hormonal changes at birth, to which some women seem especially sensitive, play a large role. Postpartum depression often goes undiagnosed and untreated across cultural groups (Dennis & Chung-Lee, 2006), but it is more likely to receive attention in societies that have regular postpartum visits from midwives or nurses. For example, in the United Kingdom, new parents receive seven visits from midwives in the first 2 weeks postpartum (Posmontier & Horowitz, 2004). Postpartum depression can be very disruptive to the early mother–infant relationship and, as discussed below, increases risk of impaired cognitive, emotional, and motor development in the infant (Wisner et al., 2006). Both social support and pharmacological interventions have been found to be helpful (Sword, Watt, & Krueger, 2006). Different cultures have different expectations for maternal adaptation, and it is important for health providers to recognize these cultural influences (Posmontier & Horowitz, 2004).

There is very little research on psychosocial and mental health issues for new fathers, but the Australian First Time Fathers Study has attempted to address this gap in knowledge (Condon, 2006). This study finds no evidence of male postnatal depression, but it does find that male partners of women with postpartum depression are at risk of depression, anxiety, and abusing alcohol. At first, most men are confused by their wives' depression, but supportive. If the depression lasts for months, which it often does, support is usually gradually withdrawn. Men report that they find their wives' irritability and lack of physical affection more troubling than the sadness and tearfulness. This study also found that male partners and other family members of depressed mothers often take on more and more of the care of the infant over time, which reinforces the mother's sense of incompetence. Communication breakdowns are very common in these situations.

RISKS TO HEALTHY INFANT AND TODDLER DEVELOPMENT

Unfortunately, not all infants and toddlers get the start they need in life. Millions of infants and toddlers around the world are impoverished, abandoned, neglected, and endangered. Collectively, the adults of the world have not ensured that every child has the opportunity for a good start in life. These adversities have consequences to the infant or toddler's immediate development, but research also indicates that adversities experienced in childhood can have negative consequences throughout the individual's life span. In a large, well-known study referred to as the adverse childhood experience (ACE) study, investigators examined the consequences of adverse childhood experiences including abuse; family violence; and parental substance abuse, mental illness, or imprisonment, on the infant's later adult physical and mental health outcomes (Felitti et al., 1998). Not only did they find a relationship between the two, but they also concluded that exposure to adversities during childhood, especially abuse and household dysfunction, increased the likelihood of developing a potentially fatal disease in adulthood. You have probably already surmised what some of the environmental factors are that inhibit healthy growth and development in infants and toddlers. This section addresses a few of those factors that social workers are especially likely to encounter: poverty, inadequate caregiving, and child maltreatment.

Poverty

Examining the social science evidence about the effects of family life on physical and mental health, Repetti, Taylor, and

> In what ways does social class affect the development of infants and toddlers?

Seeman (2002) made the following observation: "The adverse effects of low SES [socioeconomic status] on mental and physical health outcomes are as close to a universal truth as social science has offered" (p. 359). When a family is impoverished, the youngest are the most vulnerable, and, indeed, children birth to age 3 have the highest rates of impoverishment around the world (UNICEF, 2005b). Bellamy (2004) reports that 1 billion children across the world live in poverty, representing 1 in 2 children. Although children living in the poorest countries are much more likely than children living in wealthy countries to be poor (UNICEF, 2005b), the proportion of children living in poverty in 17 of the 24 wealthiest nations has been rising (UNICEF Innocenti Research Centre, 2005). Using a relative measure of poverty as income below 50% of the national median income, the UNICEF researchers found that the percentage of children living in poverty in 26 industrialized countries ranged from 2.4% in Denmark to 27.7% in Mexico. The United States had the second-highest rate, 21.9%. All of the Scandinavian countries had child poverty rates less than 5%. Most European countries had rates between 5% and 10%.

In the United States, the National Center for Children in Poverty (NCCP) (Wight, Chau, & Aratani, 2010) estimates that families need an income about twice the U.S. federal poverty level to meet basic needs, and they refer to families below this level as low-income. NCCP (2008) reports that of the more than 12 million infants and toddlers in the United States, 5.4 million (43%) live in low-income families, and 2.7 million (21%) live in families that are below the poverty level. There are racial and ethnic differences in the rates: 65% of Native American infants and toddlers live in low-income families, compared with 65% of Black infants and toddlers, 64% of Latino infants and toddlers, 27%

of Asian infants and toddlers, and 30% of White infants and toddlers. Infants and toddlers with immigrant parents are more likely than those with native-born parents to live in low-income families, 61% compared to 40%. Geographical differences also exist in the rates of infants and toddlers in low-income families: 52% of infants and toddlers living in rural areas live in low-income families, compared to 49% of those in urban areas and 35% in suburban areas. Half (49%) of infants and toddlers living in low-income families have at least one parent who works full-time, year-round.

Although some young children who live in poverty flourish, poverty presents considerable risks to children's growth and development. (That risk continues from infancy and toddlerhood into early and middle childhood, as Chapters 12 and 13 explain.) Children living in poverty often suffer the consequences of poor nutrition and inadequate health care. Many of these children do not receive proper immunizations, and many minor illnesses go untreated, increasing the potential for serious health problems. This phenomenon is particularly disturbing because many of these minor illnesses are easily treated. Most childhood ear infections, for example, are easily treated with antibiotics; left untreated, they can result in hearing loss.

In addition to inadequate health care and nutrition, children living in poverty often experience overcrowded living conditions. Overcrowding restricts opportunities for play, and thus, because most learning and development in young children takes place in the context of play, it restricts healthy development. A study of development among 12-month-old Haitian American children found that the poorer children experienced more overcrowded conditions than those not living in poverty and consequently had less play time, fewer toys, a smaller number of safe areas to play, and less private time with parents (Widmayer, Peterson, & Larner, 1990). The living conditions of the children who were poor were associated with delayed motor development and lower cognitive functioning.

Negative associations between family poverty and children's cognitive development begin to emerge by the end of the second year of life. By age 2, poor toddlers score 4.4 points lower on IQ tests than nonpoor toddlers. In addition, poor infants and toddlers are more likely to demonstrate emotional and behavioral problems than nonpoor infants and toddlers. Three-year-olds who live in deep poverty have been found to display more internalizing behavior symptoms, such as anxiety, withdrawal, and depression, than other children of the same age (Barajas et al., 2008). Children are affected not only by the direct consequences of poverty, but also by indirect factors such as family stress, parental depression, and inadequate or nonsupportive parenting (UNICEF, 2005b). For example, Irma Velasquez's depression and anxiety, noted in Case Study 11.3, will affect her relationship with her son, Henry. Poor children are also more likely to be exposed to environmental toxins (Song & Lu, 2002).

Most disturbing is the link between poverty and **infant mortality**—the death of a child before his or her first birthday. In general, infant mortality rates are the highest in the poorest countries (United Nations Development Program, 2005). Infant mortality rates in the United States are high compared to other industrialized nations (UNICEF, 2005b), but Malaysia, a country with one quarter the average income of the United States, has the same infant mortality rate as the United States (United Nations Development Program, 2005). Within the United States, mortality rates for infants are higher among the poor, and the rate among African Americans is twice that of European Americans. As discussed in Chapter 10, low birth weight (LBW) as a result of inadequate prenatal care is the primary factor that contributes to the high infant mortality rate (United Nations Development Program, 2005).

Interestingly, the infant mortality rate for children of Hispanic women is lower than that for children of European American women (Hessol & Fuentes-Afflick, 2005), even though inadequate prenatal care is prominent among Hispanic women. This fact suggests that differences in prenatal care explain only part of the disparity in infant mortality rates. The mother's diet and social support network have been suggested as other factors that may affect birth weight and infant mortality rates (Gonzalez-Quintero et al., 2006; McGlade, Saha, & Dahlstrom, 2004). One comparative study found lower rates of alcohol and tobacco use among Hispanic women than among women of other racial/ethnic groups and the presence of stronger family, cultural, and social ties (McGlade et al., 2004). These findings suggest that social support may offset the consequences of inadequate prenatal care.

Inadequate Caregiving

The most pervasive response to inadequate caregiving is nonorganic failure to thrive (NOFTT). This diagnosis is used to describe infants, usually ages 3 to 12 months, who show poor development, primarily in terms of weight gain. These infants weigh less than 80% of the ideal weight for their age. The "nonorganic" feature refers to the lack of medical causes for the poor development, and is thought to be a consequence of environmental neglect (lack of food) and stimulus deprivation (Bassali & Benjamin, 2002). Overall, NOFTT is a consequence of the infant's basic needs going unmet, primarily the needs for feeding and nurturing.

A review of the literature identified several parental factors that appear to increase the likelihood of the development of NOFTT (Bassali & Benjamin, 2002; Marino, Weinman, & Soudelier, 2001). These include maternal depression, maternal malnutrition during pregnancy, marital problems between parents, and mental illness and/or substance abuse in the primary caretaker.

Parental mental illness and depression are associated with other problems among infants and toddlers as well. For example, infants of depressed mothers demonstrate less positive expressions of mood and personality and are less attentive in play (Gomez, 2001). Overall, they demonstrate less joy, even when they are securely attached to the mother. One analysis of the literature on parental mental illness and infant development concluded the following (R. Seifer & Dickstein, 2000):

- Parental mental illness increases the likelihood of mental health problems among the children.
- Mothers who are depressed are more negative in interaction with their infants.
- Similarly, infants with depressed mothers are more negative in their exchange with their mothers.

- There is an association between parental mental illness and insecure attachment between parents and infants.
- Depressed mothers tend to view their infant's behavior as more negative than nondepressed mothers do.

Child Maltreatment

National data indicate that in 2007, a total of 794,000 children in the United States were assessed to be victims of abuse or neglect. (It is important to note that it is generally assumed that many abused and neglected children never come to the attention of government authorities.) The national data also indicate that 31.9% of all known victims of child maltreatment are younger than 4 years of age. Infants from birth to 1 year of age have the highest rate of victimization, 21.9 per 1,000 infants age birth to 1 year (U.S. Department of Health and Human Services, 2009a). For all age groups, 60% of confirmed cases of child maltreatment involved neglect, 10.8% involved physical abuse, 7.6% involved sexual abuse, and 4.2% involved psychological abuse.

> How might child abuse or neglect experienced as an infant or toddler serve as a risk factor for later development?

The effect of child maltreatment and other trauma on the brain during the first 3 years of life has been the subject of considerable study in recent years (see Rosemary Farmer's excellent discussion of this topic in Chapter 5 of her 2009 book *Neuroscience and Social Work Practice: The Missing Link*). Remember that neuroscientific research has clearly demonstrated that the brain is plastic throughout life, which means that it is shaped by experiences across the life course. Research indicates that several brain parts involved in responses to stress are especially disrupted and changed by traumatic events during the first 3 years of life. They include the brain parts that regulate *homeostasis*, or internal stability (brain stem and locus ceruleus); those that form memory systems and are involved in emotion regulation (hippocampus, amygdala, and frontal cortex); and brain parts that regulate the executive functions of planning, working memory, and impulse control (orbitofrontal cortex, cingulate and dorsolateral prefrontal cortex). In addition, the major neuroendocrine stress response system, the hypothalamic-pituitary-adrenal (HPA) axis, is also impacted by trauma. Research indicates that early life stress, such as child maltreatment, can lead to disruptions in HPA axis functioning, and may result in anxiety disorders and depression in adulthood (see Mello, Mello, Carpenter, & Price, 2003; Van Voorhees & Scarpa, 2004).

The child who experiences maltreatment or other trauma at the ages of 2, 3, or 4 is at risk of developing memory problems, difficulty regulating emotions, and problems integrating sensory experiences. Research shows that people who experienced childhood trauma are more likely to develop decreased volume in the hippocampus, a brain characteristic also found with adults experiencing post-traumatic stress disorder (PTSD). Injuries to the hippocampus have been found to be associated with cognitive impairments, memory deficits, poor coping responses, and dissociation (Farmer, 2009). When a child is exposed to extreme stress or trauma, the autonomic nervous system is activated, resulting in increased heart rate, respiration, and blood pressure. The child may freeze in place before beginning to fight. In the case of child sexual abuse, the child may dissociate, or detach from what is happening, becoming compliant and emotionally numb (B. Perry, 2002b).

As noted above, 60% of all confirmed cases of child maltreatment involve neglect. Child neglect is thought to occur when caregivers are ignorant of child development, overwhelmed by life stresses, or struggling with mental health or substance abuse problems. Children who experience neglect in the early years of life often do not thrive. Much of the early human research on child neglect focused on Romanian children who were placed in state-run institutions with few staff (staff–child ratio of 1:60) and very little sensory and emotional stimulation, as noted earlier in this chapter. At 3 years of age, these children were found to have delays in physical growth as well as in motor, cognitive, and language skills; they also had poor social skills. Preliminary research suggests that neglect leads to deficits in prefrontal cortex functioning (attention and social deficits) and executive functioning

(planning, working memory, and impulse control). Working memory is key to learning. Early evidence suggests that these changes in brain functioning are related to difficulties managing emotions, problem solving, and social relationships. Most troubling is the finding that children who are neglected early in life have smaller brains than other children; they have fewer neurons and fewer connections between neurons. Exhibit 11.9

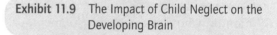

Exhibit 11.9 The Impact of Child Neglect on the Developing Brain

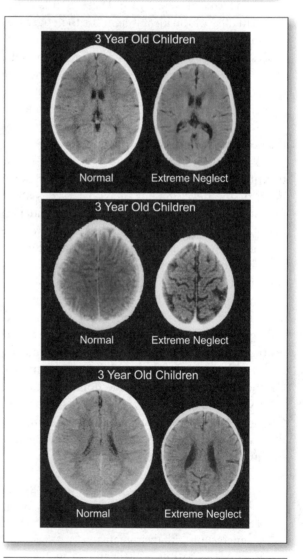

SOURCE: Adapted from Farmer (2009).

shows the brains of 3-year-old "normal" children alongside the brains of 3-year-old children who have faced extreme neglect.

An association has been found between infant temperament and abuse (Thomlison, 2004). Infants who have "difficult" temperaments are more likely to be abused and neglected, and the combination of a difficult temperament and environmental stress interact (Thomlison, 2004). Similarly, infants and toddlers with mental, physical, or behavioral abnormalities are also at a higher risk for abuse (Guterman & Embry, 2004).

Social workers need to keep abreast of the developing neuroscience research on the effects of child maltreatment on brain development, but we must also remember to put the brain in context. We must advocate for policy that ensures that parents have the best available resources to provide the type of parenting that infants and toddlers need. We must also encourage research that examines how to heal the disrupted brain.

PROTECTIVE FACTORS IN INFANCY AND TODDLERHOOD

Many young children experience healthy growth and development despite the presence of risk factors. They are said to have resilience. Several factors have been identified as mediating between the risks children experience and their growth and development (Fraser, Kirby, & Smokowski, 2004; E. E. Werner, 2000). These factors are "protective" in the sense that they shield the child from the consequences of potential hazards (Fraser et al., 2004). Following are some protective factors that help diminish the potential risks to infants and toddlers.

Education

Research indicates that the education of the mother directly affects the outcome for infants and toddlers. This effect was found even in the devastating poverty that exists in Nicaragua (Pena & Wall, 2000).

The infant mortality rate is predictably high in this country. However, investigators found that the higher the mother's level of formal education, the lower the infant mortality rate. Investigators hypothesize that mothers with higher levels of formal education provide better quality of care to their infants by feeding them more conscientiously, using available health care, keeping the household cleaner, and generally satisfying the overall needs of the infant. These mothers simply possessed better coping skills.

Similar results were found in a study of mothers and infants with two strikes against them—they are living in poverty and the infants were born premature (R. Bradley et al., 1994). Infants whose mothers had higher intellectual abilities demonstrated higher levels of cognitive and social development and were more likely to be in the normal range of physical development.

Social Support

Social support is often found in informal networks, such as friends and extended family members, or in formal support systems, such as religious organizations, community agencies, day care centers, social workers, and other professionals. The availability of social support seems to buffer against many risk factors, such as stress experienced by parents (E. E. Werner & Smith, 2001). For example, Mrs. Hicks (Case Study 11.1) could truly benefit from having the opportunity to take a break from the stresses of caring for Holly. Both formal and informal social support can fill this gap for her. Even child abuse is reduced in the presence of positive social support networks (Coohey, 1996).

Extended family members often serve as alternative caregivers when parents cannot provide care because of physical or mental illness or job demands. Reliance on an extended family is particularly important in some cultural and socioeconomic groups. Sarah's dad, Chris Johnson (Case Study 11.2), probably would not have been able to care for her without the support of his family. And it is through the support of his family that he has been able to continue his education.

Easy Temperament

Infants with a positive temperament are less likely to be affected by risk factors (Fraser et al., 2004). The association between easy temperament and "protection" is both direct and indirect. Infants with a positive temperament may simply perceive their world more positively. Infants with a positive temperament may also induce more constructive and affirming responses from those in their environment.

National and State Policies

Many social workers and others advocate for better national, state, and local policies that will enhance good health in infants and toddlers, build and support strong families, promote positive early learning experiences, and create systems that advance the development and well-being of infants and toddlers (Zero to Three, n.d.). This includes legislation and financial support to ensure things such as adequate health coverage for infants and toddlers, improved policies and programs that prevent child abuse, and development of programs and policies that promote parental and infant mental health. Also, continued support of national programs like the Women, Infants, & Children (WIC) program and the Child and Adult Care Food Program (CACFP) are considered crucial to promoting healthy physical development in infants and toddlers. Other advocates promote the improvement of existing social and educational programs. Knitzer (2007), for example, identifies what she refers to as legislation to improve the odds for young children. She suggests investing more federal and state financial resources to extend programs such as Early Head Start to incorporate home visiting, center-based instruction, and family support for all low-income babies and toddlers through (instead of up to) age 3.

Critical Thinking Questions 11.3

Why do you think that researchers consistently find a negative association between family poverty and children's cognitive development? What biological, psychological, and social factors might be involved in that association? There is growing evidence that child maltreatment has a negative impact on brain development. What role can social workers play in informing the public about the impact of the environment on brain development?

Implications for Social Work Practice

In summary, knowledge about infants and toddlers suggests a number of practice principles:

- Become well acquainted with theories and empirical research about growth and development among infants and toddlers.
- Assess infants and toddlers in the context of their environment, culture included.
- Promote continued use of formal and informal social support networks for parents with infants and toddlers.
- Continue to promote the elimination of poverty and the advancement of social justice.
- Advocate for compulsory health insurance and quality health care.
- Advocate for more affordable, quality child care.
- Collaborate with news media and other organizations to educate the public about the impact of poverty and inequality on early child development.
- Learn intervention methods to prevent and reduce substance abuse.

- Help parents understand the potential effects of inadequate caregiving on their infants, including the effects on brain development.
- Help parents and others understand the association between child development and consequential outcomes during adulthood.
- Provide support and appropriate intervention to parents to facilitate effective caregiving for infants and toddlers.

Key Terms

attachment
blooming
brain plasticity
concrete operations stage
developmental delays
developmental niche
formal operations stage
infant

infant mortality
motor skills
object permanence
preoperational stage
pruning
reflex
sensorimotor stage
sensory system

separation anxiety
stranger anxiety
symbolic functioning
temperament
toddler
transitional object
working model

Active Learning

1. Spend some time at a mall or other public place where parents and infants frequent. List behaviors that you observe that indicate attachment between the infant and caretaker. Note any evidence you observe that may indicate a lack of attachment.

2. Ask to tour a day care facility. Describe the things you observe that may have a positive influence on cognitive development for the infants and toddlers who are placed there. List those things that you think are missing from that setting that are needed to create a more stimulating environment.

3. Social support is considered to be a protective factor for individuals throughout the life course. List the forms of social support that are available to Marilyn Hicks, Chris Johnson, and Irma Velasquez. How do they help them with their parenting? In what ways could they be more helpful? How do they add to the level of stress?

Web Resources

The Clearinghouse on International Developments on Child, Youth and Family Policies

www.childpolicyintl.org

Site maintained at Columbia University, contains international comparisons of child and family policies.

Jean Piaget Society
www.piaget.org/index.html

Site presented by the Jean Piaget Society, an international interdisciplinary society of scholars, teachers, and researchers, contains information on the society, a student page, a brief biography of Piaget, and Internet links.

National Center for Children in Poverty (NCCP)

www.nccp.org

Site presented by the NCCP of the Mailman School of Public Health at Columbia University, contains media resources and child poverty facts, as well as information on child care and early education, family support, and welfare reform.

National Network for Child Care

www.nncc.org

Site presented by the Cooperative Extension System's National Network for Child Care, contains a list of over 1,000 publications and resources related to child care, an e-mail listserv, and a newsletter.

Zero to Three

www.zerotothree.org

Site presented by Zero to Three: National Center for Infants, Toddlers, and Families, a national nonprofit charitable organization with the aim to strengthen and support families. Site contains Parents' Tip of the Week, Parenting A–Z, BrainWonders, a glossary, and links to the Erikson Institute and other Internet sites.

CHAPTER 12

Early Childhood

Debra J. Woody

David Woody, III

ༀ ༝

Opening Questions

Why do social workers need to know about the ability of young children (ages 3 to 6) to express emotions and feelings?

What is the process of gender and ethnic recognition and development among young children?

What do social workers need to know about play among young children?

Key Ideas

As you read this chapter, take note of these central ideas:

1. Healthy development is in many ways defined by the environment and culture in which the child is raised. In addition, although growth and development in young children have some predictability and logic, the timing and expression of many developmental skills vary from child to child.

2. According to Piaget, preschoolers are in the preoperational stage of cognitive development and become capable of cognitive recall and symbolic functioning.

3. Erikson describes the task of children ages 3 to 6 as being the development of initiative versus guilt.

4. As young children struggle to discover stability and regularity in the environment, they are often rigid in their use of rules and stereotypes.

5. Regardless of country of residence or culture, all children ages 3 to 6 engage in spontaneous play.

6. Three types of parenting styles have been identified: authoritarian, authoritative, and permissive. Parenting styles are prescribed to some extent by the community and culture in which the parent resides, and researchers are beginning to examine the appropriateness of using this parenting style typology across cultural groups.

7. Poverty, ineffective discipline, divorce, and exposure to violence all pose special challenges for early childhood development.

CASE STUDY 12.1

Terri's Terrible Temper

Terri's mother and father, Joan and Michael Smith, really seem at a loss about what to do. They adopted Terri, age 3, when she was an infant. They describe to their social worker how happy they were to finally have a child. They had tried for many years, spent a lot of money on fertility procedures, and had almost given up on the adoption process when Terri seemed to be "sent from heaven." Their lives were going well until a year ago, when Terri turned 2. Joan Smith describes an overnight change in Terri's behavior. Terri has become a total terror at home and at preschool. In fact, the preschool has threatened to dismiss Terri if her behavior does not improve soon. Terri hits and takes toys from other children, she refuses to cooperate with the teacher, and she does "what she wants to do."

Joan and Michael admit that Terri runs their household. They spend most evenings after work coaxing Terri into eating her dinner, taking a bath, and going to bed. Any attempt at a routine is nonexistent. When they try to discipline Terri, she screams, hits them, and throws things. They have not been able to use time-outs to discipline her because Terri refuses to stay in the bathroom, the designated time-out place. She runs out of the bathroom and hides. When they attempt to hold her in the bathroom, she screams until Michael gets too tired to continue to hold her or until she falls asleep. Joan and Michael admit that they frequently let Terri have her way because it is easier than saying no or trying to discipline her.

The "straw that broke the camel's back" came during a family vacation. Joan's sister and family joined the Smiths at the beach. Michael describes the vacation as a total disaster. Terri refused to cooperate for the "entire" vacation. They were unable to eat at restaurants because of her tantrums, and they were unable to participate in family activities because Terri would not let them get her ready to go. They tried allowing her to choose the activities for the day, which worked until other family members tired of doing only the things that Terri wanted to do. Terri would scream and throw objects if the family refused to eat when and where she wanted or go to the park or the beach when she wanted. Joan's sister became so frustrated with the situation that she vowed never to vacation with them again. In fact, it was the sister who insisted that they get professional help for Terri.

CASE STUDY 12.2

Jack's Name Change

Until last month, Jack, age 4, lived with his mother, Joyce Lewis, and father, Charles Jackson Lewis, in what Joyce describes as a happy home. She was shocked when she discovered that her husband was having an affair with a woman at work. She immediately asked him to leave and has filed for divorce. Charles moved in with his girlfriend and has not contacted Joyce or Jack at this point. Joyce just can't believe that this is happening to her. Her mother had the same experience with Joyce's father but had kept the marriage going for the sake of Joyce and her siblings. Joyce, on the other hand, is determined to live a different life from the one her mother chose. She saw how depressed her mother was until her death at age 54. Joyce states that her mother died of a broken heart.

Although Joyce is determined to live without Charles, she is concerned about how she and Jack will live on her income alone. They had a comfortable life before the separation, but it took both incomes. Although she plans to seek child support, she knows she will need to move, because she cannot afford the mortgage on her own.

Joyce would prefer for Jack not to have contact with his father. In fact, she is seriously considering changing Jack's name because he was named after his father. Joyce has tried to explain the situation to Jack as best she can. However, in the social worker's presence, she told Jack that she hopes he does not grow up to be like his father. She also told Jack that his father is the devil and is now living with a witch.

Joyce also shares that Jack has had difficulty sleeping and continues to ask when his father is coming home. Joyce simply responds to Jack by telling him that they probably will never see Charles again.

CASE STUDY 12.3

A New Role for Ron and Rosiland's Grandmother

Ron, age 3, and Rosiland, age 5, have lived with Ms. Johnson, their maternal grandmother, for the last year. Prior to that time, they lived with their mother, Shirley Johnson, who has never married and had been a single mother since their birth. Shirley was sent to prison a year ago after a conviction for drug trafficking. Shirley's boyfriend, who is not the father of Ron and Rosiland, is a known drug dealer and had asked Shirley to make a "delivery" for him. Shirley was arrested as she stepped off the bus in another state where she had taken the drugs for delivery. Ron and Rosiland were with her when she was arrested, as she had taken them with her. Her boyfriend thought that a woman traveling with two young children would never be suspected of delivering drugs.

Ron and Rosiland were put into foster care by Child Protective Services until Ms. Johnson arrived to pick them up. It had taken her 2 weeks to save enough money to get to the children and fly them all home. Ms. Johnson shares with the social worker how angry she was that Shirley's boyfriend refused to help her get the children home. Shirley calls the children when she can, but because her crime was a federal offense, she has been sent to a prison far away from home. The children ask about her often and miss her terribly. Ms. Johnson has told the children that their mom is away but has not told them that she will be away for some time. She is also unsure how much they understand about what happened, even though they were present when their mom was arrested.

Ms. Johnson shares that she has no choice but to care for the children, although this is definitely not the life she had planned. She liked living alone after her husband died several years ago. With her small savings, she was planning to go see her sister in another state for an extended visit. But that money is gone now, because these funds were used to get the children home. She seems to love both of the children but confides that the children "drive her crazy." She is not accustomed to all the noise, and they seem to need so much attention from her. Getting into the habit of having a scheduled day is also difficult for Ms. Johnson. Both children attend preschool, an arrangement Shirley made before her incarceration. Ms. Johnson describes the fact that the children attend preschool as a blessing, because it gives her some relief. Her social worker suspects that preschool is a blessing for the children as well.

HEALTHY DEVELOPMENT IN EARLY CHILDHOOD

As children like Terri Smith, Jack Lewis, and Ron and Rosiland Johnson emerge from toddlerhood, they turn their attention more and more to the external environment. Just as they worked at developing some regularity in their body rhythms, attachment relationships, and emotional states in infancy and toddlerhood, they now work to discover some stability and regularity in the external world. That is not always an easy task, given their limitations in cognitive and language development.

Some children emerge from toddlerhood with a sense of confidence in the availability of support and a beginning sense of confidence in themselves. Other children, unfortunately, leave toddlerhood more challenged than when they entered that stage (Sroufe, Egeland, Carlson, & Collins, 2005). Much happens in all interrelated dimensions of development between ages 3 and 6, however, and most children emerge from early childhood with a much more sophisticated ability to understand the world and their relationships to it. They work out this understanding in an increasingly wider world, with major influences coming from family, school, peer groups, the neighborhood, and the media.

Some child development scholars still refer to the period between ages 3 and 6 as the preschool age, but others have recently begun to refer to this period as early school age, reflecting the fact that a large number of children are enrolled in some form of group-based experience during this period. In 2007, an estimated 55% of 3- and 4-year-olds in the United States were enrolled in school, at least part-time, compared with 20% in 1970 (U.S. Census Bureau, 2009c). We will simply refer to this period between 3 and 6 years of age as early childhood. Remember as you read that the various types of development discussed in this chapter under separate headings actually are interdependent, and sometimes the distinctions between the dimensions blur.

International literature criticizes the notion that there is a universal early childhood. It suggests, instead, that there are multiple and diverse early childhoods, based on class, race, gender, geography, and time (see Dahlberg, Moss, & Pence, 2007; Penn, 2005; Waller, 2009). One critic notes that more than 95% of the literature on child development comes from the United States and is, for the most part, written by men (Fawcett, 2000). There are growing criticisms that all children of the world are evaluated against Western developmental psychology science, which is a mix of statistical averages and historically and culturally specific value judgments (Dahlberg et al., 2007; Nybell, Shook, & Finn, 2009; Penn, 2005). In this chapter, we have tried to broaden the view of early childhood, where the literature allows, but please keep the above criticism in mind as you read. Also keep these data about the world's children in mind (UNICEF Canada, 2010). Of 100 children born in the world in a given year,

- Thirty would suffer malnutrition in their first 5 years of life.
- Twenty-six would not be immunized against basic childhood diseases.
- Nineteen would lack access to safe drinking water.
- Forty would lack adequate sanitation.
- Seventeen would never go to school.

Physical Development in Early Childhood

As Chapter 11 explained, infants and toddlers grow rapidly. From age 3 to 6, physical growth slows significantly. On average, height during this stage increases about 2 to 3 inches per year, and the young child adds about 5 pounds of weight per year. As a result, young children look leaner. However, there is growing global concern about increasing obesity beginning in early childhood (Keenan & Evans, 2009). At the same time, by age 4, some children in Africa and Asia weigh as much as 13 pounds less than children of the same age in Europe and America (Hendrick, 1990). Two forms of malnutrition exist: malnutrition caused by a sedentary lifestyle and eating too much processed food, and malnutrition caused by having too little to eat (McMichael, 2008). As suggested in the previous chapter, the importance of adequate nutrition cannot be overemphasized; poor nutrition is involved in at least half of the 10.9 million child deaths in the world each year. It magnifies the effect of every disease (Hunger Notes, 2011).

Great variation exists in the height and weight of young children, and racial and ethnic differences in height and weight are still evident in the early childhood years. For example, in the United States, African American children in early childhood on average are taller than White and Hispanic American children of the same age, and there is some evidence that Hispanic children weigh more on average than other young children (Dennison et al., 2006; Overpeck et al., 2000). Children of low economic status, worldwide, are more likely than other children to be overweight during early childhood, but severe food insecurity may lead to growth inhibition (Y. Wang & Zhang, 2006).

As noted in Chapter 11, the brain continues to be shaped by experience throughout early childhood and beyond. By age 5, the child's brain is 90% of its adult size. Motor and cognitive abilities grow by leaps and bounds because of increased interconnections between brain cells, which allow for more complex cognitive and motor capability. In addition, through a process called **lateralization,** the two hemispheres of the brain begin to operate slightly differently, allowing for a wider range of activity. Simply stated, brain functioning becomes more specialized. The left hemisphere is activated during tasks that require analytical skills, including speaking and reading. Tasks that involve emotional expression and spatial skills, such as visual imagery, require response from the right hemisphere. With the development of the right hemisphere and the socio-emotional components there, young children develop the ability to reflect on the feelings and thoughts of others (Beatson & Taryan, 2003). Note that this reflective function is a critical component of attachment. Brain lateralization was identified early in neuroscientific research, but current thinking is that we should avoid applying the right hemisphere/left hemisphere paradigm too rigidly. The hemispheres are in constant communication, and the tasks performed by each hemisphere are much more complex than once thought (Fogarty, 2009).

Because of other developments in the brain, children also obtain and refine some advanced motor skills during this time, such as running, jumping, and hopping, but less is known about motor development in early childhood compared to infancy and toddlerhood (Keenan & Evans, 2009). Early intervention specialists suggest the gross motor milestones presented in Exhibit 12.1. In addition to these **gross motor skills**—skills that require use of the large muscle groups—young children develop **fine motor skills,** including the ability to scribble and draw, and to cut with scissors. Suggested fine motor milestones are also presented in Exhibit 12.1. As you review these suggested milestones, remember that there is much variability in motor development in early childhood. For example, one child may be advanced in gross motor skills and lag in fine motor skills, or the opposite. In addition, different motor skills are valued in different developmental niches, and the expression of motor skills will depend on the tools available to

Photo 12.1 During early childhood, young children make advancement in the development of fine motor skills, including the ability to draw.

the child. With these cautions, parents and other adults who spend time with young children will find the milestones presented in Exhibit 12.1 to be helpful to keep in mind as they interact with young children.

Increases in fine motor skills also enable young children to become more self-sufficient. However, allowing the extra time needed for young children to perform these tasks can be frustrating to adults. Ms. Johnson, for example, has lived alone for some time now and may need to readjust to allowing extra time for the children to "do it themselves." Spills and messes, which are a part of this developmental process, are also often difficult for adults to tolerate.

Exhibit 12.1 Gross Motor and Fine Motor Skills Developed in Early Childhood

	Gross Motor Skills	Fine Motor Skills
Most 3-year-olds can	Run forward	Turn single pages
	Jump in place	Snip with scissors
	Stand on one foot with support	Hold crayons with thumb and finger
	Walk on tiptoe	Use one hand consistently
	Avoid obstacles in path	Imitate circular, vertical, and horizontal strokes
	Catch an 8-inch ball	Paint with some wrist action
	Climb and walk up stairs with alternating feet	Make dots, lines, and circular strokes
		Roll, pound, squeeze, and pull clay
		Build tower of up to nine cubes
		String ½-inch beads
		Cut along a line
		Use a fork
		Manage large buttons
		Dress self with supervision
Most 4-year-olds can	Run around obstacles	Build a tower of nine small blocks
	Walk on a line	Drive nails and pegs
	Balance on one foot for 5–10 seconds	Copy a circle
	Hop on one foot	Manipulate clay material
	Push, pull, and steer wheeled toys	Hold a pencil with appropriate grasp
	Ride a tricycle	
	Use a slide independently	
	Jump over 6-inch-high object and land on both feet	
	Throw a ball overhead	
	Catch a bouncing ball	
Most 5-year-olds can	Walk backwards toe-heel	Cut on a line
	Jump forward 10 times without falling	Copy a cross
	Walk up and down stairs independently with alternating feet	Copy a square
	Turn a somersault	Print some capital letters

SOURCE: Based on Early Intervention Support (2009).

Cognitive and Language Development

A few years ago, the first author of this chapter was at a doctor's office when a mother walked into the waiting area with her son, about age 3. The waiting area was very quiet, and the young child's voice seemed loud in the silence. The mother immediately began to "shh" her son. He responded by saying, "I don't want to shh; I want to talk." Of course, everyone laughed, which made the child talk even louder. The mother moved immediately to some chairs in the corner and attempted to get her son to sit. He refused, stating that he wanted to stand on one foot. The mother at once attempted to engage him with the toys she had with her. They played with an electronic game in which the child selects pieces to add to a face to make a complete face. This game kept the child's attention for a while until he became bored. The mother told him to "make the game stop." The child responded by yelling at the game, demanding that it stop making the face. The mother, understanding that her son had taken a literal interpretation of her comments, rephrased her directions and showed her son how to push the stop button on the game.

Next, the two decided to read a book about the Lion King. The child became very confused, because in the book, different from his memory of the movie, the main character, Simba, was already an adult at the beginning of the story. The child, looking at the pictures, argued that the adult lion was not Simba but instead was Simba's father. The mother attempted to explain that this book begins with Simba as an adult. She stated that just as her son will grow, Simba grew from a cub to an adult lion. The son looked at his mother bewildered, responding with, "I am not a cub; I am a little boy." The mother then tried to make the connection that just like the son's daddy was once a boy, Simba grew up to be a lion. The boy responded by saying that men and lions are not the same. Needless to say, the mother seemed relieved when her name was called to see the doctor.

This scene encapsulates many of the themes of cognitive and moral development in early childhood. As memory improves, and the store of information expands, young children begin to think much more in terms of categories, as the little boy in the doctor's office was doing (D. Davies, 2004; B. Newman & Newman, 2009). He was now thinking in terms of cubs, boys, lions, and men. They also begin to recognize some surprising connections between things. No doubt, in a short time, the little boy will recognize a connection between boys and cubs, men and lions, boys and men, as well as cubs and lions. Young children are full of big questions such as where do babies come from, what happens to people when they die, where does the night come from, and so on. They can think about themselves and about other people. They engage in creative and imaginative thought and begin to develop humor, empathy, and altruism (E. Marti, 2003). They make great strides in language development and the ability to communicate. And they make gradual progress in the ability to judge right and wrong and to regulate behavior in relation to that reasoning.

Piaget's Stages of Cognitive Development

In early childhood, children fit into the second stage of cognitive development described by Piaget, the preoperational stage. This stage is in turn divided into two substages:

Substage 1: Preconceptual (ages 2 to 3). The most important aspect of the preoperational stage is the development of *symbolic representation,* which occurs in the preconceptual substage. Through play, children learn to use symbols and actively engage in what Piaget labeled deferred imitation. *Deferred imitation* refers to the child's ability to view an image and then, significantly later, recall and imitate the image. For example, 3-year-old Ella, who watches the *Dora the Explorer* cartoon on TV, fills her backpack with a pretend map and other items she might need, such as a blanket and a flashlight, puts it on, creates a pretend monkey companion named Boots, and sets off on an adventure, using the kitchen as a barn and the space under the dining table as the woods, and keeping her eyes open all the while for the "mean" Swiper the Fox. Ella's cousin, Zachery, who is enthralled with the *Bob the Builder* cartoon, often pretends that he is Bob the Builder when he is playing with his toy trucks and tractors. Whenever Zachery encounters a problem, he will sing Bob's theme song, which is, "Bob the Builder, can we fix it? Yes, we can!!"

Substage 2: Intuitive (ages 4 to 7). During the second part of the preoperational stage, children use language to represent objects. During the preconceptual substage, any object with long ears may be called "bunny." During the intuitive substage, children begin to understand that the term *bunny* represents the entire animal, not just a property of it. However, although young children are able to classify objects, their classifications are based on only one attribute at a time. For example, given a set of stuffed animals with various sizes and colors, the young child will group the animals either by color or by size. In contrast, an older child who has reached the intuitive substage may sort them by both size and color.

In early childhood, children also engage in what Piaget termed **transductive reasoning,** or a way of thinking about two or more experiences without using abstract logic. This can be explained best with an illustration. Imagine that 5-year-old Sam immediately smells chicken when he enters his grandmother's home. He comments that she must be having a party and asks who is coming over for dinner. When the grandmother replies that no one is coming over and that a party is not planned, Sam shakes his head in disbelief and states that he will just wait to see when the guests arrive. Sam recalls that the last time his grandmother cooked chicken was for a party. Because the grandmother is cooking chicken again, Sam thinks another party is going to occur. This type of reasoning is also evident in the example of the mother and child in the doctor's office. Because the child saw Simba as a cub in the movie version of *The Lion King,* he reasons that the adult lion in the picture at the beginning of the book cannot possibly be Simba.

One last related preoperational concept described by Piaget is **egocentrism.** According to Piaget, in early childhood, children perceive reality only from their own experience and believe themselves to be at the center of existence. They are unable to recognize the possibility of other perspectives on a situation. For example, a 3-year-old girl who stands between her sister and the television to watch a program believes that her sister can see the television because she can. This aspect of cognitive reasoning could be problematic for most of the children described in the case examples. Jack may believe that it is his fault that his father left the family. Likewise, Ron and Rosiland may attribute their mother's absence to their behavior, especially given that they were present when she was arrested. However, some researchers have found that children are less egocentric than Piaget suggested (Borke, 1975; Wimmer & Perner, 1983).

Language Skills

Language development is included under cognitive development because it is the mechanism by which cognitive interpretations are communicated to others. Note that for language to exist, children must be able to "organize" their experiences.

At the end of toddlerhood, young children have a vocabulary of about 1,000 words, and they are increasing that store by about 7 or 8 words per day (L. Bloom, 1998b; D. Davies, 2004). They can speak in two-word sentences, and they have learned the question form of language. They are asking "why" questions, persistently and often assertively, to learn about the world. Three-year-old speech is generally clear and easy to understand.

By the fourth year of life, language development is remarkably sophisticated. The vocabulary is becoming more and more adequate for communicating ideas, and 4-year-olds are usually speaking in sentences of 8 to 10 words. They have mastered language well enough to tell a story mostly in words, rather than relying heavily on gestures, as toddlers must do. But perhaps the most remarkable aspect of language development in early childhood

> How does language development in early childhood promote human agency in making choices?

is the understanding of grammar rules. By age 4, young children in all cultures understand the basic grammar rules of their language (Gardiner & Kosmitzki, 2008). They accomplish this mostly by a figuring out process. As they figure out new grammar rules, as with other aspects of their learning, they are overly regular in using those rules, because they have not yet learned the exceptions (Santrock, 2003). So we often hear young children make statements such as "she goed to the store," or perhaps, "she wented to the store."

There has been a long-standing debate about how language is acquired. How much of language ability is a result of genetic processes, and how much of it is learned? B. F. Skinner (1957) argued that children learn language by imitating what they hear in the environment and then being reinforced for correct usage. When children utter sounds heard in their environment, Skinner contended, parents respond in a manner (smiling, laughing, clapping) that encourages young children to repeat the sounds. As children grow older, they are often corrected by caregivers and preschool teachers in the misuse of words or phrases. At the other end of the spectrum, Noam Chomsky (1968) contended that language ability is primarily a function of genetics. Although somewhat influenced by the environment, children develop language skills as long as the appropriate genetic material is in place.

There is increasing consensus that both perspectives have merit. While the physiology of language development is still poorly understood, it is thought that humans inherit, to a much higher degree than other organisms, a genetic capacity for flexible communication skills including language and speech (G. Novak & Pelaez, 2004). But many scholars also argue that language is "inherently social because it has to be learned from other persons" (L. Bloom, 1998a, p. 332). Children learn language by listening to others speak and by asking questions. Past toddlerhood, children increasingly take charge of their own language acquisition by asking questions and initiating dialogues (L. Bloom, 1998a). Parents can assist children by asking questions, eliciting details, and encouraging children to reflect on their experiences (Haden,

Haine, & Fivush, 1997). One longitudinal study found that the size of vocabulary among 3-year-olds is correlated with the size of the vocabulary spoken to them from the age of 9 months and the amount of positive feedback provided for language development (B. Hart & Risley, 1995).

It appears that the developmental niche has an impact on the development of language skills. From observation of their environment—physical

> How do social class, culture, and gender affect the "developmental niche" during early childhood?

and social surroundings, child-rearing customs, and caregiver personality—children learn a set of regulations, or rules for communication, that shape their developing language skills. Children have an innate capacity for language, but the structuring of the environment through culture is what allows language development to occur. Here are three examples of the importance of developmental niche for language development. In the first example, children whose parents ask them lots of questions and initiate frequent verbal interactions with them recognize more letters and numbers by age 5 or 6, and score higher on language proficiency tests in second grade than children whose parents do less verbal interaction with them (Mayes & Cohen, 2003). The second example involves different cultural valuing of silence. In the Colombian *mestizo* community and among Apache Native Americans, young children are expected to keep a respectful silence while interacting with others. Refraining from speaking is a form of communication, and the "useless habit" of talking too much is discouraged (Valsiner, 2000). The third example is not as straightforward. One research team found that by 5 years of age, Portuguese- and Mandarin Chinese-speaking children could distinguish the difference between the qualifiers "all" and "each," both conceptually and linguistically. English-speaking 5-year-olds do not make this distinction (Brooks, Jia, Braine, & Da Graca Dias, 1998). The researchers suggest that cultural values may play a role in this difference in language learning. They note that Portugal and China have collectivist-oriented cultures, and speculate that children in those cultures may begin to learn words and concepts that focus on the relationship between the individual and the collectivity earlier than children from more individualistic societies.

Moral Development

During early childhood, children move from a moral sense that is based on outside approval to a more internalized moral sense, with a rudimentary moral code. They engage in a process of taking society's values and standards as their own. They begin to integrate these values and standards into both their worldview and their self-concept. There are three components of moral development during early childhood (B. Newman & Newman, 2009):

1. *Knowledge* of the moral code of the community and how to use that knowledge to make moral judgments

2. *Emotions* that produce both the capacity to care about others and the capacity to feel guilt and remorse

3. *Actions* to inhibit negative impulses as well as to behave in a **prosocial,** or helpful and empathic, manner

Understanding Moral Development

Moral development has been explored from several different theoretical perspectives that have been found to have merit. Three of these approaches to moral development are explored here:

1. *Psychodynamic approach.* Sigmund Freud's psychoanalytic theory proposed that there are three distinct structures of the personality: the id, ego, and superego. According to Freud, the superego is the personality structure that guides moral development. There are two aspects to the superego: the *conscience,* which is the basis of a moral code, and the *ego ideal,* which is a set of ideals expected in a moral person. Freud (1927) thought that the superego is formed between the ages of 4 and 7, but more recent psychodynamic formulations suggest that infancy is the critical time for the beginning of moral development (Kohut, 1971). Freud thought that children would have more highly developed superegos when their parents used strict methods to inhibit the children's impulses. Contemporary research indicates the opposite, however, finding that moral behavior is associated with parental warmth, democratic decision making, and modeling of temptation resistance (Kochanska, Forman, Aksan, & Dunbar, 2005). New psychodynamic models emphasize a close, affectionate bond with the caregiver as the cornerstone of moral development. Freud also believed that males would develop stronger superegos than females, but research has not supported this idea.

2. *Social learning approach.* From the perspective of social learning theory, moral behavior is shaped by environmental reinforcements and punishments. Children are likely to repeat behaviors that are rewarded, and they are also likely to feel tension when they think about doing something that they have been punished for in the past. From this perspective, parental consistency in response to their children's behavior is important. Social learning theory also suggests that children learn moral conduct by observing models. Albert Bandura (1977a) found that children are likely to engage in behaviors for which they see a model rewarded and to avoid behaviors that they see punished. This can be problematic for children who watch a lot of television, because they may come to view violence as an acceptable way to solve interactional conflict if they see violence go unpunished.

3. *Cognitive developmental approach.* Piaget's theory of cognitive development has been the basis for stage models of moral reasoning, which assume that children's moral judgments change as their cognitive development allows them to examine the logical and abstract aspects of moral dilemmas. Moral development is assisted by opportunities to encounter new situations and different perspectives. The most frequently researched stage model is the one presented by Lawrence Kohlberg (1969a, 1976) and summarized in Chapter 4 in Exhibit 4.3. Kohlberg described three levels of moral reasoning, with two stages in each level. It was expected

that in early childhood, children will operate at the **preconventional level of moral reasoning,** with their reasoning about moral issues based, first, on what gets them rewarded or punished. This type of moral reasoning is thought to be common among toddlers. In the second stage, moral reasoning is based on what benefits either the child or someone the child cares about. This is consistent with the child's growing capacity for attachments. There is some empirical evidence that children between the ages of 3 and 6 do, indeed, begin to use the type of moral reasoning described in Stage 2 (L. Walker, 1989). The idea of a hierarchical sequence of stages of moral development has been challenged as being based on a Western cultural orientation, but longitudinal studies in a variety of countries have produced support for the idea of an evolution of moral reasoning (Gielen & Markoulis, 2001).

| Why is the development of empathy important for future capacity for relationships? |

All of the above approaches to moral development in early childhood have been criticized for leaving out two key ingredients: **empathy,** or the ability to understand another person's emotional condition, and **perspective taking,** or the ability to see a situation from another person's point of view (Eisenberg, 2000). Neuroscientific research is currently suggesting that a special type of brain cell, called a *mirror neuron,* is key to the development of empathy. Have you ever noticed how you instinctively smile when you see someone else smiling? Mirror neurons allow us to sense the move another person is about to make and the emotions he or she is experiencing. Emotion is contagious, because mirror neurons allow us to feel what the other person feels through brain-to-brain connection. Daniel Goleman (2006) calls this primal empathy; it is based on feelings, not thoughts. He has coined the phrase "social intelligence" to refer to this ability to be attuned to another person. It appears that humans have multiple systems of mirror neurons, and scientists are in the early stages of learning about them. Studies have found that people with autism have a dysfunctional mirror neuron system (Goleman, 2006).

There is growing agreement that empathy begins in infancy and grows throughout early childhood (Meltzoff, 2002). By age 3 or 4, children across cultures have been found to be able to recognize the type of emotional reaction that other children might have to different situations. Perspective taking, which is a thinking rather than feeling activity, has been found to grow gradually, beginning at about the age of 4 or 5 (Iannotti, 1985). Longitudinal research has found that children who show empathy and perspective taking at 4 and 5 years of age are more likely to exhibit prosocial behavior and sympathy during adolescence and early adulthood (Eisenberg et al., 1999).

In addition, there has been considerable examination of the degree to which Kohlberg's model is responsive to gender and cultural experience, in view of the study population upon which his theory is based—Harvard male undergraduates (Donleavy, 2008; Sherblom, 2008). Gilligan (1982) notes that gender, in American society, plays a significant role in how one experiences and acts on themes of ethical thinking, justice, and notions of individuality and connectedness. She suggests that there is strong gender bias in Kohlberg's theory, and her research indicates that women's moral thought is guided by caring and maintaining the welfare of others while men use more abstract principles of justice. As you can see from Exhibit 4.3, caring for others and maintaining harmony in relationships would put women in Stage 3, the highest stage. A similar criticism has been lodged about the poor fit of Kohlberg's theory with many non-European cultures that are more collectivist oriented than European and North American societies. Indeed, studies of Buddhist monks find that older monks barely reach Stage 4, indicating that their moral reasoning is not as well developed as Western male adolescents, by Kohlberg's model (Huebner & Garrod, 1993). The researchers suggest that the moral ideal in Western cultures is an autonomous individual with strong convictions who sticks up for those convictions. In contrast, the Buddhist moral ideal is guided by compassion and detachment from one's own individuality. How such themes are transmitted to young children can be indelible guideposts for managing and participating in interpersonal relationships (Seigfried, 1989).

One aspect of moral reasoning is *distributive justice,* or the belief about what constitutes a fair distribution of goods and resources in a society. Cross-cultural studies suggest that cultures hold different views on what constitutes a "fair" distribution of resources. Some societies, such as Sweden and Indonesia, see fairness in terms of need, while other societies, like the United States and Hong Kong, see fairness in terms of merit (Gardiner & Kosmitzki, 2008; Murphy-Berman & Berman, 2002). Reasoning about distributive justice starts in early childhood but is not well articulated until middle childhood (Gardiner & Kosmitzki, 2008).

Helping Young Children to Develop Morally

There is growing evidence that some methods work better than others for helping children develop moral reasoning and conduct. Activities that are particularly helpful are those that help children control their own behavior, help them understand how their behavior affects others, show them models of positive behavior, and get them to discuss moral issues (Arsenio & Gold, 2006; L. Walker & Taylor, 1991). It is important, however, to consider a child's temperament when undertaking disciplinary actions. Some children are more sensitive to messages of disapproval than others; sensitive children require a smaller dose of criticism and less sensitive children usually require more focused and directive discipline (Kochanska, 1997).

Although religious beliefs play a central role in most societies in clarifying moral behavior, little research has been done to explore the role of religion in moral development in young children. Research (Roof, 1999) has indicated that adults often become affiliated with a religious organization when their children are in early childhood, even if the parents later become "religious dropouts" after the children are out of the home. Religious rituals link young children to specific actions and images of the world as well as to a community that can support and facilitate their moral development. The major world religions also teach parents about how to be parents. Young children, with their comfortable embrace of magic, easily absorb religious stories on topics that may be difficult for adults to explain. Religion that emphasizes love, concern, and social justice can enrich the young child's moral development. Conversely, religion that is harsh and judgmental may produce guilt and a sense of worthlessness, which do not facilitate higher levels of moral reasoning.

Personality and Emotional Development

The key concern for Jack Lewis and for Ms. Johnson's grandchildren—Ron and Rosiland—is their emotional development. Specifically, will they grow into happy, loving, well-adjusted people despite the disruptions in their lives? Writing about the early childhood years, Sroufe and colleagues (2005) suggest that this is the period of life when a coherent personality emerges: "[I]t is no exaggeration to say that the person emerges at this time" (p. 121). Based on a longitudinal study of 180 children born into poverty, they conclude that behavior and adaptation during early childhood predict later behavior and adaptation, something that they did not find to be the case with the predictive power of behavior and adaptation in infancy and toddlerhood. They suggest that the important themes of development during this period are self-direction, agency, self-management, and self-regulation. Young children do face important developmental tasks in the emotional arena. This section addresses these tasks, drawing on Erikson's theory of psychosocial development.

Erikson's Theory of Psychosocial Development

Erikson labeled the stage of emotional development that takes place during the early childhood years as *initiative versus guilt* (ages 3 to 6). (Refer back to Exhibit 4.11 for the complete list of Erikson's stages.) Children who pass successfully through this stage learn to get satisfaction from completing tasks. They develop imagination and fantasies, and learn to handle guilt about their fantasies.

At the beginning of this stage, children's focus is on family relationships. They learn what roles are appropriate for various family members, and they learn to accept parental limits. In addition, they develop gender identity through identification with the parent of the same sex. Age and sex boundaries must be appropriately defined at this stage, and parents must be secure enough to set limits and resist the child's possessiveness.

By the end of this stage, the child's focus turns to friendships outside the family. Children engage in cooperative play and enjoy both sharing and competing with peers. Children must have the opportunity to establish peer relationships outside the family. This is one of the functions the preschool program serves for Ms. Johnson's grandchildren.

Children who become stuck in this stage are plagued with guilt about their goals and fantasies. They become confused about their gender identity and about family roles. These children are overly anxious and self-centered.

Emotions

Growing cognitive and language skills give young children the ability to understand and express their feelings and emotions. Children between the ages of 3 and 5 can recognize and label simple emotions, and they learn about themselves when they talk about their anxieties and fears (Hansen & Zambo, 2007). Children in early childhood can also identify feelings expressed by others—as the earlier discussion of empathy illustrated—and use creative ways to comfort others when they are upset. A friend describes the response of her 5-year-old son Marcus when he saw her crying about the sudden death of her brother in a car accident. Marcus hugged his mom and told her not to cry, because, although she was sad about Uncle Johnny, she still had Marcus. Marcus promised his mother to never drive a car so she would not have

to worry about the same thing happening to him. This attempt to reduce his mother's sadness is a typical response from a child of this age (Findlay, Girardi, & Coplan, 2006).

The ability to understand emotion continues to develop as young children have more opportunity to practice these skills. Children reared in homes in which emotions and feelings are openly discussed are better able to understand and express feelings (S. Bradley, 2000). Early childhood educators Cory Cooper Hansen and Debby Zambo (2007) recommend the use of children's literature to help children understand and manage emotions. Here are some of their recommendations for how to do that (p. 277):

- Respect all responses to talks about emotions.
- Ask children to describe the emotions of story characters.
- Talk about your own emotions about story characters.
- Encourage children to draw, write, or paint about the emotions of story characters, as well as their own emotional reactions.
- Sing or chant about emotions and how to handle them.
- Brainstorm ways that story characters can handle their emotions.
- Practice reading emotions from pictures in books.
- Use stuffed animals to "listen" to children's stories.

Most child development scholars agree that all emotions, including those that have been labeled "negative" (anger, sadness, guilt, disgust), are adaptive, but more needs to be learned about how the "negative" emotions can become problematic for children (P. Cole, Luby, & Sullivan, 2008). We know that by the first grade, most children can regulate their emotions well enough to learn, obey classroom rules, and develop friendships (Calkins & Hill, 2007; Shonkoff & Phillips, 2000). However, we also know that emotional

> What are our societal expectations for regulation of emotions during early childhood?

receptivity makes young children vulnerable to environmental stress, and early exposure to adverse situations can have a negative effect on the brain, cardiovascular, and endocrine processes that support emotional development (Gunnar & Quevedo, 2007). It is important to recognize when emotional development is getting off course, and researchers are at work to develop understanding of that issue. For example, we know that most young children have tantrums. For most children, anger and distress are expressed in quick peaks in anger intensity that decline into whining and comfort-seeking behavior. Researchers are finding, however, that the tantrums of depressed young children are more violent, destructive, verbally aggressive, and self-injurious; they also have a longer recovery time (Belden, Thompson, & Luby, 2008). It is important to avoid both over-reacting and under-reacting to children's difficulties in regulating their emotions, and the guidelines are getting clearer.

Aggression

One behavior that increases during the early childhood years is aggression. Two types of aggression are observed in young children: **instrumental aggression,** which occurs while fighting over toys and space, and **hostile aggression,** which is an attack meant to hurt another individual. Recently, researchers have studied another typology of aggression: physical aggression and relational aggression. **Physical aggression,** as the name suggests, involves using physical force against another person. **Relational aggression** involves behaviors that damage relationships without physical force, behaviors such as threatening to leave a relationship unless a friend complies with demands, or using social exclusion or the silent treatment to get one's way. Researchers are finding that boys make greater use of physical aggression than girls, and girls make greater use of relational aggression (Ostrov, Crick, & Stauffacher, 2006).

Although some children continue high levels of aggression into middle childhood, usually physical aggression peaks in the early childhood years

(Alink, Mesmon, & van Zeijl, 2006). By the end of the early childhood years, children learn better negotiation skills and become better at asking for what they want and using words to express feelings. Terri Smith, in the first case study in this chapter, obviously has not developed these moderating skills.

Attachment

In early childhood, children still depend on their attachment relationships for feelings of security. In particularly stressful times, the attachment behavior of the young child may look very much like the clinging behavior of the 2-year-old. For the most part, however, securely attached children will handle their anxieties by verbalizing their needs. For example, at bedtime, the 4-year-old child may say, "Please read one more story before you go." This increased ability to verbalize wants is a source of security. In addition, many young children continue to use transitional objects, such as blankets or a favorite teddy bear, to soothe themselves when they are anxious (D. Davies, 2004).

In their longitudinal study of 180 children born into poor families, Sroufe et al. (2005) examined, among other things, how attachment style in infancy and toddlerhood affected the developmental trajectory into early childhood. Here are some of the findings:

- Anxiously attached infants and toddlers were more dependent on their mothers, but performed more poorly on teaching tasks at age 3½ than either securely or avoidantly attached toddlers.
- Securely attached infants and toddlers rated higher on curiosity, agency, activity, self-esteem, and positive emotions at age 4½ than either anxiously or avoidantly attached toddlers.
- Securely attached infants and toddlers had better emotion regulation in early childhood than anxiously attached toddlers.

Sroufe and colleagues also found that temperament was not a powerful predictor of early childhood behavior.

Social Development

In early childhood, children become more socially adept than they were as toddlers, but they are still learning how to be social and how to understand the perspectives of other people. The many young children who enter group care face increasing demands for social competence.

Peer Relations

In early childhood, children form friendships with other children of the same age and gender; boys gravitate toward male playmates and girls choose girls. Across cultures, young children's friendship groups are likely to be segregated by sex (Barbu, Le Maner-Idrissi, & Jouanjean, 2000; Maccoby, 2002a). When asked about the definition of a friend, most children in this age group think of a friend as someone with whom you play (Corsaro, 2005). Our neighbor children, for example, made their initial approach to our young son by saying, "Let's be friends; let's play" and "I'll be your friend if you will be mine." Young children do not view friendship as a trusting, lasting relationship, but even this limited view of friendship is important for this age group. For example, children who enter kindergarten with identified friends adjust better to school (C. Johnson, Ironsmith, Snow, & Poteat, 2000).

Research indicates that young children are at a higher risk of being rejected by their peers if they are aggressive and comparatively more active, demonstrate a difficult temperament, are easily distracted, and demonstrate lower perseverance (S. Campbell, 2002; C. Johnson et al., 2000; S. Walker, Berthelsen, & Irving, 2001). One would wonder, then, how young peers respond to Terri Smith. The rejection of some children is long lasting; even when they change their behavior and fit better with the norm, often they continue to be rejected (S. Walker et al., 2001). It is important, therefore, to intervene early to help children like Terri Smith learn more prosocial behavior.

Self-Concept

In early childhood, the child seems to vacillate between grandiose and realistic views of the self (D. Davies, 2004). Children are aware of their growing competence, but at the same time, they have normal doubts about the self, based on realistic comparisons of their competence with the competence of adults. In early childhood, children begin to develop a self-concept, which includes a perception of oneself as a person who has desires, attributes, preferences, and abilities.

Some investigators have suggested that during early childhood, the child's ever-increasing understanding of the self in relation to the world begins to become organized into a **self-theory** (S. Epstein, 1973, 1991, 1998; S. Epstein, Lipson, Holstein, & Huh, 1993). As children develop the cognitive ability to categorize, they use categorization to think about the self. By age 2 or 3, children can identify their gender and race (discussed in greater detail shortly) as factors in understanding who they are. Between the ages of 4 and 6, young children become more aware that different people have different perspectives on situations (Ziv & Frye, 2003). This helps them to begin to understand cultural expectations and sensitizes them to the expectations that others have for them.

This growing capacity to understand the self in relation to others leads to self-evaluation, or **self-esteem.** Very early interpersonal experiences provide information that becomes incorporated into self-esteem. Messages of love, admiration, and approval lead to a positive view of the self (J. Brown, Dutton, & Cook, 2001). Messages of rejection or scorn lead to a negative view of the self (Heimpel, Wood, Marshall, & Brown, 2002). In addition to these interpersonal messages, young children observe their own competencies and attributes, and compare them with the competencies of other children as well as adults. And they are very aware of being evaluated by others, their peers as well as important adults (B. Newman & Newman, 2009).

Of course, a young child may develop a positive view of the self in one dimension, such as cognitive abilities, and a negative view of the self in another dimension, such as physical abilities (Harter, 1998). Children also learn that some abilities are more valued than others in the various environments in which they operate. For example, in individualistic-oriented societies, self-reliance, independence, autonomy, and distinctiveness are valued, while interdependence and harmony are more valued in most collectivistic-oriented societies. Self-esteem is based on different values in these different types of cultures (J. Brown, 2003; Sedikides, Gaertner, & Toguchi, 2003). It is probably the case that every culture includes both individualistic and collectivistic beliefs (Turiel, 2004), but the balance of these two belief systems varies greatly from culture to culture. An example of the way that these beliefs play out and influence self-development from an early age was described by Markus and Kitayama (2003), who noted that in U.S. coverage of the Olympics, athletes are typically asked about how they personally feel about their efforts and their success. In contrast, in Japanese coverage, athletes are typically asked, "Who helped you achieve?" This idea of an interdependent self-is consistent with cultural relational theory, as well as feminist and Afro-centric perspectives on relationships (see Chapter 4 for a discussion of these theoretical issues).

Recently, cognitive neuroscientists have been exploring the ways that the brain gives rise to development of a sense of self. They have found that a right frontoparietal network, which overlaps with mirror neurons, is activated during tasks involving self-recognition and discrimination between the self and the other (Kaplan, Aziz-Zadeh, Uddin, & Iacoboni, 2008; Uddin, Iacoboni, Lange, & Keenan, 2007). Viewing one's own face leads to greater signal changes in the inferior frontal gyrus (IFG), the inferior occipital gyrus, and the inferior parietal lobe. In addition, there is greater signal change in the right IFG when hearing one's own voice compared to hearing a friend's voice (Kaplan et al., 2008). Beginning evidence also indicates that the cortical midline structures (CMS) of the brain are involved in self-evaluation and in understanding of others' emotional states. In addition, there is beginning evidence of at least one pathway that connects the mirror neurons and the CMS, allowing for integration of self and other understanding (Uddin et al., 2007).

Gender Identity and Sexual Interests

During early childhood, gender becomes an important dimension of how children understand themselves and others. There are four components to gender identity during early childhood (B. Newman & Newman, 2009):

> How does gender influence early childhood development?

1. *Making correct use of the gender label.* By age 2, children can usually accurately identify others as either male or female, based on appearance.

2. *Understanding gender as stable.* Later, children understand that gender is stable, that boys grow up to be men and girls to be women.

3. *Understanding gender constancy.* Even with this understanding of gender stability, young children, with their imaginative thinking, continue to think that girls can turn into boys and boys into girls by changing appearance. For example, a 3-year-old given a picture of a girl is able to identify the person as a girl. But if the same girl is shown in another picture dressed as a boy, the 3-year-old will label the girl a boy. It is not until sometime between ages 4 and 7 that children understand *gender constancy,* the understanding that one's gender does not change, that the girl dressed as a boy is still a girl.

4. *Understanding the genital basis of gender.* Gender constancy has been found to be associated with an understanding of the relationship between gender and the genitals (Bem, 1998).

Before going further, it is important to differentiate among four concepts: sex, gender, gender identity, and sexual orientation. *Sex* refers to biologically linked distinctions that are determined by chromosomal information. An infant's external genitalia are usually used as the determinant of sex. In most humans, chromosomes, hormones, and genitalia are consistent, and determining sex is considered unambiguous. However, this is not always the case. Chromosomal, genetic, anatomical, and hormonal aspects of sex are sometimes not aligned (Rudacille, 2005). *Gender* is the cognitive, emotional, and social schemes that are associated with being female or male. *Gender identity* refers to one's sense of being male or female. *Sexual orientation* refers to one's preference for sexually intimate partners.

There is evidence of gender differences in multiple dimensions of human behavior, but also much debate about just how pervasive these differences are and, if they exist, how to explain them. In terms of the pervasiveness of gender differences, the findings are not at all consistent. In 1974, Eleanor Maccoby and Carol Jacklin reviewed over 2,000 studies of children, adolescents, and adults that included sex differences and concluded that there was evidence of four sex differences: (1) Girls have greater verbal abilities than boys, (2) boys excel in visual-spatial ability, (3) boys excel in mathematical ability, and (4) boys are more aggressive. Thirty years later, Janet Hyde (2005) reviewed a large number of studies (also of children, adolescents, and adults) and found that in 78% of them, gender differences were close to zero or quite small, and there was evidence of much within-group difference. In other words, the differences *among* girls were as great as or greater than the differences *between* boys and girls. There were substantial gender differences in a few areas, however: some aspects of motor performance, some sexual attitudes and behaviors, and physical

aggression. Indeed, the research subsequent to the Maccoby and Jacklin review has found that the cognitive differences that they reported are very limited. Females do seem to have an advantage in verbal fluency and writing, but not in reading comprehension. Males' visual-spatial advantage seems to only occur in tasks requiring mental rotation of a three-dimensional object. Although male children, adolescents, and adults perform better on tests of broad mathematical ability, females score better on computation (B. Garrett, 2009).

In terms of the debate about the causes of gender differences, there are two competing perspectives: the biological determination perspective and the socially constructed perspective. There is some evidence to support each of these perspectives, suggesting, not surprisingly, that behavior is multiply determined. In terms of verbal ability, there is some evidence that females use both hemispheres of the brain for solving verbal problems, while males use mostly the left hemisphere, but the findings in this regard are not consistent. Relatively strong evidence indicates that estrogen probably does contribute to women's verbal advantage. Men who take estrogen as part of transsexual treatments to become female score higher on verbal learning than men who do not take estrogen as part of their transsexual transformation. Testosterone appears to play a role in spatial ability. Males who produce low levels of testosterone during the developmental years have less well-developed spatial ability; in addition, testosterone replacement therapy in older men improves their spatial functioning. Interestingly, there is only a small sex difference in aggression when behavior is studied in the laboratory, but a very large difference outside the laboratory. That is not convincing evidence for a biological basis for the gender differences in aggression (B. Garrett, 2009).

In terms of the socially constructed perspective, we know that human societies use gender as an important category for organizing social life. There are some rather large cultural and subcultural variations in gender role definitions, however. Existing cultural standards about gender are pervasively built into adult interactions with young children and into the reward systems that are developed for shaping child behavior. Much research evidence indicates that parents begin to use gender stereotypes to respond to their children from the time of birth (Gardiner & Kosmitzki, 2008). They cuddle more with infant girls and play more actively with infant boys. Later, they talk more with young girls and expect young boys to be more independent. Recent studies have found that the nature of parental influence on children's gender role development is more complex than this. Parents may hold to stereotypical gender expectations in some domains but not in others. For example, parents may have similar expectations for boys and girls in terms of sharing or being polite (McHale, Crouter, & Whiteman, 2003).

Once toddlers understand their gender, they begin to imitate and identify with the same-sex parent, if he or she is available. Once young children begin to understand gender role standards, they become quite rigid in their playing out of gender roles—only girls cook, only men drive trucks, only girls wear pink flowers, only boys wear shirts with footballs. This gender understanding also accounts for the preference of same-sex playmates and sex-typed toys (D. Davies, 2004). Remember, though, that the exaggeration of gender stereotypes in early childhood is in keeping with the struggle during this period to discover stability and regularity in the environment.

Evidence that gender differences in verbal, visual, and mathematical skills are at least partially socially constructed can be found in data indicating that differences in all three areas have decreased over the same time period that gender roles have changed toward greater similarity. The dramatic difference in murder rates across societies suggests that there is a strong cultural influence on aggression (B. Garrett, 2009).

During early childhood, children become increasingly interested in their genitals. They are interested, in general, in how their bodies work, but the genitals seem to hold a special fascination as the young child learns through experimentation that the genitals can be a source of pleasure. Between 3 and 5, children may have some worries and questions about genital difference; little girls may think they once had a penis and wonder what happened to it. Little boys may fear that their penises will disappear, like their sister's did. During early childhood, masturbation is used both as a method of self-soothing and for pleasure. Young children also "play doctor" with each other, and often want to see and touch their parents' genitals. Many parents and other caregivers are confused about how to handle this behavior, particularly in our era of heightened awareness of childhood sexual abuse. In general, parents should not worry about genital curiosity or about children experimenting with touching their own genitals. They should remember, however, that at this age children may be confused or over-stimulated by seeing their parents' genitals. And we should always be concerned when children want to engage in more explicit adult-like sexual play that involves stimulation of each other's genitals (D. Davies, 2004; B. Newman & Newman, 2009).

Racial and Ethnic Identity

Findings from research suggest that children first learn their own racial identity before they are able to identify the race of others (Kowalski, 1996). Elements of racial/ethnic identity awareness have been found to occur as early as the age of 3. Most children begin to self-identify as a member of a racial group by age 3 to 4, but identification with an ethnic group does not usually occur until later in childhood, between 5 and 8 years of age (Blackmon & Vera, 2008). Early identification of others by race is limited to skin color, which is more easily recognized than ethnic origin. Young children may label a Latino/Latina individual, for example, as either Black or White, depending on the individual's skin color. Young children also show a preference for members of their own race over another (Katz, 1976). Perhaps this choice is similar to the preference for same-sex playmates, a result of young children attempting to learn their own identity. In a study of children in a preschool setting, the children were observed to use race and ethnicity to

> How important is racial and ethnic identity as a source of diversity of experience in early childhood?

define themselves and others, to include peers in play, and to exclude peers from stigmatized racial and ethnic groups (Van Ausdale & Feagin, 1996).

Social scientists concerned about the development of self-esteem in children of color have investigated racial bias and preference using children in early childhood as subjects. The most famous of these studies was conducted by Kenneth Clark and Mamie Clark in 1939. They presented African American children with black dolls and white dolls and concluded that African American children responded more favorably to the white dolls and had more negative reactions to the black dolls. A similar study 40 years later, observing young African American children in New York and Trinidad, reported similar results (Gopaul-McNicol, 1988). The young children from both New York and Trinidad preferred and identified with the white dolls. Interestingly, the same results have been reported more recently in studies of Taiwanese young children (Chang, 2001). Most of the Taiwanese children in the study indicated a preference for the white dolls and demonstrated a "pro-white attitude."

It is questionable, however, whether these preferences and biases are equated with self-concept and low self-esteem for children of color. Most argue that they are not. For example, color bias and self-concept were not found to be related among the young Taiwanese children (Chang, 2001). Likewise, findings from studies about young African American children indicate high levels of self-esteem despite the children's bias in favor of the White culture and values (Crain, 1996; M. B. Spencer, 1985). Spencer concludes, "Racial stereotyping in black children should be viewed as objectively held information about the environment and not as a manifestation of personal identity" (p. 220).

The Role of Play

The young child loves to play, and play is essential to all aspects of early child development. We think of the play of young children as fun-filled and lively, and yet it serves a serious purpose. Through play, children develop the motor skills essential for physical development, learn the problem-solving skills and communication skills fundamental to

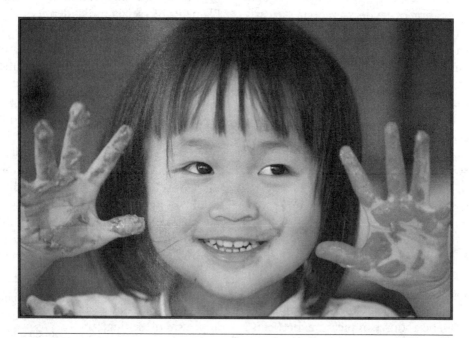

Photo 12.2 Play is one of the few elements in the development of children that is universal—regardless of culture.

Photo 12.3   During early childhood, children engage in cooperative play and enjoy sharing and competing with peers.

cognitive development, express the feelings and gain the self-confidence needed for emotional growth, and learn to cooperate and resolve social conflicts. Essentially, play is what young children are all about; it is their work.

As children develop in all areas during early childhood, their play activities and preferences for play materials change over time. Fergus Hughes (2010) makes the following recommendations about the preferred play materials at different ages during early childhood:

- Three-year-olds: props for imaginative play, such as dress-up clothes, doctor kits, and makeup; miniature toys that represent adult models, such as toy trucks, gas stations, dolls, doll houses, and airplanes; art materials, such as paint brushes, easels, marker pens, and crayons
- Four-year-olds: vehicles, such as tricycles and wagons; play materials to develop fine motor skills, such as materials for sewing, stringing beads, coloring, painting, and drawing; books that involve adventure
- Five-year-olds: play materials to develop precision in fine motor skills, such as coloring books, paints and brushes, crayons, marker pens, glue,

scissors, stencils, sequins and glitter, clay, and play dough; play materials that develop cognitive skills, such as workbenches, play cards, table games, and board games

In recent years, there has been a dramatic increase in the availability of computers and other instructional technology. These technologies have made their way into early childhood education programs, but there is controversy among early childhood educators about the positive and negative aspects of these technologies for early childhood development. There is evidence of benefits of instructional technologies in the preschool classroom. For example, 4- and 5-year-old children can use technology to develop language, art, mathematics, and science skills. Conversely, some early childhood educators are concerned that computers and other instructional technologies contribute to social isolation and limit children's creative play (F. Hughes, 2010). Adults must give serious consideration to how to balance the positive and negative aspects of these technologies.

The predominant type of play in early childhood, beginning around the age of 2, is **symbolic play,** otherwise known as fantasy play, pretend play, or imaginary play (F. Hughes, 2010; Pelligrini & Galda, 2000). Children continue to use vivid imagination in their play, as they did as toddlers, but they also begin to put more structure into their play. Thus, their play is intermediate between the fantasy play of toddlers and the structured, rules-oriented play of middle childhood. Although toddler play is primarily nonverbal, the play of young children often involves highly sophisticated verbal productions. There is some indication that this preference for symbolic play during early childhood exists across cultures, but the themes of the play reflect the culture in which it is enacted (Roopnarine, Shin, Donovan, & Suppal, 2000).

Symbolic play during early childhood has four primary functions: providing an opportunity to explore reality, contributing to cognitive development, allowing young children to gain control over their lives, and serving as a shared experience and opportunity for development of peer culture. These functions are explained in more detail below.

Play as an Opportunity to Explore Reality

Young children imitate adult behavior and try out social roles in their play (D. Davies, 2004; F. Hughes, 2010). They play house, school, doctor, police, firefighter, and so on. As they "dress up" in various guises of adult roles, or even as spiders and rabbits, they are using fantasy to explore what they might become. Their riding toys allow them to play with the experience of having greater mobility in the world.

Play's Contribution to Cognitive Development

The young child uses play to think about the world, to understand cause and effect (Roskos & Christie, 2000). Throughout early childhood, young children show increasing sophistication in using words in their dramatic play.

Some researchers have asked the question, does symbolic play facilitate cognitive development,

Photo 12.4 Young children use play to think about the world, to understand cause and effect.

or does symbolic play require mature cognitive abilities? The question is unresolved; the available evidence indicates only that cognitive development is connected with play in early childhood (Roopnarine et al., 2000). Childhood sociologists have found that children create sophisticated language games for group play that facilitate the development of language and logical thinking (Corsaro, 2005). A number of researchers have studied how young children build literacy skills through play, particularly play with books (Roskos & Christie, 2000). Play that is focused on language and thinking skills has been described as **learning play** (Meek, 2000).

Play as an Opportunity to Gain Control

In his cross-cultural study of play, William Corsaro (2005), a childhood sociologist, demonstrates that young children typically use dramatic play to cope with fears. They incorporate their fears into their group play and thus develop some mastery over stress and anxiety. This perspective on young children's play is the cornerstone of play therapy (Chethik, 2000). Anyone who has spent much time in a child care center has probably seen a group of 4-year-olds engaged in superhero play, their flowing capes improvised with towels pinned on their shirts. Such play helps the child compensate for inadequacy and fear that comes from recognizing that one is a small person in a big world (D. Davies, 2004). Corsaro suggests that the love for climbing toys that bring small children high over the heads of others serves the same purpose.

Children in preschool settings have also been observed trying to get control over their lives by subverting some of the control of adults. Corsaro (2005) describes a preschool where the children had been told that they could not bring any play items from home. The preschool teachers were trying to avoid the kinds of conflicts that can occur over toys brought from home. The children in this preschool found a way to subvert this rule, however; they began to

How does play develop skills for human agency in making choices?

bring in very small toys, such as matchbox cars, that would fit in their pockets out of sight when teachers were nearby. Corsaro provides a number of other examples from his cross-cultural research of ways that young children use play to take some control of their lives away from adults.

Play as a Shared Experience

There is increasing emphasis on the way that play in early childhood contributes to the development of peer culture. Many researchers who study the play of young children suggest that **sociodramatic play,** or group fantasy play in which children coordinate their fantasy, is the most important form of play during this time. Indeed, one researcher has reported that two thirds of the play among North American young children is sociodramatic play (K. Rubin, 1986). Young children are able to develop more elaborate fantasy play and sustain it by forming friendship groups, which in turn gives them experience with group conflict and group problem solving that carries over into the adult world (Corsaro, 2005).

As young children play in groups, they attempt to protect the opportunity to keep the play going by restricting who may enter the play field (Corsaro, 2005). Young children can often be heard making such comments as, "We're friends; we're playing, right?" Or perhaps, "You're not our friend; you can't play with us." The other side of the coin is that young children must learn how to gain access to play in progress (Garvey, 1984). An important social skill is being able to demonstrate that they can play without messing the game up. Young children learn a set of do's and don'ts to accomplish that goal (see Exhibit 12.2) and develop complex strategies for gaining access to play.

Conflict often occurs in young children's play groups, and researchers have found gender and cultural variations in how these conflicts get resolved. Young girls have been found to prefer dyadic (two-person) play interactions, and young boys enjoy larger groups (Benenson, 1993). These preferences may not hold across cultures, however. For example, White middle-class young girls in the

Exhibit 12.2 Do's and Don'ts of Getting Access to Play in Progress

Do's

Watch what's going on.

Figure out the play theme.

Enter the area.

Plug into the action.

Hold off making suggestions about how to change the action.

Don'ts

Don't ask questions for information (if you can't tell what's going on, you'll mess it up).

Don't mention yourself or your reactions to what is going on.

Don't disagree or criticize what is happening.

SOURCE: Based on Garvey (1984).

United States are less direct and assertive in challenging each other in play situations than either African American girls in the United States or young girls in an Italian preschool (Corsaro, 2005). Greater assertiveness may allow for more comfortable play in larger groups.

Play as the Route to Attachment to Fathers

Most of the efforts to understand attachment focus on the link between mothers and children, and the effect of the maternal relationship. More recently, though, there has been growing concern about and interest in the importance of fathers in the development of attachment for young children. Some suggest that father–child attachment may be promoted mainly through play, much like the mother–child relationship may be the result of caregiving activities (Laflamme, Pomerleau, & Malcuit, 2002; Roggman, 2004). Differences in play style noted for mothers versus that seen in fathers are of particular interest. Investigators conclude that more physical play is seen between fathers and young children compared to more object play and conventional play interaction between mothers and children (W. Goldberg, Clarke-Stewart, Rice, & Dellis, 2002). Both forms of play can involve the display of affection by the parent. Thus, both forms of play contribute to the development of parent–child attachment. This research broadens the notion that only certain kinds of play have the potential to effect positive attachment, and affirms the notion that there is developmental value for children in father–child physical play. In fact, physical play stimulates, arouses, and takes children out of their comfort zone. Roggman further notes that the style of play often ascribed to fathers provides opportunity for young children to overcome their limits and to experience taking chances in a context where there is some degree of confidence that they will be protected.

DEVELOPMENTAL DISRUPTIONS

Children develop at different rates. Most developmental problems in infants and young children are more accurately described as *developmental delays,* offering the hope that early intervention, or even natural processes, will mitigate the long-term effects. Developmental delays may exist in cognitive skills, communication skills, social skills, emotion regulation, behavior, and fine and gross motor skills. Developmental problems in school-age children are typically labeled disabilities and classified into groups, such as cognitive disability, learning disabilities, and motor impairment (Zipper & Simeonsson, 2004).

Many young children with developmental difficulties, including emotional and behavioral concerns, are inaccurately assessed and misdiagnosed—often because young children are assessed independently of their environment (E. Freeman & Dyer, 1993; Sameroff, Bartko, Baldwin, Baldwin, & Seifer, 1998). After interviewing professionals who work with children ages 6 and under, one research team compiled a list of traits observed in young children that indicate emotional and behavioral problems: extreme aggressive behavior, difficulty with change, invasion of others' personal space, compulsive or impulsive behavior, low ability to trust others, lack of empathy or remorse, and cruelty to animals (Schmitz & Hilton, 1996). Parents and teachers often handle these behaviors with firmer limits and more discipline. However, environmental risk factors, such as emotional abuse or neglect and domestic violence, may be the actual cause.

Given the difficulty of assessment accuracy, assessment in young children should include many disciplines, to gain as broad an understanding as possible (Zipper & Simeonsson, 2004). Assessment and service delivery should also be culturally relevant (Parette, 1995). In other words, culture and other related issues—such as family interaction patterns and stress, the social environment, ethnicity, acculturation, social influences, and developmental expectations—should all be considered when evaluating a child's developmental abilities.

For those children who have been labeled developmentally delayed, the main remedy has been social skill development. In one such program, two types of preschool classrooms were evaluated (E. Roberts, Burchinal, & Bailey, 1994). In one classroom, young developmentally delayed children were matched with non-delayed children of the same age; in another classroom, some of the "normal" children were the same age as the developmentally delayed children and some were older. Social exchange between the children with delays and those without delays was greater in the mixed-aged classroom. Another study evaluated the usefulness of providing social skills training to children with mild developmental disabilities (T. Lewis, 1994). In a preschool setting, developmentally delayed children were put in situations requiring social interaction and were praised for successful interaction. This method increased social interaction among the young children.

It is also important to recognize the parental stress that often accompanies care of children with developmental disabilities. Researchers have found that an educational intervention with parents that teaches behavioral management and how to plan activities that minimize disruptive behavior results in improved child behavior, an improved parent–child relationship, and less parental stress (Clare, Mazzucchelli, Studman, & Sanders, 2006).

In the 1980s, concern about the quality of education in the United States led to upgrades in the elementary school curriculum. Many skills previously introduced in the first grade became part of the kindergarten curriculum. This has led to increased concern about kindergarten readiness, the skills that the young child should have acquired before entering kindergarten, as well as how to provide for the needs of developmentally delayed children in the kindergarten classroom. It has also led to controversies about when to begin to think of developmental delays as disabilities. A growing concern is that children with developmental problems should not be placed in kindergarten classrooms that do not provide support for their particular developmental needs (Litty & Hatch, 2006). States vary in how much support they provide to children with developmental delays to allow them to participate in fully inclusive classrooms (classrooms where they are mainstreamed with children without developmental delays), but a growing small minority of children with developmental delays in the United States are participating as full citizens in inclusive classrooms during preschool and kindergarten (Guralnick, Neville,

Hammond, & Connor, 2008). Before leaving this discussion, we would like to emphasize one important point. When working with young children, we want to recognize and respect the variability of developmental trajectories. At the same time, however, we want to be attentive to any aspects of a child's development that may be lagging behind expected milestones, so that we can provide extra support to young children in specific areas of development.

Critical Thinking Questions 12.2

What challenges might Terri Smith, Jack Lewis, and Ron and Rosalind Johnson face in developing self-esteem? How might a social worker help each of these children to develop a positive self-evaluation? How can play be used with each of these children to foster their social development?

EARLY CHILDHOOD EDUCATION

Universal early childhood enrollment, defined as a 90% enrollment rate, begins later in the United States than in several other countries: age 5 in the United States, compared to age 3 in France and Italy, and age 4 in Japan and the United Kingdom. In France, as mentioned earlier, a large number of children below the age of 3 are enrolled in formal education (Sen, Partelow, & Miller, 2005).

Much evidence indicates that low-income and racial minority students in the United States have less access to quality early childhood education than their age peers (Education Trust, 2006b). Many poorer school districts do not provide prekindergarten programs, and there was a 13% cut in funding to Head Start between 2002 and 2008. Those cuts, along with rising unemployment, led to a growing waiting list for low-income children to get into Head Start. New funds were appropriated for Head Start programs in 2009 and 2010, but many children remain on waiting lists (National Head Start Association, 2010). With tightening budgets, some low- to middle-income districts are canceling full-day kindergarten, and some public school districts have begun to provide for-pay preschool and full-day kindergarten, a practice that clearly disadvantages low-income children. As noted in Chapter 7, wealthy families are competing for slots for their young children in expensive preschool programs, called the "baby ivies," that provide highly enriched early learning environments, further advancing opportunities for children in privileged families (Kozol, 2005). Middle-class families, as well as impoverished families, are increasingly unable to access quality early childhood education; 78% of families who earned over $100,000 per year in 2004 sent their young children to early childhood educational programs compared to less than half of families earning less than $50,000 per year (Calman & Tarr-Whelan, 2005).

In recent years, a coalition of business leaders, economists, and child development scholars has called for universal quality early childhood education in the United States, arguing that it is a wise investment (see Calman & Tarr-Whelan, 2005). Empirical evidence is mounting to support this argument. One longitudinal study has followed a group of children who attended the High/Scope Perry Preschool Program in Ypsilanti, Michigan, until they reached the age of 40 (Schweinhart et al., 2005). Between 1962 and 1967, the researchers identified a sample of 123 low-income African American children who had been assessed to be at high risk of school failure. They randomly assigned 58 of these children to attend a high-quality 2-year preschool program for 2- and 3-year-olds, while the other 65 attended no preschool program. The program met for 2.5 hours per day, 5 days a week, and teachers made home visits every 2 weeks. The teachers in the preschool program had bachelor's degrees and education certification. No more than eight children were assigned to a teacher, and the curriculum emphasized giving children the opportunity to plan and carry out their own activities. By age 40, those who had been preschool participants, on average, were doing better than the nonparticipants in several important ways:

- They were more likely to have graduated from high school (65% vs. 45%).
- They were more likely to be employed (76% vs. 62%).
- They had higher median annual earnings ($20,800 vs. $15,300).
- They were more likely to own their own home (37% vs. 28%).
- They were more likely to have a savings account (76% vs. 50%).
- They had fewer lifetime arrests (36% vs. 55% arrested five or more times).
- They were less likely to have spent time in prison or jail (52% vs. 28% never sentenced).

The researchers report that the preschool program cost $15,166 per child, and the public gained $12.90 for every dollar spent on the program by the time the participants were 40 years old. The savings came from reduced special education costs, increased taxes derived from higher earnings, reduced public assistance costs, and reduced costs to the criminal justice system.

Another longitudinal study began in North Carolina in 1972, when 112 low-income infants were randomly assigned either to a quality preschool program or to no program (Masse & Barnett, 2002). The group assigned to the preschool program was enrolled in the program for 5 years, instead of the 2 years in the High/Scope Perry study. The participants in this study were followed to the age of 21. The children who participated in the preschool program were less likely to repeat grades, less likely to be placed in special education classes, and more likely to complete high school. It is important to note that the researchers in this study also investigated the impact of the preschool program on the mothers. They found that the preschool program mothers earned $3,750 more per year than the mothers whose children did not attend the program, for a total of $78,750 more over 21 years.

The above two longitudinal studies investigated the impact of quality preschool education on low-income children, but there is also preliminary evidence of the benefit of early childhood education for all children. A study conducted at Georgetown University has examined the effect of prekindergarten (PK) programs in Tulsa, Oklahoma (Gromley, Gayer, Phillips, & Dawson, 2004). These programs are considered high quality because teachers are required to have a bachelor's degree, there are no more than 10 children per teacher, and teachers are paid on the same scale as public school teachers. The researchers found that children who attended PK scored better on letter-word identification, spelling, and applied problems than children of the same age who had not attended PK. This was true regardless of race or socioeconomic status.

These studies suggest that early childhood education programs are good for children, for families, for communities, and for society. With such evidence in hand, social workers can join with other child advocates to build broad coalitions to educate the public about the multilevel benefits and to push for public policy that guarantees universal quality early childhood education.

EARLY CHILDHOOD IN THE MULTIGENERATIONAL FAMILY

Curiosity and experimentation are the hallmarks of early childhood. Young children are sponges, soaking up information about themselves, their worlds, and their relationships. They use their families as primary sources of information and as models for relationships. Where there are older siblings, they serve as important figures of identification and imitation. Aunts, uncles, cousins, and grandparents may also fill this role, but parents are, in most families, the most important sources of information, support, and modeling for young children.

Parents play two very important roles for their 3- to 6-year-old children: those of educator and advocate (B. Newman & Newman, 2009). As educators, they answer children's big and little questions, ask questions to stimulate thinking and growth in communication skills, provide explanations, and help children figure things out. They teach children about morality and human connectedness by modeling honest, kind, thoughtful behavior, and by reading to their children about moral dilemmas and moral action. They help children develop emotional intelligence by modeling how to handle strong feelings, and by talking with children about the children's strong feelings. They take young children on excursions in their real physical worlds as well as in the fantasy worlds found in books. They give children opportunities to perform tasks that develop a sense of mastery.

Not all parents have the same resources for the educator role or the same beliefs about how children learn. And some parents take their role as educators too seriously, pushing their young children into more and more structured time with higher and higher expectations of performance (Elkind, 2001). Many of these parents are pushing their own frustrated dreams onto their young children. The concern is that these children are deprived of time for exploration, experimentation, and fantasy.

In the contemporary era, children are moving into organized child care settings at earlier ages. As they do so, parents become more important as advocates who understand their children's needs. The advocate role is particularly important for parents of young children with disabilities. These parents may need to advocate to ensure that all aspects of early childhood education programs are accessible to their children.

For some children, like Ron and Rosiland Johnson, it is the grandparent and not the parent who serves as the central figure. Estimates are that 5.8 million children live in homes headed by a grandparent or other relative, with 4.4 million in homes headed by grandparents (Children's Defense Fund, 2008). In about 50% of these families, no biological parent is present in the home. Substance abuse, divorce, teen pregnancy, the AIDS epidemic, and imprisoned mothers like Shirley account for the large number of children living in a grandparent-headed home. Some custodial grandparents describe an increased purpose for living, but others describe increased isolation, worry, physical and emotional exhaustion, and financial concerns (Clarke, 2008). These are some of the same concerns expressed by Ms. Johnson. In addition, grandparents caring for children with psychological and physical problems experience high levels of stress (Sands & Goldberg, 2000).

The literature indicates that young children often do better under the care of grandparents than in other types of homes. However, children parented by their grandparents must often overcome many difficult emotions (A. Smith, Dannison, & Vach-Hasse, 1998). These children struggle with issues of grief and loss related to loss of their parent(s) and feelings of guilt, fear, embarrassment, and anger. These feelings may be especially strong for young children who feel they are somehow responsible for the loss of their parent(s). Although children in this age group are capable of labeling their feelings, their ability to discuss these feelings with any amount of depth is very limited. In addition, grandparents may feel unsure about how to talk about the situation with their young grandchildren. Professional intervention for the children is often recommended (A. Smith et al., 1998). Some mental health practitioners have had success providing group sessions that help grandparents gain control over their grandchildren's behavior, resolve clashes in values between themselves and their grandchildren, and help grandparents avoid overindulgence and set firm limits.

Grandparents are often important figures in the lives of young children, even when they do not serve as primary caregivers; they may provide practical support, financial support, and/or emotional support. They may offer different types of practical support, coming to the aid of the family when needs arise. Or they may serve as the child care provider while parents work or provide babysitting services in the evening. They also may provide financial support, depending on their financial circumstances. They may provide cash assistance or buy things such as clothes and toys for the children; it is in fact distressing to some grandparents if they lack the financial resources to buy things for their grandchildren. Grandparents may also provide emotional support and advice to parents of young children; this is something that can be done at a distance by a variety of electronic technologies when grandparents live at some distance from their grandchildren (Clarke, 2008).

RISKS TO HEALTHY DEVELOPMENT IN EARLY CHILDHOOD _____

Why is it important to recognize risk factors and protective factors in early childhood?

This section addresses a few risk factors that social workers are likely to encounter in work with young children and their families: poverty, ineffective discipline, divorce, and violence (including child abuse). In addition, the section outlines the protective factors that can ameliorate the risks.

Poverty

As reported in Chapter 11, there are 1 billion children around the world living in poverty. Over 14 million children live in poverty in the United States—including 22% of children ages 6 and younger. About 44% of U.S. children under 6 live in low-income families, with incomes below 200% of the poverty level (defined as twice the income specified as poverty level). Sixty-nine percent of Native American children under age 6 live in low-income families, compared to 64% of African American and Latino children, 30% of White children, and 28% of Asian children (Wight & Chau, 2009b). Poverty—in the form of food insecurity, inadequate health care, and overcrowded living conditions—presents considerable risks to children's growth and development. In 2008, an estimated 22.3% of households with children under 6 years of age were food insecure. The research indicates that families with food insecurity usually attempt to provide adequate nutrition to the youngest children, with parents and older children making sacrifices to feed younger children (Nord, Andrews, & Carlson, 2009). A recent study of the Northern Cheyenne Indian Reservation in southeastern Montana found that 70% of all households were food insecure (E. Whiting & Ward, 2008). Inadequate nutrition is a serious threat to all aspects of early childhood development. Inadequate health care means that many acute conditions become chronic. Overcrowding is problematic to young children in that it restricts opportunities for play, the means through which most development occurs.

Research indicates that young children reared in poverty are significantly delayed in language and other cognitive skills (Locke, Ginsborg, & Peers, 2002). The effects of poverty on children in early childhood appear to be long lasting. Children who experience poverty during their early years are less likely to complete school than children whose initial exposure to poverty occurred in the middle childhood years or during adolescence. Researchers have also found that children who live in poverty are at high risk for low self-esteem, peer conflict, depression, and childhood psychological disorders. Poverty is often associated with other risk factors as well, such as overwhelmed parents, living in a violent setting or in deteriorated housing, and instability of frequent changes in residence and schools (Bartholomae & Fox, 2010).

Not all young children who live in poverty fare poorly, however. In their longitudinal study of 180 children born into poverty, Sroufe et al. (2005) report that four groups emerged by early childhood: They grouped 70 children into a very competent cluster who were high in enthusiasm, persistence, compliance, and affection for the mother. They grouped another 25 children into a very incompetent cluster characterized by high negativity, and low compliance and affection. The other almost half of the children were grouped into two clusters that fell between very competent and very incompetent.

Homelessness

Families with children make up one third of the homeless population, and families became more and more vulnerable to home foreclosures and unemployment during the deep recession that started in late 2007. It is estimated that 42% of homeless families have children under the age of 6. Homeless children are sick more often, are exposed to more violence, and experience more emotional and behavioral problems and more delayed development than low-income housed children. Their school attendance is often disrupted because they need to change schools, but often because of transportation problems as well (Paquette & Bassuk, 2009).

Kristen Paquette and Ellen Bassuk (2009) note that parents' identities are often closely tied to relationships they maintain, especially with their children, and that homelessness undermines their ability to protect those they have a responsibility to protect. Like all parents, homeless parents want to provide their children with basic necessities. Being homeless presents dramatic barriers and challenges for parents, who too often lose the ability to provide essentials for their children, including shelter, food, and access to education. They must look for jobs and housing while also adhering to shelter rules. Their parenting is public, easily observed and monitored by others. What they need is to be involved with a meaningful social support system which links them to organizations and professionals in the community who might offer resources and options that support them to engage in effective parenting.

Ineffective Discipline

A once-popular guidebook for parents declares, "Under no circumstances should you ever punish your child!!" (Moyer, 1974, p. 40). Punishment implies an attempt to get even with the child, whereas **discipline** involves helping the child overcome a problem. Parents often struggle with how forceful to be in response to undesired behavior. The Smiths are a good example of this struggle. And, indeed, the research on parental styles of discipline is finding that the question of appropriate style of parenting young children is very complex indeed.

A good place to begin this discussion is with the work of Diana Baumrind (1971), who, after extensive research, described three parenting styles, authoritarian, authoritative, and permissive, which use different combinations of two factors: warmth and control (see Exhibit 12.3). The **authoritarian parenting** style uses low warmth and high control. These parents favor punishment and negative reinforcement, and children are treated as submissive. Children reared under an authoritarian parenting style have been found to become hostile and moody and have difficulty managing stress (T. A. Carey, 1994; Welsh, 1985). Baumrind believed the **authoritative parenting** style, in which parents consider the child's viewpoints but remain in control, to be the most desirable approach to discipline and behavior management. The authoritative parenting style has been found to be associated with academic achievement, self-esteem, and social competence (see Domenech Rodriguez, Donovick, & Crowley, 2009). The **permissive parenting** style accepts children's behavior without attempting to modify it. Baumrind suggested that children reared from the permissive parenting orientation are cheerful but demonstrate little if any impulse control. In addition, these children are overly dependent and have low levels of self-reliance. The Smiths' style of parenting probably fits here. Certainly, Terri Smith's behavior mirrors behavior exhibited by children reared with the permissive style. Some researchers have presented a fourth parenting style, **disengaged parenting,** where parents are aloof, withdrawn, and unresponsive (G. Novak & Pelaez, 2004). Baumrind's typology of parenting styles has been the building block of much theorizing and research on parenting styles and child outcomes.

Stephen Greenspan (2006) questions Baumrind's suggestion that authoritative parenting is the best parenting. He suggests that Baumrind paid too little attention to the context in which parental discipline occurs, arguing that there are times to exercise control and times to tolerate a certain level of behavioral deviance, and that a wise parent knows the difference between these types of situations. Greenspan proposes that another dimension of parenting should be added to Baumrind's two dimensions of warmth and control. He calls this dimension "tolerance," and he

Exhibit 12.3 Three Parenting Styles

Parenting Style	Description	Type of Discipline
Authoritarian	Parents who use this type of parenting are rigid and controlling. Rules are narrow and specific, with little room for negotiation, and children are expected to follow the rules without explanation.	Cold and harsh Physical force No explanation of rules provided
Authoritative	These parents are more flexible than authoritarian parents. Their rules are more reasonable, and they leave opportunities for compromises and negotiation.	Warm and nurturing Positive reinforcement Set firm limits and provide rationale behind rules and decisions
Permissive	The parents' rules are unclear, and children are left to make their own decisions.	Warm and friendly toward their children No direction given

SOURCE: Adapted from Baumrind (1971).

recommends a style of parenting called "harmonious." He suggests that harmonious parents are warm and set limits when they feel they are called for, and overlook some child behaviors in the interests of facilitating child autonomy and family harmony. It seems that many parents, like Terri Smith's parents, struggle with knowing which situations call for firm control and which ones call for tolerating some defiance.

Parenting styles are prescribed in part by the community and the culture; therefore, it is not surprising that there is growing sentiment that Baumrind's parenting typology may be a good model for understanding parenting in White, middle-class families, but may not work as well for understanding parenting in other cultural groups. We will examine two streams of research that have explored racial and ethnic variations in parenting styles: research on Latino families and research on African American families.

Strong support has not been found for Baumrind's parenting typology in research on Latino parenting styles. Some researchers have described Latino parenting as permissive, and others have described it as authoritarian. One research team (Domenech Rodriguez et al., 2009), like Greenspan, suggests that another dimension

of parenting should be added to Baumrind's two-dimensional model of warmth and control. They call this dimension "autonomy granting," which they describe as allowing children autonomy of individual expression in the family. This seems to be very close to what Greenspan (2006) meant by "tolerance," because he writes of tolerance of emotional expression in the spirit of autonomy. Domenech Rodriguez and colleagues suggest that these three dimensions—warmth, control, and autonomy granting—can be configured in different ways to produce eight different parenting styles:

1. Authoritative: high warmth, high control, high autonomy granting

2. Authoritarian: low warmth, high control, low autonomy granting

3. Permissive: high warmth, low control, high autonomy granting

4. Neglectful: low warmth, low control, low autonomy granting

5. Protective: high warmth, high control, low autonomy granting

6. Cold: low warmth, high control, high autonomy granting

7. Affiliative: high warmth, low control, low autonomy granting

8. Neglectful II: low warmth, low control, high autonomy granting

In their preliminary research, which involved direct observation of 56 first-generation Latino American families, Domenech Rodriguez et al. (2009) found that the majority (61%) used a protective parenting style, but had different expectations for male and female children. There seems to be merit in adding the dimension of autonomy granting, because it may help to capture the parenting styles of cultural groups that are less individualistic than European American culture.

There is a relatively long line of research that has questioned the appropriateness of applying Baumrind's model to understand African American parenting, and the issues are proving to be complex. Much of this research has looked at the use of physical discipline, with the finding that physical discipline causes disruptive behaviors in White families but not in Black families (see A. Lau, Litrownik, Newton, Black, & Everson, 2006, for a review of this research). Researchers have suggested that Black children may regard physical discipline as a legitimate parenting behavior because there is a culture of using physical discipline out of "concern for the child"; high levels of firm control are used along with high levels of warmth and affection. Conversely, it is argued that White children may regard physical discipline as an act of aggression because it is often used when parents are angry and out of control (Lansford, Deater-Deckard, Dodge, Bates, & Pettit, 2004). The idea is that the context of the physical discipline and the meaning made of it will influence its impact. However, research by A. Lau et al. (2006) did not replicate earlier research that found that the effects of physical discipline differed by race. They found that for both Black and White children, physical discipline exacerbated impulsive, aggressive, and noncompliant behaviors for children who had exhibited behavioral problems at an early age. However, they also found that parental warmth protected against later problems in White children, but seemed to exacerbate early

problems in Black children. The researchers concluded that professionals must recognize that parenting may need to take different forms in different communities. Clearly, this is an issue that needs further investigation.

Research has also indicated that there are differences in parenting style based on the socioeconomic environment in which parenting occurs. Low-income parents have been noted to be more authoritarian than more economically advantaged parents. Using observation methods, one research team found that the socioeconomic differences in parenting styles are not that straightforward, however. They found that middle-class parents routinely use subtle forms of control while, at the same time, trying to instill autonomy in their children. Their children spend a large portion of their time under adult supervision, in one activity or another. The researchers also found that low-income parents tend to value conformity, but allow their school-aged children to spend considerable leisure time in settings where they do not have adult supervision, consequently affording them considerable autonomy (Weininger & Lareau, 2009).

Findings from studies about punishment and young children indicate that punishment is often used in response to early childhood behavior that is age appropriate. So rather than encouraging the independence that is otherwise expected for a child, such age-appropriate behavior is discouraged (Culp, McDonald Culp, Dengler, & Maisano, 1999). In addition, recent evidence indicates that brain development can be affected by the stress created by punishment or physical discipline (Glaser, 2000). Harsh punishment and physical discipline interfere with the neural connection process that begins in infancy and continues throughout early childhood. But for many low-income parents, harsh punishment may be less an issue of control or "bad parenting" than an effort to cope with a desperate situation.

As you can see, there are many current controversies about effective parenting for young children, and this is an issue about which parents and professionals often have strong feelings. Research is beginning to recognize that different parenting styles may work well in different developmental niches. To make the issue even more complicated, scholars like Judith Rich Harris (1998) and Steven Pinker (2002) argue that behavioral traits have such a strong genetic component that we should avoid overemphasizing the role of parenting style in behavioral outcomes. In fact, they argue that we have overemphasized the role of families in shaping behavior, other than by providing genetic heritage. Harris also argues that the peer group and community have more impact on child identity and behavior than parents. No doubt, Harris and Pinker would argue that the inconsistent findings about the impact of parenting styles are evidence that parenting style is not a supremely important variable in child development. Of course, we are learning more about the genetic component of human behavior, but we are also learning about the plasticity of the brain to be affected by experience. Parents are a very large part of that experience throughout life, but in early childhood, other people also come to be a part of the context of ongoing brain development.

Divorce

How are young children affected by this historical trend toward high rates of divorce?

The divorce rate in the United States increased steadily from the mid-19th century through the 1970s, except for a steep drop in the 1950s; it stabilized in the 1980s and has declined slightly since then (Fine, Ganong, & Demo, 2010). It is estimated that over half of the children born in the 1990s spent some of their childhood in a single-parent household (C. M. Anderson, 2005). These single-parent families often live in poverty, and as we have already mentioned, poverty can have a negative effect on children's development. Following divorce, about two thirds of children live with their mother, and most women and children experience a sharp and, unfortunately, long-term decline in economic well-being after divorce (Fine et al., 2010).

Researchers have come to very different conclusions about the effects of divorce on children. Some have found that children have severe and long-term problems following divorce (J. S. Wallerstein & Blakeslee, 1989). Others, using larger and more representative samples, have found less severe and more short-term effects of divorce on children (Barber & Demo, 2006). It has been suggested that the negative effects children experience may actually be the result of parents' responses to divorce rather than of the divorce itself (Hetherington & Kelly, 2002). After reviewing the disparate findings, Emery (1999) came to the following conclusions:

- Divorce is stressful for children.
- Divorce leads to higher levels of adjustment problems and mental health issues for children.
- Most children are resilient and adjust well to divorce.
- Children report considerable pain, unhappy memories, and continued distress about their parents' divorce.
- Post-divorce family interaction has a great influence on children's adjustment after divorce.

Several factors may protect children from long-term adjustment problems when their parents divorce. One significant parental issue is the relationship that the parents maintain with each other during and after the divorce. With minimal conflict between the parents about custody, visitation, and child-rearing issues, and with parents' positive attitude toward each other, children experience fewer negative consequences (Hetherington & Kelly, 2002). Unfortunately, many children, like Jack Lewis in the case study, end up as noncombatants in the middle of a war, trying to avoid or defuse raging anger and disagreement between the two parents. Other protective factors are higher levels of pre-divorce adjustment, adequate provision of economic resources, and nurturing relationships with both parents (Fine et al., 2010).

Children who live in families where divorce results in economic hardship are at special risk. Chronic financial stress takes its toll on the mental and physical health of the residential parent, who is usually the mother. The parent often becomes less supportive and engages in inconsistent and harsh discipline. In these situations, children become distressed, often developing difficulties in cognitive and social development (Fine et al., 2010).

In early childhood, young children are more vulnerable than older children to the emotional and psychological consequences of separation and divorce (J. S. Wallerstein & Blakeslee, 1989; J. S. Wallerstein & Corbin, 1991; J. S. Wallerstein, Corbin, & Lewis, 1988). One reason may be that young children have difficulty understanding divorce and often believe that the absent parent is no longer a member of the family and will never be seen again. In addition, because of young children's egocentrism, they often feel that the divorce is a result of their behavior and experience the absent parent's leaving as a rejection of them. One wonders if Jack Lewis thinks he not only caused his father to leave, but also caused him to become the devil.

Violence

Many parents complain that keeping violence away from children requires tremendous work, even in the best of circumstances. Children witness violence on television and through video and computer games, and they hear about it through many other sources. In the worst of circumstances, young children not only are exposed to violence, but become victims of it as well. This section discusses three types of violence experienced by many young children: community violence, domestic violence, and child abuse.

Community Violence

In some neighborhoods, acts of violence are so common that the communities are labeled "war zones." However, most residents prefer not to be combatants. When surveyed, mothers in a Chicago housing project ranked neighborhood violence as their number one concern, and as the condition that most negatively affects the quality of their life and the lives of their children (Dubrow & Garbarino, 1989). Unfortunately, neighborhood violence has become a major health issue for children (Krug, Dahlberg, Mercy, Zwi, & Lozano, 2002; Pennekamp, 1995).

A number of years ago, the first author (Debra) had the opportunity to observe the effects of community violence up close when she took her daughter to get her hair braided by someone who lived in a housing project, an acquaintance of a friend. Because the hair-braiding procedure takes several hours, she and her daughter were in the home for an extended period. While they were there, the news was released that Tupac Shakur (a popular rap singer) had died from gunshot injuries received earlier. An impromptu gathering of friends and relatives of the woman who was doing the braiding ensued. Ten men and women in their early twenties, along with their young children, gathered to discuss the shooting and to pay tribute to Tupac, who had been one of their favorite artists. As Tupac's music played in the background, Debra was struck by several themes:

- Many in the room told of a close relative who had died as a result of neighborhood violence. Debra noticed on the wall of the apartment three framed programs from funerals of young men. She later learned that these dead men were a brother and two cousins of the woman who lived in the apartment. All three had been killed in separate violent incidents in their neighborhood.
- A sense of hopelessness permeated the conversation. The men especially had little hope of a future, and most thought they would be dead by age 40. Clinicians who work with young children living in neighborhoods in which violence is prevalent relate similar comments from children (National Center for Clinical Infant Programs, 1992). When asked if he had decided what he wanted to be when he grew up, one child is quoted as saying, "Why should I? I might not grow up" (p. 25).
- Perhaps related to the sense of hopelessness was an embracing of violence. Debra observed that during lighter moments in the conversation, the guests would chuckle about physical confrontations between common acquaintances.

Ironically, as Debra and her daughter were about to leave, gunshots sounded, and the evening get-together was temporarily interrupted. Everyone, including the children, ran out of the apartment to see what had happened. For Debra, the significance of the evening was summarized in one of the last comments she heard before leaving. One of the men stated, "If all that money didn't save Tupac, what chance do we have?" It is interesting to note that Tupac's music and poetry continue to be idolized. Many still identify with his descriptions of hopelessness.

These sorts of conditions are not favorable for adequate child development (Dubrow & Garbarino, 1989; Krug et al., 2002). Investigations into the effects of living in violent neighborhoods support this claim. Children who grow up in a violent environment are reported to demonstrate low self-esteem, deficient social skills, and difficulty coping with and managing conflict (MacLennan, 1994). When Debra and her daughter visited the housing project, for example, they witnessed a 3-year-old telling her mother to "shut up." The mother and child then began hitting each other. Yes, some of this behavior is a result of parenting style, but one cannot help wondering about the influence of living in a violent community.

For many children living in violent neighborhoods, the death of a close friend or family member is commonplace. When the second author (David) was employed at a community child guidance center, he found that appointments were often canceled so the parents could attend funerals.

Living so intimately with death has detrimental effects on young children. In one study of young children whose older siblings had been victims of homicide, the surviving siblings showed symptoms of depression, anxiety, psychosocial impairment, and post-traumatic stress disorder (L. Freeman, Shaffer, & Smith, 1996). These symptoms are similar to those observed in young children in situations of political and military violence—for example, in Palestinian children in the occupied West Bank (A. Baker, 1990) and in children in South African townships during apartheid (Magwaza, Kilian, Peterson, & Pillay, 1993). Perhaps the label "war zone" is an appropriate one for violent communities. However, positive, affectionate, caregiving relationships—whether by parents or other family members or individuals in the community—can

play an important mediating role in how violence is managed by very young children (Glaser, 2000).

Domestic Violence

The family is the social group from whom we expect to receive our greatest love, support, nurturance, and acceptance. And

How does psychological age affect children's responses to domestic violence?

yet, family relationships are some of the most violent relationships in many societies. It is estimated that wife beating occurs in about 85% of the world's societies, and husband beating occurs in about 27% (D. Newman, 2008). Some suggest that physical violence between siblings may be the most common form of family violence (Gelles, 2010). Domestic violence may take the form of verbal, psychological, or physical abuse, although physical abuse is the form most often implied. It is difficult to produce accurate statistics about the amount of family violence because what happens in families is usually "behind closed doors." An estimated 3.3 million children are exposed each year to violence against their mothers by family members (American Psychological Association, 1996).

In early childhood, children respond in a number of ways during violent episodes (J. Smith, O'Connor, & Berthelsen, 1996). Some children display fright—that is, they cry and scream. Others attempt to stop the violence by ordering the abuser to stop, by physically placing themselves between the victim and the abuser, or by hitting the abuser. Many children attempt to flee by retreating to a different room, turning up the volume on the TV, or trying to ignore the violence.

The effects of domestic violence on children's development are well documented. Distress, problems with adjustment, characteristics of trauma, and increased behavior problems have all been observed in children exposed to domestic violence (H. Hughes, 1988; Perloff & Buckner, 1996; Shepard, 1992; Turner, Finkelhor, & Ormord, 2006). In addition, these children develop either aggressive behaviors or passive responses, both of which make them potential targets for abuse as teens and adults (Suh & Abel, 1990; Tutty & Wagar, 1994). Unfortunately, researchers are finding that children who witness intimate partner violence at home are also more likely to be victimized in other ways, including being victims of child maltreatment and community violence. The accumulation of victimization produces great risk for a variety of mental health problems in children (Turner et al., 2006).

In early childhood, children are more vulnerable than school-aged children to the effects of living with domestic violence (O'Keefe, 1994; J. Smith et al., 1996). Younger children simply have fewer internal resources to help them cope with the experience. In addition, older children tend to have friendships outside the family for support, whereas younger children rely primarily on the family. Many parents who are victims of domestic violence become emotionally unavailable to their young children. Battered mothers, for example, often become depressed and preoccupied with the abuse and their personal safety, leaving little time and energy for the attention and nurturing needed by young children. Another reason that young children are more vulnerable to the effects of domestic violence is that children between the ages of 3 and 6 lack the skills to verbalize their feelings and thoughts. As a result, their responses to the violence get trapped inside and continually infringe upon the child's thoughts and emotions. Finally, as in the case of divorce, because of their egocentrism, young children often blame themselves for the domestic abuse.

Domestic violence does not always affect children's long-term development, however. In one study, one third of the children seemed unaffected by the domestic violence they witnessed at home; these children were well adjusted and showed no signs of distress, anxiety, or behavior problems (J. Smith et al., 1996). Two factors may buffer the effect domestic violence has on children (O'Keefe, 1994):

1. *Amount of domestic violence witnessed by the child.* The more violent episodes children witness, the more likely they are to develop problematic behavior.

2. *Relationship between the child and the mother,* assuming the mother is the victim. If the mother–child relationship remains stable and secure, the probability of the child developing behavioral difficulties decreases significantly—even when the amount of violence witnessed by the child is relatively high.

Interestingly, the father–child relationship in cases of domestic abuse was not found to be related to the child's emotional or psychological development (O'Keefe, 1994). However, this finding should be reviewed with caution because it is often difficult to find fathers to include in this type of research, and then to accurately measure the quality of attachment a younger child in such a circumstance experiences with the father or father figure (Mackey, 2001).

Child Maltreatment

It is difficult to estimate the rate of **child maltreatment** because many incidents are never reported, and much that is reported is not determined to be child maltreatment. The most prevalent forms of child maltreatment described by the U.S. Children's Bureau included neglect, physical abuse, sexual abuse, and emotional maltreatment (U.S. Department of Health and Human Services, 2009a). About three children die from maltreatment in the United States every day, and 86% of the children who die from child maltreatment are under 6 years of age (Thomlison, 2004). Girls are most likely to be victimized overall, but boys have a higher incidence of fatal injuries than girls (Sedlak & Broadhurst, 1996). National incidence data indicate no race or ethnicity differences in maltreatment incidence, but official reports of child maltreatment include an over-representation of African Americans and American Indians/Alaska Natives (Sedlak & Broadhurst, 1996). Poverty and the lack of economic resources are correlated with abuse, especially physical abuse and neglect (Sedlak & Broadhurst, 1996). In addition, family isolation and lack of a support system, parental drug and alcohol abuse, lack of knowledge regarding child rearing, and parental difficulty in expressing feelings are all related to child abuse (Gelles, 1989; Veltkamp & Miller, 1994; Wolfner & Gelles, 1993).

An association has also been noted between abuse of young children and the overload of responsibilities that women often encounter. Mothers who work outside the home and are also responsible for most or all of the domestic responsibilities, and mothers with unemployed husbands, are more prone to abuse their young children than other groups of mothers are (Gelles & Hargreaves, 1981).

Child abuse creates risks to all aspects of growth and development, as shown in Exhibit 12.4, but children ages birth to 6 are at highest risk of having long-lasting damage (Thomlison, 2004). In their longitudinal research of 180 children born into poverty, Sroufe et al. (2005) found that young children who had been physically abused as toddlers had higher levels of negativity, noncompliance, and distractibility than other children. Those whose mothers were psychologically unavailable demonstrated more avoidance of and anger toward the mother. Children with a history of any type of

Exhibit 12.4   Some Potential Effects of Child Abuse on Growth and Development

Physical Impairments	Cognitive Impairments	Emotional Impairments
Physical Abuse and Neglect		
Burns, scars, fractures, broken bones, damage to vital organs and limbs	Delayed cognitive skills	Negative self-concept
Malnourishment	Delayed language skills	Increased aggressiveness
Physical exposure	Mental retardation	Poor peer relations
Poor skin hygiene	Delayed reality testing	Poor impulse control
Poor (if any) medical care	Overall disruption of thought processes	Anxiety
Poor (if any) dental care		Inattentiveness
Serious medical problems		Avoidant behavior
Serious dental problems		
Failure-to-thrive syndrome		
Death		
Sexual Abuse		
Trauma to mouth, anus, vaginal area	Hyperactivity	Overly adaptive behavior
Genital and rectal pain	Bizarre sexual behavior	Overly compliant behavior
Genital and rectal bleeding		Habit disorders (e.g., nail biting)
Genital and rectal tearing		Anxiety
Sexually transmitted disease		Depression
		Sleep disturbances
		Night terrors
		Self-mutilation
Psychological/Emotional Abuse		
	Pessimistic view of life	Alienation
	Anxiety and fear	Intimacy problems
	Distorted perception of world	Low self-esteem
	Deficits in moral development	Depression

maltreatment had lower self-esteem and agency and demonstrated more behavior problems than other children. Children with a history of neglect were more passive than other children.

PROTECTIVE FACTORS IN EARLY CHILDHOOD

Many of the factors listed in Chapter 11 that promote resiliency during the infant and toddler years are equally relevant during the early childhood years. Other protective factors also come into play (Fraser et al., 2004):

• *Social support.* Social support mediates many potential risks to the development of young children. The presence of social support increases the likelihood of a positive outcome for children whose parents divorce (V. Garvin, Kalter, & Hansell, 1993), moderates the effects for children who experience violence (Nettles, Mucherah, & Jones, 2000), facilitates better outcomes for children of mothers with mental illness (Oyserman, Bybee, Mowbray, & MacFarlane, 2002), and is even thought to reduce the continuation of abuse for 2- and 3-year-olds who have experienced parental abuse during the first year of life (Kotch et al., 1997). Social support aids young children in several ways (Fraser et al., 2004). Having a consistent and supportive aunt or uncle or preschool teacher who can set firm but loving limits, for example, may buffer the effects of a parent with ineffective skills. At the community level, preschools, religious programs, and the like may help to enhance physical and cognitive skills, self-esteem, and social development. Through social support from family and nonfamily relationships, young children can receive care, another identified protective factor.

• *Positive parent–child relationship.* A positive relationship with at least one parent helps children to feel secure and nurtured (Fraser et al., 2004). Remember from Chapter 11 that a sense of security is the foundation on which young children build initiative during the early childhood years. Even if Jack Lewis never has contact with his father,

Charles, a positive relationship with Joyce, his mother, can mediate this loss.

• *Effective parenting.* In early childhood, children need the opportunity to take initiative but also need firm limits, whether they are established by parents or grandparents or someone else who adopts the parent role. Terri Smith, for example, has not been able to establish self-control because her boundaries are not well defined. Effective parenting promotes self-efficacy and self-esteem and provides young children with a model of how they can take initiative within boundaries (Fraser et al., 2004).

• *Self-esteem.* A high level of self-worth may allow young children to persist in mastery of skills despite adverse conditions. Perhaps a high level of self-esteem can enhance Ron's, Rosiland's, and Jack's development despite the disruptions in their lives. In addition, research indicates that self-esteem is a protective factor against the effects of child abuse (Fraser et al., 2004).

• *Intelligence.* Even in young children, a high IQ serves as a protective factor. For example, young children with high IQs were less likely to be affected by maternal psychopathology (Tiet et al., 2001). Others suggest that intelligence results in success, which leads to higher levels of self-esteem (Fraser, 2004). For young children, then, intelligence may contribute to mastery of skills and independence, which may enhance self-esteem. Intelligence may also protect children through increased problem-solving skills, which allow for more effective responses to adverse situations.

Critical Thinking Questions 12.3

What type of parenting style do you think your parents used when you were a child? Did both parents use the same parenting style? Do you think the parenting style used by your parents was effective? How do you think your parents' parenting style was affected by culture? Would you want to use the same parenting style that your parents used if you were a parent? Why or why not?

Implications for Social Work Practice

In summary, knowledge about early childhood suggests several principles for social work practice with young children:

- Become well acquainted with theories and empirical research about growth and development among young children.
- Continue to promote the elimination of poverty and the advancement of social justice.
- Collaborate with other professionals in the creation of laws, interventions, and programs that assist in the elimination of violence.
- Create and support easy access to services for young children and their parents.
- Assess young children in the context of their environment.
- Become familiar with the physical and emotional signs of child abuse.
- Directly engage young children in an age-appropriate intervention process.
- Provide support to parents and help facilitate positive parent–child relationships.
- Encourage and engage both mothers and fathers in the intervention process.
- Provide opportunities for children to increase self-efficacy and self-esteem.
- Help parents understand the potential effects of negative environmental factors on their children.

Key Terms

authoritarian parenting
authoritative parenting
child maltreatment
discipline
disengaged parenting
egocentrism
empathy
fine motor skills
gross motor skills

hostile aggression
instrumental aggression
lateralization
learning play
permissive parenting
perspective taking
physical aggression
preconventional level of
    moral reasoning

prosocial
relational aggression
self-esteem
self-theory
sociodramatic play
symbolic play
transductive reasoning

Active Learning

1. Watch any child-oriented cartoon on television. Describe the obvious and implied messages (both positive and negative) apparent in the cartoon about race and ethnicity and gender differences. Consider how these messages might affect gender and ethnic development in young children.

2. Observe preschool-age children at play. Record the types of play that you observe. How well do your observations fit with what is described about play in this chapter?

3. The case studies at the beginning of this chapter (Terri, Jack, and Ron and Rosiland) do not specify race or ethnicity of the families. How important an omission did that appear to you? What assumptions did you make about the racial and/or ethnic background of the families? On what basis did you make those assumptions?

American Academy of Child & Adolescent Psychiatry

www.aacap.org

Site contains concise and up-to-date information on a variety of issues facing children and their families, including day care, discipline, children and divorce, child abuse, children and TV violence, and children and grief.

Children's Defense Fund

www.childrensdefense.org

Site presented by the Children's Defense Fund, a private nonprofit child advocacy organization, contains information on issues, the Black Community Crusade for Children, the Child Watch Visitation Program, and a parent resource network.

National Family Resiliency Center, Inc. (NFRC)

www.divorceabc.com

Site presented by the NFRC, contains information about support groups, resources for professionals, library of articles, news and events, KIDS Newsletter, and Frequently Asked Questions.

The Office for Studies in Moral Development and Education

http://tigger.uic.edu/~lnucci/MoralEd/

Site presented by the Office for Studies in Moral Development and Education at the College of Education at the University of Illinois, Chicago, contains an overview of Piaget's, Kohlberg's, and Gilligan's theories of moral development and the domain theory of moral development.

Play Therapy International

www.playtherapy.org

Site contains information about play therapy, reading lists, articles and research, recommended resources, and information on other related organizations.

U.S. Department of Health & Human Services

http://www.hhs.gov

Site contains information on child care, child support enforcement, and children's health insurance.

CHAPTER 13

Middle Childhood

Leanne W. Charlesworth

Jim Wood

Pamela Viggiani

附 ✿ ❧

✿ ❧

Opening Questions

How have our conceptions of middle childhood changed through time?

What types of individual, family, school, community, and other systemic qualities are most conducive to positive development during middle childhood?

During middle childhood, what factors heighten developmental risk for children, and what supports resilience?

Key Ideas

As you read this chapter, take note of these central ideas:

1. Values and beliefs regarding childhood in general, and middle childhood specifically, are shaped by historical and sociocultural context.

2. During middle childhood, a wide variety of biopsychosocial-spiritual changes take place across the developmental domains.

3. As children progress through middle childhood, the family environment remains extremely important, while the community environment—including the school—also becomes a significant factor shaping development.

4. During middle childhood, peers have an increasingly strong impact on development; peer acceptance becomes very important to well-being.

5. Poverty, family or community violence, special needs, and family disruption create developmental risk for many children.

CASE STUDY 13.1

Anthony Bryant's Impending Assessment

Anthony is a 6-year-old boy living in an impoverished section of a large city. Anthony's mother, Melissa, was 14 when Anthony was born. Anthony's father, James, who was 15 when Anthony was born, has always spent a great deal of time with Anthony. Although James now also has a 2-year-old daughter from another relationship, he has told Melissa that Anthony and Melissa are the most important people in his life. Once Anthony was out of diapers, James began spending even more time with him, taking Anthony along to visit friends and occasionally on overnight outings.

James's father was murdered when James was a toddler and he rarely sees his mother, who struggles with a serious substance addiction and is known in the neighborhood as a prostitute. James lived with his paternal grandparents until he was in his early teens, when he began to stay with a favorite uncle. Many members of James's large extended family have been incarcerated on charges related to their involvement in the local drug trade. James's favorite uncle is a well-known and widely respected dealer in the neighborhood. James himself has been arrested a few times and is currently on probation.

Melissa and Anthony live with her mother. Melissa obtained her general equivalency diploma (GED) after Anthony's birth, and she has held a variety of jobs at local fast food chains. Melissa's mother, Cynthia, receives Supplemental Social Security Income/Disability because she has been unable to work for several years due to her advanced rheumatoid arthritis, which was diagnosed when she was a teenager. Melissa remembers her father only as a loud man who often yelled at her when she made noise. He left Cynthia and Melissa when Melissa was 4 years old, and neither has seen him since. Cynthia seemed pleased when Anthony was born, and she has been a second mother to him, caring for him while Melissa attends school, works, and socializes with James and her other friends.

Anthony has always been very active and energetic, frequently breaking things and creating "messes" throughout the apartment. To punish Anthony, Cynthia spanks him with a belt or other object—and she sometimes resorts to locking him in his room until he falls asleep. Melissa and James are proud of Anthony's wiry physique and rough-and-tough play; they have encouraged him to be fearless and not to cry when he is hurt. Both Melissa and James use physical punishment as their main discipline strategy with Anthony, but he usually obeys them before it is needed.

Anthony entered kindergarten at the local public school last fall. When he started school, his teacher told Melissa that he seemed to be a very smart boy, one of the only boys in the class who already knew how to write his name and how to count to 20. It is now spring, however, and Melissa is tired of dealing with Anthony's teacher and other school staff. She has been called at work a number of times, and recently the school social worker requested a meeting with her. Anthony's teacher reports that Anthony will not listen to her and frequently starts fights with the other children in the classroom. Anthony's teacher also states that Anthony constantly violates school rules, like waiting in line and being quiet in the hallways, and he doesn't seem bothered by threats of punishment. Most recently, Anthony's teacher has told Melissa that she would like Anthony assessed by the school psychologist.

CASE STUDY 13.2

Brianna Shaw's New Self-Image

When Brianna was born, her mother, Deborah, was 31 years old with a 13-year-old daughter (Stacy) from a prior, short-lived marriage. Deborah and Michael's relationship was relatively new when Deborah became pregnant with Brianna. Shortly after Deborah announced the pregnancy, Michael moved into her mobile home. Michael and Deborah initially talked about setting a wedding date and pursuing Michael's legal adoption of Stacy, whose father had remarried and was no longer in close contact.

Michael made it clear throughout Deborah's pregnancy that he wanted a son. He seemed very content and supportive of Deborah until around the time the couple found out the baby was a girl. In Stacy's view, Michael became mean and bossy in the months that followed. He started telling Stacy what to do, criticizing Deborah's appearance, and complaining constantly that Deborah wasn't any fun anymore since she stopped drinking and smoking while she was pregnant.

(Continued)

During Brianna's infancy, the couple's relationship began to change even more rapidly. Michael was rarely home and instead spent most of his free time hanging out with old friends. When he did come by, he'd encourage Deborah to leave Brianna with Stacy so the two of them could go out like "old times." Even though her parents were Deborah's full-time day care providers and both Brianna and Stacy were thriving, Deborah was chronically exhausted from balancing parenting and her full-time job as a nursing assistant. Soon, whenever Michael came by, the couple frequently argued and their shouting matches gradually escalated to Michael threatening to take Brianna away. Michael was soon dating another woman, and his relationship with Deborah and Stacy became increasingly hostile during the following 4 years.

The summer that Brianna turned 5, the local hospital closed down and Deborah lost her job. After talking with her parents, Deborah made the decision to move with her daughters to Fairfield, a city 4 hours away from home. An old high school friend had once told Deborah that if she ever needed a job, the large hospital her friend worked for had regular openings and even offered tuition assistance. Within 2 months, Deborah had sold her mobile home, obtained a full-time position with her friend's employer, and signed a lease for a small townhouse in a suburb known for its high-quality school system.

When Brianna started kindergarten in their new town, her teacher described her to Deborah as shy and withdrawn. Deborah remembered reading something in the school newsletter about a social skills group run by a school social worker, and she asked if Brianna could be enrolled. Gradually, the group seemed to make a difference, and Brianna began to act more like her old self, forming several friendships during the following 2 years.

Today, Brianna is 8 years old and has just entered third grade. Brianna usually leaves for school on the bus at 8:00 AM, and Deborah picks her up from an after-school program at 5:45 PM. When possible, Stacy picks Brianna up earlier, after her own classes at a local community college are over. Brianna still spends summers with her grandparents in the rural area where she was born. Academically, she has thus far excelled in school, but a new concern is Brianna's weight. Brianna is 49 inches tall and weighs 72 pounds. Until the last year or so, Brianna seemed unaware of the fact that many people viewed her as overweight. In the last several months, however, Brianna has told Stacy and Deborah various stories about other children calling her "fat" and making other comments about her size. Deborah feels that Brianna is increasingly moody and angry when she is home. Brianna recently asked Deborah why she is "fat" and told Stacy that she just wishes she were dead.

Manuel Vega's Difficult Transition

A slightly built 11-year-old, Manuel Vega is in sixth grade in Greenville, Mississippi. His first language is Spanish, and he speaks English moderately well. He was born in Texas where his mother, Maria, and father, Estaban, first met. For Estaban, it has been an interesting journey from his hometown in Mexico to Mississippi. For generations, Estaban's family lived and worked near Izucar de Matamoros, a small city in Mexico on the inter-American highway. During their teen years in Izucar de Matamoros, Estaban and his four younger brothers worked on the local sugar cane farms and in the sugar refineries. By the time he was in his early twenties, Estaban began to look for better-paying work and was able to get his license to haul products from Izucar de Matamoros to larger cities, including Mexico City. Estaban and one brother eventually moved to a medium-sized city where his employer, the owner of a small trucking company, provided an apartment for several of his single truckers.

After 3 productive years in the trucking industry, the company went bankrupt. With his meager savings, Estaban made arrangements to travel to Arizona to pursue his dream of owning his own trucking company. Working as a day laborer, he eventually made his way to Laredo, Texas, where he met and married Maria. Although both Maria's and Estaban's formal schooling ended relatively early, both acquired a basic command of English while living in Laredo. During the late 1970s, Maria and Estaban requested documentation of legal status for Estaban and after a lengthy process, they were successful.

Estaban and Maria began their family while Estaban continued to work at day labor construction jobs in and around Laredo. At home and with their relatives and neighbors, Maria and Estaban spoke Spanish exclusively. In their neighborhood, Maria's many relatives not only provided social support, but also helped Maria sell tamales and other traditional Mexican foods to locals and occasional tourists. Eventually, the family saved enough money for the purchase of a small truck that Estaban used to make deliveries of Maria's specialties to more distant restaurants. However, the family faced many competitors in the local Mexican food industry. Maria's Uncle Arturo urged the family to move to the Mississippi Delta where he owns Mi Casa, a Mexican restaurant and wholesale business. Uncle Arturo was hopeful that Maria would enrich his menu with her mastery of Mexican cuisine. He promised employment for Estaban, hauling Mexican specialty food staples to the growing number of Mexican restaurants in the Delta, ranging from Memphis to Biloxi.

Almost 3 years ago, Estaban and Maria decided to take Arturo up on his offer and together with their two sons, they moved to Greenville. Their older son, Carlos, never adjusted to school life in Mississippi. Now 16, Carlos did not return to school this fall. Instead, he began working full-time for his father, loading and unloading the truck and providing his more advanced English language skills to open up new markets for the business. At first, Maria and Estaban resisted the idea of Carlos dropping out of school, but he was insistent. Carlos always struggled in school; he repeated a grade early on in his education and found most of his subjects challenging. The family's new business, after initially thriving, has struggled financially. Carlos knows the family finances have been in peril and that he is needed to help.

Carlos and his younger brother, Manuel, have always been close. Manuel yearns to be like his older brother, and Carlos has always considered it his job to protect and care for his younger brother. Carlos sees in Manuel the potential for school success that he never had. He tells Manuel that he must stay in school to acquire the "book learning" that he could never grasp. But leaving the warm embrace of their former neighborhood in Texas for the Mississippi Delta has been hard for Manuel. Their tight-knit family bonds are intact, but they are still struggling to understand how Delta culture operates. In Manuel's old school, most students and teachers spoke or knew how to speak Spanish, and Manuel always felt he fit in. Now, Manuel is one of a small percentage of Spanish-speaking students in his new school, where the vast majority of students and staff are African American and speak only English.

In the school setting, Manuel's new ESL teacher, Ms. Jones, is concerned about him. His teacher reports that he struggles academically and shows little interest in classroom activities or peers, often seeming sullen. Ms. Jones has observed that Manuel frequently appears to be daydreaming and when teachers try to talk with him, he seems to withdraw further. Ms. Jones knows that Manuel's records from Texas indicate that he was an outgoing, socially adjusted primary school student. However, his records also show that his reading and writing performance was below grade level, starting in first grade. Ms. Jones has found that if she speaks with Manuel in Spanish while taking a walk around the school, he will share stories about his family and his old neighborhood and friends. To date, no educational or psychological assessments have taken place. When Manuel meets his social worker, he avoids eye contact and appears extremely uncomfortable.

HISTORICAL PERSPECTIVE ON MIDDLE CHILDHOOD _____

Until the beginning of the 20th century, children were viewed primarily in economic terms within most European countries and the United States (Fass & Mason, 2000). Emphasis was often placed on the child's productivity and ability to contribute to the family's financial well-being. Middle childhood represented a period during which children became increasingly able to play a role in maintaining or improving the economic status of the family and community. Beginning in the early 20th century, however, a radical shift occurred in the Western world's perceptions of children. Those children passing through middle childhood became categorized as "school age," and their education became a societal priority. Child labor and compulsory education laws supported and reinforced this shift in societal values. In many parts of the nonindustrialized world, however, children continue to play important economic roles for families. In Latin America, Africa, and some parts of Asia, childhood is relatively short. Many children from the most impoverished families live and work on the streets (called "street children"). There is no time for the luxury of an indulged childhood. In rapidly industrializing countries striving toward universal primary school education, children must balance their economic productivity with time spent in school (Leeder, 2004).

The shift toward the universal public education of children is intended to be an equalizer, enabling children from a variety of economic backgrounds to become successful citizens. Historically in the United States, public schools were to be free and open to all. Instead, however, they reflected traditional public ambiguity toward poverty and diversity, and they embodied particular value systems and excluded certain groups (Allen-Meares, Washington, & Walsh, 1996). The first public schools in the United States were, in effect, open to European Americans only, and children from marginalized or nondominant groups rarely received advanced education. Today, in the United States and around the globe, schools continue to play a pivotal role in reinforcing segregation and **deculturalizing** various groups of children (Kozol, 2005; Spring, 2004). In essence, as schools pressure children from nondominant groups to assimilate or direct unequal resources toward their development (Darling-Hammond, 2007), they play a role in intentionally or unintentionally destroying or severely limiting a culture's ability to sustain itself. Most children from marginalized groups consistently achieve more poorly than the rest of the student population, a situation often referred to as the "achievement gap."

The evolution of our perceptions of middle childhood continues. Although there is incredible diversity among children, families, and communities, middle childhood has generally come to be viewed in the United States as a time when education, play, leisure, and social activities should dominate daily life (Fass & Mason, 2000). Sigmund Freud perceived middle childhood as a relatively uneventful phase of development. But in the 21st century, middle childhood is recognized as a potentially turbulent time in children's lives.

The age range classified as middle childhood is subject to debate. In the United States, it is most often defined as the period beginning at approximately age 5 or 6 and ending at approximately ages 10 to 12 (Broderick & Blewitt, 2006; Craig & Baucum, 2002). However, some assert that middle childhood begins a bit later than 6 (K. E. Allen & Marotz, 2003) and ends at the onset of puberty (D. Davies, 2004), which ranges tremendously among children.

Images of middle childhood often include children who are physically active and intellectually curious, making new friends and learning new things. But as Anthony Bryant, Brianna Shaw, and Manuel Vega demonstrate, middle childhood is filled with both opportunities and challenges. For some children, it is a period of particular vulnerability. In fact, when we think of school-aged children, images of child poverty and related school inequities; family and community violence; sexual victimization or **precociousness** (early development); learning challenges; and physical and emotional ailments like depression, asthma, and attention deficit/hyperactivity disorder (ADHD) may dominate our thoughts. In some parts of the world, children between the ages of 6 and 12 are vulnerable to war, land mines, and forced enlistment as soldiers. They are also vulnerable to slave-like labor and being sold as sex workers in an international child trafficking economy (Human Rights Watch, 2006).

MIDDLE CHILDHOOD IN THE MULTIGENERATIONAL FAMILY __

During middle childhood, the child's social world expands dramatically. Although the family is not the only relevant force in a child's life, it remains an extremely significant influence on development. Families are often in a constant state of change, and so the child's relationships with family members and the environment that the family inhabits are likely to be different from the child's first experiences of family. For example, consider the changes in Anthony Bryant's, Brianna Shaw's, and Manuel Vega's families over time and the ways in which family relationships have been continually evolving.

Despite the geographical distances that often exist between family members today, nuclear families are still emotional subsystems of extended, multigenerational family systems. The child's nuclear family is significantly shaped by past, present, and anticipated future experiences, events, and relationships (B. Carter & McGoldrick, 2005a). Profoundly important factors such as historical events, culture, and social structure often influence children through their family systems, and family members' experiences and characteristics trickle through families via generational ties. These experiences or characteristics may be biological in nature and therefore fairly obvious, or they may include more nebulous qualities such as acquired emotional strengths or wounds. For example, consider Brianna's maternal grandfather, who is African American and grew up with the legacy of slavery under Jim Crow laws and legal segregation in the United States, or Anthony's maternal grandmother, who as a child was repeatedly victimized sexually. Children become connected to events or phenomena such as a familial history of child abuse or a group history of discrimination and **oppression** (restrictions and exploitation), even in the absence of direct experiences in the present generation (see Crawford, Nobles, & Leary, 2003; McGoldrick, 2004).

Thus, the developing school-age child is shaped not only by events and individuals explicitly evident in present time and physical space, but also by those events and individuals that have more directly influenced the lives of his or her parents, grandparents, great-grandparents, and beyond. These influences—familial, cultural, and historical in nature—shape all aspects of each child's development in an abstract and complex fashion.

DEVELOPMENT IN MIDDLE CHILDHOOD __

New developmental tasks are undertaken in middle childhood, and development occurs within physical, cognitive, emotional, and social dimensions. Although each developmental domain is considered separately for our analytical purposes, changes in the developing child reflect the dynamic interaction continuously occurring across these dimensions.

Physical Development

During middle childhood, physical development typically continues steadily, but children of the same chronological age may vary greatly in stature, weight, and sexual development. For most children, height and weight begin to advance less rapidly than during prior developmental phases, but steady growth continues. The nature and pace of physical growth during this period is shaped by both genetic and environmental influences in interaction (Craig & Baucum, 2002).

As children progress from kindergarten to early adolescence, their fine and gross motor

How are Anthony, Brianna, and Manuel affected by their multigenerational families?

Photo 13.1 New developmental tasks are undertaken in middle childhood, and development occurs within physical, cognitive, emotional, and social dimensions.

skills typically advance. In the United States today, children in this age range are often encouraged to gain a high level of mastery over physical skills associated with a particular interest such as dance, sports, or music. However, medical professionals caution that school-age children continue to possess unique physical vulnerabilities related to the growth process and thus are susceptible to injuries associated with excessive physical activity or training (Craig & Baucum, 2002).

Middle childhood is a developmental phase of entrenchment or eradication of many potent risk or protective factors manifesting in this developmental domain. Focusing on risk, for children residing in chronically impoverished countries and communities, issues such as malnutrition and disease threaten physical health. Seemingly innocuous issues such as poor dental hygiene or mild visual impairment may become more serious as they begin to impact other areas of development such as cognitive, emotional, or social well-being. In the United States, health issues such as asthma and obesity are of current concern and often

either improve or become severe during middle childhood. Susceptibility to risk varies across socioeconomic and ethnic groups. In general, unintentional death and physical injury (for example, motor vehicle injuries, drowning, playground accidents, and sports-related traumatic brain injury) represent a major threat to well-being among school-age children (Borse et al., 2008). Moreover, as children move into middle childhood, they face other new risks: Approximately one third of rapes occur before age 12; homicide risk increases; and among children ages 10 to 14, suicide is a leading cause of death (CDC, 2008b). Some of the physical injuries unique to middle childhood may be indirectly facilitated by declines in adult supervision and adult overestimation of children's safety-related knowledge and ability to implement safety practices. In addition, children's continued physical and cognitive (specifically, judgment and decision-making processes) vulnerabilities combine, potentially, with an increasing propensity to engage in risk-taking activities and behaviors (Berk, 2002b).

Middle childhood is the developmental phase that leads from *prepubescence* (the period prior to commencement of the physiological processes and changes associated with puberty) to *pubescence* (the period during which the child begins to experience diverse and gradual physical processes associated with puberty). Pubescence includes the growth of pubic hair for boys and girls, breast development for girls, and genitalia development for boys. Many of us may not think of middle childhood as the developmental phase during which puberty becomes relevant. *Precocious puberty* has traditionally been defined as puberty beginning at an age that is more than 2.5 standard deviations below the population's mean age of pubertal onset. In the United States, this is approximately below age 8 in girls and below age 9 in boys (National Institute of Child Health and Human Development, 2007; Nield, Cakan, & Kamat, 2007). Ongoing consultation with a child's pediatrician or other health care provider is always recommended, but research suggests that many "early-maturing" children are simply at the early end of the normal age distribution for pubertal onset (Kaplowitz, 2006).

Focusing on racial differences, many studies have found that in the United States, non-Hispanic African American girls begin puberty earlier than other children (Adair & Gordon-Larsen, 2001; Benefice, Caius, & Garnier, 2004; Chumlea et al., 2003; National Institute of Child Health and Human Development, 2007). However, Sun et al. (2002) point out that across gender and racial groups, children continue to *complete* their **secondary sexual development,** or development of secondary sex characteristics, at approximately the same age. This issue will receive further attention in Chapter 14.

A trend toward earlier age of puberty onset, particularly among girls, has brought much attention to the potential causes. A wide variety of multidisciplinary researchers across the globe are examining available data regarding the causes of puberty onset. It is evident that a complex range of interacting factors, crossing the biopsychosocial spectrum, are relevant to understanding puberty onset. R. Wang, Needham, and Barr (2005) identify nutritional status; genetic predisposition, including race/ethnicity; and environmental chemical exposure as associated with age of puberty onset. It should be noted that careful examination of puberty onset trends suggests that the "trend toward earlier onset of puberty in U.S. girls over the past 50 years is not as strong as some reports suggested" (Kaplowitz, 2006, p. 487). Specifically, the average age of menarche (beginning of menstrual periods) decreased from approximately 14.8 years in 1877 to about 12.8 years in the mid-1960s (Kaplowitz, 2006). Most researchers have concluded that the general trend observed during this broad historical time period is the result of health and nutrition improvement within the population as a whole. An examination of available data concludes that there is little evidence to support a significant continued decline in more recent years. Nevertheless, some have suggested that our public education and health systems should reconsider the timing and nature of health education for children because the onset of puberty may impact social and emotional development and has traditionally been associated with a variety of "risky and unhealthy behaviors" (R. Wang et al., 2005, p. 1101) among children and adolescents. Indeed, a relationship, albeit complex, appears to exist between puberty and social development for both boys and girls (Felson, 2002; Kaltiala-Heino, Kosunen, & Rimpela, 2003; McCabe & Ricciardelli, 2003). During middle childhood, girls experiencing early-onset puberty may be at particular risk (American Association of University Women, 1995; Mendle, Turkheimer, & Emery, 2007). Intervention focused on self-protection and individual rights and responsibilities may be beneficial, and schools committed to the safety of their students must diligently educate staff and students about sexual development and risk.

Middle childhood is the developmental phase when increased public attention and self-awareness is directed toward various aspects of physical growth, skill, or activity patterns and levels deemed outside the normal range. Because physical development is outwardly visible, it affects perceptions of self and the way a child is viewed and treated by peers and adults. Physical development can also affect children's peer relationships. School-age children constantly compare themselves to others, and physical differences are often the topic of discussion, as Brianna Shaw is learning. Whereas "late" developers may feel inferior about their size or lack of sexual development, "early" developers may feel awkward and out of place among their peers. Many children worry about not being "normal." Reassurance by adults that physical development varies among people and that all development is "normal" is crucial.

Cognitive Development

For most children, the acquisition of cognitive abilities that occurs early in middle childhood allows the communication of thoughts with increasing complexity. Public education plays a major role in the cognitive development of children in the United States, if only because children attend school throughout the formative years of such development. When Anthony Bryant, Brianna Shaw, and Manuel Vega first entered school, their readiness to confront the challenges and opportunities that school presents was shaped by prior experiences. Anthony, for example, entered school generally prepared for the academic emphases associated with kindergarten. He was perhaps less prepared for the social expectations present in the school environment.

In Jean Piaget's (1936/1952) terms, children start school during the second stage (preoperational thought) and finish school when they are completing the fourth and final stage of cognitive development (formal operations). In the third stage (concrete operations), children are able to solve concrete problems using logical problem-solving strategies. By the end of middle childhood, they enter the formal operations stage and become able to solve hypothetical problems using abstract concepts (refer back to Exhibit 4.1 in Chapter 4 for an overview of Piaget's stages of cognitive development). Schoolchildren rapidly develop conceptual thought, enhanced ability to categorize complicated systems of objects, and the ability to solve problems. As you observe children moving into and through middle childhood, you will note these rapid gains in intellectual processes and memory (Bergen & Coscia, 2001). These brain-produced shifts in the child's understanding of him- or herself and the surrounding world are consistent with the transition into Piaget's concrete operational stage of cognitive development. Potential gains in cognitive development enable new learning in a variety of environments. For example, children gain enhanced ability to understand people, situations, and events within their surrounding environments. The task for caregivers and others within the child's environment is to recognize and respond to this ability sensitively by nurturing and supporting the child's expanding cognitive abilities.

Beyond Piaget's ideas, brain development and cognitive functioning during middle childhood have received relatively little attention when compared to research devoted to brain development in prior developmental phases. However, our ever-expanding general understanding of the human brain illuminates opportunities and vulnerabilities present throughout childhood. For example, professionals working with children are increasingly aware of the meaning and implications of brain plasticity. As pointed out in Chapter 11, infancy, toddlerhood, and early childhood appear to represent "sensitive periods" in brain development. By middle childhood, a child's brain development and functioning have been profoundly shaped by the nature of earlier experiences and development. And yet, remarkable brain plasticity continues, with brain structure and functioning capable of growth and refinement throughout life (Fogarty, 2009; Shonkoff & Phillips, 2000). The conceptual framework perhaps most useful to understanding this potential and the processes at play is *nonlinear dynamic systems theory,* also known as complexity or chaos theory (see Chapter 2 for a discussion of chaos theory) (Applegate & Shapiro, 2005). Applied to this context, this theoretical perspective

Photo 13.2 Middle childhood is a critical time for children to acquire a sense of self-confidence and develop conceptual thought.

proposes that changes in one area or aspect of the neurological system may stimulate or interact with other neurological or broader physiological system components in an unpredictable fashion, potentially leading to unanticipated outcomes. Brain development follows a coherent developmental process, but brain plasticity in particular demonstrates the role of complex, nonlinear, neurological system dynamics and processes.

At least two aspects of brain development are of particular interest when we focus on middle childhood. The first is the idea that different brain regions appear to develop according to different timelines. In other words, middle childhood may be a "sensitive period" for certain aspects of brain development not yet clearly understood. The second important idea is the notion that brain synapses (connections between cells in the nervous system) that are initially present as children enter this developmental phase may be gradually eliminated if they are not used. As reported in Chapter 11, there seems to be a pattern of *synaptogenesis,* or creation and fine-tuning of brain synapses, in the human cerebral cortex during early childhood, which

appears to be followed by a gradual pruning process that eventually reduces the overall number of synapses to their adult levels (Fogarty, 2009; Shonkoff & Phillips, 2000). The **cerebral cortex** is the outer layer of gray matter in the human brain thought to be responsible for complex, high-level intellectual functions such as memory, language, and reasoning. Ongoing positive and diverse learning opportunities during middle childhood may help facilitate continued brain growth and optimal refinement of existing structures. The National Research Council of Medicine (cited in Shonkoff & Phillips, 2000) argues that it is essential to recognize that although genetic factors and the nature and timing of early experiences matter, "more often than not, the developing child remains vulnerable to risk and open to protective influences throughout the early years of life and into adulthood" (p. 31).

Variations in brain development and functioning appear to play a critical role in learning abilities and disabilities as well as patterns of behavior (Bergen & Coscia, 2001). During middle childhood, identification and potential diagnosis of special needs, including issues such as ADHD and autism spectrum disorders, typically peak. In recent years, an area of public interest is gender or sex-based differences in brain functioning and, possibly, learning styles. This interest has been stimulated in part by evidence suggesting that in some countries such as the United States, boys are currently at higher risk than girls for poor literacy performance, special education placement, and school dropout (Weaver-Hightower, 2003).

It has been suggested that brain-based cognitive processing, behavior, and learning style differences may be responsible for the somewhat stable trends observed in gender differences in educational achievement (Fogarty, 2009; K. King & Gurian, 2006; Sax, 2005). The importance of sex, or gender, in shaping the human experience cannot be overstated. Gender is a profoundly important organizing factor shaping human development, and its biological correlates may impact behavior and learning processes in ways we do not clearly understand. In particular, the nature and causes of educational achievement differences among girls and boys are "complex and the interconnections of the causes are poorly understood" (Weaver-Hightower, 2003, p. 487). Also, it is critically important to remember that among children, gender is but one of several personal and group characteristics relevant to understanding educational privilege specifically, as well as risk and protection generally. Careful analysis of contemporary data and its shortcomings indicates that the differences between boys and girls are complex, and there simply is not clear evidence of exclusively one-sided educational advantage or disadvantage (Bailey, 2002).

Several developmental theorists, including those listed in Exhibit 13.1, have described the changes and developmental tasks associated with middle childhood. According to these traditional theorists, thinking typically becomes more complex, reasoning becomes more logical, the child's sense of morality expands and develops into a more internally based system, and the ability to understand the perspectives of others emerges. However, much developmental research historically lacked rigor and did not devote sufficient attention to females and children belonging to nondominant groups. A number of contemporary developmental theorists have focused on assessing the relevance and applicability of these developmental tasks to all children. Most agree that the central ideas of the theorists summarized in Exhibit 13.1 continue to be meaningful. For example, Erikson's thoughts remain widely recognized as relevant to our understanding of school-age children. In some areas, however, these developmental theories have been critiqued and subsequently expanded. This is particularly true in the area of moral development.

The best-known theory of moral development is Lawrence Kohlberg's stage theory (for an overview of this theory, refer back to Exhibit 4.3 in Chapter 4). Kohlberg's research on moral reasoning found that children do not enter the second level of *conventional moral reasoning,* or morality based on approval of authorities or upon upholding societal standards, until about age 9 or 10, sometime after they have the cognitive skills for such reasoning. Robert Coles (1987, 1997) expanded upon Kohlberg's work and emphasized the distinction between moral imagination—the gradually developed capacity to reflect on what is right and wrong—and moral conduct, pointing out that a "well-developed conscience does not translate, necessarily, into a morally courageous life" (p. 3). To Coles, *moral behavior* is shaped by daily experiences, developing in response to the way the child is treated in his or her various environments such as home and school. The school-age child often pays close attention to the discrepancies between the "moral voices" and actions of the adults in his or her world, including parents, friends' parents, relatives, teachers, and coaches. Each new and significant adult sets an example for the child, sometimes complementing and sometimes contradicting the values emphasized in the child's home environment.

Also, Gilligan (1982) has extensively criticized Kohlberg's theory of moral development as paying inadequate attention to girls' "ethic of care" and the keen emphasis girls often place on relationships and the emotions of others. Consistent with Gilligan's ideas, a number of developmental

Exhibit 13.1 Phases and Tasks of Middle Childhood

Theorist	Phase or Task	Description
Freud (1938/1973)	Latency	Sexual instincts become less dominant; superego develops further.
Erikson (1950)	Industry versus inferiority	Capacity to cooperate and create develops; result is sense of either mastery or incompetence.
Piaget (1936/1952)	Concrete operational	Reasoning becomes more logical but remains at concrete level; principle of conservation is learned.
Piaget (1932/1965)	Moral realism and autonomous morality	Conception of morality changes from absolute and external to relative and internal.
Kohlberg (1969a)	Preconventional and conventional morality	Reasoning based on punishment and reward is replaced by reasoning based on formal law and external opinion.
Selman (1976)	Self-reflective perspective taking	Ability develops to view own actions, thoughts, and emotions from another's perspective.

theorists have argued that girls possess heightened **interrelational intelligence,** which is based on emotional and social intelligence and is similar to Howard Gardner's concept of interpersonal intelligence (Borysenko, 1996, p. 41). Such developmentalists, drawing upon feminist scholarship, point out that both girls and boys advance rapidly in the cognitive and moral developmental domains during middle childhood, but the genders may be distinct in their approaches to social relationships and interactions, and such differences may shape the nature of development in all domains (Borysensko, 1996; Gilligan, 1982; J. M. Taylor, Gilligan, & Sullivan, 1995). It is also important to note that collectivist-oriented societies put a high value on connectedness, and research with groups from collectivist societies indicates that they do not score well on Kohlberg's model of moral development. Gardiner and Kosmitzki (2008) argue that moral thought and development must be understood in cultural context.

Developmentalists have examined the implications of advancing cognitive abilities for children's understanding of their group identities. Children become much more aware of ethnic identities and other aspects of diversity (such as socioeconomic status and gender identities) during their middle childhood years. Cultural awareness and related beliefs are shaped by the nature of experiences such as exposure to diversity within the family and community, including school contexts. Unlike the preschooler's attraction to "black and white" classifications, children progressing through middle childhood are increasingly capable of understanding the complexities of group memberships; in other words, they are cognitively capable of rejecting overly simplistic stereotypes and recognizing the complexities present within all individuals and groups (D. Davies, 2004). McAdoo (2001) asserts that, compared with children who identify with the majority group, children from nondominant groups are much more likely to possess awareness of their own group identity or identities as well as majority group characteristics. Thus, a now widely recognized developmental task associated with middle childhood is the acquisition of positive group identity or identities (D. Davies, 2004; Verkuyten, 2005). The terms *bicultural* or *multicultural competence* are used to refer to the skills children from nondominant groups must acquire in order to survive and thrive developmentally (Chestang, 1972; Lum, 2004, 2007; Norton, 1993).

Manuel speaks English as a second language and in some ways is representative of many school-age children. In the United States, approximately 20% of all children ages 5 through 17 enrolled in school speak a language other than English at home; this figure is expected to continue to increase steadily in the future (Kominski, Shin, & Marotz, 2008). Multi- and bilingual children in the United States were traditionally thought to be at risk of developmental deficits. However, significant research evidence demonstrates that bilingualism may have a positive impact on cognitive development. When controlling for socioeconomic status, bilingual children often perform better than monolingual children on tests of analytical reasoning, concept formation, and cognitive flexibility (Akbulut, 2007; Hakuta, Ferdman, & Diaz, 1987). Also, bilingual children may be more likely to acquire capacities and skills that enhance their reading achievement (R. Campbell & Sais, 1995). With growing evidence of brain plasticity and the way that environmental demands change brain structures, researchers have begun to explore the relationship between bilingualism and the brain. They have found that learning a second language increases the density of gray matter in the left inferior parietal cortex. The earlier a second language is learned and the more proficient the person becomes, the more benefit to brain development there is (Mechelli et al., 2004). Despite such findings, however, too often bilingual children receive little support for their native language and culture in the school context.

Cultural Identity Development

For many European American children, ethnicity does not lead to comparison with others or exploration of identity (Rotheram-Borus, 1993; Tatum, 2000a). But for most children who are members of nondominant groups, ethnicity or race may be a central part of the quest for identity that begins in middle childhood and continues well into adolescence and young adulthood. By

How can cultural identity serve as a protective factor for children from nondominant groups?

around age 7, cognitive advances allow children to view themselves and others as capable of belonging to more than one "category" at once, as capable of possessing two or more heritages simultaneously (Morrison & Bordere, 2001). As children mature, they may become more aware of not only dual or multiple aspects of identity, but also of the discrimination and inequality to which they may be subjected. Such issues may in fact present overwhelming challenges for the school-age child belonging to a nondominant group. At a time when development of a sense of belonging is critical, these issues set some children apart from members of dominant groups and may increase the challenges they experience.

Segregation based on ethnicity/race and social class is common in friendships at all ages, including middle childhood. Like adults, children are more likely to hold negative attitudes toward groups to which they do not belong (Haidt, 2007). However, children, like adults, vary in the extent to which they hold ethnic and social class biases. Verbalized prejudice declines during middle childhood as children learn to obey social norms against overt prejudice. However, children belonging to nondominant groups continue to face institutional discrimination and other significant challenges throughout this period of the life course (Gutierrez, 2004; Harps, 2005).

A particular challenge for children like Manuel Vega may be blending contradictory values, standards, or traditions. Some children respond to cultural contradictions by identifying with the mainstream American culture (*assimilation*) in which they are immersed or by developing negative attitudes about their subcultural group memberships, either consciously or unconsciously (*stereotype vulnerability*). Individual reactions, such as those of Manuel Vega, will be shaped by the child's unique experiences and social influences. It is a major developmental task to integrate dual or multiple identities into a consistent personal identity as well as a positive ethnic or racial identity (J. T. Gibbs & Huang, 1989; Lomsky-Feder & Leibovitz, 2010). Many models of identity exist for children of mixed ethnicity, with new ideas and theories constantly emerging. It is clear that identity development for such children is diverse, extremely complex, and not well understood. As always, however, parents and professionals must start where the child is, with a focus on facilitating understanding and appreciation of heritage in order to promote development of an integrated identity and positive self-regard (Kopola, Esquivel, & Baptiste, 1994). Children should be provided with opportunities to explore their dual or multiple heritages and to select their own terms for identifying and describing themselves (Morrison & Bordere, 2001). Although studies have produced diverse findings, positive outcomes seem to be associated with supportive family systems and involvement in social and recreational activities that expose children to their heritage and lead to self-affirmation (Fuligni, 1997; J. T. Gibbs & Huang, 1989; Guarnaccia & Lopez, 1998; Herring, 1995).

Key tasks for adults, then, include educating children about family histories and supporting the creation of an integrated sense of self. Individuals and organizations within the child's social system can provide support by being sensitive to issues related to ethnic/racial origin and ethnic/racial distinctions; they can also help by celebrating cultural diversity and trying to increase the cultural sensitivity of all children. Such interventions appear to discourage negative stereotypes of peers belonging to nondominant groups (Rotheram-Borus, 1993).

In general, it is critical to the positive identity development of all children, but particularly those from nondominant groups, that schools value diversity and offer a variety of experiences that focus on positive identity development (Morrison & Bordere, 2001). Ensuring that schools respect nondominant cultures and diverse learning styles is an important step. For schools to do this, all school staff must develop self-awareness. A variety of materials have been designed to facilitate this process among educators (see E. Lee, Menkart, & Okazawa-Rae, 1998; Matsumoto-Grah, 1992; Seefeldt, 1993) and other professionals (Fong, 2003; Lum, 2007; Sue & McGoldrick, 2005).

The family environment of course plays a critical role in shaping all aspects of development, and the family is typically the vehicle through which cultural identity is transmitted. Children typically learn through their families how to view their own ethnicity/race and that of others as well as coping strategies to respond to potential or direct exclusion, discrimination, or racism (Barbarin, McCandies, Coleman, & Atkinson, 2004).

Emotional Development

As most children move from early childhood into and through middle childhood, they experience significant gains in their ability to identify and articulate their own emotions as well as the emotions of others. Exhibit 13.2 summarizes several gains school-age children often make in the area of emotional functioning. It is important to recognize, however, that culture and other aspects of group identity may shape emotional development. For example, cultures vary in their acceptance of expressive displays of emotion.

What are our societal expectations for emotional intelligence during middle childhood?

Many children in this age range develop more advanced coping skills that help them when encountering upsetting, stressful, or traumatic situations. As defined by Daniel Goleman (1995), *emotional intelligence* refers to the ability to "motivate oneself and persist in the face of frustrations, to control impulse and delay gratification, to regulate one's moods and keep distress from swamping the ability to think, to empathize and to hope" (p. 34) (see Chapter 4 in this book for a discussion of emotional intelligence). To Goleman (2006), emotional and social intelligence are inextricably linked, and many other developmentalists agree. As a result, interventions used with children experiencing social difficulties often focus upon enhancing some aspect of emotional intelligence.

Goleman (2006) also asserts that social and emotional intelligence are key aspects of both moral reasoning and moral conduct. In other words, although often it may seem that advancing capacities in the moral domain occurs naturally for children, positive conditions and interactions

Exhibit 13.2   Common Emotional Gains During Middle Childhood

- Ability to mentally organize and articulate emotional experiences
- Cognitive control of emotional arousal
- Use of emotions as internal monitoring and guidance systems
- Ability to remain focused on goal-directed actions
- Ability to delay gratification based on cognitive evaluation
- Ability to understand and use the concept of planning
- Ability to view tasks incrementally
- Use of social comparison
- Influence of internalized feelings (e.g., self-pride, shame) on behavior
- Capacity to tolerate conflicting feelings
- Increasingly effective defense mechanisms

SOURCE: D. Davies (2004, pp. 369–372).

must exist in a child's life in order for optimal emotional and social competencies to develop. Thus, a child like Anthony Bryant, with seemingly great academic promise, may not realize his potential without timely intervention targeting the development of critical emotional competencies. These competencies include, for example, self-awareness; impulse control; and the ability to identify, express, and manage feelings, including love, jealousy, anxiety, and anger. Healthy emotional development can be threatened by a number of issues, including challenges such as significant loss and trauma. We increasingly recognize the vulnerability of school-age children to serious emotional and mental health issues. Assessment approaches that incorporate awareness of and attention to the possible existence of such issues are critical.

Fortunately, a substantial knowledge base regarding the promotion of positive emotional development exists. Many intervention strategies appear effective, particularly when they are preventive in nature and provided during or before middle childhood (see Hyson, 2004).

For example, Brianna Shaw, like too many children—particularly girls her age—is at risk of developing depression and could benefit from intervention focusing on the development of appropriate coping strategies. A number of interacting, complex biopsychosocial-spiritual factors shape vulnerability to ailments such as depression. Goleman (1995) argues that many cases of depression arise from deficits in two key areas of emotional competence: relationship skills and cognitive, or interpretive, style. In short, many children suffering from—or at risk of developing—depression likely possess a depression-promoting way of interpreting setbacks. Children with a potentially harmful outlook attribute setbacks in their lives to internal, personal flaws. Appropriate preventive intervention, based on a cognitive-behavioral approach, teaches children that their emotions are linked to the way they think and facilitates productive, healthy ways of interpreting events and viewing themselves. For Brianna, such cognitive-behavioral–oriented intervention may be helpful. Brianna also may benefit from a gender-specific intervention, perhaps with a particular focus upon relational resilience. Potter (2004) argues that gender-specific interventions are often most appropriate when the social problem is experienced primarily by one gender. She identifies eating disorders and depression as two examples of issues disproportionately impacting girls. Identifying the relevance of gender issues to Brianna's current emotional state and considering a gender-specific intervention strategy therefore may be appropriate. The concept of "relational resilience" is built upon relational-cultural theory's belief that "all psychological growth occurs in relationships"; the building blocks of relational resilience are "mutual empathy, empowerment, and the development of courage" (see Chapter 2 in this book for a discussion of relational-cultural theory) (J. V. Jordan, 2005, p. 79).

Many school-age girls and boys also experience depression and other types of emotional distress because of a variety of factors, including **trauma** (severe physical or psychological injury) or significant loss. Children with close ties to extended family are particularly likely to experience loss of a close relative at a young age and therefore are more prone to this sort of depression. Loss, trauma, and violence may present serious obstacles to healthy emotional development. Research demonstrates the remarkable potential resilience of children (see Fraser, Kirby, & Smokowski, 2004; Garmezy, 1994; S. Goldstein & Brooks, 2005; Luthar, 2003; E. E. Werner & Smith, 2001), but both personal and environmental attributes play a critical role in processes of resilience. To support the healthy emotional development of children at risk, appropriate multilevel prevention and intervention efforts are crucial.

Social Development

Perhaps the most widely recognized developmental task of this period in life is the acquisition of feelings of *self-competence*. Traditional developmentalists have pointed out that the school-age child searches for opportunities to demonstrate personal skills, abilities, and achievements. This is what Erik Erikson (1963) was referring to when he described the developmental task of middle childhood as industry versus inferiority (refer back to Exhibit 4.11 in Chapter 4 for a description of all eight of Erikson's psychosocial stages). *Industry* refers to a drive to acquire new skills and do meaningful "work."

The experiences of middle childhood may foster or thwart the child's attempts to acquire an enhanced sense of *mastery* and self-efficacy. Family, peer, and community support may enhance the child's growing sense of competence; lack of such support undermines this sense. The child's definitions of self and accomplishment vary greatly according to interpretations in the surrounding environment. But superficial, external bolstering of self-esteem is not all that children of this age group require. External appraisal must be supportive and encouraging but also genuine in order for children to value such feedback.

Some theorists argue that children of this age must learn the value of perseverance and develop an internal drive to succeed (Kindlon, 2003; Seligman, Reivich, Jaycox, & Gillham, 1995). Thus, opportunities to both fail and succeed must be provided, along with sincere feedback and support. Ideally, the developing school-age child acquires the sense of personal competence and tenacity that will serve as a protective factor during adolescence and young adulthood.

Families play a critical role in supporting development of this sense. For example, as the child learns to ride a bike or play a sport or musical instrument, adults can provide specific feedback and praise. They can counter the child's frustration by identifying and complimenting specific improvements and emphasizing the role of practice and perseverance in producing improvements. Failures and setbacks can be labeled as temporary and surmountable rather than attributed to personal flaws or deficits. The presence of such feedback loops is a key feature of high-quality adult–child relationships, in the family, school, and beyond. Middle childhood is a critical time for children to acquire a sense of competence. Each child experiences events and daily interactions that enhance or diminish feelings of self-competence.

Children are not equally positioned as they enter this developmental phase, as Anthony Bryant's, Brianna Shaw's, and Manuel Vega's stories suggest. Developmental pathways preceding entry into middle childhood are extremely diverse. Children experience this phase of life differently based not only on differences in the surrounding environment—such as family structure and socioeconomic status—but also on their personality

How does a growing sense of competence promote the capacity for human agency in making choices?

differences. A particular personality and learning style may be valued or devalued, problematic or nonproblematic, in each of the child's expanding social settings (Berk, 2002a, 2002b). Thus, although Anthony, Brianna, and Manuel are moving through the same developmental period and facing many common tasks, they experience these tasks differently and will emerge into adolescence as unique individuals. Each individual child's identity development is highly dependent upon social networks of privilege and exclusion. A direct relationship exists between the level of control and power a child experiences and the degree of balance that is achieved in the child's emerging identity between feelings of power (privilege) and powerlessness (exclusion) (A. G. Johnson, 2005; Tatum, 1992). As children move toward adolescence and early adulthood, the amount of emotional, social, spiritual, and economic **capital,** or resources, acquired determines the likelihood of socioeconomic and other types of success as well as feelings of competence to succeed. Experiencing economically and socially just support systems is critical to optimum development.

Middle childhood is an important time in moral development, a time when most children become intensely interested in moral issues. Advancing language capability serves not only as a communication tool, but also as a vehicle for more sophisticated introspection. Language is also a tool for positive assertion of self and personal opinions as the child's social world expands (R. Coles, 1987, 1997). In recent years, many elementary schools have added **character education** to their curricula. Such education often consists of direct teaching and curriculum inclusion of mainstream moral and social values thought to be universal in a community (e.g., kindness, respect, honesty). Renewed focus on children's character education is in part a response to waves of school violence and bullying. Survey research with children suggests that, compared to children in middle and high school settings, children in elementary school settings are at highest risk of experiencing bullying, either as a perpetrator or as a victim (Astor, Benbenishty, Pitner, & Meyer, 2004).

At a broader level, federal and state legislative initiatives have encouraged school personnel to confront bullying and harassment in the school setting (Limber & Small, 2003). Schools have been particularly responsive to these initiatives in the wake of well-publicized incidents of school violence. Today, most schools have policies in place designed to facilitate efficient and effective responses to aberrant behavior, including bullying and violence. The content and implementation details of such policies, of course, vary widely.

There is plentiful evidence to suggest that "the bully" or "bullying" has existed throughout modern human history (Astor et al., 2004). During the late 20th century, changes occurred within our views of and knowledge regarding bullying. In general, the public has become less tolerant of bullying, perhaps because of a fairly widespread belief that school shootings (such as the Columbine High School massacre) can be linked to bullying. Bullying is today recognized as a complex phenomenon, with both **direct bullying** (physical) and indirect bullying viewed as cause for concern (Astor et al., 2004). **Indirect bullying** is conceptualized as including verbal; psychological; and social, or "relational," bullying tactics.

In recent years, new interest has centered on the ways in which technology influences social relationships among children and youth as well as gender differences in relationships and bullying. Initially, attention was drawn to the previously under-recognized phenomenon of girls experiencing direct bullying, or physical aggression and violence, at the hands of other girls (Garbarino, 2006). Although both direct and indirect bullying cross genders, more recent attention has centered on the widespread existence of indirect, or relational, bullying, particularly among girls, and its potentially devastating consequences (R. Simmons, 2003; Underwood, 2003).

A positive outcome of recent attention to bullying is interest in establishing "best practices" in bullying prevention and intervention. Astor and colleagues (2004) argue that the United States is lagging behind other countries such as Norway, the United Kingdom, and Australia in implementing and evaluating comprehensive bullying prevention and intervention strategies; a benefit of our delayed status in the United States is our ability to learn from this international knowledge base. This knowledge base suggests that the most effective approach to reducing bullying within a school is implementation of a comprehensive, schoolwide prevention and intervention plan that addresses the contributing factors within all levels of the school environment (Espelage & Swearer, 2003; Plaford, 2006). In recent years, many school districts in the United States have implemented such initiatives and have experienced positive results (Beaudoin & Taylor, 2004).

Communities possess great potential to provide important support and structure for children. Today, however, many communities provide as many challenges as opportunities for development. Communities in which challenges outweigh opportunities have been labeled as "socially toxic," meaning that they threaten positive development (Garbarino, 1995). In contrast, within a socially supportive environment, children have access to peers and adults who can lead them toward more advanced moral and social thinking. This development occurs in part through the modeling of *prosocial behavior,* which injects moral reasoning and social sensitivity into the child's accustomed manner of reasoning and behaving. Thus, cognitive and moral development is a social issue. The failure of adults to take on moral and spiritual mentoring roles contributes significantly to the development of socially toxic environments.

This type of moral mentoring takes place in the **zone of proximal development**—the theoretical space between the child's current developmental level and the child's potential level if given access to appropriate models and developmental experiences in the social environment (Vygotsky, 1986). Thus, the child's competence alone interacts dynamically with the child's competence in the company of others. The result is developmental progress.

The Peer Group

Nearly as influential as family members during middle childhood are *peer groups:* collections of children with unique values and goals. As children progress through middle childhood, peers have an increasingly important impact on such everyday matters as social behavior, activities, and dress. By this phase of development, a desire for group belongingness is especially strong. Within peer groups, children potentially learn three important lessons. First, they learn to appreciate different points of view; second, they learn to recognize the norms and demands of their peer group; and third, they learn to have closeness to a same-sex peer (B. Newman & Newman, 2009). Whereas individual friendships facilitate the development of critical capacities such as trust and intimacy, peer groups foster learning about cooperation and leadership.

Throughout middle childhood, the importance of *group norms* is highly evident (von Salisch, 2001). Children are sensitive, sometimes exceedingly so, to their peers' standards for behavior, appearance, and attitudes. Brianna Shaw, for instance, is beginning to devalue herself because she recognizes the discrepancy between her appearance and group norms. Often, it is not until adolescence that group norms may become more flexible, allowing for more individuality. This shift reflects the complex relationship among the developmental domains. In this case, the association between social and cognitive development is illustrated by simultaneous changes in social relationships and cognitive capacities.

Gains in cognitive abilities promote more complex communication skills and greater social awareness. These developments, in turn, facilitate more complex peer interaction, which is a vital resource for the development of **social competence**—the ability to engage in sustained, positive, and mutually satisfactory peer interactions. Positive peer relationships reflect and support social competence, as they potentially discourage egocentrism, promote positive coping, and ultimately serve as a protective factor during the transition to adolescence (M. B. Spencer, Harpalani, Fegley, Dell'Angelo, & Seaton, 2003).

> What role do peer groups play in developing the capacity for meaningful relationships in middle childhood?

Gender and culture influence the quantity and nature of peer interactions observed among school-age children (Potter, 2004). Sociability, intimacy, social expectations and rules, and the value placed on various types of play and other social activities are all phenomena shaped by both gender and culture.

M. B. Spencer et al. (2003) point out that children from nondominant groups are more likely to experience dissonance across school, family, and peer settings. For example, such children may experience language differences; misunderstandings of cultural traditions or expressions; and distinct norms, or rules, regarding dating behavior, peer intimacy, or cross-gender friendships. These authors also assert that although many youth experiencing dissonance across school, family, and peer systems may suffer from negative outcomes such as peer rejection or school failure, some may learn important coping skills that will serve them well later in life. In fact, the authors argue that given the clear trend toward increasing cultural diversity around the globe, "experiences of cultural dissonance and the coping skills they allow youth to develop should not be viewed as aberrant; instead, privilege should be explored as having a 'downside' that potentially compromises the development of coping and character" (p. 137).

A persistent finding is that, across gender and culture, peer acceptance is a powerful predictor of psychological adjustment. One well-known study asked children to fit other children into particular categories. From the results, the researchers developed five general categories of social acceptance: popular, rejected, controversial, neglected, and average (Coie, Dodge, & Coppotelli, 1982). Common predictors of popular status include physical appearance and prosocial behaviors in the social setting (Rotenberg et al., 2004). Rejected children are those who are actively disliked by their peers. They are particularly likely to be unhappy and to experience achievement and self-esteem issues. Rejected status is strongly associated with poor school performance, antisocial behavior, and delinquency in adolescence (DeRosier, Kupersmidt, & Patterson, 1994; Greenman & Schneider, 2009;

Ollendick, Weist, Borden, & Greene, 1992). For this reason, we should be concerned about Brianna Shaw's growing sense of peer rejection.

Support for rejected children may include interventions to improve peer relations and psychological adjustment. Most of these interventions are based on social learning theory and involve modeling and reinforcing positive social behavior—for example, initiating interaction and responding to others positively. Several such programs have indeed helped children develop social competence and gain peer approval (Lochman, Coie, Underwood, & Terry, 1993; Wyman, Cross, & Barry, 2004; Young, Marchant, & Wilder, 2004).

Friendship and Intimacy

Throughout middle childhood, children develop their ability to look at things from others' perspectives. In turn, their capacity to develop more complex friendships—based on awareness of others' thoughts, feelings, and needs—emerges (Selman, 1976; von Salisch, 2001). Thus, complex and fairly stable friendship networks begin to form for the first time in middle childhood (Wojslawowicz Bowker, Rubin, Burgess, Booth-Laforce, Rose-Krasnor, 2006). Although skills such as cooperation and problem solving are learned in the peer group, close friendships facilitate understanding and promote trust and reciprocity. Most socially competent children maintain and nurture both close friendships and effective peer group interaction.

As children move through middle childhood, friendship begins to entail mutual trust and assistance and thus becomes more emotionally rather than behaviorally based (Asher & Paquette, 2003). In other words, school-age children may possess close friendships based on the emotional support provided for one another as much as, if not more than, common interests and activities. The concept of *friend* is transformed from the playmate of early childhood to the confidant of middle childhood. Violations of trust during this period are often perceived as serious violations of the friendship bond. As children move out of middle childhood and into adolescence, the role of intimacy and loyalty in friendship becomes even more pronounced. Moreover, children increasingly value mutual understanding and loyalty in the face of conflict among peers (Berndt, 1988).

Team Play

The overall incidence of aggression during peer activities decreases during middle childhood, and friendly rule-based play increases. This transition is due in part to the continuing development of a perspective-taking ability, the ability to see a situation from another person's point of view. In addition, most school-age children are exposed to peers who differ in a variety of ways, including personality, ethnicity, and interests.

School-age children are able to take their new understanding of others' needs and desires into account in various types of peer interaction. Thus, their communication and interaction reflect an enhanced ability to understand the role of multiple participants in activities. These developments facilitate the transition to many rule-based activities, such as team sports. Despite occasional arguments or fights with peers, involvement with team sports may provide great enjoyment and satisfaction. Participation in team sports during middle childhood may also have long-term benefits. One research team found a link between voluntary participation in team sports during middle childhood and level of physical activity in adulthood (W. Taylor, Blair, Cummings, Wun, & Malina, 1999). While participating in team sports, children also develop the capacity for interdependence, cooperation, division of labor, and competition (Van der Vegt, Eman, & Van De Vliert, 2001). In addition, participation in team sports raises issues of moral judgment and behaviors (M. Lee, Whitehead, & Ntoumanis, 2007).

Gender Identity and Gender Roles

Although most children in middle childhood have a great deal in common based upon their shared developmental phase, girls and boys differ significantly in areas ranging from their self-understanding and social relationships to school performance,

interests, and life aspirations (Potter, 2004). Among most school-age children, gender identity, or an "internalized psychological experience of being male or female," is quite well established (Diamond & Savin-Williams, 2003, p. 105).

Our understanding of the structure of gender roles is derived from various theoretical perspectives. An anthropological or social constructionist orientation illuminates the ways in which, throughout history, gender has shaped familial and societal systems and inevitably impacts individual development in an intangible yet profound fashion (Gardiner & Kosmitzki, 2008; Wertsch, del Rio, & Alvarez, 1995). Cognitive theory suggests that at the individual level, self-perceptions emerge. Gender, as one component of self-perception, joins related *cognitions* to guide children's gender-linked behaviors. A behavioral perspective suggests that gender-related *behaviors* precede self-perception in the development of gender role identity; in other words, at a very young age, girls start imitating feminine behavior and *later* begin thinking of themselves as distinctly female, and boys go through the same sequence in developing a masculine identity. Gender schema theory (see Bem, 1993, 1998), an information-processing approach to gender, combines behavioral and cognitive theories, suggesting that social pressures and children's cognition work together to perpetuate gender-linked perceptions and behaviors.

Feminist psychodynamic theorists such as Nancy Chodorow (1978, 1989) have proposed that while boys typically begin to separate psychologically from their female caregivers in early childhood, most girls deepen their connection to and identification with their female caregivers throughout childhood. Such theorists propose, then, that as girls and boys transition into adolescence and face a new level of individuation, they confront this challenge from very different psychological places, and girls are more likely to find the task emotionally confusing if not deeply overwhelming. This feminist, psychoanalytic theoretical orientation has been used to explain not only gender identity and role development, but also differences between boys and girls in their approaches to relationships and emotional expressiveness throughout childhood.

A related issue is a disturbing trend noted among girls transitioning from middle childhood to adolescence. Women's studies' experts have pointed out that school-age girls often seem to possess a "confident understanding of self," which gradually disintegrates as they increasingly "discredit their feelings and understandings, experiencing increased self-doubt" during early adolescence and subsequently becoming susceptible to a host of internalizing and externalizing disorders linked to poor self-esteem (Potter, 2004, p. 60). A number of studies and theories attempt to explain this shift in girls' self-image and mental health as they transition to adolescence (see Pipher, 1994; R. Simmons, 2003), but Potter cautions against overgeneralization of the phenomenon and in particular suggests that the trend may not apply widely across girls from differing ethnic groups, socioeconomic statuses, and sexual orientations.

During middle childhood, often boys' identification with "masculine" role attributes increases while girls' identification with "feminine" role attributes decreases (Archer, 1992; G. D. Levy, Taylor, & Gelman, 1995; Potter, 2004). For instance, boys are more likely than girls to label a chore as a "girl's job" or a "boy's job." As adults, females are the more androgynous of the two genders, and this movement toward androgyny appears to begin in middle childhood (L. M. Diamond & Savin-Williams, 2003; Serbin, Powlishta, & Gulko, 1993).

These differences have multiple causes, from social to cognitive forces. In the United States, during middle childhood and beyond, cross-gender behavior in girls is more socially acceptable than such behavior among boys. Lisa M. Diamond and Ritch Savin-Williams (2003) use the term "gender typicality," or the "degree to which one's appearance, behavior, interests, and subjective self-concept conform to conventional gender norms" (p. 105). Research to date suggests that for both genders, a traditionally "masculine" identity is associated with a higher sense of overall competence and better academic performance (Boldizar, 1991; Newcomb & Dubas, 1992). Diamond and Savin-Williams also emphasize the role of culture in this relationship, pointing out that this is likely due to the fact that

traits associated with male, or for girls, "tomboy" status are those traits most valued in many communities. These traits include qualities such as athleticism, confidence, and assertiveness. Indeed, local communities with "more entrenched sexist ideologies" regarding male versus female traits are those in which boys exhibiting feminine or "sissy" behaviors are likely to suffer (p. 107).

In general, due to expanding cognitive capacities, as children leave early childhood and progress through middle childhood, their gender stereotypes gradually become more flexible, and most school-age children begin to accept that males and females can engage in the same activities (D. B. Carter & Patterson, 1982; Sagara, 2000). The relationships among gender identity, gender stereotyping, and individual gender role adoption are not clear cut. Even children well aware of community gender norms and role expectations may not conform to gender role stereotypes in their actual behavior (L. M. Diamond & Savin-Williams, 2003; A. C. Downs & Langlois, 1988; Serbin et al., 1993). Perhaps children acquire personal gender role preferences before acquiring knowledge of gender role stereotypes, or perhaps they learn and interpret gender role stereotypes in very diverse ways. Our understanding of the complexities of gender and sexual identity development—and the relationships between the two during the life course—is in its infancy.

Spiritual Development

During the past few decades, interest in exploring the importance of spiritual development and spirituality across the life course has grown. Interdisciplinary study of spiritual development indicates that spirituality plays an important role in many if not most individuals' lives. Children are increasingly recognized as possessing awareness of spirituality and of utilizing that awareness to create meaning in their lives (B. Hyde, 2008a). Thus, spirituality in children is increasingly seen as an important dimension of development (Mercer, 2006). Early work on children's spiritual development viewed spirituality in the context of religious development (B. Hyde, 2008a). For instance, Robert Coles (1990) argued that religion and spirituality overlapped in children and that even children with no religious affiliation utilized religious language to describe their spiritual lives. It has been suggested that during this early work on the spiritual development of children, children's utilization of religious language to describe their spirituality simply mirrored the language of the researchers. Simply put, the researchers posed questions to the children in their studies utilizing religious terminology (B. Hyde, 2008a).

Subsequent research explored children's spirituality in the context of how it provided a way for children to conceptualize the meaning of life. Further, this research has examined how children's understanding of spirituality relates to an awareness of something greater at play in the course of everyday happenings (B. Hyde, 2008a). Researchers have explored the themes of transcendence and spirituality as human experience (Champagne, 2001; Hay & Nye, 2006). T. Hart (2006) argues that children's spirituality encompasses the dimensions of wonder, wisdom, and interconnectedness. He suggests that these aspects of spirituality provide a sense of hope and perspective, allow for reflection, and help shape morality. Despite the varying views regarding how children understand and utilize their spirituality, researchers agree that children in middle childhood (and younger) do have a spiritual life and that spirituality can be a protective factor in the lives of children.

Spiritual development in middle childhood has been described in a variety of ways. Some researchers have identified children in middle childhood as in the "mythic-literal" stage of spiritual development. The mythic-literal stage coincides with the cognitive and emotional developmental levels of children in middle childhood. According to Fowler and Dell (2006), children in the *mythic-literal stage* of spiritual development utilize storytelling to make sense of the world, "often along the lines of simple fairness and moral reciprocity . . . [t]he child believes that goodness is rewarded and badness is punished" (p. 39). This stage marks the beginning of ponderings and feelings about spirituality and

faith. A child at this stage of development may associate getting a physical illness like the stomach flu with having done something wrong, such as hitting a sibling.

However, children in middle childhood are also capable of going beyond a simple "good versus evil" conception of spirituality, "weave[ing] the threads of meaning" together to create a complex worldview that is meaningful to them (B. Hyde, 2008b, p. 244). For instance, when children are asked about heaven, they understand it in different ways; it has a unique meaning to each child. One interviewed child viewed heaven as "a thought. It's in your heart if you believe it's there" (B. Hyde, 2008b, p. 239). Another interviewed child thought of heaven as different for everyone based on the people, places, and things they loved or valued in life. This child explained heaven as unique, so "if a person liked painting, then they'd go to a place where you can paint all you want" (B. Hyde, 2008b, p. 239). It is apparent that children take an active role in constructing spiritual beliefs that help them make sense of their world (Mercer, 2006). Utilizing spirituality to create threads of meaning may help children cope with difficult environmental factors such as poverty, and may facilitate successful coping with challenges such as familial illness or death.

The spiritual education of children occurs in families, faith congregations/communities (e.g., churches, synagogues, mosques, temples), and schools. Families provide spiritual education in the form of family religious traditions and belief systems (Alexander & Carr, 2006). Faith congregations provide a community of members that share a common vision and tradition of spirituality as well as a space to express that spirituality (Alexander & Carr, 2006). In addition, many schools are returning to an emphasis on fostering spirituality in all of its manifestations. In secular democratic countries, the teaching of spirituality is fraught with concern regarding the separation of church and state. However, many school personnel believe it is possible that general cultivation of spirituality in schools, especially as it relates to the development of a life with meaning, purpose, and hope, as well as character development, could foster the development of caring children with a sense of interconnectedness.

Critical Thinking Questions 13.1

How would you describe the physical, cognitive, cultural identity, emotional, social, and spiritual development of Anthony Bryant, Brianna Shaw, and Manuel Vega? In what areas do they each show particular strengths? In what areas do they each show particular challenges? How could a social worker help each child to enhance development in areas where he or she is particularly challenged?

MIDDLE CHILDHOOD AND FORMAL SCHOOLING

Before discussing the role of formal schooling in the life of the school-age child in the United States and other relatively affluent societies, it is important to note that, in an era of a knowledge-based global economy, there continue to be large global gaps in opportunities for education. Although educational participation is almost universal between the age of 5 and 14 in affluent countries, 115 million of the world's children, most residing in Africa or South Asia, do not receive even a primary education and are particularly susceptible to economic downturns and environmental crises (United Nations Development Program, 2005; World Bank, 2009a). A widening gap exists in average years of education between rich and poor countries (McMichael, 2008). The average child born in Mozambique in 2005 will receive 4 years of formal education, compared with 8 years in South Asia and 15 years in France (United Nations Development Program, 2005). Females will receive 1 year less of education, on average, than males in African and Arab countries, and 2 years less in South Asia (United Nations Development Program, 2005). In sub-Saharan, Middle-Eastern/North African, and South Asian countries, primary school completion rates continue well below the United Nations' Millennium

Education goals (World Bank, 2009a). In addition, while females in most affluent industrialized countries receive higher levels of education than males, on average, females in the three mentioned geographical areas fall well below that of males (Sen et al., 2005).

The current importance of formal schooling during middle childhood in advanced industrial countries cannot be overstated. Children entering school must learn to navigate a new environment quite different from the family. In school, they are evaluated on the basis of how well they perform tasks; people outside the family—teachers and other school staff as well as peers—begin shaping the child's personality, dreams, and aspirations (Good & Nichols, 2001). For children like Manuel Vega, the environmental adjustment can be even more profound because the educational attainment of family members may be limited, and high-stakes tests place a premature burden on English-language learners (Solórzano, 2008). At the same time, the school environment has the potential to serve as an important resource for the physical, cognitive, emotional, social, and spiritual tasks of middle childhood for all children, regardless of the previous schooling available to their parents. This role for schools is particularly important to help immigrant children deal with the culture shock that many experience transitioning to their adoptive countries. In addition, schools must be aware of conditions prevalent among such children, such as traumatic stress associated with events that have occurred in their home countries or in transit to their new homes (Vaage, Garløv, Hauff, & Thomsen, 2007).

Success in the school environment is very important to the development of self-esteem. Anthony Bryant, Brianna Shaw, and Manuel Vega illustrate the potentially positive as well as painful aspects of schooling. Manuel and Brianna seem increasingly distressed by their interactions within the school environment. Often, difficulties with peers create or compound academic challenges. Brianna's school experience is becoming threatening enough that she may begin to withdraw from the environment, which would represent a serious risk to her continued cognitive, emotional, and social development.

As children move through the middle years, they become increasingly aware that they are evaluated on the basis of what they are able to do. In turn, they begin to evaluate themselves based on treatment by teachers and peers and on self-assessments of what they can and cannot do well (Skaalvik & Skaalvik, 2004). School-age children consistently rate parents, classmates, other friends, and teachers as the most important influences in their lives (Harter, 1988). Thus, children are likely to evaluate themselves in a positive manner if they receive encouraging feedback from these individuals in their academic and social environments.

Photo 13.3 As children get older, schools are the primary context for development in middle childhood.

Formal Schooling and Cognitive Development

In the past few decades, school-age children have benefited from new research and theory focusing on the concept of intelligence. Traditional views of intelligence and approaches to intelligence testing benefited European American children born in the United States. Howard Gardner's work, however, represented a paradigm shift in the field of education. He proposed that intelligence is neither unitary nor fixed, and argued that intelligence is not adequately or fully measured by IQ tests. More broadly, in his theory of multiple intelligences, intelligence is "the ability to solve problems or fashion products that are of consequence in a particular cultural setting or community" (Gardner, 1993, p. 15). Challenging the idea that individuals can be described, or categorized, by a single, quantifiable measure of intelligence, Gardner proposed that at least eight critical intelligences exist: verbal-linguistic, logical-mathematical, visual-spatial, musical-rhythmic, bodily-kinesthetic, naturalist, interpersonal, and intrapersonal (see Exhibit 4.2 for a description of these intelligences). This paradigm shift in the education field encouraged a culturally sensitive approach to students (L. Campbell, Campbell, & Dickinson, 1999) and a diminished role for standardized testing.

In its practical application, multiple intelligence theory calls for use of a wide range of instructional strategies that engage the range of strengths and intelligences of each student (S. Kagan & Kagan, 1998). Gardner (2006) specifically calls for matching instructional strategies to the needs and strengths of students, stretching the intelligences—or maximizing development of each intelligence—by transforming education curricula, and celebrating or (at a minimum) understanding the unique pattern of intelligences of each student.

> How might this increased emphasis on cognitive diversity alter the life course of students like Anthony, Brianna, and Manuel?

This last point is critical. Such understanding can facilitate self-knowledge and self-acceptance.

Understanding and celebration of cognitive diversity, Gardner believes, will come from a transformation not only of curricula, or instructional methods, but also of the fundamental way in which adults view students and students view themselves and one another. Schools help children develop a positive self-evaluation by providing a variety of activities that allow children with different strengths to succeed. For example, schools that assess children in many areas, including those described by Gardner, may help children who have a deficit in one area experience success in another realm. Children can also be encouraged to evaluate themselves positively through the creation of individual student portfolios and through school initiatives that promote new skill development. Classroom and extracurricular activities can build on children's abilities and interests and help them develop or maintain self-confidence (Barr & Parrett, 1995; Littky & Grabelle, 2004).

For example, most children benefit from diverse educational materials and varied activities that appeal to visual, auditory, and experiential learning styles. Such activities can include group work, student presentations, field trips, audiovisual presentations, written and oral skill activities, discussion, and lectures (Roueche & Baker, 1986). In recent years, *flexible grouping* is frequently employed. Grouping strategies include pairing students, forming cooperative and collaborative groups, modeling lessons for students, conducting guided practice, and setting up subject-based learning laboratories. A teacher may draw on any appropriate technique during a class period, day, or week. These approaches represent an attempt to adapt instruction to meet diverse student needs. Students such as Anthony Bryant, with more academic skill, may model effective methods of mastering academic material for less advanced students. Meanwhile, Anthony simultaneously learns more appropriate school behavior from his socially adept peers. Furthermore, this teaching method may help Anthony strengthen peer friendships—an important potential source of support as he confronts family transitions or conflict in the future.

Thus, in addition to calling for changes in instructional strategies, multiple intelligences theory calls for movement toward more comprehensive assessments of diverse areas of student performance. Such assessment includes naturalistic, across-time observation and development of self-appraisal materials such as student portfolios. This call, however, has occurred in tandem with the standards movement within the United States. Most U.S. schools and states have moved away from norm-referenced testing and toward *criterion-referenced testing*, which requires all graduating students to meet certain absolute scores and requirements. At present, all states have established some form of learning standards that all students must achieve in order to graduate from high school.

Formal Schooling and Diversity

Students such as Manuel Vega face considerable challenges in the school setting. Manuel's ability to engage in the school environment is compromised, and many schools are ill-equipped to respond to the issues confronting children like him. If Manuel is not supported and assisted by his school system, his educational experience may assault his healthy development. But if Manuel's personal and familial support systems can be tapped and mobilized, they may help him overcome his feelings of isolation in his new school environment. Carefully constructed and implemented interventions must be used to help Manuel. These interventions could include a focus on bridging the gap between his command of the rules of the informal register of English and the acquisition of formal Standard English, without destroying his Spanish language base and his Mexican cultural heritage.

Today in the United States, Manuel's situation is not rare. About 1 in 4 elementary and high school students have at least one foreign-born parent (U.S. Department of Health and Human Services, 2009b), and, in general, students are more diverse than ever before. Many challenges face children who have recently arrived in the United States, particularly those fleeing war-torn countries. Research suggests that immigrant and refugee children are at heightened risk of experiencing mental health challenges and school failure (Coughlan & Owens-Manley, 2006; Vaage et al., 2007).

Language difficulties and their consequences among such children are increasingly recognized. It has been established that children are best served when they are able to speak both their native language and the language of their host country (Moon, Kang, & An, 2008; Vuorenkoski, Kuure, Moilanen, Penninkilampi, & Myhrman, 2000). Indeed, a growing body of research indicates that learning to read in one's primary language helps a student to become more fluent in English (Watanabe, 2011). The mental health status among immigrant populations, however, appears to be dependent on a wide number of factors.

In general, *acculturation,* or a process by which two or more cultures remain distinct but exchange cultural features (such as foods, music, clothing), is easier on children than *assimilation,* or a process by which the minority culture must adapt and become incorporated into the majority culture, particularly in the school environment. Communication and interaction between families and schools is always important (Bhattacharya, 2000; U.S. Department of Health and Human Services, 2000b).

It is essential for schools and professionals to recognize the importance of language to learning. Children acquire an informal language that contains the communication rules needed to survive in the familial and cultural group to which the child belongs. Schools often ignore the potency of these informal registers as they work toward their mission of teaching the "formal register" of the dominant middle class, deemed necessary to survive in the world of work and school. The need for specific strategies to acknowledge and honor the "informal register," while teaching the formal, has been identified by several literacy researchers (see Gee, 1996; Knapp, 1995). These researchers emphasize the importance of teaching children to recognize their internal, or natural, "speech" and the "register" they use in the school environment. Identifying and mediating these processes is best accomplished in the context of a caring relationship (Noddings, 1984). By sensitively promoting an awareness of

such differences in the home and school, teachers, social workers, and other adults can help children experience less confusion and alienation.

Formal Schooling: Home and School

Indeed, parental involvement in school is associated with better school performance (Domina, 2005). Schools serving diverse populations are becoming increasingly creative in their approaches to encouraging parent involvement, including the development of sophisticated interpretation and translation infrastructures (Pardington, 2002). Unfortunately, many schools lag behind, suffering from either inadequate resources or the consequences of exclusive and racist attitudes within the school and larger community environments (see R. Jones, 2001).

The link between school and home is important in poor and affluent neighborhoods alike, because school and home are the two major spheres in which children exist. The more similar these two environments are, the more successful the child will be at school and at home. Students who experience vastly different cultures at home and at school are likely to have difficulty accommodating the two worlds (B. A. Ryan & Adams, 1995). A great deal of learning goes on before a child enters school. By the time Anthony Bryant, Brianna Shaw, and Manuel Vega began school, they had acquired routines; habits; and cognitive, social, emotional, and physical styles and skills (Kellaghan, Sloane, Alvarez, & Bloom, 1993). School is a "next step" in the educational process.

The transition is relatively easy for many students because schools typically present a mainstream model for behavior and learning. As most parents interact with their children, they model and promote the behavior that will be acceptable in school. Children from such backgrounds are often well prepared for the school environment because, quite simply, they understand the rules; as a result, the school is accepting of them (R. K. Payne, 2005). Furthermore, the school environment helps reinforce rules and skills taught in the home environment, just as the home environment helps reinforce rules and skills taught in the school environment. Research indicates that this type of home–school continuity often predicts school success (Ameta & Sherrard, 1995; Comer, 1994; J. L. Epstein & Lee, 1995; Kellaghan et al., 1993; B. A. Ryan & Adams, 1995).

In contrast, children with a distinctive background may not be fluent in mainstream speech patterns and may not have been extensively exposed to school rules or materials such as scissors and books. These children, although possessing skills and curiosity, are often viewed as inferior in some way by school personnel (Comer, 1994; Solórzano, 2008). Children viewed in this manner may begin to feel inferior and either act out or disengage from the school process (Finn, 1989). Because the school environment does not support the home environment and the home environment does not support the school environment, these children face an increased risk of poor school outcomes.

Schools that recognize the contribution of home-to-school success typically seek family involvement. Parents and other family members can help establish the motivation for learning and provide learning opportunities within the home environment (Constable & Walberg, 1996; R. Jones, 2001). Children whose parents are involved in their education typically succeed academically (Fan, 2001; Fan & Chen, 2001; Houtenville & Conway, 2008; Zellman & Waterman, 1998). Unfortunately, poor communication among parents, children, and schools may short-circuit parental involvement. Traditionally, schools asked parents only to participate in Parent Teacher Association meetings, to attend parent–teacher meetings, to act as helpers in the classroom, and to review notes and written communications sent home with the schoolchild. This sort of parental participation does not always facilitate meaningful, open communication. Schools can establish more meaningful relationships with parents by reaching out to them, involving them as partners in decision making and school governance, treating parents and other caregivers (and their children) with authentic respect, providing support and coordination to implement

and sustain parental involvement, and connecting parents with resources (see Dupper & Poertner, 1997; Patrikakou, Weisberg, Redding, & Walberg, 2005; Swap, 1993).

Formal Schooling: Schools Mirror Community

As microcosms of the larger U.S. society, schools mirror its institutional structures. Thus, schools often uphold racism, classism, and sexism (Bowles & Gintis, 1976; Harry, 2006; P. Keating, 1994; Ogbu, 1994). As discussed, cognitive development can be impacted by cultural factors specific to second-language usage and gender socialization as well as racial and class identities. Students belonging to nondominant groups have often been viewed as inherently less capable and thus failed to receive the cognitive stimulation needed for optimal growth and development. This problem has led to lowered expectations, segregation, and institutionalized mistreatment throughout the history of schooling. At the federal and state levels, from the mid-1960s through 1980, specific legislation was developed to attempt to rectify the effects of the unequal treatment of a variety of groups.

> How do racism, classism, and sexism affect middle childhood development?

In most parts of the country, however, members of historically mistreated groups (e.g., children with mental and physical challenges, children belonging to ethnic and racial minority groups) did not receive equal treatment, and they were forced to attend segregated and inferior schools throughout most of the 20th century. Over time, various court rulings, most prominently the 1954 *Brown v. Board of Education* decision (347 U.S. 483), made equal, integrated education the right of all U.S. citizens, ruling that "separate but equal" has no place in public education. However, in the past 15 years, courts at both the state and federal levels have been lifting desegregation orders, arguing that separate *can* be equal or at least "good enough." As a result, today the school systems in the United States are more segregated by race than they were 30 years ago

(Boger & Orfield, 2005; Kozol, 2005). These court rulings as well as housing patterns and social traditions work against integrated public schooling. Schools continue to mirror the social systems with which they interact and thus often fall short of their democratic ideals (Darling-Hammond, 2007). Informal segregation often persists in schools, and poor children still suffer in schools that frequently do not provide enough books, supplies, teachers, or curricula challenging enough to facilitate success in U.S. society. That has led to the achievement gap between historically underrepresented groups and the more advantaged. Gloria Ladson-Billings (2006), in her presidential address to the 2006 American Educational Research Association, identified a major cause of the gap as the nation's *education debt* for our current and past educational and political policies toward these groups of students (see also Kozol, 1991, 2005).

The juxtaposition of inner-city, rural, and suburban schools continues to point to substantial divisions between economically rich and impoverished communities. For example, although less well documented, a consistent difficulty for rural schools throughout much of the world is access to a consistent supply of teachers, especially in math and science. Many countries in the developing world offer a range of incentives to attract teachers in subject shortage areas (Ladd, 2007). Chronic teacher shortages inhibit rural children from receiving access to consistent high-quality teaching. In the United States, the challenges of rural education are compounded by the historical inability of American educational practice to provide consistent educational expertise and resources in low-wealth school districts. Often set in communities with agricultural economies, rural schools struggle to meet the language needs of migrant populations (K. Gutiérrez, 2008), overcome the legacy of historical and reconstituted segregated schooling in many southern states (Ladson-Billings, 2004), and to compensate for the isolation of remote Indigenous populations throughout the Native American reservation lands of the West. They also struggle to overcome the effects of rural poverty, which has stayed close to

20% for several decades and has remained 5% more than the percentage for urban children in poverty since the late 1990s (O'Hare, 2009). Lack of access to high-quality schooling and health care combined with high poverty rates make rural children particularly vulnerable to reduced opportunity.

During all phases of childhood, children benefit from equal treatment and attention, and they suffer when **institutional discrimination**—the systemic denial of access to assets, economic opportunities, associations, and organizations based on minority status—is in place. Indeed, even when African American and poor children, and children from predominantly Spanish-speaking populations, were integrated into public school systems in the 20th century, the process of *tracking* students assured that the vast majority of students of color and low socioeconomic status (SES) were relegated to less rigorous course sequences (Oakes, 1985; Owens, 1985). In addition, such division of students has often been based on standardized tests, which research suggests may be culturally and class biased. Students have also been divided based on school personnel reports. Such reports are often subjective and may inadvertently be based on assessments of students' dress, language, and behavior (Oakes, 1985; Oakes & Lipton, 1992). Throughout the history of public schooling, most teachers and other school staff have belonged to dominant groups, and consciously or unconsciously, they may have awarded privilege and preference to learning styles, language, and dress that they found familiar.

In short, after desegregation, tracking has traditionally served as a two-tiered system of ongoing educational inequality. Although it is necessary to understand the complexities of tracking, including both advantages and disadvantages (see Brunello & Checchi, 2007; Loveless, 1999; M. Wang, Walberg, & Reynolds, 2004), it is equally important to recognize that special education, non–college-bound, and non-accelerated classes have been disproportionately populated by historically excluded students. These classes too often prepared

> What impact have these historical trends in public education had on middle childhood development?

students to work only in low-skilled, low-paying jobs. Conversely, regular education, college-bound, and accelerated classes have been disproportionately White and middle or upper class. These classes typically prepare their members for college and leadership roles. Thus, the traditional structure of public education often both reflected and supported ethnic and class divisions within U.S. society (Kozol, 2005; Oakes & Lipton, 1992; Winters, 1993).

For an example of the dangers of tracking, consider Anthony Bryant. His behavior puts him at risk for eventual placement in specialized classes for emotionally disturbed children, even though his behavior may be a normal part of his developmental process (Hosp & Reschly, 2003). Currently, his fairly infrequent aggressive behavior seems to be dealt with by school personnel appropriately, which may prevent an escalation of the problem. Intervention with Anthony's family members may also facilitate a consistent, positive family response to Anthony's behavior. However, the professionals making decisions at Anthony's school and in his community could begin to interpret his behavior as serious and threatening. Thus, Anthony faces an increased risk of placement outside the "regular" track. What could follow, through a series of steps intended by the school system to provide special programming for Anthony, is his miseducation based on a set of faulty cultural lenses that diagnose his needs and prescribe deficient remedies. The potential miseducation of Anthony is compounded by social patterns that have persisted for years and work against the success of African American males and immigrant youth in particular.

Many school systems have now recognized their historically unequal treatment of students and taken steps to reduce discrimination. One approach is *mainstreaming,* or *inclusion,* the practice of placing all children who could be assigned to special education classrooms into regular education classrooms (Connor, Gabel, Gallagher, & Morton, 2008; Sleeter, 1995). An increasingly common and innovative approach in the disability arena is the *collaborative classroom.* Children with and without disabilities are team-taught by both a "regular" and a "special" education teacher. Heterogeneous grouping helps

prevent students of different races, socioeconomic classes, and genders from being separated and treated unequally. Different approaches to teaching academic content are used in hopes of accommodating a variety of learning styles and social backgrounds. Teachers, students, and other school personnel receive training on diversity. In addition, sexual harassment policies have slowly been implemented and enforced in public schools. The policies are enforced by the requirement that all schools receiving federal funds designate a Title IX hearing officer to inquire about and, if warranted, respond to all allegations of harassment in its many forms.

Schools have also begun to include, in their curricula, content that reflects the diversity of their students. As the topic of diversity has become prominent in academic and popular discourse, educational materials are increasingly likely to include the perspectives of traditionally nondominant groups. As a result, more literature and history lessons represent females and minorities who have contributed to U.S. life.

In the last decade, clear and consistent educational research in the fields of literacy education and educational theory has also begun to detail effective instructional strategies and methodological approaches. Implementation of such research findings has disrupted the "stand and deliver," or lecture, format as the dominant approach to teaching and knowledge acquisition.

Schools located in areas with high rates of poverty have also been targeted for extra attention. *Full-service schools* attempt to provide school-based or school-linked health and social services for schoolchildren and their families (Dryfoos, 1994; Rubenstein, 2008). Similarly, school-based family resource centers attempt to provide children, families, and communities with needed supports (L. Adler, 1993; M. Smith & Brun, 2006). Such provision of holistic family services illustrates public education's continuing effort to meet the ideal of equal and comprehensive education, allowing all U.S. children equal opportunity to achieve economic and social success.

In addition, the U.S. Department of Education launched a major initiative to close the achievement gap of historically excluded populations with the passage by Congress of the No Child Left Behind Act of 2001 (NCLB) as an extension of the Elementary and Secondary Education Act. Increasingly, schools have been refocused on English language arts and math skill development training by the national standards movement, as advanced by the requirements of NCLB and its accountability arm, but to the potential detriment of educating the whole child (Guisbond & Neill, 2004).

NCLB shifted federal focus to school and teacher accountability for higher achievement, which is monitored by annual "high stakes" tests. All children must take such standardized assessments, and schools are required to disaggregate their results for each of five subpopulations, including gender; students with disabilities; limited English proficiency; low socioeconomic status; as well as students who are Black, Hispanic, American Indian/Alaska Native, Asian/Pacific Islander, or White. Under the provisions of the law, school districts must meet adequate yearly progress (AYP) goals for both aggregated and disaggregated data sets. Districts failing to meet such goals face consequences ranging from providing extra funding for parents to acquire support services to having a school closed down for consistently missing AYP targets. As a result, educational research has been given higher status to influence educational policy than it has received in the past.

This push for educational accountability and its impact on the lives of children are complex and highly controversial. The application of the NCLB standards spurred a number of organizations and states (e.g., the National Educational Association, Michigan, Connecticut, and Utah) to either sue the federal government or sharply criticize the act for raising state achievement requirements without adequate supporting funds or as a violation of states' rights.

Nonetheless, many schools have adopted innovative practices designed to raise achievement of basic skills while attempting to meet the educational needs of all students (Sherer, 2009). However, only 10 reform programs received the highest grade (defined as moderate or limited success) by the Comprehensive School Reform Quality Center and American Institutes for Research (2006) in their federally funded 3-year study of school reform programs. Two initiatives examined within this study serve as prime examples of the variety of philosophies that drive such schools. The Knowledge Is Power Program (KIPP) follows a prescription that demands that its students strictly adhere to a regimen of social behavior development coupled with long hours dedicated to mastering content-based curricula (S. Carter, 2000). Conversely, Expeditionary Learning Schools (a consortium of 140 schools) immerse their students in problem-based learning that is linked to authentic experiences often consummated outside the walls of the school (E. Cousins, 2000; S. Levy, 2000). As this report suggests, most schools are struggling to balance a number of competing demands while meeting the standards of NCLB. Evidence regarding the effectiveness of NCLB was to be examined during congressional hearings in 2007, when the act was up for reauthorization. In 2009, the Obama administration laid out an ambitious plan to provide the financial backing to carry out several new initiatives, as well as to encourage innovative ways to meet the goals of NCLB. Money was allocated as part of the stimulus funding process to reverse the underfunding trends of the George W. Bush administration (Obama, 2009), and optimistic idea generation began anew. But, since the recession that began in 2007, states have been slashing their education budgets as part of an overall attempt to manage budget crises.

Critical Thinking Questions 13.2

Think about your own middle childhood years, between the ages of 6 and 12. What are some examples of school experiences that helped you to feel competent and confident? What are school experiences that led you to feel incompetent and inferior? What biological, family, cultural, and other environmental factors lead to success and failure in school?

SPECIAL CHALLENGES IN MIDDLE CHILDHOOD _____

In the last several decades in the United States, family structures have become more diverse than ever (Amato, 2003; Fields, 2004; Parke, 2003). The percentage of children living with both parents has steadily declined during the last four to five decades. According to the U.S. Census Bureau data, in 2007, an estimated 67.8% of children lived with married parents, 2.9% lived with two unmarried parents, 25.8% lived with one parent, and 3.5% lived with no parent present (Kreider & Elliott, 2009).

Social and economic trends have placed more parents of young children into the workforce in order to make ends meet. Legislation requires single parents who receive public assistance to remain engaged in or to reenter the workforce (Parham, Quadagno, & Brown, 2009). The school day often does not coincide with parents' work schedules, and recent research suggests that as a result of parental employment, more than half of school-age children regularly need additional forms of supervision when school is not in session. Most of these children either participate in a before- or after-school program (also known as wraparound programs) or receive care from a relative (Lerner, Castellino, Lolli, & Wan, 2003). Many low- and middle-income families struggle to find affordable child care and often are forced to sacrifice quality child care for economic reasons (National Association of Child Care Resource and Referral Agencies, 2006; Wertheimer, 2003).

Unfortunately, available data suggest that the quality of child care experienced by the average child in the United States is less than ideal (Helburn & Bergmann, 2002; Vandell & Wolfe, 2000). This fact is particularly troubling because child care quality has been linked to children's physical health as well as cognitive, emotional, and social development (Tout & Zaslow, 2003; Vandell & Wolfe, 2000). These findings apply not only to early childhood programs, but also to before- and after-school programs for older children. Moreover, as children move from the early (ages 5 to 9) to later (10 to 12) middle childhood years, they are increasingly likely to take care of themselves during the before- and after-school hours (Lerner et al., 2003). Regular participation in a high-quality before- and after-school program is positively associated with academic performance, and a significant body of research suggests that how school-age children spend their after-school hours is strongly associated with the likelihood of engaging in risky behaviors (Lerner et al., 2003).

Inadequate and low-quality child care is just one of the challenges facing school-age children—along with their families and communities—in the 21st century. Other challenges include poverty, family and community violence, mental and physical challenges, and family disruption.

Poverty

A growing international consensus indicates that poverty is the most significant human rights challenge facing the world community (Grinspun, 2004). Indeed, foremost among threats to children's healthy development is poverty, which potentially threatens positive development in all domains (Duncan, Kalil, & Ziol-Guest, 2008; D. Gordon, Nandy, Pantazis, Pemberton, & Townsend, 2003; Harper, 2004; United Nations Children's Fund, 2000a, 2000b; Vandivere, Moore, & Brown, 2000). Unfortunately, it is estimated that half of the children of the world live in poverty, many in extreme poverty (Bellamy, 2004). That children should be protected from poverty is not disputed; in the United States, this societal value dates back to the colonial period (Trattner, 1998). The nature of policies and programs targeted at ensuring the minimal daily needs of children are met, however, has shifted over time, as has our success in meeting this goal (Chase-Lansdale & Vinovskis, 1995; United Nations Children's Fund, 2000a).

In the United States, the late 20th century brought a dramatic rise in the child poverty rate, which peaked in the early 1990s, declined for approximately a decade, and has gradually increased again during the first several years of

> How does poverty serve as a risk factor in middle childhood?

the 21st century (Koball & Douglas-Hall, 2006). In 2007, the national poverty rate for the population as a whole was approximately 12.5%, and approximately 18% of the children lived in poverty. In other words, approximately 1 in 5 children live in a family with an income below the federal poverty level (National Center for Children in Poverty, 2008).

As illustrated in Exhibit 13.3, children in the middle childhood age range are less likely to live in low-income or poor families than their younger counterparts, and this trend continues as children grow toward adulthood. Caucasian children comprise the majority of poor children in the United States. Young children and children from minority groups, however, are statistically overrepresented among the population of poor children (Linver, Fuligni, Hernandez, & Brooks-Gunn, 2004; National Center for Children in Poverty, 2008). This is a persistent contemporary trend; in other words, although in absolute numbers, Caucasian children consistently compose the majority of

poor children, children from Latino and African American families are consistently significantly overrepresented among all children in poverty. Currently, the percentage of African American (61%) or Latino (62%) children living in low-income families is twice as high as the percentage of Caucasian (27%) children (National Center for Children in Poverty, 2008; Linver et al., 2004; Wight & Chau, 2009a). The child poverty rates for different racial and ethnic groups in 2008 are presented in Exhibit 13.4.

In general, the risk factors associated with child poverty are numerous, especially when poverty is sustained. Children who grow up in poverty are more likely to be born with low birth weight, to experience serious and chronic health problems, to receive poorer health care and nutrition, to be homeless or live in substandard and overcrowded housing, to live in violent communities, and to experience family turmoil than children who grow up in better financial circumstances (G. W. Evans

Exhibit 13.3 Children Living in Low-Income and Poor Families by Age, 2008

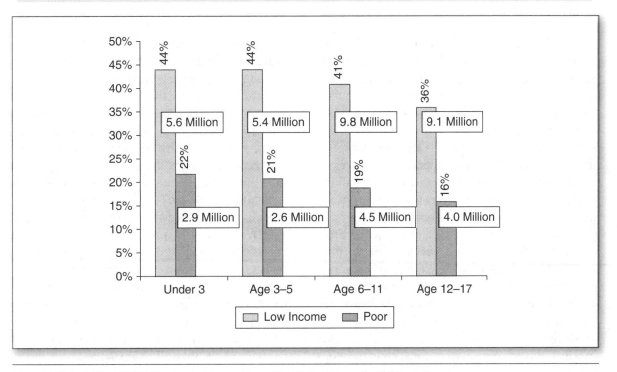

SOURCE: Wight & Chau (2009a). Reprinted with permission of the National Center for Children in Poverty.

Exhibit 13.4   Child Poverty Rates by Race/Ethnicity, 2008

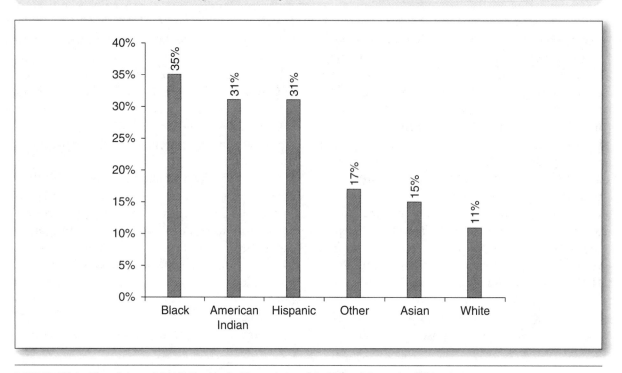

SOURCE: Wight, Chau, & Aratani (2010). Reprinted with permission of the National Center for Children in Poverty.

& English, 2002; Linver et al., 2004; United Nations Children's Fund, 2000b). Homeless children represent a small percentage of all children living in poverty and yet it is estimated that over 1 million children experience homelessness in the United States each year (Varney & van Vliet, 2008).

A number of perspectives attempt to explain the ways in which poverty impacts child development. Limited income constrains a family's ability to obtain or invest in resources that promote positive development. Poverty detrimentally impacts caregivers' emotional health and parenting practices. Individual poverty is correlated with inadequate family, school, and neighborhood resources and, thus, children experiencing family poverty are likely experiencing additional, cumulative risk factors. Each of these perspectives is valid and sheds light on the complex and synergistic ways in which poverty threatens optimal child development (Linver et al., 2004).

Children who have spent any part of their prenatal period, infancy, or early childhood in poverty have often already encountered several developmental challenges by the time middle childhood begins. Children who enter, progress through, and leave middle childhood in poverty are at much greater risk of negative developmental outcomes than those who briefly enter and then exit poverty while still in middle childhood (K. A. Moore, Redd, Burkhauser, Mbwana, & Collins, 2009).

Evidence suggests that persistent and "deep," or extreme, poverty poses the most significant threat to healthy child development (Linver et al., 2004; United Nations Children's Fund, 2000a). For example, extreme family poverty is correlated with homelessness, and poverty and homelessness combined increase a child's risk of abrupt family separation and experiencing or witnessing forms of trauma such as physical or sexual assault (Bassuk & Friedman, 2005).

But what does it actually mean, to a child, to be poor? Being poor is a relative concept, the meaning of which is defined by perceptions of and real exclusion (Dinitto & Cummins, 2006; Kozol, 2005). In most communities, one must be *not* poor in order to be fully engaged and included. Lack of income and certain goods deprive poor people of what is expected among those who belong; thus, poverty results in perceived and real inabilities and inadequacies. For example, children often participate in extracurricular activities such as sports, music, or art. These programs often involve registration, program, and equipment fees that are prohibitive to impoverished families. This is the essence of **relative poverty,** or the tendency to define one's poverty status in relation to others within one's social environment. Fundamentally, then, poverty is as much a social as an economic phenomenon. The social aspect of poverty has been extended by R. K. Payne (2005) to include emotional, spiritual, and support system impoverishment in addition to economic poverty. Such deficits in the developing child's background accumulate and result in impediments to the development of critical capacities including coping strategies. Unfortunately, income disparity—or the gap between the rich and the poor—has only continued to widen in recent years, both within and across countries around the globe (United Nations Children's Fund, 2000b, 2009).

The meaning of relative poverty for the school-age child is particularly profound. As evidence, James Garbarino (1995) points to an innocent question once asked of him by a child: "When you were growing up, were you poor or regular?" (p. 137). As the child struggles with the normal developmental tasks of feeling included and socially competent, relative poverty sends a persistent message of social exclusion and incompetence.

Family and Community Violence

Children are increasingly witness or subject to violence in their homes, schools, and neighborhoods (Hutchison, 2007). Although child maltreatment and domestic violence have always existed, they have been recognized as social problems only recently. Community violence is slowly becoming recognized as a social problem of equal magnitude, affecting a tremendous number of children and families. Exposure to violence is a particular problem in areas where a lack of economic and social resources already produces significant challenges for children (Maluccio, 2006). Among children from war-torn countries, the atrocities witnessed or experienced are often unimaginable to children and adults who have resided in the United States all of their lives (Office of the Special Representative of the Secretary-General for Children and Armed Conflict [OSRSG-CAAC] & United Nations Children's Fund, 2009).

> What protective factors can buffer the effects of neighborhood violence on school-age children?

Witnessing violence deeply affects children, particularly when the perpetrator or victim of violence is a family member. In the United States, experts estimate that anywhere between 3 and 10 million children may be impacted each year, but no consistent, valid data source exists regarding children witnessing or otherwise exposed to domestic violence (Children's Defense Fund, 2000; Fantuzzo, Mohr, & Noone, 2000).

In the United States, children appear most susceptible to nonfatal physical abuse between the ages of 6 and 12. Some speculate that in the United States, at least, this association may be due to increased likelihood of public detection of violence through school contact during these years. The number of children reported to child protective services (CPS) agencies annually is staggering. In 2007, an estimated 3.2 million referrals or reports (involving approximately 5.8 million children) were made to CPS agencies. An estimated 794,000 children were determined to be victims of at least one type of abuse or neglect, with neglect accounting for approximately 60% of confirmed maltreatment cases in 2007 (U.S. Department of Health and Human Services, 2009a). Child neglect is consistently the most common form of documented maltreatment of children, but it is important to note that victims typically experience more than one type of abuse or neglect simultaneously and therefore are appropriately included in more than one category. Maltreatment subtype trends are relatively stable over time; victims of child neglect consistently account for more than half of all child maltreatment victims (see Exhibit 13.5).

African American and Native American children are consistently overrepresented among confirmed maltreatment victims. Careful examination of this issue, however, has concluded that although children of color are disproportionately represented within the child welfare population, studies that are cognizant of the relationship between culture and parenting practices, that control for the role of poverty, and that examine child maltreatment in the general population find no association between a child's race or ethnicity and likelihood of maltreatment. Thus, it is likely that the disproportionate representation of children of color within the child welfare system is caused by the underlying relationship between poverty and race or ethnicity (Thomlison, 2004).

A variety of factors contribute to child maltreatment and family violence (Charlesworth, 2007; S. Choi & Tittle, 2002; Freisthler, Merritt, & LaScala, 2006). These factors include parental, child, family, community, and cultural characteristics. Typically, the dynamic interplay of such characteristics leads to maltreatment, with the most relevant factors varying significantly depending upon the type of maltreatment examined. Thus, multiple theoretical perspectives, particularly the life course, ecological, systems, and stress and coping perspectives, are helpful for understanding situations of child maltreatment.

Not surprisingly, children who experience abuse have been found to report more unhappiness and troubled behavior than children who only witness abuse (Maschi, Morgen, Hatcher, Rosato, & Violette, 2009). Witnesses, in turn, report more adjustment difficulties than children who have neither been abused nor witnessed domestic violence. Because of the strong association between domestic

Exhibit 13.5   Child Maltreatment Victims by Maltreatment Type, 2007

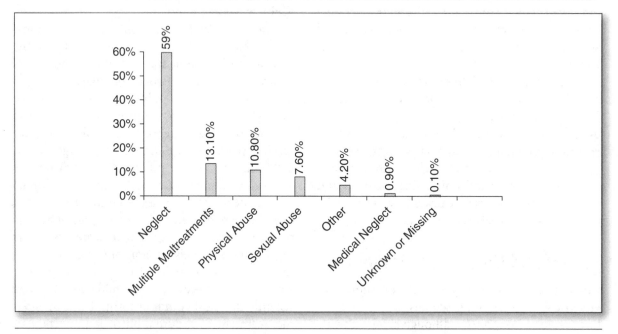

SOURCE: U.S. Department of Health & Human Services, 2009a.

NOTE: The "Unknown or Missing" category includes cases for which the type of abuse was not recorded.

violence and child maltreatment, however, many children are likely to experience these challenges to healthy development simultaneously (Crozier & Barth, 2005; V. Lee & Hoaken, 2007).

The impact of child maltreatment varies based on a number of factors including, but certainly not limited to, the type of maltreatment; the age of the child; and many other child, family, and community characteristics. The Centers for Disease Control and Prevention (CDC) National Center for Injury Prevention and Control (2010) has published a helpful overview of child maltreatment consequences, pointing out that experiencing maltreatment as a child is associated with an overwhelming number of negative health outcomes as an adult. These outcomes include an increased likelihood of using or abusing alcohol and other substances, disordered eating, depression, and susceptibility to certain chronic diseases.

Children who experience trauma, induced by either indirect or direct exposure to violence, may experience *post-traumatic stress disorder* (PTSD)—a set of symptoms that include feelings of fear and helplessness, reliving of the traumatic experience, and attempts to avoid reminders of the traumatic experience (Balaban, 2008; Farkas, 2004; Farmer, 2009). Researchers have also found changes in the brain chemistry of children exposed to chronic violence (Kowalik, 2004; J. Perry, 2006). Clearly, witnessing or experiencing violence adversely affects children in a number of areas, including the ability to function in school and the ability to establish stable social, including peer, relationships (Guterman & Embry, 2004). Children who directly experience violence are at high risk of negative outcomes, but secondary exposure to violence and trauma—such as when a child's parents are suffering from PTSD—also may lead to negative outcomes for children (Hamblen, 2002). In general, the intergenerational nature of family violence has been established (Herrenkohl et al., 2004). Childhood exposure to violence significantly increases the likelihood of mental health difficulties and violence perpetration or revictimization. Currently, the focus is on understanding the specific pathways of intergenerational processes (Coid et al., 2001; Heyman & Smith Slep, 2002;

Lang, Stein, Kennedy, & Foy, 2004). It is clear that prolonged exposure to violence has multiple implications for child development. Children are forced to learn lessons about loss and death, perhaps before they have acquired the cognitive ability to understand. They may therefore come to believe that the world is unpredictable and violent, a belief that threatens children's natural curiosity and desire to explore the social environment. Multiple experiences in which adults are unable to protect them often lead children to conclude that they must take on such responsibility for themselves, a prospect that can easily overwhelm the resources of a school-age child.

Experiencing such helplessness may also lead to feelings of incompetence and hopelessness, to which children who experience chronic violence react in diverse ways. Responses may be passive, including withdrawal symptoms and signs of depression, or they may be active, including the use of aggression as a means of coping with and transforming the overwhelming feelings of vulnerability (Charlesworth, 2007).

The emotional availability of a parent or other caretaker who can support the child's need to process traumatic events is critical. However, in situations of crisis stimulated by child maltreatment, domestic violence, and national or international violence, families are often unable to support their children psychologically. Even with the best of parental resources, moreover, children growing up in violent and chronically dangerous communities continue to experience numerous challenges to development. The child's need for autonomy and independence is directly confronted by the parent's need to protect the child's physical safety. For example, hours spent indoors to avoid danger do not promote the much-needed peer relationships and sense of accomplishment, purpose, and self-efficacy so critical during this phase of development (Hutchison, 2007).

Mental and Physical Challenges

Although the term "disability" is still widely used in academic discourse and government policy, many are actively seeking to change popular discourse to reflect the need to see all children as possessing a range of physical and mental abilities. The use of the term *disability* establishes a norm within that range and labels those with abilities outside the norm as "disabled," which implies that this group of individuals is "abnormal" and the group of individuals within the norm is "normal." In 2005, government data suggested that 6.7% of 5- to 20-year-olds, 12.7% of 21- to 64-year-olds, and 40.5% of those people 65 and older in the United States have some form of mental or physical "disability" (U.S. Census Bureau, 2005). Such a label, however, confines "normal" and "abnormal" to fixed categories that are not helpful to realizing a vision of a just and equal society. Slightly more than 1 in 10 children in the United States has difficulty performing one or more everyday activities, including, for example, learning and self-care (Emmons, 2005; Hauser-Cram & Howell, 2003). Some of these difficulties are discussed below.

Attention Deficit/Hyperactivity Disorder (ADHD)

ADHD is a commonly diagnosed childhood behavioral disorder impacting learning in the school environment. ADHD includes predominantly inattentive, predominantly impulsive-hyperactive, and combined inattentive-hyperactive forms of the disorder (American Psychiatric Association, 2000). Estimates of the prevalence of ADHD among school-age children range from 3% to 12%, with the highest incidence of ADHD diagnosis occurring between ages 5 and 10; compared with girls, boys are significantly more likely to receive a diagnosis of ADHD (Schneider & Eisenberg, 2006; Strock, 2006). ADHD is associated with school failure or academic underachievement, but the relationship is complex, in part due to the strong relationship between ADHD and a number of other factors also associated with school difficulties (Barry, Lyman, & Klinger, 2002; LeFever, Villers, Morrow, & Vaughn, 2002; Schneider & Eisenberg, 2006). Also, several studies suggest that the interpretation and evaluation of ADHD behaviors are significantly influenced by culturally linked beliefs (Glass & Wegar, 2000;

Kakouros, Maniadaki, & Papaeliou, 2004). In other words, the extent to which ADHD-linked behaviors are perceived as problematic varies according to individual and group values and norms.

Autistic Spectrum Disorders

In recent years, growing public attention and concern has focused upon autistic spectrum disorders. Among children ages 3 to 10, just over 3 per 1,000 children are diagnosed with autistic spectrum disorders; compared with girls, boys are 3 times as likely to receive such a diagnosis (Strock, 2004). Autism typically manifests and is diagnosed within the first 2 years of life; however, some children may not receive formal assessment or diagnosis until their early or middle childhood years. Like children with any special need or disability, children diagnosed with autistic spectrum disorders are extremely diverse; in particular, such children vary widely in terms of their intellectual and communicative abilities as well as the nature and severity of behavioral challenges (Volkmar, Paul, Klin, & Cohen, 2005). In general, autism consists of impairment within three major domains: reciprocal social interaction, verbal and nonverbal communication, and range of activities and interests (Holter, 2004).

Emotional/Behavioral Disorders

In many schools, the children perhaps presenting the greatest challenge to educators and administrators are those who consistently exhibit disruptive or alarming behavior yet do not clearly fit the criteria for a disability diagnosis. Although the U.S. Individuals with Disabilities Education Act (IDEA) includes a definition for "seriously emotionally disturbed" children, not all school professionals and government education agencies consistently agree with or use this definition (Brauner & Stephens, 2006; Young et al., 2004). In fact, the National Mental Health and Special Education Coalition has publicized a definition of "emotionally/behaviorally disordered" children, suggesting that this term and a set of diagnostic criteria could be used in place of the IDEA definition. Because of these definitional inconsistencies, it is extremely difficult to accurately estimate the number of school-age children falling within this population. Such estimates range from 0.05% to 6% of students.

Early identification and intervention, or provision of appropriate supportive services, are key protective factors for a child with special needs. In addition, the social environment more generally may serve as either a risk or protective factor, depending on its response to the child with a special need. Although difference of any sort is often noticed by children and adults, students with special needs or chronic illness are at particular risk for being singled out by their peers, and middle childhood is a critical time for such children. For children to acquire a clear and positive sense of self, they need positive self-regard. The positive development of all children is facilitated by support at multiple levels to promote feelings of self-competence and independence (H. Goldstein, Kaczmarek, & English, 2002). Educating all children and adults about special needs and encouraging the support of all students may help to minimize negative attitudes and incidents (Gargiulo, 2005; J. L. Garrett, 2006).

> What educational initiatives could minimize the risks associated with ADHD, autistic spectrum disorders, and other emotional/behavioral disorders?

Students who feel misunderstood by their peers are particularly likely to feel alone or isolated in the school setting. Students who are socially excluded by their peers often develop a dislike of school. Some students who are teased, isolated, or harassed on a regular basis may begin to withdraw or act out in order to cope with unpleasant experiences. Teachers, parents, and other school personnel who pay special attention to, and intervene with, students in this situation may prevent the escalation of such problems.

Children's adjustment to special needs is highly dependent on the adjustment of those around them. Families may respond in a number of ways to a diagnosis of a disability or serious illness. Often, caregivers experience loss or grief stages; these stages may include denial, withdrawal, rejection, fear, frustration, anger, sadness, adjustment, and acceptance (Boushey, 2001; E. Bruce & Schultz, 2002; Pejlert, 2001; Ziolko, 1993). The loss and grief stages are not linear, but can be experienced repeatedly as parents interface with educational, social, and medical institutions throughout their child's life (E. Bruce & Schultz, 2002; Pejlert, 2001). Awareness of and sensitivity to these stages and the ongoing nature of grief and loss is critical for those assessing the need for intervention. Typically, parents are helped by advocacy and support groups and access to information and resources.

Families of children with special needs also typically desire independence and self-determination for their children. Family empowerment was an explicit focus of the Education for All Handicapped Children Act (P.L. 94–142) of 1975, which stresses parental participation in the development of an **individual education plan** (IEP) for each child. The IEP charts a course for ensuring that each child achieves as much as possible in the academic realm. The need to include the family in decision making and planning is also embodied in the IDEA of 1990 (reauthorized in 1997 and 2004), which replaced the Education for All Handicapped Children Act (Hauser-Cram & Howell, 2003). IDEA requires that the IEP includes specific educational goals for each student classified as in need of special educational services. In addition, IDEA assures all children the right to a free and appropriate public education and supports the placement of children with disabilities into integrated settings.

Prior to this act, the education of children with disabilities was left to individual states. As a result, the population labeled "disabled" and the services provided varied greatly. Today, however, through various pieces of legislation and several court decisions, society has stated its clear preference to educate children with special needs in integrated settings (*least restrictive environment*) to the maximum extent possible.

A recent examination of the nature of inclusion nationwide concluded that during the last two decades, students with special needs (including learning disabilities) were much more likely to be formally identified, but only approximately 15 states clearly moved toward educating students with special needs in less restrictive settings (McLeskey,

Hoppey, Williamson, & Rentz, 2004). Evaluations of the impact of inclusive settings on children's school success suggest positive academic gains for children with special needs and neutral impact on academic performance for children without identified special needs (McDonnel et al., 2003).

However, some caution against a "one size fits all" model of inclusion for all students with special needs, arguing that assessment of the optimal educational setting must be thorough and individualized. For example, some within the deaf community have argued that current full inclusion programs are unable "to meet the unique communication and social development needs of solitary deaf students" (Hehir, 2003, p. 36).

Hehir (2003) explains that while inclusion in statewide assessments has been shown to improve educational opportunities and achievement for some students with disabilities, "high stakes" testing negatively impacts such progress if it alone is used as the basis for preventing students from being promoted a grade or graduating. In other words, standards-based reforms can positively impact students with disabilities if they improve the educational opportunities for all students. If such reforms, however, shift practice toward a system in which standardized testing is the only format through which student knowledge and capabilities are assessed, then many students, particularly those with special needs, are likely to suffer (Hehir, 2003, p. 40).

Family Disruption

Throughout history, most nuclear and extended families have succeeded in their endeavor to adequately protect and socialize their young. For too many children, however, the family serves as both a protective and a risk factor due to unhealthy family attributes and dynamics. In the specific realm of family disruption, divorce was traditionally viewed as a developmental risk factor for children. Today, among U.S. children with married parents, approximately one half experience the divorce of their parents (Amato, 2003). Many parents marry a second time. Thus, "in 2001, 5.4 million children lived with one biological parent and either a stepparent or adoptive

parent"; such children represent 11% of all children living with two parents (Kreider & Fields, 2005, p. 2). The likelihood of divorce is even greater for second marriages, and approximately half of these children experience the end of a parent's second marriage (Bramlett & Mosher, 2002). Many children experience the dissolution of their parents' nonmarital romantic relationships, and related attachments, without being counted in official "children of divorce" statistics or research. Although no reliable data on similar nonmarital relationship patterns exist, we can assume there are similar trends among children's nonmarried parents and other caregivers.

Divorce and other types of family disruption lead to various situations, including the introduction of new people, new housing and income arrangements, and new family roles and responsibilities (Hetherington & Jodl, 1994). Family disruption may also immerse the child in poverty (Zagorsky, 2005). As the body of research on children and divorce grows in depth and breadth, it has become apparent that divorce and other types of family disruption may detrimentally or positively impact children, depending on the circumstances preceding and following the divorce (Adam & Chase-Lansdale, 2002; Amato, 2003; Fine et al., 2010; Gilman, Kawachi, & Fitzmaurice, 2003). For example, if divorce brings an end to seriously dysfunctional spousal tension or violence and results in positive changes within the home environment, child outcomes may be positive. Alternatively, if the divorce disrupts a healthy, nurturing family system and leads to declines in the emotional and financial health of the child's primary caregiver(s), child outcomes may be negative.

Historically, many children experienced family disruption because of the death of one or both parents (Amato, 2003). Although improvements in public health have significantly reduced the likelihood of parental death, a substantial number of children continue to experience the death of a primary caregiver. Compared to adults, children have less cognitive and other resources to cope with death and loss (Saldinger, Cain, Kalter, & Lohnes, 1999). For children coping with the death of a parent, the circumstances of the death and the adjustment of the remaining caregivers are critical variables impacting child outcomes (Hope & Hodge, 2006; Kwok et al., 2005). Also, in recent years, a number of studies have focused upon "children of suicide." This literature notes the potential long-term impacts of parental suicide on surviving children and identifies the ways in which outcomes may be carried through generations (Cain, 2006).

Many school-age children experience disruption of attachment relationships through other means. For example, approximately 800,000 children in the United States spend some amount of time in foster care each year (Child Welfare League of America, 2005). A number of these children spend lengthy periods of time in some type of foster care setting, while other children enter and leave foster care rapidly and only once during their childhoods, and still other children cycle in and out of their home and foster care settings repeatedly. Approximately one third of the children in foster care at any time have been in substitute care for 3 years or more; approximately one fifth are identified as unlikely to ever return home and are awaiting a permanent plan (S. W. Downs, Moore, McFadden, Michaud, & Costin, 2004).

Family disruption is stressful for all children. Great variation exists, however, in the circumstances preceding and following the family disruption, the nature of the changes involved, and how children respond to this type of stress. Critical factors in outcomes for children include social supports within the family and surrounding community, the child's characteristics, the emotional well-being of caregivers, and in general the quality of care received following the family disruption. In addition, because middle childhood spans a wide age range, school-age children exhibit a wide range of cognitive, emotional, and behavioral responses to divorce and other types of family disruption. They may blame themselves and experience anxiety or other difficult emotions, or they may demonstrate a relatively mature understanding of the reasons behind the events.

Children experiencing family disruption without supports or those who have experienced difficulties preceding the disruption are most likely to experience long-term emotional and behavioral problems. Children placed in foster care or otherwise exposed to traumatic or multiple losses are more likely to fall into this group (N. Webb & Dumpson, 2006). These children are likely to face additional stress associated with the loss of familiar space, belongings, and social networks (Groves, 1997). However, with appropriate support and intervention as well as the presence of other protective factors, many children experiencing family disruption adjust over time.

RISK FACTORS AND PROTECTIVE FACTORS IN MIDDLE CHILDHOOD

School-age children face a variety of risks that undermine their struggles to develop a sense of purpose and self-worth. These risks include poverty, prejudice, and violence (Garbarino, 1995). More generally, risk factors are anything that increases the probability of a problem condition, its progression into a more severe state, or its maintenance (Fraser, 2004). Risk factors are moderated, however, by protective factors, either internal or external, which help children resist risk (Fraser, 2004; Garmezy, 1993, 1994; E. E. Werner & Smith, 2001). Risk and protective factors can be biological, psychological, social, and spiritual in nature, and like all influences on development, they span the micro to macro continuum (Bronfenbrenner, 1979). Dynamic, always evolving interaction occurs among risk and protective factors present in each dimension of the individual child and his or her environment.

Resilience—or "survival against the odds"—arises from an interplay of risk and protective factors and manifests as adaptive behavior producing positive outcomes (Fraser, 2004). A variety of factors influence resilience during middle childhood. Whether a factor presents risk or protection often depends on its interaction with other factors influencing the individual child. For example, a highly structured classroom environment run by a "strict" teacher may function as a protective factor for one child while simultaneously functioning as a risk factor for another child.

The life course and systems perspectives provide tools for understanding positive development during middle childhood. These perspectives also facilitate assessment and intervention efforts. As social workers, we must recognize that resilience is rarely an innate characteristic. Rather, it is a process (Egeland, Carlson, & Sroufe, 1993; Fraser, 2004) that may be facilitated by influences within the child's surrounding environment. Indeed, research suggests that high-risk behavior among children increases when they perceive declining family involvement and community support (Benson, 1990; Blyth & Roehlkepartian, 1993). In their longitudinal study of 180 children born into poor families, Sroufe et al. (2005) conclude that "Competence in elementary school is a product of early care, later care, *and* the current family supports and challenges" (p. 159).

A primary goal of the professions dedicated to child well-being must be facilitation of positive external supports for children and enhancement of the person-environment fit so as to maximize protective factors and minimize risk factors.

Critical Thinking Questions 13.3

There is general agreement that poverty and child maltreatment are among the most serious threats to healthy child development. How does poverty threaten physical, cognitive, emotional, social, and spiritual development during middle childhood? How does child maltreatment threaten physical, cognitive, emotional, social, and spiritual development during middle childhood?

Implications for Social Work Practice

This discussion of middle childhood suggests several practice principles for social workers and other professionals working with children:

- Development is multidimensional and dynamic; recognize the complex ways in which developmental influences interact, and incorporate this understanding into your work with children.
- Support parents and other family members as critically important social, emotional, and spiritual resources for their children.
- Support family, school, and community attempts to stabilize environments for children.
- Incorporate identification of multilevel risk and protective factors into assessment and intervention efforts.
- Recognize and support resilience in children and families. Support the strengths of children and families and their efforts to cope with adversity.
- Recognize the critical influence of the school environment on growth and development, and encourage attempts by school personnel to be responsive to all children and families.
- Understand the important role of peer groups in social and emotional growth and development; facilitate the development and maintenance of positive peer and other social relationships.
- Understand the ways in which the organization of schools reflects and supports the inequalities present in society. Support schools in their efforts to end practices and policies, intended or unintended, that sustain and/or reinforce inequalities based on differences such as race, ethnicity, gender, disability, and socioeconomic status.
- Facilitate meaningful teacher–family–child communication and school responsiveness to children experiencing difficulties in the school environment.
- Understand the effects of family, community, and societal violence on children, and establish prosocial, nurturing, nonviolent environments whenever possible; provide opportunities for positive nurturing and mentoring of children in the school and community environments.
- Become familiar with and implement best practices in areas such as trauma, loss and grief, social skill development, and character education.
- Promote cultural sensitivity, and help children and other adults recognize and respect all forms of diversity and difference.

capital	individual	relative poverty
cerebral cortex	education plan (IEP)	secondary
character education	institutional discrimination	sexual development
deculturalizing	interrelational intelligence	social competence
direct bullying	oppression	trauma
indirect bullying	precociousness	zone of proximal development

Active Learning

1. In small groups, compare and contrast the risk and protective factors present for Anthony Bryant, Brianna Shaw, and Manuel Vega. Brainstorm multilevel interventions you would consider if you were working with each child.

2. Assign pairs of students to the story of Anthony Bryant, Brianna Shaw, or Manuel Vega. Each pair should identify the relevance of the various developmental theorists, discussed in the chapter, to the assigned child, focusing on the theorist(s) whose idea(s) seem particularly relevant to the selected child. After approximately 20 minutes, form three small groups consisting of the pairs focusing on the same child. After comparing their similarities and differences, each group should report back to the full class.

Web Resources

American Association of University Women

www.aauw.org

Site contains information on education and equity for women and girls, including a report card on Title IX, a law that banned sex discrimination in education.

Child Trauma Academy

www.childtraumaacademy.com

Site contains information on the impact of child maltreatment on the brain and the physiological and psychological effects of trauma on children.

Child Welfare Information Gateway

www.childwelfare.gov

Site presented by the Administration for Children and Families contains information and resources to protect children and strengthen families, including statistics, prevention information, state statutes, family-centered practice, and publications.

Forum on Child and Family Statistics

www.childstats.gov

Official website of the Federal Interagency Forum on Child and Family Statistics, offers easy access to federal and state statistics and reports on children and families, including international comparisons.

Search Institute

www.search-institute.org

Site presented by Search Institute, an independent, nonprofit, nonsectarian organization with the goal of advancing the well-being of adolescents and children, contains information on 40 developmental assets and methods for building assets for child and youth development.

Adolescence

Susan Ainsley McCarter

ભ ৪০

ભ ৪০

Opening Questions

How do biological, psychological, social, and spiritual dimensions affect the adolescent phase of the life course?

Why do social workers need to understand theories of identity formation when working with adolescents?

What unique challenges do adolescents face when confronted with issues of sexuality, violence, and substance use and abuse?

Key Ideas

As you read this chapter, take note of these central ideas:

1. Adolescence is characterized by significant physical change, increased sex hormone production, sexual maturation, improved cognitive functioning, formative identity development, and increased independence.

2. During adolescence, increased sex hormone production results in a period called puberty, during which persons become capable of reproduction. Other visible physical changes during this period include skeletal, musculature, and fat distribution changes, as well as development of primary and secondary sex characteristics.

3. Unseen growth and pruning occurs in the adolescent brain.

4. Psychological changes during this period include reactions to physical, social, and cultural changes confronting the adolescent, as well as cognitive development, in which most individuals develop the abilities to contemplate the future, to comprehend the nature of human relationships, to consolidate specific knowledge into a coherent system, and to envision possible consequences from a hypothetical list of actions.

5. The greatest task of adolescence is identity formation—determining who one is and where one is going.

6. Adolescents in the United States spend nearly a third of their waking hours at school, where they should receive skills and knowledge for their next step in life, but a school that follows a Eurocentric educational model without regard for other cultures may damage the self-esteem of students from minority ethnic groups.

7. Among the physical and mental health risks to today's adolescents are violence; substance abuse; juvenile delinquency; poverty; low educational attainment; poor nutrition, obesity, and eating disorders; and depression and suicide.

CASE STUDY 14.1

David's Coming Out Process

The social worker at Jefferson High School sees many facets of adolescent life. Nothing much surprises her—especially not the way some of the kids hem and haw when they're trying to share what's really on their mind. Take David Costa, for instance. When he shows up for his first appointment, he is simply asked to tell a bit about himself.

"Let's see, I'm 17," he begins. "I'm a centerfielder on the varsity baseball team. What else do you want to know? My parents are from Bolivia and are as traditional as you can imagine. My dad, David Sr., teaches history and is the varsity soccer coach here at Jefferson. My mom is a geriatric nurse. I have a younger sister, Patti. Patti Perfect. She goes to the magnet school and is in the ninth grade."

"How are things at home?" his social worker asks.

"Whatever. Patti is perfect, and I'm a 'freak.' They think I'm 'different, arrogant, stubborn.' I don't know what they want me to be. But I don't think that's what I am. That may be because . . . because I'm gay. I haven't come out to my parents. That's all I need!"

This is obviously a difficult confession for David to make to an adult, but with a little encouragement he continues: "There are a few other athletes who are gay, and then we have some friends outside of sports. Thank God! But basically when the whole team is together or when I'm with other friends, I just act straight. I talk about girls' bodies just like the other guys. I think that is the hardest, not being able to be yourself. I'm at least glad that I've met other gay guys. It was really hard when I was about 13. I was so confused. I knew that men were supposed to be with women, not other men. What I was feeling was not 'normal,' and I thought I was the only one. I wanted to kill myself. That was a bad time."

David's tone changes. "Let's talk about something good. Let me tell you about Theo. I think Theo is hot! He's got a good body, very athletic. I wonder if he'd like to hang out together—get to know each other. He's a junior, and if we got together, the other guys I know would razz me about seeing a younger guy. But I keep thinking about him. And looking at him during school. I just need to say something to him. Some guys from the team are going out Thursday night after practice. He hasn't been invited in the past. Maybe if I invite him, he'll come."

CASE STUDY 14.2

Carl's Struggle for Identity

Whereas David seeks out the social worker, Carl Fleischer, another 17-year-old, is sent to the social worker's office at the high school. He matter-of-factly shares that he is "an underachiever." He used to get an occasional B in his classes, but now it's mostly C's with an occasional D.

When Carl is asked what he likes to do in his spare time, he replies, "I get high and surf the Net." Further probing elicits one-word answers until the social worker asks Carl about romantic interests. His face contorts as he slaps his ample belly: "I'm not exactly a sex symbol. According to my doctor, I'm a fatso. He says normal boys my age and height weigh at least 50 pounds less than I do. He also tells me to quit smoking and get some exercise. Whatever. My mom says I'm big-boned. She says my dad was the same way. I wouldn't know. I never met the scumbag. He left when my mom was pregnant. But you probably don't want to hear about that."

Carl won't say more on that topic, but with more prodding, he finally talks about his job, delivering pizzas 2 nights a week and on the weekends. "So if you need pizzas, call me at Antonio's. I always bring pies home for my mom on Tuesday and Friday nights. She works late those nights, and so we usually eat pizza and catch the Tuesday and Friday night lineups on TV. She lets me smoke in the house—cigarettes, not weed. Although I have gotten high in the house a couple times. Anyway, I am not what you would call popular. I am just a fat, slow geek and a pizza guy. But there are some heads who come into Antonio's. I exchange pies for dope. Works out pretty well: They get the munchies, and the pies keep me in with the heads."

Monica's Quest for Mastery

Monica Golden, a peer counselor at Jefferson High, hangs around to chat after a meeting of the peer counselors. Monica is the eldest and tallest daughter in a family of five kids. Monica's mother is the assistant principal at Grover Middle School, and her father works for the Internal Revenue Service. This year, Monica is the vice president of the senior class, the treasurer for the Young Republicans, a starter on the track team, a teacher at Sunday school, and a Jefferson peer counselor.

When the social worker comments on the scope of these activities, Monica replies, "I really do stay busy. I worked at the mall last year, but it was hard to keep my grades up. I'm trying to get into college, so my family and I decided I shouldn't work this year. So I just babysit sometimes. A lot of my aunts and uncles have me watch their kids, but they don't pay me. They consider it a family favor. Anyway, I am waiting to hear back from colleges. They should be sending out the letters this week. You know, the fatter the envelope the better. It doesn't take many words to say, 'No. We reject you.' And I need to either get into a state school or get a scholarship so that I can use my savings for tuition."

Next, they talk a little about Monica's options, and she shares that her first choice is Howard University. "I want to surround myself with Black scholars and role models, and my dream is to be a pediatrician, you know. I love kids," Monica says. "I tried tons of jobs—that's where I got the savings. And, well, those with kids I enjoyed the most. Like I said, I've worked retail at the mall. I've worked at the supermarket as a cashier. I've worked at the snack bar at the pool. And I've been babysitting since I was 12. That's what I like the most."

"I'd love to have kids someday. But I don't even have a boyfriend. I wear glasses. My parents say I don't need contacts; they think I'm being vain. Not that I don't have a boyfriend because I wear glasses. Guys think I'm an overachiever. They think I'm driven and demanding and incapable of having fun. That's what I've been told. I think I'm just ambitious and extroverted. But really, I just haven't had much time to date in high school. I've been so busy. Well, gotta run."

THE SOCIAL CONSTRUCTION OF ADOLESCENCE ACROSS TIME AND SPACE _____

If we were asked to describe David Costa, Carl Fleischer, and Monica Golden, attention would probably be drawn to their status as adolescents. The importance of that status has changed across time and cultures, however. Adolescence was invented as a psychosocial concept in the late 19th and early 20th centuries as the United States made the transition from an agrarian to an urban-industrial society (Fass & Mason, 2000). Prior to this time, adolescents worked beside adults, doing what adults did for the most part (Leeder, 2004). This is still the case for adolescents in many nonindustrial societies today. As the United States and other societies became urbanized and industrialized, child labor legislation and compulsory education policies were passed, and adolescents were moved from the workplace to the school and became economically dependent on parents. The juvenile justice system was developed because juvenile offenders were seen as different from adult offenders, with less culpability for their crime because of their immaturity.

In 1904, G. Stanley Hall, an American psychologist, published *Adolescence: Its Psychology and Its Relations to Physiology,*

> How have our views on adolescence changed over time?

Anthropology, Sociology, Sex, Crime, Religion, and Education. Hall proposed that adolescence is a period of "storm and stress," a period when hormones cause many psychological and social difficulties. Hall was later involved in the *eugenics* movement, a movement that intended to improve the human population by controlled selective breeding, and there is some hint of racist and classist bias in his work on adolescence, which was not unusual in his time. His discussion seemed to indicate that poor youth are at risk of trouble because of their heredity, while middle-class youth are at risk of being corrupted by the world around them (J. L. Finn, 2009). Janet Finn argues that the public, professional, and scholarly conversations about adolescence in the 20th and beginning of the 21st century have focused on adolescents as "trouble." Jane Kroger (2007) suggests that many societies are clear about what they want their adolescents to avoid (alcohol and other drugs, delinquency, and pregnancy), but not as clear about what positive things they would like their youth to achieve. There is growing agreement that the societal context in which adolescence is lived out in the United States and other wealthy nations is becoming increasingly less supportive for adolescent development (Fass & Mason, 2000). This concern has led, in recent years, to the construction of a positive youth development movement, which has focused on youth "as resources to be developed, and not as problems to be managed" (Silbereisen & Lerner, 2007b, p. 7).

Sociologists caution against thinking of a monolithic adolescence. They suggest that, unfortunately, many adults dichotomize children and adolescents as "our own" children and "other people's" children (Graff, 1995). Our own children are expected to have "an innocent and secure childhood and dependent, prolonged adolescence" (Graff, 1995, p. 332). Other people's children are expected to be resilient in their childhood and accountable for their own behavior at increasingly younger ages, as we see in the declining ages for being treated as an adult in the criminal justice system. Sociologists conclude that there are multiple adolescences, with gender, race, and class as major influences on the ways they are constructed and their realities.

Perhaps no life course phase has been the subject of more recent empirical research than adolescence. Most prominently, the National Longitudinal Study of Adolescent Health (Add Health) was initiated at the Carolina Population Center in 1994. It is a study of a representative sample of adolescents in Grades 7–12 during the 1994–1995 school year. This cohort was followed into young adulthood in 2008, when the sample was between 24 and 32 years of age. The Add Health study includes measures of social, economic, psychological, and physical well-being as well as contextual information on the family, neighborhood, community, school, friendships, peer groups, and romantic relationships. Add Health data are now generating large numbers of research reports. A partial listing of those reports can be found at www.cpc.unc.edu/projects/addhealth/pubs/.

THE TRANSITION FROM CHILDHOOD TO ADULTHOOD

In industrialized countries, adolescence is described as the transitional period between childhood and adulthood. It is more than that, of course. It is a very rich period of the life course in its own right. For many, it is a thrilling time of life, full of new experiences. The word *adolescence* originates from the Latin verb *adolescere,* which means "to grow into maturity." It is a period of life filled with transitional themes in every dimension of the configuration of person and environment: biological, psychological, social, and spiritual. These themes do not occur independently or without affecting one another. For example, David Costa's experience may be complicated because he is gay and because his family relationships are strained, but it is also strengthened by his supportive friendships and his participation in sports. Carl Fleischer's transition is marked by several challenges—his weight, his substance use, his lack of a relationship with his father, his academic performance—but also by the promise of his developing computer expertise and entrepreneurial skills. Monica Golden's movement through adolescence

Photo 14.1   Adolescence is a period of life filled with transitional themes in every dimension of life: biological, psychological, social, and spiritual.

may be eased by her academic, athletic, and social success, but it also could be taxed by her busy schedule and high expectations for herself.

Many cultures have specific **rites of passage**—ceremonies that demarcate the transition from childhood to adulthood. Often, these rites include sexual themes, marriage themes, themes of becoming a man or a woman, themes of added responsibility, or themes of increased insight or understanding. Such rites of passage are found in most nonindustrialized societies (Gardiner & Kosmitzki, 2008). For example, among the Massai ethnic group in Kenya and Tanzania, males and females are both circumcised at about age 13, and males are considered junior warriors and sent to live with other junior warriors (Leeder, 2004). For the most part, the transition from adolescence to adulthood is not marked by such clearly defined rituals in North America and many other Western countries (Gardiner & Kosmitzki, 2008). Some scholars who study adolescence have suggested that where there are no clear-cut puberty rituals, adolescents will devise their own rituals, such as "hazing, tattooing, dieting, dress, and beautification rituals" (Kroger, 2007, p. 41).

There are some groups in North America who continue to practice rites of passage, however. In the United States, some Jews celebrate the bar mitzvah for boys and bat mitzvah for girls at the age of 13 to observe their transition to adulthood and to mark their assumption of religious responsibility. Many Latino families, especially of Mexican heritage, celebrate *quinceañera,* during which families attend Mass with their 15-year-old daughter, who is dressed in white and then presented to the community as a young woman. Traditionally, she is accompanied by her *padrinos,* or godparents, who agree to support her parents in guiding her during this time. The ceremony is followed by a reception at which her father dances with her and presents her to the family's community of friends (E. Garcia, 2001; Zuniga, 1992). Among many First Nations/Native American tribes in North America, boys participate in a Vision Quest at age 14 or 15. The boy is taken into a "sweat lodge," where his body and spirit are purified by the heat. He is assisted by a medicine man who advises him and assists with ritual prayers. Later, he is taken to another place where he is left alone to fast for 4 days. Similarly, some First Nations/Native

American girls take part in a ritual that involves morning running and baking a ceremonial cake (see Gardiner & Kosmitzki, 2008).

Mainstream culture in the United States, however, has few such rites. Many young adolescents go through confirmation ceremonies in Protestant and Catholic churches. Otherwise, the closest thing to a rite of passage may be getting a driver's license, graduating from high school, registering to vote, graduating from college, or getting married. But these events all occur at different times and thus do not provide a discrete point of transition. Moreover, not all youth participate in these rites of passage.

Even without a cultural rite of passage, all adolescents experience profound biological, psychological, psychosocial, social, and spiritual changes. In advanced industrial societies, these changes have been divided into three phases: early adolescence (ages 11 to 14), middle adolescence (ages 15 to 17), and late adolescence (ages 18 to 20). Exhibit 14.1 summarizes the typical biological, psychological, and social developments in these three phases. Of course, adolescent development varies from person to person and with time, culture, and other aspects of the environment. Yet deviations from the normative patterns of adolescent change may have psychological ramifications, because adolescents are so quick to compare their own development to that of their peers, and because of the cultural messages they receive about acceptable appearance and behavior.

Exhibit 14.1 Typical Adolescent Development

Stage of Adolescence	Biological Changes	Psychological Changes	Social Changes
Early (11 to 14)	Hormonal changes Beginning of puberty Physical appearance changes Possible experimentation with sex and substances	Reactions to physical changes, including early maturation Concrete/present-oriented thought Body modesty Moodiness	Changes in relationships with parents and peers Less school structure Distancing from culture/tradition Seeking sameness
Middle (15 to 17)	Completion of puberty and physical appearance changes Possible experimentation with sex and substances	Reactions to physical changes, including late maturation Increased autonomy Increased abstract thought Beginning of identity development Preparation for college or career	Heightened social situation decision making Continued renegotiation of family relationships More focus on peer group Beginning of one-to-one romantic relationships Moving toward greater community participation
Late (18 to 22)	Slowing of physical changes Possible experimentation with sex and substances	Formal operational thought Continuation of identity development Moral reasoning	Very little school/life structure Beginning of intimate relationships Renewed interest in culture/tradition

BIOLOGICAL ASPECTS OF ADOLESCENCE _____

Adolescence is a period of great physical change, marked by a rapid growth spurt in the early years, maturation of the reproductive system, redistribution of body weight, and continuing brain development. Adequate care of the body during this exciting time is of paramount importance.

Puberty

> What is the impact of biological age on psychological age, social age, and spiritual age during adolescence?

Puberty is the period of the life course in which the reproductive system matures. It is a process that begins before any biological changes are visible and occurs through interrelated neurological and endocrinological changes that affect brain development, sexual maturation, levels and cycles of hormones, and physical growth. The hypothalamus, pituitary gland, adrenal glands, and **gonads** (ovaries and testes) begin to interact and stimulate increased hormone production. It is the increase of these hormones that leads to the biological changes. Although androgens are typically referred to as male hormones and estrogens as female hormones, males and females in fact produce all three major **sex hormones:** androgens, progestins, and estrogens. Sex hormones affect the development and functioning of the gonads (including sperm production and ova maturation) and mating and child-caring behavior.

During puberty, increased levels of androgens in males stimulate the development and functioning of the male reproductive system; increased levels of progestins and estrogens in females stimulate the development and functioning of the female reproductive system. Specifically, the androgen testosterone, which is produced in males by the testes, affects the maturation and functioning of the penis, prostate gland, and other male genitals; the secondary sex characteristics; and the sex drive. The estrogen estradiol, which is produced in females by the ovaries, affects the maturation and functioning of the ovaries, uterus, and other female genitals; the secondary sex characteristics; and child-caring behaviors.

Primary sex characteristics are those directly related to the reproductive organs and external genitalia. For boys, these include growth of the penis and scrotum. During adolescence, the penis typically doubles or triples in length. Girls' primary sex characteristics are not so visible but include growth of the ovaries, uterus, vagina, clitoris, and labia.

Secondary sex characteristics are those not directly related to the reproductive organs and external genitalia. Secondary sex characteristics are enlarged breasts and hips for girls, facial hair and deeper voices for boys, and hair and sweat gland changes for both sexes. Female breast development is distinguished by growth of the mammary glands, nipples, and areola. The tone of the male voice lowers as the larynx enlarges and the vocal cords lengthen. Both boys and girls begin to grow hair around their genitals and then under their arms. This hair begins with a fine texture and light color and then becomes curlier, coarser, and darker. During this period, the sweat glands also begin to produce noticeable odors.

Puberty is often described as beginning with the onset of menstruation in girls and production of sperm in boys, but these are not the first events in the puberty process (see following paragraph). Menstruation is the periodic sloughing off of the lining of the uterus. This lining provides nutrients for the fertilized egg. If the egg is not fertilized, the lining sloughs off and is discharged through the vagina. However, for a female to become capable of reproduction, she must not only menstruate but also ovulate. Ovulation, the release of an egg from an ovary, usually does not begin until several months after **menarche,** the onset of menstruation. For males to reproduce, **spermarche**—the onset of the ability to ejaculate mobile sperm—must occur. Spermarche does not occur until after several ejaculations.

Females typically first notice breast growth, then growth of pubic hair, then body growth, especially hips. They then experience menarche; then growth of underarm hair; and finally, an increase in production of glandular oil and sweat, possibly with body odor and acne. Males typically follow a similar pattern, first noticing growth of the testes; then growth of pubic hair; body growth; growth of penis; change in voice; growth of facial and underarm hair; and finally, an increase in the production of glandular oil and sweat, possibly with body odor and acne. Girls experience the growth spurt before they have the capacity for reproduction, but the opposite is the case for boys (Kroger, 2007).

Pubertal timing varies greatly. Generally, females begin puberty about 2 years earlier than males. Normal pubertal rates (meaning they are experienced by 95% of the population) are for girls to begin menstruating between the ages of 9 and 17 and for boys to begin producing sperm between the ages of 11 and 16 (Rew, 2005). The age at which puberty begins has been declining in this century, but there is some controversy about the extent of this shift (B. Newman & Newman, 2009).

In addition to changes instigated by sex hormones, adolescents experience growth spurts. Bones are augmented by cartilage during adolescence, and the cartilage calcifies later, during the transition to adulthood. Typically, boys develop broader shoulders, straighter hips, and longer forearms and legs; girls typically develop narrower shoulders and broader hips. These skeletal differences are then enhanced by the development of additional upper-body musculature for boys and the development of additional fat deposits on thighs, hips, and buttocks for girls. These changes account for differences in male and female weight and strength.

The Adolescent Brain

Recent magnetic resonance imaging (MRI) studies are revealing new findings regarding adolescent brain development (Giedd, 2008; Gogtay et al., 2004; S. B. Johnson, Blum, & Giedd, 2009). Contrary to previous beliefs, adolescence is a time of continued brain growth and change. As discussed in earlier chapters, researchers have known for some time that the brain overproduces gray matter from development in the womb to about 3 years old,

is highly plastic and thus shaped by experience, and goes through a pruning process. The neural connections or synapses that get exercised are retained, whereas the ones that are not exercised are eliminated. New brain research suggests that the adolescent brain undergoes another period of overproduction of gray matter just prior to puberty, peaking at about 11 years of age for girls and 12 years for boys, followed by another round of pruning. This process, like the infant's, is also affected by the individual's interactions with the outside world (S. B. Johnson et al., 2009; Sowell, Trauner, Gamst, & Jernigan, 2002).

Currently, much interest surrounds recent findings about frontal lobe development during adolescence. The pruning process described above allows the brain to be more efficient to change in response to environmental demands and also facilitates improved integration of brain activities. Recent research indicates that pruning occurs in some parts of the brain earlier than in others, in general progressing from the back to the front part of brain, with the frontal lobes among the latest to show the structural changes. The frontal lobes are key players in the "executive functions" of planning, working memory, and impulse control, and the latest research indicates that they may not be fully developed until about age 25 (S. B. Johnson et al., 2009). Because of the relatively late development of the frontal lobes, particularly the prefrontal cortex, different neuronal circuits are involved in the adolescent brain under different emotional conditions. The researchers make a distinction between "cold cognition" problem solving and "hot cognition" problem solving during adolescence. *Cold cognition* problem solving occurs when the adolescent is alone and calm, as he or she typically would be in the laboratory. Conversely, *hot cognition* problem solving occurs in situations where teens are with peers, emotions are running high, they are feeling sexual tension, and so on. The research indicates that in situations of cold cognition, adolescents or even preadolescents as young as 12 or 13 can reason and problem solve as well as adults. However, in situations of hot cognition, adolescent problem solving is more impulsive (S. B. Johnson et al., 2009).

Similar to all social mammals, human adolescents tend to demonstrate three behavior changes: increased novelty seeking, increased risk taking, and greater affiliation with peers (Giedd, 2009). Brain research does not yet allow researchers to make definitive statements about the relationship between these adolescent behavior changes and changes in the brain, but these connections are being studied.

The emerging research on the adolescent brain is raising issues about social policy related to adolescents and is being used in ways that may be both helpful and hurtful to adolescent development. This is illustrated by two recent examples. In 2005, the U.S. Supreme Court heard the case of *Roper vs. Simmons* (543 U.S. 551), involving 17-year-old Christopher Simmons who had been convicted of murdering a woman during a robbery. He had been sentenced to death for his crime. His defense team argued that his still-developing adolescent brain made him less culpable for his crime than an adult, and therefore he should not be subject to the death penalty. It is thought that the neuroscience evidence carried weight in the Supreme Court's decision to overturn the death penalty for juveniles (A. Haider, 2006). In another example, the state of Kansas used an interpretation of neuroscience research to label any consensual touching by youth under the age of 16 years as child abuse (S. B. Johnson et al., 2009).

The question being raised is, what is the extent of human agency, the capacity for decision making, among adolescents? The answer to that question will vary from adolescent to adolescent. There is great risk that neuroscience research will be overgeneralized to the detriment of adolescents. S. B. Johnson et al. (2009) caution that it is important to put the adolescent brain in context, remembering that there are complex interactions of the brain with other biological systems as well as with "multiple interactive influences including experience, parenting, socioeconomic status, individual agency and self-efficacy, nutrition,

> How do changes in the brain during adolescence affect the capacity to exercise human agency in making choices?

culture, psychological well-being, the physical and built environments, and social relationships and interactions" (p. 219). Johnson and colleagues also recommend that we should avoid focusing on pathology and deficits in adolescent development and use neuroscience to examine the unique strengths and potentials of the adolescent brain. That is in keeping with the increasing focus on positive psychology and the related positive youth development movement.

Researchers at Duke University have created an interdisciplinary team whose mission is to educate society, especially young people, about the brain—how to use it effectively and how to keep it healthy. (A link to DukeLearn appears with the web resources at the end of this chapter.) Knowing more about the neurodevelopment of their own bodies may change the behaviors of some adolescents.

Nutrition, Exercise, and Sleep

At any stage along the life course, the right balance of nutrition, exercise, and sleep is important. As the transition from childhood to adulthood begins, early adolescent bodies undergo significant biological changes, from their brains to the hair follicles on their legs and everywhere in between. Yet it appears that few adolescents maintain a healthy balance during their time in adolescent flux.

The U.S. Department of Health and Human Services (HHS) and the Department of Agriculture (USDA) (2005) have begun several campaigns aimed at adolescent nutrition. They outline some of their recommendations in their *Dietary Guidelines for Americans 2005*. For adolescents, they recommend consuming 2 cups of fruit and 2.5 cups of vegetables a day (for a 2,000 calorie intake); choosing a variety of fruits and vegetables each day from all five vegetable subgroups—dark green, orange, legumes, starchy vegetables, and other vegetables—several times a week; consuming 3 or more ounce equivalents of whole-grain products per day; consuming 3 cups per day of fat-free or low-fat milk or equivalent milk products; limiting fat intake to 25 to 35% of calories, with most fats coming from sources of polyunsaturated and monounsaturated fatty acids, such as fish, nuts, and vegetable oils; and consuming less than 2,300 mg (approximately 1 teaspoon of salt) of sodium per day.

Yet the National Youth Risk Behavior Survey for 2007 (CDC, 2008d) suggests that nationwide in the United States, only 21.4% of young people in Grades 9 to 12 had eaten at least five fruits and vegetables a day in the past 7 days. This is unfortunate, given the need for well-balanced diets and increased caloric intake during a period of rapid growth. Many U.S. youth say they don't have time to eat breakfast or that they aren't hungry in the morning. Yet the research is rather convincing, indicating that students who eat breakfast obtain higher test scores and are less likely to be tardy or absent from school (Lonzano & Ballesteros, 2006).

In terms of activity, the recommendation is for most people of every age to engage in regular physical activity and reduce sedentary activities to promote health, psychological well-being, and a healthy body weight. Physical fitness should be achieved by including cardiovascular conditioning, stretching exercises for flexibility, and resistance exercises or calisthenics for muscle strength and endurance. The specific recommendation for adolescents is to engage in at least 60 minutes of physical activity on most, preferably all, days of the week (DHHS/USDA, 2005).

Again, the data are not promising. Nationwide, 34.7% of high school students reported being physically active for a total of at least 60 minutes a day on at least 5 of the 7 days preceding the survey. Conversely, 24.9% of students played video or computer games or used the computer in some way for 3 hours or more on an average school day, and 35.4% watched television for 3 hours or more on an average school day (CDC, 2008d).

Along with other changes of puberty, there are marked changes in sleep patterns (Giedd, 2009; National Sleep Foundation, 2006). Changes in circadian rhythms create a tendency to be more alert late at night and to wake later in the morning. Given the mismatch of these sleep patterns with the timing of the school day, adolescents often doze off during the school day. Sleep researchers suggest that adolescents require 8.5 to 9.25 hours of sleep each night (National Sleep Foundation, 2006).

Researchers assert that adolescents in the United States are the most sleep-deprived segment of a very sleep-deprived society (National Institutes of Health, 2001). Survey data show that only 20% of U.S. adolescents get at least 9 hours of sleep on school nights. U.S. sixth graders get an average of 8.4 hours of sleep on school nights, and U.S. high school seniors get an average of only 6.9 hours on school nights, which gives them 12 hours of sleep deficit over the course of a week (National Sleep Foundation, 2006). School performance is affected by insufficient sleep. More than a quarter of high school students fall asleep at school at least once a week, and students who get sufficient sleep have higher grades on average than students with sleep deficit. Mood is also affected by insufficient sleep; teens who get 9 or more hours of sleep per night report more positive moods than students who get insufficient sleep (National Sleep Foundation, 2006). Indeed, sleep deprivation is associated with depression in adolescents (S. M. Holm et al., 2009).

As suggested above, the risks of sleep deprivation are varied, and they can be serious. Drowsiness or fatigue is a principal cause of at least 100,000 police-reported traffic collisions annually, killing more than 1,500 Americans and injuring 71,000 more. Drivers 25 and younger cause more than half of the crashes attributed to drowsiness (National Sleep Foundation, 2005). Sleep deficit contributes to acne, aggressive behavior, eating too much or unhealthy foods, and to illness. It also heightens the effects of alcohol and can lead to increased use of caffeine and nicotine. Sleep-deprived youth may also present with symptoms that are similar to ADHD and thus run the risk of misdiagnosis (A. Marks & Rothbart, 2003).

PSYCHOLOGICAL ASPECTS OF ADOLESCENCE

Psychological development in adolescence is multifaceted. Adolescents have psychological reactions, sometimes dramatic, to the biological, social, and cultural dimensions of their lives. They become capable of and interested in discovering and forming their psychological selves. They may show heightened creativity, as well as interest in humanitarian issues; ethics; religion; and reflection and record keeping, as in a diary (Rew, 2005). There is evidence that adolescence is a time of increased emotional complexity, and a growing capacity to understand and express a wider range of emotions and to gain insight into one's own emotions (Weissberg & O'Brien, 2004). Three areas of psychological development are particularly noteworthy: reactions to biological changes, changes in cognition, and identity development.

Psychological Reactions to Biological Changes

"Will my body ever start changing? Will my body ever stop changing? Is this normal? Am I normal? Why am I suddenly interested in girls? And why are the girls all taller (and stronger) than me? How can I ask Mom if I can shave my legs?" These are some of the questions mentioned when Jane Kroger (2007, pp. 33–34) asked a class of 12- and 13-year-old adolescents what type of questions they think most about. As you can see, themes of biological changes were pervasive. If you can remember your own puberty process, you probably are not surprised that researchers have found that pubertal adolescents are preoccupied with physical changes and appearances (McCabe & Ricciardelli, 2003). Young adolescents are able to reflect upon and give meaning to their biological transformations. Of course, responses to puberty are influenced by the way other people, including parents, siblings, teachers, and peers, respond to the adolescent's changing body. In addition, reactions to puberty are influenced by other events in the adolescent's life, such as school transition, family conflict, and peer relationships.

It appears that puberty is usually viewed more positively by males than by females, with boys focused on increased muscle mass and physical strength and girls focused on increased body weight and fat deposits (S. Phillips, 2003).

Pubescent boys tend to report an improved body image, whereas pubescent girls are more prone to depression (Benjet & Hernandez-Guzman, 2002). These reactions are rooted in European culture that values muscular males and petite, shapely females. For girls, body dissatisfaction and self-consciousness peaks between the ages of 13 and 15. There is evidence that African American adolescent girls are more satisfied with their body image and less inclined to eating disorders than Caucasian American girls, most likely due to a different cultural valuing of thinness in females (Franko & Striegel-Moore, 2002).

Reactions to menstruation are often mixed. One study of Chinese American adolescent girls found that 85% reported that they were annoyed and embarrassed by their first menstruation, but 66% also reported positive feelings (Tang, Yeung, & Lee, 2003). Reactions to menarche are greatly affected by the type of information and level of support that young women receive from parents, teachers, peers, and health advisors (Brooks-Gunn & Paikoff, 1993). Research shows that pubescent females talk with parents and friends about their first menstruation, but pubescent males do not discuss with anyone their first ejaculation, an event sometimes seen as the closest male equivalent to first menstruation (Kroger, 2007). Pubescent boys may receive less information from adults about nocturnal ejaculations than their sisters receive about menarche.

Because the onset and experience of puberty vary greatly, adolescents need reassurance regarding their own growth patterns. Some adolescents will be considered early maturers, and some will be considered late maturers. Timing and tempo of puberty are influenced by genetics, and there are ethnic differences as well. On average, African American adolescents enter puberty earlier than Mexican American adolescents, who enter puberty earlier than Caucasian Americans (Chumlea et al., 2003). There are psychological and social consequences of early and late maturing for both males and females, but the research findings are not always consistent. Previous research indicated that the impact of pubertal timing varied by gender, but more recent studies indicate similar negative outcomes of early puberty for both males and females. Early puberty has been found to be associated with more involvement in high-risk behaviors, such as smoking, experimenting with drugs, early sex, and other unhealthy behaviors in both males and females (Biehl, Natsuaki, & Ge, 2007; Cota-Robles, Neiss, & Rowe, 2002; Ge, Conger, & Elder, 2001; Richter, 2006; Wichstrom, 2001). For females, but not males, early puberty has been linked with depression, not only at puberty but across the life course (Archibald, Graber, & Brooks-Gunn, 2003). Data from the Add Health research has produced similar findings for the connection between early puberty and alcohol use, with early maturing males and females engaging in more heavy drinking than later maturing youth, and early puberty serving as a risk factor for alcohol-related problems across the life course (Biehl et al., 2007).

Changes in Cognition

During adolescence, most individuals develop cognitive abilities beyond those of childhood (D. Keating, 2004), including these:

- Contemplation of the future
- Comprehension of the nature of human relationships
- Consolidation of specific knowledge into a coherent system
- Ability to envision possible consequences from a hypothetical list of actions (foresight)
- Abstract thought
- Empathy
- Internal control

Many of these abilities are components of Jean Piaget's fourth stage of cognitive development called formal operational thought (see Exhibit 4.1 in Chapter 4 for an overview of Piaget's stages of cognitive development). *Formal operational thought* suggests the capacity to apply hypothetical reasoning to various situations and the ability to use symbols to solve problems. David Costa, for example, demonstrated formal operational thought when he considered the possibility of getting to know Theo. He considered the reactions from his other friends if he were to get together with Theo; he examined his thoughts, and he formulated a strategy based on the possibilities and on his thoughts.

Whereas younger children focus on the here-and-now world in front of them, the adolescent brain is capable of retaining larger amounts of information. Thus, adolescents are capable of hypothesizing beyond the present objects. This ability also allows adolescents to engage in decision making based on a cost-benefit analysis. As noted above, brain research indicates that adolescent problem solving is as good as adult problem solving in "cold cognition" situations, but is not equally sound in "hot cognition" situations. Furthermore, brain development alone does not result in formal operational thinking. The developing brain needs social environments that encourage hypothetical, abstract reasoning and opportunities to investigate the world (Cohen & Sandy, 2007; Gehlbach, 2006). Formal operational thinking is more imperative in some cultures than in others, but is most imperative in many fields in the changing economic base of postindustrialized societies. Although contemporary education is organized to facilitate formal operational thinking, students do not have equal access to sound curriculum and instruction.

Adolescent cognition, however, mirrors adolescence in the sense that it is multifaceted. In addition to the increased capacity for thought, adolescents also bring with them experience, culture, personality, intelligence, family values, identity, and so on. If we conceptualize adolescent cognitive development along a linear continuum from simple intuitive reasoning to advanced, computational, rational, and objective reasoning (Case, 1998; Moshman, 1998), we miss many other facets of individuals and the influences on their cognition. For example, research suggests that older adolescents may not be more objective than younger adolescents, perhaps because irrational cognitive tendencies and biases increase with age (Klaczynski, 2000; Klaczynski & Fauth, 1997). Older adolescents have more stereotypes, intuitions, memories, and self-evident truths that they may employ in processing information.

Identity Development

There is growing agreement that identity is a complex concept. From a psychological perspective, **psychological identity** is a "person's self-definition as a separate and distinct individual" (Gardiner & Kosmitzki, 2008, p. 154). From a sociological perspective, **social identity** is the part of the self-concept that comes from knowledge of one's membership in a social group and the emotional significance of that membership (Gardiner & Kosmitzki, 2008). Lene Arnett Jensen (2003) suggests that adolescents increasingly develop multicultural identities as, they are exposed to diverse cultural beliefs, either through firsthand experience or through the media. She argues that the process of developing identity presents new challenges to adolescents in a global society. Jensen gives the example of arranged marriage in India, noting that on the one hand, Indian adolescents grow up with cultural values favoring arranged marriage, but on the other hand, they are increasingly exposed to values that emphasize freedom of choice.

Theories of Self and Identity

Psychological identity is thought to have five common functions (G. R. Adams & Marshall, 1996, p. 433):

> How do factors such as gender, race, ethnicity, and social class affect identity development?

1. To provide a structure for understanding who one is

2. To provide meaning and direction through commitments, values, and goals

3. To provide a sense of personal control and free will

4. To enable one to strive for consistency, coherence, and harmony between values, beliefs, and commitments

5. To enable one to recognize one's potential through a sense of future possibilities and alternative choices

A number of prominent psychologists have put forward theories that address self or psychological identity development in adolescence. Exhibit 14.2 provides an overview of six theorists: Freud, Erikson,

Exhibit 14.2 Theories of Self or Identity in Adolescence

Theorist	Developmental Stage	Major Task or Processes
Freud	Genital stage	To develop libido capable of reproduction and sexual intimacy
Erikson	Identity versus role diffusion	To find one's place in the world through self-certainty versus apathy, role experimentation versus negative identity, and anticipation of achievement versus work paralysis
Kegan	Affiliation versus abandonment (early adolescence)	To search for membership, acceptance, and group identity, versus a sense of being left behind, rejected, and abandoned
Marcia	Ego identity statuses	To develop one of these identity statuses: identity diffusion, foreclosure, moratorium, or identity achievement
Piaget	Formal operational thought	To develop the capacity for abstract problem formulation, hypothesis development, and solution testing
Kohlberg	Postconventional morality	To develop moral principles that transcend one's own society: individual ethics, societal rights, and universal principles of right and wrong

Kegan, Marcia, Piaget, and Kohlberg. All six help to explain how a concept of self or identity develops, and all six suggest that it cannot develop fully before adolescence. Piaget and Kohlberg suggest that some individuals may not reach these higher levels of identity development at all.

Sigmund Freud (1905/1953) thought of human development as a series of five psychosexual stages in the expression of libido (sensual pleasure). The fifth stage, the genital stage, occurs in adolescence, when reproduction and sexual intimacy become possible.

Building on Freud's work, Erik Erikson (1950, 1959, 1963, 1968) proposed eight stages of psychosocial development (refer back to Exhibit 4.11 in Chapter 4 for a summary of Erikson's eight stages). He viewed psychosocial crisis as an opportunity and challenge. Each Eriksonian stage requires the mastery of a particular developmental task related to identity. Erikson's fifth stage, identity versus role diffusion, is relevant to adolescence. The developmental task is to establish a coherent sense of identity; failure to complete this task successfully leaves the adolescent without a solid sense of identity.

Robert Kegan (1982, 1994) asserts that there should be another stage between middle childhood and adolescence in Erikson's model. He suggests that before working on psychological identity, early adolescents face the psychosocial conflict of affiliation versus abandonment. The main concern is being accepted by a group, and the fear is being left behind or rejected. Successful accomplishment of group membership allows the young person to turn to the question of "Who am I?" in mid- and late adolescence.

James Marcia (1966, 1980) expounded upon Erikson's notion that adolescents struggle with the issue of identity versus role diffusion. Marcia proposed that adolescents vary in how easily they go about developing personal identity, and he described four styles of identity development in adolescents:

1. *Identity diffusion.* No exploration of, or commitment to, roles and values

2. *Foreclosure.* Commitment made to roles and values without exploration

3. *Moratorium.* Exploration of roles and values without commitment

4. *Identity achievement.* Exploration of roles and values followed by commitment

Jean Piaget proposed four major stages leading to adult thought (refer back to Exhibit 4.1 in Chapter 4 for an overview of Piaget's stages). He expected the last stage, the stage of formal operations, to occur in adolescence, enabling the adolescent to engage in more abstract thinking about "who I am." Piaget (1972) also thought that adolescents begin to use formal operational skills to think in terms of what is best for society.

Lawrence Kohlberg (1976, 1984) expanded on Piaget's ideas about moral thinking to describe three major levels of moral development (refer back to Exhibit 4.3 in Chapter 4 for an overview of Kohlberg's stage theory). Kohlberg thought that adolescents become capable of **postconventional moral reasoning,** or morality based on moral principles that transcend social rules, but that many never go beyond conventional morality, or morality based on social rules.

These theories have been influential in conceptualizations of identity development. On perhaps a more practical level, however, Morris Rosenberg, in his book *Conceiving the Self* (1986), provides a very useful model of identity to keep in mind while working with adolescents—or perhaps to share with adolescents who are in the process of identity formation. Rosenberg suggests that identity comprises three major parts:

- *Social identity* is made up of several elements derived from interaction with other people and social systems, including social statuses, membership groups, and social types.
- *Dispositions* are self-ascribed aspects of identity.
- *Physical characteristics* are simply one's physical traits, which all contribute a great deal to sense of self.

Scholars generally agree that identity formation is structured by the sociocultural context (see Gardiner & Kosmitzki, 2008; Kroger, 2007). Thus, the options offered to adolescents vary across cultures. Societies such as North American and other Western societies that put a high value on autonomy offer more options for adolescents than more collectivist-oriented societies. Some writers suggest that having a large number of options increases stress for adolescents (Gardiner & Kosmitzki, 2008). Think about the case studies of David Costa, Carl Fleischer, and Monica Golden. What is the sociocultural context of their identity struggles? What choices do they have, given their sociocultural contexts?

For those aspects of identity that we shape ourselves, individuals have four ways of trying on and developing a preference for certain identities:

1. *Future orientation.* By adolescence, youth have developed two important cognitive skills: They are able to consider the future, and they are able to construct abstract thoughts. These skills allow them to choose from a list of hypothetical behaviors based on the potential outcomes resulting from those behaviors. David Costa demonstrates future orientation in his contemplation regarding Theo. Adolescents also contemplate potential future selves.

2. *Role experimentation.* According to Erikson (1963), adolescence provides a psychosocial moratorium—a period during which youth have the latitude to experiment with social roles. Thus, adolescents typically sample membership in different cliques, build relationships with various mentors, take various academic electives, and join assorted groups and organizations—all in an attempt to further define themselves. Monica Golden, for instance, sampled various potential career paths before deciding on becoming a pediatrician.

3. *Exploration.* Whereas role experimentation is specific to trying new roles, exploration refers to the comfort an adolescent has with trying new things. The more comfortable the individual is with exploration, the easier identity formation will be.

4. *Self-evaluation.* During the quest for identity, adolescents are constantly sizing themselves up against their peers. Erikson (1968) suggested that the development of identity is a process of personal reflection and observation of oneself in relation to others. George Herbert Mead (1934) suggested that individuals create a **generalized other** to represent how others are likely to view and respond to them. The role of the generalized other in adolescents' identity formation is evident when adolescents act on the assumed reactions of their families or peers. For example, what Monica Golden (Case Study 14.3) wears to school may be based not on what she thinks would be most comfortable or look the best, but rather on what she thinks her peers expect her to wear.

Gender Identity

Adolescence, like early childhood in Chapter 12, is a time of significant gender identification, and much has been written lately in the United States about the specific experiences of either adolescent boys or adolescent girls (Garbarino, 1999, 2006; Kindlon & Thompson, 1999; Pipher, 1994; Pollack, 1999; Rimm, 1999; Wiseman, 2002). Exercise caution, however, with these types of works, as some may present an exaggerated perspective for either gender experience. The general theme of these analyses is that female adolescents are sexualized in the media and overfocused on their bodies, and that male adolescents are steered away from their emotional lives and not provided the tools to negotiate them.

Gender identity, understanding of oneself as a man or woman, is elaborated and revised during late adolescence (B. Newman & Newman, 2009). Efforts are made to integrate the biological, psychological, and social dimensions of sex and gender. Culture plays a large role in this process. All cultures have norms about gender roles, and social institutions incorporate expectations about how females and males are to behave. Gender roles are learned in many social systems, beginning with the provision of gender scripts in families. Evidence shows that mainstream U.S. culture, as well as the cultures of many other societies, is moving toward more flexible standards for gendered behavior. There is much public conversation about gender roles and considerable revision is underway, allowing for increasing diversity in the enactment of gender roles. But in many cultures of the world, very distinct gender roles are prescribed, and gender is a major category for distributing power, with males receiving more power than females. Gender roles can be a source of painful culture clash for some immigrant groups who are migrating to North America and Europe, harder for some ethnic groups than for others. But there is evidence that many immigrant families and individuals learn to be bicultural in terms of gender expectations, holding onto some traditional expectations while also innovating some new ways of doing gender roles (see Denner & Dunbar, 2004).

In most cultures, the concepts of gender and sexuality are closely related, and gender is divided into only two categories: female and male (Gardiner & Kosmitzki, 2008). Some groups have historically ascribed more than two genders, however, and there is growing recognition that chromosomal, genetic, anatomical, and hormonal aspects of sex are sometimes not aligned (Rudacille, 2005). For example, transgendered people develop a gender identity that is opposite to their biological sex. They are acutely uncomfortable with the gender assigned to them at birth, and feel certain that they were not born into the "right body." One possibility they have is to engage in a sex change through hormone treatment and surgery. One study followed the adjustment of 20 adolescent transsexuals who had sex-reassignment surgery. In the 1 to 4 years of follow-up, the adolescents were doing well, and none of them had regrets about their decision to engage in a sex change (Y. Smith, van Goozen, & Cohen-Kettenis, 2001).

As we work with adolescents and strive to be responsive to their stories, we need to begin to consider what role being female or being male may play in who they are and what may be happening in their lives. How would David Costa's situation be different if he were a lesbian versus a gay male? What if Carl Fleischer was Carol? How are weight issues different for women and men? Are they different? And do successful Black men have different experiences or expectations from successful Black women? What if Monica Golden were male?

Identity and Ethnicity

Research indicates that ethnic origin is not likely to be a key ingredient of identity for Caucasian North American adolescents, but it is often central to identity in adolescents of ethnic minority groups (Branch, Tayal, & Triplett, 2000). Considerable research indicates that adolescence is a time when young people evaluate their ethnic background and explore ethnic identity (see S. French, Seidman, Allen, & Aber, 2006; Phinney, 2006). The development of ethnic identity in adolescence has been the focus of research across Canada, the United States, and Europe in recent years, as ethnic diversity increases in all of these countries (e.g., Costigan, Su, & Hua, 2009; D. Hughes, Hagelskamp, Way, & Foust, 2009; Lam & Smith, 2009; Rivas-Drake, 2008; Street, Harris-Britt, & Walker-Barnes, 2009). Ethnic minority youth are challenged to develop a sense of themselves as members of an ethnic minority group while also coming to terms with their national identity (Lam & Smith, 2009). Adolescents tend to have wider experience with multicultural groups than when they were younger and may be exposed to ethnic discrimination, which can complicate the development of cultural pride and belonging (Costigan et al., 2009).

Evidence in the research indicates that ethnic minority adolescents tend to develop strong ethnic identity, but there is also evidence of variability within ethnic groups in terms of extent of ethnic identity. Costigan and colleagues (2009) reviewed the literature on ethnic identity among Chinese Canadian youth and concluded that the evidence indicates a strong ethnic identity among these youth. Conversely, there was much variability in the extent to which these youth reported a Canadian identity. Adolescents negotiated ethnic identity in diverse ways across different settings, with different approaches being used at home versus in public settings. Lam and Smith (2009) studied how African and Caribbean adolescents (ages 11 to 16) in Britain negotiate ethnic identity

How can social workers use research like this to understand risk and protection in minority youth?

and national identity and had similar findings to those for Chinese Canadian youth. They found that both groups of adolescents, African and Caribbean, rated their ethnic identity higher than their national identity and reported more pride in their ethnic heritage than in being British. The researchers found, however, that girls reported stronger ethnic identity than boys. Using in-depth interviews rather than standardized instruments, Rivas-Drake (2008) found three different styles of ethnic identity among Latinos in one public university in the United States. One group reported high individualistic achievement motivation and alienation from other Latinos. A second group reported strong identification with Latinos and was motivated to remove perceived barriers for the group. A third group reported strong connection to Latinos but was not motivated to work to remove barriers for the group.

Ethnic identity develops within the context of the family, and there has been a general belief that children of immigrants acculturate more quickly than their parents do, leaving parents with a stronger ethnic identity than their children. Some research in Canada questions that belief. Costigan and Dokis (2006) found that Chinese Canadian mothers and children indicated stronger ethnic identity than the fathers, and mothers and children did not differ from each other. Interestingly, they found that the adolescents tended to report stronger ethnic identity than their parents in families characterized by high levels of warmth. This finding may reflect the Canadian cultural context: Canada has an official policy of multiculturalism, which promotes the maintenance of one's cultural heritage. Conversely, researchers in the United States have found that African American parents are more likely than parents in other ethnic groups to feel the need to prepare their adolescents for racial bias as a part of their racial/ethnic socialization (D. Hughes et al., 2009). This most likely reflects a more hostile environment for African American youth in the United States than for the Chinese Canadian youth.

There are certainly added complexities for the identity formation process of minority youth. Arthur Jones (1992) suggests that "the usual rifts between young adolescents (ages 13 to 15)

and their parents are sometimes more intense in middle-class African American families, especially those in which middle-class economic status is new for the parents. This is because the generation gap is more exaggerated" (p. 29). Consider Monica Golden, who is an upper-middle-class, African American teenager in a predominantly White high school. What are some of the potential added challenges of Monica's adolescent identity formation? Is it any wonder that she is hoping to attend Howard University, a historically Black college, where she could surround herself with African American role models and professional support networks?

The available research on ethnic identity among ethnic minority youth indicates that most of these youth cope by becoming bicultural, developing skills to operate within at least two cultures. This research should alert social workers to tune into the process of ethnic identity development when they work with ethnic minority youth. It appears that ethnic identity is a theme for both David Costa and Monica Golden. They both appear to be developing some comfort with being bicultural, but they are negotiating their bicultural status in different ways. Discussion about their ethnic identity might reveal more struggle than we expected. Some youth may be more likely to withdraw from the challenges of accessing mainstream culture rather than confronting these challenges and seeking workable solutions. We must be alert to this possibility.

Critical Thinking Questions 14.1

What are the implications of recent research findings about the adolescent brain for social policy? This research is leading to a number of policy discussions about several issues, including the timing of the school day; regulations for adolescent driving, including the legal age of driving, whether evening driving should be allowed, whether other adolescents can be present in the car of an adolescent driver, and so on; and age when a juvenile can be tried as an adult in a court of law. What opinions do you hold about these issues? How are those opinions shaped by recent brain research?

SOCIAL ASPECTS OF ADOLESCENCE _____

The social environment—family, peers, organizations, communities, institutions, and so on—is a significant element of adolescent life. For one thing, as already noted, identity develops through social transactions. For another, as adolescents become more independent and move into the world, they develop their own relationships with more elements of the social environment.

Relationships With Family

Answering the question, "Who am I?" includes a consideration of the question, "How am I different from my brothers and sisters, my parents, and other family members?" For many adolescents, this question begins the process of **individuation**—the development of a self or identity that is unique and separate. David Costa seems to have started the process of individuation; he recognizes that he may not want to be what his parents want him to be. He does not yet seem comfortable with this idea, however. Carl Fleischer is not sure how he is similar to and different from his absent father. Monica Golden has begun to recognize some ways that she is different from her siblings, and she is involved in her own personal exploration of career options that fit her disposition. It would appear that she is the furthest along in the individuation process.

Separation from parents has four components (D. Moore, 1987):

1. *Functional independence.* Literally being able to function with little assistance or independently from one's parents. An example would be getting ready for school: selecting an appropriate outfit, getting dressed, gathering needed school supplies, and feeding oneself.

2. *Attitudinal independence.* Not merely having a different attitude from parents, but developing one's own set of values and beliefs. An example might be choosing a presidential candidate based not on your parents' choice, but on your values and beliefs.

3. *Emotional independence.* Not being dependent on parents for approval, intimacy, and emotional support. Emotional independence might mean discovering your own way to overcome emotional turmoil—for example, listening to your favorite CD after a fight with your girlfriend or boyfriend rather than relying on support from your parents.

4. *Conflictual independence.* Being able to recognize one's separateness from parents without guilt, resentment, anger, or other negative emotions. Conflictual independence is being comfortable with being different. Thus, instead of ridiculing your dad for wearing those shorts to the picnic, you are able to go to the picnic realizing that you would not wear those shorts but that your father's taste in shorts is not a reflection on you.

The concept of independence is largely influenced by culture, and mainstream culture in the United States places a high value on independence. However, as social workers, we need to recognize that the notion of pushing the adolescent to develop an identity separate from family is not acceptable to all cultural groups in the United States (Gardiner & Kosmitzki, 2008). Many Asian Indian families may view adolescent struggles for independence as a disloyal cutting off of family and culture (Hines et al., 2005). Peter Nguyen (2008; Nguyen & Cheung, 2009) has studied the relationships between Vietnamese American adolescents and their parents and found that a majority of the adolescents perceived their fathers as using a traditional authoritarian parenting style and see this as posing problems for their mental health in the context of the multicultural society in the United States. Our assessments of adolescent individuation should be culturally sensitive. Likewise, we must be realistic in our assessments of the functional independence of adolescents with cognitive, emotional, and physical disabilities.

Even when it is consistent with their cultural values, not all adolescents are able to achieve functional independence, attitudinal independence, emotional independence, and conflictual independence. Instead, many maintain a high level of conflict. Conflict is particularly evident in families experiencing additional stressors, such as divorce and economic difficulties (Fine et al., 2010). Conflict also plays out differently at different points in adolescence. Research suggests that conflicts with parents increase around the time of puberty but begin to decrease after that. Conflicts typically involve disagreements about chores, dress, and other daily issues (Allison & Schultz, 2004; Granic, Dishion, & Hollenstein, 2003).

> How can families stay connected to their adolescents while also honoring their struggle for independence and increased agency in making choices?

Adolescent struggles for independence can be especially potent in multigenerational contexts (Preto, 2005). These struggles typically come at a time when parents are in midlife and grandparents are entering late adulthood, and both are facing stressors of their own. Adolescent demands for independence may reignite unresolved conflicts between the parents and the grandparents and stir the pot of family discord. The challenge for the family is to stay connected while also allowing the adolescent to widen contact with the world. Most families make this adjustment well, but often after an initial period of confusion and disruption.

The Society for Research on Adolescence prepared an international perspective on adolescence in the 21st century and reached three conclusions regarding adolescents and their relationships with their families:

1. Families are and will remain a central source of support to adolescents in most parts of the world. Cultural traditions that support family cohesion, such as those in the Middle East, South Asia, and China, remain particularly strong, despite rapid change. A great majority of teenagers around the world experience close and functional relationships with their parents.

2. Adolescents are living in a wider array of diverse and fluid family situations than was true a generation ago. These include divorced, single-parent, remarried, gay and lesbian, and multilocal families. More adolescents live in households without men. As a result of AIDS, regional conflicts, and migratory labor, many adolescents do not live with their parents.

3. Many families are becoming better positioned to support their adolescents' preparation for adulthood. Smaller family sizes result in adults devoting more resources and attention to each child. Parents in many parts of the world are adopting a more responsive and communicative parenting style, which facilitates development of interpersonal skills and enhances mental health (R. W. Larson, Wilson, & Mortimer, 2002).

Relationships With Peers

In the quest for autonomy and identity, adolescents begin to differentiate themselves from their parents and associate with their peers. Early adolescents are likely to select friends that are similar to them in gender and interests, but by middle adolescence, the peer group often includes opposite-sex friends as well as same-sex friends (Kroger, 2007). Most early adolescents have one close friend, but the stability of these friendships is not high. In early adolescence, the peer group tends to be larger than in middle childhood; these larger peer groups are known as *cliques*. By mid-adolescence, the peer group is organized around common interests; these groups tend to be even larger than cliques and are generally known as *crowds* (B. B. Brown & Klute, 2003). Peer relationships contribute to adolescents' identities, behaviors, and personal and social competence.

Peer relationships are a fertile testing ground for youth and their emerging identities (B. B. Brown, 2004). Many adolescents seek out a peer group with compatible members, and inclusion or exclusion from certain groups can affect their identity and overall development. David Costa's peer groups include the baseball team and a group of gay males from school. Carl Fleischer seems to be gravitating toward the "heads" for his peer group—although this choice appears to be related to a perception of rejection by other groups. Monica Golden enjoys easy acceptance by several peer groups: the peer counselors at high school, the senior class officers, the Young Republicans, and the track team.

Photo 14.2 Peer relationships are a fertile testing ground for youth and their emerging identities.

For some adolescents, participation in certain peer groups influences their behavior negatively. Peer influence may not be strong enough to undo protective factors, but if the youth is already at risk, the influence of peers becomes that much stronger (Rew, 2005). Sexual behaviors and pregnancy status are often the same for same-sex best friends (Cavanagh, 2004). Substance use is also a behavior that most often occurs in groups of adolescents. The same is true for violent and delinquent behaviors (Garbarino, 1999; M. Klein, 1995).

Romantic Relationships

Adolescents in many cultures become involved in romantic relationships during middle school and high school. By late adolescence, the quality of these relationships becomes more intimate. Furrow and Wehner (1997, cited in B. Newman & Newman, 2009, p. 343) suggest that romantic relationships meet four needs: affiliation, attachment, caregiving, and sexual gratification. The timing and rituals for forming romantic relationships vary from culture to culture and from one age cohort to another. In some cultures, the romantic relationship develops in the context of an arranged marriage. In the United States and many other societies, romantic relationships develop through a dance of flirtation and dating. Children who have close friendships in middle school have been found to be more likely to have romantic relationships in adolescence (B. Newman & Newman, 2009).

Relationships With Organizations, Communities, and Institutions

As adolescents loosen their ties to parents, they develop more direct relationships in other arenas such as school, the broader community, employment, leisure, and the mass media, including cell phones and the Internet.

School

In the United States, as well as other wealthy nations, youth are required to stay in school through a large portion of adolescence. The situation is quite different in many poor nations, however, where children may not even receive a primary school education (United Nations Development Program, 2005).

Photo 14.3 Adolescents in many cultures become involved in romantic relationships during middle school and high school.

In their time that is spent at school, adolescents are gaining skills and knowledge for their next step in life, either moving into the workforce or continuing their education. In school, they also have the opportunity to evolve socially and emotionally; school is a fertile ground for practicing future orientation, role experimentation, exploration, and self-evaluation.

Middle schools have a very structured format and a very structured environment; high schools are less structured in both format and environment, allowing a gradual transition to greater autonomy. The school experience changes radically, however, at the college level. Many college students are away from home for the first time and are in very unstructured environments.

David Costa, Carl Fleischer, and Monica Golden have had different experiences with structure in their environments to date. David's environment has required him to move flexibly between two cultures. That experience may help to prepare him for the unstructured college environment. Carl has had the least structured home life. It remains to be seen whether that has helped him to develop skills in structuring his own environment, or left him with insufficient models for doing so. Monica is accustomed to juggling multiple commitments and should have little trouble with the competing attractions and demands of college.

School is also an institutional context where cultures intersect, which may create difficulties for students who are not familiar or comfortable with mainstream culture. That is most likely an important contributing factor to the low high school graduation rates of youth of color. Research by the Civil Rights Project at Harvard University indicates that 75% of White students graduate from high school compared to approximately half of Black, Hispanic, and Native American youth (Orfield, Losen, Wald, & Swanson, 2004). You may not realize how Eurocentric the educational model in the United States is until you view it through a different cultural lens. We can use a Native American lens as an example. Michael Walkingstick Garrett (1995) uses the experiences of the boy Wind-Wolf as an example of the incongruence between Native American culture and the typical education model:

> Wind-Wolf is required by law to attend public school. . . . He speaks softly, does not maintain eye contact with the teacher as a sign of respect, and rarely responds immediately to questions, knowing that it is good to reflect on what has been said. He may be looking out the window during class, as if daydreaming, because he has been taught to always be aware of changes in the natural world. These behaviors are interpreted by his teacher as either lack of interest or dumbness. (p. 204)

Children in the United States spend less time in school-related activities than do Chinese or Japanese children and have been noted to put less emphasis on scholastic achievement. Some

What are some ways that different cultural expectations regarding education affect adolescent development?

researchers attribute oft-noted cross-cultural differences in mathematics achievement to these national differences in emphasis on scholastics (D. Newman, 2008). For adolescents, scholastic interest, expectations, and achievements may also vary, based not only on nationality but also on gender, race, ethnicity, economic status, and expectations for the future. Girls have been found to be more invested in school activities than boys (Shanahan & Flaherty, 2001). In a study of students in 33 middle and high schools, African American and Hispanic students were found to be more disengaged from school than Asian and White students, and economically disadvantaged teenagers were found to be more disengaged than more economically advantaged students (Csikszentmihalyi & Schneider, 2000). One longitudinal research project found that adolescents with a future orientation and expectations of further schooling, marriage, and good citizenship devote a greater percentage of their time to school-related activities (Shanahan & Flaherty, 2001).

The American Youth Policy Forum (2009) reexamined a 1988 report called *The Forgotten Half*, by the William T. Grant Foundation on its study *Forgotten Half Revisited: American Youth and Young Families, 1988–2008,* and found that "the nearly ten million 18–24 year-old Americans who don't go on to college after high school aren't doing as well at the end of the 1990's as they were a decade ago" (¶1). Through the early 1990s, vocational education in the United States was stigmatized as the high school track for students with poor academic capabilities, special needs, or behavioral problems (Gamoran & Himmelfarb, 1994). Congress and most educators, however, believe that broadening the segment of the student population that participates in vocational education and adding academic achievement and postsecondary enrollment to the traditional objectives of technical competency, labor market outcomes, and general employability skills will improve the quality of these programs (R. Lynch, 2000). Moreover, the National Women's Law Center has reported that there is pervasive sex segregation in high school vocational programs in the United States, with girls clustered in programs that train them for lower-paying jobs ("Sex Bias," 2002).

The Broader Community

In the United States, the participation of high school students in volunteer work in the community is becoming common, much more so than in Europe. Indeed, community service is required in many U.S. high schools. C. Flanagan (2004) argues that community volunteer service provides structured outlets for adolescents to meet a wider circle of community people, and to experiment with new roles. The community youth development movement is based on the belief that such community service provides an opportunity to focus on the strengths and competencies of youth rather than on youth problems (see Villarruel, Perkins, Borden, & Keith, 2003). One research team found that participation in community service and volunteerism assisted in identity clarification and in the development of political and moral interests (H. McIntosh, Metz, & Youniss, 2005).

Another way that adolescents can have contact with the broader community is through a mentoring relationship with a community adult. The mentoring relationship may be either formal or informal. The mentor becomes a role model and trusted advisor. Mentors can be found in many places: in part-time work settings, in youth-serving organizations, in religious organizations, at school, in the neighborhood, and so on. There is unusually strong evidence for the positive value of mentoring for youth (S. Hamilton & Hamilton, 2004). One recent study found that perceived mentoring from an unrelated adult in the work setting was associated with psychosocial competencies and adjustment in both U.S. and European samples (Vazsonyi & Snider, 2008). Longitudinal research with foster care youth has found that youth who had been mentored had better overall health, less suicidal ideation, fewer sexually transmitted infections, and less aggression in young adulthood than foster care youth who had not been mentored (Ahrens, DuBois, Richardson, Fan, & Lozano, 2008).

Work

Like many adolescents, Carl Fleischer and Monica Golden also play the role of worker in the labor market. Work can provide an opportunity for social interaction and greater financial independence. It may also lead to personal growth by promoting notions of contribution, responsibility, egalitarianism, and self-efficacy and by helping the adolescent to develop values and preferences for future jobs—answers to questions like, "What kind of job would I like to have in the future?" and "What am I good at?" (Mortimer & Finch, 1996, p. 4). For example, Monica tried many jobs before deciding that she loves working with children and wants to become a pediatrician. In addition, employment may also offer the opportunity to develop job skills, time management skills, customer relation skills, money management skills, market knowledge, and other skills of value to future employers.

In July 2006, an estimated 21.9 million U.S. youth ages 16 to 24 were employed for an employment rate of 59.2% of the civilian noninstitutional population (U.S. Bureau of Labor Statistics, 2006). The rate fell almost 11 points between July 1989 and July 2003 but remained fairly constant from 2003 to 2006. Being in the labor force means the individual is working either full-time or part-time as a paid employee in an ongoing relationship with a particular employer, such as working in a supermarket. Individuals are not considered to be in the labor force if they work in certain "freelance jobs" that involve doing tasks without a specific employer, such as babysitting or mowing lawns. Broken down by gender and race, the employment rate for July 2006 was 61.9% for young men, 56.5% for young women, 63.3% for Whites, 43.5% for Blacks, 42.8% for Asians, and 55.2% for Latinos (U.S. Bureau of Labor Statistics, 2006).

The U.S. Department of Labor has launched a new initiative called YouthRules! that seeks to promote positive and safe work experiences for young workers. Their guidelines are the social policy result of research that suggests that for youth, work, in spite of some positive benefits, may also detract from development by cutting into time needed for sleep, exercise, maintenance of overall health, school, family relations, and peer relations. Unfortunately, the types of work that are available to adolescents are usually low-skill jobs that offer little opportunity for skill development. Adolescents who work more than 10 hours per week have been found to be at increased risk for poor academic performance; psychological problems such as depression, anxiety, fatigue, and sleep difficulties; as well as physical problems such as headaches, stomachaches, and colds. They are also more likely to use cigarettes, alcohol, or other drugs, regardless of ethnicity, socioeconomic status (SES), or age (Entwisle, Alexander, & Olson, 2005; Marsh & Kleitman, 2005). Although we cannot draw causal conclusions, Carl Fleischer is a good example of this linkage: He works more than 10 hours a week and also has declining grades and uses tobacco and marijuana.

Leisure

In wealthy nations, a sizable portion of an adolescent's life is spent in leisure pursuits. These activities often have great influence on various aspects of the individual's development, such as identity formation, and psychological and behavioral functioning (Bartko & Eccles, 2003). Cross-national research indicates that there are national differences in the way adolescents use nonschool time (Verma & Larson, 2003). For example, Korean and Japanese youth spend more time on homework and preparation for college entrance exams than U.S. or European youth (M. Lee, 2003). Compared with European teens from 12 countries, U.S. teens spend less time on schoolwork, less time in reading for leisure, more time in paid employment, and more time hanging out with friends (Flammer & Schaffner, 2003; R. M. Larson & Seepersad, 2003). Japanese and U.S. youth spend a great deal of time on extracurricular activity, particularly organized sports, based on a cultural belief that these activities build character (R. M. Larson & Seepersad, 2003; Nishino &

Photo 14.4 In wealthy nations, a sizable portion of an adolescent's life is spent in leisure pursuits.

Larson, 2003). Across national lines, girls tend to have more chores and spend more time in the arts than boys, and boys spend more time in sports and with electronic media than girls (Silbereisen, 2003).

One research team (Bartko & Eccles, 2003) examined the nonschool activity profiles of 918 adolescents from Washington, D.C., across 11 different activity domains. Using cluster analysis, the team identified a typology of six unique activity profiles:

Sports Cluster: highly involved in sports and also in spending time with friends

School Cluster: highly involved in school-based clubs, homework, and reading for pleasure

Uninvolved Cluster: activity levels below the mean in all 11 activity domains

Volunteer Cluster: highly involved in volunteer activities

High-Involved Cluster: highly involved in a range of activities, including community-based clubs, sports, homework, reading, chores, volunteering, and religious activities; low involvement in unstructured activities

Working Cluster: highly involved in paid work, and low levels of involvement in other activity domains

There were no race differences in activity choices, but there were gender differences. Males were overrepresented in the Sports Cluster and Uninvolved Cluster. Females were overrepresented in the School Cluster, Volunteer Cluster, and High-Involved Cluster. The parents of the High-Involved Cluster students had higher educational attainment than parents of students in the other clusters. Psychological and behavioral functioning was associated with the activity profiles of the respondents. Respondents in the School and High-Involved clusters had the highest grade point averages, and Uninvolved respondents had the lowest grade point averages. Behavior problems were more often reported by respondents in the Sports, Uninvolved, and Work clusters. The highest rates of depression were found in the Uninvolved Cluster.

Another study examining the relationship between leisure and identity formation for adolescents found that the patterns of influence are different for girls and boys (S. Shaw, Kleiber, &

Caldwell, 1995). Participation in sports and physical activities has a positive effect on identity development for female adolescents but shows no effect for males. Watching television has a negative effect on identity development for male adolescents but shows no effect for females. And involvement in social activities and other leisure activities was not significantly correlated with identity development for either gender.

Access to leisure activities varies. Leisure activities for rural adolescents are different from leisure activities for urban youth, for example. Adolescents living in urban areas have greater access to transportation and to public recreational activities and programs. Rural youth lack this access and thus rely more heavily on school-related leisure activities (Garton & Pratt, 1991). Access to leisure activities also increases with SES.

Cell Phones and the Internet

Nationally, the use of cell phones is not only big business, but also a cultural phenomenon whose impact remains to be seen. According to an article in *The Washington Post*, more than 75 billion text messages are sent each month in the United States, with the most prolific texters in the 13–17 age range (St. George, 2009). Adolescents average 2,272 text messages a month versus 203 calls from their cell phones. This phenomenon brings another level of connectedness—with potential benefits, such as maintaining distant relationships, keeping parents updated on their child's whereabouts or needs, and broader social networks, but also potential risks, such as driving while texting, mental and physical (primarily thumbs) fatigue, social disconnectedness, and instant gratification.

The Internet is also a relatively new vehicle for connectedness, and increasingly, teens are using the web to complete schoolwork, obtain general information, play games, and socialize. In 2004, it was estimated that two thirds of households in the United States had access to the Internet (D. Croteau & Hoynes, 2006). And with children and teenagers comprising one of the fastest-growing groups of Internet users, researchers estimate that almost 25 million youth in the United States between the ages of 10 and 17 are regular Internet users (Wolak, Mitchell, & Finkelhor, 2006). Nationwide, 24.9% of high school students said they played video or

Photo 14.5   Adolescents are prolific users of text messaging, bringing a high level of connectedness.

computer games or used a computer for something other than schoolwork for more than 3 hours on an average school day (CDC, 2008d).

Empirical evidence indicates that the Internet fosters social connections and identity development, is an important source for adolescent health information, and provides opportunities for practicing leadership skills (Borzekowski, Fobil, & Asante, 2006; P. Greenfield & Zheng, 2006; Gross, 2004). Internet social networking programs such as Facebook allow adolescents to try on various identities and create various relationships. As Bakardjieva (2004) states in the book *Community in the Digital Age: Philosophy and Practice,* social networking sites allow individuals "to traverse the social world, penetrate previously unattainable regions of anonymity" (p. 122). On the other hand, parents, school officials, and legislators have become increasingly concerned that adolescents will see sexually explicit material on the Internet, and be sexually exploited or otherwise harassed via the Internet. The Internet Crimes Against Children Task Forces (ICAC) comprise 61 federal, state, and local task forces. Since 1998, this ICAC network of task forces has reviewed more than 180,000 complaints of alleged child sexual victimization and arrested more than 16,500 individuals (ICAC, 2010). Moreover, the U.S. Department of Justice increased funding for the ICAC program from $2.4 million in 1998 to $75 million in 2009 (ICAC, 2010).

In 1999 and 2000, researchers Wolak, Mitchell, and Finkelhor (2003) conducted the first Youth Internet Safety Survey (YISS-1) with a national sample of over 1,500 youth ages 10 to 17 who used the Internet at least once a month for the past 6 months. A second Youth Internet Safety Survey (YISS-2) was conducted in 2005 by the same researchers, again using a sample of over 1,500 youth ages 10 to 17 (Wolak et al., 2006). Some of the main findings of YISS-2 are presented below:

- 91% of the youth had home Internet access, compared with 74% in YISS-1.
- 74% had access in three or more places, compared with 51% in YISS-1.

- 86% of the youth had used the Internet in the past week, compared with 76% in YISS-1.
- 23% reported using the Internet more than 2 hours at a time, compared with 13% in YISS-1.
- 49% used the Internet 5 to 7 days a week, compared with 31% in YISS-1.
- 30% visited online chat rooms, compared with 56% in YISS-1.
- 34% saw sexual material online that they did not want to see in the past year, up from 25% in YISS-1, despite the increased use of filtering, blocking, and monitoring software.
- 34% communicated online with people they did not know in person, compared to 40% in YISS-1.
- One in 7 youth received unwanted sexual solicitation, compared to 1 in 5 in YISS-1.
- 4% received aggressive sexual solicitations that attempted offline contact, compared to 3% in YISS-1.
- 4% reported that online solicitors asked them for nude or sexually explicit photographs of themselves; this information was not collected in YISS-1.
- 9% were the victims of online harassment and/or bullying, compared to 6% in YISS-1.
- 28% had made rude or nasty comments to someone on the Internet, compared to 14% in YISS-1.

YISS-2 also found a large increase in the posting or sending of personal information or pictures between 2000 and 2005. In 2005, 34% had posted their real names, home addresses, telephone numbers, or their school names; 45% had posted their date of birth or age; and 18% had posted pictures of themselves. In 2000, only 11% had posted personal information and only 5% had posted pictures of themselves. This increase reflects the rise of personal profile sites such as Facebook, MySpace, Friendster, and Xanga. Wolak, Mitchell, and Finkelhor (2003) surmise that

adolescents may be especially drawn to online relationships because of their intense interest in forming relationships, and because the expansiveness of cyberspace frees them from some of the constraints of adolescence by giving them easy access to a world beyond that of their families, schools and communities. (p. 106)

Unfortunately, adolescents are also vulnerable to unethical marketers who engage in such tactics as bundling digital pornography material with game demos and other products that youth are likely to download (Wolak et al., 2006). Researchers have also found that sex offenders target young teenagers by playing on their desire for romance and interest in sex (Wolak et al., 2006). The adolescents who are most vulnerable to these advances are girls who have high levels of conflict with their parents or who are highly troubled and boys with low levels of communication with their parents or who are highly troubled (Wolak et al., 2003).

ADOLESCENT SPIRITUALITY ____

Another potential facet of adolescent development is spirituality or religiosity. As adolescents become capable of advanced thinking and begin to contemplate their existence, identity, and future, many also undertake spiritual exploration. Sociology of religion researchers suggest that adolescents are a population that many religious organizations particularly target in order to exert influence in their lives, and adolescence and young adulthood are the life stages when religious conversion is most likely to take place (C. Smith, Denton, Faris, & Regnerus, 2002).

The National Study of Youth and Religion (NSYR) is the most comprehensive study of spirituality and religion among U.S. adolescents to date. Supported by the Lilly Endowment, this study began in August 2001 and was funded through December 2007. The first wave of data collection was conducted from July 2002 to April 2003. It was a nationally representative, random-digit dial method, telephone survey of 3,290 English- and Spanish-speaking teenagers ages 13 to 17 and of their parents living in all 50 states. It also includes more than 250 in-depth, face-to-face interviews of a subsample of survey respondents. The second wave included 78% of the original respondents and

| How important is it for social workers to assess the spirituality of adolescents with whom they work? |

was conducted from June 2005 to November 2005 (C. Smith & Denton, 2005).

The NSYR found that the vast majority of U.S. teenagers identify themselves as Christian (52% Protestant, various denominations; 23% Catholic). Sixteen percent are not religious. In addition, 2.8% identify themselves as being of two different faiths, 2.5% are Mormon, 1.5% are Jewish, and other minority faiths (Jehovah's Witness, Muslim, Eastern Orthodox, Buddhist, Pagan or Wiccan, Hindu, Christian Science, Native American, Unitarian Universalist) each comprised less than 1% of the representative sample. Four out of 10 U.S. adolescents say they attend religious services once a week or more, pray daily or more, and are currently involved in a religious youth group. Eighty-four percent of the surveyed youth believe in God, whereas 12% are unsure about belief in God, and 3% do not believe in God (C. Smith & Denton, 2005).

The bulk of the NSYR data are analyzed in the book *Soul Searching: The Religious and Spiritual Lives of American Teenagers,* by C. Smith and Denton (2005), who reached these empirical conclusions:

Religion is a significant presence in the lives of many U.S. teens today.

Teenage religiosity in the United States is extraordinarily conventional and very few youth appear to be pursuing "spiritual but not religious" personal quests.

The religious diversity represented by U.S. adolescents is no more varied today than it has been for a very long time.

The single most important social influence on the religious and spiritual lives of adolescents is their parents.

The greater the supply of religiously grounded relationships, activities, programs, opportunities, and challenges available to teenagers, the more likely teenagers will be religiously engaged and invested.

At the level of subjective consciousness, adolescent religious and spiritual understanding and concern seem to be generally very weak.

It is impossible to adequately understand the religious and spiritual lives of U.S. teenagers without framing that understanding to include the larger social and institutional contexts that form their lives.

Significant differences [exist] in a variety of important life outcomes between more and less religious teenagers in the United States. (pp. 260–263)

A growing volume of research is finding religion to be a positive force in adolescent development (P. King, 2007). Here are some of the themes found in that research: Religious participation has been found to promote civic engagement and altruism (Donnelly, Atkins, & Hart, 2005; Kerestes, Youniss, & Metz, 2004). Religion and spirituality have been found to contribute to positive identity development (Templeton & Eccles, 2006). Religion has been found to be a coping resource for adolescents in both good and ill health (A. Mahoney, Pendleton, & Ihrke, 2005). Attendance at religious services has been found to serve as a protective mechanism in high-risk neighborhoods, providing supportive relationships, moral values, and positive rituals and routines (Regenerus & Elder, 2003). Active religious participation provides adolescents with the opportunity to interact with nonparental adults (P. King & Furrow, 2004). Religious youth are less likely to engage in risky sexual behavior (Adamczyk & Felson, 2006) and to engage in other high-risk behaviors such as substance abuse and violence (Wagener, Furrow, King, Leffert, & Benson, 2003).

For many youth, spirituality may be closely connected to culture. Interventions with adolescents and their families should be consistent with their spirituality, but knowing someone's cultural heritage will not always provide understanding of their religious or spiritual beliefs. For example, it is no longer safe to assume that all Latino Americans are Catholic. Today, there is much religious diversity among Latino Americans who increasingly have membership in Protestant denominations such as Methodist, Baptist, Presbyterian, and Lutheran, as well as in such religious groups as Mormons, Seventh-Day Adventists, and Jehovah's Witnesses. Moreover, the fastest-growing religions among Latino Americans are the Pentecostal and evangelical denominations

(B. Garcia & Zuniga, 2007). Many Latino Americans, particularly Puerto Ricans, combine traditional religious beliefs with a belief in spiritualism, which is a belief that the visible world is surrounded by an invisible world made up of good and evil spirits who influence human behavior. Some Latino Americans practice Indigenous healing rituals, such as *Santeria* (Cuban American) and *curanderismo* (Mexican American). In these latter situations, it is important to know whether adolescents and their families are working with an Indigenous folk healer (Ho et al., 2004).

Although adolescents may not seem to be guided by their spirituality or religiosity, they may have underlying spiritual factors at work. As with any biological, psychological, or social aspect of the individual, the spiritual aspect of youth must be considered to gain the best understanding of the whole person.

Critical Thinking Questions 14.2

Children and adolescents in the United States spend less time on school-related activities than students in most other industrialized countries. Do you think children and adolescents in the United States should spend more time in school? How would you support your argument on this issue? How could high schools in the United States do a better job of supporting the cognitive development of adolescents? Should high schools be concerned about supporting emotional and social development of adolescents? Why or why not?

ADOLESCENT SEXUALITY

With the changes of puberty, adolescents begin to have sexual fantasies, sexual feelings, and sexual attractions. They must come to an understanding of what it means to be a sexual being, and make some decisions about which, if any, sexual behaviors to engage in. They also begin to understand the kinds of people they find sexually attractive. In their experimentation, some adolescents will contract sexually transmitted infections, and some will become pregnant. Unfortunately, some will also experience unwanted sexual attention and be victims of sexual aggression.

Sexual Decision Making

Transition into sexualized behavior is partly a result of biological changes. The amount of the sex hormone DHEA in the blood peaks between the ages of 10 and 12, a time when both boys and girls become aware of sexual feelings. The way that sexual feelings get expressed depends largely on sociocultural factors, however. Youth are influenced by the attitudes toward sexual activity that they encounter in the environment at school; among peers, siblings, and family; in their clubs/organizations; in the media; and so on. When and how they begin to engage in sexual activity are closely linked to what they perceive to be the activities of their peers (M. Henderson, Butcher, Wight, Williamson, & Raab, 2008; Ponton & Judice, 2004; Rew, 2005). Research also suggests that youth who are not performing well in school are more likely to engage in sexual activity than are those who are doing well (Rew, 2005). Finally, beliefs and behaviors regarding sexuality are also shaped by one's culture, religion/spirituality, and value system. Ponton and Judice (2004) suggest that

> a nation's attitude about adolescent sexuality plays an important role in the adolescent's sexual development and affects the laws, sexual media, sexual services, and the interaction of religion and state as well as the type of education that they receive in their schools. (p. 7)

Adolescents report a variety of social motivations for engaging in sexual intercourse, including developing new levels of intimacy, pleasing a partner, impressing peers, and gaining sexual experience (Impett & Tolman, 2006).

As the pubertal hormones cause changes throughout the body, most adolescents spend time becoming familiar with those changes. For many, exploration includes **masturbation,** the self-stimulation of the genitals for sexual pleasure. Almost 50% of boys and 30% of girls report masturbating by age 13; boys masturbate earlier and more often than girls (Leitenberg, Detzer, & Srebnik, 1993). The gender difference has been found to be even greater in Bangkok, Thailand, where 79% of male secondary students report masturbating, compared to 9% of females (O-Prasetsawat & Petchum, 2004). Masturbation has negative associations for some adolescents. Thus, masturbation may have psychological implications for adolescents, depending on the way they feel about it and how they think significant others feel about it. Female college students who are high in religiosity report more guilt about masturbation than female college students who are low in religiosity (J. Davidson, Moore, & Ullstrup, 2004).

The U.S. Youth Risk Behavior Survey suggests that nationwide 47.8% of high school students reported having had sexual intercourse during their life, 7.1% had sexual intercourse for the first time before age 13, 14.9% have had sexual intercourse with four or more persons during their life, and 35.0% were sexually active during the last 3 months (CDC, 2008d). Of the 35% of high school students who indicated that they are currently sexually active, 61.5% report that either they or their partner used a condom during last sexual intercourse, 16% reported that either they or their partner had used birth control pills to prevent pregnancy before last intercourse, and 22.5% had drunk alcohol or used drugs before their last sexual intercourse (CDC, 2008d).

Data suggest that, on average, adolescents in the United States experience first sexual intercourse slightly earlier than adolescents in other industrialized countries; the average age of first intercourse in the United States was found to be 15.8 years, compared to 16.2 in Germany, 16.8 in France, and 17.7 in the Netherlands (Berne & Huberman, 1999). In the United States, 70% of females who had sex before age 13 did so nonvoluntarily (Guttmacher Institute, 1999). One study found that the majority of teens in the United States who are sexually active wish they had waited until they were older to begin to have sexual intercourse (National Campaign to Prevent Teen Pregnancy, 2002).

As compared with the already high rates of adolescent sexual involvement in North America and Europe, recent research suggests that rates have been increasing in Latin America, sub-Saharan Africa, and East and Southeast Asia (R. W. Larson et al., 2002). In addition, although sexual relationships remain heavily sanctioned for adolescents, primarily girls, in the Middle East and South Asia, research also points to increased cross-gender interaction among urban youth in these regions (R. W. Larson et al., 2002).

Regardless of nation or milieu, there is most certainly a need for adolescents to develop skills for healthy management of sexual relationships. Early engagement in sexual intercourse has some negative consequences. The earlier a youth begins engaging in sexual intercourse, the more likely he or she is to become involved in delinquent behavior, problem drinking, and marijuana use (Armour & Haynie, 2007; F. M. Costa, Jessor, Donovan, & Fortenberry, 1995). One researcher found that while some adolescents experience mental health disruptions after first sexual intercourse, the majority do not (Meier, 2007).

Rates of sexual activity among teens in the United States are fairly comparable to those in Western Europe, yet the incidence of adolescent pregnancy, childbearing, and sexually transmitted infections in the United States far exceeds the level of most other industrialized nations (Feijoo, 2001). For instance, the Netherlands, France, and Germany have far better sexual outcomes for teens than the United States. Teens in those countries begin sexual activity at slightly later ages and have fewer sexual partners than teens in the United States. The teen pregnancy rate in the United States is 8 times greater than the pregnancy rate in the Netherlands and Japan; nearly 5 times greater than the rate in Germany; nearly 4 times greater than the rate in France; and twice as high as England, Wales, and Canada. The teenage abortion rate in the United States is nearly 7 times the rate in the Netherlands, nearly 3 times the rate in France, and nearly 8 times the rate in

Germany. There are similar differences in rates of sexually transmitted infections among teens when comparing the United States to European countries (Advocates for Youth, 2002; Guttmacher Institute, 2006a). This discrepancy is probably related to three factors: Teenagers in the United States make less use of contraception than teens in European countries, reproductive health services are more available in European countries, and sexuality education is more comprehensively integrated into all levels of education in most of Europe than in the United States (Feijoo, 2001; Huberman, 2001). It should be noted, however, that between 1995 and 2002, there was a decline in the percentage of U.S. teens having sexual intercourse before age 15, down from 19% to 13% for females and from 21% to 15% for males (Guttmacher Institute, 2006a).

The popular press, including the *New York Times* and *The Washington Post,* has reported that oral sex has gained popularity among adolescents (Jarrell, 2000; Stepp, 1999). This information has, for the most part, been anecdotal, because as adolescent sexuality researcher Lisa Remez (2000) contends, obtaining parent consent for surveys about the sexual activity of their minor children can be difficult. There is a generalized fear that asking young people about sex will somehow lead them to choose to have sex, and the federal government has been reluctant to sponsor controversial research about the noncoital (not involving heterosexual intercourse) sexual behaviors of adolescents.

However, the 2002 National Survey of Family Growth (NSFG) was able to collect data on oral sex among people ages 15 to 44, and the data have been analyzed and reanalyzed by several organizations. The consensus is that the data show that 22% of females and 24% of males ages 15 to 19 who haven't had sexual intercourse have engaged in heterosexual oral sex. In addition, 83% of females and 88% of males who have had sexual intercourse have also engaged in heterosexual oral sex. It was also found that fewer than 1 in 10 adolescents who engaged in oral sex used condoms to protect against sexually transmitted infections (Mosher, Chandra, & Jones, 2005).

Sexual Orientation

As they develop as sexual beings, adolescents begin to discover the types of people that they find sexually attractive. **Sexual orientation** refers to erotic, romantic, and affectionate attraction to people of the same sex, the opposite sex, or both sexes. It can be understood along a continuum from completely heterosexual to bisexual to completely homosexual attractions. There are also questioning adolescents who are less certain of their sexual orientation than those who label themselves as heterosexual, bisexual, or gay/lesbian (Poteat, Aragon, Espelage, & Koenig, 2009). About 6.8% of youth responding to the U.S. National Health Survey reported having experienced same-sex attractions or same-sex relationships, but only a small group reported same-sex sexual behaviors, and even fewer identified themselves as gay, lesbian, or bisexual (cited in Savin-Williams & Diamond, 2004). J. Glover, Galliher, and Lamere (2009) suggest that sexual orientation should be conceptualized as a "complex configuration of identity, attractions, behaviors, disclosure, and interpersonal explorations" (pp. 92–93).

> How does sexual orientation affect development during adolescence?

Still, adolescence is the time when most people develop some awareness of their sexual orientation. In their comprehensive investigation of gay and lesbian sexuality, Marcel Saghir and Eli Robins (1973) found that most adult gay men and lesbians reported the onset of homosexual arousal, homosexual erotic imagery, and homosexual romantic attachment during early adolescence before age 15. More recent research has produced similar findings (L. M. Diamond, 2000). Recent studies indicate, however, that gay and lesbian youth may be "coming out" and accepting their homosexual identity at earlier ages than in prior eras (Saltzburg, 2004; H. Taylor, 2000).

Gay and lesbian youth typically suffer from the awareness that they are different from most of their peers in an aspect of identity that receives a great deal of attention in our culture (J. Glover et al., 2009). Consider David Costa's conflict over his homosexuality. Dennis Anderson (1994) suggests that a "crisis of self-concept occurs because the gay adolescent senses a sudden involuntary joining to a stigmatized group" (p. 15). He goes on to elaborate, "To some gay and lesbian adolescents the experience of watching boys and girls in school walk hand-in-hand down the hallway, while their own desires must be kept secret, produces feelings of rage and sadness that are difficult to resolve" (p. 18).

Given the societal assumption of heterosexuality, many LGBQ (lesbian, gay, bisexual, questioning) youth are "creating, questioning, and sometimes even fighting their sexual identity" (Bond, Hefner, & Drogos, 2009, p. 35). In the process, they seek out information about sexual attraction, alternative sexual orientations, and the coming out process. Research is indicating that the current generation of LGBQ youth uses the Internet to get this information and to begin the coming out process. This provides a safe and anonymous venue for exploration and questioning as well as for initiating the coming out process; it can lead to greater self-acceptance before coming out to family and friends (Bond et al., 2009).

There is some question about whether research has captured the diversity within the sexual minority youth community. One research team focused on the psychosocial concerns of questioning youth and racial minority LGB youth. All LGB youth have been found to face increased victimization, but questioning youth have been found to face higher levels of victimization, substance abuse, and suicidal thoughts than other sexual minority youth (Poteat et al., 2009). It is possible that questioning youth are marginalized by both heterosexual and LGB peers. Bisexual youth also may be marginalized by the LG community. Although LGB youth of color experience discrimination based on sexual orientation, they may experience more discrimination based on race than on sexual orientation (Poteat et al., 2009).

LGB adolescents who have disclosed their sexual orientation to parents have been found to have less internalized homophobia than those who have not disclosed to their parents. However, adolescents who have disclosed to their parents report that they had to undergo a period of verbal victimization from parents before they reached a point where parents were supportive (D'Augelli, Grossman, & Starks, 2005). One research team found that higher rates of family rejection are associated with poorer health outcomes. LGB young adults who reported high levels of family rejection during adolescence were 8.4 times more likely to report suicide attempts, 5.9 times more likely to report serious depression, 3.4 times more likely to use illegal drugs, and 3.4 times more likely to report unprotected sexual intercourse than LGB young adults who reported little or no family rejection. Latino men reported the highest level of family rejection related to sexual orientation in adolescence (C. Ryan, Huebner, Diaz, & Sanchez, 2009).

To forestall potential rejection from family and friends, the Parents, Families and Friends of Lesbians and Gays (PFLAG) (2001), a social movement with the goal of promoting a more supportive environment for gay males and lesbians, produced a brochure titled *Read This Before Coming Out to Your Parents*. This brochure lists 12 questions to ponder prior to coming out, reproduced in Exhibit 14.3. These are heavy questions for any adolescent, and there are still too few nonfamilial supports available to assist adolescents in resolving their questions related to sexual orientation or easing the process of coming out.

Pregnancy and Childbearing

Approximately 750,000 adolescent girls ages 15 to 19 become pregnant each year in the United States (Guttmacher Institute, 2010). This is a pregnancy rate of 71.5 per 1,000 15- to 19-year-old women. The teen pregnancy rate declined 41% between 1990 and 2005. The majority of the decline was due to more consistent use of contraceptives, but some of the decline was due to teens delaying sexual activity. However, teen pregnancy

---

| **Exhibit 14.3** | Questions to Ponder Prior to Coming Out |

1. Are you sure about your sexual orientation?
2. Are you comfortable with your gay sexuality?
3. Do you have support?
4. Are you knowledgeable about homosexuality?
5. What's the emotional climate at home?
6. Can you be patient?
7. What's your motive for coming out now?
8. Do you have available resources?
9. Are you financially dependent on your parents?
10. What is your general relationship with your parents?
11. What is their moral societal view?
12. Is this your decision?

SOURCE: Parents, Families and Friends of Lesbians and Gays (2001).

rose in 2006, with a 3% increase over 2005. It is too early to tell if this increase will begin a new trend upward. The teen pregnancy rate varies by race and ethnicity with the pregnancy rate of Hispanic (127 per 1,000) and Black (126 per 1,000) females being almost 3 times that of non-Hispanic White females (44 per 1,000). The pregnancy rate among Black teens decreased 45% between 1990 and 2005, however. Of teen pregnancies, 57% end in birth, 29% end in abortion, and 14% end in miscarriage (Guttmacher Institute, 2006a). Two thirds of teen pregnancies occur among 18- to 19-year-olds, an age by which many adolescents are taking on adult roles (Guttmacher Institute, 2010).

Adolescent pregnancies carry increased physical risks to mother and infant, including less prenatal care and higher rates of miscarriage, anemia, toxemia, prolonged labor, premature delivery, and low birth weight. In many Asian, eastern Mediterranean, African, and Latin American countries, the physical risks of adolescent pregnancy are mitigated by social and economic support (Hao & Cherlin, 2004). In the United States, however,

What factors might be producing the recent fluctuations in the teen pregnancy rate?

adolescent mothers are more likely than their counterparts elsewhere to drop out of school, to be unemployed or underemployed, to receive public assistance, and to have subsequent pregnancies and lower educational and financial attainment. Teenage fathers may also experience lower educational and financial attainment (Bunting & McAuley, 2004).

The developmental tasks of adolescence are typically accomplished in this culture by going to school, socializing with peers, and exploring various roles. For the teenage mother, these avenues to development may be radically curtailed. The result may be long-lasting disadvantage. Consider Monica Golden's path. She obviously loves children and would like to have her own someday, but she would also like to become a pediatrician. If Monica were to become pregnant unexpectedly, an abortion would challenge her religious values, and a baby would challenge her future goals.

Sexually Transmitted Infections

Youth have always faced pregnancy as a possible consequence of their sexual activity, but other consequences now include infertility and death as a result of **sexually transmitted infections (STIs)**. The majority of sexually active adolescents used contraception the first time they have sexual intercourse, 74% of females and 82% of males. Even more did so at the most recent sexual intercourse, 83% of females and 91% of males (Guttmacher Institute, 2006a). The condom is the most common form of contraception used. However, as discussed earlier, the NSFG study found that only 1 in 10 adolescents use protection when engaging in oral sex (Mosher et al., 2005). Health and sex education at home and in the schools often does not prepare adolescents for the difficult sexual decisions they must make, and they may be particularly ill-informed about STIs (Berne & Huberman, 2000). Recent research has found several contextual and personal factors to be associated with STIs, including housing insecurity, exposure to crime, childhood sexual abuse, gang participation, frequent alcohol use, and depression. These factors all appear to increase the likelihood of risky sexual behaviors (Buffardi, Thomas, Holmes, & Manhart, 2008).

Data collection on STIs is complicated for several reasons. Only five STIs—chlamydia, gonorrhea, syphilis, hepatitis A, and hepatitis B—are required to be reported to state health departments and the U.S. Centers for Disease Control and Prevention (CDC). These conditions are not always detected and reported. Some STIs, such as chlamydia and HPV (human papillomavirus), are often asymptomatic and go undetected. In addition, many surveys are not based on representative samples (Guttmacher Institute, 2006b; Weinstock, Berman, & Cates, 2004). The best estimates available indicate that adolescents and young adults ages 15 to 24 constitute 25% of the sexually active population but account for almost half of the STI diagnoses each year (Guttmacher Institute, 2010; Weinstock et al., 2004). Although rates of gonorrhea, chlamydia, and syphilis are above average in this age group, three STIs together account for nearly 90% of the new STIs among 15- to 24-year-olds each year: HPV, trichomoniasis, and chlamydia (see Exhibit 14.4 for the age distribution of reported cases of chlamydia in 2008) (Weinstock et al., 2004).

Unfortunately, HIV/AIDS is also a growing risk to adolescent health around the world. In 2005, an estimated 50% of all newly diagnosed HIV cases globally occurred in persons between the ages of 15 and 24 (UNAIDS, 2005). In the United States in that same year, 14% of all persons with newly diagnosed infections were under 25, but the number of people living with HIV/AIDS increased for the age group 15 to 19 between 2001 and 2004 (CDC, 2006b). Exhibit 14.5 demonstrates the racial disparity in the U.S. AIDS infection rates for youth ages 13 to 19. Although White non-Hispanic youth comprise 63% of the U.S. adolescent population, they make up 13% of the adolescent AIDS cases, whereas Black non-Hispanic youth only comprise 15% of the adolescent population but make up 73% of the adolescent AIDS cases.

For AIDS information, the CDC has a confidential toll-free hotline in English and in Spanish (1-800-CDC-INFO or 1-800-232-4636).

Exhibit 14.4 Reported Cases of Chlamydia by Age, 2008

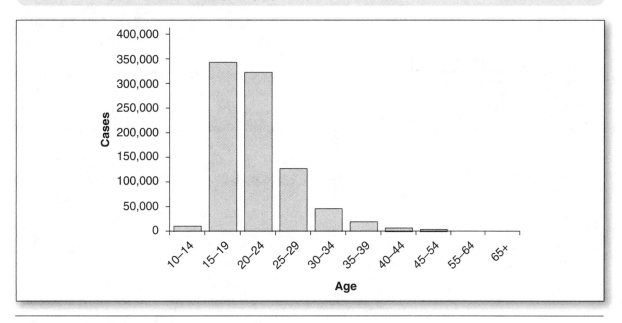

SOURCE: CDC (2009g).

Exhibit 14.5 Facts About AIDS and Adolescents

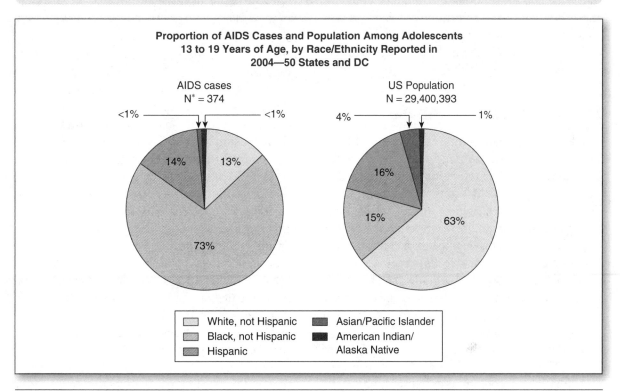

Proportion of AIDS Cases and Population Among Adolescents 13 to 19 Years of Age, by Race/Ethnicity Reported in 2004—50 States and DC

SOURCE: Centers for Disease Control and Prevention, http://www.cdc.gov/hiv/topics/surveillance/resources/slides/adolescents/index.htm.

The American Social Health Association also provides an STI resource center at 919-361-8488 or www.ashastd.org.

POTENTIAL CHALLENGES TO ADOLESCENT DEVELOPMENT

Many adjustments have to be made during adolescence in all areas of life: physical, family relationships, school transitions, and career planning. Adjustments to biological changes are a major developmental task of adolescence, family relationships are continuously renegotiated across the adolescent phase, and career planning begins in earnest for most youth in mid- to late adolescence. Most adolescents have the resources to meet these new challenges and adapt. But many adolescents engage in risky behaviors or experience other threats to physical and mental health. We have already looked at risky sexual behavior. Seven other threats to physical and mental health are discussed here: substance use and abuse, juvenile delinquency, bullying and other school and community violence, dating violence and statutory rape, poverty and low educational attainment, obesity and eating disorders, and depression and suicide.

Substance Use and Abuse

In adolescence, many youth experiment with the use of nicotine, alcohol, and other psychoactive substances with the motivation to be accepted by peers or to cope with life stresses (Weichold, 2007). For example, Carl Fleischer's use of tobacco and marijuana has several likely effects on his general behavior. Tobacco may make him feel tense, excitable, or anxious, and these feelings may amplify his concern about his weight, his grades, and his family relationships. Conversely, the marijuana may make Carl feel relaxed, and he may use it to counteract or escape from his concerns.

Although the rate of illicit drug use declined among U.S. adolescents aged 12–17 between 2002 and 2008, high school students in the United States have a higher rate of illicit drug use than youth in other industrialized countries (Johnston, O'Malley, Bachman, & Schulenberg, 2004, 2005; Substance Abuse and Mental Health Services Administration [SAMHSA], 2009b). Overall, in 2008, 9.3% of adolescents aged 12–17 were current illicit drug users: 6.7% used marijuana, 2.9% used prescription-type drugs for nonmedical purposes, 0.5% used stimulants, 0.4% used hallucinogens, 0.4% used cocaine, and 0.1% used methamphetamines (SAMHSA, 2009b). Although overall illicit drug use declined between 2002 and 2008, OxyContin (a narcotic) use increased from 1.3% to 2.6% of eighth graders. Also, 9.7% of 12th graders abuse Vicodin (another narcotic), and 7% of 12th graders abuse cold medicines (National Institute on Drug Abuse, 2006). Alcohol continues to be the most widely used of all the drugs for adolescents. Over 10 million people aged 12–20 (26.4% of this age group) reported drinking alcohol in the past month according to 2008 statistics (SAMHSA, 2009b). Furthermore, approximately 6.6 million (17.4%) considered themselves binge drinkers, and 2.1 million stated they were heavy drinkers. According to the National Survey on Drug Use and Health (SAMHSA, 2009a), for youth aged 12–17, their past month use of any tobacco product declined between 2002 and 2008, going from 15.2% to 11.4%.

When asked why youth choose to use alcohol, adolescents cite the following reasons: to have a good time with friends, to appear adult-like, to relieve tension and anxiety, to deal with the opposite sex, to get high, to cheer up, and to alleviate boredom. When asked why youth use cocaine, the additional responses were to get more energy and to get away from problems. Overall drug use at a party is also cited quite often as a reason (R. Engels & Knibbe, 2000). The following factors appear to be involved in adolescents' choice of drugs: the individual characteristics of the drug, the individual characteristics of the user, the availability of the drug, the current popularity of the drug, and the sociocultural traditions and sanctions regarding the drug (Segal & Stewart, 1996).

Adolescents who choose to abuse substances seem to differ from those who do not. In a 12-year

What are the risk factors for substance abuse in adolescence?

longitudinal study, Richard Jessor (1987) found that adolescent problem drinkers differ from other adolescents in their personal qualities, their social environment, and their other patterns of behavior. Problem drinkers are less likely to hold traditional values about education, religion, or conformity. They perceive large differences between their family's values and their peers' values, are more influenced by their peers, and have peers who are also engaged in problem drinking. Finally, problem drinkers are also more likely to participate in other risk-taking behaviors, such as sexual activity and delinquency. More recent research by Jessor and colleagues has produced similar findings (Donovan, Jessor, & Costa, 1999).

Some adolescents are clearly more at risk for substance abuse than others. American Indian youth and Alaska Native youth begin using alcohol and other drugs at a younger age than other youth, use them more frequently, use a greater amount, and use more different substances in combination with each other (L. Cameron, 1999; Novins, Beals, Shore, & Manson, 1996). The death rate due to substance abuse among American Indian youth is twice that of other youth (Pothoff et al., 1998). In response to this social need, drug treatment to Native American teens is undergoing a rapid change, with direct service provided by the tribes, employing mainly Native American staff, and using traditional Native American healing approaches in combination with standard addiction treatment approaches (Novins et al., 1996; Novins, Fleming, Beals, & Manson, 2000). It is too early to know how successful these new approaches will be.

Chemical substances pose a threat to the health of adolescents, because substance abuse affects metabolism, internal organs, the central nervous system, emotional functioning, and cognitive functioning (Segal & Stewart, 1996; Weichold, 2007). Alcohol and opiates can cause severe intoxication, coma, and withdrawal symptoms. Sedative drugs can depress the nervous and respiratory systems; withdrawal may lead to disturbances in breathing, heart function, and other basic body functions. Intravenous use of cocaine has been linked to adolescent cases of hepatitis, HIV, heart inflammation, loss of brain tissue, and abnormally high fever. Extended use of inhalants can cause irreparable neuropsychological damage. And finally, substances can weaken the immune system and increase a youth's likelihood of disease or general poor health. Preliminary evidence suggests that exposure to alcohol and other substances during adolescence, a time of rapid brain development, may alter neurocognitive functioning and lead to later misuse of substances. Indeed, most adults who are addicted to substances developed the substance abuse problem before age 25 (Spear, 2002; Weichold, 2007).

As mentioned earlier, substance use can also affect the decision to engage in sexual activity. After substance use, youth are more likely to engage in sexual activity and are less likely to use protection; thus, they are more likely to become pregnant or impregnate and to contract an STI (Brooks-Gunn & Furstenberg, 1989; Segal & Stewart, 1996; Shrier, Emans, Woods, & DuRant, 1996). In general, adolescents who use tobacco products, alcohol, marijuana, and other substances are more likely to be sexually active and to have more sexual partners (CASA, 2002; Lowry et al., 1994).

Juvenile Delinquency

Almost every adolescent breaks the rules at some time—disobeying parents or teachers, lying, cheating, and perhaps even stealing or vandalizing. Many adolescents smoke cigarettes and drink alcohol, and some skip school or stay out past curfew. For some adolescents, this behavior is a phase, passing as quickly as it appeared. Yet for others, it becomes a pattern and a probability game. Although most juvenile delinquency never meets up with law enforcement, the more times young people offend, the more likely they are to come into contact with the juvenile justice system.

In the United States, persons older than 5 but younger than 18 can be arrested for anything for which an adult can be arrested. (Children under

6 are said not to possess *mens rea,* which means "guilty mind," and thus are not considered capable of criminal intent.) In addition, they can be arrested for what are called **status offenses,** such as running away from home, skipping school, violating curfew, and possessing tobacco or alcohol—behaviors not considered crimes when engaged in by adults. When adolescents are found guilty of committing either a crime (by adult standards) or a status offense, we refer to their behavior as **juvenile delinquency.**

The Office of Juvenile Justice and Delinquency Prevention (OJJDP) reports that the number of delinquency cases, at about 1.7 million, stayed approximately the same from 2000 to 2005 (Sickmund, 2009). Although the number of delinquency cases for females has increased (from 19% in 1985 to 27% in 2005), it is still a relatively small proportion of the overall delinquency caseload at 464,700 in 2005 (as compared to 1,233,200 for males in that same year). Meanwhile, of the total U.S. population in 2005, White youth comprised 78%, Black youth comprised 17%, Asian youth (including Native Hawaiian and other Pacific Islander) comprised 4%, and Native American (including Alaska Native) comprised 1%; however, 64% of the delinquency cases handled in 2005 were for White youth, 33% were for Black youth, 1% for Asian American youth, and 1% for Native American youth. The rate at which petitioned cases were waived to criminal court was 10% greater for Black youth than the rate for White youth, and the rate at which youth in adjudicated cases were ordered to residential placement was 24% greater for Black youth than for White youth (Sickmund, 2009).

In 2008, U.S. law enforcement agencies made 2.11 million arrests of persons younger than 18, at a rate of 3.8 arrests per 100,000 juveniles ages 10–17 (Puzzanchera, 2009). Also in 2008, juveniles comprised 16% of all violent crime arrests and 26% of all property crime arrests. In addition, 11% of all murder victims were younger than 18. Although African American youth comprised 16% of the juvenile population aged 10–17, Black youth were involved in 52% of the Violent Crime Index arrests and 33% of the Property Crime Index arrests in 2008 (Puzzanchera, 2009).

In October of 2009, the National Youth Gang Center (of the OJJDP) merged with the National Gang Center (BJA) and is now recognized as the National Gang Center (2010). In 2007, the National Youth Gang Survey estimated that more than 27,000 gangs are active in the United States: 40.7% are in larger cities, 33.5% in smaller cities, 19.9% in suburban counties, and 5.9% in rural counties (National Youth Gang Center, 2009). Demographically, 49% of gang members in the United States are Hispanic/Latino, 35% are African American/Black, 9% are Caucasian/White, and 7% are "other." In 2006, 36.5% of gang members were juveniles (under 18), and 63.5% were adults (18 and over). OJJDP researchers Howard Snyder and Melissa Sickmund (2006) found that juveniles who reported belonging to a gang were twice as likely as other juveniles to have committed a major theft, 3 times more likely to have sold drugs, 4 times more likely to have committed a serious assault, and 5 times more likely to have carried a handgun (p. 72).

Bullying and Other School and Community Violence

School bullying has come to the attention of social workers because of its short- and long-term effects on children's physical and mental health. School bullying can be defined as physical or verbal attack or intimidation with the purpose of causing fear, distress, or harm to the victim (Farrington & Ttofi, 2009). The most comprehensive U.S. study of bullying reports that 13% of sixth- to tenth-grade students bully, 10% are victims, and 6% are both victims and bullies (Nansel et al., 2001). Further research suggests that bullying can be a first step to additional aggressive acts such as assault or even murder (Sampson, 2009).

In 2002, on average, four juveniles were murdered daily in the United States. That was the third leading cause of death for juveniles ages 12 to 17 with only unintentional injury and suicide killing more common among young people (H. Snyder & Sickmund, 2006). An estimated 1,600 persons under age 18 were murdered in the United States in 2002—10% of all persons murdered that year. About one third (36%) of these juvenile murder victims were female. About 1 in 10 (8%) were ages 12 to 14, and 4 in 10 (43%) were ages 15 to 17. More than half (51%) of juvenile murder victims in 2002 were White, 45% were Black, and 4% were either Native American or Asian. With White youth comprising 78% of the U.S. resident juvenile population in 2002 and Black youth comprising 16%, the murder rate for Black youth in 2002 was more than 4 times the White murder rate. This disparity was seen across victim age groups and increased with victim age. Over three quarters of juvenile homicides are committed with firearms (H. Snyder & Sickmund, 2006).

These murders are not happening at schools, however, so although school shootings have received media attention and have thus increased public concern for student safety, school-related violent deaths account for less than 1% of homicides among school-aged children and youth (M. Anderson et al., 2001). In fact, in 2001, students were safer in school and on their way to and from school than they were in 1992 because crimes against juveniles fell substantially between 1992 and 2001 both in and out of school (H. Snyder & Sickmund, 2006).

Juveniles are, however, more likely than adults to be both victims and perpetrators of violence. A 2005 Bureau of Justice Statistics (BJS) report (K. Baum, 2005) summarized National Crime Victimization Survey data for the years 1993–2003 to document the trends in nonfatal violent victimizations of youth ages 12 to 17. On average, from 1993 through 2003, juveniles ages 12 to 17 were about 2.5 times more likely than adults (i.e., ages 18 and older) to be the victim of a nonfatal violent crime. That means that in a typical group of 1,000 youth ages 12 to 17, a total of 84 experienced nonfatal violent victimizations, compared with 32 per 1,000 persons ages 18 and older (K. Baum, 2005).

Data collected in 2007 as part of the Youth Risk Behavior Survey (YRBS) reveal that on at least 1 of the 30 days preceding the survey, 18% of high school students had carried a weapon and 5.2% had carried a gun. And during the 12 months that preceded the survey, 4.2% had been in a physical fight for which they had to be treated by a doctor or nurse (CDC, 2008d).

Even if they are not perpetrators or direct victims of violence, many U.S. adolescents witness violence. One study of 935 urban and suburban youth found that over 45% had witnessed a shooting or stabbing or other serious act of violence during the previous year (O'Keefe, 1997). Moreover, participating in violence and/or witnessing violence can be a significant predictor of aggressive acting-out behavior for both male and female adolescents (O'Keefe, 1997) as well as a significant source of depression, anger, anxiety, dissociation, post-traumatic stress, and total trauma symptoms (Fitzpatrick & Boldizar, 1993; Singer, Anglin, Song, & Lunghofer, 1995).

Dating Violence and Statutory Rape

Acquaintance rape can be defined as forced, manipulated, or coerced sexual contact by someone known to the victim. Women between the ages of 16 and 24 are the primary victims of acquaintance rape, but junior high school girls are also at great risk (Bureau of Justice Statistics, 2000).

Nationwide in the United States in 2007, 9.9% of high school students responded to the YRBS that they had been hit, slapped, or physically hurt on purpose by their boyfriend or girlfriend at least once over the course of the 12 months that preceded the survey (CDC, 2008d). Young women ages 16 to 24 experience the highest rates of relationship violence (Rennison & Welchans, 2000). One study found that approximately 1 in 5 female high school students reported being physically and/or sexually abused by a dating partner (J. Silverman, Raj, Mucci, & Hathaway, 2001).

The YRBS data reveal that 7.8% of the students stated that they had been physically forced to have sexual intercourse when they did not want to. Overall, the prevalence of having been forced to have sexual intercourse was higher among Black

(10.5%) and Hispanic (8.8%) than White (7%) students. The prevalence of having been forced to have sexual intercourse was higher among 11th-grade (8.5%) and 12th-grade (8.3%) than among 9th-grade (6.6%) students (CDC, 2008d).

Because of their underreporting, date rape and dating violence may be even more prevalent among adolescents than we have data to suggest. And, unfortunately, researchers have found that adolescent girls who report a history of experiencing dating violence are more likely to exhibit other serious health risk behaviors as well (J. Silverman et al., 2001).

Statutory rape occurs when individuals have voluntary and consensual sexual relations and one individual is either too young or otherwise unable (e.g., someone with cognitive disability) to legally consent to the behavior. The majority of victims of statutory rape were females ages 14 to 15, whereas 82% of the rape perpetrators of female victims were adults ages 18 and older (H. Snyder & Sickmund, 2006). Not only were most offenders adults, but most were also substantially older than their victims. About half of the male offenders of female victims in statutory rapes reported to law enforcement were at least 6 years older than their victims. For male victims of female perpretrators, the difference was even greater; in these incidents, half of the female offenders were at least 9 years older than their victims (H. Snyder & Sickmund, 2006).

Poverty and Low Educational Attainment

Additional threats to physical and mental health may also stem from poverty and low educational attainment, both of which are rampant in the nonindustrialized world. In the United States, 12% of all persons lived at or below the poverty thresholds in 2002. This proportion was far greater for persons under age 18 (18%) than for those ages 18 to 64 (11%) and those above age 64 (10%) (H. Snyder & Sickmund, 2006).

The education institution is becoming a prime force in perpetuating, if not exacerbating, economic inequalities. A 2006 report by the Education Trust indicates that current trends in the education institution are the principal reason that there is less upward mobility in the social class structure in the United States today than there was 20 years ago, and less mobility in the United States than in any European nation except the United Kingdom (Haycock, 2006). High school graduation rates are a key measure of whether schools are making adequate yearly progress (AYP) under the provisions of the No Child Left Behind (NCLB) legislation (see Chapter 13 for a fuller discussion of NCLB). As it turns out, most school districts do not have a system for calculating graduation rates, and there are major holes in their reported data. Furthermore, researchers have analyzed the reported state data and found that all states inflated their graduation rates, ranging from a 1% to a 33% inflation rate (see D. Hall, 2005). These researchers estimate that graduation rates for students who entered high school in 2000 ranged from 51% in South Carolina to 86% in New Jersey. More than half of nongraduates were African American, Latino, or Native American, indicating an overrepresentation because these groups together comprise about one third of students in public school nationally. Even when students in impoverished rural and urban neighborhoods graduate, their high schools may not have offered the types of courses that college admissions departments require. There is also a critical shortage of teachers trained to teach English language learners who often must navigate very large high school settings (Hood, 2003).

Obesity and Eating Disorders

As suggested earlier, the dietary practices of some adolescents put them at risk for overall health problems. These practices include skipping meals, usually breakfast or lunch; snacking, especially on high-calorie, high-fat, low-nutrition snacks; eating fast foods; and dieting. Poor nutrition can affect a youth's growth and development, sleep, weight, cognition, mental health, and overall physical health.

An increasing minority of adolescents in the United States is obese, and the risks and consequences of this can be profound (Hedley et al., 2004; W. P. T. James, 2006). The 2003–2004 National Health and Nutrition Examination Survey (NHANES) found that an estimated 17% of children and adolescents (ages 2 to 19), over 12.5 million, are overweight (defined as BMI-for-age at or above the 95th percentile of the 2000 CDC BMI-for-age growth charts for the United States) (Ogden, Carroll, Curtin, Lamb, & Flegal, 2010; Ogden et al., 2006). This represents an increase from 7.2% to 13.9% among 2- to 5-year-olds, from 11% to 19% among 6- to 11-year-olds, and from 11% to 17% among 12- to 19-year-olds since the NHANES III 1988–1994 statistics (Ogden et al., 2006, 2010).

It is important to note that this is a worldwide trend. According to one report (W. P. T. James, 2006), almost half of the children in North and South America, about 38% of children in the European Union, and about 20% of children in China were expected to be overweight by 2010. Significant increases were also expected in the Middle East and Southeast Asia. Mexico, Brazil, Chile, and Egypt have rates comparable to fully industrialized countries.

Research is exposing the breadth of the problem. Almost 16% of the high school students in the nationwide sample of the YRBS are overweight (CDC, 2008d). Yet 29.3% of that same sample described themselves as slightly or very overweight, and 45.2% were trying to lose weight. Moreover, within the 30 days preceding the survey, 11.8% of the high school students had gone without eating for 24 hours or more; 5.9% had taken diet pills, powders, or liquids; and 4.3% had vomited or taken laxatives to lose weight or to keep from gaining weight (CDC, 2008d).

Girls' body dissatisfaction reflects the incongruence between the societal ideal of thinness and the beginning of normal fat deposits in pubescent girls. Body dissatisfaction is a major factor in two eating disorders, anorexia nervosa and bulimia nervosa, that often have their onset in adolescence (American Psychiatric Association [APA] Work Group on Eating Disorders, 2000).

- **Anorexia nervosa** means literally "loss of appetite due to nerves," but the disorder is actually characterized by a dysfunctional body image and voluntary starvation in the pursuit of weight loss. According to the *Diagnostic and Statistical Manual of Mental Disorders* (*DSM-IV-TR*) (APA, 2000), the essential features of anorexia nervosa are refusal to maintain minimally normal weight, fear of gaining weight, and disturbance in body image.
- **Bulimia nervosa** is characterized by a cycle of binge eating; feelings of guilt, depression, or self-disgust; and purging (producing vomiting or evacuation of the bowels). The *DSM-IV-TR* (APA, 2000) suggests that individuals with bulimia nervosa are also excessively influenced by body shape and weight, and exhibit binge eating followed by purging at least twice a week for at least 3 months.

The APA Work Group on Eating Disorders (2000) estimates that 0.5% to 3.7% of women suffer from anorexia nervosa in their lifetime, and about 1% of female adolescents have anorexia nervosa. An estimated 1.1% to 4.2% of women have bulimia nervosa in their lifetime, and 50% of people who have had anorexia nervosa develop bulimia or bulimic patterns.

Depression and Suicide

Epidemiological studies suggest that as many as 8.3% of adolescents in the United States may have a major depressive disorder, with early adolescents particularly vulnerable to depression. Parents are less likely to recognize depression in their adolescents than the adolescents themselves. Although there are no known gender differences in depression prior to adolescence, during adolescence, girls are about twice as likely as boys to have a major depressive disorder (Sadock & Sadock, 2007). Research suggests that African American and Mexican American youth may be at increased risk for depression (R. E. Roberts, Roberts, & Chen, 1997).

Adolescent depression may also be underdiagnosed, among males and females alike, because it is difficult to detect. Many parents and professionals expect adolescence to be a time of ups and downs, moodiness, melodrama, anger, rebellion, and increased sensitivity. There are, however, some reliable outward signs of depression in adolescents: poor academic performance, truancy, social withdrawal, antisocial behavior, changes in eating or sleeping patterns, changes in physical appearance, excessive boredom or activity, low self-esteem, sexual promiscuity, substance use, propensity to run away from home, and excessive family conflict. Additional symptoms of depression not unique to adolescence include pervasive inability to experience pleasure, severe psychomotor retardation, delusions, and a sense of hopelessness (Sadock & Sadock, 2007).

The many challenges of adolescence sometimes prove overwhelming. We have already discussed the risk of suicide among gay male and lesbian adolescents. Nationwide, during the 12 months preceding the 2007 YRBS survey, 28.5% of high school students reported having felt so sad or hopeless almost every day for 2 weeks or more that they stopped doing some usual activities (CDC, 2008d). Furthermore, 14.5% had seriously considered attempting suicide; 11.3% had made a suicide plan; 6.9% had actually attempted suicide; and 2.0% had made a suicide attempt that resulted in an injury, poisoning, or overdose that had to be treated by a doctor or nurse (CDC, 2008d). Overall, suicide is the third leading cause of death for adolescents in the United States (National Institute of Mental Health [NIMH], 2000). In 2001 in the United States, 3,971 youth ages 15 to 24 took their own lives (R. Anderson & Smith, 2003). Of those 3,971 deaths, 86% were male and 14% were female, and 54% used firearms. During that same year, American Indian and Alaska Natives had the highest rate of suicides (R. Anderson & Smith, 2003). Cheryl King and Christopher Merchant (2008) have analyzed the research on factors associated with adolescent suicidal thinking and behavior. They identified a number of risk factors found in the research: social isolation, low levels of perceived support, childhood abuse and neglect, and peer abuse.

RISK FACTORS AND PROTECTIVE FACTORS IN ADOLESCENCE

The U.S. Department of Health and Human Services has created 12 proposed adolescent health objectives for its Healthy People 2020 campaign (Office of Disease Prevention & Health Promotion, 2009), which attempt to minimize risk factors and maximize protective factors in adolescence. They are as follows:

1. Increase educational achievement of adolescents and young adults.

2. Increase the percentage of adolescents who participate in extracurricular and out-of-school activities.

3. Increase the percentage of adolescents who have been tested for HIV.

4. Increase the proportion of adolescents who have had a wellness checkup in the past 12 months.

5. Increase the percentage of middle and high schools that prohibit harassment based on a student's sexual orientation or gender identity.

6. Decrease the percentage of adolescents who did not go to school at least once in the past month because of safety concerns.

7. Decrease the percentage of public middle and high schools with a violent incident.

8. Increase the percentage of adolescents who are connected to a parent or other positive adult caregiver.

9. Decrease the percentage of adolescents who have been offered, sold, or given an illegal drug on school property.

10. Increase the percentage of vulnerable adolescents who are equipped with the services and skills necessary to transition into an independent and self-sufficient adulthood.

11. Decrease the proportion of adolescents and young adults who are involved with criminal activity.

12. Increase the percentage of schools with a school breakfast program.

There are many pathways through adolescence; both individual and group-based differences result in much variability. Some of the variability is related to the types of risk factors and protective factors that have accumulated prior to adolescence. Emmy Werner and associates (see E. E. Werner & Smith, 2001) have found, in their longitudinal research on risk and protection, that females have a better balance of risk and protection in childhood, but the advantage goes to males during adolescence. Their research indicates that the earlier risk factors that most predict poor adolescent adjustment are a childhood spent in chronic poverty, alcoholic and psychotic parents, moderate to severe physical disability, developmentally disabled siblings, school problems in middle childhood, conflicted relationships with peers, and family disruptions. The most important earlier protective factors are easy temperament, positive social orientation in early childhood, positive peer relationships in middle childhood, non–sex-typed extracurricular interests and hobbies in middle childhood, and nurturing from nonparental figures.

Much attention has also been paid to the increase in risk behaviors during adolescence (Silbereisen & Lerner, 2007a). In the United States, attention has been called to a set of factors that are risky to adolescent well-being and serve as risk factors for adjustment in adulthood as well. These factors include use and abuse of alcohol and other drugs; unsafe sex, teen pregnancy, and teen parenting; school underachievement, failure, and dropout; delinquency, crime, and violence; and youth poverty. The risk and resilience research indicates, however, that many youth with several of these risk factors overcome the odds. Protective factors that have been found to contribute to resilience in adolescence include family creativity in coping with adversity, good family relationships, faith and attachment to religious institutions, social support in the school setting, and school-based health services. As social workers, we will want to promote these protective factors while at the same time work to prevent or diminish risk factors.

> What are the implications of research on risk and protection for social work program development?

Critical Thinking Questions 14.3

Adolescence is a time of rapid transition in all dimensions of life—physical, emotional, cognitive, social, and spiritual. What personal, family, cultural, and other social factors help adolescents cope with all of this change? What factors lead to dissatisfaction with body image and harmful or unhealthy behaviors? How well does contemporary society support adolescent development?

Implications for Social Work Practice

Adolescence is a vulnerable period. Adolescents' bodies and psyches are changing rapidly in transition from childhood to adulthood. Youth are making some very profound decisions during this life course period. Thus, the implications for social work practice are wide-ranging.

- When working with adolescents, meet clients where they are, physically, psychologically, and socially—and be aware that that place may change frequently.

- Be familiar with typical adolescent development and with the possible consequences of deviations from developmental timelines.
- Be aware of, and respond to, the adolescent's level of cognition and comprehension. Assess the individual adolescent's ability to contemplate the future, to comprehend the nature of human relationships, to consolidate specific knowledge into a coherent system, and to envision possible consequences from a hypothetical list of actions.
- Recognize that the adolescent may see you as an authority figure who is not an ally. Develop skills in building rapport with adolescents.
- Assess the positive and negative effects of the school environment on the adolescent in relation to such issues as early or late maturation, popularity/sociability, culture, and sexual orientation.
- Where appropriate, advocate for change in maladaptive school settings, such as those with Eurocentric models or homophobic environments.
- Provide information, support, or other interventions to assist adolescents in resolving questions of sexual identity and sexual decision making.
- Where appropriate, link youth to existing resources, such as extracurricular activities, education on STIs, prenatal care, and gay and lesbian support groups.
- Provide information, support, or other interventions to assist adolescents in making decisions regarding use of tobacco, alcohol, or other drugs.
- Develop skills to assist adolescents with physical and mental health issues, such as nutritional problems, obesity, eating disorders, depression, and suicide.
- Participate in research, policy development, and advocacy on behalf of adolescents.
- Work at the community level to develop and sustain recreational and social programs and places for young people.

Key Terms

acquaintance rape	masturbation	sex hormones
anorexia nervosa	menarche	sexual orientation
bulimia nervosa	postconventional moral reasoning	sexually transmitted infections
gender identity	primary sex characteristics	(STIs)
generalized other	psychological identity	social identity
gonads	puberty	spermarche
individuation	rites of passage	status offenses
juvenile delinquency	secondary sex characteristics	statutory rape

Active Learning

1. Recalling your own high school experiences, which case study individual would you most identify with—David, Carl, or Monica? For what reasons? How could a social worker have affected your experiences?

2. Visit a public library and check out some preteen and teen popular fiction or magazines. Which topics from this chapter are discussed, and how are they dealt with?

3. Have lunch at a local high school cafeteria. Be sure to go through the line, eat the food, and enjoy conversation with some students. What are their concerns? What are their notions about social work?

ABA's Juvenile Justice Center

www.abc-directory.com/site/2790593

Site presented by the American Bar Association's Juvenile Justice Center contains links to juvenile justice–related sites.

Add Health

www.cpc.unc.edu/projects/addhealth/pubs

Site presented by the Carolina Population Center, contains a reference list of published reports of the National Longitudinal Study of Adolescent Health (Add Health), which includes measures of social, economic, psychological, and physical well-being.

Adolescent and School Health

www.cdc.gov/healthyyouth/

Site maintained by the Centers for Disease Control and Prevention, contains links to a variety of health topics related to adolescents, including alcohol and drug use, sexual behavior, nutrition, youth suicide, and youth violence.

DukeLEARN

dukebrainworks.com/

Site presented by DukeLEARN, an interdisciplinary team of neuroscientists, psychologists, physicians, and social scientists at Duke University, contains links to research and publication directed to public understanding of the brain.

Sexually Transmitted Infections Information

www.ashastd.org

Site maintained by the American Social Health Association, which is dedicated to improving the health of individuals, families, and communities, with an emphasis on sexual health and a focus on preventing sexually transmitted diseases.

Youth Risk Behavior Surveillance System (YRBSS)

www.cdc.gov/HealthyYouth/yrbs/index.htm

Site presented by the National Center for Chronic Disease Prevention and Health Promotion, contains the latest research on adolescent risk behavior.

CHAPTER 15

Young and Middle Adulthood

Elizabeth D. Hutchison and Holly C. Matto

What theories are useful for understanding adult development?

What do social workers need to know about biological, psychological, social, and spiritual stability and change in adulthood?

What are the antecedent risk factors and protective factors that affect resilience in adulthood as well as the effects of adult behavior on subsequent health and well-being?

Key Ideas

As you read this chapter, take note of these central ideas:

1. Young and middle adulthood has received less scholarly attention than other phases of the life course, but Carl Jung, Erik Erikson, and Daniel Levinson have presented important theories about this period of life.

2. A new phase called "emerging adulthood" (ages 18 to 25) has been proposed as a time when individuals explore and experiment with different life roles, occupational interests, educational pursuits, religious beliefs, and relationships—with more focus than in adolescence but without the full commitment of young adulthood.

3. Physical functioning is typically at its height during young adulthood. However, changes in physical appearance, mobility, the reproductive system, and health begin to appear in middle adulthood.

4. Cognitive capacities become more flexible in young adulthood, and there is growing evidence that cognitive performance remains stable for the majority of midlife adults.

5. Young adults struggle with the Eriksonian psychosocial crisis of intimacy versus isolation, and midlife adults struggle with the psychosocial crisis of generativity versus stagnation.

6. Identity development continues into adulthood; identity is dynamic, not static, ever evolving through significant interpersonal relationships and work experience.

7. Social relationships play a major role in life satisfaction and physical well-being across the life course. Relationships in adulthood have been shaped by relationships in earlier life phases.

8. Work has different meanings for different people: It can serve as a source of income, a life routine and way of structuring time, a source of status and identity, a context for social interaction, or a meaningful experience that provides a sense of accomplishment.

CASE STUDY 15.1

Scott Pukalski, Wanting to Work at 22

At age 22, Scott Pukalski is a handsome young man with a crop of wavy blond hair, but you first notice the fatigue on his face and the droop in his shoulders. Scott is the third and youngest son of a working-class family. His life was relatively uneventful until he was 12. His father worked at a factory, and his mother went to work at the neighborhood grocery store once the children were in school. A large extended family, including both sets of grandparents, lived in the neighborhood. Scott was friendly and outgoing, but he struggled in school and was diagnosed with a learning disability when he was in first grade. His mother sat patiently with him in the evenings as he made great effort to complete his homework.

When Scott was 12, his mother was diagnosed with colon cancer. She died 1 year later. This was a tough time for the family, both emotionally and economically. With the help of extended family and people from the church parish, Scott's father managed to hold the family together, but Scott and his brothers were suddenly expected to carry a much heavier load of housework, as well as to supplement the family income. Scott's struggles at school intensified without his mother's patient support. His father remarried when Scott was 15, and he and his brothers did not get along well with their stepmother. Scott began to spend a lot of time at the home of his girlfriend, Sonya.

When Sonya became pregnant, both families insisted that she and Scott should marry. Scott and Sonya both dropped out of high school before the baby was born, and Scott went to work for an uncle who was a carpenter. A second baby was born 2 years later. Scott, Sonya, and the children live with Sonya's parents but hope to find a place of their own. That looked promising until the recession hit. The construction business in their midwestern urban area has not yet shown any signs of recovering, and Scott has not been employed steadily for the past 2 years. Sonya now works at a fast food restaurant in the evenings, and Scott looks after the children. He loves Sonya and the children, but he feels like a failure. He realizes that, lacking high school diplomas, their future is insecure, but he is at a loss for how they can get on better footing.

CASE STUDY 15.2

Carla Aquino, Transitioning to Parenthood at 30

Carla Aquino is a 30-year-old Latina living in a large West Coast city. She graduated from the local college with a degree in business and is currently employed as an accountant. She has been married for 4 years to a man she met through her church and is 4 months pregnant with her first child.

In the midst of her excitement about the new baby, Carla is anxious about how she will juggle the new care-giving responsibilities with her career aspirations. She knows she wants both to have a meaningful career and to be a good mother but is very concerned about managing multiple demanding roles. Her husband, a consultant, works long hours and travels frequently for his job. Carla has discussed with the social worker at the company Employee Assistance Program the disruption, strain, and lack of continuity she feels in their marriage as a result of her husband's intense work schedule, but she also knows that he makes good money, and she respects the fact that he enjoys his work.

Carla and her husband are actively involved in their church group, where they meet monthly with other young adults for spirituality discussions. They also participate in the church's various outreach projects, and Carla volunteers 2 hours each week with Streetwise Partners. However, they live in a very transient part of the city, and she is struggling to develop more meaningful connections with neighbors.

Carla's mother died of liver failure the year before Carla graduated from high school, but Carla's father is still alive and is a significant support in her life. Most of Carla's extended family live nearby or in towns outside the

(Continued)

(Continued)

central city, although some relatives still live in the Dominican Republic. Carla's mother-in-law, Jan, lives close by and just recently got divorced after 27 years of marriage. Jan relies heavily on her son and daughter-in-law for emotional (and some financial) support during this life transition.

Carla and her husband both say that they are having trouble dealing with the myriad roles they are faced with (such as young professionals, marriage partners, supportive family members), and are considering how the new role of first-time parents will affect their current lives and future life choices.

CASE STUDY 15.3

Viktor Spiro, Assuming New Responsibilities as He Turns 40

Viktor Spiro was born in a village outside of Tirana, Albania, and lived most of his life, as did many Albanians in the Stalinist state, amidst very impoverished conditions. He was the youngest of four children, with two sisters and a brother 12 years his senior. Viktor describes his childhood as "normal," until he sustained a serious head injury after falling from a tractor when he was 13. He experienced an increasing depression following his hospitalization; his school performance declined, and he withdrew from his friends. When Viktor was 20, his older brother died from a rare gastrointestinal illness, another traumatic event that exacerbated Viktor's depression and substance abuse. He subsequently went absent without leave (AWOL) from his military post and fled to Greece, where he continued to drink heavily and was reportedly hospitalized at a psychiatric facility.

Because his father was a U.S. citizen, Viktor was able to immigrate to the United States in his late 20s, after the dissolution of Albania's repressive communist regime. He secured a job as a painter, but the language barrier and fast-paced life left him feeling vulnerable. Struggling to cope, Viktor made a series of suicide attempts and was arrested after lunging for the gun of a police officer who was trying to help him. Viktor claims that he did not intend to harm the officer, but that he saw the gun as a quick means to end his own life. Viktor's suicide attempts and arrest led to the beginning of a long relationship with mental health services (MHS). He was diagnosed with bipolar disorder with psychotic features, made more suicide attempts, was hospitalized, and lived in a group home.

After a few years, Viktor's father and mother, Petro and Adriana, moved to the United States to reunite with Viktor and his sister Maria. Viktor moved into an apartment with his parents and showed some signs of improved adjustment, including advances in his use of English. However, his firsthand exposure to the worsening state of Petro's vascular dementia proved very traumatic. Then, Petro broke his hip and was in a nursing home briefly. He may have benefited from more advanced care and rehabilitation in a nursing facility, but his family could not wait to get him home. Supporting an elderly family member at an institution was culturally unacceptable.

Viktor and his father were both referred to a residential program to obtain counseling and case management services. The family was transferred here approximately 8 months after Viktor's most recent suicide attempt. His social worker learned that Viktor had accrued over $140,000 in hospital bills and was still on "medical leave" from his job. The family had no significant income other than Petro's monthly $400 social security check and Adriana's stipend from Social Services to "take care" of her husband. Viktor shared that he had deep regrets about his latest suicide attempt and could not put himself or his family through this again. He felt that he was at a turning point and needed to take on more responsibility as he approaches 40, especially with caring for his ailing parents.

Viktor began to reveal a more reflective, insightful side during his recovery. He confided to his treatment team that he had been hearing voices for nearly 6 months prior to his last suicide attempt, but didn't tell anyone. He hoped the voices would just "go away." Viktor was able to communicate more freely about his emotions and no longer seemed preoccupied with past anxiety about being discovered by the military or with guilt regarding his brother's premature passing. His social worker and job coach assisted him with transition back into the workforce, and he eventually obtained the medical clearance to return to his dishwashing job, resuming the role as the primary breadwinner for the family. This was a real lift to Viktor's self-esteem. The Spiro family experienced another financial lift with the news of a total forgiveness of Viktor's outstanding hospital bills.

While the Spiro family was enjoying their improving situation, the treatment team worked with Viktor to expand his social network outside the family. Viktor had been spending all of his time with his parents in their apartment when he was not working. As his confidence grew with his psychiatric improvement, however, he became more receptive to suggestions about weekend social activities coordinated by the agency. Viktor tried out a couple of the groups and enjoyed the activities and chance to form new relationships. He quickly immersed himself in a variety of weekend activities that involved shopping, movies, athletics, and cultural events.

The social worker assisted Viktor with the long process of reapplying for naturalization, after learning that he did not provide INS (Immigration and Naturalization Service) with the required documents on his previous application. With his improved mental state, Viktor was able to concentrate on studying for the citizenship test, which he passed. His citizenship ceremony was a wonderful event for Viktor and his family, and he made a poignant speech about dreaming of this day as a teenager watching CHIPS reruns in Albania.

—Derek Morch

CASE STUDY 15.4

Phuong Le, Serving Family and Community at 57

Le Thi Phuong, or Phuong Le as she is officially known in the United States, grew up in Saigon, South Vietnam, in the midst of war and upheaval. She has some fond memories of her first few years when Saigon was beautiful and peaceful. She loves to remember riding on her father's shoulders down the streets of Saigon on a warm day and shopping with her grandmother in the herb shops. But she also has chilling memories of the military presence on the streets, the devastation caused by war, and the persistent fear that pervaded her home.

Phuong was married when she was 17, to a man chosen by her father. She smiles when she recounts the story of her future groom and his family coming to visit with the lacquered boxes full of betrothal gifts of nuts, teas, cake, and fruit. She admits that, at the time, she was not eager to marry and wondered why her father was doing this to her. But she is quick to add that her father made a wise choice, and her husband, Hien, is her best friend, and is, as his name suggests, "nice, kind, and gentle." Their first child, a son, was born just before Phuong's 19th birthday, and Phuong reveled in being a mother.

Unfortunately, on Phuong's 20th birthday, April 30, 1975, life in Saigon turned horrific. That is the day that the North Vietnamese Army overran Saigon. For Phuong and Hien, as well as for most people living in South

(Continued)

(Continued)

Vietnam, just surviving became a daily struggle. Both Phuong's father and her father-in-law were in the South Vietnamese military, and both were imprisoned by the Viet Cong for a few years. Both managed to escape, and they moved their families around until they were able to plan an escape from Vietnam by boat. Family members got separated during the escape, and others were lost when pirates attacked their boats. Phuong's father and one brother have never been heard from since the pirate attack. Phuong and Hien and their son spent more than 2 years in a refugee camp in Thailand before being resettled in Southern California. Their second child, a daughter, was born in the camp, and a second daughter was born 1 year after they resettled in California. Over time, other family members were able to join them in the large Vietnamese community where they live.

Phuong's and Hien's opportunities for education were limited during the war years, but both came from families that valued education, and both managed to receive several years of schooling. Luckily, because they were living in a large Vietnamese community, language did not serve as a major barrier to employment in the United States. Phuong found a job working evenings as a waitress at a restaurant in Little Saigon, and Hien worked two jobs, by day as dishwasher in a restaurant, and by night cleaning office buildings in Little Saigon. Phuong's mother lived with Phuong and Hien and watched after the children while the parents worked. Hien's parents lived a few blocks away, and several siblings and cousins of both Phuong and Hien were in the neighborhood. The Vietnamese community provided much social support and cultural connection. Phuong loved taking the children to visit the shops in Little Saigon and found special pleasure in visiting the herb shops where the old men sat around and spoke animatedly in Vietnamese.

Phuong grieved the loss of her beloved father and brother, but she wanted to create a positive life for her children. She was happy that she was able to stay connected to her cultural roots and happy that her children lived in a neighborhood where they did not feel like outsiders. But she also wanted her children to be able to be successful outside the Vietnamese community as well as to be a resource for the community. She was determined that her children would have the education that she and Hien had been denied. Although she could have gotten by well in her neighborhood without English, she studied English along with her children because she wanted to model for them how to live a bilingual, bicultural life. She was pleased that the children did well in school and was not surprised at how quickly the older two adapted to life in their adopted country. Sometimes there was tension in the multigenerational family about how the children were acculturating, and Phuong often served as the mediator in these tensions. She understood the desire of the older generation to keep cultural traditions, and she herself loved traditions such as the celebration of the Chinese New Year, with the colorful dresses and the little red *lai-see* envelopes of good luck money that were given to the children. She wanted her children to have these traditional experiences. But she also was tuned in to the children's desire to be connected with some aspects of the dominant culture, such as the music and other popular media. She was also aware of how hard it was for the family elders to enforce the traditional family hierarchy when they were dependent on younger family members to help them navigate life in the English-speaking world outside their cultural enclave.

When her children reached adolescence, Phuong herself was uncomfortable with the Western cultural ideal for adolescent independence from the family, but she found ways to give her children some space while also holding them close and keeping them connected to their cultural roots. Other mothers in the neighborhood began to seek her advice about how to handle the challenging adolescent years. When her own adolescent children began to be impatient with the pervasive sadness they saw in their grandparents, Phuong suggested that they do some oral history with their grandparents. This turned out to be a therapeutic experience for all involved. The grandparents were able to sift through their lives in Vietnam and the years since, give voice to all that had been lost, but also begin to recognize the strength it took to survive and their good fortune to be able to live among family and a community where much was familiar. The grandchildren were able to hear a part of their family narrative that they did not know because the family had preferred not to talk about it. Phuong was so pleased with this outcome that she asked to start a program of intergenerational dialogue at the Vietnamese Community Services Center. She thought that this might be one way to begin to heal the trauma in her community while also giving the younger generation a strong cultural identity as they struggled to live in a multicultural world. She continues to be an active force in that program, even though her own children are grown.

Their forties and early fifties brought both great sorrow and great joy to Phuong and Hien. Within a 2-year period, Phuong's mother and Hien's mother and father all died. Phuong and Hien became the family elders. They provided both economic and emotional support during times of family crisis, such as a sibling's cancer, a niece's untimely pregnancy, and a nephew's involvement with a neighborhood gang. But there was also great joy. Phuong was very good at her job and became the supervisor of the wait staff at the best restaurant in Little Saigon. Hien was able to buy his own herb shop. After attending the local community college, the children were all able to go on to university and do well. Their son became an engineer, the older daughter became a physician, and the younger daughter recently finished law school. Their son is now father to two young children, and Phuong finds great joy in being a grandmother. She is playing an important role in keeping the grandchildren connected to some Vietnamese traditions. Phuong finds this phase of life to be a time of balance in all areas of her life, and she is surprised and pleased to find renewed interest in spiritual growth through her Buddhist practices.

Phuong has come to talk to the social worker at the Vietnamese Community Services Center. Her younger daughter has recently informed Phuong that she is a lesbian. Phuong says that she has struggled with this news and has not yet told Hien. She knows that the Vietnamese community does not engage in "gay bashing" the way some communities do, but she also knows that homosexuality carries some stigma in her community. She has done much soul searching as she tries to integrate what her daughter has told her. But she knows one thing: She loves her daughter very much, and she wants her daughter to feel loved and supported by her family and her community. Her daughter plans to march with a Vietnamese gay rights group in the upcoming Tet Celebration march, and she has asked Phuong to march with her. Phuong is trying to decide what to do. She has come to ask the social worker if the Community Services Center runs any groups for parents of gays and lesbians. If not, she would like to start one.

THE MEANING OF ADULTHOOD

You have just read about four lives in process, the lives of Scott Pukalski, Carla Aquino, Viktor Spiro, and Phuong Le. With such different histories and current circumstances, they are likely to have very different futures. Despite the many differences in their life course trajectories, we think of each of them as an adult.

But what exactly does it mean to be an adult? Although much has been written about adult development in the past few decades, definitions of adulthood are rare. In an edited book (Erikson, 1978) written over three decades ago for the purpose of clarifying the meaning of adulthood, the following phrases were used, some repeatedly, by the various authors: "grown up," "a fully grown individual," "mature," "responsible," and "age of majority."

> Is it biological age, psychological age, social age, or spiritual age that best defines adulthood?

The limited attempts to define adulthood have been based on biological age, psychological age, or social age. In terms of *biological age,*

Katchadourian (1978) proposes that any definition of adulthood must include "completion of growth and reproductive capacity" (p. 54). That definition raises the question of whether Scott and Sonya should have been considered adults when Sonya became pregnant when they were in their mid-teens. Katchadourian acknowledges the difficulty with this biological definition of adulthood, commenting that a comprehensive definition will be based not only on biology but also on psychosocial characteristics and "mind and spirit that lend meaning to life." (p. 54).

And what of attempts to define *psychological* adulthood? Stegner (1978) suggests several traits that are identified with psychological adulthood: sanity, morality, rationality, sobriety, continuity, responsibility, wisdom, and conduct as opposed to mere behavior. This list, however, reflects the biases of modern Western cultures (Lapidus, 1978; Rudolph & Rudolph, 1978). Some have suggested that any listing of adult psychological qualities serves only as an ideal type; it does not accurately reflect the psychological state of many persons considered adult (for example, see Bouwsma, 1978). Indeed, governments often reserve the right to declare an age-qualified adult to be incompetent, but secular laws rely on vague, ambiguous, and unreliable psychiatric models for making evaluations of mental status (Kirk & Kutchins, 1992). For example, do you think Viktor Spiro should have been considered a competent adult during his most suicidal period?

Social definitions of adulthood focus on family and work roles. Benchmarks such as financial independence, "a place of my own," and marriage and parenthood have been a part of the informal social definition of adulthood, but these benchmarks have been shifting in recent decades (Draut, 2005; Settersten, Furstenberg, & Rumbaut, 2005). Social definitions of adulthood are also formalized by secular law, which specifies who is recognized by government as adults. To be an adult in the eyes of secular law, one must have reached the *statutory age of majority*, which is based solely on chronological age. The statutory age of majority has changed over time, varies from place to place, and sometimes varies within a given locality for different purposes. For example, the U.S. federal voting age was reduced from 21 to 18 in 1971 by the Twenty-Sixth Amendment to the Constitution, but federal legislation in the 1980s resulted in states establishing 21 as the drinking age.

Simone Scherger (2009) examined the timing of young adult transitions (moving out of parental home, marriage, becoming a parent) among 12 cohorts in West Germany. Cohorts of a 5-year range (e.g., born 1920–1924) were used for the analysis, beginning with the cohort born in 1920–1924 and ending with the cohort born in 1975–1979. This research found a greater variability in the timing of transitions among the younger cohorts than among the older cohorts. Scherger also found that the transitions were influenced by gender (men made the transitions later than women) and education level (higher education was associated with delay in the transitions). It is important to note, however, that another research team found that young adult transitions have remained stable in the Nordic countries where strong welfare institutions provide generous supports for the young adult transitions (K. Newman, 2008). It is also important to note that within cultures, there is much diversity in the sequencing and timing of adult life course markers.

Obviously, definitions of adulthood are somewhat arbitrary. In this book, we use a chronological definition that begins at approximately age 18 and ends when life ends. This is a very long period that can span 80 years and more. In this chapter, we discuss the years between approximately age 18 and age 65, covering what is usually considered young and middle adulthood. Late adulthood is discussed in Chapter 16.

THEORETICAL APPROACHES TO ADULTHOOD

Religious, philosophical, and literary texts suggest that humans have long contemplated questions about their personal biographies and the adult life course. But early psychological theorizing, influenced by Freud, paid little attention to life after adolescence, and young and middle adulthood have received less scholarly attention than other periods of life, including late adulthood. It was not until the 1960s that adulthood became the subject of scholarly inquiry. Since that time, theorizing about the adult life course has grown steadily in the behavioral sciences. This chapter will not attempt a thorough discussion of recent theorizing about adulthood but will summarize the central ideas from the theories of Carl Jung, Erik Erikson, and Daniel Levinson. It will also present recent theorizing about the transition to adulthood, Arnett's theory of emerging adulthood.

Jung's Analytic Psychology

The work of Swiss psychoanalyst Carl Jung is considered here because he played an important role in stimulating interest in adult development among behavioral scientists and has been referred to as "the father of the modern study of adult development" (cited in Austrian, 2008). Unlike his mentor, Sigmund Freud, who thought that no significant personality development happened after adolescence, Jung came to think that personality development had barely begun by the end of adolescence (Jung, 1933a, 1933b).

Although Jung may be best known for his typology of introvert and extrovert personality types and his use of the concept of collective unconscious, the concepts of differentiation and individuation are central to his theory and most pertinent to discussion of adulthood (Jung, 1939). He proposed that **differentiation** is the process by which humans develop unique patterns and traits. **Individuation** is the full development of all aspects of the self into a unique and harmonious whole that gives expression to repressed attributes and desires. Gender roles come into better balance as do introversion and extroversion. Jung believed that individuation does not happen before age 40. He thought that the adult years before age 40, by necessity, are focused on breaking away from parents and meeting responsibilities to family, work, and community. Once those tasks have been accomplished,

the individual can work on greater understanding and acceptance of the self.

Erikson's Psychosocial Life Span Theory

Erik Erikson's psychosocial theoretical framework is probably one of the most universally known approaches to understanding life course development (Erikson, 1950, 1959, 1982). As reported earlier, Erikson describes a sequence of eight psychosocial stages across the life span that result from the interaction between internal instincts and drives and external social and cultural demands. Elements of this theory have been discussed in earlier chapters and summarized in Exhibit 4.11 in Chapter 4.

A major focus of Erikson's theory is the development of **identity,** a concept that he never explicitly defines but that appears to include a sense of self that distinguishes "who I am" from other people and that is enduring over time. Identity develops as the person encounters physiological changes and the changing demands of society, demands that produce a **psychosocial crisis**—a struggle or turning point that defines the particular stage. A well-resolved psychosocial crisis leads to strength; a poorly resolved psychosocial crisis sets the stage for psychopathology. The last three stages of Erikson's theory are adult stages, generally referred to as the stage of young adulthood, middle adulthood, and later adulthood.

According to Erikson, the psychosocial struggle in young adulthood is *intimacy versus isolation.* It is the time when individuals move from the identity fragmentation, confusion, and exploration of adolescence into more intimate engagement with significant others (Erikson, 1968, 1978). **Intimacy** can be defined as a sense of warmth or closeness, and involves three components: interdependence with another person, self-disclosure, and affection (D. Perlman & Fehr, 1987). Exhibit 15.1 lists some of the tasks involved in fostering an intimate relationship with someone.

> How is the capacity for intimacy affected by earlier social relationships?

Exhibit 15.1   Tasks in Fostering Intimacy

- Effectively negotiating expectations for the relationship
- Negotiating roles and responsibilities
- Making compromises
- Prioritizing and upholding values
- Deciding how much to share of oneself
- Identifying and meeting individual needs
- Identifying and meeting partnership needs
- Renegotiating identity
- Developing trust and security
- Allowing for reciprocal communication
- Making time commitments to partner
- Effectively resolving conflict and solving problems
- Demonstrating respect, support, and care

Scott and Sonya Pukalski developed an intimate relationship while they were still adolescents and appear to have a warm and close relationship now. Erikson would suggest, however, that their premature merger led them to inadequately address the underlying psychosocial crisis of identity versus role confusion. It is not too late, of course, to work through this psychosocial crisis, and Scott's current employment problems may precipitate such a struggle for him. His relationship with Sonya and the children may need to get reworked in the context of his evolving identity. In contrast, Carla Aquino appears to have developed an intimate relationship with her husband after successful resolution of the adolescent identity crisis. Now, she is struggling to find a way to incorporate a parental role into her identity while staying intimately connected to her husband.

Individuals who successfully resolve the crisis of intimacy versus isolation are able to achieve the virtue of love. An unsuccessful effort at this stage may lead the young adult to feel alienated, disconnected, and alone. A fear that exists at the core of this crisis is that giving of oneself through a significant, committed relationship will result in a loss of self and diminution of one's constructed identity. To successfully pass through this stage, young adults must try out new relationships and

attempt to find a way to connect with others in new ways while preserving their individuality (Erikson, 1978; J. W. Fowler, 1981).

According to Erikson, the psychosocial struggle of middle adulthood is generativity versus stagnation. **Generativity** is the ability to transcend personal interests to provide care and concern for younger and older generations; it encompasses "procreation, productivity, and creativity, and thus the generation of new beings, as well as of new products and new ideas, including a kind of self-generation concerned with further identity development" (Erikson, 1982, p. 67). Generative adults provide "care, guidance, inspiration, instruction, and leadership" (McAdams, 2001, p. 395) for future generations. Failure to find a way to contribute to future generations, or to make a contribution to the general well-being, results in self-absorption and a sense of stagnation. Erikson saw generativity as an instinct that works to perpetuate society. With some help, Viktor Spiro is beginning to practice generativity in his relationship with his parents. Phuong Le is finding a variety of ways to enact generativity in both her family and her community. As a social worker, however, you will most likely encounter people who struggle with a sense of stagnation in middle adulthood.

Dan McAdams and Ed de St. Aubin (de St. Aubin, McAdams, & Kim, 2004; McAdams, 2006; McAdams & de St. Aubin, 1992, 1998) have presented a model of generativity that includes the seven components found in Exhibit 15.2. McAdams and de St. Aubin (1992, 1998) see generativity coming from both the person (personal desire) and the social and cultural environment (social roles and cultural demand).

Even though Erikson outlined middle adult generativity in 1950, generativity was not a subject of empirical investigation until the 1980s (Peterson & Duncan, 2007). There is limited longitudinal research to answer the question, Are midlife adults more generative than people in other life course phases? Most of the cross-sectional research on generativity reports greater generativity during middle adulthood than in young adulthood or late adulthood (An & Cooney, 2006; McAdams, 2001;

Exhibit 15.2 McAdams and de St. Aubin's Seven Components of Generativity

1. Inner desire for immortality and to be needed
2. Cultural demand for productivity
3. Concern for the next generation
4. Belief in the species
5. Commitment
6. Action: creating, maintaining, or offering
7. Development of a generative life story

SOURCE: Adapted from McAdams, Hart, & Maruna (1998).

Zucker, Ostrove, & Stewart, 2002), but other researchers have found that generativity continues to grow past middle adulthood (Sheldon & Kasser, 2001). Some researchers have identified three components of generativity: generative desire, generative felt capacity, and generative accomplishment, noting that some research indicates that young adults may be high in generative motivation but lack the resources for generative accomplishments (Zucker et al., 2002).

Studies have also found that generativity is associated with gender, class, and race, but the findings are inconsistent. Several researchers (N. Marks, Bumpass, & Jun, 2004; McAdams & de St. Aubin, 1992; McKeering & Pakenham, 2000) have found that men who had never been fathers scored particularly low on measures of generativity, but not being a mother did not have the same effect for women. However, An and Cooney (2006) did not find parenting to be more associated with generativity for men than women, but did find that midlife women are more involved in both private and public caring than midlife men. Phuong Le is certainly more involved in providing private and public caring than Hien, who is nevertheless active in his family and community. When Phuong sees a need in her own family, she also wants to address the need at the community level. Another recent research project found that as generativity increases for adults ages 35–74, so does psychological well-being, and this association between generativity and well-being is equally strong for childless adults as for parents (Rothrauff & Cooney, 2008). Generativity has been found to increase with educational level (Keyes & Ryff, 1998). Black adults have been found to score higher on some measures of generativity than White adults (H. Hart, McAdams, Hirsch, & Bauer, 2001).

Levinson's Theory of Seasons of Adulthood

Although Erikson's psychosocial theory has had the most influence on stage theories of adulthood, Daniel Levinson's theory of seasons of adulthood is one of the best known and most often quoted stage theories (D. Levinson, 1978, 1980, 1986, 1990, 1996). Levinson (1996) conceptualizes the life course as a sequence of eras (see Exhibit 15.3), each with its own biopsychosocial character, with major changes from one era to the next and smaller changes within eras. The eras are partially overlapping, with cross-era transitions, in which characteristics of both the old era and the new are evident, lasting about 5 years. Adult life is, therefore, composed of alternating periods of relative stability and periods of transition. Every era begins and ends at a clearly defined average age, with a range of approximately 2 years above and below this average.

Levinson (1996) postulated that the eras and the cross-transition periods are universal, found in all human lives, but they accommodate innumerable "variations related to gender, class, race, culture, historical epoch, specific circumstances, and genetics" (p. 5). Just consider the variations at age 22 among the four people whose stories you read at the beginning of the chapter. Scott Pukalski is an unemployed father of two; Carla Aquino had just completed college and started her career; Viktor Spiro had recently lost a brother, gone AWOL from the military, and was struggling with depression and substance abuse; and Phuong Le was hoping to escape Vietnam and get to a place where she could live without fear.

Exhibit 15.3   Levinson's Seasons of Adulthood

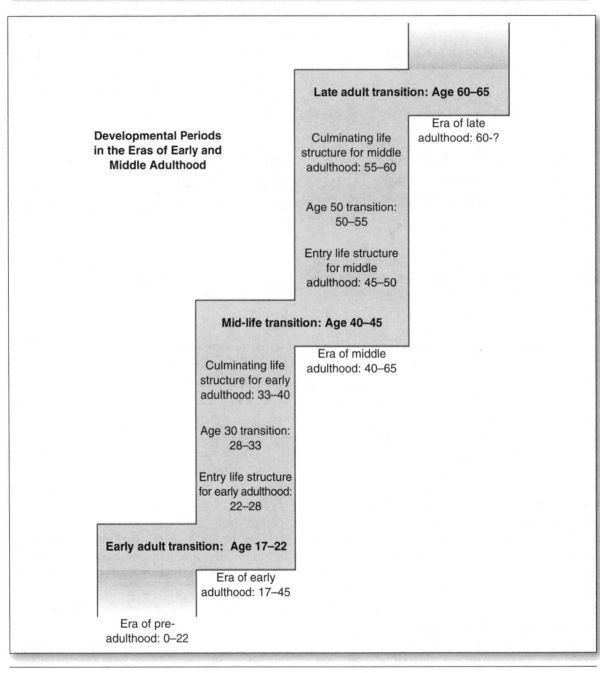

Developmental Periods in the Eras of Early and Middle Adulthood

Late adult transition: Age 60–65

Era of late adulthood: 60-?

Culminating life structure for middle adulthood: 55–60

Age 50 transition: 50–55

Entry life structure for middle adulthood: 45–50

Mid-life transition: Age 40–45

Era of middle adulthood: 40–65

Culminating life structure for early adulthood: 33–40

Age 30 transition: 28–33

Entry life structure for early adulthood: 22–28

Early adult transition: Age 17–22

Era of early adulthood: 17–45

Era of pre-adulthood: 0–22

SOURCE: Levinson (1996)

Levinson (1996) initially developed his theory based on interviews with men about their adult experiences; later, he included women in the research. From his research, he developed the concept of **life structure,** by which he means "the underlying pattern or design of a person's life at a given time" (p. 22). Levinson uses the concept *central components* to designate the relationships that have the greatest significance to a life structure. He suggests that usually no more than two central components exist in a life structure, but the structure may also have peripheral components and unfulfilled components. In most cases, family and occupation are the central components in the life structure, but people vary widely in how much weight they assign to each. These variations are quite evident in the life course trajectories of Scott Pukalski, Carla Aquino, Viktor Spiro, and Phuong Le. Work has been important to Scott in the past, and he longs to find work again. Carla is wondering how she can possibly balance parenting and work. Viktor's mental health problems have made it impossible for him to keep a sustained connection to work. Work is important to Phuong, but she is able to balance work with commitments to family and community at this point in her life.

Levinson considered the ages of 17 to 33 to be the *novice phase* of adulthood. The transition into young adulthood, which occurs during the ages of 17 to 22, includes the tasks of leaving adolescence and making preliminary decisions about relationships, career, and belief systems; the transition out of this phase, which occurs around the age of 30, marks significant changes in life structure and life course trajectory. It appears that Carla Aquino is in the midst of this transition.

During the novice phase, young persons' personalities continue to develop, and they prepare to differentiate (emotionally, geographically, financially) from their families of origin (Levinson, 1978). Levinson suggested that it may take up to 15 years for some individuals to resolve the transition to adulthood and to construct a stable adult life structure.

According to Levinson (1996), early adulthood, from about 17 to 45, is the adult era of greatest vigor but also of "greatest contradiction and stress" (p. 19). The twenties and thirties are peak years biologically. Psychosocially, early adulthood offers only limited life experience for making crucial decisions about domestic partnerships, family, work, and lifestyle. Heavy financial obligations are likely to be incurred, but earning power is still comparatively low. Both the rewards and costs of this era are enormous.

The era of middle adulthood, from about 40 to 65, is a time of reduced biological capacities but also a period when many people are energized by satisfying intimate relationships and gratifying contributions at work and in the community. This certainly seems to be the case for Phuong Le. It appears that this may be an improved era for Viktor Spiro as well. For some, however, middle adulthood is a time of progressive decline, self-absorption, and emptiness. In a similar way to Jung, Levinson suggests that during the transition to middle adulthood, individuals often try to give greater attention to previously neglected components. He sees this transition as balancing four opposing aspects of identity: young versus old, creation versus destruction, feminine versus masculine, and attachment versus separation (Levinson, 1977).

Building on Levinson's concepts, others have noted that cultural and societal factors affect life structure choices during adulthood by constraining or facilitating opportunities (B. Newman & Newman, 2009). For example, socioeconomic status, parental expectations, availability of and interactions with adult role models, neighborhood conditions, and community and peer group pressures may all contribute to a young person's decisions about whether to marry early, get a job or join the military before pursuing a college education or advanced training, or delay childbearing. Social and economic factors may directly or indirectly limit a young person's access to alternative choices, thereby rigidifying a young person's life structure. Along these lines, many researchers discuss the strong link between social capital and human capital, suggesting that a family's "wealth transfer" or extent of familial assets, such as the ability to pay for children's college education, is influential in opening up or limiting young adults' opportunities for advanced education and viable employment (Lui, Robles, Leondar-Wright, Brewer, & Adamson, 2006; Rank, 2005).

Scott Pukalski's young adult transition has been shaped by his mother's early death, adolescent fatherhood, and an economic recession, all factors that limited his choices. Carla Aquino may find herself making decisions to curtail some of her career aspirations in order to fulfill her familial obligations and responsibilities as a new parent. Viktor Spiro's young adult transition was negatively impacted by poverty and political unrest, as well as by trauma, depression, and substance abuse. War, early marriage, and limited education placed serious limits on Phuong Le's young adult transition. Especially in young adulthood, life structures are in constant motion, changing with time and evolving as new life circumstances unfold. Decisions made during the young adulthood transition, such as joining the military, foregoing postsecondary education, or delaying childbearing may not accurately or completely represent a young person's desired life structure or goals.

Arnett's "Emerging" Adulthood

A number of prominent developmental scholars who have written about the stages of adolescence and young adulthood in advanced industrial countries have described phenomena called "prolonged adolescence," "youthhood," or "psychosocial moratorium," which represent an experimentation phase of young adulthood (Arnett, 2000; Erikson, 1968; Settersten et al., 2005; Sheehy, 1995). This is consistent with Levinson's conceptualization of a novice phase of adulthood. Jeffrey Jensen Arnett has gone one step further, defining a phase he terms **emerging adulthood** in some detail (Arnett, 2000, 2004; Arnett & Tanner, 2005). He describes emerging adulthood as a developmental phase distinct from both adolescence and young adulthood, occurring between the ages of 18 and 25 in industrialized societies (Arnett, 2000, p. 470). Arnett notes that there is considerable variation in personal journeys from emerging adulthood into young adulthood, but suggests that most individuals make the transition by age 30 (Arnett, 2000). He conceptualized this new phase of life based on research showing that a majority of young persons ages 18 to 25 believe they have not yet reached adulthood and that a majority of people in their thirties do agree they have reached adulthood.

> What historical trends are producing "emerging" adulthood?

According to Arnett (2006, 2007), identity exploration has become the central focus of emerging adulthood, not of adolescence. Emerging adulthood is a period of prolonged exploration of social and economic roles where young people try out new experiences related to love, work, financial responsibilities, and educational interests without committing to any specific lasting plan. The social role experimentation of adolescence becomes further refined, more focused, and more intense, although commitment to adult roles is not yet solidified. Arnett explains this adulthood transition using an organizing framework that includes cognitive, emotional, behavioral, and role transition elements (Arnett & Taber, 1994).

Most young persons in emerging adulthood are in education, training, or apprenticeship programs working toward an occupation; most individuals in their thirties have established a more solid career path and are moving through occupational transitions (e.g., promotion to leadership positions and recognition for significant accomplishments). Studies do show more occupational instability during the ages 18 to 25 as compared to age 30 (Rindfuss, Cooksey, & Sutterlin, 1999). Indeed, Arnett (2007) suggests that emerging adulthood can be an "unstructured time" characterized by a lack of attachment to social institutions, where young people are moving out from their families of origin; have not yet formed new families of their own; and are moving out of prior educational systems and into new vocational, educational, or employment sectors (p. 25).

Although marriage has traditionally been cited as a salient marker in the adulthood transition, current research shows that marriage has not retained its high status as the critical benchmark of adulthood. Today, independent responsibility for decision making and finances seems to be more significant in marking this transition than marriage is (Arnett, 1998). Overall, the emphasis in emerging adulthood is on trying out new roles without the

> How much personal agency was involved in Scott Pukalski's, Carla Aquino's, Viktor Spiro's, and Phuong Le's transition to adulthood?

pressure of making any particular commitment (Schwartz, Cote, & Arnett, 2005). The transition, then, from *emerging* adulthood into *young* adulthood is marked by solidifying role commitments. Newer research shows that, across race and ethnicity, the difference between those who follow a **default individualization** pathway (adulthood transitions defined by circumstance and situation, rather than individual agency) and those who follow a **developmental individualization** pathway (adulthood transitions defined by personal agency and deliberately charted growth opportunities in intellectual, occupational, and psychosocial domains) is a firmer commitment to goals, values, and beliefs for those in the developmental individuation pathway (Schwartz et al., 2005, p. 204). In addition, these researchers found that personal agency, across race and ethnicity, is associated with a more flexible and exploratory orientation to adulthood commitments, and is less associated with premature closure and circumscribed commitment.

Residential stability and mobility is another theme of this transition. Emerging adults in their early twenties may find themselves at various times living with family, living on their own in independent housing arrangements yet relying on parents for instrumental support, and living with a significant partner or friends. Indeed, residential instability and mobility is typically at its height in the mid-twenties (Rindfuss et al., 1999). Thus, a traditional definition of the separation-individuation process may not be appropriately applied to emerging adulthood. True "separation" from the family of origin may appear only toward the end of young adulthood or, perhaps for some, during the transition to middle adulthood. Scott Pukalski, although he most likely considers himself an adult, is a parent still living with his in-laws. Viktor Spiro lived on his own in his twenties, but there are a number of reasons why he resides with his parents as he approaches 40.

Demographic changes over the past several decades, such as delayed marriage and childbearing, have made young adulthood a significant developmental period filled with complex changes and possibilities (Arnett, 2000; Sheehy, 1995). Current global demographic trends suggest a similar picture. Overall, globally, family size has decreased; the timing of first marriage is being delayed, including a decrease in teenage marriages; and there are overall decreases in adolescent labor accompanied by increases in educational attainment. However, in some countries like Pakistan, the delay in first marriage has been attributed to a rise in the rate of adolescent girls in the labor market (see C. B. Lloyd, Behrman, Stromquist, & Cohen, 2006; N. R. White, 2003). In addition, there is similarity in adulthood transitioning trends between developing countries and more economically developed countries, with East Asian countries showing the highest trend similarities and sub-Saharan African showing the least similarities (Behrman & Sengupta, 2006). Specifically, there has been an increased reliance on finding employment outside the family, an emphasis on more formal schooling rather than family-based learning, a decreased gender gap, and greater transiency in young adulthood (Behrman & Sengupta, 2006).

Recent fertility data reported in *The Economist* ("Go Forth and Multiply a Lot Less," 2009) suggest a worldwide trend in declining fertility rates (the number of children a woman is projected to have during her lifetime), even in poor and developing countries, which have typically yielded higher fertility rates. Scholars believe that the disparity between women's desired and actual number of children has decreased in recent years in part due to increased access to family planning and literacy programs, which have remarkably grown in countries such as Iran, where such education for women just decades ago was negligible (i.e., in 1976, 10% of rural Iranian women aged 20–24 were literate; today it is 91%) (p. 30). These changing demographic trends have other societal ramifications, one of which is the potential to make it easier for women across the globe to transition to the formal workplace. A chart in *The Economist* ("Go Forth and Multiply," 2009) article from 2007 data shows a clear association between countries' fertility rates and the economy. Countries with fertility rates above the replacement rate of 2.1 (such as Ghana and India) have lower income per person, while countries that have maintained fertility rate stability at or below the replacement rate of 2.1 (such as China, Brazil, Iran, South Korea, the United States) have higher income per person.

VARIATIONS IN THE TRANSITION TO ADULTHOOD _____

What are the sources of diversity in the transition to adulthood?

The theory of emerging adulthood recognizes that there is much diversity of experience with this transition. Individual routes of development (the timing and sequence of transitions) are contingent on socialization processes experienced within family, peer groups, school, and community. Environmental opportunities, expressed community attitudes, and family expectations may all influence the timing and sequencing of transitions during emerging adulthood. Socially constructed gauges of adulthood—such as stable and independent residence, completion of education, entry into a career path, and marriage or significant partnership—hold varying importance across families, cultures, and historical time.

For some young persons, decisions may be heavily weighted toward maintaining family equilibrium. For example, some may choose not to move out of the family home and establish their own residence in order to honor the family's expectation that children will continue to live with their parents, perhaps even into their thirties. For others, successful adult development may be defined through the lens of pragmatism; a young person may be expected to make decisions based on immediate, short-term, utilitarian outcomes. For example, he or she may be expected to enter the labor force and establish a career in order to care for a new family and release the family of origin from burden. Carla Aquino seems to be struggling to uphold several Latina social norms, as seen through her emotional and financial commitments to her immediate and extended family, efforts to maintain a meaningful connection to her church, and creation of a family of her own. However, the multiple role demands experienced are considerable, as her own personal goals of maintaining a professional identity, being a good wife, and giving back to the community compete for Carla's time and emotional energy.

One recent study examined the home-leaving behavior of poor and nonpoor emerging adults in the United States. Using a longitudinal data set and a family economic status measure that included a federal poverty line indicator and childhood public assistance receipt, the authors found significant home-leaving and returning differences between poor and nonpoor emerging adults (De Marco & Cosner Berzin, 2008). Specifically, having a family history of public welfare assistance, dropping out of high school, and becoming a teen parent were the characteristics most likely to predict leaving the family home before age 18 years. Repeated home-leaving (leaving, returning, leaving again) was more frequent for nonpoor as compared to poor emerging adults. And when they left home, nonpoor emerging adults were more likely than poor emerging adults to transition to postsecondary educational opportunities (De Marco & Cosner Berzin, 2008). Scott and Sonya Pukalski do not fit this profile. They became teen parents and dropped out of high school, but they have continued to live with Sonya's parents and have been fortunate to receive both economic and child care support from them.

International research that has focused specifically on foster youth aging out of care suggests that such youth face significant transitioning risks, such as homelessness, substance abuse, and involvement with the criminal justice system (Tweddle, 2007, p. 16). More successful transitioning outcomes for former foster youth, such as finding stable housing and employment, are associated with having had a strong social support system and problem-solving skill development before leaving care (M. Stein, 2005; Tweddle, 2007).

Culture and gender also have significant influence on young adult roles and expectations (Arnett & Taber, 1994). Social norms may sanction the postponement of traditional adult roles (such as marriage) or may promote marriage and childbearing in adolescence. There may be different family expectations about what it means to be a "good daughter" or "good son," and these expectations may be consistent or inconsistent with socially prescribed gender roles, potentially creating competing role demands. For example, examining the life course priorities of Appalachian emerging adults aged 19–24, R. A. Brown, Rehkopf, Copeland, Costello, and Worthman (2009) found that high family poverty, and particularly the combination of poverty and parental neglect, was associated with emerging adults' lower educational goals. In addition, the experience of traumatic stressors was associated with lowered economic attainment priorities.

Some environments may offer limited education and occupational opportunities. Economic structures, environmental opportunities, family characteristics, and individual abilities all contribute to variations in transitioning during emerging adulthood. Young adults with developmental disabilities tend to remain in high school during the adulthood transitioning years of 18 to 21, as compared to their peers without such disabilities who are more likely to continue on to college or enter the workforce. Research suggests that more inclusive postsecondary environments, that offer higher education opportunities for young adults with developmental disabilities, and the necessary accommodations for such adults to succeed, can increase their social and academic skills, as well as facilitate productive interactions between young adults with and without disabilities (Casale-Giannola & Kamens, 2006). Some studies have shown that Latina mothers of young adults with developmental disabilities encourage family-centered adulthood transitioning, with less emphasis on traditional markers of independence and more emphasis on the family's role in the young adults' ongoing decision making, with such mothers reporting that their young adults' social interactions were more important to them than traditional measures of productivity (Rueda, Monzo, Shapiro, Gomez, & Blacher, 2005).

Individuals who grow up in families with limited financial resources, or who are making important transitions during an economic downturn, have less time for lengthy exploration than others do and may be encouraged to make occupational commitments as soon as possible. Certainly Scott Pukalski is struggling with the financial pressure of the current economic recession and would like to quickly become reemployed. Although he enjoys caring for his children, he feels that he *should* be the breadwinner in the family, and he worries about his ability to provide for them economically in the future.

Indeed, research shows that childhood socioeconomic status is an important mediating factor in young adult transitions (Smyer, Gatz, Simi, & Pedersen, 1998). For example, Astone, Schoen, Ensminger, and Rothert (2000) examined the differences between "condensed" (or time-restricted) and "diffuse" (or time-open) human capital development, with findings suggesting that a diffuse educational system offers opportunities for school reentry across the life course, which may be beneficial to young people who do not immediately enter higher education due to family or economic reasons, such as going into the military or entering the labor force. And, more specifically, they found that military service after high school increased the probability of returning to higher education for men, but not for women.

A family's economic background and resources are strongly associated with the adult status of the family's children; high correlations exist between parents' income and occupational status and that of their children (Rank, 2005). For example, about one third (34%) of youth from low-income families go on to college compared with 83% of youth from high-income families (Hair, Ling, & Cochran, 2003). Individuals with greater financial stability often have more paths to choose from and may have more resources to negotiate the stressors associated with this developmental period.

Critical Thinking Questions 15.1

Which transitional markers do you see as the best indicators that one has become an adult? Why did you choose these particular markers? How do the stories of Scott Pukalski, Carla Aquino, Viktor Spiro, and Phuong Le fit with the developmental markers you have chosen? What societal and institutional barriers might contribute to stagnation in middle adulthood? Under what conditions, and for what groups, might these be particularly challenging barriers?

BIOLOGICAL FUNCTIONING IN YOUNG AND MIDDLE ADULTHOOD

Physical functioning is typically at its height during early adulthood. Most biological systems reach their peak performance in the mid-twenties. But as young adults enter their thirties, an increased awareness of physical changes—changes in vision, endurance, metabolism, and muscle strength—is common (e.g., Bjorklund & Bee, 2008).

There have been dramatic changes in the last few decades in the numbers of adults who enjoy healthy and active lives in the years between 45 and 65 and beyond. However, some physical and mental decline does begin to occur. Age-related changes are usually gradual, accumulating at different rates in different body systems. The changes are the result of interactions of biology with psychological, sociocultural, and spiritual factors, and individuals play a very active role in the aging process throughout adulthood. However, by the age of 50, the accumulation of biological change becomes physically noticeable in most people.

The biggest stories in biological functioning and physical and mental health in middle adulthood are changes in physical appearance; changes in mobility; changes in the reproductive system; and changes in health, more specifically the beginnings of chronic disease. There are enormous individual differences in the timing and intensity of these changes, but some changes affect almost everyone, such as *presbyopia* (difficulty seeing close objects) for both men and women and menopause for women. Typical biological changes in middle adulthood are summarized in Exhibit 15.4.

Health Maintenance in Young and Middle Adulthood

With new role responsibilities in family, parenting, and career, young adults may spend less time in exercise and sports activities than during adolescence and pay less attention to their physical health. At the same time, young adults ages 18 to 34 are the least insured when it comes to health care coverage as compared to any other age cohort (Draut, 2005). It is unclear how much this situation will improve with the Affordable Care Act enacted in 2010. One provision of this legislation requires most health insurance plans that include coverage for children on their parents' plans to extend that coverage until the "children" reach the age of 26 (HealthCare.gov, 2010). In any case, many

Exhibit 15.4 Biological Changes in Middle Adulthood

Changes in Physical Appearance	Changes in Mobility	Changes in Reproductive System & Sexuality
Skin begins to sag and wrinkle. Brown pigmentation appears in spots exposed to sunlight. Skin becomes drier. Hair on head becomes thinner and grayer. Hair may appear in unwanted places (ears, chin). Body build changes, with height loss and weight gain (increased body fat).	Progressive loss of muscles leads to loss of strength. Progressive loss of bone mineral leads to less strong, more brittle bones. Cartilage that protects joints begins to degenerate, interfering with ease of movement.	Women: Supply of egg cells is depleted, and ovarian production of hormones slows; women gradually lose capacity to conceive children, which ends with menopause (cessation of menstruation); vaginal dryness results. Men: Testes shrink gradually; volume of seminal fluid declines; testosterone level declines; frequency and intensity of orgasm decreases; erection becomes more difficult to achieve.

Photo 15.1 Young adults may choose to get more actively involved in community recreational leagues.

young adults make an effort to maintain or improve their physical health, committing to exercise regimens and participating in wellness classes (such as yoga or meditation). They may choose to get more actively involved in community recreational leagues in such sports as hockey, soccer, racquetball, and ultimate Frisbee. Sometimes physical activities are combined with participation in social causes, such as Race for the Cure runs, AIDS walks, or organized bike rides to benefit a charity.

By middle adulthood, the need for good health maintenance activities becomes more imperative. To prevent unnecessary wear and tear on joints, it is important to wear the proper footwear when engaging in exercise activities and to avoid repetitive movements of the wrists. Flexibility exercises help to expand the range of motion for stiff joints. Exercises to strengthen the muscles that support joints also help to minimize the mobility problems associated with changes in joints. By engaging in strength training, midlife adults can minimize the loss of muscle mass. An effective strength training program involves two or three workouts per week.

The physical changes in middle adulthood require some adjustments in the sexual lives of midlife men and women. Many couples adjust well to these changes, however, and with children out of the home, may find that their sexual lives become less inhibited and more passionate. The sex lives of midlife adults may benefit from improved self-esteem that typifies middle adulthood and, in relationships of some longevity, from better understanding of the desires and responses of the sexual partner.

Physical and Mental Health in Young and Middle Adulthood

Behavioral risks to health in emerging and young adulthood may include unprotected sex and substance abuse. The potential for STIs, including HIV, is related to frequent sexual experimentation, substance use (particularly binge drinking), and smoking or use of other tobacco products.

According to the Substance Abuse and Mental Health Administration's most recent data from the National Survey on Drug Use and Health, one fifth (19.6%) of young adults ages 18–25 years used illicit drugs in 2008, which was higher than the rate for youth ages 12–17 (9.3%) and for adults over the age of 26 (5.9%). The nonmedical use of pain medications for this age group during 2008 was 4.6%, up from 4.1% in 2002. Illicit drug use for adults aged 18 years and older showed highest rates for the unemployed (19.6%) and lower rates for part-time (10.2%) and full-time (8.0%) employment status (SAMHSA, 2009b).

Research has shown physical and psychosocial interactions in producing health status. For example, obesity in adolescence leads to depression and lower social attainment (i.e., educational, economic, work satisfaction) in young adulthood for females but not males (Merten, Wickrama, & Williams, 2008). There are important associations between being overweight and having depression in adolescence and young adulthood for African American and Caucasian females (Franko, Striegel-Moore, Thompson, Schreiber, & Daniels, 2005).

The changing economic environment, particularly the recent economic volatility experienced globally, has been found to affect physical health. According to a 2008 National Study of the Changing Workplace (Aumann & Galinsky, 2009), workers' overall health has declined from 2002 levels, with an increase in frequency of minor health problems (such as headaches), rising obesity rates, and rising stress levels (41% reported significant stress). Of those workers who experience chronic health problems, most often reported conditions include high blood pressure (21%), high cholesterol (14%), diabetes (7%), heart condition (3%), or a mental health disorder (4%).

In working with young adults who have a physical or mental illness, social workers will want to assess the client's relationship to the illness and evaluate how the treatments are affecting the psychosocial developmental tasks of young adulthood (Dunbar, Mueller, Medina, & Wolf, 1998). For example, an illness may increase a young person's dependence on others at a time when independence from parents is valued, and individuals may have concerns about finding a mate. Societal stigma

associated with the illness may be intense at a time when the individual is seeking more meaningful community engagements, and adjustment to the possibilities of career or parenthood delays may be difficult. Increasingly, online social networking sites like PatientsLikeMe (www.patientslikeme.com) are being used by young adults with chronic health conditions to create online communities to promote social interaction and information exchange. Users can create a shared health profile and find other users who have the same health condition to share treatment experiences. Examples of current disease communities include HIV/AIDS, fibromyalgia, mood conditions, and multiple sclerosis. Currently, about one third (34%) of the PatientsLikeMe member base is under age 39, and the majority (72%) are women.

For several years now, many young adults in the United States have been returning from war zones with a variety of serious injuries, some of which will require long-term treatment and involve chronic impairment and disability. The two most pressing concerns are for returning soldiers with traumatic brain injury and post-traumatic stress disorder. To see video testimonials of some of the challenges the returning service people and their families face, you can visit this link, sponsored by the Defense Centers of Excellence: www.dcoe.health.mil/ForWarriors/RealWarriorsCampaign.aspx.

Young adult partners who struggle with infertility problems may have to confront disappointment from family members and adjust to feelings of unfulfilled social and family expectations. Costs of treatment may be prohibitive, and couples may experience a sense of alienation from peers who are moving rapidly into parenthood and child rearing. See Chapter 10 in this book for further discussion of infertility.

Health during middle adulthood is highly variable. There are some positive changes: The frequency of accidents declines, as does susceptibility to colds and allergies. On the other hand, although many people live through middle adulthood with little

> What might be some reasons for these race and gender differences in health in middle adulthood?

disease or disability, the frequency of chronic illness, persistent symptoms, and functional disability begins to rise during this time, and the death rate increases continuously over the adult years. There are significant gender and race/ethnicity differences in the death rates in middle adulthood, with men having higher death rates than women in Black, White, and Hispanic populations, and Blacks of both genders having alarmingly higher death rates than their White and Hispanic counterparts.

In the past century, there has been a change in the types of diseases that are likely to affect health across the life course in affluent countries. In the early 1900s, when life expectancy was in the mid-forties, most deaths were caused by infectious diseases, such as pneumonia, tuberculosis, and influenza (Sapolsky, 2004). With the increase in life expectancy, chronic disease plays a more important role in the great stretch of middle adulthood and beyond. People are now living long enough to experience a chronic illness: "We are now living well enough and long enough to slowly fall apart. . . . [T]he diseases that plague us now are ones of slow accumulation of damage—heart disease, cancer, cerebrovascular disorders" (Sapolsky, 2004, p. 3).

It is important to note that there are some global differences in causes of death. The World Health Organization (WHO, 2008a) reports on the leading causes of death in low-income, middle-income, and high-income countries. In high-income countries, heart disease is the number-one cause of death, and cerebrovascular disease (stroke) is the number-two cause of death. In middle-income countries, the situation is reversed, with stroke the number-one cause and heart disease the number-two cause. In low-income countries, however, lower respiratory infection (pneumonia) is the number-one cause, followed by heart disease. In low-income countries, diarrheal disease is the number-three cause of death, and HIV/AIDS is the number-four cause. Neither of these conditions is included in the top 10 causes of death in middle-income and high-income countries. Tuberculosis, neonatal infections, and malaria are also among the top 10 causes of death in low-income countries. None of these conditions is included in the top 10

in high-income countries, and only tuberculosis is among the top 10 in middle-income countries, where it is the ninth cause. These data indicate that chronic illness is the major cause of death in high-income and middle-income countries, but infectious diseases continue to be a major challenge in less affluent nations that lack access to safe water and adequate sanitation.

Death is not the only outcome of chronic illness. As Sapolsky (2004) suggests, chronic disease often has a slow course and involves some level of disability over a number of years. WHO uses the concept of disability-adjusted life year (DALY) to measure the sum of the years lost due to premature death *plus* the number of years spent in states of poor health or disability. There is much international evidence that socioeconomic position is a powerful predictor of both mortality and poor health (morbidity) (Marmot & Fuhrer, 2004). WHO has calculated the worldwide leading causes of DALYs for males and females 15 years old and older; these are reported in Exhibit 15.5. It is important to note that the WHO data include mental health as well as physical health conditions, whereas health statistics in the United States do not. Therefore, the WHO data are useful because they give a better picture of the impact of unipolar depressive disorders (major depressive episodes that occur without a manic phase) and alcohol use disorders on global health.

The story of Viktor Spiro demonstrates the important impact that mental health conditions can have on life trajectories. There is evidence that baby boomers in the United States and Europe have higher rates of depression and substance abuse than previous generations (Piazza & Charles, 2006). A longitudinal study in the Netherlands found that mental health tends to improve across the life course, but a minority of midlife adults show persistently high levels of depressive symptoms and loneliness across the middle adult years (Deeg, 2005). These researchers, like many others who study middle adulthood, emphasize that reporting average results can mask the great variability in middle adult trajectories. Researchers have also found that "midlife is a particularly high-risk

Exhibit 15.5 Leading Causes of Disease Burden (DALYs) for Males and Females Ages 15 Years and Older, Worldwide, 2002

Males	Females
1. HIV/AIDS	1. Unipolar depressive disorders
2. Ischemic heart disease	2. HIV/AIDS
3. Cerebrovascular disease	3. Ischemic heart disease
4. Unipolar depressive disorders	4. Cerebrovascular disease
5. Road traffic injuries	5. Cataracts
6. Tuberculosis	6. Hearing loss, adult onset
7. Alcohol use disorders	7. COPD
8. Violence	8. Tuberculosis
9. COPD	9. Osteoarthritis
10. Hearing loss, adult onset	10. Diabetes mellitus

SOURCE: World Health Organization (2003).

NOTE: COPD = chronic obstructive pulmonary disease (includes chronic bronchitis and emphysema).

period for either delayed onset or reactivated PTSD" (Z. Solomon & Mikulincer, 2006, p. 664).

Viktor Spiro struggled with depression and substance abuse before he immigrated to the United States, and, as happens with many immigrants, the multiple losses and demands associated with the immigration experience exacerbated his mental health problems. As Karen Aroian and Anne E. Norris (2003) note, "Depression significantly impairs immigrants' ability to adapt to the new country and has serious emotional and economic consequences for immigrants and their families" (p. 420). Aroian and Norris found high levels of depression in a sample of immigrants from the former Soviet Union; they also found that the severity and longevity of depressive symptoms were correlated with the level of immigration-related stressors. They concluded that mental health interventions with depressed immigrants should focus on relieving these stressors by focusing on such practical issues as learning English and

obtaining employment, as well as on emotional issues like loss, trauma, and feeling at home in the new country. Viktor was lucky to find mental health professionals who did just this, assisting him to get debt forgiveness and attain citizenship, while also working on issues of emotion regulation and expanding his social network.

Phuong Le and her family saw many horrors in Saigon, both during the war and after. They suffered the loss of family members as well as their homeland. Phuong knows that many Vietnamese refugees did not fare well when they reached the United States, some falling prey to substance abuse, family violence, and suicide, and others living lives of quiet desperation. She feels lucky to have been able to settle among so many other Vietnamese people and believes that their support has been invaluable to her own well-being. She also feels that her children have given her hope and belief in the future. She has painful memories, but she feels lucky that they have not overpowered her.

COGNITION IN YOUNG AND MIDDLE ADULTHOOD _____

Young adulthood is a time when individuals expand, refine, and challenge existing belief systems, and the college environment is especially fertile ground for such broadening experiences. Late adolescents and young adults are also entering Piaget's formal operations stage, during which they begin to develop the cognitive ability to apply abstract principles to enhance problem solving and to reflect on thought processes (refer back to Exhibit 4.1 in Chapter 4 for an overview of Piaget's stages of cognitive development). These more complex cognitive capabilities, combined with a greater awareness of personal feelings, characterize cognitive development in young adulthood (Gardiner & Kosmitzki, 2008).

The abstract reasoning capabilities of adulthood and the awareness of subjective feelings can be applied to life experiences in ways that help individuals negotiate life transitions, new roles, stressors, and challenges (Labouvie-Vief, 1990, 2005). You might think of the development in cognitive processing from adolescence to young adulthood as a gradual switch from obtaining information to using that information in more applied ways (Arnett & Taber, 1994). Young adults are better able to see things from multiple viewpoints and from various perspectives than adolescents are.

With increasing cognitive flexibility, young adults begin to solidify their own values and beliefs. They may opt to retain certain traditions and values from their family of origin while letting go of others in order to make room for new ones. During this sorting out process, young adults are also defining what community means to them and what their place in the larger societal context might be like. Individuals begin establishing memberships in, and attachments to, selected social, service, recreational, and faith communities. Research indicates that religious beliefs, in particular, are reevaluated and critically examined in young adulthood, with individuals sorting out beliefs and values they desire to hold onto and those they choose to discard (Arnett & Jensen, 2002; Hodge, Johnson, & Luidens, 1993). However, there is a danger that discarded family

beliefs may not be replaced with new meaningful beliefs (Arnett, 2000). Many emerging adults view the world as cold and disheartening and are somewhat cynical about the future. With this common pitfall in mind, we can take comfort from Arnett's finding that nearly all the 18- to 24-year-olds who participated in his study believed that they would ultimately achieve their goals at some point in the future (Arnett, 2000).

Perhaps no domain of human behavior in middle adulthood arouses more concern than intellectual functioning. A trip to your local pharmacy will confront you with the variety of supplements and herbal remedies that are marketed to midlife adults with promises of maintaining mental alertness and mental acuity. And yet, middle-aged adults are often at the peak of their careers and filling leadership roles. Most of the recent presidents of the United States were men older than 50.

Research on cognitive changes in middle adulthood is recent, but there is growing and clear evidence that cognitive performance remains stable for the majority of midlife adults (M. Martin & Zimprich, 2005; S. Willis & Schaie, 2005). However, a significant subset of midlife adults shows important gain in cognitive functioning, and another significant subset shows important decline (S. Willis & Schaie, 2005). The amount of gain and decline varies across different types of cognitive functioning. For example, S. Willis and Schaie found that, depending on the specific cognitive skill, the proportion of midlife adults who were stable in performance ranged from 53% to 69%, the proportion who gained ranged from 6% to 16%, and the proportion who declined ranged from 15% to 31%.

Researchers are finding that individual differences in intellectual performance increase throughout middle adulthood (M. Martin & Zimprich, 2005). These increasing variations are related to both biological and environmental factors. Several biological risk factors have been identified for cognitive decline in midlife—including hypertension, diabetes, high cholesterol, and the APOE gene (a gene that has been associated with one type of Alzheimer's disease). Several protective factors have also been identified, most of them social in nature, including education, work or other environments that demand complex cognitive work, and physical exercise (S. Willis & Schaie, 2005). These findings are consistent with increasing evidence of brain plasticity throughout the life course, and suggest that cognitive decline can be slowed by engaging in activities that train the brain.

The Seattle Longitudinal Study (SLS) is studying intellectual changes from the early twenties to very old age by following the same individuals over time as well as drawing new samples at each test cycle. S. Willis and Schaie (2006) summarize the findings about changes for selected mental abilities across the life course, paying attention to gender differences. By incorporating data on new participants as the survey progresses, they are also able to study generational (cohort) differences, addressing the question, Is the current baby boom midlife cohort functioning at a higher intellectual level than their parents' generation?

S. Willis and Schaie (2005, 2006) summarize the findings for six mental abilities:

1. *Vocabulary:* ability to understand ideas expressed in words

2. *Verbal Memory:* ability to encode and recall language units, such as word lists

3. *Number:* ability to perform simple mathematical computations quickly and accurately

4. *Spatial Orientation:* ability to visualize stimuli in two- and three-dimensional space

5. *Inductive Reasoning:* ability to recognize and understand patterns in and relationships among variables to analyze and solve logical problems

6. *Perceptual Speed:* ability to quickly make discriminations in visual stimuli

The research shows that middle adulthood is the period of peak performance of four of the six mental abilities: inductive reasoning, spatial orientation, vocabulary, and verbal memory. Two of the six mental abilities, perceptual speed and numerical ability, show decline in middle adulthood, but the decline in perceptual speed is much more dramatic than the decline in numerical ability. The question is, "How much does the culture value speed?" In the United States, speed is highly valued, and quick thinking is typically seen as an indication of high intelligence. However, in many non-Western countries, perceptual speed is not so highly valued (Gardiner & Kosmitzki, 2008). S. Willis and Schaie (2005) note that the mental abilities that improve in middle adulthood—inductive reasoning, spatial orientation, vocabulary, and verbal memory—are among the more complex, higher-order mental abilities.

There are gender differences in the changes in mental abilities during middle adulthood. On average, men reach peak performance somewhat earlier than women. Men reach peak performance on spatial orientation, vocabulary, and verbal memory in their fifties, and women reach peak performance on these same mental abilities in their early sixties. Conversely, on average, women begin to decline in perceptual speed somewhat earlier than men, in their twenties compared to the thirties for men. The improvement in mental abilities in middle adulthood is more dramatic for women than for men. Across the adult life course, women score higher than men on vocabulary, verbal memory, perceptual speed, and inductive reasoning. Men, conversely, score higher than women across the adult life course on spatial orientation. There is some evidence that cognitive decline in middle adulthood is predictive of cognitive impairment in late adulthood (S. Willis & Schaie, 2005).

S. Willis and Schaie (2006) also report on cohort differences in the selected mental abilities. They found that the baby boom cohort scored higher on two of the abilities, verbal memory and inductive reasoning, than their parents' generation did at the same chronological age. The baby boomers also scored higher than their parents on spatial orientation, but these differences were smaller than those for verbal memory and inductive reasoning. There were virtually no cohort differences on vocabulary and perceptual speed. The boomers did not score as well as their parents' generation on numerical ability, and the authors note that this

What factors might be producing this historical trend toward declines in numerical ability?

is a continuation of a negative trend in numerical ability since the early 1900s found in other studies.

Currently, intense research efforts are exploring what is happening in the middle-aged brain (see Strauch, 2010, for a summary of the research). It is clear that some brains age better than others, resulting in much variability in middle-aged brains. Researchers are finding evidence of both loss and gain, but on balance, the news is good. Part of memory wanes, most notably the part that remembers names. But the ability to make accurate judgments about people and situations gets stronger. In summarizing this situation, Barbara Strauch notes that "this middle-aged brain . . . just as it's forgetting what it had for breakfast can still go to work and run a multinational bank or school or city . . . then return home to deal with . . . teenagers, neighbors, parents" (pp. xvi–xvii). Neuroscientists are suggesting that as we reach midlife, our brains begin to reorganize and behave in a different way. Most notably, people in middle age begin to use both sides of their brains to solve problems for which only one side was used in the past, a process called bilateralization. The two hemispheres of the brain become better integrated. Research also indicates that starting in middle age, the brain's ability to tune out irrelevant material wanes, leading to more time in daydream mode but also greater capacity to capture "the big picture." Researchers are not certain about the most protective things that can be done for the aging brain, but the best evidence to date indicates that education buffers the brain, and physical exercise is a "potent producer of new neurons" (Strauch, 2010, p. 128). The ideal dosage of physical exercise is not known.

PERSONALITY AND IDENTITY IN YOUNG AND MIDDLE ADULTHOOD

Does it appear to you that Scott Pukalski, Carla Aquino, Viktor Spiro, and Phuong Le have grown "more like themselves" over their life course trajectories, or do you see changes in their personalities as they travel the life course? Do you think their identities were fully established as they made the transition to adulthood, or is identity development—how they think about and relate to themselves in the realms of love, work, and belief systems—ongoing?

Some theorists and researchers focus on how personality changes and stays the same across adulthood. Others focus specifically on identity in adulthood. Freud's psychoanalytic theory saw personality as determined sometime in middle childhood, and personality change in middle adulthood was seen as practically impossible. Some psychoanalysts broke with Freud and proposed that personality continues to change across adulthood. Regarding identity, Erikson's work resulted in identity development being associated with adolescence and seen as a discrete developmental marker, rather than as a process spanning all stages of the life course. However, recent theorists see ongoing identity development as necessary to make adult commitments possible, to allow individuals to abandon the insular self and embrace connection with important others (see R. Glover, 1996; Kroger, 2007). Identity is further shaped by the work adults do.

Let's look first at theory and research about personality. Some psychoanalysts propose that middle adulthood is a time when the personality ripens and matures. Most notable of these are Carl Jung, Erik Erikson, and George Vaillant. Jung conceptualizes middle adulthood as a time of balance in the personality. Although Erikson sees early life as important, he suggests that societal and cultural influences call for different personal adaptations over the life course. Vaillant (1977, 2002) suggests that with age and experience, **coping mechanisms,** or the strategies we use to master the demands of life, mature. He divides coping mechanisms into *immature mechanisms* (denial, projection, passive aggression, dissociation, acting out, and fantasy) and *mature mechanisms* (sublimation, humor, altruism, and suppression). His research indicates that as we age across adulthood, we make more use of mature coping mechanisms such as altruism, sublimation, and humor and less use of immature coping mechanisms such as denial and projection. Definitions for both the immature and mature coping mechanisms are found in Exhibit 15.6.

Exhibit 15.6 Coping Mechanisms

Immature Coping Mechanisms

Acting out. Ideas and feelings are acted on impulsively rather than reflectively.

Denial. Awareness of painful aspects of reality are avoided by negating sensory information about them.

Dissociation. Painful emotions are handled by compartmentalizing perceptions and memories, and detaching from the full impact.

Fantasy. Real human relationships are replaced with imaginary friends.

Passive-aggression. Anger toward others is turned inward against the self through passivity, failure, procrastination, or masochism.

Projection. Unacknowledged feelings are attributed to others.

Mature Coping Mechanisms

Altruism. Pleasure is attained by giving pleasure to others.

Mature humor. An emotion or thought is expressed through comedy, allowing a painful situation to be faced without individual pain or social discomfort.

Sublimation. An unacceptable impulse or unattainable aim is transformed into a more acceptable or attainable aim.

Suppression. Attention to a desire or impulse is postponed.

SOURCE: Vaillant (1977, 2002).

Recent empirical studies have focused on the degree to which individuals exhibit five broad personality traits, often referred to as the Big Five personality traits (Dörner, Mickler, & Studinger, 2005; Gardiner & Kosmitzki, 2008; B. Roberts, Robins, Trzesniewski, & Caspi, 2003):

1. *Neuroticism:* tendency to be moody, anxious, hostile, self-conscious, and vulnerable

2. *Extroversion:* tendency to be energetic, outgoing, friendly, lively, talkative, and active

3. *Conscientiousness:* tendency to be organized, reliable, responsible, hardworking, persistent, and careful

4. *Agreeableness:* tendency to be cooperative, generous, cheerful, warm, caring, trusting, and gentle

5. *Openness to experience:* tendency to be curious, imaginative, creative, intelligent, adventurous, and nonconforming

Research on the Big Five personality traits suggests that there is long-term stability in terms of the ranking of traits. For example, a person who is high in agreeableness at one point in adulthood will continue to be high in agreeableness across the life course (Dörner et al., 2005; Gardiner & Kosmitzki, 2008; B. Roberts et al., 2003). However, there is some evidence that there is a slight drop in consistency during early midlife, suggesting that this might be a period of the life course that is more conducive to personality change than other adult phases (Dörner et al., 2005). Researchers have studied the genetic basis of the Big Five traits and found a small genetic contribution, particularly for neuroticism and agreeableness (Jang et al., 2001). In addition, a 40-year longitudinal study drawn from the Berkeley Guidance Study—which collected data during late childhood and again during young adulthood and middle adulthood—found a great deal of personality consistency over time (Caspi, 1987).

Nevertheless, a number of both cross-sectional and longitudinal studies report age-related changes in personality traits in middle and late adulthood (Dörner et al., 2005; McCrae et al., 1999; B. Roberts et al., 2003). Extroversion (activity and thrill seeking), neuroticism (anxiety and self-consciousness), and openness to experience have been found to decline with age starting in middle adulthood. Conversely, agreeableness has been found to increase with age, and conscientiousness and emotional stability have been found to peak in middle adulthood (Dörner et al., 2005; Lachman & Bertrand, 2001). What's more, these patterns of age-related changes in personality have been found in cross-cultural research that included samples from Germany, Italy, Portugal, Croatia, and South Korea (Gardiner & Kosmitzki, 2008). Although the research finds much individual stability in aspects of personality over adulthood, one longitudinal study of a group of college-educated women found them, as a group, to become "less compulsive, more considerate of others, more organized, and better able to adapt to institutional settings" in middle adulthood (B. Roberts, Helson, & Klohnen, 2002, p. 96). They also became more tolerant of human diversity. This greater openness to human diversity appears to be occurring with Phuong Le (Case Study 15.4) in late midlife.

Some researchers have found gender differences in personality traits to be greater than age-related differences (Lachman & Bertrand, 2001). Women score higher than men in agreeableness, conscientiousness, extroversion, and neuroticism. Men, conversely, score higher than women on openness to experience. These gender differences in personality have been found in 26 cultures, but the magnitude of differences varied across cultures. The researchers were surprised to find that the biggest gender differences occurred in European and North American cultures, where traditional gender roles are less pronounced than in many other countries (P. Costa, Terracciano, & McCrae, 2001).

In spite of these gender differences, a number of researchers have found evidence for a gender-role shift during middle adulthood, as hypothesized by Jung, who suggested that in midlife both men and women become more androgynous. In fact, one research team found that scales measuring femininity and masculinity were among those that revealed the most change between the ages of 43 and 52 (Helson & Wink, 1992). Women were found by these and other researchers to increase in decisiveness, action orientation, and assertiveness during midlife (B. Roberts et al., 2002). Men have been found by some researchers (Havighurst, Neugarten, & Tobin, 1968; Neugarten & Gutmann, 1968) to increase in nurturance and affiliation in midlife. Recent support for this idea was reported by one research team that found that in late midlife, women's emotional satisfaction was correlated with bodily sexual practices, and men's physical pleasure was associated with relationship factors, a finding that contradicts gender stereotypes (L. Carpenter, Nathanson, & Kim, 2009). Joan Borysenko (1996), a cellular biologist, provides evidence for a gender crossover in personality in midlife that she attributes to changes in levels of sex hormones. Conversely, some researchers have found no gender role crossover for men (Lowenthal, Thurnher, & Chiriboga, 1975), and recent research suggests that it is motherhood and not age that promotes femininity in women (B. Roberts et al., 2002). Bjorklund and Bee (2008) suggest that it is more accurate to talk about "expansion of gender roles" rather than "gender role crossover," as midlife adults become more open to unexpressed aspects of the self. This is consistent with Jung's theory of increased androgyny in middle adulthood.

Now, let's look at theory and research that focuses on identity. James Marcia (1966, 1993), whose identity theory we examined in Chapter 14, has stated that people revisit and redefine their commitments as they age. As a result, identity is not static, but dynamic, open, and flexible. More recently, he has suggested that during a time of great upheaval and transition in young adulthood, people are likely to regress to earlier identity modes (Marcia, 2002). You may recall from Exhibit 14.2 that Marcia defined the following types of identity formation:

- Diffused (no exploration; no commitment)
- Foreclosed (no exploration; commitment)

- Moratorium (exploration; no commitment)
- Achievement (exploration; commitment)

Research exploring this notion that identity formation is a process that continues deep into adulthood shows several interesting outcomes. In one study, the researchers interviewed women and men between the ages of 27 and 36 to explore the process of commitment in five domains of identity: religious beliefs, political ideology, occupational career, intimate relationships, and lifestyle (Pulkkinen & Kokko, 2000). Results indicated that men and women differed in their overall commitment to an identity at age 27. Women were more likely to be classified in Marcia's foreclosed identity status, and men were more likely to be classified in the diffused identity status. However, these gender differences diminished with age, and by age 36, foreclosed and achieved identity statuses were more prevalent than diffused or moratorium statuses for both men and women. This trend of increasing commitment with age held constant across all domains except political ideology, which showed increased diffusion with age. Also, across ages, women were more likely than men to be classified in the achieved identity status for intimate relationships; for men, the diffused identity status for intimate relationships was more prevalent at age 27 as compared with age 36.

Susan Whitbourne and colleagues (K. Jones, Whitbourne, & Skultety, 2006; Whitbourne, 1986; Whitbourne & Connolly, 1999) propose that identity plays a central role in adult personality stability and change. Drawing on Piaget's theory of cognitive development, they suggest that identity continues to develop throughout adulthood through the processes of assimilation and accommodation. *Assimilation* is the process through which individuals incorporate new experiences into their existing identity. *Accommodation*, on the other hand, is the process through which an individual changes some aspect of identity in response to new experiences. Three identity styles are identified in middle adulthood, based on the way that midlife individuals respond to new experiences:

1. *Assimilative identity style.* Midlife individuals see themselves as unchanging and may either deny the physical and other changes they are experiencing or rationalize them as something else.

2. *Accommodative identity style.* Midlife individuals overreact to physical and other changes, and this undermines their identity and leaves it weak and incoherent.

3. *Balanced identity style.* Midlife individuals, combining goals and inner purpose with the flexibility to adapt to new experiences, recognize the physical and other changes of aging, engage in good health maintenance to minimize risk and enhance protection, and accept what cannot be changed.

It appears that earlier losses and trauma may have predisposed Viktor Spiro to an accommodative identity style. As he enters middle adulthood, with professional help, Viktor appears to be making some movement toward a more balanced identity style. Phuong Le appears to have a balanced identity style in spite of early experiences with war and resettlement. She moved with both purpose and flexibility to help her multigenerational family adapt to resettlement in the United States, and she remains open to new ways to express generativity.

> How does a balanced identity style relate to human agency in making choices?

YOUNG AND MIDDLE ADULT SPIRITUALITY_____

The church parish was a major support to Scott Pukalski's family when his mother died. Attending church is important to Carla Aquino, and she also feels that she needs to "make a difference" through her church service projects. Viktor Spiro's mother draws strength from her Greek Orthodox faith to cope with adversity. Search for connectedness plays a major role in Phuong Le's life. There is much evidence that, as one aspect of ongoing identity development, adults explore and refine their belief systems. Part of that process is development of spirituality, a focus on that which gives meaning, purpose, and direction to one's life. Spirituality manifests itself through one's ethical obligations and behavioral commitment to values and ideologies. It is a way of integrating values relating to self, other people, the community, and a "higher being" or "ultimate reality" (Hodge, 2001). Spirituality has been found to be associated with successful marriage (Kaslow & Robison, 1996), considerate and responsible interpersonal relations (C. G. Ellison, 1992), positive self-esteem (C. G. Ellison, 1993), more adaptive approaches to coping with stress (Tartaro, Luecken, & Gunn, 2005), and general well-being (George, Larson, Koenig, & McCullough, 2000).

Spirituality develops in three dimensions (George et al., 2000; Hodge, 2001):

1. *Cognition.* Beliefs, values, perceptions, and meaning related to work, love, and life

2. *Affect.* Sense of connection and support; attachment and bonding experiences; psychological attachment to work, love, and life

3. *Behavior.* Practices, rituals, and behavioral experiences

Research has shown that religious behavioral practices are correlated with life course stages. One study found that religiosity scores (reflecting beliefs, practices, and personal meaning) were higher for a group of young adults (ages 18 to 25) than for a group of adolescents (ages 14 to 17) (R. Glover, 1996), suggesting a growing spiritual belief system with age. Individuals making the transition from adolescence into young adulthood seem to place a particularly high value on spirituality. In addition, religious participation has been found to increase with age, even within the young adulthood stage (G. Gallup & Lindsay, 1999; Stolzenberg, Blair-Loy, & Waite, 1995; Wink & Dillon, 2002). The major world religions associate spiritual growth with advancing age (see, e.g., Biggs, 1999; Wink & Dillon, 2002).

In an attempt to understand the development of spirituality, James W. Fowler (1981) articulated a theory of six stages of faith development (see Chapter 5 for a brief description). Fowler's research suggested that two of these stages occur primarily in childhood, and the other four could occur in adolescence and adulthood. Adolescents are typically in a stage characterized by **synthetic-conventional faith,** during which faith is rooted in external authority. Individuals ages 17 to 22 usually begin

Photo 15.2   Spirituality develops in three dimensions: cognition, affect, and behavior.

the transition to **individuative-reflective faith,** a stage when the person begins to let go of the idea of external authority and looks for authority within the self (Fowler, 1981). During this time, young adults establish their own belief system and evaluate personal values, exploring how those values fit with the various social institutions, groups, and individuals with whom they interact. The transition from synthetic-conventional faith to individuative-reflective faith usually occurs in the early to mid-twenties, although it may occur in the thirties and forties, or may never occur at all (Fowler, 1981).

Interestingly, Fowler's description of **conjunctive faith**—during which the person looks for balance in such polarities as independence and connection, recognizes that there are many truths, and opens out beyond the self in service to others—overlaps with theories of middle adulthood previously discussed in this chapter. Fowler suggests that many people never reach this faith stage, and if they do, they almost never reach it before middle adulthood. Fowler's reference to balance in this faith stage calls to mind the theories of Jung and Levinson, who saw middle adulthood as a time of bringing balance to personality and life structure. In addition, the idea of opening oneself in service to others is consistent with Erikson's idea of generativity as the psychosocial struggle of middle adulthood (Biggs, 1999; Dollahite, Slife, & Hawkins, 1998). Drawing on Jung, one theorist proposes that late midlife is "a time when our energy naturally moves beyond the concerns of our nuclear family into a concern with the world family" (Borysenko, 1996, p. 185). The emphasis is on spirituality as a state of "being connected." Using data from a national survey of midlife adults in the United States, one researcher found a strong correlation between regular participation in religious activities and community service, particularly in terms of making financial contributions to community organizations and charities (Rossi, 2004).

Actually, there are two different models of spiritual development in adulthood (Wink & Dillon, 2002). Fowler's theory can be called a *growth model,* an approach that sees spiritual growth as a positive outcome of a maturation process. The other model sees increased spirituality across the adult life course as an outcome of adversity (Wink and Dillon call it an *adversity model*) rather than as a natural maturation process; in this view, spirituality becomes a way to cope with losses, disappointments, and difficulties. One rare longitudinal study of spiritual development across the adult life course found evidence for both of these models (Wink & Dillon, 2002). The researchers found a strong tendency for increased spirituality beginning in late middle adulthood, something that occurred among all research participants but was more pronounced among women than men. They also found that experiencing negative life events in early adulthood was associated with higher levels of spirituality in middle and late adulthood. Phuong Le (Case Study 15.4) reports a renewed intensity to her spiritual quest, which seems to include both a drive for spiritual growth and a resource for coping with loss and difficulty.

Critical Thinking Questions 15.2

Erik Erikson suggested that identity development occurred in adolescence, but recent theory and research suggests that identity is open and flexible and continues to develop across adulthood. What do you think about this recent suggestion that identity development is an ongoing process? What types of experiences in young and middle adulthood might affect identity development? Do you think that your identity has changed since late adolescence? If so, which aspects of your identity have changed? What impact do you think that the new technologies, particularly cell phones and the Internet, have on adult identity development?

RELATIONSHIPS IN YOUNG AND MIDDLE ADULTHOOD

Social relationships play a major role in life satisfaction and physical well-being across the life course. The life course perspective reminds us that relationships in adulthood have been shaped by relationships in earlier life phases, in the attachment process in infancy, as well as in family and peer relationships in childhood and adolescence (Blieszner & Roberto, 2006; Möller & Stattin, 2001). Although current relationships are shaped by our experiences with earlier relationships, longitudinal research indicates that it is never too late to develop new relationships that can become turning points in the life course (Vaillant, 2002; E. E. Werner & Smith, 2001).

Toni Antonucci and colleagues (Antonucci & Akiyama, 1987, 1997; Antonucci, Akiyama, & Takahashi, 2004) suggest that we each travel through life with a **convoy,** or a network of social relationships that protect, defend, aid, and socialize us. They also acknowledge that the convoy can have damaging effects on individuals, contributing more stress than support, and creating problems rather than solving them. In one study, the researchers asked respondents in representative samples of people ages 8 to 93 from both the United States and Japan to map their convoys of support, using three concentric circles surrounding the individual respondent (Antonucci et al., 2004). In the inner circle, the respondents were asked to identify people who were so close and important to them that they could not imagine living without them (very close). In the middle circle, respondents were asked to name people who were not quite that close but still very close and important to them (close). In the outer circle, respondents were asked to name people who were not as close as those in the two inner circles but who were still important enough that they came to mind as members of the support network (less close).

Antonucci et al. (2004) found no differences in the composition of the convoys between the U.S. and Japanese participants. They found that the convoys of the midlife adults ages 40–59 were, on average, slightly smaller than the convoys of young adults ages 20–39 and slightly larger than the convoys of late-life adults. Women reported more very close relationships (inner circle) than men. On average, young adults reported nine close members in their convoys compared to an average of eight for midlife adults. For both groups, the inner circle

(very close) consisted of mother, spouse, daughter, and son, and the middle circle (close) included sister, brother, and female friend. Young adults listed some configuration of sister, brother, and female friend in their outer circle (less close), but midlife adults included only one person, a female friend. It is important to note that the size of the convoy does not necessarily indicate how much support is available (C. Chen, 2006a).

Other research has found racial and ethnic differences, as well as social class differences, in reported convoys in the United States. Whites have been found to have larger convoys than African Americans, and the convoys of African American adults as well as other adults with low incomes have a higher proportion of kin in them than the convoys of higher-income White adults (Ajrouch, Antonucci, & Janevic, 2001; Antonucci, Akiyama, & Merline, 2001; Montague, Magai, Consedine, & Gillespie, 2003). A study conducted in Taiwan suggests that in our very mobile times, when younger generations leave home to follow jobs in global cities, some people may have only one or two circles in their convoys (C. Chen, 2006b). Certainly, it is important to understand the very dynamic nature of convoys in the lives of many people in a globalized world. The available research indicates that the most important relationships in adulthood are romantic relationships (spouses), relationships with parents (mothers, specifically), relationships with children, relationships with siblings, and relationships with friends. There is also research evidence that relationships with grandchildren can be an important source of life satisfaction for midlife adults.

Romantic Relationships

Romantic relationships are a key element in the development of intimacy during young adulthood. **Romantic love** has been described as a relationship that is sexually oriented, is "spontaneous and voluntary," and occurs between equal partners (R. C. Solomon, 1988). Satisfaction in romantic partnerships depends on finding a delicate balance between positive and negative interactions across time (Gottman, 1994).

Photo 15.3 Research finds that family members are an important part of the social convoys of young and midlife adults.

Anthropologist Helen Fisher (2004) suggests that the choice of romantic partners is based on three distinct emotional systems: lust, attraction, and attachment. *Lust* is sexual attraction and is associated with androgen hormones. *Attraction* involves feeling great pleasure in the presence of the romantic interest and thinking of the other person all the time. Fisher suggests that attraction is associated with increased levels of dopamine and norepinephrine and decreased levels of serotonin, which are neurotransmitters in the brain. Fisher's description of *attachment* is similar to Bowlby's concept described in Chapter 11 of this book. It involves a sense of security when in the presence of the attachment figure, which is the romantic

partner in this discussion. Attachment has been associated with the hormone oxytocin.

In the United States, heterosexual romantic love has traditionally been considered a precursor to marriage. However, a recent trend in romantic relationships is to have sex earlier but marry later. For the past decade, more than half of all marriages occurred after a period of cohabitation (Heuveline & Timberlake, 2004). It is important to remember, however, that in many parts of the world and among many recent immigrant groups to the United States, marriage is arranged and not based on romantic courtship. Many other variations in relationship development exist as well. Chapter 9 in this book discusses some of these variations, including couples with no children, lone-parent families, stepfamilies, and same-sex partner families.

In the past, increasing education decreased women's likelihood of marrying, but recent data suggest a reversal of that trend, at least in the United States. The cohort of women who recently graduated from college, both Black and White, are likely to marry later than women of their cohort without a college education, but their rate of eventual marriage will be higher (J. Goldstein & Kenney, 2001). The researchers interpret this trend to indicate that marriage is increasingly becoming a choice only for the most educated members of society. Given the economic advantages of a two-earner family, this trend may contribute toward the widening economic gap in our society.

Each person brings prior relationship experiences to partner relationships of all types. Möller and Stattin (2001) reviewed the empirical literature on these relationships and identified a number of characteristics of prior relationships that have been found to influence partner relationships in adulthood. For example, affection and warmth in the household during the preschool years have been associated with long and happy partnerships in adulthood. Interactions with peers during adolescence help to build the social skills necessary to sustain partner relationships. Based on these findings, Möller and Stattin engaged in longitudinal research with a Swedish sample to investigate the links between early relationships and later partner relationships. They found that warm relationships with parents during adolescence are associated with later satisfaction in the partner relationship. Relationships with fathers were more strongly related to partner satisfaction for males than for females. Contrary to previous research, Möller and Stattin found that the quality of parents' marital relationship was not associated with the quality of later partner relationships. The parent–child relationship was a better predictor of later partner relationships than the quality of the parents' marital relationships.

For heterosexual marriages, there is a long line of research that indicates a U-shaped curve in marital happiness, with high marital satisfaction in the early years of marriage, followed by a decline that hits bottom in early midlife, but begins to rise again in the post-parental years. However, one longitudinal research project, one of the few studies to use a national representative sample, found no upturn in marital satisfaction in later life. As found in other studies, satisfaction took a steep decline over the first 5 years of marriage. This was followed by a gradual decline during the next 20 years, after which marital satisfaction leveled off for a few years, but declined again beginning at 40 years of marriage (VanLaningham, Johnson, & Amato, 2001). There was some indication that more recent cohorts have lower marital satisfaction than earlier cohorts. Other research has found that lesbian partners report no change in relationship quality in the first 10 years of partnership (Kurdek, 2004).

There is evidence that unmarried partners tend to be more egalitarian in the division of household activities than married couples (T. Simmons & O'Connell, 2003); there is also considerable evidence that African American married couples engage in more egalitarian role sharing than White married couples (Coltrane, 2000). Likewise, gay and lesbian partnerships have been found to be more egalitarian than married heterosexual couples (Kurdek, 2004).

Baby boomers are more likely to be divorced than midlife adults in earlier cohorts (Fingerman & Dolbin-MacNab, 2006). Although many marriages flourish once the children have been launched,

some marriages cannot survive without the presence of children to buffer conflicts. Men report more marital satisfaction than women in the United States and Chinese Malaysia (Mickelson, Claffey, & Williams, 2006; Ny, Loy, Gudmunson, & Cheong, 2009), and most divorces are initiated by women (Carter & McGoldrick, 2005a). Longitudinal research has found that baby boom women are less satisfied with their marriages than their mothers were at midlife (Putney & Bengtson, 2003; VanLaningham et al., 2001).

Although there is a period of adjustment to divorce, midlife adults cope better with divorce than young adults (S. Greene, Anderson, Hetherington, Forgatch, & DeGarmo, 2003). Some individuals actually report improved well-being after divorce (Antonucci et al., 2001). Women have been found to be more adversely affected by a distressed marriage and men more adversely affected by being divorced (Hetherington & Kelly, 2002). However, the financial consequences of divorce for women are negative. After divorce, men are more likely to remarry than women, and Whites are more likely to remarry than African Americans.

Relationships With Children

One of the key decisions in young adulthood is whether to have children or not. In previous chapters, you have read about the influence of parent–child relationships on child and adolescent behavior. But parenting is an interactive process, with reciprocal parent–child and child–parent influences (Maccoby, 2002b). The multiple role transitions that mark entry into parenthood during young adulthood can be both exciting and challenging, as new familial interdependencies evolve. New social obligations and responsibilities associated with caregiving affect the relationship between the young adult partners and between the young adults and their parents. Often, the nature of the partners' relationship before parenthood will determine how partners will manage the demands of these changing roles (Durkin, 1995).

In a comprehensive review of the effects of minor children on parents, Anne-Marie Ambert (2001) suggests that parent–minor child relationships are influenced by characteristics of the child, characteristics of the parent, and the ways a society is organized to meet the needs of parents and children. Ambert suggests some societal traits that will produce more positive outcomes for both children and parents: adequate, affordable, and accessible housing, child care alternatives, schools, health and mental health resources, and recreational facilities; work opportunities that do not put parents at a disadvantage; safe neighborhoods; positive peer group cultures for children and adolescents; positive mass media; and societal regard for the contributions of parents. Currently, our social institutions are falling short in many of these areas, making them fruitful areas for social work planning and advocacy.

Research about the costs and benefits of parenting indicate that the benefits are primarily cognitive and emotional, such as more hopeful anticipation of the future, more complex thinking, greater self-awareness and maturity in identity, improved emotional regulation, more sense of responsibility, more playfulness, and more physical affection. Most of the costs appear to be in three primary areas: finances, personal freedom, and time. In agrarian societies, children are financial benefits, but they become financial costs in industrialized, urbanized societies. The research currently indicates that the costs in personal freedom and time are experienced more by mothers than by fathers, because mothers continue to be the primary caregivers in most families (Ambert, 2001).

However, Ralph LaRossa's (1997) historical analysis of the social and political history of fatherhood provides evidence of an ongoing struggle throughout the 20th century to rework the gender-based division of labor that accompanied industrialization. He also provides evidence that a variety of fathering styles have coexisted at any given historical time. In the contemporary era in the United States, one fifth of children in two-parent families have their father as their primary caregiver (Halle, 2002).

Although a growing number of midlife adults are parenting young or school-age children, most midlife adults are parents of adolescents or young adults. Parenting adolescents can be a challenge, and launching young adult offspring from the nest is a happy experience for most families. It is a family transition that has been undergoing changes in the past 20 years, however, coming at a later age for the parents and becoming more fluid in its timing and progress (K. Newman, 2008).

Blieszner and Roberto (2006) argue that "lifestyles of midlife baby-boom parents revolve around their children" (p. 270). Providing support to children is associated with better psychological well-being in midlife adults. In general, mothers have closer relationships with their young adult children than fathers, and divorced fathers have been found to have weaker emotional attachments with their adult children than either married fathers or divorced mothers (Putney & Bengtson, 2003).

Research also indicates that midlife adults can be negatively affected by their relationships with their adult children. E. Greenfield and Marks (2006) found that midlife adults whose adult children have problems such as chronic disease or disability, emotional problems, problems with alcohol or other substances, financial problems, work-related problems, partner relationship problems, and so on, report lower levels of well-being than midlife adults who do not report such problems in their adult children. Ha, Hong, Seltzer, and Greenberg (2008) found that midlife parents of adult children with developmental disabilities or mental health problems were more likely than parents of nondisabled children to report higher levels of negative emotions, decreased psychological well-being, and somatic symptoms. Seltzer et al. (2009) found that midlife adults had more negative emotions, more disruption in cortisol, and more physical symptoms on the days that they spent more time with their disabled children. These findings suggest a need for social service support for midlife parents whose adult children are facing ongoing challenges.

Relationships With Parents

In the United States and the industrialized European countries, it became common for young adults to live outside the family prior to marriage in the 1960s.

Then, in the United States, in the 1980s, two trends became evident: increased age at first leaving home and increased incidence of returning home. Popular culture has used phrases such as "prolonged parenting," "cluttered nest," "boomerang generation," and "adultolescents" to describe these trends (Putney & Bengtson, 2001, 2003). Recent data indicate that 30% to 40% of parents between the ages of 40 and 60 in the United States have adult children living with them. Approximately half of these young adult children have never left home, and the other half have left home but returned one or more times. About 40% of recent cohorts of young adults have returned home at least once after leaving home (Putney & Bengtson, 2001). A very similar trend exists in Northern Europe: Of parents ages 50 to 59, 28% in Denmark, 36% in Sweden, and 48% in Germany and Austria have adult children living with them. In contrast, 79% of parents in the same age group have adult children living with them in Spain and 82% in Italy (Kohli & Künemund, 2005). In general, parents are more positive than their young adult children about living together (Blieszner & Roberto, 2006). We know that Scott and Sonya Pukalski (Case Study 15.1) are eager to establish their own home, but it is quite possible that Sonya's parents are satisfied with the current arrangements, which can have economic and intimacy benefits.

However, it is also the case that in today's society, young persons are increasingly becoming primary caretakers for elderly family members. Such responsibilities can dramatically affect a young adult's developing life structure. Family life, relationships, and career may all be affected (Dellmann-Jenkins & Blankemeyer, 2009; Dellmann-Jenkins, Blankemeyer, & Pinkard, 2001). The demographic trend of delaying childbearing, with an increase of first births for women in their thirties and forties and a decrease of first births to women in their twenties (Ashford, LeCroy, & Lortie, 2010), suggests that young adults are likely to face new and significant role challenges as primary caretakers for their own aging parents. This can result in young adults caring for the generation ahead of them as well as the generation behind them.

The concern is that young adults will face a substantial caregiving burden, trying to help their aging parents with later-in-life struggles while nurturing their own children. We might see a shorter period of "emerging" adulthood for many people, which would mean that they have less opportunity to explore, to gain a sense of independence, and to form new families themselves. There may be less support for the notion of giving young people time to get on their feet and establish a satisfactory independent adulthood. In addition, young adults may increasingly experience the emotional responsibilities of supporting late-in-life divorcing parents or parents deciding to go back to school at the same time these young adults may be considering advanced educational opportunities themselves.

Carla Aquino (Case Study 15.2) and her husband are clearly facing these multigenerational role demands as they become the main social support for Jan at the same time that they are trying to get ahead in their careers and prepare for their new baby. Luckily, Carla and her husband have the financial resources and an adequate support network themselves (Carla's father, some extended family, and their church) to help with logistical problem solving, such as finding day care, and to help them deal effectively with the emotional stressors of these role demands.

Most research shows that middle-aged adults are deeply involved with their aging parents (Kohli & Künemund, 2005; Marks et al., 2004). As suggested in the stories of Viktor Spiro (Case Study 15.3) and Phuong Le (Case Study 15.4), the nature of the relationship with aging parents changes over time. A cross-national study of adults in Norway, England, Germany, Spain, and Israel found that across countries, support was bidirectional, with aging parents providing emotional and financial support to their midlife adult children and also receiving support from them (Lowenstein & Daatland, 2006). Viktor Spiro lives with his parents and receives much emotional support from his mother. Phuong Le's mother monitored the after-school activities of Phuong's adolescent children. As the parents' health begins to deteriorate, however, they turn more to their midlife children for help, as is currently the case for Viktor and was the situation for Phuong a few years ago. In the United States, a national survey by the American Association of Retired Persons (AARP, 2001) found that about 78% of baby boomers age 45 to 55 provide some caregiving services to their own parents or to other older adults, but only 22% identify themselves as caregivers. A German study found that caring for elderly family members peaks between the ages of 50 and 54 (Kohli & Künemund, 2005).

Traditionally, caregivers to aging parents are daughters or daughters-in-law (Blacker, 2005). This continues to be the case, even though a great majority of midlife women are employed full-time (Czaja, 2006). This does not tell the whole story, however. The baby boom cohort has more siblings than earlier and later cohorts, and there is some evidence that caregiving is often shared among siblings, with sisters serving as coordinators of the care (Hequembourg & Brallier, 2005). In spite of competing demands from spouses and children, providing limited care to aging parents seems to cause little psychological distress (AARP, 2001). Extended caregiving, on the other hand, has been found to have some negative effects as midlife adults try to balance a complex mix of roles (Putney & Bengtson, 2001; Savia, Almeida, Davey, & Zant, 2008), but there is also some evidence of rewards of caregiving (S. Robertson, Zarit, Duncan, Rovine, & Femia, 2007).

Most of the research on caregiving focuses on *caregiver burden,* or the negative effects on mental and physical health caused by caregiver stress. Compared to matched comparison groups who do not have caregiving responsibilities, caregivers of elderly parents report more depressive symptoms, taking more antidepressant and antianxiety medication, poorer physical health, and lower marital satisfaction (Martire & Schulz, 2001; Sherwood, Given, Given, & Von Eye, 2005). Savia et al. (2008) found that psychological distress was greater on days that adult children provided assistance to aging parents, but they also found more distressed mood among caregivers with higher caregiving demands and lower resources.

Although this research is not as prevalent, some researchers have been interested in a phenomenon

they call *caregiver gain* or *caregiver reward.* One early proponent of this line of inquiry found that the majority of caregivers have something positive to say about their caregiving experiences (B. Kramer, 1997). One group of researchers was interested in the balance of positive and negative emotions in family caregivers of older adults with dementia (S. Robertson et al., 2007). They found considerable variation in the responses of caregivers in terms of the balance of stressful experiences of caregiving and positive experiences of caregiving. The stressful experiences included behavior problems of the care receiver; need to provide personal assistance with activities such as eating, dressing, grooming, bathing, toileting, and transferring into bed; role overload; and role captivity (feeling trapped in caregiver role). The positive experiences of caregiving included rewards such as growing personally, repaying care receiver, fulfilling duty, and getting perspective on what is important in life; sense of competence; and positive behaviors in care receiver. The researchers identified different groups of caregivers in terms of their levels of distress. The most well-adjusted group had more resources in terms of health, education, and so on, and reported fewer behavior problems and fewer needs for personal assistance of the care recipients.

Culture appears to play a role in whether providing care to aging parents is experienced as burden or gain. For example, Lowenstein and Daatland (2006) found a strong expectation of providing care for parents in Spain and Israel, but a more negotiable obligation in Northern Europe. In countries where caregiving is normalized, caregiving is often provided out of affection, not obligation; may be shared among family members; and may be less likely to be experienced as burden. This seems to have been the situation for Phuong Le. B. Evans et al. (2009) report that Hispanic caregivers have been found to have slightly less caregiver burden than Anglos. Very individualistic families value individual independence and may find elder care particularly troublesome to both caregiver and care recipient. However, there is evidence that both individualistically oriented families and collectivist-oriented families experience negative effects of long-term, intensive caregiving, especially those families with few economic and social resources (S. Robertson et al., 2007).

Relationships With Siblings

The great majority of adults have at least one living sibling, and researchers are beginning to take an interest in sibling relationships during adulthood. Adult sibling relationships can be close, distant, or conflicted, but the convoy research cited earlier (Antonucci et al., 2004) suggests that these relationships have at least moderate emotional closeness. Research in the Netherlands found that brothers provide more practical support to siblings and sisters provide more emotional support (Voorpostel & van der Lippe, 2007). In Taiwan, however, brother–brother dyads were found to provide the most companionship and emotional support of any dyad type (P. Lu, 2007). In the Netherlands, siblings seemed to overcome geographic distance to provide emotional support more easily than friends, but relationship quality was an important predictor of which sibling groups would offer emotional support (Voorpostel & van der Lippe, 2007).

One study found that sibling relationships can help to compensate for poor relationships with parents in emerging adulthood. In a study of 200 men and women between the ages of 19 and 33, Avidan Milevsky (2005) found that the young adults with low support from parents scored significantly higher on well-being if they had high levels of support from siblings. The respondents with high sibling support reported less depression and loneliness than those with low sibling support.

Baby boomers have more siblings than earlier and later cohorts, and, unlike previous cohorts, they have more siblings than children. Sibling relationships have been found to be important for the well-being of both men and women in midlife. Siblings often drift apart in young adulthood, but contact between siblings increases in late midlife (McGoldrick, Watson, & Benton, 2005). They are often brought together around the care and death of aging parents, and recent research indicates that sibling contact decreases again after the death of the last parent (Khodyakov & Carr, 2009). Sibling collaboration in the care of aging parents may bring them closer together or may stir new as well as unresolved resentments. Although step- and half-siblings tend to stay connected to each other, their contact is less frequent than the contact between full siblings.

Viktor Spiro's sister was an important lifeline for him when he immigrated to the United States, but tensions developed during the time when Viktor was suicidal. Their mutual concern about their father's health is drawing them closer again. Phuong Le has close relationships with her siblings, and these relationships have remained close since her mother died.

Relationships With Grandchildren

In the United States, about three fourths of adults become grandparents by the time they are 65 (Bjorklund & Bee, 2008). For those adults who become grandparents, the onset of the grandparent role typically occurs in their forties or fifties, or increasingly in their sixties. Grandparenthood has been reported to be among the top three most important roles among middle-aged men and women in the United States (Reitzes & Mutran, 2002). Baby boom grandparents are likely to have fewer grandchildren than their parents had; spend more years in the grandparent role; and share that role with more people, including step-grandparents (Blieszner & Roberto, 2006). Vern Bengtson (2001) asserts that grandparents play an important socializing role in families, and that this role is likely to grow in importance in the near future.

There are many styles of grandparenting and many cultures of grandparenting. In cultures with large extended families and reverence for elders—such as in Mexico, and many Asian and African countries—grandparents often live with the family, as was the case with Phuong Le's mother. In the United States, Asian American, African American, Hispanic American, and Italian American grandparents are more likely to play an active role in the lives of grandchildren than other ethnic groups (Gardiner & Kosmitzki, 2008). Research has indicated gender differences in enactment of the grandparent role as well, with most research suggesting that grandmothers, particularly maternal grandmothers, play more intimate roles in their grandchildren's lives than grandfathers (Bjorklund & Bee, 2008). However, James Bates (2009) argues that grandfathers have been underrepresented in research on grandparenting and recommends a more focused research effort to examine these relationships.

Researchers have noted two potential problems for grandparents. First, if adult children divorce, custody agreements may fail to attend to the rights of grandparents for visitation (Blieszner & Roberto, 2006). In addition, baby boom adults are often serving as step-grandparents, a role that can be quite ambiguous. Second, if adult children become incapacitated by substance abuse, illness, disability, or incarceration, grandparents may be recruited to step in to raise the grandchildren. As noted in an earlier chapter, the number of children cared for by grandparents in the United States has risen dramatically in the past 30 years. About 2.4 million baby boom grandparents are serving as the primary caregiver to grandchildren. Racial and ethnic minority grandparents are 2–3 times more likely than European American grandparents to be serving in this role (Blieszner & Roberto, 2006). Unfortunately, grandparents with the least resources are often the ones called upon to become primary caregivers to their grandchildren (Fields, 2004).

Relationships With Friends

There is some evidence that the frequency of interaction with friends declines over the course of adulthood, but closeness does not decline, and friends continue to play an important role in adult well-being (Carstensen, 1992). Opposite-sex socializing increases from late adolescence to early adulthood, and same-sex and mixed-sex socializing decreases (Reis, Lin, Bennett, & Nezlek, 1993, 2004). Young adults also report a smaller number of close friends than adolescents (Reis et al., 1993).

Midlife adults have more family members in their social convoys than do younger and older adults, but they also continue to report at least a few important friendships (Antonucci et al., 2004). Baby boom midlife adults are good friends with about seven people on average; these friends are usually of the same age, sex, race/ethnicity, social class, education, and employment status (Blieszner & Roberto, 2006). Some boomers also maintain cross-sex friendships, and these are particularly valued by men who are more likely than women to see a sexual dimension to these relationships (Monsour, 2002). It has been suggested that midlife adults have less time than other adult age groups for friendships (Antonucci et al., 2001).

Friendships appear to have an impact on midlife well-being for both men and women, although they do not seem to be as important as close familial relationships. For instance, the adequacy of social support, particularly from friends, at age 50 predicts physical health for men at age 70 (Vaillant, 2002). Likewise, midlife women who have a confidant or a close group of female friends report greater well-being than midlife women without such interpersonal resources (McQuaide, 1998). Women who report positive feelings toward their women friends also have fewer depressive symptoms and higher morale than women who report less positive feelings toward female friends (Paul, 1997). Whether good feelings toward friends protect against depression or depression impairs the quality of friendships remains to be determined, however.

Given this research, it appears that Phuong Le's wide circle of friends, as well as family, bode well for her continuing good health. Viktor Spiro's recent participation in social events is providing him an opportunity to expand his social convoy and appears to be adding an important dimension to his life circumstances.

It appears that the importance of friends in the social convoy varies by sexual orientation, race, and marital status. Friends are important sources of support in the social convoys of gay and lesbian midlife adults, often serving as an accepting "chosen family" for those who have traveled the life course in a homophobic society (T. Johnson & Colucci, 2005). These chosen families provide much care and support to each other, as evidenced by the primary caregiving they have provided in times of serious illness such as AIDS and breast cancer (McGoldrick, 2005). Friends also become family in many African American families. The literature on African American families often calls attention to the "nonblood" family members as a strength for these families (Boyd-Franklin, 2003). Friendships also serve an important role in the social convoys of single midlife adults, serving as a chosen family rather than a "poor substitute" for family (Berliner, Jacob, & Schwartzberg, 2005).

WORK IN YOUNG AND MIDDLE ADULTHOOD

In what ways can work help or hinder the opportunity for development of human agency?

Scott Pukalski's work as a carpenter allowed him to support his family and helped him to feel like a responsible adult. He feels like a failure now that he is not working and worries about the economic future of his family. Career is important to Carla Aquino, but she is concerned about how she will juggle her career with motherhood. Viktor Spiro's return to his dishwashing job has been a real lift to his self-esteem. Phuong Le takes pride in her rise to a supervisory role with the wait staff at the restaurant where she works, and she enjoys a chance to interact with both customers and the wait staff. Work has different meanings for different people. Here are some of the meanings that work can have: a source of income, a life routine and way of structuring time, a source of status and identity, a context for social interaction, or a meaningful experience that provides a sense of accomplishment (Friedmann & Havighurst, 1954). The recent economic recession produced high rates of unemployment and left many workers vulnerable, young adult workers and middle adult workers alike.

Work in Young Adulthood

The transition into the world of work is an important element of social development during young adulthood. A young adult's opportunity for successful adulthood transitioning into the labor market depends on a variety of dimensions, including **human capital** (talents, skills, intellectual capacity, social development, emotional regulatory capacity), as well as **community assets** such as public infrastructure (e.g., adequate transportation to get to work), community networks, and educational opportunities. In addition, family capital is important. "Transformative assets," or those family contributions that aid in deferring the immediate economic costs of long-term investments such as a college education or the downpayment for a house, are differentially spread across race, with half of White families giving young adults this investment edge, while data show that only 20% of Black families are able to do so (Lui et al., 2006). This, coupled with the fact that, in some states, children of undocumented immigrants do not receive in-state tuition for higher education, makes the prospects of getting into college and affording a college education out of reach for many young adults, and erodes their longer-term access to asset growth and economic stability. One report (Draut & Silva, 2004) indicates that young adults face daunting economic challenges characterized by underemployment, high cost of purchasing a first home, and rising debt from student loans and credit cards.

Given that our educational institution operates as society's gatekeeper to economic opportunities, we need to examine how our educational system is preparing our youth for future employment as well as how and to whom such opportunities are afforded. We need to examine how differential education and training tracks might be influencing lifelong economic and labor market trajectories, keeping certain groups entrenched in poverty (Lui et al., 2006; Rank, 2005).

Indeed, as important as individual factors are in the transition to work, the changing labor market and structural shifts in the economy may have an even greater influence by shaping a young person's opportunities for finding and maintaining productive work. Work in industry and manufacturing has been diminishing for four decades now, and the number of jobs in the service sector has increased (Portes & Rumbaut, 2001). Manufacturing jobs once offered unskilled youth with relatively little education an opportunity for good wages, employment benefits, and job security. However, the service sector is divided between low-wage, temporary or part-time service jobs and work opportunities that call for advanced technical skills. Today, there is a high labor market demand for low-wage, low-skill jobs as well as a high demand among employers for workers with more specialized and technical skills (Portes & Rumbaut, 2001).

Vulnerable Populations in the Transition to Work

Data suggest that youth with disabilities are at higher risk for dropping out of high school compared with youth who do not have a disability. More specifically, African American and Latino youth with disabilities are at significantly higher risk than their White counterparts (Trainor, 2008). While approximately three quarters of White youth with disabilities entered paid employment after high school, only 61.7% of African American and 65.4% of Latino youth with disabilities obtained employment after high school. Only one fifth of youth with disabilities go on to higher education opportunities (Wagner, Newman, Cameto, & Levine, 2005).

Other vulnerable youth populations, such as youth transitioning out of state care, face challenges in moving to paid employment in young adulthood. C. Reid (2007) suggests that "seven pillars" serve as a foundation for success for youth transitioning out of state care at age of majority, which include relationships, education, housing, life skills, identity, youth engagement (ownership over the transitioning plan), emotional healing, and financial support (p. 35). A recent Child Trends

> What factors put individuals at risk when making the transition to adulthood?

Photo 15.4 The changing labor market and structural shifts in the economy shape a young person's opportunities for finding and maintaining productive work.

report summarized specific empirically validated competencies that have been shown to increase high school students' success in the labor market: second language competency; ability to interact with others to problem solve and work through conflict; critical thinking skills; planfulness; good judgment; strong work ethic such as reliability and professionalism in the work environment; having had internship experience; and general self-management skills such as responsibility, initiative, and time-management skills (Lippman & Keith, 2009, pp. 1–2). Policies and programs, such as the Foster Care Independence Act (P. L. 106–169) and John H. Chafee Foster Care Independence Program (1999), provide additional support for postsecondary education, vocational training, housing, health care, and counseling until age 21, and are a good start in responding to these specific needs of youth transitioning out of state care.

Incarcerated youth who are discharged from the juvenile justice system as emerging adults also face significant labor attachment challenges. Many face uncertain outcomes upon discharge back into their preinstitutionalized communities that can include rearrest for new crimes (about one third will be rearrested) or violence from peers who vow revenge for wrongs committed before the youth were institutionalized (Inderbitzin, 2009). Difficulty in obtaining gainful employment upon release can be complicated because of deficient legitimate job skills, stigma of institutionalization, and lack of prosocial community and economic capital (Inderbitzin, 2009). Job training, transitioning to new neighborhoods, and engaging in a safety net of continuing care services are critical predictors for successful release back into the community.

Alejandro Portes and Ruben G. Rumbaut (2001), in their book *Legacies: The Story of the Immigrant Second Generation,* based on results from the Children of Immigrants Longitudinal Study (CILS), note that the structural labor market change of the past few decades disproportionately affects immigrants, particularly youth in late adolescence who will be emerging into this new occupational landscape. "Increasing labor market inequality implies that to succeed socially and economically, children of immigrants today must cross, in the span of a few years, the educational gap that took descendants of Europeans several generations to bridge" (p. 58).

The dilemma facing disadvantaged youth entering adulthood is vexing. Labor market attachment is not only the surest route to material well-being (for example, according to Shapiro [2004], once basic living expenses are accounted for, each additional dollar of annual income generates $3.26 in net worth over a person's lifetime), but labor market attachment also has been found to be significantly related to mental health and psychosocial well-being. One study looked at factors associated with well-being and adjustment between ages 16 and 21. The study found that experiences of unemployment were significantly associated with thoughts of suicide, substance abuse, and crime (Fergusson, Horwood, & Woodward, 2001). Benefits of work include increased self-esteem, increased social interaction, and external validation through social recognition. Increasingly, therefore, youths' life trajectories will be determined by access to advanced education and then good jobs.

Race, Ethnicity, and Work

The associations among race, ethnicity, and work attachment have received some attention. Although first-generation male Mexican immigrants earn incomes that are half that of White males, second-generation male immigrants typically earn three quarters that of White men and more than Black men. About 40% of first-generation Mexican immigrants ages 16 to 20 are in school or college as compared to two thirds of second-generation immigrants in this age cohort ("Of Meat, Mexicans and Social Mobility," 2006).

Unfortunately, the labor force participation among young Black men has declined since 1980. Labor force connection tends to be weakest for Black males who have little formal education and who lack work experience (Holzer, 2009). Of course, the economic restructuring of past decades has made good-quality jobs for young adults without specialized skills hard to come by. Other barriers for young Black men include discrimination in hiring, absence of adult mentors in the community who might help socialize youth toward work roles and connect them to employers, a disconnect from a good-paying job with benefits, diminished self-efficacy related to perceptions of constricted economic opportunities, hopelessness about finding quality jobs, and the presence of alternative informal and more prosperous economic options (e.g., drug dealing, gambling). All may decrease the youth's ability or motivation to pursue formal work opportunities. But that is not to say that young Black men do not want to succeed in the world of work.

Sociological studies have shown that White men with a prison record are more likely to be hired for a job than Black men without a prison record (Lui et al., 2006). Racism can directly tax individuals and families and can indirectly deplete their buffering resources and weaken solutions to managing direct stressors (Harrell, 2000). Stressors and resources change over the life course, however, and social workers need to be able to assess the ways in which individuals and families are able to adapt to such changes. It is also important for social workers to understand the range of diversity within the African American community along many social dimensions, including SES, in order to avoid perpetuating the stereotypes that further stigmatize this diverse group.

In addition, social workers should be aware of how social assistance is unequally distributed, and should work toward eliminating such disparities. For example, of those exiting welfare, White mothers are twice as likely as Black or Latina mothers to receive child care or transportation transitional assistance. In addition, the median wage for a White welfare exiter between 1997 and 1999 was $7.31/hour compared to $6.88 and $6.71 for African American and Latina exiters, respectively (Lui et al., 2006). Other research shows that when women who leave Temporary Assistance to Needy Families (TANF) are employed in steady jobs and remain employed over time, their wages increase with this longevity in the work world (M. Corcoran, Danziger, Kalil, & Seefeldt, 2000).

However, the reality is that many young women leaving TANF do not enter long-term continuous employment because of a variety of barriers, such as maternal and child physical and/or mental health problems; unaffordable, inaccessible, or poor-quality child care; or unreliable transportation (M. Corcoran et al., 2000). Without addressing these problems, the *long-term* wage stability and economic viability of these families remain in question. The living wage social movement that continues to gain momentum will help bring more public awareness and hopefully policy change to these issues.

Work in Middle Adulthood

In the deep economic recession that began in December 2007, workers age 45 had a lower unemployment rate than younger workers, but they were disproportionately represented among the long-term unemployed, out of work for an average of 22.2 weeks, compared with 16.2 weeks for younger workers (Luo, 2009). These midlife baby boomers are too young to draw a pension or to have medical coverage through Medicare.

In affluent societies, the last few decades have seen a continuing decline in the average age of retirement, particularly for men (Kim & Moen, 2001; Moen, 2003). This trend exists alongside trends of lengthening of years of both midlife and late adulthood and the fact that adults are entering midlife healthier and better educated than in previous eras. Improved pension plans are at least partially responsible for this trend, but in the United States, there is a growing gap in pension coverage. Between 1979 and 1993, the gap in pension coverage between workers with less than 12 years of education and workers with 16 years or more of education more than quadrupled (O'Rand, 2003). Governmental policies minimize the pension gap in European countries (Heinz, 2003).

Overall, the work patterns of middle-aged workers in the United States have changed considerably in the past three decades. Changes in the global economy have produced job instability for middle-aged workers. There is greater variability

Photo 15.5 Changes in the global economy have produced job instability for middle-aged workers, and job retraining often becomes essential.

in the timing of retirement; some retire in their mid- to late fifties, but many others anticipate working until their early seventies. Many people now phase into retirement, working part-time, or find reemployment with less financial reward after losing a job. Midlife workers are increasingly returning to school to retrain (Dittmann-Kohli, 2005; Luo, 2009; Moen, 2003; Sterns & Huyck, 2001).

These trends aside, there is both good news and bad news for the middle-aged worker in the beginning of the 21st century. Research indicates that middle-aged workers have greater work satisfaction, organizational commitment, and self-esteem than younger workers (Dittmann-Kohli, 2005). However, with the current changes in the labor market, employers are ambivalent about middle-aged employees. Employers may see middle-aged workers as "hard-working, reliable, and motivated" (Sterns & Huyck, 2001, p. 476). But they also often cut higher-wage older workers from the payroll as a short-range solution for reducing operating costs and staying competitive.

For some midlife adults, like Viktor Spiro, the issue is not how they will cope with loss of a good job but rather how they can become established in the labor market. In the previous industrial phase, poverty was due to unemployment. In the current era, the major issue is the growing proportion of low-wage, no-benefit jobs. Adults like Viktor, with disabilities, have an even harder time finding work that can support them. In July 2009, the unemployment rate for persons with a disability was 15.1% compared to 9.5% for persons with no disability (U.S. Bureau of Labor Statistics, 2009b). Even with the legislation of the past two decades, much remains to be done to open educational and work opportunities to persons with disabilities. In addition, Viktor has had to contend with language and cultural barriers.

Thus, middle-aged workers, like younger workers, are deeply affected by a changing labor market. Like younger workers, they must understand the patterns in those changes and be proactive in maintaining and updating their skills. As researchers are finding, however, that task is easier for middle-aged workers who arrive in middle adulthood with accumulated resources (Moen, 2003). Marginalization in the labor market in adulthood is the result of "cumulative disadvantage" over the life course. Unfortunately, adults like Scott Pukalski and Viktor

Spiro who have employment disruptions early in the adult life course tend to have more job disruption in middle adulthood as well.

RISK FACTORS AND PROTECTIVE FACTORS IN ADULTHOOD

Why is it important for social workers to understand both antecedents and consequences of young adult and middle adult behavior?

From a life course perspective, adult behavior has both antecedents and consequences. Earlier life experiences can serve either as risk factors or as protective factors for health and well-being during adulthood. And behaviors at one adult phase can serve either as risk factors or as protective factors for future health and well-being. The rapidly growing body of literature on risk, protection, and resilience based on longitudinal research has recently begun to add to our understanding of the antecedents of young adult and middle adult behavior.

One of the best-known programs of research is a longitudinal study begun by Emmy Werner and associates with a cohort born in 1955 on the island of Kauai, Hawaii. The research participants turned 40 in 1995, and Werner and Ruth Smith (2001) capture their risk factors, protective factors, and resilience in *Journeys From Childhood to Midlife*. They summarize their findings by suggesting that the participants "taught us a great deal of respect for the self-righting tendencies in human nature and for the capacity of *most* individuals who grew up in adverse circumstances to make a successful adaptation in adulthood" (p. 166). The risk factors and protective factors that influence adjustment at ages 32 and 40 are summarized in Exhibit 15.7.

Emmy Werner and Ruth Smith (2001) identified clusters of protective factors at significant points across the life course that are associated with successfully making the transition to adulthood. They identified high-risk individuals and then determined the specific factors that influenced their positive adaptation to adulthood at age 32. These protective factors are summarized under "Antecedents to Young Adult Adjustment" in Exhibit 15.7. Other researchers have identified similar protective factors associated with successful developmental transitions into emerging adulthood and young adulthood, including childhood IQ, parenting quality, and socioeconomic status. Adaptation in emerging adulthood, specifically, is associated with an individual's planning capacity, future motivation, autonomy, social support, and coping skills (Masten et al., 2004).

Emmy Werner and Ruth Smith (2001) also identify a number of risk factors that are associated with the transition to adulthood, also summarized under "Antecedents to Young Adult Adjustment" in Exhibit 15.7. Other studies have found that adolescent fatherhood can be a risk factor for delinquency, which in turn can lead to problematic entry into adulthood (Stouthamer-Loeber & Wei, 1998).

A recent study (Ringeisen, Casanueva, Urato, & Stambaugh, 2009) found that although about half (48%) of young adults with a child maltreatment history had mental health problems, only 25% of these young adults received treatment services for their problems. In particular, there was a significant decline from those receiving services in adolescence (47.6%) to those continuing to receive such services in adulthood (14.3%). Data suggest that there is a significant risk of losing continuity of mental health services when making the move out of adolescence and into young adulthood, with data showing particularly high risk for non-Whites and those without Medicaid assistance (Ringeisen et al., 2009).

Other studies of youth aging out of the foster care system have found similar declining trends in mental health service utilization during the adolescent–adult transition. A study by J. C. McMillan and Raghavan (2009) found that 60% of 19-year-old foster youth dropped out of services during the transition from pediatric system care to the adult service system. This is significant given that 20,000 youth age out of foster care each year (U.S. Department of Health and Human Services [DHHS], 2005), and that former

Exhibit 15.7   Risk Factors and Protective Factors Affecting Adjustment in Young and Middle Adulthood

Antecedents to Young Adult Adjustment		Antecedents to Middle Adult Adjustment	
Risk Factors	Protective Factors	Risk Factors	Protective Factors
Low family income during infancy Poor reading achievement by age 10 Problematic school behavior during adolescence Adolescent health problems For men: an excessive number of stressful events, living with an alcoholic or mentally ill father, and substance abuse For women: a sibling death in early childhood, living with an alcoholic or mentally ill father, and a conflicted relationship with the mother	Successful early social, language, and physical development Stable maternal employment when the child was 2 to 10 years old Access to nurturing, caring adults in the community Good problem-solving skills in middle childhood Access to a variety of social support sources, and a sense of belonging with the family unit at age 18 Educational and work expectations and plans by age 18 Social maturity and a sense of mastery and control in late adolescence	Severe perinatal trauma Small for gestational age birth weight Early childhood poverty Serious health problems in early childhood Problems in early schooling Parental alcoholism and/or serious mental illness Health problems in adolescence Health problems in the thirties	Competent, nurturing caregiver in infancy Emotional support of extended family, peers, and caring adults outside the family Continuing education at community college Military service Marriage to a stable partner Religious conversion Survival despite a life-threatening illness or accident

SOURCE: Based on E. E. Werner & Smith (2001).

foster youth (ages 19–30) have twice the rate of post-traumatic stress disorder as U.S. war veterans (Pecora et al., 2005). In addition, they have more severe mental health and behavioral problems than the general population and than children who have a maltreatment history but not foster care placement (Lawrence, Carlson, & Egeland, 2006).

A study of the effects of war on adult mental health reveals other risk factors of which social workers should be aware. Although some researchers have found that military service often provides youth with a positive opportunity to transition into adulthood (E. E. Werner & Smith, 2001) and frequently leads to facilitating a young adult's return to higher education (Astone et al., 2000), the ravages of war experienced during military

service can pose significant mental health risk. For example, Hoge, Auchterlonie, and Milliken (2006) examined the prevalence of mental health problems and service utilization among military personnel who recently returned from service in Iraq and found that one fifth (19.1%) had at least one mental health problem, with about one third (35%) of those adults accessing mental health services during their first year back home. In addition, those personnel who were assessed as having a mental health condition were more likely to subsequently leave the military as compared to those personnel who returned home without a mental health condition. Therefore, it appears that although military service can be a positive path for many transitioning youth, the nature and quality of a youth's military experience may influence later physical and mental health outcomes, as well as work trajectory decisions (e.g., to leave the military early). It appears that military service in a time of war may be a risk factor rather than protective factor. In addition, the availability of, access to, and quality of mental health care for military personnel upon their return home may also contribute to the severity of wartime service as a risk factor.

At age 40, compared to previous decades, the overwhelming majority of the participants in the Emmy Werner and Ruth Smith (2001) study reported "significant improvements" in work accomplishments, interpersonal relationships, contributions to community, and life satisfaction. Most adults who had a troubled adolescence had recovered by midlife. Many of these adults who had been troubled as youth reported that the "opening of opportunities" (p. 168) in their twenties and thirties had led to major *turning points*. Such turning points included continuing education at community college, military service, marriage to a stable partner, religious conversion, and survival despite a life-threatening illness or accident. As noted in Exhibit 15.7, at midlife, participants were still benefiting from having had a competent, nurturing caregiver in infancy, as well as from the emotional support along the way of extended family, peers, and caring adults outside the family. Although this research is hopeful, Werner and Smith also found that 1 of 6 of the study cohort was doing poorly at work and in relationships at age 40.

The earlier risk factors that E. E. Werner and Smith (2001) found to be associated with poor midlife adjustment are noted in Exhibit 15.7 under "Antecedents to Middle Adult Adjustment." Viktor Spiro's early life produced several of these risk factors: early childhood poverty, health problems in adolescence, and his father's chronic depression. It is interesting to note that Werner and Smith found that the long-term negative effects of serious health problems in early childhood and adolescence were just beginning to show up at age 40. We are also

learning that some negative effects of childhood and adolescent trauma may not present until early midlife.

Studies have also examined the effects of midlife behavior, specifically the effects on subsequent health (see Dioussé, Driver, & Gaziano, 2009). They have found a number of health behaviors that are risk factors for more severe and prolonged health and disability problems in late adulthood. These include smoking, heavy alcohol use, diet high in fats, overeating, and sedentary lifestyle. Economic deprivation and high levels of stress have also been found to be risk factors throughout the life course (Auerbach & Krimgold, 2001b; Spiro, 2001). A health behavior that is receiving much research attention as a protective factor for health and well-being in late adulthood is a physical fitness program that includes stretching exercises, weight training, and aerobic exercise (Whitbourne, 2001).

Knowledge of risk and protective factors related to the adulthood transition can help social workers assess young adult clients' current challenges, vulnerabilities, strengths, and potential. Gaining an accurate understanding of the client's developmental history provides guidance to the social worker in formulating appropriate goals and intervention strategies in work with both young and midlife adults. It is important to remember to check out your own assumptions of "risk" with clients in order to clarify the unique impact such experiences have on individual clients.

Critical Thinking Questions 15.3

What developmental risk factors do you see in the stories of Scott Pukalski, Carla Aquino, Viktor Spiro, and Phuong Le? What developmental protective factors do you see in each of their stories? How would you evaluate the balance of risk factors and protective factors in each of their lives? What evidence do you see of current behaviors that might have consequences, either positive or negative, for their future life course?

This discussion has several implications for social work practice with young and midlife adults:

- Be familiar with the unique pathways your clients have traveled to reach adulthood.
- Recognize that social roles during emerging adulthood may be different from those later in young adulthood.
- Explore cultural values, family expectations, attitudes toward gender roles, and environmental constraints/resources that may influence life structure decisions and opportunities when working with adult clients.
- Where appropriate, help young adults to master the tasks involved in developing intimate relationships.
- Help midlife clients to think about their own involvement in generative activity and the meaning that this involvement has for their lives.
- Understand the ways that social systems promote or deter people from maintaining or achieving health and well-being.
- Be aware of both stability and the capacity for change in personality in middle adulthood.
- Engage midlife clients in a mutual assessment of their involvement in a variety of relationships, including romantic relationships, relationships with parents, relationships with children, other family relationships, relationships with friends, and community/organizational relationships.
- Collaborate with social workers and other disciplines to advocate for governmental and corporate solutions to work and family life conflicts.

Key Terms

community assets	differentiation (Jung)	individuative-reflective faith
conjunctive faith	emerging adulthood	intimacy
convoy	generativity	life structure
coping mechanisms	human capital	psychosocial crisis
default individualization	identity	romantic love
developmental individualization	individuation (Jung)	synthetic-conventional faith

Active Learning

1. Choose one of the case studies at the beginning of the chapter (Scott Pukalski, Carla Aquino, Viktor Spiro, or Phuong Le). Change the gender for that case without changing any other major demographic variable. Explore how your assumptions change about the individual's problems, challenges, and potential. Now choose a different case. Change the race or ethnicity for that case and again explore your assumptions. Finally, choose a third case, change the SES, and again explore how your assumptions change.

2. Identify one current social issue as portrayed in the media (e.g., housing, immigration policies, health care access or coverage or affordability, living wage) and explore how this social issue uniquely affects young adults.

3. Draw your social convoy as it currently exists with three concentric circles:
   - Inner circle of people who are so close and important to you that you could not do without them
   - Middle circle of people who are not quite that close but are still very close and important to you

- Outer circle of people who are not as close and important as those in the two inner circles but still close enough to be considered part of your support system

What did you learn from engaging in this exercise? Do you see any changes you would like to make in your social convoy?

Web Resources

High School & Beyond
http://nces.ed.gov/surveys/hsb

Site of the National Education Longitudinal Studies program of the National Center for Education Statistics, provides data and reports from their longitudinal projects that have tracked the educational and personal development of youth transitioning into adulthood.

Max Planck Institute for Human Development
www.mpib-berlin.mpg.de/index_js.en.htm

Site presented by the Max Planck Institute for Human Development, Berlin, Germany, contains news and research about life course development.

National Survey of Family Growth
http://www.cdc.gov/nchs/nsfg.htm

Site of the National Center for Health Statistics, offers reports, other publications, and data from their CDC-sponsored survey documenting family formation issues in adulthood, such as fertility and family planning, sexual behavior, and health.

MIDMAC
midmac.med.harvard.edu/

Site presented by the John D. and Catherine T. MacArthur Foundation Research Network on Successful Midlife Development (MIDMAC), contains an overview of recent research on midlife development and links to other human development research projects.

Network on Transitions to Adulthood
http://www.transad.pop.upenn.edu/

Site examines the policies, programs, and institutions influencing the adulthood transition; contains fast facts and information on research initiatives. The network is funded by the John D. and Catherine T. MacArthur Foundation and focuses on six areas: education, labor economics, social history, changing attitudes and norms, developmental changes, and ethnography.

Seattle Longitudinal Study
http://geron.psu.edu/sls

Site at Pennsylvania State University presents information on the Seattle Longitudinal Study and publications from the study.

Sloan Work and Family Research Network
http://wfnetwork.bc.edu

Site presented by the Sloan Work and Family Research Network of Boston College, contains a literature database, research newsletter, resources for teaching, research profiles, and work and family links. Part of the network's mission is to inform policy makers on key family–work issues.

CHAPTER 16

Late Adulthood

Matthias J. Naleppa

Pamela J. Kovacs

Rosa Schnitzenbaumer

ACKNOWLEDGMENTS: The authors wish to thank Mariette Klein, Dr. Peter Maramaldi, and Dr. Michael Melendez for contributions to this chapter.

Opening Questions

How will the trend toward increased longevity affect family life and social work practice?

What do social workers need to understand about the biological, psychological, social, and spiritual changes in late adulthood and the coping mechanisms used to adapt to these changes?

When working with clients in very late adulthood, what do social workers need to know about how people respond to crises such as severe illness, acquired disability, and loss?

Key Ideas

As you read this chapter, take note of these central ideas:

1. Unlike in earlier historical eras, many people in the United States and other industrialized countries today reach the life phase of late adulthood, and the older population is a very heterogeneous group, including the young-old (65 to 74 years), the middle-old (75 to 84 years), and the oldest-old (85 and above).

2. The cumulative effect of health disparities based on race, ethnicity, gender, and socioeconomic status impacts the quality of aging for significant subpopulations of older people in the United States and around the world.

3. The most commonly discussed psychosocial theories of social gerontology are disengagement, activity, continuity, social construction, feminist, social exchange, life course, and age stratification theories.

4. All systems of the body appear to be affected during the aging process.

5. It has been difficult to understand psychological changes in late adulthood without long-term longitudinal research, but recent longitudinal research suggests that with age and experience, individuals tend to use more adaptive coping mechanisms.

6. Families play an important role in late adulthood, and as a result of increased longevity, multigenerational families are more common than ever.

7. Very late adulthood is the one life course phase when dying is considered "on time," and very late-life adults seem to have less denial about the reality of death than those in other age groups.

8. Theoreticians and researchers continue to try to understand the multidimensional process of grief.

CASE STUDY 16.1

Ms. Ruby Johnson Is Providing Care for Three Generations

Ms. Ruby Johnson is a handsome woman who describes herself as a "hard-boiled, 71-year-old African American" who spent the first 30 years of her life in Harlem, until she settled in the Bronx, New York. She married at 19 and lived with her husband until her 30th birthday. During her initial assessment for case management services, she explained her divorce with what appeared to be great pride. On her 29th birthday, Ruby told her husband that he had one more year to choose between "me and the bottle." She tolerated his daily drinking for another year, but when he came home drunk on her 30th birthday, she took their 6-year-old daughter and left him and, she explained, she "never looked back."

Ruby immediately got a relatively high-paying—albeit tedious—job working for the postal service. At the same time, she found the Bronx apartment, in which she has resided for the past 41 years. Ruby lived there with her daughter, Darlene, for 18 years until she "put that girl out" on what she describes as the saddest day of her life.

Darlene was 21 when she made Ruby the grandmother of Tiffany, a vivacious little girl in good health. A year later, Darlene began using drugs when Tiffany's father abandoned them. By the time Darlene was 24, she had a series of warnings and arrests for drug possession and prostitution. Ruby explained that it "broke my heart that my little girl was out there sellin' herself for drug money." Continuing the story in an unusually angry tone, she explained that "I wasn't gonna have no 'hoe' live in my house."

During her initial interview, Ruby's anger was betrayed by a flicker of pride when she explained that Darlene, now 46, has been drug-free for more than 20 years. Tiffany is 25 and lives with her husband and two children. They have taken Darlene into their home to help Ruby. Ruby flashed a big smile when she shared that "Tiffany and Carl [her husband] made me a great-grandma twice, and they are taking care of Darlene for me now." Darlene also has a younger daughter—Rebecca—from what Ruby describes as another "bad" relationship with a "no good man." Rebecca, age 16, has been living with Ruby for the past 2 years since she started having difficulty in school and needed more supervision than Darlene was able to provide.

In addition, about a year ago, Ruby became the care provider for her father, George. He is 89 and moved into Ruby's apartment because he was no longer able to live independently after his brother's death. On most weeknights, Ruby cooks for her father, her granddaughter, and everyone at Tiffany's house as well. Ruby says she loves having her family around, but she just doesn't have half the energy she used to have.

Ruby retired 5 years ago from the postal service, where she worked for 36 years. In addition to her pension and Social Security, she now earns a small amount for working part-time providing child care for a former coworker's daughter. Ruby explains that she has to take the extra work in order to cover her father's prescription expenses not covered by his Medicare benefits, and help pay medical/prescription bills for Tiffany's household. Tiffany and Carl receive no medical benefits from their employers and are considering lowering their income in order to qualify for Medicaid benefits. Ruby wants them to keep working, so she has been trying to use her connections to get them jobs with the postal service. Ruby reports this to be her greatest frustration, because her best postal service contacts are "either retired or dead."

Although Ruby's health is currently stable, she is particularly concerned that it may worsen. She is diabetic and insulin dependent and worries about all the family members for whom she feels responsible. During the initial interview, Ruby confided that she thinks that her physical demise has begun. Her greatest fear is death—not for herself, she says, but for the effect it would have on her family. She then asked her social worker to help her find a way to ensure their well-being after her death.

—Peter Maramaldi

CASE STUDY 16.2

Mr. and Mrs. Menzel Need Assistance

Christine, the 51-year-old daughter of Joseph and Elizabeth Menzel, came to the geriatric counseling center in a small town in Bavaria, Germany. She indicated that she could no longer provide adequate care to her parents and requested assistance from the geriatric social work team. Christine described the family situation as follows.

(Continued)

(Continued)

Her parents, Joseph and Elizabeth, live in a small house about 4 miles away from her apartment. Her brother Thomas also lives close by, but he can only provide help on the weekends because of his employment situation. The 79-year-old mother has been diagnosed with dementia of the Alzheimer's type. Her increasing forgetfulness is beginning to interfere with her mastery of the household and some other activities of daily living. The 84-year-old father's behavior is also adding to the mother's difficulties. Mr. Menzel is described as an authoritarian and very dominant person. For example, Christine says that he does not allow his wife to select which television shows to watch or what music she listens to, even though she would like to make such choices by herself. According to the daughter, his behavior seems to add to Mrs. Menzel's confusion and lack of personal confidence. At the same time, however, Mr. Menzel spends a lot of his time in bed. During those times, he does not interact much with Mrs. Menzel. Sometimes he would not get up all day and would neglect his own personal care. It was not clear how much his staying in bed was related to his general health condition; he has silicosis (a respiratory disease) and congestive heart failure.

The couple lives a fairly isolated life and has no friends. Family members, the son Thomas, the daughter Christine and her partner, four grandchildren, and a brother of Mrs. Menzel are the only occasional visitors. Christine's primary concern was with her mother's well-being. The mother needs assistance with the instrumental activities of daily living as well as with her health care. Being employed full-time, the daughter indicated that she has a hard time providing the assistance and care that she thinks would be needed. Chores like doctor visits, shopping, cleaning, and regular checking in with the parents could be done by her and her brother. However, additional care responsibilities seem to be beyond the daughter's capacity at this time. During the initial contact with the daughter, the following services were discussed:

- Applying for additional funding for dementia services through long-term care insurance (German *Pflegeversicherung*)
- Hiring a local care provider to help with managing the couple's medications
- Applying for daily lunch delivery for the parents through the local meals-on-wheels service
- Locating a volunteer through the local volunteer network to stop by 1–2 times per week to engage the mother in activities such as music, walks, playing games, or memory training
- Assessing Mrs. Menzel's interest in attending the weekly *Erzählcafé* meetings, a local group for persons with dementia
- Arranging for Mr. Menzel to receive information from the geriatric counseling center regarding how to attend to his wife's dementia
- Assessing whether Mr. Menzel has depression, and, if needed, connecting him to relevant medical services
- Inviting the daughter to participate in a support group for relatives and caregivers of persons with dementia

All of the described services and programs were secured in quick succession. After three initial visits, Mrs. Menzel had established a good relationship with the volunteer helper and indicates that she likes attending the *Erzählcafé* meetings. After the assistance for his wife started, Mr. Menzel opened up to having a conversation with the geriatric social worker. He indicated that he was thinking a lot lately about his own personal biography. He and his wife were displaced after World War II. They grew up as neighbors in Silesia (today part of Poland). Both of their families had to leave everything behind and flee overnight in October of 1946. After staying in various refugee camps, their families finally ended up in Bavaria. This is where they started dating and finally married. Having lost everything, they had to start all over again. They had to work hard for everything they have today.

Mr. Menzel worked his entire life as a miner, supplementing his income through a second job painting houses. His wife was employed as a seamstress. Respected for their hard work and engagement, they were soon accepted as members of their new community. However, Mr. Menzel says that he has never come to terms with his postwar displacement and the loss of his homeland. He had started a community group and organized regular meetings for displaced persons. Together with his daughter, he also wrote a book about his homeland. Now he feels too weak and ill to do anything. He just wants to stay at home and sit in his recliner all day. After talking with the geriatric social worker, Mr. Menzel overcame his initial reluctance and agreed to have additional contacts with the geriatric counseling center.

Soon after connecting with the geriatric counseling center, the daughter unexpectedly died during a routine surgery. After the initial shock and grieving of the sudden loss, the family began adjusting to the new situation. The brother assumed the overall coordination and management of his mother's care. Other family members, including Christine's partner, took on more responsibilities and increased the frequency of visiting Mrs. Menzel. The contacts with the volunteer proved to be a valuable support for Mrs. Menzel's work around the loss and grief topic. In spite of her dementia, she had experienced her daughter's death very intensely.

While this all was occurring, Mr. Menzel's health declined rapidly. He has been hospitalized twice for longer periods over the past few months. During this time, more intensive assistance had to be provided to his wife.

Note: Students in the United States are probably not familiar with the Bavarian Geriatric Counseling Centers. These centers were established to coordinate and provide geriatric services to older adults in the community and to create service provider networks.

CASE STUDY 16.3

Margaret Davis Stays at Home

Margaret Davis has lived in her small, rural community in southern West Virginia for all of her 85 years. It is in this Appalachian mountain town that she married her grade school sweetheart, packed his pail for long shifts in the mine, and raised their four children. It has been over 30 years since she answered the door to receive the news that her husband had perished in an accident at the mine. She remains in that same house by herself, with her daughter living in a trailer on the same property and one of her sons living just down the road. Her other son recently moved to Cleveland to find work, and her other daughter lives in the same town but has been estranged from the family for several years.

Mrs. Davis has hypertension and was recently diagnosed with type 2 diabetes. The nurse from the home health agency is assisting her and her daughter with learning to give insulin injections. It is the nurse who asks for a social work consult for Mrs. Davis. The nurse and Mrs. Davis's daughter are concerned that she is becoming increasingly forgetful with her medications and often neglects her insulin regime. They also suspect that she is experiencing some incontinence, as her living room couch and carpet smell of urine.

Mrs. Davis and her daughter Judy greet the social worker at Mrs. Davis's home. They have been baking this morning and offer a slice of peanut butter pie. Judy excuses herself to go to her trailer to make a phone call. The social worker asks Mrs. Davis about how her insulin regime has been going and if she felt that she could keep up with the injections. She responds that she has learned to give herself the shots and "feels pretty fair." The social

(Continued)

worker conveys the concern that she may be missing some of the injections and other medications as well. To this she replies, "Oh, don't worry about me. I'm fine." The social worker proceeds to ask the sensitive question as to whether she has been having trouble with her bladder or getting to the bathroom. This causes Mrs. Davis to become very quiet. Looking up at the social worker, she shares that witches have been visiting her house late at night and have been urinating in her living room. The witches are very "devious" but because she is a very religious person, she does not feel that they will harm her.

Judy returns to the home and joins her mother and the social worker. Judy voices her concern about her mother's safety, noting the problems with medications and with general forgetfulness. Judy is able to prepare meals, dispense the medications, and give insulin injections in the morning because she works evenings at a factory. Judy's daughter Tiffany has been staying overnight in the home but complains of her grandmother's wandering and confusion late at night. As a result, she is often exhausted during her day shifts at a nursing home in the next county and in caring for her small children. When asked about Mrs. Davis's son's involvement in her care, Judy responds, "He works and is in the Guard some weekends. He handles mom's money mostly and his wife, well, she has her own problems." Judy also reported that her mother has Medicare, but she was not sure if that would be sufficient to pay for all her mother's care long-term. Judy is also worried because her old car has been giving her problems lately, and the repairs are becoming expensive. She concludes by stating, "We promised Mom that she would never go to a home. . . . We take care of our own."

—Kristina Hash and Meenakshi Venkataraman

CASE STUDY 16.4

Bina Patel Outlives Her Son

Bina Patel is a 90-year-old immigrant who moved to the United States 25 years ago from India with her son and his family. Like many other South Asian older adults, Mrs. Patel prefers to reside with her adult children and values the mutual interdependency among generations common in their culture. Upon arriving in this country at age 65, Mrs. Patel, a widow, played a critical role in the family, providing child care, assisting with meals and various household tasks, and offering companionship and support for her adult children. True to her cultural tradition, Mrs. Patel expects adult children—especially sons—to provide for parents in their old age, and believes that the role of the elder is to provide crucial functions such as passing on wisdom and guidance to children and grandchildren, and being constantly available to them.

Mrs. Patel had been in remarkably good health until she had a mild stroke last year. She was managing well at home with weekly physical therapy and her family's assistance with bathing. She and her family have been unprepared for her longevity, and in fact it appears that she will outlive her son, who at age 69 was recently diagnosed with pancreatic cancer with a prognosis of 6 to 12 months to live. Her daughter-in-law is home full-time with Mrs. Patel, but does not drive and currently is emotionally distraught over her husband's rapid decline. Mrs. Patel's two grandchildren, who are in their thirties, have relocated with their own families due to employment. They are in frequent telephone contact, but they live a 2-hour plane ride away and are busy with work and children's school and activities. Although this family has traditionally handled their family needs on their own or with the help of a small South Asian network, the son's decline in health has caused tremendous concern regarding Mrs. Patel's future well-being.

The hospital social worker has been asked to meet with the son and daughter-in-law during his hospitalization to explore possible sources of assistance throughout the son's pending decline as well as to help strategize for Mrs. Patel's anticipated increased need of physical care, given her recent decline in cognitive and physical capacity.

DEMOGRAPHICS OF THE OLDER ADULT POPULATION

For Ruby Johnson, Joseph and Elizabeth Menzel, Margaret Davis, and Bina Patel, more years of life stretch behind them than ahead of them, but, like all other individuals, their day-to-day lives incorporate past, present, and future orientations (Mayer et al., 1999). Research from the longitudinal Berlin Aging Study has been able to dispel some commonly held beliefs about older adults. According to this research as well as findings from other studies, older adults

- Are not preoccupied with death and dying;
- Are able and willing to learn new things;
- Still feel that they can and want to be in control of their life;
- Still have life goals;
- Do not live primarily in the past;
- Still live an active life, their health permitting.

The term *late adulthood* covers about one quarter to one third of a person's life and includes active and less active, healthy and less healthy, working and nonworking persons. Late adulthood encompasses a wide range of cohort-related life experiences. Someone reaching the age of 65 today, if the person has lived his or her entire life in the United States, has experienced segregation and busing, Martin Luther King's "I Have a Dream" speech, but also the election of the first African American president and the appointment of the first Latina Supreme Court Justice. He or she may have experienced the Dust Bowl and two

world wars, and would have grown up listening to radio shows before TV existed. The person may have been at Woodstock and could be in the age cohort of Mick Jagger and Bob Dylan. Every client in the stories above could be considered old, and yet they are functioning in different ways and at different levels. In the context of U.S. society, the term *old* can have many meanings. These meanings reflect attitudes, assumptions, biases, and cultural interpretations of what it means to grow older. In discussing life course trajectories, we commonly use the term *older population* or *elderly persons* to refer to those over 65 years of age. But an Olympic gymnast is "old" at age 25, a president of the United States is "young" at age 50, and a 70-year-old may not consider herself "old" at all.

Late adulthood is perhaps a more precise term than old, but it can still be confusing because of the 50-year range of ages it may include. Late adulthood is considered to start at 65 and continue through to the end of life. Considering age 65 as the starting point for late adulthood is somewhat arbitrary, since there is no sudden change to our physiology, biology, or personality at this time. Rather, it can be traced back to the statesman Otto von Bismarck's social insurance schemes in Germany more than 100 years ago and the introduction of the Social Security Act in the United States in 1935. In both cases, 65 years was selected for retirement based on population statistics and expected survival rates. Many people today reach the life stage of late adulthood. In 2008, there were approximately 508 million people age 65 years or older in the world, and by 2040 this number is expected to increase to 1.3 billion

(National Institute on Aging, National Institute of Health [NIA/NIH], 2009). The United States has a fairly young population as wealthy nations go, with just over 12% of its population age 65 and older. Most European countries have an average of 15% of their population 65 or older. Japan and Italy's older population stands at 20% of the total population (Federal Interagency Forum on Aging-Related Statistics, 2008). The enormous increase in life expectancy is not unique to the United States, nor is it occurring only in the developed world. Most nations of the world have a growing older population. Currently, 62% of the population over 65 lives in nonindustrialized or newly industrializing countries, and the population growth in these countries is twice that of developed countries (NIA/NIH, 2009). Due to this trend, it is expected that 1 billion people over 65, that is, 76% of the projected world total, will live in today's developing countries (NIA/NIH, 2009). Disability rates are declining among the older population in the United States, Japan, and a number of European nations (American Association of Retired Persons, 2003).

According to the U.S. Census Bureau (2008b), the 85-and-older population is the fastest-growing segment of the aging population, projected to increase from 4.2 million in 2000 to 8.7 million in 2030. There are increasing numbers of people who are 100 years and older (called *centenarians*), a staggering 117% increase from 1990 figures (Administration on Aging, 2008). As of 2006, persons reaching age 65 have an average life expectancy of an additional 19 years (20.3 years for females and 17.4 for males). A child born in the United States in 2006 could expect to live 78.1 years, about 30 years longer than a child born in 1900 (Administration on Aging, 2008).

Increased life expectancy is a product of a number of factors: decreased mortality in children and young adults, decreased mortality among the aging, improved health technology, and other factors. Life expectancy also varies by race, gender, and socioeconomic status. On average, Whites can expect to live 5.5 years longer than minority groups in the United States. The gap is anticipated to narrow to a point where life expectancy for Whites is 1.6 years longer than for Blacks (Administration on Aging, 2008; George, 2005; Rieker & Bird, 2005; D. R. Williams, 2005).

Just a century ago, it was uncommon to reach 65. The first population census of the United States, conducted in 1870, estimated about 3% of the population to be over 65 years of age. Today, more than three fourths of all persons in the United States live to be 65 (A. Walker, Manoogian-O'Dell, McGraw, & White, 2001). The U.S. Census Bureau estimates that in the next 25 years, the elderly population will double to 72 million. By 2030, an estimated 1 in 5 people in the United States will be 65 or older. People in the United States are living longer, are more racially diverse, have lower rates of disability, are less likely to live in poverty, and on average have higher levels of education than in the past (Administration on Aging, 2008; U.S. Census Bureau, 2004b). These salutary developments are not without social and economic implications for both the aging and general population.

> What factors are leading to this trend toward increased longevity?

Age structure, the segmentation of society by age, will affect the economic and social condition of the nation, especially as it regards dependence. An interesting side effect of the growing elderly population is a shifting **dependency ratio**—a demographic indicator that expresses the degree of demand placed on society by the young and the aged combined (L. Morgan & Kunkel, 1996). There are three dependency ratios: the elderly dependency ratio, the number of elders 65 and older per 100 people ages 18 to 64; the child dependency ratio, the number of children under 18 per 100 persons ages 18 to 64; and the total dependency ratio, the combination of both of these categories (U.S. Census Bureau, 2008b).

The nature of the U.S. dependency ratio has changed gradually over the past century as the percentage of children in the population has decreased and the percentage of dependent older adults has increased. As Exhibit 16.1 demonstrates, the elderly dependency ratio is predicted to continue to increase at a fairly rapid pace in the near future.

U.S. Census projections indicate small increases of elderly dependency from 20.9 per 100 persons age 18 to 64 in 1995 to 21.2 per 100 in 2010. Steep increases are projected for 2010 to 2030, however, with stability occurring at the level of 36 per 100 by 2050. The child dependency ratio has shown a modest "U" trend. There were about 43 persons under 18 per 100 persons ages 18 to 64 in 1995 with an anticipated drop to 39 per 100 by 2010 and expected increase to 43 by 2030. The overall dependency ratio is expected to stabilize at about 80 per 100 persons ages 18 to 64 between 2030 and 2050 (Administration on Aging, 2008). The social and economic implications of this increase in the dependency ratio are the focus and concern of many scholars and policy makers.

The older population encompasses a broad age range and is often categorized into subgroups:

the young-old (age 65 to 74), the middle-old (age 75 to 84), and the oldest-old (over 85). Ruby Johnson exemplifies the young-old, the Menzels the middle-old, and Margaret Davis and Bina Patel the oldest-old.

There have always been those who outlive their cohort group, but greater numbers of people are surpassing the average life expectancy and more are becoming centenarians. Although very few 100-year-old people were known to exist in the United States in 1900, the number of centenarians doubled in the 1980s and again in the 1990s, with approximately 84,330 estimated in 2007 (W. J. Hall, 2008). In the next 50 years, midrange projections anticipate that over 800,000 people in the United States could reach the century mark. The number is expected to grow to 834,000 by 2050 and double every 10 years thereafter

Exhibit 16.1   Dependency Ratio: Percentage of Children and Elderly per 100 Ages 18 to 64 for the Years 1900, 1995, and 2030

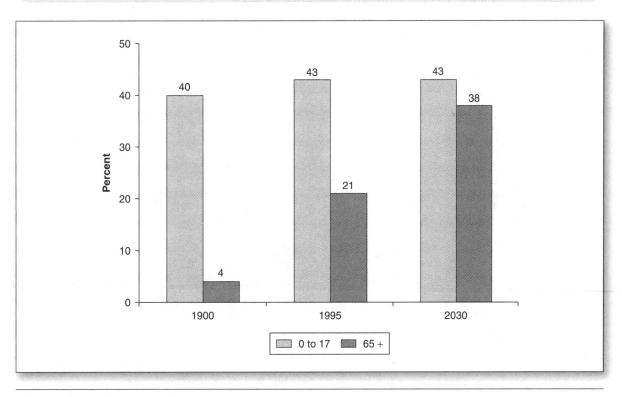

SOURCE: Administration on Aging (2006a).

(L. S. Coles, 2004). Other industrialized countries report similar trends. Future editions of human behavior textbooks might in fact report on another group that demographers are now counting—*supercentenarians,* people age 110 and over (L. S. Coles, 2004).

The U.S. society is one of the most racially and ethnically diverse societies in the world. By 2050, it has been predicted that 48% of the general population will be minorities with approximately one third of the older adults reflecting minority communities. The aging population reflects the shifting trends in the general population. The data available from 2007 indicate that 19.3% of adults over age 65 are non-White, with 8.3% non-Hispanic Black, 6.6% Hispanic, 3.2% Asian and Pacific Islander, and less than 1% Indigenous Americans (Administration on Aging, 2008). As demonstrated in Exhibit 16.2, racial and ethnic composition of older adults is projected to change profoundly by 2050. This change reflects the decline in the percentage of White elderly in the elderly population (from 83% of older Americans in 2004 to a projected 72% in the year 2030 and 66% by 2050), as well as dramatic increases in all other categories. The U.S. Census Bureau estimates that between the years 2000 and 2050, the Hispanic population will be the fastest-growing subpopulation, accounting for 19.8% of older adults by 2050. Proportionally, 6.8% of the populations of minorities are older as compared to 15% of the White population.

Among the older population in the United States, women—especially those in very late adulthood (85 and older)—continue to outnumber men across all racial and ethnic groups. In 2007, the sex ratio among older adults stood at 137 females per 100 males. The female-to-male

Exhibit 16.2 Racial Makeup of U.S. Elderly Population, 2004 and 2050

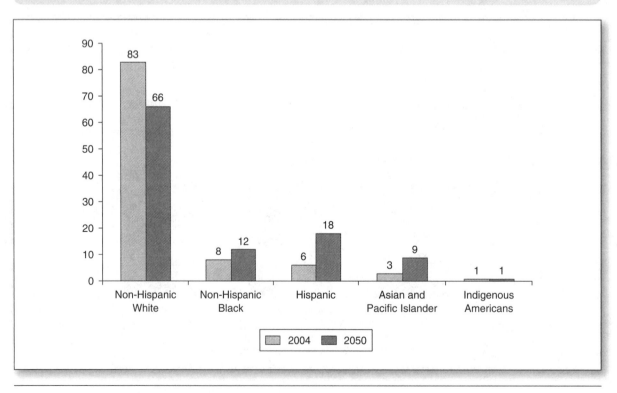

SOURCE: Administration on Aging (2006a, 2006b, 2006c).

ratio increases with age, ranging from 114 females per 100 males for the 65–69 age group to a high of 210 females per 100 males for those 85 and older (Administration on Aging, 2008). Female centenarians outnumber males 9 to 1 (Harvard Health Letter, 2002).

One of the biggest gender differences in life circumstances of older adults relates to marital status. Older men are more likely to be married than older women. According to data from 2008, 75% of men 65 and older were married as compared to 45% of women in the same age group. In the 85 and older group, 60% of men and 15% of women are married (Federal Interagency Forum on Aging-Related Statistics, 2008). This is an important consideration because marital status influences a person's emotional and economic status, living arrangement, and caregiving needs.

Gender, race, and ethnicity have a significant effect on the economic status of elderly individuals.

> How are gender, race, ethnicity, and social class related in late adulthood?

As of 2007, an estimated 9.7% of elderly persons in the United States were below the poverty level. An additional 6.4% of elderly persons are classified as "near poor" (income levels between poverty level and 125% of that level). The poverty rate increases with age from 9% for persons 65 to 74, to 12% for the population between the ages of 75 and 84, and 14% for those ages 85 and older. However, elderly men have a significantly lower poverty rate than elderly women (6.6% vs. 12%) (Administration on Aging, 2008).

Poverty rates also differ for racial groups. While 7.4% of White elderly people lived in poverty, this was the case for 23.2% of elderly African Americans, 11.3% of Asians, and 17.1% of Hispanics (Administration on Aging, 2008). Almost 40% of those older adults with the highest poverty levels were older African American and Hispanic women living alone (Administration on Aging, 2008). Although it was initially thought that trends indicated that the poverty rate was declining for all racial and ethnic groups of older adults, there is mounting evidence of increasing economic disparities across groups (Schoeni, Martin, Andreski, & Freedman, 2005; Wilmoth & Longino, 2006).

CULTURAL CONSTRUCTION OF LATE ADULTHOOD

The ethnic/racial diversity of the older population in the United States underscores the complexity and importance of taking cultural differences

> How important is social age in defining late adulthood?

in perceptions of aging into account. A salient example of cultural differences in approaches to aging is the contrast between traditional Chinese and mainstream U.S. beliefs and values. China has been described in anthropological literature as a "gerontocracy," wherein older people are venerated, given deference, and valued in nearly every task. Benefiting from the Confucian values of filial piety, older people hold a revered position in the family and society.

By contrast, consider the traditional cultural influences in the United States, where individualism, independence, and self-reliance are core values that inherently conflict with the aging process. In the United States, older people have traditionally been collectively regarded as dependent, and cultural values dictate that older people living independently are given higher regard than those requiring assistance. As people age, they strive to maintain the independence and avoid—at all costs—becoming a burden to their family. Older people in the United States typically resort to intervention from private or social programs to maintain their independence rather than turning to family. By contrast, Chinese elders traditionally looked forward to the day when they would become part of their children's household, to live out their days being venerated by their families (Gardiner & Kosmitzki, 2008).

No discussion of comparisons between cultures would be complete without mention of differences that occur within groups. An individual Chinese person might value independence, while

Photos 16.1 a & b The ethnic/racial diversity of the older population in the United States underscores the importance of taking cultural differences in perceptions of aging into account.

an individual in the United States might be closer to the Confucian value of filial piety than traditional U.S. values. In addition, processes such as acculturation, assimilation, and bicultural socialization further influence the norms, values, expectations, and beliefs of all cultural groups, including that which is considered the dominant cultural norm. Globalization of economics and information exchange also impact and change the cultural norms of all countries (Gardiner & Kosmitzki, 2008). In fact, U.S. values of aging appear to be shifting, influenced in part by political and market forces. In the United States, we are now bombarded with contradictory information about aging—media presentations of long-lived, vibrant older adults are juxtaposed with those of nursing home horror stories (Vaillant, 2002). Moreover, there is much variation in the age at which health issues take on great importance.

In his book *Aging Well,* George Vaillant (2002) raises the question, "Will the longevity granted to us by modern medicine be a curse or a blessing?" (p. 3). The answer, he suggests, is influenced by individual, societal, and cultural values, but his research makes him optimistic. Vaillant reports on the most long-term longitudinal research available, the Study of Adult Development. The study includes three separate cohorts of 824 persons, all of whom have been studied since adolescence. A significant limitation of the study is the lack of racial and ethnic diversity among the participants, who are almost exclusively White. The great strength of the study is its ability to control cohort effects by following the same participants over such a long period of time.

Much of the news from the Study of Adult Development is good news. Vaillant (2002) reminds us that Immanuel Kant wrote his first book of philosophy at 57, Titian created many artworks after 76, Ben Franklin invented bifocals at 78, Will Durant won a Pulitzer Prize for history at 83, Frank Lloyd Wright designed the Guggenheim Museum at age 90, the great surgeon Dr. Michael DeBakey obtained a patent for a surgical innovation when he was 90, Leopold Stokowski signed a 6-year recording contract at 94, and Grandma Moses was still painting at 100. Unless they develop a brain disease, the majority of older adults maintain a "modest sense of well-being" (p. 5), usually until a few months before they die. Older adults are also less

> How much agency can we exercise over the six traits for "growing old with grace"?

depressed than the general population. Many older adults acknowledge hardships of aging but also see a reason to continue to live. Vaillant (2002) concludes that "positive aging means to love, to work, to learn something we did not know yesterday, and to enjoy the remaining precious moments with loved ones" (p. 16). Although he found many paths to successful aging, Vaillant identifies six traits for "growing old with grace," found in Exhibit 16.3.

A more recent study using longitudinal data from the Americans' Changing Lives study (ACL) continues to examine the question of the impact of life expectancy and quality of life as a person ages. This is a nationally representative sample of adults age 25 years and older, first interviewed in 1986 and reinterviewed in 1989, 1994, and 2001/2002 (House, Lantz, & Herd, 2005). The ACL was designed to address one central dilemma of research on aging and health: whether increased life expectancy in the United States and other developed nations foreshadowed a scenario of longer life but worsening health as the result of increasing chronically ill and functionally limited and disabled people requiring expensive medical and long-term care—or whether, through increased understanding of psychosocial as well as biomedical risk factors, the onset of serious morbidity and attendant functional limitation and disability could be potentially postponed or "compressed."

These authors focused on socioeconomic disparities in health changes through the middle and later years. They represent a set of scholars who are examining a theoretical concept of cumulative advantage and disadvantage and its role in understanding differential aging among various populations (Hatch, 2005; Wickrama, Conger, & Abraham, 2005). **Cumulative advantage** is the accumulation of increasing advantage over the life course as early advantage positions an individual for later advantage. **Cumulative disadvantage** is the accumulation of increasing disadvantage as early disadvantage positions an individual for later disadvantage. The researchers (Hatch, 2005; Wickrama et al., 2005) argue that multiple interacting factors throughout the life course impact the quality of the health of older individuals. For example, early poverty, lifetime of poverty, poor environmental conditions, poor education, race, and gender have a direct impact on how a person will age. It is not a simple linear, causal track, but instead reflects the complexity of interacting risk and protective factors.

Reviewing research findings from the ACL study, House et al. (2005) examined the impact of two factors related to socioeconomic status (SES), education and income, on poor health. They found that overall socioeconomic disparities do impact health outcomes rather than the reverse. In addition, they found that education has a greater impact than income on the onset of functional limitations/ disabilities. Income, however, has a greater impact on the *progression* of functional limitations. Finally,

---

Exhibit 16.3   Six Traits for Growing Old With Grace

Caring about others and remaining open to new ideas

Showing cheerful tolerance of the indignities of old age

Maintaining hope

Maintaining a sense of humor and capacity for play

Taking sustenance from past accomplishments while remaining curious and continuing to learn from the next generation

Maintaining contact and intimacy with old friends

SOURCE: Vaillant (2002, pp. 310–311).

the impact of educational disparities on the onset of functional limitations increased strikingly in later middle and early old age, with more highly educated individuals postponing limitations and thus compressing the number of years spent with limitations (House et al., 2005).

PSYCHOSOCIAL THEORETICAL PERSPECTIVES ON SOCIAL GERONTOLOGY

How social workers see and interpret aging will inspire our interventions with older adults. **Social gerontology**—the social science that studies human aging—offers several theoretical perspectives that can explain the process of growing old. Eight predominant theories of social gerontology are introduced here.

1. *Disengagement theory.* Disengagement theory suggests that as elderly individuals grow older, they gradually decrease their social interactions and ties and become increasingly self-preoccupied (Cumming & Henry, 1961). This is sometimes seen as a coping mechanism in the face of ongoing deterioration and loss (Tobin, 1988). In addition, society disengages itself from older adults. While it was the first comprehensive theory trying to explain the aging process (Achenbaum & Bengtson, 1994), disengagement theory has received much criticism and little research support (see, for example, Cornwell, Laumann, & Schumm, 2008; J. Hendricks & Hatch, 2006). Disengagement theory is now widely discounted by gerontologists (Hooyman & Kiyak, 2008).

2. *Activity theory.* Activity theory states that higher levels of activity and involvement are directly related to higher levels of life satisfaction in elderly people (Havighurst, 1968). If they can, individuals stay active and involved, and carry on as many activities of middle adulthood as possible. There is growing evidence that physical activity is associated with postponing functional limitation and disability (Benjamin, Edwards, & Bharti, 2005).

Activity theory has received some criticism, however, for not addressing relatively high levels of satisfaction for individuals like Ms. Johnson, whose level of activity is declining, arguing that the theory satisfies U.S. society's view of how people *should* age (Moody, 2010). It also does not address the choice made by many older individuals to adopt a more relaxed lifestyle. Brandtstadter (2006) argues that self-efficacy is more predictive of positive aging than activity. Other critics argue that the theory does not adequately address factors such as ethnicity, lifestyle, gender, and socioeconomic status (Eliopoulus, 2010; Moody, 2010).

3. *Continuity theory.* Continuity theory was developed in response to critiques of the disengagement and activity theories. According to continuity theory, individuals adapt to changes by using the same coping styles they have used throughout the life course, and they adopt new roles that substitute for roles lost because of age (Neugarten, Havighurst, & Tobin, 1968). Individual personality differences are seen as a major influence in adaptation to old age. Current scholarship considers the interaction between personal and contextual factors that promote or impede the accomplishment of desired goals and new roles, recognizing that individuals have control over some contextual factors but not others (Brandtstadter, 2006). The theory distinguishes normal aging from pathological aging but does not sufficiently address older persons with chronic health conditions (Quadagno, 2007). Continuity theory is difficult to empirically test (Hooyman & Kiyak, 2008).

4. *Social construction theory.* Social construction theory aims to understand and explain the influence of social definitions, social interactions, and social structures on the individual elderly person. This theoretical framework suggests that ways of understanding aging are shaped by the cultural, social, historical, political, and economic conditions in which knowledge is developed, and thus values are associated with various ways of understanding (Dean, 1993). Conceptions about aging arise through interactions of an individual with the social environment (Dannefer & Perlmutter, 1990).

The recent conceptualization of "gerotranscendence" is an example of the application of social constructionist theory to aging. The idea of gerotranscendence holds that human development extends into old age and does not simply end or diminish with aging (Hooyman & Kiyak 2008; Tornstam, 2005). According to this theory, aging persons evaluate their lives in terms of the time they have ahead and try to derive a sense of identity, self, and place in the world and universe (Degges-White, 2005; Tornstam, 2005).

5. *Feminist theory.* Proponents of feminist theories of aging suggest that gender is a key factor in understanding a person's aging experience. They contend that because gender is a critical social stratification factor with attendant power, privilege, and status that produces inequalities and disparities throughout the life course, we can only understand aging by taking gender into account (Arber & Ginn, 1995). Gender is viewed as influencing the life course trajectory by impacting access and opportunity, health disparities, and disparities in socioeconomic opportunities, and by creating a lifelong condition of "constrained choice" (Rieker & Bird, 2005). Gabriela Spector-Mersel (2006) argues that in Western societies, older persons have been portrayed as "ungendered." Older men are in a paradoxical position because the metaphors for old age are the opposite of the metaphors for masculinity in these societies. Think, for example, about Mr. Menzel's experience as a caregiver to his wife and how some of his role obligations differ from his lifelong role expectations as a man. Also, consider Ms. Johnson's experience as a single older woman. How might her personal situation differ if she were a man?

6. *Social exchange theory.* Social exchange theory is built on the notion that an exchange of resources takes place in all interpersonal interactions (Blau, 1964; Homans, 1961). This theory is rooted in an analysis of values developed from a market-driven capitalist society. Individuals will only engage in an exchange if they perceive a favorable cost-benefit ratio, or if they see no better alternatives (J. Hendricks, 1987). As individuals become

older, the resources they are able to bring to the exchange begin to shift. Exchange theory bases its explanation of the realignment of roles, values, and contributions of older adults on this assumption. For example, many older persons get involved in volunteer activities; this seemingly altruistic activity may also be seen as fulfilling an emotional need that provides a personal gain. Thus, they are able to adjust and adapt to the altered exchange equation. Older individuals who withdraw from social activities may perceive their personal resources as diminished to the point where they have little left to bring to an exchange, thus leading to their increasing seclusion from social interactions. As social workers, then, it is important to explore how older couples like Mr. and Mrs. Menzel are dealing with the shift in resources within their relationship. Several studies indicate that maintaining reciprocity is important for older individuals (Fiori, Consedine, & Magai, 2008). For example, a recent study of reciprocity among residents of assisted living looked at the positive contributions of aging care recipients to their social relationships, including their interactions with caregivers (Beel-Bates, Ingersoll-Dayton, & Nelson, 2007).

7. *Life course perspective.* From the life course perspective, the conceptual framework used in this section of the book, aging is a dynamic, lifelong process (Greve & Staudinger, 2006). Individuals go through many transitions over their life course (J. Hendricks & Hatch, 2006). The era they live in, the cohort they belong to, and personal and environmental factors influence individuals during these transitions. "Life course capital" is a contemporary addition to the life course perspective. The theory states that people, over the course of their life, accumulate human capital, that is, resources that they can use to address their needs. This capital can take on various forms—for example, it may be social, biological, psychological, or developmental human capital (Hooyman & Kiyak, 2008). This accumulation of life course capital has an impact on a person's aging, for instance, on his or her health (e.g., morbidity, mortality) or wealth (e.g., standard of living in retirement).

8. *Age stratification perspective.* The framework of age stratification falls into the tradition of the life course perspective (Foner, 1995; Riley, 1971). Stratification is a sociological concept that describes a given hierarchy that exists in a given society. Social stratification is both multidimensional and interactive, as individuals occupy multiple social locations with varying amounts of power, privilege, and status. The age stratification perspective suggests that, similar to the way society is structured by socioeconomic class, it is also stratified by age. Roles and rights of individuals are assigned based on their membership in an age group or cohort. The experience of aging differs across cohorts because cohorts differ in size, composition, and experience with an ever-changing society. Hooyman and Kiyak (2008) suggest that the size of the baby boomer generation entering old age will have a significant impact on the age stratification system. For example, they will

> view retirement and leisure more positively, be physically active and healthier, be more likely to challenge restrictions on their roles as workers and community participants, live long enough to be great grandparents, [and] be more planful and proactive about aging and dying processes. (p. 316)

Critical Thinking Questions 16.1

At what age will you consider yourself old? What do you think your favorite activity will be when you are "old"? What do you think your biggest challenge will be? What do you think will be important to you when you reach old age? Where do you get your ideas about old age?

BIOLOGICAL CHANGES IN LATE ADULTHOOD

Every day, our bodies are changing. In a sense, then, our bodies are constantly aging. In general, all persons experience **primary aging,** or changes that are a normal part of the aging process. In addition, many experience **secondary aging** caused by health-compromising behaviors such as smoking or environmental factors such as pollution (Bjorklund & Bee, 2008). As social workers, however, we need not be concerned with the body's aging until it begins to affect the person's ability to function in her or his world, which typically begins to occur in late adulthood.

> How important is the impact of biological age on the experience of the late adult phase of the life course?

Age-Related Changes in Physiology

All systems of the body appear to be affected during the aging process. Consider the *nervous system.* In the brain, neurons and synapses are the transmitters of information throughout the nervous system. Because neurons are not replaced by the body after birth, the number of neurons decreases throughout the life span (NIA/NIH, 2009). The result is a slow decrease of brain mass after age 30. Because we are born with many more neurons and synapses than we need to function, problems usually do not arise, however. Also, if the older adult develops brain deficits in one area of the brain, he or she may make up for these deficits by increasing activity in other brain regions (Whitbourne, 2001). However, a neurological injury or disease may result in more permanent and serious consequences for an older person. There is also evidence of stress-related increases in norepinephrine in the aging brain, resulting in difficulty returning to baseline after stressful events (Aldwin & Gilmer, 2004). We will look more closely at changes in the brain and neurodegenerative diseases in the next section.

Our *cardiovascular system* also changes in several ways as we become older. The cardiac output—the amount of blood pumped per minute—decreases throughout adult life, and the pulse slows with age (Bjorklund & Bee, 2008). The arteries become less elastic and begin to harden, which can result in arteriosclerosis. Fatty lipids accumulate in the walls of the blood vessels and make them narrower, which can cause atherosclerosis. As a result of these changes, less oxygen is available for muscular activities (Whitbourne, 2001). With advancing age, it takes longer for the blood pressure and heart rate to return to normal resting levels after stressful events (Aldwin & Gilmer, 2004).

The *respiratory system,* too, changes with age. Beginning at about 20 years of age, a person's lung capacity decreases throughout the life span (Whitbourne, 2001). The typical decrease from age 20 to age 80 is about 40% for a healthy person. But in healthy older adults who do not smoke, respiratory function is quite good enough for daily activities (Bjorklund & Bee, 2008).

The most important age-related change in our *skeletal system* occurs after age 30, when the destruction of bones begins to outpace the reformation of bones. The gradual decrease in bone mass and bone density can cause osteoporosis. Osteoporosis occurs in 20% of women over 50 and 50% of women over 80 (Bjorklund & Bee, 2008). It is estimated that bone mineral content decreases by 5% to 12% per decade from the twenties through the nineties. One result is that we get shorter as we age. As the cartilage between the joints wears thin, arthritis, a chronic inflammation of the joints, begins to develop. Although many individuals suffer from some form of arthritis in their forties, the symptoms are often not painful until late adulthood. Some of these changes can be ameliorated by diet and exercise and by avoiding smoking and alcohol (Aldwin & Gilmer, 2004).

With increasing age, the *muscular system* declines in mass, strength, and endurance. As a consequence, an elderly person may become fatigued more easily. In addition, muscle contractions begin to slow down, which contributes to deteriorating reflexes and incontinence. However, the muscular system of older individuals can be successfully strengthened through weight training and changes in diet and lifestyle (Bjorklund & Bee, 2008).

Changes in the neurological, muscular, and skeletal systems have an impact on the *sensory system* and the sense of balance, which contributes to the increase in accidental falls and bone fractures in late adulthood. Vision decreases with age, and older persons need more light to reach the retina in order to see. The eye's adaptation to the dark slows with age, as does visual acuity, the ability to detect details (Aldwin & Gilmer, 2004). Age-related decreases in hearing are caused by degenerative changes in the spiral organ of the ear and the associated nerve cells. Many older adults have a reduced ability to hear high-pitched sounds (Aldwin & Gilmer, 2004). By age 65, about one third of adults have significant hearing loss, with men being more likely than women to suffer hearing loss (Bjorklund & Bee, 2008). Age-related changes in taste appear to be minimal. Differences may reflect individual factors, such as exposure to environmental conditions like smoking, periodontal disease, or use of medications, rather than general processes of aging. The smell receptors in the nose can decrease with age, however, and become less sensitive (Aldwin & Gilmer, 2004).

The *integumentary system* includes the skin, hair, and nails. The skin comprises an outer layer (epidermis) and an inner layer (dermis). With age, the epidermis becomes thinner, and pigment cells grow and cluster, creating age spots on the skin (Aldwin & Gilmer, 2004). The sweat and oil-secreting glands decrease, leaving the skin drier and more vulnerable to injury. Much of the fat stored in the hypodermis, the tissue beneath the skin, is lost as we age, causing wrinkles. The skin of an older person often feels cool because the blood flow to the skin is reduced (Aldwin & Gilmer, 2004).

Sexual potency begins to decline at age 20, but without disease, sexual desire and capacity continue in late adulthood. According to a 1998 survey, half of all persons in the United States age 60 or older are sexually active. Among those who are sexually active, 74% of the men and 70% of the women report that they are as satisfied or more satisfied with their sex lives now than they were in their forties (National Council on the Aging, n.d.). Vaillant (2002) reports that *frequency* of sexual activity decreases, however. He found that partners in good health at 75 to 80 often continue to have sexual relations, but that the average frequency is approximately once in every 10 weeks. Interestingly, Vaillant also found that among the women in his study, mastering the life task of generativity, rather than mastering the task of intimacy, was the predictor of regular attainment of orgasm.

Contemporary views on the physiology of aging focus on longevity. Antiaging medicine focuses on developing interventions that will delay age-related pathology or other changes that are not officially listed as disease. Science and technology are achieving gains that show great promise for the future. However, to date, there is no evidence that these gains have increased the maximum life span of humans (International Longevity Center—USA, 2002).

Health and Longevity

Mortality rates—the frequency at which death occurs within a population—have declined significantly for all segments of the population in the United States during the last century. Between 1981 and 2001, the overall age-adjusted death rates for all causes of death for individuals 65 years and older declined by 18%. In this age bracket, death rates from heart disease and stroke declined by approximately 44%. However, the death rates for some diseases increased, such as diabetes mellitus by 38% and chronic lower respiratory diseases by 53%. In 2008, the leading causes of death for people 65 and older were, in descending order, heart disease, cancer, stroke, chronic lower respiratory diseases, Alzheimer's disease, influenza/pneumonia, and diabetes. Overall death rates in 2001 were higher for older men than for older women (Federal Interagency Forum on Aging-Related Statistics, 2008; National Health Statistics, 2006). Access to health care, ample and nutritious food, safe and affordable housing, safe working conditions, and other factors that influence the quality of life also affect longevity.

As mortality has decreased, **morbidity**—the incidence of disease—has increased. In other words, the proportion of the population suffering from age-related chronic conditions has increased in tandem with the population of elderly persons. In 2006, for people 65 years or older, the most prevalent and debilitating chronic conditions in descending order were arthritis (54% of men, 43% of women), hypertension (52% of men, 54% of women), heart disease (37% of men, 26% of women), cancer (24% of men, 19% of women), and diabetes (19% of men, 17% of women). Chronic illnesses are long-term, rarely cured, and costly health conditions (Federal Interagency Forum on Aging-Related Statistics, 2008; National Health Statistics, 2006).

The prevalence of chronic conditions varies significantly by gender, race, and ethnicity. For example, older women report higher levels of hypertension, asthma, chronic bronchitis, and arthritic symptoms than older men. Older men are more likely to identify heart disease, cancer, diabetes, and emphysema. There are also racial and ethnic differences. Non-Hispanic Blacks report higher levels of hypertension (70% compared to 51%) and diabetes (29% compared with 16%) than non-Hispanic Whites. Hispanics (25%) report higher levels of diabetes than Whites (16%). Between 1992 and 2002, the prevalence of certain conditions among ethnic/racial minorities increased, including a 50% increase in hypertension and a 16% increase in diabetes (Federal Interagency Forum on Aging-Related Statistics, 2008). As of 2002, arthritis was reported by 68% of non-Hispanic African Americans, 58% of non-Hispanic Whites, and 50% of Hispanics. Interestingly, cancer is more prevalent among Whites, reported by 21% of non-Hispanic Whites, 11% of Hispanics, and 9% of non-Hispanic African Americans (Federal Interagency Forum on Aging-Related Statistics, 2004). Physical decline is also associated with SES, but it is difficult to separate SES from race and ethnicity because minority groups tend to be overrepresented in lower SES groups (George, 2005; Wilmoth & Longino, 2006). Vaillant (2002) found the physical conditions of inner-city men ages 68 to 70 to be similar to the physical conditions of the women and the Harvard men ages 78 to 80.

A chronic condition can have considerable impact on a family system. In Ms. Johnson's case, the seven people for whom she cares—including two toddlers, an adolescent, an adult daughter

Photo 16.2 Social workers need to be concerned with aging if and when it affects a person's ability to function in his or her world.

who is functionally impaired, a granddaughter and her husband who both are at risk of leaving the workforce, and an aging father—are all affected by her chronic diabetes. Mr. and Mrs. Menzel's family members have needed to provide increasing assistance as the couple's chronic conditions deteriorate. Mrs. Davis's daughter and granddaughter are working hard to manage her chronic conditions at home. These cases illustrate the untold impact of chronic conditions in aging populations that are rarely described by national trend reports.

For many people, illness and death can be postponed through lifestyle changes. In recent years, the importance of preventing illness by promoting good health has received considerable attention (Agency for Healthcare Research and Quality [AHRQ], 2006). The goals of health promotion for older adults include preventing or delaying the onset of chronic disease and disability; reducing the severity of chronic diseases; and maintaining mental health, physical health, and physical functioning as long as possible (Greve & Staudinger, 2006; J. Hendricks & Hatch, 2006; McAuley et al., 2006).

Ways to promote health in old age include improving dietary habits, increasing activity levels and physical exercise, stopping smoking, and obtaining regular health screenings (blood sampling, blood pressure measurement, cancer screening, glaucoma screening). An important finding has been the roles of self-efficacy, sense of mastery, positive attitude, and social supports in improving the quality of life and delaying functional limitation and disability (Brandtstadter, 2006; A. L. Collins & Smyer, 2005; Fiksenbaum, Greenglass, & Eaton, 2006; McAuley et al., 2006).

Functional Capacity in Very Late Adulthood

Although persons who reach 85 years of age and older demonstrate resilience in the simple fact of their longevity, they continue to face an increased incidence of chronic illness and debilitation with age. The likelihood of living in a nursing home increases with age. Among nursing home residents, about 12% are between 65 and 74 years old, 32%

are between 75 and 84, and 45% are 85 and older (Federal Interagency Forum on Aging-Related Statistics, 2008). Many late-life adults enter a nursing home for a period of convalescence after hospitalization and then return to their home or another setting.

Although trend data from a six-wave National Long Term Care Survey indicated a high level of disability among older adults 85 and over, the rate of disability declined over a 15-year period from 62.0% in 1984 to 55.5% in 1999 (Spillman, 2003). There was no decline in limitations in **activities of daily living (ADLs)**, or basic self-care activities, but declines did occur in limitations in **instrumental activities of daily living (IADLs)**, which are more complex everyday tasks. (Exhibit 16.4 lists common ADLs and IADLs.)

Although late adulthood is a time of loss of efficiency in body systems and functioning, the body is an organism that repairs and restores itself as damage occurs. Those persons who live to be 85 and older may be blessed with a favorable genetic makeup. But they may also have found ways to compensate, to prevent, to restore, and to maintain other health-promoting behaviors. One cross-sectional study of individuals age 85 and over found that most report well-being despite their physical and social losses (C. L. Johnson & Barer, 1997). Most very late-life adults come to think of themselves in ways that fit their circumstances. They narrow the scope of their activities to those that are most cherished, and they carefully schedule their activities to make the best use of their energy and talents.

Sooner or later, however, most very late-life adults come to need some assistance with ADLs and IADLs. As a society, we have to grapple with the question of who will provide that assistance. Currently, most of the assistance is provided by family members. But as families grow smaller, fewer adult children exist to provide such care. A number of family theorists have begun to wonder how multigenerational families might adjust their relationships and better meet

Exhibit 16.4   Common Activities of Daily Living (ADLs) and Instrumental Activities of Daily Living (IADLs)

Activities of Daily Living
Bathing
Dressing
Walking a short distance
Shifting from a bed to a chair
Using the toilet
Eating
Instrumental Activities of Daily Living
Doing light housework
Doing the laundry
Using transportation
Handling finances
Using the telephone
Taking medications

long-distance caregiving needs (Cagle, 2008; Harrigan & Koerin, 2007; MetLife/National Alliance for Caregiving, 2004).

The Aging Brain and Neurodegenerative Diseases

Before reading this discussion of the most common neurodegenerative diseases, dementia and Parkinson's disease, you might find it helpful to review the discussion of the nervous system in Chapter 3. Several changes occur in the brain as we age. Between ages 20 and 90, the brain loses 5 to 10% of its weight (Palmer & Francis, 2006). The areas most affected by this decrease are the frontal lobe and the hippocampus. A general loss of neurons also occurs. The transmission of information between neurons through the neurotransmitters can also decrease in some brain regions as we age. Furthermore, there is less growth of new capillaries and a reduced blood flow due to narrowing arteries in the brain. Plaques and tangles develop in and around the neurons (see discussion of Alzheimer's disease below), and inflammation and damage by free radicals increase (NIA/NIH, 2009). The normal aging brain does not appear to lose synapses, however (Palmer & Francis, 2006).

The effects of these changes on task performance and memory are generally fairly small. Scores for task performance, for example, are similar for younger and older adults, when the older group is provided with additional time. Older adults can compensate and adapt well to many age-related brain changes. Part of this adaptation occurs through changes in the brain. Neuroimaging shows that some brain functions seem to get reorganized as the brain ages (Reuter-Lorenz, 2002). Imaging results point to a process in which the aging brain starts using areas of the two hemispheres that were previously not focusing on performing those tasks to compensate for age-related loss (S.-C. Li, 2006). Negative changes can also be offset by age-related overall improvements in some cognitive areas such as verbal knowledge or vocabulary (NIA/NIH, 2009). Other brain changes, however, can become more challenging. We will now turn to some common neurodegenerative diseases.

Dementia

Dementia is the term for brain disease in which memory and cognitive abilities deteriorate over time. It may be significantly unrecognized and undiagnosed in many older adults. One research team found that in Canada as many as 64% of community-dwelling older adults with dementia are not diagnosed as such (S. Sternberg, Wolfson, & Baumgarten, 2000). The estimates available suggest that the incidence of dementia is between 0.7 and 3.5 per 1,000 per year for persons ages 65 to 69, and doubles about every 5 years (Joshi & Morley, 2006). The risk of a person over 90 years old showing signs of severe mental decline caused by some form of dementia is around 60% (Helmchen et al., 1999). *Reversible dementia* is caused by factors such as drug and alcohol use, a brain tumor, hypothyroidism, syphilis, AIDS, or severe depression, and the cognitive decline is reversible if identified and treated early enough (Joshi & Morley, 2006). *Irreversible dementia* is not curable. In the advanced stages, the person may repeat the same words over and over again, may have problems using appropriate words, and may not recognize a spouse or other family members. At the same time, the person may still be able to recall and vividly describe events that happened many years ago. Epidemiological studies indicate that Alzheimer's disease is the most common form of dementia, responsible for 75% of cases (Nourhashemi, Sinclair, & Vellas, 2006).

The initial stage of cognitive dysfunction is called *age-associated memory impairment* (AAMI). It is followed by even greater memory loss and diagnosed as *mild cognitive impairment* (MCI), which may progress to dementia. The rate of decline in cognitive and functional skills is predictive of mortality among non-demented older adults (Schupf et al., 2005). AAMI and MCI involve primarily memory loss, whereas dementia results in disruption of daily living and difficulty functioning or inability to function normally.

MCIs have been thought not to constitute dementia, but to be a transitional stage between normal cognitive functioning and Alzheimer's disease. Studies have identified a subset of amnesic MCI as evidence of the early stage of Alzheimer's disease (J. C. Morris, 2006).

Risk factors for cognitive decline and dementia include genetic factors; female gender; medical conditions including but not limited to hypertension, heart disease, and diabetes; lifestyle choices such as smoking or substance abuse; and psychological and psychosocial factors such as low educational achievement, lack of physical activity, lack of social interaction and leisure activities, and excessive response to stress (Institute for the Study of Aging, 2001).

It is important to recognize the distinction between dementia and **delirium,** which is characterized by an impairment of consciousness. Unlike dementia, delirium has a sudden onset (a few hours or days), then follows a brief and fluctuating course that includes impairment of consciousness, and has the potential for improvement when the causes are treated. Prevalent causative factors of delirium include not only central nervous system disturbances, but also outside factors such as toxicity from medications, low oxygen states, infection, retention of urine and feces, undernutrition and dehydration, and metabolic conditions (Joshi & Morley, 2006). The prevalence of delirium is high among hospitalized elderly persons, with approximately 50% of hospital patients over age 65 experiencing an episode following surgery during their hospital stay, compared to 15 to 25% of other patients (Berthold, 2009). Delirium is very common for older persons admitted to intensive care and those transferred to nursing facilities (AGS Foundation for Health in Aging, 2009). It accounts for almost half of the hospital days for older adults (Inouye, 2006).

Alzheimer's disease, the most common type of dementia, is estimated to cost up to $148 billion annually in the United States (Alzheimer's Association, 2009). It is considered the third most expensive illness in the United States (Joshi & Morley, 2006). While the numbers of death caused by heart disease, stroke, and many forms of cancer saw significant reductions during the first half decade of this century, deaths caused by Alzheimer's disease increased by 47% (Alzheimer's Association, 2009). As populations around the world age, this is a trend that can be seen on the global level as well. Alzheimer's disease is characterized by a progression of stages. A general distinction is made among mild, moderate, and severe stages of Alzheimer's, although the description of the symptoms shows that the stages are not completely distinct. Exhibit 16.5 provides an overview of the three stages of Alzheimer's disease and the related symptoms.

Early detection and diagnosis of Alzheimer's disease is still difficult, but is now recommended. The time period from the diagnosis of Alzheimer's disease to death ranges from 3 to 4 years to up to 10 years, depending on the person's age. However, it is believed that the changes in the brain that cause Alzheimer's disease begin 10 or even 20 years before its onset. Consequently, there is a strong focus on trying to find biomarkers in cerebrospinal fluids, blood, or urine that may help to detect the presence of developing Alzheimer's.

In late-stage Alzheimer's disease, a person is often bedridden and has increasing health difficulties. The most common reason for death in the late stage is aspiration pneumonia, when the person can no longer swallow properly and fluids and food end up in the lungs (NIA/NIH, 2009). Mrs. Menzel would fall under the earlier phases of the disease and would be considered to have mild- to moderate-stage dementia. It is important that Margaret Davis receive good diagnostic services to determine whether her problems in functioning are related to Alzheimer's disease or some other type of dementia.

Despite significant progress in researching the disease and trying to find possible cures, much is still unknown. Research shows that brains of persons with Alzheimer's disease have an unusual accumulation of two substances: neurofibrillary tangles and amyloidal plaques. Several medications are available for persons with Alzheimer's, including donepezil (Aricept), galantamine (Razadyne), and rivastigmine (Exelon). All of these medications

Exhibit 16.5   Stages and Symptoms of Alzheimer's Disease

Stage of Alzheimer's Disease	Typical Symptoms
Mild or Early Stage	• Memory loss • Confusion about location of familiar places • Taking longer for routine daily tasks • Trouble handling money and bills • Loss of spontaneity • Mood and personality changes • Increased anxiety and aggression
Moderate Stage	• Increased memory loss and confusion • Decreased attention span • Inappropriate outbursts of anger and irritability • Problems recognizing friends and family members • Language problems • Difficulty reading, writing, working with numbers • Difficulty organizing thoughts • Inability to cope with new or unexpected situations • Restlessness, agitation, anxiety • Wandering, especially in late afternoon and at night • Repetitive statements or movements • Hallucinations, delusions, suspiciousness, paranoia • Loss of impulse control • Inability to carry out complex tasks requiring multiple steps
Severe or Late Stage	• Weight loss • Seizures • Skin infections • Difficulty swallowing • Groaning, moaning, grunting • Increased sleeping • Lack of bladder and bowel control

SOURCE: Based on NIA/NIH (2009, pp. 30–32).

can slow the progression of the disease, but none can reverse or cure it. Currently, no cure for the disease is on the horizon.

Parkinson's Disease

Parkinson's disease is a chronic and progressive movement disorder that primarily affects older adults over the age of 70 years. However, as in the case of movie and television star Michael J. Fox, it can afflict persons earlier in life as well. It is estimated that at least 500,000 persons in the United States have Parkinson's disease, but since it is hard to diagnose, the actual number may be significantly higher (NINDS, 2010).

Symptoms of Parkinson's include tremors (arms, legs, head), rigidity (stiffness of limbs), bradykinesia (trouble with and slowness of movement), and postural instability (insecure gait and balance). It can also cause language problems and cognitive difficulties, and in extreme cases can lead to a complete loss of movement. The disease is difficult to accurately diagnose, because some features of the normal aging process can be mistaken for Parkinson's disease. Tremors, slower movements, or insecure ways of walking all may be part of normal aging, symptoms of depression, or medication-induced side effects. Consequently, A. J. Hughes et al. (2002) found that a significant error rate with the diagnosis of Parkinson's disease exists. Even though Parkinson's disease is a neurodegenerative movement disorder, it often has mental health consequences. For example, cognitive impairment, dementia, depression, and sleep disorders may be associated with or co-occur with Parkinson's disease.

Parkinson's disease is caused by a gradual loss of cells that produce dopamine in a part of the brain called the basal ganglia, which is located at the base of the frontal brain area and is involved in coordinating the body's movements. The chemical dopamine is a neurotransmitter that transmits information about movement in the brain. A decrease in neurons that transmit information with the help of dopamine alters the processing of information related to physical movement (Playfer, 2006). Losing neurons in the substantia nigra, which is a part of the basal ganglia, is part of normal aging. We are born with 400,000 neurons in this part of the brain, and at age 60 we have about 250,000 neurons left. However, research indicates that persons afflicted with Parkinson's disease may have as little as 60,000 to 120,000 neurons present in this part of the brain (Palmer & Francis, 2006).

Several drugs are available to address Parkinson's disease. A combination of these drugs with physical rehabilitation has shown great success in reducing the symptoms of the disease (Playfer, 2006). One group of medications works on increasing the dopamine levels in the brain. Levodopa is an example of such a drug. It is the most common medication for treating Parkinson's disease, and has been used with success for more than 40 years (Playfer, 2006). A second type of drug mimics dopamine (dopamine antagonists) or inhibits dopamine breakdown (NINDS, 2010). A more recent approach to treating the effects of Parkinson's disease is deep brain stimulation. Using this method, a tiny electrode is surgically implanted in the brain. Through a pulse generator, this implant then stimulates the brain and stops many of the symptoms (NINDS, 2009). Results of deep brain simulation show a positive effect on cognitive functions (Zangaglia et al., 2009).

PSYCHOLOGICAL CHANGES IN LATE ADULTHOOD

Without good longitudinal research, it has been difficult to understand psychological changes in late adulthood. Because cross-sectional research cannot control for cohort effects, we need to exercise great caution in interpreting findings of age differences in human psychology. Three areas that have received a lot of attention are changes in personality, changes in intellectual functioning, and mental health and mental disorders in late adulthood. The Berlin Aging Study, one of the largest studies of older adults, included numerous measures of psychological aging. Findings suggest that one should not think about a uniform process of psychological aging (Baltes & Mayer, 1999). Rather, changes in areas such as cognition, social relationships, self, and personality occur to a large extent independent of each other.

Personality Changes

A couple of theorists have addressed the issue of how the personality changes as individuals age. As noted in Chapter 15, Erik Erikson's (1950) life span theory proposes that the struggle of middle adulthood is one of generativity versus stagnation (refer back to Exhibit 4.11 in Chapter 4 for an overview of Erikson's stages of psychosocial development). You may recall that generativity is the ability to transcend personal interests to guide the next generation. The struggle of late adulthood, according to Erikson, is *ego integrity versus ego despair*. **Integrity** involves the ability to make peace with one's "one and only life cycle" and to find unity with the world. Erikson (1950) also noted that from middle adulthood on, adults participate in a "wider social radius," with an increasing sense of social responsibility and interconnectedness. Some support was found for this notion in a 50-year follow-up study of adult personality development (Haan, Millsap, & Hartka, 1986). The researchers found that in late adulthood, three aspects of personality increased significantly: outgoingness, self-confidence, and warmth. A more recent study examining the association of chronological aging with positive psychological change supported the idea that some forms of positive psychological change are normative across the life span, that older people know clearly what values are most important, and that they pursue these objectives with a more mature sense of purpose and ownership (Sheldon, 2006).

George Vaillant (2002) has also considered the personality changes of late adulthood. He found that for all three of the cohorts in the Study of Adult Development, mastery of generativity tripled the likelihood that men and women would find their seventies to be a time of joy instead of despair. He also proposed that another life task or role, Keeper of the Meaning, comes between generativity and integrity. The *Keeper of the Meaning* takes on the task of passing on the traditions of the past to the next generation. In addition, Vaillant (2002) suggests that humans have "elegant unconscious coping mechanisms that make lemonade out of lemons" (p. 91). As discussed in Chapter 15, Vaillant reports that with age and experience, individuals tend to use more adaptive coping mechanisms. This idea is supported by Fiksenbaum et al. (2006), who see successful coping as an essential aspect of aging.

Vaillant (2002) finds support for the proposition that coping mechanisms mature with age. He found that over a 25-year period, his sample of Harvard men made significant increases in their use of altruism and humor and significant decreases in their use of projection and passive aggression. Overall, he found that 19 of 67 Harvard men made significant gains in use of mature coping mechanisms between the ages of 50 and 75, a total of 28 men were already making strong use of mature mechanisms at age 50, use of mature mechanisms stayed the same

for 17 men, and only 4 out of the 67 men used less mature coping mechanisms with advancing age. Vaillant (1993) in part attributed this maturation in coping to the presence of positive social support and the quality of the men's marriages. These findings are consistent with results from another longitudinal study of aging that found that in late adulthood, participants became more forgiving, more able to meet adversity cheerfully, less prone to take offense, and less prone to venting frustrations on others (McCrae & Costa, 1990). Langle and Probst (2004) suggest that this might be the result of older adults being required to face fundamental questions of existence, because coping with the vicissitudes of life loom ever larger during aging.

In Chapter 15, you read that there are controversies about whether personality changes or remains stable in middle adulthood. There are similar controversies in the literature on late adulthood. Findings from the large-scale Berlin Aging Study indicate that, on the whole, self and personality change only a little with age (Staudinger, Freund, Linden, & Maas, 1999). Vaillant (2002), on the other hand, found evidence for both change and continuity. He suggests that personality has two components: temperament and character. Temperament, he concludes, does not change, and adaptation in adolescence is one of the best predictors of adaptation in late adulthood. Studies on depression, anxiety, and suicidal ideation in late adulthood support this idea that coping and adaptation in adolescence are a good predictor of later-life temperament (Cheung & Todd-Oldehaver, 2006; T. R. Lynch, Cheavens, Morse, & Rosenthal, 2004; Wickrama et al., 2005). Conversely, character, or adaptive style, does change, influenced by both experiences with the environment and the maturation process. Vaillant attributes this change in adaptive style over time to the fact that many genes are "programmed to promote plasticity," or the capacity to be shaped by experience. One personality change that was noted in Chapter 15 to occur in middle age is gender role expansion, with women becoming more dominant and men becoming more passive. This pattern has also been noted in late adulthood.

Intellectual Changes, Learning, and Memory

Answering the question about how our intellectual capabilities change in late adulthood is a complex and difficult task. One often-cited study on age-related intellectual changes found that fluid intelligence declines with age, but crystallized intelligence increases (J. L. Horn, 1982). **Fluid intelligence** is the capacity for abstract reasoning and involves such things as the ability to "respond quickly, to memorize quickly, to compute quickly with no error, and to draw rapid inferences from visual relationships" (Vaillant, 2002, p. 238). **Crystallized intelligence** is based on accumulated learning and includes the ability to reflect and recognize (e.g., similarities and differences, vocabulary) rather than to recall and remember. This theory has received much criticism, however, because it was based on a cross-sectional comparison of two different age groups who may have had very different educational experiences. Researchers who followed a single cohort over time found no general decline of intellectual abilities in late adulthood (Schaie, 1984). Rather, they found considerable individual variation. Other longitudinal research has found that fluid intelligence declines earlier than crystallized intelligence, which has been found to remain the same at 80 as at 30 in most healthy older adults (Vaillant, 2002).

Learning and memory are closely related; we must first learn before we can retain and recall. Memory performance, like the impact of aging on intelligence, demonstrates a wide degree of variability. One study suggests that the effects of aging on the underlying brain processes related to retention and recall are dependent on individual memory performance, and the researchers call for further investigation of performance variability in normal aging (Duarte, Ranganath, Trujillo, & Knight, 2006). When we process information, it moves through several stages of memory (Bjorklund & Bee, 2008; Palsson, Johansson, Berg, & Skoog, 2000; Winkler & Cowan, 2005):

- *Sensory memory.* New information is initially recorded in sensory memory. Unless the person deliberately pays attention to the information, it is lost within less than a second. There seems to be little age-related change in this type of memory.
- *Primary memory.* If the information is retained in sensory memory, it is passed on to the primary memory, also called recent or short-term memory. Primary memory has only limited capacity; it is used to organize and temporarily hold information. *Working memory* refers to the process of actively reorganizing and manipulating information that is still in primary memory. Although there are some age-related declines in working memory, there seems to be little age-related decline in primary memory.
- *Secondary memory.* Information is permanently stored in secondary memory. This is the memory we use daily when we remember an event or memorize facts for an exam. The ability to recall seems to decline with age, but recognition capabilities stay consistent.
- *Tertiary memory.* Information is stored for extended periods, several weeks or months, in tertiary memory, also called remote memory. This type of memory experiences little age-related changes.

Another way to distinguish memory is between intentional and incidental memory. **Intentional memory** relates to events that you plan to remember. **Incidental memory** relates to facts you have learned without the intention to retain and recall. Research suggests that incidental memory declines with old age, but intentional memory does not (Direnfeld & Roberts, 2006).

Another element of intellectual functioning studied in relation to aging is *brain plasticity*, the ability of the brain to change in response to stimuli. Research indicates that even older people's brains can rewire themselves to compensate for lost functioning in particular regions, and in some instances, may even be able to generate new cells. As a result, people are capable of lifelong learning, despite myths to the contrary. Adult education and intellectual stimulation in later life may actually help maintain cognitive health. Not only are humans capable of lifelong learning, but the stimulation associated with learning new things may also reduce the risk of impairments (Institute for the Study of Aging, 2001).

Mental Health and Mental Disorders

A number of longitudinal studies indicate that, without brain disease, mental health improves with age (Vaillant, 2002). Older adults have a lower prevalence of mental disorders than adults in young and middle age. This finding is supported by virtually all epidemiological studies ever conducted (Bengtson, Gans, Putney, & Silverstein, 2009). Although older adults are more predisposed to certain brain diseases such as dementia, these disorders are not a part of the normal aging process. The prevalence of mental disorders in residents of long-term care facilities is high, however, and many institutionalized individuals with mental disorders may not receive all the needed care from mental health professionals (Conn, 2001). However, many of the more common mental disorders associated with older age can be diagnosed and treated in elderly persons much as they would be in earlier adulthood (Aldwin & Gilmer, 2004). Given the aging of the population, the need for gero-psychiatric research and clinical practice is likely to increase.

SOCIAL ROLE TRANSITIONS AND LIFE EVENTS OF LATE ADULTHOOD

Transitions are at the center of the life course perspective, and people experience many of them, some very abrupt, in late adulthood. Retirement, death of a spouse or partner, institutionalization, and one's own death are among the most stressful events in human existence, and they are clustered in late adulthood. Despite the concern of the impact of the loss of social roles, studies have demonstrated that older adults generally adapt to late-life role transitions and maintain emotional well-being (Hinrichsen & Clougherty, 2006).

Social isolation is considered to be a powerful risk factor not only for the development of cognitive and intellectual decline in very late adulthood, but also for physical illness (McInnis-Dittrich, 2009). A sense of connectedness with family and friends can be achieved in person; on the phone; and more recently via e-mail, chat rooms, blogs, social networking sites, and Skype. The focus in this section is on relationships with people; however, remember that pets, plants, and other connections with nature bring comfort to any age group, including older adults.

Families in Later Life

As you saw with the case studies of Ruby Johnson, Joseph and Elizabeth Menzel, Margaret Davis, and Bina Patel, families continue to play an important role in the life of an older person. With increased longevity, however, the post–empty nest and post-retirement period lengthens (F. Walsh, 2005). Thus, the significance of the marital or partner relationship increases in late adulthood. As older individuals are released from their responsibilities as parents and members of the workforce, they are able to spend more time together. Overall satisfaction with the quality of life seems to be higher for married elderly individuals than for the widowed or never married. For married couples, the spouse is the most important source of emotional, social, and personal support in times of illness and need of care.

Thirty percent (9.7 million) of noninstitutionalized U.S. older adults live alone. The most common living arrangement for men over 65 is with their wife; in 2003, 73% of men over 65 lived with their spouse (Administration on Aging, 2005). The picture is different for older women, who are twice as likely as older men to be living alone. By age 75, over one half of women are living alone, because, on average, men die earlier than women.

Living arrangements for older adults vary by race and ethnicity in the United States. In 2004, the proportion of White and Black women living alone was similar, about 41%. Fewer older Hispanic women lived alone (25%), and even fewer Asian and Pacific Islander women lived alone (21%) (Administration on Aging, 2005). Older Black

Photo 16.3 As older adults are released from responsibilities as parents and members of the workforce, they are able to spend more time together.

and Hispanic women are less likely than White women to live with a spouse (Himes, 2001). Older Asian men and women are more likely to live with relatives than are older men and women of other ethnic groups (Federal Agency Forum on Aging-Related Statistics, 2004). A complex relationship that involves culture, socioeconomic status, and individual personality has to be considered in accounting for the ethnic and racial differences in living arrangements. Drawing inferences based solely on cultural differences is overly simplistic given the use of racial categories devised by U.S. federal agencies as proxies for cultural identity.

Family relationships have been found to be closer and more central for older women than for older men. Mother–daughter relationships have been found to be particularly strong (Silverstein & Bengtson, 2001). In addition, friendship appears to be a more important protective factor for older women than for older men. Friendships have been associated with lower levels of cognitive impairment and increased quality-of-life satisfaction (Beland, Zunzunegui, Alvarado, Otero, & del Ser, 2005).

Those who were never married constitute a very small group of the current elderly population. It will further decrease for some time as the cohort of baby boomers, with its unusually high rate of marriage, enters late adulthood (Bjorklund & Bee, 2008). However, the proportion of elderly singles and those never married will probably increase toward the middle of the next century, because the cohort that follows the baby boomers has had an increase in the number of individuals remaining single.

Singlehood due to divorce in late adulthood is increasing, however, as divorce is becoming more socially accepted in all population groups. As in all stages of life, divorce in later life may entail financial problems, especially for older women, and it may be especially difficult to recuperate financially post-retirement. Divorce also results in a change of kinship ties and social networks, which are important sources of support in later life. The incidence of remarriage after divorce or widowhood is significantly higher for older men than for older women. The fact that there are more elderly women than men contributes to this trend. Even if older adults are not themselves divorced, they may need to adjust to the enlarged and complicated family networks that come from the divorces and remarriages of their children and grandchildren (F. Walsh, 2005).

One group of older adults that has often been neglected in the discussion of late adulthood is elderly gay men and lesbians. Estimates of the proportion of gay men and lesbians among elderly persons are similar to those for younger age groups (Teitelman, 1995). Being faced not only with ageist but also with homophobic attitudes, elderly gay men and lesbians may be confronted by a double jeopardy. Eligibility requirements for many services to elderly adults continue to be based on a norm of heterosexuality. Although growing in number, services catering directly to older gay or lesbian persons are still few and far between in many parts of the country. But the most problematic aspect of being an elderly homosexual may be the lack of societal sanction to grieve openly when the partner dies (Barranti & Cohen, 2001; Humphreys & Quam, 1998; Teitelman, 1995).

Sibling relationships play a special role in the life of older adults. Siblings share childhood experiences and are often the personal tie with the longest duration. Siblings are typically not the primary source of personal care, but they often play a role in providing emotional support. Sibling relationships often change over the life course, with closer ties in pre-adulthood and later life and less involvement in early and middle adulthood. Women's ties with siblings have been found to be more involved than those of men (Bjorklund & Bee, 2008).

Relationships with children and grandchildren are also significant in late adulthood. The "myth of the golden age" in the United States suggests that in the past, older people were more likely to live in a multigenerational family, be well taken care of, and have valued emotional and economic roles. This heartwarming picture is a myth, however, because people died earlier, and multigenerational families were less prevalent than they are in our era of increased longevity (Hareven, 2000). Furthermore, even in the past, elderly individuals valued independent living, and they typically resided in separate households from their adult children, although they usually lived in close proximity.

In fact, multigenerational families have become more common in recent years, resulting in more interactions and exchanges across generations. Contrary to common belief, intergenerational exchanges between adult children and elderly parents are not one-directional. Children often take care of their elderly parents, but healthy elderly persons also provide significant assistance to their adult children, as is the case with Ms. Johnson. Research on elderly parents living with their adult children suggests that for the young-old, more assistance flows from the elderly parents to the adult children than the other way around (Speare & Avery, 1993). In another study (Ward, Logan, & Spitze, 1992), older parents living with their adult children reported doing more than three quarters of the housework. Patterns of co-residence between parents and adult children vary by race. The proportion of multigenerational relationships that involve parents living with adult children tends to be higher among some families of color, especially African Americans (Hooyman & Kiyak, 2008). Also, as in Bina Patel's case, families with a collectivist heritage prefer to have elderly parents reside with their grown children.

Grandparenthood

In some cases, older people such as Ms. Johnson are assuming full responsibility for parenting their grandchildren, because their children have problems with drugs, HIV infection or other major illness, or crime. Beginning in the early 1990s, the U.S. Census Bureau began to note an increasing number of children under 18 living with grandparents, rising from 3% of children under age 18 in 1970 to 5.5% in 1997 (Bryson & Casper, 1999). About 1.53 million older people in the United States live in a household in which a grandchild is present. Approximately 50% of this number reside in parent-maintained households (Administration on Aging, 2005). A little over one quarter are primary caregivers for their grandchildren (U.S. Census Bureau, 2004b). This has been viewed by some as a negative trend, but there is no inherent reason why grandchildren receiving care from grandparents is problematic, and, indeed, across time and place, grandparents have sometimes been seen as appropriate caregivers. Many cultural groups often have multigenerational households that are not predicated on dysfunction within the family. Large percentages of Asian, Hispanic, and Black elders live with family members, not alone or with their spouse. It does appear, however, that the current trend is influenced by the growth of drug use among parents, teen pregnancy, and the rapid rise of single-parent families (Bryson & Casper, 1999). As a result, new physical, emotional, and financial demands are placed on grandparents with already limited resources. Some speculate that custodial grandparents may also be caring for their own impaired adult child, because two thirds of grandparent-headed households have a member of the "skipped generation" in residence (Burnette, 1999). On the other hand, Margaret Davis's granddaughter, Tiffany, is an important part of Mrs. Davis's caregiving system.

Grandparenthood is a normative part of the family life cycle, but the majority of grandparents do not co-reside with their grandchildren. The timing of grandparenthood influences the way it is experienced and the roles and responsibilities that a grandparent will take on. Predominant, many first-time grandparents are middle-aged adults in their early fifties. However, the census data from 2004 indicate that grandparenthood has been documented as beginning as young as age 30 (U.S. Census Bureau, 2004b). Others do not become grandparents until they are 70 or 80 years old. Because individuals are enjoying longer lives, more and more people assume the role of grandparent, and they assume it for more years. Many spend the same number of years being a grandparent as being a parent of a child under the age of 18. As life expectancy has continued to increase, the number of great-grandparents is also expected to grow over the next decades.

In general, it appears that being a grandparent is a welcome and gratifying role for most individuals, but it may increase in significance and meaning for an older person. Family researchers have begun to take a strong interest in the grandparenting role, but little is actually known about grandparent–grandchild relationships. A classic study of middle-class grandparents in the early 1960s identified several styles of grandparents: formal grandparents, fun seekers, distant figures, surrogate parents, and mentors (Neugarten & Weinstein, 1964). More recently, another research team found five types of grandparents in their study of 451 families: influential grandparents, supportive grandparents, passive grandparents, authority-oriented grandparents, and detached grandparents (M. Mueller, Wilhelm, & Elder, 2002).

Think about your relationships with your grandparents. How would you characterize their grandparenting styles? Did you have different types of relationships with different grandparents? Did your grandparents have different types of relationships with different grandchildren? What might explain any differences?

Work and Retirement

Until the 20th century, the average worker retired about 3 years before death. In 1890, 90% of men in the United States over age 70 were still in the workforce. Increased worker productivity, mass longevity, and Social Security legislation changed that situation, however, and by 1986, only 31% of 65-year-old men were in the workforce. As of 2004, only 14.4% of U.S. adults 65 and older were still in the workforce—18% of men and 10% of women. However, in the age group 65 to 74, 25% of men and 15% of women were still in the labor force (U.S. Census Bureau, 2004b). In the past century, with the combined impact of increased longevity and earlier retirement, the average number of years spent in retirement before death is almost 15 (Vaillant, 2002).

> How do these social trends affect the late-adult phase of the life course?

Retirement patterns vary with social class. Vaillant (2002) found that only 20% of his sample of surviving inner-city men were still in the workforce at age 65, but half of the sample of Harvard men were still working full-time at 65. The inner-city men retired, on average, 5 years earlier than the Harvard men. Poor health often leads to earlier retirement among less advantaged adults (Sterns & Huyck, 2001). In addition, higher levels of education make workers eligible for more sedentary jobs, which are a better fit with the declining energy levels in late adulthood (Vaillant, 2002).

Data about retirement have been based on the work patterns of men, probably because women's labor force involvement has been less uniform. Current trends reflect the history of women's involvement in the workforce, with many "baby boomers" having never worked or worked intermittently. A trend was noted in the early 1990s, however, in which labor force participation rates for men over 50 were falling while labor force participation rates of women over 50 were increasing. The greatest increase of women workers in the 55 to 61 age range occurred between 1963 and 2003, up from 44% to 63%. During the same period, the labor force participation of women increased from 29% to 39% among women ages 62 to 64 and from 17% to 23%

for women ages 65 to 69. The gap between male and female labor participation has narrowed from 46% in 1963 to 12% in 2003 (Federal Interagency Forum on Aging-Related Statistics, 2004). The decline in labor force participation of men can be accounted for by a number of factors, including eligibility for retirement at age 62 and greater wealth generated by workers, consequently permitting retirement (Federal Interagency Forum on Aging-Related Statistics, 2004).

The "appropriate" age for retirement in the United States is currently understood to be age 65. This cultural understanding has been shaped by Social Security legislation enacted in 1935. However, the 1983 Social Security Amendments included a provision for a gradual increase in the age at which a retired person could begin receiving Social Security retirement benefits. Exhibit 16.6 shows the schedule for increasing the age for receiving full benefits. In arguing for this

Exhibit 16.6   Amended Age to Receive Full Social Security Benefits (1983)

Year of Birth	Full Retirement Age
1937 and earlier	65
1938	65 and 2 months
1939	65 and 4 months
1940	65 and 6 months
1941	65 and 8 months
1942	65 and 10 months
1943–1954	66
1955	66 and 2 months
1956	66 and 4 months
1957	66 and 6 months
1958	66 and 8 months
1959	66 and 10 months
1960 and later	67

SOURCE: Social Security Administration (2009).

legislative change, members of Congress noted increased longevity and improved health among older adults (Federal Interagency Forum on Aging-Related Statistics, 2004). In the national conversation about the future fiscal health of the Social Security program, some policy analysts are suggesting raising the age for Social Security eligibility even higher.

Certainly, some older individuals continue to work for many years after they reach age 65. Individuals who continue to work fall into two groups: those who could afford to retire but choose to continue working and those who continue to work because of a financial need. Because economic status in old age is influenced by past employment patterns and the resultant retirement benefits, the second group consists of individuals who had lower-paying employment throughout their lives. This group also includes elderly divorced or widowed women who depended on their husband's retirement income and are now faced with poverty or near poverty. Lifelong gender inequality in wages contributes to inequality in pension and retirement funds (Wilmoth & Longino, 2006). Ms. Ruby Johnson continues to be employed on a part-time basis out of financial necessity.

There are many ways of retiring from the workforce. Some individuals cease work completely, but others continue with part-time or part-year employment. Others may retire for a period and then reenter the labor market. Retirement is a socially accepted way to end an active role in the workforce. Most persons retire because of advancing age, mandatory retirement policies, health problems, a desire to pursue other interests, or simply a wish to relax and lead the life of a retiree.

Individuals vary in whether they view retirement as something to dread or something to look forward to. Most often, however, retirement is a positive experience. Vaillant (2002) found no evidence in his longitudinal research that retirement is bad for physical health. For every person who indicated that retirement was bad for her or his health, four retirees indicated that retirement had improved their health. Vaillant noted four conditions under which retirement is perceived as stressful (p. 221):

1. Retirement was involuntary or unplanned.

2. There are no other means of financial support besides salary.

3. Work provided an escape from an unhappy home life.

4. Retirement was precipitated by preexisting bad health.

These conditions are present among only a fraction of retirees, but social workers may be more likely to come into contact with these retirees.

Vaillant (2002) found that retirement has generally been rewarding for many of the participants of his study. Four basic activities appear to make retirement rewarding:

1. Replacing work mates with another social network

2. Rediscovering how to play

3. Engaging in creative endeavors

4. Continuing lifelong learning

Vaillant (2002) also suggests that retirement would be less stressful if the culture provided rituals for the transition, as it does for other life transitions. While some people with a long tenure in a job are given retirement parties by their employers, he found little evidence of significant rituals in his research.

Caregiving and Care Receiving

As retirement unfolds, declining health may usher in a period of intensive need for care. The majority of older adults with disabilities live in the community and receive predominantly informal care from spouses, children, and extended family. The percentage of older adults receiving informal or formal caregiving actually declined from 15% in 1984 to 11% in 1999. Over 90% of those older adults with disabilities who received care between 1984 and 1999 received primarily informal caregiving in combination with some formal caregiving. Two thirds of this group received only informal caregiving (Federal Interagency Forum on Aging-Related Statistics, 2004). Eighty percent of older adults who need long-term care receive that care in the community rather than in an institution. Women are the primary source of caregiving in old age (F. Walsh, 2005). As noted earlier, daughters are more likely than sons to take care of elderly parents. Moreover, elderly men tend to be married and thus are more likely to have a wife available as caregiver.

Caregiving can be an around-the-clock task and often leaves caregivers overwhelmed and exhausted. Mr. Menzel is a good example of the burden that can be experienced by an elderly spouse. Programs that can assist caregivers like him in reducing their exceptional levels of stress have received much attention. Many programs combine educational components—for example, information about and training in adaptive coping skills—with ongoing support through the opportunity to share personal feelings and experiences. Respite programs for caregivers are also available. In-home respite programs provide assistance through a home health aide or a visiting nurse. Community-based respite is often provided through adult day care and similar programs.

Based on their research on the topic, Rhonda Montgomery and Karl Kosloski (2000, 2009) developed a caregiver identity theory. Their framework consists of seven "career markers," stages that individuals typically move through in their career as caregivers. The first marker signifies the time when the dependency situation begins. One person needs assistance with routine activities and another person starts performing caregiving tasks. The second marker is reached when the self-definition as a caregiver begins; that is, the person incorporates the role of caregiver into his or her personal and social identity. The third marker is characterized by the performance of personal care tasks. At this time, caregiving family members begin to evaluate whether to continue as caregivers or seek alternatives. Although spousal caregivers may already see

themselves as such after reaching the second marker, they now begin to unambiguously identify with their new role. The next marker is reached when outside assistance is sought and formal service use is considered. Whether outside help is requested depends on factors such as seeing one's personal situation as deficient, recognizing the potential service as addressing that deficiency, and the psychological and monetary cost-benefit of using the service (Kosloski & Montgomery, 1994). Considering nursing home placement is the fifth marker. Although the institutional placement is considered at earlier phases, the decision now is more imminent. Nursing home placement is the sixth marker. When caregiving becomes too overwhelming, a nursing home placement may be pursued. Caregiving often continues after a family member enters a nursing home. Although caregivers are relieved from direct care, they continue to be involved in the emotional and social aspects of care in the nursing home (Naleppa, 1996). Although many individuals will spend some time in a nursing home, others never enter such an institution and die at home. The final marker in Montgomery and Kosloski's (2000) caregiver identity theory is the termination of the caregiver role. This may occur due to recovery or death of the care recipient or through "quitting" as a caregiver.

Stress and burden are not experienced only by the caregiver. The care recipient also experiences significant strain. Requiring care is a double loss: The person has lost the capability to perform the tasks for which he or she now needs assistance, and the person has also lost independence. Having to rely on others for activities that one has carried out independently throughout one's adult life can be the source of tremendous emotional and psychological stress. Some individuals respond by emotional withdrawal; others become agitated and start blaming others for their situation. The levels of stress that an elderly care recipient may experience depend on "(1) personal and situational characteristics of the elderly recipient; (2) characteristics of the caregiver; (3) social support provided to caregiver and recipient; (4) aspects of the relationship between family caregiver and recipient; and (5) characteristics of caregiving" (Brubaker, Gorman, & Hiestand, 1990, p. 268).

Think of Joseph Menzel. He has served as both caregiver and care recipient. His stress in both roles was probably amplified by culturally defined norms promoting independence, individuality, and pride. Helping someone like him to overcome his uneasiness about receiving assistance may include asking him to verbalize his worries, listening to him express his feelings, and looking together at ways that he could overcome his uneasiness in small steps. Margaret Davis's daughter is proud to say, "We take care of our own," but she worries about the family's economic resources to provide the level of care needed.

Institutionalization

One myth of aging is that older individuals are being abandoned and neglected by their families and being pushed into nursing homes to get them out of the way. Fewer elderly persons are institutionalized than we generally assume, but the risk for entering a nursing home increases significantly with age. During the past decade, the percentage of older people living in nursing homes actually declined from 5.1% in 1990 to 4.5% in 2000, but the total number has increased due to the rapid growth in the aged population (Federal Interagency Forum on Aging-Related Statistics, 2004). Only 1.1% of older adults between the ages of 65 and 74, compared with 18.2% of those 85 and older, live in nursing homes. In addition, 5% of older adults live in self-described senior housing, which often has supportive services (Administration on Aging, 2005). There have been many efforts to reduce disability that can result in nursing home placement (Agency for Healthcare Research and Quality, 2006). It remains to be seen whether Ms. Johnson, Mr. or Mrs. Menzel, Margaret Davis, or Bina Patel will spend some time before death in a nursing home.

Most children and spouses do not use nursing homes as a dumping ground for their elderly relatives. They turn to nursing homes only after they have exhausted all other alternatives. Nor is institutionalization a single, sudden event. It is a process that starts with the need to make a decision, continues through the placement itself, and ends in the adjustment to the placement (Naleppa, 1996).

Researchers have taken a close look at the factors that predict a person's entry into a nursing home. Among the most important are the condition and needs of the elderly individual. Functional and behavioral deficits, declining health, previous institutionalization, and advanced age all contribute to the decision to enter a nursing home. Family characteristics that are good predictors of institutionalization include the need for 24-hour caregiving, caregiver feelings of distress, caregiver health and mental status, and caregiving environment (Naleppa, 1996). Marital status is a strong predictor of institutionalization for elderly men. Unmarried and never married men have the highest risk of entering a nursing home (Dolinsky & Rosenwaike, 1988; Hanley, Alecxih, Wiener, & Kennell, 1990). Individuals without a spouse who live alone in the community are at a higher risk of entering a nursing home than those living with spouses, family members, or friends (Montgomery & Kosloski, 1994). There is evidence that very late-life adults in the United States are institutionalized more often for social reasons than for medical reasons (Hooyman & Kiyak, 2008). One reason for this is that approximately 1 in 5 women 80 and older has been childless throughout her life or has outlived her children. In addition, baby boomers and their children tended to have more divorces and fewer children, decreasing the caregiving options for their parents and grandparents (Hooyman & Kiyak, 2008).

The placement decision itself is emotionally stressful for all involved and can be viewed as a family crisis. Yet it can be considered a normative part of the family life cycle. Because many nursing home placements are arranged from the hospital for an elderly individual who entered the hospital expecting to return home, many people may not have time to come to terms with the need for institutionalization. For those who unexpectedly enter a nursing home from the hospital, it may be advisable to arrange a brief visit home to say farewell to their familiar environment, if feasible. While society has developed rituals for many occasions, unfortunately no rituals exist for this difficult life transition.

Entering a nursing home means losing control and adjusting to a new environment. How well a person adjusts depends on many factors. If the elderly individual sees entering the nursing home in a favorable light and feels in control, adjustment may proceed well. Frequent visits by relatives and friends also help in the adaptation to the new living arrangement. Despite the commonly held belief that families do not visit their relatives, continued family involvement seems to be the norm. About two thirds of nursing home residents receive one or more visitors a week, and only a very small group is never visited (Bitzan & Kruzich, 1990).

Prior to nursing home placement, some older adults use other community resources when they begin to have trouble caring for themselves. Some attend adult day care during the day and receive family care in the evening. Others enter assisted living facilities, which provide private or semi-private apartments while also offering assistance with medications, meals, personal care, and some therapeutic services. Other than skilled nursing care reimbursed by Medicare and other health insurance, the majority of assistance that people need must be paid for privately. Financing is a major problem for low-income and even many middle-income people.

Critical Thinking Questions 16.2

George Vaillant suggests that his longitudinal research indicates that humans have "elegant unconscious coping mechanisms that make lemonade out of lemons." Think of a late-life adult whom you know who has or is making lemonade out of lemons. What challenges has this person faced in earlier life or in late adulthood? What is it about this late-life adult that makes you think of her or him as making lemonade out of lemons? What types of coping mechanisms do you think this person uses to deal with adversities?

THE SEARCH FOR PERSONAL MEANING

As adults become older, they spend more time reviewing their life achievements and searching for personal meaning. In gerontology, the concept of **life review** as a developmental task of late adulthood was introduced by Robert Butler (1963). He theorized that this self-reflective review of one's life is not a sign of losing short-term memory, as had been assumed. Rather, life review is a process of evaluating and making sense of one's life. It includes a reinterpretation of past experiences and unresolved conflicts. Newer forms of clinical interventions rooted in narrative theory underscore the importance of providing structure, coherence, and opportunity for making meaning of one's experience that "storying" provides (A. Morgan, 2000). Social workers can influence a more positive outcome of a life review through relationship, empathic listening and reflection, witnessing to the story, and providing alternative reframes and interpretations of past events. For example, promoting a story of resiliency as a lifelong process helps to reframe stories that support successful mastery of challenges and compensatory recovery in the face of adversity (O'Leary & Bhaju, 2006; Wadensten, 2005).

The life review can lead to diverse outcomes, including depression, acceptance, or satisfaction (Butler, 1987). If the life review is successful, it leads the individual to personal wisdom and inner peace. But the reassessment of one's life may also lead to despair and depression. This idea that the process of a life review may lead to either acceptance or depression is similar to the eighth stage of Erikson's theory of adult development; through the life review, the individual tries to work through the conflict between ego integrity (accepting oneself and seeing one's life as meaningful) and despair (rejecting oneself and one's life).

The ways in which individuals review their lives differ considerably. Some undertake a very conscious effort of assessing and reevaluating their achievements; for others, the effort may be subtle and not very conscious. Regardless of how they pursue it, life review is believed to be a common activity for older adults that occurs across cultures and time.

The concept of **reminiscence** is closely related to life review. Most older persons have a remarkable ability to recall past events. They reminisce about the past and tell their stories to anyone who is willing to listen, but they also reminisce when they are on their own. This reminiscing can serve several functions (Sherman, 1991):

- Reminiscing may be an enjoyable activity that can lift the spirits of the listener and of the person telling the story.
- Some forms of reminiscing are directed at enhancing a person's image of self, as when individuals focus on their accomplishments.
- Reminiscing may help the person cope with current or future problems, letting her or him retreat to the safe place of a comfortable memory or recall ways of coping with past stressors.
- Reminiscing can assist in the life review, as a way to achieve ego integrity.

Reminiscing combines past, present, and future orientations (Sherman, 1991). It includes the past, which is when the reviewed events occurred. However, the construction of personal meaning is an activity that is also oriented to the present and the future, providing purpose and meaning to life. One study examined the association between reminiscence frequency, reminiscence enjoyment or regret, and psychological health outcomes. The study found that high frequency of reminiscence and having regret were associated with poor psychological health. Reminiscence enjoyment, conversely, was positively associated with psychological health outcomes (Mckee et al., 2005). The *Erzählcafé* that Elizabeth Menzel visits tries to incorporate this by regularly including group activities that foster reminiscing in a safe, positive, and fun environment.

Another factor in the search for personal meaning is religious or spiritual activity. Cross-sectional research has consistently found that humans become more religious or spiritual in late adulthood (G. Gallup & Lindsay, 1999). Vaillant's

(2002) longitudinal research did not find support for this idea, however. He found that the importance of religion and spirituality, on average, did not change in the lives of his study participants over time. He suggests that the cross-sectional finding may be picking up a cohort effect, and that subsequent cohorts of older adults may be less religious or spiritual in adolescence and young adulthood than the current cohort of older adults was. What Vaillant fails to address is whether his cohort reaches a higher faith stage in late adulthood, as developmental theorists would suggest.

There is some evidence that spirituality late in life is often associated with loss (Armatowski, 2001). According to Armatowski (p. 75), over time, losses accumulate in the following areas:

- *Relationships:* to children, spouses and partners, friends, and others
- *Status and role:* in family, work, and society
- *Health:* stamina, mobility, hearing, vision, and other physical and cognitive functions
- *Control and independence:* finances, housing, health care, and other decision-making arenas

K. Fischer (1993) suggests that for older adults, the meaning of spirituality often takes the form of these five themes of advice:

1. Embrace the moment.
2. Find meaning in past memories as part of constructing meaning in your life.
3. Confront your own limitations.
4. Seek reconciliation and forgiveness.
5. Reach out to others through prayer or service.

RESOURCES FOR MEETING THE NEEDS OF ELDERLY PERSONS ___

The persons in the case studies at the beginning of this chapter need several kinds of assistance. Ruby Johnson requires a level of assistance most practically provided by effective and comprehensive case management; she is specifically asking for help in planning for the well-being of her multigenerational family after she dies. The Menzels' needs are quite different. Elizabeth Menzel is confronted with Alzheimer's-related care and assistance needs. Much of this assistance had been provided by her daughter Christine (before her death) and by her husband, Joseph. Joseph Menzel, in turn, needs some respite services to prevent him from being overwhelmed by the demands of giving care. This respite is being provided by his wife's weekly attendance at an Alzheimer's social group meeting. Margaret Davis's daughter and granddaughter are providing assistance with her daily care, and they could use a variety of services to assist them in their attempt to care for her at home. There is a strong need for assistance in managing her multiple chronic health problems. Finding accessible, affordable services in her rural community could be a real challenge for Mrs. Davis's social worker. Until recently, Bina Patel provided as much assistance as she received, but her deteriorating health now poses a special challenge to her and her family in the face of her son's terminal illness. This family will need emotional support as well as practical assistance in planning for her future care.

The types of support and assistance that elderly persons receive can be categorized as either formal or informal resources. *Formal resources* are those provided by formal service providers. They typically have eligibility requirements that a person has to meet in order to qualify. Some formal resources are free, but others are provided on a fee-for-service basis, meaning that anyone who is able to pay can request the service. *Informal resources* are those provided through families, friends, neighbors, churches, and so forth. Elderly persons receive a considerable amount of support through these informal support networks. As the society ages, more attention will need to be paid to the interaction between the informal and formal support systems (Wacker & Roberto, 2008).

Many types of formal services are available, but the social worker's most daunting task is often assessing the elderly person's needs. It may also be a challenge, however, to find quality services that are affordable. Thus, advocacy on behalf of older adults remains a concern of the social work profession.

Some elderly persons have difficulty managing their legal and financial affairs. A **power of attorney** (**POA**) is a legal arrangement by which a person appoints another individual to manage his or her financial and legal affairs. The person given the POA should be someone the client knows and trusts. Standard POA forms are available at stationery stores, but the POA can be tailored to the individual's situation. It then needs to be notarized, a service provided by attorneys and some banks. A POA can be limited (for a limited time period), general (no restrictions), or durable (begins after the client reaches a specified level of disability) (Wacker & Roberto, 2008).

THE DYING PROCESS

The topic of death and dying is almost always in the last chapter of a human behavior textbook, reflecting the hope that death will come as late as possible in life. Obviously, people die at all stages of life, but very late adulthood is the time when dying is considered "on time."

Despite our strong cultural predisposition toward denial of the topic, and perhaps in response to this, there have been a plethora of efforts to talk about death, starting most notably with Elisabeth Kübler-Ross's book *On Death and Dying* in 1969. In recent years, efforts like the Project on Death in America (PDIA), funded by the Soros Foundation, and end-of-life initiatives funded by the Robert Wood Johnson Foundation have set out to change mainstream attitudes. The mission of PDIA was to understand and transform the culture and experience of dying and bereavement. It promoted initiatives in research, scholarship, the humanities, and the arts, and fostered innovations in the provision of care, education, and policy. Television programs such as the Public Broadcasting Service's *On Our Own Terms: Moyers on Dying* have facilitated public education and community dialogue.

On a more individual level, many factors influence the ways in which a person adjusts to death and dying, including one's religion and philosophy of life, personality, culture, and other personal traits. Adjustment may also be affected by the conditions of dying. A person with a prolonged terminal illness has more time and opportunity to accept and prepare for his or her own death than someone with an acute and fatal illness or sudden death.

The following adjectives used to describe death are found in both the professional and popular literature: good, meaningful, appropriate, timely, peaceful, sudden, and natural. One can be said to die well, on time, before one's time, and in a variety of ways and places. This terminology reflects an attempt to embrace, acknowledge, tame, and integrate death into one's life. Other language is more indirect, using euphemisms, metaphors, medical terms, and slang, reflecting a need to avoid directly talking about death—suggesting the person is "lost," has "passed away," or has "expired" (DeSpelder & Strickland, 2005). It is important for a social worker to be attentive to words that individuals and families choose because they often reflect one's culture and/or religious background and comfort level.

As with life, the richness and complexity of death is best understood from a multidimensional framework involving the biological, psychological, social, and spiritual dimensions (Bern-Klug, 2004; Bern-Klug, Gessert, & Forbes, 2001). The following conceptualizations of the dying process help capture the notion that dying and other losses, and the accompanying bereavement, are processes that differ for each unique situation, yet share some common aspects.

In *On Death and Dying,* Kübler-Ross (1969) described stages that people tend to go through in accepting their own inevitable death or that of others, summarized in Exhibit 16.7. Although these stages were written with death in mind, they have application to other loss-related experiences, including the aging process. Given time, most individuals experience these five reactions, although not necessarily in this order. People often shift back and forth between the reactions rather than experience them in a linear way, get stuck in a stage, or skip over others. Kübler-Ross suggests that, on some level, hope of survival persists through all stages.

Although these reactions may fit people in general, very late-life adults appear to experience far less denial about the reality of death than other age groups (McInnis-Dittrich, 2009). As they confront their limitations of physical health and become socialized to death with each passing friend and family member, most very late-life adults become less fearful of death. Unfortunately, some professionals and family members may not be as comfortable expressing their feelings related to death and dying, which may leave the elder feeling isolated.

Exhibit 16.7   Stages of Accepting Impending Death

Denial: The person denies that death will occur: "This is not true. It can't be me." This denial is succeeded by temporary isolation from social interactions.

Anger: The individual asks, "Why me?" The person projects his or her resentment and envy onto others and often directs the anger toward a supreme being, medical caregivers, family members, and friends.

Bargaining: The individual starts bargaining in an attempt to postpone death, proposing a series of deals with God, self, or others: "Yes, me, but I will do _____ in exchange for a few more months."

Depression: A sense of loss follows. Individuals grieve about their own end of life and about the ones that will be left behind. A frequent reaction is withdrawal from close and loved persons: "I just want to be left alone."

Acceptance: The person accepts that the end is near and the struggle is over: "It's okay. My life has been . . . "

SOURCE: Based on Kübler-Ross (1969).

In addition to expressing feelings about death, some very late-life adults have other needs related to dying. A fear of prolonged physical pain or discomfort, as well as fear of losing a sense of control and mastery, trouble very late-life adults most. Some have suggested that older adults who are dying need a safe and accepting relationship in which to express the fear, sadness, anger, resentment, or other feelings related to the pending loss of life and opportunity, especially separation from loved ones (Bowlby, 1980).

Ira Byock (1997, 2004) writes about the importance of certain tasks when facing death, as well as in everyday life, given that we never know how much time we have. These tasks address affirmation (I love you; do you love me?); reconciliation (I forgive you; do you forgive me?); and saying good-bye. Farber, Egnew, and Farber (2004) prefer the notion of a "respectful death" over a "good death," proposing a process of respectful exploration of the goals and values of individuals and families rather than a prescription for successfully achieving a "good death." This approach reminds us of the importance of a social worker's nonjudgmental recognition of the uniqueness of each person's situation.

Advance Directives

On a more concrete level, social workers can help patients and families discuss, prepare, and enact health care **advance directives,** or documents that give instructions about desired health care if, in the future, individuals cannot speak for themselves. Such discussions can provide an opportunity to clarify values and wishes regarding end-of-life treatment. Ideally, this conversation has been started prior to very late adulthood. If not, helping people to communicate their wishes regarding life-sustaining measures, who they want to act on their behalf when they are no longer competent to make these decisions, and other end-of-life concerns helps some people feel more empowered.

How do advance directives promote a continued sense of human agency in making choices?

Since the passage of the Patient Self-Determination Act in 1990, hospitals and other health care institutions receiving Medicare or Medical Assistance funds are required to inform patients that should their condition become life-threatening, they have a right to make decisions about what medical care they would wish to receive (McInnis-Dittrich, 2009). The two primary forms of advance directives are the living will and the durable power of attorney for health care.

A **living will** describes the medical procedures, drugs, and types of treatment that one would choose for oneself if able to do so in certain situations. It also describes the situations for which the patient would want treatment withheld. For example, one may instruct medical personnel not to use any artificial means or heroic measures to keep one alive if the condition is such that there is no hope for recovery. Whereas a living will allows an individual to speak for him- or herself in advance, a durable power of attorney designates someone else to speak for the individual if he or she is unable to.

The promotion of patient rights as described above has helped many patients feel empowered and has comforted some family members, but this topic is not without controversy. Because the laws vary from state to state, laypersons and professionals must inquire about the process if one relocates. Also, rather than feeling comforted by knowing a dying person's wishes, some family members experience the burden of difficult decision making that once was handled by the physician. Advance directives are not accepted or considered moral by some ethnic, racial, and religious groups. Because of historical distrust and fear that the White medical establishment will withhold treatment from them, some African American and Hispanic families have preferred life-sustaining treatment to the refusal of treatment inherent in advance directives. Among some religious groups, the personal control represented in advance directives is seen to interfere with a divine plan and is considered a form of passive suicide. As discussed below, social workers must approach each patient and family with an openness to learn about their values and wishes. Volker (2005) cautions health care providers to consider the relevancy of Western values, such as personal control over one's future, in the lives of non-Western patient groups.

Care of People Who Are Dying

Although some associate hospice and palliative care with "giving up" and there being "nothing left to do," in fact hospices provide **palliative care**—a form of care focusing on pain and symptom management as opposed to curing disease. The focus is on "caring, not curing" (National Hospice and Palliative Care Organization [NHPCO], 2008), when curative-focused treatment is no longer available or desired. Palliative care attends to the psychological, social, and spiritual issues in addition to the physical needs. The goal of palliative

care is achievement of the best possible quality of life for patients and their families.

Hospice is one model of palliative care, borrowed from the British, which began in the United States in the mid-1970s to address the needs of dying persons and their loved ones. It is more a philosophy of care than a place, with the majority of persons receiving hospice services where they live, whether that is their private residence (42%) or a nursing or residential facility (38.3%) (NHPCO, 2008). Hospice services are typically available to persons who have received a prognosis of 6 months or less and who are no longer receiving care directed toward a cure. For instance, the hospital social worker may want to give Bina Patel and her daughter-in-law information about hospice care, as an additional support during Mrs. Patel's son's illness. Exhibit 16.8

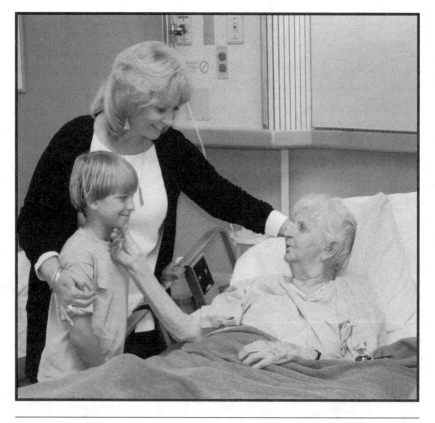

Photo 16.4 Palliative care focuses on providing pain and symptom management when cure of disease is no longer an option. The patient and the family are the unit of care.

Exhibit 16.8 Key Ideas of Hospice Care

- The patient and the family (as defined by the patient) are the unit of care.
- Care is provided by an interdisciplinary team composed of physician, nurse, nurse's aide, social worker, clergy, volunteer, and other support staff who attend to the spectrum of biopsychosocial and spiritual needs of the patient and family.
- The patient and family have chosen hospice services and are no longer pursuing aggressive, curative care, but selecting palliative care for symptom management.
- Bereavement follow-up is part of the continuum of care available to family members after the patient's death.

SOURCE: McInnis-Dittrich (2009); NHPCO (2008).

summarizes the key ideas that distinguish hospice care from more traditional care of the dying.

According to the National Hospice and Palliative Care Organization (2008), the United States had approximately 4,700 hospice programs in 2007 serving most rural, suburban, and urban communities in all 50 states. In 2007, approximately 1.4 million patients, representing about 38.8% of all deaths in the United States, received hospice services. An estimated 4 out of 5 hospice patients are 65 years of age or older, and about 37% are 85 and older. When hospice care was first established in the United States in the 1970s, cancer patients accounted for the majority of hospice admissions. Over time, hospices responded to the needs of others with end-stage disease (i.e., renal, lung, kidney, and heart disease; AIDS; and dementia), and in 2006, cancer accounted for less than half of all admissions (41.3%).

Disparities have been noted in hospice care, as in other health care settings, with persons of color historically being underserved. Initiatives through NHPCO, the Soros Foundation's Faculty Scholar program, as well as the Robert Wood Johnson Foundation's Promoting Excellence in End-of-Life Care, have focused on program development specific to the needs of patients and families in African American, Hispanic, Native American, and other communities that have been underserved by more traditional hospice programs (Crawley et al., 2000; NHPCO, 2008).

Palliative care programs are emerging in hospital settings to address pain and symptom management in patients who might not fit the hospice criteria. Some hospitals have palliative care units specializing in management of short-term, acute symptoms; others have palliative care consultative services that serve medical, oncology, pediatric, and other units throughout the hospital (Reith & Payne, 2009).

End-of-Life Signs and Symptoms

Family members and others caring for a person who is dying often experience a great deal of anxiety when they do not have adequate information about the dying process. Most families appreciate knowing what to expect, and honest, factual information can help allay their fears of the unknown (Cagle & Kovacs, 2009; Proot et al., 2004). Many hospice services provide written information about symptoms of death for those families anticipating the death of a loved one at home. Exploring how much information people have and want is an important part of the social worker's assessment.

Obviously, each individual situation will differ, but the following general information about symptoms of impending death helps people prepare (Foley, 2005; Reith & Payne, 2009):

- *Temperature and circulation changes.* The patient's arms and legs may become cool to the touch, and the underside of the body may darken in color as peripheral circulation slows down. Despite feeling cool to the touch, the patient is usually not aware of feeling cold, and light bed coverings usually provide sufficient warmth.

- *Sleeping.* The dying patient will gradually spend more time sleeping and at times may be difficult to rouse as metabolism decreases. The patient will gradually retreat from the surroundings. It is best to spend more time with the patient during the most alert times.
- *Vision and hearing.* Clarity of vision and hearing may decrease. The patient may want the lights on as vision decreases. Hearing is the last of the five senses to be lost, so it should not be assumed that an unresponsive patient cannot hear. Speech should be soft and clear, but not louder than necessary. Many patients talk until minutes before death and are reassured by the exchange of words between loved ones.
- *Secretions in the mouth and congestion.* Oral secretions may become more profuse and collect in the back of the throat. Most people are familiar with the term *death rattle,* a result of a decrease in the body's intake of fluids and inability to cough up normal saliva. Tilting the head to the side and elevating the head of the bed will ease breathing. Swabbing the mouth and lips also provides comfort.
- *Incontinence.* Loss of bowel and bladder function may occur around the time of death or as death is imminent, as the muscles begin to relax. The urine will become very dark in color. If needed, pads should be used to keep skin clean and dry.
- *Restlessness and confusion.* The patient may become restless or have visions of people or things that do not exist. These symptoms may be a result of a decrease in the oxygen circulation to the brain and a change in the body's metabolism. Someone should stay with the patient, reassuring the person in a calm voice, telling the person it is okay to let go, and using oxygen as instructed. Soft music, back rubs, and gentle touch may help soothe the patient. The patient should not be interfered with or restrained, yet should be prevented from falling.
- *Eating, drinking, and swallowing.* Patients will have decreased need for food and drink. It may be helpful to explain to families and caregivers that feeding will not improve the condition,

and in fact may exacerbate symptoms. Slight dehydration may be beneficial in reducing pulmonary secretions and easing breathing. Dehydration also generally results in mild renal insufficiency that is somewhat sedating. To withhold food and water feels counterintuitive, however, because food and water are usually equated with comfort and sustaining life. Ice chips, small sips of water, and small amounts of food that have meaning to the patient and family are more helpful than forcing food or liquids.
- *Breathing changes.* Breathing may become irregular, with periods of 10 to 30 seconds of no breathing. This symptom is very common and indicates a decrease in circulation and buildup of body waste products. Elevating the head of the bed and turning the patient on his or her side often help relieve irregular breathing patterns.
- *Pain.* Frequent observation will help determine if the patient is experiencing pain. Signs of discomfort include moaning, restlessness, and a furrowed brow. Medication should be given as instructed, or the nurse or physician should be contacted if pain persists.

Dying may take hours or days; no one can predict the time of death, even when the person is exhibiting signs and symptoms of dying. The following are signs that death has occurred:

- Breathing stops.
- Heart stops beating.
- Bowel or bladder control is lost.
- There is no response to verbal commands or shaking.
- Eyelids may be slightly open with eyes fixed on a certain spot.
- Mouth may fall open slightly as the jaw relaxes.

Such explicit discussion of death with those attending a dying family member or close friend may seem upsetting, but this knowledge is also comforting and can help ease the anxiety related to the fear of the unknown. Dying persons are also comforted knowing that their family members have the informational, medical, and social support they need to help them in their caregiving role. It is also helpful to have funeral plans in place so that one phone call to the mortuary facilitates the process, rather than facing difficult and emotional decision making at the time of death.

LOSS, GRIEF, AND BEREAVEMENT

Loss is a common human experience. There is a great deal of evidence that people of all cultures have strong, painful reactions to the death of the people to whom they are emotionally attached (Doka & Tucci, 2009). Sadness, loneliness, disbelief, and anxiety are only a few of the feelings a person may experience in times of bereavement. The challenge is to refrain from making grief the problem, thereby pathologizing someone's experience, and to understand the complexities related to death in a society that has grown increasingly old age and death avoidant (J. McKnight, 1995). So, we offer the following, cautioning against turning someone's grief into a problem, and encouraging readers to help others understand grief as a normal part of life.

Grief, bereavement, and *mourning* are words that are often used interchangeably, perhaps because no one word "reflects the fullness of what a death introduces into the life of an individual, family or community" (P. R. Silverman, 2004, p. 226). The following definitions help distinguish the various aspects of this process:

- **Loss.** The severing of an attachment an individual has with a loved one; a loved object (such as a pet, home, or country); or an aspect of one's self or identity (such as a body part or function; physical or mental capacity; or role or position in family, society, or other context) (Stroebe, Stroebe, & Hansson, 1993). P. R. Silverman (2004) suggests that loss doesn't *happen* to us; rather, it is "something we must make sense out of, give meaning to, and respond to" (p. 226).
- **Bereavement.** The state of having suffered a loss.
- **Grief.** The normal internal reaction of an individual experiencing a loss. Grief is a complex coping process, is highly individualized (Stroebe et al., 1993), and is an expected period of transition (P. R. Silverman, 2004).

- **Mourning.** The external expression of grief (Stroebe et al., 1993); the "mental work following the loss of a loved one . . . [a] social process including the cultural traditions and rituals that guide behavior after a death" (P. R. Silverman, 2004, p. 226).

The rituals associated with death vary in historical and cross-cultural context (Counts & Counts, 1991; Doka & Tucci, 2009). In some cultures, the dead are buried; in other cultures, the dead are burned and the ashes are spread. In some places and times, a surviving wife might have been burned together with her husband. In the United States, death rituals can be as different as a traditional New Orleans funeral, with street music and mourners dressed in white, or a somber and serene funeral with hushed mourners dressed in black. Some cultures prescribe more emotional expression than others. Some cultures

Photo 16.5 Many factors influence the way in which a person adjusts to death and dying, including one's religion and philosophy of life, personality, and other traits.

build ritual for expression of anger, and some do not. However, the death rituals in most cultures include the following (Counts & Counts, 1991):

- Social support provided to grievers
- Ritual and ceremony used to give meaning to death
- Visual confrontation of the dead body
- A procession

Throughout life, we are faced with many losses, some that occur by death, but many that occur in other ways as well. For example, Ruby Johnson has faced loss through divorce, disappointment and estrangement with her daughter, and retirement. Joseph and Elizabeth Menzel have recently had to cope with the untimely death of their daughter, as well as losses of physical and mental functioning and the related loss of independence. Joseph continues to struggle, many decades later, with his painful loss of homeland. Margaret Davis lost her husband to death, but she has also lost a daughter through estrangement and faced much loss of independence and privacy as she increasingly needed assistance from her children and grandchildren. Bina Patel lost her husband, lost a homeland when she immigrated to be near her children, and she lost some physical functioning after her stroke. Recently, the burgeoning literature on loss, grief, and bereavement has recognized that there may be similar processes for grieving all losses, including those that occur for reasons other than death. Loss is one of the most important themes in our work as social workers. For example, we encounter loss due to foster care placement, divorce, disease and disability, migration and immigration, unemployment, and so on.

> Do these earlier experiences with loss serve as either risk factors or protective factors for coping with current losses?

Theories and Models of Loss and Grief

A variety of theorists have sought to make sense of the complex experience of loss. Much of the literature on grief and bereavement for the past century has been influenced by Sigmund Freud's (1917/1957) classic article "Mourning and Melancholia." Freud described the "work of mourning" as a process of severing a relationship with a lost person, object, or ideal. He suggested that this happens over time as the bereaved person is repeatedly faced with situations that remind him or her that the loved person (or object or ideal) has, indeed, been lost. From this classic work came the idea of a necessary period of **grief work** to sever the attachment bond, an idea that has been the cornerstone of a number of stage models of the grief process.

In the United States, Erich Lindemann (1944) was a pioneer in grief research. Through his important study of families of people who died in a fire at the Cocoanut Grove Lounge in Boston, he conceptualized grief work as both a biological and psychological necessity. The common reactions to loss that he identified included the following:

- Somatic distress, occurring in waves lasting from 20 minutes to an hour, including tightness in throat, choking and shortness of breath, need for sighing, empty feeling in abdomen, lack of muscular power, and intense subjective distress
- Preoccupation with image of deceased, yearning for the lost one to return, wanting to see pictures of the deceased or touch items that are associated with the deceased
- Guilt
- Hostile reactions, toward the deceased as well as toward others
- Loss of patterns of conduct, where the ability to carry out routine behaviors is lost

Lindemann (1944) proposed that grief work occurs in stages, an idea that has been popular with other theorists and researchers since the 1960s. A number of stage models of grief have been proposed, and four are presented in Exhibit 16.9. As you can see, although the number and names of stages vary somewhat among theorists and researchers, in general the stage models all agree that grief work progresses from disbelief and feelings of unreality, to painful and disorganizing

Exhibit 16.9 Four Stage Models of Grief

Typical Stages of Grief	Erich Lindemann (1944)	Elisabeth Kübler-Ross (1969)	John Bowlby (1980)	Therese Rando (1993)
Disbelief and feelings of unreality	Shock and disbelief	Denial and isolation	Numbness	Avoidance
Painful and disorganizing reactions	Acute mourning	Anger Bargaining Depression	Yearning Disorganization Despair	Confrontation
A kind of "getting over" the loss	Resolution	Acceptance	Reorganization	Accommodation

reactions, to a kind of "coming to terms" with the loss. Parkes (2002) notes that stages or phases run the risk of being misused when taken too literally; however, they have served to remind us that grief is a process that people "need to pass through on the way to a new view of the world" (p. 380).

J. William Worden (2009) took a somewhat different approach, writing about the "tasks of mourning" rather than stages of mourning. He considered *task* to be more consistent with Freud's concept of grief work, given that the mourner needs to take action and do something rather than passively move through grief. Worden suggests that the following four tasks of mourning are important when a person is adapting to a loss:

Task I: To accept the reality of the loss. Working through denial takes time, because this involves an intellectual and an emotional acceptance. Some people have traditional rituals that help with this process.

Task II: To work through the pain of grief. Because people are often uncomfortable with the outward displays of grief, our society often interferes with this task. People often seek a geographic cure or quickly replace the lost person in a new relationship but often still have this task to complete.

Task III: To adjust to an environment in which the deceased is missing. This includes filling roles previously filled by the deceased and making appropriate adjustments in daily activities. In terms

of roles, many widows report being thrown the first time they have to cope with a major home repair. Regarding adjustments in daily activities, many bereaved persons report that they find themselves automatically putting the favorite foods of the deceased in their grocery carts.

Task IV: To emotionally relocate the deceased and move on with life. This task was best described by Sadie Delany after the loss of her beloved sister, Bessie: "I don't want to get over you. I just want to find a way to live without you" (Delany, 1997).

In the past couple of decades, there has been a critique of the idea of grief work. A highly influential article, "The Myths of Coping With Loss" (Wortman & Silver, 1989), disputed two major themes of the traditional view of grief work: Distress is an inevitable response to loss, and the failure to experience distress is a sign of improper grieving. In fact, a number of researchers have found that those who show the highest levels of distress immediately following a loss are more likely than those who show little distress to be depressed several years later. In another vein, P. R. Silverman (2004) challenges the notion of "tasks," which suggests something can be completed, recommending that we focus instead on "issues and processes" (p. 237).

Given the tremendous diversity among individuals based on gender, culture, personality, and life experience, as well as the various circumstances surrounding a loss, the grieving process is not easily defined, but theorists and practitioners continue to try and provide some framework for understanding the process. Camille Wortman and Roxanne Silver (1990) proposed that at least four different patterns of grieving are possible: normal, chronic, delayed, and absent. Worden (2009) elaborated on these patterns:

1. *Normal or uncomplicated grief.* Relatively high level of distress soon after the loss encompassing a broad range of feelings and behaviors, followed by a relatively rapid recovery

2. *Chronic or prolonged grief.* High level of distress continuing over a number of years without coming to a satisfactory conclusion

3. *Delayed grief (or inhibited, suppressed, or postponed grief).* Little distress in the first few months after the loss, but high levels of distress at some later point

4. *Absent grief.* No notable level of distress either soon after the loss or at some later time. Some question this notion and wonder if it is not absent, but masked or delayed; observation over time is important.

In their research, Wortman and Silver (1990) found absent grief in 26% of their bereaved participants, and other researchers have had similar findings (L. Levy, Martinkowski, & Derby, 1994). These same researchers have found a high rate (over 30%) of chronic grief.

Given these critiques of traditional models of grief, theorists and researchers have looked for other ways to understand the complex reactions to loss. Recently (see Bonanno, 2004; Boss, 2006), the study of bereavement has been influenced by developments in the study of stress and trauma reactions. Research on loss and grief has produced the following findings (Bonanno & Kaltman, 1999):

- It is the evaluation of the nature of the loss by the bereaved survivor that determines how stressful the loss is.
- How well a coping strategy works for dealing with loss depends on the context and the nature of the person-environment encounter.

- Maintaining some type of continued bond with the deceased, a strong sense of the continued presence of the deceased, may be adaptive.
- The capacity to minimize negative emotions after a loss allows the bereaved to continue to function in areas of personal importance.
- Humor can aid in the grief process by allowing the bereaved to approach the enormity of the loss without maximizing psychic pain or alienating social support.
- In situations of traumatic loss, there is a need to talk about the loss, but not all interpersonal relationships can tolerate such talk.

T. L. Martin and Doka's (2000) model of adult bereavement explores the role of gender, culture, and other characteristics that influence a person's grieving style. This model includes two adaptive grieving styles that they theorize to be at two ends of a continuum: the internal experience of loss and the outward expression relating to the loss. Doughty (2009) surveyed 20 experts in the field of thanatology (the study of death) to examine their opinions about this model. Consensus was found on the following items: the uniqueness of the griever, recognition of multiple factors influencing the grief process, the use of both cognitive and affective strategies in adapting to bereavement, and the idea that most people experience both internal and external pressures to grieve in certain ways.

In summary, grief is a multidimensional process—a normal life experience—that theorists and practitioners continue to try to understand. There seems to be general agreement that culture, past experience, gender, age, and other personal characteristics influence how one copes with loss.

Culture and Bereavement

It is important to be informed about the impact of each individual's culture and how religious and spiritual practices affect the individual bereavement process. Historically, because of sensitivity about racial issues, there has been some hesitancy to address issues of race and ethnicity in the health care arena. Unfortunately, when ethnic differences are not taken into consideration, too often it is assumed that the norm is White and middle class. As the United States becomes increasingly multiracial and ethnically diverse, you will need to continually inform yourself about cultural, ethnic, and religious traditions of individuals and families with whom you work so as to avoid becoming unintentionally ethnocentric. Del Rio (2004) reminds us that our own view of reality is "always socially constructed, does not account for all the phenomena of life, and should not take precedence over a client's view of reality" (p. 441). Given the tremendous diversity within groups as well as among them, the individual and the family are your best teachers. Ask them, "What do I need to know about you (your family, cultural, or religious and spiritual traditions) so that I can be of help to you?"

Some suggest that all people feel the same pain with grief, but that cultural differences shape our mourning rituals, traditions, and behavioral expressions of grief (Cowles, 1996). In the United States, we tend to psychologize grief, understanding it in terms of sadness, depression, anger, and other emotions (J. McKnight, 1995). There may be a cohort divide in the United States on this issue, however, and the current generation of very late-life adults are often much more matter-of-fact about death than younger adults are (Pipher, 1999). In China and other Eastern societies, grief is more often *somatized,* or expressed in terms of physical pain, weakness, and other physical discomfort (Irish, Lundquist, & Nelsen, 1993). We need to be aware of the possibility of somatization when working with many clients from different cultures, as well as with some older adults of Anglo heritage.

Cultural variation also exists regarding the acceptable degree of emotional expression of grief, from "muted" to "excessive" grief, with many variations between these two ends of the continuum. Gender differences exist in many cultures, including the dominant U.S. culture, where men have learned to be less demonstrative with emotions of grief and sadness than women (J. A. Murray, 2001).

Mourning and funeral customs also differ a great deal. For example, among African Americans, customs vary depending on whether the family is Southern Baptist, Black Catholic, northern Unitarian,

Black Muslim, or Pentecostal (H. Perry, 1993); in fact, "religion may be a stronger determining factor than race alone" (R. Barrett, 2009, p. 85). Perhaps because of some vestiges of traditional African culture and slavery, a strong desire to celebrate the person's life and build up a sense of community, funerals are important external expressions of mourning in many Black communities.

The complex and at times impersonal health care system in the United States often is insensitive to cultural traditions. In some cultures, proper handling of the body, time to sit with the deceased, and other traditions are important. For example, the Hmong believe that proper burial and worship of ancestors directly influence the safety and health of the surviving family members. They believe that the spiritual world coexists with the physical world. Because they believe that each person has several souls, it is important that the souls be "sent back appropriately" (Bliatout, 1993, p. 83).

Tremendous diversity exists within the Latino cultures in the United States, depending upon country of origin and degree of acculturation; however, for the most part these subgroups share several common Latino values, language, religion, and traditional family structure. Some Latino cultural themes that can influence care at the end of life include *familismo* (emphasis of family over individual); *personalismo* (trust building over time based on mutual respect); *jerarquismo* (respect for authority and hierarchy); *presentismo* (focus on present more than past or future); *espiritismo* (belief that good and evil spirits can impact health); and *fatalism* (fate determines life outcomes) (Sandoval-Cros, 2009).

Given the approximately 350 distinct Native American tribes in the United States and more than 596 different bands among the First Nations in Canada, and because of the differing degrees of acculturation and religious practices from one group to another, it is difficult to provide useful generalizations about this cultural group (Brokenleg & Middleton, 1993). However, honoring cultural norms of each person will help health care professionals learn about ceremonies and customs a Native American may find comforting when facing death or when grieving. Most Native Americans understand death as a natural end of life, not fearing it, and while it may be a painful separation for the living who are left behind, rituals exist to help with the transition (G. R. Cox, 2009).

These are only a few examples of the rich diversity among some of the peoples in our increasingly multiethnic society. You cannot possibly know all the specific traditions, but it is important to assume that you do not know, and therefore to inquire of the family how you can assist them.

RISK FACTORS AND PROTECTIVE FACTORS IN LATE ADULTHOOD

Chapter 15 suggests that young and middle adult behavior has both antecedents and consequences. The same can be said for late adulthood. Early life experiences can serve either as risk factors or as protective factors for health and well-being during late adulthood.

As the longest-term longitudinal research available on late-adult behavior, Vaillant's Study of Adult Development (2002) provides the clearest understanding of the antecedents of late-adult well-being. Like Emmy Werner, who has studied a cohort until midlife (see Chapter 15), Vaillant is impressed with the self-righting tendencies in human nature. He summarizes the antecedent risk factors and protective factors for late adulthood in this way: "What goes right in childhood predicts the future far better than what goes wrong" (p. 95). He also suggests that unhappy childhoods become less important over the stages of adulthood. Consequently, Vaillant asserts that it is more important to count up the protective factors than to count up the risk factors. Although he found childhood experiences to diminish in importance over time, Vaillant also found that much of the resilience, or lack thereof, in late adulthood is predicted by factors that were established by age 50. He suggests that risk factors and protective factors change over the life course.

Exhibit 16.10 lists six variables that Vaillant (2002) was surprised to find did not predict healthy aging and seven factors that he did find to predict healthy aging. Some of the factors that did not predict healthy aging *did* predict good adjustment at earlier adult stages. In terms of stress, Vaillant found that if we wait a few decades, many people recover from psychosomatic illness. In terms of parental characteristics, he found that they are still important for predicting adaptation at age 40, but not by age 70. In terms of both

Exhibit 16.10   Variables That Affect Healthy Aging

Variables That Do Not Predict Healthy Aging	Variables That Do Predict Healthy Aging
Ancestral longevity	Not smoking, or stopping young
Cholesterol	Using mature coping mechanisms
Stress	Not abusing alcohol
Parental characteristics	Healthy weight
Childhood temperament	Stable marriage
General ease in social relationships	Some exercise
	Years of education

SOURCE: Vaillant (2002).

childhood temperament and general ease in social relationships, he found that they are strong predictors of adjustment in young adulthood, but no longer important at age 70.

On the other hand, Vaillant (2002) found that the seven factors on the right side of Exhibit 16.10, collectively, are strong predictors of health 30 years in the future. He also found that each variable, individually, predicted healthy aging, even when the other six variables were statistically controlled. Vaillant has chosen to frame each of these predictive factors in terms of protection; he sees risk as the flip side of protection. He notes the danger of such a list of protective factors: that it be used to "blame the victim," rather than provide guidance for aging well. He sees the list of predictors as "good news," however, because they all represent something that can be controlled to some extent. In addition, he notes that the following personal qualities in late adulthood bode well for continued well-being:

- Good self-care
- Future orientation—ability to anticipate, plan, and hope
- Capacity for gratitude and forgiveness
- Capacity for empathy—to imagine the world as the other sees it
- Desire to do things *with* people rather than *to* them

THE LIFE COURSE COMPLETED_____

In the last seven chapters of this book, we have explored the seasons of the life course. These seasons have been and will be altered by changing demographics. Recent demographic trends have led to the following predictions about the future of the life course (Hogstel, 2001):

- The size and inevitable aging of the baby boom generation will continue to drive public policy debate and improve services for very late-life adults.
- Women will continue to live longer than men.

- Educational attainment levels of the very late-life adult will increase, with more women having been in the labor force long enough to have their own retirement income.
- Six-generation families will be common, although the generations will live in geographically dispersed settings, making care for very late-life adults difficult.
- Fewer family caregivers will be available for very late-life adults because the baby boomers and their children tended to marry later and have fewer children. At the same time, the need for informal or family caregiving to supplement formal care will be increasing.
- Assessment and management of health care, as well as health care education, will increasingly be available via telephone, computer/Internet, and television, providing greater access in remote areas but running the risk of rendering the service more impersonal.

As a society, we have a challenge ahead of us, to see that newborns begin the life course on a positive foot and that everyone reaches the end of life with the opportunity to see his or her life course as a meaningful whole. As social workers, we have a responsibility to take a look at our social institutions and evaluate how well they guarantee the opportunity for each individual to meet basic needs during each season of life, as well as whether they guarantee the opportunity for interdependence and connectedness appropriate to the season of life.

Critical Thinking Questions 16.3

What does death mean to you? Is it the final process of life, the beginning of life after death, a joining of the spirit with a cosmic consciousness, rest and peace, a continuation of the spirit, or something else? How has culture influenced your understanding of the meaning of death? How has religion influenced your understanding of the meaning of death? How might your understanding of the meaning of death affect your work with someone who is dying? What does it mean to live a good life?

Several practice principles for social work with older adults can be recommended:

- When working with an older adult, take into account the person's life history.
- Develop self-awareness of your views on aging and how different theoretical perspectives may influence your practice.
- Be conscious that age-related social roles change over time and that they vary for different cohorts.
- Identify areas in which you can assist an elderly client in preventing future problems, such as health-related difficulties.
- Develop an understanding of and skills to assess the differences among the physical, biological, psychological, and socio-emotional changes that are part of normal aging and those that are indicative of a problematic process.
- Develop an understanding of the retirement process and how individuals adjust differently to this transition.
- Carefully assess an elderly person's caregiving network. Be conscious of the difficulties that the caregiving situation poses for both the caregiver and the care recipient. Familiarize yourself with local caregiver support options.
- Develop an understanding of the process of institutionalizing an older adult. Develop an understanding of the process of adaptation to nursing home placement and skills to assist an older adult and his or her family with that adaptation.
- When assessing the need for service, be conscious of the availability of formal and informal support systems. Develop an understanding and knowledge of the formal service delivery system.
- Avoid treating older persons as if they were incapable of making decisions simply because they may not be able to carry out the decision. Rather, involve them to the maximum extent possible in any decisions relating to their personal life and care, even if they are not able to carry out the related actions.
- Assess the impact of loss in the lives of your very late-life clients—loss of partners, friends, children, and other relationships, but also loss of role, status, and physical and mental capacities.
- Be aware of your own feelings about death and dying so that you may become more comfortable being physically and emotionally present with clients and their loved ones.

Key Terms

activities of daily living (ADLs)	fluid intelligence	loss
advance directives	grief	morbidity
Alzheimer's disease	grief work	mortality rate
bereavement	hospice	mourning
crystallized intelligence	incidental memory	palliative care
cumulative advantage	instrumental activities of daily living (IADLs)	power of attorney (POA)
cumulative disadvantage	integrity	primary aging
delirium	intentional memory	reminiscence
dementia	life review	secondary aging
dependency ratio	living will	social gerontology

Active Learning

1. Think about the four case studies presented at the outset of this chapter (Johnson, Menzel, Davis, and Patel). Which theory or theories of social gerontology seem to be the best fit with each of these individuals?

2. Think about your own extended family. What roles do the members of the oldest generation play in the family? How do the different generations interact, exchange resources, and influence each other? How do the different generations deal with their role changes and life transitions as they age? In what ways do the different generations support and hinder each other in life transitions?

3. Think about possible relationships among poverty, gender, sexual orientation, and race as one ages in the United States today. Identify ways that social workers can influence policies that affect housing, health care, and other essential services directly related to quality of life in very late-life adulthood.

Web Resources

Administration on Aging

www.aoa.gov

Site accesses information about the Older Americans Act, other federal legislation, and a range of programs and statistics.

AgingStats.Gov

www.agingstats.gov

Site presented by the Federal Interagency Forum on Aging-Related Statistics covers 31 key indicators of the lives of older people in the United States and their families.

American Association of Retired Persons

www.aarp.org

Organizational site provides a wide range of resources from health technology, travel, legal, and policy and advocacy.

American Society on Aging

www.asaging.org

Site provides general information about aging-related services, including a link to the LGBT Aging Issues Network (LAIN) and LGBT Aging Resources Clearinghouse (LARC), and information on older adults, alcohol, medication, and other drugs.

Center on an Aging Society—Older Hispanic Americans

http://ihcrp.georgetown.edu/agingsociety/pubhtml/hispanics/hispanics.html

Site presents research results on chronic conditions of older Latino Americans.

Duke Institute on Care at the End of Life

www.iceol.duke.edu

Site provides information on spirituality, cultural diversity, and end-of-life care.

Hospice Foundation of America

www.hospicefoundation.org

Site contains information on locating hospice programs, a newsletter, and links to resources.

National Academy on an Aging Society

www.agingsociety.org

Organization provides clear, unbiased research and analysis focused on public policy issues arising from the aging of America's and the world's population.

National Caregivers Library

www.caregiverslibrary.org

Site maintained by FamilyCare America, Inc., makes resources available to caregivers through alliances with professionals, businesses, and other organizations serving seniors and caregivers.

National Caucus & Center on Black Aged

www.ncba-aged.org

Site contains aging news for policy makers, legislators, advocacy groups, minority professionals, and consumers that addresses finances, caregiving, intergenerational issues, and governmental programs.

National Center for Gerontological Social Work Education

http://www.cswe.org/CentersInitiatives/GeroEd Center.aspx

Site maintained by the Council on Social Work Education Gero-Ed Center (National Center for Gerontological Social Work Education) provides resources for aging and end-of-life care.

National Council on Aging

www.ncoa.org

Site contains information on advocacy, programs, publications, and a number of good links to other aging resources.

National Hospice and Palliative Care Organization

www.nhpco.org

Site contains information on the history and current development of hospice and palliative care programs, advance directives, grief and bereavement, caregiving, and other related topics.

National Institute on Aging

www.nia.nih.gov

Site contains information about the U.S. National Institutes of Health National Institute on Aging (NIA), news and events, health, research programs, research funding and training, and the National Advisory Council on Aging.

REFERENCES

A guide to African Americans and religion. (2007). Retrieved May 20, 2010, from http://www.religionlink.com/tip_070108.php

Aarnoudse-Moens, C. S., Weisglas-Kuperus, N., van Goudoever, J. B., & Oosterlaan, J. (2009). Meta-analysis of neurobehavioral outcomes in very premature and/or very low birth weight children. *Pediatrics, 124*(2), 717–728.

Abdel-Latif, M. E., Bajuk, B., Oel, J., Vincent, T., Sutton, L., & Liu, K. (2006). Does rural or urban residence make a difference to neonatal outcome in premature birth? A regional study in Australia. *Archives of Disease in Childhood: Fetal and Neonatal Edition, 91*(4), F251–F256.

Abma, J., & Martinez, G. (2006). Childlessness among older women in the United States: Trends and profiles. *Journal of Marriage and Family, 68,* 1045–1056.

Abrams, D., Hogg, M., Hinkle, S., & Otten, S. (2005). The social identity perspective on small groups. In M. Poole & A. Hollingshead (Eds.), *Theories of small groups: Interdisciplinary perspectives* (pp. 99–137). Thousand Oaks, CA: Sage.

Achenbaum, W. A., & Bengtson, V. C. (1994). Re-engaging the disengagement theory of aging: Or the history and assessment of theory development in gerontology. *The Gerontologist, 34,* 756–763.

Adair, L. S., & Gordon-Larsen, P. (2001). Maturational timing and overweight prevalence in U.S. adolescent girls. *American Journal of Public Health, 9*(4), 642–644.

Adam, E. K., & Chase-Lansdale, L. P. (2002). Home sweet home(s): Parental separations, residential moves, and adjustment problems in low-income adolescent girls. *Developmental Psychology, 38*(5), 792–805.

Adamczyk, A., & Felson, J. (2006). Friends' religiosity and first sex. *Social Science Research, 35*(4), 924–947.

Adams, B., & Trost, J. (2005). *Handbook of world families.* Thousand Oaks, CA: Sage.

Adams, G. R., & Marshall, S. K. (1996). A developmental social psychology of identity: Understanding the person-in-context. *Journal of Adolescence, 19,* 429–442.

Adelman, E. (2006). Mind–body intelligence. *Holistic Nursing Practice, 20*(3), 147–151.

Adler, J. (1995). *Arching backwards: The mystical initiation of a contemporary woman.* Rochester, VT: Inner Traditions.

Adler, L. (1993). Introduction and overview. *Journal of Education Policy, 8*(5–6), 1–16.

Adler, N. (2001). A consideration of multiple pathways from socioeconomic status to health. In J. Auerbach & B. Krimgold (Eds.), *Income, socioeconomic status, and health: Exploring the relationships* (pp. 56–66). Washington, DC: Academy for Health Services Research & Health Policy.

Adler, N. (2006, October). *Health disparities: Monitoring, mechanism, and meaning.* Paper presented at the NIH Conference on Understanding and Reducing Health Disparities: Contributions From the Behavioral and Social Sciences, Bethesda, MD.

Administration on Aging, U.S. Department of Health and Human Services. (2005). *A profile of older Americans: 2005.* Washington, DC: Author.

Administration on Aging, U.S. Department of Health and Human Services. (2006a). *Aging in the 21st century—Demography.* Washington, DC: Author.

Administration on Aging, U.S. Department of Health and Human Services. (2006b). *A statistical profile of black older Americans aged 65+.* Washington, DC: Author.

Administration on Aging, U.S. Department of Health and Human Services. (2006c). *A statistical profile of Hispanic older Americans aged 65+.* Washington, DC: Author. Retrieved July 7, 2006, from http://www/aoa/gov/aoa root/Press_Room/Products_Materials/pdf/stat_Profile_Hispanic_Aged_65.pdf

Administration on Aging, U.S. Department of Health and Human Services. (2008). *A profile of older Americans: 2008.* Retrieved July 30, 2011, from http://www.mowaa.org/Document.Doc?id=69

Advanced Fertility Center of Chicago. (2009). *Cost of IVF at the Advanced Fertility Center of Chicago.* Retrieved December 27, 2009, from http://www.advancedfertility.com/ivfprice.htm

Advocates for Youth. (2002). *Adolescent sexual health in Europe and the U.S.: Why the difference?* Retrieved June 6, 2002, from http://www.advocatesforyouth.org

Agency for Healthcare Research and Quality. (2006). Preventing disability in the elderly with chronic disease. *Research in Action, 3.* Retrieved July 7, 2006, from http://www.ahrq.gov/research/elderdis.htm

AGS Foundation for Health in Aging. (2009). *Aging in the know: Delirium (sudden confusion).* Retrieved March 3, 2010, from http://www.healthinaging.org/agingintheknow/chapters_print_ch_trial.asp?ch=57

Aguilar, M. A. (2001). Catholicism. In M. Van Hook, B. Hugen, & M. Aguilar (Eds.), *Spirituality within religious traditions in social work practice* (pp. 120–145). Pacific Grove, CA: Brooks/Cole.

Ahman, E. L., & Shah, I. H. (2006). Contraceptive use, fertility, and unsafe abortion in developing countries. *The European Journal of Contraception and Reproductive Health Care: The Official Journal of the European Society of Contraception, 11*(2), 126–131.

Ahrens, K., DuBois, D., Richardson, L., Fan, M., & Lozano, P. (2008). Youth in foster care with adult mentors during adolescence have improved adult outcomes. *Pediatrics, 121*(2), 246–252.

Ainsworth, M., Blehar, M., Waters, E., & Wall, S. (1978). *Patterns of attachment: A psychological study of the strange situation.* Hillsdale, NJ: Erlbaum.

Aitken, R. J., Baker, M. A., Doncel, G. F., Matzuk, M. M., Mauck, C. K., & Harper, M. J. K. (2008). As the world grows: Contraception in the 21st century. *Journal of Clinical Investigation, 118*(4), 1330–1343.

Aitken, R. J., Skakkebaek, N. E., & Roman, S. D. (2006). Male reproductive health and the environment. *Medical Journal of Australia, 185*(8), 414–416.

Aitken, R. J., Wingate, J. K., De Iullis, G. N., Koppers, A. J., & McLaughlin, E. A. (2006). Cis-unsaturated fatty acids stimulate reactive oxygen species generation and lipid peroxidation in human spermatozoa. *Journal of Clinical Endocrinology and Metabolism, 91*(10), 4154–4163.

Ajrouch, K., Antonucci, T., & Janevic, M. (2001). Social networks among Blacks and Whites: The interaction between race and age. *Journal of Gerontology: Social Sciences, 56,* S112–S118.

Ajzen, I., & Fishbein, M. (1977). Attitude–behavior relations: A theoretical analysis and review of empirical research. *Psychological Bulletin, 84,* 888–918.

Akande, A. (1997). Determinants of personal space among South African students. *Journal of Psychology, 131,* 569–571.

Akbulut, Y. (2007). Bilingual acquisition and cognitive development in early childhood: Challenges to the research paradigm. *Elementary Education Online, 6*(3), 422–429. Retrieved January 19, 2010, from http://ilkogretim-online .org.tr/vol6say3/v6s3m32.pdf

Al-Ansari, E. (2002). Effects of gender and education on the moral reasoning of Kuwait university students. *Social Behavior & Personality, 30*(1), 75–82.

Albrecht, G. L., Seelman, K. D., & Bury, M. (Eds.). (2001). *Handbook of disability studies.* Thousand Oaks, CA: Sage.

Aldashev, G., & Verdier, T. (2009). When NGOs go global: Competition on international markets for development donations. *Journal of International Economics, 79*(2), 198–210.

Aldwin, C. M. (2007). *Stress, coping, and development: An integrative perspective* (2nd ed.). New York: Guilford Press.

Aldwin, C. M., & Gilmer, D. (2004). *Health, illness, and optimal aging: Biological and psychosocial perspectives.* Thousand Oaks, CA: Sage.

Aldwin, C. M., & Yancura, L. A. (2004). Coping and health: A comparison of the stress and trauma literatures. In P. Schnurr & B. Green (Eds.), *Trauma and health: Physical health consequences of exposure to extreme stress* (pp. 99–125). Washington, DC: American Psychological Association.

Alexander, H. A., & Carr, D. (2006). Philosophical issues in spiritual education and development. In E. C. Roehlkepartain, P. E. King, L. Wagener, & P. L. Benson (Eds.), *The handbook of spiritual development in children and adolescence* (pp. 34–45). Thousand Oaks, CA: Sage.

Al-Hasani, S., & Zohni, K. (2008). The overlooked role of obesity in infertility. *Journal of Family and Reproductive Health, 2*(3), 115–122.

Alink, L., Mesmon, J., & van Zeijl, J. (2006). The early childhood aggression curve: Development of physical aggression in 10- to 50-month-old children. *Child Development, 77*(4), 954–966.

Allan, K. (2007). *The social lens: An invitation to social and sociological theory.* Thousand Oaks, CA: Sage.

Allen, K. E., & Marotz, L. R. (2003). *Developmental profiles: Pre-birth through twelve* (4th ed.). Clifton Park, NY: Delmar Learning/Thomson.

Allen, K. R., Lloyd, S., & Few, A. (2009). Reclaiming feminist theory, method, and praxis for family studies. In S. Lloyd, A. Few, & K. R. Allen (Eds.), *Handbook of feminist family studies* (pp. 3–17). Thousand Oaks, CA: Sage.

Allen, R. H., & Goldberg, A. B. (2007). Emergency contraception: A clinical review. *Clinical Obstetrics & Gynecology, 50*(4), 927–936.

Allen, V. M., Wilson, R. D., & Cheung, A. (2006). Pregnancy outcomes after assisted reproductive technology. *Journal of Obstetrics and Gynaecology Canada, 28*(3), 220–250.

Allen-Meares, P., Washington, R. O., & Walsh, B. (1996). *Social work services in schools* (2nd ed.). Englewood Cliffs, NJ: Prentice Hall.

Allison, B., & Schultz, J. (2004). Parent–adolescent conflict in early adolescence. *Adolescence, 39,* 101–119.

Almaas, A. H. (1995). *Luminous night's journey.* Berkeley, CA: Diamond Books.

Almaas, A. H. (1996). *The point of existence.* Berkeley, CA: Diamond Books.

Alperovitz, G. (2005). *America beyond capitalism: Reclaiming our wealth, our liberty, and our democracy.* Hoboken, NJ: Wiley.

Als, H., Heidelise, A., & Butler, S. (2008). Newborn individualized developmental care assessment program: Changing the future for infants and families in intensive care and special care nurseries. *Early Childhood Services: An Interdisciplinary Journal of Effectiveness, 2*(1), 1–19.

Al-Saleh, I., Coskun, S., Mashhour, A., Shinwari, N., El-Doush, I., Billedo, G., et al. (2008). Exposure to heavy metals (lead, cadmium and mercury) and its effects on the outcome of in-vitro fertilization treatment. *International Journal of Hygiene and Environmental Health, 211*(5–6), 560–579.

Altman, I. (1975). *The environment and social behavior: Privacy, personal space, territory, and crowding.* Monterey, CA: Brooks/Cole.

Altman, I. (1993). Dialectics, physical environments, and personal relationships. *Communication Monographs, 60,* 26–34.

Alviggi, C., Humaidan, P., Howles, C. M., Tredway, D., & Hillier, S. G. (2009). Biological versus chronological ovarian age: Implications for assisted reproductive technology. *Reproductive Biology and Endocrinology, 7,* 101.

Alwin, D., & McCammon, R. (2003). Generations, cohorts, and social change. In J. Mortimer & M. Shanahan (Eds.), *Handbook of the life course* (pp. 23–49). New York: Kluwer Academic/Plenum Publishers.

Alwin, D., McCammon, R., & Hofer, S. (2006). Studying baby boom cohorts within a demographic and developmental context: Conceptual and methodological issues. In S. Whitbourne & S. Willis (Eds.), *The baby boomers grow up: Contemporary perspectives on midlife* (pp. 45–71). Mahwah, NJ: Erlbaum.

Alzheimer's Association. (2009). *2009 Alzheimer's disease facts and figures.* Chicago: Author.

Amato, P. R. (2003). Family functioning and child development: The case of divorce. In R. M. Lerner, F. Jacobs, & D. Wertlieb (Eds.), *Handbook of applied developmental science, Vol. 1* (pp. 319–338). Thousand Oaks, CA: Sage.

Ambert, A. (2001). *Effect of children on parents* (2nd ed.). New York: Haworth.

American Academy of Family Physicians. (2005). *Natural family planning.* Retrieved August 5, 2006, from http://familydoctor.org/126.xml?printxml

American Academy of Pediatrics. (1999). *Caring for your baby and young child.* New York: Bantam.

American Academy of Pediatrics—Committee on Adolescence. (2005). Emergency contraception: Policy statement. *Pediatrics, 116*(4), 1026–1035.

American Association of Retired Persons. (2001). *In the middle: A report on multicultural boomers coping with family and aging issues.* Washington, DC: Author.

American Association of Retired Persons. (2003). *Global aging: Achieving its potential.* Washington, DC: Author.

American Association of University Women. (1995). *How schools shortchange girls.* New York: Marlowe.

American College of Nurse-Midwives. (2005). *Position statement on home birth.* Retrieved May 19, 2010, from http://www.midwife.org/siteFiles/position/homeBirth.pdf

American College of Nurse-Midwives. (2008). *Midterm Annual Report 2008.* Retrieved August 9, 2009, from http://www.midwife.org/Annual-Reports

American College of Nurse-Midwives. (2009). *American College of Nurse-Midwives responds to AMA resolutions on homebirth and physician oversight of midwives.* Retrieved August 27, 2011, from http://www.midwife.org/siteFiles/policy/ACNM_Letter_to_AMA.pdf

American Congress of Obstetricians and Gynecologists. (2008). *ACOG statement on home births* [ACOG news release]. Retrieved August 27, 2011, from http://www.medscape.com/viewarticle/725383

American Diabetes Association. (n.d.). *Direct and indirect costs of diabetes in the United States.* Retrieved October 18, 2006, from http://www.diabetes.org/linkforlife?WTLPromo=all aboutdiabetes_linkforlife

American Heart Association. (2005). *Heart disease and stroke statistics—2005 update.* Retrieved May 18, 2010, from http://www.oxysure.com

American Heart Association. (2006). *AHA statistical update. Heart disease and stroke statistics—2006 Update* [Electronic version]. *Circulation, 113,* 85–151. Retrieved August 4, 2006, from http://circ.ahajournals.org/cgi/content/short/113/6/e85

American Heart Association. (2009). *Cardiovascular disease statistics.* Retrieved December 4, 2009, from http://www.americanheart.org/presenter.jhtml?identifier=4478

American Heart Association. (2010). *Cardiovascular disease statistics.* Retrieved April 19, 2010, from http://www.americanheart.org/presenter.jhtml?identifier=4478

American Medical Association. (2002). *Emergency contraception.* Retrieved September 9, 2002, from http://www.ama-assn.org

American Medical Association House of Delegates. (2008). *Resolution 205(A-08). Home deliveries.* Retrieved May 19, 2010, from http://www.aolcdn.com/tmz_documents/0617_ricki_lake_wm.pdf

American Pregnancy Association. (2009). *Preimplantation genetic diagnosis: PGD.* Retrieved January 3, 2010, from http://www.americanpregnancy.org/infertility/preimplantiongeneticdiagnosis.html

American Psychiatric Association. (2000). *Diagnostic and statistical manual of mental disorders* (4th ed., Text Rev.). Washington, DC: Author.

American Psychiatric Association Work Group on Eating Disorders. (2000). Practice guidelines for the treatment of patients with eating disorders (revision). *American Journal of Psychiatry, 157*(1 Suppl), 1–39.

American Psychological Association. (1996). *Violence and the family: Report of the APA President Task Force on Violence and the Family.* Washington, DC: Author.

American Public Health Association. (2001). *Increasing access to out-of-hospital maternity services through state-regulated and nationally-certified direct-entry midwives.*

APHA Public Policy Statements, 1948–present, cumulative. Washington, DC: APHA. Retrieved August 27, 2011, from http://mana.org/APHAformatted.pdf

American Youth Policy Forum. (2009). *The forgotten half revisited: American youth and young families, 1988–2008.* Retrieved February 8, 2010, from http://www.aypf.org/pressreleases/pr18.htm.

Ameta, E. S., & Sherrard, P. A. (1995). Inquiring into children's social worlds: A choice of lenses. In B. A. Ryan, G. R. Adams, T. P. Gullotta, R. P. Weissberg, & R. L. Hampton (Eds.), *The family-school connection: Theory, research, and practice* (pp. 29–74). Thousand Oaks, CA: Sage.

Amole, D. (2005). Coping strategies for living in student residential facilities in Nigeria. *Environment & Behavior, 37*(2), 201–219.

An, J., & Cooney, T. (2006). Psychological well-being in mid to late life: The roles of generativity development and parent-child relationships across the lifespan. *International Journal of Behavioral Development, 30*(5), 410–421.

Anandarajah, G., & Hight, E. (2001). Spirituality and medical practice: Using the HOPE questions as a practical tool for spiritual assessment. *American Family Physician, 63*(1), 81–99.

Ananth, C. V., Liu, S., Joseph, K. S., Kramer, M. S., & Fetal and Infant Health Study Group of the Canadian Perinatal Surveillance System. (2008). A comparison of foetal and infant mortality in the United States and Canada. *International Journal of Epidemiology, 38*(2), 480–489.

Anderson, C. M. (2005). Single-parent families: Strengths, vulnerabilities, and interventions. In B. Carter & M. McGoldrick (Eds.), *The expanded family life cycle: Individual, family, and social perspectives* (3rd ed., pp. 399–416). Boston: Allyn & Bacon.

Anderson, D. A. (1994). Lesbian and gay adolescents: Social and developmental considerations. *High School Journal, 77*(1–2), 13–19.

Anderson, H. (2009). A spirituality for family living. In F. Walsh (Ed.), *Spiritual resources in family therapy* (2nd ed., pp. 194–211). New York: Guilford Press.

Anderson, M., Kaufman, J., Simon, T. R., Barrios, L., Paulozzi, L., Ryan, G., et al., & the School-Associated Violent Deaths Study Group. (2001). School-associated violent deaths in the United States, 1994–1999. *Journal of American Medical Association, 286*, 2695–2702.

Anderson, R. (2002). Deaths: Leading causes for 2000. *National Vital Statistics Report, 50*(16), 1–86. Retrieved August 4, 2006, from http://www.ncbi.nlm.nih.gov/pub/12355905

Anderson, R., & Smith, B. (2003). Deaths: Leading causes for 2001. *National Vital Statistics Report, 52*(9), 1–86.

Anderson, R. E., & Anderson, D. A. (1999). The cost-effectiveness of home birth. *Journal of Nurse Midwifery, 44*(1), 30–35.

Anderson, R. E., & Carter, I., with Lowe, G. R. (1974). *Human behavior in the social environment: A social systems approach.* Chicago: Aldine.

Angell, G. B., Dennis, B. G., & Dumain, L. E. (1998). Spirituality, resilience, and narrative: Coping with parental death. *Families in Society, 79*(6), 615–630.

Angers, M. E. (2008). Psychoanalysis, politics, and "the repressed feminine": Toward a psychoanalytically informed sociology of knowledge. *Issues in Psychoanalytic Psychology, 30*(2), 137–155.

Antonucci, T., & Akiyama, H. (1987). Social networks in adult life and a preliminary examination of the convoy model. *Journal of Gerontology: Social Sciences, 42*, S519–S527.

Antonucci, T., & Akiyama, H. (1997). Concern with others at midlife: Care, comfort, or compromise? In M. Lachman & J. James (Eds.), *Multiple paths of midlife development* (pp. 145–169). Chicago: University of Chicago Press.

Antonnuci, T., Akiyama, H., & Merline, A. (2001). Dynamics of social relationships in midlife. In M. Lachman (Ed.), *Handbook of midlife development* (pp. 571–598). New York: Wiley.

Antonucci, T., Akiyama, H., & Takahashi, K. (2004). Attachment and close relationships across the life span. *Attachment & Human Development, 6*(4), 353–370.

Appelrouth, S., & Edles, L. (2007). *Sociological theory in the contemporary era.* Thousand Oaks, CA: Pine Forge.

Applegate, J. S., & Shapiro, J. R. (2005). *Neurobiology for clinical social work: Theory and practice.* New York: Norton.

Arber, S., & Ginn, J. (1995). *Connecting gender and aging: A sociological approach.* Philadelphia: Open University Press.

Archer, J. (1992). Childhood gender roles: Social content and organization. In H. McGurk (Ed.), *Childhood social development* (pp. 31–62). Hillsdale, NJ: Erlbaum.

Archibald, A., Graber, J., & Brooks-Gunn, J. (2003). Pubertal processes and physiological growth in adolescence. In G. Adams & M. Berzonsky (Eds.), *Blackwell handbook of adolescence* (pp. 27–47). Oxford, UK: Blackwell.

Argyris, C. (1999). *On organizational learning.* Cambridge, MA: Blackwell.

Argyris, C., & Schön, D. (1978). *Organizational learning: A theory of action perspective.* Reading, MA: Addison-Wesley.

Argyris, C., & Schön, D. (1996). *Organizational learning II: Theory, method, and practice.* Reading, MA: Addison-Wesley.

Armatowski, J. (2001). Attitudes toward death and dying among persons in the fourth quarter of life. In D. O. Moberg (Ed.), *Aging and spirituality: Spiritual dimensions of aging theory, research, practice, and policy* (pp. 71–83). New York: Haworth Pastoral Press.

Armour, S., & Haynie, D. (2007). Adolescent sexual debut and later delinquency. *Journal of Youth and Adolescence, 36*(2), 141–152.

Armstrong, E. M. (2000). Lessons in control: Prenatal education in the hospital. *Social Problems, 47*(4), 583–611.

Arnett, J. J. (1998). Learning to stand alone: The contemporary American transition to adulthood in cultural and historical context. *Human Development, 41*(5), 295–297.

Arnett, J. J. (2000). Emerging adulthood: A theory of development from the late teens through the twenties. *American Psychologist, 55*(5), 469–480.

Arnett, J. J. (2004). *Emerging adulthood: The winding road from the late teens through the twenties.* New York: Oxford University Press.

Arnett, J. J. (2006). G. Stanley Hall's adolescence: Brilliance and nonsense. *History of Psychology, 9,* 186–197.

Arnett, J. J. (2007). Suffering, selfish, slackers? Myths and reality about emerging adults. *Journal of Youth and Adolescence, 36,* 23–29.

Arnett, J. J., & Jensen, L. (2002). A congregation of one. *Journal of Adolescent Research, 17*(5), 451–467.

Arnett, J. J., & Taber, S. (1994). Adolescence terminable and interminable: When does adolescence end? *Journal of Youth & Adolescence, 23*(5), 517–538.

Arnett, J. J., & Tanner, J. L. (2005). *Emerging adults in America: Coming of age in the 21st century.* Washington, DC: American Psychological Association.

Aroian, K., & Norris, A. E. (2003). Depression trajectories in relatively recent immigrants. *Comprehensive Psychiatry, 44*(5), 420–427.

Aronowitz, S. (2003). Global capital and its opponents. In S. Aronowitz & H. Gautney (Eds.), *Implicating empire: Globalization and resistance in the 21st century world order* (pp. 179–195). New York: Basic Books.

Arsenio, W., & Gold, J. (2006). The effects of social injustice and inequality on children's moral judgments and behavior: Towards a theoretical model. *Cognitive Development, 21,* 388–400.

Asher, S., & Paquette, J. (2003). Loneliness and peer relations in childhood. *Current Directions in Psychological Science, 12,* 75–78.

Ashford, J., LeCroy, C., & Lortie, K. (2010). *Human behavior in the social environment* (4th ed.). Belmont, CA: Cengage.

Ashkanani, H. R. (2009). The relationship between religiosity and subjective well-being: A case of Kuwaiti car accident victims. *Traumatology, 15*(1), 23–28.

Assagioli, R. (1965). *Psychosynthesis: A manual of principles and techniques.* New York: Viking.

Assagioli, R. (1973). *The act of will.* New York: Penguin.

Assagioli, R. (1989). Self-realization and psychological disturbances. In S. Grof & C. Grof (Eds.), *Spiritual emergency: When personal transformation becomes a crisis* (pp. 27–48). Los Angeles: Jeremy P. Tarcher.

Association for the Advancement of Social Work With Groups. (2005). *Standards for social work practice with groups* (2nd ed.). Alexandria, VA: Author.

Astone, N. M., Schoen, R., Ensminger, M., & Rothert, K. (2000). School reentry in early adulthood: The case of inner-city African Americans. *Sociology of Education, 73,* 133–154.

Astor, R. A., Benbenishty, R., Pitner, R. O., & Meyer, H. A. (2004). Bullying and peer victimization in the schools. In P. Allen-Meares & M. W. Fraser (Eds.), *Intervention with children and adolescents: An interdisciplinary perspective* (pp. 417–448). Boston: Allyn & Bacon.

Auerbach, J., & Krimgold, B. (2001a). Improving health: It doesn't take a revolution. In J. Auerbach & B. Krimgold (Eds.), *Income, socioeconomic status, and health: Exploring the relationships* (pp. 1–11). Washington, DC: Academy for Health Services Research & Health Policy.

Auerbach, J., & Krimgold, B. (Eds.). (2001b). *Income, socioeconomic status, and health.* Washington, DC: National Policy Association.

Aumann, K., & Galinsky, E. (2009). *The state of health in the American workforce: Does having an effective workplace matter?* New York: Families and Work Institute. Retrieved January 10, 2010, from http://www.families andwork.org/site/research/reports/HealthReport.pdf

Australian Government: Department of Family and Community Services, Office for Women. (2006). *What the Australian government is doing for women.* Retrieved April 10, 2010, from http://www.fahcsia.gov.au/sa/women/ pubs/govtint/budgetpubs/govt_for_women/Documents/ booklet.pdf

Austrian, S. (2008). Adulthood. In S. Austrian (Ed.), *Developmental theories through the life cycle* (pp. 201–283). New York: Columbia University Press.

Averill, J. R. (1997). The emotions: An integrative approach. In R. Hogan, J. A. Johnson, & S. R. Briggs (Eds.), *Handbook of personality psychology* (pp. 513–541). San Diego, CA: Academic Press.

Bachmann, G. A. (2007). Preventing pregnancy without hormones. *Cortlandt Forum, 20*(2), 55–56.

Bada, H. S., Das, A., Bauer, C. R., Shankaran, S., Lester, B. M., Gard, C. C., et al. (2005). Low birth weight and preterm births: Etiological fraction attributable to prenatal drug exposure. *Journal of Perinatology, 25*(10), 631–637.

Bagdikian, B. (2004). *The new media monopoly* (5th ed.). Boston: Beacon Press.

Bahrick, L., Lickliter, R., & Flom, R. (2006). Up versus down: The role of intersensory redundancy in the development of infants' sensitivity to the orientation of moving objects. *Infancy, 9,* 73–96.

Bailey, S. M. (2002). Foreword. In *The Jossey-Bass reader on gender and education* (pp. xxi–xxiv). San Francisco: Jossey-Bass.

Baillargeon, R. (1987). Object permanence in 3½ and 4½ month old infants. *Developmental Psychology, 23,* 655–664.

Baillargeon, R. (2004). Infants' physical world. *Current Directions in Psychological Science, 13,* 89–94.

Bain, M. D., Gau, D., & Reed, G. B. (1995). An introduction to antenatal and neonatal medicine, the fetal period and perinatal ethics. In G. B. Reed, A. E. Claireaux, & F. Cockburn (Eds.), *Diseases of the fetus and newborn* (2nd ed., pp. 3–23). London: Chapman & Hall.

Bakardjieva, M. (2004). Virtual togetherness: An everyday life perspective. In A. Feenberg & D. Barney (Eds.), *Community in the digital age: Philosophy and practice* (pp. 121–142). Lanham, MD: Rowman & Littlefield.

Baker, A. (1990). The psychological impact of the Intifada on Palestinian children in the occupied West Bank and Gaza: An exploratory study. *American Journal of Orthopsychiatry, 60,* 496–505.

Baker, L. (2006). Are we transferring women into the community too quickly? *British Journal of Midwifery, 14*(3), 148–149.

Baker, M., Das, D., Venugopal, K., & Howden-Chapman, P. (2008). Tuberculosis associated with household crowding in a developed country. *Journal of Epidemiology and Community Health, 62*(8), 715–721.

Bakhru, A., & Stanwood, N. (2006). Performance of contraceptive patch compared with oral contraceptive pill in a high-risk population. *Obstetrics and Gynecology, 108*(2), 378–386.

Balaban, V. (2008). Assessment of children. In E. B. Foa, T. M. Keane, M. J. Friedman, & J. A. Cohen (Eds.), *Effective treatments for PTSD: Practice guidelines from the International Society for Traumatic Stress Studies* (2nd ed., pp. 62–82). New York: Guilford Press.

Baler, R. D., Vakow, N. D., Fowler, J. S., & Benveniste, H. (2008). Is fetal brain monoamine oxidase inhibition the missing link between maternal smoking and conduct disorders? *Journal of Psychiatry and Neuroscience, 33*(3), 187–198.

Balkwell, J. W. (1994). Status. In M. Foshci & E. J. Lawler (Eds.), *Group processes: Sociological analyses* (pp. 119–148). Chicago: Nelson-Hall.

Ballantine, J., & Roberts, K. (2009). *Our social world: Introduction to sociology* (2nd ed.). Thousand Oaks, CA: Pine Forge.

Balsam, K., Beauchaine, T., Rothblum, E., & Solomon, S. (2008). Three-year follow-up of same-sex couples who had civil unions in Vermont, same-sex couples not in civil unions, and heterosexual married couples. *Developmental Psychology, 44*(1), 102–116.

Baltes, P. B., & Mayer, K. U. (Eds.). (1999). *The Berlin Aging Study: Aging from 70 to 100.* Cambridge, UK: Cambridge University Press.

Bandura, A. (1977a). Self-efficacy: Toward a unifying theory of behavioral change. *Psychological Review, 84,* 191–215.

Bandura, A. (1977b). *Social learning theory.* Englewood Cliffs, NJ: Prentice Hall.

Bandura, A. (1986). *Social foundations of thought and action: A social cognitive theory.* Englewood Cliffs, NJ: Prentice Hall.

Bandura, A. (2001). Social cognitive theory: An agentic perspective. *Annual Review of Psychology, 52,* 1–26.

Bandura, A. (2002). Social cognitive theory in cultural context. *Applied Psychology: An International Review, 51*(2), 269–290.

Bandura, A. (2006). Toward a psychology of human agency. *Perspectives on Psychological Science, 1*(2), 164–180.

Banerjee, M. M., & Canda, E. R. (2009). Spirituality as a strength of African-American women affected by welfare reform. *Social Thought, 28*(3), 239–262.

Barajas, R., Philipsen, N., & Brooks-Gunn, J. (2008). Cognitive and emotional outcomes for children in poverty. In D. Crane & T. Heaton (Eds.), *Handbook of families and poverty* (pp. 311–333). Thousand Oaks, CA: Sage.

Baranowski, T. (1983). Social support, social influence, ethnicity, and the breastfeeding decision. *Social Science & Medicine, 17,* 1599–1611.

Barbarin, O., McCandies, T., Coleman, C., & Atkinson, T. (2004). Ethnicity and culture. In P. Allen-Meares & M. W. Fraser (Eds.), *Intervention with children and adolescents: An interdisciplinary perspective* (pp. 27–53). Boston: Allyn & Bacon.

Barber, B., & Demo, D. (2006). The kids are alright (at least, most of them): Links between divorce and dissolution and child well-being. In M. Fine & J. Harvey (Eds.), *Handbook of divorce and relationship dissolution* (pp. 289–311). Mahwah, NJ: Erlbaum.

Barbu, S., Le Maner-Idrissi, G., & Jouanjean, A. (2000). The emergence of gender segregation: Towards an integrative perspective. *Current Psychology of Letters: Behavior, Brain, and Cognition, 3,* 7–18.

Barclay, L. (2009). ACOG issues guidelines for stillbirth management. *Obstetrics & Gynecology, 113,* 748–761.

Barker, K. K. (1998). "A ship upon a stormy sea": The medicalization of pregnancy. *Social Science & Medicine, 47*(8), 1067–1076.

Barker, R. G. (1968). *Ecological psychology: Concepts and methods for studying the environment of human behavior.* Palo Alto, CA: Stanford University Press.

Barnekow, K., & Kraemer, G. (2005). The psychobiological theory of attachment. A viable frame of reference for early intervention providers. *Physical & Occupational Therapy in Pediatrics, 25*(1 & 2), 3–15.

Barnes, P. M., Bloom, B., & Nahin, R. (2008, December 10). Complementary and alternative medicine use among adults and children: United States, 2007. *CDC National Health Statistics Report #12.* Retrieved April 17, 2010, from http://nccam.nih.gov/news/2008/ nhsr12.pdf

Barnett, S., & Scotch, R. (2002). *Disability protests.* Washington, DC: Gallaudet University Press.

Barnoff, L., & Moffatt, K. (2007). Contradictory tensions in anti-oppression practice in feminist social services. *Affilia, 22*(1), 56–70.

Barr, R. D., & Parrett, W. H. (1995). *Hope at last for at-risk youth.* Boston: Allyn & Bacon.

Barranti, C., & Cohen, H. (2001). Lesbian and gay elders: An invisible minority. In R. Schneider, N. Kropf, & A. Kisor (Eds.), *Gerontological social work: Knowledge, service setting, and special populations* (pp. 343–368). Belmont, CA: Brooks/Cole.

Barret, R., & Barzan, R. (1996). Spiritual experiences of gay men and lesbians. *Counseling and Values, 41,* 4–15.

Barrett, C. E., Noble, P., Hanson, E., Pine, D. S., Winslow, J. T., & Nelson, E. E. (2009). Early adverse rearing experiences alter sleep–wake patterns and plasma cortisol levels in juvenile rhesus monkeys. *Psychoneuroendocrinology, 34*(7), 1029–1040.

Barrett, M. J. (1999). Healing from trauma: The quest for spirituality. In F. Walsh (Ed.), *Spiritual resources in family therapy* (pp. 192–208). New York: Guilford Press.

Barrett, R. (2009). Sociocultural considerations: African Americans, grief, and loss. In D. J. Doka & A. S. Tucci (Eds.), *Living with grief: Diversity and end-of-life care* (pp. 79–91). Washington, DC: Hospice Foundation of America.

Barry, T. D., Lyman, R. D., & Klinger, L. G. (2002). Academic underachievement and attention-deficit/hyperactivity disorder: The negative impact of symptom severity on school performance. *Journal of School Psychology, 40*(3), 259–283.

Bartholomae, S., & Fox, J. (2010). Economic stress and families. In S. Price, C. Price, & P. McKenry (Eds.), *Families & change: Coping with stressful events and transitions* (4th ed., pp. 185–209). Thousand Oaks, CA: Sage.

Bartholomew, R. E. (2000). *Exotic deviance: Medicalizing cultural idioms—From strangeness to illness.* Boulder: University Press of Colorado.

Bartko, W. T., & Eccles, J. (2003). Adolescent participation in structured and unstructured activities: A person-oriented analysis. *Journal of Youth and Adolescence, 32*(4), 233–241.

Baskin, C. (2006). Aboriginal world views as challenges and possibilities in social work education. *Critical Social Work, 7*(2).

Bassali, R., & Benjamin, J. (2002, July 12). Failure to thrive. *EMedicine Journal, 3*(7). Retrieved August 21, 2002, from http://www.emedicine.com/PED/topic738.htm

Bassuk, E. L., & Friedman, S. M. (2005). *Facts on trauma and homeless children.* Durham, NC: National Child Traumatic Stress Network. Retrieved January 19, 2010, from http://www.nctsnet.org/nctsn_assets/pdfs/promising_practices/Facts_on_Trauma_and_Homeless_Children.pdf

Bates, J. (2009). Generative grandfathering: A conceptual framework for nurturing grandchildren. *Marriage & Family Review, 45,* 331–352.

Baum, F. (1999). The role of social capital in health promotion. Australian perspectives. *Health Promotion Journal of Australia, 9*(3), 171–178.

Baum, K. (2005, August). *Juvenile victimization and offending, 1993–2003* (Special Report, National Crime Victimization Survey, NCJ 209468). Washington, DC: U.S. Department of Justice, Office of Justice Programs, Bureau of Justice Statistics.

Bauman, L., Silver, E., & Stein, R. (2006). Cumulative social disadvantage and child health. *Pediatrics, 117*(4), 1321–1328.

Bauman, Z. (1998). *Globalization: The human consequences.* New York: Columbia University Press.

Baumrind, D. (1971). Current patterns of parental authority. *Developmental Psychology Monographs, 41*(1, Pt. 2).

Baxter, L., & Braithwaite, D. (2006). Introduction: Metatheory and theory in family communication research. In D. Braithwaite & L. Baxter (Eds.), *Engaging theories in family communication: Multiple perspectives* (pp. 1–15). Thousand Oaks, CA: Sage.

Beatson, J., & Taryan, S. (2003). Predisposition to depression: The role of attachment. *Australian and New Zealand Journal of Psychiatry, 37,* 219–225.

Beauchemin, K., & Hays, P. (1996). Sunny hospital rooms expedite recovery from severe and refractory depressions. *Journal of Affective Disorders, 40*(1–2), 49–51.

Beauchemin, K., & Hays, P. (1998). Dying in the dark: Sunshine, gender, and outcomes in myocardial infarction. *Journal of the Royal Society of Medicine, 91,* 352–354.

Beaudoin, M., & Taylor, M. (2004). *Breaking the culture of bullying and disrespect, Grades K–8: Best practices and successful strategies.* Thousand Oaks, CA: Corwin.

Bechtel, R. (2000). Assumptions, methods, and research problems of ecological psychology. In S. Wapner, J. Demick, T. Yamamoto, & H. Minami (Eds.), *Theoretical perspectives in environment–behavior research: Underlying assumptions, research problems, and methodologies* (pp. 61–66). New York: Kluwer Academic.

Beck, A. T. (1976). *Cognitive therapy and the emotional disorders.* New York: International Universities Press.

Beck, E., & Eichler, M. (2000). Consensus organizing: A practice model for community building. *Journal of Community Practice, 8*(1), 87–102.

Beck, J. S. (1995). *Cognitive therapy: Basics and beyond.* New York: Guilford Press.

Beck, U. (1992). *Risk society: Towards a new modernity.* Thousand Oaks, CA: Sage.

Beck, U. (1999). *World risk society.* Cambridge, UK: Polity.

Becker, D. (2004). Post-traumatic stress disorder. In P. J. Caplan & L. Cosgrove (Eds.), *Bias in psychiatric diagnosis* (pp. 207–212). Lanham, MD: Jason Aronson.

Becker, D. (2005). *The myth of empowerment: Women and the therapeutic culture in America*. New York: New York University Press.

Becker, G. (1981). *A treatise on the family*. Cambridge, MA: Harvard University Press.

Becker, G. (2002). Dying away from home: Quandaries of migration for elders in two ethnic groups. *Journals of Gerontology, Series B, 57*(2), S79–S95.

Becker, H. (1957). Current sacred–secular theory and its development. In H. Becker & A. Boskoff (Eds.), *Modern sociological theory in continuity and change* (pp. 137–185). New York: Dryden.

Becker, M. (1974). The health belief model and sick role behavior. *Health Education Monographs, 2,* 409–419.

Becker, M., & Joseph, J. (1988). AIDS and behavioral change to avoid risk: A review. *American Journal of Public Health, 78,* 384–410.

Becvar, D., & Becvar, R. (1996). *Family therapy: A systemic integration* (3rd ed.). Boston: Allyn & Bacon.

Beel-Bates, C. A., Ingersoll-Dayton, B., & Nelson, E. (2007). Deference as a form of reciprocity on aging. *Research on Aging, 29,* 626–643.

Behrman, J., & Sengupta, P. (2006). Documenting the changing contexts within which young people are transitioning to adulthood in developing countries: Convergence toward developed economies? In C. B. Lloyd, J. R. Behrman, N. Stromquist, & B. Cohen (Eds.), *The changing transitions to adulthood in developing countries: Selected studies* (pp. 13–55). Washington, DC: National Research Council.

Beitel, M., Genova, M., Schuman-Olivier Z., Arnold R., Avants, S. K., & Margolin A. (2007). Reflections by inner-city drug users on a Buddhist-based spirituality-focused therapy: A qualitative study. *American Journal of Orthopsychiatry, 77*(1), 1–9.

Beland, F., Zunzunegui, M., Alvarado, B., Otero, A., & del Ser, T. (2005). Trajectories of cognitive decline and social relations. *Journals of Gerontology: Series B: Psychological Sciences and Social Sciences, 60*(6), 320–330.

Belanger, K., Copeland, S., & Cheung, M. (2009). The role of faith in adoption: Achieving positive adoption outcomes for African American children. *Child Welfare, 87*(2), 99–123.

Belcher, J. R., Fandetti, D., & Cole, D. (2004). Is Christian religious conservatism compatible with the liberal social welfare state? *Social Work, 49*(2), 269–276.

Belden, A., Thompson, N., & Luby, J. (2008). Temper tantrums in healthy versus DSM-IV depressed and disruptive preschoolers: Defining tantrum behaviors associated with clinical problems. *Journal of Pedatrics, 152,* 117–122.

Belge, K. (2011). *Where can gays legally marry?* Retrieved March 21, 2011, from http://lesbianlife.about.com/cs/wedding/a/wheremarriage.htm

Bell, L. (1997). Theoretical foundations for social justice education. In M. Adams, L. Bell, & P. Griffin (Eds.), *Teaching for diversity and social justice* (pp. 1–15). New York: Routledge.

Bell, L. (2009). Mindful psychotherapy. *Journal of Spirituality in Mental Health, 11*(1–2), 126–144.

Bell, Y. R., Bouie, C. L., & Baldwin, J. (1998). Afrocentric cultural consciousness and African American male–female relationships. In J. D. Hamlet (Ed.), *Afrocentric visions: Studies in culture and communication* (pp. 47–71). Thousand Oaks, CA: Sage.

Bellamy, C. (2004). *The state of the world's children 2005*. New York: The United Nations Children's Fund.

Belsky, J. (1987). Infant day care and socioemotional development: The United States. *Journal of Child Psychology and Psychiatry, 29,* 397–406.

Belsky, J., & Braungart, J. M. (1991). Are insecure-avoidant infants with extensive day care experience less stressed by and more independent in the strange situation? *Child Development, 62,* 567–571.

Belsky, J., Campbell, S., Cohn, J., & Moore, G. (1996). Instability of infant–parent attachment security. *Developmental Psychology, 32,* 921–924.

Bem, S. L. (1993). *The lenses of gender: Transforming the debate on sexual inequality*. New Haven, CT: Yale University Press.

Bem, S. L. (1998). Gender schema theory and its implications for child development: Raising gender-aschematic children in a gender-schematic society. In D. L. Anselmi & A. L. Law (Eds.), *Questions of gender: Perspectives and paradoxes*. Boston: McGraw-Hill.

Benasich, A., & Leevers, H. (2003). Processing of rapidly presented auditory cues in infancy: Implications for later language development. In H. Hayne & J. Fagen (Eds.), *Progress in infancy research* (Vol. 3, pp. 245–288). Mahwah, NJ: Erlbaum.

Benedetti, F., Colombo, C., Barbini, B., Campori, E., & Smeraldi, E. (2001). Morning sunlight reduces length of hospitalization in bipolar depression. *Journal of Affective Disorders, 62*(3), 221–223.

Benedict, R. (1946). *The chrysanthemum and the sword*. Boston: Houghton Mifflin.

Benedict, R. (1989). *Patterns of culture*. Boston: Houghton Mifflin. (Original work published 1934)

Benefice, E., Caius, N., & Garnier, D. (2004). Cross-cultural comparison of growth, maturation, and adiposity. *Public Health Nutrition, 74*(4), 479–485.

Benenson, J. (1993). Greater preference among females than males for dyadic interaction in early childhood. *Child Development, 64,* 544–555.

Bengtson, V. L., Gans, D., Putney, N. M., & Silverstein, M. (2009). *Handbook of theories of aging* (2nd ed.). New York: Springer.

Benjamin, K., Edwards, N. C., & Bharti, V. K. (2005). Attitudinal, perceptual, and normative beliefs influencing the exercise decisions of community-dwelling physically frail seniors. *Journal of Aging and Physical Activity, 13*(3), 276–293.

Benjet, C., & Hernandez-Guzman, I. (2002). A short-term longitudinal study of pubertal change, gender, and psychological well-being of Mexican early adolescents. *Journal of Youth and Adolescence, 31,* 923–931.

Bennett, W. L. (2004). Communicating global activism: Strength and vulnerabilities of networked politics. In W. van de Donk, B. Loader, P. Nixon, & D. Rucht (Eds.), *Cyberprotest: New media, citizens and social movements* (pp. 109–126). London: Routledge.

Bennion, J. (2009, June 23). Drowning in electronics: Where the law stands on e-waste. *FrontlineWorld.* Retrieved October 17, 2009, from http://www.pbs.org/frontlineworld/stories/ghana804/resources/ewaste.html

Benokraitis, N. V. (2004). *Marriages and families: Changes, choices, and constraints* (5th ed.). Upper Saddle River, NJ: Prentice Hall.

Benson, P. L. (1990). *The troubled journey: A portrait of 6th–12th grade youth.* Minneapolis, MN: Search Institute.

Bentley, K. J., & Walsh, J. (2006). *The social worker and psychotropic medication: Toward effective collaboration with mental health clients, families, and providers* (3rd ed.). Pacific Grove, CA: Brooks/Cole.

Berck, J. (1992). *No place to be: Voices of homeless children.* Boston: Houghton Mifflin.

Berg, P., Appelbaum, E., Bailey, T., & Kalleberg, A. (2004). Contesting time: International comparisons of employee control of working time. *Industrial and Labor Relations Review, 57*(3), 331–349.

Bergen, D., & Coscia, J. (2001). *Brain research and childhood education: Implications for educators.* Olney, MD: Association for Childhood Education International.

Berger, P. L. (1969). *The sacred canopy: Elements of a sociological theory of religion.* Garden City, NY: Doubleday.

Berger, P. L., & Luckmann, T. (1966). *The social construction of reality.* Garden City, NY: Doubleday.

Berk, L. E. (2002a). *Infants and children: Prenatal through middle childhood* (4th ed.). Boston: Allyn & Bacon.

Berk, L. E. (2002b). *Infants, children, and adolescents* (4th ed.). Boston: Allyn & Bacon.

Berk, L. E. (2005). *Infants, children, and adolescents* (5th ed.). Boston: Pearson.

Berke, E., Koepsell, T., Moudon, A., Hoskins, R., & Larson, E. (2007). Association of the built environment with physical activity and obesity in older persons. *American Journal of Public Health, 97*(3), 486–492.

Berliner, K., Jacob, D., & Schwartzberg, N. (2005). The single adult and the family life cycle. In B. Carter & M. McGoldrick (Eds.), *The expanded family life cycle: Individual, family, and social perspectives* (3rd ed., pp. 362–372). Boston: Allyn & Bacon.

Berman, R. O. (2006). Perceived learning needs of minority expectant women and barriers to prenatal education. *Journal of Perinatal Education, 15*(2), 36–42.

Berndt, T. J. (1988). Friendships in childhood and adolescence. In W. Damon (Ed.), *Childhood development today and tomorrow* (pp. 332–348). San Francisco: Jossey-Bass.

Berne, L., & Huberman, B. (1999). *European approaches to adolescent sexual behavior and responsibility.* Washington, DC: Advocates for Youth.

Berne, L., & Huberman, B. (2000). Lessons learned: European approaches to adolescent sexual behavior and responsibility. *Journal of Sex Education & Therapy, 25*(2–3), 189–199.

Bern-Klug, M. (2004). The ambiguous dying syndrome. *Health and Social Work, 29*(1), 55–65.

Bern-Klug, M., Gessert, C., & Forbes, S. (2001). The need to revise assumptions about the end of life: Implications for social work practice. *Health and Social Work, 26*(1), 38–48.

Berry, M. E. (2009). *The sacred universe: Earth, spirituality, and religion in the 21st century.* New York: Columbia University Press.

Berthold, J. (2009). Dealing with delirium in older hospitalized adults. *ACP Hospitalist.* Retrieved May 16, 2010, from http://www.acphospitalist.org/archives/2009/06/delirium.htm

Besser, G. M., & Thorner, M. O. (1994). *Clinical endocrinology* (2nd ed.). London: Times Mirror International.

Best, J. (1989). Extending the constructionist perspective: A conclusion and introduction. In J. Best (Ed.), *Images of issues: Typifying contemporary social problems* (pp. 243–252). New York: Aldine de Gruyter.

Besthorn, F. H. (2001). Transpersonal psychology and deep ecology: Exploring linkages and applications for social work. In E. R. Canda & E. D. Smith (Eds.), *Transpersonal perspectives on spirituality in social work* (pp. 23–44). Binghamton, NY: Haworth Press.

Besthorn, F. H., & Canda, E. R. (2002). Revisioning environment: Deep ecology for education and teaching in social work. *Journal of Teaching in Social Work, 22*(1/2), 79–101.

Bhathena, R. K., & Guillebaud, J. (2006). Contraception for the older woman: An update. *Climacteric: The Journal of the International Menopause Society, 9*(4), 264–276.

Bhattacharya, G. (2000). The school adjustment of South Asian immigrant children in the United States. *Adolescence, 35,* 77–85.

Bidart, C., & Lavenu, D. (2005). Evolutions of personal networks and life events. *Social Networks, 27*(4), 359–376.

Biehl, M., Natsuaki, M., & Ge, X. (2007). The influence of pubertal timing on alcohol use and heavy drinking trajectories. *Journal of Youth & Adolescence, 36*(2), 153–167.

Biggs, S. (1999). *The mature imagination: Dynamics of identity in midlife and beyond*. Philadelphia: Open University Press.

Biorck, G. (1977). The essence of the clinician's art. *Acta Medica Scandinavica, 201*(3), 145–147.

Bitzan, J. E., & Kruzich, J. M. (1990). Interpersonal relationships of nursing home residents. *The Gerontologist, 30*, 385–390.

Bjorklund, B., & Bee, H. (2008). *The journey of adulthood* (6th ed.). Upper Saddle River, NJ: Pearson Prentice Hall.

Black, H. K. (1999). Life as gift: Spiritual narratives of elderly African American women living in poverty. *Journal of Aging Studies, 13*(4), 441–455.

Blacker, L. (2005). The launching phase of the life cycle. In B. Carter & M. McGoldrick (Eds.), *The expanded family life cycle: Individual, family, and social perspectives* (3rd ed., pp. 287–306). Boston: Allyn & Bacon.

Blackmon, S., & Vera, E. (2008). Ethnic and racial identity development in children of color. In J. Asamen, M. Ellis, & G. Berry (Eds.), *The SAGE handbook of child development, multiculturalism, and the media* (pp. 47–61). Thousand Oaks, CA: Sage.

Blass, E., & Ciaramitaro, V. (1994). A new look at some old mechanisms in human newborns: Taste and tactile determinants of state, affect, and action. *Monographs of the Society for Research in Child Development, 59*(1), v–81.

Blau, P. M. (1964). *Exchange and power in social life*. New York: Wiley.

Bliatout, B. (1993). Hmong death customs: Traditional and acculturated. In D. Irish, K. Lundquist, & V. Nelsen (Eds.), *Ethnic variations in dying, death, and grief: Diversity in universality* (pp. 77–99). Washington, DC: Taylor & Francis.

Blieszner, R., & Roberto, K. (2006). Perspectives on close relationships among the baby boomers. In S. Whitbourne & S. Willis (Eds.), *The baby boomers grow up: Contemporary perspectives on midlife* (pp. 261–281). Mahwah, NJ: Erlbaum.

Bloch, D. P., & Richmond, L. J. (Eds.). (1998). *Finding the work you love, loving the work you have*. Palo Alto, CA: Davies-Black.

Bloom, D. A., Yinghao, S., Sabanegh, E., De Almeida, J. C., Miner, J., & Gopalakrishan, G. (2009). Take home messages. *American Urological Association News (AUANews), 14*(5), 4–9.

Bloom, L. (1998a). Language acquisition in its developmental context. In W. Damon, D. Kuhn, & R. Siegler (Eds.), *Handbook of child psychology: Cognition, perception, and language* (5th ed., Vol. 2., pp. 309–370). New York: Wiley.

Bloom, L. (1998b). Language development: Emotional expression. *Pediatrics, 102*, 1272–1277.

Bloom, M. (1984). *Configurations of human behavior: Life span development in social environments*. New York: Macmillan.

Blyth, D. A., & Roehlkepartian, E. C. (1993). *Healthy communities, healthy youth*. Minneapolis, MN: Search Institute.

Boas, F. (1948). *Race, language and culture*. New York: Free Press. (Original work published 1940)

Boase, J., Horrigan, J., Wellman, B., & Rainie, L. (2006). The strength of Internet ties: The Internet and email aid users in maintaining their social networks and provide pathways to help when people face big decisions. Washington, DC: Pew Internet & American Life Project. Retrieved November 27, 2006, from http://www.pew internet.org

Boddie, S. C., & Cnaan, R. A. (Eds.). (2006). *Faith-based social services: Measures, assessments, and effectiveness*. Binghamton, NY: Haworth Press.

Boger, J., & Orfield, G. (2005). *School resegregation: Must the South turn back?* Chapel Hill, NC: University of North Carolina.

Boggia, B., Carbone, U., Farinari, E., Zarrilli, S., Lombardi, G., Colao, A., et al. (2009). Effects of working posture and exposure to traffic pollutants on sperm quality. *Journal of Endocrinological Investigation, 32*(5), 430–434.

Bohannan, P. (1995). *How culture works*. New York: Free Press.

Boldizar, J. P. (1991). Assessing sex typing and androgyny in children: The children's sex role inventory. *Developmental Psychology, 27*, 505–515.

Bolen, J. S. (1984). *Goddesses in every woman: A new psychology of women*. San Francisco: Harper & Row.

Bolland, K., & Atherton, C. (1999). Chaos theory: An alternative approach to social work practice and research. *Families in Society, 80*(4), 367–373.

Bonanno, G. (2004). Loss, trauma, and human resilience. *American Psychologist, 59*(1), 20–28.

Bonanno, G., & Kaltman, S. (1999). Toward an integrative perspective on bereavement. *Psychological Bulletin, 125*(6), 760–776.

Bond, B., Hefner, V., & Drogos, K. (2009). Information-seeking practices during the sexual development of lesbian, gay, and bisexual individuals: The influence and effects of coming out in a mediated environment. *Sexuality & Culture, 13*, 32–50.

Borden, W. (2009). *Contemporary psychodynamic theory and practice*. Chicago: Lyceum.

Borke, H. (1975). Piaget's mountains revisited: Changes in the egocentric landscape. *Developmental Psychology, 11*, 240–243.

Bornstein, A. (2009). N30 + 10: Global civil society, a decade after the Battle of Seattle. *Dialectical Anthropology, 33*, 97–108.

Bornstein, M., & Bradley, R. (Eds.). (2003). *Socioeconomic status, parenting, and child development*. Mahwah, NJ: Erlbaum.

Borse, N. N., Gilchrist, J., Dellinger, A. M., Rudd, R. A., Ballesteros, M. F., & Sleet, D. A. (2008). *CDC childhood injury report.* Washington, DC: Centers for Disease Control and Prevention. Retrieved January 19, 2010, from http://www.cdc.gov/safechild/images/CDC-Childhood Injury.pdf

Borysenko, J. (1996). *A woman's book of life: The biology, psychology, and spirituality of the feminine life cycle.* New York: Riverhead Books.

Borzekowski, D., Fobil, J., & Asante, O. (2006). Online access by adolescents in Accra: Ghanian teens' use of the Internet for health information. *Developmental Psychology, 42*(3), 450–458.

Bos, H., van Balan, F., & Visser, A. (2005). Social and cultural factors in infertility and childlessness. *Patient Education and Counseling, 59*(3), 223–225.

Boss, P. (2006). *Loss, trauma, and resilience: Therapeutic work with ambiguous loss.* New York: Norton.

Boubekri, M., Hull, R., & Boyer, L. (1991). Impact of window size and sunlight penetration on office workers' mood and satisfaction. *Environment and Behavior, 23,* 474–493.

Bourdieu, P. (1977). *Outline of a theory of practice.* New York: Cambridge University Press.

Boushey, A. (2001). The grief cycle—one parent's trip around. *Focus on Autism and Other Developmental Disabilities, 16*(1), 27–30.

Bouwsma, W. (1978). Christian adulthood. In E. H. Erikson (Ed.), *Adulthood* (pp. 81–96). New York: Norton & Norton.

Bowen, M. (1978). *Family therapy in clinical practice.* New York: Aronson.

Bowlby, J. (1969). *Attachment and loss.* New York: Basic Books.

Bowlby, J. (1980). *Attachment and loss: Loss, sadness, and depression* (Vol. 3). New York: Basic Books.

Bowlby, J. (1982). *Attachment and loss* (Vol. 1). New York: Basic Books.

Bowles, S., & Gintis, H. (1976). *Schooling in capitalist America: Educational reform and the contradictions of economic life.* New York: Basic Books.

Bowman, P. J. (2006). Role strain and adaptation issues in the strength-based model: Diversity, multilevel, and life-span considerations. *Counseling Psychologist, 34*(1), 118–133.

Boyatzis, R., & McKee, A. (2005). *Resonant leadership: Renewing yourself and connecting with others through mindfulness, hope, and compassion.* Boston: Harvard Business School Press.

Boyd, D., & Ellison, N. (2007). Social network sites: Definition, history, and scholarship. *Journal of Computer-Mediated Communication, 13*(1). Retrieved November 13, 2009, from http://jcmc.indiana.edu/vol13/issue1/boyd.ellison .html

Boyd-Franklin, N. (2003). Race, class, and poverty. In F. Walsh (Ed.), *Normal family processes: Growing diversity and complexity* (3rd ed., pp. 260–279). New York: Guilford Press.

Bradley, R., & Corwyn, R. (2002). Socioeconomic status and child development. *Annual Review of Psychology, 53,* 371–399.

Bradley, R., Whiteside, L., Mundfrom, D., Casey, P., Kelleher, K., & Pope, S. (1994). Early indications of resilience and their relation to experiences in the home environments of low birthweight, premature children living in poverty. *Child Development, 65,* 346–360.

Bradley, S. (2000). *Affect regulation and the development of psychopathology.* New York: Guilford Press.

Bradshaw, Y., Healey, J., & Smith, R. (2001). *Sociology for a new century.* Thousand Oaks, CA: Pine Forge.

Brain Injury Association of America. (2001). *Brain Injury Awareness Month 2001: Awareness kit.* Retrieved January 21, 2002, from http://www.biausa.org

Bramlett, M. D., & Mosher, W. D. (2002, July). Cohabitation, marriage, divorce, and remarriage in the United States. CDC National Center for Health Statistics and Vital Health Stat Series, 23(22). Retrieved January 19, 2010, from http://www.cdc.gov/nchs/data/series/sr_23/sr23_022.pdf

Branch, C., Tayal, P., & Triplett, C. (2000). The relationship of ethnic identity and ego identity status among adolescents and young adults. *International Journal of Intercultural Relations, 23,* 777–790.

Brandon, D. (1976). *Zen in the art of helping.* New York: Delta/Seymour Lawrence.

Brandon, D. H., Ryan, D. J., & Barnes, A. H. (2008). Effect of environmental changes on noise in the NICU. *Advances in Neonatal Care: Official Journal of the National Association of Neonatal Nurses, 8*(5 suppl), S5–S10.

Brandon, G. D., Adeniyl-Jones, S., Kirkby, S., Webb, D., Culhane, J., & Greenspan, J. S. (2009). Are outcomes and care processes for preterm neonates influenced by health insurance status? *Pediatrics, 124*(1), 122–127.

Brandtstadter, J. (2006). Adaptive resources in later life: Tenacious goal pursuits and flexible role adjustment. In M. Csikszentmihalyi & I. Csikszentmihalyi (Eds.), *A life worth living: Contributions to positive psychology* (pp. 143–164). New York: Oxford Press.

Brantley, J., Doucette, D., & Lindell, A. (2008). Mindfulness, meditation, and health. In A. L. Strozier & J. E. Carpenter (Eds.), *Introduction to alternative and complementary therapies* (pp. 9–29). New York: Haworth Press.

Braude, A. (1997). Women's history is American religious history. In T. A. Tweed (Ed.), *Retelling U.S. religious history* (pp. 87–107). Berkeley: University of California Press.

Brauner, C. B., & Stephens, C. B. (2006). Estimating the prevalence of early childhood serious emotional/behavioral disorders: Challenges and recommendations. *Public Health Reports, 121*(3), 303–310.

Brave Heart, M. Y. H. (2001). Clinical interventions with American Indians. In R. Fong & S. Furuto (Eds.), *Cultural competent social work practice: Practice skills, interventions, and evaluation* (pp. 285–298). New York: Longman.

Braver, S., Shapiro, J., & Goodman, M. (2006). Consequences of divorce for parents. In M. Fine & J. Harvey (Eds.), *Handbook of divorce and relationship dissolution* (pp. 313–337). Mahwah, NJ: Erlbaum.

Brawley, E. (2006). *Design innovations for aging and Alzheimer's.* Hoboken, NJ: Wiley.

Brazelton, T. B. (1983). *Infants and mothers: Differences in development.* New York: Delta/Seymour Lawrence.

Breitman, B. E. (1995). Social and spiritual reconstruction of self within a feminist Jewish community. *Woman and Therapy: A Feminist Quarterly, 16*(2/3), 73–82.

Brent, J. (1997). Community without unity. In P. Hoggett (Ed.), *Contested communities: Experiences, struggles, policies* (pp. 68–83). Bristol, UK: Policy Press.

Bridgett, D., Gartstein, M., Putnam, S., McKay, T., Iddins, E., Robertson, C., et al. (2009). Maternal and contextual influences and the effect of temperament development during infancy on parenting in toddlerhood. *Infant Behavior & Development, 32,* 103–116.

Broderick, P. C., & Blewitt, P. (2006). *The life span: Human development for helping professionals* (2nd ed.). Upper Saddle River, NJ: Pearson.

Brodsky, A., & Marx, C. (2001). Layers of identity: Multiple psychological senses of community within a community setting. *Journal of Community Psychology, 29*(2), 161–178.

Brodsky, A., O'Campo, P., & Aronson, R. (1999). PSOC in community context: Multilevel correlates of a measure of psychological sense of community in low-income, urban neighborhoods. *Journal of Community Psychology, 27,* 659–679.

Brokenleg, M., & Middleton, D. (1993). Native Americans: Adapting, yet retaining. In D. Irish, K. Lundquist, & V. Nelsen (Eds.), *Ethnic variations in dying, death, and grief: Diversity in universality* (pp. 101–112). Washington, DC: Taylor & Francis.

Bronfenbrenner, U. (1979). *The ecology of human development: Experiments by nature and design.* Cambridge, MA: Harvard University Press.

Bronfenbrenner, U. (1989). Ecological systems theory. *Annals of Child Development, 6,* 187–249.

Bronfenbrenner, U. (1993). The ecology of cognitive development: Research models and fugitive findings. In R. Wozniak & K. Fischer (Eds.), *Development in context: Acting and thinking in specific environments* (pp. 3–44). Hillsdale, NJ: Erlbaum.

Bronfenbrenner, U. (1999). Environments in developmental perspective: Theoretical and operational models. In S. Friedman & T. Wachs (Eds.), *Measuring environment across the life span* (pp. 3–28). Washington, DC: American Psychological Association.

Brooks, P., Jia., X, Braine, M., & Da Graca Dias, M. (1998). A cross-linguistic study of children's comprehension of universal quantifiers: A comparison of Mandarin Chinese, Portuguese, and English. *First Language, 18,* 33–79.

Brooks-Gunn, J., & Furstenberg, F. (1989). Adolescent sexual behavior. *American Psychologist, 44,* 249–257.

Brooks-Gunn, J., & Paikoff, R. (1993). Sex is a gamble, kissing is a game: Adolescent sexuality and health promotion. In S. Millstein, A. Petersen, & E. Nightingale (Eds.), *Promoting the health of adolescents* (pp. 180–208). New York: Oxford University Press.

Brown, B. B. (2004). Adolescent's relationships with peers. In R. M. Lerner & L. Steinberg (Eds.), *Handbook of adolescent psychology* (2nd ed., pp. 363–394). New York: Wiley.

Brown, B. B., & Klute, C. (2003). Friendships, cliques, and crowds. In G. Adams & M. Berzonsky (Eds.), *Blackwell handbook of adolescence* (pp. 330–345). Oxford, UK: Blackwell.

Brown, G. (2009). NICU noise and the preterm infant. *Neonatal Network, 28*(3), 165–173.

Brown, G., Lawrence, T., & Robinson, S. (2005). Territoriality in organizations. *Academy of Management Review, 30*(3), 577–594.

Brown, J. (2003). The self-enhancement motive in collectivistic cultures: The rumors of my death have been greatly exaggerated. *Journal of Cross-Cultural Psychology, 34,* 603–605.

Brown, J., Dutton, K., & Cook, K. (2001). From the top down: Self-esteem and self-evaluation. *Cognition and Emotion, 15,* 615–631.

Brown, K. A., Jemmott, F. F., Mitchell, H. J., & Walton, M. L. (1998). The Well: A neighborhood-based health promotion model for Black women. *Health and Social Work, 23*(2), 146–152.

Brown, L., Shepherd, M., Wituk, S., & Meissen, G. (2007). How settings change people: Applying behavior setting theory to consumer-run organizations. *Journal of Community Psychology, 35*(3), 399–416.

Brown, R. A., Rehkopf, D. H., Copeland, W. E., Costello, E. J., & Worthman, C. M. (2009). Lifecourse priorities among Appalachian emerging adults: Revisiting Wallace's organization of diversity. *ETHOS, 37*(2), 225–242.

Brown, S. G., Morrison, L. A., Larkspur, L. M., Marsh, A. L., & Nicolaisen, N. (2008). Well-being, sleep, exercise patterns, and the menstrual cycle: A comparison of natural hormones, oral contraceptive and Depo-Provera. *Women's Health, 47*(1), 105–121.

Browne, C., Mokuau, N., & Braun, K. (2009). Adversity and resiliency in lives of Native Hawaiian elders. *Social Work, 54*(3), 253–261.

Brubaker, E., Gorman, M. A., & Hiestand, M. (1990). Stress perceived by elderly recipients of family care. In T. H. Brubaker (Ed.), *Family relationships in later life* (2nd ed., pp. 267–281). Newbury Park, CA: Sage.

Bruce, E., & Schultz, C. (2002). Non-finite loss and challenges to communication between parents and professionals. *British Journal of Special Education, 29*(1), 9–14.

Bruce, S., & Muhammad, Z. (2009). The development of object permanence in children with intellectual disability, physical disability, autism, and blindness. *International Journal of Disability, Development & Education, 56*(3), 229–246.

Brunello, G., & Checchi, D. (2007). Does school tracking affect equality of opportunity? New evidence. *Economic Policy, 22,* 781–861.

Brunner, H., Larissa, R., & Huber, K. R. (2009). Contraceptive choices of women 35–44 years of age: Findings from the behavioral risk factor surveillance system. *Annals of Epidemiology, 19*(11), 823–831.

Bryson, K., & Casper, L. (1999). *Coresident grandparents and grandchildren.* Washington, DC: U.S. Census Bureau.

Bucko, R. A., & Iron Cloud, S. (2008). Lakota health and healing. *Southern Medical Journal, 101*(6), 596–598.

Buffardi, A., Thomas, K., Holmes, K., & Manhart, L. (2008). Moving upstream: Ecosocial and psychosocial correlates of sexually transmitted infections among young adults in the United States. *American Journal of Public Health, 98*(6), 1128–1136.

Bullis, R. K. (1996). *Spirituality in social work practice.* Washington, DC: Taylor & Francis.

Bullis, R. K., & Harrigan, M. (1992). Religious denominational policies on sexuality. *Families in Society, 73,* 304–312.

Bunting, L., & McAuley, C. (2004). Teenage pregnancy and motherhood: The contribution of child support. *Child and Family Social Work, 9,* 201–215.

Bureau of Justice Statistics. (2000). *Women ages 16 to 24 experience the highest rates of violence by current or former partners.* Washington, DC: Author.

Burke, M. T., Chauvin, J. C., & Miranti, J. G. (2005). *Religious and spiritual issues in counseling: Applications across diverse populations.* New York: Brunner/Routledge.

Burnette, D. (1999). Custodial grandparents in Latino families: Patterns of service use and predictors of unmet needs. *Social Work, 44*(1), 22–34.

Burrell, G., & Morgan, G. (1979). *Sociological paradigms and organizational analysis.* London: Heinemann.

Burt, M., & Katz, B. (1987). Dimensions of recovery from rape: Focus on growth outcomes. *Journal of Interpersonal Violence, 2,* 57–82.

Burtless, G. (2001). *Has widening inequality promoted or retarded U.S. growth?* Retrieved April 20, 2010, from http://www.brookings.edu/articles/2003/0901useconomics_burtless.aspx

Burton, L. (1981). *A critical analysis and review of the research on Outward Bound and related programs.* Unpublished doctoral dissertation, Rutgers University, New Brunswick, NJ.

Busato, J., & Wilson, F. S. (2009). Vasectomy reversal: A seven-year experience. *Urologia Internationalis, 82*(2),170–174.

Bush, K., Bohon, S., & Kim, H. (2010). Adaptation among immigrant families: Resources and barriers. In S. Price, C. Price, & P. McKenry (Eds.), *Families & change: Coping with stressful events and transitions* (4th ed., pp. 285–310). Thousand Oaks, CA: Sage.

Buss, L., Tolstrup, J., Munk, C., Bergholt, T., Ottesen, B., Gronbaek, M., et al. (2006). Spontaneous abortion: A prospective cohort study of younger women from the general population in Denmark: Validation, occurrence and risk determinants. *Acta Obstetricia et Gynaecologica Scandinavica, 85*(4), 467–475.

Bussolari, C., & Goodell, J. (2009). Chaos theory as a model of life transitions counseling: Nonlinear dynamics and life's changes. *Journal of Counseling & Development, 87,* 98–107.

Butler, R. N. (1963). The life review: An interpretation of reminiscence in the aged. *Psychiatry, 26,* 65–70.

Butler, R. N. (1987). Life review. In G. L. Maddox (Ed.), *The encyclopedia of aging: A comprehensive resource in gerontology and geriatrics* (2nd ed., pp. 397–398). New York: Springer.

Buzzell, L. (Ed.). (2009). *Ecotherapy: Healing with nature in mind.* San Francisco: Sierra Club Books.

Byock, I. (1997). *Dying well: Peace and possibilities at the end of life.* New York: Riverhead Books.

Byock, I. (2004). *The four things that matter most: A book about living.* New York: Free Press.

Byoung-Suk, K., Ulrich, R., Walker, V., & Tassinary, L. (2008). Anger and stress: The role of landscape posters in an office setting. *Environment & Behavior, 40*(3), 355–381.

Cacioppo, J. T., Amaral, D. G., Blancard, J. J., Cameron, J. L., Carter, C. S., Crews, D., et al. (2007). Social neuroscience: Progress and promise. *Perspectives on Psychological Science, 2,* 99–123.

Cacioppo, J. T., Bernston, G. G., Sheridan, J. F., & McClintock, M. K. (2000). Multilevel integrative analysis of human behavior: Social neuroscience and the complementary nature of social and biological approaches. *Psychological Bulletin, 126*(6), 829–843.

Cagle, J. G. (2008). Informal caregivers of advanced cancer patients: The impact of geographic proximity on social support and bereavement adjustment. Unpublished doctoral dissertation, Virginia Commonwealth University. Retrieved January 8, 2010, from https://digarchive.library.vcu.edu/bitstream/10156/1974/1/caglejg_phd.pdf

Cagle, J. G., & Kovacs, P. J. (2009). Education: A complex and empowering social work intervention at the end of life. *Health & Social Work, 34*(1), 17–27.

Cain, A. C. (2006). Parent suicide: Pathways of effects into the third generation. *Psychiatry, 69*(3), 204–227.

Cairns, D. B. (2005). The journey to resiliency: An integrative framework for treatment for victims and survivors of family violence. *Social Work & Christianity, 32*(4), 305–320.

Calkins, S. (2004). Early attachment processes and the development of emotional self-regulation. In R. Baumeister & K. Vohs (Eds.), *Handbook of self-regulation: Research, theory, and application* (pp. 324–339). New York: Guilford Press.

Calkins, S., & Hill, A. (2007). Caregiver influences on emerging emotion regulation: Biological and environmental transactions in early development. In J. Gross (Ed.), *Handbook of emotion regulation* (pp. 229–248). New York: Guilford Press.

Calman, L., & Tarr-Whelan, L. (2005). *Early childhood education for all: A wise investment.* Retrieved May 3, 2007, from http://web.mit.edu/workplacecenter/docs/Full%20Report.pdf

Cameron, J. (1992). *The artist's way: A spiritual path to higher creativity.* New York: Putnam.

Cameron, L. (1999). Understanding alcohol abuse in American Indian/Alaskan native youth. *Pediatric Nursing, 25*(3), 297.

Campbell, C., & Jovchelovitch, S. (2000). Health, community and development: Towards a social psychology of participation. *Journal of Community & Applied Social Psychology, 10,* 255–270.

Campbell, D. (1997). *The Mozart effect: Tapping the power of music to heal the body, strengthen the mind, and unlock the creative spirit.* New York: Harper Trade.

Campbell, L., Campbell, B., & Dickinson, D. (1999). *Teaching and learning through multiple intelligences* (2nd ed.). Needham Heights, MA: Allyn & Bacon.

Campbell, R., & MacFarlane, A. (1986). Place of delivery: A review. *British Journal of Obstetrics and Gynaecology, 93*(7), 675–683.

Campbell, R., & Sais, E. (1995). Accelerated metalinguistic (phonological) awareness in bilingual children. *British Journal of Developmental Psychology, 13,* 61–68.

Campbell, S. (2002). *Behavioral problems in preschool children* (2nd ed.). New York: Guilford Press.

Canadian Council on Learning. (2006). *Why is high-quality child care essential?* Retrieved February 13, 2010, from http://www.ccl-cca.ca

Canda, E. R. (1983). General implications of shamanism for clinical social work. *International Social Work, 26*(4), 14–22.

Canda, E. R. (1988). Conceptualizing spirituality for social work: Insights from diverse perspectives. *Social Thought, 14*(1), 30–46.

Canda, E. R. (1997). Spirituality. *Encyclopedia of social work: 1997 supplement* (19th ed.). Washington, DC: NASW Press.

Canda, E. R. (2001). Buddhism. In M. V. Hook, B. Hugen, & M. Aguilar (Eds.), *Spirituality within religious traditions in social work practice* (pp. 53–72). Pacific Grove, CA: Brooks/Cole.

Canda, E. R. (2005). The future of spirituality in social work: The farther reaches of human nature. *Advances in Social Work, 6*(1), 97–108.

Canda, E. R., & Furman, L. D. (1999). *Spiritual diversity in social work practice: The heart of helping.* New York: Free Press.

Canda, E. R., & Furman, L.D. (2010). *Spiritual diversity in social work practice: The heart of helping* (2nd ed.). New York: Oxford University Press.

Canda, E. R., Nakashima, M., & Furman, L. D. (2004). Ethical considerations about spirituality in social work: Insights from a national qualitative study. *Families in Society: The Journal of Contemporary Social Services, 85*(1), 27–35.

Canda, E. R., & Phaobtong, T. (1992). Buddhism as a support system for Southeast Asian refugees. *Social Work, 37,* 61–67.

Canda, E. R., Shin, S., & Canda, H. (1993). Traditional philosophies of human services in Korea and contemporary social work implications. *Social Development Issues, 15*(3), 84–104.

Canda, E. R., & Yellow Bird, M. J. (1996). Cross-tradition borrowing of spiritual practices in social work settings. *Society for Spirituality and Social Work Newsletter, 3*(1), 1–7.

Cannon, W. B. (1924). *Bodily changes in pain, hunger, fear, and rage.* New York: Appleton.

Cantor, K. (2007). PREEMIE Act passes Congress: Funding still needed to reduce preterm births. *Nursing for Women's Health, 11*(2), 129–132.

Caplan, G. (1990). Loss, stress, and mental health. *Community Mental Health Journal, 26,* 27–48.

Caplan, G., & Caplan, R. B. (2000). The future of primary prevention. *Journal of Primary Prevention, 21*(2), 131–136.

Cappeliez, P., Beaupré, M., & Robitaille, A. (2008). Characteristics and impact of life turning points for older adults. *Ageing International, 32,* 54–64.

Carey, J. (Ed.). (1990). *Brain facts: A primer on the brain and nervous system.* Washington, DC: Society for Neuroscience.

Carey, T. A. (1994). "Spare the rod and spoil the child." Is this a sensible justification for the use of punishment in child rearing? *Child Abuse and Neglect, 18,* 1005–1010.

Carley, G. (2005). An influence of spiritual narrative in community work. *Canadian Social Work, 7*(1), 81–94.

Carnes, R., & Craig, S. (1998). *Sacred circles: A guide to creating your own women's spirituality group.* San Francisco: HarperSanFrancisco.

Carolan, M. T., Bagherinia, G., Juhari, R., Himelright, J., & Mouton-Sanders, M. (2000). Contemporary Muslim families: Research and practice. *Contemporary Family Therapy, 22*(1), 67–79.

Carpenter, L., Nathanson, C., & Kim, Y. (2009). Physical women, emotional men: Gender and sexual satisfaction in midlife. *Archives of Sexual Behavior, 38*(1), 21–26.

Carpenter, M. B. (1991). *Core text of neuroanatomy* (4th ed.). Baltimore: Williams & Wilkins.

Carroll, M. (1998). Social work's conceptualization of spirituality. *Social Thought, 18*(2), 1–14.

Carstensen, L. (1992). Social and emotional patterns in adulthood: Support for socioemotional selectivity theory. *Psychology and Aging, 7,* 331–338.

Carter, B., & McGoldrick, M. (2005a). Coaching at various stages of the life cycle. In B. Carter & M. McGoldrick (Eds.), *The expanded family life cycle: Individual, family, and social perspectives* (3rd ed., pp. 436–454). New York: Pearson.

Carter, B., & McGoldrick, M. (2005b). The divorce cycle: A major variation in the American family life cycle. In B. Carter & M. McGoldrick (Eds.), *The expanded family life cycle: Individual, family, and social perspectives* (3rd ed., pp. 373–380). Boston: Allyn & Bacon.

Carter, B., & McGoldrick, M. (2005c). *The expanded family life cycle: Individual, family, and social perspectives* (3rd ed.). New York: Pearson.

Carter, D. B., & Patterson, C. J. (1982). Sex roles as social conventions: The development of children's conceptions of sex-role stereotypes. *Developmental Psychology, 18,* 812–824.

Carter, R. (2009). *The human brain book.* London: DK.

Carter, S. (2000). *No excuses: Lessons from 21 high-performing, high poverty schools.* Washington, DC: The Heritage Foundation.

Carvalho, A. E., Linhares, M. B., Padovani, F. H., & Martinez, F. E. (2009). Anxiety and depression in mothers of preterm infants and psychological intervention during hospitalization in neonatal ICU. *The Spanish Journal of Psychology, 12*(1), 161–170.

CASA. (2002). *CASA 2002 teen survey.* New York: National Center on Addiction and Substance Abuse at Columbia University (CASA).

Casale-Giannola, D., & Kamens, M. W. (2006). Inclusion at a university: Experiences of a young woman with Down syndrome. *Mental Retardation, 44*(5), 344–352.

Case, R. (1998). The development of conceptual structures. In D. Kuhn & R. Siegler (Eds.), *Handbook of child psychology: Vol. 2. Cognition, perception, and language* (5th ed., pp. 745–800). New York: Wiley.

Caspi, A. (1987). Personality in the life course. *Journal of Personality and Social Psychology, 53*(6), 1203–1213.

Castex, G. M. (1994). Providing services to Hispanic/Latino populations: Profiles in diversity. *Social Work, 39*(3), 288–296.

Cattich, J., & Knudson-Martin, C. (2009). Spirituality and relationship: A holistic analysis of how couples cope with diabetes. *Journal of Marital & Family Therapy, 35*(1), 111–124.

Cavanagh, S. (2004). The sexual debut of girls in early adolescence: The intersection of race, pubertal timing, and friendship group characteristics. *Journal of Research on Adolescence, 14,* 285–312.

Center for Health Design. (2006). *Transforming healthcare buildings into healing environments.* Retrieved August 31, 2006, from http://www.healthdesign.org

Centers for Disease Control and Prevention. (2004). *Trends in reportable sexually transmitted diseases in the United States, 2004.* Retrieved August 4, 2006, from http://www.cdc.gov/std/stats/trends2004.htm

Centers for Disease Control and Prevention. (2005a). *HIV/AIDS among African Americans.* Retrieved May 18, 2010, from http://www.cdc.gov/hiv/topics/aa/resources/fact sheets.aa.htm

Centers for Disease Control and Prevention. (2005b). *Preventing heart disease and stroke.* Retrieved October 20, 2006, from http://www.cdc.gov/nccdphp/publishers/factsheets/Prevention/cvh.htm

Centers for Disease Control and Prevention. (2005c). *Trends in reportable sexually transmitted diseases in the United States, 2004: National Surveillance Data for Chlamydia, Gonorrhea, and Syphilis.* Retrieved September 10, 2011, from http://www.cdc.gov/std/stats07/trends.htm

Centers for Disease Control and Prevention. (2006a). *Breast-feeding: Data and statistics: Breastfeeding practices—Results from the 2005 National Immunization Survey.* Retrieved December 11, 2006, from http://www.cdc.gov/breastfeedomgdat/NIS_data/data_2005.htm

Centers for Disease Control and Prevention. (2006b). *Cases of HIV infection and AIDS in the United States, 2004. HIV/AIDS surveillance report* (Vol. 16). Atlanta, GA: Author.

Centers for Disease Control and Prevention. (2006c). *Facts about traumatic brain injury.* Retrieved October 24, 2009, from http://www.biausa.org/aboutbi.htm.

Centers for Disease Control and Prevention. (2006d). State-specific prevalence of obesity among adults: United States. *Morbidity and Mortality Weekly Report, 55*(36), 985–988.

Centers for Disease Control and Prevention. (2007). *Youth Risk Behavior Surveillance System (YRBSS). 2007 national, state, and local data.* Retrieved January 1, 2010, from http://www.cdc.gov/HealthyYouth/yrbs/index.htm

Centers for Disease Control and Prevention. (2008a). *NCHS Data on teenage pregnancy.* CDC/National Center for Health Statistics. Retrieved November 1, 2009, from http://www.cdc.gov/nchs/data/infosheets/infosheet_teen_preg.htm

Centers for Disease Control and Prevention. (2008b). *Sexual violence: Facts at a glance.* Washington, DC: Author. Retrieved January 19, 2010, from http://www.cdc.gov/violenceprevention/pdf/SV-DataSheet-a.pdf

Centers for Disease Control and Prevention. (2008c). *Teen pregnancy and birth rates: Birth rates in teen girls ages 15–19, 2006.* CDC/National Center for Health Statistics. Retrieved November 1, 2009, from http://www.cdc.gov/featerues/dsteenpregnancy

Centers for Disease Control and Prevention. (2008d). *Youth risk behavior surveillance—United States, 2007.* Retrieved May 19, 2010, from http://www.cdc.gov/mmwr/preview/mmwrtml/ss5704a1.htm

Centers for Disease Control and Prevention. (2009a). *Assisted reproduction technology (ART) report: National summary and fertility clinic reports.* Retrieved August 6, 2011, from http://www.cdc.gov/art/

Centers for Disease Control and Prevention. (2009b). *Autism spectrum disorders.* Retrieved February 22, 2010, from http://www.cdc.gov/ncbddd/autism/screening.html

Centers for Disease Control and Prevention. (2009c). *Basic statistics. HIV/AIDS surveillance report: Cases of HIV infection in the United States and dependent areas, 2007.* Retrieved December 4, 2009, from http://www.cdc.gov/hiv/topics/surveillance/basic.htm#hivaidscases

Centers for Disease Control and Prevention. (2009d). *FastStats: Birthweight and gestation.* Retrieved January 17, 2010, from http://www.cdc.gov/nchs/fastats/birthwt.htm

Centers for Disease Control and Prevention. (2009e). *Life expectancy.* Retrieved February 23, 2010, from http://www.cdc.gov/nchs/fastats/lifexpect.htm

Centers for Disease Control and Prevention. (2009f). *Preventing teen pregnancy: An update in 2009.* Retrieved January 17, 2010, from http://www.cdc.gov/reproductivehealth/adolescentreprohealth/AboutTP.htm

Centers for Disease Control and Prevention. (2009g). *Sexually transmitted diseases surveillance, 2007.* Retrieved February 9, 2010, from http://www.cdc.gov/std/stats07/natoverview.htm

Centers for Disease Control and Prevention. (2009h). *Teen birth rates up again in 2007.* CDC/National Center for Health Statistics. Retrieved November 8, 2009, from http://www.cdc.gov/nchs/pressroom/09newsreleases/teenbirth2007.htm

Centers for Disease Control and Prevention. (2009i). *Teen births.* CDC/National Center for Health Statistics. Retrieved October 31, 2009, from http://www.cdc.gov/nchs/fastats/beenbrth.htm

Centers for Disease Control and Prevention. (2010). *Heart disease and stroke statistics 2010 update.* Retrieved September 14, 2011, from http://www.cdc.gov/heart disease/facts.htm

Centers for Disease Control and Prevention, National Center for Injury and Prevention and Control. (2010). *Child maltreatment: Fact sheet.* Retrieved September 14, 2011, from http://www.cdc.gov/violenceprevention/pdf/CM-FactSheet-a.pdf

Cervigni, F., Suzuki, Y., Ishii, T., & Hata, A. (2008). Spatial accessibility to pediatric services. *Journal of Community Health, 33,* 444–448.

Chachamovich, J., Chachamovich, E., Fleck, M., Cordova, F., Knauth, D., & Passos, E. (2009). Congruence of quality of life among infertile men and women: Findings from a couple-based study. *Human Reproduction, 24*(9), 2151–2157.

Challenger, Gray, & Christmas, Inc. (2006). *May 2006 Challenger employment report.* Retrieved November 12, 2006, from http://chicagobusiness.com/cgi-bin/article.pl?portal_id=131@page_id=2000

Champagne, E. (2001). Listening to . . . listening for . . . : A theological reflection on spirituality in early childhood. In J. Erriker, C. Ota, & C. Erricker (Eds.), *Spiritual education: Cultural, religious, and social differences: New perspectives for the 21st century.* Brighton, UK: Sussex Academic.

Chang, L. (2001). The development of racial attitudes and self concepts of Taiwanese preschoolers (China). *Dissertation Abstracts International: Section A: Humanities & Social Sciences, 61*(8-A), 3045.

Charles, V. E., Polis, C. B., Sridhara, S. K., & Blum, R. W. (2008). Abortion and long-term mental health outcomes: A systematic review of the evidence. *Contraception, 79*(6), 436–450.

Charlesworth, L. (2007). Child maltreatment. In E. Hutchison, H. Matto, M. Harrigan, L. Charlesworth, & P. Viggiani (Eds.), *Challenges of living: A multidimensional working model for social workers* (pp. 105–139). Thousand Oaks, CA: Sage.

Charon, J. (1998). *Symbolic interactionism: An introduction, an interpretation, and integration* (6th ed.). Englewood Cliffs, NJ: Prentice Hall.

Chase-Lansdale, P. L., & Vinovskis, M. A. (1995). Whose responsibility? An historical analysis of the changing roles of mothers, fathers, and society. In P. L. Chase-Lansdale & J. Brooks-Gunn (Eds.), *Escape from poverty: What makes a difference for children?* (pp. 11–37). New York: Cambridge University Press.

Chavarro, J. E., Rich-Edwards, J. W., Rosner, B. A., & Willett, W. C. (2007). Diet and lifestyle in the prevention of ovulatory disorder infertility. *Obstetrics and Gynecology, 110*(5), 1050–1058.

Cheap IVF needed: Editorial. (2006, August 30). *Nature, 442*(31), 958. Retrieved October 28, 2006, from http://www.nature.com/nature/journal/v442/n7106/full/442958a.html

Check, J. H. (2007). Treatment of male infertility. *Clinical and Experimental Obstetrics and Gynecology, 34*(4), 201–207.

Chen, C. (2006a). Does the completeness of a household-based convoy matter in intergenerational support exchanges? *Social Indicators Research, 79,* 117–142.

Chen, C. (2006b). A household-based convoy and the reciprocity of support exchange between adult children and noncoresiding parents. *Journal of Family Issues, 27*(8), 1100–1136.

Chen, J., Rehkopf, D., Waterman, P., Subramanian, S., Coull, B., Cohen, B., et al. (2006). Mapping and measuring social disparities in premature mortality: The impact of census tract poverty within and across Boston. *Journal of Urban Health, 83*(6), 1063–1084.

Chen, M., Harris, D., Folkoff, M., Drudge, R., & Jackson, C. (1999). Developing a collaborative GIS in social services. *Geo Info Systems, 9,* 44–47.

Chen, X. (2009). The linkage between deviant lifestyles and victimization: An examination from a life course perspective. *Journal of Interpersonal Violence, 24*(7), 1083–1110.

Chestang, L. (1972). *Character development in a hostile environment.* Chicago: University of Chicago Press.

Chethik, M. (2000). *Techniques of child therapy: Psychodynamic approaches* (2nd ed.). New York: Guilford Press.

Cheung, G., & Todd-Oldehaver, C. (2006). Personality trait of harm avoidance in late-life depression. *International Journal of Geriatric Psychiatry, 21*(2), 192–193.

Chibucos, T., & Leite, R. (2005). *Readings in family theory.* Thousand Oaks, CA: Sage.

Child Trends. (2011). *Foster care data snapshot.* Retrieved August 29, 2011, from http://www.childtrends.org/Files/Child_Trends_2011_05_31_DS_FosterCare.pdf

Child Trends Data Bank. (2010). *Education attainment (youth).* Retrieved February 22, 2010, from http://www.childtrendsdatabank.org/?q=node/182

Child Welfare League of America. (2005). Statement of the Child Welfare League of America for House Subcommittee on Human Resources of the Committee on Ways and Means for the Hearing on Federal Foster Care Financing. Retrieved December 27, 2006, from http://www.cwla.org/advocacy/fostercare050609.htm

Children's Defense Fund. (2000). *Yearbook 2000: The state of America's children.* Washington, DC: Author.

Children's Defense Fund. (2008). *The state of America's children, 2008.* Washington, DC: Author.

Childress, H. (2004). Teenagers, territory and the appropriation of space. *Childhood: A Global Journal of Child Research, 11,* 195–205.

China Education and Research Network. (2000). *Basic education in China (IV).* Retrieved November 6, 2006, from http://www.edu.cn/20010101/21778.shtml

Chodorow, N. (1978). *The reproduction of mothering: Psychoanalysis and the sociology of gender.* Berkeley: University of California Press.

Chodorow, N. (1989). *Feminism and psychoanalytic theory.* New Haven, CT: Yale University Press.

Choi, G., & Tirrito, T. (1999). The Korean church as a social service provider for older adults. *Arete, 23*(2), 69–83.

Choi, S., & Tittle, G. (2002). *Parental substance abuse and child maltreatment literature review.* Retrieved September 11, 2011, from http://www.cfrc.illinois.edu/publications/lr_20020501_ParentalSubstanceAbuseAndChildMaltreatment.pdf

Chomsky, N. (1968). *Language and mind.* New York: Harcourt Brace Jovanovich.

Christ, C. P. (1995). *Odyssey with the goddess: A spiritual quest in Crete.* New York: Continuum.

Christiansen, O. B., Nielsen, H. S., & Kolte, A. M. (2006). Future directions of failed implantation and recurrent miscarriage research. *Reproductive Biomedicine Online, 13.*

Chugani, H., Behen, M., Muzik, O., Juhasz, C., Nagy, F., & Chugani, D. (2001). Local brain functional activity following early deprivation: A study of post-institutional Romanian orphans. *Neuroimage, 14,* 1290–1301.

Chumlea, W. C., Schubert, C. M., Roche, A. F., Kulin, H. E., Lee, P. A., Himes, J. H., et al. (2003). Age at menarche and racial comparisons in U.S. girls. *Pediatrics, 111*(1), 110–113.

Chung, D. K. (2001). Confucianism. In M. V. Hook, B. Hugen, & M. Aguilar (Eds.), *Spirituality within religious traditions in social work practice* (pp. 73–97). Pacific Grove, CA: Brooks/Cole.

Chung, G., Tucker, M., & Takeuchi, D. (2008). Wives' relative income production and household male dominance: Examining violence among Asian American enduring couples. *Family Relations, 57,* 227–238.

Chung, I. W. (2006). A cultural perspective on emotions and behavior: An empathic pathway to examine intergenerational conflicts in Chinese immigrant families. *Families in Society, 87*(3), 367–376.

Cingolani, J. (1984). Social conflict perspective on work with involuntary clients. *Social Work, 29,* 442–446.

Clammer, J. (2009). Sociology and beyond: Towards a deep sociology. *Asian Journal of Social Science, 37*(3), 332–346.

Clare, R., Mazzucchelli, T., Studman, L., & Sanders, M. (2006). Behavioral family intervention for children with developmental disabilities and behavioral problems. *Journal of Clinical Child and Adolescent Psychology, 35*(2), 180–193.

Clark, C. C. (2002). *Health promotion in communities: Holistic and wellness approaches.* New York: Springer.

Clark, J. L. (2007). Listening for meaning: A research-based model for attending to spirituality, culture, and worldview in social work practice. *Critical Social Work, 7*(1). Retrieved February 26, 2010, from http://www.uwindsor.ca/criticalsocialwork/2006-volume-7-no-1

Clark, K., & Clark, M. (1939). The development of consciousness of self and the emergence of racial identification in

Negro preschool children. *Journal of Social Psychology, 10,* 591–599.

Clark, M. K., Dillon, J., Sowers, M., & Nichols, S. (2005). Weight, fat mass, and central distribution of fat increase when women use depotmedroxprogesterone acetate for contraception. *International Journal of Obesity, 29*(10), 1252–1258.

Clark, P. A. (2009). Embryo donation/adoption: Medical, legal, and ethical perspectives. *The Internet Journal of Law, Healthcare, and Ethics, 5*(2), 1–12.

Clarke, L. (2008). Grandparents: A family resource? In D. R. Crane & T. Heaton (Eds.), *Handbook of families & poverty* (pp. 365–380). Thousand Oaks, CA: Sage.

Clarke-Stewart, K. A. (1988). "The 'effects' of infant day care reconsidered" reconsidered: Risks for parents, children, and researchers. *Early Childhood Research Quarterly, 3*(3), 293–318.

Clarke-Stewart, K. A. (1989). Infant day care: Maligned or malignant? *American Psychologist, 17,* 454–462.

Clean Clothes Campaign. (2009, October 5). *Asia wage demand put to Euro retailers.* Retrieved October 23, 2009, from http://www.cleanclothes.org/media-inquiries/press-releases/asia-wage-demand-put-to-euro-retailers

Clearfield, M., & Nelson, N. (2006). Sex differences in mothers' speech and play behavior with 6-, 9-, and 14-month-old infants. *Sex Roles, 54*(1/2), 127–137.

Clearinghouse on International Developments in Child, Youth and Family Policies at Columbia University. (2002). *Child policy international.* Retrieved June 7, 2002, from http://www.childpolicyintl.org

Clearinghouse on International Developments in Child, Youth and Family Policies at Columbia University. (2004). *Maternity and parental leaves, 1999–2002.* Retrieved April 25, 2010, from http://www.childpolicyintl.org

Cleveland Clinic. (2005–2009). *Your pulse and your target heart rate.* Retrieved December 20, 2009, from http://www.cchs.net/health/health-info/docs/0900/0984.asp?index=5508

Coates, J. (2003). *Ecology and social work: Toward a new paradigm.* Halifax, NS, Canada: Fernwood.

Coates, J. (2007). From ecology to spirituality and social justice. In J. Coates, J. R. Graham, B. Swartzentruber, & B. Ouelette (Eds.), *Spirituality and social work: Selected Canadian readings* (pp. 213–227). Toronto, Ont.: Canadian Scholars' Press.

Cohen, J., & Sandy, S. (2007). The social, emotional and academic education of children: Theories, goals, methods and assessments. In R. Bar-On, J. Maree, & M. Elias (Eds.), *Educating people to be emotionally intelligent* (pp. 63–77). Westport, CT: Praeger.

Cohn, T. (1997). Art as a healing force: Creativity, healing, and spirituality. *Artweek, 28,* 15–17.

Coid, J., Petruckevitch, A., Feder, G., Chung, W. S., Richardson, J., & Moorey, S. (2001). Relation between childhood sexual and physical abuse and risk of revictimisation in women: A cross-sectional survey. *The Lancet, 358,* 450–454.

Coie, J. D., Dodge, K. A., & Coppotelli, H. (1982). Dimensions and types of social status: A cross-age perspective. *Developmental Psychology, 18,* 557–570.

Cole, P., Luby, J., & Sullivan, M. (2008). Emotions and the development of childhood depression: Bridging the gap. *Child Development Perspectives, 2*(3), 141–148.

Cole, S. (1992). *Making science: Between nature and society.* Cambridge, MA: Harvard University Press.

Coleman, J. (1990). *Foundations of social theory.* Cambridge, MA: Belknap Press.

Coles, L. S. (2004). Demography of human supercentenarians. *Journal of Gerontology: Biological Sciences, 59*(6), 579–586.

Coles, R. (1987). *The moral life of children.* Boston: Houghton Mifflin.

Coles, R. (1990). *The spiritual life of children.* Boston: Houghton Mifflin.

Coles, R. (1997). *The moral intelligence of children.* New York: Random House.

Collins, A. L., & Smyer, M. A. (2005). The resilience of self-esteem in late adulthood. *Journal of Aging and Health, 17*(4), 471–489.

Collins, G. (2009). *When everything changed: The amazing journey of American women from 1960 to the present.* New York: Little, Brown.

Collins, P. H. (1990). *Black feminist thought: Knowledge, consciousness, and empowerment.* Boston: Unwin Hyman.

Collins, P. H. (2000). It's all in the family: Intersections of gender, race, and nation. In U. Narayan & S. Harding (Eds.), *Decentering the center: Philosophy for a multicultural, postcolonial, and feminist world* (pp. 156–176). Bloomington: Indiana University Press.

Collins, R. (1981). On the micro-foundations of macrosociology. *American Journal of Sociology, 86,* 984–1014.

Collins, R. (1990). Conflict theory and the advance of macrohistorical sociology. In G. Ritzer (Ed.), *Frontiers of social theory: The new syntheses* (pp. 68–87). New York: Columbia University Press.

Collins, R. (1994). *Four sociological traditions.* New York: Oxford University Press.

Colonial Williamsburg. (n.d.). *The Native-American family.* Retrieved December 3, 2009, from http://www.history.org/almanack/life/family/first.cfm

Coltrane, S. (2000). Research on household labor: Modeling and measuring the social embeddedness of routine family work. *Journal of Marriage and the Family, 62,* 1208–1233.

Comer, J. P. (1994). Home, school, and academic learning. In K. I. Goodland & P. Keating (Eds.), *Access to knowledge:*

The continuing agenda for our nation's schools. New York: College Board.

Comprehensive School Reform Quality Center and American Institutes for Research. (2006). *CSRQ Center report on middle and high school CSR models.* Retrieved December 30, 2006, from http://www.csrq.org/MSHSreport.asp

Condon, J. (2006). What about Dad? Psychosocial and mental health issues for new fathers. *Australian Family Physician, 35*(9), 690–692.

Conger, R., & Conger, K. (2008). Understanding the processes through which economic hardship influences families and children. In D. R. Crane & T. Heaton (Eds.), *Handbook of families & poverty* (pp. 64–81). Thousand Oaks, CA: Sage.

Conger, R., & Elder, G. (1994). *Linking economic hardship to marital quality and instability. Families in troubled times: Adapting to change in rural America.* New York: Aldine De Gruyter.

Conger, R., Wallace, L., Sun, Y., Simons, R., McLoyed, V., & Brody, G. (2002). Economic pressure in African American families: A replication and extension of the family stress model. *Developmental Psychology, 38,* 179–193.

Conn, D. K. (2001). Mental health issues in long-term care facilities. In D. Conn, N. Herrmann, A. Kaye, D. Rewilak, & B. Schogt (Eds.), *Practical psychiatry in the long-term care facility: A handbook for staff* (pp. 1–16). Seattle, WA: Hogrefe & Huber.

Connor, D., Gabel, S., Gallagher, D., & Morton, M. (2008). Disability studies and inclusive education: Implications for theory, research and practice. *International Journal of Inclusive Education, 12*(5–6), 441–457.

Conrad, P. (2007). *The medicalization of society: On the transformation of human conditions into treatable disorders.* Baltimore: Johns Hopkins University Press.

Constable, R., & Walberg, H. (1996). School social work: Facilitating home–school partnerships in the 1990s. In R. Constable, J. P. Flynn, & S. McDonald (Eds.), *School social work: Practice and research perspectives* (3rd ed., pp. 182–196). Chicago: Lyceum Books.

Coohey, C. (1996). Child maltreatment: Testing the isolation hypothesis. *Child Abuse and Neglect, 20*(3), 241–254.

Cook, K. (Ed.). (1987). *Social exchange theory.* Newbury Park, CA: Sage.

Cook, K., O'Brien, J., & Kollock, P. (1990). Exchange theory: A blueprint for structure and process. In G. Ritzer (Ed.), *Frontiers of social theory: The new syntheses* (pp. 158–181). New York: Columbia University Press.

Cooley, C. (1964). *Human nature and the social order.* New York: Scribner's. (Original work published 1902)

Coombs, D., & Capper, S. (1996). Public health and mortality: Public health in the 1980s. In D. Peck & J. Hollingsworth (Eds.), *Demographic and structural change: The effects of the 1980s on American society* (pp. 101–126). Westport, CT: Greenwood.

Corbett, J. M. (1997). *Religion in America* (3rd ed.). Upper Saddle River, NJ: Prentice Hall.

Corcoran, J., & Walsh, J. (2006). *Clinical assessment and diagnosis in social work practice.* New York: Oxford University Press.

Corcoran, M., Danziger, S. K., Kalil, A., & Seefeldt, K. S. (2000). How welfare reform is affecting women's work. *Annual Review of Sociology, 26,* 241–269.

Corey, M. S., & Corey, G. (2006). *Groups: Process and practice* (7th ed.). Belmont, CA: Thomson Brooks/Cole.

Cornish, J. A., Tan, E., Simillis, C., Clark, S. K., Teare, J., & Tekkis, P. P. (2008). The risk of oral contraceptives in the etiology of inflammatory bowel disease: A meta analysis. *American Journal of Gastroenterology, 103*(9), 2394–2400.

Cornwall, M. (1989). Faith development of men and women over the life span. In S. Bahr & E. Peterson (Eds.), *Aging and the family* (pp. 115–139). Lexington, MA: Lexington Books/DC Heath.

Cornwell, B., Laumann, E. O., & Schumm, L. P. (2008). The social connectedness of older adults: A national profile. *American Sociological Review, 73*(2), 185–203.

Corsaro, W. (2005). *The sociology of childhood* (2nd ed.). Thousand Oaks, CA: Pine Forge.

Cortright, B. (1997). *Psychotherapy and spirit: Theory and practice in transpersonal psychotherapy.* Albany: State University of New York Press.

Coser, L. (1956). *The functions of conflict.* New York: Free Press.

Coser, L. (1975). Presidential address: Two methods in search of a substance. *American Sociological Review, 40,* 691–700.

Costa, F. M., Jessor, R., Donovan, J. E., & Fortenberry, J. D. (1995). Early initiation of sexual intercourse: The influence of psychosocial unconventionality. *Journal of Research on Adolescents, 5,* 93–121.

Costa, P., Terracciano, A., & McCrae, R. (2001). Gender differences in personality traits across cultures: Robust and surprising findings. *Journal of Personality and Social Psychology, 81*(2), 322.

Costas, O. E. (1991). Hispanic theology in North America. In L. M. Getz & R. O. Costa (Eds.), *Strategies for solidarity: Liberation theologies in tension* (pp. 63–74). Minneapolis, MN: Fortress Press.

Costigan, C., & Dokis, D. (2006). Similarities and differences in acculturation among mothers, fathers, and children in immigrant Chinese families. *Journal of Cross-Cultural Psychology, 37,* 723–741.

Costigan, C., Su, T., & Hua, J. (2009). Ethnic identity among Chinese Canadian youth: A review of the Canadian literature. *Canadian Psychology, 50*(4), 261–272.

Cota-Robles, S., Neiss, M., & Rowe, D. C. (2002). The role of puberty in violent and nonviolent delinquency among

Anglo American, Mexican American, and African American boys. *Journal of Adolescent Research, 17,* 364–376.

Coughlan, R., & Owens-Manley, J. (2006). *Bosnian refugees in America: New communities, new cultures.* New York: Springer Science and Business Media.

Council for a Parliament of the World's Religions. (2010). *About us: Our mission.* Retrieved February 20, 2010, from http://www.parliamentofreligions.org/index.cfm?n=1

Council on Social Work Education. (2008). *Educational policy and accreditation standards.* Alexandria, VA: Author.

Counts, D. R., & Counts, D. A. (1991). *Coping with the final tragedy: Cultural variation in dying and grieving.* Amityville, NY: Baywood.

Cousins, E. (2000). *Roots: From outward bound to expeditionary learning.* Dubuque, IA: Kendall Hunt Publishing.

Cousins, L. (1994). *Community High: The complexity of race and class in a Black urban high school.* Unpublished doctoral dissertation, University of Michigan, Ann Arbor.

Cowles, K. V. (1996). Cultural perspectives of grief: An expanded concept analysis. *Journal of Advanced Nursing, 23,* 287–294.

Cowley, A. S. (1993). Transpersonal social work: A theory for the 1990s. *Social Work, 38,* 527–534.

Cowley, A. S. (1996). Transpersonal social work. In F. J. Turner (Ed.), *Social work treatment: Interlocking theoretical approaches* (4th ed., pp. 663–698). New York: Free Press.

Cowley, A. S. (1999). Transpersonal theory and social work practice with couples and families. *Journal of Family Social Work, 3*(20), 5–21.

Cowley, A. S., & Derezotes, D. (1994). Transpersonal psychology and social work education. *Journal of Social Work Education, 30,* 32–39.

Cox, G. R. (2000). Death, dying, and end of life in American-Indian communities. In D. J. Doka & A. S. Tucci, *Living with grief: Diversity and end-of-life care* (pp. 107–115). Washington, DC: Hospice Foundation of America.

Cox, T., Jr. (1993). *Cultural diversity in organizations: Theory, research, and practice.* San Francisco: Berrett-Koehler.

Cox, T., Jr. (2001). *Creating a multicultural organization: A strategy for capturing the power of diversity.* San Francisco: Jossey-Bass.

Crabtree, S. A., Husain, F., & Spalek, B. (2008). *Islam and social work: Debating values, transforming practice.* Bristol, UK: Policy Press.

Craig, G. J., & Baucum, D. (2002). *Human development* (9th ed.). Upper Saddle River, NJ: Prentice Hall.

Crain, R. (1996). The influences of age, race, and gender on child and adolescent multidimensional self-concept. In B. Bracken (Ed.), *Handbook of self-concept* (pp. 395–420). New York: Wiley.

Crane, J., & Winsler, A. (2008). Early autism detection: Implications for pediatric practice and public policy. *Journal of Disability Policy Studies, 18*(4), 245–253.

Crawford, J. J., Nobles, W. W., & Leary, J. D. (2003). Reparations and healthcare for African Americans: Repairing the damage from the legacy of slavery. In R. Winbush (Ed.), *Should America pay? Slavery and the raging debate on reparations* (pp. 251–281). New York: HarperCollins.

Crawley, L., Payne, R., Bolden, J., Payne, T., Washington, P., & Williams, S. (2000). Palliative and end-of-life care in the African American community. *Journal of the American Medical Association, 284*(19), 2518–2521.

Cressey, T., & Lallemant, M. (2007). Pharmacogenetics of antiretroviral drugs for the treatment of HIV-infected patients: An update. *Infection, Genetics and Evolution, 7*(2), 333–342.

Critchley, H. O., & Wallace, W. H. (2005). Impact of cancer treatment on uterine function. *Journal of the National Cancer Institute, 34,* 64–68.

Crompton, R. (2006). *Employment and the family: The reconfiguration of work and family life in contemporary societies.* Cambridge, UK: Cambridge University Press.

Crook, W. (2001). Trickle-down bureaucracy: Does the organization affect client responses to programs? *Administration in Social Work, 26*(1), 37–59.

Cross, W., Parham, T., & Black, E. (1991). The stages of Black identity development: Nigrescence models. In R. Jones (Ed.), *Black psychology* (3rd ed., pp. 319–338). Berkeley, CA: Cobb & Henry.

Croteau, A., Marcoux, S., & Brisson, C. (2007). Work activity in pregnancy, preventative measures, and the risk of preterm delivery. *American Journal of Epidemiology, 166*(8), 951–966.

Croteau, D., & Hoynes, W. (2006). *The business of media: Corporate media and the public interest* (2nd ed.). Thousand Oaks, CA: Pine Forge.

Croxatto, H. B., Brache, V., Massai, R., Ivarez, F., Forcelledo, M. L., Pavez, M., et al. (2005). Feasibility study of Nestorone-ethinylestradiol vaginal contraceptive ring for emergency contraception. *Contraception, 73*(1), 46–52.

Crozier, J. C., & Barth, R. P. (2005). Cognitive and academic functioning in maltreated children. *Children & Schools, 27*(4), 197–206.

Csikszentmihalyi, M., & Schneider, B. (2000). *Becoming adult: How teenagers prepare for the world of work.* New York: Basic Books.

Cuba, L., & Hummon, D. (1993). A place to call home: Identification with dwelling, community, and region. *Sociological Quarterly, 34*(1), 111–131.

Culhane, D., Lee, C., & Wachter, S. (1997). Where the homeless come from: A study of the prior address distribution of families admitted to public shelters in New York City and Philadelphia. In D. Culhane & S. Hornburg (Eds.), *Understanding homelessness: New policy and research perspectives* (pp. 225–263). Washington, DC: Fannie Mae Foundation.

Culp, R., McDonald Culp, A., Dengler, B., & Maisano, P. (1999). First-time young mothers living in rural communities use of corporal punishment with their toddlers. *Journal of Community Psychology, 27*(4), 503–509.

Cumes, D. (1998). Nature as medicine: The healing power of the wilderness. *Alternative Therapies, 4,* 79–86.

Cumming, E., & Henry, W. (1961). *Growing old.* New York: Basic Books.

Curtis, S. (2004). *Health and inequality: Geographical perspectives.* London: Sage.

Czaja, S. (2006). Employment and the baby boomers: What can we expect in the future? In S. Whitbourne & S. Willis (Eds.), *The baby boomers grow up: Contemporary perspectives on midlife* (pp. 283–298). Mahwah, NJ: Erlbaum.

Czarniawska, B. (2007). Has organization theory a tomorrow? *Organization Studies, 28,* 27–29.

Dahlberg, G., Moss, P., & Pence, A. (2007). *Beyond quality in early childhood education and care: Postmodern perspectives* (2nd ed.). New York: Routledge Falmer.

Dainton, M., & Zelley, E. (2006). Social exchange theories: Interdependence and equity. In D. Braithwaite & L. Baxter (Eds.), *Engaging theories in family communication: Multiple perspectives* (pp. 243–259). Thousand Oaks, CA: Sage.

Damus, K. (2008). Prevention of premature births: A renewed national priority. *Current Opinions in Obstetrics and Gynecology, 20,* 590–596.

D'Andrade, R. G. (1995). Cultural meaning systems. In R. Shweder & R. LeVine (Eds.), *Culture theory: Essays on mind, self, and emotion* (pp. 88–122). New York: Cambridge University Press. (Original work published 1984)

Dannefer, D. (2003a). Toward a global geography of the life course: Challenges of late modernity for life course theory. In J. Mortimer & M. Shanahan (Eds.), *Handbook of the life course* (pp. 647–659). New York: Kluwer Academic/ Plenum.

Dannefer, D. (2003b). Whose life course is it, anyway? Diversity and "linked lives" in global perspective. In R. Settersten, Jr. (Ed.), *Invitation to the life course: Toward new understandings of later life* (pp. 259–268). Amityville, NY: Baywood.

Dannefer, D., & Perlmutter, M. (1990). Development as a multidimensional process: Individuals and social constituents. *Human Development, 33,* 108–137.

Danto, E. (2008). Same words, different meanings: Notes toward a typology of postmodern social work education. *Social Work Education, 27*(7), 710–722.

Darcy, A. E. (2009). Complications of the late preterm infant. *Journal of Perinatal and Neonatal Nursing, 23*(1), 78–86.

Darling-Hammond, L. (2007). The flat earth and education: How America's commitment to equity will determine our future. *Educational Researcher, 36*(6), 318–334.

Das, A., & Harries, B. (1996). Validating Fowler's theory of faith development with college students. *Psychological Reports, 78,* 675–679.

Datar, A., & Jacknowitz, A. (2009). Birth weight effects on children's mental, motor, and physical development. *Maternal and Child Health Journal, 13*(6), 780–794.

D'Augelli, A., Grossman, A., & Starks, M. (2005). Parents' awareness of lesbian, gay, and bisexual youths' sexual orientation. *Journal of Marriage and Family, 67,* 474–482.

David, H. P. (1996). Induced abortion: Psychosocial aspects. In J. J. Sciarra (Ed.), *Gynecology and obstetrics* (Vol. 6, pp. 1–8). Philadelphia: Lippincott-Raven.

Davidoff, A., & Kenney, G. (2005). *Uninsured Americans with chronic health conditions: Key findings from the National Health Interview Survey.* Retrieved April 25, 2010, from http://www.urban.org/UploadedPDF/411161_uninsured_americans.pdf

Davidson, J., Moore, N., & Ullstrup, L. (2004). Religiosity and sexual responsibilities: Relationships of choice. *Journal of Health Behavior, 28*(4), 335–346.

Davidson, R. J., Kabat-Zinn, J., Schumacher, J., Rosenkranz, M., Muller, D., Santorelli, S. F., et al. (2003). Alterations in brain and immune function produced by mindfulness meditation. *Psychosomatic Medicine, 65*(4), 564–570.

Davies, D. (2004). *Child development: A practitioner's guide* (2nd ed.). New York: Guilford Press.

Davies, S. (2006). *Challenging gender norms: Five genders among the Bugis in Indonesia.* Belmont, CA: Wadsworth.

Davis, B., & Jocoy, S. (2008). In vitro fertilization for infertility. *WebMD.* Retrieved December 27, 2009, from http://www.webmd.com/infertility-and-reproduction/invitro-fertilization-for-infertility

Davis, G., McAdam, D., Scott, W. R., & Zald, M. (2005). *Social movements and organization theory.* Cambridge, UK: Cambridge University Press.

Davis, L. E. (1984). Essential components of group work with Black Americans. *Social Work With Groups, 7*(3), 97–109.

Davis, S., Greenstein, T., & Marks, J. (2007). Effects of union type on division of household labor: Do cohabiting men really perform more housework? *Journal of Family Issues, 28*(9), 1246–1272.

Day, P., & Schuler, D. (2004). *Community practice in the network society: Local action/global interaction.* New York: Routledge.

De Brucker, M., Haentjens, P., Evenepoel, J., Devroey, P., Collins, J., & Tournaye, H. (2009). Cumulative delivery rates in different age groups after artificial insemination with donor sperm. *Human Reproduction, 24*(8), 1891–1899.

de Escobar, G. M., Ares, S., Berbel, P., Obregon, M. J., & del Rey, F. E. (2008). The changing role of maternal thyroid hormone in fetal brain development. *Seminars in Perinatology, 32*(6), 380–386.

de Jonge, A., van der Goes, B. Y., Ravelli, A. C. J., Amelink-Verbury, M. P., Mol, B. W., Nijhuis, J. G., et al. (2009). Prenatal mortality and morbidity in a nationwide cohort of 529,688 low-risk, planned home and hospital births. *BJOG: An International Journal of Obstetrics and Gynaecology, 116*(9), 1177–1184.

De Marco, A. C., & Cosner Berzin, S. (2008). The influence of family economic status on home-leaving patterns during emerging adulthood. *Families in Society, 89*(2), 208–218.

De Schipper, J., Tavecchio, L., & Van IJzendoorn, M. (2008). Children's attachment relationship with day care caregivers: Associations with positive caregiving and the child's temperament. *Social Development, 17*(3), 454–470.

de St. Aubin, E., McAdams, D., & Kim, T. (2004). *The generative society: Caring for future generations.* Washington, DC: American Psychological Association.

Dean, R. G. (1993). Teaching a constructivist approach to clinical practice. In J. Laird (Ed.), *Revisioning social work education: A social constructionist approach* (pp. 55–75). New York: Haworth Press.

Dean, R. G. (2001). The myth of cross-cultural competence. *Families in Society, 82*(6), 623–630.

Deeg, D. (2005). The development of physical and mental health from late midlife to early old age. In S. Willis & M. Martin (Eds.), *Middle adulthood: A lifespan perspective* (pp. 209–241). Thousand Oaks, CA: Sage.

Degges-White, S. (2005). Understanding gerotranscendence in older adults: A new perspective for counselors. *Adultspan Journal, 4*(1), 36–48.

DeHart, G. B., Sroufe, L. A., & Cooper, R. G. (2000). *Child development: Its nature and course* (4th ed.). Boston: McGraw-Hill.

Del Rio, N. (2004). A framework for multicultural end-of-life care: Enhancing social work practice. In J. Berzoff & P. R. Silverman (Eds.), *Living with dying: A handbook for end-of-life healthcare practitioners* (pp. 439–461). New York: Columbia University Press.

Delany, S., with Hearth, A. (1997). *On my own at 107: Reflections on life without Bessie.* New York: HarperCollins.

Delaunay-El Allam, M., Marlier, L., & Schaal, B. (2006). Learning at the breast: Preference formation for the artificial scent and its attraction against the odor of maternal milk. *Infant Behavior and Development, 29*(3), 308–321.

Delgado, C. E. F., Vagi, S. J., & Scott, K. G. (2007). Identification of early risk factors for developmental delay. *Exceptionality, 15*(2), 119–136.

Delgado, M. (1988). Groups in Puerto Rican spiritism: Implications for clinicians. In C. Jacobs & D. D. Bowles (Eds.), *Ethnicity and race: Critical concepts in social work* (pp. 34–37). Silver Spring, MD: NASW Press.

Delgado, M. (2000). *New arenas for community social work practice with urban youth: Use of arts, humanities, and sports.* New York: Columbia University Press.

Delgado, M., & Humm-Delgado, D. (1982). Natural support systems: Sources of strength in Hispanic communities. *Social Work, 27,* 83–89.

della Porta, D. (1996). Social movements and the state: Thoughts on the policing of protest. In D. McAdam, J. McCarthy, & M. Zald (Eds.), *Comparative perspectives on social movements* (pp. 62–92). New York: Cambridge University Press.

della Porta, D., & Diani, M. (2006). *Social movements: An introduction* (2nd ed.). Malden, MA: Blackwell.

Dellmann-Jenkins, M., & Blankemeyer, M. (2009). Emerging and young adulthood and caregiving. In K. Shifren (Ed.), *How caregiving affects development: Psychological implications for child, adolescent, and adult caregivers* (pp. 93–117). Washington, DC: American Psychological Association.

Dellmann-Jenkins, M., Blankemeyer, M., & Pinkard, O. (2001). Incorporating the elder caregiving role into the developmental tasks of young adulthood. *International Journal of Aging and Human Development, 52*(1), 1.

Deloria, V., Jr. (1994). *God is red: A native view of religion.* Golden, CO: Fulcrum.

DeNavas-Walt, C., Proctor, B., & Hill Lee, C. (2006). *Income, poverty, and health insurance coverage in the United States: 2005.* Washington, DC: U.S. Census Bureau.

DeNavas-Walt, C., Proctor, B., & Smith, J. (2009). *Income, poverty, and health insurance coverage in the United States: 2008.* Washington, DC: U.S. Census Bureau.

Denner, J., & Dunbar, N. (2004). Negotiating femininity: Power and strategies of Mexican American girls. *Sex Roles, 50,* 301–314.

Dennis, C., & Chung-Lee, L. (2006). Postpartum depression help-seeking barriers and maternal treatment preferences: A qualitative systematic review. *Birth, 33*(4), 323–331.

Dennison, B., Edmunds, J., & Stratton, H. (2006). Rapid infant weight gain predicts childhood overweight. *Obesity, 14*(3), 491–499.

DePoy, E., & Gilson, S. F. (2004). *Rethinking disability: Principles for professional and social change.* Belmont, CA: Wadsworth.

DePoy, E., & Gilson, S. F. (2007). *The human experience: Description, explanation, and judgment.* New York: Rowman & Littlefield.

DePoy, E., & Gilson, S. F. (2008). Healing the disjuncture: Social work disability practice. In K. Sowers & C. Dulmus

(Series Eds.) & B. White (Vol. Ed.), *Comprehensive handbook of social work and social welfare: The profession of social work* (Vol. 1, pp. 267–282). Hoboken, NJ: Wiley.

DePoy, E., & Gilson, S. F. (2010). *Studying disability: Multiple theories and responses.* Thousand Oaks, CA: Sage.

DePree, M. (1997). *Leading without power.* San Francisco: Jossey-Bass.

Derezotes, D. S. (2001). Transpersonal social work with couples: A compatibility-intimacy model. In E. R. Canda & E. D. Smith (Eds.), *Transpersonal perspectives on spirituality in social work* (pp. 163–174). Binghamton, NY: Haworth Press.

Derezotes, D. S. (2006). *Spiritually oriented social work practice.* Boston: Pearson Education.

Derman, S. G., & Seifer, D. B. (2003). In vitro fertilization in the older patient. *Current Women's Health Reports, 3*(5), 275–283.

DeRosier, M. E., Kupersmidt, J. B., & Patterson, C. J. (1994). Children's academic and behavioral adjustment as a function of the chronicity and proximity of peer rejection. *Child Development, 65,* 1799–1813.

DeSpelder, L. A., & Strickland, A. L. (2005). *The last dance: Encountering death and dying* (7th ed.). Boston: McGraw-Hill.

Devereux. E. (2008). *Understanding the media* (2nd ed.). Thousand Oaks, CA: Sage.

Devine-Wright, P. (2009). Rethinking NIMYism: The role of place attachment and place identity in explaining place-protective action. *Journal of Community & Applied Social Psychology, 19*(6), 426–441.

Devlin, A. (1992). Psychiatric ward renovation: Staff perception and patient behavior. *Environment and Behavior, 24,* 66–84.

Diamond, J. (1999). *Guns, germs, and steel: The fates of human societies.* New York: Norton.

Diamond, L. M. (2000). Passionate friendships among adolescent sexual-minority women. *Journal of Research on Adolescence, 10,* 191–209.

Diamond, L. M., & Savin-Williams, R. C. (2003). Gender and sexual identity. In R. M. Lerner, F. Jacobs, & D. Wertlieb (Eds.), *Handbook of applied developmental science* (Vol. 1, pp. 101–121). Thousand Oaks, CA: Sage.

Dickason, E., Silverman, B., & Kaplan, J. (1998). *Maternal-infant nursing care* (3rd ed.). St. Louis, MO: Mosby.

Dick-Read, G. (1944). *Childbirth without fear: Principles and practices of natural childbirth.* New York: Harper & Row.

Diekema, D. S. (2003). Involuntary sterilization of persons with mental retardation: An ethical analysis. *Mental Retardation and Developmental Disabilities Research Reviews, 9*(1), 21–26.

Dinitto, D. M., & Cummins, L. K. (2006). *Social welfare: Politics and public policy* (6th ed.). Boston: Allyn & Bacon.

Dioussé, L., Driver, J., & Gaziano, J. (2009). Relation between modifiable lifestyle factors and lifetime risk of heart failure. *Journal of American Medical Association, 302*(4), 394–400.

Direnfeld, D., & Roberts, J. (2006). Mood congruent memory in dysphoria: The roles of state affect and cognitive style. *Behavior Research and Therapy, 44*(9), 1275–1285.

Dirubbo, N. E. (2006). Counsel your patients about contraceptive options. *The Nurse Practitioner, 31*(4), 40–44.

Disabled Peoples' International. (2005). *DPI home page—DPI at a glance.* Retrieved September 5, 2006, from http://v1.dpi.org/lang-en/index

Dittmann-Kohli, F. (2005). Middle age and identity in a cultural and lifespan perspective. In S. Willis & M. Martin (Eds.), *Middle adulthood: A lifespan perspective* (pp. 319–353). Thousand Oaks, CA: Sage.

Dixon, J., Dogan, R., & Sanderson, A. (2005). Community and communitarianism: A philosophical investigation. *Community Development Journal, 40*(1), 4–16.

Doka, K. J., & Tucci, A. S. (2009). *Living with grief: Diversity and end-of-life care.* Washington, DC: Hospice Foundation of America.

Dolinsky, A. L., & Rosenwaike, I. (1988). The role of demographic factors in the institutionalization of the elderly. *Research on Aging, 10,* 235–257.

Dollahite, D., Slife, B., & Hawkins, A. (1998). Family generativity and generative counseling: Helping families keep faith with the next generation. In D. McAdams & E. de St. Aubin (Eds.), *Generativity and adult development: How and why we care for the next generation* (pp. 449–481). Washington, DC: American Psychological Association.

Domenech Rodriguez, M., Donovick, M., & Crowley, S. (2009). Parenting styles in a cultural context: Observations of "protective parenting" in first-generation Latinos. *Family Process, 48*(2), 195–210.

Domina, T. (2005). Leveling the home advantage: Assessing the effectiveness of parental involvement in elementary school. *Sociology of Education, 78*(3), 233–249.

DONA International. (n.d.). *For mothers & families.* Retrieved May 20, 2010, from http://www.dona.org/mothers/index.php

Donleavy, G. (2008). No man's land: Exploring the space between Gilligan and Kohlberg. *Journal of Business Ethics, 80,* 807–822.

Donnelly, T., Atkins, R., Hart, D. (2005). The relationship between spiritual development and civic engagement. In P. Benson, E. Roehlkepartain, P. King, & L. Wagener (Eds.), *The handbook of spiritual development in childhood and adolescence.* Thousand Oaks, CA: Sage.

Donovan, J., Jessor, R., & Costa, F. (1999). Adolescent problem drinking: Stability of psychosocial and behavioral correlates across a generation. *Journal of Studies on Alcohol, 60*(3), 352–361.

Dörner, J., Mickler, C., & Studinger, U. (2005). Self-development at midlife: Lifespan perspectives on adjustment and growth. In S. Willis & M. Martin (Eds.), *Middle adulthood: A lifespan perspective* (pp. 277–317). Thousand Oaks, CA: Sage.

Dosser, D. A., Smith, A. L., Markowski, E. W., & Cain, H. I. (2001). Including families' spiritual beliefs and their faith communities in systems of care. *Journal of Family Social Work, 5*(3), 63–78.

Doughty, E. A. (2009). Investigating adaptive grieving styles: A delphi study. *Death Studies, 33,* 462–480.

Downes, D. M., & Rock, P. (2003). *Understanding deviance: A guide to the sociology of crime and rule-breaking.* New York: Oxford University Press.

Downs, A. C., & Langlois, J. H. (1988). Sex typing: Construct and measurement issues. *Sex Roles, 18*(1–2), 87–100.

Downs, S. W., Moore, E., McFadden, E. J., Michaud, S. M., & Costin, L. B. (2004). *Child welfare and family services: Policies and practice* (7th ed.). Boston: Pearson.

Draper, L. (2006). Working women and contraception: History, health, and choices. *American Association of Occupational Health Nurses Journal, 54*(7), 317–326.

Draut, T. (2005). *Strapped: Why America's 20- and 30-somethings can't get ahead.* New York: Doubleday.

Draut, T., & Silva, J. (2004). *Generation broke: The growth of debt among young Americans. Borrowing to make ends meet series.* Retrieved January 5, 2010, from http://archive.demos.org/Pubs/Generation_Broke.pdf

Drescher, K. D, Burgoyne, M., Casas, E., Lovato, L., Curran, E., Pivar, I., et al. (2009). Issues of grief, loss, honor, and remembrance: Spirituality and work with military personnel and their families. In S. M. Freeman, B. A. Moore, & A. Freeman (Eds.), *Living and surviving in harm's way: A psychological treatment handbook for pre- and post-deployment of military personnel* (pp. 437–466). New York: Routledge.

Drosdzol, A., & Skrzypulec, V. (2008). Quality of life and sexual function of Polish infertile couples. *European Journal of Contraceptive and Reproductive Health Care, 13,* 271–281.

Dryfoos, J. G. (1994). *Full-service schools: A revolution in health and social services for children, youth, and families.* San Francisco: Jossey-Bass.

Duarte, A., Ranganath, C., Trujillo, C., & Knight, R. T. (2006). Intact recollection memory in high-performing older-adults: RP and behavioral evidence. *Journal of Cognitive Neuroscience, 18*(1), 33–47.

Duba, J. D., & Watts, R. E. (2009). Therapy with religious couples. *Journal of Clinical Psychology, 65*(2), 210–223.

Dubrow, N., & Garbarino, J. (1989). Living in the war zone: Mothers and young children in a public housing development. *Child Welfare, 68,* 3–20.

Dunbar, H. T., Mueller, C. W., Medina, C., & Wolf, T. (1998). Psychological and spiritual growth in women living with HIV. *Social Work, 43,* 144–154.

Duncan, G., Kalil, A., & Ziol-Guest, K. (2008). *Economic costs of early childhood poverty* (Issue Paper #4). Retrieved January 19, 2010, from http://www.partnershipforsuccess.org/docs/researchproject_duncan_200802_paper.pdf

Dupper, D. R., & Poertner, J. (1997). Public schools and the revitalization of impoverished communities: School-linked, family resource centers. *Social Work, 42,* 415–422.

Duran, E., & Duran, B. (1995). *Native American postcolonial psychology.* Albany: State University of New York Press.

Durkin, K. (1995). *Developmental social psychology.* Malden, MA: Blackwell.

Duvall-Early, K., & Benedict, J. (1992). The relationship between privacy and different components of job satisfaction. *Environment and Behavior, 24,* 670–679.

Dybicz, P. (2004). An inquiry into practice wisdom. *Families in Society, 85*(2), 197–203.

Eagle, M., & Wolitzky, D. L. (2009). Adult psychotherapy from the perspectives of attachment theory and psychoanalysis. In J. H. Obegi & E. Berant (Eds.), *Attachment theory and research in clinical work with adults* (pp. 351–378). New York: Guilford Press.

Earle, A. M. (1987). *An outline of neuroanatomy.* Omaha: University of Nebraska Medical Center.

Early Intervention Support. (2009). *Child development.* Retrieved February 15, 2010, from http://www.earlyinterventionsupport.com/development/

Edin, K., Kefalas, M., & Reed, J. (2004). A peek inside the black box: What marriage means for poor unmarried parents. *Journal of Marriage and the Family, 66,* 1007–1014.

Edin, K., & Reed, J. (2005). Why don't they just get married? Barriers to marriage among the disadvantaged. *The Future of Children, 15*(5), 117–137.

Edlich, R. F., Winters, K. L., Long, W. B., III, & Gubler, K. D. (2005). Rubella and congenital rubella. *Journal of Long-Term Effects of Medical Implants, 15*(3), 319–328.

Education Trust. (2006a). *Missing the mark: An Education Trust analysis of teacher-equity plans.* Retrieved April 28, 2010, from http://www.edtrust.org/print/525

Education Trust. (2006b, September 1). *Yes we can: Telling truths and dispelling myths about race and education in America.* Retrieved April 28, 2010, from http://www.edtrust.org/print/159

Edwards, C. (1992). Normal development in the preschool years. In E. V. Nuttall, I. Romero, & J. Kalesnik (Eds.), *Assessing and screening preschoolers* (pp. 9–22). Boston: Allyn & Bacon.

Edwards, E., Eiden, R., & Leonard, K. (2006). Behavior problems in 18–36-month-old children of alcoholic fathers: Secure mother–father attachment as a protective factor. *Developmental Psychopathology, 18*(2), 395–407.

Egeland, B., Carlson, E., & Sroufe, L. A. (1993). Resilience as process. *Development and Psychopathology, 5,* 517–528.

Eisenberg, N. (2000). Emotion, regulation, and moral development. *Annual Review of Psychology, 51,* 665–697.

Eisenberg, N., Guthrie, I., Murphy, B., Shepard, S., Cumberland, A., & Carlo, G. (1999). Consistency and development of prosocial dispositions: A longitudinal study. *Child Development, 70,* 1360–1372.

Eitzen, D. S., & Zinn, B. C. (Eds.). (2006). *Globalization: The transformation of social worlds.* Belmont, CA: Wadsworth.

Ekeh, P. (1974). *Social exchange theory: The two traditions.* Cambridge, MA: Harvard University Press.

Elder, G. H., Jr. (1974). *Children of the Great Depression: Social change in life experience.* Chicago: University of Chicago Press.

Elder, G., Jr. (1992). Life course. In E. Borgatta & M. Borgatta (Eds.), *Encyclopedia of sociology* (pp. 1120–1130). New York: Macmillan.

Elder, G., Jr. (1994). Time, human agency, and social change: Perspectives on the life course. *Social Psychology Quarterly, 57*(1), 4–15.

Elder, G., Jr. (1998). The life course as developmental theory. *Child Development, 69*(1), 1–12.

Elder, G. H., Jr., & Giele, J. (Eds.). (2009a). *The craft of life course research.* New York: Guilford Press.

Elder, G., & Giele, J. (2009b). Life course studies: An evolving field. In G. Edler & J. Giele (Eds.), *The craft of life course research* (pp. 1–24). New York: Guilford.

Elder, G., Jr., & Kirkpatrick Johnson, M. (2003). The life course and aging: Challenges, lessons, and new directions. In R. Settersten, Jr. (Ed.), *Invitation to the life course: Toward new understandings of later life* (pp. 49–81). Amityville, NY: Baywood.

Eliopoulus, C. (2010). *Gerontological nursing* (7th ed.). Philadelphia: Lippincott, Williams & Wilkins.

Elkind, D. (2001). *The hurried child: Growing up too fast too soon* (3rd ed.). Reading, MA: Addison-Wesley.

Elley, N. (2001). Early birds, too early: Prematurity may mean poor performance. *Psychology Today, 34*(15), 28.

Ellis, A. (1989). Is rational emotive therapy (RET) "rationalist or constructivist"? In W. Dryden (Ed.), *The essential Albert Ellis* (pp. 199–233). New York: Springer.

Ellison, C. G. (1992). Are religious people nice? Evidence from a national survey of Black Americans. *Social Forces, 71*(2), 411–430.

Ellison, C. G. (1993). Religious involvement and self-perception among Black Americans. *Social Forces, 71*(4), 1027–1055.

Ellison, C. G., & Levin, J. S. (1998). The religion–health connection: Evidence, theory, and future directions. *Health, Education, and Behavior, 25*(6), 700–720.

Ellison, J. W., & Plaskow, J. (Eds.). (2007). *Heterosexism in contemporary world religion: Problem and prospect.* Cleveland, OH: Pilgrim Press.

Ellison, N., Steinfield, C., & Lampe, C. (2007). The benefits of Facebook "friends": Social capital and college students' use of online social network sites. *Journal of Computer-Mediated Communication, 12,* 1143–1168.

El-Messidi, A., Al-Fozan, H., Lin Tan, S., Farag, R., & Tulandi, T. (2004). Effects of repeated treatment failure on the quality of life of couples with infertility. *Journal of Obstetrics and Gynaecology Canada, 26,* 333–336.

Elwan, A. (1999). *Poverty and disability: A survey of the literature.* Retrieved April 28, 2010, from http://asksource.ids.ac.uk/cf/display/bibliodisplay.cfm?ID=26550&topic=dis&Search=QL%5FDISPOV05&display=full

Emerson, R. (1972a). Exchange theory: Part I. A psychological basis for social exchange. In J. Berger, M. Zelditch Jr., & B. Anderson (Eds.), *Sociological theories in progress* (Vol. 2, pp. 38–57). Boston: Houghton Mifflin.

Emerson, R. (1972b). Exchange theory: Part II. Exchange relations and networks. In J. Berger, M. Zelditch Jr., & B. Anderson (Eds.), *Sociological theories in progress* (Vol. 2, pp. 58–87). Boston: Houghton Mifflin.

Emery, R. (1999). *Marriage, divorce, and children's adjustment* (2nd ed.). Thousand Oaks, CA: Sage.

Emirbayer, M., & Goodwin, J. (1994). Network analysis, culture, and the problem of agency. *American Journal of Sociology, 99,* 1411–1454.

Emmons, P. G. (2005). *Understanding sensory dysfunction: Learning, development and sensory dysfunction in autism spectrum disorders, ADHD, learning disabilities and bipolar disorder.* London: Jessica Kingsley.

Engel, G. (1977). The need for a new medical model: A challenge for biomedicine. *Science, 196,* 129–136.

Engels, F. (1892). *The condition of the working class in England in 1844* (F. K. Wischnewtzky, Trans.). London: Sonnenschein.

Engels, F. (1970). *The origins of the family, private property and the state.* New York: International. (Original work published 1884)

Engels, R., & Knibbe, R. (2000). Alcohol use and intimate relationships in adolescence: When love comes to town. *Addictive Behavior, 25,* 435–439.

Engle, J., & Theokas, C. (2010). College results online brief: *Top gainers: Some public four-year colleges and universities make big improvements in minority graduation rates.* Retrieved February 21, 2010, from http://www.edtrust.org/dc/publication/college-results-online-brief-top-gainers

Entwisle, D., Alexander, K., & Olson, L. (2005). Urban teenagers: Work and dropout. *Youth and Society, 37,* 3–32.

Epel, E., Wilhelm, F., Wolkowitz, O., Cawthorn, R., Adler, N., Dolbier, C., et al. (2006). Cell aging in relation to stress arousal and cardiovascular disease risk factors. *Psychoneuroendocrinology, 31*(3), 277–287.

Epstein, J. L., & Lee, S. (1995). National patterns of school and family connections in the middle grades. In B. A. Ryan, G. R. Adams, T. P. Gullotta, R. P. Weissberg, & R. L. Hampton (Eds.), *The family–school connection: Theory, research, and practice* (pp. 108–154). Thousand Oaks, CA: Sage.

Epstein, S. (1973). The self-concept revisited: Or, a theory of a theory. *American Psychologist, 28,* 404–416.

Epstein, S. (1991). Cognitive-experiential self-theory: An integrative theory of personality. In R. Cutis (Ed.), *The self with others: Convergences in psychoanalytic, social, and personality psychology* (pp. 111–137). New York: Guilford Press.

Epstein, S. (1998). Cognitive-experiential self-theory. In D. Barone & M. Hersen (Eds.), *Advanced personality* (pp. 211–238). New York: Plenum.

Epstein, S., Lipson, A., Holstein, C., & Huh, E. (1993). Irrational reactions to negative outcomes: Evidence for two conceptual systems. *Journal of Personality and Social Psychology, 62,* 328–339.

Erikson, E. (1950). *Childhood and society.* New York: Norton.

Erikson, E. (1959). The problem of ego identity. *Psychological Issues, 1,* 101–164.

Erikson, E. (1963). *Childhood and society* (2nd ed.). New York: Norton.

Erikson, E. (1968). *Identity: Youth and crisis.* New York: Norton.

Erikson, E. (Ed.). (1978). *Adulthood.* New York: Norton.

Erikson, E. (1982). *The life cycle completed.* New York: Norton.

Ernst, J. (2000). Mapping child maltreatment: Looking at neighborhoods in a suburban county. *Child Welfare, 79,* 555–572.

Espelage, D. L., & Swearer, S. M. (Ed.). (2003). *Bullying in American schools: A social-ecological perspective on prevention and intervention.* Mahwah, NJ: Erlbaum.

Evans, B., Crogan, N., Belyea, M., & Coon, D. (2009). Utility of the life course perspective in research with Mexican American caregivers of older adults. *Journal of Transcultural Nursing, 20*(1), 5–14.

Evans, C. J., Boustead, R. S., & Owens, C. (2008). Expressions of spirituality in parents with at-risk children. *Families in Society: The Journal of Contemporary Social Services, 89*(2), 245–252.

Evans, G. W., & English, K. (2002). The environment of poverty: Multiple stressor exposure, psychophysiological stress and socioemotional adjustment. *Child Development, 73*(4), 1238–1248.

Evans, G. W., Lepore, S., & Allen, K. (2000). Cross-cultural differences in tolerance for crowding: Fact or fiction? *Journal of Personality and Social Psychology, 79*(2), 204–210.

Evans, G. W., & Saegert, S. (2000). Residential crowding in the context of inner city poverty. In S. Wapner, J. Demick, T. Yamamoto, & H. Minami (Eds.), *Theoretical perspectives in environment-behavior research: Underlying assumptions research problems, and methodologies* (pp. 247–267). New York: Kluwer Academic.

Ewert, A., & Heywood, J. (1991). Group development in the natural environment: Expectations, outcomes, and techniques. *Environment and Behavior, 23,* 529–615.

Ewing, R., Schmid, T., Killingsworth, R., Zlot, A., & Raudenbush, S. (2003). Relationship between urban sprawl and physical activity, obesity, and morbidity. *American Journal of Health Promotion, 18*(1), 47–57.

Faber, A., Willerton, E., Clymer, S., MacDermid, S., & Weiss, H. (2008). Ambiguous absence, ambiguous presence: A qualitative study of military reserve families in wartime. *Journal of Family Psychology, 22*(2), 222–230.

Fadiman, A. (1998). *The spirit catches you and you fall down: A Hmong child, her American doctors, and the collision of two cultures.* New York: Farrar, Straus and Giroux.

Faiola, A. (2006, July 28). The face of poverty ages in rapidly graying Japan. *The Washington Post,* p. A01.

Falicov, C. J. (2003). Immigrant family processes. In F. Walsh (Ed.), *Normal family processes: Growing diversity and complexity* (3rd ed., pp. 280–300). New York: Guilford Press.

Family Health International. (2006). *FHI research briefs on the female condom. No. 2: Effectiveness for preventing pregnancy and sexually transmitted infections.* Retrieved September 12, 2011, from http://www.fhi.org/en/RH/Pubs/Briefs/FemCondom/EffectiveSTIs.htm

Fan, X. (2001). Parental involvement and students' academic achievement: A growth modeling analysis. *Journal of Experimental Education, 70,* 27–61.

Fan, X., & Chen, M. (2001). Parental involvement and students' academic achievement: A meta-analysis. *Educational Psychology Review, 13*(1), 1–22.

Fantuzzo, J. W., Mohr, W. K., & Noone, M. J. (2000). Making the invisible victims of violence against women visible through university/community partnerships. In R. A. Geffner, P. G. Jaffe, & M. Suderman (Eds.), *Children exposed to domestic violence: Current issues in research, intervention, prevention, and policy development* (pp. 9–24). New York: Haworth Press.

Farber, S., Egnew, T., & Farber, A. (2004). What is a respectful death? In J. Berzoff & P. R. Silverman (Eds.), *Living with dying: A handbook for end-of-life healthcare professionals* (pp. 102–127). New York: Columbia University Press.

Farkas, B. (2004). Etiology and pathogenesis of PTSD in children and adolescents. In R. R. Silva (Ed.), *Posttraumatic stress disorders in children and adolescents* (pp. 123–140). New York: Norton.

Farmer, R. (2009). *Neuroscience and social work practice: The missing link.* Thousand Oaks, CA: Sage.

Farrell, M. (2009, September 19). ACORN scandal: How much federal funding does it get? *The Christian Science Monitor.* Retrieved April 28, 2010, from http://www.csmonitor.com/USA/2009/0919/p02s13-usgn.html

Farrelly-Hansen, M. (2009). *Spirituality and art therapy: Living the connection.* London: Jessica Kingsley.

Farrington, D. P., & Ttofi, M. M. (2009). *School-based programs to reduce bullying and victimization.* Rockville,

MD: Campbell Collaboration Crime and Justice Group and the U.S. Department of Justice (NCJ 229377). Retrieved February 9, 2010, from http://www.ncjrs.gov/pdffiles1/nij/grants/229377.pdf

Fass, P., & Mason, M. (Eds.). (2000). *Childhood in America.* New York: New York University Press.

Faull, K., & Hills, M. (2006). The role of the spiritual dimensions of the self as the prime determinant of health. *Disability and Rehabilitation, 28*(11), 729–740.

Fauri, D. P. (1988). Applying historical themes of the profession in the foundation curriculum. *Journal of Teaching in Social Work, 2,* 17–31.

Faver, C. A., & Trachte, B. L. (2005). Religion and spirituality at the border: A survey of Mexican-American social work students. *Social Thought, 24*(4), 3–18.

Fawcett, M. (2000). Historical views of childhood. In M. Boushel, M. Fawcett, & J. Selwyn (Eds.), *Focus on early childhood: Principles and realities* (pp. 7–20). Oxford, UK: Blackwell.

Federal Interagency Forum on Aging-Related Statistics. (2004). *Older Americans 2004: Key indicators of well-being.* Washington, DC: U.S. Government Printing Office.

Federal Interagency Forum on Aging-Related Statistics. (2008). *Older Americans 2008: Key indicators of well-being.* Retrieved September 12, 2011, from http://www.agingstats.gov/Main_Site/Data/Data_2008.aspx

Feijoo, A. (2001). Adolescent pregnancy, birth, and abortion rates in Western Europe far outshine U.S. rates. *Transitions, 14*(2), 4–5.

Feldman, R. (1990). Settlement-identity: Psychological bonds with home places in a mobile society. *Environment and Behavior, 22*(2), 183–229.

Feldman, R. (2004). Mother–infant skin-to-skin contact and the development of emotion regulation. In S. Shohov (Ed.), *Advances in psychology research* (Vol. 27, pp. 113–131). Hauppauge, NY: Nova Science.

Feldman, R., & Edelman, A. (2003). Mother–infant skin-to-skin contact (Kangaroo Care) accelerates autonomic and neurobehavioral maturation in premature infants. *Developmental Medicine and Child Neurology, 45*(4), 274–281.

Felitti, V., Anda, R., Nordenburg, D., Williamson, D., Spitz, A., Edwards, V., et al. (1998). Relationship of childhood abuse and household dysfunction to many of the leading causes of death in adults: The Adverse Childhood Experiences (ACE) study. *American Journal of Preventive Medicine, 14*(4), 245–258.

Felson, R. B. (2002). Pubertal development, social factors, and delinquency among adolescent boys. *Criminology, 40*(4), 967–988.

Felty, K., & Poloma, M. (1991). From sex differences to gender role beliefs: Exploring effects on six dimensions of religiosity. *Sex Roles, 23,* 181–193.

Ferguson, K. M., Wu, Q., Dryrness, G., & Spruijt-Metz, D. (2007). Perceptions of faith and outcomes in faith-based programs for homeless youth: A grounded theory approach. *Journal of Social Service Research, 33*(4), 25–43.

Fergusson, D. M., Horwood, L. J., & Woodward, L. J. (2001). Unemployment and psychosocial adjustment in young adults: Causation or selection? *Social Science & Medicine, 53*(3), 305.

Ferlin, A., Arredi, B., & Foresta, C. (2006). Genetic causes of male infertility. *Reproductive Technology, 22*(2), 133–141.

Ferraro, K., & Shippee, T. (2009). Aging and cumulative inequality: How does inequality get under the skin? *The Gerontologist, 49*(3), 333–343.

Field, T., Woodson, R., Greenberg, R., & Cohen, C. (1982). Discrimination and imitation of facial expressions by neonates. *Science, 218,* 179–181.

Fields, J. (2004). *America's families and living arrangements: 2003. U.S. Census Bureau Current Population Reports.* Retrieved December 3, 2006, from http://www.census.gov/prod/2004pubs/p20-553.pdf

Figley, C. R. (2002). Compassion fatigue: Psychotherapists' chronic lack of self care. *Journal of Clinical Psychology, 58*(11), 1433–1441.

Figueira-McDonough, J. (1990). Abortion: Ambiguous criteria and confusing policies. *Affilia, 5*(4), 27–54.

Fiksenbaum, L. M., Greenglass, E. R., & Eaton, J. (2006). Perceived social support, hassles, and coping among the elderly. *Journal of Applied Gerontology, 25*(1), 17–30.

Findlay, L., Girardi, A., & Coplan, R. (2006). Links between empathy, social behavior, and social understanding in early childhood. *Early Childhood Research Quarterly, 21*(3), 347–359.

Fine, M., Ganong, L., & Demo, D. (2010). Divorce: A risk and resilience perspective. In S. Price, C. Price, & P. McKenry (Eds.), *Families & change: Coping with stressful events and transitions* (4th ed., pp. 211–233). Thousand Oaks, CA: Sage.

Finer, L., & Henshaw, S. (2006). Disparities in rates of unintended pregnancy in the United States, 1994 and 2001. *Perspectives on Sexual and Reproductive Health, 38*(2), 90–96.

Finger, W., & Arnold, E. M. (2002). Mind–body interventions: Applications for social work practice. *Social Work in Health Care, 35*(4), 57–78.

Fingerman, K., & Dolbin-MacNab, M. (2006). The baby boomers and their parents: Cohort influences and intergenerational ties. In S. Whitbourne & S. Willis (Eds.), *The baby boomers grow up: Contemporary perspectives on midlife* (pp. 237–259). Mahwah, NJ: Erlbaum.

Finn, J. D. (1989). Withdrawing from school. *Review of Educational Research, 59,* 117–142.

Finn, J. L. (2009). Making trouble. In L. Nybell, J. Shook, & J. Finn (Eds.), *Childhood, youth, and social work* in transformation: Implications for policy and practice (pp. 37–66). New York: Columbia University Press.

Finn, J. L., & Checkoway, B. (1998). Young people as competent community builders: A challenge to social work. *Social Work, 43*(4), 335–345.

Fiori, J. L., Consedine, N. S., & Magai, C. (2008). Ethnic differences in patterns of social exchange among older adults: The role of resource context. *Ageing & Society, 28*, 495–524.

Firebaugh, G., & Goesling, B. (2004). Accounting for the recent decline in global income inequality. *American Journal of Sociology, 110*(2), 283–312.

Fischer, D. (1989). *Albion's seed: Four British folkways in America*. New York: Oxford University Press.

Fischer, K. (1993). Aging. In M. Downey (Ed.), *The new dictionary of Catholic spirituality* (pp. 31–33). Collegeville, MN: Liturgical Press.

Fisek, M. H., Berger, J., & Moore, J. (2002). Evaluations, enactment, and expectations. *Social Psychology Quarterly, 65*(4), 329–345.

Fisher, H. (2004). *Why we love: The nature and chemistry of romantic love*. New York: Holt.

Fisher, R., & Shragge, E. (2000). Challenging community organizing: Facing the 21st century. *Journal of Community Practice, 8*(3), 1–19.

Fitzgerald, J. (1997). Reclaiming the whole: Self, spirit, and society. *Disability and Rehabilitation, 19*(10), 407–413.

Fitzpatrick, K. M., & Boldizar, J. P. (1993). The prevalence and consequences of exposure to violence among African American youth. *Journal of the American Academy of Child and Adolescent Psychiatry, 56*, 22–34.

Fjerstad, M., Truissell, J., Sivin, I., Lichtenberg, S., & Cullins, V. (2009). Rates of serious infection after changes in regimens for medical abortion. *New England Journal of Medicine, 361*(2), 145–151.

Flacks, R. (2004). Knowledge for what? Thoughts on the state of social movement studies. In J. Goodwin & J. Jasper (Eds.), *Rethinking social movements: Structure, meaning, and emotion* (pp. 135–153). Lanham, MD: Rowman & Littlefield.

Flake, E., Davis, B., Johnson, P., & Middleton, L. (2009). The psychosocial effects of deployment on military children. *Journal of Developmental & Behavioral Pediatrics, 30*(4), 271–278.

Flammer, A., & Schaffner, B. (2003). Adolescent leisure across European nations. In S. Verma & R. Larson (Eds.), *Examining adolescent leisure time across culture: New directions for child and adolescent development, No. 99* (pp. 65–77). San Francisco: Jossey-Bass.

Flanagan, C. (2004). Institutional support for morality: Community-based and neighborhood organizations. In T. A. Thorkildsen & H. Walberg (Eds.), *Nurturing morality* (pp. 173–183). New York: Kluwer Academic/Plenum.

Flanagan, L. M. (2008). Object relations theory. In J. Berzoff, L. M. Flanagan, & L. Melano (Eds.), *Inside out and outside in: Psychodynamic clinical theory and psychopathology in contemporary multicultural contexts* (2nd ed., pp. 121–169). Lanham, MD: Jason Aronson.

Floyd, K., & Morman, M. (Eds.). (2006). *Widening the family circle: New research on family communication*. Thousand Oaks, CA: Sage.

Fogarty, R. (2009). *Brain-compatible classrooms* (3rd ed.). Thousand Oaks, CA: Corwin.

Foley, K. M. (Ed.). (2005). *When the focus is on care: Palliative care and cancer*. Atlanta, GA: American Cancer Society.

Fonagy, P. (2003). The development of psychopathology from infancy to adulthood: The mysterious unfolding of disturbance in time. *Infant Mental Health Journal, 24*, 212–239.

Foner, A. (1995). Social stratification. In G. L. Maddox (Ed.), *The encyclopedia of aging: A comprehensive resource in gerontology and geriatrics* (2nd ed., pp. 887–890). New York: Springer.

Fong, R. (Ed.). (2003). *Culturally competent practice with immigrant and refugee children and families*. New York: Guilford Press.

Fong, R., & Furuto, S. B. C. L. (Eds.). (2001). *Culturally competent practice: Skills, interventions, and evaluations*. Boston: Allyn & Bacon.

Fontana, A. (1984). Introduction: Existential sociology and the self. In J. Kotarba & A. Fontana (Eds.), *The existential self in society* (pp. 3–17). Chicago: University of Chicago Press.

Ford, D., & Lerner, R. (1992). *Developmental systems theory: An integrative approach*. Newbury Park, CA: Sage.

Fordham, S. (1996). *Blacked out: Dilemmas of race, identity, and success at Capital High*. Chicago: University of Chicago Press.

Foster, D. G., Rostovtseva, D. P., Brindis, C. D., Biggs, M.A., Hulett, D., & Darney, P. D. (2009). Cost savings from the provision of specific methods of contraception in a publically funded program. *American Journal of Public Health, 99*(3), 446–451.

Foucault, M. (1969). *The archaeology of knowledge and the discourse on language*. New York: Harper Colophon.

Fowler, J. W. (1981). *Stages of faith: The psychology of human development and the quest for meaning*. San Francisco: Harper.

Fowler, J. W. (1995). *Stages of faith: The psychology of human development and the quest for meaning*. New York: HarperCollins.

Fowler, J. W. (1996). *Faithful change: The personal and public challenges of postmodern life*. Nashville, TN: Abingdon Press.

Fowler, J. W., & Dell, M. L. (2006). Stages of faith from infancy through adolescence: Reflections on three decades of faith development theory. In E. C. Roehlkepartain, P. E. King, L. Wagener, & P. L. Benson (Eds.), *The handbook of spiritual development in children and adolescence* (pp. 34–45). Thousand Oaks, CA: Sage.

Fox, C., & Miller, H. (1995). *Postmodern public administration: Toward discourse.* Thousand Oaks, CA: Sage.

Fox, M. (1994). *The reinvention of work: A new vision of livelihood for our time.* San Francisco: HarperSanFrancisco.

Frame, M. W. (2003). *Integrating religion and spirituality into counseling: A comprehensive approach.* Pacific Grove, CA: Brooks/Cole Thompson Learning.

Francescato, D., & Tomai, M. (2001). Community psychology: Should there be a European perspective? *Journal of Community & Applied Social Psychology, 11,* 371–380.

Frank, A. (1967). *Capitalism and development in Latin America.* New York: Monthly Review Press.

Frank, L., Andresen, M., & Schmid, T. (2004). Obesity relationships with community design, physical activity, and time spent in cars. *American Journal of Preventive Medicine, 27*(2), 87–96.

Franklin, C. (1995). Expanding the vision of the social constructionist debates: Creating relevance for practitioners. *Families in Society, 76,* 395–407.

Franklin, R. M. (1994). The safest place on earth: The culture of Black congregations. In J. P. Wind & J. W. Lewis (Eds.), *American congregations* (Vol. 2, pp. 257–260). Chicago: University of Chicago Press.

Franko, D. L., & Striegel-Moore, R. (2002). The role of body dissatisfaction as a risk factor for depression in adolescent girls: Are the differences Black and White? *Journal of Psychosomatic Research, 53,* 975–983.

Franko, D. L., Striegel-Moore, R. H., Thompson, D., Schreiber, G. B., & Daniels, S. R. (2005). Does adolescent depression predict obesity in Black and White young adult women? *Psychological Medicine, 35,* 1505–1513.

Fraser, M. (2004). *Risk and resilience in childhood: An ecological perspective* (2nd ed.). Washington, DC: NASW Press.

Fraser, M., Kirby, L., & Smokowski, P. (2004). Risk and resilience in childhood. In M. Fraser (Ed.), *Risk and resilience in childhood: An ecological perspective* (2nd ed., pp. 13–66). Washington, DC: NASW Press.

Freedberg, S. (2007). Re-examining empathy: A relational-feminist point of view. *Social Work, 52*(3), 251–259.

Freedom House. (2010). *Freedom of the press.* Retrieved February 23, 2010, from http://www.freedomhouse.org/template.cfm?page=16

Freeman, D. R. (2006). Spirituality in violent and substance-abusing African American men: An untapped resource in healing. *Social Thought, 25*(1), 3–22.

Freeman, E., & Couchonnal, G. (2006). Narrative and culturally based approaches in practice with families. *Families in Society: The Journal of Contemporary Social Services, 87*(2), 198–208.

Freeman, E., & Dyer, L. (1993). High-risk children and adolescents: Family and community environments. *Families in Society, 74,* 422–431.

Freeman, L., Shaffer, D., & Smith, H. (1996). Neglected victims of homicide: The needs of young siblings of murder victims. *American Journal of Orthopsychiatry, 66,* 337–345.

Freeman, S. (2004). Nondaily hormonal contraception: Considerations in contraceptive choice and patient counseling. *Journal of the American Academy of Nurse Practitioners, 16*(6), 226–238.

Freisthler, B., Merritt, D. H., & LaScala, E. A. (2006). Understanding the ecology of child maltreatment: A review of the literature and directions for future research. *Child Maltreatment, 11*(3), 263–280.

Fremeaux, I. (2005). New labour's appropriation of the concept of community: A critique. *Community Development Journal, 40*(3), 265–274.

French, L. A., & White, W. L. (2004). Alcohol and other drug addictions among Native Americans: The movement toward tribal-centric treatment programs. *Alcoholism Treatment Quarterly, 22*(1), 81–91.

French, S., Seidman, E., Allen, L., & Aber, J. (2006). The development of ethnic identity during adolescence. *Developmental Psychology, 42,* 1–10.

Freud, S. (1927). Some psychological consequences of the anatomical distinction between the sexes. *International Journal of Psycho-Analysis, 8,* 133–142.

Freud, S. (1928). *The future of an illusion.* London: Hogarth Press and Institute of Psychoanalysis.

Freud, S. (1938). *An outline of psychoanalysis.* London: Hogarth Press. (Original work published 1973)

Freud, S. (1953). Three essays on the theory of sexuality. In J. Strachey (Ed. & Trans.), *The standard edition of the complete psychological works of Sigmund Freud* (Vol. 7, pp. 135–245). London: Hogarth Press. (Original work published 1905)

Freud, S. (1957). Mourning and melancholia. In J. Strachey (Ed. & Trans.), *The standard edition of the complete psychological works of Sigmund Freud* (Vol. 14, pp. 237–258). London: Hogarth. (Original work published 1917)

Freud, S. (1978). *The interpretation of dreams* (A. A. Brill, Trans.). New York: Modern Library. (Original work published 1899)

Freundl, G., Sivin, I., & Batár, I. (2010). State of the art of nonhormonal methods of contraception: IV. Natural family planning. *European Journal of Contraceptive and Reproductive Health Care, 15*(2), 113–123.

Frey, L., & Sunwolf. (2005). The symbolic-interpretive perspective of group life. In M. Poole & A. Hollingshead (Eds.), *Theories of small groups: Interdisciplinary perspectives* (pp. 185–239). Thousand Oaks, CA: Sage.

Friedman, B., Kahn, P., Hagman, J., Severson, R., & Gill, B. (2006). The watcher and the watched: Social judgments about privacy in a public place. *Human–Computer Interaction, 21*(2), 235–272.

Friedman, S. H., Kessler, A. R., & Martin, R. (2009). Psychiatric help for caregivers of infants in neonatal intensive care. *Psychiatric Services, 60*(4), 554.

Friedmann, E., & Havighurst, R. (1954). *The meaning of work and retirement.* Chicago: University of Chicago Press.

Frith, U., & Frith, C. (2010). The social brain: Allowing humans to boldly go where no other species has been. *Philosophical Transactions of the Royal Society B: Biological Science, 365*(1537), 165–176.

Fromm, E. (1941). *Escape from freedom.* New York: Avon.

Fromm, E., & Maccoby, M. (1970). *Social character in a Mexican village.* Englewood Cliffs, NJ: Prentice Hall.

Frumkin, H. (2001). Beyond toxicity: Human health and the natural environment. *American Journal of Preventive Medicine, 20*(3), 234–240.

Frumkin, H. (2003). Healthy places: Exploring the evidence. *American Journal of Public Health, 93*(9), 1451–1456.

Frumkin, P. (2002). Service contracting with nonprofit and for-profit providers. In J. D. Donahue & J. S. Nye Jr. (Eds.), *Market-based governance* (pp. 66–87). Washington, DC: Brookings Institution Press.

Fu, H., Darroch, J., Haas, T., & Ranjit, N. (1999). Contraceptive failure rates: New estimates from the 1995 National Survey of Family Growth. *Family Planning Perspectives, 31*(2), 52–58.

Fukuyama, M. A., & Sevig, T. D. (1999). *Integrating spirituality into multicultural counseling.* Thousand Oaks, CA: Sage.

Fuligni, A. (1997). The academic achievement of adolescents from immigrant families: The roles of family background, attitudes, and behavior. *Child Development, 68*(2), 351–363.

Furman, L. E., & Chandy, J. M. (1994). Religion and spirituality: A long-neglected cultural component of rural social work practice. *Human Services in the Rural Environment, 17*(3/4), 21–26.

Furushima, R. Y. (1983). Faith development in a cross-cultural perspective. *Religious Education, 80,* 414–420.

Galambos, C. (2001). Community healing rituals for survivors of rape. *Smith College Studies in Social Work, 71*(3), 441–457.

Gale, J. (2009). Meditation and relational connectedness: Practices for couples and families. In F. Walsh (Ed.), *Spiritual resources in family therapy* (2nd ed., pp. 247–266). New York: Guilford Press.

Galinsky, E., Aumann, K., & Bond, J. (2009). *Times are changing: Gender and generation at work and at home.* Washington, DC: Families and Work Institute. Retrieved December 3, 2009, from http://www.familiesandwork.org

Galinsky, M. J., Schopler, J. H., & Abell, M. D. (1997). Connecting group members through telephone and computer groups. *Health & Social Work, 22,* 181–188.

Gallagher, W. (1993). *The power of place: How our surroundings shape our thoughts, emotions, and actions.* New York: Poseidon.

Gallup. (2008). *Religion.* Retrieved February, 26, 2010, from http://www.gallup.com/poll/1690/religion.aspx

Gallup, G., & Jones, T. (2000). *The next American spirituality: Finding God in the twenty-first century.* Colorado Springs, CO: Cook Communication Ministries.

Gallup, G., & Lindsay, D. M. (1999). *Surveying the religious landscape: Trends in U.S. beliefs.* Harrisburg, PA: Morehouse.

Galotti, K. M. (1989). Gender differences in self-reported moral reasoning: A review and new evidence. *Journal of Youth and Adolescence, 18,* 475–488.

Galvin, K. (2006). Joined by hearts and words: Adoptive family relationships. In K. Floyd & M. Morman (Eds.), *Widening the family circle: New research on family communication* (pp. 137–152). Thousand Oaks, CA: Sage.

Galvin, K., Bylund, C., & Brommel, B. (2003). *Family communication: Cohesion and change* (6th ed.). New York: Allyn & Bacon.

Galvin, K., Dickson, F., & Marrow, S. (2006). Systems theory: Patterns and wholes in family communication. In D. Braithwaite & L. Baxter (Eds.), *Engaging theories in family communication: Multiple perspectives* (pp. 309–324). Thousand Oaks, CA: Sage.

Gambrill, E. (2006). *Critical thinking in clinical practice: Improving the quality of judgments and decisions* (2nd ed.). Hoboken, NJ: Wiley.

Gamoran, A., & Himmelfarb, H. (1994). *The quality of vocational education.* Washington, DC: U.S. Department of Education.

Gamson, W., & Meyer, D. (1996). Framing political opportunity. In D. McAdam, J. McCarthy, & M. Zald (Eds.), *Comparative perspectives on social movements* (pp. 273–290). New York: Cambridge University Press.

Garbarino, J. (1995). *Raising children in a socially toxic environment.* San Francisco: Jossey-Bass.

Garbarino, J. (1999). *Lost boys: Why our sons turn violent and how we can save them.* New York: Free Press.

Garbarino, J. (2006). *See Jane hit: Why girls are growing more violent and what we can do about it.* New York: Penguin.

Garbarino, J., & Bedard, C. (1997). Spiritual challenges to children facing violent trauma. *Childhood: A Global Journal of Child Research, 3*(4), 467–478.

Garcia, B., & Zuniga, M. (2007). Cultural competence with Latino Americans. In D. Lum (Ed.), *Culturally competent practice: A framework for understanding diverse groups and justice issues* (3rd ed., pp. 299–327). Belmont, CA: Thomson Brooks/Cole.

Garcia, E. (2001). Parenting in Mexican American families. In N. Boyd Webb (Ed.), *Culturally diverse parent–child and family relationships: A guide for social workers and other practitioners* (pp. 157–179). New York: Columbia University Press.

Garden, F., & Jalaludin, B. (2009). Impact of urban sprawl on overweight, obesity, and physical activity in Sydney, Australia. *Journal of Urban Health, 86*(1), 19–30.

Gardiner, H. W., & Kosmitzki, C. (2008). *Lives across cultures: Cross-cultural human development* (4th ed.). Boston: Pearson.

Gardner, H. E. (1993). *Multiple intelligences: The theory in practice.* New York: Basic Books.

Gardner, H. E. (1999). *Intelligence reframed: Multiple intelligences for the 21st century.* New York: Basic Books.

Gardner, H. E. (2006). *Multiple intelligences: New horizons.* New York: Basic Books.

Gargiulo, R. M. (2005). *Young children with special needs.* Albany, NY: Thomson/Delmar Learning.

Gargus, R. A., Vohr, B. R., Tyson, J. E., High, P., Higgins, R. D., Wrage, L. A., et al. (2009). Unimpaired outcomes for extremely low birth weight infants at 18 and 22 months. *Pediatrics, 124*(1), 112–121.

Garland, D. R., Myers, D. M., & Wolfer, T. A. (2008). Social work with religious volunteers: Activating and sustaining community involvement. *Social Work, 53*(3), 255–265.

Garland, E., & Howard, O. (2009). Neuroplasticity, psychosocial genomics, and the biopsychosocial paradigm in the 21st century. *Health & Social Work, 34*(3), 191–199.

Garmezy, N. (1993). Vulnerability and resilience. In D. C. Funder, R. D. Parke, C. Tomlinson-Keasey, & K. Widaman (Eds.), *Studying lives through time* (pp. 377–398). Washington, DC: American Psychological Association.

Garmezy, N. (1994). Reflections and commentary on risk, resilience, and development. In R. J. Haggerty, L. R. Sherrod, N. Garmezy, & M. Rutter (Eds.), *Stress, risk, and resilience in children and adolescents: Processes, mechanisms, and interventions* (pp. 1–18). New York: Cambridge University Press.

Garrett, B. (2009). *Brain and behavior: An introduction to biological psychology* (2nd ed.). Thousand Oaks, CA: Sage.

Garrett, J. L. (2006). Educating the whole child. *Kappa Delta Pi Record, 42*(4), 154–155.

Garrett, K. (2004). Use of groups in school social work: Group work and group processes. *Social Work With Groups, 27*(2/3), 75–92.

Garrett, M. W. (1995). Between two worlds: Cultural discontinuity in the dropout of Native American youth. *The School Counselor, 10*, 199–208.

Garrow, E., & Hasenfeld, Y. (2010). Theoretical approaches to human service organizations. In Y. Hasenfeld (Ed.), *Human services as complex organizations* (2nd ed., pp. 33–57). Thousand Oaks, CA: Sage.

Garton, A. F., & Pratt, C. (1991). Leisure activities of adolescent school students: Predictors of participation and interest. *Journal of Adolescence, 14*, 305–321.

Gartstein, M., Gonzales, C., Carranza, J., Adaho, S., Rothbart, M., & Yang, S. (2006). Studying cross-cultural differences in the development of infant temperament: People's Republic of China, the United States of America, and Spain. *Child Psychiatry and Human Development, 37*, 145–161.

Gartstein, M., Knyazev, G., & Slobodskaya, H. (2005). Cross-cultural differences in the structure of temperament: United States of America (U.S.) and Russia. *Infant Behavior and Development, 28*, 54–61.

Gartstein, M., Peleg, Y., Young, B., & Slobodskaya, H. (2009). Infant temperament in Russia, United States of America, and Israel: Differences and similarities between Russian-speaking families. *Child Psychiatry and Human Development, 40*, 241–256.

Garver, K. L. (1995). Genetic counseling. In G. B. Reed, A. E. Claireaux, & F. Cockburn (Eds.), *Diseases of the fetus and newborn* (2nd ed., pp. 1007–1012). London: Chapman & Hall.

Garvey, C. (1984). *Children's talk.* Cambridge, MA: Harvard University Press.

Garvin, C. D., & Reed, B. G. (1983). Gender issues in social group work: An overview. *Social Work With Groups, 6*(3/4), 5–18.

Garvin, V., Kalter, N., & Hansell, J. (1993). Divorced women: Factors contributing to resiliency and vulnerability. *Journal of Divorce and Remarriage, 21*(1/2), 21–39.

Gates, G., & Ost, J. (2004). *The gay and lesbian atlas.* Washington, DC: The Urban Institute.

Gaylord, M., Greer, M., & Botti, J. (2008). Improving perinatal health: A novel approach to improve community and adult health. *Journal of Perinatology, 28*, 91–96.

Ge, X., Conger, R. D., & Elder, G. H., Jr. (2001). The relation between puberty and psychological distress in adolescent boys. *Journal of Research on Adolescence, 11*, 49–70.

Gee, J. P. (1996). Social linguistics and literacies: Ideology in discourses (2nd ed.). London: Falmer.

Geertz, C. (1983). Common sense as a cultural system. In C. Geertz, *Local knowledge: Further essays in interpretive anthropology* (pp. 73–93). New York: Basic Books.

Gehlbach, H. (2006). How changes in students' goal orientations relate to outcomes in social studies. *Journal of Education Research, 99*, 358–370.

Geiger, B. (1996). *Fathers as primary caregivers.* Westport, CT: Greenwood.

Gelberg, L., & Linn, L. S. (1988). Social and physical health of homeless adults previously treated for mental health problems. *Hospital and Community Psychiatry, 39*, 510–516.

Gelles, R. (1989). Child abuse and violence in single-parent families: Parent absence and economic deprivation. *American Journal of Orthopsychiatry, 59*, 492–501.

Gelles, R. (2010). Violence, abuse, and neglect in families and intimate relationships. In S. Price, C. Price, & P. McKenry (Eds.), *Families & change: Coping with* stressful events and transitions (4th ed., pp. 119–139). Thousand Oaks, CA: Sage.

Gelles, R., & Hargreaves, E. (1981). Maternal employment and violence toward children. *Journal of Family Issues, 2*, 509–530.

George, L. K. (1993). Sociological perspectives on life transitions. *Annual Review of Sociology, 19*, 353–373.

George, L. K. (2003). What life-course perspective offers the study of aging and health. In R. Settersten, Jr. (Ed.), *Invitation to the life course: Toward new understandings of later life* (pp. 161–188). Amityville, NY: Baywood Publishing.

George, L. K. (2005). Socioeconomic status and health across the life course: Progress and prospects. *The Journal of Gerontology: Series B: Psychological Sciences and Social Sciences, 60B*, 135–139.

George, L. K., Larson, D. B., Koenig, H. G., & McCullough, M. E. (2000). Spirituality and health: What we know, what we need to know. *Journal of Social & Clinical Psychology, 19*, 102–116.

Georgieff, M. K. (2007). Nutrition and the developing brain: Nutrient priorities and measurement. *American Journal of Clinical Nutrition, 85*(2), 614S–620S.

Gergen, K. (1985). The social constructionist movement in modern psychology. *American Psychologist, 40*, 266–275.

Gerhardt, S. (2004). *Why love matters: How affection shapes a baby's brain*. Philadelphia: Routledge/Taylor & Francis.

Germain, C. (1973). An ecological perspective in casework practice. *Social Casework, 54*, 323–330.

Germain, C. (1978). Space: An ecological variable in social work practice. *Social Casework, 59*, 515–522.

Germain, C. (1994). Human behavior and the social environment. In R. Reamer (Ed.), *The foundations of social work knowledge* (pp. 88–121). New York: Columbia University Press.

Germain, C., & Gitterman, A. (1980). *The life model of social work practice*. New York: Columbia University Press.

Gevirtz, C. (2006). Managing postpolio syndrome pain. *Nursing, 36*(12), 17.

Gibbs, J. T., & Huang, L. N. (1989). A conceptual framework for assessing and treating minority youth. In J. T. Gibbs & L. N. Huang (Eds.), *Children of color: Psychological interventions with minority youth* (pp. 1–29). San Francisco: Jossey-Bass.

Gibbs, N. (2009, October 14). What women want now. *Time*. Retrieved December 3, 2009, from http://www.time.com/time/specials/packages/article/0,28804,1930277_1930145,00.html

Gibson, M. (1988). *Accommodation without assimilation: Sikh immigrants in an American high school*. Ithaca, NY: Cornell University Press.

Gibson-Davis, C., Edin, K., & McLanahan, S. (2005). High hopes but even higher expectations: The retreat from marriage among low-income couples. *Journal of Marriage and Family, 65*(5), 1301–1312.

Giddens, A. (1979). *Central problems in social theory: Action, structure, and contradiction in social analysis*. Berkeley: University of California Press.

Giddens, A. (2000). *Runaway world: How globalization is reshaping our lives*. New York: Routledge.

Giedd, J. (2008). The teen brain: Insights from neuroimaging. *Journal of Adolescent Health, 42*, 335–343.

Giedd, J. (2009). Editorial: Linking adolescent sleep, brain maturation, and behavior. *Journal of Adolescent Health, 45*, 319–320.

Gielen, U., & Markoulis, D. (2001). Preference for principled moral reasoning: A developmental and cross-cultural perspective. In L. Adler & U. Gielen (Eds.), *Cross-cultural topics in psychology* (2nd ed., pp. 81–101). Westport, CT: Praeger/Greenwood.

Gifford, R. (2007). *Environmental psychology: Principles and practice* (4th ed.). Colville, WA: Optimal Books.

Gill, S. (2010). *Developing a learning culture in nonprofit organizations*. Thousand Oaks, CA: Sage.

Gilligan, C. (1982). *In a different voice: Psychological theory and women's development*. Cambridge, MA: Harvard University Press.

Gilligan, C. (1988). Remapping the moral domain: New images of self in relationship. In C. Gilligan, J. V. Ward, & J. M. Taylor (Eds.), *Mapping the moral domain* (pp. 3–20). Cambridge, MA: Harvard University Press.

Gilman, S. E., Kawachi, I., & Fitzmaurice, G. M. (2003). Family disruption in childhood and risk of adult depression. *American Journal of Psychiatry, 160*(5), 939–946.

Gilson, S. F. (1996). *The disability movement and federal legislation*. Unpublished manuscript.

Gilson, S. F., & DePoy, E. (2000). Multiculturalism and disability: A critical perspective. *Disability & Society, 15*(2), 207–218.

Gilson, S. F., & DePoy, E. (2002). Theoretical approaches to disability content in social work education. *Journal of Social Work Education, 37*, 153–165.

Gitterman, A. (2009). The life model. In A. R. Roberts (Ed.), *Social workers' desk reference* (2nd ed., pp. 231–235). New York: Oxford University Press.

Giudice, L. C. (2006). Infertility and the environment: The medical context. *Seminars in Reproductive Medicine, 24*(5), 1039–1048.

Glaser, D. (2000). Child abuse and neglect and the brain—A review. *Journal of Child Psychology and Psychiatry, 41*(1), 97–116.

Glass, C. S., & Wegar, K. (2000). Teacher perceptions of the incidence and management of attention deficit hyperactivity disorder. *Education, 121*(2), 412–420.

Glover, J., Galliher, R., & Lamere, T. (2009). Identity development and exploration among sexual minority adolescents: Examination of a multidimensional model. *Journal of Homosexuality, 56*, 77–101.

Glover, R. (1996). Religiosity in adolescence and young adulthood: Implications for identity formation. *Psychological Reports, 78*, 427–431.

Glynn M., & Rhodes P. (2005, June). *Estimated HIV prevalence in the United States at the end of 2003.* Paper presented at the National HIV Prevention Conference, Atlanta, GA. Retrieved August 4, 2006, from http://www.cdc.gov/hiv/topics/surveillance/basic.htm

Go Forth and Multiply a Lot Less. (2009, October 29). *The Economist.* Retrieved May 20, 2010, from http://www.econo.hit-u.ac.jp/~makoto/education/economist_fertility_20091031.pdf

Goffman, E. (1959). *Presentation of self in everyday life.* Garden City, NY: Archer.

Gogtay, N., Giedd, J., Lusk, L., Hyashi, K., Greenstein, D., Vaituzis, A. C., et al. (2004). Dynamic mapping of human cortical development during childhood through early adulthood. *Proceedings of the National Academy of Science, 101*(21), 8174–8179.

Gold, K. J., Dalton, V. K., Schwenk, T. L., & Hayward, R. A., (2007). What causes pregnancy loss? Preexisting mental illness as an independent risk factor. *General Hospital Psychiatry, 29*(3), 207–213.

Goldberg, A. (2010). Lesbian- and gay-parent families: Development and functioning. In S. Price, C. Price, & P. McKenry (Eds.), *Families & change: Coping with stressful events and transitions* (pp. 263–284). Thousand Oaks, CA: Sage.

Goldberg, W., Clarke-Stewart, K., Rice, J., & Dellis, E. (2002). Emotional energy as an explanatory construct for fathers' engagement with their infants. *Parenting: Science & Practice, 2*, 379–408.

Goldenberg, R. L., Hauth, J. C., & Andrews, W. W. (2000). Intrauterine infection and premature delivery. *New England Journal of Medicine, 342*(20), 1500–1508.

Goldenberg, R. L., & Jobe, A. H. (2001). Prospects for research in reproductive health and birth outcomes. *Journal of the American Medical Association, 285*(5), 633–642.

Goldman, J. (1996). *Healing sounds: The power of harmonics.* Rockport, MA: Element Books.

Goldstein, A. (2006, August 7). Welfare changes a burden to states: Work rules also threaten study, health programs. *The Washington Post*, p. A01.

Goldstein, C. (n.d.). *Spiritual activism: Co-creating the world we seek.* Retrieved February 26, 2010, from http://www.feminist.com/activism/spiritualactivism1.html

Goldstein, D. (1996). Ego psychology theory. In F. Turner (Ed.), *Social work treatment* (4th ed., pp. 191–217). New York: Free Press.

Goldstein, E. (1995). *Ego psychology and social work practice* (2nd ed.). New York: Free Press.

Goldstein, E. (2001). *Object relations theory and self psychology in social work practice.* New York: Free Press.

Goldstein, E. (2008). Ego psychology theory. In B. A. Thyer, K. M. Sowers, & C. N. D. Dulmus (Eds.), *Comprehensive handbook of social work and social welfare, Vol. 2: Human behavior in the social environment* (pp.135–162). Hoboken, NJ: Wiley.

Goldstein, H., Kaczmarek, L. A., & English, K. M. (2002). *Promoting social communication: Children with developmental disabilities from birth to adolescence.* Baltimore: Paul H. Brookes.

Goldstein, J., & Kenney, C. (2001). Marriage delayed or marriage forgone? New cohort forecasts of first marriage for U.S. women. *American Sociological Review, 66*(4), 506–519.

Goldstein, S., & Brooks, R. B. (2005). Why study resilience? In S. Goldstein & R. B. Brooks (Eds.), *Handbook of resilience in children* (pp. 3–15). New York: Kluwer Academic/Plenum.

Goleman, D. (1995). *Emotional intelligence.* New York: Bantam.

Goleman, D. (2005). *Emotional intelligence* (10th anniv. ed.). New York: Bantam.

Goleman, D. (2006). *Social intelligence: The new science of human relationships.* New York: Bantam.

Golsworthy, R., & Coyle, A. (1999). Spiritual beliefs and the search for meaning among older adults following partner loss. *Mortality, 4*(1), 21–40.

Gomez, N. (2001). EEG during different emotions in 10-month-old infants of depressed mothers. *Journal of Reproductive and Infant Psychology, 19*(4), 295–313.

Gonzalez-Quintero, V., Tolaymat, L., Luke, B., Gonzalez-Garcia, A., Duthely, L., & O'Sullivan, M. (2006). Outcomes of pregnancies among Hispanics: Revisiting the epidemiologic paradox. *Journal of Reproductive Medicine, 51*(1), 10–14.

Good, T., & Nichols, S. (2001). Expectancy effects in the classroom: A special focus on improving the reading performance of minority students in first-grade classrooms. *Educational Psychologist, 36*, 113–126.

Goodenough, W. (1996). Culture. In D. Levinson & M. Ember (Eds.), *Encyclopedia of cultural anthropology* (Vol. 1, pp. 291–298). New York: Holt.

Goodson-Lawes, J. (1994). Ethnicity and poverty as research variables: Family studies with Mexican and Vietnamese newcomers. In E. Sherman & W. Reid (Eds.), *Qualitative research in social work* (pp. 22–31). New York: Columbia University Press.

Goodwin, J., & Jasper, J. (Eds.). (2004). *Rethinking social movements: Structure, meaning, and emotion.* Lanham, MD: Rowman & Littlefield.

Gopaul-McNicol, S. (1988). Racial identification and racial preference of Black preschool children in New York and Trinidad. *Journal of Black Psychology, 14*(2), 65–68.

Gordon, D., Nandy, S., Pantazis, C., Pemberton, S., & Townsend, P. (2003). *Child poverty in the developing world*. Bristol, UK: The Policy Press.

Gordon, L., Thakur, M., & Atlas, M. (2007). What hormonal contraception is most effective for obese women? *Journal of Family Practice, 56*(6), 471–475.

Gordon, M. (1964*). Assimilation in American life: The role of race, religion, and national origins*. New York: Oxford University Press.

Gordon, W., Zafonte, R., Cicerone, K., Cantor, J., Brown, M., Lombard, L., et al. (2006). Traumatic brain injury rehabilitation: State of the science. *American Journal of Physical Medicine & Rehabilitation, 85*(4), 343–382.

Gosten, L. O. (2007). Abortion politics: Clinical freedom, trust in the judiciary, and the autonomy of women, *Journal of the American Medical Association, 298*(13), 1562–1564.

Gottman, J. M. (1994, May/June). Why marriages fail. *Family Therapy Networker*, 41–48.

Gould, D. (2004). Passionate political processes: Bring emotions back into the study of social movements. In J. Goodwin & J. Jasper (Eds.), *Rethinking social movements: Structure, meaning, and emotion* (pp. 155–175). Lanham, MD: Rowman & Littlefield.

Gould, S. (1981). *The mismeasure of man*. New York: Norton.

Gourevitch, A. (2001, May 30). Awakening the giant: How the living wage movement can revive progressive politics. *American Prospect Online*. Retrieved May 5, 2010, from http://www.prospect.org/cs/articles?article=awakening_the_giant

Grady, D. (2009, November 3). Premature rates are fueling higher rate of infant mortality in U.S., report says. *New York Times, A15*. Retrieved January 17, 2010, from http://www.nytimes.com/2009/11/04/health/04infant.html

Graff, H. (1995). *Conflicting paths: Growing up in America*. Cambridge, MA: Harvard University Press.

Grainger, D. A., Frazier, L. M., & Rowland, C. A. (2006). Preconception care and treatment with assisted reproductive technologies. *Maternal and Child Health Journal, 10* (Suppl 7), 161–164.

Granic, I., Dishion, T., & Hollenstein, T. (2003). The family ecology of adolescence: A dynamic systems perspective on normative development. In G. Adams & M. Berzonsky (Eds.), *Blackwell handbook of adolescence* (pp. 60–91). Oxford, UK: Blackwell.

Greeff, A. P., & Fillis, A. J. (2009). Resiliency in poor single-parent families. *Families in Society: The Journal of Contemporary Social Services, 90*(3), 279–285.

Greenberg, L. S. (2008). The clinical application of emotion in psychotherapy. In M. Lewis, J. M. Havilland-Jones, & L. F. Barrett (Eds.), *Handbook of emotions* (3rd ed., pp. 88–101). New York: Guilford Press.

Greene, R. R., & Cohen, H. L. (2005). Social work with older adults and their families: Changing practice paradigms. *Families in Society, 86*(3), 367–373.

Greene, S., Anderson, E., Hetherington, E., Forgatch, M., & DeGarmo, D. (2003). Risk and resilience after divorce. In F. Walsh (Ed.), *Normal family processes: Growing diversity and complexity* (3rd ed., pp. 96–120). New York: Guilford Press.

Greenfield, E., & Marks, N. (2006). Linked lives: Adult children's problems and their parents' psychological and relational well-being. *Journal of Marriage and Family, 68*, 442–454.

Greenfield, P., Keller, H., Fuglini, A., & Maynard, A. (2003). Cultural pathways through universal development. *Annual Review of Psychology, 54*, 461–490.

Greenfield, P., & Zheng, Y. (2006). Children, adolescents, and the Internet: A new field of inquiry in developmental psychology. *Developmental Psychology, 42*(3), 391–394.

Greenman, P., & Schneider, B. (2009). Stability and change in patterns of peer rejection: Implications for children's academic performance over time. *School Psychology International, 30*(2), 163–183.

Greenspan, S. (2006). Rethinking "harmonious parenting" using a three-factor discipline model. *Child Care in Practice, 12*(1), 5–12.

Greenwald, H. (2008). *Organizations: Management without control*. Thousand Oaks, CA: Sage.

Greve, W., & Staudinger, U. M. (2006). Resilience in later adulthood and old age: Resources and potentials for successful aging. In D. Cicchetti & D. J. Cohen (Eds.), *Developmental psychopathology, Vol. 3: Risk, disorder and adaptation* (pp. 796–840). Hoboken, NJ: Wiley.

Griffith, S. (1996). *Amending attachment theory: Ambiguities among maternal care, day care peer group experience, general security and altruistic prosocial proclivities in 3, 4 and 5 year old children*. Unpublished doctoral dissertation, Adelphi University, New York.

Grimes, D.A., Lopez, L., Raymond, E. G., Halpern, V., Nanda, K., & Schulz, K. F. (2005). Spermicide used alone for contraception. *Cochrane Database of Systematic Review, 19*(4), CD005218.

Grinspun, A. (2004, March). From the editor. *In Focus*. Retrieved January 19, 2010, from http://www.ipc-undp.org/pub/IPCPovertyInFocus2.pdf

Griswold, W. (2008). *Cultures and societies in a changing world* (3rd ed.). Thousand Oaks, CA: Pine Forge.

Grof, S. (1988). *The adventure of self-discovery*. New York: State University of New York Press.

Grof, S. (2003). Physical manifestations of emotional disorders: Observations from the study of non-ordinary states of consciousness. In K. Taylor (Ed.), *Exploring holotropic breathwork: Selected articles from a decade of The Inner Door.* Santa Cruz, CA: Hanford Mead Publishers.

Grof, S., & Bennett, H. Z. (1992). *The holotropic mind: The three levels of human consciousness and how they shape our lives.* New York: HarperCollins.

Gromley, W., Gayer, T., Phillips, D., & Dawson, B. (2004). *The effects of universal pre-K on cognitive development.* Retrieved May 21, 2010, from http://www.crocus .georgetown.edu/reports/oklahoma9z.pdf

Gross, E. (2004). Adolescent Internet use: What we expect, what teens report. *Applied Developmental Psychology, 25,* 633–649.

Grossman, P., Niemann, I., Schmidt, S., & Walach, H. (2004). Mindfulness-based stress reduction and health benefits: A meta-analysis. *Journal of Psychosomatic Research, 57*(1), 35–43.

Groves, B. M. (1997). Growing up in a violent world: The impact of family and community violence on young children and their families. *Topics in Early Childhood Special Education, 17*(1), 74–102.

Guarnaccia, P., & Lopez, S. (1998). The mental health and adjustment of immigrant and refugee children. *Child and Adolescent Psychiatric Clinic of North America, 7*(3), 537–553.

Gudmunson, C., Beutler, I., Israelsen, C., McCoy, J., & Hill, E. (2007). Linking financial strain to marital instability: Examining the roles of emotional distress and marital interaction. *Journal of Family and Economic Issues, 28*(3), 357–376.

Guillory, V. J., Cai, J., & Hoff, G. L. (2008). Secular trends in excess fetal and infant mortality using perinatal periods of risk analysis. *Journal of the National Medical Association, 100*(12), 1450–1456.

Guisbond, L., & Neill, M. (2004, September/October). Failing our children: No Child Left Behind undermines quality and equity in education. *Clearing House, 78*(1), 12.

Gunnar, M. R., Broderson, L., Nachimas, M., Buss, K., & Rigatuso, J. (1996). Stress reactivity and attachment security. *Developmental Psychobiology, 29*(3), 191–204.

Gunnar, M. R., & Quevedo, K. (2007). The neurobiology of stress and development. *Annual Review of Psychology, 58,* 145–173.

Guralnick, M., Neville, B., Hammond, M., & Connor, R. (2008). Continuity and change from full-inclusion early childhood programs through the early elementary period. *Journal of Early Intervention, 30*(3), 237–250.

Gurgan, T., & Demiro, A. (2007). Unresolved issues regarding assisted reproductive technology. *Reproductive BioMedicine Online, Supp 1*(14), 40–43.

Guterman, N., & Embry, R. (2004). Prevention and treatment strategies targeting physical child abuse and neglect. In P. Allen-Meares & M. Fraser (Eds.), *Intervention with children and adolescents: An interdisciplinary perspective* (pp. 130–158). Boston: Allyn & Bacon.

Gutheil, I. (1991). The physical environment and quality of life in residential facilities for frail elders. *Adult Residential Care Journal, 5,* 131–145.

Gutheil, I. (1992). Considering the physical environment: An essential component of good practice. *Social Work, 37,* 391–396.

Gutiérrez, K. (2008). Developing a sociocritical literacy in the third space. *Reading Research Quarterly, 43*(2), 148–164.

Gutiérrez, L. (1990). Working with women of color: An empowerment perspective. *Social Work, 35*(2), 149–153.

Gutiérrez, L. (1994). Beyond coping: An empowerment perspective on stressful life events. *Journal of Sociology and Social Welfare, 21*(3), 201–219.

Gutierrez, R. A. (2004). Internal colonialism: An American theory of race. *Social Science Research on Race, 1*(2), 281–295.

Gutman, L., McLoyd, V., & Tokoyawa, T. (2005). Financial strain, neighborhood stress, parenting behaviors, and adolescent adjustment in urban African American families. *Journal of Research on Adolescence, 15*(4), 425–449.

Guttmacher Institute. (1999). *Teen sex and pregnancy.* Retrieved June 6, 2006, from http://www.agi-usa.org/ pubs/fb_teen_sex.html

Guttmacher Institute. (2002a). *Sexuality education.* Retrieved October 24, 2006, from http://www.guttmacher.org

Guttmacher Institute. (2002b). *Teenagers' sexual and reproductive health: Developed countries.* Retrieved October 24, 2006, from http://www.guttmacher.org

Guttmacher Institute. (2005). *Facts in brief: Contraceptive use.* Retrieved December 13, 2006, from http://www.guttm acher.org/pubs/fb_const_use.html

Guttmacher Institute. (2006a). *Facts on American teens' sexual and reproductive health.* Retrieved September 12, 2011, from http://www.guttmacher.org/pubs/FB-ATSRH.html

Guttmacher Institute. (2006b). *Facts on sexually transmitted infections in the United States.* Retrieved November 20, 2006, from http://www.guttmacher.org

Guttmacher Institute. (2009). *Facts on induced abortion world-wide.* Retrieved November 20, 2009, from http:// www.guttmacher.org/pubs/fb_IAW.pdf

Guttmacher Institute. (2010). *Facts on American teens' sexual and reproductive health.* Retrieved February 2, 2010, from http://www.guttmacher.org/pubs/FB-ATSRH.html

Ha, J., Hong, J., Seltzer, M., & Greenberg, J. (2008). Age and gender differences in the well-being of midlife and aging parents with children with mental health or developmental problems: Report of a national study. *Journal of Health and Social Behavior, 49,* 310–316.

Haan, N. (1991). Moral development and action from a social constructivist perspective. In W. Kurtines & J. Gewirtz (Eds.), *Handbook of moral behavior and development: Theory* (Vol. 1, pp. 251–273). Hillsdale, NJ: Erlbaum.

Haan, N., Millsap, R., & Hartka, E. (1986). As time goes by: Change and stability in personality over fifty years. *Psychology and Aging, 1*, 220–232.

Habash, A. (2008). *Counting on graduation: An agenda for state leadership.* Retrieved May 5, 2010, from http://www.closing theachievementgap.org/cs/ctag/view/resources/125

Habash Rowan, A., Hall, D., & Haycock, K. (2010). *Gauging the gaps: A deeper look at student achievement.* Retrieved February 21, 2010, from http://www.edtrust.org/sites/edtrust.org/files/publications/files/NAEP%20_0.pdf

Habermas, J. (1984). *The theory of communicative action, Vol. 1: Reason and the rationalization of society.* Boston: Beacon Press.

Habermas, J. (1987). *The theory of communicative action, Vol. 2: Lifeworld and system: A critique of functionalist reason* (T. McCarthy, Trans.). Boston: Beacon Press. (Original work published 1981)

Haddad, Y. Y. (1997). Make room for the Muslims? In W. H. Conser Jr., & S. B. Twiss (Eds.), *Religious diversity and American religious history: Studies in traditions and cultures* (pp. 218–261). Athens: University of Georgia Press.

Haden, C., Haine, R., & Fivush, R. (1997). Developing narrative structure in parent–child reminiscing across the preschool years. *Developmental Psychology, 33*, 295–307.

Hagan, J. (1994). *Crime and disrepute.* Thousand Oaks, CA: Pine Forge.

Hagestad, G. (2003). Interdependent lives and relationships in changing times: A life-course view of families and aging. In R. Settersten, Jr. (Ed.), *Invitation to the life course: Toward new understandings of later life* (pp. 135–159). Amityville, NY: Baywood Publishing.

Hahn, S., Haselhorst, U., Quadbeck, B., Tan, S., Kimming, R., Mann, K., et al. (2006). Decreased soluble leptin receptor levels in women with polycystic ovarian syndrome. *European Journal of Endocrinology, 154*(2), 287–294.

Haider, A. (2006). *Roper v. Simmons*: The role of the science brief. *Ohio State Journal of Criminal Law, 375*, 369–377.

Haider, S., & Darney, P. D. (2007). Injectable contraception. *Clinical Obstetrics and Gynecology, 50*(4), 898–906.

Haidt, J. (2007). The new synthesis in moral psychology. *Science, 316*, 998–1002.

Haig-Brown, C. (1988). *Resistance and renewal: Surviving the Indian residential school.* Vancouver, BC, Canada: Tillacum Library.

Hair, E., Ling, T., & Cochran, S. W. (2003). *Youth development programs and educationally disadvantaged older youths: A synthesis.* Washington, DC: Child Trends.

Hakuta, K., Ferdman, B. M., & Diaz, R. M. (1987). Bilingualism and cognitive development: Three perspectives. In S. Rosenberg (Ed.), *Advances in applied psycholinguistics: Vol. 2. Reading, writing, and language learning* (pp. 284–319). New York: Cambridge University Press.

Hale, R. (2007). Choices in contraception. *British Journal of Midwifery, 15*(5), 305–309.

Hall, D. (2005, June). Getting honest about grad rates: How states play the numbers and students lose. *The Education Trust.* Retrieved May 5, 2010, from http://www.ccsso .org/content/pdfs/GettingHonestAboutGradRates.pdf

Hall, E. (1966). *The hidden dimension.* New York: Doubleday.

Hall, G. S. (1904). *Adolescence: Its psychology and its relations to physiology, anthropology, sociology, sex, crime, religion, and education.* New York: Appleton.

Hall, W. J. (2008). Centenarians: Metaphor becomes reality. *Archives of Internal Medicine, 168*(3), 262–263.

Halle, T. (2002). *Charting parenthood: A statistical portrait of fathers and mothers in America.* Washington, DC: Child Trends.

Halperin, D. (2001). The play's the thing: How social group work and theatre transformed a group into a community. *Social Work With Groups, 24*(2), 27–46.

Hamblen, J. (2002). *Terrorism and children.* Retrieved January 23, 2002, from http://www.ncptsd.org/facts/disasters/fs_children_disaster.html

Hames, A. M., & Godwin, M. C. (2008). The "out of control" balloon: Using spirituality as a coping resource. In C. F. Sori, & L. L. Hecker (Eds.), *The therapist's notebook: More homework, handouts, and activities for use in psychotherapy* (pp. 171–176). New York: Routledge/Taylor & Francis.

Hamilton, B. E., Martin, J., & Ventura, S. (2009, March 18). Births: Preliminary data for 2007. *National Vital Statistics Reports, 57*(12). Hyattsville, MD: National Center for Health Statistics.

Hamilton, S., & Hamilton, M. (2004). Implications for youth development practices. In S. Hamilton & M. Hamilton (Eds.), *The youth development handbook: Coming of age in American communities* (pp. 351–371). Thousand Oaks, CA: Sage.

Hampton, K., Sessions, L., Her, E. J., & Rainie, L. (2009, November 4). *Social isolation and new technology.* Washington, DC: Pew Internet & American Life Project.

Hampton, K., & Wellman, B. (2003). Neighboring in Netville: How the Internet supports community and social capital in a wired suburb. *City & Community, 2*(4), 277–311.

Hannerz, U. (1992). *Cultural complexity: Studies in the social organization of meaning.* New York: Columbia University Press.

Hansen, C., & Zambo, D. (2007). Loving and learning with Wemberly and David: Fostering emotional development in early childhood education. *Early Childhood Education Journal, 34*(4), 273–278.

Hansen, L. B., Saseen, J. J., & Teal, S. B. (2007). Levonorgestrel-only dosing strategies for emergency contraception. *Pharmacotherapy, 27*(2), 278–284.

Hansen, L. S. (1997). *Integrative life planning: Critical tasks for career development and changing life patterns.* San Francisco: Jossey-Bass.

Hao, L., & Cherlin, A. J. (2004). Welfare reform and teenage pregnancy, childbirth, and school dropout. *Journal of Marriage and Family, 66,* 179–184.

Hareven, T. (Ed.). (1978). *Transitions: The family and the life course in historical perspective.* New York: Academic Press.

Hareven, T. (1982a). American families in transition: Historical perspectives on change. In F. Walsh (Ed.), *Normal family processes* (pp. 446–466). New York: Guilford Press.

Hareven, T. (1982b). *Family time and industrial time: The relationship between the family and work in a New England industrial community.* New York: Cambridge University Press.

Hareven, T. (Ed.). (1996). *Aging and generation relations over the life course: A historical and cross-cultural perspective.* New York: Walter de Gruyter.

Hareven, T. K. (2000). *Families, history, and social change: Life-course and cross-cultural perspectives.* Boulder, CO: Westview Press.

Harkness, S., & Super, C. (2003). Culture and parenting. In M. Bornstein (Ed.), *Handbook of parenting* (2nd ed., Vol. 2, pp. 253–280). Mahwah, NJ: Erlbaum.

Harkness, S., & Super, C. (2006). Themes and variations: Parental ethnotheories in Western cultures. In K. Rubin (Ed.), *Parental beliefs, parenting, and child development in cross-cultural perspectives* (pp. 61–80). New York: Psychology Press.

Harper, C. (2004, March). Escaping poverty cycles. *In Focus.* Retrieved January 19, 2010, from http://www.undp.org/

Harps, S. N. (2005). Race-related stress, racial socialization, and African American adolescent adjustment: Examining the mediating role of racial identity. *Dissertation Abstracts International: The Humanities and Social Sciences, 66*(5), November 1975-A.

Harrell, S. P. (2000). A multidimensional conceptualization of racism-related stress: Implications for the well-being of people of color. *American Journal of Orthopsychiatry, 70*(1), 42–57.

Harrigan, M. P., & Koerin, B. B. (2007). Long-distance caregiving: Personal realities and practice implications. *Reflections, 13*(2), 5–16.

Harris, J. R. (1998). *The nurture assumption: Why children turn out the way they do.* New York: Touchstone.

Harrison, R., & Thomas, M. (2009). Identity in online communities: Social networking sites and language learning. *International Journal of Emerging Technologies & Society, 7*(2), 109–124.

Harry, B. (2006). *Why are so many minority students in special education? Understanding race and disability in schools.* New York: Teachers College Press.

Hart, B., & Risley, T. (1995). *Meaningful differences in the everyday experiences of young American children.* Baltimore: Paul H. Brookes.

Hart, H., McAdams, D., Hirsch, B., & Bauer, J. (2001). Generativity and social involvements among African-American and among Euro-American adults. *Journal of Research in Personality, 3*(2), 208–230.

Hart, J. (1970). The development of client-centered therapy. In J. T. Hart & T. M. Tomlinson (Eds.), *New directions in client-centered therapy* (pp. 3–22). Boston: Houghton Mifflin.

Hart, T. (2006). Spirituality experiences and capacities of children and youth. In E. C. Roehlkepartain, P. E. King, L. Wagener, & P. L. Benson (Eds.), *The handbook of spiritual development in children and adolescence* (pp. 34–45). Thousand Oaks, CA: Sage.

Harter, S. (1988). Developmental processes in the construction of self. In T. D. Yawkey & J. E. Johnson (Eds.), *Integrative processes and socialization: Early to middle childhood* (pp. 45–78). Hillsdale, NJ: Erlbaum.

Harter, S. (1998). The development of self-representations. In W. Damon & N. Eisenberg (Eds.), *Handbook of social development: Vol. 3. Social, emotional and personality development* (pp. 553–618). New York: Wiley.

Hartig, T., Evans, G., Jamner, L., Davis, D., & Gärling, T. (2003). Tracking restoration in natural and urban field settings. *Journal of Environmental Psychology, 23*(2), 109–123.

Hartig, T., Mang, M., & Evans, G. (1991). Restorative effects of natural environment experiences. *Environment and Behavior, 23,* 3–26.

Hartig, T., & Staats, H. (2006). The need for psychological restoration as a determinant of environmental preferences. *Journal of Environmental Psychology, 26*(3), 215–226.

Hartman, A. (1970). To think about the unthinkable. *Social Casework, 51,* 467–474.

Hartman, A. (1995). Diagrammatic assessment of family relationships. *Families in Society, 76,* 111–122.

Hartman, A., & Laird, J. (1983). *Family-centered social work practice.* New York: Free Press.

Harvard Health Letter. (2002). Aging—living to 100: What's the secret? *Harvard Health Letter, 27*(3), 1–3.

Harvey, S. M., Beckman, L. J., Sherman, C., & Petitti, D. (1999). Women's experience and satisfaction with emergency contraception. *Family Planning Perspectives, 31,* 237–240, 260.

Harwood, R. (1992). The influence of culturally derived values on Anglo and Puerto Rican mothers' perceptions of attachment behavior. *Child Development, 63,* 822–839.

Hasenfeld, Y. (2010a). The attributes of human service organizations. In Y. Hasenfeld (Ed.), *Human services as complex organizations* (2nd ed., pp. 9–32). Thousand Oaks, CA: Sage.

Hastings, M. (1998). Theoretical perspectives on social movements. *New Zealand Sociology, 13*(2), 208–238.

Hatch, S. L. (2005). Conceptualizing and identifying: Cumulative adversity and protective resources: Implications for understanding health inequalities. *The Journal of Gerontology: Series B: Psychological Sciences and Social Sciences, 60B*, 130–135.

Hatecher, R. A., Trussel, J., Stewart, F., Stewart, G. K., Kowal, D., Guest, F., et al. (1994). *Contraception technology* (16th ed.). New York: Irvington.

Hauser, M., Cushman, F., Young, L., Mikhail, J., & Jin, R. K. (2007). A dissociation between moral judgments and justifications. *Mind & Language, 22*(1), 1–21.

Hauser-Cram, P., & Howell, A. (2003). The development of young children with disabilities and their families: Implications for policies and programs. In R. M. Lerner, F. Jacobs, & D. Wertlieb (Eds.), *Handbook of applied developmental science, Vol. 1* (pp. 259–279). Thousand Oaks, CA: Sage.

Havighurst, R. J. (1968). Personality and patterns of aging. *The Gerontologist, 8*, 20–23.

Havighurst, R. J., Neugarten, B., & Tobin, S. (1968). Personality and patterns of aging. In B. L. Neugarten (Ed.), *Middle age and aging* (pp. 173–177). Chicago: University of Chicago Press.

Hay, D., & Nye, R. (2006). *The spirit of the child* (Rev. ed.). London: Jessica Kingsley.

Hay, D., Nye, R., & Murphy, R. (1996). Thinking about childhood spirituality: Review of research and current directions. In L. J. Francis, W. K. Kay, & W. S. Campbell (Eds.), *Research in religious education* (pp. 47–71). Macon, GA: Smyth & Helwys.

Haycock, K. (2006, August 1). *Promise abandoned: How policy choices and institutional practices restrict college opportunities.* Retrieved May 5, 2010, from http://www.edtrust.org/dc/publication/promise-abandoned-how-policy-choices-and-institutional-practices-restrict-college-opp

Haynie, D., Petts, R., Maimon, D., & Piquero, A. (2009). Exposure to violence in adolescence and precocious role exits. *Journal of Youth and Adolescence, 38*, 269–286.

Healey, J. F. (2010). *Race, ethnicity, gender, and class: The sociology of group conflict and change* (5th ed.). Thousand Oaks, CA: Pine Forge.

HealthCare.gov. (2010). *Young adult coverage until age 26.* Retrieved June 5, 2011, from http://www.healthcare.gov/law/provisions/youngadult/index.html

Hearn, G. (1969). *The general systems approach: Contributions toward an holistic conception of social work.* New York: Council on Social Work Education.

Hearn, J., & Parkin, W. (1993). Organizations, multiple oppressions and postmodernism. In J. Hassard & M. Parker (Eds.), *Postmodernism and organizations* (pp. 148–162). Newbury Park, CA: Sage.

Heck, K. E., Schoendorf, K. C., & Chavez, G. F. (2002). The influence of proximity of prenatal services on small-for-gestational-age birth. *Journal of Community Health, 27*(1), 15–27.

Hedberg, P., Brulin C., & Alex, L. (2009). Experiences of purpose in life when becoming and being a very old woman. *Journal of Women & Aging, 21*(2), 125–137.

Hedley, A. A., Ogden, C. L., Johnson, C. L., Carroll, M. D., Curtin, L. R., & Flegal, K. M. (2004). Prevalence of overweight and obesity among U.S. children, adolescents, and adults, 1999–2002. *Journal of American Medical Association, 291*, 2847–2850.

Hegtvedt, K. A. (1994). Justice. In M. Foshci & E. J. Lawler (Eds.), *Group processes: Sociological analyses* (pp. 177–204). Chicago: Nelson-Hall.

Hehir, T. (2003). Beyond inclusion. *School Administrator, 60*(3), 36–40.

Heimpel, S., Wood, J., Marshall, J., & Brown, J. (2002). Do people with low self-esteem really feel better? Self-esteem differences in motivation to repair negative moods. *Journal of Personality and Social Psychology, 82*, 128–147.

Heinz, W. (2003). From work trajectories to negotiated careers: The contingent work life course. In J. Mortimer & M. Shanahan (Eds.), *Handbook of the life course* (pp. 185–204). New York: Kluwer Academic/Plenum.

Helburn, S., & Bergmann, B. (2002). *America's child care problem: The way out.* New York: Palgrave Macmillan.

Helmchen, H., Baltes, M. M., Geiselmann, S., Kanowski, S., Linden, M., Reischies, E. M., et al. (1999). Psychiatric illness in old age. In P. B. Baltes & K. U. Mayer (Eds.), *The Berlin Aging Study: Aging from 70 to 100* (pp. 167–196). Cambridge: Cambridge University Press.

Helson, R., & Wink, P. (1992). Personality change in women from the early 40s to the early 50s. *Psychology and Aging, 7*, 46–55.

Henderson, L. (2000). The knowledge and use of alternative therapeutic techniques by social work practitioners: A descriptive study. *Social Work in Health Care, 30*(3), 55–71.

Henderson, M., Butcher, I., Wight, D., Williamson, L., & Raab, G. (2008). What explains between-school differences in rates of sexual experience? *BMC Public Health, 8*(8), 53.

Hendrick, J. (1990). Early childhood. In R. Thomas (Ed.), *The encyclopedia of human development and education: Theory, research, and studies.* Oxford, UK: Pergamon.

Hendricks, C., & Rudich, G. (2000). A community-building perspective in social work education. *Journal of Community Practice, 8*(3), 21–36.

Hendricks, J. (1987). Exchange theory in aging. In G. L. Maddox (Ed.), *The encyclopedia of aging* (pp. 238–239). New York: Springer.

Hendricks, J., & Hatch, L. R. (2006). Lifestyle and aging. In R. H. Binstock & L. K. George (Eds.), *Handbook of aging and the social sciences* (pp. 301–319). Amsterdam: Elsevier.

Hepp, S. M., & Meuleman, E. J. (2006). Vasectomy: Indications and implementation in historic perspective. *Nederlands Tijdschrift Voor Geneeskunde, 150*(11), 611–614.

Hepworth, D., Rooney, R., Rooney, G. D., Strom-Gottfried, K., & Larsen, J. (2010). *Direct social work practice: Theory and skills* (8th ed.). Belmont, CA: Brooks/Cole.

Hequembourg, A., & Brallier, S. (2005). Gendered stories of parental caregiving among siblings. *Journal of Aging Studies, 19,* 53–71.

Herrenkohl, T. I., Mason, W. A., Kosterman, R., Lengua, L. J., Hawkins, J. D., & Abbott, R. D. (2004). Pathways from physical childhood abuse to partner violence in young adulthood. *Violence and Victims, 19*(2), 123–145.

Herring, R. D. (1995). Developing biracial ethnic identity: A review of the increasing dilemma. *Journal of Multicultural Counseling and Development, 23*(1), 29–38.

Herzog, T., Herbert, E., Kaplan, R., & Crooks, C. (2000). Cultural and developmental comparisons of landscape perceptions and preferences. *Environment and Behavior, 32*(3), 323–346.

Hessol, N., & Fuentes-Afflick, E. (2005). Ethnic differences in neonatal and postneonatal mortality. *Pediatrics, 115*(1), 164.

Hetherington, E. M., & Jodl, K. M. (1994). Stepfamilies as settings for child development. In A. Booth & J. Dunn (Eds.), *Stepfamilies: Who benefits? Who does not?* (pp. 55–79). Hillsdale, NJ: Erlbaum.

Hetherington, E. M., & Kelly, J. (2002). *For better or for worse: Divorce reconsidered.* New York: Norton.

Heuveline, P., & Timberlake, J. (2004). The role of cohabitation in family formation: The United States in comparative perspective. *Journal of Marriage and Family, 66,* 1214–1230.

Heyman, R. E., & Smith Slep, A. M. (2002). Do child abuse and interparental violence lead to adulthood violence? *Journal of Marriage and Family, 64*(4), 864–871.

Hickson, J., & Phelps, A. (1998). Women's spirituality: A proposed practice model. In D. S. Becvar (Ed.), *The family, spirituality, and social work* (pp. 43–57). Binghamton, NY: Haworth Press.

Hidalgo, M., & Hernandez, B. (2001). Place attachment: Conceptual and empirical questions. *Journal of Environmental Psychology, 21,* 273–281.

Hilger, N. (2003, May). *Market liberalization, labor unions and real wages in Mexico, 1984–1998.* Honors thesis in economics, Stanford University, Palo Alto, California.

Retrieved November 9, 2006, from http://economics.stanford.edu/files/Theses/Theses_2004/Hilger.pdf

Hill, R. (1949). *Families under stress.* Westport, CT: Greenwood.

Hill, R. (1958). Generic features of families under stress. *Social Casework, 49,* 139–150.

Hillier, A. (2007). Why social work needs mapping. *Journal of Social Work Education, 43*(2), 205–221.

Himes, C. (2001). Social demography of contemporary families and aging. In A. Walker, M. Manoogian-O'Dell, L. McGraw, & D. L. White (Eds.), *Families in later life: Connections and transitions* (pp. 47–50). Thousand Oaks, CA: Pine Forge Press.

Himmelstein, D., Thorne, D., Warren, E., & Woolhandler, S. (2009). Medical bankruptcy in the United States, 2007: Results of a national study. *American Journal of Medicine, 122*(8), 741–746.

Hines, P. M., Preto, N. G., McGoldrick, M., Almeida, R., & Weltman, S. (2005). Culture and the family life cycle. In B. Carter & M. McGoldrick (Eds.), *The expanded family life cycle: Individual, family, and social perspectives* (3rd ed., pp. 69–87). Boston: Allyn & Bacon.

Hing, B. (2004). *Defining America through immigration policy.* Philadelphia: Temple University Press.

Hinrichsen, G. A., & Clougherty, K. F. (2006). Role transitions. In *Interpersonal psychotherapy for depressed older adults* (pp. 133–152). Washington, DC: American Psychological Association.

Hitchcock, J. (2006). *Net crimes and misdemeanors: Outmaneuvering web spammers, stalkers, and con artists.* Medford, NJ: CyberAge Books.

Hitlin, S., & Elder, G., Jr. (2007). Time, self, and the curiously abstract concept of agency. *Sociological Theory, 25*(2), 170–191.

Hitti, M. (2009, May 28). Health and pregnancy, pregnancy weight gain: New guidelines. *WebMD.* Retrieved January 19, 2010, from http://www.webmd.com/baby/news/20090528/pregnancy-weight-gain-new-guidelines

Ho, M., Rasheed, J., & Rasheed, M. (2004). *Family therapy with ethnic minorities* (2nd ed.). Thousand Oaks, CA: Sage.

Hobfoll, S. E. (1996). Social support: Will you be there when I need you? In N. Vanzetti & S. Duck (Eds.), *A lifetime of relationships* (pp. 46–74). Belmont, CA: Thomson Brooks/Cole.

Hobsbawm, E. (1983). Introduction: Inventing tradition. In E. Hobsbawm & T. Ranger (Eds.), *The invention of tradition* (pp. 1–14). New York: Cambridge University Press.

Hodge, D. R. (2001). Spiritual assessment: A review of major qualitative methods and a new framework for assessing spirituality. *Social Work, 46*(3), 203–214.

Hodge, D. R. (2002). Does social work oppress evangelical Christians? A new class analysis of society and social work. *Social Work, 47,* 401–414.

Hodge, D. R. (2003). Differences in worldviews between social workers and people of faith. *Families in Society: The Journal of Contemporary Social Services, 84,* 285–295.

Hodge, D. R. (2004). Working with Hindu clients in a spiritually sensitive manner. *Social Work, 49*(1), 27–38.

Hodge, D. R. (2005a). Developing a spiritual assessment toolbox: A discussion of the strengths and limitation of five different assessment methods. *Health & Social Work, 30*(4), 314–323.

Hodge, D. R. (2005b). Social work and the House of Islam: Orienting practitioners to the beliefs and values of Muslims in the United States. *Social Work, 50*(2), 162–173.

Hodge, D. R., Cardenas, P., & Montoya, H. (2001). Substance use: Spirituality and religious participation as protective factors among rural youths. *Social Work Research, 25*(3), 153–161.

Hodge, D. R., Johnson, B., & Luidens, D. (1993). Determinants of church involvement of young adults who grew up in Presbyterian churches. *Journal for the Scientific Study of Religion, 32*(3), 242–255.

Hodnett, E. D., Downe, S., Edwards, N., & Walsh, D. (2005, January 25). Home-like versus conventional institutional settings for birth (Cochrane Review). *The Cochrane Database of Systematic Reviews,* Issue 1, CD000012.

Hoff, E. (2009). *Language development* (4th ed.). Pacific Grove, CA: Cengage.

Hofstede, G. (1996). An American in Paris: The influence of nationality on organization theories. *Organization Studies, 17*(13), 525–537.

Hofstede, G. (1998). A case for comparing apples with oranges: International differences in values. *International Journal of Comparative Sociology, 39,* 16–31.

Hoge, C. W., Auchterlonie, J. L., & Milliken, C. S. (2006). Mental health problems, use of mental health services, and attrition from military service after returning from deployment to Iraq or Afghanistan. *Journal of the American Medical Association, 295*(9), 1023–1032.

Hogg, M. (2005). The social identity perspective. In S. Wheelan (Ed.), *The handbook of group research and practice* (pp. 133–157). Thousand Oaks, CA: Sage.

Hogstel, M. (2001). *Gerontology: Nursing care of the older adult.* Albany, NY: Delma-Thompson Learning.

Holder, D. W., Durant, R. H., Harris, T. L., Daniel, J., Obeidallah, D., & Goodman, E. (2000). The association between adolescent spirituality and voluntary sexual activity. *Journal of Adolescent Health, 26*(4), 295–302.

Hollander, D. (2008). FYI. *Perspectives on Sexual & Reproductive Health, 40*(3), 128–129.

Hollinghurst, S., Kessler, D., Peters, T., & Gunnell, D. (2005). Opportunity cost of antidepressant prescribing in England: Analysis of routine data. *British Medical Journal, 330*(7948), 999–1000.

Holm, J., & Bowker, J. (Eds.). (1994). *Women in religion.* New York: Pinter.

Holm, S. M., Forbes, E. E., Ryan, N. D., Phillips, M. L., Tarr, J. A., & Dahl, R. E. (2009). Reward-related brain function and sleep in pre/early pubertal and mid/late pubertal adolescents. *Journal of Adolescent Health, 45*(4), 326–334.

Holman, A., & Silver, R. (1998). Getting "stuck" in the past: Temporal orientation and coping with trauma. *Journal of Personality and Social Psychology, 74*(5), 1146–1163.

Holter, M. C. (2004). Autistic spectrum disorders: Assessment and intervention. In P. Allen-Meares & M. W. Fraser (Eds.), *Intervention with children and adolescents: An interdisciplinary perspective* (pp. 205–228). Boston: Allyn & Bacon.

Holzer, H. (2009). The labor market and young Black men: Updating Moynihan's perspective. *Annals of the American Academy of Political and Social Science, 621,* 47–69.

Homans, G. (1958). Social behavior as exchange. *American Journal of Sociology, 63,* 597–606.

Homans, G. (1961). *Social behavior: Its elementary forms.* New York: Harcourt Brace Jovanovich.

Hood, L. (2003). *Immigrant students, urban high schools: The challenge continues.* New York: Carnegie Corporation of New York. Retrieved May 17, 2010, from http://carnegie.org/fileadmin/Media/Publications/PDF/immigrantstudents.pdf

Hooyman, N. R., & Kiyak, H. A. (2008). *Social gerontology: A multidisciplinary perspective.* Boston: Allyn & Bacon.

Hope, R. M., & Hodge, D. M. (2006). Factors affecting children's adjustment to the death of a parent: The social work professional's point of view. *Child and Adolescent Social Work Journal, 23*(1), 107–126.

Horn, A. W., & Alexander, C. I. (2005). Recurrent miscarriage. *Journal of Family Planning and Reproductive Health Care, 31*(2), 103–107.

Horn, J. L. (1982). The theory of fluid and crystallized intelligence in relation to concepts of cognitive psychology and aging in adulthood. In F. I. M. Craik & S. Trehub (Eds.), *Aging and cognitive processes* (pp. 237–278). New York: Plenum.

Horney, K. (1939). *New ways in psychoanalysis.* New York: Norton.

Horney, K. (1967). *Feminine psychology.* New York: Norton.

Hornik, R. (1991). Alternative models of behavior change. In J. Wasserheit, S. Aral, K. Holmes, & P. Hitchcock (Eds.), *Research issues in human behavior and sexually transmitted diseases in the AIDS era* (pp. 201–218). Washington, DC: American Society for Microbiology.

Hornsey, M. J. (2008). Social identity theory and self-categorization theory: A historical review. *Social and Personality Psychology Compass, 2*(1), 204–222.

Hosmer, L. (2001). Home birth, alternative medicine, and obstetrics. *Clinical Obstetrics and Gynecology, 44*(4), 671–680.

Hosp, J. L., & Reschly, D. J. (2003). Referral rates for intervention or assessment: A meta-analysis of racial differences. *Journal of Special Education, 37*(2), 67–80.

House, J. S., Lantz, P. M., & Herd, P. (2005). Continuity and change in the social stratification of aging and health over the life course: Evidence from a nationally representative longitudinal study from 1986 to 2001/2002 (Americans' Changing Lives Study). *The Journal of Gerontology: Series B: Psychological Sciences and Social Sciences, 60B*, 15–26.

Houston, J. B., Pfefferbaum, B., Sherman, M., Meison, A., Jeon-Slaughter, H., Brand, M., et al. (2009). Children of deployed National Guard troops: Perceptions of parental deployment to Operation Iraqi Freedom. *Psychiatric Annals, 39*(8), 805–811.

Houtenville, A., & Conway, K. (2008). Parental effort, school resources, and student achievement. *Journal of Human Resources, 43*(2), 437–453.

Hoyert, D. L., Matthews, T. J., Menacker, F., Strobino, D. M., & Guyer, B. (2006). Annual summary of vital statistics: 2004. *Pediatrics, 117*(10), 168–183.

Hser, Y., Longshore, D., & Anglin, M. (2007). The life course perspective on drug use. *Evaluation Review, 31*(6), 515–547.

Hsu, S. H., Grow, J., Marlatt, A., Galanter, M., & Kaskutas, L. A. (Eds.). (2008). *Research on Alcoholics Anonymous and spirituality in addiction recovery*. New York: Springer Science.

Huang, L. Z., & Winzer-Serhan, U. H. (2006). Chronic neonatal nicotine upregulates heteromeric nicotinic acetylcholine receptor binding without change in subunit mRNA expression. *Brain Research, 1113*(1), 94–109.

Huber, M. S., Egeren, L., Pierce, S., & Foster-Fishman, P. (2009). GIS applications for community-based research and action: Mapping change in a community-building initiative. *Journal of Prevention & Intervention in the Community, 27*, 5–20.

Huberman, B. (2001). The lessons learned: A model to improve adolescent sexual health in the United States. *Transitions, 14*(2), 6.

Hudson, C. (2000). At the edge of chaos: A new paradigm for social work? *Journal of Social Work Education, 36*(2), 215–230.

Huebner, A., & Garrod, A. (1993). Moral reasoning among Tibetan monks. A study of Buddhist adolescents and young adults in Nepal. *Journal of Cross-Cultural Psychology, 24*, 167–185.

Hughes, A. J., Daniel, S. E., Ben Shlmo, Y., & Lees, A. J. (2002). The accuracy of diagnosis of Parkinsonian syndromes in a specialist movement disorder service. *Brain, 125*(part 4), 861–870.

Hughes, B. (2009). Disability activisms: Social model stalwarts and biological citizens. *Disability & Society, 24*(6), 677–688.

Hughes, D., Hagelskamp, C., Way, N., & Foust, M. (2009). The role of mothers' and adolescents' perceptions of ethnic-racial socialization in shaping ethnic-racial identity among early adolescent boys and girls. *Journal of Youth and Adolescence, 38*, 605–626.

Hughes, F. (2010). *Children, play, and development* (4th ed.). Thousand Oaks, CA: Sage.

Hughes, H. (1988). Psychological and behavioral correlates of family violence in child witnesses and victims. *American Journal of Orthopsychiatry, 58*, 77–90.

Hughes, S., Williams, B., Molina, L., Bayles, C., Bryant, L., Harris, J., et al. (2005). Characteristics of physical activity programs for older adults: Results of a multisite survey. *The Gerontologist, 45*(5), 667–675.

Huinink, J., & Feldhaus, M. (2009). Family research from the life course perspective. *International Sociology, 24*(3), 299–324.

Human Genome Project. (2009a). *Human Genome project legislation*. Retrieved December 2, 2009, from http://www.ornl.gov/hgmis

Human Genome Project. (2009b). *Genetics privacy and legislation*. Retrieved December 2, 2009, from http://www.ornl.gov/sci/techresources/Human_Genome/elsi/legislat.shtml

Human Rights Campaign. (2009). *Statewide marriage prohibitions*. Retrieved May 11, 2010, from http://www.hrc.org/documents/marriage_prohibitions.pdf

Human Rights Campaign. (2011a). *Latest on DOMA*. Retrieved March 21, 2011, from http://www.hrc.org/issues/marriage.asp

Human Rights Campaign. (2011b). *Marriage equality & other relationship recognition laws*. Retrieved March 21, 2011, from http://www.hrc.org/documents/Relationship_Recognition_Laws_Map.pdf

Human Rights Watch. (2006). *Child labor*. Retrieved January 13, 2007, from http://hrw.org/children/labor.htm

Humphreys, N. A., & Quam, J. K. (1998). Middle-aged and old gay, lesbian, and bisexual adults. In G. A. Appleby & J. W. Anastas (Eds.), *Not just a passing phase: Social work with gay, lesbian, bisexual people* (pp. 243–267). New York: Columbia University Press.

Hunger Notes. (2011). *2011 world hunger and poverty facts and statistics*. Retrieved September 14, 2011, from http://www.worldhunger.org/articles/Learn/world%20hunger%20facts%202002.htm

Hunler, O. S., & Gencoz, T. (2005). The effect of religiousness on marital satisfaction: Testing the mediator role of marital problem solving between religiousness and marital satisfaction relationship. *Contemporary Family Therapy, 27*(1), 123–136.

Hunter, A., & Riger, S. (1986). The meaning of community in community mental health. *Journal of Community Psychology, 14,* 55–71.

Hunter, J. D. (1994*). Before the shooting begins: Searching for democracy in America's culture wars.* New York: Free Press.

Huntington, S. (1996). *The clash of civilizations and the remaking of world order.* New York: Simon & Schuster.

Hurdle, D. E. (2002). Hawaiian traditional healing: Culturally based interventions for social work practice. *Social Work, 47*(2), 183–192.

Hurdle, S. (2001). "Less is best"—A group-based treatment program for persons with personality disorders. *Social Work With Groups, 23*(4), 71–80.

Hurst, J. (2007). Disability and spirituality in social work practice. *Journal of Social Work in Disability & Rehabilitation, 6*(1/2), 179–194.

Hutchison, E. (1987). Use of authority in direct social work practice with mandated clients. *Social Service Review, 61*(4), 581–598.

Hutchison, E. (2007). Community violence. In E. Hutchison, H. Matto, M. Harrigan, L. Charlesworth, & P. Viggiani (Eds.), *Challenges of living: A multidimensional working model for social workers* (pp. 71–104). Thousand Oaks, CA: Sage.

Hutchison, E. (2011). A life course perspective. In E. Hutchison (Ed.), *Dimensions of human behaviour: The changing life course* (4th ed., pp. 1–38). Thousand Oaks, CA: Sage.

Hutchison, E., & Charlesworth, L. (2000). Securing the welfare of children: Policies past, present, and future. *Families in Society, 81*(6), 576–586.

Hutchison, E., Charlesworth, L., Matto, H., Harrigan, M., & Viggiani, P. (2007). Elements of knowing and doing in social work. In E. Hutchison, H. Matto, M. Harrigan, L. Charlesworth, & P. Viggiani, *Challenges of living: A multidimensional working model for social workers* (pp. 13–33). Thousand Oaks, CA: Sage.

Hutchison, E., Matto, H., Harrigan, M., Charlesworth, L., & Viggiani, P. (2007). *Challenges of living: A multidimensional working model for social workers.* Thousand Oaks, CA: Sage.

Huttenlocher, P., & Kabholkar, A. (1997). Regional differences in synaptogenesis in human cerebral cortex. *Journal of Comparative Neurology, 387,* 167–178.

Huynh-Nhu, L., Ceballo, R., Chao, R., Hill, N., Murry, V., & Pinderhughes, E. E. (2008). Excavating culture: Disentangling ethnic differences from contextual influences in parenting. *Applied Developmental Science, 12*(4), 163–175.

Hyde, B. (2008a). Children and spirituality: Searching for meaning and connectedness. Philadelphia, PA: Jessica Kingsley.

Hyde, B. (2008b). Weaving the threads of meaning: A characteristic of children's spirituality and its implications for religious education. *British Journal of Religious Education, 30(3),* 235–245.

Hyde, J. (2005). The gender similarities hypothesis. *American Psychologist, 60,* 581–592.

Hyson, M. (2004). *The emotional development of young children: Building an emotion-centered curriculum.* New York: Teachers College Press.

Iannello, K. (1992). *Decisions without hierarchy: Feminist interventions in organization theory and practice.* New York: Routledge.

Iannotti, R. (1985). Naturalistic and structured assessments of prosocial behavior in preschool children: The influence of empathy and perspective taking. *Developmental Psychology, 21,* 46–55.

Impett, E., & Tolman, D. (2006). Late adolescent girls' sexual experiences and sexual satisfaction. *Journal of Adolescent Research, 21, 628–646.*

Imre, R. (1984). The nature of knowledge in social work. *Social Work, 29,* 41–45.

Inderbitzin, M. (2009). Reentry of emerging adults: Adolescent inmates' transition back into the community. *Journal of Adolescent Research, 24,* 453–476.

Ingram, R. E., & Luxton, D. D. (2005). Vulnerability-stress models. In B. L. Hankin & J. R. Z. Abela (Eds.), *Development of psychopathology: A vulnerability-stress perspective* (pp. 32–46). Thousand Oaks, CA: Sage.

Ingstad, B., & Whyte, S. (Eds.). (1995). *Disability and culture.* Berkeley: University of California Press.

Inhorn, M. C. (2003). Global infertility and the globalization of the new reproductive technologies: Illustrations from Egypt. *Social Science and Medicine, 56*(9), 1837–1852.

Inouye, S. K. (2006). Delirium in older persons. *New England Journal of Medicine, 354*(11), 1157–1165.

Institute for the Study of Aging. (2001). *Achieving and maintaining cognitive vitality with aging* (International Longevity Center Workshop Report). New York: Author.

Institute of Medicine of the National Academies. (2006). *Preterm birth: Causes, consequences and prevention.* Washington, DC: National Academies Press.

Institute of Medicine of the National Academies. (2009). *Weight gain during pregnancy: Reexamining the guidelines.* Retrieved January 19, 2010, from http://www.iom.edu/Reports/2009/Weight-Gain-During-Pregnancy-Reexamining-the-Guidelines.aspx

International Longevity Center—USA. (2002). *Is there an "anti-aging" medicine?* (Workshop Report D17692). New York: Author.

International Telecommunications Union. (2008). *Global ICT developments.* Retrieved May 17, 2010, from http://www.itu.int/ITU-D/ict/statistics/ict/index.html

Internet World Stats. (2010). *Internet usage statistics: The Internet big picture.* Retrieved February 23, 2010, from http://www.internetworldstats.com/stats.htm

Irish, D., Lundquist, K., & Nelsen, V. (1993). *Ethnic variations in dying, death, and grief: Diversity in universality.* Washington, DC: Taylor & Francis.

Jackson, J. (2006, October). *Capstone presentation.* Paper presented at the NIH Conference on Understanding and Reducing Health Disparities: Contributions From the Behavioral and Social Sciences, Bethesda, MD.

Jackson, K. M., & Nazar, A. M. (2006). Breastfeeding, the immune response, and long-term health. *Journal of the American Osteopathic Association, 106,* 203–207.

Jackson, M. A. (2002). Christian womanist spirituality: Implications for social work practice. *Social Thought, 21*(1), 63–76.

Jackson, R. L. (Ed.). (2004). *African American communication and identities: Essential readings.* Thousand Oaks, CA: Sage.

Jaddoe, V. W., Troe, E. J., Hofman, A., Mackenbach, J. P., Moll, H. A., Steegers, E. A., et al. (2008). Active and passive maternal smoking during pregnancy and the risks of low birthweight and preterm birth: The generation R study. *Paediatric and Perinatal Epidemiology, 22*(2), 162–171.

Jahromi, L., Putnam, S., & Stifter, C. (2004). Maternal regulation of infant reactivity from 2 to 6 months. *Developmental Psychology, 40,* 477–487.

Jain, T. (2006). Socioeconomic and racial disparities among infertility patients seeking care. *Fertility and Sterility, 85*(4), 876–881.

Jain, T., & Gupta, R. S. (2007). Trends in the use of intracytoplasmic sperm injection in the United States. *New England Journal of Medicine, 357*(3), 251–257.

James, R. K., & Gilliland, B. E. (2001). *Crisis intervention strategies* (4th ed.). Pacific Grove, CA: Brooks/Cole.

James, W. (1890). *Principles of psychology.* New York: Holt.

James, W. P. T. (2006). The challenge of childhood obesity. *The International Journal of Pediatric Obesity, 1*(1), 7–10.

Jandt, F. (2010). *An introduction to intercultural communication: Identities in a global community* (6th ed.). Thousand Oaks, CA: Sage.

Jang, K., Liveseley, J., Riemann, R., Vernon, P., Hu, S., Angleirner, A., et al. (2001). Covariance structure of neuroticism and agreeableness: A twin and molecular genetic analysis of the role of the serotonin transporter gene. *Journal of Personality and Social Psychology, 81*(2), 295.

Jansen, P., Raat, H., Mackenbach, J., Jaddoe, V., Hofman, A., Verhulst, F., et al. (2009). Socioeconomic inequalities in infant temperament. *Social Psychiatry and Psychiatric Epidemiology, 44,* 87–95.

Janssen, R., Saxell, L., Page, L. A., Klein, M. C., Liston, R. M., & Lee, S. K. (2009). Outcomes of planned home birth with registered midwife versus planned hospital birth with midwife or physician. *Canadian Medical Association Journal, 191*(6–7), 377–383.

Jarrell, A. (2000, April 2). The face of teenage sex grows younger. *New York Times,* Section 9, p. 1, Column 1.

Jenkins, R. (Ed.). (1998). *Questions of competence: Culture, classification and intellectual disability.* New York: Cambridge University Press.

Jenkins, W. (2008). *Ecologies of grace: Environmental ethics and Christian theology.* Oxford, UK: Oxford University Press.

Jensen, L. A. (2003). Coming of age in a multicultural world: Globalization and adolescent cultural identity formation. *Applied Developmental Science, 7,* 188–195.

Jessor, R. (1987). Problem-behavior theory, psychosocial development, and adolescent problem drinking. *British Journal of Addiction, 82,* 331–342.

Johanson, R., Newburn, M., & Macfarlane, A. (2002). Has the medicalisation of childbirth gone too far? *British Medical Journal, 324*(7342), 892–895.

Johnson, A. G. (2005). *Privilege, power and difference.* New York: McGraw-Hill.

Johnson, A. N. (2008). Engaging fathers in the NICU: Taking down the barriers to the baby. *Journal of Perinatal and Neonatal Nursing, 22*(4), 302–306.

Johnson, B., & Chavkin, W. (2007). Policy efforts to prevent ART-related preterm birth. *Maternal Child Health Journal, 11,* 219–225.

Johnson, C., Ironsmith, M., Snow, C., & Poteat, M. (2000). Peer acceptance and social adjustment in preschool and kindergarten. *Early Childhood Education Journal, 27*(4), 207–212.

Johnson, C. L., & Barer, B. M. (1997). *Life beyond 85 years: The aura of survivorship.* New York: Springer.

Johnson, D. W., & Johnson, F. P. (1994). *Joining together: Group theory and skills* (5th ed.). Boston: Allyn & Bacon.

Johnson, G. R., Jang, S. J., Larsen, D. B., & De Li, S. (2001). Does adolescent religious commitment matter? A re-examination of the effects of religiosity on delinquency. *Journal on Research in Crime and Delinquency, 38*(1), 22–43.

Johnson, H. C. (2001). Neuroscience in social work practice and education. *Journal of Social Work Practice in the Addictions, 1*(3), 81–102.

Johnson, K. C., & Davis, B. (2005). Outcomes of planned home-births with certified professional midwives: Large prospective study in North America. *British Medical Journal, 330*(7505), 1416.

Johnson, K. D., Whitbeck, L., & Hoyt, D. (2005). Predictors of social network composition among homeless and runaway adolescents. *Journal of Adolescence, 28*(2), 231–248.

Johnson, M. (Ed.). (1992). *People with disabilities explain it all for you.* Louisville, KY: Advocado Press.

Johnson, M. P. (2002). An exploration of men's experience and role at childbirth. *Journal of Men's Studies, 10*(12), 165–183.

Johnson, R., Browne, K., & Hamilton-Giachritsis, C. (2006). Young children in institutional care at risk of harm. *Trauma, Violence & Abuse, 7*(1), 34–60.

Johnson, S. B., Blum, R., & Giedd, J. (2009). Adolescent maturity and the brain: The promise and pitfalls of neuroscience research in adolescent health policy. *Journal of Adolescent Health, 45,* 216–221.

Johnson, S. K. (1997). Does spirituality have a place in rural social work? *Social Work and Christianity, 24*(1), 58–66.

Johnson, T., & Colucci, P. (2005). Lesbians, gay men, and the family life cycle. In B. Carter & M. McGoldrick (Eds.), *The expanded family life cycle: Individual, family, and social perspectives* (3rd ed., pp. 346–361). Boston: Allyn & Bacon.

Johnston, L., O'Malley, P., Bachman, J., & Schulenberg, J. (2004). *Monitoring the future national results on adolescent drug use: Overview of key findings, 2003* (NIH Publication No. 04–5506). Bethesda, MD: National Institute on Drug Abuse.

Johnston, L., O'Malley, P., Bachman, J., & Schulenberg, J. (2005). *Monitoring the future national results on adolescent drug use: Overview of key findings, 2004* (NIH Publication No. 04–5506). Bethesda, MD: National Institute on Drug Abuse.

Johnston, L., O'Malley, P., Bachman, J., & Schulenberg, J. (2006). *Monitoring the future national results on drug use: Overview of key findings, 2005* (NIH Publication No. 06–5882). Bethesda, MD: National Institute on Drug Abuse.

Johnstone, B., Yoon, D. P., Rupright, J., & Reid-Arndt, S. (2009). Relationships among spiritual beliefs, religious practices, congregational support and health for individuals with traumatic brain injury. *Brain Injury, 23*(5), 411–419.

Joint United Nations Programme on HIV/AIDS (UNAIDS). (2009). *Eight-year trend shows new HIV infections down by 17%—Most progress seen in sub-Saharan Africa.* Retrieved December 4, 2009, from http://www.unaids .org/en/KnowledgeCentre/Resources/FeatureStories/ archive/2009/20091124_pr_EpiUpdate.asp

Jones, A. (1992). Self-esteem and identity in psychotherapy with adolescents from upwardly mobile middle-class African American families. In L. Vargas & J. Koss-Chioino (Eds.), *Working with culture: Psychotherapeutic interventions with ethnic minority children and adolescents.* San Francisco: Jossey-Bass.

Jones, J. (2009). Who adopts? Characteristics of women and men who have adopted children. *NCHS Data Brief, 12,* 1–8.

Jones, K., Whitbourne, S., & Skultety, K. (2006). Identity processes and the transition to midlife among baby boomers. In S. Whitbourne & S. Willis (Eds.), *The baby boomers grow up: Contemporary perspectives on midlife* (pp. 149–164). Mahwah, NJ: Erlbaum.

Jones, R. (2001). How parents can support learning: Not all parent involvement programs are equal, but research shows what works. *American School Board Journal, 188*(9), 18–22.

Jones, R. K., Zolna, M. R., Henshaw, S. K., & Finer, L. B. (2008). Abortion in the United States: Incidence and access to services, 2005. *Perspectives on Sexual and Reproductive Health, 40*(1), 6–16.

Jones, S., & Fernyhough, C. (2007). A new look at the neural diathesis-stress model of schizophrenia: The primacy of social-evaluative and uncontrollable situations. *Schizophrenia Bulletin, 33*(5), 1171–1177.

Jones, T. (2005). Mediating intragroup and intergroup conflict. In S. Wheelan (Ed.), *The handbook of group research and practice* (pp. 463–483). Thousand Oaks, CA: Sage.

Jordan, J. V. (2005). Relational resilience in girls. In S. Goldstein & R. B. Brooks (Eds.), *Handbook of resilience in children* (pp. 79–90). New York: Kluwer Academic/Plenum.

Jordan, M. (2009). Back to nature. *Therapy Today, 20*(3), 26–28.

Jordon, C. B., & Ferguson, R. J. (2006). Infertility-related concerns in two family practice sites. *Family, Systems, and Health, 24*(1), 28–32.

Joseph, K. S., Allen, A. C., Dodd, S. C., Turner, L. A., Scott, H., & Liston, R. (2005). The perinatal effects of delayed childbearing. *Obstetrics and Gynecology, 105*(6), 1410–1418.

Joseph, M. V. (1988). Religion and social work practice. *Social Casework, 69,* 443–452.

Joshi, S., & Morley, J. (2006). Cognitive impairment. *Medical Clinics of North America, 90*(5), 769–787.

Joss-Moore, L., & Lane, R. (2009). The developmental origins of adult diseases. *Current Opinions in Pediatrics, 21*(2), 230–234.

Joye, Y. (2007). Architectural lessons from environmental psychology: The case of biophilic architecture. *Review of General Psychology, 11*(4), 305–328.

Jung, C. (1933a). *Modern man in search of a soul.* New York: Harcourt, Brace & World.

Jung, C. (1933b). *Psychological types.* New York: Harcourt, Brace.

Jung, C. (1939). Conscious, unconscious and individuation. In *The collected works of C. G. Jung* (Vol. 9i). Princeton, NJ: Princeton University Press.

Jung, C. (1969). *The archetypes and the collective unconscious* (R. F. C. Hull, Trans.). Princeton, NJ: Princeton University Press. (Original work published 1959)

Jung, C. (1971). *The portable Jung.* New York: Viking Press.

Kagan, J. (2007). *What is emotion? History, measures, and meanings.* New Haven, CT: Yale University Press.

Kagan, S., & Kagan, M. (1998). *Multiple intelligences: The complete multiple intelligences book.* San Clemente, CA: Kagan Cooperative Learning.

Kahana, B. (1992). Late-life adaptation in the aftermath of extreme stress. In M. Wykel, E. Kahana, & J. Kowal (Eds.), *Stress and health among the elderly* (pp. 5–34). New York: Springer.

Kahn, J., & Pearlin, L. (2006). Financial strain over the life course and health among older adults. *Journal of Health & Social Behavior, 47*(1), 17–31.

Kahn, M., & Scher, S. (2002). Infusing content on the physical environment into the BSW curriculum. *Journal of Baccalaureate Social Work, 7*(2), 1–14.

Kahn, P. (1999). *The human relationship with nature: Development and culture.* Cambridge: MIT Press.

Kahneman, D., & Tversky, A. (1982). The psychology of preferences. *Scientific American, 246,* 160–173.

Kahneman, D., & Tversky, A. (1984). Choices, values, and frames. *American Psychologist, 39,* 341–350.

Kaiser Family Foundation. (2008). *Fact sheet: Abortion in the U.S.: Utilization, financing, and access* (#3269–02). Retrieved November 20, 2009, from http://www.kff.org

Kaitz, M., Bar-Haim, Y., Lehrer, M., & Grossman, E. (2004). Adult attachment style and interpersonal distance. *Attachment & Human Development, 6*(3), 285–304.

Kakouros, E., Maniadaki, K., & Papaeliou, C. (2004). How Greek teachers perceive functioning of pupils with ADHD. *Emotional and Behavioural Difficulties, 9*(1), 41–53.

Kalia, J. L., Visintainer, P., Brumberg, H. L., Pici, M., & Kase, J. (2009). Comparison of enrollment in interventional therapies between late-preterm and very preterm infants at 12 months corrected age. *Pediatrics, 123*(3), 804–809.

Kalkhoff, W., & Barnum, C. (2000). The effects of status-organizing and social identity processes on patterns of social influence. *Social Psychology Quarterly, 63,* 95–115.

Kaltiala-Heino, R., Kosunen, E., & Rimpela, M. (2003). Pubertal timing, sexual behaviour and self-reported depression in middle adolescence. *Journal of Adolescence, 26*(5), 531–454.

Kamerman, S. (1996). Child and family policies: An international overview. In E. Zigler, S. Kagan, & N. Hall (Eds.), *Children, families, and government: Preparing for the twenty-first century* (pp. 31–48). New York: Cambridge University Press.

Kamerman, S., & Kahn, A. (1995). Innovations in toddler day care and family support services: An international overview. *Child Welfare, 74*(6), 1281–1300.

Kamp Dush, C., & Amato, P. (2005). Consequences of relationship status and quality for subjective well-being. *Journal of Social and Personal Relationship, 22*(5), 607–627.

Kapit, W., Macey, R. I., & Meisami, E. (2000). *The physiology coloring book* (2nd ed.). Cambridge, MA: HarperCollins.

Kaplan, B., Nahum, R., Yairi, Y., Hirsch, M., Pardo, J., & Orvieto, R. (2005). Use of various contraceptive methods and time of contraception in a community-based population. *European Journal of Obstetrics, Gynecology, and Reproductive Biology, 123*(1), 72–76.

Kaplan, C. (2006). Special issues in contraception: Caring for women with disabilities. *Journal of Midwifery & Women's Health, 51*(6), 450–457.

Kaplan, J., Aziz-Zadeh, L., Uddin, L., & Iacoboni, M. (2008). The self across the sense: An fMRI study of self-face and self-voice recognition. *Social Cognitive & Affective Neuroscience, 3,* 218–223.

Kaplan, R. (1983). The role of nature in the urban context. In I. Altman & J. F. Wohlwill (Eds.), *Behavior and the natural environment* (pp. 127–161). New York: Plenum.

Kaplan, R., & Kaplan, S. (1989). *The experience of nature: A psychological perspective.* New York: Cambridge University Press.

Kaplan, S. (1995). The restorative benefits of nature: Toward an integrative framework. *Journal of Environmental Psychology, 15,* 169–182.

Kaplowitz, P. (2006). Pubertal development in girls: Secular trends. *Current Opinions in Obstetrics and Gynecology, 18,* 487–491.

Karenga, M. (1995). Making the past meaningful: Kwanzaa and the concept of Sankofa. *Reflections: Narratives of Professional Helping, 1*(4), 36–46.

Karls, J. M., & O'Keefe, M. (2008). *Person-in-environment system manual* (2nd ed.). Washington, DC: NASW Press.

Karpa, K. D. (2006). Pharmacist critique was ill-informed. *Annals of Pharmacotherapy, 40*(7–8), 1441–1444.

Kasee, C. R. (1995). Identity, recovery, and religious imperialism: Native American women and the New Age. *Women and Therapy: A Feminist Quarterly, 16*(2/3), 83–93.

Kaslow, F., & Robison, J. A. (1996). Long-term satisfying marriages: Perceptions of contributing factors. *The American Journal of Family Therapy, 24*(2), 153–170.

Katchadourian, H. (1978). Medical perspectives on adulthood. In E. H. Erikson (Ed.), *Adulthood* (pp. 33–60). New York: Norton & Norton.

Katz, P. (1976). *Toward the elimination of racism.* New York: Pergamon Press.

Kavanaugh, M. L., & Schwarz, E. B. (2008). Counseling about and use of emergency contraception in the United States. *Perspectives on Sexual and Reproductive Health, 40*(2), 81–86.

Kawachi, I., & Kennedy, B. (2001). How income inequality affects health: Evidence from research in the United States. In J. Auerbach & B. Krimgold (Eds.), *Income, socioeconomic status, and health: Exploring the relationships* (pp. 16–28). Washington, DC: National Policy

Association, Academy for Health Services Research and Health Policy.

Kay, A. (2006). Social capital, the social economy and community development. *Community Development Journal, 41*(2), 160–173.

Kaya, N., & Burgess, B. (2007). Territoriality: Seat preferences in different types of classroom arrangements. *Environment & Behavior, 39*(6), 859–876.

Kaya, N., & Weber, M. (2003). Territorial behavior in residence halls: A cross-cultural study. *Environment and Behavior, 35*(3), 400–414.

Kaye, H. S. (2000). *Computer and Internet use among people with disabilities*. Washington, DC: National Institute on Disability and Rehabilitation Research.

Kayne, M., Greulich, M., & Albers, L. (2001). Doulas: An alternative yet complementary addition to care during childbirth. *Clinical Obstetrics and Gynecology, 44*(4), 692–703.

Kdous, M., Fadhlaoui, A., Boubaker, M., Youssef, A., Chaker, A., Ferchious, M., et al. (2007). Intrauterine insemination with conjoint semen: How to increase the success rate? *La Tunisie Medicale, 85*(9), 781–787.

Keane, C. (1991). Socioenvironmental determinants of community formation. *Environment and Behavior, 23*(1), 27–46.

Kearney, A. (2006). Residential development patterns and neighborhood satisfaction: Impacts of density and nearby nature. *Environment and Behavior, 38*(1), 112–139.

Keating, D. (2004). Cognitive and brain development. In R. M. Learner & L. Steinberg (Eds.), *Handbook of adolescent psychology* (2nd ed., pp. 45–84). New York: Wiley.

Keating, P. (1994). Striving for sex equity in schools. In K. I. Goodland & P. Keating (Eds.), *Access to knowledge: The continuing agenda for our nation's schools* (pp. 91–106). New York: The College Board.

Keefe, T. (1996). Meditation and social work treatment. In F. J. Turner (Ed.), *Social work treatment: Interlocking theoretical approaches* (4th ed., pp. 434–460). New York: Free Press.

Keenan, T., & Evans, S. (2009). *An introduction to child development* (2nd ed.). Thousand Oaks, CA: Sage.

Kefer, J. C., Agarwal, A., & Sabenegh, E. (2009). Role of antioxidants in the treatment of male infertility. *International Journal of Urology, 16*(5), 449–457.

Kegan, R. (1982). *The evolving self: Problem and process in human development*. Cambridge, MA: Harvard University Press.

Kegan, R. (1994). *In over our heads: The mental demands of modern life*. Cambridge, MA: Harvard University Press.

Kellaghan, T., Sloane, K., Alvarez, B., & Bloom, B. S. (1993). *The home environment and school learning: Promoting parental involvement in the education of children*. San Francisco: Jossey-Bass.

Kellert, S., & Wilson, E. (Eds.). (1993). *The biophilia hypothesis*. Washington, DC: Island Press.

Kelley, H., & Thibaut, J. (1978). *Interpersonal relations: A theory of interdependence*. New York: Wiley.

Kelly, Y., Sacker, A., Schoon, I., & Nazroo, J. (2006). Ethnic differences in achievement of developmental milestones by 9 months of age: The Millennium Cohort Study. *Developmental Medicine & Child Neurology, 48,* 825–830.

Kelly-Weeder, S., & O'Connor, A. (2006). Modifiable risk factors for impaired fertility in women: What nurse practitioners need to know. *Journal of the American Academy of Nurse Practitioners, 18,* 268–276.

Kendler, K. S., Gardner, C., & Prescott. C. (1997). Religion, psychopathology and substance use and misuse: A multimeasure, genetic-epidemiology study. *American Journal of Psychiatry, 154*(3), 322–329.

Kendler, K. S., Liu, X. Q., Gardner, C. O., McCullough, M. E., Larson, D., & Prescott, C. A. (2003). Dimensions of religiosity and their relationship to lifetime psychiatric and substance use disorders. *The American Journal of Psychiatry, 160*(3), 496–503.

Kennedy, S., Kiecolt-Glaser, J. K., & Glaser, R. (1988). Immunological consequences of acute and chronic stressors: Mediating role of interpersonal relationships. *British Journal of Medical Psychology, 61,* 77–85.

Kent, M. M. (2009). *Premature births help explain higher U.S. infant mortality*. Retrieved January 17, 2010, from http://www.prb.org/Articles/2009/prematurebirths.aspx

Kent, S. (1991). Partitioning space: Cross-cultural factors influencing domestic spatial segmentation. *Environment and Behavior, 23,* 438–473.

Kerestes, M., Youniss, J., & Metz, E. (2004). Longitudinal patterns of religious perspective and civic integration. *Applied Developmental Science, 8*(1), 39–46.

Keutzer, C. (1982). Physics and consciousness. *Journal of Humanistic Psychology, 22,* 74–90.

Keyes, C., & Ryff, C. (1998). Generativity in adult lives: Social structural contours and quality of life consequences. In D. McAdams & E. de St. Aubin (Eds.), *Generativity and adult development: How and why we care for the next generation* (pp. 227–263). Washington, DC: American Psychological Association.

Khawaja, U. B., Khawaja, A. A., Gowani, S. A., Shoukat, S., Ejaz, S., Ali, F. N., et al. (2009). Frequency of endometriosis among infertile women and association of clinical signs and symptoms with the laparoscopic staging of endometriosis. *Journal of Pakistan Medical Association, 59*(1), 30–34.

Kher, U. (2008). Outsourcing your heart. In S. Sernau (Ed.), *Contemporary readings in globalization* (pp. 143–145). Thousand Oaks, CA: Pine Forge.

Khodyakov, D., & Carr, D. (2009). The impact of late-life parental death on adult sibling relationships. *Research on Aging, 31*(5), 495–519.

Kidd, S. M. (1996). *The dance of the dissident daughter: A woman's journey from Christian tradition to the sacred feminine.* New York: HarperCollins.

Kilbury, R., Bordieri, J., & Wong, H. (1996). Impact of physical disability and gender on personal space. *Journal of Rehabilitation, 62*(2), 59–61.

Kim, J., & Moen, P. (2001). Moving into retirement: Preparation and transitions in late midlife. In M. Lachman (Ed.), *Handbook of midlife development* (pp. 487–527). New York: Wiley.

Kim, J., Siegel, S., & Patenall, V. (1999). Drug-onset cues as signals: Intraadministration associations and tolerance. *Journal of Experimental Psychology: Animal Behavior Processes, 25*(4), 491–504.

Kimura, H., Nagao, F., Tanaka, Y., Sakai, S., Ohnishi, S., & Okumura, K. (2005). Beneficial effects of the Nishino breathing method on immune activity and stress level. *Journal of Alternative and Complementary Medicine, 11*(2), 285–291.

Kindlon, D. J. (2003). *Too much of a good thing: Raising children of character in an indulgent age.* New York: Miramax Books.

Kindlon, D. J., & Thompson, M. (1999). *Raising Cain: Protecting the emotional life of boys.* New York: Random House.

King, C., & Merchant, C. (2008). Social and interpersonal factors relating to adolescent suicidality: A review of the literature. *Archives of Suicide Research, 12*, 181–196.

King, K., & Gurian, M. (2006). With boys in mind: Teaching to the minds of boys. *Educational Leadership, 64*(1), 56–61.

King, P. (2007). Adolescent spirituality and positive youth development: A look at religion, social capital, and moral functioning. In R. Silbereisen & R. Lerner (Eds.), *Approaches to positive youth development* (pp. 227–242). Thousand Oaks, CA: Sage.

King, P., & Furrow, J. (2004). Religion as a resource for positive youth development: Religion, social capital, and moral outcomes. *Developmental Psychology, 40*(5), 703–713.

King, W. (2009). Toward a life-course perspective of police organizations. *Journal of Research in Crime and Delinquency, 46*(2), 213–244.

Kinkade, K. (1973). *A Walden Two experiment: The first five years of Twin Oaks Community.* New York: Morrow.

Kinnunen, U., & Feldt, T. (2004). Economic stress and marital adjustment among couples: Analyses at the dyadic level. *European Journal of Social Psychology, 34*(5), 519–532.

Kirk, S., & Kutchins, H. (1992). *The selling of DSM: The rhetoric of science in psychiatry.* New York: Aldine de Gruyter.

Kirk, S., & Reid, W. (2002). *Science and social work: A critical appraisal.* New York: Columbia University Press.

Kissman, K., & Maurer, L. (2002). East meets West: Therapeutic aspects of spirituality in health, mental health and addiction recovery. *International Social Work, 45*(1), 35–43.

Kitayama, S., Karasawa, M., & Mesquita, B. (2004). Collective and personal processes in regulating emotions: Emotion and self in Japan and the United States. In P. Philippot & R. Feldman (Eds.), *The regulation of emotion* (pp. 251–276). Mahwah, NJ: Erlbaum.

Kivel, P. (1991). Men, spirituality, and violence. *Creation Spirituality, 7*(4), 12–14, 50.

Kiwi, R. (2006). Recurrent pregnancy loss: Evaluation and discussion of the causes and their management. *Cleveland Clinic Journal of Medicine, 73*(10), 913–991.

Klaczynski, P. (2000). Motivated scientific reasoning biases, epistemological beliefs, and theory polarization: A two-process approach to adolescent cognition. *Child Development, 71*(5).

Klaczynski, P., & Fauth, J. (1997). Developmental differences in memory-based intrusions and self-serving statistical reasoning biases. *Merrill-Palmer Quarterly, 43*, 539–566.

Klapper, B. (2006, September 25). Swiss voters toughen asylum, immigration laws. *The Washington Post*, p. A16.

Klein, M. (1995). *The American street gang: Its nature, prevalence, and control.* New York: Oxford University Press.

Kline, G., Stanley, S., Markman, H., Olmos-Gallo, P. A., Peters, M., Whitton, S., et al. (2004). Timing is everything: Pre-engagement cohabitation and increased risk for poor marital outcomes. *Journal of Family Psychology, 18*(2), 311–318.

Knapp, M. S. (1995). *Teaching for meaning in high-poverty classrooms.* New York: Teachers College Press.

Knitzer, J. (2007). Putting knowledge into policy: Toward an infant-toddler policy agenda. *Infant Mental Health Journal, 28*(2), 237–245.

Knudsen, E. I. (2004). Sensitive periods in the development of the brain and behavior. *Journal of Cognitive Neuroscience, 16*(8), 1412–1425.

Koball, H., & Douglas-Hall, A. (2006). *The new poor: Regional trends in child poverty since 2000.* Retrieved November 13, 2006, from http://www.nccp.org/pub_npr06.html

Kobayashi, M., & Miura, K. (2000). Natural disaster and restoration housings. In S. Wapner, J. Demick, T. Yamamoto, & H. Minami (Eds.), *Theoretical perspectives in environment-behavior research: Underlying assumptions, research problems, and methodologies* (pp. 39–49). New York: Kluwer Academic.

Kochanska, G. (1997). Multiple pathways to conscience for children with different temperaments: From toddlerhood to age 5. *Developmental Psychology, 33*, 228–240.

Kochanska, G., Aksan, N., & Joy, M. (2007). Children's fearfulness as a moderator of parenting in early socialization: Two longitudinal studies. *Developmental Psychology, 43*, 222–237.

Kochanska, G., Forman, D., Aksan, N., & Dunbar, S. (2005). Pathways to conscience: Early mother–child mutually responsive orientation and children's moral emotion, conduct, and cognition. *Journal of Child Psychology and Psychiatry, 46,* 19–34.

Koenig, H. G. (1999). *The healing power of faith: Science explores medicine's last great frontier.* New York: Simon & Schuster.

Koenig, H. G. (2001a). Religion and medicine IV: Religion, physical health, and clinical implications. *International Journal of Psychiatry in Medicine, 31*(3), 321–336.

Koenig, H. G. (2001b). Religion and mental health II: Religion, mental health, and related behaviors. *International Journal of Psychiatry in Medicine, 31*(10), 97–109.

Koenig, H. G. (2005). *Faith and mental health: Religious sources for healing.* Philadelphia: Templeton Foundation Press.

Koenig, H. G., Larson, D. B., & Larson, S. S. (2001). Religion and coping with serious medical illness. *Annals of Pharmacotherapy, 35*(3), 352–359.

Koenig, H. G., McCullough, M. E., & Larson, D. B. (2000). *Handbook of religion and health.* New York: Oxford University Press.

Kohlberg, L. (1969a). Stage and sequence: The cognitive developmental approach to socialization. In D. A. Goslin (Ed.), *Handbook of socialization theory and research* (pp. 347–480). Chicago: Rand McNally.

Kohlberg, L. (1969b). *Stages in the development of moral thought and action.* New York: Holt, Rinehart and Winston.

Kohlberg, L. (1976). Moral stages and moralization: The cognitive-developmental approach. In T. Lickona (Ed.), *Moral development and behavior: Theory, research, and social issues* (pp. 31–53). New York: Holt.

Kohlberg, L. (1984). Essays on moral development: Vol. 2. The psychology of moral development. San Francisco: Harper & Row.

Kohli, M., & Albertini, M. (2009). Childlessness and intergenerational transfers: What is at stake? *Ageing & Society, 29,* 1171–1183.

Kohli, M., & Künemund, H. (2005). The midlife generation in the family: Patterns of exchange and support. In S. Willis & M. Martin (Eds.), *Middle adulthood: A lifespan perspective* (pp. 35–61). Thousand Oaks, CA: Sage.

Kohut, H. (1971). *The analysis of the self.* New York: International Universities Press.

Kominski, R., Shin, H., & Marotz, K. (2008, April 16–19). *Language needs of school-age children.* Paper presented at the Annual Meeting of the Population Association of America, New Orleans, LA. Retrieved January 19, 2010, from http://www.census.gov/population/www/socdemo/lang_use.html

Kondrat, M. E. (1999). Who is the "self" in self-aware: Professional self-awareness from a critical theory perspective. *Social Service Review, 73*(4), 451–477.

Koopmans, R. (2004). Political opportunity structure: Some splitting to balance the lumping. In J. Goodwin & J. Jasper (Eds.), *Rethinking social movements: Structure, meaning, and emotion* (pp. 61–73). Lanham, MD: Rowman & Littlefield.

Kopola, M., Esquivel, G., & Baptiste, L. (1994). Counseling approaches for immigrant children: Facilitating the acculturative process. *The School Counselor, 41,* 352–359.

Koppel, G., & Kaiser, D. (2001). Fathers at the end of their rope: A brief report on fathers abandoned in the perinatal situation. *Journal of Reproductive and Infant Psychology, 19*(3), 249–251.

Kosmin, B., & Keysar, A. (2009). *American Religious Identification Survey (ARIS 2008).* Retrieved August 18, 2011, from http://www.amercianreligionsurvey-aris.org/reports/ARIS_Report_2008.pdf

Kotch, J., Browne, D., Ringwalt, C., Dufort, V., Ruina, E., Stewart, P., et al. (1997). Stress, social support, and substantiated maltreatment in the second and third years of life. *Child Abuse and Neglect, 21*(11), 1026–1037.

Kottak, C. P. (2008). *Anthropology: The exploration of human diversity* (12th ed.). Boston: McGraw-Hill.

Kottak, C. P., & Kozaitis, K. (2008). *On being different: Diversity and multiculturalism in the North American mainstream.* Boston: McGraw-Hill.

Kottler, J., & Englar-Carlson, M. (2010). *Learning group leadership: An experiential approach.* Thousand Oaks, CA: Sage.

Kovács, Á., & Mehler, J. (2009). Flexible learning of multiple speech structures in bilingual infants. *Science, 325,* 611–612,

Kowalik, S. C. (2004). Neurobiology of PTSD in children and adolescents. In R. Silva (Ed.), *Posttraumatic stress disorders in children and adolescents* (pp. 83–122). New York: Norton.

Kowalski, K. (1996). The emergence of ethnic/racial attitudes in preschool-age children. *Dissertation Abstracts International: Section B: The Sciences & Engineering, 56*(8-B), 4604.

Kozol, J. (1991). *Savage inequalities: Children in America's schools.* New York: HarperPerennial.

Kozol, J. (2000). *Ordinary resurrections: Children in the years of hope.* New York: Harper Perennial.

Kozol, J. (2005). *The shame of the nation: The restoration of apartheid schooling in America.* New York: Crown.

Kraemer, G. (1992). A psychobiological theory of attachment. *Behavioral and Brain Sciences, 15*(3), 493–511.

Kramer, B. (1997). Gain in the caregiving experience: Where are we? What next? *The Gerontologist, 37,* 218–232.

Kramer, M. R., & Hogue, C. R. (2009). What causes racial disparities in very preterm birth? A biosocial perspective. *Epidemiological Reviews, 31,* 84–98.

Kravetz, D. (2004). *Tales from the trenches: Politics and practice in feminist service organizations.* Lanham, MD: University Press of America.

Kreider, R. M., & Elliott, D. B. (2009). *America's families and living arrangements: 2007.* Washington, DC: U.S. Census Bureau. Retrieved May 21, 2010, from http://www.census .gov/prod/2009pubs/p20-561.pdf

Kreider, R. M., & Fields, J. (2005). Living arrangements of children: 2001. *Current Population Reports,* pp. 70–104. Retrieved September 13, 2011, from http://www.census .gov/prod/2005pubs/p70-104.pdf

Kriesi, H. (1996). The organizational structure of new social movements in a political context. In D. McAdam, J. McCarthy, & M. Zald (Eds.), *Comparative perspectives on social movements* (pp. 152–184). New York: Cambridge University Press.

Krill, D. (1986). Existential social work. In F. Turner (Ed.), *Social work treatment: Interlocking theoretical approaches* (pp. 181–217). New York: Free Press.

Krill, D. (1996). Existential social work. In E. J. Turner (Ed.), *Social work treatment* (4th ed., pp. 250–281). New York: Free Press.

Krisberg, K. (2006). Emergency contraception now available prescription-free. *Nation's Health, 36*(8), 6–8.

Kroeber, A., & Kluckhohn, C. (1963). *Culture: A critical review of concepts and definitions.* New York: Vintage.

Kroeber, A., & Kluckhohn, C. (1978). *Culture: A critical review of concepts and definitions.* Cambridge, MA: Peabody Museum. (Original work published 1952)

Kroger, J. (2007). *Identity development: Adolescence through adulthood* (2nd ed.). Thousand Oaks, CA: Sage.

Kroon, L. A. (2007). Drug interactions with smoking. *American Journal of Health-System Pharmacy, 64*(18), 1917–1921.

Kruel, M. (1995). Women's spirituality and healing in Germany. *Women and Therapy: A Feminist Quarterly, 16*(2/3), 135–147.

Krug, E., Dahlberg, L., Mercy, J., Zwi, A., & Lozano, R. (2002). *World report on violence and health.* Geneva, Switzerland: World Health Organization.

Kübler-Ross, E. (1969). *On death and dying.* New York: Macmillan.

Kuo, F., Bacaicoa, M., & Sullivan, W. (1998). Transforming inner-city landscapes: Trees, sense of safety, and preference. *Environment and Behavior, 30,* 28–59.

Kuo, F., & Faber Taylor, A. (2004). A potential treatment for attention deficit/hyperactivity disorder: Evidence from a national study. *American Journal of Public Health, 94*(9), 1580–1586.

Kupritz, V. (2003). Accommodating privacy to facilitate new ways of working. *Journal of Architectural and Planning Research, 20*(2), 122–135.

Kurdek, L. (2004). Are gay and lesbian cohabiting couples *really* different from heterosexual married couples? *Journal of Marriage and the Family, 66,* 880–900.

Kurdek, L. (2006). Differences between partners from heterosexual, gay, and lesbian cohabiting couples. *Journal of Marriage and Family, 68,* 509–528.

Kurjak, A., Pooh, R. K., Merce, L. T., Carrera, J. M., Salihagic-Kadic, A., & Andonotopo, W. (2005). Structural and functional early human development assessed by three-dimensional and four-dimensional sonography. *Fertility and Sterility, 84*(5), 1285–1299.

Kurtz, L. (2007). *Gods in the global village: The world's religions in sociological perspective* (2nd ed.). Thousand Oaks, CA: Pine Forge.

Kurtz, S. (2002). *Workplace justice: Organizing multi-identity movements.* Minneapolis: University of Minnesota Press.

Kvarfordt, C., & Sheridan, M. J. (2007). The role of religion and spirituality in working with children and adolescents: Results of a national survey. *Social Thought, 26*(3), 1–23.

Kwok, O., Haine, R. A., Sandler, I. N., Ayers, T. S., Wolchik, S. A., & Tein, J. Y. (2005). Positive parenting as a mediator of the relations between parental psychological distress and mental health problems of parentally bereaved children. *Journal of Clinical Child and Adolescent Psychology, 34*(2), 260–271.

Kyle, G., Graefe, A., Manning, R., & Bacon, J. (2004). Effect of activity involvement and place attachment on recreationists' perceptions of setting density. *Journal of Leisure Research, 36*(2), 209–231.

Labor Law Center. (2009). *Federal minimum wage increase for 2007, 2008, & 2009.* Retrieved October 26, 2009, from http://www.laborlawcenter.com/t-federal-minimum-wage.aspx

Labouvie-Vief, G. (1990). Modes of knowledge and the organization of development. In M. Commons, L. Kohlberg, R. Richards, & S. Sinnott (Eds.), *Beyond formal operations: Vol. 2. Models and methods in the study of adult and adolescent thought* (pp. 43–62). New York: Praeger.

Labouvie-Vief, G. (2005). Self-with-other representations and the organization of the self. *Journal of Research in Personality, 39,* 185–205.

Lachman, M. (2004). Development in midlife. *Annual Review of Psychology, 55,* 305–331.

Lachman, M., & Bertrand, R. (2001). Personality and the self in midlife. In M. Lachman (Ed.), *Handbook of midlife development* (pp. 279–309). New York: Wiley.

Ladd, H. (2007). Teacher labor markets in developed countries. *The Future of Children: Excellence in the Classroom, 17*(1), 201–217.

Ladson-Billings, G. (2004). Landing on the wrong note: The price we paid for *Brown. Educational Researcher, 33*(7), 3–13.

Ladson-Billings, G. (2006). From the achievement gap to educational debt: Understanding achievement in U.S. schools. *Educational Researcher, 35*(7), 3–12.

Laflamme, D., Pomerleau, A., & Malcuit, G. (2002). A comparison of fathers' and mothers' involvement in childcare and stimulation behaviors during free play with their infants at 9 and 15 months. *Sex Roles, 47,* 507–518.

Laing, R. D. (1967). *The politics of experience.* New York: Ballantine.

Laing, R. D. (1969). *The politics of the family.* New York: Pantheon.

Laird, J. (1994). Changing women's narratives: Taking back the discourse. In L. Davis (Ed.), *Building on women's strengths: A social work agenda for the twenty-first century* (pp. 179–210). New York: Haworth.

Lajoie, D. H., & Shapiro, S. I. (1992). Definitions of transpersonal psychology: The first twenty-three years. *Journal of Transpersonal Psychology, 4,* 79–98.

Lakoff, G. (2006). *Whose freedom? The battle over America's most important ideas.* New York: Farrar, Straus & Giroux.

Lam, V., & Smith, G. (2009). African and Caribbean adolescents in Britain: Ethnic identity and Britishness. *Ethnic and Racial Studies, 32*(7), 1248–1270.

Lamaze, F. (1958). *Painless childbirth: Psychoprophylactic method* (L. R. Celestin, Trans.). London: Burke.

Landau, E. (2008). *Report: Teen pregnancies up for first time in 15 years.* Atlanta, GA: CNN. Retrieved October 31, 2009, from http://www.cnn.com/2008/HEALTH/07/10/teen.pregnancy/index.html

Lane, C. (2007). *Shyness: How normal behavior became a sickness.* New Haven, CT: Yale University Press.

Lang, A. J., Stein, M. B., Kennedy, C. M., & Foy, D. W. (2004). Adult psychopathology and intimate partner violence among survivors of childhood maltreatment. *Journal of Interpersonal Violence, 19*(10), 1102–1118.

Langer, E., Fiske, S., Taylor, S., & Chanowitz, B. (1976). Stigma, staring, and discomfort: A novel-stimulus hypothesis. *Journal of Experimental Social Psychology, 12,* 451–463.

Langle, A., & Probst, C. (2004). Existential questions of the elderly. *Archives of Psychiatry and Psychotherapy, 6*(2), 15–20.

Lansford, J., Deater-Deckard, K., Dodge, K., Bates, J., & Pettit, G. (2004). Ethnic differences in the link between physical discipline and later adolescent externalizing behaviors. *Journal of Child Psychology and Psychiatry, 45,* 801–812.

Lantz, J., & Walsh, J. (2007). *Short-term existential intervention in clinical practice.* Chicago: Lyceum.

Lapidus, I. (1978). Adulthood in Islam: Religious maturing in the Islamic tradition. In E. H. Erikson (Ed.), *Adulthood* (pp. 97–112). New York: Norton & Norton.

LaRossa, R. (1997). *The modernization of fatherhood: A social and political history.* Chicago: University of Chicago Press.

Larson, R. M., & Seepersad, S. (2003). Adolescents' leisure time in the United States: Partying, sports, and the American experiment. In S. Verma & R. Larson (Eds.), *Examining adolescent leisure time across cultures: New directions for child and adolescent development* (No. 99, pp. 53–64). San Francisco: Jossey-Bass.

Larson, R. W., Wilson, S., & Mortimer, J. T. (2002). Adolescence in the 21st century: An international perspective—Adolescents' preparation for the future. *Journal of Research on Adolescence, 12*(1), 159–166.

Latva, R., Lehtonen, L., Salmelin, R. K., & Tamminen, T. (2007). Visits by the family to the neonatal intensive care. *Acta Paediatrica, 96*(2), 215–220.

Lau, A., Litrownik, A., Newton, R., Black, M., & Everson, M. (2006). Factors affecting the link between physical discipline and child externalizing problems in Black and White families. *Journal of Community Psychology, 34*(1), 89–103.

Lau, J. T., Wang, Q., Cheng, Y., Kim, J., Yang, X., & Tsui, H. (2008). Infertility-related perceptions and responses and their associations with quality of life among rural Chinese infertile couples. *Journal of Sexual and Marital Therapy, 34,* 248–267.

Lau, J. Y. F., Eley, T. C., & Stevenson, J. (2006). Examining the state–trait anxiety relationship: A behavioural genetic approach. *Journal of Abnormal Child Psychology, 34*(1), 19–27.

Lauer, R. (1981). *Temporal man: The meaning and uses of social time.* New York: Praeger.

Laurino, M. Y., Bennett, R. L., Sariya, D. S., Baumeister, L., Doyle, D. L., Leppig, K., et al. (2005). Genetic evaluation and counseling of couples with recurrent miscarriage: Recommendations of the National Society of Genetic Counselors. *Journal of Genetic Counseling, 14*(3), 165–181.

Lawrence, C., & Andrews, K. (2004). The influence of perceived prison crowding on male inmates' perception of aggressive events. *Aggressive Behavior, 30*(4), 273–283.

Lawrence, C. R., Carlson, E. A., & Egeland, B. (2006). The impact of foster care on development. *Development and Psychopathology, 18*(1), 57–76.

Lazarus, R. S. (2001). Relational meaning and discrete emotions. In K. R. Scherer, A. Schorr, & T. Johnstone (Eds.), *Appraisal processes in emotion: Theory, methods, research* (pp. 37–67). New York: Oxford University Press.

Lazarus, R. S. (2007). Stress and emotion: A new synthesis. In A. Monat, R. S. Lazarus, & G. Reevy (Eds.), *The Praeger* handbook on stress and coping (Vol. 1, pp. 33–51). Westport, CT: Praeger/Greenwood.

LeCroy, C. W. (1992). *Case studies in social work practice.* Belmont, CA: Wadsworth.

Lederberg, J. (2001). The meaning of epigenetics. *The Scientist, 15*(18), 6.

LeDoux, J. E., &. Phelps, E. A. (2008). Emotional networks in the brain. In M. Lewis, J. M. Havilland-Jones, & L. F. Barrett (Eds.), *Handbook of emotions* (3rd ed., pp. 159–179). New York: Guilford Press.

Lee, B., & Campbell, K. (1999). Neighbor networks of Black and White Americans. In B. Wellman (Ed.), *Networks in the global village* (pp. 119–146). Boulder, CO: Westview Press.

Lee, E., Menkart, D., & Okazawa-Rae, M. (1998). *Beyond holidays and heroes: A practical guide to K–12 anti-racist multicultural education and staff development.* Washington, DC: Network of Educators in the Americas.

Lee, J. (2001). *The empowerment approach to social work practice: Building the beloved community.* New York: Columbia University Press.

Lee, K. (2009). Infant reflexes. *MedlinePlus.* Retrieved February 12, 2010, from http://www.nlm.nih.gov/med lineplus/ency/article/003292.htm

Lee, M. (2003). Korean adolescents' "examination hell" and their use of free time. In S. Verma & R. Larson (Eds.), *Examining adolescent leisure time across cultures: New directions for child and adolescent development* (No. 99, pp. 9–21). San Francisco: Jossey-Bass.

Lee, M. (2008). A small act of creativity: Fostering creativity in clinical social work practice. *Families in Society, 89*(1), 19–31.

Lee, M., Whitehead, J., & Ntoumanis, N. (2007). The measurement of the attitudes to moral decision-making in youth sport questionnaire. *Psychology of Sport and Exercise, 8,* 369–392.

Lee, M. Y., Ng, S., Leung, P. P. Y., & Chan, C. L. W. (2009). *Integrative body-mind-spirit social work: An empirically based approach to assessment and treatment.* New York: Oxford University Press.

Lee, V., & Hoaken, P. N. S. (2007). Cognitive, emotion, and neurobiological development: Mediating the relation between maltreatment and aggression. *Child Maltreatment, 12*(3), 281–298.

Leeder, E. (2004). *The family in global perspective: A gendered journey.* Thousand Oaks, CA: Sage.

LeFever, G. B., Villers, M. S., Morrow, A. L., & Vaughn, E. S. (2002). Parental perceptions of adverse educational outcomes among children diagnosed and treated for ADHD: A call for improved school/provider collaboration. *Psychology in the Schools, 39*(1), 63–71.

Leiby, J. (1985). Moral foundations of social welfare and social work: A historical view. *Social Work, 30,* 323–330.

Leitenberg, H., Detzer, M. J., & Srebnik, D. (1993). Gender differences in masturbation and the relationship of masturbation experience in preadolescence and/or early adolescence and sexual behavior and sexual adjustment in young adulthood. *Archives of Sexual Behavior, 22,* 299–313.

Lengermann, P., & Niebrugge-Brantley, G. (2007). Contemporary feminist theories. In G. Ritzer (Ed.), *Contemporary sociological theory and its classical roots* (2nd ed., pp. 185–214). Boston: McGraw-Hill.

Lenski, G. (1966). *Power and privilege.* New York: McGraw-Hill.

LePoire, B. (2006). *Family communication: Nurturing and control in a changing world.* Thousand Oaks, CA: Sage.

Lerner, J. V., Castellino, D. R., Lolli, E., & Wan, S. (2003). Children, families, and work: Research findings and implications for policies and programs. In R. M. Lerner, F. Jacobs, & D. Wertlieb (Eds.), *Handbook of applied developmental science* (Vol. 1, pp. 281–304). Thousand Oaks, CA: Sage.

Levi, M., Cook, K., O'Brien, J., & Faye, H. (1990). The limits of rationality. In K. Cook & M. Levi (Eds.), *The limits of rationality* (pp. 1–16). Chicago: University of Chicago Press.

Levine, R. (2006). A geography of time. In D. Newman & J. O'Brien (Eds.), *Sociology: Exploring the architecture of everyday life: Readings* (6th ed., pp. 73–83). Thousand Oaks, CA: Pine Forge.

Levine, S. (1999). Children's cognition as the foundation of spirituality. *International Journal of Children's Spirituality, 4*(2), 121–140.

Levinson, D. (1977). The mid-life transition. *Psychiatry, 40,* 99–112.

Levinson, D. (1978). *The seasons of a man's life.* New York: Knopf.

Levinson, D. (1980). Toward a conception of the adult life course. In N. J. Smelser & E. H. Erikson (Eds.), *Themes of work and love in adulthood* (pp. 265–290). Cambridge, MA: Harvard University Press.

Levinson, D. (1986). A conception of adult development. *American Psychologist, 41*(1), 3–13.

Levinson, D. (1990). A theory of life structure development in adulthood. In C. N. Alexander & E. J. Langer (Eds.), *Higher stages of human development* (pp. 35–54). New York: Oxford University Press.

Levinson, D., with Levinson, J. (1996). *The seasons of a woman's life.* New York: Ballantine Books.

Levy, G. D., Taylor, M. G., & Gelman, S. A. (1995). Traditional and evaluative aspects of flexibility in gender roles, social conventions, moral rules and physical laws. *Child Development, 66,* 515–531.

Levy, L., Martinkowski, K., & Derby, J. (1994). Differences in patterns of adaptation in conjugal bereavement: Their sources and potential significance. *Omega, 29,* 71–87.

Levy, S. (2000). Still confused after all these years. *Fieldwork, 13*(2).

Lewandowski, C. A., & Canda, E. R. (1995). A typological model for the assessment of religious groups. *Social Thought, 18*(1), 17–38.

Lewis, C. (1979). Healing in the urban environment: A person/plant viewpoint. *Journal of American Planning Association, 45,* 330–338.

Lewis, C. (1996). *Green nature/human nature: The meaning of plants in our lives.* Urbana: University of Illinois Press.

Lewis, M. (2005). The child and its family: The social network model. *Human Development, 48,* 8–27.

Lewis, T. (1994). A comparative analysis of the effects of social skills training and teacher-directed contingencies on social behavior of preschool children with disabilities. *Journal of Behavioral Education, 4,* 267–281.

Li, S.-C. (2006). Biocultural co-construction of life span development. In P. B. Baltes, P. A. Reuter-Lorenz, & F. Rössler (Eds.), *Life span development and the brain: The perspective of biocultural co-constructivism* (pp. 40–60). Cambridge, UK: Cambridge University Press.

Lichter, D., & Qian, Z. (2008). Serial cohabitation and the marital life course. *Journal of Marriage and Family, 70,* 861–878.

Lightfoot, C., Lalonde, C., & Chandler, M. (Eds.). (2004). *Changing conceptions of psychological life.* Mahwah, NJ: Erlbaum.

Limb, G. E., & Hodge, D. R. (2008). Developing spiritual competency with Native Americans: Promoting wellness through balance and harmony. *Families in Society: The Journal of Contemporary Social Services, 89*(4), 615–622.

Limber, S. P., & Small, M. A. (2003). State laws and policies to address bullying in schools. *School Psychology Review, 32*(3), 445–455.

Lincoln, Y., & Guba, E. (1985). *Naturalistic inquiry.* Beverly Hills, CA: Sage.

Lindell, S. G. (1988). Education for childbirth: A time for change. *Journal of Gynecologic and Neonatal Nursing, 17*(2), 108–112.

Lindemann, E. (1944). Symptomatology and management of acute grief. *American Journal of Psychiatry, 101,* 141–148.

Lindsey, D. (2004). *The welfare of children* (2nd ed.). New York: Oxford.

Lindsey, E. W., Kurtz, P. D., Jarvis, S., Williams, N. R., & Nackerud, L. (2000). How runaway and homeless youth navigate troubled waters: Personal strengths and resources. *Clinical and Adolescent Social Work Journal, 17*(2), 115–140.

Ling, Z. J., Lian, W. B., Ho, S. K., & Yeo, C. L. (2009). Parental knowledge of prematurity and related issues. *Singapore Medical Journal, 50*(3), 270–277.

Link, A. L. (1997). *Group work with elders: 50 therapeutic exercises for reminiscence, validation, and remotivation.* Sarasota, FL: Professional Resource Press.

Linver, M. R., Brooks-Gunn, J., & Kohen, D. (2002). Family processes as pathways from income to young children's development. *Developmental Psychology, 38,* 719–734.

Linver, M. R., Fuligni, A. S., Hernandez, M., & Brooks-Gunn, J. (2004). Poverty and child development. In P. Allen-Meares & M. W. Fraser (Eds.), *Intervention with children and adolescents: An interdisciplinary perspective* (pp. 106–129). Boston: Allyn & Bacon.

Lippa, R. A. (2005). *Gender, nature, and nurture* (2nd ed.). Mahwah, NJ: Erlbaum.

Lippman, L., & Keith, J. (2009). *A developmental perspective on workplace readiness: Preparing high school students for success.* Washington, DC: Child Trends. Retrieved January 5, 2009, from http://www.childtrends.org/Files//Child_Trends-2009_04_28_RB_WorkReady.pdf

Littky, D., & Grabelle, S. (2004). *The big picture: Education is everyone's business.* Alexandria, VA: Association for Supervision and Curriculum Development.

Litty, C., & Hatch, J. A. (2006). Hurry up and wait: Rethinking special education identification in kindergarten. *Early Childhood Education Journal, 33*(4), 203–208.

Liu, S., Hearman, M., Kramer, M. S., Demissie, K., Wen, S. W., & Marcoux, S. (2002). Length of hospital stay, obstetric conditions at childbirth, and maternal admission: A population-based cohort study. *American Journal of Obstetrics and Gynecology, 187*(3), 681–687.

Liu, Z., Liu., L., Owens, J., & Kaplan, D. (2005). Sleep patterns and sleep problems among school children in the United States and China. *Pediatrics, 115,* 241–249.

Living Wage Resource Center. (2006). *The living wage resource center: Introduction.* Retrieved May 17, 2010, from http://highboldtage.wordpress.com/2008/03/12/acorns-living-wage-resource-center/

Lloyd, C. B., Behrman, J. R., Stromquist, N. P., & Cohen, B. (2006). *The changing transitions to adulthood in developing countries: Selected studies.* Washington, DC: National Research Council.

Lloyd, S., Few, A., & Allen, K. (2009). Preface. In S. Lloyd, A. Few, & K. Allen (Eds.), *Handbook of feminist family studies.* Thousand Oaks, CA: Sage.

Lochman, J. E., Coie, J. D., Underwood, M. K., & Terry, R. (1993). Effectiveness of a social relationship intervention program for aggressive and nonaggressive, rejected children. *Journal of Consulting and Clinical Psychology, 61,* 1053–1058.

Locke, A., Ginsborg, J., & Peers, I. (2002). Development and disadvantage: Implications for the early years and beyond. *International Journal of Language & Communication Disorders, 37*(1), 3–15.

Lodhi, F., Fattah, A., Abozaid, T., Murphy, J., Formantini, E., Sasy, M., et al. (2004). Gamete intra-fallopian transfer or intrauterine insemination after controlled ovarian hyperstimulation for treatment of infertility due to endometriosis. *Gynecological Endocrinology, 152*(8), 152–160.

Logan, G. (2000). Information-processing theories. In A. E. Kazdi (Ed.), *Encyclopedia of psychology* (Vol. 4, pp. 294–297). Washington, DC: American Psychological Association.

Logan, S. L. (1997). Meditation as a tool that links the personal and the professional. *Reflections: Narratives of Professional Helping, 3*(1), 38–44.

Logan, S. L. (Ed.). (2001). *The Black family: Strengths, self-help, and positive change* (2nd ed.). Boulder, CO: Westview Press.

Lohmann, R., & McNutt, J. (2005). Practice in the electronic community. In M. Weil (Ed.), *The handbook of community practice* (pp. 636–646). Thousand Oaks, CA: Sage.

Lomsky-Feder, E., & Leibovitz, T. (2010). Inter-ethnic encounters within the family: Competing cultural models and social exchange. *Journal of Ethnic & Migration Studies, 36*(1), 107–124.

Lonzano, H., & Ballesteros, F. (2006). A study on breakfast and school performance in a group of adolescents. *Nutrition Hospital, 21*(3), 346–352.

Lopez, R. (2004). Urban sprawl and risk for being overweight or obese. *Research and Practice, 94*(9), 1574–1579.

Lopez, R., & Hynes, P. (2006). Obesity, physical activity, and the urban environment: Public health research needs. *Environmental Health: A Global Access Science Source, 5*, 25. Retrieved October 15, 2009, from http://www.ehjournal.net/content/5/1/25

Lovaglia, M. (1995). Power and status: Exchange, attribution, and expectation states. *Small Group Research, 26*, 400–426.

Lovaglia, M., Mannix, E., Samuelson, C., Sell, J., & Wilson, R. (2005). Conflict, power, and status in groups. In M. Poole & A. Hollingshead (Eds.), *Theories of small groups: Interdisciplinary perspectives* (pp. 63–97). Thousand Oaks, CA: Sage.

Loveless, T. (1999). *The tracking wars: State reform meets school policy.* Washington, DC: Brookings Institution Press.

Low, S., & Altman, I. (1992). Place attachment: A conceptual inquiry. In I. Altman & S. Low (Eds.), *Place attachment* (pp. 1–12). New York: Plenum.

Lowe, J. (1997). A social-health model: A paradigm for social work in health care. In M. Reisch & E. Gambrill (Eds.), *Social work in the 21st century* (pp. 209–218). Thousand Oaks, CA: Pine Forge.

Lowe, J., Erickson, S., MacLean, P., & Duvall, S. (2009). Early working memory and maternal communication in toddlers born very low birth weight. *Acta Paediatrica, 98*, 660–663.

Lowenberg, F. M. (1988). *Religion and social work practice in contemporary American society.* New York: Columbia University Press.

Lowenstein, A., & Daatland, S. (2006). Filial norms and family support in a comparative cross-national context: Evidence from the OASIS study. *Ageing and Society, 26*, 203–223.

Lowenthal, M., Thurnher, M., & Chiriboga, D. (1975). *Four stages of life: A comparative study of women and men facing transition.* San Francisco: Jossey-Bass.

Lownsdale, S. (1997). Faith development across the lifespan: Fowler's integrative work. *Journal of Psychology and Theology, 25*, 49–63.

Lowry, R., Holtzman, D., Truman, B. I., Kann, L., Collins, J. L., & Kolbe, L. J. (1994). Substance use and HIV-related sexual behaviors among U.S. high school students: Are they related? *American Journal of Public Health, 84*, 1116–1120.

Lu, M. C., Prentice, J., Yu, S. M., Inkelas, M., Lange, L. O., & Halfon, N. (2003). Childbirth education classes: Sociodemographic disparities in attendance and the association of attendance with breastfeeding initiation. *Maternal and Child Health Journal, 7*(2), 87–93.

Lu, P. (2007). Sibling relationships in adulthood and old age: A case study in Taiwan. *Current Sociology, 55*(4), 621–637.

Lubin, H., & Johnson, D. R. (1998). Healing ceremonies. *Family Networker, 22*(5), 38–39, 64–67.

Lucille Packard Children's Hospital. (2010). *Very low birthweight.* Retrieved January 17, 2010, from http://www.lpch.org/DiseaseHealthInfo/HealthLibrary/hrnewborn/vlbw.html

Luhmann, N. (1987). Modern systems theory and the theory of society. In V. Meja, D. Misgeld, & N. Stehr (Eds.), *Modern German sociology* (pp. 173–186). New York: Columbia University Press.

Lui, M., Robles, B., Leondar-Wright, B., Brewer, R., & Adamson, R. (2006). *The color of wealth.* New York: The New Press.

Lum, D. (2004). *Social work practice and people of color: A process state approach* (5th ed.). Belmont, CA: Wadsworth.

Lum, D. (2007). *Culturally competent practice: A framework for understanding diverse groups and justice issues* (3rd ed.). Belmont, CA: Thomson.

Luo, M. (2009, April 12). Longer unemployment for those 45 and older. *New York Times.* Retrieved September 3, 2009, from http://www.nytimes.com/2009/04/13/us/13age.html

Luthar, S. (Ed.). (2003). *Resilience and vulnerability: Adaptation in the context of childhood adversities.* New York: Cambridge University Press.

Lutz, A., Dunne, J. D., & Davidson, R. J. (2007). Meditation and the neuroscience of consciousness. In P. Zelazo, M. Moscovitch, & E. Thompson (Eds.), *The Cambridge handbook of consciousness* (pp. 499–552). Cambridge, UK: Cambridge University Press.

Lynch, R. (2000). *New directions for high school career and technical education in the 21st century*. Washington, DC: U.S. Department of Education.

Lynch, T. R., Cheavens, J. S., Morse, J. Q., & Rosenthal, M. Z. (2004). A model predicting suicidal ideation and hopelessness in depressed older adults: The impact of emotion inhibition and affect intensity. *Aging and Mental Health, 8*(6), 486–497.

Lynn, L. (2002). Social services and the state: The public appropriation of private charity. *Social Service Review, 76*(1), 58–83.

Lyon, L. (1987). *The community in urban society*. Philadelphia: Temple University Press.

Lyons-Ruth, K., Lyubchik, A., Wolfe, R., & Bronfman, E. (2002). Parental depression and child attachment: Hostile and helpless profiles of parent and child behavior among families at risk. In S. Goodman & I. Gotlib (Eds.), *Children of depressed parents: Mechanisms of risk and implications for treatment* (pp. 89–120). Washington, DC: American Psychological Association.

Lyotard, J. (1984). *The postmodern condition*. Minneapolis: University of Minnesota Press.

MacArthur Network on Mind–Body Interactions. (2001). *Vital connections: Science of mind–body interactions: A report on the interdisciplinary conference held at NIH, March 26–28, 2001*. Chicago: Author.

Maccoby, E. (2002a). Gender and group processes: A developmental perspective. *Current Directions in Psychological Science, 11*, 55–58.

Maccoby, E. (2002b). Parenting effects: Issues and controversies. In J. G. Borkowski, S. Landesman Ramey, & M. Bristol-Power (Eds.), *Parenting and the child's world* (pp. 35–45). Mahwah, NJ: Erlbaum.

MacDonald, C., & Mikes-Liu, K. (2009). Is there a place for biopsychosocial formulation in a systemic practice? *Australian & New Zealand Journal of Family Therapy, 30*(4), 269–283.

MacDonald, D. (2000). Spirituality: Description, measurement, and relation to the five factor model of personality. *Journal of Personality, 68*, 157–197.

MacDorman, M. F., & Mathews, T. J. (2009). The challenge of infant mortality: Have we reached a plateau? *Public Health Reports, 124*(5), 670–681.

MacDorman, M. F., Menacker, F., & Declercq, E. (2008). Cesarean birth in the United States: Epidemiology, trends, and outcomes. *Clinics in Perinatology, 35*(2), 293–307.

Mackey, W. C. (2001). Support for the existence of an independent man-(to)-child affiliative bond. *Psychology of Men and Masculinity, 2*, 51–66.

MacKinlay, E. (Ed.). (2006). *Aging, spirituality and palliative care*. Binghamton, MA: Haworth Press.

MacLennan, B. (1994). Groups for poorly socialized children in the elementary school. *Journal of Child and Adolescent Group Therapy, 4*, 243–250.

MacMillan, R., & Copher, R. (2005). Families in the life course: Interdependency of roles, role configurations, and pathways. *Journal of Marriage and Family, 67*, 858–879.

Mader, S. M. (2003). *Biology* (8th ed). New York: McGraw-Hill.

Madigan, S., Moran, G., & Pederson, D. R. (2006). Unresolved states of mind, disorganized attachment relationships, and disrupted interactions of adolescent mothers and their infants. *Developmental Psychology, 42*(2), 293–304.

Magai, C. (2001). Emotions over the life span. In J. E. Birren & K. W. Schale (Eds.), *Handbook of the psychology of aging* (5th ed., pp. 399–426). San Diego, CA: Academic Press.

Magwaza, A., Kilian, B., Peterson, I., & Pillay, Y. (1993). The effects of chronic violence on preschool children living in South African townships. *Child Abuse and Neglect, 17*, 795–803.

Mahendru, A., Putran, J., & Khaled, M. A. (2009). Contraceptive methods. *Foundation Years Journal, 3*(3), 9–13.

Mahoney, A., Pendleton, S., & Ihrke, H. (2005). Religious coping by children and adolescents: Unexplored territory in the realm of spiritual development. In G. Roehlkepartain, P. King, L. Wagener, & P. Benson (Eds.), *The handbook of spiritual development in childhood and adolescence* (pp. 341–353). Thousand Oaks, CA: Sage.

Mahoney, M. (1991). *Human change processes: The scientific foundations of psychotherapy*. New York: Basic Books.

Main, M., & Hesse, E. (1990). Parents' unresolved traumatic experiences are related to infant disorganized attachment status: Is frightened and/or frightening parental behavior the linking mechanism? In M. Greenberg, D. Cicchetti, & E. M. Cumming (Eds.), *Attachment in the preschool years: Theory, research and intervention* (pp. 161–182). Chicago: University of Chicago Press.

Major branches of religions ranked by number of adherents. (2005). Retrieved May 20, 2007, from http://www.adherents.com/adh_branches.html

Major religions of the world ranked by numbers of adherents. (2005). Retrieved July 10, 2006, from http://www.adherents.com/Religions_By_Adherents.html

Mak, W., Cheung, R., & Law, L. (2009). Sense of community in Hong Kong: Relations with community-level characteristics and residents' well-being. *American Journal of Community Psychology, 44*, 80–92.

Malanga, S. (2003, Winter). How the "living wage" sneaks socialism into cities. *City Journal*, 1–8 [Electronic version]. Retrieved May 17, 2010, from http://www.city-journal.org/html/13_1_how_the_living_wage.html

Malinger, G., Lev, D., & Lerman-Sagie, T. (2006). Normal and abnormal fetal brain development during the third trimester as demonstrated by neurosonography. *European Journal of Radiology, 57*(22), 226–232.

Maller, C., Townsend, M., Pryor, A., Brown, P., & St. Leger, L. (2005). Healthy nature, healthy people: "Contact with nature" as an upstream health promotion intervention for populations. *Health Promotion International, 21*(1), 45–54.

Mallon, B., & Houtstra, T. (2007). Telephone technology in social work group treatment. *Health & Social Work, 32*, 139–141.

Malti, T., Gasser, L., & Buchmann, M. (2009). Aggressive and prosocial children's emotion attributions and moral reasoning. *Aggressive Behavior, 35*(1), 90–102.

Maluccio, A. N. (2006). The nature and scope of the problem. In N. B. Webb (Ed.), *Working with traumatized youth in child welfare* (pp. 3–12). New York: Guilford Press.

Mann, M. (1986). *The sources of social power* (Vol. 1). New York: Cambridge University Press.

Manning, M., Cornelius, L., & Okundaye, J. (2004). Empowering African Americans through social work practice: Integrating an Afrocentric perspective, ego psychology, and spirituality. *Families in Society: The Journal of Contemporary Social Services, 85*(2), 229–235.

Manzo, L., & Perkins, S. (2006). Finding common ground: The importance of place attachment to community participation and planning. *Journal of Planning Literature, 20*(4), 335–350.

Mapp, S. (2008). *Human rights and social justice in a global perspective: An introduction to international social work.* New York: Oxford University Press.

March, J., & Simon, H. (1958). *Organizations.* New York: Wiley.

March of Dimes. (2005). *The growing problem of prematurity.* Retrieved August 29, 2011, from http://www.smfm.org/attachedfileds/PrematurityFact.pdf

March of Dimes. (2009). *Quick reference: Facts sheet.* Retrieved January 17, 2010, from http://www.marchofdimes.com/professionals/14332_1157.asp

March of Dimes. (2010). *Nation gets a "D" as March of Dimes releases premature birth report card.* Retrieved May 21, 2010, from http://www.marchofdimes.com/aboutus/22684_42538.asp

Marcia, J. E. (1966). Development and validation of ego-identity status. *Journal of Personality and Social Psychology, 3*, 551–558.

Marcia, J. E. (1980). Identity in adolescence. In J. Adelson (Ed.), *Handbook of adolescent psychology* (pp. 159–187). New York: Wiley.

Marcia, J. E. (1993). The ego identity status approach to ego identity. In J. E. Marcia, A. S. Waterman, D. R. Mattesson, S. L. Arcjer, & J. L. Orlofksy (Eds.), *Ego identity: A handbook for psychosocial research.* New York: Springer.

Marcia, J. E. (2002). Identity and psychosocial development in adulthood. *Identity: An International Journal of Theory and Research, 2*, 7–28.

Marecek, J., Kimmel, E. B., Crawford, M., & Hare-Mustin, R. T. (2003). Psychology of women and gender. In D. K. Freedheim (Ed.), *Handbook of psychology: History of psychology* (Vol. 1, pp. 249–268). Hoboken, NJ: Wiley.

Margolin, A., Beitel, M., Schuman-Olivier, Z., & Avants, S. K. (2006). A controlled study of a spirituality-focused intervention for increasing motivation for HIV prevention among drug users. *AIDS Education and Prevention, 18*(4), 311–322.

Marino, R., Weinman, M. L., & Soudelier, K. (2001). Social work intervention and failure to thrive in infants and children. *Health and Social Work, 26*(2), 90–97.

Markovitzky, G., & Mosek, A. (2005). The role of symbolic resources in coping with immigration. *Journal of Ethnic & Cultural Diversity in Social Work, 14*(1/2), 145–158.

Markovsky, B. (2005). Network exchange theory. In G. Ritzer (Ed.), *Encyclopedia of social theory* (pp. 530–534). Thousand Oaks, CA: Sage.

Markowitz, M. (1997). HIV infection: An oncologic model of pathogenesis and treatment. *Oncologist, 2*(3), 187.

Marks, A., & Rothbart, B. (2003). *Healthy teens, body and soul: A parent's complete guide.* New York: Simon & Schuster.

Marks, N., Bumpass, L., & Jun, H. (2004). Family roles and well-being during the middle life course. In O. Brim, C. Ryff, & R. Kessler (Eds.), *How healthy are we? A national study of well-being at midlife* (pp. 514–549). Chicago: University of Chicago Press.

Markus, H., & Kitayama, S. (2003). Models of agency: Sociocultural diversity in the construction of action. In G. Berman & J. Berman (Eds.), *Cross-cultural differences in perspectives on the self* (pp. 2–57). Lincoln: University of Nebraska Press.

Markus, H., & Kitayama, S. (2009). Culture and the self: Implications for cognition, emotion, and motivation. In P. Smith & D. Best (Eds.), *Cross-cultural psychology.* (Vol. 1, pp. 265–320). Thousand Oaks, CA: Sage.

Marmot, M., & Fuhrer, R. (2004). Socioeconomic position and health across midlife. In O. Brim, C. Ryff, & R. Kessler (Eds.), *How healthy are we? A national study of well-being at midlife* (pp. 64–89). Chicago: University of Chicago Press.

Marsh, H., & Kleitman, S. (2005). Consequences of employment during high school: Character building, subversion of academic goals, or a threshold? *American Educational Research Journal, 42*, 331–370.

Marti, E. (2003). Strengths and weaknesses of cognition over preschool years. In J. Valsiner & K. Connolly (Eds.), *Handbook of development psychology* (pp. 257–275). Thousand Oaks, CA: Sage.

Marti, I., Etzion, D., & Leca, B. (2008). Theoretical approaches for studying corporations, democracy, and the public good. *Journal of Management Inquiry, 17*, 148–151.

Martin, E. P., & Martin, J. M. (2002). *Spirituality and the Black helping tradition in social work.* Washington, DC: NASW Press.

Martin, J. A., Kirmeyer, S., Osterman, M., & Shepherd, R. A. (2009). Born a bit too early: Recent trends in late preterm births. *NCHS Brief, 24*, 1–8.

Martin, J. A., & Sherman, M. (2010). The impact of military duty and military life on individuals and families.

In S. Price, C. Price, & P. McKenry (Eds.), *Families & Change: Coping with stressful events and transitions* (4th ed., pp. 381–397). Thousand Oaks, CA: Sage.

Martin, J. G. (1993). Why women need a feminist spirituality. *Women's Studies Quarterly, 1,* 106–120.

Martin, M., & Zimprich, D. (2005). Cognitive development in midlife. In S. Willis & M. Martin (Eds.), *Middle adulthood: A lifespan perspective* (pp. 179–206). Thousand Oaks, CA: Sage.

Martin, P. Y., & O'Connor, G. G. (1989). *The social environment: Open systems applications.* New York: Longman.

Martin, T. L., & Doka, K. J. (2000). *Men don't cry . . . women do: Transcending gender stereotypes of grief.* Philadelphia: Brunner/Mazel.

Martinez-Brawley, E. (2000). *Close to home: Human services and the small community.* Washington, DC: NASW Press.

Martire, L., & Schulz, R. (2001). Informal caregiving to older adults: Health effects of providing and receiving care. In A. Baum, T. Revenson, & J. Singer (Eds.), *Handbook of health psychology* (pp. 477–493). Mahwah, NJ: Erlbaum.

Marty, M. (1980). Social service: Godly and godless. *Social Service Review, 54,* 463–481.

Martz, E. (2004). Do reactions of adaptation to disability influence the fluctuation of future time orientation among individuals with spinal cord injuries? *Rehabilitation Counseling Bulletin, 47*(2), 86–95.

Martz, M. (2009, June 18). Internet access widespread in Va. *Richmond Times-Dispatch,* p. B5.

Marx, G., & McAdam, D. (1994). *Collective behavior and social movements: Process and structure.* Englewood Cliffs, NJ: Prentice Hall.

Marx, K. (1967). *Capital: A critique of political economy* (S. Moore & E. Aveling, Trans; Vol. 1). New York: International. (Original work published 1887)

Maschi, T., Morgen, K., Hatcher, S. S., Rosato, N. S., Violette, N. M. (2009). Maltreated children's thoughts and emotions as behavioral predictors: Evidence for social work action. *Social Work, 54*(2), 135–143.

Maslow, A. (1954). *Motivation and personality.* New York: Harper.

Maslow, A. (1962). *Toward a psychology of being.* New York: Van Nostrand.

Maslow, A. (1971). *Farther reaches of human nature.* New York: Viking.

Massaro, M., Rothbaum, R., & Aly, H. (2006). Fetal brain development: The role of maternal nutrition, exposures, and behaviors. *Journal of Pediatric Neurology, 4*(1), 1–9.

Masse, L., & Barnett, W. S. (2002). *A benefit cost analysis of the Abecedarian Early Childhood Intervention.* Retrieved September 13, 2011, from http://nieer.org/docs/?DocID=57

Masten, A. S., Burt, K. B., Roisman, G. I., Obradovic, J., Long, J. D., & Tellegen, A. (2004). Resources and resilience in the transition to adulthood: Continuity and change. *Development and Psychopathology, 16,* 1071–1094.

Mathambo, V., & Gibbs, A. (2009). Extended family childcare arrangements in a context of AIDS: Collapse or adaptation? *AIDS Care, 21,* 22–27.

Matheson, L. (1996). Valuing spirituality among Native American populations. *Counseling and Values, 41,* 51–58.

Mathew, P., & Mathew, J. (2003). Assessment and management of pain in infants. *Postgraduate Medical Journal, 79,* 438–443.

Matsumoto, D. (2007). Culture, context, and behavior. *Journal of Personality, 75*(6), 1285–1320.

Matsumoto-Grah, K. (1992). Diversity in the classroom: A checklist. In D. Byrnes & G. Kiger (Eds.), *Common bonds: Anti-bias teaching in a diverse society* (pp. 105–108). Olney, MD: Association for Childhood Education International.

Mattaini, M. (1997). *Clinical practice with individuals.* Washington, DC: NASW Press.

Matthews, D. A., McCullough, M. E., Larson, D. B., Koenig, H. G., Swyers, J. P., & Milano, M. G. (1998). Religious commitment and health status: A review of the research and implications for family medicine. *Archives of Family Medicine, 7*(2), 118–124.

Matto, H., Berry-Edwards, J., Hutchison, E. D., Bryant, S. A., & Waldbillig, A. (2006). An exploratory study on multiple intelligences and social work education. *Journal of Social Work Education, 42*(2), 405–416.

Maturana, H. (1988). Reality: The search for objectivity or the question for a compelling argument. *Irish Journal of Psychology, 9,* 25–82.

Maxwell, L. (2003). Home and school density effects on elementary school children: The role of spatial density. *Environment and Behavior, 35*(4), 566–578.

Mayer, K. U., Baltes, P. B., Baltes, M., Borchelt, M., Delius, J., Helmchen, H., et al. (1999). What do we know about old age and aging? Conclusions from the Berlin Aging Study. In P. B. Baltes & K. U. Mayer (Eds.), *The Berlin Aging Study: Aging from 70 to 100* (pp. 475–519). Cambridge, UK: Cambridge University Press.

Mayes, L., & Cohen, D. (2003). *The Yale child study guide to understanding your child's health and development from birth to adolescence.* New York: Little, Brown.

Mayo, K. R. (2009). *Creativity, spirituality, and mental health: Exploring connections.* Surrey, UK: Ashgate.

Mbori-Ngacha, D., Nduati, R., John, G., Reilly, M., Richardson, B., Mwatha, A., et al. (2001). Morbidity and mortality in breastfed and formula-fed infants of HIV-1-infected women: A randomized clinical trial. *Journal of the American Medical Association, 286*(19), 2413–2420.

McAdam, D. (1996a). Conceptual origins, current problems, future directions. In D. McAdam, J. McCarthy, & M. Zald (Eds.), *Comparative perspectives on social movements* (pp. 23–40). New York: Cambridge University Press.

McAdam, D. (1996b). The framing function of movement tactics: Strategic dramaturgy in the American civil rights movement. In D. McAdam, J. McCarthy, & M. Zald (Eds.), *Comparative perspectives on social movements* (pp. 338–355). New York: Cambridge University Press.

McAdam, D., McCarthy, J., & Zald, M. (1996). Introduction: Opportunities, mobilizing structures, and framing processes: Toward a synthetic, comparative perspective on social movements. In D. McAdam, J. McCarthy, & M. Zald (Eds.), *Comparative perspectives on social movements* (pp. 1–20). New York: Cambridge University Press.

McAdams, D. (2001). Generativity in midlife. In M. Lachman (Ed.), *Handbook of midlife development* (pp. 395–443). New York: Wiley.

McAdams, D. (2006). *The redemptive self: Stories Americans live by.* New York: Oxford University Press.

McAdams, D., & de St. Aubin, E. (1992). A theory of generativity and its assessment through self-report, behavioral acts, and narrative themes in autobiography. *Journal of Personality and Social Psychology, 62,* 1003–1015.

McAdams, D., & de St. Aubin, E. (Eds.). (1998). *Generativity and adult development: How and why we care for the next generation.* Washington, DC: American Psychological Association.

McAdams, D., Hart, H., & Maruna, S. (1998). The anatomy of generativity. In D. McAdams & E. de St. Aubin (Eds.), *Generativity and adult development: How and why we care for the next generation* (pp. 7–43). Washington, DC: American Psychological Association.

McAdoo, H. P. (2001). Parent and child relationships in African American families. In N. B. Webb (Ed.), *Culturally diverse parent–child and family relationships: A guide for social workers and other practitioners* (pp. 89–106). New York: Columbia University Press.

McAuley, E., Konopack, J. F., Motl, R. W., Morris, S., Doerksen, S., & Rosengren, K. (2006). Physical activity and quality of life in older adults: Influence of health status and self-efficacy. *Annuals of Behavioral Medicine, 31*(1), 99–103.

McAvoy, M. (1999). *The profession of ignorance: With constant reference to Socrates.* Lanham, NY: University Press of America.

McBee, L., Westreich, L., & Likourezos, A. (2004). A psychoeducational relaxation group for pain and stress management in the nursing home. *Journal of Social Work in Long-Term Care, 3*(1), 15–28.

McCabe, M. P., & Ricciardelli, L. A. (2003). Sociocultural influences on body image and body changes among adolescent boys and girls. *Journal of Social Psychology, 143*(1), 5–26.

McCarthy, J., & Zald, M. (1977). Resource mobilization in social movements: A partial theory. *American Journal of Sociology, 82,* 1212–1239.

McClure, E. B. (2000). A meta-analytic review of sex differences in facial expression processing and their development in infants, children and adolescents. *Psychological Bulletin, 126,* 424–453.

McClure, E. M., Nalubamba-Phiri, M., & Goldenberg, R. L. (2006). Stillbirth in developing countries. *International Journal of Gynaecology and Obstetrics: The Official Organ of the International Federation of Gynaecology and Obstetrics, 94*(2), 82–90.

McCrae, R., & Costa, P., Jr. (1990). *Personality in adulthood.* New York: Guilford Press.

McCrae, R., Costa, P., Jr., Ostendorf, F., Angleitner, A., Caprara, G., Barbaranelli, C., et al. (1999). Age differences in personality across the adult life span: Parallels in five cultures. *Developmental Psychology, 35*(2), 466.

McCreary, L., & Dancy, B. (2004). Dimensions of family functioning: Perspectives on low-income African American single-parent families. *Journal of Marriage and Family, 66,* 690–701.

McCubbin, H. I., & Figley, C. R. (1983). *Stress and the family, Vol. 1: Coping with normative transitions.* New York: Brunner/ Mazel.

McCubbin, H. I., & Patterson, J. M. (1983). The family stress process: The double ABCX model of adjustment and adaptation. In H. I. McCubbin, M. B. Sussman, & J. M. Patterson (Eds.), *Social stress and the family: Advances and developments in family stress theory and research* (pp. 7–37). New York: Haworth.

McDermott, M. L. (1997). Voting cues in low-information elections: Candidate gender as a social information variable in contemporary United States elections. *American Journal of Political Science, 41*(1), 270–283.

McDiarmid, M. A., Gardiner, P. M., & Jack, B. W. (2008, Supp. B). The clinical content of preconception care: Environmental exposure. *American Journal of Obstetrics and Gynecology, 199*(s6), S357–S361.

McDonnell, J., Thorson, N., Disher, S., Mathot-Buckner, C., Mendel, J., & Ray, L. (2003). The achievement of students with developmental disabilities and their peers without disabilities in inclusive settings: An exploratory study. *Education and Treatment of Children, 26*(3), 224–236.

McFague, S. (2001). *Life abundant: Rethinking theology and economy for a planet in peril.* Minneapolis, MN: Fortress Press.

McGlade, M., Saha, S., & Dahlstrom, M. (2004). The Latina paradox: An opportunity for restructuring prenatal care delivery. *American Journal of Public Health, 94*(12), 2062–2065.

McGoldrick, M. (2004). Legacies of loss: Multigenerational ripple effects. In F. Walsh & M. McGoldrick (Eds.), *Living beyond loss: Death in the family* (2nd ed., pp. 61–84). New York: Norton.

McGoldrick, M. (2005). Becoming a couple. In B. Carter & M. McGoldrick (Eds.), *The expanded family life cycle: Individual, family, and social perspectives* (3rd ed., pp. 231–248). Boston: Allyn & Bacon.

McGoldrick, M., Watson, M., & Benton, W. (2005). Siblings through the life cycle. In B. Carter & M. McGoldrick (Eds.), *The expanded family life cycle* (3rd ed., pp. 153–168). Boston: Allyn & Bacon.

McGovern, P. G., Legro, R. S., Myers, E. R., Bamhart, H. X., Carson, S. A., Diamond, M. P., et al. (2007). Utility of screening for other causes of infertility in women with "known" polycystic ovary syndrome. *Fertility and Sterility, 87*(2), 442–444.

McGregor, D. (1960). *The human side of enterprise.* New York: McGraw-Hill.

McHale, S., Crouter, A., & Whiteman, S. (2003). The family contexts of gender development in childhood and adolescence. *Social Development, 12,* 125–148.

McHale, S., Updegraff, K., Ji-Yeon, K., & Cansler, E. (2009). Cultural orientations, daily activities, and adjustment in Mexican American youth. *Journal of Youth and Adolescence, 38*(5), 627–641.

McInnis-Dittrich, K. (2009). *Social work with elders: A biopsychosocial approach to assessment and intervention* (2nd ed.). Boston: Allyn & Bacon.

McIntosh, H., Metz, E., & Youniss, J. (2005). Community service and identity formation in adolescence. In J. Mahoney, R. Larson, & J. Eccles (Eds.), *Organized activities as contexts of development: Extracurricular activities, after-school and community programs* (pp. 331–351). Mahwah, NJ: Erlbaum.

McIntosh, P. (2007). White privilege: Unpacking the invisible knapsack. In P. Rothenberg (Ed.), *Race, class, and gender in the United States* (6th ed., pp. 177–182). New York: Worth.

Mckee, K. J., Wilson, F., Chung, C. M., Hinchliff, S., Goudie, F., Elford, H., et al. (2005). Reminiscence, regrets and activity in older people in residential care: Associations with psychological health. *British Journal of Clinical Psychology, 44*(4), 543–561.

McKee-Ryan, F., Song, Z., Wanberg, C., & Kinicki, A. (2005). Psychological and physical well-being during unemployment: A meta-analytic study. *Journal of Applied Psychology, 90*(1), 53–76.

McKenna, J. (2002). Breastfeeding and bedsharing: Still useful (and important) after all these years. *Mothering, 114,* 28–37.

McKnight, J. (1995). *The careless society.* New York: Basic Books.

McKnight, P., Snyder, C., & Lopez, S. (2007). Western perspectives on positive psychology. In C. Snyder & S. Lopez (Eds.), *Positive psychology: The scientific and practical explorations of human strengths* (pp. 23–35). Thousand Oaks, CA: Sage.

McLachlan, H., & Forster, D. (2009). The safety of home birth: Is the evidence good enough? *Canadian Medical Association Journal, 181,* 6–7.

McLaurin, K. K., Hall, C. B., Jackson, E. A., Owens, O. V., & Mahadevia, P. J. (2009). Persistence of morbidity and cost differences between late-preterm and term infants during the first year of life. *Pediatrics, 123*(2), 653–659.

McLeod, J., & Almazan, E. (2003). Connections between childhood and adulthood. In J. Mortimer & M. Shanahan (Eds.), *Handbook of the life course* (pp. 391–411). New York: Kluwer.

McLeod, P., & Kettner-Polley, R. (2005). Psychodynamic perspectives on small groups. In M. S. Poole & A. B. Hollingshead (Eds.), *Theories of small groups* (pp. 63–99). Thousand Oaks, CA: Sage.

McLeskey, J., Hoppey, D., Williamson, P., & Rentz, T. (2004). Is inclusion an illusion? An examination of national and state trends toward the education of students with learning disabilities in general education classrooms. *Learning Disabilities Research & Practice, 19*(2), 109–115.

McMichael, P. (2004). *Development and social change: A global perspective* (3rd ed.). Thousand Oaks, CA: Pine Forge.

McMichael, P. (2008). *Development and social change: A global perspective* (4th ed.). Thousand Oaks, CA: Pine Forge.

McMillan, D. (1996). Sense of community. *Journal of Community Psychology, 24,* 315–325.

McMillan, D., & Chavis, D. (1986). Sense of community: A definition and theory. *Journal of Community Psychology, 14,* 6–23.

McMillan, J. C., & Raghavan, R. (2009). Pediatric to adult mental health service use of young people leaving the foster care system. *Journal of Adolescent Health, 44,* 7–13.

McPherson, M., Smith-Lovin, L., & Brashears, M. (2006). Social isolation in America: Changes in core discussion networks over two decades. *American Sociological Review, 71*(3), 353–375.

McQuaide, S. (1998). Women at midlife. *Social Work, 43*(1), 21–31.

McWhorter, J. (2000). *Losing the race: Self-sabotage in Black America.* New York: Free Press.

Meacham, R. B., Joyce, G. F., Wise, M., Kparker, A., & Niederberger, C. (2007). Male infertility. *Journal of Urology, 177*(6), 2058–2067.

Mead, G. H. (1934). *Mind, self and society.* Chicago: University of Chicago Press.

Mead, G. H. (1959). *The philosophy of the present.* LaSalle, IL: Open Court.

Mechelli, A., Crinion, J., Noppeney, U., O'Doherty, J., Ashburner, J., Frackowiak, R. S., et al. (2004). Structural plasticity in the bilingual brain. *Science, 431*(7010), 757.

Medical Glossary. (2011). *Genetic heterogeneity.* Retrieved April 6, 2011, from http://www.medicalglossary.org/variation_genetics_genetic_heterogeneity_definitions.html

Meek, M. (2000). Foreword. In K. Roskos & J. Christie (Ed.), *Play and literacy in early childhood: Research from multiple perspectives* (pp. vii–xiii). Mahwah, NJ: Erlbaum.

Mehall, K., Spinrad, T., Eisenberg, N., & Gaertner, B. (2009). Examining the relations of infant temperament and couples' marital satisfaction to mother and father involvement: A longitudinal study. *Fathering, 7*(1), 23–48.

Meier, A. (2007). Adolescent first sex and subsequent mental health. *American Journal of Sociology, 112*(6), 1811–1847.

Meinert, R. G., Pardeck, J. T., & Murphy, J. W. (Eds.). (1998). *Postmodernism, religion, and the future of social work.* Binghamton, NY: Haworth Press.

Meisenhelder, J. B., & Marcum, J. P. (2009). Terrorism, post-traumatic stress, coping strategies, and spiritual outcomes. *Journal of Religion and Health, 48*(1), 46–57.

Melby, T. (2009). Emergency contraception: Living up to its promise? *Contemporary Sexuality, 43*(5), 1–6.

Melchior, A., & Telle, K. (2001). Global income distribution, 1965–98: Convergence and marginalization. *Forum for Development Studies, 1,* 75–98.

Mello, A., Mello, M., Carpenter, L., & Price, L. (2003). Update on stress and depression: The role of the hypothalamic-pituitary-adrenal (HPA) axis. *Review of Brasilian Psychiatry, 25*(4), 231–238.

Melton, J. G. (1993). *Encyclopedia of American religion.* Detroit, MI: Gale Research.

Meltzoff, A. (2002). Imitation as a mechanism of social cognition: Origins of empathy theory of mind, and the representation of action. In U. Goswami (Ed.), *Blackwell handbook of childhood cognitive development* (pp. 6–25). Malden, MA: Blackwell.

Memmi, D. (2006). The nature of virtual communities. *AI & Society: Journal of Knowledge, Culture and Communication, 20,* 288–300.

Mendle, J., Turkheimer, E., & Emery, R. E. (2007). Detrimental psychological outcomes associated with early pubertal timing in adolescent girls. *Developmental Review, 27*(2), 151–171.

Mendola, P., Messer, L. C., & Rappazzo, K. (2008). Science linking environmental contaminant exposures with fertility and reproductive health impacts in the adult female. *Fertility and Sterility, 89*(2 Suppl), e81–94.

Menezes, P., Scazufca, M., Rodrigues, L., & Mann, A. (2000). Household crowding and compliance with outpatient treatment in patients with non-affective functional psychoses. *Social Psychiatry and Psychiatric Epidemiology, 35*(3), 116–120.

Merce, L. T., Barco, M. J., Alcazar, J. L., Sabatel, R., & Trojano, J. (2009). Intervillous and uteroplacental circulation in normal early pregnancy and early pregnancy loss assessed by 3-dimensional power Doppler angiography. *Journal of Obstetrics and Gynecology, 200*(3), 315.e1–8.

Mercer, J. A. (2006). Children as mystics, sages, and holy fools: Understanding the spirituality of children and its significance for clinical work. *Pastoral Psychology, 54*(5), 497–515.

Merten, J., Wickrama, K. A. S., & Williams, A. L. (2008). Adolescent obesity and young adult psychosocial outcomes: Gender and racial differences. *Journal of Youth & Adolescence, 37,* 1111–1122.

Messinger, L. (2004). Comprehensive community initiatives: A rural perspective. *Social Work, 49*(4), 529–624.

MetLife/National Alliance for Caregiving. (2004). *Miles away: The MetLife study of long-distance caregiving.* West Point, CT: MetLife.

Meyer, C. (1976). *Social work practice* (2nd ed.). New York: Free Press.

Meyer, C. (Ed.). (1983). *Clinical social work in an eco-systems perspective.* New York: Columbia University Press.

Meyer, C. (1993). *Assessment in social work practice.* New York: Columbia University Press.

Meyer, D. (2004). Tending the vineyard: Cultivating political process research. In J. Goodwin & J. Jasper (Eds.), *Rethinking social movements: Structure, meaning, and emotion* (pp. 47–59). Lanham, MD: Rowman & Littlefield.

Mickelson, K., Claffey, S., & Williams, S. (2006). The moderating role of gender and gender role attitudes on the link between spousal support and marital quality. *Sex Roles, 55,* 73–82.

Miers, R., & Fisher, A. (2002). Being church and community: Psychological sense of community in a local parish. In A. T. Fisher, C. C. Sonn, & B. J. Bishop (Eds.), *Psychological sense of community: Research applications and implications* (pp. 123–140). New York: Plenum.

Mijares, S. G., & Khalsa, G. S. (2005). *The psychospiritual clinician's handbook: Alternative methods for understanding and treating mental disorders.* New York: Haworth Reference Press.

Mikulas, W. L. (2002). *The integrative helper: Convergence of Eastern and Western traditions.* Pacific Grove, CA: Brooks/Cole Thompson Learning.

Mikulincer, M. (1994). *Human learned helplessness: A coping perspective.* New York: Plenum.

Miles, M. (1995). Disability in an Eastern religious context: Historical perspectives. *Disability and Society, 10,* 49–69.

Milevsky, A. (2005). Compensatory patterns of sibling support in emerging adulthood: Variations in loneliness, self-esteem, depression, and life satisfaction. *Journal of Social and Personal Relationships, 22,* 743–755.

Millennium Ecosystem Assessment. (2005). *Ecosystems and human well-being: Synthesis.* Washington, DC: Island Press.

Miller, J., & Holman, J. R. (2006). Contraception: The state of the art. *Consultant, 46*(4), 28.

Miller, L., Davies, M., & Greenwald, S. (2000). Religiosity and substance use and abuse among adolescents in the National Comorbidity Survey. *Journal of the American Academy of Child and Adolescent Psychiatry, 19*(9), 1190–1197.

Minami, H., & Tanaka, K. (1995). Social and environmental psychology: Transaction between physical space and group-dynamic processes. *Environment and Behavior, 27,* 43–55.

Minami, H., & Yamamoto, T. (2000). Cultural assumptions underlying concept-formation and theory building in environment-behavior research. In S. Wapner, J. Demick, T. Yamamoto, & H. Minami (Eds.), *Theoretical perspectives in environment-behavior research: Underlying assumptions, research problems, and methodologies* (pp. 237–246). New York: Kluwer Academic.

Mind. (2007). *Ecotherapy: The green agenda for mental health.* Retrieved October 9, 2009, from http://www.mind.org.uk/mindweek

Miringoff, M. (2003). *2003 Index of Social Health: Monitoring the social well-being of the nation.* Unpublished paper. Tarrytown, NY: Fordham Institute for Innovation in Social Policy.

Miringoff, M. L., & Miringoff, M. (1999). *The social health of the nation: How America is really doing.* New York: Oxford University Press.

Miringoff, M. L., Miringoff, M., & Opdycke, S. (1996). The growing gap between standard economic indicators and the nation's social health. *Challenge,* 17–22.

Miringoff, M. L., & Opdycke, S. (2008). *America's social health: Putting social issues back on the public agenda.* Armonk, NY: M.E. Sharpe.

Mischey, E. J. (1981). Faith, identity, and personality in late adolescence. *Character Potential: A Record of Research, 9*(4), 175–185.

Mishel, L., Bernstein, J., & Allegretto, S. (2006). *The state of working America 2006/2007.* Washington, DC: Economic Policy Institute.

Mistry, R., Lowe, D., Renner, A., & Chien, N. (2008). Expanding the Family Economic Stress Model: Insights from a mixed-methods approach. *Journal of Marriage and Family, 70*(1), 196–209.

Mistry, R., Vandewater, E., Huston, A., & McLoyd, V. (2002). Economic well-being and children's social adjustment: The role of family process in an ethnically diverse low-income sample. *Child Development, 73,* 935–951.

Miyake, K., Campos, J., Kagan, J., & Bradshaw, D. (1986). Issues in socioemotional development in Japan. In H. Azuma, I. Hakuta, & H. Stevenson (Eds.), *Dodoma: Child development and education in Japan* (pp. 239–261). New York: W. H. Freeman.

Moen, P. (2003). Midcourse: Navigating retirement and a new life stage. In J. Mortimer & M. Shanahan (Eds.), *Handbook of the life course* (pp. 269–291). New York: Kluwer Academic/Plenum.

Mohai, P., & Saha, R. (2007). Racial inequality in the distribution of hazardous waste: A national-level reassessment. *Social Problems, 54*(3), 343–370.

Möller, K., & Stattin, H. (2001). Are close relationships in adolescence linked with partner relationships in midlife? A longitudinal prospective study. *International Journal of Behavioral Development, 25*(1), 69–77.

Monette, D., Sullivan, T., & DeJong, C. (2008). *Applied social research: A tool for the human services* (7th ed.). Belmont, CA: Brooks/Cole.

Monsour, M. (2002). *Women and men as friends: Relationships across the life span in the 21st century.* Mahwah, NJ: Erlbaum.

Montague, D., Magai, C., Consedine, N., & Gillespie, M. (2003). Attachment in African American and European American older adults: The roles of early life socialization and religiosity. *Attachment and Human Development, 5,* 188–214.

Monte, C., & Sollod, R. (2003). *Beneath the mask: An introduction to theories of personality* (7th ed.). Hoboken, NJ: Wiley.

Montgomery, R. J. V., & Kosloski, K. (1994). A longitudinal analysis of nursing home placement for dependent elders cared for by spouses vs. adult children. *Journal of Gerontology: Social Science, 49,* S62–S74.

Montgomery, R. J. V., & Kosloski, K. (2000). Family caregiving: Change, continuity and diversity. In P. Lawton & R. Bubenstein (Eds.), *Alzheimer's disease and related dementias: Strategies in care and research.* New York: Springer.

Montgomery, R. J. V., & Kosloski, K. (2009). Caregiving as a process of changing identity: Implications for caregiver support. *Generations, 33,* 47–52.

Moody, H. R. (2010). *Aging: Concepts and controversies* (6th ed.). Thousand Oaks, CA: Pine Forge.

Moon, S., Kang, S., & An, S. (2008). Predictors of immigrant children's school achievement: A comparative study. *Research in Childhood Education, 23*(3), 278–289.

Moore, D. (1987). Parent–adolescent separation: The construction of adulthood by late adolescents. *Developmental Psychology, 23,* 298–307.

Moore, E. (1981). A prison environment's effect on health care service demands. *Journal of Environmental Systems, 11,* 17–34.

Moore, K. A., Redd, Z., Burkhauser, M, Mbwana, K., & Collins, A. (2009). *Children in poverty: Trends, consequences, and policy options.* Washington, DC: Child Trends. Retrieved January 19, 2010, from http://www.childtrends.org/Files/Child_Trends-2009_04_07_RB_ChildreninPoverty.pdf

Mor Barak, M. (2005). *Managing diversity: Toward a globally inclusive workplace.* Thousand Oaks, CA: Sage.

Mor Barak, M., & Travis, D. (2010). Diversity and organizational performance. In Y. Hasenfeld (Ed.), *Human services as complex organizations* (2nd ed., pp. 341–378). Thousand Oaks, CA: Sage.

Moreau, C., Cleland, K., & Trussell, J. (2007). Contraceptive discontinuation attributed to method dissatisfaction in the United States. *Contraception, 76*(4), 267–272.

Moren-Cross, J. L., & Lin, N. (2006). Social networks and health. In R. H. Binstock & L. K. George (Eds.), *Handbook of aging and the social sciences* (6th ed., pp. 111–126). Amsterdam: Elsevier.

Morgan, A. (2000). *What is narrative therapy?* Adelaide, South Australia: Dulwich Centre Publications.

Morgan, G. (2006). *Images of organizations* (Updated ed.). Thousand Oaks, CA: Sage.

Morgan, J. P. (2002). Dying and grieving are journeys of the spirit. In R. B. Gilbert (Ed.), *Health care and spirituality: Listening, assessing, caring* (pp. 53–64). Amityville, NY: Baywood.

Morgan, L., & Kunkel, S. (1996). *Aging: The social context.* Thousand Oaks, CA: Pine Forge.

Morreale, D. (Ed.). (1998). *The complete guide to Buddhist America.* Boston: Shambhala.

Morris, A. (2000). Reflections on social movement theory: Criticisms and proposals. *Contemporary Sociology, 29*(3), 445–454.

Morris, A. (2004). Reflections on social movement theory: Criticisms and proposals. In J. Goodwin & J. Jasper (Eds.), *Rethinking social movements* (pp. 233–246). Lanham, MD: Rowman & Littlefield.

Morris, J. C. (2006). Mild cognitive impairment in early-stage Alzheimer disease. *Archives of Neurology, 63*(1), 15–16.

Morrison, J. W., & Bordere, T. (2001). Supporting biracial children's identity development. *Childhood Education, 77*(3), 134–138.

Mortimer, J. T., & Finch, M. D. (1996). *Adolescents, work, and family: An intergenerational developmental analysis.* Thousand Oaks, CA: Sage.

Morton, C. H., & Hsu, C. (2007). Contemporary dilemmas in American childbirth education: Findings from a comparative ethnographic study. *Contemporary Dilemmas, 16*(4), 25–37.

Mosher, W., Chandra, A., & Jones, J. (2005, September 15). Sexual behavior and selected measures. Men and women 15–44 years of age, United States, 2002. *Vital and Health Statistics, 362,* 1–56. Retrieved November 20, 2006, from http://www.cdc.gov/nchs/data/ad/ad362.pdf

Moshman, D. (1998). Cognitive development beyond childhood. In D. Kuhn & R. Siegler (Eds.), *Handbook of child psychology: Vol. 2. Cognition, perception, and language* (5th ed., pp. 947–978). New York: Wiley.

Moss, T. (2004, November). *Adolescent pregnancy and childbearing in the United States.* Retrieved August 4, 2006, from http://www.advocatesforyouth.org/PUBLICATIONS/factsheet/fsprechd.htm

Moyer, K. (1974). Discipline. In K. Moyer, *You and your child: A primer for parents* (pp. 40–61). Chicago: Nelson-Hall.

Moyers, B. (1993). *Healing and the mind.* New York: Doubleday.

Mueller, M., Wilhelm, B., & Elder, G. (2002). Variations in grandparenting. *Research on Aging, 24*(3), 360–388.

Mueller, P. C., Plevak, D. J., & Rummans, T. A. (2001). Religious involvement, spirituality, and medicine: Implications for clinical practice. *Mayo Clinical Proceedings, 76*(12), 1225–1235.

Muir, D., & Lee, K. (2003). The still face effect: Methodological issues and new applications. *Infancy, 4,* 483–491.

Mullings, L. (2005). Interrogating racism: Toward an antiracist anthropology. *Annual Review of Anthropology, 34,* 667–693.

Munakata, Y., McClelland, J., Johnson, M., & Siegler, R. (1997). Rethinking infant knowledge: Toward an adaptive process account of successes and failures in object permanence tasks. *Psychological Review, 104*(4), 618–713.

Murphy-Berman, V., & Berman, J. (2002). Cross-cultural differences in perception of distribution of justice: A comparison of Hong Kong and Indonesia. *Journal of Cross-Cultural Psychology, 33,* 1157–1170.

Murray, B. (2001). Living wage comes of age: An increasingly sophisticated movement has put opponents on the defense. *The Nation, 273*(4), 24.

Murray, C., & Herrnstein, R. (1994). *The bell curve: Intelligence and class structure in American life.* New York: Free Press.

Murray, J. A. (2001). Loss as a universal concept: A review of the literature to identify common aspects of loss in diverse situations. *Journal of Loss and Trauma, 6,* 219–241.

Myers, B. K. (1997). *Young children and spirituality.* New York: Routledge.

Naidoo, R., & Adamowicz, W. (2006). Modeling opportunity costs of conservation in transitional landscapes. *Conservation Biology, 20*(2), 490–500.

Nair, A., Stega, J., Smith, R. J., & Del Priore, G. (2008). Uterus transplant. *Annals of the New York Academy of Sciences, 1127,* 83–91.

Naleppa, M. J. (1996). Families and the institutionalized elderly: A review. *Journal of Gerontological Social Work, 27,* 87–111.

Nansel, T., Overpeck, M., Pilla, R., Ruan, W., Simons-Morton, B., & Scheidt, P. (2001). Bullying behaviors among U.S. youth: Prevalence and association with psychosocial adjustment. *Journal of the American Medical Association, 285*(16), 2094–2100.

Narberhaus, A., Segarra, D., Caldu, X., Gimenez, M., Junque, C., Pueyo, R., et al. (2007). Gestational age at preterm birth in relation to corpus callosum and general cognitive outcome in adolescents. *Journal of Child Neurology, 22*(6), 761–765.

Natale, S. M., & Neher, J. C. (1997). Inspiriting the workplace: Developing a values-based management system. In D. P. Bloch & L. J. Richmond (Eds.), *Connections between spirit and work in career development: New approaches and practical perspectives* (pp. 237–255). Palo Alto, CA: Davies-Black.

Nathanson, I. G. (1995). Divorce and women's spirituality. *Journal of Divorce and Remarriage, 22,* 179–188.

National Alliance to End Homelessness. (2005, May 16). *Alliance online news.* Retrieved August 31, 2006, from http://www.endhomelessness.org

National Alliance to End Homelessness. (2009). *Geography of Homelessness, Part 1: Defining the spectrum.* Retrieved October 16, 2009, from http://www.endhomelessness.org/content/article/detail/2437

National Association of Child Care Resource and Referral Agencies. (2006). *Piggy bank: Parents and the high price of child care.* Retrieved December 30, 2006, from http://www.naccrra.org/docs/policy/breaking_the_piggy_bank.pdf

National Association of Social Workers. (1996). *Code of ethics.* Washington, DC: Author.

National Association of Social Workers. (1999). *Code of ethics* (Rev. ed.). Washington, DC: Author.

National Association of Social Workers. (2002). *NASW priorities on faith-based human services initiatives.* Retrieved February 26, 2010, from http://www.socialworkers.org/advocacy/positions/faith.asp

National Campaign to Prevent Teen Pregnancy. (2002). *General facts and stats.* Retrieved August 26, 2002, from http://www.teenpregnancy.org/resources/data/genlfact.asp

National Campaign to Prevent Teen and Unplanned Pregnancy. (2008). *Unplanned pregnancy in the United States.* Washington, DC: Author.

National Center for Children in Poverty. (2008). *Low-income children in the United States.* Retrieved January 19, 2010, from http://www.nccp.org/publications/pub_851.html

National Center for Clinical Infant Programs. (1992). How community violence affects children, parents, and practitioners. *Public Welfare, 50*(4), 25–35.

National Center for Complementary and Alternative Medicine. (n.d.). *What is CAM?* Retrieved February 26, 2010, from http://nccam.nih.gov/health/whatiscam/overview.htm

National Center for Education Statistics. (2011). *Trends in high school dropout and completion rates in the United States: 1972–2008.* Retrieved August 22, from http://nces.ed.gov/pubs2011/droput08/index.asp

National Center for Health Statistics (NCHS). (2004, October 6). Obesity still a major problem, New data show: Prevalence of overweight and obesity among children and adolescents: United States, 1999–2002. Atlanta: Author.

National Coalition for the Homeless. (2009a). *How many people experience homelessness?* Retrieved May 17, 2010, from http://www.nationalhomeless.org/factsheets/How_Many.html

National Coalition for the Homeless. (2009b). *Who is homeless?* Retrieved October 16, 2009, from http://www.nationalhomeless.org/factsheets/who.html

National Coalition for the Homeless. (2009c). *Why are people homeless?* Retrieved October 16, 2009, from http://www.nationalhomeless.org/factsheets/why.html

National Conference of State Legislatures. (2009). *State laws regarding marriages between first cousins.* Retrieved December 9, 2009, from http://www.ncsl.org/default.aspx?tabid=4266

National Council on the Aging. (n.d.). *Facts about older Americans.* Retrieved June 29, 2002, from http://www.ncoa.org/press/facts.html

National Gang Center. (2010). *About the National Gang Center.* Retrieved February 8, 2010, from http://www.nationalgangcenter.gov

National Head Start Association. (2010). *National Head Start Association 2010 policy agenda.* Retrieved September 13, 2011, from http://www.nhsa.org/files/static_page_files/8E79264A-1D09-3519-AD3D253EB15B8028/Final_NHSA_Three_Year_Research_Agenda.pdf

National Health Statistics. (2006). *Health United States 2005 with chartbook on trends in the health of Americans.* Hyattsville, MD: Centers for Disease Control and Prevention.

National Hospice and Palliative Care Organization. (2008). *NHPCO facts and figures.* Retrieved July 10, 2009, from http://www.nhpco.org

National Institute of Child Health and Human Development. (2007). *What is puberty?* Retrieved January 19, 2010, from http://www.nichd.nih.gov/health/topics/puberty.cfm

National Institute of Diabetes and Digestive and Kidney Diseases (NIDDK), National Diabetes Information Clearing House (NDIC). (2008, June). *National Diabetes statistics, 2007.*

Retrieved December 4, 2009, from http://diabetes.niddk.nih.gov/dm/pubs/statistics/index.htm#allages

National Institute of Diabetes and Digestive and Kidney Diseases (NIDDK). (2011, July). *National diabetes statistics, 2011*. Retrieved August 16, 2011, from http://diabetes.niddk.nih.gov/dm/pubs/statistics.Index.aspy

National Institute of Mental Health. (2000). *Depression in children and adolescents*. Bethesda, MD: Author.

National Institute of Neurological Disorders and Stroke. (2006). *Post-polio syndrome fact sheet* (NIH Publication No. 06–4030) [Electronic version]. Bethesda, MD: Author. Retrieved October 20, 2006, from http://www.ninds.nih.gov/disorders/post_polio/detail_post_polio.htm

National Institute of Neurological Disorders and Stroke. (2010). *Parkinson's disease: Hope through research*. Retrieved May 21, 2010, from http://www.ninds.nih.gov/disorders/parkinsons_disease/detail_parkinsons_disease.htm

National Institute on Aging. (2011). *Alzheimer's disease genetics fact sheet*. Retrieved April 6, 2011, from http://www.nia.nih.gov/Alzheimers/Publications/geneticsfs.htm

National Institute on Aging, National Institute of Health (NIA/NIH). (2009). *An aging world*. Retrieved May 21, 2010, from http://www.nia.nih.gov/ResearchInformation/ExtramuralPrograms/BehavioralAndSocialResearch/an-aging-world.htm

National Institute on Drug Abuse. (2006). *Monitoring the Future survey: Overview of key findings 2006*. Retrieved September 13, 2011, from http://www.monitoringthefuture.org/pubs/monographs/overview2006.pdf

National Institutes of Health. (2001). *Vital connections: Science of mind–body interactions*. A report on the interdisciplinary conference held at NIH March 26–28, 2001. Bethesda, MD: Author.

National Marriage Project. (2006). *The state of our unions 2006: The social health of marriage in America*. Piscataway, NJ: Rutgers, The State University of New Jersey: Author.

National Network of Libraries of Medicine. (2008). *Health literacy*. Retrieved January 1, 2010, from http://nnlm.gov/outreach/consumer/hlthlit.html

National Religious Partnership for the Environment. (n.d.). *What is the partnership?* Retrieved May 17, 2010, from http://www.nrpe.org/whatisthepartnership/index.html

National Research Council. (1990). *Who cares for America's children?* Washington, DC: Author.

National Sleep Foundation. (2005). *Drowsy driving: Facts and stats*. Retrieved November 15, 2006, from http://www.sleepfoundation.org

National Sleep Foundation. (2006). *2006 sleep in America poll: Highlights and key findings*. Retrieved November 15, 2006, from http://www.sleepfoundation.org

National Women's Health Information Center. (2009). *Infertility*. Retrieved March 30, 2011, from http://www.womenshealth.gov/faq/infertility.cfm

National Youth Gang Center. (2009). *National Youth Gang Survey analysis*. Retrieved January 21, 2010, from http://www.nationalgangcenter.gov/Survey-Analysis

Navarro, V., Muntaner, C., Borrell, C., Benach, J., Quiroga, A., Rodriguez-Manz, M., et al. (2006). Politics and health outcomes. *The Lancet, 368*(9540), 1033–1037.

Nazzi, T., & Gopnik, A. (2001). Linguistic cognitive abilities in infancy: When does language become a tool for categorization? *Cognition, 80*, B11–B20.

Needham, A. (2001). Object recognition and object segregation in 4.5-month-old infants. *Journal of Experimental Child Psychology, 78*, 3–24.

Nelson, C. A. (1999). How important are the first three years of life? *Applied Developmental Science, 3*(4), 235–238.

Nelson, C. A. (2000). The neurobiological basis of early intervention. In J. P. Shonkoff & S. J. Meisels (Eds.), *Handbook of early childhood intervention* (2nd ed., pp. 204–227). New York: Cambridge University Press.

Nelson, C. A. (2001). The development and neural bases of face recognition. *Infant and Child Development, 10*, 3–18.

Nelson-Becker, H. B. (2006). Voices of resilience: Older adults in hospice care. *Journal of Social Work in End-of-Life & Palliative Care, 2*(3), 87–106.

Nepomnaschy, P., Welch, K., McConnell, D., Low, B., Strassmann, B., & England, B. (2006). Cortisol levels and very early pregnancy loss in humans. *Proceedings of National Academy of Science USA, 103*(10), 3938–3942.

Nesdale, D. (2004). Social identity processes and children's ethnic prejudice. In M. Bennett & M. Sani (Eds.), *The development of the social self* (pp. 219–245). New York: Psychology Press.

Netting, F. E., O'Connor, M. K., & Singletary, J. (2007). Finding homes for their dreams: Strategies founders and program initiators use to position and sustain faith-based programs. *Families in Society: The Journal of Contemporary Social Services, 88*(1), 19–29.

Nettles, S., Mucherah, W., & Jones, D. (2000). Understanding resilience: The role of social resources. *Journal of Education for Students Placed at Risk, 5*(1&2), 47–60.

Neufeld, P., & Knipemann, K. (2001). Gateway to wellness: An occupational therapy collaboration with the National Multiple Sclerosis Society. *Occupational Therapy in Health Care, 12*(3/4), 67–84.

Neugarten, B. L., & Gutmann, D. (1968). Age-sex roles and personality in middle age: A thematic apperception study. In B. L. Neugarten (Ed.), *Middle age and aging* (pp. 58–71). Chicago: University of Chicago Press.

Neugarten, B. L., Havighurst, R. J., & Tobin, S. S. (1968). Personality and patterns of aging. In B. L. Neugarten

(Ed.), *Middle age and aging*. Chicago: University of Chicago Press.

Neugarten, B. L., & Weinstein, K. K. (1964). The changing American grandparent. *Journal of Marriage and the Family, 26,* 199–204.

Neugebauer, R., Kline, J., Markowitz, J. C., Blelerg, K. L., Baxi, L., Rosing, M. A., et al. (2006). Pilot randomized controlled trial of interpersonal counseling for subsyndromal depression following miscarriage. *The Journal of Clinical Psychiatry, 67*(8), 1299–1304.

New concepts on the causes of recurrent miscarriages. (2006). *Reproductive Biomedicine Online, 12*(3), 291–291. Retrieved September 13, 2011, from http://www.ncbi.nlm.nih.gov/pubmed/16569313

New York City Commission on Human Rights. (2003, Summer). *Discrimination against Muslims, Arabs, and South Asians in New York City since 9/11*. Retrieved February 26, 2010, from http://www.nyc.gov/html/cchr/pdf/sur_report.pdf

Newcomb, N., & Dubas, J. S. (1992). A longitudinal study of predictors of spatial ability in adolescent females. *Child Development, 63,* 37–46.

Newell, P. (1997). A cross-cultural examination of favorite places. *Environment and Behavior, 29,* 495–514.

Newman, B., & Newman, P. (2009). *Development through life: A psychosocial approach* (10th ed.). Belmont, CA: Thomson.

Newman, D. (2006). *Sociology: Exploring the architecture of everyday life* (6th ed.). Thousand Oaks, CA: Pine Forge.

Newman, D. (2008). *Sociology: Exploring the architecture of everyday life* (7th ed.). Thousand Oaks, CA: Sage.

Newman, K. (2008). Ties that bind: Cultural interpretations of delayed adulthood in Western Europe and Japan. *Sociological Forum, 23*(4), 645–669.

News Corporation. (2006). News Corporation: Creating and distributing top-quality news, sports and entertainment around the world. Retrieved October 13, 2006, from http://www.newscorp.com/operations

News Corporation. (2010). *News Corporation: Operations*. Retrieved February 23, 2010, from http://www.newscorp.com/operations

Nguyen, P. (2008). Perceptions of Vietnamese fathers' acculturation levels, parenting styles, and mental health outcome in Vietnamese American adolescent immigrants. *Social Work, 53*(4), 337–346.

Nguyen, P., & Cheung, M. (2009). Parenting styles as perceived by Vietnamese American adolescents. *Child and Adolescent Social Work Journal, 26,* 505–581.

Nhu, T. N., Merialdi, M., Abdel-Aleem, H., Carroli, G., Purwar, M., Zavaleta, N., et al. (2006). Causes of stillbirth and early neonatal deaths: Data from 7993 pregnancies in six developing countries. *Bulletin of the World Health Organization, 84,* 699–705.

Nichols, M., & Schwartz, R. (2006). *Family therapy: Concepts and methods* (7th ed.). Boston: Allyn & Bacon.

Nicotera, N. (2005). The child's view of neighborhood: Assessing a neglected element in direct social work practice. *Journal of Human Behavior in the Social Environment, 11*(3/4), 105–133.

Niculescu, M. D., & Lupu, D. S. (2009). High fat diet–induced maternal obesity alters fetal hippocampal development. *International Journal of Developmental Neuroscience, 27*(7), 627–633.

Nield, L. S., Cakan, N., & Kamat, D. (2007). A practical approach to precocious puberty. *Clinical Pediatrics, 46*(4), 299–306.

Niemann, S. (2005). Persons with disabilities. In M. T. Burke, J. C. Chauvin, & J. G. Miranti (Eds.), *Religious and spiritual issues in counseling: Applications across diverse populations* (pp. 105–133). New York: Brunner-Routledge.

Nishino, H., & Larson, R. (2003). Japanese adolescents' free time: Juku, Bakatsu, and government efforts to create more meaningful leisure. In S. Verma & R. Larson (Eds.), *Examining adolescent leisure time across cultures: New directions for child and adolescent development* (No. 99, pp. 23–35). San Francisco: Jossey-Bass.

Nishitani, S., Miyamura, T., Tagawa, M., Sumi, M., Takase, R., Doi, H., et al. (2009). The calming effect of a maternal breast milk odor on the human newborn infant. *Neuroscience Research, 63*(1), 66–71.

Nobles, W. W. (1980). African philosophy: Foundations for Black psychology. In R. L. Jones (Ed.), *Black psychology* (2nd ed., pp. 23–36). New York: Harper & Row.

Noddings, N. (1984). *Caring: A feminine approach to ethics and moral education*. Berkeley: University of California Press.

Noddings, N. (2002). *Starting at home: Caring and social policy*. Berkeley: University of California Press.

Noddings, N. (2005). *Educating citizens for global awareness*. New York: Teacher's College Press.

Nojomi, M., Akbarian, A., & Ashory-Moghadam, S. (2006). Burden of abortion: Induced or spontaneous. *Archives of Iranian Medicine, 9*(10), 39–45.

Nomaguchi, K., & Milkie, M. (2005). Costs and rewards of children: The effects of becoming a parent on adults' lives. In T. Chibucos & R. Leite, with D. Weis (Eds.), *Readings in family theory* (pp. 140–164). Thousand Oaks, CA: Sage.

Nord, M., Andrews, M., & Carlson, S. (2009). *Household food insecurity in the United States, 2008*. Washington, DC: U.S. Department of Agriculture. Retrieved February 17, 2010, from http://www.thefoodbank.org/documents/usdafoodinsecurity08.pdf

Northcut, T. (2000). Constructing a place for religion and spirituality in psychodynamic practice. *Clinical Social Work Journal, 28*(2), 155–169.

Northridge, M., & Sclar, E. (2003). A joint urban planning and public health framework: Contributions to health impact assessment. *American Journal of Public Health, 93,* 118–121.

Norton, D. (1993). Diversity, early socialization, and temporal development: The dual perspective revisited. *Social Work, 38*(1), 82–90.

Nourhashemi, F., Sinclair, A., & Vellas, B. (2006). *Clinical aspects of Alzheimer's disease: Principles and practice of geriatric medicine* (4th ed.). Sussex, UK: Wiley.

Novak, G., & Pelaez, M. (2004). *Child and adolescent development: A behavioral system approach.* Thousand Oaks, CA: Sage.

Novak, J. C., & Broom, B. (1995). *Maternal and child health nursing.* St. Louis, MO: Mosby.

Novins, D., Beals, J., Shore, J., & Manson, S. (1996). Substance abuse treatment of American Indian adolescents: Comorbid symptomatology, gender differences, and treatment patterns. *Child & Adolescent Psychiatry, 35*(12), 1593–1601.

Novins, D., Fleming, C., Beals, J., & Manson, S. (2000). Commentary: Quality of alcohol, drug, and mental health services for American Indian children and adolescents. *American Journal of Medicine Quarterly, 15*(4), 148–156.

Nowell, B., Berkowitz, S., Deacon, Z., & Foster-Fishman, P. (2006). Revealing the cues within community places: Stories of identity, history, and possibility. *American Journal of Community Psychology, 37*(1/2), 29–46.

Nursing. (2005). Clinical rounds: Maladies by the numbers. *Nursing, 35*(9), 35.

Ny, K., Loy, J., Gudmunson, C., & Cheong, W. (2009). Gender differences in marital and life satisfaction among Chinese Malaysians. *Sex Roles, 60,* 33–43.

Nyamathi, A., Leake, B., Keenan, C., & Gelberg, L. (2000). Type of social support among homeless women: Its impact on psychosocial resources, health and health resources, and the use of health services. *Nursing Research, 49*(6), 318–326.

Nybell, L., Shook, J., & Finn, J. (Eds.). (2009). *Childhood, youth, and social work in transformation: Implications for policy and practice.* New York: Columbia University Press.

Nye, I. (Ed.). (1982). *Family relationships: Rewards and costs.* Beverly Hills, CA: Sage.

Nye, R., & Hay, D. (1996). Identifying children's spirituality: How do you start without a starting point? *British Journal of Religious Education, 18*(3), 144–154.

Oakes, J. (1985). *Keeping track of tracking: How schools structure inequality.* New Haven, CT: Yale University Press.

Oakes, J., & Lipton, M. (1992). Detracking schools: Early lessons from the field. *Phi Delta Kappan, 73,* 448–454.

Oates, S. (2008). *Introduction to media and politics.* London: Sage.

Obama, B. (2009). *Taking on education.* Retrieved May 21, 2009, from http://www.whitehouse.gov/blog/09/03/10/taking-on-education

Oberschall, A. (1996). Opportunities and framing in the Eastern European revolts of 1989. In D. McAdam, J. McCarthy, & M. Zald (Eds.), *Comparative perspectives on social movements: Political opportunities, mobilizing structures, and cultural framings* (pp. 93–121). New York: Cambridge University Press.

O'Brien, P. (1992). Social work and spirituality: Clarifying the concept for practice. *Spirituality and Social Work Journal, 3*(1), 2–5.

O'Brien, P. (2001). Claiming our soul: An empowerment group for African-American women in prison. *Journal of Progressive Human Services, 12*(1), 35–51.

Obst, P., & Tham, N. (2009). Helping the soul: The relationship between connectivity and well-being within a church community. *Journal of Community Psychology, 37*(3), 342–361.

Obst, P., & White, K. (2004). Revisiting the Sense of Community Index: A confirmatory factor analysis. *Journal of Community Psychology, 32*(6), 691–705.

Obst, P., & White, K. (2007). Choosing to belong: The influence of choice on social identification and psychological sense of community. *Journal of Community Psychology, 35*(1), 77–90.

Obst, P., Zinkiewicz, L., & Smith, S. (2002a). Sense of community in science fiction fandom, Part 1. Understanding sense of community in an international community of interest. *Journal of Community Psychology, 30*(1), 87–103.

Obst, P., Zinkiewicz, L., & Smith, S. (2002b). Sense of community in science fiction fandom, Part 2. Comparing neighborhood and interest group sense of community. *Journal of Community Psychology, 30*(1), 105–117.

Ochshorn, J., & Cole, E. (Eds.). (1995). *Women's spirituality, women's lives.* Binghamton, NY: Haworth Press.

O'Connor, M. K., & Netting, F. E. (2009). *Organization practice: A guide to understanding human service organizations* (2nd ed.). Hoboken, NJ: Wiley.

Odent, M. (1998). *Men's role in the labour room.* Conference presentation at the Royal Society of Medicine, London.

Odent, M. (1999). Is the participation of the father at birth dangerous? *Midwifery Today, 51,* 23–24.

Odgers, C. Moffitt, T., Tach, L., Sampson, R., Taylor, A., Matthews, C., et al. (2009). The protective effects of neighborhood collective efficacy on British children growing up in deprivation: A developmental analysis. *Developmental Psychology, 45*(4), 942–957.

OECD Family Database. (2008a). *Cohabitation rate and prevalence of other forms of partnership.* Retrieved December 8, 2009, from http://www.oecd.org/els/social/family/database

OECD Family Database. (2008b, December 15). *SF6: Share of births outside marriage and teenage births.* Organisation for Economic Co-operation and Development: Social Policy Division Directorate of Employment, Labour, and Social Affairs. Retrieved November 1, 2009, from http://www.oecd.org/dataoecd/38/6/40278615.pdf

Of Meat, Mexicans and Social Mobility. (2006, June 17). *The Economist, 379*(8482), 31–32.

Office of Disease Prevention & Health Promotion, U.S. Department of Health and Human Services. (2009). *Adolescent health.* Retrieved February 8, 2010, from http://www.healthypeople.gov/hp2020/Objectives/TopicArea.aspx?id=11&TopicArea=Adolescence

Office of Faith-based and Neighborhood Partnerships. (2009). *The work of the office: Office of Faith-Based and Neighborhood Partnerships.* Retrieved May 17, 2010, from http://www.whitehouse.gov/blog/2009/11/12/work-office-white-house-office-faith-based-and-neighborhood-partnerships

Office of the Special Representative of the Secretary-General for Children and Armed Conflict (OSRSG-CAAC) & United Nations Children's Fund. (2009). *Machel Study 10-year strategic review: Children and conflict in a changing world.* New York: UNICEF. Retrieved January 19, 2010, from http://www.unicef.org/publications/index_49985.html

Ogbu, J. U. (1994). Overcoming racial barriers to equal access. In K. I. Goodland & P. Keating (Eds.), *Access to knowledge: The continuing agenda for our nation's schools* (pp. 59–90). New York: The College Board.

Ogbu, J. U. (2003). *Black American students in an affluent suburb: A study of academic disengagement.* Mahwah, NJ: Erlbaum.

Ogden, C., Carroll, M., Curtin, L., Lamb, M., & Flegal, K. (2010). Prevalence of high body mass index in U.S. children and adolescents, 2007–2008. *Journal of the American Medical Association, 303*(3), 242–249.

Ogden, C., Carroll, M. D., Curtin, L. R., McDowell, M. A., Tabak, C. J., & Flegal, K. M. (2006). Prevalence of overweight and obesity in the United States, 1999–2004. *Journal of the American Medical Association, 295,* 1549–1555.

O'Hare, W. (2009). The forgotten fifth: Child poverty in rural America. *Carsey Institute Report, No. 10.* University of New Hampshire. Retrieved January 19, 2010, from http://www.carseyinstitute.unh.edu/publications/Report-OHare-ForgottenFifth.pdf

O'Keefe, M. (1994). Adjustment of children from maritally violent homes. *Families in Society, 75,* 403–415.

O'Keefe, M. (1997). Adolescents' exposure to community and school violence: Prevalence and behavioral correlates. *Journal of Adolescent Health, 20,* 368–376.

Oken, E., Wright, R. O., Kleinman, K. P., Bellinger, D., Amarasiriwardena, H. H., Rich-Edwards, J. W., et al. (2005). Maternal fish consumption, hair mercury, and infant cognition in a U.S. cohort. *Environmental Health Perspectives, 113*(10), 1376–1381.

Oldmeadow, J., Platow, M., Foddy, M., & Anderson, D. (2003). Self-categorization, status, and social influence. *Social Psychology Quarterly, 66*(2), 138–152.

O'Leary, V. E., & Bhaju, J. (2006). Resilience and empowerment. In J. Worell & C. D. Goodheart (Eds.), *Handbook of girls' and women's psychological health: Gender and well-being across the life span* (pp. 157–165). New York: Oxford Press.

Oliver, R. (2005). Birth: Hospital or home: That is the question. *Journal of Prenatal and Perinatal Psychology and Health, 19*(4), 341–348.

Ollendick, T. H., Weist, M. D., Borden, M. C., & Greene, R. W. (1992). Sociometric status and academic, behavioral, and psychological adjustment: A five-year longitudinal study. *Journal of Consulting and Clinical Psychology, 60,* 80–87.

Opitz, J. M. (1996). Origins of birth defects. In J. J. Sciarra (Ed.), *Gynecology and obstetrics* (Rev. ed., pp. 23–30). Philadelphia: Lippincott-Raven.

O-Prasetsawat, P., & Petchum, S. (2004). Sexual behavior of secondary school students in Bangkok metropolis. *Journal of the Medical Association of Thailand, 87*(7), 755–759.

O'Rand, A. (2003). The future of the life course: Late modernity and life course risks. In J. Mortimer & M. Shanahan (Eds.), *Handbook of the life course* (pp. 693–701). New York: Kluwer Academic/Plenum.

O'Rand, A. (2009). Cumulative processes in the life course. In G. Elder & J. Giele (Eds.), *The craft of life course research* (pp. 121–140). New York: Guilford.

O'Reilly, B. (2007). *Culture warrior.* New York: Broadway Books.

Orfield, G., Losen, D., Wald, J., & Swanson, C. (2004). *How minority youth are being left behind by the graduation rate crisis.* Cambridge, MA: The Civil Rights Project at Harvard University.

Organisation for Economic Co-operation and Development. (2006a). *OECD health data 2006: Statistics and indicators for 30 countries.* Retrieved November 3, 2006, from http://www.ecosante.org/OCDEENG68.html

Organisation for Economic Co-operation and Development. (2006b). Social Expenditure Database. Retrieved May 17, 2010, from http://www.oecd.org/document/9/0,3343,en_2649_34637_38141385_1_1_1_1,00.html

Ortiz-Mantilla, S., Choudhury, N., Leevers, H., & Benasich, A. A. (2008). Understanding language and cognitive deficits in very low birth weight children. *Developmental Psychobiology, 50*(2), 107–126.

Ortner, S. B. (1973). On key symbols. *American Anthropologist, 75,* 1338–1346.

Ortner, S. B. (1984). Theory in anthropology since the sixties. *Comparative Studies in History and Society, 26*(1), 126–166.

Ortner, S. B. (1989). *High religion: A cultural and political history of Sherpa Buddhism.* Princeton, NJ: Princeton University Press.

Ortner, S. B. (1996). *Making gender: The politics and erotics of culture.* Boston: Beacon Press.

Ortner, S. B. (Ed.). (1999). *The fate of culture: Geertz and beyond.* Berkeley: University of California Press.

Ortner, S. B. (2006). *Anthropology and social theory: Culture, power, and the acting subject.* Durham, NC: Duke University Press.

Osler, M. (2006). The life course perspective: A challenge for public health research and prevention. *European Journal of Public Health, 16*(3), 230.

Ostrov, J., Crick, N., & Stauffacher, K. (2006). Relational aggression in sibling and peer relationships during early childhood. *Journal of Developmental Psychology, 27*(3), 241–253.

Overpeck, M., Hediger, M., Ruan, W., Davis, W., Maurer, K., Troendle, J., et al. (2000). Stature, weight, and body mass among U.S. children born with appropriate birth weights. *Journal of Pediatrics, 137*(2), 205–213.

Owens, D. (1985). *None of the above.* New York: Houghton Mifflin.

Oyserman, D., Bybee, D., Mowbray, C., & MacFarlane, P. (2002). Positive parenting among African American mothers with a serious mental illness. *Journal of Marriage and Family, 65,* 65–77.

Ozdemir, A. (2008). Shopping malls: Measuring interpersonal distance under changing conditions and cultures. *Field Methods, 20*(3), 226–248.

Ozorak, E. W. (1996). The power, but not the glory: How women empower themselves through religion. *Journal for the Scientific Study of Religion, 35*(1), 17–29.

Palmer, A. M., & Francis, P. T. (2006). Neurochemistry of aging. In J. Pathy, A. J. Sinclair, & E. J. Morley (Eds.), *Principles and practice of geriatric medicine* (4th ed., pp. 59–67). Chichester, UK: Wiley.

Pals, D. L. (1996). *Seven theories of religion.* New York: Oxford University Press.

Palsson, S., Johansson, B., Berg, B., & Skoog, I. (2000). A population study on the influence of depression on neuropsychological functions in 85-year-olds. *Acta Psychiatrica Scandinavica, 101*(3), 185–193.

Pan, P. (2002, December 28). Three Chinese workers: Jail, betrayal and fear; Government stifles labor movement. *The Washington Post,* p. A01.

Pandian, Z., Bhattacharya, S., Vale, L., & Templeton, A. (2005). In vitro fertilization for unexplained subfertility. *Cochrane Database of Systematic Reviews, 2.*

Panksepp, J. (2008). The affective brain and core consciousness: How does neural activity generate emotional feelings? In M. Lewis, J. M. Havilland-Jones, & L. F. Barrett (Eds.), *Handbook of emotions* (3rd ed., pp. 47–67). New York: Guilford Press.

Paquette, K., & Bassuk, E. (2009). Parenting and homelessness: Overview and introduction to the special edition. *American Journal of Orthopsychiatry, 79*(3), 292–298.

Paradies, Y. (2006). A systematic review of empirical research on self-reported racism and health. *International Journal of Epidemiology, 35*(4), 888–901.

Parappully, J., Rosenbaum, R., van den Daele, L., & Nzewi, E. (2002). Thriving after trauma: The experience of parents of murdered children. *Journal of Humanistic Psychology, 42*(1), 33–70.

Pardington, S. (2002, January 13). Multilingual pupils pose a challenge to educators. *Contra Costa Times.*

Pardini, D. A., Plante, T. G., Sherman, A., & Stump, J. E. (2000). Religious faith and spirituality in substance abuse recovery: Determining the mental health benefits. *Journal of Substance Abuse Treatment, 19,* 347–354.

Parents, Families and Friends of Lesbians and Gays (PFLAG). (2001). *Read this before coming out to your parents.* Washington, DC: Sauerman.

Parette, H. (1995, November). *Culturally sensitive family-focused assistive technology assessment strategies.* Paper presented at the DEC Early Childhood Conference on Children with Special Needs, Orlando, FL.

Pargament, K. I. (1997). *The psychology of religious coping: Theory, research, practice.* New York: Guilford Press.

Pargament, K. I. (2007). *Spiritually integrated psychotherapy: Understanding and addressing the sacred.* New York: Guilford Press.

Pargament, K. I. (2008). The sacred character of community life. *American Journal of Community Psychology, 41*(1–2), 22–34.

Pargament, K. I., Koenig, H. G., & Perez, L. M. (2000). The many methods of religious coping: Development and initial validation of the RCOPE. *Journal of Clinical Psychology, 56,* 519–543.

Parham, L., Quadagno, J., & Brown, J. (2009). Race, politics, and social policy. In J. Midgley & M. Livermore (Eds.), *The handbook of social policy* (2nd ed., pp. 263–278). Thousand Oaks, CA: Sage.

Paris, P. J. (1995). *The spirituality of African peoples: The search for a common moral discourse.* Minneapolis, MN: Fortress Press.

Parish, S. L., Magana S., & Cassiman, S. A. (2008). It's just that much harder: Multi-layered hardship experiences of low-income mothers with disabilities. *AFFILIA: Journal of Women and Social Work, 23*(1) 51–65.

Park, C., Edmondson, D., Hale-Smith, A., & Blank, T. (2009). Religiousness/spirituality and health behaviors in younger adult cancer survivors: Does faith promote a healthier lifestyle? *Journal of Behavioral Medicine, 32*(6), 582–591.

Park, R. (1936). Human ecology. *American Journal of Sociology, 17,* 1–15.

Parke, M. (2003). Are married parents really better for children? What research says about the effects of family structure on well-being. *CLASP Couples and Marriage Series,*

Brief #2. Retrieved January 15, 2007, from http://www .clasp.org/publications/marriage_brief3_annotated.pdf

Parkes, C. M. (2002). Grief: Lessons from the past, visions for the future. *Death Studies, 26*, 367–385.

Parkinson, B., Fischer, A. H., & Manstead, A. S. R. (2005). *Emotion in social relations: Cultural, group, and interpersonal processes.* New York: Psychology Press.

Parrenas, R. (2001). *Servants of globalization: Women, migration, and domestic work.* Palo Alto, CA: Stanford University Press.

Parrillo, V. (2009). *Diversity in America* (3rd ed.). Thousand Oaks, CA: Pine Forge.

Parsons, R., Tassinary, L. Ulrich, R., Hebl, M., & Grossman-Alexander, M. (1998). The view from the road: Implications for stress recovery and immunization. *Journal of Environmental Psychology, 18*, 113–140.

Pascoe, J., Pletta, K., Beasley, J., & Schellpfeffer, M. (2002). Best Start Breastfeeding promotion campaign. *Pediatrics, 109*(1), 170.

Pasley, K., & Lee, M. (2010). Stress and coping within the context of stepfamily life. In S. Price, C. Price, & P. McKenry (Eds.), *Families & change: Coping with stressful events and transitions* (4th ed., pp. 235–261). Thousand Oaks, CA: Sage.

Pasquali, R., Gambineri, A., & Pagotto, U. (2006). The impact of obesity on reproduction in women with polycystic ovary syndrome. *British Journal of Gynaecology: An International Journal of Obstetrics and Gynaecology, 113*(10), 1148–1159.

Patel, D., Patel, S., Steinkampf, M. P., Whitten, S. J., & Malizia, B. A. (2008). Robotic tubal anastomosis: Surgical technique and cost effectiveness. *Fertility and Sterility, 90*(4), 1175–1179.

Patrikakou, E. N., Weisberg, R. P., Redding, S., & Walberg, H. J. (2005). (Eds.). *School–family partnerships for children's success.* New York: Teachers College Press.

Patterson, T., Shaw, W., Semple, S., Cherner, M., McCutchan, J., Atkinson, K., et al. (1996). Relationship of psychosocial factors to HIV disease progression. *Annals of Behavioral Medicine, 18*, 30–39.

Paul, E. (1997). A longitudinal analysis of midlife interpersonal relationships and well-being. In M. Lachman & J. James (Eds.), *Multiple paths of midlife development* (pp. 171–206). Chicago: University of Chicago Press.

Paulino, A. (1995). Spiritism, santeria, brujeria, and voodooism: A comparative view of indigenous healing systems. *Journal of Teaching in Social Work, 12*(1/2), 105–124.

Paulino, A. (1998). Dominican immigrant elders: Social service needs, utilization patterns, and challenges. *Journal of Gerontological Social Work, 30*(1/2), 61–74.

Payne, R. A. (2000). *Relaxation techniques: A practical handbook for the health care professional* (2nd ed.). Edinburgh, NY: Churchill Livingstone.

Payne, R. K. (2005). *A framework for understanding poverty* (2nd ed.). Highlands, TX: aha! Process, Inc.

Pearson, J. (1996). *Discovering the self through drama and movement: The Sesame Approach.* London: Jessica Kingsley.

Pecora, P. J., Kessler, R. C., Williams, J., O'Brien, K., Downs, A. C., English, D., et al. (2005). *Improving family foster care: Findings from the Northwest Foster Care Alumni Study.* Seattle, WA: Casey Family Programs.

Pedrotti, J., Snyder, C., & Lopez, S. (2007). Eastern perspectives on positive psychology. In C. Snyder & S. Lopez (Eds.), *Positive psychology: The scientific and practice explorations of human strengths* (pp. 37–50). Thousand Oaks, CA: Sage.

Pejlert, A. (2001). Being a parent of an adult son or daughter with severe mental illness receiving professional care: Parents' narrative. *Health and Social Care in the Community, 9*(4), 194–204.

Pelligrini, A., & Galda, L. (2000). Cognitive development, play, and literacy: Issues of definition and developmental function. In K. Roskos & J. Christie (Eds.), *Play and literacy in early childhood: Research from multiple perspectives* (pp. 63–76). Mahwah, NJ: Erlbaum.

Pena, R., & Wall, S. (2000). Effects of poverty, social inequality and maternal education on infant mortality in Nicaragua, 1988–1993. *American Journal of Public Health, 90*(1), 64–69.

Penn, H. (2005). *Understanding early childhood: Issues and controversies.* Maidenhead, UK: Open University Press and McGraw-Hill Education.

Pennekamp, M. (1995). Response to violence. *Social Work in Education, 17*, 199–200.

Peplau, L., & Fingerhut, A. (2007). The close relationships of lesbians and gay men. *Annual Review of Psychology, 58*, 373–408.

Perlman, D., & Fehr, B. (1987). The development of intimate relationships. In D. Perlman & S. Duck (Eds.), *Intimate relationships: Development, dynamics, and deterioration* (pp. 13–42). Newbury Park, CA: Sage.

Perlman, J. M. (2001). Neurobehavioral deficits in premature graduates of intensive care—Potential medical and neonatal environmental risk factors. *Pediatrics, 108*(16), 1339–1449.

Perloff, J., & Buckner, J. (1996). Fathers of children on welfare: Their impact on child well-being. *American Journal of Orthopsychiatry, 66*, 557–571.

Perry, A. V., & Rolland, J. S. (2009). The therapeutic benefits of a justice-seeking spirituality: Empowerment, healing, and hope. In F. Walsh (Ed.), *Spiritual resources in family therapy* (2nd ed., pp. 379–396). New York: Guilford Press.

Perry, B. (2002a). Childhood experience and the expression of genetic potential: What childhood neglect tells us about nature and nurture. *Brain & Mind, 3*(1), 79–100.

Perry, B. (2002b). Helping traumatized children: A brief overview for caregivers. *The Child Trauma Academy.* Retrieved February 12, 2010, from http://www.childtrauma.org

Perry, B. G. F. (1998). The relationship between faith and well-being. *Journal of Religion and Health, 37*(2), 125–136.

Perry, H. (1993). Mourning and funeral customs of African Americans. In D. Irish, K. Lundquist, & V. Nelsen (Eds.), *Ethnic variations in dying, death, and grief: Diversity in universality* (pp. 51–65). Washington, DC: Taylor & Francis.

Perry, J. (2006). Applying principles of neurodevelopment to clinical work with maltreated and traumatized children: The neurosequential model of therapeutics. In N. B. Webb (Ed.), *Working with traumatized youth in child welfare* (pp. 27–52). New York: Guilford Press.

Pert, C. (1997). *Molecules of emotion: Why you feel the way you feel.* New York: Scribner.

Pestvenidze, E., & Bohrer, M. (2007). Finally, daddies in the delivery room: Parents' education in Georgia. *Global Public Health, 2*(2), 169–183.

Peterson, B., & Duncan, L. (2007). Midlife women's generativity and authoritarianism: Marriage, motherhood, and 10 years of aging. *Psychology and Aging, 22*(3), 411–419.

Peterson, B., Newton, C., & Rosen, K. (2003). Examining congruence between partners' perceived infertility-related stress and its relationship to marital adjustment and depression in infertile couples. *Family process, 42,* 59–70.

Petrini, J. R., Dias, T., McCormick, M. C., Massolo, M. L., Green, N. S., & Escobar, G. J. (2009). Increased risk of adverse neurological development for late preterm infants. *Journal of Pediatrics, 154*(2), 169–176.

Pew Forum on Religion & Public Life. (2008). *U.S. religious landscape survey: Religious affiliation—diverse and dynamic.* Washington, DC: Author.

Pew Forum on Religion & Public Life. (n.d.). *Religion and public life.* Retrieved February 26, 2010, from http://www.pewtrusts.org/our_work_category.aspx?id=318

Pew Research Center. (2009, November 16). *Faith-based programs still popular, less visible.* Retrieved February 23, 2010, from http://people-press.org/report/563/faith-based-programs

Pfeffer, J. (1982). *Organizations and organization theory.* Boston: Pitman.

Pharr, S. (1988). *Homophobia: A weapon of sexism.* Inverness, CA: Chardon Press.

Phillips, J., & Sweeny, M. (2005). Premarital cohabitation and marital disruption among White, Black, and Mexican American women. *Journal of Marriage and Family, 67,* 296–314.

Phillips, K. P., & Tanphaichitr, N. (2008). Human exposure to endocrine disrupters and semen quality. *Journal of Toxicology and Environmental Health: Part B, 11*(3/4), 188–220.

Phillips, S. (2003). Adolescent health. In I. Weiner (Ed.), *Handbook of psychology: Health psychology* (Vol. 9, pp. 465–485). New York: Wiley.

Phinney, J. (2006). Ethnic identity exploration in emerging adulthood. In J. Arnett & J. Tanner (Eds.), *Emerging adults in America: Coming of age in the 21st century* (pp. 117–134). Washington, DC: American Psychological Association.

Piaget, J. (1952). *The origins of intelligence in children.* New York: International Universities Press. (Original work published 1936)

Piaget, J. (1965). *The moral judgment of the child.* New York: Free Press. (Original work published 1932)

Piaget, J. (1972). Intellectual evolution from adolescence to adulthood. *Human Development, 15,* 1–12.

Piazza, J., & Charles, S. (2006). Mental health among baby boomers. In S. Whitbourne & S. Willis (Eds.), *The baby boomers grow up: Contemporary perspectives on midlife* (pp. 111–146). Mahwah, NJ: Erlbaum.

Pincus, A., & Minahan, A. (1973). *Social work practice: Model and method.* Itasca, IL: Peacock.

Pinker, S. (2002). *The blank slate: The modern denial of human nature.* New York: Penguin.

Pinto, R. (2006). Using social network interventions to improve mentally ill clients' well-being. *Clinical Social Work Journal, 34*(1), 83–100.

Pipher, M. (1994). *Reviving Ophelia: Saving the selves of adolescent girls.* New York: Ballantine.

Pipher, M. (1999). *Another country: Navigating the emotional terrain of our elders.* New York: Riverhead Books.

Piven, F., & Cloward, R. (1977). *Poor people's movements: Why they succeed, how they fail.* New York: Pantheon.

Piwoz, E., Ross, J., & Humphrey, J. (2004). Human immunodeficiency virus transmission during breastfeeding: Knowledge, gaps, and challenges for the future. *Advances in Experimental Medical Biology, 554,* 195–210.

Plaford, G. (2006). *Bullying and the brain: Using cognitive and emotional intelligence to help kids cope.* Lanham, MD: Rowman & Littlefield Education.

Plante, M. (2000). Fertility preservation in the management of gynecological cancers. *Current Opinion in Oncology, 12*(5), 497–507.

Plante, M. (2006). Fertility-preserving options for cervical cancer. *Oncology, 20*(6), 479.

Plasse, B. R. (2001). A stress reduction and self-care group for homeless and addicted women: Meditation, relaxation and cognitive methods. *Social Work With Groups, 24*(3/4), 117–133.

Playfer, J. R. (2006). Parkinson's disease and Parkinsonism in the elderly. In J. Pathy, A. J. Sinclair, & E. J. Morley (Eds.), *Principles and practice of geriatric medicine* (4th ed., pp. 765–776). Chichester, UK: Wiley.

Plutchik, R. (2005). The nature of emotions. In P. W. Sherman & J. Alcock (Eds.), *Exploring animal behavior: Readings from American Scientist* (4th ed., pp. 85–91). Sunderland, MA: Sinauer Associates.

Pollack, W. (1999). *Real boys: Rescuing our sons from the myths of boyhood.* New York: Henry Holt.

Polletta, F. (2004). Culture is not just in your head. In J. Goodwin & J. Jasper (Eds.), *Rethinking social movements* (pp. 97–110). Lanham, MD: Rowman & Littlefield.

Pollio, D. E. (1995). Hoops group: Group work with young "street" men. *Social Work With Groups, 18*(2/3), 107–116.

Pons, F., Laroche, M., & Mourali, M. (2006). Consumer reactions to crowded retail settings: Cross-cultural differences between North America and Middle East. *Psychology & Marketing, 23*(7), 555–572.

Ponton, L., & Judice, S. (2004). Typical adolescent sexual development. *Child and Adolescent Psychiatric Clinics of North America, 13*(3), 497–511.

Popple, P., & Leighninger, L. (2001). *The policy-based profession: An introduction to social welfare policy analysis for social workers* (2nd ed.). Boston: Allyn & Bacon.

Popple, P., & Leighninger, L. (2005). *Social work, social welfare, and American society* (6th ed.). Boston: Allyn & Bacon.

Porcaro, C., Zappasodi, F., Barbati, G., Salustri, C. Pizzella, V., Rossini, P., et al. (2006). Fetal auditory responses to external sounds and mother's heart beat: Detection improved by Independent Component Analysis. *Brain Research, 1101,* 51–58.

Portes, A., & Rumbaut, R. G. (2001). *Legacies: The story of the immigrant second generation.* Berkeley: University of California Press.

Posmontier, B., & Horowitz, J. (2004). Postpartum practices and depression prevalences: Technocentric and ethnokinship cultural perspectives. *Journal of Transcultural Nursing, 15,* 34–43.

Poteat, V. P., Aragon, S., Espelage, D., & Koenig, B. (2009). Psychosocial concerns of sexual minority youth: Complexity and caution in group differences. *Journal of Consulting and Clinical Psychology, 77*(1), 196–201.

Pothoff, S., Bearinger, L., Skay, C., Cassuto, N., Blum, R., & Resnick, M. (1998). Dimensions of risk behaviors among American Indian youth. *Archives of Pediatric & Adolescent Medicine, 152,* 157–163.

Potocky-Tripodi, M. (2004). The role of social capital in immigrant and refugee economic adaptation. *Journal of Social Service Research, 31*(1), 59–91.

Potter, C. C. (2004). Gender differences in childhood and adolescence. In P. Allen-Meares & M. W. Fraser (Eds.), *Intervention with children and adolescents: An interdisciplinary perspective* (pp. 54–79). Boston: Allyn & Bacon.

Prabhakaran, S. (2008). Self-administration of injectable contraceptives. *Contraception, 77*(5), 315–317.

Praglin, L. (2004). Spirituality, religion, and social work: An effort towards interdisciplinary conversation. *Social Thought, 23,* 67–84.

Prata, N. (2009). Making family planning accessible in resource-poor settings. *Philosophical Transactions of the Royal Society of London, Series B, Biological Sciences, 364*(1532), 3093–3099.

Preto, N. (2005). Transformation of the family system during adolescence. In B. Carter & M. McGoldrick (Eds.), *The expanded family life cycle: Individual, family, and social perspectives* (3rd ed., pp. 274–286). Boston: Allyn & Bacon.

Pretty, G. (1990). Relating psychological sense of community to social climate characteristics. *Journal of Community Psychology, 18,* 60–65.

Pretty, G., & McCarthy, M. (1991). Exploring psychological sense of community among men and women of the corporation. *Journal of Community Psychology, 19,* 351–361.

Prewitt, K. (2000, October). Census 2000: *A new picture of America.* Plenary Session at George Warren Brown School of Social Work 75th Anniversary Celebration, St. Louis, MO.

Price, S. J., Price, C., & McKenry, P. (2010). *Families & change: Coping with stressful events and transitions* (4th ed.). Thousand Oaks, CA: Sage.

Price, S. K. (2006). Prevalence and correlates of pregnancy loss history in a national sample of children and families. *Maternal and Child Health Journal, 10*(6), 489–500.

Procidano, M. E., & Smith, W. W. (1997). Assessing perceived social support: The importance of context. In G. R. Pierce, B. Lakey, & B. R. Sarason (Eds.), *Sourcebook of social support and personality* (pp. 93–106). New York: Plenum.

Proescholdbell, R., Roosa, M., & Nemeroff, C. (2006). Component measures of psychological sense of community among gay men. *Journal of Community Psychology, 34*(1), 9–24.

Proot, I. M., Abu-Saad, H. H., ter Meulen, R. H. J., Goldsteen, M., Spreeuwenberg, C., & Widdershoven, G. A. M. (2004). The needs of terminally ill patients at home: Directing one's life, health and things related to beloved others. *Palliative Medicine, 18,* 53–61.

Puchalski, C., & Romer, A. L. (2000). Taking a spiritual history allows clinicians to understand patients more fully. *Journal of Palliative Medicine, 3*(1), 129–137.

Pulkkinen, L., & Kokko, K. (2000). Identity development in adulthood: A longitudinal study. *Journal of Research in Personality, 34,* 445–470.

Putnam, R. (1993). *Making democracy work.* Princeton, NJ: Princeton University Press.

Putnam, R. (2000). *Bowling alone: The collapse and revival of American community.* New York: Simon & Schuster.

Putney, N., & Bengtson, V. (2001). Families, intergenerational relationships, and kinkeeping in midlife. In M. Lachmann (Ed.), *Handbook of midlife development* (pp. 528–570). New York: Wiley.

Putney, N., & Bengtson, V. (2003). Intergenerational relations in changing times. In J. Mortimer & M. Shanahan (Eds.),

Handbook of the life course (pp. 149–164). New York: Kluwer Academic/Plenum.

Puzzanchera, C. (2009). Juvenile arrests 2008. *Juvenile Justice Bulletin.* Washington, DC: U.S. Department of Justice, Office of Justice Programs, Office of Juvenile Justice and Delinquency Prevention. Retrieved February 9, 2010, from http://www.ojp.usdoj.gov

Quadagno, J. (2007). *Aging and the life course: An introduction to social gerontology* (4th ed.). Hightstown, NJ: McGraw-Hill.

Queralt, M., & Witte, A. (1998a). Influences on neighborhood supply of child care in Massachusetts. *Social Service Review, 72*(1), 17–46.

Queralt, M., & Witte, A. (1998b). A map for you? Geographic information systems in the social services. *Social Work, 43*(5), 455–469.

Quigley, B. (2001). The living wage movement. *Blueprint for Social Justice, LIV*(9), 1–7.

Rabin, R. C. (2009, November 24). Childbirth: Earning a low grade for premature births. *New York Times,* p. 6.

Ragland, D., Krause, N., Greiner, B., & Fisher, J. (1998). Studies of health outcomes in transit operators: Policy implications of the current scientific database. *Journal of Occupational Health Psychology, 3*(2), 172–187.

Rai, S. (2006, February 10). Labor rigidity in India stirs investors' doubts. *The International Herald Tribune,* p. 14.

Raines, J. (1997). Co-constructing the spiritual tree. *Society for Social Work and Social Work Newsletter, 4*(1), 3, 8.

Rainie, L. (2010, January 5). *Internet, broadband, and cell phone statistics.* Retrieved February 23, 2010, from http://www.pewinternet.org/~/media/Files/Reports/2010/PIP_December09_update.pdf

Rakison, D., & Poulin-Dubois, D. (2001). Developmental origin of the animate-inanimate distinction. *Psychological Bulletin, 127*, 209–228.

Ramirez, R. (1985). Hispanic spirituality. *Social Thought, 11*(3), 6–13.

Ramos, B., Siegel, S., & Bueno, J. (2002). Occasion setting and drug tolerance. *Integrative Physiological & Behavioral Science, 37*(3), 165–177.

Rampell, C. (2010, February 6). Women now a majority in American workplaces. *New York Times,* p. A10.

Ramsey, J., Langlois, J., Hoss, R., Rubenstein, A., & Griffin, A. (2004). Origins of a stereotype: Categorization of facial attractiveness by 6-month-old infants. *Developmental Science, 7*, 201–211.

Rando, T. (1993). *Treatment of complicated mourning.* Champaign: Research Press.

Rank, M. R. (2005). *One nation, underprivileged: Why American poverty affects us all.* New York: Oxford University Press.

Rapoport, A. (1990). *Meaning of the built environment.* Tucson: University of Arizona Press.

Rappaport, H., Enrich, K., & Wilson, A. (1985). Relation between ego identity and temporal perspective. *Journal of Personality and Social Psychology, 48*(6), 1609–1620.

Rathus, S., Nevid, J., & Fichner-Rathus, L. (1998). *Essentials of human sexuality.* Boston: Allyn & Bacon.

Rauch, J. (1988). Social work and the genetics revolution: Genetic services. *Social Work, 9/10,* 389–395.

Raustiala, K. (2005). The evolution of territoriality. *International Studies Review, 7,* 515–519.

Ray, L. (1993). *Rethinking critical theory: Emancipation in the age of global social movements.* Newbury Park, CA: Sage.

Ray, O. (2004). How the mind hurts and heals the body. *American Psychologist, 59*(1), 29–40.

Ray, R., Gornick, J., & Schmitt, J. (2009). *Parental leave policies in 21 countries: Assessing generosity and gender equality.* Washington, DC: Center for Economic and Policy Research. Retrieved May 17, 2010, from http://www.cepr.net/index.php/publications/reports/plp/

Raza, M., & Velez, P. (Directors). (2002). *Occupation: The Harvard University living wage sit-in* [Motion picture]. Waterville, ME: EnMasse Films.

Rector, R., & Hederman, R. (1999). *Income inequality: How census data misrepresent income distribution.* Retrieved May 17, 2010, from http://www.heritage.org/Research/Reports/1999/09/Income-Inequality

Rector, R., Johnson, K., & Fagan, P. (2008). Increasing marriage would dramatically reduce child poverty. In D. R. Crane & T. Heaton (Eds.), *Handbook of families & poverty* (pp. 457–470). Thousand Oaks, CA: Sage.

Redman, D. (2008). Stressful life experiences and the roles of spirituality among people with a history of substance abuse and incarceration. *Social Thought, 27*(1–2), 47–67.

Reed, G. B. (1996). Introduction to genetic screening and prenatal diagnoses. In J. J. Sciarra (Ed.), *Gynecology and obstetrics* (Rev. ed., pp. 999–1003). Philadelphia: Lippincott-Raven.

Reed, M. (1993). Organizations and modernity: Continuity and discontinuity in organization theory. In J. Hassard & M. Parker (Eds.), *Postmodernism and organizations* (pp. 163–182). Newbury Park, CA: Sage.

Reed, R. K. (2005). *Birthing fathers: The transformation of men in American rites of birth.* New Brunswick. NJ: Rutgers University Press.

Reedy, N. J. (2007). Born too soon: The continuing challenge of preterm labor and birth in the United States. *Journal of Midwifery & Women's Health, 52*(3), 281–290.

Reedy, N. J. (2008). The challenge of preterm birth. *Journal of Midwifery & Women's Health, 53*(1), 281–290.

Reese, D. J., & Kaplan, M. S. (2000). Spirituality, social support, and worry about health: Relationships in a sample of HIV+ women. *Social Thought, 19*(4), 37–52.

Reeves, T. C. (1998). *The empty church: Does organized religion matter anymore?* New York: Simon & Schuster.

Regenerus, M., & Elder, G. (2003). Staying on track in school: Religious influences in high and low-risk settings. *Journal for the Scientific Study of Religion, 42*(4), 633–649.

Regoeczi, W. (2008). Crowding in context: An examination of the differential responses of men and women to high-density living environments. *Journal of Health and Social Behavior, 49*(3), 254–268.

Reichert, E. (2006). *Understanding human rights: An exercise book.* Thousand Oaks, CA: Sage.

Reid, C. (2007). The transition from state care to adulthood: International examples of best practices. *New Directions for Youth Development, 113,* 33–49.

Reid, K. E. (1997). *Social work practice with groups: A clinical perspective* (2nd ed.). Pacific Grove, CA: Wadsworth/ Thomson Learning.

Reid, T. R. (2004). *The United States of Europe: The new superpower and the end of American supremacy.* New York: Penguin.

Reid, W., & Smith, A. (1989). *Research in social work* (2nd ed.). New York: Columbia University Press.

Reilly, P. (1995). The religious wounding of women. *Creation Spirituality, 11*(1), 41–45.

Reinhardt, U., Hussey, P., & Anderson, G. (2002). Cross-national comparisons of health systems using OECD data, 1999. *Health Affairs, 21*(3), 169–181.

Reinhardt, U., Hussey, P., & Anderson, G. (2004). U.S. health care spending in an international context. *Health Affairs, 23*(3), 10–25.

Reis, H. (2006). Implications of attachment theory for research on intimacy. In M. Mikulincer & G. Goodman (Eds.), *Dynamics of romantic love: Attachment, caregiving, and sex* (pp. 383–403). New York: Guilford Press.

Reis, H., Lin, Y., Bennett, M., & Nezlek, J. (1993). Change and consistency in social participation during early adulthood. *Developmental Psychology, 29,* 633–645.

Reis, H., Lin, Y. Bennett, M., & Nezlek, J. (2004). Change and consistency in social participation during early adulthood. In H. Reis & C. Busbult (Eds.), *Close relationships.* New York: Psychology Press.

Reisch, M. (1997). The political context of social work. In M. Reisch & E. Gambrill (Eds.), *Social work in the 21st century* (pp. 80–92). Thousand Oaks, CA: Pine Forge.

Reith, M., & Payne, M. (2009). *Social work in end-of-life and palliative care.* Chicago: Lyceum Books.

Reitzes, D., & Mutran, E. (2002). Grandparenthood: Factors influencing frequency of grandparent–grandchildren contact and grandparent role satisfaction. *Journals of Gerontology: Social Sciences, 59B,* S9-S16.

Remez, L. (2000). Oral sex among adolescents: Is it sex or is it abstinence? *Family Planning Perspectives, 32*(6), 298–304.

Rennison, C. M., & Welchans, S. (2000). *Intimate partner violence* (Special Report). Washington, DC: U.S. Bureau of Justice Statistics, National Institute of Justice. (NCJ 178247)

Repetti, R., Taylor, S., & Seeman, T. (2002). Risky families: Family social environments and the mental and physical health of offspring. *Psychological Bulletin, 18,* 330–366.

Reporters Without Borders. (2010). *World Press Freedom Index 2009.* Retrieved May 17, 2010, from http://en.rsf .org/IMG/pdf/classement_en.pdf

Resnick, H., & Jaffee, B. (1982). The physical environment and social welfare. *Social Casework, 63,* 354–362.

Ressler, L. E., & Hodge, D. R. (2003). Silenced voices: Social work and the oppression of conservative narratives. *Social Thought, 22,* 125–142.

Reuter-Lorenz, P. A. (2002). New visions of the aging mind and brain. *Trends in Cognitive Sciences, 6,* 394–400.

Reuther, R. (1983). *Sexism and God-talk: Toward a feminist theology.* Boston: Beacon Press.

Rew, L. (2005). *Adolescent health: A multidisciplinary approach to theory, research, and intervention.* Thousand Oaks, CA: Sage.

Richards, M. (2005). Spirituality and social work in long-term care. *Journal of Gerontological Social Work, 45*(1/2), 173–183.

Richman, J. M., Rosenfeld, L. B., & Hardy, C. J. (1993). The Social Support Survey: A validation study of a clinical measure of the social support process. *Research on Social Work Practice, 3,* 288–311.

Richmond, M. (1901). Charitable cooperation. In *Proceedings of the National Conference of Charities and Corrections* (pp. 298–313). Boston: George H. Elles.

Richmond, M. (1917). *Social diagnosis.* New York: Russell Sage Foundation.

Richter, L. (2006). Studying adolescence. *Science, 312,* 1902–1905.

Rieker, P. R., & Bird, C. E. (2005). Rethinking gender differences in health: Why we need to integrate social and biological perspectives. *The Journal of Gerontology: Series B, Psychological Sciences and Social Sciences, 60B,* 40–47.

Riera, C. (2005). Social policy and community development in multicultural contexts. *Community Development Journal, 40*(4), 433–438.

Rieser-Danner, L. (2003). Individual differences in infant fearfulness and cognitive performance: A testing, performance, or competence effect? *Genetic, Social, and General Psychology Monographs, 129*(1), 41–71.

Rifas-Shiman, S. L., Rich-Edwards, J. W., Willett, W. C., Kleinman, K. P., Oken, E., & Gillman, M. W. (2006). Changes in dietary intake from first to second trimester of pregnancy. *Perinatal Epidemiology, 20*(1), 35–42.

Riley, M. W. (1971). Social gerontology and the age stratification of society. *The Gerontologist, 11,* 79–87.

Rimm, S. (1999). *See Jane win.* New York: Three Rivers Press.

Rindfuss, R. R., Cooksey, E. C., & Sutterlin, R. L. (1999). Young adult occupational achievement: Early expectations versus behavioral reality. *Work & Occupations, 26*(2), 220–263.

Ringeisen, H., Casanueva, C. E., Urato, M., & Stambaugh, L. F. (2009). Mental health service use during the transition to adulthood for adolescents reported to the child welfare system. *Psychiatric Services, 60*(8), 1084–1091.

Riordan, J., & Auerbach, K. (1999). *Breastfeeding and human lactation* (2nd ed.). Sudbury, MA: Jones & Bartlett.

Ritzer, G. (2008a). *The McDonaldization of society* (5th ed.). Thousand Oaks, CA: Pine Forge.

Ritzer, G. (2008b). *Sociological theory* (7th ed.). Boston: McGraw-Hill.

Ritzer, G., & Goodman, D. (2004). *Modern sociological theory* (6th ed.). Boston: McGraw-Hill.

Rivas-Drake, D. (2008). Perceived opportunity, ethnic identity, and achievement motivation among Latinos at a selective public university. *Journal of Latinos and Education, 7*(2), 113–128.

Robbins, S., Chatterjee, P., & Canda, E. (2006a). *Contemporary human behavior theory: A critical perspective for social work* (2nd ed.). Boston: Pearson.

Robbins, S., Chatterjee, P., & Canda, E. (2006b). Theories of assimilation, acculturation, bicultural socialization, and ethnic minority identity. In *Contemporary human behavior theory: A critical perspective for social work* (2nd ed., pp. 126–161). Boston: Allyn & Bacon.

Roberson, W. W. (2004). *Life and livelihood: A handbook for spirituality at work.* Harrison, PA: Morehouse Publishing.

Roberts, B., Helson, R., & Klohnen, E. (2002). Personality development and growth in women across 30 years: Three perspectives. *Journal of Personality, 70,* 79–102.

Roberts, B., Robins, R., Trzesniewski, K., & Caspi, A. (2003). Personality trait development in adulthood. In J. Mortimer & M. Shanahan (Eds.), *Handbook of the life course* (pp. 579–595). New York: Kluwer Academic/Plenum.

Roberts, E., Burchinal, M., & Bailey, D. (1994). Communication among preschoolers with and without disabilities in same-age and mixed-age classes. *American Journal on Mental Retardation, 99,* 231–249.

Roberts, K. A. (2004). *Religion in sociological perspective* (4th ed.). Belmont, CA: Wadsworth.

Roberts, R. E., Roberts, C. R., & Chen, Y. R. (1997). Ethnocultural differences in prevalence of adolescent depression. *American Journal of Community Psychology, 25*(1), 95–111.

Robertson, R. (1992). *Globalization.* London: Sage.

Robertson, S., Zarit, S., Duncan, L., Rovine, M., & Femia, E. (2007). Family caregivers' patterns of positive and negative affect. *Family Relations, 56,* 12–23.

Robinson, G. E., Stotland, N. L., Russo, N. F., Lang, J. A., & Occhiogrosso, M. (2009). Is there an "abortion trauma syndrome"? Critiquing the evidence. *Harvard Review Psychiatry, 17*(4), 266–290.

Robinson, T. L. (2000). Making the hurt go away: Psychological and spiritual healing for African American women survivors of childhood incest. *Journal of Multicultural Counseling and Development, 28*(3), 160–176.

Roehlkepartain, E. C., King, P. E., Wagener, L., & Benson, P. L. (2006). *Spiritual development in childhood and adolescence.* Thousand Oaks, CA: Sage.

Roff, S. (2004). Nongovernmental organizations: The strengths perspective at work. *International Social Work, 47*(2), 202–212.

Rogers, C. (1951). *Client-centered therapy.* Boston: Houghton Mifflin.

Rogge, M. (1993). Social work, disenfranchised communities, and the natural environment: Field education opportunities. *Journal of Social Work Education, 29,* 111–120.

Roggman, L. (2004). Do fathers just want to have fun? *Human Development, 47,* 228–236.

Roggman, L., Boyce, L., Cook, G., Christiansen, K., & Jones, D. (2004). Playing with daddy: Social toy play, early head start, and developmental outcomes. *Fathering, 2,* 83–108.

Rogoff, B. (2003). *The cultural nature of human development.* New York: Oxford University Press.

Rogoff, B., & Chavajay, P. (1995). What's become of research on the cultural basis of cognitive development? *American Psychologist, 50,* 859–873.

Roller, B. (1997). *The promise of group therapy: How to build a vigorous training and organizational base for group therapy in managed behavioral health care.* San Francisco: Jossey-Bass.

Ronen, T., & Freeman, A. (Eds.). (2007). *Cognitive behavior therapy in clinical social work practice.* New York: Springer.

Rönkä, A., Oravala, S., & Pulkkinen, L. (2003). Turning points in adults' lives: The effects of gender and amount of choice. *Journal of Adult Development, 10*(3), 203–215.

Roof, W. C. (1993). *A generation of seekers: The spiritual journeys of the baby boom generation.* San Francisco: HarperCollins.

Roof, W. C. (1999). *Spiritual marketplace: Baby boomers and the remaking of American religion.* Princeton, NJ: Princeton University Press.

Roopnarine, J., Shin, M., Donovan, B., & Suppal, P. (2000). Sociocultural contexts of dramatic play: Implications for early education. In K. Roskos & J. Christie (Eds.), *Play and literacy in early childhood: Research from multiple perspectives* (pp. 205–220). Mahwah, NJ: Erlbaum.

Roper v. Simmons, 543 U.S. 551 (2005).

Rose, S. (1992). *Case management and social work practice.* White Plains, NY: Longman.

Rose, S. (1994). Defining empowerment: A value-based approach. In S. P. Robbins (Ed.), *Melding the personal and the political: Advocacy and empowerment in clinical and community practice. Proceedings of the Eighth Annual Social Work Futures Conference,* May 13–14, 1993 (pp. 17–24), Houston, TX: University of Houston Graduate School of Social Work.

Rosen, R. (2004). *Time and temporality in the ancient world.* Philadelphia: University of Pennsylvania Museum of Archaeology and Anthropology.

Rosenberg, M. (1986). *Conceiving the self*. Malabar, FL: Robert E. Krieger.

Rosenzweig, M. R., Breedlove, S. M., & Watson, N. W. (2004). *Biological psychology: An introduction to behavioral and cognitive neuroscience* (4th ed.). Sunderland, MA: Sinauer Associates.

Rosenzweig, M. R., & Leiman, A. L. (1989). *Physiological psychology* (2nd ed.). Lexington, MA: Heath.

Roskos, K., & Christie, J. (2000). *Play and literacy in early childhood: Research from multiple perspectives*. Mahwah, NJ: Erlbaum.

Ross, L., & Coleman, M. (2000). Urban community action planning inspires teenagers to transform their community and their identity. *Journal of Community Practice, 7*(2), 29–45.

Ross, M., & Holmberg, D. (1992). Are wives' memories for events in relationships more vivid than their husbands' memories? *Journal of Social and Personal Relationships, 9*, 585–604.

Rossi, A. (2004). Social responsibility to family and community. In O. Brim, C. Ryff, & R. Kessler (Eds.), *How healthy are we? A national study of well-being at midlife* (pp. 550–585). Chicago: University of Chicago Press.

Rostow, W. (1990). *The stages of economic growth: A noncommunist manifesto*. Cambridge, UK: Cambridge University Press.

Rotenberg, K., McDougall, P., Boulton, M., Vaillancourt, T., Fox, C., & Hymel, S. (2004). Cross-sectional and longitudinal relations among peer-reported trustworthiness, social relationships, and psychological adjustment in children and early adolescents from the United Kingdom and Canada. *Journal of Experimental Child Psychology, 88*, 46–67.

Rothenberg, P. (2006). Preface. In P. Rothenberg (Ed.), *Beyond borders: Thinking critically about global issues* (pp. xv–xvii). New York: W. H. Freeman.

Rothenberg, P. (2007). *Race, class, and gender in the United States* (7th ed.). New York: Worth.

Rotheram-Borus, M. J. (1993). Biculturalism among adolescents. In M. Bernal & G. Knight (Eds.), *Ethnic identity* (pp. 81–102). Albany: State University of New York Press.

Rothman, B. K. (1991). *In labor: Women and power in the birthplace* (2nd ed.). New York: Norton.

Rothman, J. (2008). *Cultural competence in process and practice: Building bridges*. Boston: Pearson.

Rothrauff, T., & Cooney, T. (2008). The role of generativity in psychological well-being. Does it differ for childless adults and parents? *Journal of Adult Development, 15*, 148–159.

Rothschild-Whitt, J., & Whitt, J. (1986). *The cooperative workplace*. Cambridge, UK: Cambridge University Press.

Roueche, J. E., & Baker, G. A., III. (1986). *Profiling excellence in America's schools*. Arlington, VA: American Association of School Administrators.

Roulstone, A. (2004). Employment barriers and inclusive futures? In *Disabling barriers—Enabling environments* (2nd ed., pp. 195–200). Thousand Oaks, CA: Sage.

Roumen, F. J., Op Ten Berg, M. M., & Hoomans, E. H. (2006). The combined contraceptive vaginal ring (NuvaRign®): First experience in daily clinical practice in the Netherlands. *The European Journal of Contraception and Reproductive Health: The Official Journal of the European Society of Contraception, 11*(1), 14–22.

Rovee-Collier, C. (1999). The development of infant memory. *Current Directions in Psychological Science, 8*(3), 80–85.

Rowlands, S. (2009). New technologies in contraception. *BJOG: An International Journal of Obstetrics & Gynaecology, 116*(2), 230–239.

Rubenstein, G. (2008). *Full-service schools: Where success is more than academic*. Retrieved May 21, 2010, from http://www.edutopia.org/whats-next-2008-community-services

Rubin, A., & Babbie, E. (1993). *Research methods for social work* (2nd ed.). New York: Columbia University Press.

Rubin, K. (1986). Play, peer interaction, and social development. In A. Gottfried & C. Brown (Eds.), *Play interactions: The contribution of play materials and parental involvement to children's development* (pp. 163–174). Lexington, MA: Heath.

Rubin, K., Fein, G., & Vandenberg, B. (1983). Play. In E. M. Hetherington (Ed.), *Handbook of child psychology: Vol. 4, Socialization, personality, and social development* (4th ed., pp. 693–744). New York: Wiley.

Rudacille, D. (2005). *The riddle of gender: Science, activism, and transgender rights*. New York: Pantheon.

Rudolph, S., & Rudolph, L. (1978). Rajput adulthood: Reflections on the Amar Singh Diary. In E. H. Erikson (Ed.), *Adulthood* (pp. 149–171). New York: Norton & Norton.

Rue, V., Coleman, P., Rue, J., & Reardon, D. (2004). Induced abortion and traumatic stress: A preliminary comparison of American and Russian women. *Medical Science Monitor, 10*(10), SR5–SR16.

Rueda, R., Monzo, L., Shapiro, J., Gomez, J., & Blacher, J. (2005). Cultural models of transition: Latina mothers of young adults with developmental disabilities. *Exceptional Children, 71*(4), 401–414.

Ruffman, T., Slade, L. & Redman, J. (2005). Young infants' expectations about hidden objects. *Cognitive, 97*, B35–B43.

Ruger, J. A., Moser, S. E., & Frisch, L. (2000). Smokers over 35 continue to receive oral contraceptives: Survey of patients in a family practice residency practice. *Scandinavian Journal of Primary Health Care, 18*(2), 113–114.

Ruger, J. P., & Kim, H. (2006). Global health inequalities: An international comparison. *Journal of Epidemiology and Community Health, 60*, 928–936.

Russel, R. (1998). Spirituality and religion in graduate social work education. *Social Thought, 18*(2), 15–29.

Ryan, B. A., & Adams, G. R. (1995). The family–school relationships model. In B. A. Ryan, G. R. Adams, T. P. Gullotta, R. P. Weissberg, & R. L. Hampton (Eds.), *The family–school connection: Theory, research, and practice* (pp. 3–28). Thousand Oaks, CA: Sage.

Ryan, C., Huebner, D., Diaz, R., & Sanchez, J. (2009). Family rejection as a predictor of negative health outcomes in White and Latino lesbian, gay, and bisexual young adults. *Pediatrics: Official Journal of the American Academy of Pediatrics, 123*, 346–352.

Ryan, M., David, B., & Reynolds, K. (2004). Who cares? The effect of gender and context on the self and moral reasoning. *Psychology of Women Quarterly, 28*(3), 246–255.

Ryan, P. L. (1998). Spirituality among adult survivors of childhood violence: A literature review. *Journal of Transpersonal Psychology, 30*(1), 39–51.

Ryan, W. (1999). The new landscape for nonprofits. *Harvard Business Review, 77*(1), 127–136.

Sabatelli, R. (1984). The Marital Comparison Level Index: A measure for assessing outcomes relative to expectations. *Journal of Marriage and the Family, 46*, 651–662.

Sabbagh, M., & Baldwin, D. (2001). Learning words from knowledgeable versus ignorant speakers: Links between preschoolers' theory of mind and semantic development. *Child Development, 72*, 1054–1070.

Sadock, B., & Sadock, V. (2007). *Kaplan & Sadock's synopsis of psychiatry: Behavioral sciences/clinical psychiatry* (10th ed.).Baltimore: Wolters Kluwer.

Saez, E. (2009). *Striking it richer: The evolution of top incomes in the United States* (Update with 2007 estimates). Retrieved February 20, 2010, from http://elsa.berkeley.edu/~saez

Safyer, A. W., & Spies-Karotkin, G. (1988). The biology of AIDS. *Health and Social Work, 13*, 251–258.

Sagara, J. (2000). Development of attitudes toward gender roles in children: Stereotypes and flexibility. *Japanese Journal of Educational Psychology, 48*(2), 174–181.

Saghir, M. T., & Robins, E. (1973). *Male and female homosexuality: A comprehensive examination.* Baltimore: Williams & Wilkins.

Sagi, A., Koren-Karie, N., Gini, M., Ziv, Y., & Joels, T. (2002). Shedding further light on the effects of various types and quality of early child care on infant–mother attachment relationships: The Haifa study of early child care. *Child Development, 73*, 1166–1186.

Sahlins, M. (1981). *Historical metaphors and mythical realities: Structure in the early history of the Sandwich Islands kingdom.* Ann Arbor: University of Michigan Press.

Saigal, S., Stoskopf, B., Streiner, D., Boyles, M., Pinelli, J., Paneth, N., et al. (2006). Transition of extremely low birth weight infants from adolescent to young adulthood. *Journal of American Medical Association, 295*(6), 667–675.

Saint Louis Healthy Families. (2009). *Stepfamilies in the United States: A fact sheet.* Retrieved September 15, 2011, from http://www.stlhealthyfamilies.org/announcements/step families-in-the-united-states-a-fact-sheet

Salamon, L., Anheier, H., List, R., Toepler, S., & Sokolowski, W. (1999). *Global civil society: Dimensions of the nonprofit sector.* Baltimore: The Johns Hopkins Comparative Center for Civil Society Studies.

Saldinger, M. A., Cain, A., Kalter, N., & Lohnes, K. (1999). Anticipating parental death in families with young children. *American Journal of Orthopsychiatry, 69*(1), 39–48.

Saleebey, D. (1994). Culture, theory, and narrative: The intersection of meanings in practice. *Social Work, 39*, 351–359.

Saleebey, D. (1996). The strengths perspective in social work practice: Extensions and cautions. *Social Work, 41*(3), 296–304.

Saleebey, D. (2001). *Human behavior and social environments: A biopsychosocial approach* (3rd ed.). New York: Columbia University Press.

Saleebey, D. (2006). *The strengths perspective in social work practice.* Boston: Pearson/Allyn & Bacon.

Saltzburg, S. (2004). Learning that an adolescent child is gay and lesbian: The parent experience. *Social Work, 49*, 109–119.

Sameroff, A., Bartko, W., Baldwin, A., Baldwin, C., & Seifer, R. (1998). Family and social influences on the development of child competence. In M. Lewis & C. Feiring (Eds.), *Families, risk, and competence* (pp. 161–186). Mahwah, NJ: Erlbaum.

Sampson, R. (2003). The neighborhood context of well-being. *Perspectives in Biology and Medicine, 46*(3), S53–S65.

Sampson, R. (2009). *Bullying in schools. Problem-oriented guides for police. Problem-specific guides series No. 12.* Washington, DC: U.S. Department of Justice. Office of Community Oriented Policing Services. Retrieved February 9, 2010, from http://www.cops.usdoj.gov/files/RIC/Publications/e07063414-guide.pdf

Sampson, R., Morenoff, J., & Earls, F. (1999). Beyond social capital: Spatial dynamics of collective efficacy for children. *Science, 277*, 918–924.

Sanders, S. (2005). Is the glass half empty or half full? Reflections on strain and gain in caregivers of individuals with Alzheimer's disease. *Social Work in Health Care, 40*(3), 57–73.

Sandoval-Cros, C. (2009). Hispanic cultural issues in end-of-life care. In D. J. Doka & A. S. Tucci, *Living with grief: Diversity and end-of-life care* (pp. 117–126). Washington, DC: Hospice Foundation of America.

Sands, R., & Goldberg, G. (2000). Factors associated with stress among grandparents raising their grandchildren. *Family Relations, 49*(1), 97–105.

Santrock, J. (2003). *Life-span development* (8th ed.). New York: McGraw-Hill.

Saperstein, A. (1996). The prediction of unpredictability: Applications of the new paradigm of chaos in dynamical systems to the old problem of the stability of a system of hostile nations. In L. D. Kiel & E. Elliott (Eds.), *Chaos theory in the social sciences: Foundations and applications* (pp. 139–163). Ann Arbor: University of Michigan Press.

Sapolsky, R. (2004). *Why zebras don't get ulcers* (3rd ed.). New York: Henry Holt.

Sapolsky, R. (2005). Sick of poverty. *Scientific American, 293*(6), 92–99.

Sarafino, E. P. (2008). *Health psychology: Biopsychosocial implications* (6th ed.). Belmont, CA: Wiley.

Sarason, S. (1974). *The psychological sense of community: Prospects for a community psychology.* San Francisco: Jossey-Bass.

Satir, V. (1983). *Conjoint family therapy* (3rd ed.). Palo Alto, CA: Science and Behavior Books.

Savia, J., Almeida, D., Davey, A., & Zant, S. (2008). Routine assistance to parents: Effects on daily mood and other stressors. *Journals of Gerontology Series B, Psychological Sciences & Social Sciences, 36B*(3), S154–S161.

Savin-Williams, R. (2008). Then and now: Recruitment, definition, diversity, and positive attributes of same-sex populations. *Developmental Psychology, 44,* 135–138.

Savin-Williams, R., & Diamond, L. (2004). Sex. In R. Lerner & L. Steinberg (Eds.), *Handbook of adolescent psychology* (2nd ed., pp. 189–231). New York: Wiley.

Sax, L. (2005). *Why gender matters: What parents and teachers need to know about the emerging science of sex differences.* New York: Random House.

Scales, T. L., Wolfer, T. A., Sherwood, D. A., Garland, D. R., Hugen, B., & Pittman, S. W. (2002). *Spirituality and religion in social work practice: Decision cases with teaching notes.* Alexandria, VA: Council on Social Work Education.

Scanzoni, J., & Szinovacz, M. (1980). *Family decision-making: A developmental sex role model.* Beverly Hills, CA: Sage.

Scarlett, A. G., Naudeau, S., Salonius-Pasternak, D., & Ponte, I. (2005). *Children's play.* Thousand Oaks, CA: Sage.

Schachere, K. (1990). Attachment between working mothers and their infants: The influence of family processes. *American Journal of Orthopsychiatry, 60,* 19–34.

Schackman, B. R., Gebo, K. A., Walensky, R. P., Losina, E. L., Muccio, T., Sax, P. E., et al. (2006). The lifetime cost of current Human Immunodeficiency Virus care in the United States. *Medical Care, 44*(11), 990–997.

Schacter, S., & Singer, J. E. (1962). Cognitive, social, and physiological determinants of emotional states. *Psychological Review, 69,* 379–399.

Schafer, J. E., Osborne, L. M., Davis, A. R., & Westhoff, C. (2006). Acceptability and satisfaction using Quick Start with the contraceptive vaginal ring versus an oral contraceptive. *Contraception, 73*(5), 488–492.

Schaie, K. W. (1984). The Seattle Longitudinal Study: A 21-year exploration of psychometric intelligence in adulthood. In K. W. Schaie (Ed.), *Longitudinal studies of adult psychological development* (pp. 64–135). New York: Guilford.

Schein, E. (1992). *Organizational culture and leadership* (2nd ed.). San Francisco: Jossey-Bass.

Scherger, S. (2009). Social change and the timing of family transitions in West Germany: Evidence from cohort comparisons. *Time & Society, 18*(1), 106–129.

Schmid, H. (2004). The role of nonprofit human service organizations in providing social services: A prefatory essay. *Administration in Social Work, 28*(3/4), 1–21.

Schmitz, C., & Hilton, A. (1996). Combining mental health treatment with education for preschool children with severe emotional and behavioral problems. *Social Work in Education, 18,* 237–249.

Schneider, H., & Eisenberg, D. (2006). Who receives a diagnosis of attention deficit/hyperactivity disorder in the United States elementary school population? *Pediatrics, 117*(4), 601–609.

Schneider, J., & Cook, K. (1995). Status inconsistency and gender: Combining revisited. *Small Group Research, 26,* 372–399.

Schoeni, R. F., Martin, L. G., Andreski, P. A., & Freedman, V. A. (2005). Persistent and growing socioeconomic disparities in disability among the elderly: 1982–2002. *American Journal of Public Health, 95*(11), 2065–2072.

Schore, A. N. (2001). The effects of a secure attachment relationship on right brain development, affect regulation, and infant mental health. *Infant Mental Health Journal, 22,* 7–66.

Schore, A. N. (2002). Dysregulation of the right brain: A fundamental mechanism of traumatic attachment and the psychopathogenesis of post-traumatic stress disorder. *Australian and New Zealand Journal of Psychiatry, 36,* 9–30.

Schriver, J. (2011). *Human behavior and the social environment: Shifting paradigms in essential knowledge for social work practice* (5th ed.). Boston: Pearson.

Schuetze, P., Lewis, A., & DiMartino, D. (1999). Relation between time spent in daycare and exploratory behavior. *Infant Behavior & Development Special Issue, 22*(2), 267–276.

Schumm, W. R., Bell, D. B., & Knott, B. (2000). Characteristics of families of soldiers who return prematurely from overseas deployments: An assessment from Operation Restore Hope (Somalia). *Psychological Reports, 86*(3 pt 2), 1267–1272.

Schupf, N., Tang, M., Albert, S., Costa, A. R., Andrews, H., Lee, J., et al. (2005). Decline in cognitive and functional skills increases mortality risk in nondemented elderly. *Neurology, 65*(8), 1218–1226.

Schuster, M. A., Stein, B. P., Jaycox, L. H., Collins, R. L., Marshall, G. N., Zhou, A. J., et al. (2001). A national survey of stress reactions after the September 11, 2001, terrorist attacks. *New England Journal of Medicine, 345*(20), 1507–1512.

Schutt, R. (2009). *Investigating the social world: The process and practice of research* (6th ed.). Thousand Oaks, CA: Sage.

Schutz, A. (1967). *The phenomenology of the social world* (G. Walsh & F. Lehnert, Trans.). Evanston, IL: Northwestern University Press. (Original work published 1932)

Schwalbe, M. (2006). Afterword: The costs of American privilege. In P. Rothenberg (Ed.), *Beyond borders: Thinking critically about global issues* (pp. 603–605). New York: Worth.

Schwartz, S., Cote, J., & Arnett, J. (2005). Identity and agency in emerging adulthood: Two developmental routes in the individualization process. *Youth and Society, 37*(2), 201–229.

Schweinhart, L., Montie, J., Xiang, Z., Barnett, W., Belfield, C., & Nores, M. (2005). *Lifetime effects: The High/Scope Perry preschool study through age 40*. Ypsilanti, MI: High/Scope Educational Research Foundation.

Sclowitz, I. K., & Santos, I. S. (2006). Risk factors for repetition of low birth weight, intrauterine growth retardation, and prematurity in subsequent pregnancies: A systematic review. *Cadernos De Saude Publica, 22*(6), 1129–1136.

Scott, A. H., Butin, D. N., Tewfik, D., Burkhardt, A., Mandel, D., & Nelson, L. (2001). Occupational therapy as a means to wellness with the elderly. *Physical and Occupational Therapy in Geriatrics, 18*(4), 3–22.

Scott, K. D., Klaus, P. H., & Klaus, M. H. (1999). The obstetrical and postpartum benefits of continuous support during childbirth. *Journal of Women's Health and Gender-Based Medicine, 8*(10), 1257–1264.

Scott, M. (2005). A powerful theory and a paradox: Ecological psychologists after Barker. *Environment and Behavior, 37*(3), 295–329.

Scott, W. R. (2008). *Institutions and organizations: Ideas and interests* (3rd ed.). Thousand Oaks, CA: Sage.

Seabury, B. (1971). Arrangement of physical space in social work settings. *Social Work, 16*, 43–49.

Sebba, R. (1991). The landscapes of childhood: The reflection of childhood's environment in adult memories and in children's attitudes. *Environment and Behavior, 23*, 395–422.

Seccombe, K., & Warner, R. (2004). *Marriages and families: Relationships in social context*. New York: Thomson Learning.

Sedikides, C., Gaertner, L., & Toguchi, Y. (2003). Pancultural self-enhancement. *Journal of Personality and Social Psychology, 84*, 60–69.

Sedlak, A., & Broadhurst, D. (1996). *Third national incidence study of child abuse and neglect: Final report*. Washington, DC: U.S. Department of Human Services.

Seefeldt, C. (1993). Educating yourself about diverse cultural groups in our country by reading. *Young Children, 48*, 13–16.

Segal, B. M., & Stewart, J. C. (1996). Substance use and abuse in adolescence: An overview. *Child Psychiatry and Human Development, 26*(4), 193–210.

Segall, M., Dasen, P., Berry, J., & Poortinga, Y. (1999). *Human behavior in global perspective* (2nd ed.). Boston: Allyn & Bacon.

Segerstrom, S. S., & Miller, G. E. (2004). Psychological stress and the human immune system: A meta-analytic study of 30 years of inquiry. *Psychological Bulletin, 130*(4), 601–630.

Seibert, S., & Gruenfeld, L. (1992). Masculinity, femininity, and behavior in groups. *Small Group Research, 23*, 95–112.

Seifer, D. B., Frazier, L. M., & Grainger, D. A. (2008). Disparity in assisted reproductive technologies outcomes in Black women compared to White women. *Fertility and Sterility, 90*(5), 1701–1710.

Seifer, R., & Dickstein, S. (2000). Paternal mental illness and infant development. In C. Zeanah (Ed.), *Handbook of infant mental health* (2nd ed., pp. 145–160). New York: Guilford Press.

Seigfried, C. (1989). Pragmatism, feminism and sensitivity to context. In M. M. Brabeck (Ed.), *Who cares? Theory, research and educational implications of the ethic of care* (pp. 63–83). New York: Praeger.

Seligman, M. (1991). *Learned optimism*. New York: Knopf.

Seligman, M. (1992). *Helplessness: On depression, development, and death*. New York: Freeman.

Seligman, M. (1998). *Learned optimism: How to change your mind and your life* (2nd ed.). New York: Pocket Books.

Seligman, M. (2002). *Authentic happiness: Using the new positive psychology to realize your potential for lasting fulfillment*. New York: Free Press.

Seligman, M., Reivich, K., Jaycox, L., & Gillham, J. (1995). *The optimistic child*. New York: Houghton Mifflin.

Selman, R. L. (1976). Social-cognitive understanding: A guide to educational and clinical practice. In T. Lickona (Ed.), *Moral development and behavior: Theory, research, and social issues* (pp. 219–316). New York: Holt, Rinehart & Winston.

Seltzer, M., Almeida, D., Greenberg, J., Savla, J., Stawski, R., Hong, J., et al. (2009). Psychosocial and biological markers of daily lives of midlife parents of children with disabilities. *Journal of Health and Social Behavior, 50*, 1–15.

Selye, H. (1991). History and present status of the stress concept. In A. Monat & R. S. Lazarus (Eds.), *Stress and coping: An anthology* (3rd ed., pp. 21–35). New York: Columbia University Press.

Sen, A., Partelow, L., & Miller, D. (2005). *Comparative indicators of education in the United States and other G8 countries: 2004* (NCES 2005–021). U.S. Department of Education, National Center for Education Statistics. Washington, DC: U.S. Government Printing Office.

Senge, P. (1990). *The fifth discipline.* New York: Doubleday.

Sennett, R. (2006). *The culture of the new capitalism.* New Haven, CT: Yale University Press.

Serbin, L. A., Powlishta, K. K., & Gulko, J. (1993). The development of sex typing in middle childhood. *Monographs of the Society for Research in Child Development, 58*(2), Serial No. 232.

Sernau, S. (2006). *Worlds apart: Social inequalities in a global economy* (2nd ed.). Thousand Oaks, CA: Pine Forge.

Serrant-Green, L. (2008). Review: Contraceptive patch and vaginal ring are as effective as oral contraceptives. *Evidence-Based Nursing, 11*(4), 108.

Sethi, V. (2004). Iodine deficiency and development of brain. *Indian Journal of Pediatrics, 71*(4), 325–329.

Settersten, R. A., Jr. (2003a). Age structuring and the rhythm of the life course. In J. Mortimer & M. Shanhan (Eds.), *Handbook of the life course* (pp. 81–98). New York: Kluwer Academic/Plenum.

Settersten, R. A., Jr. (2003b). Introduction: Invitation to the life course: The promise. In R. Settersten, Jr. (Ed.), *Invitation to the life course: Toward new understandings of later life* (pp. 1–12). Amityville, NY: Baywood Publishing.

Settersten, R. A., Jr., Furstenberg, F. F., & Rumbaut, R. G. (2005). *On the frontier of adulthood: Theory, research, and public policy.* Chicago: University of Chicago Press.

Severy, L. J., & Spieler, J. (2000). New methods of family planning: Implications for intimate behavior. *Journal of Sex Research, 37*(3), 258–265.

Sex Bias Cited in Vocational Ed. (2002, June 6). *The Washington Post,* pp. 18–19.

Sexton, M. B., Byrd, M. R., & Von Kluge, S. (2010). Measuring resilience in women experiencing infertility using the CD-RISC: Examining infertility-related stress, general distress, and coping styles. *Journal of Psychiatric Research, 44*(4), 236–241.

Shanahan, M. (2000). Pathways to adulthood in changing societies: Variability and mechanisms in life course perspective. *Annual Review of Sociology, 27*, 667–692.

Shanahan, M., & Flaherty, B. (2001). Dynamic patterns of time use in adolescence. *Child Development, 72*(2), 385–401.

Shapiro, T. (2004). *The hidden cost of being African-American: How wealth perpetuates inequality.* New York: Oxford University Press.

Sharma, S., Mittal, S., & Aggarwal, P. (2009). Management of infertility in low resource countries. *BJOG: An International Journal of Obstetrics & Gynaecology, 116*, 71–76.

Shaw, M. E. (1981). *Group dynamics: The psychology of small group behavior* (3rd ed.). New York: McGraw-Hill.

Shaw, S., Kleiber, D., & Caldwell, L. (1995). Leisure and identity formation in male and female adolescents: A preliminary examination. *Journal of Leisure Research, 27*, 245–263.

Sheehy, G. (1995). *New passages.* New York: Random House.

Sheets, V., & Manzer, C. (1991). Affect, cognition, and urban vegetation: Some effects of adding trees along city streets. *Environment and Behavior, 23*, 285–304.

Sheiner, E. K., Sheiner, E., Hammei, R. D., Potashnik, G., & Carel, R. (2003). Effect of occupational exposures on male fertility: Literature review. *Industrial Health, 41*(2), 55–62.

Shek, D. (2003). Economic stress, psychological well-being and problem behavior in Chinese adolescents with economic disadvantage. *Journal of Youth and Adolescence, 32*(4), 259–266.

Sheldon, K. (2006). Getting older, getting better? Recent psychological evidence. In M. Csikszentmihalyi & I. Csiksezentmihali (Eds.), *A life worth living: Contributions to positive psychology* (pp. 215–229). New York: Oxford University Press.

Sheldon, K., & Kasser, T. (2001). Getting older, getting better? Personal striving and psychological maturity across the life span. *Developmental Psychology, 37*, 491–501.

Shepard, M. (1992). Child visiting and domestic abuse. *Child Welfare, 71*, 357–367.

Shephard, B. (2005). Play, creativity, and the new community organizing. *Journal of Progressive Human Services, 16*(2), 47–69.

Sherblom, S. (2008). The legacy of the "care challenge": Re-envisioning the outcome of the justice-care debate. *Journal of Moral Education, 37*(1), 81–98.

Sherer, M. (2009). *Challenging the whole child: Reflections on best practices in learning, teaching and leadership.* Alexandria, VA: Association for Supervision & Curriculum Development.

Sheridan, M. J. (1995). Honoring angels in my path: Spiritually sensitive group work with persons who are incarcerated. *Reflections: Narratives of Professional Helping, 1*(4), 5–16.

Sheridan, M. J. (2002). Spiritual and religious issues in practice. In A. R. Roberts & G. J. Greene (Eds.), *Social workers' desk reference* (pp. 567–571). New York: Oxford University Press.

Sheridan, M. J. (2004). Predictors of use of spiritually-derived interventions in social work practice: A survey of practitioners. *Journal of Spirituality and Religion in Social Work: Social Thought, 23*(4), 5–25.

Sheridan, M. J. (2009). Ethical issues in the use of spiritually-based interventions in social work practice: What are we doing and why? *Social Thought, 28*(1/2), 99–126.

Sheridan, M. J., & Amato-von Hemert, K. (1999). The role of religion and spirituality in social work education and practice: A survey of student views and experiences. *Journal of Social Work Education, 35*(1), 125–141.

Sheridan, M. J., & Bullis, R. K. (1991). Practitioners' views on religion and spirituality: A qualitative study. *Spirituality and Social Work Journal, 2*(2), 2–10.

Sheridan, M. J., Bullis, R. K., Adcock, C. R., Berlin, S. D., & Miller, P. C. (1992). Practitioners' personal and professional attitudes and behaviors toward religion and spirituality: Issues for social work education and practice. *Journal of Social Work Education, 28*(2), 190–203.

Sheridan, M. J., Wilmer, C., & Atcheson, L. (1994). Inclusion of content on religion and spirituality in the social work curriculum: A study of faculty views. *Journal of Social Work Education, 30,* 363–376.

Sherman, E. (1991). *Reminiscence and the self in old age.* New York: Springer.

Sherwood, P., Given, C., Given, B., & Von Eye, A. (2005). Caregiver burden and depressive symptoms: Analysis of common outcomes in caregivers of elderly patients. *Journal of Aging Health, 17,* 125–147.

Shilts, R. (1987). *And the band played on.* New York: St. Martin's Press.

Shmotkin, D. (1991). The role of time orientation in life satisfaction across the life span. *Journal of Gerontology, 46*(5), 243–250.

Shonkoff, J., Hauser-Cram, P., Krauss, M., & Upshur, C. (1992). Development of infants with disabilities and their families: Implications for theory and service delivery. *Monographs of the Society for Research in Child Development, 57*(6), 230–239.

Shonkoff, J., & Phillips, D. (Eds.). (2000). *From neurons to neighborhoods: The science of early childhood development.* Washington, DC: National Academies Press.

Shore, R., & Shore, B. (2009). *Increasing the percentage of children living in two-parent families.* Baltimore: The Annie E. Casey Foundation. Retrieved December 9, 2009, from http://www.kidscount.org

Shorey, H. S., & Snyder, C. R. (2006). The role of adult attachment styles in psychopathology and psychotherapy outcomes. *Review of General Psychology, 10*(1), 1–20.

Shrier, L., Emans, S., Woods, E., & DuRant, R. (1996). The association of sexual risk behaviors and problem drug behaviors in high school students. *Journal of Adolescent Health, 20,* 377–383.

Shu, L., & Li, Y. (2007). How far is enough? A measure of information privacy in terms of interpersonal distance. *Environment & Behavior, 39*(3), 317–331.

Shweder, R. (1995). Anthropology's Romantic rebellion against the Enlightenment, or there's more to thinking than reason and evidence. In R. Shweder & R. LeVine (Eds.), *Culture theory: Essays on mind, self, and emotion* (pp. 27–66). New York: Cambridge University Press. (Original work published 1984)

Shweder, R., & LeVine, R. (Eds.). (1995). *Culture theory: Essays on mind, self, and emotion.* New York: Cambridge University Press. (Original work published 1984)

Sickmund, M. (2009, June). *Delinquency cases in Juvenile Court, 2005.* U.S. Department of Justice, Office of Justice Programs, Office of Juvenile Justice and Delinquency Prevention. Retrieved February 9, 2010, from http://www.ncjrs.gov/pdffiles1/ojjdp/224538.pdf

Sideridis, G. D. (2006). Coping is not an "either" "or": The interaction of coping strategies in regulating affect, arousal and performance. *Stress and Health: Journal of the International Society for the Investigation of Stress, 22*(5), 315–327.

Siegel, D. (1999). *The developing mind: Toward a neurobiology of interpersonal experience.* New York: Guilford Press.

Siegel, S. (1991). Feedforward processes in drug tolerance and dependence. In R. Lister & H. Weingartner (Eds.), *Perspectives on cognitive neuroscience* (pp. 405–416). New York: Oxford University Press.

Siegel, S. (2001). Pavlovian conditioning and drug overdose: When tolerance fails. *Addiction Research & Theory, 9*(5), 503–513.

Siegel, S. (2005). Drug tolerance, drug addiction, and drug anticipation. *Current Directions in Psychological Science, 14*(6), 296–300.

Siegel, S., & Allan, L. (1998). Learning and homeostasis: Drug addiction and the McCollough effect. *Psychological Bulletin, 124*(2), 230–239.

Siegel, S., Hinson, R., Krank, M., & McCully, J. (1982). Heroin "overdose" death: Contribution of drug-associated environmental cues. *Science, 216,* 436–437.

Silbereisen, R. (2003). Contextual constraints on adolescents' leisure. In S. Verma & R. Larson (Eds.), *Examining adolescent leisure time across cultures: New directions for child and adolescent development* (No. 99, pp. 95–102). San Francisco: Jossey-Bass.

Silbereisen, R., & Lerner, R. (2007a). *Approaches to positive youth development.* Thousand Oaks, CA: Sage.

Silbereisen, R., & Lerner, R. (2007b). Approaches to positive youth development: A view of the issues. In R. Silbereisen & R. Lerner (Eds.), *Approaches to positive youth development* (pp. 3–30). Thousand Oaks, CA: Sage.

Silverman, D. (1971). *The theory of organizations: A sociological framework.* New York: Basic Books.

Silverman, D. (1994). On throwing away ladders: Re-writing the theory of organizations. In J. Hassard & M. Parker (Eds.), *Towards a new theory of organizations* (pp. 1–23). New York: Routledge.

Silverman, J., Raj, A., Mucci, L., & Hathaway, J. (2001). Dating violence against adolescent girls and associated substance use, unhealthy weight control, sexual risk behavior, pregnancy, and suicidality. *Journal of the American Medical Association, 286*(5), 572–579.

Silverman, P. R. (2004). Bereavement: A time of transition and changing relationships. In J. Berzoff & P. R. Silverman (Eds.), *Living with dying: A handbook for end-of-life healthcare practitioners* (pp. 226–241). New York: Columbia University Press.

Silverstein, M., & Bengtson, V. (2001). Intergenerational solidarity and the structure of adult child–parent relationships in American families. In A. Walker, M. Manoogian-O'Dell, L. McGraw, & D. L. White (Eds.), *Families in later life: Connections and transitions* (pp. 53–61). Thousand Oaks, CA: Pine Forge.

Simmons, R. (2003). *Odd girl out: The hidden culture of aggression in girls.* Orlando, FL: Harcourt Trade.

Simmons, T., & O'Connell, M. (2003). *Married-couple and unmarried-partner households: 2000.* Washington, DC: U.S. Census Bureau.

Simon, H., & Zieve, D. (2008). Vasectomy and vasectomy reversal. *Vasectomy and Vasovasostomy (Reversal Surgery),* 1–6.

Singer, M. I., Anglin, T. M., Song, L. Y., & Lunghofer, L. (1995). Adolescents' exposure to violence and associated symptoms of psychological trauma. *Journal of the American Medical Association, 273*(6), 477–482.

Singh, L., Morgan, J., & Best, C. (2002). Infants' listening preferences: Baby talk or happy talk? *Infancy, 3,* 365–394.

Singh, R. (2001). Hinduism. In M. V. Hook, B. Hugen, & M. Aguilar (Eds.), *Spirituality within religious traditions in social work practice* (pp. 34–52). Pacific Grove, CA: Brooks/Cole.

Singh-Manoux, A., Marmot, M., & Adler, N. (2005). Does subjective social status predict health and change in health status better than objective status? *Psychosomatic Medicine, 67*(6), 855–861.

Single-rod etonogestrel implant safe and efficacious. (2009, June 15). *Fertility Weekly,* pp. 4–5.

Sinha, S., & Mukherjee, N. (1996). The effect of perceived cooperation on personal space requirements. *Journal of Social Psychology, 136,* 655–657.

Sinha, S., & Nayyar, P. (2000). Crowding effects of density and personal space requirements among older people: The impact of self-control and social support. *Journal of Social Psychology, 140*(6), 721–726.

Siporin, M. (1975). *Introduction to social work practice.* New York: Macmillan.

Siporin, M. (1986). Contribution of religious values to social work and the law. *Social Thought, 12*(4), 35–50.

Siragusa, N. (2001). *The language of gender* [Electronic version]. New York: Gay Lesbian Straight Education Network. Retrieved December 29, 2006, from http://www.glsen.org/cgi-bin/iowa/all/libarary/record/811.html

Skaalvik, S., & Skaalvik, E. (2004). Frames of reference for self-evaluation of ability in mathematics. *Psychological Reports, 94,* 619–632.

Skinner, B. F. (1948). *Walden two.* New York: Macmillan.

Skinner, B. F. (1957). *Verbal behavior.* Englewood Cliffs, NJ: Prentice Hall.

Skocpol, T. (1979). *States and social revolutions.* New York: Cambridge University Press.

Skocpol, T. (2003). *Diminished democracy: From membership to management in American civil life.* New York: Cambridge University Press.

Skye, W. (2002). E.L.D.E.R.S. gathering for Native American youth: Continuing Native American traditions and curbing substance abuse in Native American youth. *Journal of Sociology and Social Welfare, 24*(1), 117–135.

Sleeter, C. (1995). White pre-service students and multicultural education coursework. In J. M. Larkin & C. E. Sleeter (Eds.), *Developing multicultural teacher education curricula* (pp. 17–30). Albany: State University of New York Press.

Sloter, E., Schmid, T. E., Marchetti, F., Eskenazi, B., Nath, J., & Wyrobek, A. J. (2006). Quantitative effects of male age on sperm motion. *Human Reproduction, 21*(11), 2868–2875.

Smith, A., Dannison, L., & Vach-Hasse, T. (1998). When Grandma is Mom. *Childhood Education, 75*(1), 12–16.

Smith, B., & Blass, E. (1996). Taste-mediated calming in premature, preterm, and full-term human infants. *Developmental Psychology, 32,* 1084–1089.

Smith, C., & Denton, M. L. (2005). *Soul searching: The religious and spiritual lives of American teenagers.* New York: Oxford University Press.

Smith, C., Denton, M. L., Faris, R., & Regnerus, M. (2002). Mapping American adolescent religious participation. *Journal for the Scientific Study of Religion, 41*(4), 597–612.

Smith, D., Stormshak, E., Chamberlain, P., & Whaley, R. (2001). Placement disruption in foster care. *Journal of Emotional and Behavioral Disorders, 9,* 200–211.

Smith, E. D. (1995). Addressing the psychospiritual distress of death as reality: A transpersonal approach. *Social Work, 40,* 402–413.

Smith, E. D., & Gray, C. (1995). Integrating and transcending divorce: A transpersonal model. *Social Thought, 18*(1), 57–74.

Smith, G. (1996). Ties, nets and an elastic bund: Community in the postmodern city. *Community Development Journal, 31*(3), 250–259.

Smith, J., Chatfield, C., & Pagnucco, R. (1997). *Transnational social movements and global politics: Solidarity beyond the state.* Syracuse, NY: Syracuse University Press.

Smith, J., O'Connor, I., & Berthelsen, D. (1996). The effects of witnessing domestic violence on young children's psycho-social adjustment. *Australian Social Work, 49*(4), 3–10.

Smith, M., & Brun, C. (2006). An analysis of selected measures of child well-being for use at school- and community-based family resource centers. *Child Welfare, 85*(6), 985–1010.

Smith, M. A., Acheson, L. S., Byrd, J. E., Curtis, P., Day, T. W., Frank, S. H., et al. (1991). A critical review of labor and birth care. *Journal of Family Practice, 33*(3), 281–293.

Smith, N. R. (2006). *Workplace spirituality: A complete guide for business leaders*. Lynn, MA: Axial Age.

Smith, S. (2010). The political economy of contracting and competition. In Y. Hasenfeld (Ed.), *Human services as complex organizations* (2nd ed., pp. 139–160). Thousand Oaks, CA: Sage.

Smith, Y., van Goozen, S., & Cohen-Kettenis, P. (2001). Adolescents with gender identity disorder who were accepted or rejected for sex assignment surgery: A prospective follow-up study. *Journal of the American Academy of Child and Adolescent Psychiatry, 40,* 472–481.

Smyer, M. A., Gatz, M., Simi, N. L., & Pedersen, N. L. (1998). Childhood adoption: Long-term effects in adulthood. *Psychiatry: Interpersonal and Biological Processes, 61*(3), 191.

Snipp, C. M. (1998). The first Americans: American Indians. In M. L. Andersen & P. H. Collins (Eds.), *Race, class, and gender: An anthology* (pp. 357–364). Belmont, CA: Wadsworth.

Snyder, C., & Lopez, S. (2007). *Positive psychology: The scientific and practical explorations of human strengths*. Thousand Oaks, CA: Sage.

Snyder, H., & Sickmund, M. (2006). *Juvenile offenders and victims: 2006 national report*. Washington, DC: U.S. Department of Justice, Office of Justice Programs, Office of Juvenile Justice and Delinquency Prevention.

Snyder, S., & Mitchell, D. (2001). Re-engaging the body: Disability studies and the resistance to embodiment. *Public Culture, 13*(3), 367–389.

Social Security Administration. (2009). *Retirement age*. Retrieved September 15, 2011, from http://ssa.gov/pubs/retirechart.htm

Sokol, R. J., Janisse, J. J., Louis, J. M., Bailey, B. N., Ager, J., Jacobson, S. W., et al. (2007). Extreme prematurity: An alcohol-related birth effect. *Alcoholism: Clinical and Experimental Research, 31*(6), 1031–1037.

Solantaus, T., Leinonen, J., & Punamaki, R. (2004). Children's mental health in times of economic recession: Replication and extension of the Family Economic Stress Model in Finland. *Developmental Psychology, 40*(3), 412–429.

Sollod, R., Wilson, J., & Monte, C. (2009). *Beneath the mask: An introduction to theories of personality* (8th ed.). Hoboken, NJ: Wiley.

Solomon, B. (1976). *Black empowerment: Social work in oppressed communities*. New York: Columbia University Press.

Solomon, B. (1987). Empowerment: Social work in oppressed communities. *Journal of Social Work Practice, 2*(4), 79–91.

Solomon, R. C. (1988). *About love: Reinventing romance for modern times*. New York: Simon & Schuster.

Solomon, Z., Helvitz, H., & Zerach, G. (2009). Subjective age, PTSD and physical health among war veterans. *Aging & Mental Health, 13*(3), 405–413.

Solomon, Z., & Mikulincer, M. (2006). Trajectories of PTSD: A 20-year longitudinal study. *American Journal of Psychiatry, 163*(4), 659–666.

Solórzano, R. (2008). High-stakes testing: Issues, implications, and remedies for English language learners. *Review of Educational Research, 78*(2), 260–329.

Sommer, R. (1969). *Personal space: The behavioral basis of design*. Englewood Cliffs, NJ: Prentice Hall.

Sommer, R. (2002). Personal space in a digital age. In R. Bechtel & A. Churchman (Eds.), *Handbook of environmental psychology* (pp. 647–660). New York: Wiley.

Song, Y., & Lu, H. (2002). *Early childhood poverty: A statistical profile (March 2002)*. New York: National Center for Children in Poverty. Retrieved August 21, 2002, from http://cpmcnet.columbia.edu/dept/nccp/ecp302.html

Sonn, C. (2002). Immigrant adaptation: Understanding the process through the sense of community. In A. T. Fisher, C. S. Sonn, & B. J. Bishop (Eds.), *Psychological sense of community: Research, applications, and implications* (pp. 205–222). New York: Plenum.

Sonn, C., & Fisher, A. (1996). Psychological sense of community in a politically constructed group. *Journal of Community Psychology, 24,* 417–430.

Soulsby, A., & Clark, E. (2007). Organization theory and the post-socialist transformation: Contributions to organizational knowledge. *Human Relations, 60*(10), 1419–1442.

Sowell, E., Trauner, D., Gamst, A., & Jernigan, T. (2002). Development of cortical and subcortical brain structures in childhood and adolescence: A structural MRI study. *Developmental Medicine and Child Neurobiology, 44,* 4–16.

Spear, L. (2002). The adolescent brain and the college drinker: Biological basis of propensity to use and misuse alcohol. *Journal of Studies on Alcohol, 63*(Suppl.), 71–81.

Speare, A., Jr., & Avery, R. (1993). Who helps whom in older parent–child families? *Journal of Gerontology, 48,* S64–S73.

Specht, H., & Courtney, M. E. (1994). *Unfaithful angels: How social work has abandoned its mission*. New York: Free Press.

Spector-Mersel, G. (2006). Never-aging stories: Western hegemonic masculinity scripts. *Journal of Gender Studies, 15*(1), 67–82.

Spencer, M. B. (1985). Black children's race awareness, racial attitudes and self concept: A reinterpretation. *Annual Progress in Child Psychiatry & Child Development,* 616–630.

Spencer, M. B., Harpalani, V., Fegley, S., Dell'Angelo, T., & Seaton, G. (2003). Identity, self, and peers in context: A culturally sensitive, developmental framework for analysis. In R. M. Lerner, F. Jacobs, & D. Wertlieb (Eds.), *Handbook of applied developmental science* (Vol. 1, pp. 123–142). Thousand Oaks, CA: Sage.

Spencer, N., & Logan, S. (2002). Social influences on birth weight: Risk factors for low birth weight are strongly influenced by the social environment. *Archives of Disease in Childhood: Fetal and Neonatal Edition, 86*(1), 6–8.

Spiegel, D., & Classen, C. (2000). *Group therapy for cancer patients: A research-based handbook of psychosocial care.* New York: Basic Books.

Spieker, S., Nelson, D., & Petras, A. (2003). Joint influence of child care and infant attachment security for cognitive and language outcomes of low-income toddlers. *Infant Behavior & Development, 26*(3), 326–344.

Spillman, B. (2003). *Changes in elderly disability rates and the implications for health care utilization and cost.* Washington, DC: Urban Institute.

Spiro, A. (2001). Health in midlife: Toward a life-span view. In M. Lachmann (Ed.), *Handbook of midlife development* (pp. 156–187). New York: Wiley.

Spitz, I. M., Bardin, C. W., Benton, L., & Robbins, A. (1998). Early pregnancy termination with mifepristone and misoprostol in the United States. *New England Journal of Medicine, 338*(18), 983–987.

Sprecher, S. (2005). Equity and social exchange in dating couples: Associations with satisfaction, commitment, and stability. In T. Chibucos & R. Leite, with D. Weis (Eds.), *Readings in family theory* (pp. 165–182). Thousand Oaks, CA: Sage.

Sprent, J., & Surth, C. (2001). Generation and maintenance of memory T cells. *Current Opinion in Immunology, 13*(2), 248–254.

Spring, J. (2004). *Deculturalization and the struggle for educational equality.* New York: McGraw-Hill.

Sroufe, L. A., Egeland, B., Carlson, E., & Collins, W. A. (2005). The development of the person: The Minnesota study of risk and adaptation from birth to adulthood. New York: Guilford Press.

St. George, D. (2009, February 22). 6,473 texts a month, but at what cost? Constant cellphone messaging keeps kids connected, parents concerned. *The Washington Post.* Retrieved February 9, 2010, from http://www.washingtonpost.com/wp-dyn/content/article/2009/02/21/AR2009022101863.html

Staats, H., Kieviet, A., & Hartig, T. (2003). Where to recover from attentional fatigue: An expectancy-value analysis of environmental preference. *Journal of Environmental Psychology, 23*(2), 147–157.

Stanley, S., Markman, H., & Whitton, S. (2002). Communication, conflict, and commitment: Insights on the foundations for relationship success from a national survey. *Family Process, 41,* 659–675.

Stansfeld, S., Head, J., Bartley, M., & Fonagy, P. (2008). Social position, early deprivation and the development of attachment. *Social Psychiatry and Psychiatric Epidemiology, 43*(7), 516–526.

Staral, J. M. (2000). Building on mutual goals: The intersection of community practice and church-based organizing. *Journal of Community, 7*(3), 85–95.

Starhawk. (1979). *The spiral dance: A rebirth of the ancient religion of the great Goddess.* San Francisco: Harper & Row.

Staudinger, U. M., Freund, A. M., Linden, M., & Maas, I. (1999). Self, personality, and life regulation: Facets of psychological resilience in old age. In P. B. Baltes & K. U. Mayer (Eds.), *The Berlin Aging Study: Aging from 70 to 100* (pp. 302–328). Cambridge, UK: Cambridge University Press.

Stegner, W. (1978). The writer and the concept of adulthood. In E. H. Erikson (Ed.), *Adulthood* (pp. 227–336). New York: Norton & Norton.

Stein, L. (2009). Social movement web use in theory and practice: A content analysis of U.S. movement websites. *New Media & Society, 11*(5), 749–771.

Stein, M. (2005). Resilience and young people leaving care: Implications for child welfare policy and practice in the UK. In R. J. Flynn, P. M. Dudding, & J. G. Barber (Eds.), *Promoting resilience in child welfare* (pp. 264–278). Ottawa, Ont., Canada: University of Ottawa Press.

Stephens, K., & Clark, D. (1987). A pilot study on the effect of visible stigma on personal space. *Journal of Applied Rehabilitation Counseling, 18,* 52–54.

Stepp, L. S. (1999, July 8). Parents are alarmed by an unsettling new fad in middle schools: Oral sex. *The Washington Post,* p. A1.

Sternberg, E. (2009). *Healing spaces: The science of place and well-being.* Cambridge, MA: Belknap Press.

Sternberg, S., Wolfson, C., & Baumgarten, M. (2000). Undetected dementia in community-dwelling older people. *Journal of the American Geriatrics Society, 48*(11), 1430–1434.

Sterns, H., & Huyck, M. (2001). The role of work in midlife. In M. Lachman (Ed.), *Handbook of midlife development* (pp. 447–486). New York: Wiley.

Stewart, C., Koeske, G., & Pringle, J. L. (2007). Religiosity as a predictor of successful post-treatment abstinence for African-American clients. *Journal of Social Work Practice in the Addictions, 7*(4), 75–92.

Stewart, J. (2001). Radical constructivism in biology and cognitive science. *Foundations of Science, 6*(1–3), 99–124.

Stirling, K., & Aldrich, T. (2008). Child support: Who bears the burden? *Family Relations, 57,* 376–389.

Stokols, D., & Montero, M. (2002). Toward an environmental psychology of the Internet. In R. Bechtel & A. Churchman (Eds.), *Handbook of environmental psychology* (pp. 661–675). New York: Wiley.

Stolte, J. F. (1994). Power. In M. Foshci & E. J. Lawler (Eds.), *Group processes: Sociological analyses* (pp. 149–176). Chicago: Nelson-Hall.

Stolzenberg, R. M., Blair-Loy, M., & Waite, L. J. (1995). Religious participation in early adulthood: Age and family life cycle effects on church membership. *American Sociological Review, 60*(1), 84–104.

Stone, D. (2002). *Policy paradox: The art of political decision making* (Rev. ed.). New York: Norton.

Stouthamer-Loeber, M., & Wei, E. H. (1998). The precursors of young fatherhood and its effect on delinquency of teenage males. *Journal of Adolescent Health, 22,* 56–65.

Stovall, K., & Dozier, M. (1998). Infants in foster care: An attachment theory perspective. *Adoption Quarterly, 2*(1), 55–88.

Strauch, B. (2010). *The secret life of the grown-up brain: The surprising talents of the middle-aged mind.* London: Viking.

Strauss, L. T., Herndon, J., Chang, J., Parker, W. Y., Bowens, S. V., & Berg, C. J. (2002). *Abortion surveillance—United States, 2002.* Retrieved November 15, 2006, from http://www.cdc .gov/mmwr/preview/mmwrhtml/ss5407a1.htm

Street, J., Harris-Britt, A., & Walker-Barnes, C. (2009). Examining relationships between ethnic identity, family environment, and psychological outcomes for African American adolescents. *Journal of Child and Family Studies, 18,* 412–420.

Streeter, C., & Gillespie, D. (1992). Social network analysis. *Journal of Social Service Research, 16,* 201–221.

Streifel, C., & Servaty-Seib, H. L. (2009). Recovering from alcohol and other drug dependency: Loss and spirituality in a 12-step context. *Alcoholism Treatment Quarterly, 27*(2), 184–198.

Streri, A. (2005). Touching for knowing in infancy: The development of manual abilities in very young infants. *European Journal of Developmental Psychology, 2,* 325–343.

Strock, M. (2004). *Autism spectrum disorders (pervasive developmental disorders)* (NIH Publication No. NIH-04-5511). Bethesda, MD: National Institute of Mental Health. Retrieved January 15, 2007, from http://www .nimh.nih.gov/publicat/autism.cfm

Strock, M. (2006). *Attention deficit hyperactivity disorder.* Bethesda, MD: National Institute of Mental Health. Retrieved December 5, 2006, from http://www.nimh .nih.gov/publicat/NIMHadhdpub.pdf

Stroebe, M., Stroebe, W., & Hansson, R. (1993). *Handbook on bereavement: Theory, research and intervention.* New York: Cambridge University Press.

Stuart, R. (1989). Social learning theory: A vanishing or expanding presence? *Psychology: A Journal of Human Behavior, 26,* 35–50.

Substance Abuse and Mental Health Services Administration (SAMHSA), Office of Applied Studies. (2009a). *The NSDUH Report: Trends in tobacco use among adolescents: 2002 to 2008.* Rockville, MD: Author. Retrieved February 9, 2009, from http://www.oas.samhsa.gov/2k9/ 152/152Trends.htm

Substance Abuse and Mental Health Services Administration (SAMHSA). (2009b). *Results from the 2008 National Survey on Drug Use and Health: National findings* (Office of Applied Studies, NSDUH Series H-36, HHS Publication No. SMA 09-4434). Rockville, MD: Author. Retrieved February 9, 2009, from http://www.oas.samhsa .gov/nsduh/2k7nsduh/2k7Results.pdf

Sue, D. W., & McGoldrick, M. (2005). *Multicultural social work practice.* Hoboken, NJ: Wiley.

Suh, E., & Abel, E. (1990). The impact of violence on the children of the abused. *Journal of Independent Social Work, 4*(4), 27–43.

Sullivan, W., Kuo, F., & DePooter, S. (2004). The fruit of urban nature: Vital neighborhood spaces. *Environment and Behavior, 36*(5), 678–700.

Sun, S. S., Schubert, C. M., Chumlea, W. C., Roche, A. F., Kulin, H. E., Lee, P. A., et al. (2002). National estimates of the timing of sexual maturation and racial differences among U.S. children. *Pediatrics, 110*(5), 911–919.

Sunderman, G. (2006). *The unraveling of No Child Left Behind: How negotiated changes transform the law.* Cambridge, MA: The Civil Rights Project at Harvard University.

Suzuki, K., Tanaka, T., Kondo, N., Minai, J., Sato, M., & Yamagata, Z. (2008). Is maternal smoking during early pregnancy a risk factor for all low birth weight infants? *Journal of Epidemiology, 18*(3), 89–96.

Swain, J., French, S., Barnes, C., & Thomas, C. (2004). *Disabling barriers—Enabling environments* (2nd ed.). Thousand Oaks, CA: Sage.

Swap, S. M. (1993). *Developing home–school partnerships: From concepts to practice.* New York: Teachers College Press.

Swatos, W. H. (2005). Globalization theory and religious fundamentalism. In P. Kivisto (Ed.), *Illuminating social life: Classical and contemporary theory revisited* (3rd ed., pp. 319–339). Thousand Oaks, CA: Pine Forge.

Swenson, C. H., Fuller, S., & Clements, R. (1993). Stage of religious faith and reactions to terminal cancer. *Journal of Psychology and Theology, 21,* 238–245.

Swidler, A. (1986). Culture in action: Symbols and strategies. *American Sociological Review, 51,* 273–286.

Swift, D. C. (1998). *Religion and the American experience.* Armonk, NY: M.E. Sharpe.

Swinton, J. (1997). Restoring the image: Spirituality, faith, and cognitive disability. *Journal of Religion and Health, 36*(1), 21–27.

Sword, W., Watt, S., & Krueger, P. (2006). Postpartum health, service needs, and access to care experiences of immigrant and Canadian-born women. *Journal of Obstetric Gynecological and Neonatal Nurses, 35*(6), 717–727.

Taddio, A., Shah, V., Gilbert-Macleod, C., & Katz, J. (2002). Conditioning and hyperalgesia in newborns exposed to repeated heel lances. *Journal of the American Medical Association, 288*(7), 857–861.

Takahashi, E. A., & Turnbull, J. E. (1994). New findings in psychiatric genetics: Implications for social work practice. *Social Work in Health Care, 20*(2), 1–21.

Takahashi, K. (1990). Are the key assumptions of the "strange situation" procedure universal? A view from Japanese research. *Human Development, 33,* 23–30.

Takano, T., Nakamura, K., & Watanabe, M. (2002). Urban residential environments and senior citizens' longevity in megacity areas: The importance of walkable green spaces. *Journal of Epidemiology and Community Health, 56*(12), 913–918.

Tan, H., & Loth, S. (2010). Microsurgical reversal of sterilization—is this still clinically relevant today? *Annals: Academy of Medicine Singapore, 39*(1), 22–26.

Tan, P. P. (2006). Spirituality and religious beliefs among South-East Asians. *Reflections: Narratives of Professional Helping, 12*(3), 44–47.

Tang, C., Yeung, D., & Lee, A. (2003). Psychosocial correlates of emotional responses to menarche among Chinese adolescent girls. *Journal of Adolescent Health, 33,* 193–201.

Tangenberg, K. M. (2008). Saddleback Church and the P.E.A.C.E. plan: Implications for social work. *Social Work & Christianity, 35*(4), 391–412.

Tangenberg, K. M., & Kemp, S. (2002). Embodied practice: Claiming the body's experience, agency, and knowledge for social work. *Social Work, 47*(1), 9–18.

Tanielian, T., & Jaycox, L. (Eds.). (2008). *Invisible wounds of war: Psychological and cognitive injuries, their consequences, and services to assist recovery.* Santa Monica, CA: RAND Corporation.

Tanner, J. (2002). Do laws requiring higher wages cause unemployment? *CQ Researcher, 12*(33), 769–786.

Tarrow, S. (1994). *Power in movement: Social movements, collective action, and politics.* New York: Cambridge University Press.

Tarrow, S. (1998). *Pover in movement: Social movements and contentious politics* (2nd ed.). New York: Cambridge University Press.

Tarrow, S. (2006). *The new transnational activism.* New York: Cambridge University Press.

Tartaro, J., Luecken, L., & Gunn, H. (2005). Exploring heart and soul: Effects of religiosity/spirituality and gender on blood pressure and cortisol stress response. *Journal of Health Psychology, 10,* 753–766.

Tate, A., Dezateux, C., Cole, T., & the Millennium Cohort Study Child Health Group. (2006). Is infant growth changing? *International Journal of Obesity, 30,* 1094–1096.

Tatum, B. D. (1992). Talking about race, learning about racism: The application of racial identity development in the classroom. *Harvard Educational Review, 62*(1), 1–24.

Tatum, B. D. (2000a). The complexity of identity: Who am I? In M. Adams, W. Blumenfeld, R. Castañeda, H. Hackman, M. Peters, & X. Zúñiga (Eds.), *Readings for diversity and social justice: An anthology on racism, anti-Semitism, sexism, heterosexism, ableism, and classism* (pp. 9–14). New York: Routledge.

Tatum, B. D. (2000b). *Why are all the Black kids sitting together in the cafeteria? And other conversations about race* (Rev. ed.). New York: Basic Books.

Taylor, A. (2003). Extent of the problem. *British Medical Journal, 327*(7412), 434–436.

Taylor, A., Kuo, F., Sullivan, W. (2002). Views of nature and self-discipline: Evidence from inner city children. *Journal of Environmental Psychology, 22*(1–2), 49–63.

Taylor, A., Wiley, A., Kuo, F., & Sullivan, W. (1998). Growing up in the inner city: Green spaces as places to grow. *Environment and Behavior, 30,* 3–27.

Taylor, F. W. (1911). *Principles of scientific management.* New York: Harper & Row.

Taylor, H. (2000). Meeting the needs of lesbian and gay young adolescents. *Clearing House, 73*(4), 221–224.

Taylor, J. M., Gilligan, C., & Sullivan, A. M. (1995). *Between voice and silence: Women and girls, race and relationship.* Cambridge, MA: Harvard University Press.

Taylor, M. Y., Wyatt-Asmead, J. W., Gray, J., Bofill, J. A., Martin, R., & Morrison, J. C. (2006). Pregnancy loss after first-trimester viability in women with sickle cell trait: Time for a reappraisal? *American Journal of Obstetrics and Gynecology, 194*(6), 1604–1609.

Taylor, R. B. (1988). *Human territorial functioning: An empirical, evolutionary perspective on individual and small group territorial cognitions, behaviors, and consequences.* Cambridge, UK: Cambridge University Press.

Taylor, R. J., Ellison, C. G., Chatters, L. M., Levin, J. S., & Lincoln, D. L. (2000). Mental health services in faith communities: The role of clergy in Black churches. *Social Work, 45*(1), 73–87.

Taylor, S. E., Lewis, B., Gruenewald, T., Gurung, R., Updegraff, J., & Klein, L. (2002). Sex differences in biobehavioral responses to threat. *Psychological Review, 109*(4), 751–753.

Taylor, S. E., & Stanton, A. L. (2007). Coping resources, coping processes, and mental health. *Annual Review of Clinical Psychology, 3,* 377–401.

Taylor, W., Blair, S., Cummings, S., Wun, C., & Malina, R. (1999). Childhood and adolescent physical activity patterns and adult physical activity. *Medicine and Science in Sports and Exercise, 31,* 118–123.

Teachman, J. (2003). Premarital sex, premarital cohabitation, and the risk of subsequent marital dissolution among women. *Journal of Marriage and Family, 65*(2), 444–455.

Teeple, G. (2000). *Globalization and the decline of social reform: Into the twenty-first century.* Aurora, Ont., Canada: Garamond Press.

Teicher, M. (2002). Scars that won't heal: The neurobiology of child abuse. *Scientific American, 286*(3), 68–75.

Teitelman, J. L. (1995). Homosexuality. In G. L. Maddox (Ed.), *The encyclopedia of aging: A comprehensive resource in gerontology and geriatrics* (2nd ed., p. 270). New York: Springer.

Templeton, J., & Eccles, J. (2006). The relationship between spiritual development and identity processes. In G. Roelkepartain, P. King, L. Wagener, & P. Benson (Eds.), *The handbook of spiritual development in childhood and adolescence* (pp. 252–265). Thousand Oaks, CA: Sage.

Tennessen, C., & Cimprich, B. (1995). Views to nature: Effects on attention. *Journal of Environmental Psychology, 15,* 77–85.

Terkel, S. (2003). *Hope dies last: Keeping the faith in difficult times.* New York: The New Press.

Thibaut, J. W., & Kelley, H. H. (1959). *The social psychology of groups.* New York: Wiley.

Thomas, A., & Chess, S. (1986). The New York longitudinal study: From infancy to early adult life. In R. Plomin & J. Dunn (Eds.), *The study of temperament: Changes, continuities, and challenges* (pp. 39–52). Hillside, NJ: Erlbaum.

Thomas, A., Chess, S., & Birch, H. G. (1968). *Temperament and behavior disorders in children.* New York: New York University Press.

Thomas, A., Chess, S., & Birch, H. G. (1970). The origin of personality. *Scientific American, 223,* 102–109.

Thomas, M. L. (2009). Faith collaboration: A qualitative analysis of faith-based social service programs in organizational relationships. *Administration in Social Work, 33*(1), 40–60.

Thomas, W. I., & Thomas, D. S. (1928). *The child in America: Behavior problems and programs.* New York: Knopf.

Thomlison, B. (2004). Child maltreatment: A risk and protective factor perspective. In M. F. (Ed.), *Risk and resilience in childhood: An ecological perspective* (2nd ed., pp. 89–131). Washington, DC: NASW.

Thompson, P. (1993). Postmodernism: Fatal distraction. In J. Hassard & M. Parker (Eds.), *Postmodernism and organizations* (pp. 183–203). Newbury Park, CA: Sage.

Thompson, R. A., & Nelson, C. (2001). Developmental science and the media: Early brain development. *American Psychologist, 56*(1), 5–15.

Thomson, R. G. (Ed.). (1996). *Freakery: Cultural spectacles of the extraordinary body.* New York: New York University Press.

Thyer, B. A. (2005). The misfortunes of behavioral social work: Misprized, misread, and misconstrued. In S. A. Kirk (Ed.), *Mental disorders in the social environment: Critical perspectives* (pp. 330–343). New York: Columbia University Press.

Thyer, B., & Wodarski, J. (2007). *Social work in mental health: An evidence-based approach.* Hoboken, NJ: Wiley.

Tiet, A., Bird, H., Hoven, C., Wu, P., Moore, R., & Davies, M. (2001). Resilience in the face of maternal psychopathology and adverse life events. *Journal of Child and Family Studies, 10*(3), 347–365.

Tilley, I. B., Shaaban, O. M., Wilson, M., Glasier, A., & Mishell, D. R. (2009). Breastfeeding and contraception use among women with unplanned pregnancies less than two years after delivery. *International Journal of Gynaecology and Obstetrics: The Official Organ of the International Federation of Gynaecology and Obstetrics, 105*(2), 127–130.

Tilly, C. (2004). *Social movements, 1768–2004.* Boulder, CO: Paradigm.

Tilton, J. (2009). Youth uprising: Gritty youth leadership development and communal transformation. In L. Nybell, J. Shook, & J. Finn (Eds.), *Childhood, youth, & social work in transformation: Implications for policy & practice* (pp. 385–400). New York: Columbia University Press.

Timberlake, E. M., & Cook, K. O. (1984). Social work and the Vietnamese refugee. *Social Work, 29*(2), 108–114.

Tindall, D. (2004). Social movement participation over time: An ego-network approach to micro-mobilization. *Sociological Focus, 37,* 163–184.

Titone, A. M. (1991). Spirituality and psychotherapy in social work practice. *Spirituality and Social Work Communicator, 2*(1), 7–9.

Tobin, S. (1988). Preservation of the self in old age. *Social Casework: The Journal of Contemporary Social Work, 66* (9), 550–555.

Tolliver, D. E. (2001). African-American female caregivers of family members living with HIV/AIDS. *Families in Society, 82*(2), 145–156.

Tomai, M., Veronica, R., Mebane, M., D'Acunti, A., Benedetti, M., & Francescato, D. (2010). Virtual communities in schools as tools to promote social capital with high school students. *Computers & Education, 54,* 265–274.

Toner, J. P. (2002). Progress we can be proud of: U.S. trends in assisted reproduction over the first 20 years. *Fertility and Sterility, 78,* 943–950.

Tonnies, F. (1963). *Community and society* (C. P. Loomis, Ed.). New York: Harper & Row. (Original work published 1887)

Tornstam, L. (2005). *Gerotranscendence: A developmental theory of positive aging.* New York: Springer.

Torrez, E. (1984). *The folk-healer: The Mexican-American tradition of curanderismo.* Kingsville, TX: Nieves Press.

Toseland, R. W., & Rivas, R. F. (2009). *An introduction to group work practice* (6th ed.). New York: Pearson.

Tout, K., & Zaslow, M. (2003). Public investments in child care quality: Needs, challenges, and opportunities. In R. M. Lerner, F. Jacobs, & D. Wertlieb (Eds.), *Handbook of applied developmental science* (Vol. 1, pp. 339–366). Thousand Oaks, CA: Sage.

Tracy, E., & Johnson, P. (2007). Personal social networks of women with co-occurring substance use and mental disorders. *Journal of Social Work Practice in Addictions, 7*(1/2), 69–70.

Trainor, A. A. (2008). Using cultural and social capital to improve postsecondary outcomes and expand transition models for youth with disabilities. *Journal of Special Education, 42*(3), 148–162.

Trattner, W. (1998). *From poor law to welfare state: A history of social welfare in America* (6th ed.). New York: Free Press.

Trees, A. (2006). Attachment theory: The reciprocal relationship between family communication and attachment patterns. In D. Braithwaite & L. Baxter (Eds.), *Engaging theories in family communication: Multiple perspectives* (pp. 165–180). Thousand Oaks, CA: Sage.

Tripses, J., & Scroggs, L. (2009). Spirituality and respect: Study of a model school–church–community collaboration. *School Community Journal, 19*(1), 77–97.

Troiden, R. (1989). The formation of homosexual identities. *Journal of Homosexuality, 17,* 43–73.

Trussell, J. (2004). Contraceptive failure in the United States. *Contraception, 70*(2), 89–96.

Turiel, E. (2004). Commentary: Beyond individualism and collectivism: A problem or progress? *New Directions in Child and Adolescent Development, 104,* 91–100.

Turner, H., Finkelhor, D., & Ormrod, R. (2006). The effect of lifetime victimization on the mental health of children and adolescents. *Social Science & Medicine, 62*(1), 13–27.

Turner, R. P., Lukoff, D., Barnhouse, R. T., & Lu, F. G. (1995). Religious or spiritual problem: A culturally sensitive diagnostic category in the DSM–IV. *Journal of Nervous and Mental Disease, 183,* 435–444.

Tutty, L., & Wagar, J. (1994). The evolution of a group for young children who have witnessed family violence. *Social Work With Groups, 17*(1/2), 89–104.

Tweddle, A. (2007). Youth leaving care: How do they fare? *New Directions for Youth Development, 113,* 15–31.

Tweed, T. T. (1997). Asian religions in the United States. In W. H. Conser, Jr., & S. B. Twiss (Eds.), *Religious diversity and American religious history: Studies in traditions and cultures* (pp. 189–217). Athens: University of Georgia Press.

Twiss, P., & Cooper, P. (2000). Youths revitalizing Main Street: A case study. *Social Work in Education, 22*(3), 162–176.

Uchino, B. N. (2009). Understanding the links between social support and physical health: A life-span perspective with emphasis on the separability of perceived and received support. *Perspectives on Psychological Science, 4*(3), 236–255.

Uddin, L., Iacoboni, M., Lange, C., & Keenan, J. (2007). The self and social cognition: The role of cortical midline structures and mirror neurons. *Trends in Cognitive Sciences, 11*(4), 153–157.

Uhlenbruck, K., Meyer, K., & Hitt, M. (2003). Organizational transformation in transition economies: Resource based and organizational learning perspectives. *Journal of Management Studies, 40,* 257–282.

Ulrich, R. (1984). View through a window may influence recovery from surgery. *Science, 224,* 420–421.

Ulrich, R. (1993). Biophilia, biophobia, and natural landscapes. In S. Kellert & E. Wilson (Eds.), *The biophilia hypothesis* (pp. 73–137). Washington, DC: Island Press.

Ulrich, R. (2006). Evidence-based health-care architecture. *The Lancet, 368,* 538–539.

Ulrich, R., & Zimring, C. (2005). *The role of the physical environment in the hospital of the 21st century: A once-in-a-lifetime opportunity.* Retrieved September 14, 2011, from http://www.rwjf.org/files/publications/other/RoleofthePhysicalEnvironment.pdf

UNAIDS. (2005). *Global summary of the HIV and AIDS epidemic, December 2004.* Retrieved April 24, 2005, from http://whqlibdoc.who.int/unaids/2004/a62410_intro.pdf

Underwood, M. K. (2003). *Social aggression among girls.* New York: Guilford Press.

UNESCO. (2010). *Education for All global monitoring report 2010: Summary.* Paris: Author.

Ungar, M. (2002). A deeper, more social ecological social work practice. *Social Service Review, 76*(3), 480–497.

UNICEF. (2000). *Child poverty in rich nations.* Florence, Italy: United Nations Children's Fund.

UNICEF. (2005a). *Child poverty in rich countries 2005: Report card no. 6.* Florence, Italy: UNICEF Innocenti Research Centre.

UNICEF. (2005b). *The state of the world's children 2006: Excluded and invisible.* New York: Author.

UNICEF. (2007). *Child poverty in perspective: An overview of child well-being in rich countries.* Florence, Italy: United Nations Children's Fund.

UNICEF. (2009a). *The state of the world's children: Special edition statistical tables.* New York: Author.

UNICEF. (2009b). *Tracking progress in child and maternal nutrition.* Retrieved February 12, 2010, from http://www.unicef.org/media/files/Tracking_Progress_on_Child_and_Maternal_Nutrition_EN_110309.pdf

UNICEF. (2011, January 1). *Facts on children: Early childhood.* Retrieved August 1, 2011, from http://www.unicef.org/earlychildhood/9475.html

UNICEF. (n.d.). *Information by country and programme.* Retrieved January 13, 2010, from http://www.unicef.org/infobycountry/index.html

UNICEF Canada. (2010). *Early child development.* Retrieved September 2, 2011, from http://www.unicef.ca./portal/SmartDefault.aspx?at=1285

UNICEF Innocenti Research Centre. (2005). *Child poverty in rich countries 2005* (Innocenti Report Card No. 6). Florence, Italy: Author.

United Nations. (1948). *The universal declaration of human rights.* Retrieved January 14, 2010, from http://www.un.org/Overview/rights.html

United Nations Children's Fund. (2000a). *A league table of child poverty in rich nations. Innocenti Report Card (1).* Retrieved December 3, 2006, from http://www.unicef-icdc.org/publications/pdf/repcard1e.pdf

United Nations Children's Fund. (2000b). *Poverty reduction begins with children.* New York: Author. Retrieved January 15, 2007, from http://www.unicef.org/publications/index_5616.html

United Nations Children's Fund (2009, July). *Economic update: Countries' evolving vulnerability from a child's* perspective. (Social and Economic Working Brief). New York: Author. Retrieved January 19, 2010, from http://www.unicef.org/socialpolicy/files/Countries_Evolving_Vulnerability_final.pdf

United Nations Development Program. (2005). *Human development report 2005: International cooperation at the crossroads: Aid, trade, and security in an unequal world.* New York: Oxford University Press.

University of Cincinnati. (2001–2010). *About COM. Polio.* Cincinnati, OH: University of Cincinnati, College of Medicine. Retrieved January 1, 2010, from http://www.med.uc.edu/about/history/htmlversion/polio.cfm

Upadhyay, U. D. (2005). *New contraceptives choices* (Population Reports, Series M, No. 19). Baltimore: The John Hopkins Bloomberg School of Public Health.

Urban Institute. (2006). *Welfare reform: Ten years later.* Retrieved May 17, 2010, from http://www.urban.org/toolkit/issues/welfarereform.cfm

Urbina, I. (2010, March 23). Acorn to shut all offices by April 1. *New York Times,* p. A17.

U.S. Bureau of Labor Statistics. (2006, August 25). *Bureau of Labor Statistics News: Employment and unemployment among youth summary.* Washington, DC: Author.

U.S. Bureau of Labor Statistics. (2008). *Employment and earnings, 2008 annual averages and the monthly labor review.* Retrieved December 3, 2009, from http://www.dol.gov/wb/stats/main.htm

U.S. Bureau of Labor Statistics. (2009a). *Labor force statistics from the current population.* Retrieved January 5, 2010, from http://www.bls.gov/cps/

U.S. Bureau of Labor Statistics. (2009b). *New monthly data series on the employment status of people with a disability.* Retrieved September 3, 2009, from http://www.bls.gov/cps/cpsdisability.htm

U.S. Bureau of Labor Statistics. (2010). *Economic news release: Employment situation summary.* Retrieved February 20, 2010, from http://www.bls.gov/news.release/empsit.nr0.htm

U.S. Census Bureau. (1999). *Statistical abstract of the United States.* Washington, DC: U.S. Government.

U.S. Census Bureau. (2002a). *Census brief. Coming to America: A profile of the nation's foreign born* (2000 update). Washington, DC: Author

U.S. Census Bureau. (2002b). *Current population survey.* Washington, DC: Author.

U.S. Census Bureau. (2004a). *The foreign born population 2004.* Washington, DC: Author.

U.S. Census Bureau. (2004b). *We the people: Aging in the United States* (Census 2000 Special Report). Washington, DC: U.S. Department of Commerce.

U.S. Census Bureau. (2005). *2005 American community survey.* Retrieved January 14, 2007, from http://www.census.gov/hhes/www/disability/2005acs.html

U.S. Census Bureau. (2008a). *Population estimates.* Retrieved September 15, 2011, from http://www.census.gov/popest/states/NST-ann-est.html

U.S. Census Bureau. (2008b). *Table 2: Projections of population by selected age and sex for groups in the U.S. from 2010 to 2030.* Retrieved March 3, 2010, from http://www.census.gov/population/www/projections

U.S. Census Bureau (2009a). *America's families and living arrangements: 2007.* Retrieved December 9, 2009, from http://www.census.gov/

U.S. Census Bureau. (2009b). *Definition: Household and family.* Retrieved November 30, 2009, from http://www.census.gov/

U.S. Census Bureau. (2009c). *Facts for features.* Retrieved September 15, 2011, from http://www.census.gov/newsroom/releases/archives/facts_for_features_special_editions/cb09-ff14.html

U.S. Census Bureau. (2009d). *Population estimates program: National characteristics.* Retrieved July 23, 2009, from http://www.census.gov/popest/national/asrh/NC-EST2008-srh.html

U.S. Census Bureau. (2009e). *U.S. POPClock projection.* Retrieved July 23, 2009, from http://www.census.gov/population/www/popclockus.html

U.S. Census Bureau. (n.d.). *The living arrangements of children in 2005. Population profile of the United States: Dynamic version.* Washington, DC: Author. Retrieved November 15, 2006, from http://www.census.gov/population/pop-profile/dynamic/LivArrChildren.pdf

U.S. Commission on Human Rights. (1998). Indian tribes: A continuing quest for survival. In P. S. Rothenberg (Ed.), *Race, class and gender in the United States: An integrated study* (4th ed., pp. 378–382). New York: St. Martin's Press.

U.S. Conference of Mayors. (2007). *A hunger and homelessness survey, 2007.* Retrieved October 16, 2009, from http://usmayors.org/uscm/home.asp

U.S. Department of Health and Human Services. (2000a). *Tracking healthy people 2010.* Washington, DC: U.S. Government Printing Office.

U.S. Department of Health and Human Services. (2000b). *Trends in the well-being of America's children and youth.* Washington, DC: U.S. Government Printing Office.

U.S. Department of Health and Human Services. (2005). *Child maltreatment 2003.* Washington, DC: U.S. Government Printing Office.

U.S. Department of Health and Human Services. (2009a). *Child maltreatment 2007.* Retrieved February 13, 2010, from http://www.acf.hhs.gov/programs/cb/pubs/cm07/cm07.pdf

U.S. Department of Health and Human Services. (2009b). *Children of foreign-born parents.* Retrieved March 3, 2010, from http://mchb.hrsa.gov/chus08/popchar/pages/102fbp.html

U.S. Department of Health and Human Services/U.S. Department of Agriculture. (2005). *Dietary guidelines for Americans 2005.* Retrieved November 15, 2006, from http://www.healthierus.gov/dietaryguidelines

U.S. Department of Housing and Urban Development. (2009). *Federal definition of homeless.* Retrieved October 16, 2009, from http://www.hud.gov/homeless/definition.cfm

U.S. Department of Labor, Bureau of Labor Statistics. (2008). *Employment and earnings, 2008 annual averages and the monthly labor review.* Retrieved December 3, 2009, from http://www.dol.gov/wb/stats/main.htm

Vaage, A. B., Garløv, C., Hauff, E., & Thomsen, P. H. (2007). Psychiatric symptoms and service utilization among refugee children referred to a child psychiatry department: A retrospective comparative case note study. *Transcultural Psychiatry, 44*(3), 440–458.

Vaillant, G. (1977). *Adaptation to life.* Boston: Little, Brown.

Vaillant, G. (1993). *The wisdom of the ego.* Cambridge, MA: Harvard University Press.

Vaillant, G. (2002). *Aging well: Surprising guideposts to a happier life from the Landmark Harvard Study of Adult Development.* Boston: Little, Brown.

Valsiner, J. (1989). *Human development and culture: The social nature of personality and its study.* Lexington, MA: Lexington Books.

Valsiner, J. (2000). *Culture and human development.* Thousand Oaks, CA: Sage.

Van Aelst, P., & Walgrave, S. (2004). New media, new movements? The role of the Internet in shaping the "anti-globalization" movement. In W. van de Donk, B. Loader, P. Nixon, & D. Rucht (Eds.), *Cyberprotest: New media, citizens and social movements* (pp. 87–108). London: Routledge.

Van Ausdale, D., & Feagin, J. (1996). Using racial and ethnic concepts: The critical case of very young children. *American Sociological Review, 61,* 119–269.

van de Beek, C., Thijssen, J. H., Cohen-Kettenis, P. T., van Goozen, S. H., & Buitelaar, J. K. (2004). Relationships between sex hormones assessed in amniotic fluid, and maternal and umbilical cord serum: What is the best source of information to investigate the effects of fetal hormonal exposure? *Hormones and Behavior, 46*(5), 663–669.

van der Spuy, Z. M., & Dyer, S. J. (2004). The pathogenesis of infertility and early pregnancy loss in polycystic ovary syndrome. *Best Practice and Research: Clinical Obstetrics and Gynaecology, 18*(5), 755–771.

Van der Vegt, G., Eman, B., & Van De Vliert, E. (2001). Patterns of interdependence in work teams: A two-level investigation of the relations with job and team satisfaction. *Personnel Psychology, 54,* 51–69.

Van der Wijden, C. A., Kleijnen, J., & Van den Berk, T. (2003). Lactational amenorrhea for family planning. *Cochrane Database Systematic Review,* Issue 3, CD001329.

Van Hook, M., Hugen, B., & Aguilar, M. (Eds.). (2001). *Spirituality within religious traditions in social work practice.* Pacific Grove, CA: Brooks/Cole.

Van Voorhees, E., & Scarpa, A. (2004). The effects of child maltreatment on the hypothalamic-pituitary-adrenal axis. *Trauma Violence Abuse, 5*(4), 333–352.

Van Voorhis, B. (2006). Outcomes from assisted reproductive technology. *Obstetrics & Gynecology, 107*(1), 183–200.

Vandell, D. L., & Wolfe, B. (2000). *Child care quality: Does it matter and does it need to be improved?* (Special Report #78). Madison, WI: Institute for Research on Poverty.

Vanden Heuvel, K., & Graham-Felsen, S. (2006). Chicago's living wage. *The Nation, 283*(9), 8–9.

Vandivere, S., Moore, K. A., & Brown, B. (2000). Child well-being at the outset of welfare reform: An overview of the nation and 13 states. *New Federalism, National Survey of American Families,* Series B, No. B-23. Washington, DC: The Urban Institute.

VanLaningham, J., Johnson, D., & Amato, P. (2001). Marital happiness, marital duration, and the U-shaped curve: Evidence from a five-wave panel study. *Social Forces, 78*(4), 1313–1341.

Vansteelandt, S., Goetgeluk, S., Lutz, S., Waldman, I., Lyon, H., Schadt, E. et al. (2009). On the adjustment for covariates in genetic association analysis: A novel, simple principle to infer direct causal effects. *Genetic Epidemiology, 33*(5), 394–405.

Varela, F. (1989). Reflections on the circulation of concepts between the biology of cognition and systemic family therapy. *Family Process, 28,* 15–24.

Varney, D., & van Vliet, W. (2008). Homelessness, children, and youth: Research in the United States and Canada. *American Behavioral Scientist, 51,* 715–720.

Vaughn, B., & Bost, K. (1999). Attachment and temperament. In J. Cassidy & P. Shaver (Eds.), *Handbook of attachment: Theory, research, and clinical applications* (pp. 198–225). New York: Guilford Press.

Vazsonyi, S., & Snider, J. B. (2008). Mentoring, competencies, and adjustment in adolescents: American part-time employment and European apprenticeships. *International Journal of Behavioral Development, 32*(1), 46–55.

Vekemans, M. (1996). Cytogenetics. In J. J. Sciarra (Ed.), *Gynecology and obstetrics* (Rev. ed., pp. 57–66). Philadelphia: Lippincott-Raven.

Veltkamp, L., & Miller, T. (1994). *Clinical handbook of child abuse and neglect.* Madison, CT: International Universities Press.

Ventura, S. J., Martin, J. A., Curtin, S. C., & Mathews, T. J. (1998). Report of final natality statistics: 1996. *Monthly Vital Statistics Report, 46*(225), 1–99.

Verity, F., & King, S. (2007). Responding to intercommunal conflict—What can restorative justice offer? *Community Development Journal, 43*(4), 470–482.

Verkuyten, M. (2005). Ethnic group identification and group evaluation among minority and majority groups: Testing the multiculturalism hypothesis. *Journal of Personality and Social Psychology, 88*(1), 121–138.

Verma, S., & Larson, R. (Eds.). (2003, Spring). Examining adolescent leisure time across cultures. *New Directions for Child and Adolescent Development, 99.*

Vetere, A. (2005). Structural family therapy. In T. Chibucos & R. Leite (Eds.), *Readings in family theory* (pp. 293–302). Thousand Oaks, CA: Sage.

Viacom. (2006). *Viacom fact sheet.* Retrieved October 13, 2006, from http://www.viacom.com/2006/pdf/viacom FactSheet%20_915_%without_contacts.pdf

Vickrey, B. G., Strickland, T. L., Fitten, L. J., Admas, G. R., Ortiz, F., & Hays, R. D. (2007). Ethnic variations in dementia caregiving experiences: Insights from focus groups. *Journal of Human Behavior in the Social Environment, 15*(2/3), 233–249.

Villarruel, F., Perkins, D., Borden, L., & Keith, J. (2003). *Community youth development: Programs, policies, and practice.* Thousand Oaks, CA: Sage.

Virilio, P. (2000). *The information bomb.* London: Verso.

Vlahov, D., Galea, S., & Freudenberg, N. (2005). The urban health "advantage." *Journal of Urban Health, 82*(1), 1–4.

Vohra-Gupta, S., Russell, A., & Lo, E. (2007). Meditation: The adoption of Eastern thought to Western social practices. *Social Thought, 26*(2), 49–61.

Volgt, M., Hermanussen, M., Wittwer-Backofen, U., Fusch, C., & Hesse, V. (2006). Sex-specific differences in birth weight due to maternal smoking during pregnancy. *European Journal of Pediatrics, 165*(110), 757–761.

Volker, D. L. (2005). Control and end-of-life care: Does ethnicity matter? *American Journal of Hospice & Palliative Care, 22*(6), 442–446.

Volkmar, F. R., Paul, R., Klin, A., & Cohen, D. J. (2005). *Handbook of autism and pervasive developmental disorders.* Hoboken, NJ: Wiley.

Volling, B., Blandon, A., & Kolak, A. (2006). Marriage, parenting, and the emergence of early self-regulation in the family system. *Journal of Child and Family Studies, 15*(4), 493–506.

von Salisch, M. (2001). Children's emotional development: Challenges in their relationships to parents, peers, and friends. *International Journal of Behavioral Development, 25,* 310–319.

Voorpostel, M., & van der Lippe, T. (2007). Support between siblings and between friends: Two worlds apart? *Journal of Marriage and Family, 69,* 1271–1282.

Vosler, N. R. (1996). *New approaches to family practice: Confronting economic stress.* Thousand Oaks, CA: Sage.

Voss, K. (1996). The collapse of a social movement: The interplay of mobilizing structures, framing, and political opportunities in the Knights of Labor. In D. McAdams, J. McCarthy, & M. Zald (Eds.), *Comparative perspectives on social movements* (pp. 227–258). New York: Cambridge University Press.

Voss, R. W., Douville, V., Little Soldier, A., & Twiss, G. (1999). Tribal and shamanic-based social work practice: A Lakota perspective. *Social Work, 44*(3), 228–241.

Vranic, A. (2003). Personal space in physically abused children. *Environment and Behavior, 35*(4), 550–565.

Vuorenkoski, L., Kuure, O., Moilanen, I., Penninkilampi, V., & Myhrman, A. (2000). Bilingualism, school achievement, and mental well-being: A follow-up study of return migrant children. *Journal of Child Psychology and Psychiatry and Allied Disciplines, 41*(2), 261–266.

Vygotsky, L. (1986). *Thought and language.* Cambridge: MIT Press.

Waanders, C., Mendez, J., & Downer, J. (2007). Parent characteristics, economic stress and neighborhood context as predictors of parent involvement in preschool children's education. *Journal of School Psychology, 45*(6), 619–636.

Wachs, T. (1992). *The nature of nurture.* Newbury Park, CA: Sage.

Wacker, R., & Roberto, K. (2008). *Community resources for older adults: Programs and services in an era of change* (3rd ed.). Thousand Oaks, CA: Sage.

Wadensten, B. (2005). Introducing older people to the theory of gerotranscendence. *Journal of Advanced Nursing, 52*(4), 381–388.

Wadsworth, M., & Santiago, C. (2008). Risk and resiliency processes in ethnically diverse families in poverty. *Journal of Family Psychology, 22*(3), 399–410.

Wagener, L., Furrow, J., King, P., Leffert, N., & Benson, P. (2003). Religion and developmental resources. *Review of Religious Research, 44*(3), 271–284.

Wagner, M., Newman, L., Cameto, R., & Levine, P. (2005). *Changes over time in the early postschool outcomes of youth with disabilities.* Menlo Park, CA: SRI International.

Wainright, J., Russell, S., & Patterson, C. (2004). Psychosocial adjustment, school outcomes, and romantic relationships of adolescents with same-sex parents. *Child Development, 75,* 1886–1898.

Walch, J., Day, R., & Kang, J. (2005). The effect of sunlight on postoperative analgesic medication use: A prospective study of patients undergoing spinal surgery. *Psychosomatic Medicine, 67,* 156–163.

Waldron-Hennessey, R., & Sabatelli, R. (1997). The Parental Comparison Level Index: A measure for assessing parental rewards and costs relative to expectations. *Journal of Marriage and the Family, 59,* 823–833.

Walker, A., Manoogian-O'Dell, M., McGraw, L., & White, D. (2001). *Families in later life: Connections and transitions.* Thousand Oaks, CA: Pine Forge.

Walker, D. F., Reid, H. W., O'Neill, T., & Brown, L. (2009). Changes in personal religion/spirituality during and after childhood abuse: A review and synthesis. *Psychological Trauma: Theory, Research, Practice, and Policy, 1*(2), 130–145.

Walker, L. (1989). A longitudinal study of moral reasoning. *Child Development, 5,* 33–78.

Walker, L., & Taylor, J. (1991). Family interactions and the development of moral reasoning. *Child Development, 62,* 262–283.

Walker, S., Berthelsen, D., & Irving, K. (2001). Temperament and peer acceptance in early childhood: Sex and social status differences. *Child Study Journal, 31*(3), 177–192.

Waller, T. (2009). Modern childhood: Contemporary theories and children's lives. In T. Waller (Ed.), *An introduction to early childhood* (2nd ed., pp. 2–15). Thousand Oaks, CA: Sage.

Wallerstein, I. (1974). *The modern world system: Capitalist agriculture and the origins of the European world economy in the 16th century.* New York: Academic Press.

Wallerstein, I. (1979). *The capitalist world economy.* London: Cambridge University Press.

Wallerstein, I. (1980). *The modern world-system: Mercantilism and the consolidation of the European world economy, 1600–1750.* New York: Academic Press.

Wallerstein, I. (1989). *The modern world-system: The second great expansion of the capitalist world-economy, 1730–1840's.* San Diego: Academic Press.

Wallerstein, J. S., & Blakeslee, S. (1989). *Second chances: Men, women and children a decade after divorce.* New York: Ticknor & Fields.

Wallerstein, J. S., & Corbin, S. (1991). The child and the vicissitudes of divorce. In M. Lewis (Ed.), *Child and adolescent psychiatry: A comprehensive textbook* (pp. 1108–1118). Baltimore: Williams & Wilkins.

Wallerstein, J. S., Corbin, S., & Lewis, J. (1988). Children of divorce: A ten-year study. In E. Hetherington & J. Arasteh (Eds.), *Impact of divorce, single-parenting and step-parenting on children* (pp. 198–214). Hillsdale, NJ: Erlbaum.

Walsh, F. (2003a). Changing families in a changing world: Reconstructing family normality. In F. Walsh (Ed.), *Normal family processes: Growing diversity and complexity* (3rd ed., pp. 3–26). New York: Guilford Press.

Walsh, F. (2003b). Family resilience: Strengths forged through adversity. In F. Walsh (Ed.), *Normal family processes: Growing diversity and complexity* (3rd ed., pp. 399–423). New York: Guilford Press.

Walsh, F. (2005). Families in later life: Challenges and opportunities. In B. Carter & M. McGoldrick (Eds.), *The expanded family life style: Individual, family, and social perspectives* (3rd ed., pp. 307–326). Boston: Allyn & Bacon.

Walsh, F. (2006). *Strengthening family resilience* (2nd ed.). New York: Guilford Press.

Walsh, F. (2009a). Integrating spirituality in family therapy: Wellsprings for health, healing, and resilience. In F. Walsh (Ed.), *Spiritual resources in family therapy* (2nd ed., pp. 31–61). New York: Guilford Press.

Walsh, F. (2009b). Spiritual resources in family adaptation to death and loss. In F. Walsh (Ed.), *Spiritual resources in family therapy* (2nd ed., pp. 81–102). New York: Guilford Press.

Walsh, J. (2000). *Clinical case management with persons having mental illness: A relationship-based perspective.* Pacific Gove: Brooks/Cole.

Walsh, J. (2010). *Theories for direct social work practice* (2nd ed.). Belmont, CA: Wadsworth.

Walsh, J., Meyer, A., & Schoonhoven, C. (2006). A future for organization theory: Living in and living with changing organizations. *Organization Science, 17*(5), 657–671.

Walsh, J., & Zacharias-Walsh, A. (2008). Working longer, living less: Understanding Marx through the workplace today. In P. Kivisto (Ed.), *Illuminating social life* (4th ed., pp. 5–40). Thousand Oaks, CA: Sage.

Wamsley, G., & Zald, M. (1973). *The political economy of public organizations.* Lexington, MA: Heath.

Wang, M., Walberg, H., & Reynolds, A. (2004). *Can unlike students learn together? Grade retention, tracking, and grouping.* Charlotte, NC: Information Age Publishing.

Wang, R., Needham, L., & Barr, D. (2005). Effects of environmental agents on attainment of puberty: Considerations when assessing exposure to environmental chemicals in the National Children's Study. *Environmental Health Perspectives, 113*(8), 1100–1107.

Wang, Y., & Zhang, Q. (2006). Are American children and adolescents of low socioeconomic status at increased risk of obesity? Changes in the association between overweight and family income between 1971 and 2002. *American Journal of Clinical Nutrition, 84*(4), 707–716.

Wanyeki, I., Olson, S., Brassard, P., Menzies, D., Ross, N., Behr, M., et al. (2006). Dwellings, crowding, and tuberculosis in Montreal. *Social Science & Medicine, 63*(2), 501–511.

Wapner, S. (1995). Toward integration: Environmental psychology in relation to other subfields of psychology. *Environment and Behavior, 27,* 9–32.

Ward, R. R., Logan, J., & Spitze, G. (1992). The influence of parent and child needs on coresidence in middle and later life. *Journal of Marriage and the Family, 54,* 209–221.

Warner, S. R. (1993). Work in progress: Toward a new paradigm for the sociological study of religion in the United States. *American Journal of Sociology, 98,* 1044–1093.

Warren, K., Franklin, C., & Streeter, C. (1998). New directions in systems theory: Chaos and complexity. *Social Work, 43*(4), 357–372.

Warren, R. (1963). *The community in America.* Chicago: Rand McNally.

Warren, R. (1978). *The community in America* (2nd ed.) Chicago: Rand McNally.

Warren, R. (1987). *The community in America* (3rd ed.). Chicago: Rand McNally.

Warwick, L. L. (1995). Feminist Wicca: Paths to empowerment. *Women and Therapy: A Feminist Quarterly, 16*(2/3), 121–133.

Watanabe, T. (2011, May 9). New approach to bilingual teaching. *Los Angeles Times,* pp. A1, A14.

Watson, J., & Crick, F. (1953). Molecular structure of nucleic acids. *Nature, 171,* 737–738.

Watters, E. (2010). *Crazy like us: The globalization of the American psyche.* New York: Free Press.

Watts, F., Dutton, K., & Gulliford, L. (2006). Human spiritual qualities: Integrating psychology and religion. *Mental Health, Religion & Culture, 9*(3), 277–289.

Weaver, H. (1999). Indigenous people and the social work profession: Defining culturally competent services. *Social Work, 44*(3), 217–225.

Weaver, H. (2007). Cultural competence with First Nations peoples. In D. Lum (Ed.), *Culturally competent practice: A framework for understanding diverse groups and justice issues* (3rd ed., pp. 254–275). Belmont, CA: Thomson.

Weaver-Hightower, M. (2003). The "boy turn" in research on gender and education. *Review of Educational Research, 73*(4), 471–498.

Webb, J., & Weber, M. (2003). Influence of sensory abilities on the interpersonal distance of the elderly. *Environment and Behavior, 35*(5), 695–711.

Webb, N., & Dumpson, J. (2006). *Working with traumatized youth in child welfare.* New York: Guilford Press.

Weber, M. (1947). *The theory of economic and social organization.* New York: Free Press.

Weber, M. (1958). *The Protestant ethic and the spirit of capitalism* (T. Parsons, Trans.). New York: Scribner's. (Original work published 1904–1905)

WebUrbanDesign. (2009). *New urbanism & urban design.* Retrieved October 15, 2009, from http://www.web urbandesign.com

Weichold, K. (2007). Prevention against substance misuse: Life skills and positive youth development. In R. Silbereisen & R. Lerner (Ed.), *Approaches to positive youth development* (pp. 293–310). Thousand Oaks, CA: Sage.

Weiner, B. (2008). Reflections on the history of attribution theory and research: People, personalities, publications, problems. *Social Psychology, 39*(3), 151–156.

Weininger, E., & Lareau, A. (2009). Paradoxical pathways: An ethnographic extension of Kohn's findings on class and childrearing. *Journal of Marriage and Family, 71,* 680–695.

Weinstock, H., Berman, S., & Cates, W. (2004). Sexually transmitted diseases among American youth: Incidence and prevalence estimates, 2000. *Perspectives on Sexual and Reproductive Health, 36*(1), 6–10.

Weisberg, R. (Producer/Director). (2006). *Waging a living* [Motion picture]. New York: Public Policy Productions.

Weisglas-Kuperus, N., Hille, E. T., Duivenboorden. H. J., Finken, M. J., Wit, J. M., Van Buuren, S., et al. (2009). Intelligence of very preterm or very low birthweight infants in young adulthood. *Archives of Disease in Childhood, 94*(3), 196–200.

Weisman, G. (1981). Modeling environment–behavior systems: A brief note. *Journal of Man–Environment Relations, 1*(2), 32–41.

Weisner, T. (2005). Attachment as cultural and ecological problem with pluralistic solutions. *Human Development, 48,* 89–94.

Weissberg, R., & O'Brien, M. (2004). What works in school-based social and emotional learning programs for positive youth development. *Annals of the American Academy of Political and Social Science, 591,* 86–97.

Weitz, R. (2009). *The sociology of health, illness, and health care: A critical approach* (5th ed.). Beverly, MA: Wadsworth.

Wellman, B. (1979). The community question. *American Journal of Sociology, 84,* 1201–1231.

Wellman, B. (1982). Studying personal communities. In P. Marsden & N. Lin (Eds.), *Social structure and network analysis* (pp. 61–80). Beverly Hills, CA: Sage.

Wellman, B. (1996). Are personal communities local? A Dumptarian reconsideration. *Social Networks, 18,* 347–354.

Wellman, B. (1999). The network community: An introduction. In B. Wellman (Ed.), *Networks in the global village* (pp. 1–47). Boulder, CO: Westview Press.

Wellman, B. (2001). *The persistence and transformation of community: From neighborhood groups to social networks: Report to the Law Commission of Canada.* Retrieved November 13, 2009, from http://www.chass.utoronto .ca/~wellman/publications/index.html

Wellman, B. (2005). Community: From neighborhood to network. *Communications of the ACM, 48*(10), 53–55.

Wellman, B., & Potter, S. (1999). The elements of personal communities. In B. Wellman (Ed.), *Networks in the global village* (pp. 49–81). Boulder, CO: Westview Press.

Wellman, B., & Wortley, S. (1990). Different strokes from different folks: Community ties and social support. *American Journal of Sociology, 96,* 558–588.

Wellons, M. F., Lewis, C. E., Schwartz, S. M., Gunderson, E. P., Schreiner, P. J., Sternfeld, B., et al. (2008). Racial differences in self-reported infertility and risk factors for infertility in a cohort of Black and White women: The CARDIA women's study. *Fertility and Sterility, 90*(5), 1640–1648.

Welner, S. L. (1997). Gynecologic care and sexuality issues for women with disabilities. *Sexuality and Disability, 15*(10), 33–40.

Welsh, R. (1985). Spanking: A grand old American tradition? *Children Today, 14*(1), 25–29.

Welwood, J. (2000). *Toward a psychology of awakening: Buddhism, psychotherapy, and the path of personal and spiritual transformation.* Boston: Shambhala.

Wenger, G. C. (2009). Childlessness at the end of life: Evidence from rural Wales. *Ageing and Society, 29*(8), 1243–1259.

Wenstrom, K. D. (2009). A randomized, controlled trial of magnesium sulfate for the prevention of cerebral palsy. *Obstetrical and Gynecological Survey, 65*(10), 15–17.

Werner, C., & Altman, I. (2000). Humans and nature: Insights from a transactional view. In S. Wapner, J. Demick, T. Yamamoto, & H. Minami (Eds.), *Theoretical perspectives in environment-behavior research: Underlying assumptions, research problems, and methodologies* (pp. 21–37). New York: Kluwer Academic.

Werner, C., Altman, I., & Oxley, D. (1985). Temporal aspects of homes: A transactional perspective. In I. Altman & C. Werner (Eds.), *Home environments* (pp. 1–32). New York: Plenum.

Werner, C., Brown, B., & Altman, I. (2002). Transactionally oriented research: Examples and strategies. In R. Bechtel & A. Churchman, *Handbook of environmental psychology* (pp. 203–221). Hoboken, NJ: Wiley.

Werner, E., Dawson, G., Osterling, J., & Dinno, N. (2000). Brief report: Recognition of autism spectrum disorder before one year of age: A retrospective study based on home videotapes. *Journal of Autism & Developmental Disorders, 30*(2), 157–162.

Werner, E. E. (2000). Protective factors and individual resilience. In J. Shonkoff & S. Meisels (Eds.), *Handbook of early childhood intervention* (2nd ed., pp. 115–132). New York: Cambridge University Press.

Werner, E. E., & Smith, R. S. (1992). *Overcoming the odds: High-risk children from birth to adulthood*. Ithaca, NY: Cornell University Press.

Werner, E. E., & Smith, R. S. (2001). *Journeys from childhood to midlife*. Ithaca, NY: Cornell University Press.

Wertheimer, R. (2003). *Poor families in 2001: Parents working less and children continue to lag behind*. Washington, DC: Child Trends. Retrieved January 15, 2007, from http://www.childtrends.org/Files/PoorFamiliesRB.pdf

Wertsch, J. V., del Rio, P., & Alvarez, A. (Eds.). (1995). *Sociocultural studies of the mind*. New York: Cambridge University Press.

West, M. (1986). *Landscape views and stress responses in the prison environment*. Unpublished master's thesis, University of Washington, Seattle.

Westrin, A., & Lam, R. (2007). Seasonal affective disorder: A clinical update. *Annals of Clinical Psychiatry, 19*(4), 239–246.

Wetherby, A., Woods, J., Allen, L., Cleary, J., Dickinson, H., & Lord, C. (2004). Early indicators of autism spectrum disorders in the second year of life. *Journal of Autism & Developmental Disorders, 34*(5), 473–493.

Wethington, E., Moen, P., Glasgow, N., & Pillemer, K. (2000). Multiple roles, social integration, and health. In K. Pillemer, P. Moen, & N. Glasgow (Eds.), *Social integration in the second half of life* (pp. 48–71). Baltimore: Johns Hopkins University Press.

Wettenhall, R. (1999). Privatization in Australia: How much and what impacts? *Asian Review of Public Administration, 10*(1–2), 144–158.

Weyermann, M., Beermann, C., Brenner, H., & Rothenbacher, D. (2006). Adponectin and leptin in maternal serum, cord blood, and breast milk. *Clinical Chemistry, 52*(11), 2095–2102.

Wheeler, H. (Ed.). (1973). *Beyond the punitive society*. San Francisco: Freeman.

Whitbourne, S. (1986). *The me I know: A study of adult identity*. New York: Springer Verlag.

Whitbourne, S. (2001). The physical aging process in midlife: Interactions with psychological and sociocultural factors. In M. Lachman (Ed.), *Handbook of midlife development* (pp. 109–155). New York: Wiley.

Whitbourne, S., & Connolly, L. (1999). The developing self in midlife. In S. Willis & J. Reid (Eds.), *Life in the middle: Psychological and social development in middle age* (pp. 25–45). San Diego, CA: Academic Press.

White, J., & Klein, D. (2002). *Family theories* (2nd ed.). Thousand Oaks, CA: Sage.

White, J., & Klein, D. (2008a). The conflict framework. In *Family theories* (3rd ed., pp. 179–204). Thousand Oaks, CA: Sage.

White, J., & Klein, D. (2008b). The feminist framework and poststructuralism. In J. White & D. Klein, *Family theories* (3rd ed., pp. 205–240). Thousand Oaks, CA: Sage.

White, J., & Klein, D. (2008c). The social exchange and rational choice framework. In *Family theories* (3rd ed., pp. 65–92). Thousand Oaks, CA: Sage.

White, J., & Klein, D. (2008d). The systems framework. In *Family theories* (3rd ed., pp. 151–177). Thousand Oaks, CA: Sage.

White, N. R. (2003). Changing conceptions: Young people's views of partnering & parenting. *Journal of Sociology, 39*(2), 149–164.

White, P. (Ed.). (2005). *Biopsychosocial medicine: An integrated approach to understanding illness*. Oxford, UK: Oxford University Press.

Whitehouse.gov. (2010). *Health care*. Retrieved May 8, 2010, from http://www.whitehouse.gov/issues/health-care

Whiting, B., & Whiting, J. (1975). *Children of six cultures: Studies of childrearing*. Cambridge, MA: Harvard University Press.

Whiting, E., & Ward, C. (2008). Food insecurity and provisioning. In D. R. Crane & T. Heaton (Eds.), *Handbook of families & poverty* (pp. 198–219). Thousand Oaks, CA: Sage.

Wichstrom, L. (2001). The impact of pubertal timing on adolescents' alcohol use. *Journal of Research on Adolescence, 11,* 130–150.

Wicker, A. (1979). *An introduction to ecological psychology.* Monterey, CA: Brooks/Cole.

Wicker, A. (1987). Behavior settings reconsidered: Temporal stages, resources, internal dynamics, context. In D. Stokols & I. Altman (Eds.), *Handbook of environmental psychology* (Vol. 1, pp. 613–654). New York: Wiley.

Wickrama, K. A. S., Conger, R. D., & Abraham, W. T. (2005). Early adversity and later health: The intergenerational transmission of adversity through mental disorder and physical illness. *The Journal of Gerontology: Series B, Psychological Sciences and Social Sciences, 60B,* 125–129.

Widmayer, S., Peterson, L., & Larner, M. (1990). Predictors of Haitian-American infant development at twelve months. *Child Development, 61,* 410–415.

Wigert, H., Johannson, R., Berg, M., & Hellstrom, A. L. (2006). Mothers' experiences of having their children in a neonatal intensive care unit. *Scandinavian Journal of Caring Sciences, 20*(10), 35–41.

Wight, V., & Chau, M. (2009a). *Basic facts about low-income children: Children under age 18.* New York: National Center for Children in Poverty. Retrieved February 17, 2010, from http://www.nccp.org/publications/pub_892.html

Wight, V., & Chau, M. (2009b). *Basic facts about low-income children, 2008: Children under age 6.* National Center for Children in Poverty. Retrieved February 17, 2010, from http://www.nccp.org/publications/pdf.text_896.pdf

Wight, V., Chau, M., & Aratani, Y. (2010). *Who are America's poor children? The official story.* New York: National Center for Children in Poverty. Retrieved February 13, 2010, from http://www.nccp.org/publications/pdf/text_912.pdf

Wilber, K. (1977). *The spectrum of consciousness.* Adyar, India: Quest Books.

Wilber, K. (1995). *Sex, ecology, spirituality: The spirit of evolution.* Boston: Shambhala.

Wilber, K. (1996). *A brief history of everything.* Boston: Shambhala.

Wilber, K. (1997a). *The eye of spirit: An integral vision for a world gone slightly mad.* Boston: Shambhala.

Wilber, K. (1997b). An integral theory of consciousness. *Journal of Consciousness Studies, 4*(1), 71–93.

Wilber, K. (2000a). *Integral psychology: Consciousness, spirit, psychology, therapy.* Boston: Shambhala.

Wilber, K. (2000b). *Sex, ecology, spirituality: The spirit of evolution* (2nd ed.). Boston: Shambhala.

Wilber, K. (2001). *A theory of everything: An integral vision for business, politics, science, and spirituality.* Boston: Shambhala.

Wilber, K. (2006). *Integral spirituality.* Boston: Integral Books.

Wilcox, T., Woods, R., Tuggy, L., & Napoli, R. (2006). Shake, rattle, and . . . one or two objects? Young infants' use of auditory information to individuate objects. *Infancy, 9,* 97–123.

Wilde-Mathews, A. (2009, May 7). Tallying the cost to bring baby home. *Wall Street Journal, 253*(106), pp. D1–D7.

Wilkes, S., & Murdoch, A. (2009). Obesity and female fertility: A primary care perspective. *Journal of Family Planning and Reproductive Health Care, 35*(5), 181–185.

Wilkin, A. C. (2009). Masculinity dilemmas: Sexuality and intimacy talk among Christians and Goths. *Signs, 34*(2), 343–368.

Wilkinson, R. (2001). Why is inequality bad for health? In J. Auerbach & B. Krimgold (Eds.), *Income, socioeconomic status, and health: Exploring the relationships* (pp. 29–43). Washington, DC: National Policy Association, Academy for Health Services Research and Health Policy.

Willer, D. (1987). *Theory and the experimental investigation of social structures.* New York: Gordon and Breach.

Williams, A., & Nussbaum, J. (2001). *Intergenerational communication across the life span.* Mahwah, NJ: Erlbaum.

Williams, C. (2006). The epistemology of cultural competence. *Families in Society: The Journal of Contemporary Social Services, 87*(2), 209–220.

Williams, D. R. (2005). The health of U.S. racial and ethnic populations. *The Journal of Gerontology: Series B, Psychological Sciences and Social Sciences, 60B,* 53–63.

Williams, M., Teasdale, J. D., Segal, Z., & Kabat-Zinn, J. (2007). *The mindful way through depression: Freeing yourself from unhappiness.* New York: Guilford Press.

Williams, R. (1977). *Marxism and literature.* Oxford, UK: Oxford University Press.

Williams, R. (1983). *Key words: A vocabulary of culture and society* (Rev. ed.). New York: Oxford University Press.

Williamson, J. S., & Wyandt, C. M. (2001). New perspectives on alternative medicines. *Drug Topics, 145*(1), 57–66.

Willinger, M., Ko., C., & Reddy, U. (2009). Racial disparities in stillbirth across gestation in the United States. *American Journal of Obstetrics and Gynecology, 201*(5), 469.e1–469.e8.

Willis, J. (2010). *Researching London's Living Wage Campaign.* Retrieved October 23, 2009, from http://www.geog/qmul.ac.uk/livingwage/

Willis, S., & Schaie, K. W. (2005). Cognitive trajectories in midlife and cognitive functioning in old age. In S. Willis & M. Martin (Eds.), *Middle adulthood: A lifespan perspective* (pp. 243–275). Thousand Oaks, CA: Sage.

Willis, S., & Schaie, K. W. (2006). Cognitive functioning in the baby boomers: Longitudinal and cohort effects. In S. Whitbourne & S. Willis (Eds.), *The baby boomers grow up: Contemporary perspectives on midlife* (pp. 205–234). Mahwah, NJ: Erlbaum.

Wills, T. A., Yaeger, A. M., & Sandy, J. M. (2003). Buffering effect of religiosity for adolescent substance abuse. *Psychology of Addictive Behaviors, 17*(1), 24–31.

Wilmoth, J. M., & Longino, C. F. (2006). Demographic trends that will shape U.S. policy in the twenty-first century. *Research on Aging, 28*(3), 269–288.

Wilson, E. (1984). *Biophilia*. Cambridge, MA: Harvard University Press.

Wilson, E. (2007). Biophilia and the conservation ethic. In D. Penn & I. Mysterud (Eds.), *Evolutionary perspectives on environmental problems* (pp. 249–257). New Brunswick, NJ: Transaction Publishers.

Wilson, G., & Baldassare, M. (1996). Overall "sense of community" in a suburban region: The effects of localism, privacy, and urbanization. *Environment and Behavior, 28*(1), 27–43.

Wilson, J. Q. (1995). *On character*. Washington, DC: AIE Press.

Wilson, S. (2009). *Fallopian tubes and intrafallopian transfer*. Retrieved May 21, 2010, from http://ezinearticles.com/?Fallopian-Tubes-and-Intrafallopian-Transfer=2875716

Wimmer, H., & Perner, J. (1983). Beliefs about beliefs: Representation and constraining function of wrong beliefs in young children's understanding of deception. *Cognition, 13*, 104–128.

Wimpory, D., Hobson, R., Williams, J., & Nash, S. (2000). Are infants with autism socially engaged? A study of recent retrospective parental reports. *Journal of Autism & Developmental Disorders, 30*, 525–536.

Winant, H. (2004). *The new politics of race: Globalism, difference, justice*. Minneapolis: University of Minnesota Press.

Wingate, M. S., & Alexander, G. R. (2006). Racial and ethnic differences in perinatal mortality: The role of fetal death. *Annals of Epidemiology, 16*(6), 485–491.

Wink, P., & Dillon, M. (2002). Spiritual development across the adult life course: Findings from a longitudinal study. *Journal of Adult Development, 9*(1), 79–94.

Winkler, I., & Cowan, N. (2005). From sensory to long-term memory: Evidence from auditory memory reactivation studies. *Experimental Psychology, 52*(1), 3–20.

Winnicott, D. W. (1975). *Collected papers: From paediatrics to psycho-analysis*. New York: Basic Books.

Winston, C. A. (2006). African American grandmothers parenting AIDS orphans: Grieving and coping. *Qualitative Social Work, 5*(1), 33–43.

Winters, W. G. (1993). *African American mothers and urban schools: The power of participation*. New York: Lexington Books.

Wirth, J. (2009). The function of social work. *Journal of Social Work, 9*(4), 405–419.

Wiseman, R. (2002). *Queen bees and wannabes: Helping your daughter survive cliques, gossip, boyfriends, and other realities of adolescence*. New York: Crown Publishers.

Wisner, K., Chambers, C., & Sit, D. (2006). Postpartum depression: A major public health problem. *Journal of American Medical Association, 296*(21), 2616–2618.

Wisniewski, C. (2008). Applying complementary and alternative medicine practices in a social work context: A focus on mindfulness meditation. *Praxis, 8*, 13–22.

Witkin, S., & Gottschalk, S. (1988). Alternative criteria for theory evaluation. *Social Service Review, 62*, 211–224.

Wittine, B. (1987, September/October). Beyond ego. *Yoga Journal*, pp. 51–57.

Wockel, A., Schafer, E., Beggel, A., & Abou-Dakn, M. (2007). Getting ready for birth: Impending fatherhood. *British Journal of Midwifery, 15*(6), 344–348.

Wojslawowicz Bowker, J., Rubin, K., Burgess, K., Booth-Laforce, C., & Rose-Krasnor, L. (2006). Behavioral characteristics associated with stable and fluid best friendship patterns in middle childhood. *Merrill-Palmer Quarterly, 52*(4), 671–693.

Wolak, J., Mitchell, K. J., & Finkelhor, D. (2003). Escaping or connecting? Characteristics of youth who form close online relationships. *Journal of Adolescence, 26*, 105–119.

Wolak, J., Mitchell, K. J., & Finkelhor, D. (2006). *Online victimization of youth: Five years later*. Retrieved November 15, 2006, from http://www.unh.edu/ccrc/pdf/CV138.pdf

Wolfner, G., & Gelles, R. (1993). A profile of violence toward children: A national study. *Child Abuse and Neglect, 17*, 197–212.

Wong, Y., & Hillier, A. (2001). Evaluating a community-based homelessness prevention program: A geographic information system approach. *Administration in Social Work, 25*(4), 21–45.

Wood, J. (2006). Critical feminist theories: A provocative perspective on families. In D. Braithwaite & L. Baxter (Eds.), *Engaging theories in family communication: Multiple perspectives* (pp. 197–212). Thousand Oaks, CA: Sage.

Woods, T., Antoni, M., Ironson, G., & Kling, D. (1999). Religiosity is associated with affective and immune status in symptomatic HIV-infected gay men. *Journal of Psychosomatic Research, 46*(2), 165–176.

Woolever, C. (1992). A contextual approach to neighbourhood attachment. *Urban Studies, 29*(1), 99–116.

Woollett, A., Dosanjh-Matwala, N., Nicolson, P., Marshall, H., Djhanbakhch, O., & Hadlow, J. (1995). The ideas and experiences of pregnancy and childbirth of Asian and non-Asian women in East London. *British Journal of Medical Psychology, 68*, 65–84.

Worden, J. W. (2009). *Grief counseling and grief therapy: A handbook for the mental health practitioner* (4th ed.). New York: Springer.

World Bank. (2009a). *Global monitoring report, 2009: A development emergency*. New York: Author. Retrieved January 19, 2010, from http://go.worldbank.org/AR2V89HT70

World Bank. (2009b). *Social capital implementation framework*. Retrieved November 16, 2009, from http://www.worldbank.org/

World Health Organization. (2003). *The world health report 2003*. Geneva, Switzerland: Author.

World Health Organization. (2004). *Unsafe abortion: Global and regional estimates of unsafe abortion and associated mortality in 2000.* Retrieved September 14, 2011, from http://www.who.int/reproductivehealth/publications/unsafe_abortion/9241591803/en/

World Health Organization. (2006a). *Countries.* Retrieved November 3, 2006, from http://www.who.int/countries/

World Health Organization. (2006b). *Global access to HIV therapy tripled in past two years, but significant challenges remain.* Retrieved June 24, 2006, from http://www.who.int/hiv/mediacentre/news57/en/index.html

World Health Organization. (2006c). *Global polio eradication initiative strategic plan 2004–2008. Polio case count.* Retrieved May 17, 2010, from http://www.comminit.com/en/node/267428/292

World Health Organization. (2006d). *The world health report 2006.* Retrieved November 3, 2006, from http://www.who.int/whr/2006/

World Health Organization. (2008a). *Global burden of disease 2004 update.* Retrieved September 14, 2011, from http://www.who.int/healthinfo/global_burden_disease/2004_report_update/en/

World Health Organization. (2008b). Poliomyelitis. *Fact Sheet No. 114.* Retrieved January 1, 2010, from http://www.who.int/mediacentre/factsheets/fs114/en/index.html

World Health Organization. (2008c). *Primary health care: Now more than ever.* Geneva, Switzerland: Author. Retrieved February 22, 2010, from http://www.who.int/whr/2008/whr08_en.pdf

World Health Organization. (2010, November). *Poliomyelitis.* Retrieved August 16, 2011, from http://www.who.int/mediacentre/factsheets/fs114/en/

World Health Organization Multicentre Growth Reference Study Group. (2006a). Assessment of differences in linear growth among populations in the WHO Multicentre Growth Reference Study. *Acta Paediatrica, Supplement, 450,* 56–65.

World Health Organization Multicentre Growth Reference Study Group. (2006b). Assessment of sex differences and heterogeneity in motor milestone attainment among populations in the WHO Multicentre Growth Reference Study. *Acta Paediatrica, Supplement, 450,* 66–75.

World Health Organization Multicentre Growth Reference Study Group. (2006c). WHO motor development study: Windows of achievement for six gross motor developmental milestones. *Acta Paediatrica, Supplement, 450,* 86–95.

Wortman, C., & Silver, R. (1989). The myths of coping with loss. *Journal of Consulting and Clinical Psychology, 57,* 349–357.

Wortman, C., & Silver, R. (1990). Successful mastery of bereavement and widowhood. A life course perspective. In P. Baltes & M. Baltes (Eds.), *Successful aging: Perspectives from the behavioral sciences* (pp. 225–264). Cambridge, UK: Cambridge University Press.

Wright, V. H. (2005). *The soul tells a story: Engaging spirituality with creativity in the writing life.* Downers Grove, IL: InterVarsity Press.

Wronka, J. (2008). *Human rights and social justice: Social action and service for the helping and health professions.* Thousand Oaks, CA: Sage.

Wuthnow, R. (2001). *Creative spirituality: The way of the artist.* Berkeley: University of California Press.

Wuthnow, R. (2003). Studying religion, making it sociological. In M. Dillon (Ed.), *Handbook of the sociology of religion* (pp. 17–30). Cambridge, UK: Cambridge University Press.

Wyman, P. A., Cross, W., & Barry, J. (2004). Applying research on resilience to enhance school-based prevention: The promoting resilient children initiative. In C. S. Clauss-Ehlers & M. D. Weist (Eds.), *Community planning to foster resilience in children* (pp. 249–266). New York: Kluwer Academic/Plenum.

Yalom, I. D. (1995). *The theory and practice of group psychotherapy* (4th ed.). New York: Basic Books.

Yang, B., & Brown, J. (1992). A cross-cultural comparison of preferences for landscape styles and landscape elements. *Environment and Behavior, 24,* 471–507.

Yellow Bird, M. J. (1995). Spirituality in First Nations story telling: A Sahnish-Hidatsa approach to narrative. *Reflections: Narratives of Professional Helping, 1*(4), 65–72.

Yoon, D. P., & Lee, E. K. O. (2004). Religiousness/spirituality and subjective well-being among rural elderly whites, African Americans, and Native Americans. *Journal of Human Behavior in the Social Environment, 10*(1), 191–211.

Young, K. R., Marchant, M., & Wilder, L. K. (2004). School-based interventions for students with emotional and behavioral disorders. In P. Allen-Meares & M. W. Fraser (Eds.), *Intervention with children and adolescents: An interdisciplinary perspective* (pp. 175–204). Boston: Allyn & Bacon.

Yu, C. K., Teoh, T. G., & Robinson, S. (2006). Obesity in pregnancy. *British Journal and Obstetrics and Gynaecology: An International Journal of Obstetrics and Gynaecology, 113*(10), 1117–1125.

Zachary, E. (2000). Grassroots leadership training: A case study of an effort to integrate theory and method. *Journal of Community Practice, 7*(1), 71–93.

Zagorsky, J. (2005). Marriage and divorce's impact on wealth. *Journal of Sociology, 41*(4), 406–424.

Zangaglia, R., Pacchetti, C., Pasotti, C., Mancini, F., Servello, D., Sinforiani, E., et al. (2009). Deep brain stimulation and cognitive functions in Parkinson's disease: A three-year controlled study. *Movement Disorder, 11,* 1621–1628.

Zautra, A. (2003). *Emotions, stress, and health.* New York: Oxford University Press.

Zeisel, J. (2006). *Inquiry by design: Environment/behavior/neuroscience in architecture, interiors, landscape, and planning* (Rev. ed.). New York: Norton.

Zellman, G. L., & Waterman, J. M. (1998). Understanding the impact of parent school involvement on children's educational outcomes. *Journal of Educational Research, 91*(6), 370–380.

Zero to Three. (n.d.). *Baby matters: A gateway to state policies and initiatives.* Retrieved September 14, 2011, from http://sparkaction.org/node/6883

Zigler, E., Finn-Stevenson, M., & Hall, N. (2002). *The first three years and beyond: Brain development and social policy.* Chicago: R. R. Donnelly.

Zimbardo, P. (2007). *The Lucifer effect.* New York: Random House.

Zimmerman, S. (2001). *Family policy: Constructed solutions to family problems.* Thousand Oaks, CA: Sage.

Zimmet, P., Alberti, K., & Shaw, J. (2001). Global and societal implications of the diabetes epidemic. *Nature, 414,* 782–787.

Zinnbauer, B., Pargament, K., Cole, B., Rye, M., Butter, E., & Belavich, T. (1997). Religion and spirituality: Unfuzzying the fuzzy. *Journal for the Scientific Study of Religion, 36,* 549–564.

Ziolko, M. E. (1993). Counseling parents of children with disabilities: A review of the literature and implications for practice. In M. Nagler (Ed.), *Perspectives on disability* (2nd ed., pp. 185–193). Palo Alto, CA: Health Markets Research.

Zipper, I., & Simeonsson, R. (2004). Developmental vulnerability in young children with disabilities. In M. Fraser (Ed.), *Risk and resilience in childhood: An ecological perspective* (2nd ed., pp. 161–181). Washington, DC: NASW.

Ziv, M., & Frye, D. (2003). The relation between desire and false belief in children's theory of mind: No satisfaction? *Developmental Psychology, 39,* 859–876.

Zucca, P., Milos, N., & Vallortigara, G. (2007). Piagetian object permanence and its development in Eurasian jays. *Animal Cognition, 10*(2), 243–258.

Zucker, A., Ostrove, J., & Stewart, A. (2002). College-educated women's personality development in adulthood: Perceptions and age differences. *Psychology and Aging, 17*(2), 236–244.

Zuniga, M. (1992). Families with Latino roots. In E. Lynch & M. Hanson (Eds.), *Developing cross-cultural competence: A guide for working with young children and their families* (pp. 151–179). Baltimore: Paul H. Brookes.

Zunkel, G. (2002). Relational coping processes: Couples' response to a diagnosis of early stage breast cancer. *Journal of Psychosocial Oncology, 20*(4), 39–55.

Zwelling, E. (1996). Childbirth education in the 1990s and beyond. *Journal of Gynecologic and Neonatal Nursing, 17*(2), 108–112.

GLOSSARY

ABC-X model of family stress and coping A way of viewing families that focuses on stressor events and crises, family resources, family definitions and beliefs, and outcomes of stress pileup

Accommodation (cognitive) The process of altering a schema when a new situation cannot be incorporated within an existing schema

Accommodation (cultural) Process of partial or selective cultural change in which members of nondominant groups follow the norms, rules, and standards of the dominant culture only in specific circumstances and contexts

Acculturation A process of changing one's culture by incorporating elements of another culture; a mutual sharing of culture

Acquaintance rape Forced, manipulated, or coerced sexual contact by someone who is known to the victim

Acquired immunodeficiency syndrome (AIDS) Disease caused by the human immunodeficiency virus (HIV); involves breakdown of the immune system

Activities of daily living (ADLs) Basic self-care activities, such as bathing, dressing, walking a short distance, shifting from a bed to a chair, using the toilet, and eating

Adaptation A change in functioning or coping style that results in a better adjustment of a person to his or her environment

Advance directives Documents that give instructions about desired health care if, in the future, an individual cannot speak for herself or himself

Alzheimer's disease The most common type of dementia; a progressive and incurable deterioration of key areas of the brain

Anorexia nervosa An eating disorder characterized by a dysfunctional body image and voluntary starvation in the pursuit of weight loss

Antibodies Protein molecules that attach to the surface of specific antigens in an effort to destroy them

Antigens Foreign substances such as bacteria, fungi, protozoa, and viruses that cause the immune system to react

Assimilation (cognitive) In cognitive theory, the incorporation of new experiences into an existing schema

Assimilation (cultural) The process of change whereby individuals of one society or ethnic group are culturally incorporated or absorbed into another by adopting the patterns and norms of the host culture

Assisted reproductive technologies (ART) A range of techniques to help women who are infertile to conceive and give birth

Assistive devices Devices that allow a person with a disability to communicate, see, hear, or maneuver. Examples include wheelchairs, motorized scooters, hearing aids, and telephone communications devices (TTD/TTY)

Assumption Something taken to be true without testing or proof

Atria (singular: atrium) The two upper, thin-walled chambers of the heart

Attachment An enduring emotional bond between two people who are important to each other. Provides affection and a sense of security

Authoritarian parenting A parenting style, identified by Baumrind, that involves unresponsive, inflexible, harsh, and controlling interactions with the child

Authoritative parenting A parenting style, identified by Baumrind, that involves responsive and supportive interactions with the child while also setting firm limits. Thought to be the most effective parenting style

Autoimmune diseases Diseases that occur when the immune system wrongly attacks systems that it should be protecting

Axon A conduction fiber that conducts impulses away from the body of a nerve cell

Behavior settings theories Theories that propose that consistent, uniform patterns of behavior occur in particular places, or behavior settings

Bereavement The state of having suffered a loss

Bifurcate Divide into two branches, as in labor force bifurcation into a core of stable, well-paid labor and a periphery of casual, low-wage labor

Biophilia A genetically based need of humans to affiliate with nature

Biopsychosocial approach An approach that considers human behavior to be the result of interactions of integrated biological, psychological, and social systems

Blood pressure Measure of the pressure of the blood against the walls of a blood vessel

Blooming A period of overproduction of brain synapses during infancy, followed by a period of synapse pruning

Bonding social capital Community relationships that are inward looking and tend to mobilize solidarity and in-group loyalty; they lead to exclusive identities and homogenous communities

Boundary An imaginary line of demarcation that defines which human and nonhuman elements are included in a given system and which elements are outside the system

Brain injury (BI) Damage to the brain arising from head trauma (falls, automobile accidents), infections (encephalitis), insufficient oxygen (stroke), or poisoning

Brain plasticity The ability of the brain to change in response to stimuli

Bridging social capital Community relationships that are outward looking and diverse and that link community members to assets and information across community boundaries

Built environment The portion of the physical environment attributable solely to human effort

Bulimia nervosa An eating disorder characterized by a cycle of binge eating; feelings of guilt, depression, or self-disgust; and purging

Bureaucracy A form of organization, considered by Max Weber to be the most efficient form for goal accomplishment, based on formal rationality

Capital A term used in different ways by different disciplines, but generally refers to having the potential, capacity, and resources to function, produce, or succeed; in the social sciences, refers to possession of attributes associated with civic engagement and economic success

Cardiovascular system Biological system made up of the heart and the blood circulatory system

Cerebral cortex The outer layer of gray matter in the human brain thought to be responsible for complex, high-level intellectual functions such as memory, language, and reasoning

Chaos theory A theory that emphasizes systems processes that produce change, even sudden, rapid change

Character education The direct teaching and curriculum inclusions of mainstream values thought to be universal by a community (e.g., kindness, respect, tolerance, and honesty)

Child maltreatment Physical, emotional, and sexual abuse and neglect of children, most often by adult caregivers. Definitions vary by culture and professional discipline but typically entail harm, or threatened harm, to the child

Chromosomes Threadlike structures composed of DNA and proteins that carry genes and that are found within each body cell nucleus

Classical conditioning theory A theory in the social behavioral perspective that sees behavior as the result of the association of a conditioned stimulus with an unconditioned stimulus

Cognition Conscious thinking processes; mental activities of which the individual is fully aware. These processes include taking in information from the environment, synthesizing that information, and formulating plans of action based on that synthesis

Cognitive social learning theory A theory in the social behavioral perspective that sees behavior as learned by imitation and through cognitive processes

Cohort Group of persons who are born in the same time period and who are of the same age group at the time of specific historical events and social changes

Cohort effects The effects of social change on a specific cohort

Collective efficacy The ability of community residents to engage in collective action to gain control of the neighborhood

Colonialism The practice of dominant and powerful nations going beyond their boundaries; using military force to occupy and claim less dominant and powerful nations; imposing their culture, laws, and language upon the occupied nation

Common sense Shared ways of perceiving reality and shared conclusions drawn from lived experience; an organized body of culture-bound beliefs that members of a community or society believe to be second nature, plain, obvious, and self-evident

Community People bound either by geography or by webs of communication, sharing common ties, and interacting with one another

Community assets Community resources such as public infrastructure (e.g., adequate transportation to get to work), community networks, and educational opportunities

Concept A word or phrase that serves as an abstract description, or mental image, of some phenomenon

Concrete operations stage The third stage in Piaget's theory of cognitive development. School-age children (ages 7 to 11) begin to use logical reasoning at this stage, but their thinking is not yet abstract

Conflict perspective An approach to human behavior that draws attention to conflict, dominance, and oppression in social life

Conjunctive faith The fifth faith stage in James Fowler's theory of faith development, a stage when individuals look for balance among competing moral systems, recognize that there are many truths, and open themselves in service to others

Conservative thesis A philosophy that inequality is the natural, divine order, and no efforts should be made to alter it

Control theories Theories that focus on the issue of how much control we have over our physical environment and the attempts we make to gain control

Convoy A person's network of social relationships that protect, defend, aid, and socialize

Coping A person's efforts to master the demands of stress, including the thoughts, feelings, and actions that constitute those efforts

Coping mechanisms Strategies used to master the demands of life

Countermovement A social movement that arises to oppose a successful social movement

Crisis A major upset in psychological equilibrium as a result of some hazardous event, experienced as a threat or loss, with which the person cannot cope

Critical consciousness The ongoing process of reflection and knowledge seeking about mechanisms and outcomes of social, political, and economic oppression; requires taking personal and collective action toward fairness and social justice

Critical perspective on organizations A perspective that sees formal organizations as instruments of domination

Critical theorists Theorists who argue that as capitalism underwent change, people were more likely to be controlled by culture and their consumer role than by their work position

Critical thinking Engaging in a thoughtful and reflective judgment about alternative views and contradictory information; involves thinking about your own thinking and the influences on that thinking, as well as a willingness to change your mind

Crowding Unpleasant experience of feeling spatially cramped

Crystallized intelligence The ability to use knowledge from accumulated learning

Cultural framing (CF) perspective on social movements An approach to social movements that asserts that they can be successful only when participants develop shared understandings and definitions of some situation that impels the participants to feel aggrieved or outraged, motivating them to action

Cultural hegemony The all-encompassing dominance of particular structures in society. Not limited to political control, but includes a way of seeing the world that includes cultural and political dominance

Cultural innovation A process of adapting, modifying, and changing culture through interaction over time

Cultural relativism The position that behavior in a particular culture should not be judged by the standards of another culture

Culture Shared cognitive and emotional frames and lenses that serve as the bases for an evolving map for living. It is constructed from the entire spectrum of human actions and the material circumstances of people in societies as they attempt to create order, meaning, and value.

Culture of poverty A term coined by Oscar Lewis to describe the unique culture and ways of those who are impoverished; it has been used over time to look at impoverished people as having cultural deficits

Cumulative advantage The accumulation of increasing advantage as early advantage positions an individual for later advantage

Cumulative disadvantage The accumulation of increasing disadvantage as early disadvantage positions an individual for later disadvantage

Customs Beliefs, values, and behaviors, such as marriage practices, child-rearing practices, dietary preferences, and attire, that are handed down through generations and become a part of a people's traditions

Deculturalizing The intentional or unintentional process that results in the destruction, or severe limitation, of a culture's ability to sustain itself (language, customs, rituals, and so forth)

Deductive reasoning A method of reasoning that lays out general, abstract propositions that can be used to generate specific hypotheses to test in unique situations

Default individualization One possible pathway in young adulthood, which involves making transitions defined by circumstance and situation

Defense mechanisms Unconscious, automatic responses that enable a person to minimize perceived threats or keep them out of awareness entirely

Defensive social movement A social movement with the goal of defending traditional values and social arrangements

Delirium Syndrome characterized by an impairment of consciousness. It has a sudden onset (a few hours or days), follows a brief and fluctuating course that includes impairment of consciousness, and has the potential for improvement when causes are treated. Prevalence of delirium is high among hospitalized elderly persons; toxicity from prescribed medications is a common cause.

Dementia Impairment or loss of cognitive functioning caused by damage in the brain tissue. Dementia is not part of the brain's normal aging process, but its prevalence increases with age.

Density Ratio of persons per unit area of a space

Dependency ratio A demographic indicator expressing the degree of demand placed on society by the dependent young and the dependent elderly combined

Determinism A belief that persons are passive products of their circumstances, external forces, or internal urges

Developmental delays Delays in developing skills and abilities in infants and preschoolers

Developmental individualization One possible pathway in young adulthood, which involves making transitions defined by personal agency and deliberately charted growth opportunities in intellectual, occupational, and psychosocial domains

Developmental niche The cultural context into which a particular child is born; guides every aspect of the developmental process

Developmental perspective An approach that focuses on how human behavior changes and stays the same across stages of the life cycle

Diabetes mellitus A disease of the endocrine system resulting from insulin deficiency or resistance to insulin's effects

Differentiation (Jung) The process by which humans develop unique patterns and traits

Dimension A feature that can be focused on separately, but that cannot be understood without considering its embeddedness with other features

Direct bullying Intentionally inflicting emotional or physical harm on another person through fairly explicit physical or verbal harassment, assault, or injury

Discipline Action taken by a child's caretaker to help the child correct behavioral problems

Disengaged parenting Aloof, withdrawn, and unresponsive parenting

Diversity Patterns of group differences

Dominant genes Genes that express themselves if present on one or both chromosomes in a pair

Downsizing Corporate layoff of workers for the purpose of greater efficiency

Ecocentric Perspective that the ecosphere and everything on earth has its own intrinsic worth, and should be valued and cared for, including earth (Gaia) itself; recognition that humans are only one part of the interconnected web of life

Ecomaps Visual representations of the relations between social network members. Members of the network are represented by points, and lines are drawn between pairs of points to demonstrate a relationship between them; also called a sociogram

Economic institution The social institution with primary responsibility for regulating the production, distribution, and consumption of goods and services

Ecotherapy Exposure to nature and the outdoors as a component of psychotherapy

Educational institution The social institution responsible for passing along formal knowledge from one generation to the next

Efficacy expectation In cognitive social learning theory, the expectation that one can personally accomplish a goal

Ego A mental structure of personality that is responsible for negotiating between internal needs of the individual and the outside world

Ego psychology A theory of human behavior and clinical practice that views activities of the ego as the primary determinants of behavior

Egocentrism The assumption by children in the preoperational stage of cognitive development that others perceive, think, and feel just the way they do. Inability to recognize the possibility of other perspectives

Embryo The stage of prenatal development beginning in the second week and lasting through the eighth week

Emerging adulthood A developmental phase distinct from both adolescence and young adulthood, occurring between the ages of 18 and 25 in industrialized societies

Emotion A feeling state characterized by one's appraisal of a stimulus, changes in bodily sensations, and expressive gestures

Emotional intelligence A person's ability to process information about emotions accurately and effectively, and consequently to regulate emotions in an optimal manner

Emotion-focused coping Coping efforts in which a person attempts to change either the way a stressful situation is attended to (by vigilance or avoidance) or the meaning of what is happening. Most effective when situations are not readily controllable by action

Empathy Ability to understand another person's emotional condition

Empirical research A careful, purposeful, and systematic observation of events with the intent to note and record them in terms of their attributes, to look for patterns in those events, and to make one's methods and observations public

Empowerment theories Theories that focus on processes by which individuals and collectivities can recognize patterns of inequality and injustice and take action to increase their own power

Endocrine system The biological system that is involved in growth, metabolism, development, learning, and memory. Made up of glands that secrete hormones into the blood system

Ethnocentrism Considering one's own culture as superior, and judging culturally different practices (beliefs, values, behavior) by the standards and norms of one's own culture

Exchange theory (small groups) Focuses on power issues in small groups, who gets valued resources and how fairly they are perceived as being distributed

Faith As defined in Fowler's theory of faith development, a generic feature of the human search for meaning that provides a centering orientation from which to live one's life. May or may not be based in religious expression

Faith stages Distinct levels of faith development, each with particular characteristics, emerging strengths, and potential dangers. Fowler identifies seven faith stages in his theory of faith development.

Family A social group of two or more persons, characterized by ongoing interdependence with long-term commitments that stem from blood, law, or affection

Family and kinship institution The social institution primarily responsible for the regulation of procreation, for the initial socialization of new members of society, and for mutual support

Family economic stress model A model of family stress that suggests that economic hardship leads to economic pressure, which leads to parent distress, which leads to disrupted family relationships, which leads to child and adolescent adjustment problems

Family investment model Theoretical model that proposes that families with greater economic resources can afford to make large investments in the development of their children

Family life cycle perspective An approach that looks at how families change over time and proposes normative changes and tasks at different stages

Family of origin The family into which we were born and in which we were raised, when the two are the same

Family resilience perspective An approach to family that seeks to identify and strengthen family processes that allow families to bear up under and rebound from distressing life experiences

Family systems perspective A way of understanding families that focuses on the family as a social system, with patterns of interaction and relationships, and on changes in these patterns over time

Family timeline A visual representation of important dates and events in a family's life over time

Feedback control mechanism The mechanism by which the body controls the secretion of hormones and therefore their actions on target tissues

Feedback mechanism A process by which information about past behaviors in a system is fed back into the system in a circular manner

Feminist perspective on families A perspective that proposes that families should not be studied as whole systems, with the lens on the family level, but rather as patterns of dominance, subjugation, and oppression, particularly as those patterns are tied to gender

Feminist theories Theories that focus on male domination of the major social institutions and present a vision of a just world based on gender equity

Fertilization The penetration of an ovum by a spermatozoon, usually occurring in the fallopian tube

Fetal viability The capability of the fetus to survive outside the womb, typically requiring at least 25 weeks' gestation

Fetus The developing organism from the ninth week of pregnancy to birth

Fine motor skills Skills based on small muscle movements, particularly in the hands, as well as eye–hand coordination

First Force therapies Therapies based on dynamic theories of human behavior, with the prime concern being about repression and solving instinctual conflicts by developing insights

Fluid intelligence Abstract reasoning skills

Formal operations stage The fourth and final stage in Piaget's theory of cognitive development, generally experienced in adolescence. Involves the capacity to apply hypothetical reasoning and to use symbols to solve problems

Formal organization A collectivity of people, with a high degree of formality of structure, working together to meet a goal or goals

Four quadrants From Wilber's integral theory, the four most important dimensions of existence. The upper-left quadrant represents the interior of individuals, or the subjective aspects of consciousness or awareness; the upper-right quadrant represents the exterior of individuals, including the objective biological and behavioral aspects; the lower-left quadrant represents the interior of collectives, or the values, meanings, worldviews, and ethics that are shared by groups of individuals; the lower-right quadrant represents the exterior, material dimensions of collectives, including social systems and the environment

Fourth Force therapies Therapies that specifically target the spiritual dimension, focusing on helping the person let go of ego attachments and transcend the self through various spiritually based practices

Fulcrum In Wilber's full-spectrum model of consciousness, a specific turning point in development, where the person must go through a three-step process of fusion/differentiation/integration in order to move from one level of consciousness to another

Gender identity Understanding of oneself as a male or female

Generalized other A construction that represents how others might view and respond to our behavior

Generativity The ability to transcend personal interests to provide care and have concern for generations to come

Genes Basic units of heredity, made of DNA, and found on chromosomes

Genogram A visual representation of the multigenerational family system, using squares, circles, and relationship lines

Genotype The totality of the hereditary information present in an organism

Gestation The length of maturation time from conception to birth. In humans, it averages 280 days, with a range of 259 to 287 days

Gini index An index that measures the extent to which the distribution of income within a country deviates from a perfectly equal distribution; scores range from 0 (perfect equality) to 100 (perfect inequality)

Globalization The process by which the world's people are becoming more interconnected economically, politically, environmentally, and culturally

Gonads Sex glands—ovaries in females and testes in males

Government and political institution The social institution responsible for how decisions are made and enforced for the society as a whole

Grief The normal internal reaction of an individual experiencing a loss, a complex process that is highly individualized

Grief work A necessary period of working to sever the attachment bond to a lost person or object

Gross motor skills Skills based upon large muscle group movements and most easily observed during whole-body movements, such as hopping, skipping, and running

Group cohesiveness A sense of solidarity or "we-ness" felt by group members toward the group

Group work A recognized social work method that involves teaching and practicing social work with groups

Health care institution The social institution with primary responsibility for promoting the general health of a society

Heterogeneity Individual-level variations, differences among individuals

Hierarchy of needs Abraham Maslow's humanistic theory that suggests that higher needs cannot emerge until lower needs have been satisfied; the hierarchy runs from physiological needs at the bottom, to safety needs, belongingness and love needs, and esteem needs, with self-actualization needs at the top

High blood pressure (hypertension) Blood pressure greater than 140/90; the leading cause of strokes and a major risk factor for heart attacks and kidney failure

Hospice Program that provides care to the terminally ill. Patients typically receive treatment by a team of doctors, nurses, social workers, and care staff through inpatient or outpatient care

Hostile aggression Aggression that is an attack meant to hurt another individual

Human agency The use of personal power to achieve one's goals

Human capital Individual assets such as talents, skills, intellectual capacity, social development, and emotional regulatory capacity

Human immunodeficiency virus (HIV) The virus that causes acquired immunodeficiency syndrome (AIDS)

Humanistic perspective An approach that sees human behavior as based on freedom of action of the individual and focuses on the human search for meaning

Hypotheses Tentative statements to be explored and tested

Identity A sense of self that distinguishes "who I am" from other people and that is enduring over time

Ideology (personal) A particular body of ideas or outlook; a person's specific worldview

Immune system Organs and cells that interact and work together to defend the body against disease

Incidental memory Memory that relates to facts a person has learned without the intention to retain and recall

Indirect bullying Less explicit and less detectable than direct bullying, including more subtle verbal, psychological, and social or "relational" bullying tactics

Individual education plan (IEP) An individualized, collaboratively developed plan that focuses on facilitating achievement and is designed to respond to the unique needs of a child with a disability in the school setting. Such plans are mandated by the Individuals with Disabilities Education Act of 1990

Individuation (Jung) The full development of all aspects of the self into a unique and harmonious whole that gives expression to repressed attributes and desires; does not occur before age 40

Individuation The development of a self and identity that are unique and separate

Individuative-reflective faith The fourth stage of James Fowler's six-stage model of faith development, a stage when adults no longer rely on outside authority and look instead for authority within the self

Infant A young child in the first year of life

Infant mortality The death of a child before his or her first birthday

Infertility The inability to create a viable embryo; can also include situations where women can get pregnant but are unable to stay pregnant

Institutional discrimination The systematic denial of access to assets, economic opportunities, associations, and organizations based on minority status

Instrumental activities of daily living (IADLs) More complex everyday tasks such as doing light housework, doing the laundry, using transportation, handling finances, using the telephone, and taking medications

Instrumental aggression Aggression that occurs while fighting over toys and space, etc.

Integrity The ability to make peace with one's "one and only life cycle" and to find unity with the world; the task Erik Erikson associated with late adulthood (integrity versus despair)

Intentional memory Memory that relates to events that a person plans to remember

Interpretist perspective Ways of understanding human behavior that share the assumption that reality is based on people's definition of it

Interpretive perspective on organizations A perspective that sees formal organizations as social constructions of reality

Interrelational intelligence Based on emotional and social intelligence and similar to Howard Gardner's concept of interpersonal intelligence

Intersectionality feminist theory A feminist theory that suggests that no single category is sufficient to understand social oppression, and that categories such as gender, race, and class intersect to produce different experiences for women of various races and classes

Intimacy Characteristic of close interpersonal relationships, includes interdependence, self-disclosure, and affection

Juvenile delinquency Acts that, if committed by an adult, would be considered crimes, plus status offenses such as running away from home, skipping school, violating curfew, and possession of tobacco or alcohol

Lateralization Process in which the two hemispheres of the brain begin to operate slightly differently during early childhood

Learned helplessness In cognitive social learning theory, a situation in which a person's prior experience with environmental forces has led to low self-efficacy and efficacy expectation

Learning play Play that is focused on language and thinking skills

Levels of consciousness From Wilber's integral theory, overall stages of awareness and being; moving from the pre-personal to the personal and transpersonal phases, each with multiple levels of development

Life course perspective An approach to human behavior that recognizes the influence of age but also acknowledges the influences of historical time and culture

Life event Incident or event that is brief in scope but is influential on human behavior

Life review A process of evaluating and making sense of one's life. It includes a reinterpretation of past experiences and unresolved conflicts. The process of life review relates to the eighth stage of Erikson's theory of adult development (ego integrity versus ego despair).

Life structure In Levinson's seasons of adulthood theory, the patterns and central components of a person's life at a particular point in time

Linear time Time based on past, present, and future

Lines of consciousness From Wilber's integral theory, the approximately two dozen relatively independent developmental lines or streams that can evolve at different rates, with different dynamics, and on different time schedules; examples include cognitive, moral, interpersonal, self-identity, and socio-emotional capacity

Living will A document that describes the medical procedures, drugs, and types of treatment that an individual would choose for oneself if able to do so in certain situations. It also describes the situations for which this individual would want treatment withheld

Loss The severing of an attachment an individual has with a loved one, a love object, or an aspect of one's self or identity

Lymphocytes White blood cells, which fight infection in the body

Mass media institution In a democratic society, the social institution responsible for managing the flow of information, images, and ideas

Masturbation Self-stimulation of the genitals for sexual pleasure

Menarche The onset of menstruation

Mobilizing structures (MS) perspective An approach to social movements that suggests that they develop out of existing networks and formal organizations

Morbidity The incidence of disease and illness in a population group

Mortality rate The incidence of death in a population group

Motor skills Control over movements of body parts

Mourning The external expression of grief, also a process, influenced by the customs of one's culture

Multidetermined behavior A view that human behavior is developed as a result of many causes

Multidimensional Having several identifiable dimensions

Multiple intelligences The eight distinct biopsychosocial potentials, as identified by Howard Gardner, with which people process information that can be activated in cultural settings to solve problems or create products that are of value in the culture

Musculoskeletal system Muscles that are attached to bone and cross a joint. Their contraction and relaxation are the basis for voluntary movements

Natural environment The portion of the environment influenced primarily by geological and nonhuman biological forces

Neocolonialism The practice of dominant and powerful nations going beyond their boundaries, utilizing international financial institutions such as the World Bank and the International Monetary Fund to exert influence over impoverished nations and to impose their culture, laws, and language upon the occupied nation through the use of financial incentives (loans) and disincentives

Neoliberal philosophy A philosophy that governments should keep their hands off the economic institution

Neonate Infant up to 1 month of age

Nervous system The biological system responsible for processing and integrating incoming sensory information; it influences and directs reactions to that information

Neural plasticity The capacity of the nervous system to be modified by experience

Neuron Nerve cell that is the basic working unit of the nervous system. Composed of a cell body, dendrites (receptive extensions), and an axon

Neurotransmitters Messenger molecules that transfer chemical and electrical messages from one neuron to another

New federalism The downward movement of policy responsibilities from federal to state and local governments

Nonspecific immunity Immunity that includes physical barriers to infection, inflammation, and phagocytosis. Does not include antibodies or cell-mediated immunity

Object permanence The ability to understand that objects exist even when they cannot be seen

Object relations theory A psychodynamic theory that considers that our ability to form lasting attachments is based on early experiences of separation from and connection with our primary caregivers

Objective reality The belief that phenomena exist and have influence, whether or not we are aware of them

Offensive social movement A social movement with the goal of changing traditional social arrangements

Operant conditioning theory A theory in the social behavioral perspective that sees behavior as the result of reinforcement

Oppression The intentional or unintentional act or process of placing restrictions on an individual, group, or institution; may include observable actions, but more typically refers to complex, covert, interconnected processes and practices (such as discriminating, devaluing, and exploiting a group of individuals) reflected in and perpetuating exclusion and inequalities over time

Palliative care Active care of patients who have received a diagnosis of a serious, life-threatening illness; a form of care focusing on pain and symptom management as opposed to curing disease

Performance expectations The expectations group members have of other group members in terms of how they will act or behave in the group or how well they will perform a task

Permissive parenting A parenting style, identified by Baumrind, that involves no limit setting on the part of the parent

Personal space The physical distance we choose to maintain in interpersonal relationships

Perspective taking The ability to see a situation from another person's point of view

Phenomenal self An individual's subjectively felt and interpreted experience of "who I am"

Phenotype The expression of genetic traits in an individual

Physical aggression Aggression against another person using physical force

Place attachment A process in which individuals and groups form bonds with places

Place identity A process in which the meaning of a place merges with one's self-identity

Pluralistic theory of social conflict A theory that suggests that there is more than one social conflict going on at all times, that individuals often hold cross-cutting and overlapping memberships in status groups, and that these cross-cutting memberships prevent the development of solidarity among oppressed groups

Political opportunities (PO) perspective An approach to social movements that suggests that they develop when windows of political opportunity are open

Positive psychology An approach to psychology that focuses on people's strengths and virtues and promotes optimal functioning of individuals and communities

Positivist perspective The perspective on which modern science is based. Assumes objective reality, that findings of one study should be applicable to other groups, that complex phenomena can be studied by reducing them to some component part, and that scientific methods are value-free

Postconventional moral reasoning Third and final level of Lawrence Kohlberg's stage theory of moral development; morality based on moral principles that transcend societal rules

Postmodernism A term used to describe contemporary culture as a postindustrial culture in which people are connected across time and place through global electronic communications; emphasis is on the existence of different worldviews and concepts of reality

Post-poliomyelitis syndrome (PPS) Progressive atrophy of muscles that can occur in those who once had polio

Postpositivism A philosophical position that recognizes the complexity of reality and the limitations of human observers; proposes that scientists can never develop more than a partial understanding of human behavior

Power of attorney (POA) A person appointed by an individual to manage his or her financial and legal affairs. A POA can be limited (for a limited time period), general (no restrictions), or durable (begins after the individual reaches a specified level of disability)

Practice orientation A way of thinking about culture that recognizes the relationships and mutual influences among structures of society and culture, the impact of history, and the nature and impact of human action

Precociousness Early development; most often refers to a rare level of intelligence at an early age, but may refer to "premature" ability or development in a number of areas

Preconscious Mental activity that is outside of awareness but can be brought into awareness with prompting

Preconventional level of moral reasoning First level of moral reasoning in Lawrence Kohlberg's stage theory of moral reasoning; morality based on what gets rewarded or punished or what benefits either the child or someone the child cares about

Preoperational stage The second stage in Piaget's theory of cognitive development. Young children (ages 2 to 7) use symbols to represent their earlier sensorimotor experiences. Thinking is not yet logical at this stage.

Primary aging Changes that are a normal part of the aging process

Primary emotions Emotions that developed as specific reactions and signals with survival value for the human species. They serve to mobilize an individual, focus attention, and signal one's state of mind to others; examples include anger, fear, sadness, joy, and anticipation.

Primary sex characteristics Physical characteristics that are directly related to maturation of the reproductive organs and external genitalia

Privilege Unearned advantage enjoyed by members of some social categories

Problem-focused coping Coping efforts in which the person attempts to change a stress situation by acting on the environment. Most effective when situations are controllable by action

Propositions Assertions about a concept or about the relationship between concepts

Prosocial Behaving in a helpful or empathic manner

Protective factors Personal and societal factors that reduce or protect against risk

Pruning Reduction of brain synapses to improve the efficiency of brain functioning; follows a period of blooming of synapses

Psychoanalytic theory A theory of human behavior and clinical intervention that assumes the primacy of internal drives and unconscious mental activity in determining human behavior

Psychodynamic perspective An approach that focuses on how internal processes motivate human behavior

Psychodynamic perspective on families Assumes that current personal and interpersonal problems are the result of unresolved problems in the family of origin

Psychodynamic theory (small groups) Focuses on the relationship between emotional unconscious processes and the nature and quality of interpersonal communication in the group

Psychological identity Self-definition as a separate and distinct person

Psychology The study of the mind and mental processes

Psychosocial crisis A struggle or turning point that defines a particular stage in Erik Erikson's developmental model

Puberty Stage during which individuals become capable of reproduction

Qualitative methods of research Research methods that use flexible modes of data collection, seek holistic understanding, present findings in words rather than numbers, and attempt to account for the influence of the research setting and process on the findings

Quantitative methods of research Research methods, based on the tenets of modern science, that use quantifiable measures of concepts, standardize the collection of data, attend only to preselected variables, and use statistical methods to look for patterns and associations

Race A system of social identity based on biological markers such as skin color that influence economic, social, and political relations

Radical antithesis Philosophy that equality is the natural, divine order, and that inequality is based on abuse of privilege and should be minimized

Rational choice perspective An approach that sees human behavior as based in self-interest and rational choices about effective goal accomplishment

Rational perspective on organizations A perspective that sees formal organizations as goal-directed, purposefully designed machines that maximize efficiency and effectiveness

Recessive genes Genes that express themselves only if present on both chromosomes in a pair

Reflex An involuntary response to a simple stimulus

Relational aggression Aggression that involves behaviors that damage relationships without physical force, such as threatening to leave a relationship unless a friend complies with demands, or using social exclusion or the silent treatment to get one's way

Relational community A community based on voluntary association rather than geography

Relational coping Coping that takes into account actions that maximize the survival of others as well as oneself

Relational theory A theory that proposes that the basic human tendency is relationships with others, and that our personalities are formed through ongoing interactions with others

Relative poverty A conceptualization of poverty that emphasizes the tendency to define one's poverty status in relation to others within one's social environment

Religion A systematic set of beliefs, practices, and traditions experienced within a particular social institution over time

Religious institution The social institution with primary responsibility for answering questions about the meaning and purpose of life

Reminiscence Recalling and recounting past events. Reminiscing serves several functions: It may be an enjoyable activity, it may be directed at enhancing a person's self-image, it may serve as a way to cope with current or future problems, and it may assist in the life review as a way to achieve ego integrity.

Resilience Healthy development in the face of risk factors; thought to be the result of protective factors that shield the individual from the consequences of potential hazards

Risk factors Personal or social factors that increase the likelihood of a problem occurring

Rites of passage Ceremonies that demarcate transition from one role or status to another

Role A set of usual behaviors of persons occupying a particular social position

Romantic love An intimate relationship that is sexually oriented

Schema (plural: schemata) An internalized representation of the world, including systematic patterns of thought, action, and problem solving

Science A set of logical, systematic, documented methods for answering questions about the world

Second Force therapies Therapies based on behavioral theories; they focus on learned habits and seek to remove symptoms through various processes of direct learning.

Secondary aging Changes caused by health-compromising behaviors such as smoking or environmental factors such as pollution

Secondary emotions Emotions that are socially acquired. They evolved as humans developed more sophisticated means of learning, controlling, and managing emotions to promote flexible cohesion in social groups. Examples include envy, jealousy, anxiety, guilt, shame, relief, hope, depression, pride, love, gratitude, and compassion.

Secondary sex characteristics Physical characteristics associated with sexual maturation that are not directly related to the reproductive organs and external genitalia

Secondary sexual development Associated with puberty and referring to the development of secondary sex characteristics such as the growth of

pubic, chest, and facial hair in males and the growth of pubic hair and breasts in females

Self An essence of who we are that is more or less enduring

Self-categorization theory A theory of small groups that proposes that in the process of social identity development, we come to divide the world into in-groups (those to which we belong) and out-groups (those to which we do not belong) and to be biased toward in-groups

Self-efficacy A sense of personal competence

Self-esteem The way one evaluates the self in relation to others

Self-system In Wilber's full-spectrum model of consciousness, the active self or person who moves through the stages of consciousness and mediates between the basic and transitional structures of development

Self-theory An organized understanding of the self in relation to others; begins to develop in early childhood

Sense of community A feeling of belonging and mutual commitment

Sensorimotor stage The first stage in Piaget's theory of cognitive development. Infants (ages 0 to 2 years) learn through sensory awareness and motor activities

Sensory system The system of senses: hearing, sight, taste, smell, touch, responsiveness to the body's position, and sensitivity to pain

Separation anxiety When an infant becomes anxious at the signs of an impending separation from parents, at about 9 months of age

Sex hormones Hormones that affect the development of the gonads, functioning of the gonads, and mating and child-caring behavior; includes androgens, progestins, and estrogens

Sexual orientation Erotic, romantic, and affectionate attraction to people of the same sex, the opposite sex, or both sexes

Sexually transmitted infections (STIs) Infectious diseases that are most often contracted through oral, anal, or vaginal sexual contact. Also called venereal diseases

Small group A small collection of individuals who interact with each other, perceive themselves as belonging to a group, are interdependent, join together to accomplish a goal, fulfill a need through joint association, or are influenced by a set of rules and norms

Social behavioral perspective An approach that sees human behavior as learned when individuals interact with their environments

Social capital Connections among individuals based on reciprocity and trustworthiness

Social class A particular position in a societal structure of inequality

Social competence The ability to engage in sustained, positive, and mutually satisfactory peer interactions

Social constructionist perspective An approach that focuses on how people learn, through their interactions with each other, to classify the world and their place in it

Social exchange theory A theory in the rational choice perspective that sees human behavior as based on the desire to maximize benefits and minimize costs in social interactions

Social gerontology The social science that studies human aging

Social identity The part of the self-concept that comes from knowledge of one's membership in a social group and the emotional significance of that membership

Social institutions Patterned ways of organizing social relations in a particular sector of social life

Social movements Large-scale collective actions to make change, or resist change, in specific social institutions

Social network The people with whom a person routinely interacts; the patterns of interaction that result from exchanging resources with others

Social network theory A developing theory in the rational choice perspective that focuses on the pattern of ties that link persons and collectivities

Social structure A set of interrelated social institutions developed by humans to impose constraints on human interaction for the purpose of the survival and well-being of the collectivity

Social support The interpersonal interactions and relationships that provide people with assistance or feelings of attachment to others they perceive as caring

Social welfare institution The social institution in modern industrial societies that promotes interdependence and provides assistance for issues of dependency

Sociodramatic play Fantasy play in a group, with the group coordinating fantasies; important type of play in early childhood

Specific immunity Immunity that involves cells (lymphocytes) that not only respond to an infection, but also develop a memory of that infection and allow the body to defend against it rapidly during subsequent exposure

Spermarche Onset of the ability to ejaculate mobile sperm

Spiritual bypassing Use of spiritual beliefs or practices to avoid dealing in any significant depth with unresolved issues and related emotional and behavioral problems; includes attempts to prematurely transcend the ego

Spirituality A search for purpose, meaning, and connection between oneself other people, the universe, and the ultimate reality, which can be experienced within either a religious or a nonreligious framework

State A personality characteristic that changes over time, depending on the social or stress context

States of consciousness From Wilber's integral theory, an understanding of experience that includes both ordinary (waking, sleeping, and dreaming)

and non-ordinary experiences (peak experiences, religious experiences, altered states, and meditative or contemplative states)

Status A specific social position

Status characteristics In status characteristics and expectation states theory, any characteristics that are evaluated in the broader society to be associated with competence

Status characteristics and expectation states theory A theory of basic group process that assumes that the influence and participation of group members during initial interactions are related to their status and to expectations others hold about their ability to help the group accomplish tasks

Status offenses Behaviors that would not be considered criminal if committed by an adult, but are considered delinquent if committed by an adolescent—for example, running away from home, skipping school, violating curfew, and possessing tobacco or alcohol

Statutory rape A criminal offense that involves an adult engaging in sexual activities with a minor or a mentally incapacitated person

Stimulation theories Theories that focus on the physical environment as a source of sensory information that is necessary for human well-being

Stranger anxiety When an infant reacts with fear and withdrawal to unfamiliar persons, at about 9 months of age

Stress Any biological, psychological, or social event in which environmental demands or internal demands, or both, tax or exceed the adaptive resources of the individual

Subjective reality The belief that reality is created by personal perception and does not exist outside that perception; the same as the interpretist perspective

Symbol Something verbal (language, words) or nonverbal (such as a flag) that comes to stand for something else; a way of expressing meaning

Symbolic functioning The ability to think using symbols to represent what is not present

Symbolic interaction theory (small groups) Focuses on the small group as a place where symbols are created, exchanged, and interpreted

Symbolic play Fantasy play; begins around the age of 2

Synapse In the nervous system, the gap between an axon and a dendrite; the site at which chemical and electrical communication occurs

Synthetic-conventional faith The third stage of James Fowler's six-stage model of faith development; faith that is rooted in external authority

Systems perspective An approach that sees human behavior as the outcome of reciprocal interactions of persons operating within organized and integrated social systems

Systems perspective on organizations A perspective that focuses on formal organizations in constant interaction with multiple environments

Temperament A person's disposition and primary behavioral characteristics

Teratogen Anything present during prenatal life that adversely affects normal cellular development in form or function in the embryo or fetus

Territorial community A community based on geography

Territoriality A pattern of behavior of a group or individual that involves marking or personalizing a territory to signify ownership and engaging in behaviors to protect it from invasion

Testes Male gonads, primarily responsible for producing sperm (mature germ cells that fertilize the female egg) and secreting male hormones called androgens

Theory A logically interrelated set of concepts and propositions, organized into a deductive system, that explains relationships among aspects of our world

Therapeutic medicine An approach to medicine that focuses on diagnosing and treating disease

Third Force therapies Therapies rooted in experiential/humanistic/existential theories that focus on helping a person deal with existential despair, and that seek the actualization of the person's potential through techniques grounded in immediate experiencing

Time orientation The extent to which individuals and collectivities are invested in three temporal zones: past, present, and future time

Toddler A young child from about 12 to 36 months of age

Tradition A process of handing down from one generation to another certain cultural beliefs and practices. In particular, a process of ratifying certain beliefs and practices by connecting them to selected social, economic, and political practices

Trait A stable personality characteristic

Trajectories Long-term patterns of stability and change based on unique person-environment configurations over time

Transductive reasoning Reasoning from one particular event to another particular event rather than in a logical, causal manner

Transitional object Comfort object, such as a favorite blanket or stuffed animal, that toddlers often use to help them cope with separations from parents

Transitions Changes in roles and statuses that represent a distinct departure from prior roles and statuses

Transnational corporation (TNC) A very large company that carries on production and distribution activities in many nations

Transpersonal approach An approach to human behavior that includes levels of consciousness or spiritual development that move beyond rational-individuated-personal personhood to a sense of self that transcends the mind/body ego—a self-identity also referred to as transegoic

Trauma A physical or mental injury generally associated with violence, shock, or an unanticipated situation

Traumatic stress Stress associated with events that involve actual or threatened severe injury or death of oneself or significant others

Turning point A special event that produces a lasting shift in the life course trajectory

Ultimate environment Conceptualizations of the highest level of reality, understood differently by persons at various levels of spiritual development or consciousness

Unconscious Mental activities of which one is not aware but that influence behavior

Uterus Also called the womb, serves as the pear-shaped home for the fetus for the 9 months between implantation and birth

Ventricles The two lower, thick-walled chambers of the heart

Voluntarism The belief that persons are free and active agents in the creation of their behaviors

Working model Model for relationships developed in the earliest attachment relationship

Worldcentric Identification beyond the "me" (egocentric), or the "us" (ethnocentric), to identification and concern for "all of us" (worldcentric), or the entire global human family; a moral stance that is characteristic of higher levels of spiritual development

Zone of proximal development According to Vygotsky, the theoretical space between the child's current developmental level (or performance) and the child's potential level (or performance) if given access to appropriate models and developmental experiences in the social environment

Zygote A fertilized ovum cell

INDEX

Averill, J., 125
Axons, 85, 85 (exhibit)

Babbie, E., 27
Baby boomer generation, 163, 623, 627, 654, 666, 687
Bakardjieve, M., 571
Ballantine, J., 260
Bandura, A., 57, 63, 64, 65, 115, 471
Barker, R., 223
Barr, D., 509
Barret, R., 186
Barrett, R., 685
Barzan, R., 186
Bassuk, E., 490
Baum, F., 309
Baumrind, D., 490, 491, 492
Baxter, L., 342
Beck, U., 163
Becker, H., 302
Behavior modification, 65
Behavior. *See* Behavior settings theories; Human behavior
Behavior settings theories, 223–224
 behavior programs, generation of, 223
 life histories of behavior settings and, 223–224
 setting size and, 224
 social work assessment/intervention and, 224
 staffing, level of, 224
 substance addictions and, 230
 virtual behavior settings and, 223
 See also Built environment; Physical environment
Bell, D. B., 388
Bell, L., 20
Bellamy, C., 453
Belyea, M., 626
Ben Shlmo, Y., 662
Benbenishty, R., 518
Benedetti, M., 305
Bengtson, V., 627
Bennett, H. Z., 178
Berck, J., 231
Bereavement, 681, 682, 684
 culture and, 684–686
 model of adult bereavement, 684
 See also Grief; Grief work
Berger, P., 52, 165
Berkeley Guidance Study, 616
Berlin Aging Study, 645, 662, 663
Best practices, 291
Bicultural competence, 513–514
Bicultural socialization, 216, 650
Bifurcation of labor, 252–253
Big Five personality traits, 616–617
Bioethical concerns, 395
Biological citizens, 320

Biological determinism, 207–208, 478
Biological person, 10–11 (exhibits)
 amino acids and, 86
 brain injury case study and, 76–77
 cardiovascular system and, 93–96, 95 (exhibit)
 circadian rhythms, 555
 conflict perspective and, 96
 developmental perspective and, 92
 diabetes diagnosis case study and, 77
 diversity, legitimate communities and, 82
 endocrine system and, 86, 87–89, 87–88 (exhibits)
 health status, socioeconomic factors and, 104–106
 high blood pressure case study and, 78
 HIV diagnosis case study, 77–78
 immune system and, 89–93
 interior biological environment, exterior environmental
  factors and, 80–82
 late adulthood and, 654–662
 medicalization of lived experience and, 81
 mind-body interactions, integrative mechanisms and, 81
 musculoskeletal system and, 96–99, 98 (exhibit)
 nervous system and, 83–87, 84–85 (exhibits)
 peptides and, 86
 post-polio syndrome case study and, 79
 rational choice perspective and, 89
 reproductive health case study and, 79–80
 reproductive system and, 99–104, 101–103 (exhibits)
 sex, 350
 social constructionist perspective and, 82
 social work practice and, 80–81, 82
 systems perspective and, 81–82, 83, 96
 See also Fetal development; Genetics; Human procreation
Biology, 12
 biological coping, 139–140
 constructivist biology, 54
 homeostasis and, 120, 139
 See also Biological person; Brain function
Biology-as-destiny approach, 68
Biophilia, 225
Biopsychosocial approach, 12–13
 biopsychosocial disease model, 39
 person-in-environment classification system and,
  148, 149 (exhibit)
 spiritual dimension and, 158–159, 204
 See also Psychobiological theory of attachment
Biorck, G., 25
Birth. *See* Contraceptive methods; Human procreation;
 Postpartum depression; Reproductive system
Black, M., 492
Blaming the victim, 22 (exhibit)
Blau, P., 48, 50
Blehar, M., 131
Bliatout, B., 685
Blieszner, R., 624

Blood pressure. *See* Cardiovascular system; High blood pressure

Bloom, L., 470

Blooming, 432

Blum, R., 554

Blumer, H., 52

Boas, F., 208

Bohannan, P., 204

Bond, B., 576

Bond, J., 315, 345

Bonding social capital, 305, 306

Boomerang generation, 625

Borysenko, J., 60

Bos, H., 388

Bould, D., 322

Boundaries:
    boundary regulating mechanisms and, 220
    impermeable cultural boundaries, 41
    imposed national boundaries, 248
    labor flow, control of, 250
    systems configuration and, 39, 41, 41 (exhibit)
    theoretical synthesizing and, 39

Bowen, M., 346

Bowlby, J., 56, 441, 442, 683

Boyd, D., 299

Brain function:
    acquired brain injury and, 83
    adolescent brain and, 553–554
    amygdala, 121–122, 135
    areas of the brain and, 84–85, 84 (exhibit)
    attachment, brain development and, 444–445
    bilingualism and, 514
    blooming of synapses and, 432
    brain injury outcomes and, 83–84
    cerebellum and, 85
    cerebral cortex and, 84, 84–85 (exhibits), 85, 511
    child maltreatment/trauma, brain development and, 455–457, 456 (exhibit)
    cold/hot cognition and, 553
    cortical midline structures and, 477
    early nurturing, neurological development and, 134–135, 432
    emotional processing and, 121–122
    environmental stimulation and, 219
    forebrain and, 84
    frontal lobe and, 85 (exhibit)
    genetic processes, brain development and, 432
    hemispheres of the brain and, 84
    hindbrain and, 84, 85
    infant self-regulatory functions and, 426
    infant/toddler brain development and, 426, 431–433, 444–445, 455–457, 456 (exhibit)
    late adulthood, neurodegenerative diseases, 659–662, 661 (exhibit)
    midbrain and, 84
    mirror neurons and, 477
    movement, control of, 84, 85
    neural plasticity and, 86, 134, 189, 432, 493, 510, 664–665
    neural schemata, patterns of information processing and, 122
    neurons and, 84, 85, 85 (exhibit), 431, 432
    neurotransmitters and, 85–86
    occipital lobe and, 85 (exhibit)
    orbital frontal cortex and, 135
    parietal lobes and, 85 (exhibit)
    pathways of the brain, 84
    plasticity and, 86, 134, 189, 432, 493, 510, 664–665
    pruning of synapses and, 432
    psychodynamic theories and, 57
    psychotropic medications and, 86
    sense of self and, 477
    social brain and, 13
    stress, brain development and, 135
    temporal lobe and, 85 (exhibit)
    thalamus, 121, 122
    traumatic brain injury and, 83, 86, 610

Brain injury (BI), 76–77, 83–84

Brain plasticity, 86, 134, 189, 432, 493, 510, 664–665

Braithwaite, D., 342

Brandtstadter, J., 652

Brashears, M., 299

Brazelton, T. B., 431

Breastfeeding, 396, 397, 426, 451–452

Brent, J., 310, 427

Brich, H., 440

Bridging social capital, 305, 306

Brommel, B., 342

Bronfenbrenner, U., 13, 40

Brown, R. A., 607

Brown v. Board of Education (1954), 256, 528

Brubaker, E., 672

Bruce, S., 435

Buber, M., 66

Buchanan, J., 48

Built environment, 227
    evidence-based design and, 227–228
    healing environments, physical/mental health and, 227–229
    inner-city neighborhoods, ill health in, 230
    obesity and, 229, 230
    sociality, social interaction/physical environment and, 227
    sociofugal spaces and, 227
    sociopetal spaces and, 227
    sunlight, healing properties of, 229
    toxic waste problem and, 227
    urban design, health status and, 229–230
    urban sprawl, suburban environments and, 229
    See also Physical environment

Bulimia nervosa, 585

Bullis, R. K., 191

Bullying, 518–519, 582
    direct bullying, 518

paid child care, 450
quality day care services, 450
staff training and, 450
staff-child ratio and, 450
universal child care, 450
See also Infant/toddler development
Child maltreatment, 134, 221
child neglect and, 535–536
early childhood development and, 496–498, 497 (Exhibit)
infant/toddler development and, 455–457, 456(Exhibit)
middle childhood development and, 535–537, 536 (Exhibit)
Child Protective Services (CPS), 239, 421–422, 535
Child Trends report, 630–631
Child Welfare League of America, 541
Child welfare system, 444
Childbearing. *See* Fetal development; Human procreation;
    Reproductive system; Young/middle adulthood
Childhood:
bone growth and, 97
cognitive development, sequential unfolding of, 114
early nurturing, long term effects of, 134–135
early positive environment, physical/mental health and, 262
faith development stages in, 168
gender-based child rearing environment and, 58
immune system function and, 92
object relations, development of, 130
parent-child attachment model and, 130–131
parent-child relationships, power dynamics in, 58
poverty, vulnerability to, 246, 263
psychosexual stage theory of development and, 56, 59
schema, psychological equilibrium and, 113
social health indicators and, 246 (exhibit)
traumatic brain injury and, 83
See also Adolescence; Early childhood development;
    Education institution; Infancy; Infant/toddler
    development; Middle childhood
Children of Immigrants Longitudinal Study (CILS), 631
Children's Comprehensive Services, 265
Chinese Exclusion Act of 1882, 215–216
Chodorow, N., 521
Chomsky, N., 470
Chromosomes, 392, 393 (exhibit)
Circadian rhythms, 555
Circulatory system, 94, 95 (exhibit)
Citizenship:
melting pot metaphor and, 18
pluralistic society and, 18
vulnerability to poverty and, 246
Civil Rights Act of 1964, 314
Civil rights movement, 314, 315–316
Civil Rights Project, 566
Clammer, J., 41
Clark, J. L., 178
Clark, K., 480

Clark, M., 480
Class. *See* Social class; Social structure
Class consciousness, 44, 273
Classical conditioning theory, 62–63
Clearinghouse on International Developments in Child, Youth
    and Family Policies, 449
Clock time, 10 (exhibit), 12 (exhibit), 16, 17
Cluttered nest, 625
Code of Ethics, 21, 25–26, 25 (exhibit), 45, 186, 210
Cognition, 12, 112, 113, 433
adolescence and, 557
cognitive development, sequential unfolding of, 114
cold/hot cognition, 553, 557
constructivism and, 53, 54
dopamine and, 86
early childhood development and, 465–466
emotions, influence of, 121
human agency and, 115
infant/toddler cognitive development and, 433–436,
    433 (exhibit)
metacognition and, 25
middle childhood development and, 510–514
moral development, cognitive developmental approach and,
    471–472
stages of cognitive operations, 113, 113 (exhibit), 114
young/middle adulthood and, 613–615
See also Psychological person; Theories of cognition
Cognitive accommodation, 113–114
Cognitive assimilation, 113
Cognitive development stages theory, 433–434, 510, 559, 618
categorization skill and, 435–436
concrete operations stage, 434
criticisms of, 435
cultural differences and, 435
deferred imitation and, 468–469
formal operations stage, 434, 557
object permanence and, 434, 435
pre-language skills and, 436
preoperational stage, 434, 468–469
sensorimotor stage, 434, 435
separation anxiety and, 434
stranger anxiety and, 434
substages in sensorimotor development, 434–435
transductive reasoning and, 469
Cognitive social learning theory, 63–64
Cognitive theory, 113, 114
See also Cognitive development stages theory; Theories of
    cognition
Cohabitation, 356–357, 623
Cohort, 384, 647
Cohort effects, 60, 386, 650, 662
Cold War, 248
Coleman, J., 48, 49, 50, 51
Coles, R., 24, 512, 523

Collective agency, 64
Collective efficacy, 308
Collective responsibility/solutions, 22 (exhibit)
Collins, P. H., 45, 351
Collins, R., 46, 51, 52
Collins, W. A., 473, 475, 489, 497, 542
Colonialism:
    global political landscape and, 247–248
    globalization process and, 252
    imperialism, contemporary global inequalities and, 274
    intersectionality theory and, 351
    neocolonialism and, 247–248, 274
    Third World nations and, 20
Colucci, P., 362
Common sense, 213
Communication technology, 18
    access inequalities and, 300
    computer-mediated communication, 318–319
    Internet use and, 268, 270, 306
    new media and, 267
    personal space requirements and, 221
    postgesellschaft community and, 302
    postmodern culture and, 208
    privacy concerns and, 220
    relational communities and, 299–300
    small group sessions and, 333, 335
    social isolation and, 299–300
    social movement action and, 316, 318–319
    social networking sites and, 298–300
    solidarity community and, 306
    transnational communities and, 297, 298–299, 300
    transnational computer-based networks, 318–319
    virtual behavior settings and, 223
    world systems and, 41, 42
    See also Internet; Mass media; Mass media institution
Community, 10–11 (exhibits), 13, 202, 297
    access to new technologies, inequalities in, 300
    communication technologies and, 297, 298–299, 300, 302
    community building and, 309
    comprehensive community initiatives and, 304
    conflict approach to, 301 (exhibit), 309–311
    contacts and, 299
    contrasting types approach to, 301–302, 301 (exhibit)
    definition of, 287 (exhibit)
    diversity in, 19
    domestic labor's transnational community case study, 282–284
    elements of communities and, 302
    gemeinschaft vs. gesellscahft and, 301–302, 301 (exhibit)
    geographic information system and, 304
    Internet use, active neighboring and, 299
    legitimate communities, 82
    local ties, social connections and, 299, 300
    middle childhood development and, 519

    personal community, 306
    postgesellschaft community and, 302
    relational community and, 298, 299–300
    sense of community and, 298, 307
    social capital approach to, 301 (exhibit), 307–309
    social networking sites and, 298–300
    social systems approach to, 301 (exhibit), 304–307
    social work practice and, 302
    solidarity community, 306
    spatial arrangements approach to, 301 (exhibit), 302–304
    territorial community and, 298–299, 300, 302
    theoretical approaches to, 301, 301 (exhibit)
    ties and, 299
    transformation of, 302
    transnational communities, 297, 298–299, 300
    urban community gardening projects, 225
Community assets, 629
Community youth development movement, 567
Community-based wellness initiatives, 190
Compassion stress, 138
Complementary and alternative medicine (CAM), 188
Complexity theory, 40, 42
Comprehensive community initiatives (CCIs), 304
Computer-mediated communication (CMC), 318–319, 333
Concepts, 27, 38
Concrete operations stage, 434, 513
Conflict approach to community, 301 (exhibit), 309–310
    community psychology, European perspective and, 310
    Intercultural Mediation Program and, 310, 311
    restorative justice programs and, 311
    social capital approach, criticism of, 310
    United States social work perspective and, 311
Conflict perspective, 43–47, 43 (exhibit)
    capitalist economic system and, 44
    class consciousness and, 44
    coherence/conceptual clarity of, 46
    comprehensiveness of, 46
    contemporary theory, roots of, 44
    cultural conflict and, 210
    culture industry, domination by, 44
    diversity and, 46
    empirical support for, 46
    empowerment theories and, 45, 46, 47
    inequality, creation of, 44–45
    inevitability of conflict and, 44
    multidimensional perspective on inequality and, 44
    negative health report and, 96
    oppression and, 45
    pluralistic theory of social conflict and, 44–45
    power dynamics and, 44, 46
    privilege, dynamics of, 45
    social inequality and, 274
    social work practice, usefulness for, 46–47
    status group membership and, 44–45

postmodern contemporary culture, 204, 208, 209 (exhibit), 210–212

powerful influence of, 7–9

practice orientation and, 211–212

premodern traditional culture, 208, 209 (exhibit)

Romantic intellectual orientation and, 206, 207–208, 207 (exhibit)

social work assessment and, 204, 216

social work, history of, 205

social work practice and, 210, 211 (exhibit), 216

time orientation and, 17

United States' tradition and, 204

Western vs. Eastern regions and, 21

worldview and, 209–210

See also Diversity; Physical environment

Culture industry, 44

Culture of poverty, 210–211

Cumulative advantage/disadvantage, 651–652

Curriculum Policy Statement, 179–180

Customs, 213–214

Cyberstalking, 335

Daatland, S., 626

D'Acunti, A., 305

Daily hassles, 136

Daniel, S. E., 662

Dating violence, 583–584

Davey, A., 626

Davies, D., 437, 438, 516

Davis, G., 319

Day care. See Child care arrangements

de Beauvoir, S., 66

de St. Aubin, E., 600

Death/dying, 675–676

adjectives for, 676

advance directives and, 677–678

causes, global differences in, 611

death rattle and, 680

dehydration and, 680

denial about, 676

end-of-life signs/symptoms and, 679–681

fears about, 677

good death ideal and, 677

hospice services and, 678–679, 679 (exhibit)

living will and, 677

mortality rates and, 656

palliative care and, 678

parental death, child outcomes and, 540–541

patients' rights, promotion of, 677–678

rituals associated with, 681–682

spirituality and, 188

stages of acceptance and, 676, 676 (exhibit)

See also Bereavement; Grief; Grief work; Loss; Mourning

Debt crisis, 250, 252

Deculturalizing, 506

Deductive reasoning, 27

Deep ecology, 41

Default individualization, 605

Defense Centers of Excellence, 610

Defense of Marriage Act (DOMA) of 1996, 361

Defense mechanisms, 56, 140, 141–142 (exhibit)

Defensive social movement, 311–312

Dehumanization, 68, 289

Deity mysticism, 175

DeJong, C., 31

Del Rio, N., 685

Delirium, 660

Dell, M. L., 523

della Porta, D., 312

Dementia, 626, 659

age-associated memory impairment and, 659–660

Alzheimer's disease, 219, 613, 659, 660–661, 661 (Exhibit)

delirium and, 660

irreversible dementia, 659

mild cognitive impairment and, 659–660

reversible dementia, 659

risk factors for, 660

See also Aging; Late adulthood

Democratic management, 291

DeNavas-Walt, C., 244

Density ratio, 222

Denton, M. L., 572

Dependency ratio, 646–647, 647 (Exhibit)

Dependency theory, 274

DePoy, E., 80, 81, 82

Determinism, 27

See also Biological determinism

Developed nations, 21

Developing nations, 21

Developmental crises, 137

Developmental delays, 447

accurate assessment, need for, 447, 485

autism spectrum disorders and, 447–448

crowding and, 223

developmental trajectories, variability of, 486

early childhood development and, 484–486

early detection/diagnosis, improved outcomes and, 448

education settings, inclusive classrooms and, 485–486

infant/toddler development and, 477–478

parental stress and, 485

social skill development and, 485

See also Infant/toddler development

Developmental Disabilities Assistance and Bill of Rights Act of 1963/2000, 447

Developmental individualization, 605

Developmental niche, 424–425, 424 (exhibit), 441, 470

Developmental perspective, 58–62, 59 (exhibit)

coherence/conceptual clarity of, 61

Galileo, 163
Galinsky, E., 345
Gallagher, W., 230
Galliher, R., 576
Gallup, G., 160, 163
Gallup Polls, 160, 162
Galvin, K., 342
Gambrill, E., 69
Gamete intrafallopian tube transfer (GIFT), 403
Gamma aminobutyric acid (GABA), 86
Gamson, W., 321
Gang activity, 210, 582
Garbarino, J., 535
Gardiner, H. W., 117, 424, 513, 558
Gardner, H., 115, 116, 525
Garfinkel, H., 52
Garrett, M. W., 566
Garrow, E., 292
Garvey, C., 483, 484
Gay/lesbian/bisexual/transgender (GLBT) population:
    adolescent youth and, 576–577, 577 (exhibit)
    baby dykes and, 339
    bicultural nature of, 362
    civil unions and, 361
    coming out case study, 546–547
    Defense of Marriage Act, repeal efforts and, 361
    family, definition of, 342
    late adulthood and, 667
    marriage equality issue and, 361
    parenting and, 362
    questioning youth and, 576
    religious teachings and, 340
    same-sex marriage, legalization of, 361
    same-sex partner families, 355, 361–362
    same-sex partner families, child well-being and, 362
    same-sex partnership, characteristics of, 361–362, 623
    social work practice and, 185–186
    spirituality and, 184–186
    supportive environment for, 577
    See also Sexual orientation
Gemeinschaft, 301, 301 (exhibit)
Gender, 478
    biologically described genders, 100
    crowding, response to, 222–223
    culture-based gender differences, 68, 100
    diffuse status characteristic of, 339
    family, gender roles within, 345, 346, 350
    glass ceiling and, 345
    homelessness and, 232
    hostile environments and, 58
    interpersonal distance and, 221
    late adulthood and, 648–649
    learned helplessness and, 65
    male domination and, 45

poverty, vulnerability to, 246
    relational coping and, 142
    social service organizations and, 296
    spirituality and, 184
    stress response and, 140
    symbol of, 209
    women, moral deficits in, 58
    women's development, gender power differentials and, 61–62
    See also Gay/lesbian/bisexual/transgender (GLBT)
        population; Gender identity
Gender equity, 45
Gender feminists, 132–133
Gender identity, 478
    adolescence and, 560–561
    cross-gender behavior, 522
    early childhood development and, 477–479
    gender constancy and, 477
    gender differences, causal perspectives on, 478–479
    genital basis of, 478
    hierarchical social structures and, 20
    male privilege and, 20
    middle childhood development and, 521–522
    See also Gender
Gender schema theory, 521
General Agreement on Tariffs and Trade (GATT), 249
General Social Survey (GSS), 181
General systems theory, 41
Generalized other, 560
Generation, 385
Generativity, 600–601, 601 (Exhibit), 662
Genes, 392, 394
    dominant genes, 394
    recessive genes, 394
    See also Genetics
Genetics:
    bioethical concerns and, 395
    brain development and, 432
    chromosomal aberration, 411, 411 (exhibit)
    chromosomes, 392, 394
    congenital anomalies and, 409–413, 410–412 (exhibits)
    dominant genes and, 394
    epigenetics and, 60, 410
    fertilization and, 392
    genes and, 392, 394
    genetic heterogeneity, 410
    genetic inheritance, mechanisms of, 392, 393 (exhibit)
    genetic liability, 411
    genetic testing/genetic counseling and, 394–395, 413
    genotype and, 394
    germ cells and, 392
    Human Genome Project and, 392, 394
    language ability and, 470
    multifactorial inheritance and, 410 (exhibit), 411
    phenotype and, 394

Greenberg, J., 624
Greenberg, L. S., 125
Greenfield, E., 624
Greenglass, E. R., 663
Greenspan, S., 490, 491
Grief, 24, 681
    death-related rituals and, 681–682
    middle childhood development and, 539
    multidimensional process of, 684
    theories/models of, 682–684
    See also Death/dying; Grief work; Loss; Mourning
Grief work, 682
    critique of, 683
    individual diversity and, 683–684
    model of adult bereavement and, 684
    patterns of grieving and, 684
    spiritual sensitivity and, 188
    stages of, 682–683, 683 (exhibit)
    stress/trauma reactions and, 684
    tasks of mourning, 683
    See also Bereavement; Death/dying; Grief; Mourning
Griswold, W., 300
Grof, S., 178
Gross motor skills, 430, 466, 467 (exhibit)
Group cohesiveness, 336
Group work, 47, 333
    social constructionist perspective and, 55
    See also Small groups
Gruenewald, T., 140, 142
Gurung, R., 140, 142

Ha, J., 624
Haan, N., 118
Habermas, J., 44, 311
Hall, D., 258
Hall, E., 221
Hall, G. S., 548, 549
Hansen, C. C., 474
Hareven, T., 60, 384
Harris, J. R., 493
Hart, H., 601
Hart, T., 523
Hartmann, H., 55
Harvard Living Wage Campaign, 315
Harwood, R., 439
Hasenfeld, Y., 292
Havighurst, R., 60
Haycock, K., 257
Head Start programs, 450, 458, 486
Healing environments, 227–229
Health belief model (HBM), 48
Health Care and Education Reconciliation Act of 2010, 261
Health care institution, 258–259
    aggressive treatments, reimbursement system and, 261

antiretroviral therapy, access to, 260
cost of health care, 260, 261
health care, human right to, 261
health care legislation and, 261
infectious/parasitic diseases and, 259–260
insurance coverage and, 260
life expectancy and, 260
medical tourism and, 261
mortality rates and, 259–260, 261
national health care systems and, 261
personal bankruptcies, health care costs and, 260
poor nations, basic prevention/treatment services and, 259–260
satisfaction levels and, 260–261
system fragmentation and, 261
therapeutic medicine and, 261
traditional healing practices and, 261
United States health system and, 260–261
universal health plans and, 260, 261
within-country health disparities and, 260–261
    See also Mental health; Physical health; Social institutions
Health care referral program, 96
Health literacy, 106
Healthy People 2010 campaign, 451
Healthy People 2020 campaign, 586–587
Healthy People's Initiative, 413
Hearn, J., 296
Hechter, M., 48
Hefner, V., 576
Hegel, G., 43
Hehir, T., 540
Heidegger, M., 66
Herd, P., 651
Heterogeneity, 19
Heuveline, P., 356
Hickson, J., 178
Hierarchy of needs, 66
Hiestand, M., 672
High blood pressure, 78, 93–94, 105
Higher thinking skills, 84
Highly active antiretroviral therapy (HAART), 90, 92
Hill Lee, C., 244
Hillier, A., 304
Hispanics. *See* Latino Americans
Hitt, M., 293
HIV/AIDS, 92, 260, 323, 356, 396, 452, 578–579, 579 (exhibit), 609, 611
Hodge, D. R., 619
Hoge, C. W., 635
Holarchical spectrum of consciousness, 172–173
Holotropic Breathwork model, 178
Homans, G., 48, 50
Homelessness, 231–232, 232 (exhibit), 489–490
Homeostasis, 120, 139, 455

Human relations theory, 290 (Exhibit), 291–292
Human rights, 18
  barriers to, 23
  global social justice and, 23
  Universal Declaration of Human Rights, 23
Humanistic perspective, 65–69, 66 (exhibit)
  alienating contexts and, 68
  coherence/conceptual clarity of, 67
  comprehensiveness of, 67–68
  dehumanizing world and, 68
  diversity and, 68
  empirical support for, 67
  existential psychology and, 65, 66
  existential sociology tradition and, 65–66
  fourth force of psychology and, 66
  hierarchy of needs theory and, 66
  humanistic psychology and, 65
  nondominant groups, preferential input of, 68
  organizational humanism, 292
  peak experiences concept and, 66
  phenomenal self and, 67, 68
  positive psychology and, 67, 68
  power dynamics and, 68
  roots of, 66
  social work practice, usefulness for, 68–69
  strengths vs. pathology approaches and, 68–69
  testability of, 67
  theory evaluation criteria and, 67–69
  therapeutic process, core conditions of, 67
  third force of psychology and, 65
  transcendent self-actualization and, 166
  transpersonal psychology and, 66, 165–167
Humanistic psychology, 65
Husserl, E., 52, 66
Hyde Amendment, 399
Hyde, B., 523
Hyde, J., 478
Hynes, P., 229
Hypertension. *See* High blood pressure
Hypotheses, 26

Iannello, K., 297
Id, 56, 471
Ideal-type bureaucracy, 289, 290 (exhibit), 291
Identity:
  accommodative identity style and, 618
  adolescent identity development, 558–562
  assimilative identity style and, 618
  balanced identity style and, 618
  dispositions and, 559
  emerging adulthood and, 604
  ethnicity and, 561–562
  exploration and, 560
  foreclosure and, 559

  future orientation and, 560
  identity achievement and, 559
  identity diffusion and, 559
  individuation process and, 166, 438, 521, 563
  middle adulthood and, 618
  moratorium and, 559
  physical characteristics and, 559
  place identity, 231
  psychological identity, 558–559
  role experimentation and, 146–147, 560
  self-evaluation and, 560
  self/identity, theoretical perspectives on, 558–560, 558 (exhibit)
  social identity, 20, 558, 559, 560
  sociocultural context and, 560–561
  young/middle adulthood and, 617–618
  See also Gender identity
Ideology, 208
  See also Personal ideology
Immigrant families, 365
  challenges to, 369–370
  characteristics of, 368–370
  clinical models for family practice and, 367
  cultural diversity and, 366–368
  cultural groups, variability within, 368
  culturally sensitive practice principles and, 368
  culturally variant families, context of, 367–368
  first-generation immigrants, 369
  formal schooling and, 524, 526–527
  informed-not-knowing stance and, 367
  involuntary immigrants, 369
  labor market, structural changes in, 631
  loss, experience of, 369
  second-generation immigrants, 369
  sequential migration and, 369
  third-generation immigrants, 369
  transnational families and, 369
  See also Diversity of family life; Families
Immigration, 24
  anti-immigrant legislation, 215–216
  anti-immigrant sentiment and, 19, 271, 307
  cultural diversity and, 214–215
  economic opportunity and, 215
  economically marginal immigrants, 215
  life expectancy of immigrants, 104
  mass cross-national migration and, 250, 271
  new policies for, 18–19
  oppression and, 45
  othering tendency and, 208
  place identity and, 231
  struggles in settling case study, 238–240
  United States, nation of immigrants, 18–19, 104
  See also Immigrant families
Immigration Act of 1990, 369

individuation process and, 438

infant, definition of, 423

language skill development and, 433 (exhibit), 436

maternal education level and, 457

motor skills and, 428–431, 431 (exhibit)

multigenerational family environment and, 450–452

neural plasticity and, 432

nonorganic failure to thrive and, 455

nutrition and, 425, 426

overprotective parenting case study, 422

pain perception and, 428

parental mental illness/depression and, 452, 455

physical development and, 425–433

play, role of, 445–447, 445–446 (exhibit)

policies, pro-child support and, 458

postpartum depression and, 452

poverty and, 453–455

premature birth case study, 420–421

premature/low birth weight infants and, 414–415, 420–421, 428, 432–433

protective factors and, 457–458

psychosocial development stages and, 437–438

reflexes and, 428, 429 (exhibit), 434

risks for sub-optimal development and, 453–457

self-regulatory functions and, 426–427

sensory abilities and, 427–428

social supports and, 452, 454–455, 457

socioemotional development, 436–445, 437 (exhibit)

teen parents case study, 421–422

temperament and, 439–441, 458

toddler, definition of, 423

toilet training and, 431

touch, importance of, 427–428

trust development and, 437

See also Childhood; Early childhood development; Fetal development; Infancy

Infertility, 358, 379–381

female infertility, 401, 402 (exhibit)

male infertility, 401–402, 402 (exhibit)

stress and, 402

young adults and, 610

See also Infertility treatments

Infertility treatments, 401

adoption and, 404

assisted reproductive technologies and, 402–404

gamete intrafallopian tube transfer, 403

gestational surrogacy, 404

intrauterine insemination, 403

in vitro fertilization, 380–381, 403

ovulation, problems with, 401

polycystic ovarian syndrome and, 401

preservation of embryos, 403–404

primary ovarian insufficiency and, 401

risks of, 404

uterine transplant and, 404

See also Infertility

Information processing theory, 114

Injustice. See Oppression; Social justice; Social movements

Instinct theory, 55, 56

Institutional discrimination, 529

Instrumental activities of daily living (IADLs), 658, 658 (exhibit)

Instrumental aggression, 475

Instrumental conditioning, 63

Integral theory of consciousness, 171–172

deity mysticism and, 175

emptiness as pure consciousness and, 175

formless mysticism and, 175

four quadrants of consciousness and, 171–173, 172 (exhibit)

fulcrum/switch point and, 173–174

holarchical spectrum of consciousness and, 172–173

human development, ultimate goal of, 172, 175

interior consciousness, components of, 173–174

levels of consciousness and, 173

lines of consciousness and, 173

nature mysticism and, 174

nondual mysticism and, 175

phases of development and, 174–176

psychic disorders/causal pathologies, treatment modalities and, 175–176

quadrants/levels of consciousness and, 171–172, 172 (exhibit)

self differentiation/dis-identification and, 174, 175

self-system and, 173

spectrum of consciousness, chain of being and, 172–173

states of consciousness and, 173

Wilber's theory, summary/critique of, 176–178

witness, inner sense of, 174, 175

See also Spiritual person; Transpersonal theories

Integrity, 662–663

Intelligence:

crystallized intelligence and, 664

definition of, 115

early childhood protective factor, 498

emotional intelligence, 124–125, 515–516

fluid intelligence and, 664

interrelational intelligence, 513

late adulthood and, 664

multiple intelligences theory, 115, 116 (exhibit), 525–526

social intelligence, 515–516

Intentional memory, 664

Intercultural Mediation Programme, 310, 311

Intergenerational stresses case study, 36–37

Internalized oppression, 22 (exhibit)

International Association of Schools of Social Work (IASSW), 180

International Federation of Social Workers (IFSW), 180

International Monetary Fund (IMF), 248, 249, 250, 251, 252, 262, 274

Internet, 268, 270, 306, 318–319, 322, 335, 570–572

age-related pathology and, 656
Alzheimer's disease and, 219, 613, 659, 660–661, 661 (exhibit)
biological changes in, 654–662
brain plasticity and, 664–665
cardiovascular system changes and, 654–655
caregiving/care receiving and, 670–672
centenarians and, 646, 647
chronic conditions and, 656–657
coping mechanisms and, 663
cross-generational caregiving case study, 640–641
cultural construction of, 649–652
cumulative advantage/disadvantage, differential aging and, 651–652
dementia and, 659–661
demographics of older adult population and, 645–649, 647–648 (exhibits)
dependency ratio and, 646–647, 647 (exhibit)
divorce and, 666–667
economic status/poverty rates in, 649
family relationships in, 665–667
family systems, impact on, 656–657
formal resources and, 675
functional capacity, very late adulthood and, 657–659
gay/lesbian elders, 667
gender differences and, 648–649, 653
geriatric counseling case study, 641–643
gerontocracy and, 649
gerotranscendence and, 653
grandparenthood and, 667–668
in-place aging case study, 643–644
independence/self-reliance and, 649
informal resources and, 675
institutional placement decisions and, 672–673
integumentary system changes and, 655
intelligence in, 664
learning process and, 664
life expectancy and, 646, 647–648
long-distance caregiving and, 658–659
memory capacity and, 664
mental health/disorders and, 665
morbidity and, 656
mortality rates and, 656
musculoskeletal system and, 655
nervous system changes and, 654
neurodegenerative diseases and, 659–662
osteoporosis and, 655
parent outliving child case study, 644–645
Parkinson's disease and, 661–662
personal meaning, search for, 673–674
personality changes and, 652, 662–663
physiological changes in, 654–656
positive aging and, 650–651, 651 (exhibit)
power of attorney and, 675
protective factors and, 686–687, 686 (exhibit)

psychological changes in, 662–665
race/ethnicity and, 648, 648 (exhibit)
resources for, 674–675
respiratory system changes and, 655
risk factors and, 686–687, 686 (exhibit)
sensory system changes and, 655
sexual desire/capacity and, 655–656
sibling relationships and, 667
social role/life event transitions and, 665–673
subgroups of old age, 647
supercentenarians and, 648
within-group differences in, 649–650
See also Aging; Death/dying; Social gerontology
Latency phase of development, 56, 513
Latino Americans:
    bereavement customs and, 685
    biological determinism and, 208
    browning effect and, 215
    crowding, response to, 222
    graduation rates and, 258
    historical plight of, 205
    immigration and, 214, 215
    schooling experience and, 213
    spirituality and, 181–182
    unemployment rate and, 254
    See also Culture; Ethnic groups; Social inequality
Lau, A., 492
Lazarus, R., 123, 136
Learned behavior. See Learned helplessness; Social behavioral perspective
Learned helplessness, 65, 67
Learned optimism, 67
Learning:
    direct learning, 113
    learned helplessness, 65, 67
    social learning, 113
Learning organization theory, 290 (exhibit), 293
Learning play, 483
Least restrictive environment, 539
Lee, B., 307
Lee, M. Y., 42, 43
Leeder, E., 26
Lees, A. J., 662
Legitimate communities, 82
Leighninger, L., 262
Lenski, G., 273
Lepore, S., 222
Lerner, R., 549
Lesbians. See Gay/lesbian/bisexual/transgender (GLBT) population
Levels of consciousness, 173
Lévi-Strauss, C., 48
Levin, J. D., 128
Levinson, D., 60, 61, 599, 601, 602, 603

McAdams, D., 600, 601
McAdoo, H. P., 513
McAvoy, M., 29
McCarthy, J., 319
McCullough, M. E., 619
McDonaldization of society, 291
McGoldrick, M., 346, 349
McGregor, D., 68
McInnis-Dittrich, K., 679
McIntosh, P., 20
McLeod, P., 337
McMichael, P., 241, 251
McMillan, D., 308, 309
McMillan, J. C., 634
McPherson, M., 299
Mead, G. H., 52, 53, 125, 560
Mebane, M., 305
Media. *See* Communication technology; Mass media; Mass media institution
Medical diagnostic perspective, 86
Medical model, 136
Medical tourism, 261
Medicare program, 262, 677
Medications:
    diuretics, 105
    HIV/AIDS and, 92, 260
    psychotropic medications, 86
    side effects of, 92
Meditation, 143, 189
Meisami, E., 94
Melting pot metaphor, 18
Memmi, D., 302
Memory:
    childhood trauma and, 456
    forebrain and, 84
    implicit/automatic memory, 135
    incidental memory, 664
    infant cognitive development and, 434
    information processing theory and, 114
    intentional memory, 664
    internalized attachments and, 130
    late adulthood and, 659–660
    learning and, 664
    norepinephrine and, 86
    primary memory, 664
    secondary memory, 664
    sensory memory, 664
    stages of, 664
    tertiary memory, 664
    See also Reminiscence
Menarche, 552, 556
Menstruation, 552, 556
Mental health:
    cognitive/emotional disorders, 127–128, 127 (exhibit)

healing environments and, 227–229
human strength/competence, promotion of, 67
late adulthood and, 665
learned optimism and, 67
life trajectories and, 611–612
natural environments and, 225
positive psychology approach and, 67
psychotropic medications and, 86
spirituality/religiosity and, 13, 187
stress/diathesis models of mental illness and, 138
thankfulness and, 13
See also Mental illness; Physical health; Well-being
Mental illness:
    cognitive/emotional disorders, 127–128, 127 (exhibit)
    crowding and, 223
    definition of, 146
    eating disorders and, 584–585
    infant/toddler development and, 455
    late adulthood and, 665
    postpartum depression, 452
Mentoring, 567–568
Merchant, C., 586
Merton, R., 40
Mesosystems, 13
Messinger, L., 304
Metacognition, 25
Meyer, C., 23
Meyer, D., 321
Meyer, H. A., 518
Meyer, K., 293
Microsystems, 13
Middle childhood:
    aggression and, 475
    challenges in, 532–541
    historical perspective on, 506–507
    multigenerational family environment and, 507
    risk factors in, 508
    See also Childhood; Early childhood development; Middle childhood development; Middle childhood education
Middle childhood development, 507
    aggression and, 521
    attention deficit/hyperactivity disorder and, 538
    autism spectrum disorders and, 538
    bicultural/multicultural competence and, 513–514
    challenges in, 532–541
    character education and, 518
    child maltreatment and, 535–537, 536 (exhibit)
    cognitive development and, 510–514, 519
    community support/structure and, 519
    community violence and, 535
    cultural identity development and, 514–515
    depression, emotional competence deficits and, 516–517
    diverse developmental pathways and, 517–518

divorce and, 540
domestic violence and, 535, 536–537
emotional development and, 515–517, 516 (exhibit)
emotional intelligence and, 515–516
emotional/behavioral disorders and, 538–540, 541
family disruption and, 540–541
family environment and, 515, 517
foster care and, 541
friendship/intimacy and, 520–521
gender differences in, 512–513
gender identity/gender roles and, 521–522
grief/loss stages and, 539
group norms and, 519
individuation and, 521
industry task and, 517
mastery and, 517
mental/physical challenges and, 537–540
moral development/moral behavior and, 512, 518
new self-image case study, 503–504
nonlinear dynamic systems theory and, 510–511
peer relationships and, 510, 519–520
phases/tasks in, 512, 513 (exhibit)
physical development and, 507–510
physical vulnerabilities and, 508
poverty and, 532–535, 533–534 (exhibits), 540
precocious puberty and, 509
prepubescence and, 509
prosocial behaviors and, 519, 520
protective factors and, 541–542
pubescence and, 509
relational resilience and, 516–517
resilience and, 541
risk, susceptibility to, 508
risks for sub-optimal development and, 532–541
secondary sexual development and, 509
self-awareness and, 509–510
self-doubt, increase in, 522
self-perceptions, emergence of, 521
sensitive periods of brain development and, 510
social competence, development of, 519
social development and, 517–522
social intelligence and, 515–516
special needs, identification of, 511–512
spiritual development and, 522–524
stereotype vulnerability and, 514, 522
team play and, 521
trauma, depression and, 517
zone of proximal development and, 519
See also Middle childhood; Middle childhood education
Middle childhood education, 524
acculturation process and, 527
achievement gap and, 530–531
assessment case study, 502–503
assimilation process and, 527
bullying/harassment and, 518–519
character education and, 518
cognitive development and, 525–526
collaborative classrooms and, 530
community institutional structures, reflection/reproduction of, 528–531
comprehensive assessments and, 526
cultural transition case study, 504–505
diverse educational materials/activities and, 526, 530
diverse student body and, 526–527, 530
evidence-based practice and, 530, 531
flexible grouping and, 526
formal schooling, importance of, 524
full-service schools and, 530
home-to-school success and, 527–528
inclusion/mainstreaming and, 530, 539–540
institutional discrimination and, 529
language challenges and, 526, 527
multiple intelligences and, 525–526
nondominant cultures, respect for, 515
parental involvement in, 527, 528
refugee/immigrant children and, 526–527
school violence, responses to, 518
self-assessment and, 525
self-esteem, school success and, 524–525
special needs, identification of, 511–512
tracking practices and, 529–530
wraparound programs and, 532
See also Middle childhood; Middle childhood development
Midwifery, 389–390
Migrations, 250, 271
Mikulas, W. L., 178
Mikulincer, M., 612
Mild cognitive impairment (MCI), 659–660
Milevsky, A., 627
Military personnel:
adult mental health and, 635, 636
military families, 362–365
time orientation and, 17
unemployment rate among, 254
See also War
Millennium Cohort Study Child Health Group, 425
Milliken, C. S., 635
Mind-body interactions, 81, 188–189
Mindfulness practices, 17, 187, 190
Miringoff, M. L., 245, 246
Miscarriage, 408–409
Mitchell, K. J., 571
Mobilizing structures (MS) perspective, 313 (exhibit), 316–317
coalitions of organizations and, 318
computer-mediated communication and, 318–319
flexible structures and, 318
informal/formal structures and, 317–318
life course of social movements and, 318

local progressive networks and, 316–317

network model, natural networks and, 317, 323

organization vs. spontaneity and, 318

preexisting structure/networks and, 317–318

resource mobilization and, 317, 323

social movement organizations and, 317, 318

transnational social movement organizations and, 317

unrest, window of opportunity and, 318

See also Social movements

Model of case coordination, 13, 14 (exhibit)

Models, 26

Modernism:

    bureaucracies and, 289

    classifications of nations and, 20–21

    modern culture and, 208

    religious conflict and, 163, 165

    sacred-secular continuum and, 302

    See also Postmodernism

Modernization theory, 274

Modified consensual organization model, 297

Möller, K., 622, 623

Monette, D., 31

Monogamy, 342–343

Monte, C., 64

Montgomery, R., 671

Mood, 112, 128, 555

    See also Emotion; Temperament

Moore, D., 563

Moore, K. L., 412

Mor Barak, M., 295

Moral development, 471, 559

    autonomous morality, 513 (exhibit)

    caregiver bond and, 471

    character education and, 518

    cognitive developmental approach and, 471–472

    conscience/superego and, 471, 512

    conventional stage of moral reasoning and, 117 (exhibit)

    distributive justice and, 473

    early childhood development and, 471

    ego ideal and, 471

    empathy and, 472–473

    ethic of care and, 512

    facilitation strategies for, 473

    interrelational intelligence and, 513

    Kohlberg's stages of moral reasoning and, 116–118, 471–472

    middle childhood development and, 512–513, 518

    perspective taking and, 472–473

    preconventional level of moral reasoning and, 117 (exhibit), 472, 513 (exhibit)

    postconventional stage of moral reasoning and, 117 (exhibit)

    prosocial behaviors and, 471

    psychodynamic approach and, 471

    social learning approach and, 471

theoretical approaches to, 116–118, 471–472

    See also Early childhood development

Morality, 116

    conventional morality, 117

    cultural influence on, 117–118, 119

    ethic of care and, 117

    fundamentalist religious movements and, 320

    Gilligan's stages of moral development, 117, 118 (exhibit)

    justice-oriented approach to, 117

    Kohlberg's stages of moral development, 117, 117 (exhibit)

    moral development, social constructionist theory of, 118

    postconventional morality, 117

    poverty and, 210

    preconventional morality, 117

    rational choice models of organizations and, 292

    women, moral deficits in, 58

    See also Moral development

Morbidity, 656

Morenoff, J., 308

Mortality rate, 259–260, 261, 656

    See also Death/dying; Infant mortality

Mortimer, J. T., 568

Motor skills:

    continuous development process for, 431

    culture/ethnicity, influence of, 430

    early childhood development, 466, 467 (exhibit)

    fine motor skills, 430, 466, 467 (exhibit)

    gross motor skills, 430, 466, 467 (exhibit)

    infant development and, 428–431

    toilet training and, 431

    windows of milestone achievement and, 429–430, 431 (exhibit)

Motor theory, 114

Mourning, 681

    death-related rituals and, 681–682

    spiritual sensitivity and, 188

    tasks of mourning, 683

    work of mourning and, 682–683

    See also Bereavement; Grief work

Moyer, K., 490

Muhammad, Z., 435

Multicentre Growth Reference Study (MGRS), 425–426, 429, 430

Multicultural competence, 513–514

Multiculturalism, 165

Multidetermined behavior, 10, 12

Multidimensional approach, 7, 10, 38–39

    case study for, 4–6

    culture, powerful influence of, 7–9

    dimension, definition of, 10

    ecological theory and, 9–10

    environmental dimensions and, 7–9, 10–12 (exhibits), 13, 15

    inequality, creation of, 44

    multidetermined behavior and, 10, 12

    personal dimensions and, 7, 10–11 (exhibits), 12–13

social theories of emotion and, 125
social work practice, theories of cognition and, 118–120
social work practice, theories of emotion and, 125–126, 126 (exhibit)
stages of cognitive operations and, 113, 113 (exhibit)
transition to college life case study, 110–112
See also Coping; Stress
Psychological sense of community (PSOC), 308–309
Psychological theories of emotion, 122
attribution theory, 123–124
ego psychology, 123
emotional intelligence theory, 124–125
psychoanalytic theory, 122–123
See also Theories of emotion
Psychology, 12
analytic psychology, 599
definition of, 112
existential psychology, 65, 66
First Force therapies and, 166
Fourth Force therapies and, 66, 167
humanistic psychology, 65
positive psychology, 67, 68
Second Force therapies and, 166
self psychology, 55, 56, 129
Third Force therapies and, 65, 166
See also Humanistic perspective; Psychological person
Psychosexual stage theory, 55, 56, 59
Psychosocial approach, 12
Psychosocial crisis, 60, 599
Psychosocial development, 146, 147 (exhibit), 559
anxiety, sources of, 438, 438 (exhibit)
autonomy vs. shame/doubt stage and, 437–438
early childhood development and, 473–474
family relationships and, 474
friendships/peer relations and, 474
infant/toddler development stages and, 437–438
trust vs. mistrust stage and, 437
Psychosocial life span theory, 599–601, 600–601 (Exhibits)
Psychosynthesis, 166
Psychotropic medications, 86
Puberty stage, 552–553, 556–557, 574
Public choice theory, 48
Public health practice, 106, 309
Public Law 101–336, 233
Public territories, 222
Putnam, R., 305, 307, 308, 309, 310, 323, 332

Qian, Z., 357
Qualitative research, 28
Quantitative research, 28

Race:
biological determinism and, 207–208
college education and, 258, 259 (exhibit)

early childhood development and, 479–480
health disparities and, 46, 260
labor force participation and, 631–632
late adulthood and, 648, 648 (exhibit)
new technologies, access to, 300
spirituality and, 181–184
symbol of, 209
terminology for, 19–20
White privilege, 20
See also African Americans; Culture; Diversity; Ethnic groups
Radical antithesis, 273
Raghavan, R., 634
Rando, T., 683
Rape:
acquaintance rape, 583–584
adolescents and, 582–583
middle childhood and, 508
statutory rape, 584
Rapoport, A., 223
Rational perspective of organizations, 48, 289, 290 (exhibit)
best practices and, 291
boards of directors, legal immunity for, 48
evidence-based practice and, 291
human relations theory and, 290 (exhibit), 291–292
ideal-type bureaucracy and, 289, 290 (exhibit), 291
organizational actors, rational capacity of, 292
organizational humanism and, 292
scientific management and, 290 (exhibit), 291
See also Formal organizations
Rational choice perspective, 47–48, 47 (exhibit)
coherence/conceptual clarity of, 49
comparison level alternative and, 49
comparison level standard and, 49
comprehensiveness of, 50–51
disease information/knowledge and, 89
diversity and, 51
ecomap tool and, 49, 50 (exhibit)
empirical support for, 49
health belief model and, 48
interdisciplinary nature of, 47
opportunity costs and, 49
power dynamics and, 51
social exchange theory and, 48–49
social network theory and, 48, 49, 51
social work practice, usefulness for, 51
testability of, 49
theory evaluation criteria and, 49–51
theory of reasoned action and, 48
utilitarian perspective and, 47
See also Rational choice models of organizations
Rationality, 208
Ray, L., 311
Ray, O., 189
Reagan, R. W., 315

Recessive genes, 394
Redlining, 211
Reflexes of infants, 428, 429 (exhibit), 434
Refugee Assistance Extension Act of 1986, 369
Refugees:
    case study analysis, 7–9
    case study of, 4–6
    formal schooling and, 526–527
    mass cross-national migration and, 250, 271
    place identity and, 231
    resettlement/shared journey case study, 378–379
    rural communities, exclusionary/punitive reactions of, 311
    time orientation and, 17
Regulatory processes, 241
Rehabilitation Act of 1973, 98, 233
Rehkopf, D. H., 607
Reich, R., 315
Reid, C., 630
Reid, K. E., 336
Reid, T. R., 248
Reid, W., 10, 26, 29
Reinforcement, 63
Reisch, M., 250
Relational aggression, 475
Relational community, 298, 299–300
Relational coping, 142
Relational feminist theory, 56
Relational resilience, 516–517
Relational theory, 131–132
Relational-cultural theory, 55, 56, 517
Relative poverty, 535
Religion, 159
    affiliation, rationales for, 165
    fundamentalist religious movements, 320
    global experience of, 160–165, 162 (exhibit), 164 (exhibit)
    mental health and, 13
    modernism and, 163, 165
    moral development and, 473
    multiculturalism and, 165
    public life, role in, 190
    racial/ethnic groups and, 181–184
    religion switching, generation of *See*kers and, 163
    religious conflict, 163, 165
    religious dropouts and, 473
    sacred canopy and, 165
    social justice and, 180
    social support role of, 145
    spiritual bypassing and:
    warfare, modern technological advances in, 165
    See also Faith; Faith development stages; Religious institution;
        Spiritual person; Spirituality; Well-being
Religious institution, 265
    diverse religious traditions, unified ethical code and, 265
    genocide/ethnic cleansing and, 265

global religious landscape and, 266
globalization, coexisting religious communities and, 265
modernist branches and, 266–267
pacifist motif and, 266
Parliament of the World's Religions and, 265–266
religions, internal culture wars in, 266–267
resilience of, 266–267
social work practice and, 267
traditionalist branches and, 266–267
warrior motif and, 266
See also Social institutions
Remez, L., 575
Reminiscence, 333, 674
Repetti, R., 453
Reproductive system, 99
    androgens and, 100, 552
    breasts, function of, 103–104
    contraception use and, 99
    ejaculation and, 101
    estrogen and, 103
    female sexual organs and, 101–103, 102–103 (exhibits)
    gender/sexuality, social constructionist perspective and, 100
    male sexual organs and, 100–101, 101 (exhibit)
    ova and, 101, 103
    ovulation and, 103
    penis and, 100, 101 (exhibit), 102
    progesterone and, 103
    puberty and, 552–553
    replacement rate reproduction and, 18
    reproductive health case study and, 79–80, 104
    sex education and, 99–100
    sexual arousal and, 100, 102
    sexually transmitted disease and, 99
    social work practice and, 100, 104
    spermatocyte/spermatozoan and, 100–101
    teen pregnancy and, 99
    testes and, 100
    testosterone and, 100
    uterus and, 103, 103 (exhibit)
    vagina and, 102–103, 103 (exhibit)
    See also Human procreation
Research. *See* Empirical research
Resilience, 387
    adaptive behaviors/positive outcomes and, 541
    early life traumas and, 135
    family resilience perspective, 352–354
    other people's children and, 549
    relational resilience, 516–517
    See also Family resilience perspective
Respondent conditioning, 62–63
Restorative justice programs, 311
Retirement, 632–633, 668–670, 669 (Exhibit)
Rewards, 63
Rhodes, P., 90

for-profit organizations and, 264–265
industrial capitalism, social inequalities of, 263
interdependence, promotion of, 262
labor market insecurities and, 262, 263
neoliberal political philosophy and, 263
nongovernmental organizations and, 264
parental leave policies and, 263–264
policy development and, 262
public assistance programs and, 264
public expenditure on social welfare, 263
public-private partnerships and, 264
purchase of service contract agreements and, 264
social control function and, 265
United States social welfare system, 262, 263–264
vulnerability to poverty and, 263
welfare reform and, 210, 263, 264
See also Social institutions
Social work, 6
biopsychosocial approach and, 12–13
case coordination model and, 13, 14 (exhibit)
case, knowledge about, 23–24
case study and, 4–6
Code of Ethics for, 21, 25–26, 25 (exhibit)
cognition, theories of, 118–120, 119–120 (exhibits)
critical use of theory/research and, 29–31, 30 (exhibit)
culturally sensitive practice and, 25, 115
curriculum/educational policy for, 179–180
diversity issues and, 18–20
dyadic relationships and, 10 (exhibit), 12 (exhibit), 15
ecological perspective and, 9–10, 13
educational policy/accreditation standards and, 180
emotion, theories of, 125–126, 126 (exhibit)
empirical research and, 27–31, 30 (exhibit)
environmental dimensions and, 7–9, 10–12 (exhibits), 13, 15
functionalist sociology and, 40, 41
global perspective and, 17–23
history of, 205
human behavior/social environment curriculum and, 6–7, 9
human rights, concern for, 18
knowing/doing social work, ingredients in, 23–31
literature on theory/research and, 10
medical diagnostic perspective and, 86
person-environment interactions and, 9
personal dimensions and, 7, 10–11 (exhibits), 12–13
physical environment dimension and, 10–11 (exhibits), 13
power relations, inequalities and, 20–21
psychiatric model of, 40
psychodynamic theory and, 9
psychosocial approach and, 12
public health research/practice and, 106
purpose of, 6
scientific knowledge and, 26–31
self, knowledge about, 24–25
social justice and, 21–23, 22 (exhibit)

social location and, 21, 25
social systems approach and, 13
social worker-client relationship and, 24
spiritual person dimension and, 13
spirituality-social work linkages, historical phases of, 178–180
strengths vs. pathology approaches and, 68–69
theory and, 26–27, 29–31, 30 (exhibit)
time dimensions and, 9, 10 (exhibit), 12 (exhibit), 15–17
time orientations and, 17
values of, 25–26, 25 (exhibit)
See also Council on Social Work Education (CSWE); Human behavior/theoretical perspectives; Multidimensional approach
Socialization:
bicultural socialization, 216, 650
labor force participation and, 632
toilet training and, 431
Society:
McDonaldization of, 291
pluralist society, 18
social structure and, 241
See also Social class
Society for Research on Adolescence, 564
Society for Spirituality and Social Work (SSSW), 179
Sociodramatic play, 483
Socioeconomic status (SES), 104, 105, 106, 227, 453
See also Social inequality
Sociograms, 49
Solidarity community, 306
Sollod, R., 64
Solomon, Z., 612
Sommer, R., 220, 221
Soul, 128
Spatial arrangements approach to community, 301 (exhibit), 302–304
comprehensive community initiatives and, 304
distressed neighborhoods, resident interpretation of, 303
environmental design, social interactions/sense of control and, 303–304
human ecology theory and, 303
mapping social/economic injustices and, 304
symbolic images of communities and, 303
See also Community
Special education. *See* Disabled individuals
Specific immunity, 91–92
Spector-Mersel, G., 653
Spencer, M. B., 520
Spermarche, 552
Spiritual activism movement, 190
Spiritual bypassing, 176
Spiritual person, 10–11 (exhibits), 13, 154
challenging questions case study, 154–155
faith journey case study, 156
Fowler's stages of faith development and, 167–171, 176–178

Structural adjustment programs, 274
Structural determinism, 274–275
Structural model of the mind, 55, 56
Structuration theory, 275
Stuart, R., 65
Study of Adult Development, 650–651, 663, 686
Subjective reality, 27, 52
Substance abuse:
    adolescents and, 580–581
    behavior settings and, 230
    fetal effects of, 411, 412 (exhibit)
    military personnel and, 365
    recovery, spiritual dimension and, 187
    tolerance and, 230
    young adults and, 609–610
Substance Abuse and Mental Health Services Administration
    (SAMHSA), 580, 609
Sudden infant death syndrome (SIDS), 426
Suffering, 66
Suffrage movement, 316
Suicide risk, 508, 541, 586
Sullivan, H. S., 60
Sullivan, T., 31
Superego, 56, 471
Swatos, W. H., 163
Symbolic functioning, 434
Symbolic interaction theory, 48, 125
    community culture and, 305
    deviance and, 147–148
Symbolic interaction theory for small groups, 337–338
Symbolic play, 481–482, 483
Symbols, 53, 209
Sympathetic system, 95
Synapses, 85, 85 (exhibit), 431
Synthetic-conventional faith, 168, 169–170, 171, 619–620
Systems perspective, 13, 39–43, 39 (exhibit)
    autopoietic systems and, 41
    biological person/environmental context and, 81–82, 83, 96
    boundaries and, 39
    chaos theory and, 40–41, 42, 43
    closed systems and, 41, 41 (exhibit)
    coherence/conceptual clarity of, 42
    complexity theory and, 40, 42
    comprehensiveness of, 42
    deep ecology and, 41
    diversity and, 42
    ecological/dynamic systems approaches and, 40, 42
    empirical support for, 42
    feedback mechanisms and, 39, 40–41, 41 (exhibit)
    functional sociology and, 40, 41, 42
    general systems theory and, 41
    globalization theories and, 41, 42
    homeostasis/equilibrium and, 40
    interdisciplinary nature of, 39

linked social systems, reciprocal interactions and, 39
    negative feedback loops and, 40–41
    open systems and, 41, 41 (exhibit)
    positive feedback loops and, 41
    power differentials and, 42
    role structure, system balance and, 40
    social work practice, usefulness for, 42–43
    social worker dissatisfaction with, 40
    stability vs. change in, 40–41
    subsystems, state of flux and, 41
    testability of, 42
    theory evaluation criteria and, 42–43
    See also Family systems perspective; Social systems approach
        to community; Systems perspective on organizations
Systems perspective on organizations, 290 (exhibit), 292–293
    equifinality and, 292
    learning organization theory and, 290 (exhibit), 293
    multiple environments, continuous interaction of, 292
    political economy model and, 290 (exhibit), 293
    See also Formal organizations
Szinovacz, M., 45

Takahashi, E. A., 411
Tarrow, S., 319
Task groups, 333, 334 (exhibit)
Taylor, F. W., 291
Taylor, S., 453
Taylor, S. E., 140, 142
Technological disasters, 138
Technological revolution, 68, 163, 165
    assisted reproductive technologies, 402–404
    geographic information system, 304
    personal space requirements and, 221
    virtual behavior settings and, 223
    See also Communication technology
Teen pregnancy, 99, 395, 421–422, 577–578
Telecommunications Act of 1996, 269
Temperament, 439–441
    child abuse/maltreatment and, 457
    cross-cultural differences and, 441
    difficult temperament and, 440
    feedback loops and, 440, 441
    genetics/development niche and, 441
    goodness of fit, temperament type and, 440
    infant regulatory capacity, marital satisfaction and, 440–441
    protective factor of, 458
    slow to warm up infants and, 440
    socioeconomic status and, 441
    stable patterns of, 440
Temporary Assistance to Needy Families (TANF), 264, 632
Tend-and-befriend response, 140
Teratogens, 405–406, 405 (exhibit), 411, 411 (exhibit)
Terkel, S., 323
Territorial community, 298–299, 300, 302

transition points and, 349
transition to work, vulnerable populations and, 630–631
Transnational corporations (TNCs), 248, 250, 251, 274
Transnational social movement organizations (TSMOs), 317
Transpersonal psychology, 65, 66
Transpersonal theories, 66, 165–166
    consciousness, evolution of, 166
    Fourth Psychology and, 166
    higher unconscious, creativity/spirituality and, 166
    psychosynthesis and, 166
    spiritual outlook, development of, 166
    therapeutic approaches and, 166–167
    transcendent self-actualization and, 166
    See also Integral theory of consciousness; Spiritual person
Trauma, 135, 138, 517, 583, 684
Trauma survivors:
    coping mechanisms and, 143
    early life trauma, resilience and, 135
    post-traumatic stress disorder and, 143–144
    spirituality and, 187–188
    time orientation and, 17
Traumatic brain injury (TBI), 83, 86, 610
Traumatic stress, 138, 143–144
Travis, D., 295
Triangulation, 347
Trickle-down bureaucracy, 291, 292
Turnbull, J. E., 411
Turning point, 386, 636
Tversky, A., 49

Uhlenbruck, K., 293
Ulrich, R., 227
Ultimate environment, 168
Unconsciousness, 56, 112
United Nations Children's Fund (UNICEF), 358, 359, 426, 453, 534
United Nations Development Program, 242–243, 244, 255, 260, 454
United Nations Education, Scientific, and Cultural Organization (UNESCO), 255
United Nations High Commissioner for Refugees (UNHCR), 8, 12
United Nations (UN):
    development of, 249
    homeless population statistics and, 231
    Joint United Nations Programme on HIV/AIDS, 90
    Universal Declaration of Human Rights, 23
United States:
    AIDS deaths in, 90
    anti-immigrant sentiment and, 19
    browning of, 215
    cardiovascular disease in, 93, 94
    diversity in, 18
    education in, 256–258

Enlightenment/Romanticism, conflict between, 207–208
    family leave policy in, 448–449, 449 (Exhibit)
    health care system in, 260–261
    health status, socioeconomic factors and, 104–106
    immigrant populations in, 18–19, 214–215, 368–369
    income gap and, 243, 244 (exhibit)
    melting pot metaphor and, 18
    per capita income in, 20
    polio/post-poliomyelitis syndrome and, 96–97
    sexual activity in, 99
    social health in, 245, 246 (exhibit)
    social welfare institution in, 262, 263–264
    spirituality and, 160–163, 162 (exhibit)
    United States privilege and, 20
    welfare reform and, 210, 263
    See also Social institutions
Universal child care, 450
Universal Declaration of Human Rights (UDHR), 23
Universal early childhood education, 256
Universal franchise, 314
Updegraff, J., 140, 142
Urbanization:
    classifications of nations and, 20–21
    environmental hazards and, 105
    gesellschaft and, 302
    inner-city neighborhoods, characteristics of, 230
    modern culture and, 208
    urban community gardening projects and, 225
    urban design, health status and, 229
    urban penalty, public health and, 229
    urban sprawl/suburban design features and, 229
U.S. Census Bureau, 19, 202, 215, 243, 335, 341, 342, 646
U.S. Citizenship and Immigration Services (USCIS), 238
U.S. Department of Agriculture (USDA), 554
U.S. Department of Health and Human Services (HHS), 554, 634
U.S. Department of Housing and Urban Development, 232
U.S. Environmental Protection Agency (EPA), 227
U.S. National Health Survey, 576
Uterus, 103, 103 (exhibit)

Vaillant, G., 60, 68, 615, 616, 650, 651, 663, 664, 668, 670, 686, 687
Value-free research, 28, 273
Values:
    core values of social work practice, 25–26, 25 (exhibit)
    spirituality and, 166
    symbols and, 209
van Balan, F., 388
Vandenberg, G., 446
Ventricles, 94
Veronica, R., 305
Vertical linkage, 305, 306
Very low birth weight (VLBW) infants, 414–415

ABOUT THE AUTHOR

Elizabeth D. Hutchison, MSW, PhD, received her MSW from the George Warren Brown School of Social Work at Washington University in St. Louis and her PhD from the State University of New York at Albany. She was on the faculty in the Social Work Department at Elms College from 1980 to 1987, and was chair of the department from 1982 to 1987. She was on the faculty in the School of Social Work at Virginia Commonwealth University from 1987 to 2009, where she taught courses in human behavior and the social environment, social work and social justice, and child and family policy; she also served as field practicum liaison. She has been a social worker in health, mental health, aging, and child and family welfare settings. She is committed to providing social workers with comprehensive, current, and useful frameworks for thinking about human behavior. Her other research interests focus on child and family welfare. She currently lives in Rancho Mirage, California.

ABOUT THE CONTRIBUTORS

Suzanne M. Baldwin, PhD, LCSW, MSW, BSN, RN, received her PhD in social work from the School of Social Work at Virginia Commonwealth University. She works as a clinical social worker in private practice with families and spent almost two decades working as a clinical nurse specialist in newborn intensive care. Her major areas of interest are working with families involved with the court system and military family issues. She has taught human behavior, practice, communications, and research courses at Old Dominion University and at the School of Social Work at Virginia Commonwealth University. She is the mother of three adult children. Her oldest daughter was a patient in the NICU, and her grandson spent a month in the NICU after his birth in 2009.

Leanne W. Charlesworth, LMSW, PhD, is Associate Professor in the Department of Social Work at Nazareth College of Rochester, New York. She has practiced within child welfare systems, and her areas of service and research interest include poverty and child and family well-being. She has taught human behavior and research at the undergraduate and graduate levels.

Linwood Cousins, MSW, MA, PhD, is Professor and Director of the School of Social Work at Western Michigan University. He is a social worker and an anthropologist who has practiced in child welfare and family services. His research, teaching, and practice interests include the sociocultural manifestations of race, ethnicity, and social class as well as other aspects of human diversity in the community life and schooling of African Americans and other ethnic and economic minorities.

Elizabeth P. Cramer, MSW, PhD, LCSW, ACSW, is Professor in the School of Social Work at Virginia Commonwealth University. Her primary scholarship and service areas are domestic violence, lesbian and gay male issues, and group work. She is editor of the book *Addressing Homophobia and Heterosexism on College Campuses* (2002). She teaches in the areas of foundation practice, social justice, oppressed groups, and lesbian and bisexual women.

Stephen French Gilson, MSW, PhD, is Professor and Coordinator of Interdisciplinary Disability Studies at the Center for Community Inclusion and Disability Studies; Professor at the School of Social Work at the University of Maine; and Senior Research Fellow at Ono Academic College Research Institute for Health and Medical Professions, Kiryat Ono, Israel. After he completed his undergraduate degree in art, he shifted his career to social justice, pursuing a master's in social work. Realizing that knowledge of human biology and physiology was foundational to his work, he completed a PhD in medical sciences. Synthesizing the diversity and richness of this scholarly background, Dr. Gilson engages in research in disability theory, disability as diversity, design and access, social justice, health and disability policy, and the atypical body. He serves on the Board of Directors of the Disability Rights Center of Maine and is Chair of the Disability Section of the American Public Health Association. He teaches courses in disability as diversity, policy, and human behavior from a legitimacy perspective. Along with Liz DePoy, his wife, Stephen is the owner of an adapted rescue farm in Maine. Living his passion of full access, he has adapted the barn and farm area not only to better ensure human access and animal caretaking, but also to respond to the needs of the disabled and medically involved animals that live on the farm. Two other major influences on

Dr. Gilson's writing, research, and work include his passion for and involvement in adaptive alpine skiing and dressage.

Marcia P. Harrigan, MSW, PhD, is Associate Professor Emeritus and former Associate Dean of Student and Academic Affairs in the School of Social Work at Virginia Commonwealth University. She has practiced in child welfare, juvenile justice, and mental health. Her major areas of interest are nontraditional family structures, family assessment, multigenerational households, and long-distance family caregiving. She has taught human behavior and practice courses.

Pamela J. Kovacs, MSW, PhD, is Associate Professor in the School of Social Work at Virginia Commonwealth University. Her practice experience includes work with individuals, families, and groups in oncology, hospice, and mental health settings. Her major areas of interest are HIV/AIDS, hospice and palliative care, volunteerism, caregiving, and preparing social workers for health care and other settings serving older adults. She teaches clinical practice, social work practice and health care, and qualitative research, and she additionally serves as a field liaison.

Holly C. Matto, MSW, PhD, LCSW-C, is Associate Professor in the Social Work Program at George Mason University. Her research focuses on substance abuse assessment and treatment. She has taught courses in human behavior, social work practice, art therapy in social work practice, and research methodology. She is currently conducting a clinical trial with Inova Fairfax Hospital and Georgetown University that uses neuroimaging technology to examine functional and structural brain change associated with behavioral health interventions for substance-dependent adults.

Susan Ainsley McCarter, MS, MSW, PhD, is Assistant Professor in the Department of Social Work at the University of North Carolina at Charlotte. She has worked as a juvenile probation officer; mental health counselor for children, adolescents, and families; social policy advocate; and mother. Her major area of interest is risk and protective factors for adolescents, specifically the overrepresentation of youth of color in the juvenile justice system. She currently teaches research methods and the MSW capstone course, and has taught human behavior, social policy, social work and criminal justice, and sociology courses at both the undergraduate and graduate levels.

Matthias J. Naleppa, MSW, PhD, is Associate Professor in the School of Social Work at Virginia Commonwealth University (VCU) and a Hartford Geriatric Social Work Scholar. His research focuses on geriatric social work, short-term treatment, and international social work. He teaches philosophy of science, practice, and research in the MSW and doctoral programs at VCU. Over the past years, he has regularly conducted workshops on task-centered practice and geriatric social work in Europe and Asia. He holds an MSW from the Catholic School of Social Work in Munich and a PhD from the University at Albany.

Rosa Schnitzenbaumer is a graduate of the Catholic School of Social Work, Munich, Germany. She works as a geriatric social worker and licensed practical nurse for the Caritas Welfare Organization in Miesbach, Germany. She teaches as adjunct faculty for the School for Care Management at the University of Applied Sciences in Innsbruck, Austria, and is a board member of the Adelheid Stein Institute for Therapeutic Roleplay. Throughout her career, she has been involved in developing and managing programs for older adults, including a regional outpatient gero-psychiatric counseling center, individualized service systems for older adults, a senior volunteer network, and caregiver training programs. She has also initiated *Erzählcafés*, volunteer-led groups for persons with dementia.

Michael J. Sheridan, MSW, PhD, is currently Research Associate Professor at the National Catholic School of Social Service (NCSSS) of the Catholic University of America. Her practice experience includes work in mental health, health, corrections, and youth and family services. Her major areas of interest are spirituality and social work and issues related to diversity, oppression, and social and economic justice. She teaches courses on diversity and social justice, spirituality and social work, transpersonal theory, human behavior, international social development, and conflict resolution and peacebuilding at the BSW, MSW, and doctoral levels. She is also the Director of Research for NCSSS's Center for Spirituality and Social Work.

Pamela Viggiani, MSW, PhD, is Assistant Professor in the Department of Social Work at Nazareth College of Rochester. Her research focuses on oppression, social justice, and pedagogy. She teaches courses in social justice, social advocacy, diversity, policy, and social work methods. She serves on the New York State Social Work Board. In the past, she was an evaluator and consultant for grants funding public child welfare professionalization.

Joseph Walsh, MSW, PhD, LCSW, is Professor in the School of Social Work at Virginia Commonwealth University. He was educated at Ohio State University and has worked for 30 years in community mental health settings. His major areas of interest are clinical social work, serious mental illness, and psychopharmacology. He teaches courses in social work practice, human behavior and the social environment, and research while maintaining a small clinical practice.

Jim Wood, EdD, is a 33-year veteran of teaching and administration at all levels of public schooling and is currently Associate Professor of Childhood Education at the Ralph C. Wilson, Jr. School of Education at St. John Fisher College in Rochester, New York. His areas of interest include social justice education, integrated school environments, achievement gap issues, and diverse school cultures.

David Woody, III, PhD, LCSW, is currently Director of Program Services at the Salvation Army, DFW Metroplex Command. After several years in academia at the University of Texas at Arlington and Baylor University, Dr. Woody has returned to work in the local community, focused on economic self-sufficiency, clinical counseling for those in poverty, and establishing low-cost medical homes for those without health insurance. In addition to issues related to poverty, Dr. Woody's major areas of interest include research exploring strengths of African American single mothers, and initiatives enhancing the significance of fatherhood in the African American community.

Debra J. Woody, PhD, LMSW, is Associate Dean for Academic Affairs in the School of Social Work at the University of Texas at Arlington. Her areas of research and practice interests focus upon child and family issues related to drug and alcohol use. She is the principal investigator for several grants that support a drug and alcohol intervention program called New Connections, providing services to mothers and their drug-exposed infants and toddlers. She currently teaches both undergraduate and graduate research and practice courses.

PHOTO CREDITS

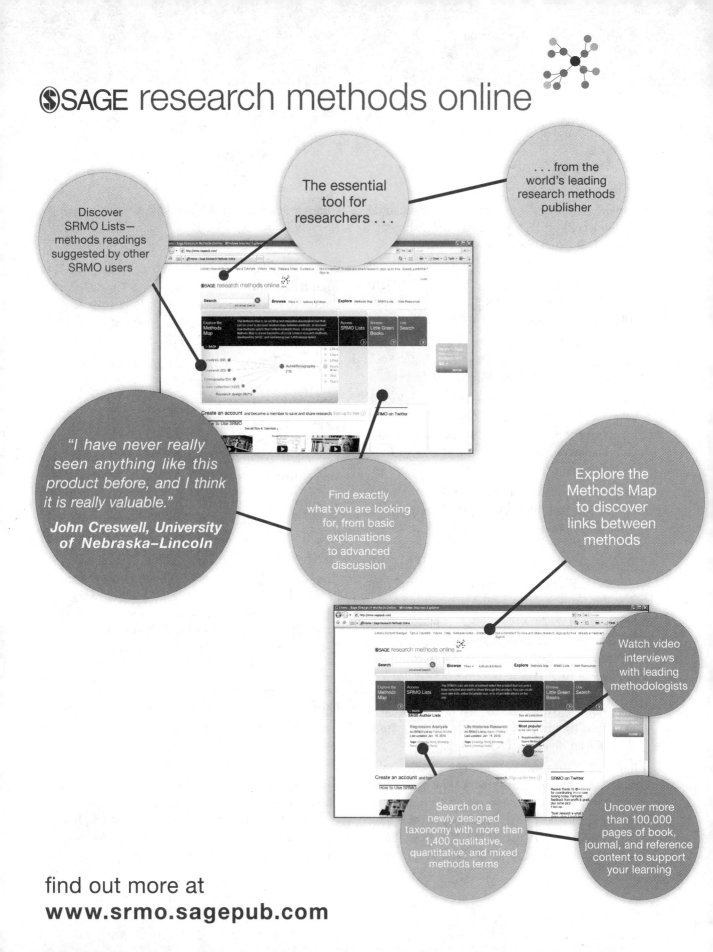